...rißion, socios III. scholares IV. una cum inferiorum Ordinum Officiarijs. Exinde vero elegantibus Ædificijs, annivog reditu multo auctius est factum pia ejusd. Regi
...ifica rentione recitantur) adeo ut jam numerent, ibid Socij 14 Schol:ve studentes juxta 30 Fuatores 10. etc 4 Colleg: hodie, licet recentiùs paulo fundatu, Claros Viros et Scrip-
...aritha Profeßor Ant. Tuckney Regius Profeß. Mathæus Poel Synopseos (vitæ sacr Author Laboriosiß. Præter quos gessit idem Coll: hodie inter suos numerare post p ædictum
...Consultiß omniq laude majores. Asserit queq sibi D: Wilhel:Temple varijs pro Reg Majestate CAROLI II Elegationib apud exteros functi Edm:Castle S.T.P. hodiernum li in Archi...
...M.D. apud Londin. cum alijs quam plurimis, quorum nomina jam nunc in honore sunt, et apud posteros erunt in perpetuum.

A HISTORY OF
EMMANUEL COLLEGE,
CAMBRIDGE

Cicero's *De Officiis* (Mainz, Fust and Schoeffer, 1465), illuminated for Prince Arthur *c.* 1500, presented to the College before 1597.

A HISTORY OF EMMANUEL COLLEGE, CAMBRIDGE

Sarah Bendall
Christopher Brooke
Patrick Collinson

THE BOYDELL PRESS

First published 1999
The Boydell Press, Woodbridge

ISBN 0 85115 393 3

The Boydell Press is an imprint of Boydell & Brewer Ltd
PO Box 9, Woodbridge, Suffolk IP12 3DF, UK
and of Boydell & Brewer Inc.
PO Box 41026, Rochester, NY 14604–4126, USA
website: http://www.boydell.co.uk

A catalogue record for this book is available
from the British Library

Library of Congress Cataloging-in-Publication Data
applied for

This publication is printed on acid-free paper

Printed in Great Britain by
St Edmundsbury Press Ltd, Bury St Edmunds, Suffolk

Contents

Chapters 4–5, 12 and 17 are by Sarah Bendall; chapters 1, 10–11, 13–16, 18–21 by Christopher Brooke; chapters 2–3, 6–9 by Patrick Collinson. The Epilogue is by the Master, J. E. Ffowcs Williams. Appendices 1, 2 and 5 are by Sarah Bendall; 3 and 4 by Christopher Brooke.

CONTENTS

Illustrations

Front Endpaper Emmanuel College *c*. 1690, from David Loggan, *Cantabrigia Illustrata* (ECL Prints no. PR. c. 10)

Frontispiece Cicero's *De Officiis* (Mainz, Fust and Schoeffer, 1465), illuminated for Prince Arthur *c*. 1500, presented to the College before 1597 (ECL, MS 5.3.11)

Plates (between pages 394 and 395)

1 Miniature of Queen Elizabeth on her Letters Patent of 11 January 1584, granting licence to Sir Walter Mildmay for the foundation of the College. Most probably by Nicholas Hilliard (ECA)
2 The Westmorland Building – a reconstruction of the 'Founder's Range' begun in 1719 (photo F. H. Stubbings)
3 The west front of the College; architect James Essex, completed 1775. Coloured aquatint from Ackermann's *Cambridge*, 1815 (ECL, GI.L1.2)
4 The Chapel and Gallery from the south-west; architect Sir Christopher Wren, completed *c*. 1677 (photo Wim Swaan)
5 The Great Pond, formerly the Dominicans' fishpond, with Emmanuel House (1894) and part of the Hostel (1886–94) (photo Wim Swaan)
6a The Hall roof-trusses (photo R. Fuerni)
 b The original Hall screens, masked by the eighteenth-century panelling (photo Reeve Photography Ltd)
 c Screens in the Old Library, originally the Chapel (photo F. H. Stubbings)
 All of the late sixteenth century
7 The Hall, interior
8a The Chapel, interior, after the refurbishment by A. W. Blomfield in 1884
 b The Master's Lodge of 1874, by A. W. Blomfield
9a The Chapel ceiling, designed by James Grove (photo Edward Leigh)
 b Detail of the communion rail in the Chapel (photo F. H. Stubbings)
10a The Elizabethan pulpit from the original Chapel (now the Old Library), now in Trumpington Church (photo by courtesy of the Royal Commission on Historical Monuments for England: Crown Copyright)
 b The gable end of the Brick Building of the 1630s, commonly called Old Court (photo F. H. Stubbings)

11a Lime-wood carving over the Gallery entrance-door, showing the arms of John Breton (Master 1665–75), William Sancroft (Master 1662–5) and Thomas Holbech (Master 1675–80) (photo by courtesy of the Royal Commission on Historical Monuments for England: Crown Copyright)

  b Silver caudle-cup and cover, 1677, given by Sir William Temple

12 North Court. One of several alternative designs by Leonard Stokes, c. 1910. As built, the gate-tower was omitted, and the left-hand range reduced to one storey (Emmanuel College Drawings, no. 519)

13 The Founder's Tomb in St Bartholomew the Great, Smithfield, City of London. Drawing by John Carter, 1784 (Emmanuel College Drawings, no. 502)

14a The Founder, from the full-length portrait painted for the College in 1588, now in the Old Library (ECP 18; photo Stearn and Sons)

  b Binding, by Jean de Planche, of Theodore Beza, *Tractationes Theologicae*, vol. II (Geneva, 1573). The book, dedicated to Mildmay, is shown in the Founder's portrait

  c Inscription in the Founder's hand on the title page of the French Bible (Geneva, 1588: ECL FB.1), presented to him by the ministers of the church at Geneva

15a Ralph Symons, architect of the original buildings of the College (ECP 7)

  b Joseph Hall, Bishop of Exeter (1627–41) and Norwich (1641–56). Engraving by John Payne, 1628. Reproduced from vol. II of Hall's collected *Works*, 1647 (ECL 305.3.2)

  c William Sancroft, by Bernard Lens the elder, painted in 1650 (ECP 83)

  d William Bennet, Bishop of Cork (1790–4), and Cloyne (1794–1820), probably by G. C. Stuart (ECP 23)

16a Silhouette of Robert Towerson Cory, Master, 1797–1835. By Auguste Édouart, 1829 (ECP 101)

  b Caricatures in the margin of Psalm 106 in a Prayer Book of 1829 from the College Chapel, now owned by Mr John Harding (photo by courtesy of the Royal Commission on Historical Monuments for England: Crown Copyright)

  c Sketch of George Archdall-Gratwicke, Master, 1835–71, made in 1859 by Frank Besant, then an undergraduate at Emmanuel (ECP 107)

  d James Bennet Peace as rowing coach; from Herbert G. Jones, *Friends in Pencil*, Cambridge, 1893 (ECL, Welbourn 987.2.12)

17a Edward Welbourne, Master 1951–64

  b Richard Farmer, Master 1775–97. Drawing by John Downman, 1778, in the Fitzwilliam Museum (J. W. Goodison, *Catalogue of Cambridge Portraits*, Cambridge, 1935, no. 122: photo by courtesy of the Syndics of the Fitzwilliam Museum)

  c Leonard Hugh Graham Greenwood, Fellow 1909–1965. Chalk drawing by Luis Vargas, 1959 (ECP 87)

  d Sir Frederick Gowland Hopkins (1861–1947). Charcoal drawing by Edmond Kapp, 1943, in the Fitzwilliam Museum, no. 2511 (Goodison, *Catalogue*, no.221; photo by courtesy of the Syndics of the Fitzwilliam Museum)

18a The Founder's Cup: silver-gilt tazza, made at Antwerp, 1541. The finial is enamelled with the Founder's arms on one side and his monogram on the other.

  b The Founder's Cup: repoussé decoration inside the bowl, showing the poet Arion being rescued by a dolphin, surrounded by a frieze of fantastic sea-creatures.

19 The Chapel Plate of 1637: all except the first were purchased from the legacy of the elder William Sancroft (Master 1628–37)

  a One of a pair of double-gilt chalices, with paten covers; and one of three 'livery-stoops' (i.e. serving-flagons)

  b One of two parcel-gilt alms-dishes; and one of two silver-gilt patens

20 Silver tea service, made by Paul Storr, 1817: the tea-pot was given by George Porcher, the sugar-basin and cream-jug by George Collins Poore

21a College Orders of 10 December 1588, signed by Laurence Chaderton, first Master, and the first twelve Fellows of the College (ECA COL.14.1)

  b Entries in the College Admissions Register. The second line reads 'John Harvard Midlsex: Decemb: 19 [fee paid] £0 - 10s - 0d.' (ECA CHA.1.4)

  c A first list, in William Sancroft's hand, of subscriptions towards the building of the Wren Chapel (ECA CHA.1.2.1.6)

22a Samuel Parr's German silver tobacco pipe, *c*. 1790

  b Samuel Blackall's woods (perhaps *c*. 1795), still used for playing bowls in the Fellows' Garden

23 The Four Swans Inn, Bishopsgate, London, given to the College by the Founder in 1585. From a drawing of *c*. 1850 (Emmanuel College Drawings, no. 516)

24 Map of Chequer Court Farm, Ash, Kent, part of the property bequeathed to the College by George Thorpe, D.D. (1638–1719). Drawn in 1824 by George Quested, surveyor, tenant of the farm (ECA KE.5)

Final Endpaper Plan of the College, by Hugh Richmond

ECA – Emmanuel College Archives

ECL – Emmanuel College Library

ECP – Unpublished Catalogue of Emmanuel College Portraits, by F. H. Stubbings

Maps

Figures and Tables

Tables

Preface

Thomas Fuller is noted for weaving charming anecdotes into his dry-as-dust books of historical reference. Thus he wrote in 1655, during the reign of Oliver Cromwell, on Sir Walter Mildmay and Queen Elizabeth I:

> Coming to Court after he had founded his Colledge, the Queen told him, Sir Walter I hear you have erected a Puritan Foundation. No, Madam, saith he, farre be it from me to countenance any thing contrary to your established Lawes, but I have set an Acorn, which when it becomes an Oake, God alone knows what will be the fruit thereof. Sure I am [adds Fuller] at this day it hath overshadowed all the University, more than a moyety of the present Masters of Colledges being bred therein. . . .[1]

In 1984 Emmanuel celebrated its fourth centenary, and Frank Stubbings adorned the occasion with a splendid edition of Mildmay's Statutes and a delightful presentation of *Forty-Nine Lives*.[2] But he lamented to one of us at the time that the College had not succeeded – as had been hoped – in producing a full-length history. A seed of some kind had been planted, and it occurred to Christopher Brooke – as a Dixie Professor living *in partibus infidelium* as a fellow of Caius – that it might be a hopeful task for him to propagate it. A friendly reviewer of his *History of Gonville and Caius College* had indeed drawn the moral that college histories ought to be written from outside; yet there is a paradox here, for some intimacy with a College is essential to the understanding of a complex historical organism. It has been resolved in this instance in a book which is at once and equally from without and from within.

From without – for Patrick Collinson had recently returned to Cambridge, and joined with Christopher Brooke to expound the origin and transformation of a great Protestant foundation between its birth in 1584 and the age of William Law in the early eighteenth century. This was the period when it might be said that the history of Emmanuel was the history of Protestant England.

From within, for Sarah Bendall, already Research Fellow and Archivist of the College, was appointed to write the history of Emmanuel's estates and finances. All three authors have been supported by many Emmanuel

---

[1] Fuller 1655, p. 147.
[2] Stubbings 1983a, 1983b.

folk – above all by Frank Stubbings, whose knowledge of every branch of the tree has been most generously and cordially at our disposal throughout; whose words are frequently echoed and quoted in it, who has helped in collecting the material for the text and above all in choosing and gathering the plates.

Support also came from Derek Brewer, Master when the enterprise began, whose warm welcome above all encouraged us to proceed – a welcome most kindly echoed by his three successors; and Professor Brewer and the Governing Body responded very generously to our request for help. The authors also give hearty thanks to the staff of the Archives and Library, and especially to Janet Morris, Margaret Farrar, Rhiannon Jones and Norma Searby, who have given constant aid and support; and additionally to Neville Morley, Niall Murphy and Frances Willmoth, who helped with the compilation of a complete biographical register of those who attended Emmanuel, from 1584 to 1990.

Writing the history of modern Emmanuel from without has been a task of peculiar delicacy: in a similar predicament King Agag (it will be recalled) trod delicately – before being hewn in pieces by the prophet Samuel. If Christopher Brooke and Sarah Bendall escape the fate of Agag, it will be entirely the work of their many friends within the covenant, who have helped, advised and written for them: the Masters, Professor Brewer, Lord St John of Fawsley, Professor Ffowcs Williams; Vice-Masters, Brian Thrush and Alan Baker; Senior Tutors, David Newsome and Gerard Evans; Bursars, David Livesey, Stephen Brooker and Michael Gross; Life Fellows, Frank Stubbings and Ronald Gray; alumni, Graham Watson, Harry Whitcut, Peter Bayley. Christopher Brooke is also very grateful to his oldest friends in the Emmanuel community, Priscilla Hele and her sister the late Carroll Holland, daughters of a former Master, and Jacqueline Line, daughter of a former Fellow. He owes special thanks to John Manning, former groundsman, and his wife, for a delightful afternoon on college sports. Patrick Collinson's chapters owe much to the generous aid of Bruce Barker-Benfield, Mary Clapinson, Seán Hughes, Arnold Hunt, Peter Lake, the late Jeremy Maule, Jonathan Moore, Glyn Parry, Alex Shepard, Kenneth Shipps, Margo Todd, Nicholas Tyacke, Alex Walsham, and Tom Webster.

We are indebted to Hugh Richmond, formerly Head of Architecture in the Royal Commission on Historical Monuments for England, who has drawn the maps and advised on the architectural history of his own College; and to Michael Young, yet another Emmanuel man, who drew the map of the College estates. We also thank many other friends and colleagues, including Elisabeth Leedham-Green, Peter Searby and Malcolm Underwood.

The first draft of Sarah Bendall's chapters was completed in 1993, of Christopher Brooke's in 1994. We have revised them and the

Bibliography in 1998. But we have not attempted detailed references to the recent literature.

We sowed a seed some years ago: we are not botanists enough to be sure what manner of plant has grown – but such as it is, we offer it in homage to the men and women of Mildmay's heritage.

Sarah Bendall
Christopher Brooke
Patrick Collinson

December 1998

DATES

In all cases, the year has been taken as beginning on 1 January.

A NOTE ON TRANSCRIPTION IN CHAPTERS 4, 5 and 12

Spelling and punctuation have been preserved; words in small capitals have been transcribed in lower case.

<u>letters underlined</u>   expansions of abbreviations (some standard abbreviations have not been expanded)
[ ]   editorial insertions
< >   material deleted in MS
\ /   material inserted in MS
{ }   MS defective
( )   parenthesis in MS
~   hyphen in MS

1

Prologue: The Friars Preachers of St Dominic

In the early 1580s Sir Walter Mildmay purchased the site and precinct of the Dominican friary in Cambridge, suppressed in 1538, for his new college for the training of protestant preachers, to be called Emmanuel, 'God with us'.[1] To the Dominicans, the Order of Friars Preachers, the Black Friars, Emmanuel owes the scale of its precinct – eight or so acres in the heart of Cambridge – similar to that of Sidney Sussex, founded ten years later on the site of the house of the Franciscan friars. The walls of the nave of the Dominican church survive largely intact in the college's hall and parlour, and much of the Front Court occupies the site of the Dominican cloister.[2] More than that, the houses of friars were precursors, in a sense the models, for the early colleges; and the orders of friars, especially the Franciscans – clearly much aided by the Dominicans – probably founded the Faculty of Theology and enhanced the modest academic pretensions of early Cambridge so as to make it a viable university.[3] In a variety of senses, the house of the Friars Preachers was a prologue to the College.

The Dominican Order was formally inaugurated in 1216, when St Dominic and a tiny band of about sixteen friars won recognition from the Pope for an Order of canons, following the old established Rule of St Augustine, with a special mission to preach, and particularly to preach to the heretics – as they appeared to the Catholic Church of the day – in the south of France.[4] Dominic had made Toulouse his headquarters, Simon de Montfort, count of Toulouse, his patron. Simon was the father of another Simon de Montfort, celebrated in English history of the mid-thirteenth century. The elder Simon was a devout and sadistic crusader against the heretics, leader, under papal authority, of the Crusade against

---

[1] See below, pp. 22–3. The account which follows is especially indebted to Zutshi and Ombres 1990, which contains virtually all that is known of the medieval Cambridge Dominican house. There is much of value also in Hinnebusch 1951; for the buildings, see esp. Stubbings 1984a; and for the background, Knowles 1948, esp. chaps. 13–14.

[2] Stubbings 1984a; below, pp. 8–9.

[3] Little 1943; Zutshi and Ombres 1990, pp. 324–5; Leader 1988, p. 33 and n.50.

[4] For this interpretation of Dominican origins, see Brooke (R.B.) 1975, chap. 6 and cf. p. 170 for the number of friars; Brooke (C.N.L.) 1971, chap. 11. For a more detailed account, see Vicaire 1964.

the Cathars or Albigensians. By war and persecution he had won the county of Toulouse; and he had encountered Dominic, already dedicated to converting the Cathars by more peaceful means. But in 1217 the power of Count Simon began to founder, and in 1218 he died. Dominic meanwhile was discovering a new vocation. In 1216, it seems, he had met St Francis, and been deeply moved by the inspiration of a different type of religious, and a different approach to the heretic.[5] In the event, Dominic followed Francis in seeking to make poverty an essential element in his Order, and in directing his mission, not to the obdurate heretic, but to the ignorant, apathetic catholic – to the whole world indeed. Late in 1217, acting on an impulse as wilful as any of Francis's, he abandoned Toulouse, sent his tiny band of followers out into the world two by two, and bade them make Paris and Bologna their headquarters.[6]

Paris and Bologna, the two pioneer university cities of the twelfth century, to which students had flocked from every corner of Europe: it was here that Dominic sought his vocation, here and in Rome – where he was a frequent visitor to the papal Curia.[7] From Rome came his authority, from the student centres the best of his recruits. His friars settled in Paris and Bologna in 1217–18; by 1221 they were in Oxford, and by 1238 in Cambridge.[8] The growth of this tiny band into a great Order spread all over Christendom was exceedingly rapid, its speed only paralleled by that of their brothers and rivals the Franciscans. The most ardent religious impulses of the twelfth and thirteenth centuries could be summed up as the pursuit of poverty and of the apostolic life, as then interpreted. The avant-garde religious of the twelfth century, such as the Cistercian monks, had been country dwellers – they had gone out in search of solitude and self-sufficiency. The new movements of the early thirteenth century were city-based; their mission was to the rapidly growing towns of the urban renaissance;[9] they lived among or near the new urban proletariat. But they lived their own lives too. They sought and found ample precincts, in which they could follow the regular life – for the Dominicans, according to the Rule of St Augustine enlarged by the Dominican constitutions – and with large churches with ample space to gather audiences to hear their sermons.[10] The friars' churches needed choirs in which the community could celebrate their masses and sing their offices, and large naves in which they could preach; hence they

[5] Brooke 1971, pp. 222–6.
[6] Jordan of Saxony, *Libellus de principiis Ordinis Praedicatorum*, in Scheeben 1935, cc. 46–55; Eng.trans. in Brooke 1975, pp. 170–2.
[7] Brooke 1971, pp. 223–4.
[8] Hinnebusch 1951, pp. 493–7.
[9] For this concept see Brooke and Keir 1975, chaps. 1, 3 and refs.
[10] For a detailed account of the Dominican Constitution, see Galbraith 1925; on Dominican architecture, see Meersseman 1946.

tended to be long and relatively narrow, like that at Cambridge. The speed of their success and the resources put at their disposal are astonishing.

Dominic, like Francis, had tried to insist on modest, humble buildings, in conformity with the Order's ideal of poverty.[11] But both Orders rapidly became the victims of their own success. For the very reason that they had modest resources – the Franciscans none, the Dominicans only a little they could call their own – they were at the mercy of their patrons, or anyway allowed themselves to become so. The growth of the Orders testifies as much to their success in search of patrons as of recruits. But that is not the whole story. The Order continued to curb excesses in building – in 1250, when the General Chapter of the Order was held in London, the English provincial and the prior of Newcastle-on-Tyne were set to penance 'for excessive building ventures'.[12] And yet by 1300 the Dominican friars had 52 houses in England, a number at least with ample complexes capable of housing 40–70 friars, those at Oxford and London over 90.[13] Few communities of monks or canons comprised numbers on this scale in the thirteenth century, and – if we look forward to the fourteenth and fifteenth centuries – only two colleges in Oxford and two in Cambridge had as many as 70 on their foundations.[14]

Every English town, indeed – with very few exceptions – had houses of both Dominicans and Franciscans; and not a few had Carmelites and Austin Friars as well. Cambridge boasted six or seven houses of friars, though only the 'orders four' survived for more than a generation.[15] It is astonishing that Orders so young could command recruits and patrons in such plenty. It was characteristic of the Church's hierarchy in the thirteenth century, for all its involvement in politics and its grandeur, to remain in the closest contact with the most avant-garde and charismatic religious movements of the day. Many who know nothing else of Pope Innocent III have contemplated his dream of a humble friar who would save the Church from collapse in the celebrated fresco in the Upper Church of the Basilica of St Francis at Assisi.[16]

Dominic was a beggar, but not – in the Franciscan sense – a charismatic. He and his successors aimed to provide an ordered, disciplined way of life, poor and simple in living standards indeed, but provided with books and teachers and guided and governed by a rational

---

[11] Hinnebusch 1951, pp. 126–8.
[12] Hinnebusch 1951, p. 128.
[13] Hinnebusch 1951, pp. 493–5; Knowles and Hadcock 1971, pp. 213–20 (ibid., pp. 215–20 give the numbers of friars, where known).
[14] New College and Magdalen, Oxford; the King's Hall and King's College, Cambridge.
[15] Brooke 1985a, pp. 60–1, 73–4.
[16] Reproduced in *Giotto. Frescoes in the Upper Church, Assisi*, photos by A. Belli (London–Paris, 1954), pl. VI.

constitution. Dominic died in 1221, the year in which the friars first came to England and settled in Oxford, only three and a half years after the move from Toulouse to Paris and Bologna. How much should be attributed to him personally is not clear: perhaps as much was due to his successor, Jordan of Saxony, who commanded precisely the mixture of charisma and orderliness the development of the Dominican constitution required.[17] Under his leadership the hierarchy of committees was formed which ruled the Order. The Dominican General Chapter became a committee of thirteen, including the Master General: two years out of three the twelve were elected representatives or *diffinitores* of the provinces, the third the heads or priors of the provinces formed the chapter.[18] There were many sophistications and provincial chapters were larger bodies; but in general, at every level, there was a mixture of authority and representation. Among the Preachers, declared Humbert de Romans, Master General of the Order from 1254 to 1263, 'there is an abundance of wisdom even among the subject friars' – that is to say, wisdom is sought in the elected priors 'and also among subject friars selected by their brethren.'[19] In due course a whole hierarchy of committees was formed, to run convents, and groups of convents called 'Visitations', and provinces and the whole Order. The Visitation came last: by 1300 the Cambridge house itself was the centre of one of four Visitations covering the English province. Dominic and Jordan were the apostles of committee government, and it has been thought that they inspired ideas of representative government and so of clerical convocations and parliaments.[20] The truth seems to be that parliaments and estates of the realm and representation – quintessential products, like the friars, of the thirteenth century – were already in the wind when Dominic was young, especially in his native Castile;[21] what is remarkable among the Dominicans is the combination of advanced and highly sophisticated political thought with shrewd experience of the government of other orders and probably also of the Italian cities. There were to be many differences in Oxford and Cambridge between convents and colleges; but the young colleges of the

---

[17] The essential problem is that the earliest surviving text of the Dominican Constitutions represents their state after the *Generalissimum* Chapter of 1228, which evidently completed a process of modification of the constitutional organisation which obscures its earliest features. On the Dominican Constitution see Brooke (R.B.) 1959, pp. 225–31 and 193 for the texts; Galbraith 1925. On Jordan see Brooke (C.N.L.) 1971, chap. 11.

[18] Hinnebusch 1951, pp. 30–1, cites Matthew Paris to the effect that 400 friars or more attended the General Chapter in London in 1250, and the better evidence of the Close Rolls that 700 were reckoned to be present at the same occasion in London in 1263. But serious discussion and decision lay with the thirteen persons including the Master General, who formed the official General Chapter.

[19] Berthier 1889, II, 61, quoted in Knowles 1948, p. 158 n.1. For the Cambridge Visitation (below), see Zutshi and Ombres 1990, p. 316.

[20] So Barker 1913, an ingenious and suggestive study which has not won acceptance.

[21] For a general view of medieval parliaments, see Myers 1975.

fourteenth and fifteenth centuries grew up under the shadow of the religious rules, and perhaps particularly of the Dominican;[22] and they owed to them that strange combination of authority and democracy – of rule by a patriarchal head of house over a group of fellows who yet had equal votes in electing the head and in making major decisions – which came to be, not the universal form, but the common practice, the model, of college government.

One of Dominic's notable recruits had been the lady Diana Dandolo, who became the central figure in the Dominican community of nuns in Bologna; and to her Brother Jordan wrote regularly on his travels in the 1220s and 30s.

'Fare well in Christ Jesus always. I write to you from England before Candlemas [2 February] in good health. Pray for me without ceasing to the Lord, that He may open His hand to us generously always, and direct His Word in our mouth to His honour, to the Church's profit and the growth of the Order. I was then at the schools at Oxford; and the Lord gave us ample hope of a good catch...'[23] The friars were indeed a miraculous draught of fishes. One of the witnesses to the canonization process for St Dominic described how he himself had been caught by St Dominic while a student at Bologna: while he was pondering on his vocation, Dominic suddenly summoned him and clothed him in the friar's habit before he could hesitate any longer.[24] We have no such vivid stories of the making of the Cambridge community; but one of the first friars there described how he had been inspired to join the Order by a vision while a student at Cambridge.[25] The application of reason to the Order affected their constitution and, above all, their schools. They were to be an Order of preachers, trained to the task. Every community was in some sense a school, but especially those in the University towns. The Dominicans led the way in establishing the strange relationship which made the presence of the friars in the universities so stimulating and yet so galling to their secular colleagues: galling at first because of their practice of landing so many of the best students in their nets; both stimulating and galling because they founded schools of theology and fructified the universities, while claiming all manner of privileges, especially that of completing their courses much more rapidly than secular masters. They could not wait the seven years that it took for an arts degree and the many more for theology thereafter.[26] There developed a relationship of love and hate between the secular masters and the friars. Sometimes the

---

[22] But see Mayr-Harting 1988 on the influence of the Rule of St Benedict on the statutes of Peterhouse.

[23] Brooke (R.B.) 1975, p. 188 (from Walz 1951, no. 16).

[24] Brooke (R.B.) 1975, p. 180: cf. Brooke (C.N.L.) 1971, pp. 221–2.

[25] Zutshi and Ombres 1990, p. 316 and n.12.

[26] For all this, and esp. for Cambridge, see Leader 1988, pp. 50–8.

greatest secular masters joined hands with the friars, as did Robert Grosseteste – who was deeply influenced by his friendship with the Dominican Jordan of Saxony – when he became *lector* (reader or lecturer) to the Franciscans in Oxford in the 1220s.[27] But the success and the privileges of the friars led to an explosive argument in Paris in the mid-thirteenth century – when the University was winning immortal fame as the home of St Thomas Aquinas the Dominican and St Bonaventure the Franciscan; and the University of Cambridge was sufficiently mature in 1303 to quarrel with the friars in like manner. The outcome then – and again in 1366, after royal and papal intervention – was a compromise: the friars were allowed some exemptions from university rules, and to preach the sermons which were essential to their courses in their own churches.[28] Meanwhile, if it be true that the Franciscan Duns Scotus studied and taught in Cambridge, as well as in Oxford and Paris, then the most notable luminary of medieval Cambridge was a friar.[29] The friars were central to the academic and spiritual life of medieval Cambridge.

The Dominicans needed not only recruits, but patrons. They begged alms from rich and poor alike, and the spread of the Order and the scale of their buildings reveals their extraordinary success. Readers of Langland's *Piers Plowman* or Chaucer's *Canterbury Tales* are inclined to picture the friars, at least in the fourteenth century, as venal and corrupt, targets of satire and scorn. Yet they flourished in England until the 1530s, and even if there was a decline in numbers on the eve of the dissolution and a marked division of theological opinion among them in the 1530s, the evidence is abundant, especially in the lists of bequests, that the Cambridge Dominicans remained successful beggars – that is to say, still very popular with many folk – down to the day in 1538 when they suddenly vanished. The lists suggest 'an upsurge in support for them as late as the early sixteenth century'.[30]

The Dominican friars came to England in 1221 and settled first in Oxford. We first hear of them in Cambridge in 1238, in a very characteristic way: King Henry III, who befriended all manner of communities of friars, gave them three oaks in the forest of Weybridge in Surrey towards the building of their chapel.[31] If we had to give a short answer to the question, why is there a university in Cambridge? it might well be: because King Henry III willed it. The king's political record was

---

[27] Southern 1986, pp. 74–5.
[28] Leader 1988, pp. 54–7.
[29] Leader 1988, p. 170n.; Emden 1963, pp. 198–201.
[30] Zutshi and Ombres 1990, p. 349; Knowles 1959, pp. 52–61. The lists are discussed, with references, in Zutshi and Ombres 1990, p. 340 and n.113. For wills see ibid. pp. 339–40. Some houses were dissolved in 1539; the Oxford and Cambridge houses, with the majority, in 1538 (Knowles and Hadcock 1971, pp. 213–14).
[31] *Close Rolls 1237–42* (Public Record Office Texts and Calendars, 1911), p. 61; Zutshi and Ombres 1990, p. 315 and n.5.

ambiguous at best, but he was a very notable patron of the friars and the arts. His gifts inspired and encouraged others to support the friars; and his writs laid down that there should be no more than two universities in England, at Oxford and Cambridge.[32]

Henry III's privilege of 1231 extended to both Oxford and Cambridge, and is to us a first indication that Cambridge might survive as a university after its very modest beginnings from about 1209 onwards. The Dominicans may have come to Cambridge in the early 1230s or even earlier; by 1238 they were building; in 1240 they were extending their precinct and were allowed to close a lane to enlarge it.[33] The Hundred Roll of 1279 records that 'The house comprises eight acres and more in length and breadth; on that site there used to be divers dwellings in which many people dwelt who were wont to pay geld and aid to the town; now the friars hold the land in perpetual alms [that is, free of geld and aids and other taxes] from their purchases and the gifts of many donors.'[34] The Hundred Rolls are a notoriously slippery source; but we may presume that the site was cleared – at least along what is now St Andrew's Street – by a complex series of transactions in which great and small benefactors, and the Preachers' own initiatives, were involved. The greatest of the benefactors, according to later report, was Alice, widow of Robert de Vere, fifth earl of Oxford, of the mid-thirteenth century;[35] but the size of the precinct, so near the centre of a thriving town, and the scale of the buildings presuppose highly successful fund-raising, partly at least among well-to do citizens, over a long period. The precinct allowed room for ample buildings in the corner where the College still stands, and gardens and fish ponds: the college lily pond is evidently the lineal successor of the Dominicans' principal fish pond.[36]

The remains of the nave of the Dominican church are incorporated in the present College Hall and Parlour, and the analysis of them by Frank Stubbings and Hugh Richmond suggests that the fabric was probably mainly of the thirteenth century, which we may reckon the heyday of the Cambridge Dominican community – obscure as its history is to us.[37] 'The pattern of the surviving medieval fabric in the Hall range,' writes Hugh Richmond, 'particularly the disposition of the surviving buttresses of the north wall, suggests that the Nave of the Friary church extended to the east wall of the Parlour.' In Loggan's engraving of c. 1690 the outline of a

---

[32] Leader 1988, p. 2.
[33] *Close Rolls 1237–42*, p. 185, cited e.g. by Zutshi and Ombres 1990, p. 315 and n.6.
[34] Quoted Zutshi and Ombres 1990, p. 317 n.15.
[35] Hinnebusch 1951, p. 89; Zutshi and Ombres 1990, p. 339; on Alice, see *Complete Peerage*, X, 217–18.
[36] Its shape was altered in the 1960s from the rectangle shown in Loggan (Welbourne 1963–4).
[37] Stubbings 1984a.

large west window is clearly visible, presumably an insertion of the four-teenth or fifteenth centuries, very likely adorned with stained glass such as we know was common in friars' churches.[38] The gorgeous retable at Thornham Parva and its counterpart the altar frontal now in the Musée de Cluny in Paris are thought to come from the Dominican friary at Thetford, founded in 1335 by a syndicate inspired by Edmund Gonville, country parson, entrepreneur of religious foundations, founder also of

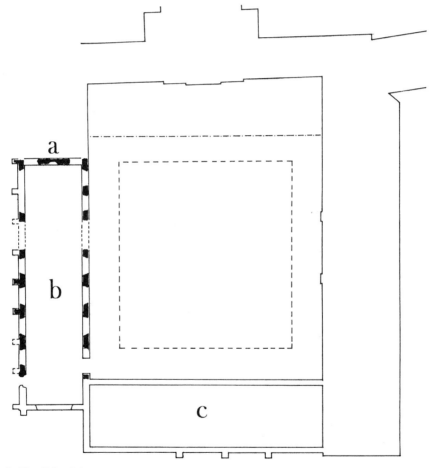

1 The Friars' Cloister, by Hugh Richmond.
   a, passage east of nave altar; b, the Friars' nave; c, the west range.

---

[38] Though it very rarely survives, and the only fragments of glass from Cambridge friaries known to exist are those from the Carmelite convent now in the Old Library at Queens' and possibly from the Franciscans in Sidney Sussex. For Loggan's engraving, see front endpapers.

Gonville Hall, now Gonville and Caius College. But it has been suggested that a possible alternative is the Cambridge friary; if so, it was most splendidly adorned.[39] For the rest, the surviving structure suggests solid, commodious but not luxurious buildings, such as one would expect. The main walls of the church evidently survived the Dissolution and were in place in the 1580s to be incorporated in Mildmay's new buildings. All known analogies, and the lay-out of the very ample precinct, suggest that the cloister lay to the south of the nave, in what is now Front Court, and

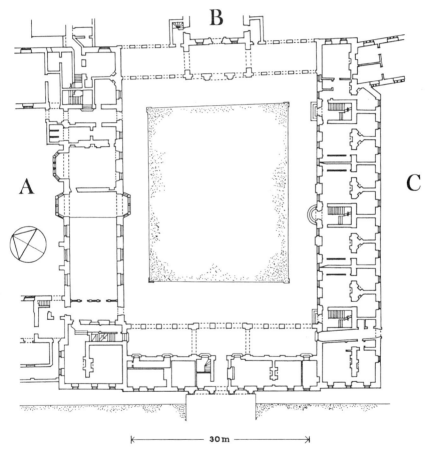

B

A

C

|← 30m →|

2 The Front Court in the 1950s, by Hugh Richmond.
A, Hall and Parlour; B, Chapel; C, Westmorland Building.

---

[39] Norton, Park and Binski 1987; for the suggestion of Cambridge as a possible alternative, see the review by Pamela Tudor-Craig (Lady Wedgwood) in *Antiquaries Journal*, 68 (1988), 367–8.

may have been almost as large as the present court. Loggan's engraving and a plan of the College by James Essex of 1746 show a western range running at right-angles from the west end of the church – and now obliterated by Essex's new buildings of the eighteenth century – having some medieval windows and doors, and supported by buttresses which have all the appearance of medieval construction. We may be sure that Mildmay used part of this building relatively little altered; but we can be less sure of its original function. The Dominicans followed their forebears, the Augustinian canons, in preserving the basic arrangement of church and cloister, even in the crowded conditions of a city centre – and assuredly in the ample space of their precinct in Cambridge.[40] Thus Hugh Richmond writes: 'The medieval ranges visible in 1690 and 1746 appear to have defined the north and west sides of a court in the position normally occupied by the cloister and suggest that it was approximately square in plan, having sides of just over 100 feet. The dotted lines on map 1 show a possible outline for the open area. This interpretation is supported by a resistivity survey carried out in 1993 over the grassed area of the court, when no evidence for significant structures resulted.' The few surviving fragments of English Dominican houses, however, suggest that the buildings round the cloister followed a pattern in some respects peculiar to the Dominicans. They needed chapter house, dormitory, refectory and library above all, and these were common features of, for example, late medieval Benedictine houses; but they had their special features. The community in Cambridge was large, sometimes as large as 75, but averaging about 60 in the late thirteenth and early fourteenth centuries. There is little reason to suppose that the numbers of friars in Cambridge fell after the Black Death of 1348–9, and the Cambridge Dominicans remained numerous and popular till shortly before the Dissolution in 1538.[41] The most remarkable feature of the Dominican buildings was the dormitory, which seems normally to have combined accommodation for sleep and study: an open space in the centre for beds and along the walls enclosed carrels, well lit by windows. It has been suggested that the dormitory replaced the cloister as the main place of study.[42] This may be so, but even on the most generous interpretation, the dormitory at Cambridge could hardly have housed more than about two-thirds of the community at its height; one suspects that the dormitory was a

---

[40] On all this I owe much to the advice of Hugh Richmond (whom I quote in the text); and on Dominican architecture, of Dr Lucy Vinten Mattich (see now Vinten Mattich 1995). For the general background, see Brooke 1987; on Dominican architecture in general, see the fundamental article Meersseman 1946. On the surviving evidence of Dominican architecture in England, there is valuable material in Hinnebusch 1951, chaps. 7–10.

[41] Knowles and Hadcock 1971, p. 215; Zutshi and Ombres 1990, p. 349. For estimates of total numbers in the province, see Knowles and Hadcock 1971, p. 492.

[42] On the Dormitory, see Hinnebusch 1951, pp. 163–80.

supplement to other places of study, not a substitute. In some sense, this combination of bedroom and study anticipated the college chambers of the fourteenth and later centuries. Indeed, the two may have grown up together, for the earliest chambers may well go back into the thirteenth century. The chamber for three or four fellows and students, with common sleeping space in its centre and individual studies by windows on the sides of the room, was well established by the time New College, Oxford, was built in the later fourteenth century – and survived until the sharp decline in college numbers in the mid-seventeenth century: long enough to flourish and multiply in the Founder's Range and the Brick Building of Emmanuel.[43] We may conjecture that the refectory abutted the western side of the cloister, the dormitory the southern and the chapter house the eastern side, as at Gloucester; and it is estimated that in the dormitory there one can see space for about 26 carrels – for a community varying from 30 to 40.[44] At Cambridge we may conjecture a dormitory with perhaps 40 carrels, and about 150 feet long.

We know the names of 9 friars of the thirteenth century, 109 of the fourteenth, 183 of the fifteenth and 85 of the sixteenth;[45] but the vast majority of these are names only. We can only sketch in outline the life they led and the work they did. They combined study and scholarship with preaching and pastoral work: they served the townsfolk and others who came to them for confession and attended their sermons; they welcomed the pilgrims and the bequests to the image of Our Lady of Grace.[46] For a brief period in the 1330s and 1340s the place which Fenton Hort was to adorn from 1872 to 1892 was the scene of some of the outstanding biblical study of the fourteenth century. Here worked Robert Holcot, 'artistic, cultured and affable', author of a celebrated commentary on Wisdom; and his disciples, who included Thomas de Ryngstede, who wrote on Proverbs and rose to be bishop of Bangor.[47] Less affable, perhaps, were the inquisitors, who lived in the cloister from time to time. In the 1370s Cambridge rang with the argument whether or not the Carmelites had been founded by Elijah on Mount Carmel. John Stokes, O.P., denied the claim; but the masters of the University solemnly decided in favour of the Carmelites and Elijah.[48] At the very end, in the 1530s, the house was still very active intellectually. When Latimer preached in St Edward's church in 1529, William Buckenam, prior of the

[43] Brooke 1989, p. 164 and note on p. 165.
[44] Hinnebusch 1951, p. 173; cf. Knowles and Hadcock 1971, p. 216. It has been alternatively interpreted as the Library – but Hinnebusch's evidence strongly confirms the notion of it as a study-dormitory.
[45] Zutshi and Ombres 1990, pp. 363–70, in large part based on Emden 1963 but with much detail added, including a list of priors, pp. 371–3.
[46] Zutshi and Ombres 1990, pp. 332, 339–40.
[47] Zutshi and Omnbres 1990, pp. 336–8; Smalley 1960, esp. chap. 7.
[48] Zutshi and Ombres 1990, p. 342.

Black Friars, came into the same pulpit early in 1530 to denounce Latimer and to defend in particular the inexpediency of studying the Scriptures in English.[49] In 1534 he was succeeded by William Olyver, another conservative. A report had gone to Cranmer that Buckenam 'will do mischief wherever he is . . .' and Cranmer himself wrote to Thomas Cromwell in the same year that Olyver 'is a man of little learning and ill qualities. He also preached against the King's cause [i.e. Henry VIII's divorce from Catherine of Aragon] and defended the authority of the bishop of Rome' – a judgement doubtless biassed.[50] But there were men of a different cast of mind in the community. In the same letter Cranmer added: 'There are in the house of Black Friars men of good study and learning'. Among those who subscribed the deed of surrender one John Scory went on to become chaplain to Cranmer and rather too Protestant for safety in Henry VIII's last years; but he survived to continue a chequered career in which he was at one time or another bishop of Rochester, Chichester and Hereford.[51] The last prior, Gregory Dodds, 'went on to become dean of Exeter and subscribed to the Thirty-Nine Articles'.[52] Thus the last generation of friars prepared for the coming of Emmanuel; and when John Scory died on 25 June 1585, the College was already a thriving community as large as the Black Friars had ever been.[53]

[49] Zutshi and Ombres 1990, p. 347. Buckenam subsequently fled to Scotland and Louvain (ibid. p. 345).
[50] Zutshi and Ombres 1990, pp. 346–7.
[51] Zutshi and Ombres 1990, pp. 348, 370 n.42; Shuckburgh 1904, p. 3. On Scory, see also DNB.
[52] Zutshi and Ombres 1990, p. 348.
[53] Shuckburgh 1904, pp. 4–5, reckons it comprised 80 persons by 1 July 1585.

2

The Foundation and Beginnings

The Ingoldsby Legend

It is almost mandatory to begin any historical account of Emmanuel College with that pleasant little fiction according to which the founder, charged by Queen Elizabeth I with having 'erected a puritan foundation', replied that he had merely set an acorn, and that God alone knew what would be the fruit thereof. The reader turns the page and soon comes upon the poet-bishop Richard Corbet's satirical verses about 'the pure house of Emmanuel'. We shall make a start with a fiction, or semi-fiction, of a different kind, planting in the mind of the reader the seed of an idea that the received history of Emmanuel may itself contain elements of fiction, one of those invented traditions. It will be an exercise in debunking, rather as if Lytton Strachey were to have written, not *Eminent Victorians*, but the history of our college.

The year is 1618, and Emmanuel, already one of the largest of Cambridge colleges and about to be absolutely the largest, a spreading oak tree indeed, is more than thirty years old. It is late on the evening of December 15th and a group of Emmanuel men, not rowdy undergraduates but B.A.s, are engaged in some serious drinking at the sign of the Red Lion in Petty Cury. There is plenty of drink on the table, and the revellers are buying rounds, engaging in the newly introduced Dutch custom of drinking healths, 'in a most luxurious bowsing and deboshed manner'. (Soon the town preacher of Ipswich would denounce 'that foolish and vicious custom of drinking healths'.[1]) Presently the junior proctor's deputy arrives to investigate this noisy little party, only to lay down his staff of office and join in. Later, he marches the whole company off to the vice-chancellor's prison, the Tolbooth, where he locks them up for the night.

There was more to this small riot than meets the eye, or so according to a piece of fiction in the archives, a bill of information exhibited by the

---

[1] Samuel Ward, *Woe to drunkards* (1622), p. 47.

attorney general in the Court of Star Chamber.[2] All the healths had been drunk by way of congratulation to a young man called William Ingoldsby. Emmanuel was about to elect to two vacant fellowships, and Ingoldsby had a letter in his pocket from no less a patron than King James I, a mandate which ought to have secured his election, regardless of his youth and lack of statutory qualifications. Ingoldsby had graduated in the previous summer, had not been seen in Cambridge since, was not a member of any college, but had sought election in more than one. In due course we shall hear more about Ingoldsby's ticket back to Cambridge, these royal mandates.

The Court of Star Chamber heard that young Ingoldsby had been the victim of a 'crafty, deceitful and ungodly device and invention'. Most of the fellowship were allegedly complicit, the intention being to keep Ingoldsby out, royal letter or no royal letter, and to secure the election of Samuel Hildersham, son of a well-known puritan minister and otherwise well qualified for a fellowship. Hildersham and one Richard Hunt were duly chosen between eleven and twelve o'clock on Thursday December 16th, which was the morning after the night before. (Whether Hildersham was subsequently a success, or popular, may be another story. Encouraging the elder William Sancroft to take on the mastership in 1628, a correspondent wrote: 'I pray conceal my desires towards the cause and your self from Mr Hildersham': who perhaps nursed ambitions of his own.[3])

The 'invention' of Hildersham's supporters in 1618 was to have a party call on him at the Red Lion, where he was lodged on his arrival from the Court at Newmarket, still booted and spurred, with his horse in the stable. Under the pretence of offering congratulations, the idea was to make him so drunk that he would finish the night in the lock-up and so miss the election, which, as part of the plot, the fellows had cunningly brought forward to the next morning. Michael Drake of St Catharine's, the vice-proctor, was a party to the conspiracy. 'With a palliated and masked show and pretence of a public going abroad', he entered the Red Lion with a little posse, armed with weapons 'as well invasive as defensive', to play his part in the charade. This was why he laid down his staff, 'purposing with a fresh supply to drive the said Ingoldsby

---

[2] PRO, STAC 8 28/2. The Star Chamber documents were digested in an article by H. S. Bennett, 'Election by Royal Mandate', *ECM*, 29 (1934–5), 81–90. By implication, I refer to Natalie Zemon Davis, *Fiction in the Archives* (Princeton, 1987), a seminal study in the historical postmodernism of facts turned into fictions.

[3] BL, MS Harl. 3783, fol. 11. Throughout the chapters which follow, I shall refer to the third master of the college as William Sancroft the elder, to distinguish him from the seventh master and archbishop of Canterbury, his nephew and namesake William Sancroft. My practice departs from the tradition of referring to the elder Sancroft in the earlier form of the name, Sandcroft, which some writers (e.g. Willis and Clark 1886 (1988)) use for the younger Sancroft.

into further distemper'. Only when the young man was judged to be 'sufficiently foxed' did Drake conduct him and the rest to the Tolbooth, keeping a firm grip of Ingoldsby's arm. All requests for bail were refused.

The night was still young. Although it was now four hours after his bedtime, Drake went to Emmanuel to report to the fellows (were they all roused from their beds?); then back to the Tolbooth for further conference with the conspirators, two of whom had been locked up with Ingoldsby for appearance sake. This called for another celebration. Fresh supplies were summoned up and more toasts drunk. Ingoldsby may have dropped off, but was 'nothing so far spent with drink' as were the others, hearing and understanding everything, which was how it was that Drake, Hildersham and others found themselves co-defendants in Star Chamber, charged with having treated a royal letter with contempt. By now, insult had been added to injury. The conspirators were further charged with having bragged about their exploit, not only in various hostelries but in public orations and declamations in the schools of the university.

Earlier proceedings in the vice-chancellor's own court,[4] undertaken on Ingoldsby's formal complaint (he had been 'very much wronged'), suggest that this story had improved with the telling. Ingoldsby had sued only after the Red Lion affair had been alluded to in the logic schools by one individual, albeit 'after a disgraceful, abusive and scoffing manner'. Already the evidence begins to shrink before our eyes into proportion. This was what the vice-chancellor might have made of the whole business, as he tried to sort out much conflicting evidence. Dr John Preston of Queens', who would become master of Emmanuel a little after these events, a leading puritan divine and courtier with some well-connected pupils, had heard from one of these pupils about goings-on at Newmarket and about Ingoldsby's mandate, a rumour which he passed on 'occasionally' and 'accidentally' as a piece of gossip to Samuel Hildersham who, as we know, was an interested party. 'I hear that Sir Ingoldsby endeavoureth to get a mandate for Emmanuel College...' According to the Ingoldsby camp, the master and fellows, 'or some of them', now plotted to frustrate Ingoldsby's ambition. But all eleven fellows, including Hildersham and Hunt, the two elected on December 16th, would later testify that they had received no information from Preston.

Enter the actors, the 'three bachelors' John Browne, Nathaniel Fowle and Francis Rivett, all of Emmanuel, and Mr Drake of St Catharine's, late of Emmanuel. Browne and Ingoldsby were both from Lincolnshire and bosom pals as undergraduates. So at one level this was a prank between friends, and it was Browne who laughed loudest and longest over its

---

4 CUL, MS V.C.Ct.III 23, fols. 190–212(vi). I owe this reference to the kindness of Dr Alex Shepard.

success. Fowle's part was to rouse Drake, telling him that there was trouble at the Red Lion and that there was a wager. If he told him more than that, it was as they made their way to Petty Cury, Drake having alerted the junior proctor and borrowed his staff, the proctor promising that 'he would follow after'.

The barmen at the Red Lion and Mr Slegg the jailor and his assistants take up the story. There does not seem to have been an orgy as such: only beer and tobacco in the public bar, followed by a quart of sack in Ingoldsby's chamber, and then another round of pints when Drake arrived. Witnesses were unable to agree on the extent of Ingoldsby's inebriation by the time he reached the Tolbooth, which was no grim dungeon but 'Clegg's college', more like an after-hours club than a prison, where Slegg and his wife made up a bed for Ingoldsby. Slegg's offsider denied that Ingoldsby was drunk, and said that all the young men behaved 'very sensible'. As for the fellows of Emmanuel, they stood to their side of the story. The election had proceeded regularly, according to statute. If Ingoldsby really had a mandate, he could have produced it before or after his night on the town.

This may not have been the whole story. The role of Preston, a great fixer, looks suspicious, as does the circumstance that Preston was in touch with John Cotton, the soon-to-be-famous preacher at Boston in Lincolnshire (Ingoldsby's country) and at another Boston, putting pressure on Ingoldsby to back off from an affair which, said Preston, was 'very inordinate'. Improbable though it may seem, this unsavoury affair had something to do with the machinations of that 'godly' spider's web whose hub was Emmanuel.

The fact that such a tale could be told about Emmanuel, indeed by Emmanuel, may offset the story of the acorn and the oak and so prepare the reader for a college history which will contain its full share of what Marxists used to call internal contradictions. Many of those contradictions represented the frustration of the founder's intentions, as expressed in his statutes for the college, while others arose from the perverse contents of the statutes themselves. It is reasonably clear what those statutes intended, but how far Sir Walter Mildmay's aspirations were to be fulfilled is something which, as he told Queen Elizabeth, only God was in a position to know, but which these pages will seek to decipher. But, first, to the founder himself.

Wait a moment, the reader may ask. What happened to those conspirators of 1618? Well, Ingoldsby became a country clergyman. Nathaniel Fowle made it into an Emmanuel fellowship in 1621 and became rector of St Ives in Cornwall, where he died young in 1630. Michael Drake, though a fellow of St Catharine's at the time of these events, was really an Emmanuel man, one of the same year as the 'three bachelors'. Poor Drake was buried at St Botolph's in April 1622, when he cannot have been much more than twenty-five. To quote the title of a radio series, he had been famous for five minutes.[5]

The Founder[1]

Six weeks after Queen Elizabeth came to the throne in November 1558, Sir Walter Mildmay was made Chancellor of the Exchequer (not quite equivalent to the modern office of that name), and he was to remain Chancellor for the last thirty of almost fifty years of uninterrupted public service. From 1566 until his death in 1589, he was also a Privy Councillor, like his brother-in-law, the Secretary of State Sir Francis Walsingham, a permanent lynchpin of the remarkably cohesive and stable government which England enjoyed in the middle decades of Elizabeth's reign. It was a solid rather than glittering or ambitious career. According to his daughter-in-law, he deliberately evaded higher promotions.[2] But under the Lord Treasurership of the grandees, the Marquis of Winchester and Lord Burghley, there is no doubt that it was Mildmay who effectively ran the Elizabethan Exchequer. His tomb in the great church of his London parish, St Bartholomew the Great, at once austere and ornate (no funeral effigy, but plastered with somewhat spurious heraldry and exquisite in a kind of Stoic high Renaissance taste: see Plate 13), measures the distance travelled by this son of a Chelmsford shopkeeper who had been born across the street from the smelly fish market of that modest market town, and who died in his stately Northamptonshire home of Apethorpe. Towards the end, and at the age of sixty-four, Mildmay founded Emmanuel College. No amount of gratitude for his noble foundation should inhibit his beneficiaries from asking why.

William Paulet, marquis of Winchester, under whose long shadow Mildmay's career had prospered (Winchester nominated him for the office of Chancellor) had contrived to remain Lord Treasurer for forty-two years, surviving four changes of government and two of religion. Winchester put this down to his ability to bend with the winds of change, more willow than oak.[3] To persist with this sylvan metaphor, Mildmay was both willow and oak. Unlike Winchester, he was a deeply convinced, unbending Protestant, so unbending that posterity has regarded him as a member of that more defined and extreme species, a Puritan. His

---

[5] Venn, Part I, II, 448, 167, 64.

[1] This account of Mildmay is naturally much indebted to the only modern full-length study, Lehmberg 1964. All information derives from Lehmberg unless otherwise indicated.

[2] Pollock 1993, pp. 31–2.

[3] Sir Robert Naunton reported his elegant humanistic *impresa*: 'Ortus sum ex salice, non ex quercu.' (*Fragmenta Regalia* (1641), p. 12).

personal archive is stuffed with rare and important papers relating to the
aspirations and trials of Elizabethan clergymen who certainly were
Puritans, if that name means anything;[4] as well as documents of the
adversarial dealings of Archbishop John Whitgift with groups of 'godly
ministers', and of successive parliamentary campaigns for 'further
reformation', with which Mildmay was closely connected.[5]

And yet this was the Privy Councillor who was obliged to summarise
the queen's case against Whitgift's almost puritan predecessor, Archbishop Grindal (they had briefly shared the same college at Cambridge),
after Grindal had resisted a royal demand that he suppress the preaching
conferences called 'prophesyings'.[6] It was the same Mildmay who in 1587
roundly denounced the lunatic fringery of a radical presbyterian measure
which had somehow found its way onto the floor of the House of
Commons, backed by men with whom he privately sympathised;[7] and
who in the same year prosecuted William Davison (whose son was an
undergraduate at Emmanuel at the time), the scapegoat for Elizabeth's
displeasure at the execution of Mary Queen of Scots.[8] This was the
queen's good servant, but not an uncritical servant, nor, as we might say,
his own man so much as a man who lived to serve the commonwealth. It
was this same Mildmay who opposed plans for any royal marriage which
might threaten the protestant settlement, and whose concern for the
safety of the state seems to have transcended his personal devotion to a
monarch whose lifespan inevitably had a term placed upon it.[9] When the
French duke of Alençon courted Elizabeth in 1573, Mildmay did not
mince his words in detailing the suitor's qualities: 'His fame fraud, . . .
ignorance of God, papistry, looseness of God, papistry, looseness of life';
son of 'a most subtile Italian [Queen Catherine de Medici], having no fear
of God.' When the French prince (now styled Anjou) renewed the suit in
1578, Mildmay spoke publicly, in the Privy Council, of 'the offence to
God' if the queen, 'being patroness of the Gospel' should be 'coupled
with a papist'; and of the evident risk that she would lose the goodwill of
her subjects.[10] For words hardly as strong as these, Sir Philip Sidney was
to forfeit his political career.

---

[4] Northamptonshire Record Office, Fitzwilliam of Milton Papers, F.(M).P.55a, 62, 139. I am
grateful to the Trustees of the Fitzwilliam of Milton estate for permission to cite these
documents.

[5] Ibid., F.(M).P. 53, 63, 193: papers relating to, to quote Mildmay's description of one of
them, 'matters touchinge the Archbishop of Caunterburye and the Ministers', and
resembling the materials gathered by the ministers themselves in *The Seconde Parte of a
Register*, ed. A. Peel, 2 vols. (Cambridge, 1915); ibid., F.(M).P. 5, 60, 148, 162.

[6] Ibid., F.(M).P. 70, 70a, 70b, 70c; Lehmberg 1964, pp. 147–53; Collinson 1979, pp. 233–65.

[7] Collinson 1967, pp. 303–13; Neale 1957, pp. 148–64, esp. 161.

[8] Lehmberg 1964, pp. 278–81; Ibish 1985, pp. 397–8.

[9] Collinson 1994a.

[10] Northamptonshire Record Office, F.(M).P.11. This is a paper book with a title (in

A godly man indeed! His papers contain some verses of scriptural paraphrase, perhaps his own composition:

> The woorde of god ys lyvely ever
> in workinge mighty and more clever
> Then any sworde too edges beringe . . .[11]

Mildmay's daughter-in-law, Lady Grace (the earliest English woman diarist), recorded an unqualified eulogy of the private and public life of the man who had chosen her to marry his son, whether he liked it or not. She was ready to forgive even the distressing fact that Sir Walter for many years had kept the young couple on a very short financial shoestring.[12]

The key to those religious and educational aspirations which Sir Walter Mildmay sank in his foundation of Emmanuel is to be found in his own Cambridge college, Christ's. Here he had spent a couple of years in the late 1530s, before leaving without a degree (common enough) to join his older and already successful brother Thomas in that part of the newly reconstructed royal bureaucracy which was charged with the administration of the dissolved monastic properties now coming into the hands of the Crown (including the house of the Dominican friars in Cambridge): the Court of Augmentations. Although it is likely that Mildmay was converted to his ardent Protestantism at Cambridge, the Reformation had hardly begun to bite in his time and it was more than twenty years later that Christ's became a forcing ground of evangelical religion. This development was by no means inconsistent with the original intentions of its founders, Bishop St John Fisher and his patron Lady Margaret Beaufort, although they would have deplored the sour, protestant grapes which their vineyard yielded.[13] By the same token, the history of the site of Emmanuel, before and after its foundation, was not wholly discontinuous. The site, after all, had long stood on 'Preachers' Street'. The Reformation was as much a fulfilment as a denial of pre-Reformation religious values.

In the first decade of Elizabeth's reign, Christ's, or several of its fellows, became committed to the nurture of what Elizabethan Protestants called 'the godly preaching ministry', with a special emphasis on 'godly'.[14] Insofar as we may regard it as a puritan college (and such was its

---

Mildmay's hand): 'Discoorses of hir Ma[jesty']s marryag and succession'. See also Mildmay's copies of papers relating to a critical moment in the reign, the perceived threat to the queen's safety in 1584–5, the Bond of Association and the scheme for an interregnum. (Ibid., F.(M).P. 96, 155, 184.)

[11] Ibid., F.(M).P.7.
[12] Pollock 1993, pp. 31–42.
[13] Porter 1958, p. 3.
[14] Ibid., *passim*; Collinson 1967, pp. 124–8; Morgan 1986 *passim*.

reputation for forty or fifty years) the Puritanism of Christ's was a resolve to convert all England to the protestant Gospel through first converting its clergy into a new order of preachers. John More, later known as 'The Apostle of Norwich', who took his B.A. from Christ's in 1562, told a congregation of Norfolk country gentlemen and justices: 'But alas, I cannot preach to the whole land.' 'Wherefore (good brethren) if ye will be saved, get you preachers in your parishes, ... bestow your labour, cost and travail to get them. Ride for them, run for them, stretch your purses to maintain them. We shall begin to be rich in the Lord Jesus.'[15] 'Without this preaching of the word we can never have faith', proclaimed a best-selling catechism written by More in collaboration with another Christ's man, Edward Dering, who graduated in 1560 and held a fellowship through the sixties.[16]

Dering was the pattern and paragon of Elizabethan Puritanism, more concerned with the main chance of preaching to the unconverted than with ceremonies and church order, but a doughty enemy of these and any other church ordinances, institutions and abuses, insofar as they frustrated that cause. Towards 1570, he threw away the prospect of an ecclesiastical career by playing the role of Nathan the Prophet to the three notables upon whom his preferment depended: Mr Secretary Cecil (later Lord Burghley), Archbishop Parker and Queen Elizabeth. What was left to Dering was a magnetic London pulpit, more trouble with the authorities, and an early and consumptive death. But when he told Cecil 'I have never broken the peace of the Church neither for cap nor surplice, for archbishop nor bishop', he placed pragmatic, pastoral limits on the puritan conscience which the first master of Emmanuel Laurence Chaderton, himself for some years a fellow and tutor at Christ's, would make the special hallmark of Mildmay's foundation.

Mildmay no doubt knew and approved of the evangelical reputation of his old college. In 1569 he made a generous gift to Christ's of rents worth £20 a year, with which to found not only the stipend of a preacher and six scholarships but a lectureship in Greek. For 'godly learning' was not only godly. It was also learning. Mildmay's gifts to the college included a small library of Greek and Latin texts, including copies of Aristotle and Plutarch in Greek which survive to this day, and which bear his signature.[17]

So, to repeat our question, why Emmanuel, rather than the further enrichment of Christ's? Mildmay's colleague Lord Burghley was so dedicated over a long lifetime to his own *alma mater*, St John's, that it is hard to imagine him setting up a rival show. There is no single, simple answer. Emmanuel was not created in opposition to Christ's, or even in rivalry. Its

[15] Collinson 1983, pp. 296–8.
[16] Patrick Collinson, 'A Mirror of Elizabethan Puritanism: The Life and Letters of "Godly Master Dering"', Collinson 1983, pp. 288–324.
[17] Lehmberg 1964, pp. 222–3; Peile 1910–13, p. 24.

statutes were modelled on those of the older foundation, its first master had his roots in the college, and what modern university administrators would call the 'aims and objectives' of Emmanuel were similar, if accentuated. The answer, for public consumption, may be that Mildmay wanted a super-Christ's, where nothing would interfere with the role of the college as seminary. There is evidence that Mildmay lacked confidence in a new master of Christ's, elected a year before the decision was taken to found Emmanuel.[18] Indeed, it had always been the fellows of Christ's, not its successive masters, who had created and guarded its godly reputation. The need for a preaching ministry had never seemed more urgent than it did in 1583–4, with the forces of the Counter-Reformation gathering against protestant England and an archbishop in charge of the destiny of the Church of England who set more store by conformity than 'godliness'. This was a matter touching the security of the state as much as the needs of the soul. But privately we may also suspect that the foundation was all of a piece with that armorial tomb in St Bartholomew's, and with the vanity of Mildmay's quest for a thoroughly bogus noble ancestry, in the very year that the plans for Emmanuel were laid on the table.[19] An old man was contemplating the future, his posterity. He wished to be remembered, not in the old-fashioned and popish way, with masses and months' minds and obits; merely remembered – but not by name.

Like some other Elizabethan founders and benefactors (including his neighbour in St Bartholomew's, the judge Sir Roger Manwood[20]), Mildmay was content, and shrewd enough, to play the part of *primus inter pares* in his foundation. He enlisted the support and opened the purses of several of his colleagues in government, as well as the encouragement of the godly mafia which, by the 1580s, had infiltrated the upper reaches of metropolitan society, the interconnected worlds of politics, the law and the city. To one such hoped-for benefactor, Mildmay wrote: 'Sir, being informed of your godly disposition and intent to bestow some portion of land for the maintenance of scholars in the university: I am bold to move you, that your good purpose therein may be employed upon a poor college lately erected in Cambridge called Emmanuel College . . .'[21] An essential part in this strategy was played by the wealthy merchant banker Richard Culverwell, the leading figure in a potent and

[18] Shuckburgh 1904, p. 26; Porter 1958, p. 236.
[19] Lehmberg 1964, pp. 3–4.
[20] Manwood founded the grammar school at Sandwich, Kent, by augmenting his own endowment with the voluntary subscriptions of the townspeople, thus limiting his outlay but securing his name for the school (Jordan 1961, pp. 78–9).
[21] Mildmay to 'Mr Covert', BL, MS Harl. 703, fol. 17v. We owe this reference to Ibish 1895, pp. 52–3. The date is likely to have been 8 March 1584(/5), not 1584, as Ibish suggests. Mr Covert was Walter Covert of Slaugham Sussex (*c.* 1549–1631), a long-serving M.P. and a man of some substance. (Hasler 1981, I, pp. 665–6.) See below, pp. 102–3.

conspicuously godly clan with Christ's connections, uncle by marriage of both Chaderton and the ranking English Calvinist divine, William Whitaker.[22] It was Culverwell who put up most of the capital which secured the site and remaining buildings of the Dominican Friary.[23] Further details of this collaborative work of benefaction will be found in Sarah Bendall's first chapter.[24]

But we may bring this section to an end with a little essay on the name 'Emmanuel'. This was presumably Mildmay's personal choice and not the decision of a committee. It is a remarkable fact, and one that we should not overlook, that while Cambridge has a Sidney Sussex College and, for that matter, a Robinson College, there is no Mildmay College. Generations of Commentators, with a vague memory of Shakespeare in their heads,[25] have seen in the name a kind of puritan talisman, proof of the college's embarrassingly sectarian origins. True enough, and it may be significant, when the extreme puritan activist John Field (well known to Richard Culverwell) wrote to the martyrologist John Foxe or to the famous divine Anthony Gilby at Ashby-de-la-Zouch in Leicestershire in the early 1570s, he invariably began his letters with the pious motto 'Immanuell'.[26] Ashby-de-la-Zouch was the seat of Henry Hastings, 3rd earl of Huntingdon, Gilby's patron, who endowed Emmanuel with four livings. And from Ashby came both Gilby's son Nathaniel, first to Christ's and then to a fellowship at Emmanuel, and his illustrious pupil, Joseph Hall. But the president of Magdalen College Oxford, an early example of the 'establishment' puritan type, also headed his letters to 'Father Gilby' 'Immanuel',[27] and the practice was not necessarily deeply sectarian, although it may have been idiosyncratic and personal. Most of the letters from the Emmanuel tutor Elias Travers to the grandmother of his pupil, Thomas Knyvett, dated 1612–13, are headed 'Immanuel', and also, occasionally, 'Grace and peace'.[28] As late as 1658, a Latin letter

---

[22] I am indebted to Brett Usher for allowing me to consult an unpublished work, 'The Culverwells 1550–1630'. See also Usher's account of the worldly, ostentatious godliness of the Culverwells: Usher 1992. The Culverwells were linked in cousinage with Mildmay, and Sir Francis Walsingham. Usher describes them as 'the major financial force behind the Puritan campaigns' of Elizabeth's reign.

[23] Willis and Clark 1886, II, pp. 687–8.

[24] And in Ibish 1985, chapter II 'Benefactors 1584–1624'.

[25] See *Henry VI*, pt 1, 4, 2, 95–7: 'Cade: What is your name? / Clerk of Chatham: Emmanuel. / Dick the Butcher: They used to write it on top of letters: 'twill go hard with you'.

[26] BL, MS Harl. 416, fol. 185r; CUL. MS Mm.1.43, pp. 442, 444, 447.

[27] Ibid., p. 427. John Ireton, a fellow of Christ's later to be beneficed in Leicestershire, wrote to Gilby about the placement of his son in the college and headed his letter 'Grace and Peace'. (Ibid., pp. 437–8.) For the Hastings connection with Emmanuel, see Ibish 1985, pp. 78–83.

[28] BL, MS Egerton 2715, fols. 137–83. I owe my knowledge of the Travers-Knyvett correspondence to the late Jeremy Maule. Among John Foxe's correspondence are letters headed 'Grace and peace from God the father etc.', and 'Jesus'. A letter from John Knox of 18 May 1558 is headed 'The mighty comfort of the Holy Ghost for salvation'. (BL, MS Harl. 416, fols. 208r, 210r, 70r.)

from one Justus Dozen of Amsterdam to Samuel Hartlib was headed 'Emmanuel'.[29]

The Statutes[1]

In 1662 William Sancroft, the future archbishop of Canterbury, was elected to the mastership of Emmanuel. Since he had been effectively appointed by the Crown, it was an offer hard to refuse. And yet Sancroft hesitated. 'There are many things that discourage me . . . The statutes are very odd and strict in point of residence, and otherwise.'[2] What 'discouraged' Sancroft and in what ways were the Statutes of Emmanuel College perceived to be 'odd'? What did 'otherwise' mean?

We may listen, momentarily, to the well-informed but prejudiced voice of the learned eighteenth-century annalist of the college, William Bennet, tutor of Emmanuel and later bishop of Cloyne: 'The truth of the matter is, that our Founder being an Enemy to some part of the doctrine and discipline of the English Church, intended his College as a nursery for what we now call the Presbyterians. This is the key to all our statutes'; and there followed a list of particular if, in Bennet's jaundiced perception, connected grievances.[3]

Bennet makes one expostulate and insist that the founder, whatever he was, was not a Presbyterian, and to beg the bishop of Cloyne to slow down a little so that we can sort out the rights and the wrongs of Mildmay's statutes. We may begin with Sancroft's complaint about residence. This refers to Statute 2 'Of the residence of the master', but also to Statute 26, which regulated the absences of fellows. The master could not be absent from the college for more than a month each quarter without *ipso facto* suffering deprivation. Fellows, except for some urgent cause, were not to be away for more than twenty days in the year. These statutes were not so very odd, and they followed the equivalent provisions for Christ's pretty closely. But whereas at Christ's a fellow enjoying a certain income from some other source forfeited his stipend, at Emmanuel he ceased to be a fellow: a critical and characteristic difference.[4]

---

[29] Justus Dozen to Samuel Hartlib, 10 May 1658; Sheffield University Library, Hartlib Papers 49/6/1.

[1] It goes without saying that this section is heavily indebted to Frank Stubbings' edition of *The Statutes of Sir Walter Mildmay for Emmanuel College* (Cambridge, 1983), to his *glosses* and *scholia* no less than to the text.

[2] Bodleian Library, MS Tanner 48, fol. 52. For Sancroft's abortive attempts at reform, or amelioration, of the statutes, see pp. 28–9, 266–70 below. In 1663 he thought that without such a reform 'we are remediless'. (ECA, COL.9.1(A), pp. 222–3.)

[3] ECA, COL.9.1(B), Bennet's 'Register', no. 2. On Bennet, see below, pp. 302–4.

[4] Stubbings 1983a, p. 64.

These statutes were meant to make it impossible to combine senior membership of the college with preferment in the Church at large; difficult even to put oneself in the way of preferment by serving as some nobleman's chaplain or otherwise coming to public attention. And here was the rub, since it was the founder's intention that Emmanuel men should not enjoy what is now called an academic career but should, after perhaps seventeen or eighteen years in the university, make themselves useful in the pastoral ministry of the wider Church. It was as if a girl (or rather a no longer very young woman in her early thirties) should be told both that she must marry, since there would soon be no place for her at home, but that in the meantime she must on no account go out for the evening with the prospect of meeting a husband. Hence some of Sancroft's misgivings. When he was given the mastership, a post worth a paltry £30 a year, he was already dean of York and a prebendary of Durham, rich preferments both. At Christ's there would have been no difficulty. But with Emmanuel Sancroft found himself in the awkward position of the Rich Young Ruler, rescued only by the royal power of dispensing from statute. The rub of rubs was the extraordinary, supplementary statute *De mora sociorum*, 'Of the tarrying in the College of the Fellows, and of their proceeding to the degree of Doctor of Divinity': which while no longer in force after 1660 left a bitter taste in Bishop Bennet's mouth.[5] To this particular sour grape we shall return.

But first we should take stock of the main body of the statutes, to get the measure of the founder's intentions. The Preface makes clear that Mildmay had no interest in providing for what the sixteenth century called the 'mere scholar'. It speaks in biblical language of 'the sons of the prophets', and of 'seed-plots' of theology and 'right good learning', from which those grown to maturity might be 'transplanted to all parts of the Church'. Statute 21 declares, in the audible tones of the founder:

> In establishing this College we have set before us this one aim, of rendering as many persons as possible fit for the sacred ministry of the Word and the Sacraments; so that from this seminary the Church of England [not, we may notice, some sect within, let alone outside, the Church of England] might have men whom it may call forth to instruct the people and undertake the duty of pastors (a matter of all things most necessary).

This was fundamental. Anyone entering the college for any other purpose than to study Theology 'and in due time to labour in preaching the Word' rendered Mildmay's hope 'vain', enjoying the place of scholar or fellow 'contrary to our institution'. All fellows at their inception took an oath to ensure, collectively, that no member of the society should remove

[5] ECA, COL.9.1(B), pp. 38–9.

to any other faculty than that of Theology (Statute 19).

Sancroft, who as master elect had contemplated the 'oddness' of the statutes, wrote when in post: 'Our over rigorous statutes pinch us.'[6] Indeed, they seem to define a pinching seminary of a strict and Tridentine variety rather than any Oxbridge college which we should recognise. Pupils were to be 'always occupied, so far as they may be, either in the worship of God, or in the study of good learning, or in the cultivation of distinguished manners', distinguished, that is, for modesty of countenance, deportment and apparel (Statute 34). There was to be no idleness, no meeting in rooms for play, feasting, or even 'conversation', and to enforce this rule the fellows in pairs were to visit and inspect the chambers of undergraduates at least twice a week (Statute 28). Mildmay's statutes were in advance of those of any other college in formalising the tutorial system. Tutors were responsible for the 'morals and diligence' of their pupils, who were to sleep in their chambers and never to go into town without tutorial consent, except to lectures and other academic exercises (Statute 27).[7] Scholars were permitted no more than twenty days' absence a year (increased to nine weeks in 1598) with no provision (unlike Christ's) for a Christmas holiday. They were to dress uniformly in clothing provided, in a 'set colour' (Statute 36).[8] 'In criminal matters', there was a novel provision for the expulsion of both fellows and scholars (Statute 3). The life of fellows living strictly by the book would have been Spartan indeed, if their annual stipends were no more than thirty shillings, half the wages fixed at Christ's at the other end of the sixteenth century, before the so-called 'price revolution' of the intervening decades.[9]

The sterner features of Mildmay's intended regime were doubtless hard to enforce; especially since, as we shall see, the college would rapidly take shape not so much as a seminary as a kind of finishing school for the sons of the godly aristocracy, whose personal godliness

---

6   ECA, COL.9.1(A), pp. 222–3. In the context of this letter, it was the financial pinch which most concerned Sancroft.

7   For the rise of the tutorial system, the essence of the pedagogical regime in collegiate Cambridge, see Cobban 1969, pp. 66–85 and other studies cited in Brooke, Highfield and Swaan 1988, p. 139 n. 60.

8   Stubbings 1983a, p. 79. At Christ's it was the fellows who were to spend their clothing allowance at Stourbridge Fair on cloth of a single colour, 'so that all may go attired alike when the honour of the College demands it.' (Ibid., p. 63.)

9   Statute 23 states that each fellow should 'each year at the customary times receive as his stipend thirty shillings' and Stubbings 1983a (p. 63) assumed that this indicates the whole amount of the annual stipend. But 'customary times' suggests half-yearly or quarterly payments of £3 or £6 yearly. In 1630 fellows seem to have received £4.16s annually. (ECA, BUR.8.2, 20 April 1630.) Even at that rate, they were hardly over-paid. In 1663 Sancroft wrote of the 'statutable allowance' being 'so miserably scant'. He thought it impossible for the college ever to flourish again unless fellowships and scholarships were made 'competent', and supplemented with liberal allowances. (ECA, COL.9.1(A), pp. 222–3.)

could not always be guaranteed. And the sharp edges of discipline may have become rounded with the passage of time. What later generations of college statesmen and barrack room lawyers objected to was less all this than those 'presbyterian' features of the foundation which affected the seniority in its conduct of college business and prospects beyond the university.

Statute 19 was one of those presbyterian measures in Bennet's book. Whereas heads of houses in Tudor and Stuart Cambridge were bishops in embryo, ruling in their colleges as monarchs, the master of Emmanuel was most explicitly denied a negative voice in college business – that is, a veto – and especially in the election of fellows. And fellows were bound by oath to an unusual measure of secrecy (Statute 19). This was a recipe for 'faction'. Still more troublesome were arrangements to ensure that the whole of God's vineyard should be evenly refreshed from this seed-bed. Although some preference was given to the founder's native and adoptive counties of Essex and Northampton, at any one time no single county was to be represented by more than one fellow or three scholars (Statutes 17 and 32). Bennet called these provisions 'most unfortunate', since they obliged the college to prefer the unworthy to the worthy, while in the seventeenth century Benjamin Whichcote had equally complained that Statute 17 favoured the undeserving, or threatened to leave fellowships vacant.[10]

And what about the apportionment of college livings, the readiest means for fellows to comply with the founder's will that they deploy themselves in the Lord's vineyard when fully qualified? Human nature would suggest the sovereignty of Buggins's turn, the law of seniority. And so it often was, but only by turning a half-blind eye to Statute 38, which required the choice of the man 'best endowed with those gifts which the Holy Spirit bestows upon the true pastor'; who might or might not be one and the same as the senior fellow. Bennet reported that in the seventeenth century (as we should expect) this had played into the hands of 'party', so that after 1688, as in all other colleges, the principle of seniority obtained.[11]

And so back to *De mora sociorum*, which stored up more trouble for the future than all the other statutes put together. The story may be tedious to the modern reader, but earlier generations would not forgive us if this thorny issue were not to figure prominently in the annals of Emmanuel.

[10] ECA, COL.9.1(B), pp. 2, 32; COL.9.1(A), p. 79.
[11] ECA, COL.9.1(B), p. 33. As early as 1616, a Kentish gentleman and *alumnus* was inclined to grant the college the right of next presentation to his living of West Wickham, but troubled by reports that it was customary to bestow the next available benefice on the most senior fellow. Chaderton's means of reassuring his correspondent was to tell him that he had the ideal man for the job, William Sancroft (the elder), the future master. (Ibid., pp. 67–8.)

'Seeing that we have founded our College to the intent that it might be by the grace of God a seminary of learned men', and since over-long residence in the university was 'useless', *De mora* requires the fellows to proceed as soon as the statutes of the university permit to the degree of Doctor of Divinity (ten years from commencing M.A.); and that one year after that 'they shall permanently cease to be Fellows', having no further claim on the college beyond, on various conditions, a preferential right to any of the college livings which might conveniently happen to lie vacant.

'The truth is', reflected Bennet, reviewing the chequered history of the founder's 'afterthought', 'the Plan of a Presbyterian Seminary would have been incomplete without it.' Bennet shed tears over the fate imposed on poor men 'who had spent the flower of their lives in the service of the College', who must have been poor or they never could have become fellows, and whose strict terms of residence having cut them off from all connection with the outside world, were to be 'turned out to starve with the title of Doctor'.[12]

If Bennet overdid the personal tragedies which *De mora* entailed, he would have been hard put to have exaggerated its contentiousness. It was first challenged in 1595, when the senior fellow, Charles Chadwick (an M.A. for twelve years but as yet no Doctor) tried to hang on to his place on the ground that the statute was of doubtful validity, an argument to be used again and again in future years. But Chadwick lost his appeal and left the college, forced to wait six years in the wilderness for his Essex living.[13]

In 1627 the fellows formally petitioned Charles I for relief from this 'very hard' statute, 'a grievance to our society', questioning its validity and pointing out that Sidney Sussex had already succeeded in getting rid of a similar statute, derivative from the Emmanuel statutes. This démarche was well timed. The chancellor of the university was now the duke of Buckingham, an old patron of Emmanuel's politically well-connected master, John Preston. On reference to the vice-chancellor and heads, there followed a series of meetings. After the first, the vice-chancellor, Dr Smyth of Magdalene, drafted a letter which went against the petitioning fellows. Smyth had been impressed by testimony from the aged and now retired Laurence Chaderton, who recalled that the founder had written

---

[12] Ibid., pp. 38–9.

[13] Bennet's 'Some account of the disputes relative to the Statute at Emmanuel entitled de Mora Sociorum', ECA, COL.9.1(A), pp. 200–9; Cambridge University Library, MS Mm.1.38 (Baker 27), no. 4, pp. 60–71. Bennet suggests that during the lifetime of the founder, 'decency' had prevented a challenge to the statute. Chadwick was hardly consistent. Eight years earlier, he had been prosecuted in the vice-chancellor's court for an intemperate sermon in which he had denounced those living in the university on the proceeds of benefices, and especially heads of houses, as murderers of thousands of souls. (Cambridge University Library, MS Add. 10, no. 94.) For Chadwick's C.V., see Ibish 1985, pp. 381–2.

the statute himself, and with particular care, often telling Chaderton 'that he had rather not have founded the College than have omitted this statute.' Meanwhile, the founder's grandson, Sir Henry Mildmay, said to have been 'violently opposed' to the change, offered to reduce the risk of doctoral starvation with five or six additional and 'competent' benefices. But two days later the argument swung the other way, the heads perhaps outvoting the vice-chancellor, and it was decided that the pastoral condition of the Church had so far improved that the statute was now doing more harm than good. The king responded by suspending *De mora*, while promising to revoke his suspension within six years if Mildmay proved to be as good as his word.[14] Presently the master (by now William Sancroft the elder) and six of the fellows petitioned the chancellor (now the earl of Holland) against the suspension, claiming that the statute had almost never resulted in the involuntary termination of a fellowship, whereas its suspension was liable to clog the wheels of internal academic preferment, and lay behind certain recent 'disturbances' of the peace of the college.[15] Perhaps, in the political climate of the 1630s, there was a sub-text: an objection to the royal suspending power itself. But in the event, Sir Henry failed to come up to scratch and *De mora* remained suspended until the early 1640s, when, with everything in a state of revolutionary flux, the founder's kin petitioned Parliament for its restitution, it appears successfully.[16] *De mora* was by now a piece of political ballast.

It is assumed that the statute simply lapsed with the Restoration. But it

---

[14] Petition from the fellows of Emmanuel, undated, Cambridge University Library, MS. Add. 22, fol. 15v; Henry Smyth to chancellor, undated, ibid., fol. 16r; Chaderton's 'reasons', 14 April 1627, ibid., fol. 26r; the heads to the chancellor, 16 April 1627, Cambridge University Library, MS Mm.1.38, p. 67; Charles I to the vice-chancellor and heads, 5 May 1627, ibid., p. 69. The politics of all this are hard to fathom. Shuckburgh 1904 (p. 64) thinks that the vice-chancellor and heads may have changed their tune on receiving a hint from Buckingham. But Ball 1677 (quoted by Shuckburgh, p. 66) reports that Preston was vehemently opposed to the relaxation of the statute. In 1627 Chancellor Buckingham and Master Preston no longer saw eye to eye on many matters. The apparent interest of the king, Buckingham and Bishop Matthew Wren (see above, p. 220) in suspending the statute suggests that Bennet was not wrong to suggest that *De mora* was *perceived* to be a piece of Puritanism. A letter from Sir Henry Mildmay to William Sancroft, the master, contains further evidence of the strength of his opposition to the suspension, and of his conviction that even a royal letter had less force than a statute which the fellows had sworn to observe. (Mildmay (to Sancroft), 30 Jan. 1629, BL, MS Harl. 3783, fol. 17.)

[15] Bennet's copy of the petition, which he dated 'about 1630', in ECA, COL.9.1(A), pp. 80–1. The six petitioning fellows were Anthony Tuckney (a future master), Thomas Hill, William Bridge, Samuel Bowles, David Ensign and Anthony Burgess. Bennet connected this episode with evidence in a letter from Tuckney to Sancroft of unhappiness in the society under Sancroft's government. (See pp. 220, 223 below.)

[16] Stubbings 1983a p. 98; Twigg 1990, pp. 55–6, whose account of transactions in 1640–2 suggests that the reinstatement of *De mora sociorum* may have been less tidy and conclusive than Stubbings (and Shuckburgh) suggest.

may not have been as simple as that. Sancroft's reflections on the matter in 1663 deserve quoting in full:

> I am clearly convinced of what you wisely and solidly suggest [Sancroft was writing to his old tutor, Ezekiel Wright] concerning the intended Statute (for truly I cannot look upon it as of the same authority with the rest) De mora sociorum. Something I had done in it before you wrote. The Kings suspension of it for ought I can learn is lost during these late times, you will easily guess how. But I have recovered both the first draft of it under my Lord of Elies [i.e., Bishop Matthew Wren's] own hand (whom the King appointed to pen it) and a Copie of it which I found among my Uncle Sancrofts papers. If I cannot enquire out the original, I will if I live get it to pass the seal once more, to facilitate which design I desire, sir, you would furnish me with your Copie, if you have one, and what memories besides you have concerning the whole affair.[17]

What, the reader may ask, if the master and fellows were to fall out among themselves irreparably, or if they failed to agree on the terms of such awkward statutes? Who, for that matter, with Mildmay dead and gone, apart from his kin, was to ensure that they were duly observed? Was there no provision for an external visitor? There was none. However, Statute 41 provided a mechanism for interpreting 'ambiguities and obscurities', by appeal to the master of Christ's and the two senior Doctors of Divinity of the university. Doubtless this machinery eventually found its own modalities, in the event of its occasional use, but at first it appears to have been a recipe for chaos. When, in 1592, an appeal was lodged by six or seven fellows to these visitors (strengthened by the presence of the vice-chancellor's deputy) for an interpretation of certain statutes (which we don't know), the master and remaining fellows, led by the litigious Charles Chadwick, complained of irregularities in the procedure. The debate 'did grow both tedious and confused, many of the said fellows speaking at once'. Chadwick and the other dissidents, who included the master, entered a formal protest and defence of the statutory liberties of the college, willing and requiring the visitors 'not to intrude or offer your sense in this action'. Laurence Chaderton was Laurence Chaderton, but medievalists may confirm that on the evidence of this little storm in a Cambridge teacup, the Middle Ages were not yet over.[18]

In practice, and increasingly, as in the matter of De mora sociorum, it was

---

[17] Sancroft to Ezekiel Wright, 17 June 1663, ECA, COL.9.1(A), pp. 222–3. For the later history of De mora sociorum, which remained de facto nugatory but was only legally ruled to be defunct by the University Commissioners in 1856–61, see Shuckburgh 1904, pp. 65–6.

[18] Cambridge University Library, Registry Guard Book xcv, nos. 3–7; copies in MS Mm.1.38, pp. 60–5. Those protesting, besides the master, were Chadwick, John Richardson, Nathaniel Gilby, Richard Rolfe and John Gray.

the higher and remote authority of Crown or chancellor which disposed, whatever the society might propose. When, in 1665, William Sancroft was replaced as master by royal mandate, the senior fellow observed: 'This I think was the only way to preserve unity among us . . . It is easier to obey than to choose.' That, as we shall see, sums up much of the public history of seventeenth-century Emmanuel, of seventeenth-century Cambridge, and, why do we not say it, of the entire seventeenth century.[19]

Laurence Chaderton (1)[1]

Wert thou ere young? for truth I hold,
And do believe thou wert born old,
There's none alive I'm sure can say
They knew thee young, but always gray.

So ran an elegy upon Laurence Chaderton, composed for his 'long-deferred funeral'. Chaderton was a centenarian when he died in November 1640, but whether aged 104 or a mere 102 or 3 (as his simple memorial in the chapel states) no-one was, or is, sure. He used to say that he was eight when the English took Boulogne. That was in 1544, which would make him 48 at the beginning of his mastership (old for a head of house in the sixteenth century) and 86 at the time of his resignation in 1622.[2] In later years, 'the old Doctor' was one of the treasured antiquities of Cambridge. On the first warm day in April 1631, when he was in his early nineties, we catch a glimpse of him walking out to inspect the new ditch which was to bring water to the college.[3] He could still read every prick in his Hebrew Bible without the aid of spectacles. At the age of about a hundred, he annotated a book with which he disagreed, writing in a tremulous hand and largish letters, but with all his wits about him, as if correcting a student exercise: 'Who can prove this?' 'What's this?' 'Show examples'.[4] At last, Chaderton died 'merely through age'. His

---

[19] Robert Alefounder to William Sancroft, 'Trinity even', 1665, BL, MS Harl. 3784, fol. 276.

[1] This section is much indebted to the fullest modern study of Chaderton, contained in Lake 1982. I am grateful for the comments on an earlier draft of Professor Lake, and of Arnold Hunt and Seán Hughes.

[2] But Chaderton is also said to have remembered that when he went up to Cambridge in 1563 or 4, he was 24 or 25, which would date his birth to 1537 or 8. In fact he went up in 1562. Baptismal registers, introduced a year or two too late for Chaderton, have proved a useful invention.

[3] Joseph Mede to Sir Martin Stuteville, 2 April 1631, BL, MS Harl. 390, fol. 549r. The master, the elder Sancroft, accompanied Chaderton on this walk.

[4] Chaderton's annotated copy of A *soveraigne antidote against Sabbatarian error* (1636) (attributed in a MS note in this copy and elsewhere to Robert Sanderson) is in the Library of Trinity College Cambridge, C.26.34. See n. 20 below.

daughter recalled how he was walking up and down in his chamber, 'swinging about his stick', when it struck his legs and brought him down. But even after that mishap he still got up every day at 5 a.m.

The fourth, fifth, sixth and seventh masters of the college accumulated a legendary body of biographical material from which no subsequent historian has strayed very far.[5] First Richard Holdsworth (1637–1644) prepared his sermon for the great funeral which, in the turbulent month of Chaderton's death, had been postponed for twenty years, setting down 'what particulars he could learn from the kindred or the ancient men of the university in scattered bits and fragments of paper'. William Sancroft (1662–1665) found these notes in Holdsworth's study, together with a 'more methodical account' in Latin by Anthony Tuckney (1644–1653). Sancroft 'digested' this material and sent it to William Dillingham (1653–1662), a relative of Chaderton's by marriage, with access of his own to family traditions. Dillingham wrote a Latin life, of which Evelyn Shuckburgh would publish an abridged translation in 1884.

These masters were men of very different tempers and tendencies. Tuckney had secured the mastership after Holdsworth's removal by Parliament. He and Dillingham were acceptable to the interregnal regimes of Commonwealth and Protectorate, a vile usurpation in the perception of Sancroft who, as an undergraduate, had shared a chamber with Dillingham. When Dillingham was in his turn ejected by the restored monarchy, Sancroft succeeded him.[6] Yet all four were hewn from the same old block and all four had known the first master personally. It was a very tangled skein, the threads that connected the puritan Chaderton, born in the reign of Henry VIII, to Sancroft, the non-juring high churchman who died resisting the usurpation of William and Mary: 150 years of turbulent ideological history, which we must begin to unravel.

Chaderton came from a small country estate near Oldham. His parents, Edmund and Joan, daughter of Lawrence Tetloe of Oldham, were minor gentry. Laurence enjoyed the sporting life so characteristic of Tudor and Stuart Lancashire, and he retained a lifelong zest for archery, tennis and fives. Nor did he ever lose a countryman's sympathy for growing things.

---

5 Among the Sancroft MSS in the Bodleian Library, MS Sancroft 79 includes (pp. 11–19) an account of Chaderton which is doubly useful, since it contains both Sancroft's own contribution to the Life and his explanation of how the various ingredients of Dillingham's pudding were brought together. Dillingham's *Vita Laurentii Chadertoni* was published in 1700, along with his *Vita Jacobi Usserii Archiepiscopi Armachani*. E. S. Shuckburgh published in Cambridge in 1884 his translation, *Lawrence Chaderton, D.D. (First Master of Emmanuel)*. All material in this section derives from Sancroft-Dillingham-Shuckburgh, unless otherwise indicated.

6 For evidence of Sancroft's and Dillingham's literary friendship in the Restoration years, see p. 268n. 20 below.

We are told that 'he delighted himself in simpling and gathering plants', being a 'skilful herbalist'; and that both at Christ's and Emmanuel he planted trees for posterity, only to see them mature and decay in his own long lifetime.

As a somewhat mature student, Chaderton fell into the hands of Laurence Vaux, a good scholar who, as a recusant exile from Elizabethan England, would later write and publish at Louvain the standard catholic catechism. It must have been the influence of Vaux which sent Chaderton to Christ's in his mid-twenties. He was still an unreconstructed Lancashire Catholic, a wrestler and a brawler. Part of the legendary mosaic tells how this future Puritan was mixed up in a town and gown riot in which he saved the life (or at least the limbs) of his Christ's contemporary, Richard Bancroft, the future hammer of the Puritans and destined to be archbishop of Canterbury. Bancroft and Chaderton are said to have remained fast friends for life, which may (or may not) account for episodes otherwise hard to explain.

No-one had warned Chaderton's father of what might happen to his son in Cambridge. The circumstances of his conversion to a fervent, intensely evangelical Protestantism are unknown, but are likely to have implicated Edward Dering, who had been elected to his fellowship a year or two before Chaderton went up. Chaderton was to play Elisha to Dering's Elijah, and in his turn would shape the mind and vocation of the most influential of all the puritanical divines of Elizabethan Cambridge, William Perkins. This was the godly Christ's succession, from which Emmanuel, that mighty oak, was, so to say, a cutting.

Chaderton's father reacted violently to his son's change of religion, threatening to cut him off with, literally, a shilling: a threat which may not have been carried out to the letter. Like Martin Luther's father, he had intended to make his clever son a lawyer. But Chaderton was by now hooked on scholarship and on the fast track to becoming an accomplished divine, teaching to make ends meet and acquiring a formidable array of rhetorical and philological skills. He was elected a fellow of Christ's hard on the heels of his bachelor's degree, successfully competing against his seniors. It is said that Dering could have voted for one of his own pupils but abstained, acknowledging Chaderton's superior merit.

From the first moment at which we hear his voice, and he was already middle-aged, Chaderton expressed Edward Dering's urgent sense of God's majesty and providence, knocking at the door of England and its people, demanding attention, repentance, obedience. The occasion was a sermon delivered from the national pulpit of Paul's Cross, the year was 1579, and Dering had been dead for three years.[7] Paul's Cross sermons

[7] Laurence Chaderton, *An excellent and godly sermon . . . preached at Paules Cross* (London, 1580); especially Sigs. F2, C3, F6v–7.

were conventional occasions for breast-beating, rousing calls to national repentance. This was no exception, the great congregation being warned of such recent 'signs and forerunners of God's wrath' as comets, floods, earthquakes (this was a few months before a famous earthquake was to hit southern England in April 1580), and the plague even then stalking the streets of London. In almost the same words which Dering had been wont to use from the pulpit, Chaderton blamed this general delinquency of the nation on the unworthy clergy of the Church of England, castigating 'whole swarms of idle, ignorant and ungodly curates and readers', while reserving even harsher words for those preachers who, replete with worldly learning, stuffed their sermons with the vapid matter of 'curious, affected figures'.

Out of this angry and zealous passion arose both Emmanuel College and Chaderton's Puritanism, indeed what Professor Peter Lake has called 'the subtle but all pervading influence of his puritanism on Emmanuel College'.[8] Emmanuel was, from the point of view of its first master, the logical outcome of what had begun at Christ's, a kind of engine to train preachers and to feed them into the parishes and pulpits of the Church of England, something which the official leadership of the Church, royal and episcopal, had conspicuously failed to do: indeed, could not do without the human material which only the universities, suitably dedicated, could produce.

Chaderton set an example by his own incessant preaching: for half a century a lecturer in the parish of St Clement's in Bridge Street. When he gave up this weekly lecture, at the age of 82, forty divines signed a testimonial to the effect that they owed their conversion to Chaderton. Since St Clement's was and is a very small church, this may suggest that Chaderton's sermons were delivered *ad clerum*, and that it was from this pulpit that he exercised his moral and spiritual ascendancy over the Cambridge scene. Long vacations were spent preaching in the country, and especially in Lancashire. Chaderton became a hook on which to hang that timeless anecdote, that when on one occasion he offered to leave off preaching after a mere two hours, his hearers cried: 'For God's sake, sir, go on!'

In 1576, Chaderton married Cecily, one of the daughters of the seriously rich London haberdasher Nicholas Culverwell, the financial mainstay of the early Elizabethan preaching ministry and other good causes, who had died in 1569.[9] Culverwell left behind, among other imaginative bequests, a trust fund to support two poor and godly preachers in

---

[8] Lake 1982, p. 49.
[9] The historian of the Culverwells is Brett Usher, author of the as yet unpublished 'The Culverwells 1550–1630'. I am grateful for a sight of this. See also Usher 1992. Further information (relating, for example, to Susan Culverwell's first marriage) has been privately communicated by Mr Usher.

Christ's College, where his son Samuel and a much younger brother (godly to be sure but not poor) were to be students. Chaderton may have been one of the first beneficiaries of this charity, and he later joined with other leading Cambridge lights, William Whitaker and Richard Greenham, in commending to various members of the Elizabethan establishment a similar scheme, to raise funds for 'poor, learned and godly students'. In that this appeal reached Mildmay, amongst others, it may have served as a prompt for the foundation of Emmanuel itself.[10] When Nicholas Culverwell's equally rich brother, the mercer Richard Culverwell, died in 1584, he left the considerable sum of £350 in trust to Chaderton, Whitaker, Greenham and other ministers to distribute to 'the sincerest and poorest', 'whether preachers or other'. They could, if they so chose, use the money themselves.[11] Richard Culverwell was closely associated with his nephew, Chaderton, in the complex process of cross-conveyancing which made available to the founder the site of Emmanuel.

According to legend, on the same day that Chaderton was married, his close colleague William Whitaker, later to be master of St John's and the most celebrated of the divines and controversialists of late Elizabethan Cambridge, married another Culverwell daughter, Susan. A nasty accident at the double wedding ceremony was narrowly averted, Laurence protesting, 'No, no, it is Cecilia I want.' In fact the Whitaker-Culverwell marriage took place a year later. This by no means exhausts the godly capital in the Culverwell bank. At the time of her marriage to Whitaker, Susan was the young widow of Cuthbert Fuller, brother of a famous puritan lawyer, Nicholas Fuller, who proves (of course) to have been a Christ's man in Edward Dering's time, and was an early benefactor of Emmanuel. After Whitaker's death, she married the radical Kentish minister Josias Nicholls,[12] Chaderton officiating at the wedding. The oft-repeated statement that another sister was the wife of Arthur Dent, another Christ's man who wrote that model for *Pilgrim's Progress*, *The plain mans pathway to heaven*, is, according to the historian of the Culverwells, Brett Usher, unfounded. But one of Chaderton's sisters-in-law was the mother of the great Jacobean preacher, William Gouge,

---

[10] Richard Greenham, *Workes* (5th edn, London, 1612), Sig. 4E6v. The evidence (which I owe to Arnold Hunt) is contained in a letter from Greenham (the godly preacher of Dry Drayton near Cambridge) to an unnamed nobleman, referring to similar appeals to be sent to Sir Francis Walsingham, Secretary William Davison, Mildmay and 'others of your most Honourable society'.

[11] Will of Richard Culverwell, PRO, PCC wills, 9 Windsor, 1585.

[12] Fuller's bequest consisted of two houses in Smithfield, valued at £8. He was also much involved in other pieces of conveyancing on behalf of the college. ('Emmanueliana', *ECM*, 21, 49.) On Nicholls, see *DNB: Missing Persons*, pp. 494–5. See also Lake 1982, p. 39; and, for Nicholls's later years in London, Brett Usher, 'The Cosyns and the Galliardellos: Two Elizabethan Musical Dynasties', *Consort: European Journal of Early Music*, 1 (1994), 95–110.

while one of the two divines who were his brothers-in-law, sons of Nicholas Culverwell, married the daughter of the early Elizabethan non-conformist, Thomas Sampson. It was an apostolic succession and one sees why the enemies of the Puritans complained of that 'tribe'. Usher writes of 'a puritan peerage'.

As a married man, Chaderton resigned his fellowship, but continued to play the college system like a skilled organist at his instrument. In 1578, a fellow of Christ's informed 'Father' Anthony Gilby in Leicestershire that although 'Mr Chaderton taketh none to his tuition', he had been instrumental in placing Gilby's son Nathaniel (destined to be a foundation fellow of Emmanuel) under 'Mr Dickinson, a Lancashire man, a young man, very godly and learned'.[13] So began the manipulative habits of a lifetime, the entire Church of England, its parishes and schools, Chaderton's chessboard, his pieces young men 'very godly and learned'.[14]

In a later chapter, we shall have occasion to observe how judiciously Chaderton moderated his Puritanism and that of his college for the sake of that main chance, the promotion of a godly, converting, preaching ministry. How much of a Puritan was the Elizabethan Chaderton, the pre-Emmanuel Chaderton? And, in particular, was he, like Thomas Cartwright, a presbyterian, convinced on scriptural authority that there ought to be no bishops, committed to a ministry and polity of ministerial parity: pastors, doctors, elders and deacons, the polity of other Reformed churches, Scotland included?[15]

Cambridge was an environment sympathetic to presbyterianism as it would be congenial to the political left in the circumstances of the 1930s. A roll-call of Chaderton's contemporaries and juniors at Christ's reveals many fellow travellers, among them his cousin by marriage Samuel Culverwell and the Essex preacher Robert Wright, who were both students at Heidelberg with Thomas Cartwright, companions in a kind of presbyterian exile, in the early 1570s.[16] Wright was made a minister in Antwerp without episcopal ordination and would preach in the radically puritan household of the Rich family, another link with the Emmanuel

---

[13] CUL, MS Mm.i.43 (Baker 32), pp. 437–8.

[14] For Chaderton's involvement as (at the very least) a referee in the placement of puritan preachers and schoolmasters, see Lake 1982, pp. 38–40; and Collinson 1957, pp. 598–605, 1019.

[15] 'Presbyterians' in an Elizabethan context is mildly anachronistic, since a distinctively presbyterian ecclesiology was defined only in the 1640s (in contradistinction to the independent or congregational way). For Elizabethan presbyterianism, see Scott Pearson 1926, Collinson 1967, Lake 1982.

[16] Brett Usher has drawn attention to the convergence of these three on Heidelberg, a political and academic point of focus for the Reformed churches, in his unpublished monograph on the Culverwells. See also Collinson 1967, pp. 152–3.

future.[17] But that was in the clear-cut 1570s and early 1580s, and if Wright never lost his youthful radicalism, Samuel Culverwell did.

As for Chaderton, at the Commencement in July 1573 he formally opposed a proposition advanced by John Whitgift of Trinity and Andrew Perne of Peterhouse that ministers should not be chosen by their congregations.[18] That, to be sure, was an academic exercise and William Sancroft later reported that Chaderton had remained on good terms with both Cartwright and his arch-opponent Whitgift, and that 'he often professed that they who dislike the government by bishops would bring in a far worse both for Church and State'.[19] Well, perhaps Sancroft would say that. Chaderton is not on public record as having said anything of the sort, and his private reflections, as he read and annotated some of the controversial literature on the subject, tell another story.[20] Reading the arguments in favour of episcopacy as a divinely ordained and absolutely indispensable institution, Chaderton was laconic but caustic in his criticism. The early Church in Chaderton's estimation was a society in which the Apostles ruled 'with others, not by themselves', there being no distinction of spiritual function between bishops and presbyters.[21] This was not altogether incompatible with a pragmatic and political tolerance of hierarchy such as Sancroft attributed to Chaderton.

The closest we come to publicly stated anti-episcopal statements which we can be sure were Chaderton's are some acerbic remarks about scribes and pharisees to be found in the notes of some lectures which he gave in 1590–1.[22] Here we find him complaining that the adversaries of true religion were to be found 'yea even among the learned and those that are of great authority in the church'. If the pharisees could err in making

---

[17] Ibid., pp. 342–4. Wright's dealings in the Rich household are documented in proceedings against Richard Rich, bastard uncle of the Elizabethan Lord Rich and great uncle of the earl of Holland (chancellor of the university). (Cambridgeshire Record Office, MS M32/8/13/15.)

[18] BL, MS Cotton Titus C VI, fols. 18v–22v. This circumstance was brought to the attention of Lord Burghley, chancellor of the university, by Lord Henry Howard, later earl of Northampton and sometime public orator in Cambridge. In 1573–4 the crypto-catholic Howard was currying favour at Court, partly by writing a book against Cartwright.

[19] Bodleian Library, MS Sancroft 79, p. 18.

[20] Chaderton's annotations to his copies of Matthew Sutcliffe, *A treatise of ecclesiastical discipline* (London, 1591) and William Barlow, *One of foure sermons* (London, 1606): Trinity College Cambridge Library, C.9.11, Sig. Tr, C.9.113, Sigs. B2v, B3r, C2v. C3r. Chaderton's annotations to the Barlow sermon are critical of the *iure divino* views on episcopacy of Bishop Thomas Bilson and Hadrian Saravia, and some comments are explicitly presbyterian. I am indebted to Dr Arnold Hunt for introducing me to these annotations. See his essay 'Laurence Chaderton and the Hampton Court Conference', in Wabuda and Litzenberger 1998, pp. 207–28. It is, of course, possible that Sancroft was accurately reporting the views of Chaderton's old age, having known him no earlier.

[21] Chaderton's (undated) critical comments on the *Ordinal* of 1559 are extant. (Lambeth Palace Library, MS 2550, fols. 200–1, 207r, 210r.) See Hunt in Wabuda and Litzenberger, p. 215.

[22] Pembroke College, Cambridge, MS LC.II.2.164. See Lake 1982, pp. 49–52.

constitutions for the Church, 'then others may err as they did'. It would have been impossible to have heard these words and not to have applied them to Archbishop Whitgift.

However, the only unambiguously presbyterian utterances attributed to Chaderton occur in a sermon first published in 1584 as *A Fruitful Sermon* on certain verses of the 12th chapter of the Epistle to the Romans, a passage widely regarded as a proof-text for presbyterianism.[23] Here the preacher lamented the Church's lack of 'pastors, teachers, elders, deacons', 'those parts which are wanting', and spoke of the Church abhorring and loathing such as were 'abounding', 'as namely the calling of Archbishop, Bishop, Deans' (etc.), 'and all such as be rather members and parts of the whore and strumpet of Rome'.[24]

This was strong stuff. Did Chaderton preach this sermon, which was published anonymously? If so, where and when did he preach it? (It could as well have been in 1574 as in 1584.) And, most to the point, was he responsible for the version of the sermon as printed, which was the product of a partisan publishing enterprise capable, on at least one other occasion, of hi-jacking and distorting the work of another respectable Cambridge figure?[25] The best evidence that Chaderton was indeed the author is contained in the confessions made by certain Londoners in 1593 that they had been persuaded to separate from the Church of England and to form a gathered and schismatic congregation by some of the learned preachers, specifying this *Fruitful sermon* and naming Chaderton as its author.[26] However, these confessions were not unprompted. Among those doing the prompting was Chaderton's old friend, Richard Bancroft. Not only Bancroft but Richard Hooker was at this very moment arguing (in his *Laws of Ecclesiastical Polity*) that the Puritans had bought a ticket on a line which led straight to Separatism.[27]

In Bury St Edmunds in March 1590 there was a great deal of fuss after more preaching on Romans 12. This was in the setting of a preaching

---

[23] *A fruitful sermon upon the 3.4.5.6.7 and 8 verses of the 12 ch. of the Epistle to the Romans,* printed by Robert Waldegrave in 1584 but entered in the Stationers' Register only on 22 August 1586; further editions (by Waldegrave) in 1586 and 1589; attributed to Chaderton in the *Revised Short-Title Catalogue* (and in various library catalogues) but, strictly speaking, incorrectly.

[24] Quoted, Lake 1982, p. 30.

[25] William Fulke, in his post-presbyterian phase master of Pembroke, had written, in the early 1570s, a presbyterian manifesto, a *Learned discourse of ecclesiastical government* which was hijacked by the radical preacher John Field and Waldegrave in 1584, and published as *A briefe and plaine declaration.* According to the anti-puritan press, Fulke was not best pleased. (Collinson 1967, pp. 108, 274.) The almost simultaneous publication in 1584 of presbyterian manifestoes widely attributed to Fulke and Chaderton, and by the Walde-grave press, could have been part of a strategy to frustrate the retreat of the Cambridge great and good into moderation, if not conformity.

[26] BL., MS Harl. 6848, fols. 32–6, 45–80.

[27] See Collinson 1997.

conference or 'combination' which was the major cultural asset of late Elizabethan Suffolk, a county with which the infant Emmanuel already had strong ties. The Bury ministers were preaching their way through Romans and had already disposed of those awkward verses in chapter 12, making sure that they were handled by 'the ancientest and discreetest of our company', when, on the next lecture day, the pulpit was occupied by Thomas Rogers, an Oxford man destined to make his mark opposing those 'Cambridge boys', the Suffolk Puritans. Instead of proceeding, Rogers chose to go back to those same disputed verses, pulling out of his bosom a sermon composed for that purpose 'long ago'. The text from which he read was already set up for the printer, for it would be published in London within a matter of weeks.

The other ministers were scandalised, insisting that the author of the *Fruitful Sermon* (not identified) was 'a godly and learned man', and they succeeded in getting Rogers excluded from the Bury combination. Rogers fought back, denying that the author could have been learned and godly when he uttered that sermon. From his own sermon of confutation we learn that there had been 'divers impressions' of the *Fruitful Sermon* since its first appearance in 1584, 'that fertile year of contentious writings'. He made rhetorical play of his ignorance of and indifference to the sermon's authorship ('I have none eye to his person, but to his doctrine') but observed that the printer, Robert Waldegrave, was 'a man well known'. Now Waldegrave was at this moment a wanted man as the printer of those notorious anti-episcopal satires the Marprelate Tracts, and Rogers's Bury sermon was part of the spin-off from the Marprelate affair. Rogers would later serve as chaplain to Archbishop Bancroft, who made his name in organising the response of the establishment to Martin Marprelate.[28]

A footnote is provided by a certain Henoch Clapham, a radical and even eccentric Emmanuel Puritan and Separatist who came out of the cold into full conformity with the Church of England and wrote *Errour on the right hand*, a dialogic satire on 'preposterous zeal'. 'Flyer' (a Separatist) tells 'Malcontent' (a non-separated Puritan) that he had been a member of his 'classis' 'when you in Cambridge (in secret) chattered out that Sermon upon Rom. 12, which afterwards was published without name, because (it seemeth) you were not minded for it publicly to take up Christ's cross,

---

[28] J. S. Craig, 'The "Cambridge Boies": Thomas Rogers and the "Brethren" in Bury St Edmunds', in Wabuda and Litzenberger 1998, pp. 154–76. Rogers's sermon was published as *A sermon vpon the 6.7. and 8. verses of the 12 Chapter of S. Pauls Epistle vnto the Romanes; Made to the confutation of so much of another sermon* (etc.) by John Windet (printer of Bancroft's anti-puritan books) and dated 13 April 1590.

and so to follow him'. This was to identify 'Chatterton' as 'Malcontent', a representative but compromised Puritan.[29]

What did Clapham mean by Chaderton's 'classis'? In the 1580s a network of puritan ministers in London, East Anglia and the midlands, organised by the radical London preacher John Field, had met in conferences resembling and perhaps aspiring already to constitute the 'classes' and synods which were the building-blocks of a presbyterian church order. In these meetings work had been done on a presbyterian church constitution or 'Book of Discipline'. Chaderton was involved in these clandestine activities, both as Field's correspondent for Cambridge and as a participant in meetings held in Cambridge in 1587 and 1589 which were timed to coincide with the crowds attending the nearby Stourbridge Fair in September. Much of what we know of this movement was researched by Bancroft as evidence for the prosecution in a state trial of some of the ministers involved.[30]

On the basis of these manipulated sources we cannot be sure precisely what Chaderton's role in the classis movement may have been, let alone that he was actively plotting ecclesiastical revolution. But in an atmosphere ideologically resembling that of Cambridge left wing politics in the 1930s he may have been, if only in his head. At Oxford, his opposite number, John Rainolds, a formidable academic and controversialist, seems to have played a similar role.[31] Both Chaderton and Rainolds contrived to maintain a certain distance between their covert presbyterianism and their great and good public *personae*, as well as what we have called the main chance of the pastoral and evangelical imperative. As for Bancroft, his part in all this looks more devious still. It seems to have suited his purpose to exploit Chaderton's involvement, but not by openly naming him. Evidently Chaderton was the fourth, or fifth, or umpteenth man in a presbyterian conspiracy of the 1580s, his destination

[29] Henoch Clapham, *Errour on the right hand, through a preposterous zeale* (London, 1608), pp. 3–4. I have written on Clapham in 'Sects and the Evolution of Puritanism', Bremer 1993, pp. 161–2, and in 'Separating In and Out of the Church: the Consistency of Barrow and Greenwood', *Journal of the United Reformed Church History Society*, 5, 5 (November, 1994), 239–58. Clapham does not appear in Ibish's lists, but his presence at Emmanuel and the fact that his tutor was William Jones was established by W.C.B., 'Henoch Clapham', *Notes and Queries*, 10th ser. 4 (November 1905), 362–3. I owe this reference to the kindness of Dr Michael Moody.

[30] Collinson 1967, pp. 320–1, 325–6, 400–2, 412, 428. The impression that the 1589 Cambridge meeting, held in St John's master's lodge, was some kind of 'presbytery' was spread for an allegedly malicious purpose by the anti-puritan faction in the college, opposing the master, William Whitaker. The rumour was described as 'a discredit to the whole university' in a letter to Burghley from the vice-chancellor and six heads, backed up by a testimonial from thirty-four fellows of St John's offering to testify that they did not know of 'any such presbytery as hath been reported'. That was the end of the matter until further hostile evidence was given in the Star Chamber in 1591 (Collinson 1957, pp. 1012–18).

[31] Collinson 1997.

a master's lodge rather than, shall we say, Moscow.

In the early years of Emmanuel not only the main chance but the very title deeds of protestant orthodoxy itself appeared to be threatened by doctrinal subversion, elements in Cambridge which, said some of the heads of houses in writing to the chancellor, Lord Burghley, were 'lurking in the colleges amongst us'.

We have said 'appeared to be threatened'. This was the perception of the dominant theological tendency in the university, which included a majority of the heads and, very conspicuously, those brothers-in-law, Chaderton and Whitaker. Those said to be 'lurking' were numerically and politically in a weak position, but were seen by their powerful opponents to be aggressive. One recalls that wicked animal in the Paris zoo which, when attacked, defends itself. Burghley was obliged to pay attention to these troublesome matters, but complained of 'too high mysteries for his understanding', which prompted his long-time client Whitaker to speak tactfully of his 'weakness' in that regard.

The reader of this story may well share Burghley's 'weakness'. How little does one need to know to make sense of certain critical theological events in 1595–6? These 'high mysteries' concerned salvation, grace and predestination, and they were contained in these and cognate propositions: that salvation is limited to those whom God has unconditionally and of his absolute will and pleasure elected to that end, for whose redemption alone Christ's death was effectual; that the remainder of mankind was absolutely reprobate; that it was no more possible for the elect to lose their faith or fall finally and irrevocably from the state of grace than for the reprobate to be saved; that true believers were assured, by faith, of their salvation. Such was the essence of what is conventionally but not altogether properly called 'Calvinism', 'the truth of religion publicly and generally received', and the motive force of that main chance which was the evangelical and pastoral drive of Chaderton's kind of Puritanism.

When William Barrett, a young fellow of Caius, attacked some of the implications of these positions (and particularly the point of assurance, as if it were the same thing as a presumptuous 'security') he was, according to Professor Peter Lake, fighting a rearguard action against those he called 'puritanissimi', and in defence of a latitude on these matters which the Thirty-Nine Articles appeared to allow, but which the dominant party was determined to exclude. In the perception of the heads it was Barrett who was provocative (and they did not mistake his character), a 'Pelagian' whose doctrine made God's sovereign will dependent upon man's response, and a secret papist to boot, 'strongly savouring of the leaven of popery'. Chaderton interviewed Barrett on several occasions. 'I pray you tell me', he asked, 'bona fide', seeing that your opinion that faith may be lost and that there is no certainty of salvation is one which Lutherans and Catholics share, which opinion do you hold? Barrett confessed, according to Chaderton's notes of the meeting, that he held the opinion of the Church of Rome.[32] Not long after this, Barrett left Cambridge and converted to Catholicism.

Out of this academic storm came the Lambeth Articles of 1595, an attempt on the part of Archbishop Whitgift, himself in theological sympathy with the heads but distrustful of their heresy-hunting motives and methods, to settle the matter by defining the doctrine of the Church of England in a 'Calvinist' (or, better, Reformed) sense. But constitutionally Whitgift had no power so to act and his Articles were promptly repudiated by the queen, prompted, it appears, by the affronted 'weakness' of the undogmatic Burghley.

With the collapse of the Lambeth Articles, the position of the heads was more directly challenged, this time by a divine and academic of French origin, Peter Baro, for whom Barrett had been a stalking-horse. Baro was a man in his sixties who had taught in Cambridge for more than twenty years, having held the Lady Margaret chair since 1574. He was a client of that ambivalent figure, Andrew Perne of Peterhouse,[33] and an intellectual confidante of the Danish theologian Hemmingsen, a pupil of Melanchthon and a modified Lutheran of international standing. As early as 1583, Baro had been perceived by the vigilantly orthodox circles in which Chaderton moved as a problem requiring attention, a boil ripe for lancing.[34] After renewed ructions, Baro too was now forced out of Cambridge. However, the attempt to make the university and the Church at large waterproof against any deviation from Calvinist orthodoxy had come unstuck, with momentous consequences in the seventeenth century for the fortunes of both institutions. We shall encounter some of those consequences in due course, under the heading of 'Arminianism'.[35]

This may explain how it was that Chaderton, an establishment figure, remained embattled. As late as 1613 he would publish some of the defensive Calvinist pronouncements, his own included, which the events of 1595–6 had provoked.[36]

---

[32] Lambeth Palace Library, MS 2550, fol. 164v.

[33] Patrick Collinson, 'Perne the Turncoat: an Elizabethan Reputation', in Collinson 1994, pp. 179–217.

[34] Collinson 1967, pp. 235–6. The orthodox extrusion of Baro as a kind of foreign body closely resembles the treatment meted out to the heterodox Spaniard Antonio del Corro in Oxford and London. (Collinson 1983, pp. 237–43.)

[35] My account has followed Lake 1982, chapter 9, which substantially modifies the account in Porter 1958 (pp. 314–90), especially in its assessment of the dispositions and relative strengths of the embattled parties, and on the theology of the Lambeth Articles. On English 'Calvinism' more generally and in the years following this episode, see Seán Hughes, ' "The Problem of Calvinism": English Theologies of Predestination c. 1580–1630', in Wabuda and Litzenberger 1998, pp. 229–49.

[36] Chaderton's *De justificationis perseverentia non intercisa* was included in the *Brevis et dilucida explicatio* of 1613 which, as Lake persuasively argues (Lake 1982, pp. 223–4, 331) Chaderton edited.

When the niggardly Sir Walter Mildmay offered Chaderton the mastership of his college, the stipend a mere £15 a year, he had the prospect of a benefice worth ten times as much. Was this another part of the legendary history of Emmanuel? While he hesitated, perhaps thinking of his growing family, Mildmay told him: 'If you will be no Master, I will be no Founder.' Evidently Chaderton was as indispensable to the great design as the statute *de mora sociorum*.

This design was the capture of the Church of England by a kind of Trojan horse strategy of insidious infiltration which, instead of a politically imposed and revolutionary change of structure (presbyterianism), would make use of legitimate and regular means within the existing structure to bring about its reforming purpose. This was something like that strategy which Jesus, in an enigmatic parable, had called 'making friends of the Mammon of Unrighteousness'. But it was aimed not so much at the unrighteous as at the great and the good, and even more at the formation of the great and the good of the future, the coming generation of rich young rulers, some of whom were indeed called Rich.

In the early days of Emmanuel, the married Chaderton lived outside the college, first in a house which the Chadertons and Whitakers shared, then in purpose-built premises on the site of the old St Nicholas Hostel (on the far side of the modern Emmanuel Street), and here he accommodated as boarders fellow commoners from leading puritan families. Here lived Henry Rich (admitted 1603), the future earl of Holland and chancellor of the university, and John Finch (admitted 1590), Charles I's chief justice and lord keeper. Both these great men would publicly honour their old master in the days of their greatness, before the Civil War, Finch ordering the Great Seal to be carried before Chaderton as they processed into Hall, calling him 'the father of my soul'. Chaderton had come a long way from the chattering classes of his thirties and forties.

The Early Years of Emmanuel

Sir Walter Mildmay's deed of foundation was dated May 25th 1584, his statutes for the college, October 1st 1585. No time was lost in providing the fabric and the human resources to make the founder's vision concrete. By December 1587, it was possible to clear away the builders' rubble and to hold a ceremony of dedication, with Mildmay present to receive a congratulatory address from the vice-chancellor.[1] This cannot have been an entirely secular occasion, but what kind of religious service there may

[1] J. B. Peace in *ECM* 6 (1894–5), 10–11.

have been we are unable to say. Whatever happened would have taken place in the Hall, where 'prayers' had been said in the preceding months. The first college communion was held in the following year, presumably in the now completed chapel.[2]

By then the college was, in a sense, finished. Its physical fabric, consisting in large part of remodelled portions of the Dominican Priory, the Black Friars, comprised two courts which were entered, not, as today, from St Andrew's Street (Preachers' Street in the sixteenth century) but from Emmanuel Lane (now Emmanuel Street), to the north. Over the gate stood the inscription: 'Sacrae Theologiae Studiosis posuit Gualterus Mildmaius A° Dni. 1584'. On your left, as you entered what is now New Court, was the Chapel, an unconsecrated building, oriented north-south, and scarcely recognisable for what it was, with chambers in the roof void above. It was inconveniently small for what would rapidly grow into a very large college: 68 feet by 28 feet, austerely furnished with pulpit, hour-glass and communion table, with forms for sitting, the queen's arms dominant in the window at the (north) end. This building would be known to future generations as the Old Library. Straight ahead stood the Hall, with Buttery and Fellows' Parlour, the Master's Lodging abutting on Hall and Chapel to the left. Archaeological evidence confirmed, in the eighteenth century and in more recent investigations, that the Hall was adapted from the great church of the Dominicans, facts tastefully concealed by James Essex's stone facings of 1760, with the contemporaneous improvements to the interior, plaster ceiling and panelling. To the right were the kitchens.

In the larger court, now Front Court, the range on the right, flanking Preachers' Street, provided accommodation out of the remains of what had perhaps been the friars' refectory. (Professor Brooke suggests to me that this may have also contained working and sleeping quarters quite similar to those adopted in secular Oxbridge colleges.) This was the 'Old Building', with a new, purpose-built range of chambers to the south, 'Founder's Range', so named because this building contained a set of rooms, overlooking the garden and pond, reserved for the founder's kin. (This part of the college would be demolished in 1721.) To the east, where Wren's and Archbishop Sancroft's Chapel now stands, there was an open, arcaded aspect towards what Hamond's 1592 map calls 'Emmanuel College Walks', the arena for Laurence Chaderton's strenuous tree-planting. Willis and Clark believed that all the principal buildings (Hall, Chapel, Kitchens, Gallery, Master's Lodging, Founder's Range) were complete some time before Mildmay's death in May 1589. And what about the Library? It seems to have found its first home in a small range, dating from the early seventeenth century and demolished in 1828, which ran

---

[2] Ibid., 74–5; CUL, MS Mm.2.23, p. 74/70 (sic).

out from the kitchen range to Preachers' Street, forming one side of a little space called Bungay Court. These original buildings were the achievement of Ralph Symons, the great Cambridge builder of his day, described as 'architectus sua aetate peritissimus' in the inscription on the portrait which hangs in the Gallery of the college. 'Architect' should not be read anachronistically, and Symons would have been a stone mason by trade.[3]

There is some irony in the fact (to return to the ceremonies of December 1587) that the vice-chancellor who congratulated the founder for his benefaction was the long-serving master of Caius, Thomas Legge, for Legge's conduct of his own college was a contradiction of everything that Mildmay and Chaderton held dear.[4] A civil lawyer and dramatist rather than divine (he was the author of *Richardus Tertius*), Legge was easy-going about matters of religion. In the prevailing climate of opinion, pragmatic tolerance was readily mistaken for crypto-catholicism, and Legge's own fellows had recently risen in rebellion against a complacent regime which sheltered Catholics and was said to have made the college a place of 'lewd singing and organs'. Chaderton knew all about this. Now Legge extolled Emmanuel as 'such a beauty and ornament to the university'; while privately he may have resented it as a cuckoo in the nest, entrenching and propagating values which were not his values.[5]

The first three of Emmanuel's fellows were Charles Chadwick, a Christ's man, and William Jones and Lawrence Pickering, both recruited from Clare. Chadwick should have been another transplanted sprig from the Dering tradition of applied godliness, but in character he was not a Dering, still less a Chaderton. To be sure, he would soon be in trouble for an extravagant university sermon in the Dering tradition, which denounced non-resident clergy as soul-murderers, and he would count some of the more puritanical of the early students among his pupils. But he was also an active college politician, the first fellow to challenge the statute *de mora sociorum* in his own interest.[6] Jones would duly conform to the disagreeable statute, leaving the college to marry and settle down to a forty-five year ministry at East Bergholt, in the puritan heartland of the Suffolk-Essex borders, where he wrote biblical commentaries. Pickering, too, observed the statute and disappeared into total obscurity.[7]

Within four years, the fellowship stood at the statutory twelve and included Nathaniel Gilby, son of the puritan 'father' Anthony Gilby of Ashby-de-la-Zouch (another recruit from Christ's) who was to be Joseph

---

[3] Willis and Clark 1886 (1988), II, 687–94; *ECM* 6, 2–18; Stubbings 1984a, 14–23. See C. N. L. Brooke above, pp. 9–11; also Plate 15a.

[4] Brooke 1985, pp. 84–93.

[5] *ECM* 6 (1894–5), 10.

[6] CUL, MS. Add. 10, no. 94; Porter 1958, p. 137; CUL, Registry Guard Book vol. 95, nos. 3–7; CUL, MS Mm.1.38, pp. 60–3; ECA, COL.9.1(A), p. 200. Stubbings 1983a, p. 97.

[7] Ibish 1985, pp. 470–1, 515.

Hall's tutor, and two men destined to be heads of houses: William Branthwaite, one of the translators of the Authorised Version, made master of Caius by royal mandate in 1607,[8] and John Richardson, his fellow-translator, a future regius professor of divinity and master first of Peterhouse and later of Trinity. Richardson's divergence from Emmanuel orthodoxy in the direction of what would later be called Arminianism was apparent even before the disputes about the doctrine of grace which led to the Lambeth Articles of 1595. It was an undergraduate from a godly gentry background, aged perhaps sixteen, John Sammes, who in 1590 complained of the future regius and master of Trinity for defending 'three absurdities and false points of doctrine' in his lectures: before going on to the inns of court and the life of an Essex J.P.[9]

The new foundation set off at once on a growth curve which would make it the largest college in Cambridge within forty years of its founda-tion.[10] More than fifty students were admitted in the first eighteen months of the college's existence. By 1604, according to Dr Joan Ibish's calculations, 832 Emmanuel men had passed through the college, a figure arrived at by adding to the data collected by the Cambridge prosopographer J. A. Venn (787 names) forty-five additional names, mostly derived from communion lists dating from these early years.[11]

To provide a meaningful analysis of these bare statistics we have first to distinguish between the various categories under which students were admitted, indicative of the status which they enjoyed within the society.[12] Scholars, of whom there were at first half-a-dozen, were, like fellows, beneficiaries of the foundation. Fellow commoners, the sons of nobility and affluent gentry, enjoyed a life-style comparable to that of senior members, paying double fees and costing their fathers forty or fifty pounds a year.[13] Pensioners, too, were often the sons of gentry or clergy and were in principle adequately provided for. Sizars were at the bottom of the heap, student-servants on reduced fees who worked their passage,

---

[8] Brooke 1985, pp. 104–10.
[9] ECA, CHA 1.4(A), fol. lv; Ibish 1985, pp. 539–40.
[10] For the statistics underpinning the paragraphs which follow, I am dependent upon Tyler 1975 and Ibish 1985.
[11] CUL, MS Mm.2.23, pp. 74/70(sic)–78.
[12] See John Venn's pioneering work on the gradations of student status, based on the admissions registers of Gonville and Caius College, in Venn, *Caius* III and Venn 1913; and refinements and debates in Joan Simon, 'The Social Origins of Cambridge Students 1603–1640', *Past and Present*, no. 26 (November 1963), pp. 58–67, and David Cressy, 'The Social Composition of Caius College, Cambridge, 1580–1640', *Past and Present*, no. 47 (May 1970), pp. 113–15. See also relevant material and discussion in Lawrence Stone, ed., *The University in Society*, 2 vols. (Princeton, 1974), Curtis 1959, and Heal and Holmes 1994.
[13] For evidence that in 1613 a fellow commoner was expected by his family to live on £40 a year, but disappointed their expectations, see p. 53 below. Sir Simonds D'Ewes, a fellow commoner at St John's between 1617 and 1620, found it hard to manage on £50 (D'Ewes 1845, I, 118–19).

although some sizars improved their lot and advanced within this mini-hierarchy which to be sure had some ameliorating features. 'Good child', wrote a Norfolk gentlewoman to her son, 'let not a poor hungry sizar want a reward from thee.'[14] (In Emmanuel's early years, professional servants were beginning to displace sizars.) Fellow commoners often failed to matriculate, rarely proceeded to a degree, and commonly went on from university to the inns of court, having used it as a kind of finishing school. Ordination and the life of a clergyman or (if unlucky) schoolmaster was the predestination of most sizars and many pensioners. Scholars had the prospect of finding their way into the fast lane of ecclesiastical and academic preferment.

The earliest cohort of alumni, and their subsequent careers, conformed to something like the Cambridge norm. Of the first fifty or so admitted, no more than a dozen or so were the sons of gentlemen of whom only seven were fellow commoners. At the other extreme, the number of sizars was relatively small, no more than fifteen. But at least twelve of the fifteen were to pursue a clerical career, many as beneficed clergy. With nine of a larger group of twenty-six pensioners and three of the six scholars also entering the ministry, at least twenty-four or 48% of the intake of the first two years answered to the founder's expectations in this regard.

But the small initial group of fellow commoners and more privileged pensioners pointed to a pattern of growth which on the face of it ran counter to what Mildmay intended, although it may have answered to a less explicit agenda. Many of these socially well-connected students found their way to Emmanuel from godly gentry families where a protestant, not to say puritan, magistracy was already in the ascendant and able through its power of ecclesiastical patronage to populate the parishes with a godly preaching ministry: Essex, Suffolk, Northamptonshire, Cornwall.

From Suffolk came Thomas Jermyn, son of that East Anglian Joshua, Sir Robert Jermyn of Rushbrooke, and William Copinger, another scion of the godly Jermyn clan. A little later, the college admitted two sons and a nephew of the ardent Suffolk puritan magistrate and M.P., Sir Edward Lewkenor. Lewkenor's mother-in-law, Martha Higham, was Sir Robert Jermyn's aunt, a formidably religious matriarch and, with other Jermyns, a benefactress of the college. It was Martha who despatched to Emmanuel the son of the Lewkenors' curate, Timothy Pricke alias Oldmayne, endowing a scholarship on condition that he should be the first to enjoy it. Timothy followed his father, Robert Pricke, in ministering to this exemplary family, living in a parsonage paid for and built by Martha Higham. No less than twelve members of the Jermyn-Higham-Lewkenor

---

[14] Hughey 1941, p. 72.

connection attended Emmanuel in the first twenty years of its existence, not to speak of such sons of the prophets as Timothy Pricke.[15]

From Essex came young John Sammes, Dr Richardson's outspoken critic; from Cornwall, a county conspicuous for an interconnected network of protestant gentry families, Jonathan Trelawney of Fowey, ward and later son-in-law of the famous Cornishman and diplomat Sir Henry Killigrew, Lord Burghley's brother-in-law and Mildmay's friend and colleague, one of Emmanuel's original benefactors. Trelawney arrived in company with Killigrew's nephew, William Godolphin, and yet another young Cornishman called Trevisa, evidently part of this same Killigrew connection.[16]

Before long, young men like these would dominate the college. Of the 832 members of the society in the first twenty years, no less than 125 were fellow commoners, only 243 sizars, while fellow commoners and pensioners (378) together (503) outnumbered the sizars two to one. Relying on the younger (J.A.) Venn's incomplete data, so that all figures are likely to be underestimates, Dr Richard Tyler has studied the social composition of the early Emmanuel between 1596 and 1645, against a control group in three other colleges, Jesus, King's and St John's.[17] Within the fifty years in question, all four colleges admitted a total of 7,039 students. Emmanuel, by a small margin, admitted the most: 2,606. In 1621 the college was said to have had 260 members and in 1624, the peak year, it opened its doors to 82 freshmen.

Dr Tyler finds that the sons of the gentry, fellow commoners and pensioners, were proportionately more numerous than in the other three colleges in his sample, and much more so than in St John's: perhaps 63%, compared with less than 53% in the other colleges, 48% in St John's. Emmanuel admitted a correspondingly low percentage of sizars, and, for the students whose social origins are known or inferrable, a smaller number from social levels below the gentry and professional classes. Dr Ibish concurs. Emmanuel had rather more fellow commoners than other colleges, a great many more pensioners, and many fewer sizars.[18]

It follows almost logically from these statistics that a relatively low number of Emmanuel men matriculated or took degrees. Of the students of known gentry origin, 71.8% failed to graduate (compared with 60.1% in the control group) and 26.6% to matriculate (compared with 11%). 14%

---

[15] 'Puritanism and the Gentry in Suffolk, 1575–1585: A Case-Study', chapter 9 of Collinson 1957; Collinson 1982, pp. 156–64; 'Magistracy and Ministry: A Suffolk Miniature', in Collinson 1983, pp. 445–66; Ibish 1985, pp. 240–6, 520.

[16] Ibish 1985, pp. 238–40; Hasler 1981, III, 525–6, II, 198. For some details of puritan networks in Elizabethan Cornwall, see Patrick Collinson, 'The Elizabethan Exclusion Crisis and the Elizabethan Polity', *Proceedings of the British Academy*, 84 (1994).

[17] Tyler 1975, pp. 40–4, 72, 99–163, 242.

[18] Ibish 1985, p. 201.

of these Emmanuel students went on from Cambridge to the inns of court, compared with 8% from the other colleges.

Above all, it almost necessarily follows from the social profile of its intake that proportionately fewer members of Emmanuel entered the ordained ministry: some 38%, compared with perhaps 43% in the other colleges. In the quinquennium 1596–1600, almost 50% of the members of Jesus, King's and St John's were to become clerics, only 35% of Emmanuel men. In the first twenty years, well under 50% of Emmanuel men graduated and less than a third were ordained. Was that what Mildmay had wanted?

Although it was a commonplace that Emmanuel was 'a nursery of preachers', 'a famous seminary'[19] it never was, least of all in these early years, simply, or even predominantly, a seminary, still less a puritan seminary. This is not to say that its significance, for the history of the seventeenth century on both sides of the Atlantic, has been misunderstood. Emmanuel in its first half-century nourished a puritan élite, always a minority of the society as a whole, but a hugely important minority, composed in roughly equal numbers of future clerics and laymen, lawyers and magistrates, that formidable amd mutually supportive combination of 'ministry and magistracy' which shaped the politics and culture of the English provinces in the decades preceding the Civil War and, almost incidentally, invented American civilization.

Why the élitism? There seem to be two explanations. Emmanuel was poorly endowed, could not afford too many sizars and needed all the wealthy and landed alumni and alumni's fathers it could get, if only to provide the ex-sizars with livings through the ecclesiastical patronage they dispensed. This was an indirect way of achieving the founder's objectives. In the second place, the country gentry who took their religion seriously to heart were anxious to place their sons in Emmanuel, quite simply to ensure the salvation of their souls, or at least to keep them well clear of 'evil courses'. In 1634, someone wrote that the godly reputation of the college 'makes every man that looketh Heaven-ward anxious to crowd his children into it'.[20]

It was a crowded college, and as a social and pedagogical experiment by no means consistent with the declared aims of Mildmay's statutes, and not necessarily a happy place. The inadequacy of the endowment required a complement of twelve fellows on slender stipends to look after far too many undergraduates, in modern terms a staff-student ratio of one to fifteen or even twenty, and this in a college which placed a premium on the tutorial system, its essence the cohabitation of tutor and pupil and

[19] John Ward (of Norwich) to William Sancroft (the elder), 19 October 1634, BL, MS Harl. 3783, fol. 39.
[20] Ibid.

round-the-clock surveillance. In practice, the system broke down, with many undergraduates living off-limits in rented and improvised accommodation. In 1636 Archbishop Laud was told: 'Many of their scholars live and lodge in the town houses, and from thence they come through the street with surplices upon them to chapel, and in the night time have opportunity to go abroad and be where they please. The cause hereof is for they admit many more into the college than it is able to hold.'[21]

As for the fellows and tutors, their situation was not unlike that of underpaid university teachers in a modern system of higher education artificially extended beyond its appropriate funding base. Many years later Benjamin Whichcote, the distinguished Cambridge Platonist and by then provost of King's, would tell Anthony Tuckney that during his time as a tutor of Emmanuel (1633–43) 'employment with pupils took my time from me. I have not read many books.'[22] And, not unlike their more recent successors, today's 'academics', seventeenth-century fellows of Emmanuel were neither secure in their tenure nor confident about future employment.

The archives of the early years convey something of the tension between the austerity of the seminarian ideal and the more diverse and irrepressible reality of a community of over a hundred adolescents drawn from a variety of social and cultural backgrounds. College communions, held in principle once a term, were divisive rather than uniting occasions, since it was by no means assumed that all members of the society were fit to take part. 'Discipline' on the Calvinist model ensured that there would be some absentees, while the limited success of that discipline added to their number. At the first recorded communion, on May 26th 1588, there were seventy-nine communicants, including the master and fellows, but no less than forty non-communicants, including sixteen excluded for lack of adequate knowledge, nine as under age, and twelve recorded as merely absent. Subsequently, about a third of the college would be non-communicants, and there would always be some exclusions 'for want of knowledge' or 'other defects', or as 'unfit' or, significantly, 'unprepared'. In 1600 (ninety communicants, fifty-two non-communicants) the fourteen 'unprepared' included the most senior fellow, Dr Richardson.[23]

Some of those deemed unfit to receive the sacrament found their way into the Admonition Book, a document which suggests that the real

---

[21] CUL, Baker MS 45, fol. 73. The lecturer of Dedham, John Rogers, told the master of Emmanuel, William Sancroft the elder, that no chamber could be found for his step-son when he first came to the college, so that he 'kept' in a house over against Emmanuel for the year, where he contracted smallpox. (BL, MS Harl. 3783, fol. 52.)

[22] Whichcote 1753, p. 54. It must be admitted that Whichcote was here responding to the accusation that he had been reading the wrong kinds of books, leading to his heterodox deviation from 'orthodox' Calvinism.

[23] CUL, MS Mm.2.23, pp. 74/70(sic)–77.

Emmanuel was never simply the pious hothouse of legend. Henry Duckett was already a B.A. when he was admonished for 'wearing great ruffs' and for neglecting prayers in the chapel. Duckett was no casual absentee from communion. He was duly returned by two of the fellows as a (presumably popish) recusant. A note in the record reads 'he is gone', but apparently no further than Clare, where he proceeded M.A. in 1593.[24] Among the disorderly there were a few upper-class 'hooray Henrys' (in modern parlance), including two fellow commoners, Denis Hartridge and George Catesby, who came from godly Northamptonshire stock. Hartridge and Catesby misspent their time in hunting, frequenting the forbidden maygames on the Gogmagog Hills, and quarrelling with the servants of the earl of Rutland. Now the earl of Rutland was sixteen years of age, and a student at Corpus Christi. Hunting 'contrary to the master's commandment' seems to have been the favourite occupation of this fast set. But humble sizars could be unruly too, in their own way. In 1586 John Cook and Robert Tomson were both implicated in verbal and physical abuse against other students. Both would finish up as rectors of parishes in deepest Leicestershire.[25]

The other side of the coin was represented by an institution called 'a mutual conference in communication of gifts among students of divinity'.[26] This exercise was either an Emmanuel peculiarity or, more probably, part of the Christ's legacy. The Emmanuel arrangements, part of a set of orders dated 1588 and supplementing the statutes, closely resemble 'an order to be used for the training up and exercising of students in divinity, whereby they may be made fit and meet to discharge the duties belonging to that profession'; which is attributed in a contemporary MS copy to 'Mr Chaderton of Cambridge'.[27] Both schemes had an affinity to the exercise of 'prophesying' which was widely practised in the early Elizabethan Church but suppressed in its original form by the queen in person, after disciplining her archbishop of Canterbury, Edmund Grindal, for his conscientious refusal to be party to the suppression.[28]

'Prophesying', a less exotic and chiliastic affair than its name might suggest, derived from St Paul's discussion of church offices and functions in his correspondence with the early Christians of Corinth. More immediately, it was modelled on the practice of the Swiss and south German reformed churches. The basic principle was one of a 'conference',

[24] ECA, CHA.1.4(A), fol. 2r; CUL, Registry Guard Book 4, 1d, 1dd; Ibish 1985, p. 402.
[25] ECA, CHA 1.4(A), fols. 2v, 1r; Ibish 1985, pp. 388–9, 563.
[26] ECA, COL.14.1, fols. 3–8v; printed, Stubbings 1983, pp. 106–11.
[27] Dr Williams's Library, MS Morrice A, fol. 191 (calendared, Peel 1915, I, 133–4; printed, H. C. Porter, *Puritanism in Tudor England* (London, 1970), pp. 195–7). There is no reason to suppose, as some have, that the 'Mr Chaderton of Cambridge' referred to was William Chaderton, bishop of Chester.
[28] Collinson 1967, pp. 168–76, 191–201; Collinson 1979, pp. 233–65.

consisting of two or three sermons addressed to the same text, with one and another of the company bringing their particular gifts, whether linguistic or rhetorical, to the enterprise of shared exposition. In the market towns of Elizabethan England, prophesying provided a kind of open university or seminary without walls. Its prime function was to turn non-graduate, non-preaching clerics into preachers and evangelists. But the proceedings were originally public, in church, and served to edify the population at large (on the basis of voluntary attendance) and to compensate for a general dearth of sermons. Chaderton's orders brought prophesying back within *academe*.

Prophesying was not incompatible with episcopacy. Indeed, many bishops, like Grindal, approved of the practice and had authorised it. Under the at least nominal authority of the bishop, the presiding moderators exercised a quasi-episcopal, referred superintendency over the less qualified clergy. But after the queen's intervention, there was a tendency for the sectarian, 'godly' potential of the exercises to be accentuated, as they went underground, turned in upon themselves, and developed in a direction which was at least implicitly presbyterian.[29] This is reflected in the Emmanuel orders, where the rules for formal 'censure' or criticism of the doctrine delivered respected the rights of all present, 'because the judgment is the judgment of all and not of any one alone'; and where it is explicitly stated, as in the rules for the conference of ministers meeting at this time in and around Dedham on the Suffolk-Essex border[30], 'that no man which is not of the company be made party to that which is done amongst us.'

Whether undergraduate students took an active part in these meetings or were merely a passive audience, like the laity in the country prophesyings, we do not know. But we have already heard one former undergraduate's memory of the Emmanuel 'classis' in Henoch Clapham's words: 'when you in Cambridge (in secret) chattered out that Sermon upon Rom. 12.' And there is a fuller account of conferences of this kind in details of the *Life* of a graduate of Clare, John Carter (later a minister in Suffolk), which seems to belong to the years around 1580, before the foundation of Emmanuel. Carter was said to have taken part in weekly conferences with Chaderton, Lancelot Andrewes of Pembroke, Mr Culverwell (presumably Ezekiel Culverwell), John Knewstub of St John's (later doyen, not to say pope, of the Suffolk ministers) and others, 'whom God raised up and fitted to send forth into his Harvest, to gather his Corn, then ripe for the Sickle, into his Barn.' 'One was for the *Original Languages*, anothers task was for the *Grammatical* Interpretation; anothers

---

[29] Collinson 1967, pp. 208–39.
[30] *The Presbyterian Movement in the Reign of Queen Elizabeth as Illustrated by the Minute Book of the Dedham Classis, 1582–1589*, ed. R. G. Usher, Camden 3rd ser. 8 (1905).

for the *Logical Analysis*; anothers for the true sense, and meaning of the Text; another gathered the Doctrines . . . ' 'Till at last they went out, like *Apollos*, eloquent men, and mighty in the Scriptures.'[31] There are references to these 'exercises' from the early years of the seventeenth century and from the 1630s. Unanimity of 'judgment' was not always easy to achieve. In 1595, Chaderton was obliged to ask twelve students to sign an order binding them to refrain from contention in the exercises, and a few years later the exercises witnessed a lively debate about how the Sabbath should be observed, and whether it should begin on Sunday morning or Saturday evening.[32]

Thirty years after Mildmay planted his acorn, the themes of this chapter were captured in a mirror, the mirror of an Emmanuel tutor's correspondence with a Norfolk gentlewoman, the grandmother of his prize pupil.[33] Elias Travers, the tutor in question, was the son on the one hand of a radical Devon puritan minister, John Travers, who was the brother of the famous Walter Travers; and on the other of the sister of Travers's even more formidable opponent, Richard Hooker.[34]

In 1612–13, Travers had in his charge a sixteen-year-old fellow commoner and heir to a considerable Norfolk estate, Thomas Knyvett. It will come as no surprise to learn that Knyvett's mother was the daughter of the godliest gentleman in Norfolk, Sir Nathaniel Bacon of Stiffkey.[35] But it was his grandmother, Lady Meriel Knyvett, who made the young Thomas her responsibility, held the purse strings, and carefully filed the correspondence relating to his education.[36] First we hear from Knyvett's Norfolk schoolmaster, who packed him off to Cambridge with Polonius-like advice to take heed especially of his 'consorts', and neither a borrower nor a lender be.[37] The university to which he consigned this

---

[31] Clarke 1677, pp. 132–3. Those named in the *Life* of Carter as participating in these meetings suggest that Chaderton began them in his days as a fellow of Christ's, before the foundation of Emmanuel. The inclusion of Lancelot Andrewes's name is some of the best evidence of, if not his early 'Puritanism', his acquaintance with the godly, which has sometimes been doubted.

[32] Webster 1997, pp. 17–21.

[33] BL, MS Egerton 2715, fols. 137–83. The letters are discussed and excerpted in the Introduction to *The Knyvett Letters (1620–1644)*, ed. Bertram Schofield (Norfolk Record Soc. 1949), pp. 19–22. It was the late Jeremy Maule who drew this correspondence to my attention.

[34] Collinson 1967, pp. 441–3, 454.

[35] *The Knyvett Letters*, p. 19. For Bacon and his conspicuous godliness, see A. Hassell Smith, G. M. Baker and R. W. Kenny, eds., *The Papers of Nathaniel Bacon of Stiffkey*, I, Norfolk Record Society (Norwich, 1979), pp. xvii, 289–90.

[36] The first of Elias Travers's letters in MS Egerton 2715 (which are evidently not foliated in chronological order) is endorsed, in a woman's hand which was doubtless Lady Knyvett's: 'Letters from September the 17 1612 to august 1613 the second yere of toms being at Cambrigg' (fol. 137v).

[37] John Rawlyns (from Attleborough) to Lady Meriel Knyvett, 23 October 1611, BL, MS Egerton 2715, fol. 126.

very special pupil was, according to Sir Simonds D'Ewes, at this time swarming with 'the debauched and atheistical'.[38]

But Knyvett seems to have kept clear of the fast and dangerous set, and Travers could report that he had been hitherto preserved from 'falling into these blind by-paths of the errors of youth', not to speak of 'that fatal conceit gentlemen have taken up, they need not study so much nor apply their time so frugally nor aspire to that sufficiency that other scholars do, who mean to make a fortune out of their learning'.[39] So Knyvett was not extravagant, but he was nevertheless unable to manage on his annual allowance of £40. Travers wrote: 'It is impossible in my sense to devise a more frugal manner of living for him in any seemly fashion suitable to his place and rank.'[40] Felicity Heal and Clive Holmes remark of this 'expensive and morally threatening environment': 'An archive could be constructed out of the anxious correspondence between parents, boys and tutors on the financing of the young.'[41]

Knyvett's rank required expenditure on lace, silk, satin, cuffs, four dozen long buttons and three dozen black buttons.[42] His tutor was expected to look after these things, as well as his pupil's account with the college; until, in despair, Travers told the grandmother that he could no longer 'bring the two ends together', and that in future she must be directly responsible for the young man's dealings with his tailor and other things of that kind.[43] Travers was expected as a matter of course to convey his charge to and from Norfolk, and to accept the elder Knyvetts' hospitality.[44] Evidently, Lady Meriel regarded the university as an extension to family life and household education. If Travers had other pupils and more pressing concerns, these were no concern of hers.[45]

---

[38] Heal and Holmes 1994, p. 262.

[39] Travers to Lady Knyvett, 9 December n.y., BL, MS Egerton 2715, fol. 145.

[40] Travers to Lady Knyvett, 12 October n.y., ibid., fol. 140. Simonds D'Ewes as a fellow commoner at St John's paid £2.2s. for a pair of silk stockings with garters and roses to match, and £4.7s. for his gown. (Marsden 1851, p. 2.) Cf. Joseph Mede, fellow of Christ's, to Sir Martin Stuteville, 25 May 1625: 'When your letter was delivered me, I was paying the Draper for your sons gown and suit.' (BL, MS. Harl. 389, fol. 446.) Accounts survive from 1582 detailing the anticipated annual expenditure in Cambridge of two young men (Thomas Sisley and Thomas Campion) of a lower social rank than Knyvett or D'Ewes. 'Diet', rent, tuition and other items came to £20 for the two, and the yearly clothing allowance consisted for each of a gown, a cap, a hat, two doublets, two pairs of hose, four pairs of 'netherstocks', six pairs of shoes, two shirts and three bands; together with 'all such books as they shall need from time to time'. (BL, MS Egerton 2599, fol. 233v.) Medical bills were another necessary expense. In the summer of 1618 they came to more than £4 for a student of Christ's, mostly for laxatives, electuaries and suppositories. (CUL, CUA, MS V.C. Ct. III 23, fol. 225(ii).)

[41] Heal and Holmes 1994, p. 264.

[42] Travers to Lady Knyvett, 14 March n.y., BL, MS Egerton 2715, fol. 175.

[43] Travers to Lady Knyvett, 6 August 1613, ibid., fol. 161.

[44] Travers to Lady Knyvett, 6 December n.y., 18 December n.y., undated, 3 May 1613, 6 August 1613, 9 February n.y.; ibid., fols. 145v, 146r, 149r, 158v, 161, 173r.

[45] Heal and Holmes 1994, p. 263.

This could have been the path to a preferment which would more than repay so much effort devoted to a single pupil. But Travers had no other connection with Norfolk, was reluctant to look in that direction, and regularly made his excuses. And when Lady Meriel invited him for a more extended stay, perhaps to serve as her chaplain, he had to explain that the statutes of Emmanuel made this impossible.[46] Altogether, the life of a fellow of Emmanuel consisted of more snakes than ladders. At one point, Lady Knyvett, who liked her clergymen to be 'neither over precise nor yet dissolute',[47] listened to damaging rumours about her grandson's tutor, particularly concerning his use of tobacco, a notorious badge of a dissolute life in Jacobean Cambridge, and she threatened to remove young Knyvett to another college. Travers used the occasion to send into Norfolk a rather risky little essay on the theme of Christian liberty.[48] And perhaps Lady Knyvett had heard of worse things than addiction to the weed. At about this time, Travers was forced to go into the vice-chancellor's court to defend himself against a rhyming libel which was being repeated all over the college and left for anyone to read in the chapel. The insinuation of this 'Skeltonical salutation' was that Travers had been 'dishonest of his body' with 'some wench or woman'; leading to much conjecture 'what woman or wench'. These verses, which the court proceedings have preserved, are not proof of 'taunting Travers's' immorality, but they are evidence of unpopularity:

> Us schollers pore
> Thou makes us rore
> punishing soe sore.[49]

Poor Travers! Forced by the statute *De mora* to leave the college without a living, he moved to a fellowship at Christ's and waited for Chaderton to die. The final disappointment came in 1622 when the old man (with eighteen years of life still in him) was persuaded to resign and the fellows, with remarkable unanimity and still more subtlety, determined that not Travers but John Preston of Queens' should be their second

---

[46] Travers to Lady Knyvett, 14 March n.y.; BL, MS Egerton 2715, fol. 175v.

[47] Ibid., p. 333.

[48] 'If a free use of a liberal condition of life hath occasioned offence and opened her mouth, it is my fate rather than fault . . . What you have wrote of the counsel you have been advised by, to change your son's college, though I am loath there should be just cause given, yet I assure you it may be without touch of want of discretion to any, or discredit to me.' (Travers to Lady Knyvett, 23 April n.y.; BL, MS Egerton 2715, fol. 178.)

[49] CUL, CUA, MS V.C. Ct. III, 19, fols. 38–41. I owe this reference to Dr Alex Shepard. The composition, repetition and public display of libellous 'ballads' was a prominent feature of early modern culture and local politics. See Adam Fox, 'Ballads, Libels and Popular Ridicule in Jacobean England', *Past and Present*, no. 145 (1994), 47–83; Adam Fox, 'Religious Satire in English Towns, 1570–1640', in Patrick Collinson and John Craig, eds., *The Reformation in English Towns, 1500–1640* (Basingstoke, 1998), pp. 221–40.

master.[50] Now Preston was the greatest pupil monger in Cambridge, with more fellow commoners on his books than he could count. His arrival in Emmanuel brought a still young college to the apogee of its fortunes, as measured by socially advantageous admissions. For Elias Travers there was only the consolation prize of the Leicestershire living of Thurcaston, part of Emmanuel's dowry provided by Mildmay's brother-in-law, the Elizabethan foreign secretary, Sir Francis Walsingham.[51]

---

[50] Joseph Mede wrote to Sir Martin Stuteville: 'Dr Travers himself whom some might suppose likely to hear of such a matter heard not the least jot of it till all was past, notwithstanding all the acquaintance and relations he left behind him.' (BL, MS Harl. 389, fol. 127.) The full story is told in Thomas Ball's 'Life of Dr Preston', Clarke 1677, pp. 92–5.

[51] Ibish 1985, pp. 564–5, 77–8.

3

Emmanuel and Cambridge: The Early Seventeenth-century Heyday

The Society: Life in a Seventeenth-century College

The seventeenth-century college was more of a monastery than its modern successor, reserved and almost embattled against the world and even the university outside. The great gatehouses of the wealthier and more established colleges, Queens', St John's, Trinity, were symbols of a kind of splendid and sovereign isolation. In the Great Gate riot of 1611, Trinity men hurled down missiles on to the skulls and shoulders of invading Johnians, 'sturdye northerne fellowes', 'tuff laddes'.[1] The young Simonds D'Ewes, a Johnian but not especially 'tuffe', returned from a 'hot' football match with Trinity with a broken shin and shared in the general punishment which followed an invasion of Trinity by the back gates in which even M.A.s were offered violence.[2] The Crown and the ministry of the day were kept at bay by the seniors with more sophisticated weapons.[3] Most physical, spiritual and even pedagogical needs were met within the college. The public schools of the university were primarily arenas for the performance of 'acts', rites of academic passage, and, as with some arts subjects today, college tuition counted for more than university lectures.

It was on those occasions when the university and town were invaded by plague that the capacity of a college to seal itself off from the outside world was most effectively demonstrated. In the visitation of 1629–30, we hear from Joseph Mede of Christ's (in his letters to his friend, the Suffolk gentleman Sir Martin Stuteville, our best informant on early seventeenth-century Cambridge): 'Our gates strictly kept, none but fellows to go forth or any to be lett in . . . Only a sizar may go with his Tutors ticket upon an errand.' (Sizars, like infantry, were dispensable.) Tradesmen left their supplies at the gates and college officers and even laundresses and bedmakers (in breach of statute) moved in. 'Thus we live as close

---

[1] Nelson 1989, I, 425–86; Clark 1906.
[2] Marsden 1851, pp. 94–6.
[3] See pp. 208–14 below.

prisoners.'[4] When the emergency was over, Mede recorded the deaths of those beyond the college gates: an under cook and some of his family, the college gardiner and all of his family, the college butcher and three of his children, two of the baker's children. 'Dr Chadderton tells me there hath dyed of the whole number about 108 in our parish.'[5] But there were no fatalities within the college.

The strict letter of the statutes of Emmanuel made its inmates prisoners, if not close prisoners, at the best and most of times. Scholars were allowed no more than twenty days' absence in a year (increased to nine weeks by a college order of 1598). Fellows were worse off, with no more than twenty days' annual holiday, 'at discretion', with another thirty days allowed exceptionally for urgent cause.[6] When in 1641 Ralph Cudworth produced medical certificates as his warrant for a visit to Tunbridge Wells, he was told by one of the fellowship 'that the same reason and certificate might be efforced for other fellows in the like case.'[7] Mildmay's Statutes insisted that fellows, no less than their pupils, should be within the college gates by nine ('let none be a walker by night nor sleep abroad at night'), that they should not frequent pubs 'or any improper place', or hold secret converse with women anywhere, especially in their rooms, where there were to be no pets or unlawful games, such as cards and dice.[8]

Fellows in their turn were to inspect the chambers of scholars twice a week, 'the ordinary visiting of chambers', to ensure that there were no 'meetings' for play, feasting and 'conversation'. Scholars who played informers on other scholars for making water or emptying chamber pots in unsuitable places were rewarded with the fine of twopence. In the assignment of rooms, preference was to be given to those scholars who had proved 'more diligent'. Recreation was allowed in three separate hours of the day, after dinner at eleven, and before and after supper at six. (But what was 'recreation'?) 'All other times should be spent in their

---

4 The Mede-Stuteville correspondence is in BL, MS Harl. 389 and 390. See D. A. J. Cockburn, 'A Critical Edition of the Letters of the Reverend Joseph Mead, 1626–1627, Contained in British Library Harleian MS 390', unpublished Cambridge Ph.D. thesis, 1994. These letters are dated 24 April, 20 Oct. and 27 Nov. 1630 and are in MS Harl. 390, fols. 516, 518 and 522–3. Of the breach of statutes, Mede wrote whimsically: 'We have taken 3 women into our College and appointed them a Chamber to lye in together . . . two are bedmakers and a Landresse . . . I hope the next parlament will include us in the generall pardon.'
5 Fuller reported that, in all, 347 townspeople died: perhaps 10–15% of the population. (Fuller 1840, p. 314.)
6 Statutes 36, 26; Stubbings 1983a, pp. 79, 66.
7 ECA, CHA.1.4.A, fol. 11r. The fact that the day was Christmas Eve and the year 1641 suggests that Cudworth had a genuine medical reason for his journey, which only one fellow opposed.
8 Statute 22; Stubbings 1983a, p. 62.

calling.'[9] In some colleges, informal allowance was made for youthful high spirits in occasional episodes of what anthropologically-minded historians call 'licensed misrule': for example, in the humiliating initiation rite known as 'salting and tucking'.[10] But in Emmanuel, salting was a cause for 'admonition'.[11]

So much for Statutes and Orders, which, suggests Dr Victor Morgan, were 'mainly directed at controlling the offspring of the elite'.[12] Reality was naturally somewhat different. Choices, and compromises, had to be made, at all levels. At St John's, in 1618–19, the young Simonds D'Ewes took exception to the common 'swearing, drinking, rioting and hatred of all piety and virtue'. 'Nay, the very sin of lust began to be known and practised by very boys.' By his own account, he began to live almost as a recluse, keeping to the college and conversing only with some of the 'honester' fellows. But D'Ewes also played football, tennis, bowls and cards. He swam in the river daily and enjoyed fishing and boat-rides.[13]

At Emmanuel, the unique 'Admonition Book' records disciplinary appearances before the master and dean, after tutorial punishment had failed. It details in roughly equal measure offences committed within the somewhat claustrophobic environment of the college and transgressions across and beyond its boundary walls.[14] On the one hand, students (not all students – these are isolated cases) call each other such names as 'rake-hell', fight amongst themselves with fists, cudgels and knives, use catapults, tear each other's gowns and ruffs; or they 'pump the skull' (i.e. put the kitchen boy or scullion under the pump) and let off fireworks at Candlemas. On the other hand, they stay out of college after the gates are locked (8 o'clock in winter, 9 in summer), or even all night, drinking and frequenting 'suspicious' or 'scandalous' houses, 'drinking wine and clamorous singinge'.[15] In 1602, the chancellor condemned 'common

---

[9] Statute 28, 'Decrees agreed upon by the Master and Fellows for the better government of the Colledge'; Stubbings 1983a, pp. 69, 103–5.

[10] Freshmen were summoned to hall to meet with their seniors, and were obliged to pronounce a witticism. If the audience laughed, they were rewarded with beer. If not, they had to consume a salt-based concoction and were 'tucked', which involved making an incision in the lip and an abrasion from lip to chin. (Morgan 1983, pp. 231–2; Marsden 1851, pp. 14–15.) See Keith Thomas, *Rule and Misrule in the Schools of Early Modern England* (Reading, 1975).

[11] ECA, CHA.1.4.A, fol. 4r.

[12] Morgan 1983, p. 219.

[13] At high table, D'Ewes, as a fellow commoner, 'sorted' himself with the fellows, and especially those of 'honest and scholar-like' conversation. (Marsden 1851, pp. 43, 96–7; Halliwell 1845, I, 141–2.)

[14] ECA, CHA.1.4.A. In the hundred years from 1586 to 1686, there were 102 cases of endogamous, 118 of exogenous misbehaviour, the latter classified as absence at night (47 cases), drinking in public places (4), visiting scandalous houses (11), going to the fair (4), riding and hunting (11). I owe this analysis to Alex Shepard, who is investigating the varieties of young masculine identity and behaviour in early modern Cambridge.

[15] ECA, CHA.1.4.A, fols. 1–12, *passim*.

frequenting of the Town by day or nighte, sitting and drinking in Taverns and other houses', 'idle common wandring about' in the fields with dogs and guns.[16] The commonest of all offences at Emmanuel was 'being out of the college and coming over the walls'. There was annual misbehaviour at the midsummer games at the Gogmagog Hills and at Stourbridge Fair in September. Bear-baiting at Chesterton brought the students out in droves, 'a great multitude of younge schollers', although this was forbidden fruit, as were the itinerant stage-plays.[17]

In 1621, two fellow commoners were said to have been drinking excessively 'in a chamber next to the open street', to the offence not only of the college but 'also of the town'.[18] Social interaction with townsmen was officially discouraged. Yet students were not monks and at home and in their grammar schools they had grown up with the young men who were now on the other side of the fence, and perhaps knew something about young women. Much interaction was aggressively adversarial, in the age-old tradition of town and gown. Emmanuel had been founded five years after a notorious Shrove Tuesday football match at Chesterton when the locals had ambushed their student opponents and many heads had been broken.[19] In 1611, six Emmanuel fellow commoners were threatened with expulsion for 'riding the horses in Mr Woolfes close [at night] and making some of them breake out into the corne.'[20]

But in other circumstances there was cooperation, and town and gown literally hunted together. Two other fellow commoners climbed back into college with the aid of a ladder 'borrowed of Manning's wife'.[21] In November 1592 there was an affray in the fields of Coton, just outside Cambridge, when a hunting party tangled with a local farmer and other villagers, and weapons were used, a sword and a dagger on the one side, pitchforks and flails on the other. When news of the affair reached a football match back in Cambridge, some of the players set out with clubs, intent on revenge. This required the weighty intervention of the vice-chancellor's court. The leading figure was the Kentish fellow commoner of Emmanuel, Denis Hartridge, whom we have already met, quarrelling with the youthful earl of Rutland.[22] Hartridge admitted that he had kept greyhounds, beagles and a horse 'ever since he came to the town', where he lived not in college but in private lodgings. From the evidence given, we gain a vivid impression of confrontation. The Coton farmer called

[16] CUL, CUA Lett.9.B.24.
[17] Nelson 1989, I, 298, 311, 339–43, 346–9, and (on the visiting troupes of players) almost *passim*. See Patrick Collinson, 'Perne the Turncoat: An Elizabethan Reputation', in Collinson 1994, pp. 204–5, 215.
[18] ECA, CHA.1.4.A, fol. 8r.
[19] BL, MS Lansdowne 33, nos. 34, 35, fols. 67, 69.
[20] ECA, CHA.1.4.A, fol. 3v.
[21] Ibid., fol. 2r.
[22] See p. 50 above.

Hartridge 'a dark knave with the gold lace'. The scholars were conducted to the village stocks and in a mocking ritual made to doff their caps and 'honour' the stocks. After this there was said to have been 'friendly conference' and a wrestling match. But this was not so much town versus gown as town against country. The hunting party included bakers and tailors, the clerk of the court noting with sadness: 'Thus townsmen and their sons keep misrule in the fields as well as scholars, but all goeth in the name and slander of scholars and the university.'[23]

The obverse of social isolation beyond the college gates was an intensification of relations within the walls of a kind which, in a post-Freudian and permissive age, we must make a deliberate effort to understand and interpret as the seventeenth century would have interpreted it, and not anachronistically. These relations, close and even intimate, existed between tutors and their pupils, and among the scholars themselves, especially in the hugger-mugger cohabitation of 'chamber fellows' and even 'bedfellows'. According to statute, scholars slept four to a room; while at Christ's, and perhaps at Emmanuel, each chamber was partitioned into, or had attached to it, four 'studies'.[24] We may take as representative of the first relationship the tutorial experience of Joseph Mede of Emmanuel's sister (or mother) college of Christ's; of the second, the touching Emmanuel story of the love affair between the future archbishop, William Sancroft, and his chamber fellow, Arthur Bownest.

Joseph Mede of Christ's had a choice and favourite pupil, Justinian Isham, the nephew of his great friend Martin Stuteville and a young Northamptonshire gentleman of promise and, indeed, future fame.[25] We learn from Mede's correspondence that it was necessary to attract such prizes by securing the best chambers, preferably close to the tutor's own rooms, a matter of competition within the fellowship; and with the master too, who in Christ's as in some other colleges (but not Emmanuel) had absolute power in this respect, a significant means of redressing the political weakness of the head's isolation.[26] To provide adequate accommodation for Justinian Isham necessitated face to face confrontation with the master, a business which made Mede 'almost sick'.[27]

---

[23] CUL, CUA V.C. Ct. III, 2/233, 234, 237, 238. I owe this reference to the kindness of Dr Alex Shepard.

[24] Statute 4; Stubbings 1983a, p. 32; Joseph Mede to Sir Martin Stuteville, 23 April 1625, BL, MS Harl. 389, fol. 428.

[25] See Sir Gyles Isham, ed., *The Correspondence of Bishop Brian Duppa and Sir Justinian Isham 1650–1660*, Northamptonshire Record Society, 17 (1951).

[26] Mede to Stuteville, 17 Feb., 10 March, 17 March 1627; BL, MS Harl. 390, fols. 206, 221, 225.

[27] Mede wrote on 17 February: 'I have not yet spoken to our Master because it is a little Hell to me to go about it . . . And I am so proud that I cannot humble my selfe to sue for a toy as some would scarce perhaps do for a Bishoprick.' On the politics and psychology of the power of heads of houses in this respect, see Morgan 1983, p. 303.

Presently there was more to be sick about. Isham, whom Mede confessed to loving 'with some degree more than a Tutor's affection', began to receive advances, including a 'panderlike' letter, from Mede's great enemy in the fellowship, William Power, a 'son of Belliall' whose practice it was (or so says Mede) 'to send for boyes and bring them out of conceit and love of their Tutors, and so to make them his own.' There were visits, Nicodemus-like, at night. Mede looked out of his window and saw Isham headed for Power's chamber, 'his man going and a sizar before him'. The seduction which Mede feared was perhaps no more than professional and theological, Power being of the other party religiously in a deeply divided college. Yet he writes of his 'jealousy' and 'passion', and of his fear that Power intended to engage the 'boys' 'in some wickedness', to make them 'little better than Filii Gehenne'.[28]

The danger seems to have passed and Mede's responsibilities towards Justinian Isham came to a satisfactory conclusion, as, over in Emmanuel, did those of the elder Ralph Cudworth, when his pupil William Sancroft the elder, a future master, won his fellowship in 1603: 'Now seeing your sonne hath served out a prentisship with me, he is at length become a freeman.' A dozen years later, when Sancroft was himself a tutor, one of his erstwhile pupils wrote: 'I think often upon that which once you said, that I was the worst pupil that ever you had.'[29] It was a settled convention for sometime pupils to refer to or address their old tutors as 'loving tutor', or perhaps 'honoured tutor'.[30]

William Sancroft the younger, the future master and archbishop of Canterbury, came up to Emmanuel in 1633, Arthur Bownest, a pensioner from a family of minor gentry in Hertfordshire, two years later. They became chamber fellows who read and studied together and became friends in a manner of friendship familiar to both young men from its models in Ovid and other pieces of classical literature. These were scenarios which many young men in the seventeenth century reenacted,

[28] Mede to Stuteville, 19 May, 26 May 1627; BL, MS Harl. 390, fols. 253, 257. On Power, see Peile 1910–13, I, 209. Thomas Leigh, scholar of Christ's and fellow of Emmanuel, reported that 'Power's pupils, thought too loose like their Tutor, were called Powritans; Chappel's, thought too precise, called Puritans; Mede's that kept the median between both, Medians'. Power was a notorious anti-Puritan who, towards the end of his forty-five year fellowship, was pursued in Cambridge market place by parliamentary soldiers with cries of 'A Pope, A Pope'.

[29] Ralph Cudworth the elder to William Sancroft the elder, 20 March (1603), BL, MS Harl. 3783, fols. 3–4; John Stoughton to William Sancroft the elder, 13 Nov. 1615, ibid., fols. 8–9. Stoughton succeeded Cudworth as rector of Aller, Somerset, and married his widow, the widow of his tutor's tutor!

[30] Over many years, Archbishop Sancroft's sometime pupil Henry Paman invariably addressed him, in all the changing scenes of his life, as 'honoured tutor'.

amongst them John Milton and Charles Diodati, for whom the poet wrote 'Epitaphium Damonis'.[31] As the academic careers of these two exceedingly diligent scholars began to burgeon (Sancroft was about to be elected to his fellowship), Bownest succumbed to what sounds like tuberculosis and went home to the country. Sancroft wrote to Bownest: 'I had a colleague in my studies, with whom I could communicate both my reading, and my doubts . . . But now . . . I sitt alone.' 'Friendships (as one said well) are but Elemented in an Universitie, and soe was ours, but they are best tried in the countrie, in absence I meane.' Bownest agreed. 'Thou art oftener in my thoughts than ever; thou art nearer mee then when I embraced thee.' He wrote to 'Will' at Emmanuel: 'Thou saiest thou lovest me: good, well repeat it againe and againe.' Will wrote to Arthur: 'Oh lett me bosome thee, lett me preserve thee next to my heart and give thee so large an interest there, that nothing may supplant thee.'

Arthur Bownest died in May 1641. His mother, who (unlike Mr Bownest) was very fond of Sancroft, described the last moments in a woman's letter, without punctuation: 'Now at last death hath opened the gate of life to my most deare sonne he departed this morning abought 4 of the clocke his departure was very quiet.' Sancroft quoted 2 Samuel 1. 26. 'I am distressed for thee, my brother Jonathan, very pleasant hast thou been unto me, thy love to me was wonderful, surpassing the love of women.' A year later, he wrote to his father: 'His converse was so sweet and so full of affection that methinks an university life hath not been to me so desirable since I lost him as before.'[32]

We may end this section with Simonds D'Ewes's farewell to Cambridge: 'So then, farewell dear Mother! – farewell dear Schools! – farewell happy lectures! – farewell faithful friends!'[33]

[31] *Works of Milton*, XII, *Miscellaneous Correspondence* (New York, 1936). The late Jeremy Maule helped me to place the Sancroft-Bownest correspondence in its literary-generical context.

[32] The Sancroft-Bownest correspondence consists of 28 items, 18 letters from Sancroft to Bownest, 10 from Bownest to Sancroft: Bodl. Libr., MSS Tanner 65, nos. 2, 13, fols. 2, 26, Tanner 67, nos. 13, 50, 68, 78, fols. 32, 125, 173, 191, Tanner 467, no. 3, fols. 20, 23–36, 38, 40–2, 44–5, 47. The preservation of the bulk of the correspondence, out of chronological sequence, in MS Tanner 467, may suggest recognition at some stage of the collation of this material of the intimate nature of the letters. There are also two letters from Sancroft to his father, reflecting on his loss, 27 May 1641, 4 April 1642; MS Tanner 66, fol. 116, MS Tanner 63, fol. 3. Both are printed in D'Oyly 1821, I, 11–14. Bownest's mother's letter to Sancroft, reporting her son's death, is written on the *verso* of a letter to Arthur from Arthur Jackson, 'your loving Brother', 10 July 1640. (BL, MS Harl. 3783, fol. 56.)

[33] Marsden 1851, p. 122.

Between Two Worlds: Country, College and Career

As Simonds D'Ewes's farewell to Cambridge reminds us, students are transitory comets, flashing across the everlasting firmament of the university. Nor, in their brief sojourn in Cambridge, were they lost to their families and friends at home. This section explores, from an Emmanuel perspective, some of the strands and networks connecting the university and its colleges with the country, in the company of the historian who has made this subject his own, Dr Victor Morgan.[1]

In seventeenth-century England, 'country' was a resonant but deeply ambiguous word, evoking both the burgeoning nation-state of England and its constituent counties; and even those microcosmic 'countries' which were all those market towns with their surrounding villages, where the majority of English people still lived out their entire lives. The historical debate about which of these senses of 'country' was the most compelling, largely prompted by the urge to explain that 'revolt of the provinces', the Civil War, has sometimes overlooked the obvious fact that it was possible to entertain multiple, or concentric patriotisms, simultaneously to identify with family, neighbourhood, county and nation; and with such artificial communities as university and college. The university itself was at one and the same time a melting pot, imposing a common formative experience on young men from diverse backgrounds and different regions, while actually consolidating county identities and contributing to regional differentiation.

This was one consequence of the growth of the collegiate system with its local roots and connections. For early modern England was the sum of its provincialities. There was no state provider to fund a system of higher education through national taxation: only the land and its produce. Cambridge and Emmanuel were literally earthed in a society the governing principle of which was, to borrow an ugly European word of our own time, subsidiarity. St John's was the college of northerners. Magdalene recruited from Lincolnshire. Corpus Christi and Gonville and Caius had all-important East Anglian connections, and at Corpus it was the rule that Norwich scholars should be taught by Norwich fellows, reading books and sleeping in bedding inherited from their Norwich predecessors. At Jesus, a fellow was supported out of income from lands held by the college in his native county.[2] Paradoxically, even the rule which prevailed at Emmanuel, that no two fellows could hail from the same county, enhanced the awareness of county origins. To be a Leicestershire or an Essex man was not an identity shed on arriving in Cambridge.

---

[1] Morgan 1974; Morgan 1983.
[2] Morgan 1974, pp. 218–19.

The invasion of the university by the sons of the gentry with their particularly strong sense of county as country was a major factor binding the colleges to their country constituencies, bonds consolidated in the embossed plate which gentlemen commoners were expected to present on going down, and by the heraldic shields which multiplied in the windows of college halls. The founder's great-grandson, the earl of Westmorland, wrote to William Sancroft the elder on the eve of a royal visit to the university, addressing him as 'Master, for so I must style you, as being a member of the college still, though discontinuance perhaps hath wiped my name out of the buttery tables or racked it quite out of the manciple's books.' Westmorland hoped to find a guest room in college 'for I would be loth to lodge in any other than where I sucked my first milk'.[3] Like modern alumni, gentlemen who had spent time in the university were looked to for benefactions. They remembered their old tutors, sent their sons to Cambridge to follow in their footsteps under carefully selected tutors; and as patrons presented men they knew through university and college connections, perhaps those very tutors, to livings in their gift.

In 1631, the Suffolk magnate Sir William Spring, sometime sheriff and M.P. for his county, wrote with false modesty to the master of Emmanuel and his fellow-countryman, the elder Sancroft. He had once been his pupil (Spring had been admitted a fellow commoner in 1603) but Sancroft would hardly remember him, 'for I was altogether obscure'. (Did not Sancroft also hail from Suffolk?) Now he was ready to send his only son to Emmanuel, to be 'under your government'. The master would oblige him if he would select a tutor 'both fit and honest to undertake the peculiar care and trust of a Jewel, so dear to me, in whose well or ill doing consists the sole hopes, or fears, of my happy, or miserable age'. 'I chiefly beg of God he may above all learn to be good and religious, and so the better able to do good service to God and his Country.'[4] Presently, Sancroft's brother wrote to announce the imminent arrival of his sons, the future Archbishop Sancroft and his brother. 'I have presumed to send them, leaving them to you to be furnished of such necessaries for the present as you shall think fit and please to direct.'[5]

The evidence for all this survives in the great seventeenth-century letter collections, letters carried to and from Cambridge by the country carriers, 'the young student's joy and expectation'; for it was the carrier who brought clean linen, home cooking, and, above all, money. Forth Winthrop wrote from Emmanuel to his father, the future governor of

---

[3] BL, MS Harl. 3783, fol. 28.

[4] Ibid., fol. 22. Spring's hopes were amply fulfilled. His son became in his turn a most religious country gentleman, sat in the Long Parliament, and served as a committee man for Suffolk and as a presbyterian church elder. (Cliffe 1984, pp. 96–7.)

[5] BL, MS Harl. 3783, fol. 24.

Massachusetts: 'You may safely deliver it to Hobson the Cambridge carrier.'[6] With the cash came anxious letters from mothers, warning against vice and the consumption of too much soft fruit. In August 1597, which saw a surfeit in Emmanuel orchard, it was Sancroft's tutor who wrote to warn his father in Suffolk that his son was eating too much fruit.[7] For those who could afford it, there was a way of getting in and out of Cambridge, another service provided by that public-spirited man Thomas Hobson in the shape of his horse hire or 'hackney' business, the famous precursor of the twentieth-century empire built on the internal combustion engine by the Marshall family. Everyone has heard of 'Hobson's choice'.

The Norfolk family of Paston, who for two hundred years never threw away a letter, has left us the fullest record of what the country carrier carried in the correspondence of the future Sir William Paston Bart., an undergraduate at Corpus, with his mother, Lady Katherine Paston. Lady Katherine and 'Will' wrote to each other two or three times a week, vying with each other to be the better correspondent. 'I do like this strife if I may so call it exceedingly well.' The carrier was kept busy transporting turkey pies and pasties, cheese and 'a few puddings', 'some marmalade'; satin suits and silk stockings, for 'it is a great commendation to see a young man spincs [sic] and neat'. With these good things came a regular flow of country news, illnesses, deaths and marriages, the threat to the coast of the Dunkirk pirates, election news; and a great deal of advice: 'Meddle not good child with any of the townsmen'; 'beware of violent tennising and leaping'; 'take heed of fruit of all sorts'; 'good child let not a poor hungry sizar want a reward from thee.' 'I hope to hear that you still hate the very smell of tobacco.'[8]

It was to Cambridge, as it were along the A11, that all traffic from London, and all the London and continental news, came first, before fanning out into the East Anglian hinterland. We know about this in great detail from the newsletters received by Joseph Mede at Christ's and passed on to Sir Martin Stuteville in Suffolk.[9] But there are several hints in Mede's correspondence that Chaderton at Emmanuel was even better informed than he was about the world beyond the university.[10] Writing from London in 1621, John Davenant wrote: 'I perceive it is lost labour to

---

[6] Morgan 1974, pp. 229–30; *Winthrop Papers*, I, 348.
[7] BL, MS Harl. 3783, fol. 1.
[8] Hughey 1941, 64–103 *passim*.
[9] See pp. 56–7 and 57n. 4 above.
[10] Mede to Stuteville, 16 August 1623: 'For news, Dr Chaderton hath been absent ever since I went, and so Dr Meddus [Mede's and Chaderton's London informant] hath not written all this time.' (BL, MS Harl. 389, fol. 352.) In October 1630, Mede reported that it was Chaderton who had been informed by Meddus of the death of the Spanish general Spinola. (BL, MS Harl. 390, fol. 518r.)

write news unto Cambridge, for you know it sooner there than we do here.'[11]

So much for our sources. But what the sources tell us is that the inter-weaving of university and country entailed more than correspondence. It was a matter of face-to-face socialising and hospitality, all set in the context of what Dr Morgan calls 'the rhythm of a provincial year'.[12] In early July, the country came to Cambridge for the Great Commencement, the formalities of graduation. Part of the light relief on these occasions was the performance of that carnivalesque figure, the praevaricator, or academic jester. On one occasion this clown alarmed the university authorities by proposing that they should serve up free roast beef to all the country clergy present, which tells us something about where the East Anglian clergy were to be found in the first week of July.[13] Then came the as yet unofficial but widely appropriated Long Vac (called by the vice-chancellor and heads in 1568 'a time of breathing'[14]). The younger Sancroft was a fellow of Emmanuel when he wrote, on 10 July 1650: ''Tis vacation with us and all weeks and days in the week are indifferent to us': a delicious moment in the year, as all university teachers know.[15]

Now was the time for the university in the shape of pupils and their tutors to go out into the country, savouring the social round of visiting and sporting and musical occasions which accompanied and followed the harvest. And then the country came back to Cambridge in September for the great Stourbridge Fair. In mid-August 1635, the young Sancroft wrote to his father to say that he hoped to see him at the fair. 'I pray forget not to send our shoes, my brother Thomas his cheese.'[16] There would be more country visits at Christmas. Elias Travers wrote from Emmanuel to the grandmother of his prize Norfolk pupil, Thomas Knyvett: 'I am well con-tented with it, to see your ladyship and his grandfather this Christide [note the Emmanuel touch], if it please your ladyship to send for him.' But there was a change of plan, Travers writing to say that he was expected to spend the festive season with another gentry family, and rather than leave the young Knyvett in college, 'I purpose to carry him together with me.'[17]

Tutors often accompanied their more valuable pupils to and from their homes in the country. When the future master of Emmanuel, Richard Holdsworth, took his pupil Simonds D'Ewes back to his Suffolk home, the young man was delighted with the sermon which he preached for his

---

[11] Morgan 1983, p. 160.
[12] Morgan 1974, p. 227.
[13] Ibid.
[14] Morgan 1983, p. 158.
[15] Bodl. Libr., MS Tanner 56, fol. 216.
[16] Bodl. Libr., MS Tanner 467, fol. 48.
[17] BL, MS Egerton 2715, fols. 145–6.

father, 'so sweetly and profitably' that he 'began to love him better than ever.' When D'Ewes went down for the last time, Holdsworth went with him and tactfully avoided any mention of the £13 his pupil owed him until he and D'Ewes *père* were together in the coach on the way to the Bury lecture.[18]

The Sancroft-Bownest correspondence, referred to in the previous section, is full of clues about these country itineraries and their significance. 'I am sorry your father opposeth your going into Suffolk with me.' 'I am here in the bosom of my dear parents, in the embrace of my loving brothers and sisters, in the midst of my kind friends and acquaintance, ... and yet the absence of my Arthur takes from the lustre of them all and oft times bemidnights my thoughts in a melancholy discontent.' 'The old cow's nurse is to be married on Thursday. There are to be 100 messes at her wedding and nothing to be wanting but thy dear company.' 'Everyone I meet poseth me with this question: "Why came not your chamberfellow with you?" '[19] One hot summer, Sancroft wrote to Bownest after a Suffolk jaunt: 'On Thursday afternoon I went to Mendham to my brother Jacob's house; on Friday to my brother Tie's house; on Saturday to Mr Bloys his house; and the Monday following we met all at Fressingfield.' And here, he added, is a pair of gloves from my sister Deb (a significant token?).[20]

At other seasons, the country experience could be less agreeable. At home in Fressingfield in a wet October, Sancroft wrote from 'sloughland in the midst of quicks and quagmires'. ''Tis so lewd a place to sojourn in ... You might justly wonder what detains me here so long.' But in truth Sancroft was in love with Fressingfield.[21] Such a love-hate relationship with 'the country' was somewhere near the heart of seventeenth-century civilisation.

There is sadly a more sombre story to tell about early seventeenth-century Emmanuel and the Suffolk rural scene. Like the unfortunate Arthur Bownest, students often went home to recover from the illnesses so easily contracted in Cambridge, or to escape them. In the summer of 1604, the young sons of Sir Edward Lewkenor of Denham came home from Emmanuel to avoid the plague, bringing with them a college friend who went down with smallpox. Both the Lewkenor parents were infected and both died, within twenty-four hours. Cambridge was enormously affected by this country tragedy and prepared a copious collection of epitaphs in Greek, Latin, Hebrew and English, a *Threnodia*, or *Funerall verses upon the death of the right worshipfull Sir Edward Lewkenor knight and*

---

[18] Marsden 1851, pp. 35, 124–5; Halliwell 1845, I, 148.
[19] Bodl. Libr., MSS Tanner 65, fol. 26, Tanner 67, fol. 32, Tanner 467, fol. 17.
[20] Bodl. Libr., MS Tanner 467, fol. 29.
[21] Bodl. Libr., MS Tanner 57, fol. 384. See p. 249 below.

Madame Susan his lady. Among the contributors were both the two future Emmanuel bishops, William Bedell and Joseph Hall.[22]

As for the career and life destinations of those whose student days were done for ever, that is a matter which ought to concern the historian of any university or college, if he aspires to transcend the normally rather narrow in-house confines of his art, for no university or college lives only in and for itself. But in its sheer prosopographical complexity, the task may be beyond him. In general, it would be good to know how far university and college acted like points of the railway of a man's life, sending him in unpredictable directions and making his career. At one extreme, we have the gentleman commoner who, having spent an agreeable year or two in Cambridge, proceeds to the inns of court and back to his native soil; on the other, the clever and aspiring scholar, perhaps from the north, who uses his success at Cambridge, and those new contacts in the country which Cambridge made possible, to find a living and a career in the ministry far from home, like John Knewstub, the leading figure among the godly clergy of early seventeenth-century Suffolk. Knewstub came to Suffolk from Westmorland, via St John's. John More, Edward Dering's closest colleague at Christ's, became the famous puritan 'apostle of Norwich', but began life in the far north-west of Yorkshire.[23] It was almost the function of colleges like St John's, or Pembroke, to provide career opportunities in the affluent south-east for clever boys from the north. For young men of a different class and aspirations, the university could open up exciting if risky opportunities at Court, or in the service of some great man. That was part of the hidden agenda of the college plays which will be touched on in the next section, for these were not the least important points of contact between Cambridge and the outside world.

For two or three generations, from about the time of Emmanuel's foundation to the Civil War, the close alliance of 'magistracy and ministry' was a striking feature of the puritan ascendancy in counties like Essex, Suffolk and Northamptonshire.[24] Some of these bonds were formed in Emmanuel, or arose from the Emmanuel connection. Thus, Sir Robert Brooke of Blythburgh, Suffolk (fellow commoner 1588), like Sir William Spring the elder a sheriff of Suffolk and like the younger Spring a presbyterian elder in the 1640s, made his contemporary John King his household chaplain. Sir Henry Mildmay, grandson of the founder, presented Humphrey Maddison (sizar 1610) to his rectory at Wanstead. The four sons of Brampton Gurdon of Assington, Suffolk, were all in residence at Emmanuel in the second decade of the seventeenth century, William for a

---

[22] Collinson 1983, p. 461.
[23] For Knewstub, an important point of reference for Emmanuel in Suffolk, see Collinson 1983, pp. 438–9, 449, 451–2, 456–7, 539; for More, ibid., pp. 296–8.
[24] Collinson 1982, pp. 141–88.

few brief months, for 'this most hopeful young gentleman' died in college within months of his arrival. John, the eldest (pensioner 1611), would be M.P. for Suffolk in both the Short and Long Parliaments. The father presented to Assington his sons' contemporary, Nathaniel Rogers (sizar 1614), who would leave for New England in 1636.[25]

Emmanuel, particularly in its East Anglian and especially Suffolk connections, presents its own scenario. Humphrey Maddison, Mildmay's minister at Wanstead, came out of Essex to Emmanuel and returned to Essex. Nathaniel Rogers came out of Suffolk and by means of Gurdon's patronage returned to Suffolk. In the case of these careers, the college may be seen as a resource for the fulfilment and consolidation of certain aspirations of those coming out of the country and going back into it, like the young William Spring, a future parliamentarian, whose father hoped that Emmanuel would make him 'better able to do good service to God and his Country'. In that perception of what a life was for, Emmanuel was as much a reinforcing part of that country which was at once Suffolk and England as the grammar school at Bury St Edmunds through which some of its students, like William Sancroft, and the Johnian D'Ewes, progressed in order to reach the university. For the fiercely royalist Sancroft, Emmanuel was the springboard which launched him into ultimate greatness, archbishop of Canterbury and the second person in precedence in the kingdom. But when all this was taken from him, it was to Suffolk and his beloved Fressingfield that he reverted, his last days spent in building a new house within sight of the house in which he was born.

Exercises, Tutorials and Comedies: the Curriculum and the Public Culture of Seventeenth-century Cambridge

Mildmay's statutes required Emmanuel students to shun 'idleness and inaction' and to 'be always occupied'; but in what? Mildmay specified the worship of God, 'the study of good learning' ('bonarum artium studiis'), and 'the cultivation of distinguished manners'. The worship of God included not only that but frequent attendance at sermons, the students busily 'diting' them in their notebooks.[1] But what in late Elizabethan and early Stuart Cambridge was 'good learning' and how was it acquired?

We have to distinguish between a kind of shell, or framework, the curriculum prescribed by the university statutes, and a rather more

---

[25] Cliffe 1984, pp. 94–5; Ibish 1985, p. 370.

[1] The future Archbishop William Sancroft's student sermon notes are in Bodleian Library, MS Sancroft 62.

elusive pedagogical reality. The shell remained formally scholastic, and the systematic ordering of knowledge invented by Aristotle still reigned supreme. So far as concerned the undergraduate course leading to the B.A. and further studies for the M.A. (with which this chapter is mainly concerned), the university statutes demanded a strict progression, year on year: according to the *Ratio Studiorum* of Edward VI (1549), a year of mathematics, designed as shock treatment for mere grammarians, then a year of dialectic (logic), followed by two of philosophy, consisting of metaphysics, physics and ethics. Elizabeth I changed this (and we shall see that this was significant) to a first year of rhetoric, followed by two years of dialectic and a fourth of philosophy.[2]

These studies, the 'arts', were concerned less with content than with method and the training of the mind. They were pursued in formal lectures in the 'schools' of the university, in which topics were pursued, scholastically, by questions, one question leading to another; in dialectical disputations, logical contests between answerers or defenders of theses and objectors, subject to formal moderation; and 'declamations', set-piece rhetorical performances, progenitors of the modern weekly 'essay'.

These were all, in the language of the day, 'exercises', and as intellectual exercises disputations, often disparaged in the sixteenth century, as now, for their 'sophistry', were superior to any written examinations, when it came to testing a student's mettle. They were conducted according to the formal rules of logic, which knew no less than forty-five illegitimate forms of syllogism or 'logical fallacies' (one of them called *'baroco'*, from which we derive 'baroque'), all of which the aspiring sophister needed to master, as well as the legitimate ones. These were also formidable tests of memory. Disputations were adversarial occasions, on which the object was to defeat, not to say humiliate, the other side. In the only complete transcription of a Cambridge disputation of the period to have come down to us, the opponent cries out at one point: 'I will slit your throat with your own sword!' ('tuo gladio jugulabo').[3] Aspirants for the B.A. were required to dispute four times in their four undergraduate years, twice as defendants, twice as opponents. More frequent disputations in college halls and chapels were warming-up sessions for the more public and intimidating encounters in the schools.[4]

---

[2] Costello 1958, Chapter One, 'The Framework of Scholasticism', Chapter Two, 'The Undergraduate Curriculum: The Arts'.

[3] Ibid., pp. 19–24. At the Marburg summit of the Protestant reformers in 1529, Zwingli exulted: 'This verse will break your neck.' Luther retorted: 'Don't be so sure! Necks don't break that easily.' Zwingli: 'I'm sorry . . . It's just a Swiss expression.' (*Documents on the Continental Reformation*, ed. William G. Naphy (Basingstoke, 1996), p. 99.) Costello remarks (p. 15): 'To call these disputations merely debates between students . . . is like describing a Spanish bullfight as the killing of a cow.'

[4] Costello 1958, pp. 14–15.

At a more senior level, disputations were a demonstration, often laid on for the benefit of visiting dignitaries, of what scholars in the university got up to. Disputations in divinity, law, physic and philosophy were the central 'acts' at the graduation ceremonies (or 'commencements') of the summer, enlivened by the antics of the carnivalesque 'praevaricator', who did his best to send the whole affair up. On one famous occasion, when the praevaricator was hardly needed, King James I much enjoyed a lively debate on the question 'whether dogs can make syllogisms', which pitted a future master of Emmanuel, John Preston, against the later bishop of Ely, Matthew Wren.[5]

But it is a good question how far these set pieces remained the sinews and life of a university education. The statutory curriculum has even been called 'moribund'.[6] However it is a moot point how far university lectures were still attended, or honoured in the breach. Then, as now, we hear complaints about lecturing to bare walls,[7] and while this appears to have been a trope, it happened literally in the still unofficial long vacation, when the statutes required lectures to continue. (Long Vacation lecturers were called 'wall' lecturers.) On the other hand, there is conflicting evidence (two lists of 1575 and 1588) that all students did indeed attend the prescribed number of lectures.[8] It is a little like the uncertainty surrounding church attendance in the same period.

What is certain is that much pedagogical activity had been displaced into the colleges, some of which were almost self-sufficient for the purposes of an undergraduate education. And the education of undergraduates now reigned supreme, as an end in itself. In Emmanuel's first five years, the university awarded 177 B.A. degrees and 128 M.A.s, but only twenty-two degrees in the higher faculties of medicine, law and divinity (none in music), a mere 7% of the total; while a high proportion of students, fellow commoners and pensioners, took no degree at all. The higher degrees in divinity might be a ticket to a fellowship, but fellows spent much of their time teaching undergraduates.[9]

The Emmanuel statutes provided for the appointment of a dean and catechist, who presided over weekly disputations in theology and every Saturday afternoon lectured on 'some article of the Christian religion'; and for a college lecturer, with a fixed stipend, assisted by an unspecified number of sub-lecturers, whose remuneration was discretionary. The

---

[5] Ibid., pp. 24–6. John Ball's *Life* of John Preston includes a full and circumstantial account of the Visitation. (Clarke, 1677, pp. 79–81.)

[6] Curtis 1959, pp. 96–7, and *passim*.

[7] Rowland Taylor, the Marian martyr and a civil lawyer, remembered 'I have read the Institutes to bare walls.' (J. S. Craig, 'The Marginalia of Dr Rowland Taylor', *Historical Research*, 64 (1991), 411–20).

[8] Feingold 1984, pp. 46 7.

[9] Curtis 1959, pp. 150–2, and *passim*.

books prescribed for these lectures were the standard texts.[10] In the seventeenth century, Emmanuel rewarded the 'head lecturer' with the statutory £2.12s.4d, and found £2 each for lecturers in Greek and Hebrew.[11]

College lectures and disputations did not necessarily conflict with the university timetable. Yet attendance at lectures and performance in disputations, whether in college hall or schools, were evidently for many undergraduates less rewarding ways of spending time than constant, even daily, exposure to one-to-one or small group instruction by their tutors. To understand this, the heart of the real academic culture of seventeenth-century Cambridge, we have to take account of several factors. These included the increased pressure from well-born students with no interest in qualifying for a degree, and the quasi-parental role of tutors in the care of these precious charges; the full impact of printing, making affordable books which to some degree rendered lectures redundant; and the ascendancy, which we may attribute to Renaissance humanism, of those skills of persuasive communication which were categorised as rhetoric, partially displacing scholastic logic, at least in fashionable esteem. The premium now placed on rhetoric takes us back to our first factor: the function of a collegiate education in 'the virtuous education of youth', more than in training professional scholars, now sometimes disparaged as 'mere scholars', which we may contrast with our expression, 'mere rhetoric'.[12]

Rhetoric, to which students arriving from the better grammar schools had already been exposed, had its own intricate and formal rules, which were learned from such classical models as the pseudo-Ciceronian *Rhetorica ad Herennium* and from ancient and modern textbooks on the subject, Quintilian's *Institutio oratoria*, Thomas Wilson's *The arte of rhetorique*. But rhetoric led by a pleasant if exacting path into a variety of literary pursuits, including poetry, history and moral and political philosophy. This was an education consisting of 'set books'. 'A training in the humanities can virtually be equated with a study of the classical languages': which meant a great deal of Latin and rather less (sometimes only a smattering) of Greek. In all this there was 'little or no connection with the discovery of new knowledge', and no sense that the modern world had in any way progressed, or could progress, beyond the world inhabited by Virgil and Horace, Cicero and Seneca.[13] The end product

---

[10] Stubbings 1983a, chapters 14, 29, 30.

[11] The bursarial accounts record payments (presumably half-yearly) of £1.6s.8d to the head lecturer; and of £2 (which dropped to £1.6s.8d between 1632 and 1636) (presumably annually) to the Greek and Hebrew lecturers. (ECA, BUR.8.2.)

[12] Curtis 1959, Chapter 4 'The Virtuous Education of Youth'.

[13] I follow the best account of the Renaissance rhetorical tradition now available, Quentin Skinner, *Reason and Rhetoric in the Philosophy of Hobbes* (Cambridge, 1996), ch. 1, 'The Study of Rhetoric'. See also T. W. Baldwin, *William Shakespere's Small Latine and Lesse Greeke*, 2 vols. (Urbana, Illinois, 1944).

was not dialectical conquest in disputation but elegant and persuasive speech, to be deployed in Parliament and other political fora, in the law courts, in the pulpit, in letter writing.

The method consisted of reading and re-reading the set texts, not a solitary reading but a reading shared with the tutor and perhaps with a chamber fellow[14]; the taking of notes or remembering 'without book'; and 'commonplacing', the collection in notebooks large and small of choice passages from the texts. Such was the essence of the formation of a public man of the seventeenth century. Often Latin fluency was later lost. That great Emmanuel worthy, Bishop Joseph Hall, wrote in his old age: 'My Latin style is rusty with want of use.'[15] But the mental habits which went with the Latin style died hard.

Surviving commonplace books from the seventeenth century are to be found in all our great libraries and archives. But the most remarkable and telling evidence for the lifelong persistence of these disciplines and habits has been left behind by Emmanuel's William Sancroft (the future arch-bishop).[16] In the Bodleian Library will be found scores of Sancroft's notebooks and commonplace books, closely written in his distinctive miniscule, some of them containing hundreds of thousands of words.[17] They take us from Sancroft's Bury St Edmunds schoolboy essays through the sermons he 'dited' as a student to notebooks apparently dating from his old age, as a deprived archbishop of Canterbury: literature (MS Sancroft 29 contains a great deal of Shakespeare)[18], scientific memorabilia, dreams and divinations, jests and scurrilous satires, like the Great Parliament Fart of 1607: 'Reader, I was born and cry'd/Crackt so, smelt so, and so dy'd.'[19]

William Holdsworth, the elder Sancroft's successor and fourth master of Emmanuel, had migrated from St John's, where he was Simonds

---

[14] Lisa Jardine and Anthony Grafton, ' "Studied for Action": How Gabriel Harvey Read His Livy', *Past and Present*, 129 (November, 1990), 30–78; William H. Sherman, *John Dee: The Politics of Reading and Writing in the English Renaissance* (Amherst, Mass., 1995).

[15] Bishop Joseph Hall to Samuel Hartlib, 5 June n.y. (1642 or later?), Sheffield University Library, Hartlib Papers, 5/2/11B.

[16] There are 145 volumes of Sancroft MSS in the Bodleian Library, most of them notebooks of one kind or another. See the *Summary Catalogue of Western Manuscripts*, III, nos. 10302 ff. See also Bodleian Library, MS Rawlinson D 816. See especially MS Sancroft 87 for lecture notes and academic commonplaces.

[17] MS Sancroft 28 contains 411 closely written pages, perhaps 300,000 words; MS Sancroft 27 286 pages, or 220,000 words. But other MSS contain blank pages, 'multa vacua' in the words of the Catalogue.

[18] The schoolboy exercises are in Bodleian Library, MS Tanner 467. The 'dited' sermons are in MS Sancroft 62. There are further literary collections in MSS Tanner 465 and 466, including Milton's 'Let us with a gladsome mind', noted by Sancroft as 'done at 15 years old'. (MS Tanner 466, fols 20v–1r.)

[19] MS Sancroft 55. MS Sancroft 31 (200 folios) contains 64 of William Sancroft the elder's sermons, perhaps preached in Emmanuel.

D'Ewes's 'loving tutor'.[20] It was probably in that college that he compiled his 'Directions for Students in the Universitie', which are preserved in Emmanuel College MS 48.[21] Holdsworth was an academic Polonius whose moral exhortations were predictable and timeless: 'Many loose a great deale of time in visiting . . . a little acquaintance in the University is enough.' Resist the temptation to lie in. 'Step but out of bed and the danger is over.' His practical advice, which related only to the studies overseen by the tutor and ignored altogether the more public dimension of lectures and disputations, defined in the greatest detail the long haul of a four-year reading course in the set books, laying down the order of subjects to be studied and distinguishing between books to be tasted and those to be thoroughly absorbed and digested. Holdsworth (who died possessed of a library of some 10,000 books, now dispersed in the University Library collections) betrays a considerable rhetorical and literary bias. The strategy was to progress from 'a plain, easy and familiar style' to something 'more raised and polished'; and to be furnished in the formal university acts 'with quaint and handsome expressions'. These and 'many choice and witty sayings, sentences and passages' were to be stored in a commonplace book, with detailed advice on how to organise such a book. A literary syllabus without tears, and with most texts to be read in English, was realistically prescribed for those who had no intention of making scholarship their profession, 'but only to gett such learning as may serve to delight and ornament'.

But the most interesting feature of Holdsworth's Directions, and its most radical departure from the statutory curriculum, was in substituting for a horizontal allocation of a student's time by year and subject a vertical scheme which distinguished between morning and afternoon studies: a varied day, with morning devoted to a progressively more advanced course in logic and philosophy, afternoons to the more relaxed arts of expression, poetry, classical oratory and history. William Sancroft, who took his B.A. in 1637, the year in which Holdsworth became master of Emmanuel, and won his fellowship five years later, made Holdsworth his model. 'Your counsel was both card and compasse.' It was his only hope to live under Holdsworth's 'happy discipline' to receive his directions 'for study, for life, for all'.[22] It is therefore interesting to find Sancroft prescribing for himself (in 1636) an exacting vacation routine of unrelenting and mostly private study. 'Breakfasts are breakestudies. I'll abjure

---

[20] Marsden 1851, p. 37, and *passim*; Halliwell 1845, *passim*.
[21] Printed in *ECM* I, no. 2 (1889), IV, no. 1 (1892) and IV, no. 3 (1893).
[22] William Sancroft to Richard Holdsworth, 19 August n.y., Bodleian Library, MS Tanner 61, fol. 64v; William Sancroft to Bishop Ralph Brownrigg of Exeter, 14 August 1649, MS Tanner 56, no. 52, fol. 94.

them.'[23] Later he prescribed for one of his own pupils a plan closely resembling Holdsworth's: 'First in the morning steps forth holy Hebrew in an antique but grave matronlike garbe to perfume the aire ... Then forth comes Seneca ... with his Philosophicall beesome ... At last enters Horace ... with his basket of flowers to deck and garnish all.'[24] An early eighteenth-century Emmanuel MS merely renews Holdsworth's Directions, which perhaps remained the tutorial norm.[25]

Holdsworth's scheme, which mingled logic and rhetoric on a daily basis, was designed to bring the two disciplines into fruitful conjunction. 'Logic without Oratory is drye and unpleasing, and Oratory without Logicke is but empty babling.' Something of the same desire for a practical simplification and mutual penetration of the reasoning and persuasive arts explains the appeal in late sixteenth-century Cambridge (but not in Oxford) of the French *savant* Pierre de la Rame (Ramus) (*c.* 1515–1572).[26] Ramus had boldly declared in his M.A. thesis that 'everything affirmed on the authority of Aristotle is artificial and contrived.' This was the start of 'a career of unremitting polemical violence'[27], which forced the Protestant academies of Europe (Ramus was a Huguenot who perished in the St Bartholomew massacre in 1572) to choose between the Aristotelian and Ramist systems of both logic and rhetoric. Ramus rearranged the relative dispositions of the two disciplines (his logic is sometimes said to have been no more than a form of rhetoric), and simplified the structural composition of both. As a *méthode* we may compare its attractions to those of structuralism or post-modernism or other forms of 'theory' in the modern world.

Ramism, which proceeds like a modern computer through a relentless series of binary divisions and choices, is thought to have held particular attractions for advanced Calvinists, and to have had something to do with 'the rise of Puritanism'.[28] Certainly it was favoured in the colleges of that persuasion, Emmanuel included, as we learn from the book inventories of members of the college who died in 1593 and 1621, each

---

[23] Bodl., MS Sancroft 80, p. 3. I am grateful to the Keeper of Western MSS at the Bodleian, Mrs Mary Clapinson, and to Dr Bruce Barker-Benfield, for a transcript of this portion of a notebook 'in a pitiful state, its pages blackened by acid corrosion'. (Letter to the author, 5 May 1994.) Sancroft wrote to Bownest: 'Thou biddest me take heed of studying too much. That bridle was ill bestowed on me, that wants a spurre.' (MS Tanner 467, fol. 23.)

[24] Addressed to 'Jacobissimo suo'; Bodl., MS Tanner 467, fol. 60v.

[25] ECL, MS 179. (See Curtis 1959, p. 134.)

[26] W. J. Ong, *Ramus, Method and the Decay of Dialogue* (Cambridge, Mass., 1958); Lisa Jardine, 'Humanistic Logic', in *The Cambridge History of Renaissance Philosophy*, ed. Charles B. Schmitt *et al.* (Cambridge 1988), pp. 173–98.

[27] Skinner 1996, p. 59.

[28] Miller and Johnson 1938, pp. 28–41; also H. Kearney, *Scholars and Gentlemen* (London, 1970), ch. 3.

containing several texts of Ramus.[29] At the turn of the century, the Philosophy School was disturbed by violent clashes between Aristotelians and Ramists. Some 'made bitter invectives agaynst Aristotle', while two scholars of Clare, including Thomas Paske, a future master, hung up a picture of Ramus on a rope and 'did rayle uppon Christs College, Emmanuel and Kynges College.' 'The company beganne to knock and from knocking they came to blowes.' A Kingsman and later a famous puritan divine, William Gouge, was involved in this fracas as a champion for Ramus. It appears from his 'Life' that it was a quarrel between young sophisters (Paske and Gouge were both very junior), and was prompted by the thesis proposed for debate: 'No-one will be great for whom Ramus is great.' The Vice-Chancellor's Court did its best to impose peace. 'Albeyt wee of the universitye for Philosophye matters have preferred Aristotle, yet Ramus ys not to be abused with reprochefull words.'[30]

There is a conventional view that with the undergraduate syllabus dominated by a blend of old scholasticism and new humanism, and theology queening it over the other higher faculties, there was no room in early seventeenth-century Cambridge for mathematical and scientific pursuits, so that the roots of the so-called scientific revolution have to be looked for elsewhere, and mainly in London.[31] This is not the whole truth, and certainly not the truth about Emmanuel, even if mathematical and scientific texts are noticeable by their absence from the early library catalogues of the college.[32] The false notion of a 'mathematical desert' in which the flowering of Isaac Newton was improbable[33] owes much to the testimony of John Wallis, who came up to Emmanuel in 1632, and who later participated with Robert Boyle and others in scientific meetings in London which were the germ of the Royal Society.[34] Wallis claimed that before he came to Cambridge mathematics was for him but 'a pleasing Diversion at spare hours', and was generally disparaged as a mechanical rather than academical study. Among the 200 students at Emmanuel in his time, there were no more than two, 'perhaps not any', who knew more of mathematics than he did.

But this testimony is most unreliable. Wallis's contemporaries in the 1630s included that 'very curious astronomer' Jeremiah Horrox of Toxteth, who accurately predicted and on 24 November 1639 with his friend William Crabtree was the first to witness and describe the transit of

[29] John Cocke, fellow, d. 1593; Alexander Clugh, M.A. 1610, d. 1621. (Leedham-Green 1986, I, nos. 173, 193, pp. 528, 574.)
[30] CUL, CUA MS V.C. Ct. II 3, fols. 95v–7, III 8, fol. 83 (a reference I owe to the kindness of Dr Alex Shepard); Clarke 1677, p. 235.
[31] Costello 1958, Chapter Three 'The Undergraduate Sciences'.
[32] Bush and Rasmussen 1986.
[33] Costello 1958, pp. 103–4; a notion, and an over-view of early seventeenth-century Cambridge, learnedly refuted in Feingold 1984.
[34] Feingold 1984, pp. 86–8; DNB, art. Wallis.

Venus; and John Worthington, a future master of Jesus, who in 1659 sent Samuel Hartlib a copy of Horrox's *Venus in sole vista* and reported on the contents of his astronomical papers.[35] Wallis's tutor was Benjamin Whichcote, who had in common with his fellow Cambridge Platonists, John Smith and Ralph Cudworth, many scientific interests, which were shared by another contemporary of the 1630s, William Sancroft, or so his library lists and notebooks suggest.[36] Wallis's generation was preceded by John Bainbridge (M.A. 1607), part of the godly stock of Ashby-de-la-Zouch, and the first Savilian professor of astronomy at Oxford (1619), who in that same year published an astronomical description of Halley's Comet which had appeared in 1618, and had 'turned almost everyone into an astronomer'.[37] There was also Samuel Foster, a fellow of Emmanuel in the 1620s, who became professor of astronomy at Gresham College. It was in Foster's rooms that the founders of the Royal Society held their early meetings. All these Emmanuel men were familiar with the work of the innovatory giants, Copernicus, Galileo and Kepler.[38] Admittedly some of this science was of a visionary kind. John Sadler, another of the cohort of the 1630s and, in 1650, master of Magdalene, sat bolt upright in his bed in Dorset in 1661 and accurately prognosticated the Great Plague and Great Fire of London, the rebellion of the duke of Monmouth and the Revolution of 1688.[39]

Any account of the public culture of early seventeenth-century Cambridge which omitted any mention of the 'comedies' performed in many of the colleges (and most accounts do) would be sadly deficient, even more deficient than a history of modern Cambridge which failed to mention the Footlights.[40] There is no doubt that college plays, usually called comedies on the pattern of the Latin dramatist Terence, were the most popular and well-attended public events of early modern Cambridge, on the success or failure of which individual and corporate reputations depended heavily. A large part of the rationale for the

---

[35] Feingold 1984, p. 105; *DNB*, arts. Horrox and Crabtree; John Worthington to Samuel Hartlib, 28 April 1695, BL, MS Harl. 7033, fol. 85v.

[36] Feingold 1984, p. 88; 'A Catalogue of my bookes in mine owne study', Bodl., MS Sancroft 122; Sancroft's books in Emmanuel College Library. MS Sancroft 28 (pp. 190 ff.) contains notes on fossils, crabs and lobsters, extracted from a Venetian work of 1646 by Alessandro Tasdoni.

[37] Feingold 1984, pp. 113–14, 143–52, 162; *DNB*, art. Bainbridge.

[38] Feingold 1984, p. 114; *DNB*, art. Foster. In 1635 Jeremiah Horrox purchased Lansberg's *Tabulae Motuum coelestium perpetuae* (1632), and on the last leaf recorded the titles of works by Copernicus, Kepler, Brahe and others. (Ibid., p. 105.)

[39] *DNB*, art. Sadler; ECA, COL.9.1A (William Bennet's book). And should we mention Frost, the Emmanuel manciple, who had 'all manner of Mathematicall Instruments', and who was credited with the invention of a perpetual motion machine? 'For by it the use of Horses will be taken away . . . By it may be made to flye throughout the aire.' (Sheffield University Library, Hartlib Papers, Hartlib's Ephemerides, 30/4/9, 28/2/38B. See B. Capp, *Astrology and the Popular Press* (London, 1979); below, pp. 129, 272–3.

[40] For much of what follows, see Nelson 1989 and Nelson 1994.

building of the great hall at Trinity seems to have been theatrical, to steal the thunder of St John's, which had the strongest dramatic culture in Cambridge in the sixteenth century,[41] and to put Trinity in the forefront of attention on the occasion of royal visits. Completed under Thomas Neville's mastership in 1608, this is England's oldest surviving theatre.[42] The comedies were an important point of contact between the colleges and the Court, and a star performance could be the first step to a glittering career.[43] Sometimes colleges called back from London their 'auncient good actors', like Oxford today hiring American postgraduates for its blue boat. Plays were defended as an important academic adjunct, 'for the emboldening of their Iunior schollers, to arme them with audacity'.[44]

But the comedies could also be very riotous, even violent affairs. It was not unusual to have to repair broken windows on the morning after the night before. In 1606, we hear of 'fowle and greate disorder comitted in the time of a Comedy in Kings College by most rude and barbarous throwinge of many greate stones at and thorow the hall windowes with loud outcryes and showtinge by multitude of schollars'.[45] The most dramatic of these disturbances was the riot at the Great Gate of Trinity which lasted for two nights in February 1611.[46] The Trinity men, and especially the stage-keepers (stewards and 'bouncers', but also M.A.s of the college), were determined to exclude the Johnians, 'divers northern tuff laddes', 'Yorkeshyre men', who were equally intent on getting in. The Johnians carried clubs and used them. The Trinity stage-keepers thrust their burning links into the chests of their opponents, while stones and brickbats were hurled down from the battlements of the Great Gate on to the dense crowd trapped in the narrow passage which at that time led to it. Others proceeded to demolish the battlements. St John's was in no doubt that Trinity 'intended the quarrel', Trinity that it was 'before intended by Saint Iohns men'.[47] At one point the vice-chancellor arrived to observe the disturbances but prudently retreated.

---

[41] At the time of James I's visit to Cambridge, and mainly to Trinity, in 1614, it was said, ruefully, by a Johnian that 'the tyme was when St Iohns had the best actors and teachers in all the universitye'. Note the order. Thomas Legge's *Richardus Tertius*, a Latin play of 10,000 lines by the Master of Caius, had been played at St John's in 1578–9. (Nelson 1989, p. 713; Nelson 1994, p. 61.)

[42] Ibid., pp. 39–40.

[43] In 1614, the future preacher, Samuel Fairclough, who had scruples about acting a part in female costume in the play *Ignoramus*, was advised that 'by his acting he would become known to the Court . . . and get preferment'. Another puritan with scruples was told that 'if he played this game well, he might winne more then could be hoped for elsewhere'. (Nelson 1989, pp. 543, 544.)

[44] Ibid., pp. 853–4.

[45] Ibid., p. 411. See also pp. 361, 407–9, 491, 499.

[46] Ibid., pp. 425–86; Clark 1906.

[47] Nelson 1989, pp. 432, 472.

The root cause of such riotous scenes as this was a shortage of tickets.[48] It was those who could not get in who threw the stones which broke windows. Yet at Trinity, as many as 2000 spectators could be crammed into Neville's hall.[49] Why the comedies were so popular is a little mysterious. Many of them were in Latin and they could last for four or five hours, and sometimes seven or eight. When Prince Charles and the Elector Palatine attended the Trinity comedy in 1612 (Samuel Brooke's *Adelphe and Scyros*) the play was said to be tedious, two or three hours too long.[50] In 1614 James I came across from Newmarket in wintry weather to see four plays on four nights, including George Ruggle's *Ignoramus*, a farcical attack on the common lawyers. Although John Chamberlain thought the play 'more then half marred with extreme length', the king loved it, 'laughed exceedingly and offentymes with his handes and by wordes applauded it.' Later he returned for a repeat performance. This would be remembered many years after the event as a 'famous day', and from its reverberations we derive our word 'ignoramus'.[51]

There were no Emmanuel men implicated in the Great Gate riot[52] and there were few comedies at Emmanuel, although some Emmanuel men wrote plays[53] and Emmanuel regularly contributed to the costs incurred in staging plays for royal visitors.[54] William Sancroft was an avid play-goer and made his own copies of many plays (sometimes with the cast list), including William Johnson's anti-puritanical *Valetudinarium*, performed at Queens' in February 1638.[55] In February 1640, Sancroft wrote to Bownest: 'I gott a good place at Emmanuel College commedy', and went on with some pleasant gossip about the leading actor missing his cue because he was passing water. 'The audience expecting, actors stamping and raging.'[56] This performance, the only one we know of in Emmanuel itself, appears to be otherwise unrecorded. And soon the gathering storm clouds of the English revolution would put a stop to comedy throughout Cambridge.

---

[48] Clark 1906, pp. viii–x.

[49] Nelson 1989, p. 540.

[50] Ibid., pp. 515, 713. See also p. 640.

[51] Ibid., pp. 542, 638, 714, 861–4.

[52] Clark 1906, p. xx. Well over a hundred names appear in court proceedings.

[53] William Ainsworth's *Clytophon c.* 1625 and William Mew's *Pseudomagia c.* 1626. (Nelson 1989, p. 753.)

[54] In 1614–15, 1629, 1632, 1635. (Ibid., p. 753; ECA, BUR.8.2.)

[55] ECL, MS 52. See *Renaissance Latin Drama in England*, 2nd ser. 18 (1991), ed. H. J. Wechermann. (I owe this reference to the late Jeremy Maule.) See also Nelson 1989, pp. 925–6, 961–2, Nelson 1994, p. 35.

[56] William Sancroft to Arthur Bownest, 23 February 1639(40); Bodleian Library, MS Tanner 67, no. 50, fol. 125.

The Great Worthies of the First Age: Ward, Bedell and Hall

In this section, we leave the company of the gentlemen commoners, with their greyhounds and beagles and sights set on success in Court and Country, and we turn our attention to those dedicated scholars and budding divines for whom Emmanuel was founded, most of them bound, not only by statute but also by economic necessity, to look for a vocation beyond the university, in the ministry of the Church.

Everyone who graduated into the ministry from Emmanuel had been nurtured in the same tradition and exposed to a common experience: in a word, to the Puritanism to be further explored in chapter 6. But thereafter their lives took a variety of trajectories, and they assumed some surprising identities. Thomas Bywater (at Emmanuel in 1601) was implicated with the minor Northamptonshire gentleman Lewis Pickering (admitted 1587)[1] in the curious non-conspiracy known as the 'Bywater Plot'. It was all about an indiscreet petition to the king, 'the most saucy and dangerous thing that ever I saw', as someone wrote, and deemed seditious. Bywater disappeared into the Tower of London, never to be heard of again.[2] If that was to take Emmanuel religion to unacceptable extremes, others reacted violently against it. In the same year that Bywater went to gaol, Oliver Ormerod (admitted 1596) perpetrated an anti-Emmanuel satire, *The Picture of a Puritane.*[3]

James Wadsworth (admitted 1586) was a more drastic reactionary. A prosperous Suffolk clergyman with two or three livings and a wife and four children, he seems to have been already a secret catholic convert when, in 1605, he went as a chaplain to the English embassy in Madrid. Here he came out, fell in with the Jesuits, found employment with the Spanish Inquisition, and became English tutor to the Infanta at about the time of the abortive Spanish Match. In 1615 he discussed his conversion with the world at large in *The contrition of a protestant preacher*. 'I was a swyneheard, a protestant minister, feeding my selfe and others with the huskes of heresye.' This led to a famous triangular correspondence with Wadsworth's old Emmanuel contemporaries, the two future bishops, William Bedell and Joseph Hall. His son, James Wadsworth the younger,

---

[1] Ibish 1985, pp. 373–4.

[2] *HMC Report, Hatfield MSS.*, xvii. *passim*; W. J. Sheils, *The Puritans in the Diocese of Peterborough 1558–1610*, Publications of the Northamptonshire Record Society 30 (1979), 110–11. There is a copy of Bywater's petition in Bodl., MS Rawlinson B 151, fol. 95v. The 'someone' was James Montague, master of Sidney Sussex College.

[3] Oliver Ormerod, *The picture of a puritane: or, a relation of the opinions, and practises of the Anabaptists in Germanie, and of the puritanes in England. Wherunto is annexed Puritano-papismus* (*STC* no. 18851) (London, 1605).

reconverted to Protestantism, and made a dubious name for himself with picaresque accounts of his adventures in the world of 'Spanish Popery and Iesuiticall Strategems'.[4]

There was worse to come. Richard Kilby (admitted 1593), though a clergyman, lost his faith and caused a minor sensation by publishing, anonymously, *The burthen of a loaden conscience* (ten editions, 1608–1630), in which he confessed to living a lie. 'I have no power to turn unto God.' 'This hath been the inside of my life.'[5] It begins to look as if Emmanuel, and perhaps William Perkins, had much to answer for.

But most of the men whom Emmanuel sent out into the early Stuart Church fell into two less bizarre categories. A minority remained radical and unreconstructed Puritans, unemployable or deployed on the fringes of the establishment and in pockets of private puritan patronage. Such were William Bradshaw (admitted 1588), author of *English Puritanisme* (Amsterdam, 1605), and in his ecclesiology a founding father of Congregationalism[6]; Josias Nicholls of Kent (admitted 1590), namesake of a no less radical father who, like other extreme Puritans, was forced to make his living as a schoolmaster[7]; and John Rogers (admitted 1588), the famous lecturer of Dedham, to whom the sermon-gadders of Ipswich flocked, saying 'let's go to Dedham to get a little fire'.[8]

The majority moderated their Puritanism (without necessarily losing its essence), and some became serviceable and successful pillars of the

---

[4] James Wadsworth (the elder), *The contrition of a protestant preacher, converted to be a catholique scholar* (St Omer, 1615); *The copies of certaine letters which have passed betweene Spaine and England in matters of religion* (London, 1624), reprinted in successive editions of Gilbert Burnet's *The Life of William Bedell* (London 1685 (anonymously, at a delicate moment politically), 1692, 1736); James Wadsworth (the younger), *The English Spanishe pilgrime, or, a new discoveries of Spanish popery and Iesuiticall Stratagems* (London, 1629, 1630); *Further observations of the English Spanish pilgrims* (London, 1630). The 1629 edn of *The English Spanishe pilgrime* was dedicated to the earl of Pembroke, chancellor of the University of Oxford, the 1630 edn. to the chancellor, vice-chancellor, heads of houses and other members of the University of Cambridge.

[5] Kilby, a Derby curate, subsequently (1618) published a far from reassuring account of his spiritual deliverance: *Hallelu-iah: praise yee the Lord, for the unburdening of a loaden conscience*. Simonds D'Ewes found Kilby's *Burthen* 'ridiculous' and 'sottish', and wondered whether it was a stunt. Nevertheless, it 'almost scared' him out of keeping his own diary. (Marsden 1851, p. 70.) See Peter Lake, 'Richard Kilby: A Study in Personal Failure', in W. J. Sheils and Diana Wood, eds., *The Ministry: Clerical and Lay, Studies in Church History*, 26 (Oxford, 1989), pp. 221–35.

[6] Thomas Gataker, 'The Life and Death of Master William Bradshaw', in Clarke 1677, pp. 25–60; Lake 1982, pp. 262–78.

[7] Ibish 1985, p. 503; Peter Clark, 'Josias Nicholls and Religious Radicalism, 1553–1639', *Journal of Ecclesiastical History*, 28 (1977) 133–50; *DNB, Missing Persons*, pp. 494–5. Josias Nicholls senior became a schoolmaster after his deprivation, and all three of his sons, Suretonhie and Repentance, as well as Josias junior, laboured in the same profession. The Elizabethan preacher John Field wrote: 'Through the over-much tyranny of those that should be my encouragers, I am compelled instead to teach children, so that I cannot employ myself wholly unto that which I am bent most earnestly.' (Collinson 1983, p. 341.)

[8] Ibid., p. 544.

establishment. Such was Thomas Jackson (admitted 1589), who was a minister at Wye in Kent where the incorrigible Nicholls was schoolmaster, but who went on to become a prebendary and a famous preacher in Canterbury Cathedral, where he was characterised as 'fluviosus', for the volume and fluency of his pulpit utterances. Many of these were hotly judgmental, in the prophetic manner of his mentor, William Perkins. One such sermon, on a text in Jeremiah, was called *Judah must into captivity*: 'Pray not for this people . . . for I will not hear thee.' God really meant it, but, 'how ever thinges goe, it shall be well with the just'. 'Things' went so well for just Prebendary Jackson that he became a millionaire (in seventeenth-century values), disposing of thousands of pounds entirely within his own family, without a thought for the poor.[9] All these were products of Emmanuel in its first twenty years.

Of those who compromised, three of Emmanuel's early *alumni* entered the ranks of the great and the good of early Stuart England, and they deserve more than a passing mention. These were Samuel Ward, master of Emmanuel's little sister, Sidney Sussex; and the only two Emmanuel men to become bishops before the Civil War: William Bedell and the great Joseph Hall, a cedar towering above his contemporaries, but blasted by the storm which struck the Church and nation, just as his career reached its natural zenith. Indeed, all three of our great worthies, Ward, Bedell and Hall, came to unmerited grief in those violently pregnant years, 1641–1643.

Samuel Ward, like the obscure Richard Kilby, tells us about the 'inside' of his life in a diary which is among the most celebrated of puritan documents.[10] Like other anxious Calvinists, the young Ward used his diary-keeping as a kind of quasi-confessional religious discipline, daily monitoring small faults and failings, and taking his spiritual temperature in a generally self-reproachful tone which was as conventional as it may have been heartfelt. Recurrent words are 'pride', 'negligence', 'slackness', 'unthankfulness'. 'Oh, what a wretch am I, who will not serve God and rely on him who filleth my hart with spirituall comfort, when I deserve nothing by my hardness of hart, but his wrath.'[11]

Reflecting more positively on 'Godes Benefites', Ward marvelled that God had brought him to Cambridge, and to Christ's College, and that in the last years of the great William Perkins, the spiritual and theological prince of late Elizabethan Cambridge. 'That in Mr P. his time I should be here.'[12] Ward came from impoverished gentry stock in Durham, and the

---

[9] Patrick Collinson, Nigel Ramsay and Margaret Sparks, eds., *A History of Canterbury Cathedral* (Oxford, 1995), pp. 180–2.

[10] Extracts (from the original in Sidney Sussex College) printed in Knappen 1933. The modern authority on Ward is Professor Margo Todd, who is mining the vast deposits of Ward materials in Sidney.

[11] Knappen 1933, p. 119.

[12] Ibid., pp. 119, 127, 130.

need to provide for his 'poor kindred' may explain his somewhat worldly pluralism, and why he delayed his marriage until he was in his fifties.

Ward's career began uncertainly. Apart from the ordinary anxieties about a fellowship ('the running of my mynd upon the Fellowship, all the day long'[13]), a speech impediment raised serious doubts about his fitness for the ministry. But in 1598, Ward gained a fellowship not at Christ's but at Emmanuel, the first to be elected from outside the society. Ward was always a scholar rather than a preacher, the quality of his learning acknowledged when he was appointed to the panel revising the Apocrypha for the 1611 Authorised Version of the Bible.

Thereafter, Ward never looked back. His patron was the greatest and goodest of Jacobean churchmen, James Montague, the first master of Sidney Sussex College and subsequently bishop in turn of Bath and Wells and Winchester, a favourite churchman with James I and the editor of his published works. Montague's own background was in Northampton-shire puritan stock, he had preached Perkins's funeral sermon, and he proved to be adept at turning puritan poachers into establishment game-keepers, building up both in Somerset and at Winchester pockets of staunchly Calvinist ex-puritan churchmanship.[14] Ward rose in the great man's shadow. In 1610 he succeeded Montague as master of Sidney and he would remain in that college for thirty-three years. For twenty of those years, he was Lady Margaret Professor. As we shall see[15], in the 1620s and 1630s Ward was sheet anchor of Cambridge 'orthodoxy' in the face of Arminian revisionism. With Joseph Hall he defended the same cause on the international stage as one of the English delegates at the Synod of Dort. Montague made him archdeacon of Taunton, and he added to his portfolio of preferments a couple of country livings and a prebend in York minster. He was perhaps more anxious than a 'Puritan' should have been to avoid the obligations of residence. But whether or not he sought it, nothing better came his way. As with Bedell and Hall, it was Ward's misfortune to live on into interesting times. Towards the end, he found himself a royalist Puritan who spent some of his last weeks in custody, by order of Oliver Cromwell, who had lived under his authority as a student at Sidney Sussex.[16] Another Sidney man, Thomas Fuller, who was devoted to Ward's memory, wrote: 'He turned with the Times as a Rock riseth with the Tide.'[17]

William Bedell (who should be pronounced 'Beadle'), the son of an Essex yeoman farmer (and of a mother who practised as an amateur surgeon), was one of the first students to be admitted to Emmanuel, in

[13] Ibid., p. 110.
[14] Tyacke 1973, p. 123; Collinson 1982, pp. 85–9; Fincham 1990, pp. 229–30, 267.
[15] See p. 205.
[16] Knappen 1933, pp. 48–9.
[17] Thomas Fuller, *The Worthies of England*, quoted, Knappen 1933, p. 48.

1584, at the tender age of twelve.[18] He became the lifelong friend of Samuel Ward (they were both born in 1572 and died within a year of each other), shared and indeed exceeded his advanced proficiency in the ancient tongues, and was elected a fellow somewhat ahead of him, in 1593.[19] He seems to have acquired William Perkins's library.[20] In 1601, the statute *De mora* sent Bedell out into the ministry and to Bury St Edmunds, where he became town preacher. In frequent letters between Cambridge and Bury, Bedell and Ward talked themselves into the pragmatic advantages of ritual conformity. 'A likely matter', wrote Bedell, that they would persuade the new king 'in the twinckling of an eye' to change his religious policy. He was 'more vehement for these ceremonyes then the bishops themselves.' But Bedell's position in the heartland of Puritanism was exposed. He was accused of being 'a patron and persuader to the ceremonies', and yet, in deference to the consciences of others, withheld subscription. In a sermon before the bishop he 'wished the names of Puritan and precisian cast to hell, that we might be knowne only by the name of Christians'.[21]

That was the beginning of the reconstruction of a Puritan. The next stage took Bedell to the exotic setting of Venice, where he served as chaplain to Sir Henry Wootton, who at about this time invented the celebrated witticism about the ambassador sent to lie abroad for the good of his country. It was a time when the papal interdict against Venice and the activities of Paolo Sarpi, historian of the Council of Trent, raised false hopes that the republic was about to turn protestant. That did not happen, but Bedell became Sarpi's bosom friend, translated the Prayer Book into Italian (and would later render Sarpi's *History* into Latin), and learned that Roman Catholics are Christians too.[22]

After a trip to Constantinople, Bedell returned to Suffolk and to considerable obscurity, first back in Bury, where he settled another great Italian friend, Dr Despotino, and acted as the interpreter between the doctor and his patients; and then in the living of Horningsheath (or Horringer) where he succeeded the contentious Thomas Rogers, preacher

---

[18] *Two Biographies* of Bedell, by his son William Bedell (taken from Bodl., MS Sancroft 278), and by Alexander Clogie, who married his step-daughter, are printed, with a large appendix of letters and other documents, in Shuckburgh 1902. The first of these had earlier been published by Jones 1872. Gilbert Burnet's *The Life of William Bedell* (1685 (anonymously), 1692, 1736) derives from Clogie, and Clogie's papers. There is a memoir in the form of a commemoration lecture, Rupp 1972.

[19] Ibish 1985, p. 353.

[20] Shuckburgh 1902, pp. 6, 223.

[21] Bedell's letters to Ward are scattered through the Tanner MSS in the Bodl. Library and many of them are printed in Shuckburgh 1902. These extracts are from letters of 16 Oct. 1604 and 11 March 1605, Shuckburgh 1902, pp. 214–22.

[22] See Bedell's letters from Venice to Adam Newton, 1 Jan. 1608, 1 Jan. 1609, ibid., pp. 226–38, 256–8. Bedell defended 'the Churches in Italy and Spain' as true, visible churches in a letter to Ward, 17 Feb. 1619, ibid., pp. 256–8.

of that Bury sermon of 1590.[23] It was fifteen years before a chance encounter in London and the influence of his Suffolk patron, Sir Thomas Jermyn, a person of substance at the Court of Charles I, brought Bedell back into the public eye, but in Ireland rather than England.[24]

In 1627, with the blessing of Archbishop James Ussher of Armagh, Bedell became provost of Trinity College Dublin, a kind of institutional clone of Emmanuel, the university as seminary. And then, within two years, hardly time to set the college statutes in order and to institute Trinity's own version of *De mora*, Bedell was preferred to two Irish bishoprics, Kilmore and Ardagh. (The pluralism made him uncomfortable, and he presently jettisoned Ardagh.)

Bedell's Herculean labours in the Augean stables of the Irish Church ('dilapidations upon dilapidations, such disorders . . . of all sorts'[25]) made him the ideal subject for near hagiographical treatment in a distinctive seventeenth-century literary genre, the *Speculum Episcoporum*, a pattern of 'primitive', 'apostolic' episcopacy, which made the best of all arguments, according to Bishop Gilbert Burnet, for the lawfulness and usefulness of episcopal government.[26]

Bedell's apostolic *vita* was complete with the *via dolorosa* and Calvary of its ending. In October 1641 he found himself in the eye of a totally unexpected storm, the catastrophic Irish rebellion. First his house became a safe haven for the fleeing and terrified colonists, and then was itself invaded. The catholic bishop took possession and Bedell's papers and great library were dispersed. Bedell himself fell into rebel hands, where he soon succumbed to 'the Irish ague', which sounds like typhus, three months after the outbreak of the rebellion. In a scene proleptic of the twentieth century, his sons and their wives joined a refugee caravan escorted to the coast by the rebel soldiery. 'A sad company of poore people we were.'[27]

Moderation, in substance and in manner, and mere humanity, were the defining characteristics of Bishop Bedell. Finding himself at odds with both the Puritans and the bishop's party in Suffolk in 1604, he wrote:

---

[23] See above, pp. 37–8.

[24] But Bedell was briefly in the public eye in 1624 as a proctor in Convocation, sending Ward parliament news. (Shuckburgh 1902, pp. 22, 261–2.)

[25] Bedell wrote to Archbishop Laud, 10 August 1630: 'My Lord, I do thus account that amongst all the impediments to the worke of God amongst us, there is not any greater than the abuse of Ecclesiasticall Jurisdiction' – referring particularly to his long-running dispute with the diocesan chancellor, Dr Alan Cooke. (Shuckburgh 1902, pp. 98, 311, 31–2, 36, 50–1, 120–3, 311–18, 354–60.) See John MacCafferty, 'John Bramhall and the Church of Ireland in the 1630s', in Alan Ford, James McGuire and Kenneth Milne, eds., *As By Law Established: the Church of Ireland Since the Reformation* (Dublin, 1995), pp. 100–11.

[26] Collinson 1982, pp. 83–9; Clogie's Life, entitled *Speculum Episcoporum: Or the Apostolick Bishop*; Burnet's 1685 Preface.

[27] Shuckburgh 1902, pp. 57–75, 165–213. A rare survival from Bedell's library, still preserved in Emmanuel, is his MS Hebrew Bible, acquired in Venice.

'Thus it is, moderate courses are subject to the calumniations of both extremes.'[28] This was how it would be with Bedell for the next forty years. In Italy and Ireland, he made many catholic friends and was accused of being 'a papist, an arminian, a politician, an Italian, a neuter'.[29] On arriving in his Irish diocese, he offered (in vain) 'some intercourse' with the catholic bishop who lived only two miles away, 'as I see the African Churches and Bishops did to the Donatists'.[30]

Bedell's correspondence with James Wadsworth, his old chamber-fellow, the Emmanuel man turned papist and Spaniard, became famous for the polemical effectiveness of its eirenicism. In contrast to Joseph Hall's withering contempt for the man ('I profess, I doe hartily *pittie him*'), Bedell wrote as a friend: 'I am the same to you that I was when we were either *Scholars* together in *Emmanuell Colledge*, or Ministers in *Suffolk*.' But, 'you say *you are become Catholick*. Were you not so before?'[31]

In Ireland, 'primitive' episcopacy meant walking rather than riding the streets of Dublin, digging his own garden, and holding diocesan synods, to which Archbishop Laud and others took great exception.[32] Like some seventeenth-century Trevor Huddlestone, Bishop Bedell interposed himself between the natives and the colonists, and earned some mistrust from both. We know that he admired the missionary strategy of Matteo Ricci and other Jesuits in China.[33]

But there was more to this than pastoral and missionary strategy. Bedell was a brilliant linguist, whose experiences in Venice (with Jewish Hebraists as well as Italians) had prepared him for the challenge of communicating across a linguistic divide. At Trinity College, he insisted that his students learn Irish and take it out into the parishes. He learned the language himself and took an active part in the project to translate the Old Testament into Irish. If John Eliot (a Cambridge contemporary) won the title of 'Apostle of the Indians', Bedell should be known (if it were not somewhat politically incorrect) as 'the Apostle of the Irish'.

Out of this grew a greater if abortive ambition: to invent a universal written language which would serve the same ecumenical function as mathematical symbols. He put one of his clever Trinity colleagues, John Johnson, on to this experiment (later to be parodied by that other Dubliner, Jonathan Swift, in *Gullivers Travels*). Johnson had begun to

---

[28] Shuckburgh 1902, p. 218.
[29] Ibid., p. 30.
[30] Bedell to Ward, 6 Oct. 1629, ibid., pp. 299–300.
[31] *The copies of certaine letters*, pp. 32–3, 36, 41. Izaak Walton thought that in the Bedell-Wadsworth correspondence, there was a controversy 'who should answer each other with most love and meekness.' (*Walton's Lives*, ed. S. B. Carter (London, 1951) pp. 107–8.) By contrast, a letter of stern rebuke to Wadsworth was placed first in Joseph Hall's *Epistles* of 1608.
[32] Shuckburgh 1902, pp. 28–9, 17, 156, 38, 110–14, 349–51, 354–6, 358–60.
[33] Rupp 1972, p. 10.

publish in 'real character' when he too was caught up in the troubles, his work destroyed and he himself killed. This takes us into the wonderful world of the Hartlib circle and its projects, with which Bedell, like other Emmanuel products, had some affinity.[34]

Of his Irish flock, Bedell wrote, memorably: 'Those people had souls which ought not to be neglected till they would learn English.' It was, wrote his step-son and biographer, Alexander Clogie, 'as if he had been the first and only man that ever God sent into Ireland to seek their national good, their spiritual and eternal welfare.'[35] Gilbert Burnet found in Bedell 'all that is great in a Man, in a Christian, and in a Bishop', 'the most extraordinary person that has been in the Church since miracles ceased', 'one of the greatest men that is in all Church History'. One token of that greatness is that Bedell aroused the admiration of two such opposites as Burnet and Archbishop Sancroft.[36]

How can one do justice, in a few paragraphs, to the career and achievements of Joseph Hall?[37] Whether or not he was 'all that is great' in a bishop (and as a bishop he was perhaps good rather than great), he was one of the greatest English writers of the seventeenth century, underrated and eclipsed by Andrewes and Donne, the ten fat volumes of his collected *Works* nowadays rarely disturbed.[38] But Hall never underrated himself. With a high degree of self-consciousness, this 'English Seneca' (as Thomas Fuller tells us he was known) pioneered a succession of new literary genres: the first formal verse satires in English (*Virgidemarium*, 1597–8)[39], the first Theophrastan characters (*Characters of vertues and vices*, 1608), the first authorised English letter collection (*Epistles* 1608), and a novel style of spiritual and contemplative writing, embodying what Hall claimed to be a new method for

---

[34] Vivian Salmon, 'William Bedell and the Universal Language Movement in Seventeenth-Century Ireland', *Essays and Studies* 1983, 'collected by Beatrice White', pp. 27–39. I owe this reference to the kindness of the late Jeremy Maule. On the Hartlib circle, see Mark Greengrass, Michael Leslie and Timothy Raylor, eds., *Samuel Hartlib and Universal Reformation: Studies in Intellectual Communication* (Cambridge, 1994); and the Hartlib Papers themselves (on deposit in Sheffield University Library), now electronically published in their entirety.

[35] Shuckburgh 1902, pp. 41, 133.

[36] Burnet wrote his *Life* from materials supplied by Clogie. See Burnet's letters to William Dillingham, seeking further information (undated as to year), BL, MS Sloane 1710, fols. 221–3. Sancroft was responsible for the retrieval of the Life by William Bedell the younger, and for its preservation in MS Tanner 278.

[37] T. F. Kinloch, *The Life and Works of Joseph Hall 1574–1656* (London, 1951); F. L. Huntley, *Bishop Joseph Hall 1574–1656: A Critical Study* (Cambridge, 1979); R. A. McCabe, *Joseph Hall: A Study in Satire and Meditation* (Oxford, 1982) (the best of these studies).

[38] *Works*, ed. Philip Wynter (Oxford, 1863). Hall's published writings account for 141 entries in the *Revised STC*, 8 columns: more than for any other author and exceeding (by a narrow margin) the entries for William Perkins.

[39] There was also Hall's antipodean/utopian/dystopian satire, *Mundus alter et idem* (1605), written in his Emmanuel years.

conveying scriptural truth, for which he was most celebrated.[40] In *Virgidemarium* (six rods for whipping) he wrote:

> I first adventure: follow me who list,
> And be the second English Satyrist.

These notable *juvenilia* behind him, Hall became one of the greatest preachers of the age, and knew it. He was one of the most prolific of anti-catholic polemicists, while the opening salvoes of what was to become the English Revolution found him the principal defender of the episcopal order against an anti-episcopal consortium which included John Milton. Richard McCabe writes of the 'powerful sense of personal assurance and destiny' which accompanied him through all his literary encounters and adventures.[41]

Like William Bradshaw, Joseph Hall sprang from sanctified puritan stock at Ashby-de-la-Zouch in Leicestershire, his father being a factor of the Hastings family, earls of Huntingdon. This was some of the turf from which Emmanuel was cut. It was Nathaniel Gilby, son of the radical Anthony Gilby of Ashby, who got him to Emmanuel (in 1589), became his tutor and returned to Leicestershire and to service with the Hastings family in order to release the fellowship to which Hall was elected in 1595.[42] Thereafter, *De mora* imposed an early career which exactly paralleled those of Bedell and Wadsworth: a Suffolk living (Hawstead, 1601–8, followed by Waltham in Essex), and foreign travel (with Sir Edmund Bacon to Spain, 1605, and later with James Hay, Viscount Doncaster and later earl of Carlisle, to France in 1616).[43] Emmanuel men were never in the fast lane of high preferment and promotion came slowly, assisted by the royal patronage, first of Prince Henry (whose premature death dashed many hopes), and then of King James himself, who in 1618 sent Hall, with Samuel Ward, to the Synod of Dort, and who gave him the deanery of Worcester. But it was Charles I who in 1627 made Hall bishop of Exeter at the already advanced age of fifty-three (he had earlier refused Gloucester), and who in 1641 found it expedient to translate this leading Calvinist and lifelong moderate to Norwich.

Hall's moderation, lived out in increasingly immoderate times, was a special kind of moderation, a moderation proactive and controversial

---

[40] *Meditations and vowes divine and morall* (1605); *Contemplations upon the principall passages of the holie storie* (1611–1634). Perhaps the most attractive of Hall's writings in this vein are his little essays on natural objects, 'meditations of the creatures', including 'Vpon occasion of a Redbreast coming into his Chamber', and 'Vpon Gnates in the Sun': *Occasionall meditations* (1630).

[41] McCabe, *Joseph Hall*, p. 5.

[42] Hall's biographers, and Ibish 1985, pp. 437–8, 428–9.

[43] It was a classical commonplace as old as Homer: learn another language, visit a foreign country. Walton commented on this strange parallelism: *Walton's Lives* (n.31), p. 107.

rather than passive, and having little to do with compromise and everything to do with defending his own position and opinions with implicit
aggression and on the most favourable terms, outflanking opponents of
all kinds as extreme and disruptive, if not schismatic. This strategy began
with the *Epistles* of 1611, which, whether writing to Wadsworth or Bedell,
were a careful and public exercise in positioning.[44] When Hall called for
unity and sweet reasonableness, 'let us all sweetly incline our hearts to
peace and unity', 'let us affect nothing but Jesus Christ', we need to know
what he was really up to. Professor Peter Lake calls this 'the moderate
and irenic case for religious war', whether against papists, or protestant
sectaries, or the deviance of crypto-popery and Arminianism within the
Church. For all his dulcet tones, Hall was 'rabidly anti-catholic'.[45]

As bishop of Exeter, Hall trod a moderate tightrope between the
extremes in the English Church, in the increasingly polarised 1630s. Archbishop Laud and his party, 'some that sate at the stern of the Church',[46]
regarded him with deep suspicion as 'a favourer of puritans'. His defence
against this charge, which was made semi-public, was typical of his
sharp-edged moderation, and skilfully exploited the advantage of what
for Bedell had been a mere burden: 'the calumniations of both extremes',
or what Hall called 'the mixed noyse of these 2 angry opposites'. 'Both
my cheeks must glow for I am buffeted on both sides.'[47]

Laud played a clever card in response, as the storm clouds gathered
against the Caroline regime in church and state. He put up Hall of all
people to write the Church's defence of the divine right of episcopacy,
and this led to pamphlet wars with the presbyterians in which few holds
were barred.[48] This was the beginning of fifteen years of what Hall in a
bitterly self-defensive autobiography called *Hard Measure*: a sojourn, with
his episcopal brethren, in the Tower, deprivation, effectively, of his
bishopric and its revenues, a long retirement in a humble cottage (later a
pub) in a Norfolk village, where he died aged 82 in 1656. Of the millions

---

[44] Hall 1863, X, 41, 43–4, V, 283.
[45] Peter Lake, 'The Moderate and Irenic Case for Religious War: Joseph Hall's *Via Media* in
Context' (forthcoming). I am grateful to Professor Lake for showing me this essay. See
also Anthony Milton, 'The Church of England, Rome and the True Church: the Demise of
a Jacobean Consensus', in Fincham 1993, pp. 187–210; and Milton 1995, almost *passim*.
[46] McCabe 1982, p. 3.
[47] Fincham and Lake 1996, 'Popularity, Prelacy and Puritanism in the 1630s: Joseph Hall
Explains Himself' (*English Historical Review*, III (1996) 856–81). I am grateful to Dr
Fincham and Professor Lake for sharing this article with me before publication. Hall's
semi-open letter is in the Somerset Record Office, MS DD/PH 221, no. 40. See also K.
Fincham, 'Episcopal Government, 1603–1640', in Fincham 1993, pp. 85–7, 91.
[48] Hall's principal opponents were 'SMECTYMNUUS', a consortium consisting of Stephen
Marshall, Edmund Calamy, Thomas Young, Matthew Newcomen and William Spurstowe,
to whom Hall replied in a *Defence of that remonstrance* (1641); which drew in Milton (*Of
reformation touching church discipline in England*).

of words which Hall wrote, these stand out, a good motto for Emmanuel men in any age: 'What if we cannot turne the streame? Yet wee must swim against it.'[49]

---

[49] McCabe 1982, p. 3.

4

The Endowment

For an acorn to germinate and grow, it must be fed and nurtured; so, too, Mildmay's foundation. The endowment provided the College with its income and enabled it to function, and thus financial and estate management were of central importance to the institution. To what extent, though, were these issues recognised, what controls were there over the management of the College's resources, who were the College officers who were involved, and how did they function? These questions will be considered before looking at the endowment in greater detail and at Mildmay's role in building it up. The following chapter considers the management of the estates; the success and failure of the College in providing itself with sufficient income to meet its demands; and the relationship between the 'dead' and the 'living' College, or the fabric and its inhabitants, the Fellows, and their dividends.

Statutes

College statutes, in many cases, laid down the bare bones of the ways in which an institution's finances were to be managed and created a climate within which finances and estates were administered.[1] Thus, they enabled members of a new institution to form habits which were then followed by subsequent generations.

Responsibility for the daily administration of a college's finances varied from college to college. At St John's College, Cambridge, for example, the 1516 statutes vested the main administrative authority of the College in the Master, who was responsible for the production of an annual statement of the financial situation of the College, together with yearly accounts of the bailiffs and farmers, and quarterly accounts of receipts, expenditure and debts. The statutes that were made eight years later, in 1524, declared that the less the Master acted on his own unassisted judgement the better it would be; two Bursars were to be elected

---

[1] The founder's statutes of St Catharine's College, Cambridge in the late 1470s, however, made no arrangements for the management of the College's property or for the care of its finances (Jones 1936, p. 223).

each year as the main accountants. Soon afterwards, in 1530, the requirement for an annual change of office was dropped.[2] Later in the century, in
1549, the Edwardian statutes of St Catharine's likewise established the
office of Bursar,[3] but at Jesus in 1559 there was no similar provision.[4]

At many colleges, the statutes ordained that accounts should be presented half-yearly at Michaelmas and at Easter. In Cambridge, this was
the case at Trinity Hall, where two copies of the accounts were to be
made, one to be kept in the College Chest and the other by the Master.
The statutes continued to stipulate that any surplus funds must be used
for the common purposes for the College and not for individuals, that no
loans of College monies should be made, and that no College property
might be alienated or sold.[5] God's House, later to become Christ's
College, similarly had a statutory twice-yearly audit.[6]

Estate management featured in the regulations of some colleges. Thus,
in Oxford, the thirteenth-century statutes of Merton College laid down
that the Warden should visit all the estates and value the farm stock each
year after the harvest,[7] and Balliol – whose statutes were based on
Merton's – New College and Corpus Christi had similar requirements.[8]
These annual progresses could become regular features of a college's
calendar: the Warden of New College, for example, made yearly visits to
his College's property between 1659 and 1675.[9] In Cambridge, too, estate
administration was an evident concern in collegiate statutes: the 1524
statutes of St John's, for example, stipulated the length of leases, that a
register be kept of College property, that estate terriers[10] be renewed at
least every 20 years and preferably every 12, and that estates be inspected
regularly to collect arrears of rent and to ensure that necessary repairs
had been carried out.[11] The 1559 statutes of Queens' College demonstrated a similar interest,[12] and the 1557–73 statutes of Gonville and Caius
were especially detailed, with regulations concerning the duties of the
Bursar, the regular payment to the College of monies collected by him,
the letting of lands, the rents of certain properties, the nature of tenants
and the inspection of the estates.[13]

---

[2] Howard 1935, pp. 10–11.
[3] Jones 1936, p. 55.
[4] Gray and Brittain 1960, p. 48.
[5] Crawley 1977, p. 13.
[6] Rackham 1927, p. 15.
[7] Brodrick 1885, p. 9.
[8] Aston and Faith 1984, p. 294; Storey 1979, p. 11; Duncan 1986, p. 574.
[9] Eland 1935.
[10] Written descriptions of landed property usually detailing, for each plot, such characteristics as boundaries, acreages, tenants and land use.
[11] Howard 1935, p. 15.
[12] Twigg 1987, p. 114.
[13] Venn, *Caius*, III, pp. 372–86. I am grateful to Mrs Janet Morris and Mrs Margaret Farrar
for their help in translating these statutes.

Emmanuel's statutes, modelled as they were on those of Christ's, showed very little change from them or indeed from the medieval statutes of God's House (made c. 1448) or of Clare Hall (made 1359), on which the Christ's statutes were based. Thus, there was to be a twice-yearly audit within one month of Easter and Michaelmas, at which time the Master was to show his accounts together with the contents of the Treasury, and the bailiffs and tenants were to present their accounts. Two indentures were to be made, setting forth the state of the College, one copy to be kept in the common chest and the other by the Master. There were no detailed regulations concerning the estate and financial adminis-tration of the College. The only way in which Emmanuel's statutes differed from those of Christ's was that a clause had been introduced allowing the Master to delegate bursarial business to a Fellow (but not named 'Bursar' in the statutes), perhaps reflecting the introduction of bursars into several colleges since Christ's statutes were enacted in 1506.[14] Thus, Sir Walter Mildmay's College had no particularly unusual statutory regulations concerning its finances and estates, though the decrees were at the less detailed rather than more highly specified end of the spectrum. The degree to which this level of control is reflected in the College's attitude towards its property is a subject of the following chapter.

Statutes, however, reflect intentions rather than deeds and there is no guarantee that particular regulations were obeyed. Indeed, at St John's College, Cambridge, leases were sometimes let for longer than the pre-scribed number of years, and it is doubtful whether annual progresses were carried out at Queens' College as stipulated in its 1529 statutes.[15] How, then, did colleges manage their affairs in practice?

Masters and Bursars

A Master who took an active interest in his college's finances and property could be a great asset. At Pembroke College, Cambridge, for example, Lancelot Andrewes built up the College's finances during his Mastership from 1589 to 1606. He clearly became familiar with the College's estates and advised Matthew Wren, the President who in 1616 started to put the College's records and finances into order, about docu-ments pertaining to a particular estate.[16] Other Masters of Pembroke followed the good example of their predecessors, and examples of estate-minded Masters elsewhere include Henry James at Queens' (1675–1717)[17] and Michael Woodward at New College, Oxford.[18]

[14] Rackham 1927; Stubbings 1983a, p. 33.
[15] Howard 1935, p. 29; Twigg 1987, p. 114.
[16] Attwater 1936, pp. 55, 66.
[17] Twigg 1987, pp. 179, 301.
[18] McIntosh 1987, pp. 175–81.

Other Masters, however, could be liabilities. Lancelot Andrewes' brother, Roger, Master of Jesus College, provoked a petition by the Fellows in 1628. Among their complaints were those that their Master had detained various sums of College money, he had not given an account of the Treasury for the past two years, he had tried to make the Fellows sign false statements, wages had not been paid, local tradesmen did not trust the College, the estates had not been inspected and discipline had not been maintained.[19] It was clearly highly unsatisfactory. Some Fellows of Gonville and Caius, too, accused their Master of incompetent management in 1582,[20] and Samuel Harsnett was not in favour in Pembroke in 1615 (though with hindsight his estate management was not as ill-advised as his colleagues feared).[21] Fortunately for Emmanuel, there seem to have been no similar problems and all appears to have been harmonious.

Bursars were by no means ubiquitous, but they were to be found in many colleges. At Oxford, it was common to find a pair of Bursars at each college, who were elected annually and who could be assisted by a retained lawyer.[22] All Souls College, for instance, adopted such a system;[23] at Christ Church, however, there was only one Bursar from 1620.[24] At Cambridge, the picture is more varied. St John's followed the usual Oxford practice;[25] Gonville and Caius had one Bursar who changed annually in the 1590s but who served for longer periods in the seventeenth century. The Master did, however, assume responsibility for his College's finances at times of great stress in the College such as those following the resignation of the Master John Caius (who had run most of the College's affairs himself) and during the Commonwealth. In smaller colleges, the Master acted as Bursar.[26]

Emmanuel oscillated between having a Bursar and managing without one (see Appendix 2). Much presumably depended on the inclinations of the Master and the amount of time that he was prepared to devote to his duties. The first three Masters all acted as Bursars apart from the appointment of William Bedell as Bursar in 1601[27] (and Bedell left the College in the following year).[28] Indeed, Laurence Chaderton continued to be actively concerned with the College's finances after he resigned the Mastership: on 7 May 1628, in the last months of John Preston's reign, he was sent £40

[19] Gray and Brittain 1960, pp. 62–5.
[20] Brooke 1985, pp. 89–91.
[21] Attwater 1936, p. 62.
[22] Doolittle 1986, pp. 249–50.
[23] Blackstone 1898.
[24] Bill 1956, p. 1.
[25] Howard 1935, pp. 281–5.
[26] Hall 1990a.
[27] ECA COL.9.19(A).
[28] Venn.

of rents due from estates in London and Surrey in a box of sugar (for security reasons, perhaps?).[29] Richard Holdsworth and Anthony Tuckney, on the other hand, were both assisted by Bursars; though Tuckney signed the audit indentures during his period of office, Dillingham was paid the Bursar's annual stipend of £8.[30] Dillingham was then elected to the Mastership and continued as his own Bursar, but William Sancroft (the younger), his successor, had a Bursar as did John Breton. When Michael Stukeley, Breton's last Bursar, was appointed Rector of Preston, Suffolk, however, Breton did not replace him but acted as his own Bursar for his last 18 months or so as Master. Thomas Holbech was similarly his own Bursar for 18 months, but then John Balderston was appointed to the Bursarship and later succeeded him as Master.

William Dillingham is notable as another Master, like Chaderton, who continued to take an interest in the College's affairs after his resignation. He gave advice on several occasions. On the death in 1664 of Christopher Rose, tenant of the College at the Catherine Wheel in Smithfield, he wrote to remind his successor as Bursar, Robert Alefounder, about the counter-part of a lease which Rose had failed to return to the College. Dillingham suggested that the lease be searched for among Rose's papers; either this advice was not taken or it was unsuccessful as there is no evidence that the deed ever returned to the College.[31] About one month later, Dillingham was writing to the Master, William Sancroft, in answer to a query about the procuring of a Statute of Mortmain,[32] and in 1685 he advised John Balderston, then Master, about a quit rent which was being claimed from the College on its lands at Hyde Farm in Surrey.[33]

The duties of a Bursar were seen as custodial, aiming to maintain the status quo. Thus, the Bursar at St Catharine's College in Cambridge was to receive the revenues of the College, to purchase materials for repairs and carry them out, to keep an inventory of the College's possessions in the Treasury, and to render annual accounts.[34] Avoidance of embezzle-ment and debt were all-important; the Bursar was not expected to be an entrepreneur, to increase the College's revenues or to monitor expendi-ture under various heads.[35]

This emphasis on the Bursar as a caretaker is also reflected in the accounting practices at many colleges, and at Emmanuel *par excellence*. In general in the seventeenth and eighteenth centuries, as in the Middle Ages, accounting among landowners was primarily concerned with

---

[29] ECA BUR.0.9.
[30] ECA BUR.0.2; BUR.8.2.
[31] ECA Box 25.F1.
[32] ECA COL.9.10.17.
[33] ECA BUR.0.9, letter of 19 November 1685.
[34] Jones 1936, p. 224.
[35] Bill 1956, p. 5.

checking against fraud and with giving an overall picture,[36] and systems were haphazard and unreliable.[37] Among the colleges, the situation was no better. Accounts had no common format and varied widely in their degree of comprehensiveness; not even the most detailed were a complete record of all transactions.[38] The accounts of each trust estate[39] were usually kept completely separate from the main body of accounts,[40] and in general sums that were to be passed on to members of the College, such as their share of the income from the sale of wood, sealing fees and entry fines levied at the renewal of leases, do not appear in the main college accounts.

Record keeping at Emmanuel was unsophisticated. Receipts were mainly from land and were entered in the rentals. For most of the first rental, tenants were not listed in any meaningful order, by estate or even by county, and tenants of newly-acquired properties were simply added at the end of the list. The only exception was for the time between the Michaelmas audit of 1590 and the Easter audit of 1602. During this period and then from 1653, when the second rental started with the Easter audit, and onwards, tenants were listed by the county of their estate.[41] Other income from, for example, cash donations, the College's share of entry fines, chamber rents and sales of miscellaneous items, was added at the end of the rental. Expenditure was entered chronologically in the Bursar's Long Book[42] and summed up at the Easter and Michaelmas audits. At audit, an indenture was drawn up, signed by the Master or Bursar, giving total income, total expenditure, the balance and, until 1744, arrears.[43] At times, balances were transferred into and out of the Treasury, where reserves were kept in the 'parva cista', and cash was kept in leather bags.[44] Audit day was marked by expenditure on the 'accompte cheare': wine, perhaps.[45] The accounts were not, therefore, presented in such a way as to show clearly either how particular estates were faring, or how expenditure was distributed among various heads.

Documents were kept in the Treasury, as prescribed in the statutes,[46] and a deed box was allotted to each estate. For example, an account of the repairs to the College property at Holborn was kept in the Holborn Box in

---

[36] Pollard 1965, pp. 210–11.
[37] Clay 1985, p. 245.
[38] Dunbabin 1986, p. 271; Aylmer 1986, pp. 527–9.
[39] Estates that were given so that income from them could be used for a specific purpose, usually endowing Fellowships or scholarships, rather than for the general running of the college.
[40] For example, at Gonville and Caius College (Brooke 1985, p. 102).
[41] ECA BUR.11.1–2.
[42] ECA BUR.8.1–11.
[43] ECA BUR.0.2.
[44] A new leather bag was bought for three pence in 1631 (ECA BUR.8.2).
[45] For example, 38s 6d was spent in such a way on 23 April 1594 (ECA BUR.8.1 p. 9).
[46] Stubbings 1983a, pp. 35–6.

1710.[47] Transcripts of leases and other important documents were made into a large register, the earliest extant volume of which dates from 1676.[48] It all seems to have got into some degree of disarray, for in 1683 a Fellow, George Green, and Mr Woodham were paid £16 (a substantial sum of money) for 'regulating the Writings in the Treasury'.[49] Despite, or because of, this expenditure, Emmanuel does not seem to have had too many problems in finding its documents; New College, Oxford, however, struggled as its deeds were not well indexed or listed, and so it was difficult even to establish what rents were due on its Hornchurch estate in the mid-seventeenth century.[50]

The overall scene suggested by the documents, therefore, is one of rudimentary accountancy and management which at its best checked fraudulent behaviour, and at its worst was little more than chaotic. The system encouraged conservative attitudes and approaches, and beneficial leasing allowed conditions on estates to ride so long as fines were paid.[51] In reality, much depended on individuals and their idiosyncrasies; there were some very able estate managers, and some colleges managed better than others. Emmanuel was clearly no star and no revolutionary leader, but it survived and kept going.

The Estates and their Endowment

There was little choice for colleges in the sixteenth and seventeenth centuries as to how they should invest their capital: land was the only realistic option. Among private landowners, lending money at interest on bond was an alternative, especially for shorter-term investments. After the Restoration these landlords diversified their portfolios, they also lent money on mortgage[52] and, from 1690, they began to move into securities. Investment in stocks, however, did not become at all common until well into the eighteenth century, and colleges were not among the forerunners of change.[53] An order was passed at Pembroke College in 1707 to invest money in land and securities;[54] Emmanuel received its first income from stocks in 1732, a date beyond the scope of this chapter.[55] The present discussion is concerned with the College's holdings related to land (estates,

---

[47] ECA SCH.1.1 note, 5 December 1710, concerning the Whichcote and Sudbury estate.
[48] ECA BUR.6.3.
[49] ECA BUR.8.2.
[50] McIntosh 1987, p. 176.
[51] See below, pp. 129–30, 170–2.
[52] Anderson 1969.
[53] Clay 1985, pp. 178–9.
[54] Attwater 1936, p. 86.
[55] ECA FEL.5.7.

manors, tithes and rent charges),[56] with the sources of the benefactions and the influence of the founder, and with the logistics of realising the generous intentions of the donors. The holding of landed property by colleges was, however, subject to a number of legal controls, and in particular there were restrictions on the acquisition of land and its sale.[57]

The legal framework

All corporations were subject to Statutes of Mortmain and these controlled the expansion of a college's rental income. As corporations were perpetual, the Crown did not receive the dues that accrued on the death of private landowners, and so the Statutes forbade alienation, or transfer of property, to corporations except by licence.[58] Permission was either granted to hold land up to a limited annual value, or to acquire a named property. The limit imposed reflected the size and importance of the foundation and the intentions of the benefactor.

Emmanuel's foundation Charter granted a licence of mortmain to purchase or hold land to the annual value of £400;[59] by 1621, this ceiling had been reached and it was necessary to obtain permission to increase the limit by another £400.[60] In 1654, there were doubts as to whether Francis Ash's gift of the estate at Shernborne in Norfolk would exceed the current permitted annual income and to be on the safe side a new licence was obtained to hold land worth a further £500.[61] William Dillingham, as Master, was involved in seeking this licence, and on 19 January 1665 he wrote to explain the complexities of the business to the then Master, William Sancroft (the younger):

> As to the busines of mortmain procured from Oliver [Cromwell], it was the best remedy which those times afforded for the salving of a doubt (whether the Colledge was then by the 800 li mortmaine formerly granted capeable of Mr Ash his Gift, which we understood would all of it require mortmaine, though most of it would not concern the Colledge but as Trustee) now we reckoned that the

---

[56] Tithes were one-tenth of the annual increase of the produce of the soil. They were payable to the rector of a parish; an absentee rector normally appointed a vicar to perform the parochial services and allotted to him a portion of the tithes, usually the small tithes (all except for those of grain, hay and wood, which were the great tithes and generally reserved for the rector). A rent charge was a sum of money, usually an annual payment, which was tied to a particular piece of land.

[57] Much of what follows is based on Shadwell 1898. Precise details of individual benefactions are given in Appendix 5.

[58] 'Mortmain' means the alienation of property to a corporation, a 'dead hand'. For further details, see Raban 1982.

[59] Bendall and Stubbings 1989–90.

[60] ECA BUR.8.1 p. 103; ECA Charter Cabinet drawer 7 (10 June 1621).

[61] ECA BUR.8.2 records expenditure of £20 in obtaining this licence, paid on 4 October 1654; the licence is in ECA Charter Cabinet drawer 6 (31 July 1654).

Colledges revenues did already ammount unto about 550 li (as I remember) or thereabouts, and Mr Ash his Gift was purchased by him (after the rent it was then racked unto) at 280 li per annum, which would have more then filled our Mortmain with the Colledge lands; but the Gift is shrunk within compasse, under 200 li but a further doubt there was about the Colledge livings, whether they tooke up any mortmaine, which was not at that time much inquired into, because it was thought that Mr Ashe's Gift without them would have overrun the mortmaine; & upon these grounds there was more procured from Oliver; which upon his Majestyes returne I easily saw was not worth a straw any longer, & Mr Ash his Gift was by that time shrunk sufficiently, but then I thought necessary to inquire further into the case about the College livings; and although I had at that time my hands full of other busines, yet I advised with two of the Judges & 2 other able Lawyers, whom I found differing in theire judgements about it, some thinking that they did fill mortmaine according to theire full annuall valew, others according to what land the purchase valew of them would buy; all aggreed that the case would require a special verdict, if ever it should come to triall. The consideration wherof made it seeme expedient that with the first opportunity the Colledge should seek to . . . gett theire mortmaine enlarged; but at that time it seemed not so seasonable to move in it, there being so many hungry stomachs then at Court who would bee ready to catch at any advantage, which might have proved still more dangerous for the Colledge interest in regard that although the livings should not be accounted at all, yet Mr Ashe's deed making recitall of Olivers mortmaine (which was done utterly against my mind at first) it might be questioned whether that estate could be founded upon the old mortmaine, had wee had never so much to spare . . .

Dillingham therefore decided to let sleeping dogs lie, as the deed was inrolled in the King's bench 'where seldome search is made, and so not liable to an easy discovery', and when the time was right to apply for a new licence of mortmain, the permit should be expressed in such terms as to overcome any problems incurred by the reference to a licence granted by Oliver Cromwell.[62] By 1672, a further licence of £300 had to be obtained.[63]

Just as there were controls over how much land a college could acquire, there were also restrictions over the sale of estates. Until the late sixteenth century, colleges could sell one property and buy another as they wished: St Catharine's did so during a financial crisis in the

[62] ECA COL.9.10.17.
[63] ECA Charter Cabinet drawer 5 (10 February 1672).

mid-sixteenth century and exchanged tenements near the College for agricultural holdings.[64] After the Act of 13 Elizabeth Cap.10 (1571), however, all such activity had to stop, as it became illegal for a college to alienate or to mortgage any part of its real estate. Collegiate hands were thus tied until the nineteenth century. Queens' chose to ignore the law in 1598 when it sold its estate at Babraham (Cambridgeshire) in all but name by charging a rent, not collecting it and allowing the tenant to run the estate as if it were his own.[65] Emmanuel does not appear to have resorted to similar tactics.

The initial foundation and Mildmay's gifts
The usual pattern of endowment of a college before Emmanuel's foundation was for it to be established with a relatively insignificant source of income and for a short period of intensive activity to follow thereafter. During this period, estates were purchased and given, and a college could receive many benefactions. There might, from time to time, be a subsequent gift. Christ's, for example, was founded in 1505, and acquired 12 manors and estates in Cambridgeshire alone between 1510 and 1595; afterwards, it was given little more in the county and acquisition of land elsewhere was spasmodic.[66] Much depended on the precise nature of the foundation, the founder and his or her generosity, and the success of the college in attracting donations in the succeeding years.

Emmanuel was fortunate in being founded by Sir Walter Mildmay. He himself was generous: besides giving the College its site, its Master, magnificent plate and some books,[67] he also donated estates. On 8 May 1585, he purchased from John Digge 23 acres of marshland at Ripple in Barking, Essex.[68] Five days later the land, which was worth £20 a year, was conveyed to the College.[69] Mildmay was probably not aware that six of these acres were leasehold from the Crown, as the College was soon to learn to its cost.[70] In June of the same year, he bought the Horseshoe Inn and a tenement in West Street, Godmanchester (Huntingdonshire), and gave them to the College on 1 August.[71] These two properties had annual values of £22 and £26 13s 4d respectively (though the Horseshoe Inn estate was liable to a payment of £20 a year to maintain the Grammar School in the town).[72] November saw him purchasing the Four Swans and the tenement to the North in Bishopsgate Street, London for £200

---

[64] Jones 1936, p. 220.
[65] Twigg 1987, p. 112.
[66] Postgate 1964, p. 148; *VCH Cambs*, III, 430.
[67] See pp. 17–23.
[68] ECA Box 15.A3.
[69] ECA Box 15.A4.
[70] ECA Box 15.A8.
[71] ECA Box 13.A13; Box 13.A22.
[72] ECA BUR.11.0.A f. 3r.

from John Morley and Roger Rant; the gift of these properties increased the College's annual income by a further £18 a year.[73] Thus, within a year of his purchase of the site of the College, he had bought and donated lands which yielded 62% (£86 13s 4d) of his foundation's annual income.

Further gifts from Mildmay followed three years later. In April 1588, he conveyed to the College the remainder of a 60-year lease of the Pensionary, on the corner of Emmanuel Street and St Andrew's Street and opposite the College.[74] This gift marked the end of a complicated series of transactions. Edward Leeds, former Master of Clare College (and who features in the next section), received the property from his College in an exchange on 20 April 1585.[75] Eighteen months later, on 21 October 1586, Leeds let it to Ralph Symons, the architect of Emmanuel, for 60 years from the preceding Lady Day at an annual rent of ten shillings, with a covenant that:

> the said Raphe his Executors and assignes shall and will at all tymes hereafter during the said terme, kepe beare and doe almaner of Reperacions in and by all thinges in and upon the premysses and everie parte and parcell thereof, and in and upon all howses and buildinges which the said Raphe Symondes \hath alreadye builded/ & intendeth to builde and sett up theare.

The terms of the lease were generous:

> inconsideracon that the said Raphe Symondes is a well mynded man towardes Emanuell Colledge in Cambridge latelie founded and newlie buylded, The workemanship wheareof touching the stone worke hath ben wrought and perfourmed by the said Raphe, whearein he hath shewed him selfe verie dilligent and carefull.[76]

Symons sub-let part of the property, and an occupier of two rooms was Richard Brigg, under-cook at Emmanuel.[77] On 24 July 1587, Leeds conveyed the site of the Pensionary to the College;[78] on 2 February in the following year, Mildmay bought the remainder of Symons' building lease for £120[79] and so was in a position to grant it to the College two months later.[80] By this time, Symons had built six tenements worth £12 a year on

---

[73] ECA Box 26.E7–8; ECA BUR.11.0.A ff. 3v–4r.
[74] ECA Box 4.D10.
[75] ECA Box 4.D3.
[76] ECA Box 4.D4.
[77] Brigg's rooms were sub-let by Symons to Andrew Symonds of Sonning (Berkshire), also a freemason and perhaps a relative of Ralph, on 10 January 1587 for ten years from Christmas 1586 (ECA Box 4.D5); this under-lease was assigned to the College on 4 December 1594 (Box 4.D11). The other tenant of Ralph Symons was Robert Serle (Box 4.D6).
[78] ECA Box 4.D7.
[79] ECA Box 4.D9.
[80] On 12 April 1588 (ECA Box 4.D10).

the site.[81] Then on 1 July, Sir Walter gave to the College Whipples Farm at Stondon in Essex,[82] and his final gift was on 25 October 1588 when he gave the advowson of Stanground and Farcet in Huntingdonshire and a rent charge of £8 a year.[83] Thus, the Founder endowed his College with lands worth £116 13s 4d, which represented nearly half of the establishment's annual income in 1588.[84]

Mildmay's influence during his lifetime

Mildmay's contribution to the endowment of the College, however, was far greater than the gifts that he made personally. He also encouraged others to follow his example: it is notable that of the 56 benefactions to the College during its first four decades, 26 were made before Mildmay's death on 31 May 1589. Furthermore, it is remarkable that so many gifts were made during the lifetime of the donors; in the sixteenth and seventeenth centuries, the preferred way of giving was by will. Bequests were made to the College (and as there could be a long delay between the making of a will and its administration, reasons for donations may not now be immediately obvious), but the significant contributions from the living must surely reflect both the ability of the College and Mildmay to obtain them and also the immediate needs of the new institution.[85]

The Founder encouraged donations through his influence in Government circles, from fellow evangelical protestants and from his friends and acquaintances, and some gifts he solicited directly. For example, on 8 March 1585, he wrote to Walter Covert of Slaugham in Sussex, one of the evangelical protestant gentry in the county:

> Sir beinge enformed of your good disposicion and intent to bestowe some porcion of Lande for the mainteyninge of schollers in the vniversitie: I am bold to move you, that your good purpose therin maie be imployed vppon a poore College latelie erected in Cambridge, called Emanuell College, which beinge but nowe begone, hath most neede to be releued. And the principall scope of the College beinge, to breede devines to serve in the Churche: there is no dowbte, but god will so blesse theire studies that shall continew there, as you shall finde your liberalitie well bestowed, and shall receive great comeforte therof in your owne time. For the which as theis poore schollers shalbe bounde to praie for you, so I wilbe

---

[81] ECA BUR.11.0.B f. 4v.

[82] ECA Box 15.D5; Reeve 1890, p. 122. Mildmay had bought the farm for £260 on 7 June 1588 (Box 15.D2); it was worth £10 a year.

[83] ECA Box 1.A5.

[84] From calculations based on ECA BUR.11.0.B.

[85] This, and much of the following discussion, is based on Ibish 1985. She incorporates the donation of advowsons and of miscellaneous items such as plate and a clock in her figures, but excludes gifts by Mildmay himself.

alwaies thanckefull to you for the same, and requite that with anie thinge that maie lye within the compasse of my smale habilitie. So commendinge you to the protection of the Lord Almightie this viijth of marche 1584 [i.e. 1585] . . .[86]

As it happened, this letter did not bear fruit, but others may well have done so. Many of those who did help to endow the College were, demonstrably, well known to the Founder.

Mildmay's position as Chancellor of the Exchequer gave him many contacts that proved useful to the College. The securing of a rent charge from the Crown was a notable *coup* for a number of reasons. Of the three colleges at Oxford and Cambridge that were founded during the reign of Elizabeth I, Emmanuel was the only one to be so honoured. In conjunction with this, the Queen was notoriously parsimonious: while she favoured the expansion of education, she preferred to enable others to perform charitable acts rather than to do so herself (though she was not averse to claiming the credit where possible). Characteristically, therefore, the rent charge of £16 13s 4d that she gave to Emmanuel was merely a transfer to Cambridge of half of a sum that had been given to Oxford University before the Reformation from lands then owned by Glastonbury Abbey. In addition, the purpose of Mildmay's foundation would not have aroused much sympathy with the sovereign: the Church did not, she felt, need large numbers of learned preachers; clergy who were able to read the homilies were perfectly adequate. Thus, this evangelical protestant foundation was potentially subversive. All of these points strongly suggest that the annuity from the Crown was primarily a personal gift to Sir Walter, a recognition of Her Majesty's satisfaction with his long and devoted service as Chancellor of the Exchequer.[87]

Six of Mildmay's colleagues at the Exchequer gave to the College during his lifetime (five were employed by him, one was the son of a former employee). Several gave during the College's first year. Sir Henry Killigrew was an evangelical protestant, Teller of the Exchequer and recipient of £10 in plate by Mildmay's will. He gave to the College £140 of the total sum of £150 which was paid for the purchase of St Nicholas Hostel.[88] Robert Taylor, another Teller with similar religious leanings, was the purchaser of the future site of the College in 1581;[89] he sold it on 12 June 1583 to Laurence Chaderton and Richard Culverwell[90] and then they resold it to Mildmay on 23 November.[91] By conveying the property

[86] British Library Harleian MSS 703 f. 17v.
[87] Ibish 1985, pp. 59–61.
[88] ECA COL.9.1A p. 110.
[89] ECA Box 1.E5, dated 29 September 1581.
[90] ECA Box 1.E8.
[91] ECA Box 1.E11.

through a third party in this way, the legality of the College's title to it was ensured.[92] On 8 May 1585, Taylor conveyed to the College a rent charge of £20 per annum arising from lands which he then owned at Babraham near Cambridge.[93] Thomas Smith, a wealthy London merchant and one of Mildmay's oldest associates, was another early donor. Apart from his gift to the College, he does not seem to have been an active supporter of education or a donor to charity. He might, however, have been indebted to Mildmay, who possibly turned a blind eye to Smith's embezzlement of a substantial part of the customs revenue, and he gave the College two houses in Gracechurch Street.[94] John Morley, a friend and colleague of Mildmay's, was another benefactor in 1585: the sale of his property of the Four Swans and the tenement to the North in Bishopsgate to Sir Walter on 7 November has already been noted, and Morley gave the tenement to the West directly to the College on 14 November.[95] A final example of a gift from someone connected with the Exchequer which arrived at the College during Mildmay's lifetime is that of seven tenements in Threadneedle Street, which were left by the will of John Barnes to one of the colleges in Oxford or Cambridge.[96] An executor to the will was his nephew Walter Dunch, son of William, Auditor of the Mint, and Dunch chose Emmanuel as the lucky recipient.[97]

A further six Government officials made benefactions to the College during Mildmay's lifetime, and he knew all of them. Three gave land or rent charges. Sir Francis Hastings, an active evangelical protestant Member of Parliament, gave a rent charge of £8 per annum arising from his lands in Leicestershire, including the manor of Market Bosworth, on 24 June 1585.[98] Mildmay was acquainted with two other evangelical protestants, both lawyers, who gave to the College in its first few years: Robert Snagge (who gave an annual rent charge of £6 13s 4d issuing from estates at Letchworth in Hertfordshire on 6 November 1586),[99] and Nicholas Fuller (donor on 19 May 1587 of the Catherine Wheel and two tenements at West Smithfield in London, worth £8 a year).[100]

The London merchants were also part of Mildmay's constituency. He lived to see benefactions from six with whom he was connected: three

---

[92] The legality of the transaction in 1581 had been assured by the use of three means of conveyance: bargain and sale, feoffment and final concord (ECA Box 1.E4–6).
[93] ECA BUR.11.0.A f. 1v; BUR.2.6 f. 257r (description of deed at ECA Box 1.A2).
[94] Ibish 1985, p. 71; ECA Box 25.A6.
[95] ECA Box 26.E9; Mildmay's conveyance to the College, likewise on 14 November, is at Box 26.E8.
[96] Will dated 4 June 1588 (ECA Box 27.A24).
[97] The property was conveyed to the College on 27 September 1588 (ECA Box 27.A26). The sixth donor was William Neale, who gave two advowsons in Somerset: Brompton Regis and Winsford (Box 7 Brompton Regis).
[98] ECA BUR.11.0.A f. 2r; ECA Box 1.A10.
[99] ECA Box 1.A4.
[100] ECA BUR.11.0.A f. 4v.

gave land or rent charges, the rest were donors of sums of money. A childless clothworker, John Howson, gave ten houses in St Dunstan's Alley, Chancery Lane, to Sir Walter and his 'man of business' Edmund Downing (an Exchequer official and rent collector for the College) on 22 January 1586.[101] The annual income of £7 was to be reserved to himself and his wife during their lives; his will was proved on 31 March 1586, and his wife's on 29 March in the following year.[102] Another clothworker, Thomas Skinner, gave the College an annuity of £8 issuing from the manors of Lavenham in Suffolk and Fowlmere in Cambridgeshire on 2 March 1588.[103] His connection with Mildmay is not proven, but it is possible that Sir Walter was influential in releasing him from imprisonment in 1581 or again in 1588.[104] Mildmay was one of the overseers of the will of Mrs Joyce Frankland, a wealthy widow of London origins, a philanthropist and daughter of a goldsmith. As a result of the untimely death of her only son, who was thrown from an unbroken horse and died of his injuries, she made benefactions to Lincoln and Brasenose colleges in Oxford and to Gonville and Caius and Emmanuel in Cambridge. Through Mrs Frankland's connection with Mildmay, Emmanuel received a handsome benefaction (though her bequests to Brasenose and Caius were even more generous): her executors were to purchase land and houses worth £20 a year, though they were not to spend more than £440 in so doing, and were also to give her portrait to the College.[105] The Hyde Farm Estate at Mitcham and Clapham, Surrey, was bought on 17 July for £500 10s: Mildmay gave £60 to augment Mrs Frankland's £440, and the College made up the shortfall of ten shillings.[106] All of the three donors of money were evangelical protestants. Mrs Elizabeth Walter, widow of Richard, a puritan girdler, left £400 to establish fellowships and scholarships in divinity; two fellowships were thus endowed.[107] Richard Culverwell, uncle-in-law of Laurence Chaderton (and co-purchaser of the site of the College with him in 1583) gave £200 and many books; this sum is not entered in the accounts of the income of the College.[108] Finally, Walter Fish, Master of the Merchant Taylors' Company, gave £20.[109]

Mildmay can be connected with four further benefactions which were made during his lifetime. Members of the evangelical protestant Jermyn family of Rushbrooke in Suffolk made one donation at this time and two in the subsequent two decades. Sir Robert was acquainted with Mildmay

---

[101] ECA COL.8.1; ECA BUR.11.0.A f. 5r; Gray 1992, p. 119.
[102] Proved in Consistory Court of London, cited by Ibish 1985, p. 95.
[103] ECA Box 1.A6.
[104] Ibish 1985, p. 96.
[105] PCC 17 Spencer, proved 1 April 1587, cited by Ibish 1985, p. 98; Brooke 1985, pp. 95–6.
[106] ECA Box 28.A7.
[107] ECA COL.9.10.2.
[108] ECA COL.20.1; ECA BUR.11.1.
[109] ECA COL.20.1.

and gave a rent charge of £8 arising from land at Little Welnetham in Suffolk on 27 March 1585,[110] and two or three of his sons were educated at Emmanuel. Later, Sir Robert's aunt, Martha Higham, left £100 to found a scholarship on her death in 1593; his younger brother, Anthony, bequeathed 100 marks[111] to endow another scholarship in 1606; and another brother, William, bought five acres at Badwell Ash, Suffolk, for 100 marks to augment this scholarship on 20 February 1640.[112] Second, Mildmay's son-in-law, William Fitzwilliam, was executor of the will of John Spenluffe, who gave the College an annuity of £4 issuing from Skendleby, Lincolnshire, shortly before he died in 1589.[113] Third, Sir Richard Ashton of Middleton in Lancashire, another evangelical protestant, gave £13 6s 8d for fittings for the library at an unknown date, but probably early on.[114] When the school at Middleton was refounded in 1572, Mildmay assisted, for which help Ashton must have been grateful.[115] Finally, Henry Harvey, Master of Trinity Hall, bequeathed the Chalice (21 St Andrew's Street) to the College on his death in 1585.[116] Though at best a lukewarm evangelical protestant, he had acted as a lawyer for Mildmay and the College; hence, perhaps, his benefaction.[117]

Sir Walter Mildmay and his associates account for all but three of those who gave estates to the College during his lifetime. One of those omitted is Francis Chamberlain, the first donor to the College, who on 29 May 1584, four days after the deed of foundation was signed, gave the impropriated rectory and advowson of Little Melton in Norfolk and lands in Great and Little Melton and Hethersett.[118] Mrs Ibish was unable to discover much about this donor in her exhaustive study of the foundation of the College. More is known about Edward Leeds, Master of Clare College from 1562 to 1571, after which date he retired to his manor at Croxton near Cambridge. He retained his interest in the University and showered Sir Walter Mildmay's foundation with gifts. Why Leeds did so is not easy to explain: perhaps he knew Sir Walter through Thomas Byng, a friend of Mildmay's who was Leeds' successor as Master of Clare.[119] Leeds' conveyance of the Pensionary to the College in 1587 has already

---

[110] ECA Box 1.A1.

[111] One mark was 13s 4d.

[112] Ibish 1985, pp. 124–7; ECA Box 1.A1*. When the scholarship next became vacant, preference was to be given to the son and heir, Samuel, of the vendor, Richard Chamberlayne. Samuel was duly admitted on 30 June 1640 (Venn).

[113] The gift was made on 12 January 1589 (ECA BUR.11.0.B f. 5r); his will was made on 12 April 1588 and proved on 10 June 1589 (Ibish 1985, p. 145). A draft of the conveyance is at BUR.0.9.

[114] ECA COL.20.1.

[115] Ibish 1985, p. 153.

[116] ECA Box 2.A5; the property was conveyed to the College on 12 May 1585 (Box 2.A6).

[117] Ibish 1985, p. 162.

[118] ECA COL.8.1 ff. 6v–7r.

[119] Stubbings 1971, pp. 193, 198.

been mentioned; this followed the donation of a rent charge of £16 arising from his manor and lands at Great Gransden, Huntingdonshire, on 6 June 1585,[120] and 1000 marks towards the new building in the following year.[121] There is also the possibility that he gave the College another house in St Andrew's Street by his will which was made on 10 October 1588 (though he might have been referring to the Pensionary); he certainly gave £160 6s 8d of rents due to him from the prebend of Itchington in Warwickshire at Michaelmas 1588 (though there is no evidence that this sum ever arrived), a gold ring to Mildmay, a piece of plate to Mildmay's man of business Edmund Downing (who was also a supervisor of the will), one of his best gowns to the Master, Laurence Chaderton and, by a codicil dated 5 February 1589, £20 worth of his books and a tablecloth and linen towel to the College.[122] Finally, on 3 October 1588, Lady Mary Darrell of Essex, the daughter of a London merchant, gave £146 13s 4d to endow two scholarships, each of the annual value of £3 6s 8d. Twenty pounds of her gift were to be used to purchase land, the rent from which was to pay for coals for the College.[123] The money did not arrive straightaway: in 1592, Chaderton visited her on two separate occasions and eventually collected her donation.[124]

The continuing influence of the founder
As Mildmay's influence during his lifetime was very considerable indeed, it is hardly surprising that it continued after his death. Two of his former colleagues at the Exchequer added to the College's endowment: Henry Billingsley, by his will of 1606, gave £66 13s 4d to found a scholarship,[125] and Edmund English by his will, made on 1 April 1602 and proved on 28 April 1603,[126] left £1000 to the College to found two fellowships of £10 per annum each and six scholarships of £5 per annum. This bequest was not trouble-free, but it was eventually used to purchase the tithes of Pinchbeck in Lincolnshire in 1617.[127] An associate of the Founder in Government circles was Sir John Popham, a high-ranking lawyer. He chose the College to be a beneficiary under the will of Peter Blundell, who had bequeathed £2000 to establish six scholarships at Oxford and Cambridge. Two were offered to Balliol College, Oxford (Popham's college) and four to Cambridge: two to Sidney Sussex, two to Emmanuel. Popham insisted, however, that each senior scholar should receive £15 a year and

---

[120] ECA Box 1.A3.
[121] ECA COL.20.1.
[122] The will, PCC 39 Leicester, was proved on 10 April 1589; see Ibish 1985, pp. 163–7.
[123] ECA BUR.2.6 f. 131r; Ibish 1985, pp. 138–44.
[124] ECA BUR.8.1 p. 4.
[125] Ibish 1985, pp. 72–3.
[126] PCC 25 Bolein, cited by Ibish 1985, p. 73; ECA Box 18.B2.
[127] ECA BUR.8.1 p. 88.

be given the privileges and income of a Fellow; these conditions were unacceptable to Emmanuel, and the benefaction passed to Sidney Sussex instead.[128] As a last example the executor of Walter Travers, an Elizabethan Presbyterian and acquaintance of both Mildmay and Laurence Chaderton, wrote to the College in 1635 with the news that Travers had left £100 to found divinity scholarships worth £4 yearly.[129]

Rather more surprisingly, perhaps, Sir Walter did not encourage other members of his family to give estates to his College. One did so, his daughter-in-law Lady Grace. By her will of 12 December 1618, she left a rent charge of £8 a year arising from lands at Leesthorpe in Leicestershire to maintain four poor scholars.[130]

Mildmay's legacy of a College with a reputation for evangelical protestantism led to a number of bequests. One of the messages of Godly preachers was that charity 'is the best kinde of thrift or husbandry . . . it is not giving, but lending, and that to the Lord, who in his good time will return the gift with increase'.[131] For those who were anxious about their salvation, it was necessary to go forth to do good works. Thus was demonstrated the superiority of the Godly: popery, on the other hand, fed on ignorance, which itself stemmed from poverty. The elimination of poverty and ignorance, therefore was, in the opinion of many, essential for the Gospel to triumph.[132] Arising from this, a new educational institution was an attractive charity; indeed, Jordan has suggested that more than one-quarter of all charitable giving from 1480–1660 was for educational purposes.[133]

How some evangelical protestants gave to the College during Mildmay's lifetime has already been demonstrated; others followed suit in later years, so that during the first 40 years of the College's existence, about half of the gifts to it came from those with puritan sympathies.[134] Rebecca Romney, for example, widow of the evangelical protestant merchant William (who himself had given the advowson of North Luffenham, Rutland, to the College in 1591),[135] died in 1643 and left £500 to the Haberdashers' Company to found four divinity scholarships at Cambridge: the Company chose Emmanuel and Sidney Sussex Colleges.[136] An evangelical protestant merchant of King's Lynn, Norfolk, John Titley and his wife Elizabeth, also increased the College's endowment. The eventual outcome was the establishment of two scholarships, worth £4 a

---

128 Ibish 1985, pp. 87–90.
129 ECA Box 9.Oa30; ECA SCH.1.1.
130 ECA Box 9.Oa10.
131 William Perkins, quoted by Archer 1991, p. 77 (who makes the elision).
132 Archer 1991, p. 79.
133 Jordan 1959, p. 368.
134 Ibish 1985, p. 320.
135 ECA Box 8.D6(1).
136 Jordan 1960, pp. 255, 398; ECA SCH.1.23E.

year each, for students from King's Lynn grammar school, and annuities of £2 to be paid to the Master and Fellows and £1 to the College. A contract with King's Lynn Corporation was finally signed on 27 August 1607; the journey to this agreement had been long and tortuous.[137] Sir John Hart of London was another evangelical protestant merchant; he gave £50 towards building the College walls in 1594 (and made a handsome benefaction to Emmanuel's evangelical protestant poor relation, Sidney Sussex College, by his will of 1604).[138] Sir Wolstan Dixie, Master of the Skinners' Company and Lord Mayor of London, was possibly another person with leanings towards evangelical protestantism. He might have contributed £50 to the building fund of the College, he certainly bequeathed £600 to purchase property to support two scholars and two Fellows who were studying divinity. One of each of these was to come from his projected school at Market Bosworth in Leicestershire. He died in January 1594, the College received his bequest on 17 July 1594,[139] and on 16 November it was used to purchase land at Sutton Coldfield in Warwickshire for £500.[140] Also in 1594 (on 20 April), Dixie's widow, Lady Agnes, gave a rent charge of £8 a year from houses and a wharf, Drapers' Key, in Thames Street, London, to endow lectureships in Greek and Hebrew.[141] Later, in 1632, Thomas Hobbes bequeathed the remainder of rents from lands at Braintree in Essex, in part to maintain two or three scholars at St Catharine's College or at Emmanuel, with preference to the sons of 'godly poor ministers'.[142] His executor allotted two scholarships to each college.[143]

Evangelical protestant ministers were also benefactors to the College. Moses Wilton, for instance, Rector of Fleet in Lincolnshire, died in 1609 and left 20 acres of land to support two scholars from Moulton School.[144] Richard Dawson, a graduate of the College and subsequently Vicar of Pinchbeck, also in Lincolnshire, bequeathed the remainder of his lease of the impropriation to his *alma mater* on condition that the College paid to his widow £61 10s still outstanding from the lease. He also desired the College to purchase the advowson. The College did not do this; Dymoke Walpole settled the advowson shortly afterwards.[145] Dawson's will is

---

[137] ECA BUR.2.6 ff. 133–4; ECA COL.9.2 p. 56; Ibish 1985, pp. 128–32.

[138] ECA COL.20.1; Ibish 1985, pp. 115–17.

[139] PCC 1 Dixy, made 15 May 1592, codicil 21 December 1593, proved 28 January 1594 (cited by Ibish 1985, p. 111); ECA COL.9.10.102.

[140] Ibish 1985, pp. 111–15; ECA Box 29.B1.

[141] ECA Box 1.A7.

[142] Jones 1936, p. 238. The will was dated 21 February 1632.

[143] ECA SCH.1.1.

[144] The will was made on 10 April 1609 and proved on 21 November (Maddison 1891, pp. 31–4). There is no evidence in the rentals that the bequest ever reached the College (ECA BUR.11.0.C; BUR.11.1).

[145] ECA Box 18.B12, letter of 15 March 1625 from Walpole to Chaderton.

dated 7 February 1618;[146] the previous autumn, the College had bought the tithes of corn, wool and lamb of Pinchbeck from the legacy of Edmund English.[147] A few years later, Emmanuel was a joint beneficiary with St John's, Clare and Sidney Sussex colleges of the will of the evangelical protestant Archdeacon Robert Johnson of Leicester: in 1625, he bequeathed £25 a year to each college arising as a rent charge on lands at Witham on the Hill in Lincolnshire.[148] Johnson was the first prominent evangelical protestant to be presented to a living in the diocese of Peterborough, that of North Luffenham, in 1574. His connections with Emmanuel were many. When Johnson was presented to North Luffenham, the living was in the patronage of the Crown; he was on close terms with Sir Walter Mildmay, who might well have been his patron. Johnson was related by marriage to William Romney. Romney's gift of the advowson of North Luffenham to Emmanuel in 1591 has already been mentioned; in the same year, he sold his land there to Johnson (who in fact thought he had bought the advowson as well). Johnson sent his son, Abraham, to Emmanuel in 1591, and Abraham's second marriage was to the daughter of the Master, Elizabeth Chaderton. Johnson's bequest was to endow scholarships with preference to those who had been educated at the schools he had established in the 1580s, with evangelical protestant trustees, at Oakham and Uppingham.[149]

Members of Mildmay's College also helped to endow it. William Branthwaite was one of the founding Fellows; despite the College Statutes, he managed to retain his position at Emmanuel until 1607, when he became Master of Gonville and Caius, which was to be the chief beneficiary from his will. However, he did not forget his former College, and left it £200 to found two scholarships, £20 for books and memorial rings to his colleagues Laurence Chaderton and John Richardson.[150] The money went towards the cost of buying the Unicorn in Petty Cury, Cambridge, for £480 on 12 December 1621.[151] Mildmay appointed William Bright a Fellow in 1587;[152] Bright left the College in 1597 and died in 1618, when he bequeathed £30 to it.[153] Walter Richards matriculated at Emmanuel in 1589, the year of Mildmay's death;[154] his benefaction, however, did not reach the College until 1650. By his will of 25 July 1639, Walter left about 37 acres at Lydden and Ewell in Kent to endow two exhibitions, though

---

146 ECA Box 9.Oa8.
147 ECA BUR.8.1 p. 88.
148 ECA Box 9.Ma2.
149 Sheils 1979, pp. 3, 38, 62, 99; *VCH Rutland*, p. 203; Ibish 1985, pp. 106–7; Venn.
150 ECA Box 9.Oa9.
151 ECA Box 3.A18.
152 ECA Box 1.NOM.3.
153 PCC 6 Parker, made 10 August 1618 and proved 26 January 1619 (cited by Ibish 1985, p. 178).
154 Venn.

his widow was to enjoy the property for her life. She died in 1650 and the College immediately sent the Manciple to take possession of the land.[155] Laurence Chaderton himself was a benefactor: he returned St Nicholas Hostel, of which he was the lessee, to the College in 1603. In 1585, the College had bought the property; on 2 December 1594, it was sold for £200, and made over to Chaderton on the 11th. In effect, the College thus received a loan of £200 which it used to purchase a rent charge at Woodham Ferrers in Essex, and Chaderton converted this loan into an outright gift.[156]

During Chaderton's Mastership and that of his successor, John Preston, more members of the College made benefactions to it. William Bradish, for example, was admitted in 1594, was a Fellow from 1601 to 1611 and then became Vicar of Puddletown in Dorset. He left, by his will of 9 October 1638, £200 to purchase a rent charge to finance three scholarships in Greek.[157] Thomas Aldridge migrated from Jesus College to Emmanuel in 1595; in 1640, he bequeathed a lease to Edward Plumme of Hawkedon in Suffolk on condition that he paid £3 a year for an exhibition during his tenancy.[158] John Preston himself made a benefaction to his College: he left on his death in 1628 £200 to buy lands to maintain two poor scholars. His executor, Lord Saye and Sele, however, paid for the scholars himself and it was not until the Mastership of John Breton that Saye and Sele's heir, James, was requested to make a settlement upon the College. Thus was received, on 4 May 1668, a rent charge of £12 per annum arising from about 20 acres of meadowland at Drayton in Oxfordshire.[159]

Some benefactions failed to arrive. The rejection of Sir John Popham's gift, and the possible non-arrival of Richard Culverwell's, have already been mentioned. John Bilbie, an evangelical protestant member of the Drapers' Company, left £100 to endow a fellowship or scholarship by his will which was written and proved in 1598, but neither Emmanuel nor the Drapers' Company, another beneficiary, received their legacies.[160] Philip Harris' intended gift of an annuity of £3 6s 8d towards a scholarship met a curious fate. In 1597, he heard William Bedell, Fellow of the College, preach and was much impressed by him. Harris spent the night with Bedell's father, John and, it was alleged, thrice asked for the name of William's college. Nevertheless, when he made his will in 1589 Harris wrote Trinity College instead, and Chaderton did not manage to convince

---

[155] ECA Box 17.A12, A14; ECA SCH.1.23F.
[156] ECA Box 4.H12, H15–16.
[157] Venn; ECA Box 9.Oa11. There is no record of receipt of this sum, nor of its deployment.
[158] Venn; ECA Box 9.Oa12 (will made 1 September 1640, proved 25 February 1641). The lease was dated 24 May 1630. Plumme was exempted from payment of the £3 in the last year of the lease.
[159] ECA SCH.1.1; ECA Box 1.B2; ECA BUR.6.3 pp. 371–2; SCH.1.23D2–3.
[160] ECA Box 9.Oa4; PCC 56 Lewyn (cited by Ibish 1985, pp. 118–19).

the Vice-Chancellor's Court that this was an error. The benefaction thus passed to Trinity.[161] John Freston's benefaction of £500 to buy lands with an income of £25 per annum to provide one fellowship of £10, two scholarships of £5 each, and £5 towards the maintenance and repairs of the College, was refused.[162] Freston was a lawyer of Altofts in Yorkshire and was persuaded to make his bequest to Emmanuel by William West, father of William (who came to the College in 1586) and Thomas (admitted in 1595). Freston died in 1594, but as ten pounds yearly was felt to be insufficient to endow a fellowship, the gift passed to Sidney Sussex College in 1607.[163]

During the tenure of Mildmay's chosen Master, who was succeeded by John Preston in 1622, the College's endowment was increased by a variety of other donors. Their connections with the Founder were far more tenuous, if they existed at all. A Mr Ellis of Yorkshire gave either 100 or 400 marks at an unspecified date.[164] In 1590, the lawyer John Sleigh bequeathed the lease of the impropriated revenues of the rectory of Caxton, Cambridgeshire, and £50 towards the renewal of the lease (though it seems that only £40 10s of this sum was in fact received and that the lease was not renewed in 1605).[165] Thomas Popeson, schoolmaster of Bungay in Suffolk, and the feoffees of the town each granted annuities of £6 on 16 January 1592 to pay four pence a week to ten scholars, seven of whom were to come from the school there.[166] The following April, Popeson gave 'The Monckys', in Bungay, to the feoffees of the school in return for which the schoolmaster was to be paid £3 6s 8d a year and to have rent-free accommodation.[167] A merchant, William Elkin, left £100 in 1593 to purchase lands to maintain a scholarship of £5 a year;[168] when the money was given to the College on 20 June 1594 by his widow Alice, she augmented the sum by a further £40, so that two exhibitions could be supported.[169]

---

[161] Cambridge University Archives, CUR 95, Emmanuel College, nos 1–2; Harris' will is in the Essex Record Office D/ABW 19/167 (cited by Ibish 1985, p. 145).

[162] ECA Box 9.Oa3.

[163] Ibish 1985, pp. 148–51; Venn. The College was also to receive benefactions from two members of it, if all else failed. If the sons of John Josceline (who was admitted in 1616) died without heirs, Emmanuel was to receive four-fifths of the revenue of lands near Sturmer in Essex to maintain four scholars from Sawbridgeworth, and Queens' College (the college of John's father) was to receive the rest (Venn; ECA Box 9.Oa14, will made 26 May 1668 and proved 21 November 1670). If the children of Ezekiel Wright, sometime Fellow, died, the College was to receive his estate and use it to endow two Fellowships and two scholarships (ECA Box 9.Oa13, will made 1668).

[164] ECA COL.9.2 p. 158; COL.20.1.

[165] ECA BUR.11.1; BUR.8.1; Ibish 1985, pp. 104–6.

[166] ECA Box 19.A2.

[167] ECA Box 19.A4 (dated 20 April 1592); Ibish 1985, pp. 168–9.

[168] PCC 78 Nevell made 22 August and proved 13 November 1593 (cited by Ibish 1985, p. 108).

[169] ECA BUR.2.6 f. 131r; Ibish 1985, pp. 108–11; at BUR.8.1 p. 9 is a record of payment of 43s 4d for receipt of £100 in the half year after Michaelmas 1594.

Anthony Radcliffe, Master of the Merchant Taylors' Company, gave £100 before his death in about 1603,[170] and a Skinner with leanings towards evangelical protestantism, Randall Manning, left £100 to his widow to provide an annuity of £2 to each of four poor scholars at Christ's and Emmanuel colleges during the next 30 years.[171] John Parker left an annuity of £20 to the College arising from lands at Radwell, Hertfordshire: £10 was to support a Fellow and two scholars were to receive the remainder. The gift was conveyed to the College on 15 December 1606.[172] While Chaderton was a Fellow of Christ's College, William Haynes was a student there. He subsequently became headmaster of Merchant Taylors' School, and in 1621 gave £20 to Chaderton's College.[173] This sum joined Branthwaite's gift to help to buy the Unicorn in that year.

The purchase of estates by the College

Of the various sums of money that were received during Chaderton's Mastership, some were used to buy estates for the College. By Michaelmas 1593, the College was in a position to buy about 200 acres of land at Eltisley in Cambridgeshire from William Marshall for £900.[174] Six years later, the manor of Great Gransden and lands in Huntingdonshire were purchased from Edward Leeds for £340.[175] Michael Wolfe sold to the College his property opposite it in St Andrew's Street (now numbers 11–12) on 12 March 1607 for £130,[176] John Atkinson sold nine messuages and gardens and two barns in Emmanuel Street to his neighbour on 13 July 1612 for £400,[177] and the College contributed £260 towards the cost of purchasing the Unicorn in Petty Cury from Nathaniel Harrison on 12 December 1621.[178]

The purchase of estates from cash bequests could be a complex process: property had to be found that was free from encumbrances and possible legal challenges and, as licences to hold property in mortmain became filled, new ones had to be sought.[179] Some of these concerns can be seen in a letter written by two of the governors of Uppingham School to a Fellow, Abel Bunning, on 22 September 1708, about the purchase of an estate in Whaplode and Holbeach, Lincolnshire, in connection with Archdeacon

---

[170] ECA COL.20.1; Ibish 1985, pp. 119–20.
[171] PCC 5 Fenner, made and proved in January 1612 (cited by Ibish 1985, pp. 120–1).
[172] ECA Box 9.Oa6; a copy of the relevant part of his will is at Box 9.Oa5; Box 1.A8.
[173] ECA BUR.11.1
[174] ECA BUR.2.11, reference to deed, now lost, at ECA Box 12.B (unnumbered); Box 12.B17.
[175] ECA Box 14.A11 (13 October 1599).
[176] ECA Box 2.D5.
[177] ECA Box 4.A14.
[178] ECA Box 3.A18.
[179] Archer 1991, p. 82.

Johnson's exhibitions at Emmanuel, Clare, Sidney Sussex and St John's colleges:

> According to what was desired by you from the Severall Masters, we . . . have been to see the Estate, which they are about to purchase for the Exhibitions belonging to Our schoole; And we desire you to Communicate to them the Following Account which upon sight & upon Enquirie, we have found of it viz: That the Estate is all freehold & that it conteins 234Ac:3R:0P that we cannot think it in any danger of being flooded since notwithstanding the long Raines that have fallen very \few/ Acres of it not above 4 or 5 are under water. That the Land is very good & easie rented & that the Tenents are willing to Lease & are Responsible. That the severall parcells lie near to the Tenents Houses which is a great advantage to the Tenents. That the present rent is £103-12s-00d out of which (besides the Queens Taxes) there is only 14s 4d payable by the Landlord as Quit Rent And that the Land is not chargeable to any Sewers or any other parish dues, but what the Tenents have hitherto payed & are still willing to pay. That there are 3 Houses upon the Estate with some Outhouses which want but little repaireing & that undertaken by Sir Edwards Agent in a short time to be made good which will be continued by the Tenents. As to the title all the Account we can give of that is, that not only Sir Edward Erby him[self] is reputed in his Country an Honest Gentleman But that Mr Johnson also, his Agent in the saile of the Estate is a Man of as good Reputation for just & faire practice, as anyone whosoever of his profession . . .[180]

The only drawback was that the estate was mortgaged; because of this, the purchase price was reduced from £2000 to £1940, and the conveyance was sealed on 5 March 1709.[181]

One way of evading the Statutes of Mortmain was to buy lay impropriations, or rectorial tithes. Puritans, however, argued in favour of the restoration of impropriations to the Church, as their sale meant that much of the value of livings passed into the hands of laymen, who need not put anything into the community except to pay the poor rate.[182] This theory was all very well, but in practice the attitude of the reformers was ambivalent and many puritan ministers found themselves in alliance both with impropriators and enemies of tithes. To deny lay rectors their property rights would have created widespread financial and political problems. After all, the clergy were educated at Oxford and Cambridge, at colleges which depended on income from tithes for a substantial part

---

[180] ECA BUR.6.3 p. 370.
[181] Documents at ECA SCH.1.24.
[182] Hill 1956, pp. 134–46.

of their revenues. Indeed, the puritan Henry Burton recommended in 1624 that impropriations should be bequeathed to the colleges of Oxford and Cambridge.[183]

The purchase by Emmanuel of the tithes of Pinchbeck in Lincolnshire, from Edmund English's bequest of £1000, illustrates many of the problems that could be encountered in choosing and buying an estate. English's will was proved in 1603, but the tithes were not bought for another 14 years. The executors, it seems, desired the College to find a suitable estate, to Emmanuel's displeasure. In 1611, the Master and Mr Butler (an agent) went to view land at Haddenham and Witchford near Ely.[184] This is the land that was referred in a letter to one of the executors of the will in 1616 (though the proximity of the estate to Cambridge was exaggerated), in which it appears that the College's choice of land did not meet with approval:

> Mr Pytt we perceive by Mr Butlar that youe are unwilling to convey the legacie to our college enles we will seeke out the land it should bye which we think is but a taken occasion of further delay for we found out an excellent peece of land within 4 myles of Cambridg most commodious in all respectes \to/ . . . our Colleg. Yet you (for some odd respecte) mislyked, & refused to pay us the monie for it so we lost our expenses & labor about that, and therefore meane not in that kynd to trie you agayne, seeing you, not we, by the will are bound to seek out landes for the College. Yet the same land synce hath bene sould for 100 li more then we should have payed which is our loss and the scholers that should long before this have bene mayntayned at their learning. We think \the answeare geven to Mr Butler/ unreasonable . . . that yeu should require us to seeke out landes at our owne charges you having all the money in your owne hands, & we none. Yf you will deliver the monie into our handes, we will give the bond within two years following to seek and bye landes . . . hytherto your usage \of his gift/ hath bene . . . such, as hath caused us to spend more about this legacie than ever we dyd about all that formerlie we have received. In consideration whereof we desyre to be Allowed what we have expended and what we shall further expend about the obtayning the \same/ . . . together with the Arrerages therof . . .[185]

From an entry in the rental for 23 November 1617, it appears that the College's request led to £110 being paid as a first instalment.[186] In May

---

[183] Hill 1956, pp. 150–5, 273.
[184] ECA BUR.8.1 p. 59.
[185] ECA Box 18.B3, 11 June 1616.
[186] ECA BUR.11.1.

1617, a decree was made by the Lord Keeper in Chancery that the terms of the benefaction could be altered to provide nine scholarships instead of two fellowships and six scholarships, and that the remainder of the bequest be paid over to the College. The interest that had accrued on the £1000, however, was to remain with the executors to pay for their expenses in trying to find suitable lands for investment and for keeping the £1000 available for use 'saving that 200 li was in July 1612 sent uppon the request of the Mr of the sayd Colledg for a Speciall occasion of goode & benefit to the sayd Colledg'.[187] A sigh of relief must have been breathed in June 1617, when Chaderton received a letter from the executors agreeing that, despite slight reservations that two of the pieces of property were rather expensive, the College might purchase three free-hold plots of land; these were probably in Northamptonshire or Lincolnshire since the Master visited these counties to buy land for the College after the Easter Audit of that year.[188]

All was, however, not over, for then the executors suggested that instead the College should buy an impropriation in Lincolnshire. This presented a moral dilemma for a puritan college, as Chaderton's reply pointed out:

> I have by Mr Foxton [the College's attorney] received your lettre & particular being gladd that you are willing to deliver the mony . . . We have therfor thereby Authorized Mr Browne our receiver, to receive of you 890 li & to geve you an acquittance for it. We have spent, about the obteyning of this legacie, out of our College stock one way and other 100 marks at the least, besyde an 100 li that we lost upon your denyall to buy the landes at Wytfford within 4 myles of Cambridg.[189] in consideration whereof we presume that eyther now, or hereafter, when God shall . . . move & touch your con-sciences with a due sense hereof, you will be verie willing . . . at least to recompense this loss.[190] Concerning your particular (<which I have herein returned>) I can now say nothing, but acknowledge your due respect unto us therein, because \diverse of/ our fellows being gone to Oxfordes commencement are not yet returned. We that are at home having dulie considered of it, (thoughe we have no affection to impropriations), (as we have eftsones wrytten to you) yet, yf we might \be/ secured, that there weare a . . . sufficient competencie . . . to mayntayne a precher in liberall maner, we would

---

[187] ECA Box 18.B4, 31 May 1617. This £200 is mysterious; it might have been sent to the College in connection with the proposed purchase of land near Ely, but there is no record of its arrival at Emmanuel and it is not accounted for in the payment of the remainder of the bequest on 23 November 1617.

[188] ECA Box 18.B5, 28 June 1617; ECA BUR.8.1 p. 86.

[189] Witchford, 3 miles from Ely, 13 miles from Cambridge.

[190] There is no evidence that the College was ever so reimbursed.

advise of it, the rather because all our fellows and scholars being by our statute assigned to divinitie, might with . . . better conscience participate with these kyndes of church lyvinges wherfore we pray you 1 to signifie what certayne mayntenance is yearlie comming to the vicar. 2. . . . to whom belongs the gift therof, 3. who is the seller of the rectorie 4 what paymentes goe out of it 5. to what religious howse it dyd \once/ belong, or to whom 6 whether Sr William Pelam dwell in great limbergh or els where And upon receipt of your Answer, by the returne of the fellows, you shall receive our direct answeare. Our Vicechancelare Archdeacon of Lincolne tells me that Impropriations in Lincolnshire are sould some for 10, some for 12 & \some/ for 13th \or 14/ at the most. I pray you \send us/ . . . the lowest price of this . . .[191]

After discovering that the Rectory had also been offered to the Vice-Chancellor at a lower price than that at which it had been advertised to the College, Chaderton managed to secure a better deal. He requested that the chancel be put into good repair (for, as lay rector, maintenance of the chancel would be the College's responsibility),[192] and then the College evidently decided that it could buy such a property. On 21 November 1617, it bought the tithes of wool and lamb for £555 from Anthony Oldfield,[193] and the tithe of corn was sold by Mr Robinson for £600 at about the same time.[194] The tithes were leased out for £80 a year, so the College had paid about 14½ years' purchase for them: a relatively high price, considering Chaderton's letter, but still below the average price of 16 years' purchase in 1629.[195] Clearly, then, the purchase of an estate from a cash bequest could be troublesome; in this instance, the end result was significant, with a puritan college buying an impropriated rectory.[196]

Mildmay's contribution to the endowment of his College was, therefore, considerable. First, he gave estates himself. Second, he encouraged others to follow his example, sometimes by direct solicitation. Thus Emmanuel received a large number of gifts, many of which were, unusually, made in the donor's lifetime. Sir Walter's friends and acquaintances at the Exchequer and other Government departments, his contacts among the London merchants, fellow evangelical protestants and others who knew him for a variety of reasons all made donations to the College. After his death, the magnetism of the Founder continued. His appointed

---

[191] ECA Box 18.B6. The Vice-Chancellor was John Hills of St Catharine's College (Venn).
[192] ECA Box 18.B7, 19 August 1617.
[193] ECA Box 18.B8.
[194] ECA BUR.8.1 p. 88.
[195] Hill 1956, p. 138.
[196] The College was already responsible for the chancel at Little Melton, Norfolk, and was to become responsible for that at Rushall in the same county in 1738 and for Ash, Kent, in 1859 (see Appendix 5).

Master remained in office and the College attracted further gifts and bequests from evangelical protestants, from members of the College and from those who had come across Mildmay in earlier years.

Later endowments

As time passed, however, Sir Walter's influence inevitably waned. The initial flood of gifts and bequests abated and, as in other colleges, many of the later donations were to found new fellowships or scholarships.[197] As in earlier years, gifts were of land, rent charges or money to purchase them, but apart from the possibility of a joint purchase with Clare, St John's and Sidney Sussex colleges of the impropriation of Melton Mowbray in Leicestershire for the Johnson exhibition in 1698,[198] no estates were paid for from the general funds of the College. Happily, there is no evidence of any repetition of experiences such as the protracted dealings over the purchase of the tithes at Pinchbeck.

Some of the gifts were bequests, either directly from Emmanuel men or their close relatives, or indirectly through the influence of members of the College. The only bequest from a former Fellow or Master that was to yield an annual income was that of Thomas Holbech. Admitted to the College in 1622, he was elected a Fellow in 1629 and was Master from 1675 until his death in 1680.[199] He settled on the College some fee-farm rents[200] to the annual value of £50 13s 5d, £9 of which arose from lands called Highelman and Lowelman which were part of the manors of Denny and Waterbeach near Cambridge, the rest issued from the manor of Littleport. These rents, which were conveyed to the College on 18 April 1681, were to endow a Catechist and an Ecclesiastical Lecturer with annual stipends of £20 each; of the remaining income, half was to augment the stipend of the Master, and half was to be a contribution towards the repairs of the College.[201]

Close relatives of members of the College were responsible for two bequests to it, though in the event only one of these arrived. Anne Hunt made her will on 20 December 1671 and it was proved three years later on 24 April 1674. She left a small estate – two acres of arable land at Pakefield in Suffolk – which was formerly owned by her late son John Collins. John was admitted to Emmanuel in 1664 as a pensioner and proceeded to the

---

[197] For example, at Balliol College, Oxford (Duncan 1986a, p. 562).

[198] ECA BUR.6.3 p. 250, grant of power of attorney to some of the governors of Oakham School to buy the impropriation, 16 November 1698. The purchase was considered because it had been agreed in the Court of Chancery on 6 December 1694 to commute the rent charge on land at Witham on the Hill, which had fallen into arrears, for £2100. Eventually, an estate was bought at Whaplode and Holbeach in 1708 (ECA SCH.1.24).

[199] Venn.

[200] Those for land held in fee-simple (absolute possession) subject to perpetual fixed rents.

[201] ECA Box 1.C6–7.

degree of LL.B. in 1670.[202] He must have died shortly afterwards, and his widowed mother made the bequest according to his instructions. Two poor scholars were to be the beneficiaries, with preference for those born in the hundreds of Mutford and Lothingland in Suffolk, or for the kin of John Collins.[203] There is no evidence that the other donor, John Hill, Rector of Preston in Rutland, was connected with Emmanuel. Nevertheless, by his will dated 20 January 1691 and proved the following July, he left two houses in Shoe Lane, London, with an annual rental income of £13, to found two exhibitions at the College. The houses were only to come to the College, however, if John's son and heir, John, died before he came of age. The son, who was born on 8 August 1691 (and thus after his father's death), did survive: he matriculated at Emmanuel in 1709.[204]

Other bequests came to the College though the testators were only indirectly connected with it. Thus, John Wells, Rector of the parish of Thurning in Northamptonshire, was friendly with William Dillingham, who had retired from the Mastership to the nearby town of Oundle in 1662.[205] Two years later, on 4 October 1664, Wells died. He left the advowson of Thurning to Emmanuel, 'although', said Dillingham, 'his education did forespeak him for the other University, yet for some respects (which I shall not mention) he was pleased to fix upon Emmanuel Colledge'. Wells also endowed an exhibition of the annual value of £5 by giving 30 acres to the Rector, on condition that £1 5s was paid each quarter to the exhibitioner. Wells asked that the first exhibition be granted to a kinsman, John Richardson, who was admitted in 1665 and was later a Fellow of the College.[206] This benefaction, therefore, probably came through Dillingham's influence.

Dillingham could well have steered another bequest in the direction of Emmanuel. Henry Gale, minister of Hemmington in Northamptonshire, left £50 for 'pious and charitable uses' by his will of 13 August 1656 and proved on 18 February in the following year.[207] The executors were two Emmanuel men, Edward Cawthorne and William Vinter, and the Vicar of Oundle Richard Resbury, who had attended Emmanuel's puritan sister, Sidney Sussex College. They decided to endow an exhibition of £3 per annum for a scholar from Oundle School and, with the collegiate bias of the executors, the puritanism of Resbury (he was puritan Lecturer at Oundle before becoming the Vicar there) and possibly with the

[202] ECA CHA.1.4 f. 156r; Venn.
[203] ECA Box 9.Oa17; ECA SCH.1.1 (which says, erroneously, that Collins was a Fellow Commoner).
[204] ECA Box 25.G1; Venn. Shortly after John senior's death, the College paid 13 shillings for copies of the deeds of the houses; the originals were kept by the widow (ECA BUR.8.2, expenditure after 27 October 1691).
[205] Shuckburgh 1904, p. 103.
[206] ECA COL.9.10.18; COL.9.1(A) p. 237.
[207] Longden 1940, p. 157.

connections of Dillingham (then Master) with the town, Emmanuel was the obvious choice.[208] Indeed, three of Resbury's sons attended Emmanuel and the youngest of them, Samuel, became a Gale exhibitioner in 1669.[209] Deployment of the £50 was controversial. The decision was made to use it to renew a lease of six acres of marshland at Ripple in Essex that had then expired. Control of this land was important as the College owned the adjoining 17 acres and needed to secure access and prevent trespass.[210] There was, however, some discussion as to whether the College should lease the six acres from Sir Thomas Fanshaw, paying a fine of £100 and £5 yearly in rent, or whether the fee-simple should be bought for £270. In the end, it was decided not to buy the land outright but to sub-let it, charging a £50 fine and £8 per annum in rent. Thus, Gale's bequest paid for half of the fine, and of the annual income from the land, £5 was paid in rent and £3 to the exhibitioner.[211] The disadvantage of this decision was that the College leased the estate for 31 years from Fanshaw, but could only sub-let it for 21 years. As the fine from the sub-tenant was used to pay that of the landlord, the system had complications built in and indeed caused trouble in the future.[212]

Emmanuel was named as the legatee of last resort by two testators whose connections with the College have not been discovered. In 1636, the lawyer Sir Robert Hitcham died, and by his will of 8 August he left the castle, manor and advowson of Framlingham in Suffolk to his former College, Pembroke. Hitcham died one week later,[213] but before he did so he added a codicil to the effect that if Pembroke were to refuse the bequest, it should come to Emmanuel.[214] Pembroke College experienced difficulty over the benefaction and it was not finally settled until the Mastership of William Moses (elected in 1655),[215] and as late as 1677 William Balderston and Thomas Nettleton from Emmanuel travelled to Bury St Edmunds about the will.[216] Another possibility of a donation of property in Suffolk came to nothing. Richard Peacock of Lavenham's connection with the College is not known, but £4 a year was already paid thence to Emmanuel from Thomas Skinner's benefaction. By his will of 4 September 1647, Peacock left a rent charge arising from lands at Little Waldingfield to pay, after the death of his wife, £5 a year to educate five children at Lavenham Grammar School. If, however, there were no school there, the bequest should be used to enable a student from Lavenham,

[208] ECA COL.9.10.13; Venn.
[209] Venn; ECA COL.9.10.22.
[210] ECA Box 15.A16.
[211] ECA Box 15.A17.
[212] ECA COL.9.10.22; ECA Box 15.A22.
[213] *DNB*.
[214] ECA Box 9.Oa15.
[215] Attwater 1936, pp. 72–3, 76.
[216] ECA BUR.8.2, expenditure after 3 May 1677. The journey cost two guineas.

Little Waldingfield or Brent Eleigh (in that order of preference), or, failing that, chosen by Lavenham town, to attend Emmanuel. Peacock's will seems to have concentrated the minds of the authorities at Lavenham: his widow, Joan, was buried on Christmas Day 1659 and the first school-master was appointed in the following year.[217]

Fewer benefactions were made by the living in the second half of the seventeenth century, though they were especially welcome. As Fuller said,

> To Francis Ash of London, Esquire.

> It is the life of a Gift to be done in the life of the Giver, farre better than funeral Legacies . . . For, it is not so kindly charity, for men to give what they can keep no longer: besides, such donations are most subject to abuses;

> Silver in the living,
> Is Gold in the giving;
> Gold in the dying,
> Is but Silver a flying;
> Gold and Silver in the dead,
> Turn too often into Lead.

> But you have made your own hands, Executors; and eyes, Over-seers; so bountifull to a flourishing foundation in Cambridge, that you are above the standard of a Benefactor. Longer may you live for the glory of God, and good of his servants.[218]

Francis Ash, Alderman of the City of London, Governor of the Muscovy or Russia Company and sometime Prime Warden of the Goldsmiths' Company was exceptional, for all of the other lifetime donations were made by members of the College. Ash combined his wealth with gener-osity: he was a man 'to whom God hath given a full hand, and free heart, to be bountifull on all good occasions',[219] and according to Anthony Tuckney (Master 1645–53), he gave nearly £300 to charity each year. Many of Ash's gifts were to educational and religious causes.[220] Why Emmanuel was a beneficiary is not clear: perhaps Ash was related to the nonconformist divine Simeon Ash, who was admitted to the College in 1613, to Nathaniel Ash, who matriculated in 1652 and came from one of Francis' counties, Leicestershire, or to another Simeon, from the county of Francis' birth, Derbyshire, and who matriculated in 1680.[221] In any case,

---

[217] McKeon 1829, pp. 51–2.
[218] Fuller 1655, p. 137.
[219] Fuller 1655, p. 148.
[220] Oates 1986, pp. 273–4.
[221] Venn.

he was well known to the College by the time he made his gift as he had been entertained annually there from 1651 to 1654 and was presented with a Bible by it.[222] Ash's visits were presumably connected with his conveyance of the manor of Shernborne in Norfolk to the College on 12 September 1654. The estate was worth £225 per annum;[223] from it, payments of £194 were to be made: various sums to the Master, the Fellows, the College Library and the College staff, £10 each to ten exhibitioners (preferably from the schools at Derby, where Ash was born, or at Ashby-de-la-Zouch, where he was educated), and to lecturers and teachers at these schools and in Aldermanbury in London.[224] Ironically, ownership of the Shernborne estate was to prove troublesome, and Ash's gift could very well have appeared leaden rather than golden from time to time.

Members of the College also gave to it and the building of the chapel was made possible by such support. Three of those who helped in this way were former or future Masters and two of them gave land: Thomas Holbech and William Sancroft (the younger). Holbech's bequest of a rent charge in 1681 has already been mentioned. A former Fellow and Master from 1675 to 1680, he also supported the new chapel during his lifetime by giving a lease of the 'Sempire Lands', 21 acres of arable and pasture to the South of Cambridge, including Coe Fen Leys. Peterhouse was the landlord and Holbech made over to Emmanuel on 17 March 1668 the rents that were derived from sub-letting the property.[225] The College thus received an annual income of £10 10s in return for an outlay of 19s 6d, six bushels of wheat and one quarter each of malt and oats, so the chapel did not fare badly.[226] William Sancroft, the prime promoter of the chapel, also helped to endow its maintenance. On 22 December 1671, he purchased rents from the manor of Fleet in Lincolnshire;[227] on 17 February 1674, they were conveyed to the College. Emmanuel was to enjoy the annual income of £20 17s 9½d after Sancroft's death, with instructions that the College 'shall from tyme to tyme for ever after expend and imploy the same for and towards the building furnishing adorneing and repaireing of the Chapell and Library'.[228] Sancroft's successor as Master, John Breton, bequeathed, *inter alia*, £400 towards the new chapel when he died on 2 March 1676.[229] Both were also donors of advowsons.

At the end of this long list of additions to the College's endowment comes the acquisition of one further estate, again made possible by

[222] ECA BUR.8.2. On 14 February 1654, £3 5s was paid for annotations on the Bible presented to him, and for carriage of it (BUR.8.2).
[223] ECA Box 22.A4.
[224] ECA Box 9.Ma3.
[225] ECA BUR.8.2; BUR.36.2 f. 2.
[226] ECA Box 2.J2(1); ECA BUR.6.3 pp. 190–2.
[227] ECA Box 1.B5.
[228] ECA Box 1.B7–8; Stubbings 1987–8.
[229] ECA Box 9.Oa32.

donations by members of the College while they were still alive. Benjamin Whichcote was a Fellow from 1633 to 1643 and Provost of King's College from 1645 to 1660. He was executor of the will of William Larkin and was entrusted with a substantial sum of money 'to dispose of to pious uses at his own discretion'.[230] On 18 March 1670, the College bought several tenements in Holborn for £1350,[231] and this purchase was followed by that of property in the Old Bailey for £160 by 22 September in the same year.[232] The monies so deployed were £1006 13s 4d from Larkin's bequest and £503 6s 8d given by John Sudbury.[233] This second donor matriculated at Emmanuel in 1621 and at the time of his benefaction was Dean of Durham. The income from the estate amounted to £80 and agreements were drawn up with Whichcote and Sudbury as to its disposal. Two-thirds were to be regarded as Whichcote's gift and divided between the Master and Fellows, the College, and four scholars. Half of the remaining third, Dean Sudbury's donation, was to support a Greek Lecturer, and the remainder was to be divided amongst the Master, the College and the provision of a piece of plate to the 'most worthy' of the commencing Bachelors of Arts.[234] Whichcote was canny: he dated the deeds in such a way as to ensure that the College received its rents before making the necessary payments from them and always had one quarter's rent in hand.[235]

Reduction in the value of the endowments

The picture of a steadily growing rental income, however, needs to be modified slightly: first, there were delays in obtaining the income. There is, for example, no record of receipts from Francis Chamberlain's gift of property at Great and Little Melton for the first 16 years of its ownership by the College.[236] In 1598, the College had to resort to the law courts to force the argumentative tenants at Sutton Coldfield to start paying their rents, and claimed £233 in arrears and legal costs.[237] In the late seventeenth century, too, the College had to be patient: Thomas Holbech kept the rents of the Sempire Lands for his own use from 1669 until Christmas 1671.[238]

---

[230] *DNB.*

[231] ECA BUR.2.6 f. 209r.

[232] ECA BUR.2.6 f. 207r.

[233] ECA SCH.1.11.

[234] The agreements were drawn up on 21 September 1670 (ECA BUR.2.6 ff. 209–11; ECA Box 21.B10).

[235] ECA Box 21.B11.

[236] Income first arrived at the College in the half year after the audit of 29 March 1601 (ECA BUR.11.1).

[237] ECA Box 29.B22(v). As a result of this action, the first income from the estate was paid to the College on 26 September 1598 (ECA BUR.11.1).

[238] ECA BUR.8.2; BUR.36.2 f. 2.

Second, rental income was increasingly subject to charges on it. Some estates were liable to particular dues: at Godmanchester, £20 had to be paid to the schoolmaster each year; the tithes at Pinchbeck were subject to the annual payment of a tenth, £5 12s, to the Crown; and a chief rent of 19s 4d was charged each year on the Sutton Coldfield estate.[239] All in all, £29 4s 6d was paid annually in such a way in about 1630.[240] The Hyde Farm estate, too, was liable to an annual charge of 11s 2d and in 1685 it was erroneously claimed that an additional eight shillings should be paid each year. The College paid £7 19s to settle the arrears that were being asked for and costs, because this was cheaper than contesting the case which, it was estimated, would have cost about £10.[241] Estates were increasingly liable to national and local taxes. The colleges at Oxford and Cambridge were exempt from ecclesiastical taxes before the Civil War and entry fines were similarly not taxed.[242] Thenceforwards, however, taxation increased. Poor rates and other parochial and county dues were commonly paid by the tenants whereas Parliamentary and extraordinary taxes were met by the landlord. If a tenant paid on the landlord's behalf, he was compensated by a reduction in rent.[243] The land tax, levied from 1692, rapidly became a tax on rents and owners failed to shift its payment on to their tenants.[244] Taxation could, therefore, be a great burden to a landowner. Indeed, during the Civil War and Interregnum, the Haberdashers' Company was greatly affected in this way;[245] whether Emmanuel suffered from similar causes will be seen in the following chapter.

Emmanuel and its neighbours

The viability of Mildmay's foundation was thus assured, and indeed the process of endowment of the College was noteworthy. Usually, the establishment of a college took some decades. At Sidney Sussex College, founded only 12 years after Emmanuel and similarly enjoying a reputation for inclinations towards evangelical protestantism, far fewer initial benefactions were attracted. Indeed, it took seven years for the foundress' bequest to be realised in the laying of a foundation stone for the College.[246] Within this space of time Emmanuel's future had been well secured, and by 1601 the College was sufficiently well endowed to be able to turn aside Popham's gift, which would have caused problems in its

---

[239] ECA BUR.11.0.C.
[240] ECA BUR.8.2.
[241] ECA Box 28.A21; ECA BUR.8.2, expenditure since 22 April 1686.
[242] Hill 1956, p. 193.
[243] Clay 1985, p. 224.
[244] Habakkuk 1940, p. 9.
[245] Archer 1991, p. 83.
[246] Scott-Giles 1975, p. 20; Wyatt 1996, pp. 52–3.

administration. St John's, too, was a college with leanings towards evangelical protestantism in the late sixteenth and early seventeenth centuries; it took from 1511 to 1622, nearly three times as long, to attract the same number of donations as Emmanuel did in almost 40 years.[247] The Elizabethan foundation in Oxford, Jesus College, was slow to become established. Founded in 1571, it still had an annual income of only a little more than £100 by 1620.[248] Emmanuel was clearly unusual, and much must be attributed to the zeal and enthusiasm of its founder. Both directly and indirectly, he attracted donations to the College: from personal contacts, fellow evangelical protestants, and members of the College. Only well into the seventeenth century did his influence begin to decrease; thereafter, Emmanuel conformed to the more typical pattern of receiving a few, spasmodic, donations, largely by bequest and mostly from members of the College or their close relatives.

The nature of the holdings and their geographical distribution was less remarkable. A mixture of urban and rural property, of large and small estates and of income from land, tithes, manors and rent charges was found in many colleges. Colleges in Cambridge tended to have most of their property in Eastern England: Clare and St John's colleges both did so.[249] Map 3 at the start of Appendix 5 demonstrates how Emmanuel's endowment was similarly in land located in Eastern England, with the Sutton Coldfield estate being the main exception. Other colleges had land further afield – Dr Caius, for instance, acquired an estate at Bincombe in Dorset for Gonville and Caius College in 1570[250] – but the overall geographical spread of estates was narrower than among colleges in Oxford.[251] Much depended on particular circumstances and the connections of a college, for the Elizabethan legislation meant that these institutions were largely at the donors' mercy.

---

[247] Ibish 1985, p. 183.
[248] Baker 1971, p. 10.
[249] Forbes 1928, p. 73; Howard 1935, map between pp. 382–3.
[250] Gross 1912, p. 8.
[251] Bendall (forthcoming).

5

Estate Management and Finances 1584–1719

Estate Management

Estate management in the sixteenth and seventeenth centuries

As activities of landowners were intimately related to their income, the ways in which the potential of their estates was realised are of central importance. The management of estates was, in the sixteenth century as at other times, carried out with varying degrees of efficiency. There are many examples of highly competent estate stewards and agents who worked for employers who took a great interest in their property. Among others, it was usual to do little more than ensure that rents were collected and that tenants did not run up arrears.[1] Some landlords were simply not interested in their estates: an easy-going attitude could, however, reflect neglect rather than any conscious decision to behave in this way. Perhaps such owners were not interested in estate development; leases tended to reflect local customs and practices and were rarely innovative.[2] Owners could delegate the detailed administration of their finances and businesses to agents who were not necessarily competent or honest. Thus, the day-to-day administration of a property was sometimes carried out by a motley collection of bailiffs, tenant farmers, part-time agents and stewards.[3] Much did, however, depend on the type of landlord: whether the estate was owned by an individual or by an institution, and the proximity of the land to where the owner spent most of his time.

Some absentee private owners played a less active role in estate management than those who lived on or near their property, whilst the survival of letters between other landowners and their stewards shows how control over estates could be maintained from a distance. In seventeenth-century Glamorganshire, for example, aristocratic landlords with their main seats elsewhere took far less interest in their Welsh property than those who spent much time in the county and showed a great concern in the running of their estates.[4] On the other hand, detailed

---

[1] Martin 1979, p. 22.
[2] Clay 1985, pp. 215, 242–3.
[3] Beckett 1986, p. 155.
[4] Martin 1979, p. 12.

correspondence between the third Lord Fitzwilliam and his estate steward, Francis Guybon, demonstrates how Fitzwilliam played an important role in the running of his Northamptonshire property though he lived in London. Between 1697 and 1709, he never visited his country seat; nevertheless, through letters, he influenced the choice of tenants, controlled the bargaining processes in the renewal of leases, was concerned with maintaining the productivity of the soil, and advised Guybon on which tenant knew a particular piece of ground well and could be trusted to give an unbiased valuation of it.[5] At about the same time, Sir James Lowther had a similarly close relationship with the steward of his estates in Cumberland, John Spedding.[6]

Institutional landowners were like their absentee aristocratic counterparts in many ways. They, too, frequently had large and scattered estates that covered wide areas, were partially or continuously absentee, and relied on employees to manage their property for them. Establishment of the titles to their land and securing an income from it were major interests. The Oxford colleges, the Duchy of Cornwall and the Crown are all examples of institutional owners with such attitudes towards their estates.[7] They had their land surveyed from time to time: King James I did so from 1603, in an attempt to rectify his poor financial position.[8] The remedy was not straightforward: as tenants believed that negligent administration displayed their landlord's love for them, they naturally resisted change as much as possible.[9] Surveyors were regarded with suspicion, as their activities could lead to sales of land or raised rents.[10] Financial management was always very varied; St Catharine's College, Cambridge, improved its methods in the late sixteenth century.[11] One hundred years later, both New College in Oxford and Queens' College, Cambridge, tried to tighten up their estate administration and improved their record keeping so that there was less opportunity for fraud.[12]

New tools of estate administration started to develop from the mid-sixteenth century. The concept of a survey was not novel, but in the medieval period such a document was usually a lengthy verbal description of an estate, its boundaries, its extent, its tenants, customs and practices. It was mainly concerned with value, which was not revealed by measurement of area and so accurate dimensions of the land were rarely included, although nominal acreages were often given. These means of

---

[5] Hainsworth and Walker 1990.
[6] Beckett 1990.
[7] Dunbabin 1986, p. 302; Haslam 1991, pp. 58–62; Hoyle 1990, p. 76.
[8] Lawrence 1985.
[9] Hoyle 1990, pp. 93–4.
[10] The surveyor in John Norden's *Surveyors Dialogue* (1607), for example, sets out to allay the fears of farmers and tenants.
[11] Jones 1936, p. 222.
[12] McIntosh 1987, pp. 175–81; Twigg 1987, p. 301.

estate management continued to be produced, but they came to be supplemented by the introduction of estate maps. The ninth Earl of Northumberland, for example, advised his son in 1609 that the first principle of estate management was that 'you understand your estate generally better than any one of your officers'; he went on to stress the importance of good record keeping and was an early promoter of the use of estate maps:

> The first of these [principles] I have so explained and laboured by books of surveys, plots of manors, and records, that the fault will be your own, if you understand them not in a very short time better than any servant you have. They are not difficult now they are done, they are easy and yet cost me much time and much expense to reduce them into order; by them shall you direct and see when your causes proceed well or evil, slowly or swiftly. And it is not my meaning to make you a slave to your wealth, or a whole acting instrument to your profit; for that were base, too much tasting of the clown, and loss of time from more worthy matters that your calling and place would move you to. For you to sit at the helm of your own estate, to direct well with expedition and ease, will be a means of upholding your honour with a good report, without the dislike of your neighbours, whose goods otherwise necessity will cause you to covet.[13]

Late sixteenth-century and early seventeenth-century Essex, with many large magnates, was an especially precocious county in the use of estate maps.[14] Institutional owners, too, began to appreciate the value of maps and plans: in the early seventeenth century, Christ's Hospital and the Clothworkers' Company in London, became increasingly concerned that they should have written and, if possible, drawn surveys of their estates.[15] In about 1616, John Norden recommended that demesne land and improvable waste of Crown manors should be mapped; written surveys of the remainder of the land would suffice.[16] Although many of the Oxford colleges, such as All Souls, Brasenose, Merton, New College and Corpus Christi commissioned maps at this time,[17] few Cambridge colleges followed their example.[18] In both universities, it was the Restoration that heralded a new era in which cartography played a more evident part of estate administration.[19]

Treatises on estate management, accounting, surveying and map-

---

[13] Harrison 1930, pp. 75, 77–8.
[14] Hull 1987.
[15] Schofield 1987, pp. 3–4.
[16] Lawrence 1985, p. 84.
[17] Eden 1983; Connor 1987, p. 49.
[18] Bendall (forthcoming).
[19] Dunbabin 1986, pp. 283–4; Bendall 1992, Chapter 7.

making were published in increasing numbers, starting with Fitzherbert's *Boke of Husbandry* of 1523. This first book shows affinity with the thirteenth-century treatise on husbandry by Walter of Henley,[20] but through subsequent publications landowners became acquainted with modern ideas and methods.[21] Such works were owned by both individuals and institutions in the sixteenth and seventeenth centuries, and there is evidence that members of Cambridge University were no exception.[22] Emmanuel College was connected with one of the leading authors on surveying in the mid-seventeenth century: George Atwell. Born in 1576–7, he was a teacher of mathematics and instrument-maker in Cambridge by 1624.[23] His *Faithfull Surveyor*, published in 1658 (the year of his death), was dedicated to the Master of Emmanuel, William Dillingham. In it, Atwell praises the Manciple of the College, Walter Frost, as an excellent mathematician and responsible for bringing Hobson's Conduit to the College. This took place between 1631 and 1636; Frost became Manciple between 1622 and 1628 and remained as such until 1639.[24] He later became sword-bearer to the Lord Mayor of London and a secretary to the Council of State, and his son was admitted to the College in 1636.[25] Thus, within Emmanuel in the seventeenth century, were men with interests and skills in practical mathematics.[26]

Therefore the seventeenth century heralded the introduction of new practices and techniques of estate administration by both private and institutional landlords. This is the general context against which developments in Emmanuel must be judged: the letting practices and control of estates through covenants in leases, estate repairs, collection of rents, visits to estates, and the relationship of the College with its tenants.

Leases and their making

Until the nineteenth century, Oxford and Cambridge colleges, as well as the Church, usually let their estates by granting beneficial leases. Some private owners, too, used such a method of letting, although by the mid-seventeenth century it was becoming increasingly modified.[27] Estates were let for a number of years, or lives, at low annual rents. Fines were levied at each renewal; these were the means by which the full value of the land was realised, and therefore successful estate management hinged on setting a realistic fine.[28] Typically, in rural areas, a lease was for

---

[20] Oschinsky 1971, pp. 142–3.
[21] Charlton 1965, pp. 290–1; Bendall 1992, pp. 119–21.
[22] Bendall 1992, pp. 143–50.
[23] Bendall 1997, A197; Feingold 1984, p. 85.
[24] ECA BUR.8.2.
[25] Atwell 1658, p. 81; Bushell 1938, p. 54; Venn.
[26] Bendall (forthcoming); Cormack 1997; Curtis 1959, p. 242.
[27] Bowden 1967, p. 686.
[28] Duncan 1986a, p. 568.

21 years and was renewed at seven-year intervals. As fines increased rapidly as a lease drew near its end, it was advantageous to the tenant to renew fairly frequently. Beneficial leases had various advantages over letting estates at rack-rent for a landlord who wanted to save agents' and lawyers' fees. The estate only had to be valued when a lease was up for renewal; in the meantime, the tenant was liable for repairs and was unlikely to fall into severe arrears because his annual commitments to the landlord were low. The system, however, also had its drawbacks. It had little regard for posterity and for the long-term well-being of an estate as it did not encourage the landlord to develop his property or to invest capital in it.[29] Nor did it guarantee to the landlord an assured income that kept pace with inflation: fines were irregular and frequently, in fact, did not reflect the true value of an estate. Tenants, however, were happy: they had a guarantee of a property to enjoy at a low annual rent, there was little interference from the landlord and, if they sub-let the estate, they could realise a handsome profit.

Emmanuel's foundation took place shortly after the introduction of legislation that was designed to improve the financial situation and prospects of colleges and similar institutions, and reveals a fairly sophisticated view of estate management by the leaders in Oxford and Cambridge. Two Acts, 13 Elizabeth Cap.10 (1571) and 14 Elizabeth Cap.11 (1572) guaranteed colleges a regular, and relatively frequent, chance to renew their leases and to revise their rents: the first Act limited the length of leases of agricultural property to three lives or 21 years, the second limited leases of urban property to 40 years. (Hitherto, leases had sometimes been made out for much longer periods and 99-year leases had not been unusual.) The chance to increase rents to reflect inflation was, however, rarely taken, and four years later in 1576 the Corn Rent Act (18 Elizabeth Cap.6) was passed in an attempt to remedy this. By this statute, one-third of the existing rent was to be reserved and paid either in kind in a combination of wheat and malt barley, or in the cash equivalent, using the current market prices for corn at Cambridge, Oxford or Winchester. The initial amount of grain that was due was calculated at the rate of 6s 8d a quarter for wheat and 5s a quarter for malt. In this way, part of the rental income was index-linked, and the increase that thereby accrued was to be applied to the commons and diet of the institutions. A loophole had been left by these Acts, however, and a further statute was passed in the same year (18 Elizabeth Cap.11) to prevent over-frequent renewals: a new lease could not be made to the same tenant if over three years remained to run of the existing lease. Surpluses from the corn rents and income from entry fines came to be divided among the Master and Fellowship as their dividend.[30]

[29] Cooke 1962, pp. 517–18.
[30] Aylmer 1986, pp. 534–7; Shadwell 1898, pp. 9–11; Collinson 1991, p. 19.

The legislation thus provided a framework within which institutions could operate and some adhered to it more closely than others. The statutes of both Gonville and Caius and St John's colleges, for example, limited the length of leases to 20 years, and at the former college the renewal of leases before their expiry was prohibited.[31] On occasions, external pressures made it difficult or even impossible to keep within the law. At Queens' College, for example, Her Majesty's tailor demanded a lease in reversion (that is, a lease that would only be effective on the expiry of the current lease, which could be some time off)[32] for 40 years. As Queen Elizabeth had written a letter in her tailor's support, the College could hardly refuse.[33] Ecclesiastical landowners, too, managed to find pretexts for evading the law.[34]

Emmanuel, however, appears to have been more law-abiding in the granting of leases. Almost all of its rural property was let for 21 years, the troubled Shernborne estate in the late seventeenth century being the main exception. The College's urban property was let for varying numbers of years, and in 1651 it was decided that houses, too, should only be let for 21 years.[35] The effect was short-lived; though some urban properties were let for 21 years for a while, variation soon set in and indeed as early as 1652, houses in London were let for 31 years.[36] Nevertheless, leases only exceeded the statutory length of 40 years by express legal decree for those premises that were affected by the Great Fire of London in 1666.[37] The record is not without blemish, however. The most notable lapse was disobedience to the terms of the Dixie trust and the disposal of the income from the associated estate at Sutton Coldfield. In 1678, an action was taken in Chancery against the College. The essence of the justifiable complaint was that the Master and Fellows had let the premises:

> upon Leases att great Fynes and small Rents and haue shared and devided the sayd Fynes amongst themselues and haue allowed to the sayd New Fellowshipps and Schollershipps soe very little yearely that they should not bee worth acceptance and by that meanes haue endeauoured to sincke the said yearely Rents reserued into the Treasury of the sayd Colledge to bee shared and divided amongst the said Master and other the Fellowes and Schollers of the sayd Colledge . . .

---

[31] Venn, *Caius*, III, pp. 380–1; Howard 1935, p. 14.
[32] Atherton 1996, p. 668.
[33] Twigg 1987, p. 116.
[34] Hill 1956, pp. 30–1.
[35] ECA COL.14.1 p. 57.
[36] In Threadneedle Street (ECA Box 27.B12). The houses in St Dunstan's Alley were let for 40 years in 1653 (Box 25.E2).
[37] See, for example, the lease of the Old Bailey property made on 25 January 1695 (ECA Box 25.E4).

so that for the past 30 years or so there had been few Dixie Fellows or Scholars, and those who had come to the College had been meanly supported.[38]

When an estate was given to the College the existing lease frequently had some years to run; after the necessary amount of time had passed, the process of renewal could be embarked upon. This involved some effort and expenditure by the landlord. A lawyer was retained by the College and he looked after the legal aspects of the business. Thus, an annual fee of £2 13s 4d was paid to Mr Butler from 1605 to 1612 (a Mr Bridges also acted for the College between 1604 and 1618), to Mr Foxton from 1617 to 1650, when Mr Rose succeeded him, and to Mr Jacob in 1667.[39] Much depended on the lawyer's ability; in 1640, William Ivatt wrote about the renewal of his lease of the tenement that he occupied in Threadneedle Street: 'I suppose your Regester sufficiently understandeth the drawinge of a Lease without any errors'.[40]

The estate that was to be re-let could be inspected on the College's behalf, perhaps by the person who collected the rents. Detailed valuations and surveys were, it seems, rarely drawn up before the eighteenth century; they were only necessary if a particular problem had to be resolved. Probably the first map drawn on renewal of a lease was made in 1702, for tenements in Threadneedle Street.[41] A plan was necessary to establish the boundaries of the College's property there as this was the first time the lease had been renewed since the Fire of London and one of the tenements had been partly built on land that was not owned by Emmanuel. A Fellow of the College, William Savage, was involved in London with the renewal and wrote to his colleague William Peirs in Cambridge:

> I waited upon him [Mr Layfield] in Limestreet but he tells me he can do us no service, for that he does not understand surveying, & as to the value of the Lease, Mr Austin, being a lawyer, is a much properer Judge of That. He would have us inquire out the surveyor after the fire, & the Builder, & see what intelligence we can gain from them about the extent of our ground. You say you are assured we may have a sight of the writings, of the adjacent houses, but you don't tell us where we may meet with em nor how your assurance is grounded that those owners will show their writings, since it seems to me that if they have incroached upon us, that producing their writings may ingage them in a lawsuit with the College. In short, all that I conceive is to be done, is to have an Artist measure our 3

---

[38] ECA Box 29.B14; see also pp. 138, 169.
[39] See ECA BUR.8.1–2.
[40] ECA Box 27.B9–10.
[41] The lease was made on 24 June 1703 and has a map on it (ECA Box 27.C1–2).

houses, & see whether they stand upon 2010 foot, which you say were assigned us after the fire . . .[42]

A few years later, in 1712, part of the Hyde Farm estate was measured and a map or terrier made before the lease was renewed. This might have been thought necessary because the tenant, who had died, had mortgaged the estate.[43] Terms for the new lease had to be determined; marginal notes in the Register of Leases indicate that these were based on those of the existing lease.[44] This is unsurprising; All Souls College, Oxford behaved in a similar way, to ensure that the reserved rents agreed.[45] Once all had been settled, the old lease surrendered and cancelled, the fine, sealing fees and any arrears of rent paid, and a bond for the performance of covenants drawn up,[46] the lease was sealed. Sealing took place in College, in the presence of the Master and Fellows (this practice was statutory at Queens' College),[47] and was marked by the consumption of wine.[48] Finally, the lease was delivered to the tenant and the College kept the counterpart.

Normally all went smoothly, but on occasion the letting of an estate could be very troublesome indeed. Emmanuel was introduced early on to some of the problems which could arise when it negotiated to let the Sutton Coldfield estate. The College purchased the land in 1594,[49] and soon became aware of difficulties concerning it. Attempts were made to demonstrate that a £200 debt of a former owner, Simon Perrot, had not been satisfied, and rents that were due to the College were diverted to meet these alleged liabilities.[50] A legal judgement settled this problem in Emmanuel's favour, but did not solve that of deciding how to let the estate. The tenants bombarded the College with claims and counter-claims, some wanting individual leases, others asking to be head tenant and to sub-let land to the existing tenants.[51] One letter even told tales of 'monstrous and manifold wrongs' which had been committed by the eventual tenant, Marmaduke Dawney (who had married Perrot's widow, Alice) and his fellow conspirator William Gardiner. The author, Francis Saunders, alleged forcible entry to property, hunting, chasing and killing cattle, breaking-down walls and windows, threats of arson, wrongful

---

[42] ECA Box 27.B15.
[43] ECA BUR.6.3 pp. 451–7.
[44] For example, in the renewal of a lease of the White Hart, Sutton Coldfield, on 6 July 1699 (ECA BUR.6.3 pp. 254–7).
[45] Blackstone 1898, p. 42.
[46] Brooks 1986, p. 68.
[47] Twigg 1987, p. 116.
[48] Ten shillings was spent at the sealing of Mr Houghton's lease of the Shernborne estate in 1693, for example (ECA SCH.1.1).
[49] ECA Box 29.B1.
[50] ECA Box 29.B24.
[51] ECA Box 29.B22.

imprisonment, practising and conspiring to bring about the death of men and women, hurling young children out of their beds, threatening to throw them out of windows, and needless assembly of two to three hundred inhabitants in the dead of night.[52] When Marmaduke Dawney at one stage suggested that the lease be made out to William Gardiner, proceedings were set in motion; then Dawney changed his mind and the College clearly began to lose its patience.[53] At various times, Chaderton and other Fellows visited Sutton Coldfield,[54] but eventually Sir Anthony Mildmay (Sir Walter's son and heir) was called in to arbitrate.[55] It was not until 1602, eight years after the estate was bought, that all was eventually settled and the land was let, after a considerable expenditure of time and trouble.[56]

Not even the delivery of a lease always went smoothly. When William Bedell, Bursar, delivered a lease of Little Melton in 1602, he claimed that he carried it between his cassock and his doublet, wrapped up in paper which defaced the seal. A year or two later, it was pointed out that the absence of a seal invalidated the lease, and the tenant tried to extract better terms. When J. B. Peace read of this story during his Bursarship (1893–1920), he inspected the deed and said that it looked 'as if rain had penetrated the cassock & doublet'.[57]

Covenants in leases
Covenants were built into leases, and tenants usually signed bonds that they would either keep them or pay a sum of money which could be quite considerable.[58] Terms tended not to vary in any important way between the different colleges at Oxford,[59] and Cambridge colleges, too, seem to have had largely similar conditions and obligations. The main purpose of covenants was to ensure that tenants adhered to normally accepted local customs of husbandry, and to provide the landlord with a basis for claiming financial compensation or to end a tenancy. Thus the leases of absentee owners, such as colleges, tended to be far more detailed than those of private owners who, resident on small estates, could keep a close watch on the practices themselves. It was necessary to be flexible, however, in insisting on performance of covenants in certain circumstances. In times of agricultural depression, for instance, it was unrealistic to demand that a tenant should be responsible for all repairs and not to

---

[52] ECA Box 29.B22(lxxv).
[53] ECA Box 29.B22(liv, lvi).
[54] ECA Box 29.B22(xxx, xxxiii, liv).
[55] ECA Box 29.B22(lxxviii).
[56] ECA Box 29.B25/6.
[57] ECA REF.1.1 f. 14. It is not known where Peace found this deed.
[58] £300 in the case of the property in the Old Bailey in 1694 (ECA Box 25.E4) and Shernborne, Norfolk, in 1686 (ECA BUR.6.3 pp. 136–43).
[59] Aylmer 1986, p. 525.

allow him to fall into arrears: eviction of one tenant under such financial conditions would not guarantee replacement by another better able to comply.[60] Four main classes of covenant can be identified: those that ordained the administration of property, the methods of farming, the performance of repairs and the choice of tenant. These groups can be examined to see how Emmanuel made use of such controls.

Administrative covenants: courts, visits, terriers

Covenants that regulated the administration of an estate were numerous and varied according to the type of property. For manors, for example, provisions were commonly made for keeping courts. At Balliol College, Oxford, the tenants were to keep the courts and to provide accommodation for visits by College officers.[61] Emmanuel was the owner of the manor of Great Gransden; the College kept the court itself but the tenant of 18 acres and a messuage there was to accommodate and refresh up to six people in 1601. The terms varied slightly over the years, which might reflect adaptation to changing circumstances: in 1629, six to seven people were to be given one meal, whilst in 1689 the number of those partaking of refreshments was to include the steward and other officers.[62] There are references to expenditure on journeys to Gransden every few years, so it seems that the tenant was required to meet his obligations of providing appropriate hospitality.[63] Two Fellows were to be accommodated at the manor house at Shernborne in Norfolk for 14 days a year, presumably, though not explicitly, in connection with manorial business.[64] Where the landlord owned tithes, his legal rights might have to be defended by the tenant. Covenants for such purposes were introduced into leases of tithes at Pinchbeck in 1687 and 1714;[65] at Little Melton in Norfolk, the earliest leases of the property by the College included such an obligation, together with responsibility for the repair of the chancel.[66] Balliol and New College in Oxford protected their tithes in a similar way.[67]

The right to inspect an estate was another covenant concerned with estate administration. Most leases did include the right of access for the landlord to inspect his property without let or hindrance; the precise details and frequency varied from estate to estate and there was no clear difference between urban and rural land. Thus the Ball in Gracechurch Street could be inspected twice-yearly from 1656, whereas at the Harrow

---

[60] Clay 1985, pp. 216, 224, 229–30.
[61] Duncan 1986a, p. 571.
[62] ECA Box 14.D1, D4, D16–17.
[63] ECA BUR.8.1–2.
[64] ECA BUR.6.3 pp. 51–8.
[65] ECA Box 18.A5–6.
[66] ECA Box 20.D1–4.
[67] Dunbabin 1986, p. 286.

nearby, inspections could only be annual until 1708; thereafter there, too, visits were permitted twice a year.[68] The Hyde Farm estate was similarly liable to inspections twice a year.[69] On the other hand, the College's property at Stondon, Essex, could be inspected at any time.[70] Rights of inspection became more usual over time: they were, for instance, first introduced into leases of the marsh at Ripple in Essex in 1713.[71] By the early eighteenth century, the leases of many estates included such covenants, but they were still not ubiquitous: at Eltisley, Godmanchester, Gransden, Little Melton and Pakefield, there were no conditions of this nature. No particular significance can be attached to the presence or absence of rights of inspection and their introduction cannot be attributed to any particular development or problem on an estate. Nor did proximity to Cambridge make it more or less usual to find such covenants: while many of the distant estates and urban properties did have rights of inspection, the main estate at Sutton Coldfield did not do so by 1710.[72] The increased likelihood of finding such rights probably reflects changing attitudes to land and its management in the seventeenth century: an important way of keeping control over property was to visit it from time to time.

Whether or not these rights of inspection were practised is a different issue. Some colleges had a tradition of frequent visits to estates: New College in Oxford and Queens' in Cambridge, for instance, both did so.[73] These habits often arose out of statutory obligations, as at St John's in Cambridge.[74] John Caius' statutes for Gonville and Caius College in the mid-sixteenth century gave an unusual amount of detail about the overseeing of lands by the Master, a Fellow and a servant, though the regulations were more concerned about which expenses would be paid by the College and which were not to be allowed, rather than what inspection of an estate actually involved.[75] Visits were most usually connected with the keeping of manorial courts or the selling of timber,[76] not with a regular cycle of inspection of all of a college's property: at Caius College in the sixteenth century, for example, it was the College's manors in Cambridgeshire and Norfolk that were visited annually rather than its property elsewhere.[77] At those colleges in Oxford that maintained a tradition of annual progresses, such visits largely ceased during the period of

---

[68] ECA Box 25.B2; Box 25.C2–4; ECA BUR.6.3 pp. 372–8.
[69] ECA Box 28.A5.
[70] ECA Box 15.D11.
[71] ECA Box 15.A23.
[72] ECA Box 29.B25/12.
[73] Eland 1935, pp. 81–2; Twigg 1987, p. 114.
[74] Howard 1935, p. 15.
[75] Venn, *Caius*, III, p. 386.
[76] Dunbabin 1986, p. 288.
[77] Venn, *Caius*, III, p. 240.

the Civil War.[78] Although inspection of estates was therefore largely spasmodic, it was still regarded as important: at Jesus College, Cambridge, in 1628, one of the charges against the Master, Dr Roger Andrewes, was that he did not view or send Fellows to inspect the College estates.[79]

At Emmanuel, there was no tradition of annual progresses and the Statutes were silent on the matter. From numerous references in the College's accounts, however, it appears that estates were visited from time to time. In 1642, the Eltisley estate was inspected, and visits there followed in 1647, 1653, 1662, 1679, 1680 and 1681. Many of these visits, however, were not by Fellows but by William Chapman – the Manciple and Porter – and were presumably in connection with the selling of timber or the collection of rents. Other estates were visited, too, but again either for similar purposes or to oversee repairs; journeys to keep courts have already been discussed.[80]

An estate that was visited relatively frequently, but always for a specific reason, was the College's land at Sutton Coldfield. The disputes with the tenants over the initial letting of the estate have already been mentioned: the main visit was by Laurence Chaderton in 1598 to try to sort out all of the problems.[81] Visits then continued, however: Francis Gough went there in 1605 and Chaderton returned, with two men, in 1621.[82] In 1624, the new tenant there, Edward Willoughby, requested another visit: he wrote to the then Master, John Preston, on 16 October saying that he had been expecting a magisterial visit all summer to see what Willoughby had done to the lands and how he was managing the property, and asking that a journey be made.[83] One year later, on 12 November 1625, he wrote again in a similar vein: he had hoped to have seen Preston with Chaderton and others before then to view what he had performed, and now he had received word that the visit would not take place until Christmas.[84] Indeed, from the College accounts, there is no evidence that such a journey ever took place. It is not until 1637 that the next visit is recorded, by Malachi Harris (a Fellow), and Thomas Holbech followed him in the next year to survey the land. The Manciple, William Chapman, went in 1646, 1650 and 1651. For the next 30 years, there is no evidence that the estate was inspected by the College.[85] Indeed, mismanagement of the property there was the subject of the legal suit by Sir Wolstan Dixie which was resolved on 17 March

---

[78] Twigg 1997, p. 779.
[79] Gray and Brittain 1960, pp. 63–4.
[80] See especially references in ECA BUR.8.2 for most years.
[81] ECA Box 29.B22(xxxiii).
[82] ECA BUR.8.1 pp. 29, 107.
[83] ECA Box 29.B22(xic).
[84] ECA Box 29.B22(xc). Willoughby's lease ran from 27 February 1624 (ECA BUR.11.0.C f. 6r).
[85] ECA BUR.8.2.

1701:[86] visits in connection with Dixie's complaints and later charges took place in 1682 and then in many years in the 1690s.[87]

Estate business did, therefore, entail visits by the Master and Fellows to the College's property, but they were organised on an *ad hoc* basis as the need arose, there was no regular programme of inspection, there is no evidence at all that covenants which permitted twice-yearly inspections were ever realised, and estates that yielded a high income and therefore might be thought to have been more important were not necessarily visited more frequently. It is, perhaps, more likely that College agents and rent collectors visited on its behalf. Again, there is no evidence that they did so, though the lack of detailed correspondence and accounts from agents makes it difficult to form an impression of their exact duties on behalf of the College.

Another means of keeping track of property was to demand that written surveys or terriers of an estate be made every few years. Most of the rural lands owned by the College had covenants in their leases that a terrier be provided: at seven-yearly intervals (for example, at Berry Closes in Gransden), every ten years (as at Little Melton) or within a certain number of years of the date of the lease (as at Stondon). At Ripple in 1620 the College was bound, in its lease of six acres from the Crown, to provide a sealed list of the number of great trees and timber trees of oak, elm, ash and others within one year.[88] Acquisition of an estate entailed the making of a terrier of the new property as, for example, at Sutton Coldfield in 1594 or at Shernborne in 1654.[89] Other terriers were made when an estate was let: those of the Horseshoe estate at Godmanchester in 1641 and 1660,[90] and of Little Melton in Norfolk in 1685 and 1719, were drawn up as part of the process of renewal of leases.[91] A terrier formed part of the lease of 38 acres at Gransden to William Hatley from Lady Day 1607.[92] Only one terrier now remaining, however, seems to have been drawn up in response to a covenant in a lease: the description, dated 13 August 1634, of lands at Stondon.[93] The lease to William Hubbard ran from Michaelmas 1628, and within five years a terrier had to be provided.[94] It was slightly late, but there is no other obvious reason why it was drawn up. Unless each terrier was destroyed as it was superseded, which seems unlikely, it does not appear that they were drawn up as frequently as the leases dictated.

[86] ECA Box 29.B21; see also pp. 132, 169.
[87] ECA BUR.8.2.
[88] ECA Box 15.A13.
[89] ECA Box 29.B13; Box 22.A4.
[90] ECA Box 13.B3.
[91] ECA Box 20.C2.
[92] ECA Box 14.D2; the terrier has been separated from the deed and is at Box 14.A18.
[93] ECA Box 15.D9.
[94] ECA Box 15.D6–7.

Terriers were, however, useful tools of estate management and were made from time to time for specific reasons.

Administrative covenants: rents and their collection
The other main group of administrative covenants in leases were those that concerned the payment of rents. Stipulations were very commonly made that the rent had to be paid within a certain period of time, usually 28 days, and normally in the College Hall. If not, the College could reenter upon the property. The Shernborne estate differed slightly: rents were due by 1 August after Lady Day and 2 February after Michaelmas, presumably a customary arrangement for the property.[95] In practice, at Emmanuel rents were usually received by rent collectors instead of being brought to the College by the tenants themselves. There was no uniform system, even among private owners who took an interest in their estates. The Dukes of Bedford in the early eighteenth century, for example, had a Receiver-General in London who collected rents from local receivers and bailiffs, but some tenants ignored the procedure and paid directly to the Dukes' bankers.[96] At Balliol College in Oxford, rents were only collected from properties in Oxford itself and in London; in all other cases, the money was brought to the College by the tenants.[97] Emmanuel, on the other hand, seems to have made extensive use of official collectors. The receiver in London collected monies from many estates, including those as far distant from both London and Cambridge as Sutton Coldfield. He was paid an annual salary of £2, which rose to £4 with a change of collector in 1701, and submitted his accounts from time to time.[98] In addition, judging from a letter from the tenant at Sutton Coldfield to the Master in 1631, the collector issued the tenant with a receipt, who then passed it on to the College.[99] In this way, the College knew which rents had been paid at any one time. In the early days of the ownership of this estate, Chaderton had decreed that the rent should be brought twice-yearly to Cambridge (perhaps a change of mind, since London had previously been written and crossed out); it was claimed that he had said that the tenants would have to bear the costs if they were robbed or otherwise lost their money on the way.[100]

Rent collectors could be Fellows of the College, a job that rotated

---

[95] ECA BUR.6.3 pp. 51–8.
[96] Thomson 1940, p. 304.
[97] Duncan 1986a, p. 571.
[98] ECA BUR.8.1: payments to Mr Browne 1609–19 and to Robert Washbourne 1620. BUR.8.2: payments to Robert Washbourne 1628–34, Mr Woodcock 1637–8, James Clark 1642–52, Mr Honiwood 1652–62, Mr Bembow 1666–8, Mr Browne 1671–83, Mr Millett 1685–91, John Austen 1701–19.
[99] Letter from Edward Willoughby to William Sancroft the elder, 19 November 1631 (ECA Box 29.B22(viic)).
[100] ECA Box 29.B22(xxvii, xxxiv).

annually in St Catharine's College in the sixteenth century.[101] Laurence Chaderton was collecting rents for Emmanuel in 1600,[102] and he continued to do so well into his retirement. In the 1620s, he was involved in receiving rents and arrears from the Eltisley estate;[103] in 1628, he was the person to whom the London receiver, Robert Washbourne, sent his accounts, and was paid 17s 5d for an excess of expenditure over income.[104] Other Fellows, too, became involved in the collection of rents; evidence for this is more abundant in the later seventeenth century than for earlier years. In March 1678, letters of attorney were sealed for Thomas Nettleton and James Wolfenden to receive arrears of rent at Pinchbeck and to arrest the tenant, and George Green was granted power of attorney in 1684 to receive rents (and he transferred to the College 'a bill upon Mr John Tassell Goldsmith in Lumbard Street [London] for 65£ from Mr John Stafford of Bury [St Edmunds]' for the Shernborne rent).[105]

Other members of the College or their descendants collected rents for it: in 1697, Charles Chadwick of Sutton Coldfield (either the father who matriculated in 1657 or his son who attended the College in 1692) was given authority to oversee and govern the College's estate there, to receive arrears, to evict the tenant if necessary, to give acquittances and to appoint one deputy.[106] Joseph Gurnall, the collector of quit rents from Lavenham in 1701,[107] was the son of William, who had been admitted to the College in 1632. In 1711, Joseph fell on hard times: his wife and two children had died and he was in debt and in 'declining years'. He hoped for employment by Emmanuel once again, though there is no evidence that he was so assisted.[108]

A variety of other persons collected rents for the College. Tenants sometimes did so: farmers collected rents and manorial fines for ecclesiastical estates.[109] Emmanuel employed Robert Washbourne as receiver in London from 1620 to 1634; he leased two tenements in Threadneedle Street from the College from 1622 and sub-let them to Henry Bishop.[110] Similarly, James Rawlett, tenant at Pinchbeck, was paid for collecting the tithes there from 1644 to 1651.[111] Friends of the College received rents for it: Edmund Downing, Sir Walter Mildmay's assistant at the Exchequer

---

[101] Jones 1936, p. 223.
[102] ECA BUR.8.1 p. 16.
[103] ECA Box 12.C3.
[104] Letter of 11 October 1628 from Robert Washbourne to William Sancroft the elder (ECA BUR.0.9); BUR.8.2.
[105] ECA BUR.6.3 pp. 35–6, 104; ECA SCH.1.1, accounts since Lady Day 1685.
[106] ECA BUR.6.3 pp. 233–4.
[107] ECA BUR.6.3 p. 287.
[108] ECA COL.9.10.30.
[109] Hill 1956, p. 11.
[110] ECA Box 27.B6, B6(a); ECA BUR.0.9, accounts of 21 February 1628.
[111] ECA BUR.8.2; ECA Box 18.A11–15.

and executor of his will, received rents for the College in London, Essex and Surrey from 1588 to 1590. He also acted as attorney for the College, and other lawyers, too, received rents.[112] Members of the College staff collected rents for it: the Manciple and Porter, William Chapman, went to Suffolk to do so in 1646, for instance.[113] Collectors often came from the locality: John Sawkins of Canterbury received the rents from Lydden and Ewell in Kent and let the estate in 1694, Richard Dodwell of Oxford was given authority to receive £138 in arrears from the rent charge at Drayton in Oxfordshire in 1708, and John Weyman junior of Spalding received the rents from Fleet from 1716 to 1719.[114] The background of others is not known, but many must have formed part of the changing profession of estate stewards.[115]

As well as receiving monies due from tenants (including arrears), rent collectors also acted for the College in other capacities. For instance, they received annuities for which various bodies were liable. The Crown's rent charge was, on occasion, troublesome to collect: almost every year from 1706 to 1717, when Lionel Herne and then, from 1715, Francis Herne, received it on behalf of the College, they had to ask several times for the money. In 1709, Lionel wrote:

> I attended my Lord Treasurer warrant for one years anuitie due at Michaelmas last the gift of Queene Elizabeth to your Colledge which my Lord has not yet signed, by reason of the multiplicity of the Publique affairs, but I dayly expect it.

The following year, too, Herne encountered difficulties:

> I doe assure you I have not been wanting to solicite [for the annuity], and for six months an order \for one year/ has layn ready for my Lord to signe but for want of mony it has not yet been signed nor has any person that has right to Payments of the same nature received any mony since you received your last.[116]

Rent collectors were also involved in the setting up of new trusts. For example, the receiver at London, Mr Browne, drew up the agreement for the Whichcote and Sudbury exhibitions in 1671. He was so able, that he was offered a gratuity greater than the £5 that had originally been put aside for him, but he refused the increase. Benjamin Whichcote said that 'he seemes to haue a great regard for the College So I only gratified his

---

[112] Ibish 1985, p. 95; ECA BUR.11.1.
[113] ECA BUR.8.2.
[114] ECA BUR.6.3 pp. 204, 371–2, 483; BUR.0.9 (Fleet rents).
[115] Hainsworth 1987.
[116] ECA BUR.0.8, letters of 26 February 1709 and 11 July 1710. Herne received the payment due at Michaelmas 1709 at Michaelmas 1710, and that due at Christmas 1710 at Lady Day 1711 (BUR.11.2).

Clerkes . . .'.[117] Collectors also inspected property and advised on its letting. A successor to Mr Browne as receiver in London, John Austen, viewed houses in Threadneedle Street, measured their frontages and assessed their rents and fines before a new lease was granted to Ann Lee in 1703.[118]

Clearly, the College depended on having reliable and honest collectors. Occasionally, a bad appointment was made. The most notorious case at Emmanuel in the sixteenth and seventeenth centuries was that of James Clark, receiver in London for ten years from 1642. He was always in arrears with his payments, by over £60 in 1649,[119] and in 1652 he was sacked, and was paid £4 6s 8d for letters and his 'paynes' on 29 December.[120] On other occasions, things could go slightly awry. Mr Woodcock's son, William, wrote on behalf of his father in 1630 to send a corrected account of his activities, errors having been made by the young scribe who had written out the accounts. William conveyed his father's apologies, 'who desireth to bee excused for not writinge to your worship beinge constrayned to yeeld vnto age which doth much disable him for worldlie imployments'.[121] If a receiver died in office, problems could arise. In 1701, John Austen sent accounts of rents received and sums paid, but said that 'I cannot be so possitive of the truth of the Account as those formerly sent Mr Browne haveing before he dyed taken the papers to peruse and locked them \upp/ since when they have not beene opened'. He continued, 'I understand Dr Little informed the Colledge as I desired the favour . . . that the Colledge thought fitt to Imploy me to receive theire rents . . .',[122] which indeed it did. The College was pleased to recognise good service, and if a collector excelled himself he might be given a gratuity. Joseph Gurnall, for example, was paid £5 7s 6d in 1709 in acknowledgement of his efforts in a Chancery suit to receive arrears of the Lavenham quit rents.[123]

Covenants were made to apportion the responsibility for payment of taxes. It has already been shown how landowners normally paid Parliamentary taxes and chief rents; the tenant was liable for all other rates.[124] This was the case at Emmanuel. At Ripple in Essex, the estate was charged with drainage taxes,[125] and at Little Melton in Norfolk in 1622, the tenant had to augment the vicar's stipend so as to make it up to £20 a

---

[117] ECA Box 21.B11.
[118] Letter from John Austen to John Balderston, 15 August 1702 (ECA Box 27.B15); the lease was made on 24 June 1703 (Box 27.C1–2).
[119] ECA BUR.11.1.
[120] ECA BUR.8.2.
[121] ECA BUR.0.9, letter dated 30 November 1630.
[122] ECA BUR.0.9, letter dated 15 August 1701.
[123] ECA BUR.8.2.
[124] Clay 1985, p. 224.
[125] ECA Box 15.A15.

year.[126] There were variations, however. At the Four Swans in Bishops-gate Street in London in 1704, the tenant could opt to pay an additional five shillings in a pound rent instead of paying taxes,[127] and at Pinchbeck in Lincolnshire the College was liable for all taxes until the lease of 1687, when the tenant became responsible for all except for the fee-farm rent.[128] Despite the covenants in the leases of the Hyde Farm estate that the tenant was to pay all dues, the College in fact paid the chief rent, albeit not very regularly. Indeed, the lease of 1644 said quite explicitly that the College had to pay the arrears due to the Crown.[129] An exception was the Sutton Coldfield estate in 1598, when Chaderton ordained that the tenants there should pay the chief rent themselves and laid out the pro-portion which should be paid by each of them.[130]

Rents were usually set in leases; on rare occasions, the statutes of a college mentioned levels of rents as, for example, in the 1557–73 statutes for Gonville and Caius College which set the rents for the manors of Runcton, Croxley and Burnham Thorpe in Norfolk.[131] For private owners, rents tended to be highest on leasehold farms, especially those near London and areas of high population density. Meadowland often com-manded rents two to three times as high as common-field land, and enclosed arable was more valuable than that in the open fields. With the inflation of the late sixteenth century, rents rose. The situation of institu-tional owners was rather different. The system of beneficial leases and a relative lack of interest in their estates meant that many properties were under-let and rents rose far more slowly if at all.[132] The value of the Hornchurch estate of New College, Oxford, for example, grew between 1391 and 1675, as general prices rose and demand for land near London increased. Rents, however, remained level and both the tenants and the College came to believe that they were frozen because the land was an ancient demesne.[133] At St John's College, Cambridge, in 1627, it was decided to allow six weeks between the propounding and granting of leases so as to give time to enquire about the true value of the land; this, though, seems to have been in connection with setting the level of entry fines rather than of rents.[134]

Emmanuel conformed to the practice of other institutional owners in most respects. As in other colleges, rents tended to remain level. Clearly, if an estate had a lease with time to run when it came into the College's

[126] ECA Box 20.D1. Slightly later, disputes arose over the payment (see Appendix 5).
[127] ECA BUR.6.3 pp. 302–6.
[128] ECA Box 18.A5.
[129] ECA Box 28.Aa6; see entries in ECA BUR.8.1–2.
[130] ECA Box 29.B22(xxxiv).
[131] Venn, *Caius*, III, pp. 382–3.
[132] Bowden 1967, pp. 689–92.
[133] McIntosh 1987, p. 172.
[134] Howard 1935, p. 55.

hands, nothing could be changed until the next renewal. The Four Swans in Bishopsgate Street in London, for example, was let on a 99-year lease in 1576 and the first lease by the College appears to have been made in 1662.[135] No change in rent was made, though capons were added to the payments. The rent was raised from 1703,[136] but even so a note on a transcript of the lease that was made in the following year remarked that the estate was much under-let: the fine (£53 15s) was £150 too low and the tenant sub-let the property for £200 a year (the College had just raised the rent to £30).[137] Indeed, with the agricultural depression of the late seventeenth century, the rents of many rural properties fell, as at Lydden and Ewell in Kent, Pinchbeck and Shernborne (where there were particular difficulties).

Emmanuel was unusual, though, in that the only estate that was let according to the Corn Rent Act of 1576 was Little Melton in Norfolk. For that estate from 1613, the lease determined that the rent be £8 per annum plus 12 quarters of wheat and one quarter of malt, or the best market price for them on the preceding Saturday,[138] and the rent increased to £12 and 16 quarters of wheat and one of malt in 1677.[139] Elsewhere, corn rents were not collected. From 1649 onwards, leases included capons (usually two) or payment of five shillings in lieu of each one,[140] but as the monetary substitute was always the same, this did not represent index-linking in the same way as corn rents did. It is difficult to think of a reason for this anomaly: as Sidney Sussex College, too, does not seem to have charged corn rents, perhaps the explanation lies in the date of foundation or its leanings towards evangelical protestantism. Other colleges certainly charged corn rents; Emmanuel and Sidney were founded shortly after the Act, just as other colleges were gradually changing the terms of their leases, and the newly founded colleges must have been well aware of current legislation and practices.

The administration of an estate, therefore, was partly controlled by leases and by covenants within them. In practice, however, covenants about the keeping of courts, visits to estates and their inspection, the making of terriers, the level of rents and their payment and collection were all disregarded to greater or lesser extents. Only in the payment of taxes were the formal requirements largely adhered to.

---

[135] ECA Box 26.D3; Box 26.F7–8.
[136] ECA Box 26.F9–10.
[137] ECA BUR.6.3 pp. 302–6.
[138] ECA Box 20.D1.
[139] ECA BUR.6.3 pp. 39–43.
[140] The first mention of capons was in a lease of Eltisley in 1649, where after seven years the rent was to be reduced by £2 and two fat capons or five shillings each per audit paid instead (ECA Box 12.C4); the first capon money was due to be paid in 1652 from the lease which was made in that year of the tithes at Pinchbeck (Box 18.A2).

Husbandry covenants

Husbandry covenants were included in many of the leases of rural property. Frequently, the balance of arable and pasture was to be preserved, as at Eltisley,[141] or payment was to be made for each acre of meadow ploughed up (at the Horseshoe estate at Godmanchester and at Shernborne, for example)[142] or, as the end of a lease drew near, pasture was not to be ploughed up (for example, at Hyde Farm).[143] Maintenance of soil fertility was a concern: at Pakefield in Suffolk, 12 loads of muck had to be spread on the land each year,[144] and at Lydden and Ewell in Kent, dung had to be put on the fields.[145] Crop rotations were occasionally mentioned: leases of Lydden in 1673 and 1694 stipulated that wheat was not to be sown after wheat, nor barley after barley, nor oats after oats, but these conditions disappeared from the lease of 1697.[146] At Shernborne in Norfolk in 1679, the College agreed to pay the legal costs if anyone ploughed pasture contrary to the rotation, and to pay damages to the tenant.[147]

Many of the husbandry covenants were concerned with timber. At Gransden in 1619, the tenant had to plant 252 willow trees, and a further 240 trees seven feet high within ten years of the leases made in 1634 and 1644. Thereafter, the trees had to be maintained and replaced when necessary.[148] At Godmanchester, the tenant of the Horseshoe estate similarly had to maintain the stock: he had to plant two new sets of willows for each tree that died or was blown down from 1641 onwards.[149] Frequently, a certain number of years' growth had to be left on trees at the end of a lease: four at the Hyde Farm estate in 1594, for example.[150] Earlier on that estate, in 1589, the tenant, John King, had entered into an agreement with two yeomen from Southwark, as to who was to sell the wood, underwood, wood from hedgerows, coppices and bushes, thorn trees and loppings of trees (except for those from the elms and apples), how the coppice was to be stocked, that it was to be hedged and inclosed, and that the cut wood was to be removed from the ground by next Michaelmas.[151]

The significance of these husbandry covenants varies and many simply

---

[141] ECA Box 12.C4, C6–7; ECA BUR.6.3 pp. 330–6, 439–42, ff. 501v–504.
[142] ECA Box 13.B2; ECA BUR.6.3 pp. 51–8.
[143] ECA Box 28.Aa1.
[144] ECA BUR.6.3 pp. 70–2.
[145] ECA Box 17.A15.
[146] ECA Box 17.A15; ECA BUR.6.3 pp. 205–8, 243–5.
[147] ECA BUR.6.3 pp. 51–8.
[148] ECA BUR.11.0.C f. 3r; ECA Box 14.D6, D8–9, D12.
[149] ECA Box 13.B2.
[150] ECA Box 28.Aa1.
[151] ECA Box 28.Aa21.

reflected local customs.[152] This can be seen in three main ways. First, from references to customary practices in the leases themselves: at Stondon, for example, timber was allowed to the tenant for repairs as by custom from 1687.[153] Second, by the use of local dialect words. at Lydden and Ewell in Kent, ten acres 'podder grotten[154] or somer land'[155] had to be left fit for planting with wheat in the season after the end of the lease, and at Shernborne, too, local terms are found in the leases.[156] Finally, the continuation of covenants that governed the practices of tenants before the College came to own the estate, shows an adherence to local customs. Earlier leases of the properties are not numerous in the College archives today, but where they do exist they show that many items have not been changed.[157] The covenants were seen as a means of protection. Thus, they were an insurance against unscrupulous tenants: the breaking-up of pasture, for example, was a serious crime as it took time and money to repair the damage.[158]

Other covenants, however, were seen as agendas for action. At Eltisley, for example, the first lease of the woods from the College in 1593 gave the tenant permission to stub up the trees within the moat adjoining the manor within three years, to plant an orchard.[159] Similarly, in the lease by the College of six acres at Ripple in Essex in 1682, Emmanuel had to divide and ditch the land from the estate that the College owned itself.[160] Certain covenants were not made automatically. The appearance and disappearance of various clauses clearly were the result of conscious decisions: at Eltisley, the acreage of pasture that could not be ploughed up in the last ten years of the lease was increased from 28 in 1593 to 36 in 1649. Does the insertion at the latter date of a clause that no arable may be ploughed up unless an equivalent acreage is put to pasture, reflect a malpractice by the tenant?[161] At Pinchbeck between about 1644 and 1653 the rent collector there, James Rawlett, wrote to the Master: 'I feare you haue still mistaken you selves in drawing up mr Castle \Lease/ wherin you haue only excepted the South fen & left out the North fen which is thonely fen fitt to be plowed'.[162] This covenant, then, was intended to mean something. At Shernborne in Norfolk, more detailed husbandry

---

152 Clay 1985, p. 215.
153 ECA BUR.6.3 pp. 148–51.
154 Stubble of beans, peas, tares, vetches or vegetables with pods (*OED*; Wright 1898–1905).
155 Ploughed land which lies fallow during the summer (Wright 1898–1905).
156 ECA Box 17.A15; ECA BUR.6.3 pp. 51–8.
157 For example, at The Ball in Gracechurch Street (ECA Box 25.A5, B1) and Lydden and Ewell in Kent (Box 17.A13, A15).
158 Clay 1985, p. 220.
159 ECA Box 12.B19.
160 ECA Box 15.A21.
161 ECA Box 12.B19; Box 12.C4.
162 ECA BUR.0.9, letter to Dr Tuckney, dated 1 January [no year given].

covenants were included in 1691 after the farm had been in hand for nearly two years, presumably in an attempt to avoid another recurrence of acute difficulties.[163] Importance, too, was attached by landowners to timber, as the money from its sale was usually paid to them:[164] Emmanuel was no exception and wood money provided the Fellows with a source of income. Covenants about the running of the College brew-house were carefully examined: in 1710, the lease was never sealed because the covenant that the College tried to insert to guarantee a supply of good drink (the right to inspect the malt and hops at any time) was never agreed to.[165] Much, therefore, depended on the type of covenant: some were significant, others were less so.

Repairs

Under the system of beneficial leases, tenants were liable for repairs,[166] and thus in theory the landlord was saved a great expense. Responsibility was so apportioned in leases from Emmanuel. Sometimes, covenants were explicit: the tenant of 11–12 St Andrew's Street, Cambridge, in 1630 had to spend £100 on building within three years, for example.[167] Similarly, in 1608 the tenant of the tenement to the West of the Four Swans in Bishopsgate Street had to spend £140 on rebuilding the tenement within three years,[168] and at Sutton Coldfield in 1648, £25 was to be spent on repairs to the mansion house which was 'now in decay' and other buildings within two years.[169] The White Hart, which was let separately, had been rebuilt in stone at the tenant's expense by 1623, after a fire there.[170] Three hundred pounds were spent by the tenant of the Unicorn in Cambridge in 1662 on rebuilding the premises.[171] At Shernborne in Norfolk, the tenant had to pay for ten days' work from a thatcher each year in leases of 1679 and 1686; in 1691, the requirement was reduced to seven days' work and in 1707 the precise number of days was not specified.[172] At Little Melton, where the College was the lay rector, it passed responsibility for the repair of the chancel on to the tenant there.[173] Tenants were normally allowed timber for repairs; at Hyde Farm, however, it was necessary to ask for permission to use any other than hedgebote (the right to take wood from the common to make

---

[163] ECA BUR.6.3 pp. 193–202.
[164] Clay 1985, p. 224.
[165] ECA BUR.6.3 pp. 422–7.
[166] Shadwell 1898, p. 13.
[167] ECA BUR.11.0.C f. 1v.
[168] ECA Box 26.F1.
[169] ECA Box 29.B25/7.
[170] ECA Box 29.B25/1.
[171] ECA BUR.11.0.C f. 1r.
[172] ECA BUR.6.3 pp. 51–8, 136–43, 193–202, 258–65, 362–9.
[173] ECA Box 20.D1.

or repair fences).[174] A variant on demanding repairs by covenant was that of allowing demolition: the tenant of Lydden and Ewell in Kent was permitted to take down the messuage there in 1673, for example.[175]

It must not, however, be assumed that therefore the College did not spend any money itself on repairs, for it certainly did so, both directly and indirectly. In 1640, shortly before new leases were to be made, the College was exhorted by Sir Wolstan Dixie to put its Sutton Coldfield estate into good repair, as had been agreed in 1607.[176] The Shernborne estate in Norfolk was one of the properties that required the most direct expenditure by the College. In 1661, the tenant was allowed £92 17s 5d for repairs, which he had carried out by 5 July 1662 when he received the money for them.[177] In leases of the estate, the College was responsible for repairs, apart from those to the glass windows (and for thatching, as mentioned above). It spent fairly large sums accordingly, including £75 18s 3d for repairs to the dairy and manor house and taxes in 1700,[178] but more substantial expenditure was involved in 1713. The lease that was made in that year said that the College was to put the premises (apart from the dove-house) into repair within two years, to provide workmen and materials, and to spend up to £101 16s 2d. The tenant, Thomas Hoogan, was to pay the surplus expense and to rebuild the dove-house within the same space of time. The College agreed to pay half of the cost of this building up to a maximum of £37 16s 9½d. Even so, the tenant laid out the capital for the entire expenditure; the College reimbursed him through abatements of £24 per year out of his rent.[179] This expenditure by the College was, however, insufficient: in 1715, an additional £40 was needed from the landlord.[180] The Unicorn in Petty Cury, too, cost the College money. A tenant, William Bridge, spent at least £10 on repairs to the yard, cellar, walls and shop, and about £4 10s on a lean-to ('now a very prety rome', albeit an illegal one) on an adjoining house which was also owned by the College.[181] Entries in the Bursar's accounts for 1640 and 1641 show that he was reimbursed for much of this expense.[182]

Much expenditure on repairs by the College, however, was indirect, through subsidies and allowances to rents and fines. An early example is that of the estate at Eltisley. On 20 September 1593, it was let by William

---

[174] ECA Box 28.Aa2.
[175] ECA Box 17.A15.
[176] ECA Box 29.B11.
[177] ECA Box 22.A5.
[178] ECA SCH.1.1.
[179] ECA BUR.6.3 pp. 443–51.
[180] ECA Box 22.A11.
[181] ECA BUR.0.9, letter of 3 January 1639 to the College. Lean-tos were prohibited in the town at that time, in an attempt to avoid over-crowding and its consequences of disease and fire (E. S. Leedham-Green, personal communication).
[182] ECA BUR.8.2.

Marshall to Gawan Pelset for 61 years from that Michaelmas, and the rent of £30 was to be paid to the College. Nine days later, as part of the same transaction, the College bought the land; the house, larder, dairy, bakehouse, malt-house, barns and other parts of the premises were repaired or rebuilt at a cost to the tenant of about £103. The details were given in a note attached to the counterpart of the lease, so that an allowance could be made when it was re-let.[183] Similar cases occurred on other estates. At Hyde Farm in Surrey in 1658, the tenant spent over £200 on building a house, barn and stable (there had been none before), and the fine was reduced to £10 in consequence.[184] At West Street, Godmanchester, in 1656, £100 was spent in building and again a lower fine than normal was levied.[185] In 1679, the College agreed to grant a new lease of St Nicholas Hostel in St Andrew's Street as soon as the tenant had spent £30 on the barn and stable, and decided that no fine would be charged. In fact the tenant, Sir Thomas Slater, and his predecessor William Lyndall, spent over £200 between them on repairs to the premises.[186] As a final example of an indirect subsidy by the College, the re-letting of the Sutton Coldfield estate in 1710 was made on the following terms. The tenant was to put the buildings into repair within one year, and in recompense a peppercorn rent would be charged for that year. The next year, £10 in rent and £30 as half of the fine had to be paid; then the rent was to be increased to £40 a year.[187]

One of the main ways in which the College assisted tenants in repairs to their property was in the aftermath of the Great Fire of London in 1666. The College was badly affected: it lost its two houses in Gracechurch Street, ten in St Dunstan's Alley, and only one of its tenements in Threadneedle Street survived. Emmanuel was, of course, not alone in its predicament. The Rebuilding Act of 19 Charles II Cap.3 (1667) regulated the ways in which the restoration took place. Three surveyors were appointed, Robert Hooke, John Oliver and Peter Mills, who were responsible for measuring and marking out the sites for houses. Those desiring to rebuild, who were usually tenants or sub-tenants rather than landlords, had to have the necessary money and pay a fee of 6s 8d to the Chamber of London for a survey. The receipt for payment gave the surveyor authority to lay out the foundations, which he did as soon as possible; then the builders could take over and properties were usually rebuilt within nine months.[188]

Rebuilding the first of Emmanuel's properties got under way on

[183] ECA Box 12.B17.
[184] ECA Box 28.Aa5.
[185] ECA Box 13.B4; ECA BUR.11.2.
[186] ECA Box 4.K1; ECA COL.14.1 preliminary pp. 15–16.
[187] ECA Box 29.B25/12.
[188] Mills and Oliver 1967, pp. x–xxxii.

28 April 1668, when the Courts ordained that the tenant, Robert Reynolds, should rebuild in St Dunstan's Alley at his own expense, but that the lease should be made up to 60 years and the rent and conditions should remain unchanged. The impetus, however, fell away and Reynolds did not pay for his survey until 20 April 1670; the ten messuages were rebuilt as six.[189] Next on the list were the two tenements fronting Threadneedle Street: Thomas Williamson was ordered to rebuild on 16 December 1668 and was in recompense to enjoy a tenure of an additional 40 years for one of the houses and of 32 for the other. He had already paid for his survey, on 25 November. The two tenements were rebuilt as one, but double sealing fees were to be charged in future (these fees were divided among the Fellows, who were concerned to ensure that their income from this source did not fall as a result of the amalgamation of properties).[190] The Ball in Gracechurch Street was next. At Cliffords Inn on 19 December, John Wing was allowed to have 40 years added to his lease and to enjoy an unchanged rent. He paid for his survey on 13 February following; the tenant of the Harrow, Thomas Salter, had paid for his nine days beforehand and his lease was made up to 60 years.[191] Finally, the remaining houses in Threadneedle Street were considered. On 21 December, the court decreed that the lease should be made up to 50 years and after 40 two pairs of capons or ten shillings should be added to the rent. The tenant, William Ivatt, encountered problems. He was advised by the surveyor that in order to make the house uniform it was necessary to take in a corner of land from the adjoining house, also owned by the College. The court, however, declared that Ivatt had to pay most of the rent of the adjacent property in compensation. Because Ivatt would have been prejudiced by waiting until the agreement was formally made, he went ahead with the building. One house was built, for which the sealing fees were to be increased four-fold. Ivatt's decision turned out to be a mistake as the tenant of the adjacent land died and his daughter tried to make Ivatt a sub-tenant to her, and for a shorter term. It was clearly all rather a muddle and was not sorted out until 1672.[192]

The Fire of London had a corresponding effect on other landowners. Other colleges, such as Pembroke and Trinity Hall, proceeded in similar ways;[193] as, however, rents tended to remain static, it was the loss of entry fines that probably affected the colleges most. The Haberdashers' Company suffered in a different way, as the court decreed that rents of its property should be reduced from £100 to £65.[194] Private landlords, too,

---

[189] ECA Box 25.E4; Mills and Oliver 1967, p. 55.
[190] ECA BUR.6.3 pp. 336–44; Mills and Oliver 1967, p. 72.
[191] ECA Box 25.B3; Box 25.C4; Mills and Oliver 1967, p. 40.
[192] ECA Box 27.B15; Box 27.C1–2.
[193] Mills and Oliver 1967, p. xxix; Crawley 1977, p. 74.
[194] Archer 1991, p. 92.

were hampered by the imposition of building leases on favourable terms which precluded rises in rent until well into the eighteenth century.[195]

Tenants

As covenants about repairs only told part of the story, so too did those about tenants. The only proviso in the leases themselves was that permission had to be sought if the tenant wished to assign the holding to someone else. His widow and children, however, were usually excepted. From the absence of evidence to the contrary, it appears that the College rarely refused such a request; it did, though, charge sealing fees. Other colleges behaved in similar ways: Emmanuel was given a licence to alienate its lease of the Sempire Land from Peterhouse to anyone it wished in 1715.[196]

College statutes rarely mentioned tenants; the most notable exception was Gonville and Caius College. There, the 1557–73 statutes went into a considerable degree of detail. The tenants were to be honest and able to look after the interests of the College; they were not to own the adjacent land so as to prevent the intermixing of their own and collegiate land (this was a common problem); and they were, preferably, to have proven themselves already as good lessees.[197] Emmanuel's statutes were silent on the matter. Clearly, though, a good tenant was an estate's most valuable asset.[198]

Colleges wanted an easy life. They liked their estates to run themselves and their tenants to choose themselves. A result was that, on the principle that there was less security in the unknown, estates tended to remain in the hands of the same family for long periods. Colleges also felt some degree of obligation to renew tenancies: under beneficial leases the tenants had no right to renewal, but their landlords felt paternal responsibilities towards them.[199] Balliol and Magdalen colleges in Oxford, for example, often let their estates to the same family for generations.[200] At Emmanuel, several properties passed from one member of a family to another. At Gransden, the messuage and 18 acres there were let to James and then Timothy Kettle from 1629. Timothy Kettle also became the tenant of Berry Closes nearby in 1709; these lands had been in the hands of Timothy and then Charles Griffin since 1634.[201] The Sandars family were tenants at Stondon in Essex from 1639 (though as Sarah Sandars

---

[195] Clay 1985, p. 190.
[196] Cooke 1962, p. 519; ECA BUR.6.3 pp. 190–2, 473–6.
[197] Venn, *Caius*, III, pp. 383–4.
[198] Clay 1985, p. 231.
[199] Thompson 1976, pp. 335–6.
[200] Duncan 1986a, p. 567; Cooke 1962, p. 518.
[201] Leases at ECA Box 14.D and Box 14.E1–2. See Appendix 5 for later tenancies by the family.

married John Bridges, the name changes in the leases from 1687);[202] the Horseshoe estate at Godmanchester was let to the Conny family from 1629 to 1698;[203] West Street, Godmanchester was let to John Shepherd in 1612, and then to his brother Thomas from 1634 to 1700.[204] At Pinchbeck, John Wimberley was the tenant in 1670, his son Bevil leased the tithes in 1678 and his son, also Bevil, became the lessee in 1714.[205] The Four Swans in Bishopsgate Street was let to Elizabeth Brand in 1675, to Benjamin Brand in 1701 and to Isaac Brand in 1709;[206] and as a final example, John Benton, tenant at Little Melton in Norfolk from 1649, was succeeeded by his widow Susan in 1686. She, in her turn, was followed by her son-in-law John Back in 1695.[207]

It is, perhaps, hardly surprising that estates passed from generation to generation in this way, when it is considered how they were let. In some instances, the tenant was offered a new lease by the college: this was the practice at All Souls College, Oxford in the eighteenth century.[208] Alternatively, tenants wrote to request that their leases be renewed. This occurred in 1629, when Margaret Perkins asked for a renewal of her lease of the Ball in Gracechurch Street. She used emotive language:

> I desire your favourable respects vnto me in regarde I am a widowe & haue the charge of two small children & that the rente of the same howse though it be but small is the chefeste parte of the meanes I haue to maintaine my selfe & them & for that my father & mother & my selfe for theis many yeres haue bene your Tenaunts & haue iustlie & truelie paid your rente since from tyme to tyme & haue bestowed much money in the repracons thereof I desire I may still contynue your tenaunt . . .

She continued to ask that her fine be reduced from £60 for 30 years either to £40 or to £50 for 40 years. Her lease was renewed as she requested and the fine was £45 for 32 years: a compromise.[209] Similarly, Edward Willoughby asked to renew his lease of the estate at Sutton Coldfield in 1640. He confessed that he had been slack in the past and promised to mend his faults but, 'on the word of a gentleman', the rent had simply not been there to pay. His assurance was, it seems, insufficient. The White Hart was let to William Pargiter from Lady Day 1641 and there is no evidence that Willoughby remained the tenant of the rest

---

[202] ECA Box 15.D10–13; ECA BUR.6.3 pp. 148–51.
[203] ECA BUR.11.0.C f. 3v; ECA Box 13.B2, B7–10; BUR.6.3 pp. 245–9.
[204] ECA Box 13.D2; Box 13.B4, B11–12; ECA COL.9.1(A) p. 107.
[205] ECA Box.18.A3–6.
[206] ECA COL.9.1(A) p. 103; ECA Box 26.F10; ECA BUR.6.3 pp. 302–6.
[207] ECA COL.9.1(A) p. 101; ECA Box 20.D2–3; ECA BUR.11.2 (1695). See Appendix 5 for later tenancies by the family.
[208] Blackstone 1898, p. 42.
[209] ECA BUR.0.9, letter of 18 July 1629; BUR.11.1 (1629); BUR.11.0.C f. 5r.

of the estate.[210] Tenants also asked for leases of adjoining property: on 27 January 1637, William Ivatt wrote to the Master: 'One Mr Macroe hath a house of yours adioyninge unto myne [in Threadneedle Street] which if it bee out of Lease & you deale not with him I desyre the refusall of it . . .', and Ivatt's bid was successful.[211]

The outcome of the College's policy in choice of tenants can be seen from rentals and correspondence. Without a detailed reconstruction of rental income from each estate, tenant by tenant and half-year by half-year, it is difficult to say whether particular rent collectors were zealous or otherwise, and whether estates closest to Cambridge were better governed and run. The College did, however, enjoy apparently peaceful periods as regards many estates: rents were paid, more or less on time, and nothing untoward occurred. Elsewhere, things were different. Many tenants fell into arrears at some time, partly a result of factors beyond their control (such as the Civil War, or the agricultural depression of the late seventeenth century), but also from circumstances particular to individuals. The plague, too, was used as an excuse for late payment: George Smith, tenant of Hyde Farm, blamed the sickness for being one year behindhand in sending his rent in 1631. Despite his assurances that he would never fail in this way again, the estate was let in the following year to John Morton (though it is not known why the tenant was replaced).[212] Tenants and their arrears will be discussed in more detail later in this chapter. Occasionally, letters of complaint were received about tenants. Sir Wolstan Dixie who, by a decree of Lord Keeper Wright in 1701, was allowed to recommend a new tenant of the Sutton Coldfield estate shortly before a lease expired,[213] exercised his right in 1710. He could not agree that the present tenant, Thomas Freeman, was fit. He had taken down several buildings and left others ruinous, sold the materials from them, hindered improvements, felled two acres of woodland, sold most of the timber and made charcoal from young wood. None of the sub-tenants had a good word for him; all were agreed on the suitability of Sir William Wilson. Although Dixie's advice was heeded to some extent, the estate was let to John Davis instead.[214]

Who were the College's tenants? Some were members of the College. Sir John North was admitted to Emmanuel as a Fellow Commoner on 15 July 1602; that Michaelmas, his mother Dorothy, Lady North, became the tenant of Ripple Marsh in Essex. She had inherited the tenancy from her father Valentine Dale, who was Master of the Requests during Sir Walter Mildmay's time as Chancellor of the Exchequer (and presumably,

---

[210] ECA Box 29.B22(vic); ECA COL.9.1(A) p. 119.
[211] ECA Box 27.B7, B15.
[212] ECA BUR.0.9, letter from George Smith to William Sancroft the elder, 9 May 1631; ECA Box 28.Aa4.
[213] ECA Box 29.B21 p. 23.
[214] ECA Box 29.B26(lxv); Box 29.B25/12.

therefore, they were acquainted).[215] Sir John's lease was renewed in 1622 and he wrote to the College expressing his gratitude:

> with my speciall thankes to you for your willingnes to pleasure mee, I request you to let the fellows of your house vnderstand from mee that this their kindnes toward mee, or any other heereafter doth, or shall engage mee to a reall requitall when they shall haue occasion to vse my poore seruice. This I write not as a Courtier, but as one that acknowledgeth the bond of mutuall socyety, wherof I must always professe my selfe a member . . .[216]

Laurence Chaderton himself was a tenant of the College: he leased St Nicholas Hostel during his Mastership and his daughter Elizabeth Johnson inherited the lease on her father's death and remained the tenant until 1677.[217] Elizabeth also inherited her father's tenancy of the Harrow in Gracechurch Street, London, which he had held from 1629. She continued as lessee there until 1668.[218] William Whitaker, who held the Hyde Farm estate in 1650, matriculated at Emmanuel in 1639, and later became a Fellow of Queens'. He was Minister of Hornchurch in Essex when he became the College's tenant; in 1654, he succeeded his father as Rector of St Mary Magdalene, Bermondsey and he remained at Bermondsey after his ejection in 1662. He died ten years later in 1672, but the Hyde Farm estate was let to his widow Elizabeth until 1681.[219] Other tenants were local men: George Couleson, yeoman of Wimpole, for example, was tenant at Gransden in 1704.[220] Samuel Lucas, tenant of Lydden and Ewell in Kent in 1673, was a baker in Dover,[221] and William Evans, draper of London, was the lessee of St Dunstan's Alley in the Old Bailey in 1653.[222] The estates at Little Melton and Shernborne in Norfolk and Pakefield in Suffolk were similarly let to locals.[223] Others, however, came from further afield. William Winch of St Faith's Parish, London, a silkman, rented the Chalice – 21 St Andrew's Street, Cambridge – from 1641;[224] William Otter of Boston in Lincolnshire was the tenant of one messuage in Threadneedle Street in 1662,[225] and George Smith of Broughton in Oxfordshire was the lessee of the Hyde Farm estate in 1629.[226]

---

[215] Venn; ECA Box 15.A6(1); *Complete Peerage*, IX, p. 654; *DNB*.
[216] ECA BUR.0.9, letter to Laurence Chaderton; ECA Box 15.A15.
[217] ECA BUR.11.1 p. 5; BUR.11.0.C f. 1v; ECA COL.9.1(A) p. 111.
[218] ECA Box 25.C2–3.
[219] Venn; ECA COL.9.1(A) p. 97; ECA Box 28.Aa5, Aa8–9, Aa12.
[220] ECA BUR.6.3 pp. 300–2.
[221] ECA Box 17.A15.
[222] ECA Box 25.E2.
[223] See Appendix 5 for details.
[224] ECA Box 2.A10.
[225] ECA Box 27.B14.
[226] ECA Box 28.Aa21.

Some tenants sent their sons to the College. The tithes at Pinchbeck were let to Joshua Cust in 1652. In 1659, his son, Samuel, was admitted to the College. The children of Samuel's cousin, Richard, followed: Richard was admitted in 1669 and Pury in 1670. Finally, Pury's son Richard matriculated in 1697, and so the Cust dynasty's connection with the College ended.[227]

The list of College tenants, however, should not be taken at face value, for many of the properties were sub-let. While private owners usually included covenants in their leases that permission had to be obtained for such practices,[228] and Balliol College in Oxford did likewise,[229] St John's College in Cambridge included no such restrictions.[230] Nor did Emmanuel: sub-letting was common and, under the system of beneficial leases, tenants could under-let at greatly enhanced rents.[231] The six acres at Ripple in Essex, for example, were leased by the College for £5 a year in 1660. The College sub-let the property to Sir Laurence Smith for £8 a year, and he in his turn let it for £13.[232] Similarly, at Threadneedle Street in 1703, the College was advised that a lease for 40 years was worth £2000 and the property was sub-let for £126 a year, though it was only let by the College for £16 13s 4d a year with a £220 fine.[233] The holding of a beneficial lease was thus seen as a form of investment by the tenant.[234]

For the sixteenth and seventeenth centuries, therefore, although details of under-tenants and their rents are few, it seems that sub-letting was common. Indeed, part of the problems in the initial letting of the Sutton Coldfield estate arose because of this custom: some of the tenants wanted to have their leases directly from the College, but their wishes were not granted.[235] Leases occasionally mentioned sub-tenants: the White Hart at Sutton Coldfield was under-let to William Spooner, blacksmith, and John Underhill in 1623,[236] and in 1712 the Hyde Farm estate was let to John Hall, citizen and draper of London, and occupied by Jacob Collins and his undertenants.[237] In 1708 the step was taken, unusual at that time, of attaching a plan to the lease of six tenements in St Dunstan's Alley to

[227] ECA Box 18.A2; Venn.
[228] Clay 1985, p. 223.
[229] Duncan 1986a, p. 570.
[230] Howard 1935, p. 27.
[231] Bowden 1967, p. 689.
[232] ECA COL.9.10.22.
[233] ECA Box 27.B15 (letters from John Austen to John Balderston, 15 August 1702, and from William Savage to William Peirs, 17 October 1702); Box 27.C1–2.
[234] See above, p. 152 for the claim by Margaret Perkins in 1629 that she was dependent on her lease of the Ball in Gracechurch Street to provide her with a source of income.
[235] ECA Box 29.B22.
[236] ECA Box 29.B25/1.
[237] ECA BUR.6.3 pp. 451–7.

show the various occupiers of the premises.[238] If there were problems or delays in renewing a lease, then the lessee could encounter difficulties with his tenants: in 1637, William Ivatt implored William Sancroft (the elder) to let him have his lease of tenements in Threadneedle Street forthwith, for he was 'bound in a bond of 100£ to make a lease of the house to a Marchant before our Lady day next or else I shall forfeit my bond & loose my tennant . . .'.[239] Evidence for sub-letting in Cambridge in the 1630s is provided by the Thatched House Survey which was carried out in 1632. Richard Austin, for example, sub-let his tenement in Emmanuel Street to six people at that time.[240]

The College therefore had a symbiotic relationship with its tenants. It did not over-exert itself on their behalf, but equally it relied on a thriving and contented tenantry. On their part, tenants rarely asked for the College to take an interest in their affairs except when they had to carry out burdensome repairs or were unable to pay their rents. For those who sub-let, renting a property from a college was an attractive form of investment.

In these ways, colleges in general and Emmanuel in particular administered their estates. As with all landlords, leases were just legally enforceable weapons of the last resort, they provided a loose framework within which an estate was run, and they were only resorted to when serious disputes arose. Supervision and control were far more important means of land management.[241] Apart from the absence of corn rents, Emmanuel seems to have been a typical collegiate landlord. It was not one of the colleges that showed greatest concern about its property; the system for so doing was not well developed and much, clearly, depended on individual circumstances and personalities.

Finances: Success or Failure?

The financial health of any landowner in the sixteenth and seventeenth centuries was partly a reflection of external circumstances, but it also depended on his own expertise. Clearly, some fared better than others and the degree of success can be measured in a variety of ways. What were the results of Emmanuel's management of its land: what was the picture overall, were there any particular problems, and what were the effects on the College and its Fellows?

Income, expenditure and prices all varied according to the inflation rates at the time. In the country as a whole, the late sixteenth and early

---

[238] ECA BUR.6.3 pp. 396–400. It is unfortunate that the counterpart of the lease is not in the College Archives today.

[239] ECA Box 27.B15, letter of 9 February 1637.

[240] Cambridge University Archives, CUR 37.3 (128).

[241] Clay 1985, pp. 228–9.

seventeenth centuries were times of inflation. By 1620, circumstances had begun to change and the Civil War and Interregnum were periods of difficulty for landowners, with high taxation and falling rents, disruption, damage and sequestration, and poor harvests. Until the mid-eighteenth century, landlords found it difficult to collect their rents in full, and land taxes were especially heavy in the 1660s and 1670s and between 1692 and 1713. As the value of land became much more volatile, it was far less attractive as a form of investment except for large landowners who were cushioned against economic depression and who took a long-term view.[242] The colleges of Oxford and Cambridge were such owners and as land was the only realistic form of investment available to them, there was little alternative but to weather any storms that blew up.

To try to compare the financial health of Emmanuel at different times, therefore, it is necessary to correct figures for inflation. The only index that runs throughout the history of the College is that by E. H. Phelps Brown and S. V. Hopkins. The index is based on a composite unit of consumables, made up of grains, meat and fish, butter and cheese, drink, fuel and light, and textiles, and was compiled mainly from contract prices paid by institutions. It therefore has a number of limitations: it is not a cost-of-living index, it does not include rents, and it uses wholesale rather than retail prices. It does, however, provide a yardstick against which changes can be compared and because it enables all periods in the College's history to be treated in the same way, it has been used in the current study. Prices have been adjusted to those in 1700: an arbitrary date had to be chosen and as this one was used in a previous study of the finances of various colleges in Cambridge, especially in the eighteenth and early nineteenth centuries, selection of the same date enables the situation at Emmanuel to be compared more easily with that elsewhere.[243]

The balance sheet

To obtain a clear picture of a college's prosperity is not at all straightforward.[244] Accounts were not drawn up with this aim in mind, though at audit the overall balance was calculated. Figure 1 shows the result of plotting these balances for Emmanuel: the graph demonstrates that the College did not always live within its means, and that circumstances fluctuated wildly from year to year. The Civil War adversely affected college finances in both Oxford and Cambridge;[245] Emmanuel was not alone in appearing to have entered the Restoration period scathed by the troubles. It had, for instance, to pay £100 directly to the Crown in 1642 in addition

---

[242] Clay 1985, pp. 177–8.
[243] Munby 1989, pp. 25–8; Bendall 1992.
[244] Twigg 1987, p. 112.
[245] Twigg 1997.

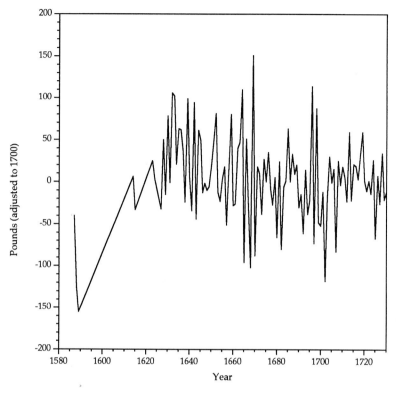

Figure 1 Balance at audit of income over expenditure to 1720. *Source*: ECA BUR.0.2, BUR.8.1–2, BUR.11.1–2.

to more general problems arising from the Civil War;[246] in the 1660s, problems continued, exacerbated by the plague. In 1665 alone, the College paid about £61 on account of the sickness.[247]

The balance of income over expenditure is, however, only a partial picture. It includes income that has been generated within the College, especially from study rents, and income taken out of reserves. On the other hand, it does not include rents received from the trust estates, of which there were many. Nor does it show total receipts from fines, as that portion which passed to the Fellows did not go through the College's books. On the expenditure side, it includes the building-up of reserves and purchase of investments (land, at this period), but does not include costs of the trust estates. Nor does it show the allowances made to

[246] ECA BUR.0.8, receipt by John Poley.
[247] ECA BUR.8.2.

individual Fellows beyond their stipends, or payments of scholarships or exhibitions. In addition, the account books normally (but not always) carry surpluses and deficits forward from year to year; this factor at least has been corrected for in the graph. It is, therefore, necessary to look elsewhere to obtain an index of Emmanuel's prosperity: at sources of income and at success and failure at realising them; at the matching of income with levels of expenditure; and at that element of most direct interest to the Fellows, the entry fines and fellowship dividends.

Income

The total income received by the College from its estates (including the trust estates) before 1720 is shown in Fig. 2. Again, the scene is one of fluctuation. As the College's endowment was being built up in the first two decades or so, income increased. As has already been pointed out, there was often a time-lag between endowment of an estate and receipt of income from it, and so the rise in income was less dramatic than the flood of gifts to the College that has been outlined. Thereafter for the following century, despite further increases in the College's property holdings, receipts only grew marginally, if at all, and the decade of the 1640s seems

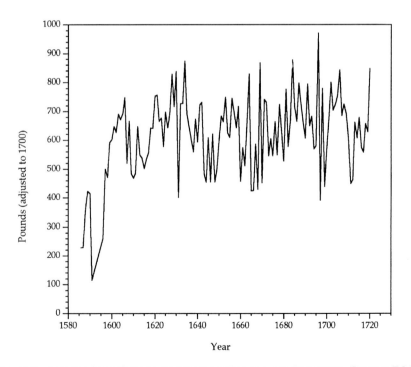

Figure 2   Income from College and trust estates to Lady Day 1720. *Source*: ECA BUR.11.1–2, SCH.1.1–2.

to have been a period of reduced rents, as would be expected from the country-wide troubles of the time. There does not, therefore, appear to have been a period of continually and markedly rising receipts for the College to enjoy.

Although the College's estates were its main source of income, the rentals included other receipts too. Of these, the most regular was income from chamber and study rents. Vacant Fellowships and scholarships and occasional cash donations also helped to increase the contents of the coffers from time to time. No other sources of revenue accrued directly to the College itself: tuition fees were paid to tutors and did not pass through the College's books, and the steward kept his own accounts.

Arrears and their recovery

Income from estates never achieved the possible maximum: always there were arrears to collect. Arrears might not be expected to be a significant problem on estates that were let under beneficial leases and therefore had low rents.[248] In Emmanuel however, as Fig. 3 shows, arrears were massive. Arrears rose in the 1620s: in February 1625, Laurence Chaderton wrote round to the College's debtors to ask for payment, at John Preston's request.[249] Outstanding sums were even higher in the late 1640s, and in the 1660s and 1670s, between about 60% and 80% of the total expected income was in arrears. These percentages represent accumulation of old debts as well as the occurrence of new ones. Data are not available for later years, but with the poor harvests of the 1690s, these levels could be expected to have continued. Perhaps, therefore, rents were either not low enough, or their collection was not sufficiently prompt or efficient. Colleges at Oxford also had difficulty in collecting rents during the 1640s and the Haberdashers' Company suffered in a similar way in the late seventeenth century.[250]

Some estates suffered more than others. The Unicorn in Petty Cury was beset with difficulties: goods were distrained by the College on four occasions between 1628 and 1634, and then in 1637 the College had to release William Bridge from his debts.[251] On several occasions, the College must have despaired of ever extracting rent from its tenants at Sutton Coldfield. On 29 November 1596 a Fellow, Richard Lyster, reentered on part of the property for non-payment of rent and a barrister was given power of attorney to receive rent from another tenant. Not until 1598 was income finally received from the estate.[252] The granting of a lease to

---

248 Clay 1985, p. 203.
249 ECA Box 18.B11.
250 Twigg 1997, pp. 785–7; Archer 1991, p. 93.
251 ECA Box 3.A20; Cambridge University Archives CUR 95, Emmanuel College, no. 11; ECA COL.9.10.103.
252 ECA Box 29.B2–3; ECA BUR.11.1.

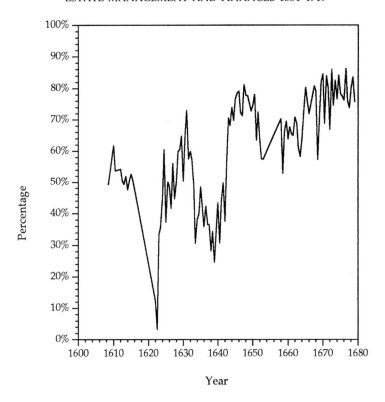

Figure 3 Indebtedness to the College to 1720 (as a percentage of total of income and sums in arrear). *Source*: ECA BUR.0.1, BUR.11.1–2.

Marmaduke Dawney in 1601 made little difference, for by 1604 it was necessary for William Bridge to reenter on the property on 20 October; only ten years later in 1614, the College reminded him of an outstanding debt of £23 10s. In addition, Dawney tried to persuade the College to borrow money itself against further receipts at Easter rent day (Dawney would pay the interest for such a loan) and to ask the Lord Chancellor for a further sum which, it was claimed, he held and was due to the College. Dawney failed to impress his landlords and received a strongly-worded rebuff in reply.[253] Power of attorney to reenter on Dawney's property had to be granted yet again on 1 July 1621, and was executed on the 30th.[254] He was clearly an unsatisfactory tenant.

In 1635, a tenant at Hyde Farm in Surrey was troublesome, too. Forty pounds were demanded for two years' arrears from William Weller. He

[253] ECA Box 29.B22(lxxxv–lxxxvi).
[254] ECA Box 29.B8.

161

was a relation of the wife of Peter White, who in his turn was guardian of the orphans of William Matthew, a previous tenant, under whose tenure the arrears accrued. As these children could have been liable, White became involved. Settlement became urgent as White was about to go on a voyage with the navy on H.M.S. *Swiftsure*. From the ship, he wrote to the College's lawyer, claiming that Matthew had been promised a renewal of the lease by Chaderton in return for which he would pay his arrears and an entry fine; the College, however, had sold the lease to someone else and the sub-tenant was evicted, refusing to pay any rent and thus preventing Matthew from paying his debts. The outcome was that White's wife offered £20, 'more', said her husband, 'than I showld have donn', to settle the whole business. Richard Foxton, the College's lawyer, advised William Sancroft (the elder) to accept this sum for 'Weller he is (say they) soe poore that nothing can be gotten at his hand he being ould & of a crasye condicion in every way I haue considered of all the occurrences in this behalfe & think it better to treate vppon the offer before peter White departe for the voyage least some misaventure at sea distourne his purpose . . .'. The College accepted this advice.[255]

Recovery of arrears could involve the College in considerable expenditure in legal suits, though costs were often awarded against the defendants. Nevertheless, law suits involved journeys and the employment of lawyers and advisers. Defendants often asked for legal proceedings to be stopped. Dymoke Walpole pleaded for clemency from the College in 1625 in his slowness in bringing rents from Pinchbeck to Cambridge; he had no excuse, but asked that he be so favoured as he had settled the advowson of the vicarage on the College's behalf. In 1632, however, he was in trouble again and the College sued him and Thomas Ogle. In 1638, Walpole was issued with a subpoena to continue with the Chancery suit, but asked for more time as he had to carry out some business for the Crown.[256] Sutton Coldfield again caused trouble: in 1653, the College sued for arrears but the defendants' attorney asked for leniency: they were too poor to pay and any charges would fall on the lawyer, whose practice would suffer.[257] In 1703, the College had to pay its share, 18s 6d, for the costs of suing for the rent charge for the Johnson Exhibitions.[258] The College tried to avoid legal expenses by making the tenant of the Ball in Gracechurch Street liable for costs of recovery of arrears; in return, he was allowed the property for five years at a peppercorn rent. In the end, however, the College did have to pay half of the costs.[259] Obtaining the quit rents from Lavenham was not easy, either: at least £12 was spent in

[255] Letters and documents at ECA BUR.0.9; BUR.11.1.
[256] ECA Box 18.B12–14.
[257] ECA Box 29.B22(iiic).
[258] ECA BUR.6.3 pp. 412–18; ECA SCH.1.1.
[259] ECA BUR.6.3 pp. 477, 480–3; BUR.0.9, arbitration dated 28 December 1720.

distraining in 1617, 1618 and 1619, and £2 had already been spent in 1612.[260] In 1705, however, the College had to lay out £128 16s 1d in Chancery proceedings against the tenants at Lavenham for arrears. Costs were awarded against the defendants but, despite a subpoena for part of the costs in 1708, the College was never fully reimbursed. Indeed, it remained out of pocket to the order of £49 18s 6d: a heavy expenditure to recover £27 16s 5d in rent. As the tenant whose arrears covered the longest period (36 years), Thomas Bird, paid £41 1s 4d in costs of recovering only £9 18s in rent, it would have been far more economical for all concerned if he and his colleagues had simply paid up.[261]

Other difficulties in the collection of rents

In addition to reduced income because of arrears, abatements were allowed for various reasons. In 1672, for example, £4 9s was remitted to the tenant at Lydden and Ewell in Kent because of his poverty.[262] A fire at Bungay in Suffolk led to £24 being allowed from the rent in 1694;[263] and at Pakefield in Suffolk £3 was abated from the rent in 1702, partly because of repairs and also since erosion by the sea had led to a reduction in the area of the estate.[264] Expenditure on repairs through reductions in rent has already been mentioned.

Particular estates encountered their own difficulties. An extreme case is that of the Shernborne estate in Norfolk. In 1658, shortly after it was given to the College, it was valued as yielding an annual income of £225 6s 10d.[265] This comfortably allowed the yearly expenditure of £194 as specified by Francis Ash.[266] By 1661, however, the annual income was only £185, and legal advice had to be taken on how to divide the money: the outcome was that the payments should be abated proportionally.[267] The tenant had difficulty in paying his rent, and in 1672 the College was forced to evict him and to farm the estate itself. This involved several Fellows in journeys to the property: Samuel Richardson and Thomas Nettleton went to hire a bailiff, Robert Moor. Nettleton and John Kent visited at seed time and Nettleton returned at the sheep-shearing. Michael Stukeley travelled there at Midsummer, and was followed by John Kent at harvest time. While at Shernborne, he paid £66 12s 4d in wages. The manor house, outbuildings, fences and gates had to be rebuilt or repaired: this cost £189 and involved the Master and two Fellows in

---

[260] ECA Box 22.C9; ECA BUR.8.1.
[261] ECA Box 22.C23, C26.
[262] ECA SCH.1.1.
[263] ECA BUR.11.2.
[264] ECA SCH.1.1.
[265] ECA Box 22.A4.
[266] ECA Box 9.Ma3.
[267] ECA BUR.6.3 f. 242r.

spending six weeks on the estate. One final journey was then made by Mr Richardson and Mr Nettleton. Over the two years in which the farm was in hand, income exceeded expenditure by nearly £240, which represented an annual income of only £120. The estate was then re-let in 1673, at an annual rent of £150.[268] When the next lease was sealed, however, in 1679, the rent was reduced to £145.[269] Even this reduction did not prevent the farm from having to be taken in hand yet again: the College's bailiff ran the estate for nearly two years. Perhaps the previous experience of running a farm helped, as this time a slight profit, of £17 11s 4d, was made.[270] Thomas Houghton became the tenant in 1691 and paid £120 a year rent; when his lease was renewed in 1698, the rent was increased to £130.[271] Ash's gift must have seemed more of a liability than an asset in the late seventeenth century.

Some of the College's problems in collecting rent charges became so acute that they were commuted. The rent charge of £13 6s 8d which the College had bought from William Fludd at Woodham Ferrers in Essex in 1594, using the money from Laurence Chaderton and the dealings over St Nicholas Hostel, was only received for 14 years. William Fludd repaid his bond of £35, which had presumably been a guarantee for the rents for the following five years from 1609 to 1613; thereafter, the annuity disappeared.[272] After the bond had been repaid, John Spenluffe's rent charge of £4 per annum was sold, and the rent of the Hostel raised from ten shillings to £7 a year in compensation.[273] John Parker's gift of an annuity of £20 arising from land at Radwell in Hertfordshire was commuted for 200 marks on 29 June 1613, only six and a half years after it had been conveyed to the College.[274]

It must have seemed at times that Sir Francis Hastings' donation of a rent charge of £8 issuing from lands in Leicestershire would never be enjoyed at all. It is a sad story. Hastings bought two yardlands[275] and three cottages in Market Bosworth in 1579; two years later, he became indebted to Mr Smith of London for £250, and the lands were charged with a bond of £500 in case of non-payment. In 1585, Hastings gave a rent charge of £8 to Emmanuel, which issued partly from these same lands. Sir Wolstan Dixie became involved when he bought the lands in Bosworth in 1589 for £200 and was misled as he was told that they were free from all

---

[268] ECA SCH.1.1.

[269] ECA BUR.6.3 pp. 51–8.

[270] ECA SCH.1.1.

[271] ECA BUR.6.3 pp. 193–202, 258–65.

[272] ECA Box 4.H12; ECA BUR.11.1.

[273] ECA BUR.11.1.

[274] ECA Box 1.A9(1).

[275] A variable measure depending on soil quality and normally about 30 acres. One-quarter of a hide, originally the amount of land that could be ploughed in a year with one plough and support a family.

incumbrances. The College was not blameless either, for it did not claim payment of the rent charge for eight years while Hastings was alive (and would therefore have been liable for the payment of it). Within one month of Hastings' death, however, the College made its claim against Dixie, who must have had a nasty shock. He generously assured the College that he would not 'wronge the deade', but, 'for the love I beare to the Colledge' offered to commute his proportion of the rent charge for £40. If this amount was unacceptable, he was willing to accept whatever sum the Lord Keeper decreed, though clearly application to the law courts would involve both him and the College in some expenditure. Dixie's offer was accepted by the College and the entire rent charge was commuted for £100 in 1617. For Dixie, however, the matter was not over: he was likely to lose the lands as well since Hastings had not settled his debt and the bond of £500 was more than the lands were worth. The purchase had been most unfortunate.[276]

Some time later, Archdeacon Johnson's rent charge on land at Witham on the Hill was commuted for £2100 as it had fallen into arrears. Various purchases were considered after this decision by the Court of Chancery on 6 December 1694 and eventually, as has been shown, an estate was bought at Whaplode and Holbeach in 1709.[277]

Expenditure: financial hardship?
There is, therefore, considerable evidence that the College experienced difficulty in collecting its rents at various times; how good was it at matching this income to its expenditure? There was a mechanism for the accumulation of reserves so as to be able to save against times of need. At Emmanuel, this was called the 'Parva Cista', the small chest that was kept in the Treasury, and surplus balances were transferred into it from time to time. Its contents are shown in Fig. 4: from 1629 to 1632, funds accumulated therein, to be used in the next few years to help to finance the building of the 'Brick Building' (Old Court). The chest was partly replenished in 1636 and thereafter its wealth fluctuated. At most of the audits from 1637 to 1652, and again from 1657 to 1667, positive balances were left in the Master or Bursar's hands to pay for College expenses, repairs and wages. In addition, sums were taken out of the chest in 1638, from 1643 to 1645 and in 1652 for the same purposes. The chest was emptied in 1661, partly to pay wages; it was replenished in 1663 from a modest surplus of £50 and from income from fines, its contents fluctuated during the rest of the decade until it was emptied once again in 1668. In 1671, £100 was transferred to refill it and was taken out again the following

---

[276] ECA Box 1.A10, A11 (5–7).
[277] ECA SCH.1.24.

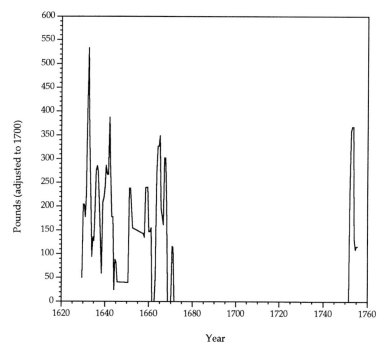

Figure 4   The contents of the Parva Cista. *Source*: ECA BUR.0.2.

year, and there is no further evidence of use of the chest until a brief revival from 1751 to 1755.[278]

From an examination of a combination of Figs 1 to 4, therefore, it appears that the College managed fairly satisfactorily until the early 1640s, though there was concern about the rising arrears of the mid-1620s. Then, however, income fell, arrears rose, balances became negative and the reserves were emptied during the Civil War period. The Interregnum years were slightly better; during the brief Mastership of William Sancroft (the younger), positive balances eventually enabled a build-up of reserves but these soon disappeared in the middle 1660s and whilst estate income rose slightly, so did arrears and expenditure (partly on the new chapel), so as not to make it a period of great prosperity. Data for the 1680s and thereafter are insufficient to enable detailed analysis in this way.

Corroboration of this summary can be seen from other evidence. It has,

---

[278] Information from the audit indentures at ECA BUR.0.2. While there are gaps in the indentures from 1679 to 1693, and from 1694 to 1735, the documents immediately before and after these years stated explicitly that the Parva Cista was empty.

for instance, already been shown how there were sufficient funds for the College to buy land at Eltisley in 1593, Gransden in 1599, St Andrew's Street in 1607, Emmanuel Street in 1612 and Petty Cury in 1621. Purchase of lands from the College's own resources then ceased, perhaps an indication of a lack of large surpluses requiring investment. Arrears of payments by the College also occurred. Indeed in 1666, as financial difficulties increased, Sir Thomas Fanshaw reentered upon the six acres at Ripple in Essex that the College leased from him because of a default in payment of rent. As a result the Master, John Breton, agreed to pay the arrears and to cause a ditch to be made to divide Fanshaw's land from that of the College. A gate to enable passage between the two properties would also be constructed. The tenant, Mr Whyte, was to carry out this work at his own expense, and by recompense for this and for damages sustained by him from the reentry, he was to be allowed £3 from the next half-year's rent.[279]

Further evidence for financial hardship comes from the practice of keeping Fellowships and scholarships vacant. By this means, both the College and the remainder of the Fellowship benefited. The absence of a Fellow or scholar meant that there were fewer charges on the College's general resources, and that the income that was to have maintained the person passed to the College. In addition, income from fines was divided by a smaller number, so both the College and the Fellowship enjoyed larger sums. Overall, however, income from vacancies was not a significant amount until after about 1710 (see Fig. 5).

A few decisions to keep Fellowships vacant were recorded. In 1613, for example, William Barrowe died and it was decided to keep his Fellowship vacant because of the arrears that had accrued on Sir Francis Hastings' rent charge (£88 for 11 years was owed at this time) and since expenditure had exceeded receipts by £29 at the Michaelmas audit in that year.[280] In 1680, another Fellow, William Mackernesse, died, and it was decided not to fill his place for one year so as to alleviate the financial difficulties that his demise caused the College.[281] Problems of the brewhouse in 1714 contributed to the need for dramatic action by the College in the following year. Mary Terry and John Brooke, the tenants of the College brew-house, were declared bankrupt shortly after their lease was sealed on 31 July 1713.[282] The brewing vessels were seized by H.M. Customs for arrears of excise duty, and the College had to pay £37 to redeem them. This occurred at about the same time as the death of the Steward, Mr Potter, which it was thought was likely to cause a debt to the College of £94. In addition, the College buildings were in need of

[279] ECA Box 15.A19.
[280] ECA COL.14.1 p. 19.
[281] ECA COL.14.1 p. 107.
[282] ECA BUR.6.3 pp. 457–62; ECA COL.9.10.31.

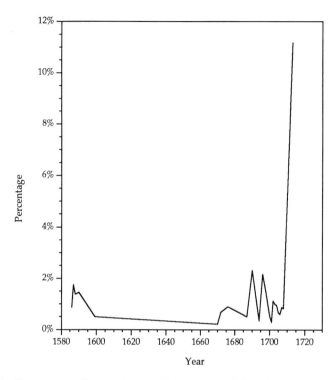

Figure 5   Percentage of estate income from vacant Fellowships and scholarships to 1720. *Source*: ECA BUR.11.1–2, SCH.1.1–2.

substantial repairs. The combination of these three factors led to a decision to keep five Fellowships vacant until times improved.[283]

Vacancies in scholarships also arose. Though these vacancies, too, led to a saving of money, their use was more discriminating. Indeed, William Sancroft (the younger) lamented vacancies in 1663 in a letter to his former tutor, Ezekiel Wright, on the state of Emmanuel. The College was not attractive to prospective scholars: it took longer at Emmanuel than elsewhere to become a Fellow, examinations were rigid and allowances to scholars were scanty. Thus, there were too few students and none was capable of succeeding to a Fellowship: seven new Fellows were about to be elected, but most of them were from elsewhere, so that half of the Fellowship would be foreigners. The College, he felt, would not flourish again until liberal allowances were given to Fellows and scholars.[284] Evidence for the low value of scholarships comes, for example, from the

[283] ECA COL.14.1 pp. 121–2.
[284] ECA COL.9.10.16.

estate at Lydden and Ewell in Kent. In 1676, it failed to yield its full annual income of £19 to maintain two scholars, paying them £6 a year each plus allowances towards the costs of the degrees and books. As the income had shrunk to £10 a year, the value of the scholarships had to be reduced commensurately.[285]

An element that was built into the terms of the Dixie benefaction allowed the College to benefit from vacant scholarships: an agreement of 1607 allowed for there to be a gap of six months between each holder, and for the money that would have been paid to the scholar to go to the College. If the scholarship remained vacant, the College would continue to enjoy its income. In addition, £4 a year would be paid from the estate towards the repair of the College.[286] From about 1670, the temptation to keep scholarships vacant unnecessarily proved irresistible, and the Dixies (who, since 1605, had the right to nominate Dixie Fellows and scholars)[287] filed bills against the College in Chancery in 1678[288] and again in 1696. The plaintiffs complained that the Dixie Fellows and scholars had not been allowed their privileges and free rooms and tuition, that the value of the Fellowships and scholarships had not been improved as income from the estate rose and that income from fines had been misapplied.[289] After lengthy negotiations, a new agreement was drawn up that put the management of the estate on a more secure footing. The College still enjoyed the income from vacancies and £4 a year was still to be paid to the College for repairs. If the Fellowships or scholarships remained vacant after their half year, then the profits would go towards the purchase of lands to augment the annual payments in the future, and then to buy advowsons.[290]

Emmanuel's problems and its ways of dealing with them can be compared with those of other colleges. At Oxford, cash reserves accumulated in a number of colleges in the 1620s and 1630s; these vanished during the Civil War but then conditions gradually improved, though some colleges emerged from the Commonwealth with debts.[291] At Cambridge, St John's College, too, enjoyed cash surpluses. Here, they were at a quite different level from those at Emmanuel: frequently, sums of about £1400 were regarded as the dead stock of the College and were, it seems, used for building and repairs. Property was purchased, too, in contrast to Emmanuel: a moiety of the manor of Rawreth in Essex was bought for £830 in 1684, in 1715, £2300 was invested in a farm at Somersham, Huntingdonshire, and other examples can be cited,

---

[285] ECA SCH.1.1.
[286] ECA Box 29.B26(vii).
[287] ECA Box 29.B22(lxxxi).
[288] ECA Box 29.B14.
[289] ECA Box 29.B26.
[290] ECA Box 29.B21; see also pp. 132, 138.
[291] Aylmer 1986, p. 549; Dunbabin 1986, p. 269; Twigg 1997, p. 773.

too.[292] Other colleges were hard-hit financially by the Civil War; Queens' suffered, though during the rest of the seventeenth century average annual income and expenditure rose, more or less hand in hand. Fellowships were left vacant in the 1650s and again from the 1680s, when things were less rosy and reserves almost exhausted.[293] Finances at Sidney Sussex, too, were at a low ebb in the mid-seventeenth century.[294] Without a detailed examination of other Cambridge colleges it is hard to say more, but the general impression is that Emmanuel was not particularly unusual in its relative prosperity in the early seventeenth century, and in having less healthy finances thereafter, though they never descended to disaster levels. Emmanuel was not one of the richer colleges.

Entry fines

The effects of the College's financial management on its Fellows, however, depended on one further factor: the levying of entry fines on the issue and renewal of leases. Fines were an important part of the system of beneficial leases: as rents were relatively low and, in the Oxford and Cambridge colleges at least, barely rose, it was the fines that reflected changing land values. In general, the longer the lease and the lower the rent, the higher the fine that was charged on entry. Other factors too, however, affected the levels of fines: the full rental value of the estate, whether or not the existing tenant was to be given the first option on renewal,[295] and the rate of interest.

In the seventeenth century, colleges tended to set fines at one year's value of the reserved rent if a lease for 21 years was renewed after seven.[296] Texts described how to calculate fines;[297] by the eighteenth century, colleges were claimed to be setting fines at rather low levels. Changes in the value of land and interest rates had not been taken into account, and perhaps colleges were less effective negotiators than private landlords. In 1718, when interest rates were 5% and private landowners were charging accordingly for renewal of their leases, colleges still assumed the rates to be about 10%. Rates had in fact fallen from 10% to 8% in 1625, and to 6% in 1651. Thus, colleges were charging only about half of the fines to which they were entitled.[298] This, however, assumed that realistic fines were set in the late sixteenth century: at St John's College in Cambridge, however, fines were low even then.[299]

[292] Howard 1935, pp. 73, 76–7.
[293] Twigg 1987, pp. 58–9, 300–2.
[294] Scott-Giles 1975, pp. 71–2.
[295] Aylmer 1986, p. 534.
[296] Dunbabin 1986, p. 277.
[297] For example, Mabbut 1700.
[298] Manningham 1722, pp. 8–14; Habbakuk 1952–3, p. 27.
[299] Howard 1935, p. 26.

At Emmanuel, fines were certainly lower than they would have been if the current interest rates had been applied. At Stondon in Essex, for example, the following comparison can be made:

Date	Fine Levied	Fine According to 6% Interest Rates
1639	15	30
1652	20	55
1666	30	60
1679	24	50
1687	11	25
1699	17	50
1717	40	90

Here, then, fines were set at approximately half the level at which they could have been levied. On other estates, too, fines were low: usually, in fact, rather lower than at Stondon and often at one-third of the expected level. The value of fines did start to rise from the early eighteenth century, to one-and-a-quarter and one-and-a-half years' value by mid-century,[300] and even to two years' purchase in some cases.[301] An early glimpse of the increases to come was provided for Emmanuel in the decree as to the proper running of the Dixie estate in 1701. The College was empowered to charge fines of up to one-and-a-half years' value, though in 1710 Sir Wolstan Dixie advised that it would be difficult to find a tenant willing to pay £60 as a fine and £42 for a reserved rent, as the estate was in so bad a state of disrepair. Dixie pointed out that the periodic vacancies of half a year would soon pay what was being asked for a fine; in the event, the fine of £60 was levied, though it was allowed to be paid by two equal instalments in the second and third years of the lease. In the first year, the rent was just one peppercorn and in the second year, it was only £10. Thereafter, the full rent of £40 was charged.[302]

In general, income from fines tended to rise in the late seventeenth and early eighteenth centuries. At Oxford, income appears to have increased substantially in the 1660s and 1670s, and thereafter to have risen more gently.[303] St John's College in Cambridge, however, saw no marked increase in proceeds from fines in the seventeenth century; it experienced a set-back during the Civil War, and the cheapness of grain and falling rents thereafter did not encourage rises in fines. Not until the eighteenth

---

[300] Dunbabin 1986, p. 277.
[301] Shadwell 1898, p. 13.
[302] ECA Box 29.B26(lxv); Box 29.B25/12.
[303] Dunbabin 1986, p. 277.

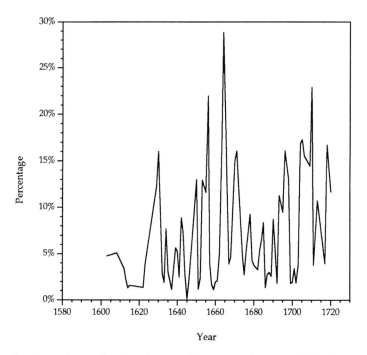

Figure 6   Percentage of estate income from entry fines to 1720. *Source*: ECA BUR.11.1–2.

century did fine income increase.[304] At Emmanuel, income from fines increased in the late 1650s and early 1660s; then it fell, and started to rise again in the last decade of the century. As Fig. 6 shows, however, the arrival of such money was spasmodic and unreliable, and in part just reflects which leases came up for renewal at a particular time.

Figure 6 demonstrates that at no time was income from fines a very large proportion of the overall yield of the College estates: rents were far more important. This is, perhaps, surprising, given the emphasis in the literature on the importance of fines. The graph, however, only shows the proportion of the fines that went into the College coffers and there is another aspect that has to be considered: the contribution of fines to the Fellowship dividend.

The Fellowship dividend
Fellows of colleges (and, in the Church, the Deans and Chapters) attached great importance to entry fines, for it was from these that the incumbents benefited directly. In the mid-sixteenth century, Caius' statutes decreed

[304] Howard 1935, pp. 67–70.

that in most cases the entire fines should be paid to the College.[305] By the end of the sixteenth century, however, things had begun to change. At Sidney Sussex College, Fellows received a proportion of the fines in 1604,[306] and at St John's, the first dividends from fines were recorded as being paid out in January 1629.[307] Other profits, too, were divided: as early as 1560, the Fellows of St Catharine's College decided that all of the profits of the dove-house were to be divided.[308] Corn rents were also divided as, for example, at Clare College in the seventeenth century.[309] Varying proportions of the fines were divided among the Fellowship. At Oxford, between one-ninth and three-quarters went to the college,[310] while at Jesus College in Cambridge, one-tenth of the entry fines went to the College.[311]

At Emmanuel, the Fellowship dividend developed early. In 1592, the College decided that all ingress money, or admission fees, should be divided among the Master and 12 Fellows, and that in consequence the Fellowship should forego its rights to income from renting the brew-house and bake-house.[312] Income from corn rents (such as it was)[313] was first divided in 1610, and from wood sales in the following year.[314] In 1617, the purchase of the tithes at Pinchbeck led to an increased rental by £80, whereas the value of the estate had only been expected to be £60. It was consequently decided by the Fellowship (not by the Master), that two-thirds of the income should go towards the costs of running the College, and that one-third should be divided among the 'living body, and publike society'. This order was, however, never enacted, and Dr Chaderton claimed in April 1632 that he had: 'never seene nor heard of it before'.[315] Clearly the proportion of fines that should be divided among the Fellowship was causing some concern, for in 1621 the Society decided, 'for the quite removeing of all such doubtes hereafter', that one-quarter of the fine should be divided amongst the Master and Fellows, and that three-quarters should be used for the general purposes of the College. By comparison with some other colleges, therefore, the demands by Emmanuel's Fellows were modest.

The decision in 1621 did not solve the matter, because the Fellows, not the Master, agreed that if the rent was raised, 'valueable alloweance be

---

[305] Venn, *Caius*, III, p. 384.
[306] Salt 1992, p. 148.
[307] Howard 1935, p. 58.
[308] Jones 1936, p. 221.
[309] Harrison 1958, p. 83.
[310] Aylmer 1986, p. 528.
[311] Gray and Brittain 1960, p. 73.
[312] ECA BUR.11.1; ECA COL.14.1 p. 19.
[313] See above, p. 144.
[314] ECA BUR.11.1.
[315] ECA COL.14.1 p. 26.

made according to this proportion'.[316] For the next 13 years, fines continued to be levied and there are records of their receipt in the rentals. In 1634, the division amongst the Master and Fellows of one-quarter of the fines was confirmed.[317] The first indication in the rentals that the sums entered therein did not represent the full amount of the fine was in the following year, when a fine of £25 was levied for renewal of a lease of part of the Hyde Farm Estate and only £9 4s 8d went to the College.[318]

From 1635, the system of dividing fines at Emmanuel became established. There were teething troubles, however. In 1637, a tenant at Threadneedle Street, William Ivatt, was negotiating to renew his lease. Proceedings were protracted through disagreements among the Fellowship as to how the fine of £20 should be divided, much to Ivatt's vexation. Indeed, Ivatt claimed that:

> if I might bee the meanes of makeing peace & unity betwixt you & the Fellowes though with the expence of five pounds out of my owne purce soe much exhausted by the soe trobelsome worke yet it shall noe wayes repent mee thereof.

This letter was written on 27 January 1637, he tried again on 9 February and all was finally settled later in the month.[319] Shortly afterwards, in 1638, comes the first reference to the College receiving three-quarters of a fine, when a lease of the tenement to the North of the Four Swans in Bishopsgate Street, London, was renewed.[320] The practice became established whereby for fines not exceeding £10, the entire sum was paid to the Master and Fellows; they received one-quarter of fines over £10. If rents were raised, an allowance was made to the Fellowship. In 1695 and 1704, for example, only two-thirds of each fine was paid to the College on the renewal of the Catherine Wheel in Smithfield and Four Swans in Bishopsgate respectively, because the rent had been raised.[321]

Fees from sealing leases were always entirely divided amongst the Master and Fellows; money from capons and the sale of timber was, too, and of the corn money, three-quarters were allocated to the Master and Fellows and one-quarter was paid to the scholars.[322] In 1651, the times at which dividends were to be paid were set down: corn and wood money were to be divided on the last Saturday in the month after the Michaelmas audit, ingress money was to be divided at the audit, the remainder from 'Bachelors feasting money' (money paid by those who

---

[316] ECA COL.14.1 ff. 24a, 25.
[317] ECA COL.9.10.9.
[318] ECA BUR.11.1.
[319] ECA Box 27.B15.
[320] ECA BUR.11.1.
[321] ECA BUR.11.2.
[322] ECA BUR.3.1–2.

were graduating Bachelor of Arts) was to be divided on the Saturday after audit, and the residue from 'Inceptors, Midsummer-Bachelors & other commencers' on the Saturday in Commencement Week.[323] Fines and sealing monies were also divided at audit.

The system was, however, not rigid. It was still open to abuse. In 1641, the entire fine of £20 from renewing the lease of the Sutton Coldfield estate was divided among the Master, Fellows and two Dixie Fellows.[324] Irregularities in the division of the fines from the Dixie estate were one of the factors that led to Lord Keeper Wright's decree of 1701, wherein it was ordained that half of the fines should be divided amongst the Master, Fellows and Dixie Fellows, and that the remainder should be put to the use of the Dixie Foundation.[325] Apart from this estate, however, there are no other recorded instances of malpractice. Although at Pembroke College in 1718, the Master and Fellows agreed to give up the greater part of their dividends towards building work in the College,[326] the Fellows of Emmanuel were reluctant to forego their portions when times became hard.

Emmanuel, therefore, like other colleges, attached great importance to entry fines. The Fellows received a relatively low proportion of the fines compared with some other colleges and so were less dependent on the income from them. Indeed, the College itself cannot have relied very heavily on income from fines: they were set at a low level, the income was variable, and was never a significant proportion of the overall produce from an estate.

The early history of Emmanuel's estates and finances can thus be drawn. The College was unusual in that its Founder played a large part, both directly and indirectly, in securing its endowment. Once it had received its land, Emmanuel does not seem to have been very go-ahead in its management of it, though from time to time there were men like William Dillingham who paid more interest in the endowment than his near contemporaries. Emmanuel was not alone; like other colleges, all that was required was sufficient income to keep going. There is little evidence of severe financial difficulty, though there were plenty of minor problems. Apart from the surprising absence of corn-rents, the College seems to have conformed, more or less, to current practices. Some other colleges, however, were more highly organised, had more detailed statutory provision for the running of their estates, kept better records of their property and appear to have taken a greater active interest in it. None,

---

[323] ECA COL.14.1.
[324] ECA BUR.11.1.
[325] ECA Box 29.B21 p. 25.
[326] Attwater 1936, p. 87.

however, would have dissented from Sir William Blackstone's good wishes to the incoming bursar at All Souls College, Oxford, in 1753:

> My hearty wishes, & I dare answer those of the whole Society, are, that your Year may be rich & peaceable; attended with a moderate Expense Roll; with good, tho' not extravagant, Price-Days; large Fines, & chearfully paid; pleasant progresses, & many Alienations; a comfortable share of Underwood, & abundance of Timber that will not improve by standing. And for your own particular, I wish You large Rags [odd monies, such as those left over from divisions], & small Tres Billae [arrears]; many Leases, & few Letters; a prodigious Increase of Bread, & a mighty Consumption of Ale; & to crown all, a clear Exoneration, without fear of Drawbacks; & a sociable Evening to celebrate the End of all things.[327]

The Bursars of Emmanuel would certainly have concurred.

---

[327] Blackstone 1898, p. 50.

6

Puritan Emmanuel

Laurence Chaderton, 2: Puritan Conformity and the Greater Good[1]

Everyone knows that Laurence Chaderton was the puritan master of a puritan college. But now the time has come to define more closely the inconsistent consistencies of Chaderton's evolving Puritanism, and thus to characterise the Puritanism of Emmanuel. Puritanism, in its original sense, meant something more concrete, more historically contingent, than that perennial puritan 'spirit' which we uncover in the young Samuel Ward's anxious scruples,[2] which were no doubt as troublesome to others as to himself:

> Pride, desire of vainglory, yea in little things . . . Thy little affection in hearing Mr Chatterton's good sermon . . . Oh the grievous sins in Trinity College which had a woman which was carried from chamber to chamber on the night time. My adulterous dream that night . . . O, that I could be so sorry for my sins as at my outward afflictions . . . Also my longing after damsons . . . Oh that I could so long after God's graces.[3]

This was what the world beyond the puritan conscience would learn to call cant.[4]

The something more which Puritanism entailed was nonconformity, a principled reluctance to be subject, whether as an individual, a congregation, or a college, to the laws and prescribed liturgy of the Church of

---

[1] I have benefited from the critical comments of Seán Hughes, Professor Peter Lake and Dr Arnold Hunt; and from Arnold Hunt's essay, 'Laurence Chaderton and the Hampton Court Conference', in Wabuda and Litzenberger, 1998, pp. 207–28. Hunt uses the materials discussed in his essay, and in this chapter, to argue more forcefully than I have done for Chaderton's continuing 'radicalism', into great old age.

[2] See above, pp. 30–42.

[3] Knappen 1933, pp. 103, 111, 112, 114.

[4] See, for example, H. R. Trevor-Roper's amused but disgusted reaction to Ward's self-confessed gluttony in the consumption of fruit, nuts and cheese (*Catholics, Anglicans and Puritans* (London, 1987), pp. 49, 82).

177

England, as established within the terms of the Elizabethan settlement of religion, a reluctance which imposed severe limits on the scope of human authority in matters of religion and which was consequently a political matter. Alienation from the church of the Elizabethan settlement could be as profound as total rejection of its two principal pillars: episcopacy and the Prayer Book, matters on which a civil war would one day be fought. Puritans as radical as that hung on by the skin of their teeth to their pews in the parish church or, if ministers, to their professional role within it, relying upon a measure of casuistry and the sense that they and their godly brethren constituted the Church of God in a special sense, a church within the Church, leavening the whole unsavoury lump.[5]

We have already considered evidence that Chaderton was intellectually a presbyterian who, like some other leading Cambridge Calvinists, suppressed his convictions for the sake of the greater good of working within the established system.[6] However, it is difficult to think of Chaderton as a bishop. By a similar token, Chaderton, who would not have composed the Book of Common Prayer if it had been left to him, and who for twenty years at least presided over a college which honoured the Prayer Book in the breach of its rubrics, would urge on nonconformists more intransigent than himself the virtues of conformity.

In the archiepiscopates of John Whitgift and Richard Bancroft (1583–1604, 1604–10), which coincided with Emmanuel's first quarter-century, it was not enough to be generally conformable. Under this relatively rigorous regime, the Church demanded not only conformity to the prescribed liturgies in the jot and tittle of every rubric, but that its ministers should formally subscribe to the proposition, one of three articles which were the shibboleth of conformity, that the Prayer Book contained nothing contrary to the Word of God.

Puritans did not believe that this was the case, which made it nearly impossible so to subscribe. Moreover, the essence of their Puritanism was the doctrine that nothing should be used or done in the service of God which was not positively commanded in (rather than merely not contrary to) God's Word, or at least generally warranted by Scripture.[7] A number of Prayer Book ceremonies and ornaments fell foul of this principle, to the extent that they were perceived as so many relics and vestiges of the old 'popish' religion, erected on fundamentally Antichristian principles. Either the disputed ceremonies lacked that neutrality or quality of 'indifference'

---

[5] The literature on English Puritanism is almost limitless. See the bibliography appended to my Historical Association pamphlet *English Puritanism* (revised edn., 1987); and more recently, Patrick Collinson, *The Puritan Character: Polemics and Polarities in Early Seventeenth-Century English Culture* (William Andrews Clark Memorial Library, University of California, 1989); and the essays in Bremer 1993.

[6] See above, pp. 35–40. The case is constructed in Lake 1982.

[7] Coolidge 1970.

which for non-Puritans made their use lawful and, when endorsed by due authority, obligatory; or the principle of 'things indifferent' itself evaporated when such things were enforced.

The particulars may appear trivial, especially to an almost post-Christian and instinctively latitudinarian age: as small as the wearing or not wearing of the white linen surplice, a garment of no particular significance and objectionable only on account of its 'popish' associations; or the 'superstitious' making of the sign of the cross on the infant's forehead in baptism; or the posture of kneeling to receive communion, implying an 'idolatrous' veneration of the sacrament. Yet for these and even smaller ritual details, hardline bishops were prepared to suspend and in the last resort deprive of their livelihoods nonconforming ministers, and nonconformists to suffer suspension, deprivation and worse; with consequences which were alienating for those tightly-knit networks of 'the godly' which made up the puritan presence within the parish churches. These issues would split English Protestantism, opening up narrow fissures which were destined to become denominational chasms. Eventually 'nonconformity' would become, not a minor scruple about a piece of white linen cloth, but a different conception of what it was to be a Christian, and an Englishman.

So these matters were not in the least trivial in their long term consequences and not trivial, more immediately, for Emmanuel. An account of 'public disorders as touching church causes in Emmanuel College'[8] describes the practice of its unconsecrated chapel, of which the very orientation differed from 'the uniform order of all Christendom'. Emmanuel, far from obeying the Prayer Book forms, followed 'a private course of public prayer, after their own fashion.' The surplice was never worn, nor the gowns and square caps of prescribed clerical and academical attire. The practice of Emmanuel was not to kneel to receive the sacrament but to be seated on forms around the communion table, passing from hand to hand both bread and cup, 'one drinking as it were to another, like good fellows.'

The motive of this report was manifestly unfriendly, but only in its rhetorical top-dressing did it exaggerate. The surplice was not worn in Emmanuel and communion was received in a sitting position. The year was 1603 and puritan hopes of negotiating a new and more favourable religious settlement were aroused by the advent of James I, who as James VI of Scotland was accustomed to a form of worship and a church polity more akin to English puritan aspirations than the Prayer Book, narrowly interpreted. Presently, a conference would be held at Hampton Court to consider, among other ecclesiastical matters, the carefully moderated puritan demand for a measure of further reformation: James as

---

[8] BL, MS Harl. 7033, fol. 98.

arbitrator, bishops and deans confronting representative spokesmen for the reformist party.[9] With the militant tendency kept firmly in the background, these representatives were extreme moderates: John Knewstub of Suffolk, who was probably behind the discreet manoeuvres at Bury St Edmunds in 1590 which we have already observed[10]; Thomas Sparke, who would soon announce his capitulation into conformity, publicly and fulsomely[11]; John Rainolds, Chaderton's counterpart in Oxford; and Chaderton himself.

The intention of the denunciation of 'public disorders' at Emmanuel must have been to discredit Chaderton and his college in advance of the Hampton Court Conference. James wrote that the puritan Millenary Petition (so-called from the thousand names supposedly attached to it, preceding and partly occasioning the Conference) was framed by one 'so near of kin to Emmanuel as I shall distrust that race the more while I live.'[12] Chaderton's conduct at Hampton Court (where little enough was achieved) had more to do with damage limitation than with the seizing of a golden opportunity. One account of the Conference describes him as 'mute as any fish'.[13] When a complaint was made about Emmanuel's sitting communions, Chaderton offered the implausible explanation that communicants were bound to sit, 'the seats so placed as they be'.[14]

A hostile report of the Conference has it that 'Chaderton must conform, and his irregular College wear the surplice, and receive the communion kneeling, or else be put out of it.' Robert Cecil, as chancellor of the university, wrote demanding the exemplary conformity of heads of

---

[9] Modern interpretations of the Hampton Court Conference include Mark H. Curtis, 'Hampton Court Conference and its Aftermath', *History*, 46 (1961), 1–16, Patrick Collinson, 'The Jacobean Religious Settlement: the Hampton Court Conference', in *Before the English Civil War*, ed. H. Tomlinson (1983), pp. 27–51 and K. C. Fincham and P. Lake, 'The Ecclesiastical Policy of King James I', *Journal of British Studies*, 24 (1985), pp. 169–207, and, by the same authors, 'The Ecclesiastical Policies of James I and Charles I', in *The Early Stuart Church, 1603–1642*, ed. Kenneth Fincham (Basingstoke, 1993) pp. 23–49. William Barlow's *The summe and substance of the conference* was included by Edward Cardwell in his *History of Conferences . . . Connected with the Revision of the Book of Common Prayer* (Oxford, 1849), pp. 167–212; and has consequently exerted a disproportionate influence among historians. R. G. Usher printed some other accounts in his *The Reconstruction of the English Church* (London and New York, 1910), II, pp. 331–54.

[10] See above, pp. 37–8.

[11] Thomas Sparke, *A brotherly perswasion to unitie, and uniformitie in iudgment, and practise touching the received, and present ecclesiastical government, and the authorised rites and ceremonies of the Church of England* (London, 1607).

[12] *HMC Report, Hatfield MSS*, XVI 363.

[13] Usher 1910, II, p. 337. This dismissive remark occurs in the context of a series of 'characters' of 'puritan actors in these points', part of an account of the Conference favourable to the bishops. But it is true that in all accounts Chaderton remains silent, but for a single intervention in favour of the ministers in Lancashire, that they should not be pressed to wear the surplice or use the sign of the cross. (Usher 1910, II, p. 353; Cardwell, 1849, pp. 210–11.) John Rainolds, Chaderton's Oxford counterpart, by contrast played an active and leading role throughout the proceedings.

[14] Cardwell, 1849, p. 212.

houses and other leading figures. Chaderton promptly advised Cecil's chaplain, Richard Neile, who was doing his master's hatchet work, that in Emmanuel they had 'begun' to reduce the college to conformity, and that he and the fellows and scholars now used the communion book 'daily', knelt to receive the sacrament, and wore the surplice. Samuel Ward noted that 18 January 1605 was the day when the surplice as first 'urged' in Emmanuel, and he hoped that it was not a portent of worse things. 'Alas, we little expected that King James would have been the first permitter of it to be brought into our college, to make us a derision to so many that bear us no good will.' So it was partly a matter of face.[15]

However, from the king himself Cecil heard that Chaderton had not in fact conformed 'as he seemed to promise at the conference', continuing to give 'ill example'. James thought that the chancellor should 'remove' him 'if he continue obstinate'. Chaderton was between a rock and a hard place. Puritans more faithful than he to the good old cause felt abandoned, one of them writing to Chaderton that he should not 'betray their cause'. There probably was no formal betrayal. In that same month of January 1605, evidence was heard in the bishop's consistory court that both Chaderton and Ward were preaching in St Clement's church without a licence, evidence of a failure to subscribe. It is probable that Chaderton never subscribed to the three conformist articles and was not pressed to do so. Rainolds in Oxford seems to have been treated with the same indulgence. But the price of this concession was that the formally non-compliant Chaderton had now to advise the consciences of other nonconformists for whom no such allowance had been made.[16]

So it was that in these highly public circumstances, Chaderton became that contradiction in terms, a kind of nonconformable conformist. There was everything to play for and the very future of Emmanuel and its mission depended upon a carefully calculated capitulation. All eyes were now on Emmanuel. A Kentish correspondent told Chaderton that London was full of ministers, all negotiating their futures as subscribers or non-subscribers, and that 'many did talk of you'. Their first instinct was to head for Cambridge to consult Chaderton face to face. But Chaderton's old friend and adversary Bancroft, now archbishop, dissuaded them. 'We would there meet to no good.'[17]

---

[15] Usher 1910, II, p. 338; *HMC Report, Hatfield MSS*, XVI, pp. 389–91, 381–2; Knappen 1933, p. 130. On these negotiations, see Pauline Croft, 'The Religion of Robert Cecil', *Historical Journal*, 34 (1991), 778–9.

[16] *HMC Report, Hatfield MSS*, XXXIV, p. 367; Collinson 1967, pp. 462–3; Lake 1982, pp. 252–6; CUL, EDR D/2/24, fol. 56r. I owe the last reference to the kindness of Peter Lake. The formality of the St Clement's case was that the churchwardens and questmen were cited for permitting Chaderton and Ward to preach without licence, and for allowing the bell to be rung to summon the congregation to their sermons.

[17] Walter Jones, 'pastor of Gods church which is at Benenden in Kent' to Chaderton, 21 August 1605, Lambeth Palace Library, MS 2550, fols. 1r–2v.

As it happens, we have in the greatest detail a series of more or less private insights into Laurence Chaderton's mind as, in the aftermath of Hampton Court, Emmanuel and the Church at large came to terms with the disciplinary code known as the Constitutions and Canons of 1604. These disclosures consist, in part, of Chaderton's adversarial annotations of a number of books, now preserved in the Library of Trinity College Cambridge[18]; in part, of a collection of casuistical letters and papers acquired in our own time by Lambeth Palace Library[19]: written evidence which we owe to Bancroft's 'misliking' of personal encounters with the master of Emmanuel. Chaderton's Kentish correspondent wrote: 'As you have been always a very loving friend and father unto me, so vouchsafe to direct me in the right way.'[20] Chaderton treated both such correspondents and the books that he read as he might have handled some semi-competent student as he scribbled in the margins of his faltering essay: sharp retorts, rigorous syllogistic logic, a total command of the apposite biblical texts.

We begin with the annotations. They include Chaderton's spare but revealing notes on the semi-official but biassed account of Hampton Court composed by William Barlow, soon to be a bishop: *The summe and substance of the conference*.[21] Reading Barlow, as at the Conference itself, Chaderton was almost as mute as the proverbial fish, except on a point of honour. Barlow denigrated the Puritans as a defeated faction, their four representatives at Hampton Court 'agents for the millenary plaintiffs'. Chaderton was stung by this aspersion, insisting that he and the other spokesmen had been invited to take part on the same terms as all other participants. 'Being summoned, how agents? or plaintiffs?'[22] Modern scholarship bears Chaderton out. All participants at Hampton Court were there by virtue of the same form of royal summons. Much of the proceedings resembled a round table conference on the future of the Church rather than Barlow's eyeball-to-eyeball confrontation of irreconcileables, the Church triumphant versus error dejected.[23]

Chaderton annotated two controversial works of 1605 relating to the contested ceremonies: a radical puritan publication called *Certaine demandes* (propounded to the bishops), and an irenical dialogue by

---

[18] These annotated books are the important discovery of Arnold Hunt. In every case a seventeenth-century hand has identified the annotations as Chaderton's, a fact which can be confirmed from other examples of Chaderton's handwriting. See p. 36 n.20 above.

[19] Lambeth Palace Library, MS 2550. The papers are discussed in Lake 1982, chapter 10, 'Conformity: Chaderton's Response to the Hampton Court Conference'; and in Rolph 1979, chapter 2, 'Laurence Chaderton: Profile of a Moderate Puritan'.

[20] Lambeth Palace Library, MS 2550, fols. 1r–2v.

[21] Trinity College Library, C.9.125.

[22] Ibid., annotations on Sig. D4r. Chaderton recorded similar reactions on Sigs. B1v and D3r.

[23] Collinson, 1983a.

Samuel Gardiner, *About the rites and ceremonies of the Church of England*.[24] From these *marginalia* it is clear that Chaderton was opposing himself to puritan hardliners by insisting on the principle of Christian liberty in the use of things indifferent. Against the author of *Certaine demandes*, he denied that the surplice was a 'popish' 'accessory, appendix and appurtenance' of the mass. Where the author had written that the surplice had been called indifferent 'falsely', Chaderton retorted: 'Prove this "falsely" and take all.'[25] But Chaderton was an unrepentant Puritan in objecting to the imposition of the surplice on innocently offended consciences. The conformist in Gardiner's dialogue, 'an absolute formalist', would have it that ceremonies were not only lawful but necessary, when commanded by the magistrate. Chaderton asked: 'Doth not this necessity remove th'indifference?' The conformist interlocutor said (and it could have been Grindal or some other early Elizabethan bishop talking) that he would never have wished to have the ceremonial laws made but, being made, he would not be one to mar them. Chaderton underlined 'never' and remarked: 'Nor I, but to pray for the change.'[26]

Chaderton's moderated Puritanism, a halfway house between simple conformity and outright nonconformity, is more fully developed in the Lambeth papers. To a Kentish minister, Walter Jones, deeply troubled by Archbishop Bancroft's demand for conformity and subscription, Chaderton paraphrased his notes on the Gardiner dialogue. He would never (again that word) have advised a church to bring in and retain such signs and ceremonies, nor (and here was the crunch) 'urge the observation of them of necessity', 'for being indifferent things they should be permitted to be used indifferently'.[27] Nevertheless, Chaderton's prime concern was to convince Jones that the sign of the cross, the particular point at issue in this correspondence, was indeed an indifferent thing which would not, as it were, bite. Similarly, the surplice was lawful, and so too kneeling.[28] However, quite what 'indifferent' meant needed some sorting out. In one of these papers, Chaderton argued that the surplice and cross were not unlawful in themselves, although they might be in the service of God. Chaderton may have had in mind a legitimate use of the surplice as academic rather than liturgical dress. All the same, one may imagine that at this point the Joneses of this troubled ecclesiastical scene may have been tempted to look for a second opinion. But lawful or

---

[24] *Certaine demandes with their grounds, drawne out of holy writ, and propounded* in foro conscientiae *by some religious gentle[man] vnto the reverend fathers* (Schilders, Middelburg, 1605); Samuel Gardiner, *A dialogue or conference betweene Irenaeus and Antimachus about the rites and ceremonies of the Church of England* (London, 1605).

[25] Trinity College Library, C.9.126, Sigs. A2v, B2r, B3r, C1v, C2r, B4r.

[26] Trinity College Library, C.9.132, Sig. E3v.

[27] Lambeth Palace Library, MS 2550, fols. 3r–5r; Lake 1982, pp. 250–2.

[28] Lambeth Palace Library, MS 2550, fols. 40r–49v (a paper headed 'The Surplis is Lawfull'); ibid., fol. 12.

unlawful, Chaderton was 'verily persuaded' the ceremonies could be used 'without sin'.[29] In yet another paper, Chaderton took refuge in the hopeful rather than reliable principle that the Church did not urge the 'religious' use of the ceremonies (a use which would have to be resisted), but only as 'matters of order, conformity and testifications of obedience to the Church and prince'.[30] In these casuistical essays Chaderton was by no means suggesting that his correspondents should bury their conscientious scruples in order to protect their livelihoods, or even for the sake of what we have called 'the greater good' of their pastoral usefulness. He was telling them that their scruples were luxuries which they had no need to afford.

But everything depended upon circumstances. The biblical key was contained in St Paul's advice to the Corinthian Christians, who thought it a question of conscience whether they should eat meat offered to idols. 'All things are lawful, but all are not profitable.' The principle was one not of law but of expediency. 'For what is more lawful than to eat and drink, or more unlawful than to be drunk?' (Chaderton rather than Paul).[31] Who was to judge what was expedient? At stake were the consciences of those 'weaker brethren' for whose sake St Paul's casuistry had been constructed. The minister was charged with the instruction of those weak consciences, but so long as they remained weak, he alone was the judge of how far they should be favoured. Expediency was local and circumstantial and only those ministers 'to whom God hath given in any measure a spirit of wisdom spiritually to discern the difference' between expediency and inexpediency could be the judge of those local circumstances.[32] This is telling evidence of Chaderton's enduring presbyterianism, an ideology of subsidiarity, consensual decision-making, consistent with the Statutes and Orders of Emmanuel College. Even the Apostles ruled 'with others, not by themselves'.[33] It was to a close friend and relative, Ezekiel Culverwell, that Chaderton disclosed these still fundamentally radical views.[34]

Professor Peter Lake's comments are characteristically shrewd and penetrating. Chaderton was critical of the hardliners on both sides. But, like the guns of Singapore, his letters and position papers, and even his

---

[29] 'An examination of 14 reasons seeming to prove that the cross and surpliss are unlawfull', ibid., fols. 9r–12v; Rolph 1979, pp. 54–6.

[30] Thomas Brightman to Chaderton, 10 January 1605(/6?), Lambeth Palace Library, MS 2550, fols. 176–8, incorporating Chaderton's theses on ceremonies, in response; Lake 1982, pp. 252–4; Rolph 1979, pp. 58–60.

[31] 'De licitis', Lambeth Palace Library, MS 2550, fols. 51r–60v; Lake 1982, pp. 244–7.

[32] This corrects Lake, who reads 'a spirit of wisdom spiritually to discern' as 'a spirit of wisdom or spirituality to discern'.

[33] See above, p. 26.

[34] Lambeth Palace Library, MS 2550, fols. 28r–29v, endorsed 'Answer to E. Culverwell 1607 Jan 27 Matters of Divinitie'; Lake 1982, pp. 257–61; Rolph 1979, pp. 63–5.

private interactions with the books in his study, pointed in one direction only, towards the puritan intransigents, with the aim of reconciling them to the idea of conformity. After all, Chaderton had some hope of persuading his fellow Puritans, whereas he had no purchase with the establishment. As helpful casuistry, his advice depended upon a reasonable and sympathetic handling of tender conscience by the bishops, which, under James and Bancroft, was not always forthcoming. Chaderton was not resolving the moderate puritan dilemma, only exposing it.[35]

Whether or not Chaderton's casuistry held water, the water of consistency, pragmatically it was a brilliant success, at least in the short to middle term. Puritanism was defused without losing its potency. Out in the field, in the Suffolk parishes, the Chadertonian strategy was working out in practice, but dividing the puritan ranks as it did so. William Bedell wrote from Bury St Edmunds to Samuel Ward at Emmanuel: could he supply a curate for John Knewstub who would be willing, as Knewstub evidently was not, to wear a surplice? Bedell, the future bishop, deplored the line taken by some Suffolk ministers (including Sir Edward Lewkenor's minister Robert Pricke, father of an Emmanuel scholar) who had ceased to preach rather than subscribe. The only beneficiary would be 'the enemy'. Bedell sympathised with the nonconformists, but wished that 'we might all yeild and goe together'. As for his own preaching, 'yt hath never bene of these matters.'[36]

Chaderton wrote in the Lambeth papers: 'We may and ought to use them [the ceremonies] to purchase and procure liberty to win souls by preaching the Gospel.'[37] That was the Emmanuel strategy which worked well for thirty years or so. Not all Emmanuel men were nonconformists. Some never had to confront the issue, while others put it behind them. The Jacobean Church contained its safe havens, where the luxury of nonconformity could still be enjoyed. There were grey areas, like Knewstub's Suffolk parish. The conditions of 1605 were not in the least typical, especially under Bancroft's successor as archbishop, George Abbot, whose brother of York, Archbishop Tobie Matthew, was both an indefatigable preacher in his own right and a patron of preachers.[38] Intelligent anti-puritans knew that they had been outflanked.[39] Militant conformists like Bishop Samuel Harsnet and Peter Heylyn would write bitterly of 'conformable puritans', leopards who only appeared to have changed

---

[35] Lake 1982, 'Chaderton's Response to Hampton Court', *passim*.

[36] William Bedell to Samuel Ward, 26 Nov. 1604, undated, 14 Oct. 1604; Bodl., MS Tanner 75, fols. 129, 130v, 126.

[37] Lambeth Palace Library, MS 2550, fol. 59r.

[38] Fincham 1990; Collinson 1982.

[39] Milton 1995, pp. 13–27. The kind of case here argued in respect of Chaderton is proposed by Dr Anthony Milton for another leading Calvinist moderate and intellectual, Andrew Willet.

their spots. On the other hand, the re-invention of 'Puritanism' in order to catch within the anti-puritan net such under-the-skin dissidents would be criticised as 'modern puritanism' by sympathetic moderates such as that good Emmanuel man, Joseph Hall. We are referring to the 1620s and 1630s.[40]

In the later years of James I, and with the succession of Charles I, a new page was turned. Under William Laud and a new establishment sufficiently in tune with Laud's aspirations to be called Laudian, a new and more determined anti-Puritanism penetrated all over again the exposed, undefended under-belly of Chadertonian Puritanism. Chaderton's chickens were forced all over again to consider whether they were nonconformists or not, and where they and their ministry stood, vis à vis the Church of England by law established. One might say that the Emmanuel Trojan horse was rumbled; except that the discovery of subversive puritan dissidence within the horse's belly depended upon the typically Laudian perception that it was there to be rumbled, just as beds are made to conceal reds. By the time this happened, all too many of Emmanuel's Greek warriors had already left the horse's belly and had dispersed into the city. In counties like Essex, Suffolk and Northamptonshire, the Chadertonian strategy had so far succeeded in converting the Church to a moderate puritan model of evangelical and practical godliness, the golden prize snatched from the jaws of defeat in 1603–5, that it proved beyond the powers of the Laudians, more even than Charles I could hope to achieve, to convert it back again. To that extent, the description of the events of the mid-seventeenth century as a Puritan Revolution is correct, and the extreme moderate, Laurence Chaderton, was England's inadvertent revolutionary.

Emmanuel and the Godly Mafia[1]

A gentleman once told Richard Rogers, the Essex preacher who was one of the godfathers of our godly mafia: 'Mr Rogers, I like you and your company very well, but you are so precise. O Sir, said he, I serve a precise God.'[2] So far this history may have read like a piece of that revisionism which afflicts so much modern historiography, a corrosive process

---

[40] Fincham and Lake 1996.

[1] This chapter is much indebted to the Cambridge Ph.D. thesis by Tom Webster, 'The Godly of Goshen Scattered: An Essex Clerical Conference in the 1620s and Its Diaspora', 1993; and to his monograph, Webster 1997. I am grateful to Dr Webster for allowing me to consult his work.

[2] Firmin 1670, p. 67.

whereby familiar historical landmarks are removed and whole land-scapes wrecked, as if by a kind of anti-Capability Brown. This has happened to the English Reformation and to the English Revolution and the reader may think that Emmanuel College has now gone the same way. We have encountered more anti-heroes than saints and have shared in some pretty unedifying episodes, of which there will be more to come.

But in this section the balance will be redressed and we will bring back into the frame the Emmanuel of nobly pious tradition, a singular college which, in full accordance with its founder's wishes, sent out into the nation cohorts of godly preachers, men like Samuel Crook, the first Dixie fellow and then rector of the rural Somerset parish of Wrington for half a century. It was said that Crook was the first to have preached the Gospel in 'the whole country adjacent', discovering to the inhabitants 'the Heavenly Canaan which before was to most of them a *Terra incognita*.'[3]

These preachers, and especially those who settled closer to Emmanuel in Essex and neighbouring parts of Suffolk, brought a special quality to the ministry and religious life, a 'practical divinity' which was unique in Europe, let alone England, and which was to cross the Atlantic, with momentous consequences for world history: a living legend written in exemplary lives and then set in stone in Cotton Mather's Eusebian book about how America began, *Magnalia Christi Americana*.[4] This was the great oak tree which grew from Mildmay's acorn, in Mather's words, 'those blessed old planters which laid the foundations of a remarkable country'.[5]

In 1630 the Scottish ecumenical enthusiast John Dury arrived in England to further his plan for the ecclesiastical pacification of Protestant Europe, the reconciliation of Lutherans and Calvinists. Dury believed that England, and especially the county of Essex, possessed resources which, once communicated to other churches, would put an end to all 'needlesse controversies'. These were 'the Principles and Doctrines of Practical Divinitie, which were more distinctly and plainly delivered in those Churches of Great Britain then in all the rest of the Christian world besides.'[6] The plan was to reduce and translate this body of divinity into a compendious book which could be communicated to the neighbouring churches. But, unlike America, this was part of the Emmanuel legacy which was never delivered, thanks in part to the singularity of the divinity. As one of them wrote: 'The preaching eloquence of English

---

[3] Clarke 1677, p. 204.
[4] First published in 1702. I follow the third edition (Hartford, U.S.A., 1852) as reprinted by the Banner of Truth Trust, 1979.
[5] Mather 1852, p. 529.
[6] Thomas Hooker wrote to John Cotton from Rotterdam: 'The power of godliness for ought I can see or hear, they know not.' (Ibid., p. 340.)

divines is very hard to bee exprest. For they have made a new language as it were.[7] What was this new language, and who were these divines?

It is Emmanuel and Emmanuel men who will supply the answers. William Haller, in the most celebrated book on the subject, *The Rise of Puritanism* (1938), dated the rise of what he called 'a spiritual brotherhood' from the beginning of the reign of James I. That was a little late (we recall that Edward Dering, the prototypical puritan divine, had died thirty years earlier), and Haller seemed strangely unaware that this perspective owed much to the gathering of exemplary *Lives* of his brotherhood, derived from their funeral sermons, and that these were first collected for the generation leaving the university and entering the preaching ministry in the early 1600s, the first Emmanuel generation. The principal gatherer, who published large collections of these *Lives* later in the seventeenth century, the Old English counterpart to Mather's *Magnalia*, was himself an Emmanuel man (1617–1620), Samuel Clarke.[8]

Here we are concerned primarily with the godly Emmanuel mafia of 'painful preachers' which spread itself across Essex and its borders. Spread itself? Much of the spreading was done by the great patrons of godly religion in Essex, Robert Rich, second earl of Warwick (Emmanuel 1603) and his cousin Nathaniel Rich (Emmanuel 1601). (We shall meet Robert's brother Henry Rich, earl of Holland and chancellor of the university (Emmanuel 1603), in a later section.) Other influential patrons were the Barringtons of Hatfield Broadoak, clients and allies of the Riches. Warwick presented to no less than twenty-four Essex livings. These were godly friends as well as patrons.[9] The painful preachers included various members of the Rogers and Ward clans, all those confusing Johns, Nathaniels, Samuels and Daniels; together with Thomas Hooker, Thomas Shepard and Stephen Marshall; not forgetting John Cotton (Cotton Mather's grandfather), who was to make history in two Bostons, separated by 3,000 miles. With Cotton the exception to prove the geographical rule, these were the 'old Essex Christians' whom Giles Firmin (Emmanuel 1629) remembered with critical affection in his circumstantial, back-projected

---

[7] Webster 1997, Chapter 3, 'John Dury and the Godly Ministers', esp. pp. 259–60.

[8] Full references to Clarke's eight compilations, published between 1650 and 1683, will be found in my ' "A Magazine of Religious Patterns": An Erasmian Topic Transposed in English Protestantism', Collinson 1983, pp. 499–526. Clarke wrote to Thomas Hill, his contemporary at Emmanuel, who was later abortively elected master of Emmanuel but exchanged Emmanuel for Trinity: 'He was a great friend to the publication of the lives of Godly and eminent Ministers, and Christians, and assisting to me in procuring information concerning the Lives of some of those Worthies whom I have formerly printed.' (Clarke 1677, p. 234.)

[9] K. W. Shipps, 'Lay Patronage of East Anglian Puritan Clerics in Pre-Revolutionary England' (unpublished Yale University Ph.D. thesis, 1971); Hunt 1983, p. 104; Bremer 1994, pp. 43–6.

book *The Real Christian* (1670).[10] These were certainly almost dauntingly real Christians, alienated and self-excluded from the society and culture of most Englishmen of their generation: in the words of John Winthrop, the Suffolk gentleman who became the first governor of Massachusetts, 'despised, pointed at, hated of the world, made a byword, reviled, slandered, rebuked, made a gazing stock, called Puritans . . .'[11] The intensity of shared religious experience which was of the essence of Puritanism was both cause and effect of this alienation. So-called 'Puritans' most commonly called themselves 'Christians', but did so, like some modern Evangelicals, in a special and exclusive sense.[12]

In the first three decades of the seventeenth century, Essex, together with neighbouring parts of Suffolk, was turned into a kind of extension of Emmanuel, a constellation of townships penetrated and partly appropriated by the godly ministers, which became a spiritual laboratory and a refuge, or cave of Adullam. Later, in the 1630s, many of these ministers with 'companies' of their 'people', migrated 3,000 miles across the Atlantic in order to preserve and perpetuate their spiritual experience and their safety. We can trace more than one cord in the network of Essex godliness: in addition to the umbilical cord of Emmanuel, and the Emmanuel instinct for fellowship and conference, which became the habit of a lifetime's quest for spiritual assurance and professional fulfilment; the cord of kinship, the ties of blood relationship and marriage; and a spiritual affinity and genealogy of converting influences.

Let us begin with ties of blood of the kind which we have already encountered in exploring the extended kindred by marriage of Laurence Chaderton, the remarkable Culverwell connection.[13] 'Tribe' was a word often used of Puritans, pejoratively, but not unfairly. It is simplest to pick out first the clerical stem of Rogers and its side-shoots.[14] John Rogers, like his father before him, was a Chelmsford carpenter and joiner, whose plebeian genes seem to have been one of the determinants of the Rogers style of ministry. John's son Richard was at Christ's in the time of Dering and Chaderton, a little ahead of William Perkins. After an interesting episode as curate to the Elizabethan antiquarian William Harrison in the Essex parish of Radwinter, which introduced the older man to a new and

---

[10] See Susan Hardman Moore, 'Arguing for Peace: Giles Firmin on New England and Godly Unity', in *Unity and Diversity in the Church, Studies in Church History*, 32, ed. R. N. Swanson (Oxford, 1996), pp. 251–61.

[11] Quoted, Bremer 1994, p. 41.

[12] Hunt 1983, p. 91.

[13] See above, pp. 33–5.

[14] See M. M. Knappen's Introduction to *Two Elizabethan Puritan Diaries*, Knappen 1933. The wills of Richard Rogers and John Rogers are printed in *The New England Historical and Genealogical Register*, 17 (1863), 326–30.

more dynamic pastoral style[15], Rogers settled as a lecturer at Wethersfield, near Braintree, and spent the rest of his life there, perhaps forty years, the ancientest of the ancient Essex ministers. His brother John remained a Chelmsford tradesman, like his father and grandfather, but sent his son, another John, helped and encouraged by Uncle Richard, to Emmanuel which he entered as a sizar in 1588. John Rogers was to be lecturer of Dedham, in the Stour valley, for more than thirty years (1605–1637), one of the most 'powerful' and histrionic of seventeenth-century preachers. Students would make the journey from Cambridge, 'to get a little fire'.[16] John's son Nathaniel Rogers (Emmanuel 1614) preached from a number of Essex and Suffolk pulpits before leaving for New England in 1636, taking with him yet another John Rogers, his son, who would become president of Harvard, and whose three sons and three grandsons all became New England ministers.[17]

We return to Richard Rogers of Wethersfield, famous as a pioneering puritan diarist and author of the most influential of all works of practical divinity, *Seven Treatises* (editions 1602, 1604, 1605, 1610, 1616, 1627, 1630). Richard's eldest son was Daniel, who followed his father to Christ's and would later become in his turn lecturer at Wethersfield. Daniel's son Samuel (Emmanuel 1629) we shall soon meet as another puritan minister-diarist.[18] Daniel's younger brother Ezekiel Rogers (M.A. Christ's, 1604) became chaplain to the Barringtons at Hatfield Broadoak, was placed by them in the living of Rowley in Yorkshire, and, after a ministry in the spectacular Rogers style, in 1639 took himself and the place-name of Rowley to New England.[19] Richard Rogers had married the widow of a pioneer of Elizabethan Puritanism, John Ward, preacher at Haverhill in Suffolk. Ward's three sons, Rogers's step-sons, all became ministers: Samuel (not to be confused with Samuel Ward of Sidney Sussex) was a famous town preacher at Ipswich for thirty-four years; John Ward (Emmanuel 1610) was rector of Dennington, Suffolk; and Nathaniel

---

[15] This is the discovery, so far unpublished, of Dr Glyn Parry of the Victoria University of Wellington, New Zealand.

[16] John Howe, *Works* (London, 1834), VI, 493. Oliver Heywood's Life of John Angier, a Dedham boy who became a preacher in Lancashire, records some details of Rogers's remarkable pulpit style, such as 'his taking hold with both hands of the Canopy of the Pulpit, and roaring hideously, to represent the torments of the damned', which 'had an awakening force attending to it.' (*Oliver Heywood's Life of John Angier of Denton*, ed. E. Axon, Chetham Society New Series 97 (1937), p. 50.)

[17] Mather 1852, pp. 414–22.

[18] Of his demanding, somewhat melancholic father, Samuel wrote: 'I will looke up to see if by the eye of faith I can discerne the bowells of my fathers love, under an angry countenance.' (Queen's University Belfast, Percy MS 7, fol. 210, a reference I owe to Kenneth Shipps and Tom Webster.)

[19] Mather 1852, pp. 408–13. Ezekiel Rogers's letters to Lady Joan Barrington are in *Barrington Family Letters*, ed. Arthur Searle, Camden 4th ser. 28 (1983), pp. 128–30, 167–8, 225–6.

(Emmanuel 1596) was rector of Stondon Massey in Essex until his departure in 1637 for New England, where he wrote a celebrated satire, *The Simple Cobbler of Aggawam* (the Indian name for Ipswich, Massachusetts). Nathaniel's son John Ward (Emmanuel 1622) followed him in 1639.[20] Nathaniel's daughter married Giles Firmin (Emmanuel 1629), whom Daniel Rogers called 'cousin',[21] and Firmin was the source of numerous Rogers and Ward anecdotes in his book *The Real Christian*. It is not possible to plug Thomas Hooker, Thomas Shepard and Stephen Marshall, the remaining great names in the Emmanuel-Essex story, into the Rogers-Ward cousinage. But Marshall was Richard Rogers's immediate successor at Wethersfield; while Hooker 'grew into a most intimate acquaintance with Mr Rogers at Dedham', and called him 'the prince of all the preachers in England'. His first published work was an Introduction to John Rogers's influential *The Doctrine of Faith* (1629).[22] Shepard married Hooker's daughter. Shepard and Firmin were both taught at a famous puritan academy run at Felstead, under the benevolent eye of the Riches, by Martin Holbech, who also taught Chaderton's (and the Culverwells') nephew William Gouge, as well as four sons of Oliver Cromwell. (Samuel Hartlib noted that Holbech 'hath sent forth many hundreds of converted soules by the way of schooling'.) Ezekiel Culverwell was Richard Rogers's closest friend.[23]

So much for the bloodstock. But water (so to speak), that is, the spirit, was thicker than blood. Indeed, blood counted for little where there was no spiritual affinity. Puritan writers taught their readers not to rely upon 'carnall friends', but on 'godly men, for they will proove our surest friends. Vicinitie and neighbourhood will faile, and alliance and kindred will faile, but grace and religion will never faile.' When it came to charity, charity did not begin at home. According to the London preacher, John Downame, we are to prefer 'our spiritual kindred' before 'those who are only a kinne unto us in the flesh'.[24]

Within our godly mafia, spiritual kinship was a matter of father to son relationships. We might say, in biblical language, that Richard Rogers begat Paul Baynes, who begat Richard Sibbes, who, with William Perkins, begat John Cotton, who begat John Preston, who begat Thomas Shepard,

---

[20] Mather 1852, I, pp. 521–5. For Samuel Ward of Ipswich, see Collinson 1982, pp. 175–7.

[21] Firmin 1670, Epistle.

[22] Webster 1993, p. 112; A. R. Pennie, 'The Evolution of Puritan Mentality in an Essex Cloth Town: Dedham and the Stour Valley 1560–1640', unpublished Ph.D., University of Sheffield, 1991, chapter 4, ' "God's Counsell and the Narrow Way". Spiritual Warfare Divinity in Dedham and Essex, 1600–40'; Bush 1980, p. 31.

[23] Webster 1997, pp. 13, 33, 136; Sheffield University Library, Hartlib MS 28/1/15B.

[24] John Dod and Robert Cleaver, quoted in Collinson 1983, p. 547; John Downame, *The plea of the poore* (1616), p. 133.

and so on.[25] According to Mather, the preaching of Perkins had so stung the conscience of Cotton that when the great man died in 1602 (a little before Cotton's migration from Trinity to Emmanuel) 'his mind secretly rejoiced' to hear the bell toll. But the influence of Sibbes soon made him 'a thoroughly renewed Christian'. Cotton's conversion altered the preaching style of one of Cambridge's budding rhetoricians. A surprisingly 'plain' sermon of 'over-arching gravity and Majesty' so affected John Preston, then a fellow of Queens', that 'pierced at the heart' he came knocking on Cotton's door, just as Hugh Latimer had come to Thomas Bilney's rooms in Trinity Hall, eighty years before, to 'hear his confession'.[26] At first, 'few knew how Master *Cottons* Sermon' had wrought upon this ambitious academic and courtier. But no-one was destined to have more spiritual progeny, pupils and clients, than the mature Preston, Chaderton's successor as master of Emmanuel. And, as with Chaderton, the young preachers emerging from Emmanuel were so many godly chess-pieces, carefully placed on the board by Preston, who liaised closely with local puritan networks.

In both university and country, the intensely shared experience of conversion and the relentless struggle for assurance of salvation and spiritual growth which followed initial conversion spun tight webs of mutual recognition and dependence which excluded the unconverted. Preston's pupil Thomas Cawton (by reputation an ultra-Puritan) made sure that his own pupils should not become 'intangled or infected with bad company'.[27] The spiritual networks connected admired preachers and teachers in Cambridge and the country, especially in the accessible country of Essex and East Anglia. If the country ministers regularly returned to Cambridge to recharge their batteries, especially at the seasonal reunions of Commencement and Stourbridge Fair, young scholars, still finding their spiritual and career path, sought inspiration from the Rogers powerhouses of Dedham and Wethersfield. As the old standards threatened to slip in the university, the older men in the country considered themselves guardians of traditional godliness.[28]

---

[25] See, for example, the Life of Sibbes: 'It pleased God to convert him by the Ministry of Master *Paul Baines*.' (Clarke 1677, p. 143.) Baynes was the natural successor to Perkins, as fellow of Christ's and as lecturer at St Andrew's church. For Preston's effect on Shepard, see McGiffert 1972, pp. 41, 45, 47, 53. Shepard wrote that Preston's first sermon as master of Emmanuel 'so bored my ears as that I understood what he spake and the secrets of my soul were laid open befor me ... I thought he was the most searching preacher in the world.' See also Mather 1852, pp. 380–1.

[26] Ibid., pp. 252–6; Ziff 1962, pp. 18–33; Bremer 1994, pp. 30–1; Clarke 1677, pp. 79, 218–19. For the Bilney-Latimer story, see Porter 1958, p. 44.

[27] Webster 1997, p. 21. See also *DNB*, art. Cawton. Frank Bremer writes of a rediscovery of the communion of saints, with 'saints' exclusively defined; according to Paul Baynes 'a point of practice, as well as an article of belief'. (Bremer 1994, pp. xii, 5–6.)

[28] Mather 1852, pp. 302–20. John Wilson made a 'pilgrimage' to Richard Rogers at

Until the nineteenth century, there were almost no institutional seminaries (or 'theological colleges') for the professional formation of the Anglican ministry. Neither a university degree nor even three or four years' immersion in a college like Emmanuel added up to a pastoral qualification. But in puritan East Anglia a regular practice was established of training young preachers in the households of older and more experienced men. This was made a rule and obligation by the ministers who met for conference in and around Dedham in the 1580s.[29] There were household seminaries at Richard Greenham's parish of Dry Drayton, just outside Cambridge, and later at Barking in south Essex, where Alexander Richardson taught Thomas Hooker and the great William Ames. The most celebrated of these establishments was conducted at Ashen on the Suffolk–Essex border by Richard Blackerby, who took in 'divers young students', and gave them 'excellent advice for Learning, Doctrine and Life'. Such was Blackerby's charisma that it was said that even Rogers of Dedham could not enter his presence 'without some kind of trembling upon him; because of the Divine Majesty and Holiness' which seemed to shine within him. Mather called him 'Saint Blackerby'.[30] Blackerby's (informal) successor was Thomas Hooker, who in the years around 1630 was described as the 'oracle' of the younger Essex ministers in cases of conscience and points of divinity, and their 'principal library'. Like the 'practical divinity' itself, these teachers became internationally known and attracted a number of Dutch and other foreign students, who were 'finished' in these little seminaries as a twentieth-century engineer might make tracks for the Massachusetts Institute of Technology.[31]

But to seek out the most influential of all 'oracles' it was necessary to turn one's back on Essex and set out for Boston in Lincolnshire and John Cotton. John Preston used to advise his 'near fledg'd Pupils' to 'go live with Mr Cotton', so that it became almost a proverb, 'Mr Cotton was Dr Preston's seasoning vessell.' Cotton taught two future grandees of puritan Cambridge, Anthony Tuckney, fifth master of Emmanuel, and Thomas Hill, translated from Emmanuel to the master's lodge at Trinity.

Wethersfield. A generation later, Thomas Goodwin, Jeremiah Burroughes and William Bridges, who had 'travelled from Cambridge into Essex, on purpose to observe the Ministers in that Country', were impressed with John Wilson's lecture at Sudbury, while John Rogers's electrifying performance at Dedham convinced Goodwin of the virtues of 'powerful preaching'. Goodwin found that 'to those that came not early there was no possibility of getting room in that spacious large church'. (Bremer 1994, p. 39; Webster 1997, pp. 22–3.) On the anxiety expressed by Rogers on developments in Cambridge, see pp. 221–2 below.

[29] R. G. Usher, ed., *The Presbyterian Movement in the Reign of Queen Elizabeth as Illustrated by the Minute Book of the Dedham Classis* 1582–89, Camden 3rd ser. 8 (1905), p. 93; Collinson 1982, pp. 118–19; Webster 1997, pp. 23–35; Morgan 1986, pp. 293–300.

[30] Mather 1852, pp. 334, 336, 434; Samuel Clarke, *The Lives of Sundry Eminent Persons* (London, 1683), p. 58; Webster 1997, pp. 31–2.

[31] Mather 1852, p. 336; Webster 1997, pp. 24, 27.

Oracles also received and wrote letters. Cotton's first biographer, a fellow New England migrant, wrote that 'he answered many letters that were sent far and near, wherein were handled many difficult cases of conscience, and many doubts by him cleared to the greatest satisfaction'. One of Cotton's quondam students, by then a domestic chaplain in a Lincolnshire gentry family, wrote (in 1626) to ask advice about card-playing, mixed dancing and the drawing of names for Valentines 'so they terme it'. Cotton could not approve carding and Valentines, but allowed some sorts of dancing while not permitting 'lascivious dauncinge to wanton dittyes'.[32]

The formal 'exercises' for pious and aspiring students of divinity instituted by Chaderton even before Emmanuel began[33] seem to have been kept alive from generation to generation. In 1634 the Emmanuel student Samuel Rogers (grandson of Richard and son of Daniel) noted that 'a companye of us have ioined together to meet often to pray together and discourse', under the supervision of his tutor.[34] Prayer and discourse was regularly intensified by the practice of fasting, a distinctive puritan institution which entailed not only personal self-discipline but a prolonged and shared exposure to preaching and extempore prayer, often related to a perceived crisis or some pressing choice or decision.[35] In December 1624 such a fast was held at the home of the Barringtons at Hatfield Broadoak, with the preaching entrusted to John Preston and the newly promoted archbishop of Armagh, James Ussher. The Barringtons' chaplain observed that fasts were called for 'when great things are undertaken, when any judgment is imminent, . . . when the Church is in danger and when affliction is upon the Church'. Among other matters discussed at Hatfield Broadoak was the professional placement of Thomas Hooker.[36] Preston had asked Ussher some years earlier: 'What say you to Mr Hookers; his employment is too narrow here, and not adequate to his parts.'[37]

The location of preaching ministers was a principal concern of the semi-official ministerial conferences which began in the eastern counties no later than the 1580s, when such a conference met in and around Dedham in the Stour valley and kept minutes of its proceedings. It was 'conference' which 'settled' Stephen Marshall at Finchingfield, releasing the lectureship at Wethersfield for Daniel Rogers, the son of Richard; and Thomas Shepard at Earls Colne rather than Coggeshall, a matter

---

[32] Ibid., pp. 259–60; Sargent Bush, Jr., 'Epistolary Counselling in the Puritan Movement: The Example of John Cotton', in Bremer 1993, pp. 127–46.

[33] See pp. 50–2 above.

[34] Queen's University Belfast, MS Percy 7, fols. 15, 22. I owe this reference to Kenneth Shipps and Tom Webster.

[35] On the Elizabethan roots of the puritan fast, see Collinson 1967, pp. 214–19; and on fasts in early seventeenth-century Essex, Webster 1997, pp. 9–14, 60–73.

[36] Ibid., pp. 9–13.

[37] Ibid., p. 10.

determined 'amongst those worthies in Essex where we had monthly fasts.' It was Hooker who thought Shepard too inexperienced for Coggeshall, 'a great town'. Shepard had been trained at Terling under Thomas Weld (soon to leave for New England), and was a member of Hooker's Chelmsford conference. The Earls Colne people came to Terling 'where the ministers met' to secure Shepard's appointment, approved by the ministers 'with one joint consent'. Shepard wrote: 'And thus I ... was called out by twelve or sixteen ministers of Christ ... The Lord sent me to the best county in England, *viz.* to Essex, and set me in the midst of the best ministry in the country, by whose monthly fasts and conferences I found much of God.'[38]

According to the laws and canons of the Church of England, such matters should have been 'settled' differently, by bishops. So ecclesiastical historians have understandably regarded these networks and conferences as experiments in presbyterianism, a deliberate challenge to the established constitution of the Church. While it would be innocent to suppose that Puritanism of this kind offered no threat to the ecclesiastical *status quo* and no response to a threatening conformist establishment (the history of the 1640s suggests otherwise) there is little evidence that the networks and meetings of the early seventeenth century took shape in response to some ecclesiological dogma about the ministry and discipline of the Church. These were not (yet) 'Presbyterians' and 'Congregationalists'.

It is more likely that the whole complex engine of puritan godliness and edification, the dynamo of our 'godly mafia', was an urgent and shared concern with the saving of souls, not least the souls of those charged with the ministry of saving others. In 1632 Ezekiel Rogers wrote to his patron, Lady Barrington: 'I much advise you to seeke helpe by the communion of the saintes.'[39]

What kind of help was needed? William Perkins, the taproot of so much of this anxious, exacting religiosity, had written of the greatest case of conscience of all: how a man might know that he was of God's Elect. And to be one of the Elect was to be separated from a reprobate world which one preacher defined as 'a sea of glasse, a pageant of foolish delight, a Theatre of vanitie, a labyrynth of error, a gulf of griefe, a stie of filthiness' – and so on, for some lines.[40]

Perkins's question was either unanswerable, or, since it could only be answered by the power of faith and not reason, the presence or absence of true faith being the heart of the problem, answerable in so many ways that it led to endless debate and individual soul-searching about the

---

[38] Webster 1997, pp. 38–9; Tom Webster, *Stephen Marshall and Finchingfield* (Chelmsford, 1994); Bremer 1994, p. 59; Mather 1852, p. 382; McGiffert 1972, pp. 46–7.

[39] Barrington 1983, p. 226. Webster 1997, chs. 2, 6.

[40] Quoted, Morgan 1986, p. 21.

order and significance of the various stages in the process of salvation: even whether they were temporally related stages at all. Perkins had provided a 'practical syllogism': 'Everyone that beleeves is a child of God: but I do beleeve: Therefore I am the child of God.' But how do I *know* that I believe? How can I be sure that my faith is not temporary, or counterfeit?[41]

It would not be appropriate, in the context of a college history, to even attempt to unravel this tangled skein, although it was the very rationale for our college's existence. It is sufficient to report that, from the evidence of the self-monitoring of spiritual states which we find in puritan diaries, letters and other personal records, such questions were not easily resolved, and perhaps seldom resolved once for all. So to talk, as we have done, about personal 'conversions' may mislead. If John Cotton was 'converted' at Emmanuel, it was not until some years later, and as an already famous minister at Boston, and it was his wedding day, that he received assurance of God's love and forgiveness. And we have no reason to believe that that was the end of the matter.[42] It is also a mistake to suppose that the spiritual athleticism of puritan religion turned on the single point, or problem, of predestination. If it had been possible to prove an effectual calling beyond all possible doubt, the result would not have been a happy relaxation of spiritual endeavour.[43]

Consequently we find some of the leading athletes living (as St Paul, after all, told them they should) an incessant spiritual warfare, struggling every day until their last for proven godliness, suspecting in themselves the opposite, godlessness. A middle-aged Thomas Shepard, years after his Emmanuel conversion and by now a founding father of Harvard College, could write in his Journal: 'the Lord let me see I was nothing else but a mass of sin and that all that I did was very vile'; 'I saw how I was without all sense as well as sight of God, estranged from the life of God'; 'I saw my soul . . . in a manner, as good as in hell'; 'I felt a wonderful cloud of darkness and atheism over my head'; 'I considered the evil (1) of my ministry, (2) of my Christianity'; 'I saw God was gone . . . no faith; knew not what it was'. These entries run from 1641 to 1643, when Shepard was approaching forty, had less than ten years to live, and had been a minister for fifteen years or so. The editor of his Journal comments that through it his suspicions of his own hypocrisy 'run like threads of

---

[41] Kendall 1979, p. 71 and *passim*.

[42] Mather 1852, p. 258.

[43] It is a fundamental error of Kendall's *Calvin and English Calvinism to 1649* (Oxford, 1979), and an imbalance in many other accounts of puritan divinity, to exaggerate the centrality in puritan religious experience of predestinarian dogma. See forthcoming work by Jason Yiannikkou of Queens' College Cambridge. On the evidence of 'puritan' diaries and their introspective religiosity, see Tom Webster, 'Writing to Redundancy: Approaches to Spiritual Journals and Early Modern Spirituality', *Historical Journal*, 39 (1996), 33–56.

fire'. His perception of his hypocrisy was perhaps itself hypocritical, destroying any cognitive basis of assurance.[44]

The diary of Samuel Rogers, a Rogers of the third generation, monitored his erratic spiritual progress in a spirit no less negative, conforming, the cynic might think, to a kind of literary convention. We may quote one entry: 'Sweetly touched by Mr [Stephen] Marshalls sermon but readye to drop againe, I have need of continual underproppings, to hold up my tottering soule.'[45]

Giles Firmin, who entered Emmanuel in 1629, published in 1670 a brilliant critique of this divinity, in his book called *The Real Christian*, addressed to 'they that read our English practical divines'. Firmin identified Hooker, Shepard and Daniel Rogers as those who by their writings had 'caused the most trouble', trouble which could be traced back to Perkins and John Rogers. The 'trouble' was that the insistence of these writers on 'preparation' had brought their readers into a state of almost incurable doubt about the validity of their own faith. Firmin was afraid to read Daniel Rogers and Shepard. God had handled Rogers 'strangely' and he had failed to find 'full assurance'. Nathaniel Rogers had differed from his father John Rogers on these matters, publicly dissenting from the pulpit. His father 'stood by and heard him with great attention, the people, they heard him with some amazement'.

Shepard wrote to Firmin urging a preaching which would humiliate the hearers. 'If Axes and Wedges withall be not used to humiliate and breake this rough, unhewn, bold, yet professing Age', the fruit of all their ministry would be 'mere hypocrisy'. Firmin thought that if Rogers had been in St Paul's shoes when the Philippian jailor asked what he must do to be saved, he would have confronted him with 'harsh conditions'. Firmin knew of a maid-servant who was so cast down by one of Shepard's books 'that all the Christians that came to her could not quiet her spirit'. He had met people who could not be resolved that their faith was true because of what Daniel Rogers had written. Of the little flock of Christ, and Firmin was in no doubt that it was a very small flock indeed, many would sit down dismayed, unable to go the pace their shepherds drove them.[46]

Was this no more than a caricature? A letter to the progressive puritan projector Samuel Hartlib from Thomas Goodwin (another very famous divine) appears to confirm Firmin's judgment: 'Hooker is a severe and crule man like John Baptist, urges too much and too farre the Worke of

---

[44] McGiffert 1972, pp. 88, 98, 133, 135, 143–5, 210, 18. Shepard was perhaps an exceptional case. When his religious conscience was first aroused he became suicidal. 'I had some strong temptations to run my head against walls and brain and kill myself.' (Ibid., p. 43.) See also Webster 1997, pp. 111–12, 122.

[45] I owe this (unfoliated) extract from Rogers's diary to the kindness of Dr Webster.

[46] Firmin 1670, *passim*.

Humiliation.'[47] Modern scholarly opinion is divided over something which in the nature of things is unknowable: whether Emmanuel-style practical divinity induced an almost chronic anxiety, even a state of despair, or a calm, settled, if strenuous assurance of spiritual safety (we dare not say 'security' which was a negative, loaded word in this religious discourse, full of spiritual peril). On the one hand John Stachniewski has written an account of *The Persecutory Imagination*, sub-titled *English Puritans and the Literature of Religious Despair* (1991). He opens with a quotation from Professor Blair Worden: 'The volume of despair engendered by Puritan teaching on predestination is incalculable.' On the other, we have Charles Cohen's *God's Caress: the Psychology of Puritan Religious Experience* (1986). Cohen agrees that Puritans 'excelled at dissecting the psychology of religious experience' (p. 9). But Cohen's Puritans were able 'to transform a weakling into a dynamo' (pp. 272–3). The Saints had a renewed sense of spiritual self-worth which had a huge potential for political and social activism. Another student of the subject remarks, simply: 'Godliness worked.'[48] What, how and why it worked occupied the mind of the great German social thinker, Max Weber.[49]

What need not be in doubt is that individual self-worth, often caricatured in accounts of protestant and puritan religion as 'individualism', depended critically on the fellowship of the holy huddle. Francis Bremer has written perceptively of the especial importance of social reinforcement for religious ideas which by their very nature do not lend themselves to empirical verification.[50] The young Samuel Rogers fantasised in the 1630s about going to New England (it was no more than a fantasy for him, since his father, Daniel Rogers, strongly opposed it). Dr Tom Webster, editor of Rogers's Diary, finds that Rogers's dream had little to do with either 'persecution' or a preference for Congregationalism as a way of constituting the Church. It had everything to do with saving his own soul. For it was New England where Rogers could hope to find that critical godly mass in which his deep religious fears might be assuaged. 'I sigh after N. E.: and the more I thinke of that, I thinke I find the more of God.'[51]

---

[47] Sheffield University Library, Hartlib MS 29/2/56A. Richard Rogers had observed: 'Blessed is the man the feareth always.' (Quoted, Hunt 1983, p. 122.)

[48] Ibid., p. 129.

[49] Max Weber, *The Protestant Ethic and the Spirit of Capitalism*, tr. Talcott Parsons (London, 1991: most recent edn.) – and an apparently endless flow of derivative literature.

[50] Bremer 1994, pp. 11–12.

[51] Webster 1997, pp. 281–5. Dr Webster will publish an edition of Rogers's Diary in the Church of England Record Society series, utilising earlier work on the text by Dr Kenneth Shipps, who was the first to discover and make use of a manuscript acquired by the Queen's University Belfast in the 1960s.

The Anti-Calvinist Reaction and Odium Theologicum

In Emmanuel's early years, a crack began to appear in the façade, if not the edifice, of Elizabethan Protestantism, a small fissure which can be seen as a reaction against the Reformed or 'Calvinist' orthodoxy which had hitherto formally, and even actually, prevailed in the church and nation; or as developing tensions within that tradition itself; or, a very different perception, as the reassertion of older religious habits of mind and behaviour, rather as ancient features of a building will begin to reveal themselves from behind a superficial layer of stucco. The issue, whether there ever was a kind of Calvinist consensus, rather than an Anglican compromise to which Calvinism had always been alien and marginal, continues to divide religious historians of the period.[1]

For much of the reign of James I, Emmanuel's heyday, the cracks were papered over, which may be to undervalue that monarch's capacity to play the broad middle ground against the narrower extremes and to hold the ring,[2] deliberately entertaining and hearing preachers of both or all tendencies in his Chapel Royal,[3] just as he aspired to hold the ring on a larger scale, a royal ecumenist in religiously divided Europe.[4] Under James's successor, religious division became more pronounced, harder to contain, impossible to suppress. Again, historians cannot agree whether these conflicts, which were proleptic to the greater conflict of the Civil War, were inevitable, written, as it were, into the script, or should be laid at the door of Charles I, or of his archbishop of Canterbury, William Laud. And if blame is to be attached, contingently, to Charles or to Laud, what kind of blame, what degree of responsibility, are we talking about? Was Laud provoked by the Puritans, or was he himself provocative? Are the momentous events of the 1640s, which brought Laud to the scaffold, to be understood as religious revolution, or as counter-revolution (or, more plausibly, partaking of both)? Were Laud's puritan enemies conservative defenders of a status quo which novel Laudian courses had disturbed, needlessly, or radical innovators who, like Samson in Gaza, wilfully pulled the temple down around their ears? Did Laud ruin the Church of England, or only fail to save it?[5]

---

[1] On the one hand, Tyacke 1990, Peter Lake, 'Calvinism and the English Church, 1570–1635', *Past and Present*, no. 114 (1987), 32–76, Lake 1995; on the other, White 1992, Kevin Sharpe, *The Personal Rule of Charles I* (New Haven, 1992), Bernard 1990.
I am grateful for Arnold Hunt's critical comments on this section.
[2] Fincham and Lake 1985; Fincham and Lake 1993.
[3] McCullough 1998.
[4] Patterson 1997.
[5] Tyacke 1973; Collinson 1982; Kevin Sharpe, 'Archbishop Laud and the University of

Already the reader has had more than enough of metaphors, but let us add one more. Historians of the English religious scene between, say, 1590 and 1640 are playing three-dimensional, even multi-dimensional chess. This was not a simple matter of church parties, as in the Victorian age, Evangelical, Catholic, Broad. There were parties, or at least more or less organised bodies of opinion. But the polemical need to deny flagrant partisanship, and to head for the safe middle ground, meant that all positions were more or less nuanced and moderated. Calvinism and Anticalvinism may have been the underlying rationale, but the surface appearance was more complicated.[6] Ordinary church-goers were not supposed to know that such differences existed, and the overwhelming evidence of the thousands of catechisms from which they were instructed is that, indeed, such things were not much discussed in front of the children: which is not to say that the underlying and implied orthodoxy was not, if you will, Calvinist.[7]

And then there was the royal interest, which arguably was, and always had been, paramount, for the rock on which the Church of England was built, quite literally an alternative foundation to St Peter, was the crown.[8] Moreover, the Church of England was one of a family of churches in all of which the crown had an interest, which it assumed to be a controlling interest, although this was contested, especially in Scotland. If historians can agree on one thing, it is that it was Charles I's attempt to impose a new and essentially Anglican model on Scotland which fatally destabilised church and state in England; and that even then it would not have come to civil war in England if there had been no Ireland, where the established Church was weak and ineffective and the majority of the population Catholic.[9]

But we have hardly begun. The British monarchies and churches were part of a Europe in which religious differences were a constituent of almost endemic conflict, both within and between states, especially after the outbreak of the Thirty Years War in 1618. James I's diplomacy, which was conducted, in traditional style, by means of dynastic marriages and proposals of marriage, was meant to help the cause of peace, but led to an

---

Oxford', in Hugh Lloyd Jones *et al.*, eds., *History and Imagination: Essays in Honour of H. R. Trevor-Roper* (London, 1981), pp. 146–64; Davies 1992.

[6] The issue runs through the studies listed in n.1 above, to which add Tyacke 1993, Lake, 'The Laudian Style: Order, Uniformity and the Pursuit of Beauty and Holiness in the 1630s', Fincham 1993, pp. 161–85; and Andrew Foster 'The Clerical Estate Revitalised', in Collinson 1995.

[7] Ian Green, *The Christian's ABC: Catechisms and Catechizing in England c.1530–1740* (Oxford, 1996).

[8] Bernard 1990.

[9] Peter Donald, *An Uncounselled King: Charles I and the Scottish Troubles 1637–1641* (Cambridge, 1990); Conrad Russell, *The Causes of the English Civil War* (Oxford, 1990); Russell 1991; J. S. Morrill, *The Nature of the English Civil War* (London, 1993).

involvement in continental conflicts which was full of contradictions and a major cause of domestic division and instability. Increasingly, it became an issue whether the Church of England regarded Roman Catholics as the opposite of Christians, with the Pope Antichrist, or as fellow Christians with whom Protestants had serious and justified differences.[10] Nor was this a remote and theoretical problem, safely distanced behind the fog which so often isolated the Continent. There were plenty of English Catholics, some of them in positions of power and responsibility. Even James I's queen, Anne of Denmark, was discreetly catholic. In the 1620s, England was threatened with one catholic queen (Spanish) and got another (French). The mother of the royal favourite, George Villiers, duke of Buckingham, was only one of many notable converts to Rome. The membrane between catholic and protestant was very permeable.[11] But how were Catholics ('papists') to be defined, or recognised? For every Catholic who 'outed', many more remained within the closet.[12] The greyness of a religious landscape which two or three generations of Protestants had been taught to see in black and white was a cause of deep anxiety and insecurity. To undermine the Calvinist doctrine of predestinate grace by suggesting that free will could have anything to do with salvation, or to exalt in worship the ceremonialism which Archbishop Laud called 'the beauty of holiness', was suspected as covert popery: and anti-popery was the strongest of all political emotions, throughout the seventeenth century.[13]

We have now begun to address the issues. The religions of Europe in 1600 were shaped in contradistinction to their opposites. The religion of the English Church as publicly stated and defended was defined by its denial of Catholicism, the only subject on which its clergy were legally obliged to preach.[14] Leaving aside the papacy, to which royal supremacy was sufficient response, English Protestants affirmed salvation by faith alone, the logical corollary of which was denial of free will and affirmation of predestination, with salvation intended only for the elect. Whether or not we talk of 'Calvinism' (and purists are aware of good reasons why we should not),[15] this was at the formal heart of much of

---

[10] Milton 1995.

[11] Michael C. Questier, *Conversion, Politics and Religion in England, 1580–1625* (Cambridge, 1996).

[12] Alexandra Walsham, *Church Papists: Catholicism, Conformity and Confessional Polemic in Early Modern England* (London, 1993).

[13] Peter Lake, 'Anti-Popery: the Structure of a Prejudice', in Cust and Hughes 1989, pp. 72–106; Jonathan Scott, 'England's Troubles: Exhuming the Popish Plot', in M. Goldie *et al.*, eds., *The Politics of Religion in Restoration England* (Oxford, 1990), pp. 107–31.

[14] This was the subject prescribed for quarterly sermons in the Royal Injunctions of 1559, which may have lapsed but were never rescinded.

[15] Seán Hughes, 'The Problem of "Calvinism" in the Elizabethan and Stuart Church of England', in Wabuda and Litzenberger 1998, pp. 229–49.

European Protestantism, denying the whole religious economy of good and pious works, including the invocation of saints and the doctrine and practice of eucharistic sacrifice, the Mass. It is a serious mistake to suppose that Protestants, if you will Calvinists, were indifferent to the sacraments, as if they had room only for sermons.[16] But they were nervous about any attempt to sever sacrament from word, or to reinstate the catholic altar (rather than the holy table, 'God's board'), or to exalt it above the pulpit. 'Ceremony' was a word with mostly negative connotations.

In the perception of many contemporaries, and of some historians, differences over the theology of grace were the fundamental rationale of the tensions and conflicts which began to appear in the higher echelons of English Protestantism, and especially in the universities, from the 1590s onwards.[17] A number of theological milestones punctuated the decades which followed, occasions when it could be said of both Calvinists and their opponents what visitors to the Jardin des Plantes were warned: 'This animal is wicked. When it is attacked, it defends itself.' In 1595 and 1596 the wicked animals in Cambridge were a majority of Calvinist doctors and heads of houses, including Laurence Chaderton and mar-shalled by his brother-in-law, William Whitaker of St John's, confronting some individuals whose views from the Calvinist point of view were sub-versive of the very title deeds of faith, and in some respects anticipated those soon associated with the Dutch theologian, Jacobus Arminius. The outcome for Calvinist orthodoxy was unfortunate. Archbishop Whitgift, having been persuaded to publish his Lambeth Articles, which for the most part upheld the Calvinist position, found that he had acted *ultra vires* and that the Articles could not be enforced.[18] Subsequent attempts to give the Lambeth Articles the status of orthodoxy failed and there remained a dangerous area of doctrinal greyness. Nevertheless, a spectrum of broadly Calvinist doctrine was apparently the strongest tendency in the early Stuart Church, and enjoyed the approval of James I, who sent an English delegation to the Synod of Dort (1618–19), called to resolve a major religious and political crisis in the Netherlands. The English delegates took up a moderate Calvinist position, its moderation designed to protect upholders of this orthodoxy from charges of extremism. We are talking about the fine distinction between grace sufficient for salvation (unrestricted – 'for all') and efficacious grace (restricted – 'for some'). These were not inconsistent concepts, but the distinction allowed for

---

[16] Arnold Hunt, 'The Lord's Supper in Early Modern England', *Past and Present*, no. 161 (1998), 39–83.

[17] The view especially of Tyacke. See above, n.1.

[18] Lake 1982, pp. 201–42, refines and corrects the argument of Porter 1958, pp. 314–90.

divisive differences of emphasis.[19] Cambridge in the second decade of the seventeenth century was still a Calvinist stronghold.[20] But in the early 1620s, Richard Montague, in a double-bladed attack on both Catholics and 'Puritans', denied that what had been defined and defended at Dort was the doctrine of the Church of England. The *furore* over 'Arminianism' which ensued led, early in the reign of Charles I, to the York House Conference, where John Preston played an important if mysterious role.[21] The outcome of York House was that the king and his favourite the duke of Buckingham soon indicated their preference for Arminian doctrine. By 1630 public debate about these matters, for example, in university disputations and sermons, was forbidden, and the effect of these orders was not neutral but came close to making Anticalvinism the new orthodoxy.

For other historians, the issue of predestination was only one of a number of fault lines running through the English Church. If 'Arminianism' seemed to be the burning issue of the 1620s it was no longer such a prominent concern in the 1630s. It has been rightly said that the Civil War was not a war about predestination and was not fought between Calvinists and Arminians.[22] If Archbishop Laud was an Arminian, he concealed that fact with a good deal of success.[23] Laud's agenda had more to do with the enforcement of ceremonial uniformity, both a novel enforcement of old but widely disregarded ceremonies, such as kneeling to receive communion, and the introduction of ceremonies which were in themselves novel and of dubious legality, such as the requirement to kneel at rails surrounding and safeguarding the sanctity of the holy table, now positioned as an altar. These policies, which were as much royal as archiepiscopal,[24] alienated not only Puritans, whose voluntaristic and exclusionist religion of Sabbatarianism, sermons, lectures, days of fasting and so-called 'conventicles' Laud and like-minded bishops were determined to suppress and eradicate,[25] but a very broad body of relatively conservative churchmanship, which would resist any attempt

---

[19] Tyacke 1990, pp. 87–180; Patterson 1997, pp. 260–92. We await the publication by Anthony Milton for the Church of England Record Society of documents connected with the English delegation at Dort.

[20] Hoyle 1991, p. 109. And Oxford, contrary to what some might suppose, was an even stronger stronghold, its divinity 'militantly protestant, generally Calvinist, in the sense of adhering to the Reformed theology of grace, and strongly evangelical' (Tyacke 1997a, p. 569). This was the environment against which William Laud reacted.

[21] See p. 219 below. Nicholas Tyacke has helpfully observed that the writings of Arminius were 'more important as a defining label than as a direct source' of English 'Arminianism' (Tyacke 1997a, p. 578).

[22] Lake 1995, p. 121.

[23] Tyacke 1990, pp. 266–70; Tyacke 1993; Collinson 1995.

[24] Davies 1992. The point, however, is contentious, and will be challenged by Fincham and Tyacke, with particular reference to the issue of altar rails.

[25] Patrick Collinson, 'The English Conventicle', in W. J. Sheils and Diana Wood, eds., *Voluntary Religion, Studies in Church History* 23 (Oxford, 1986), pp. 223–59.

to tamper with what were by now the long accustomed ways in worship, from what ever quarter: Laudian in the 1630s, puritan in the 1640s.[26] But it is not plausible to separate matters of ceremony from matters of doctrine. In the writings of Richard Hooker and the sermons of Lancelot Andrewes it is possible to see the link between a theology which came close to affirming the universality of saving grace, and a religious economy which emphasised the sacraments as channels of grace and tended to elevate prayer and sacrament above soul-saving preaching. According to some scholars, what we are witnessing, especially in Hooker, is not the defence of Anglicanism but something like its invention.[27] There were loose coalitions of early Stuart churchmen united and somewhat embattled in their dislike of the divisive enthusiasm and low churchmanship of what looks like the Calvinist majority. Before Laud's rise to great power in the Church, their Cave of Adullam was Durham House, the London residence of Richard Neile as bishop of Durham, a circle which included Richard Montague and Neile's lieutenant at Durham, the future Bishop John Cosin, who was about to introduce Cambridge to the whole panoply of the new ceremonialism as Master of Peterhouse.[28] But there is no agreement what to call these churchmen: 'Anglican' is full of anachronism and will not serve. 'Laudian' is not very satisfactory. 'Avant-garde conformist' is unlikely to spread far beyond the specialised language of refined scholarship.[29]

All of the issues we have briefly addressed erupted in Cambridge from time to time, often in the forum of the vice-chancellor's court, where the preachers of offending sermons regularly found themselves.[30] These stirs and troubles underlie the sense of unease in Emmanuel and among Emmanuel men in the country which was registered when John Preston, the second master, was chosen to succeed Chaderton, and when William Sancroft the Elder was with equal haste brought in to replace Preston.[31] It would be a mistake to suppose that Emmanuel in these years was intellectually a landlocked Calvinist seminary. The library was well stocked and nothing if not eclectic, including not only the Genevan works of John Calvin and Theodore Beza, but a representative collection of Lutheran authors, including the writings of the Danish theologian Nicholas Hemmingsen, often seen as a significant taproot of Arminian doctrine, as well as medieval scholastics (Aquinas) and Counter-

---

[26] Judith Maltby, *Prayer Book and People in Elizabethan and Early Stuart England* (Cambridge, 1998).

[27] Lake 1988, pp. 145–238.

[28] Tyacke 1990; Andrew Foster, 'Church Policies of the 1630s', in Cust and Hughes 1989, pp. 193–223.

[29] 'Avant-garde conformist' is a term coined by Peter Lake.

[30] Most of these cases are fully discussed in Hoyle 1991. Some of the documentation will be found in Cooper 1845 and Heywood and Wright 1854.

[31] See pp. 221–2 below.

Reformation controversialists (Bellarmine).[32] While it is, of course, impossible to know to what extent such authors were consulted primarily for the
purpose of confuting them, the resources of the College certainly provided
for theological diversity and originality, and this would come. Witness the
intellectual trajectories of Sancroft the Younger, or of Ralph Cudworth, or
Benjamin Whichcote. Many flowers could bloom in this soil.[33]

Nevertheless, there is no reason to doubt that Emmanuel under the
masterships of Sancroft the Elder and Richard Holdsworth would have
been broadly 'orthodox', in the Reformed sense of orthodoxy. But by the
1630s the threat to this tradition seemed very real. Samuel Ward of Sidney
Sussex had written in 1628: 'Why that should now be esteemed puritane
doctrine which those hold who have done the Church the greatest service
in beating down Puritanism, or why men should be restrained from
teaching that Doctrine hereafter, which hitherto has been generally and
publiquely mainteined wise men perhapps may but I cannot understand.'[34] What Cambridge was now to witness has been called 'a protracted and wide-ranging assault on the English reformation settlement'.[35]
In the mid-1630s it appeared that that assault would be mounted by none
other than Archbishop Laud himself, who held no office in the University
(he was Chancellor of Oxford) but who insisted on his metropolitan right
to visit it. Ostensibly, the University, headed by its own Chancellor, the
earl of Holland, presented a solid front of resistance. But heads of houses of
the new tendency gave the archbishop private encouragement. Backed by
the king Laud successfully asserted his rights of visitation: but then proved
to be too busy and distracted to exercise them.[36]

In 1633, John Normanton of Caius preached Arminian doctrine in a
university sermon in which he was clearly in breach of the royal declaration forbidding the public handling of such matters. He got away with it,
and worse was to follow. In 1636, Normanton was again university
preacher and mounted a wide-ranging and provocative attack on many
fundamental protestant doctrines, including justification by faith alone, a
word he said only to be found in Luther's 'idle Dutch translation'. He
poured scorn on the proposition that the Pope is Antichrist, attacked
clerical marriage, called Thomas Aquinas 'Saint', and praised Cardinal
Bellarmine. Normanton was in the business of preaching himself 'clean
out of the Church of England', and he soon arrived at a Roman destination.
But what was surprising, and scandalous, about these very protracted proceedings was that the heads of houses were divided – not quite evenly –
for and against dealing with the matter with the seriousness it deserved;

---

[32] Bush and Rassmussen 1986.
[33] See pp. 247–64 below.
[34] Quoted (from Bodl., MS Tanner 72, fol. 298) by Hoyle 1991, p. 164.
[35] Ibid., p. 228.
[36] Heywood and Wright 1854, pp. 407–27; Twigg 1990, pp. 38–41.

and so with most of the cases of these years. A slight majority of the heads of houses did not consider the doctrine of justification by faith alone, in the terms of the Articles of the Church of England, to be worth fighting for.[37]

The real riposte to the Normanton tendency came from a fellow of Emmanuel, Nathaniel Barnard, who pulled out all the stops in a sermon in Great St Mary's in 1632, preached on a text from 1 Samuel, 'the glory is departed from Israel'. The glory of a nation was defined as conformity to God's ordinances, and anyone who went about to deprive a nation of any of God's ordinances was a traitor to his church and nation. Such were those who endeavoured to quench the light and abate the glory of Israel by bringing in (and note the linkage in Barnard's thought and rhetoric) 'Pelagian errors' ('Arminianism') and 'the superstitions of the Church of Rome into our worship of God, as high Altars, Crucifixes and bowing to them, i.e. (in plaine English) worshipping them'. Barnard had attacked the queen's religion in a London sermon, and now there were other nearly treasonable words about a king who did nothing to preserve the glory of his nation. Traitors against the state and nation were worse than traitors against the king. 'Against all such traytors, then, let us take up armes (*there he made a good long pause*) – I mean, the armes of our church, our prayers . . .' It is perhaps hardly surprising that whereas Normanton was allowed to remain in Cambridge until he converted and voluntarily withdrew himself, Barnard fell into the hands of the High Commission and ended his days, or so Parliament was later informed, in prison, neither the first nor the last of Emmanuel's martyrs.[38]

It was not necessary to leave the environment of the Cambridge college chapels to encounter the plain idolatry of which Barnard's rash and self-destructive sermon had complained. Much of our evidence, inevitably highly coloured, comes from evidence later given to a Committee of the Long Parliament, 'Innovations in Religion and abuses in Government in the University of Cambridge'.[39] Peterhouse under Matthew Wren and John Cosin was the showcase for the new style of devotion, created between 1628 and 1632: a marble floor before the altar on which the officiating clergy only trod when covered with a turkey carpet, or in slippers; the altar itself, surrounded with coloured silks and bearing two great gilt

---

[37] The Normanton case is extensively documented in the university archives (see especially CUL, CUA, Com. Ct. I.18) and in BL, MS Harl. 7019, fol. 55, as well as in the papers of Samuel Ward at Sidney Sussex; all of which have been employed by Margo Todd in her essay ' "All One With Tom Thumb": Arminianism, Popery and the Story of the Reformation in Early Stuart Cambridge', *Church History*, 64 (1995), 563–79. See also Milton 1995, pp. 75–6.

[38] Documents relating to the Barnard case in Heywood and Wright 1854, pp. 392–403; and in BL, MS Harl. 7019, fol. 91.

[39] Discussed by David Hoyle, 'A Commons Investigation of Arminianism and Popery in Cambridge on the Eve of the Civil War', *Historical Journal*, 29 (1986), 419–25.

candlesticks, above it a dove to represent the Holy Ghost and painted cherubims, behind, a stained glass representation of the crucifixion and 'divers pictures of the history of Christ'; at the end of every seat a cross; incense mingling with the music of the organs and voices raised in the revived polyphonic pricksong on which Cosin was particularly keen. Everyone bowed to the altar on entering and leaving, 'divers bowings and cringeings'. 'It is credibly reported that there are divers private oratories and Altars in the Colledge with crucifixes and severall other popish pictures.' St John's under William Beale, 'dressed up after a new fashion' was not far behind Peterhouse. Beale was later credited with being 'the sole encourager of Dr Cozins in his vice chancellorship, to tyranize in that jesuiticall, popish and canterburian religion'. In addition to similar altar arrangements, the roof of the chapel was painted sky blue 'and set full of gilt starrs', with the words set in gold letters through the whole roof JESUS CHRISTUS DOMINUS NOSTER. At Trinity too £1000 was spent to give the chapel 'a new dresse'. There were similar if less spectacular innovations at Caius, Jesus, Pembroke Hall and Christ's.[40]

Many readers of this *History*, not Calvinists or Puritans, would have appreciated, even delighted in, the aesthetics of Arminianism-Laudianism, and they must be asked to exercise their historical empathy to appreciate how deeply offensive to old-fashioned Calvinists like Samuel Ward and Simonds D'Ewes all such things were. The new fashions even rubbed off on to Emmanuel, where 'some of the schollers have received harme by their frequent goeinge to Peterhouse Chappel, contrary to the orders and government of the College'. Hence their 'novel gestures' in their own chapel, and evidence of crucifixes in some of their chambers. Two fellows, Nicholas Hall and the future Master, Thomas Holbech, soon to be identified to the Long Parliament as *personae non gratae*, set a dangerous example through bowing at ingress and egress out of the chapel, and at the name of Jesus. Emmanuel was clearly confused and in a state of flux.[41] But then came the deluge of 1640. The English Revolution had begun, and presently the semi-official iconoclast William Dowsing was taking a particularly unfriendly interest in the college chapels of Cambridge. However, when he came to Emmanuel from the holocaust he had ordered in other college chapels, Dowsing merely noted: 'There is nothing to be done.'[42]

---

[40] BL, MS Harl. 7019, fols. 71–3, 74, 77, 79, 80, 81, 83. Some of these details with much other Cambridge material were included in the case against Archbishop Laud at his trial. (William Prynne, *Canterburies Doome* (1646), pp. 73 f.).

[41] BL, MS Harl. 7019, fol. 82.

[42] J. S. Morrill, 'William Dowsing, the Bureaucratic Puritan', in John Morrill, Paul Slack and Daniel Woolf, eds., *Public Duty and Private Conscience in Seventeenth-Century England*: *Essays Presented to G. E. Aylmer* (Oxford, 1993), pp. 173–203. And see Trevor Cooper's forthcoming edition of Dowsing's Cambridge visitations for the Ecclesiological Society.

A Death, A Murder, and A Suicide:
Buckingham and Holland: Cambridge and the Caroline Court

Thomas Howard, earl of Suffolk, chancellor of Cambridge University, chose a very inconvenient moment to die. The date was Sunday 28 May 1626, the time 2 a.m., the place Charing Cross. By noon on Monday, the University was in receipt of a message indicating that it was the desire of Charles I, to put it no more strongly, that they should elect as Suffolk's successor the duke of Buckingham. Cambridge was at once in turmoil. Joseph Mede, our principal informant, conveys the atmosphere brilliantly. The masters of colleges were for the most part inclined to comply, but 'we of the Body murmur, we run one to another to complaine, we say the Heads in this Election have no more to do then any of us.'[1] Minds were seriously disturbed: by the 'special admonition' of the discovery of some old protestant books in the belly of a codfish in Cambridge market, by a whirpool on the Thames which smashed into Buckingham's garden wall at York House.[2] Parliament had been in session since February, the attempted impeachment of the increasingly unpopular Buckingham its main business.[3] If the scholars of Cambridge elected Buckingham, they would please the king but earn the contempt of Parliament for, in Mede's words, 'men of most prostitute flatteries'. If they rejected Buckingham, they would suffer the royal displeasure. Either way, the privileges of the University were at risk: a hiding to nothing, as we say nowadays. The news of Buckingham's success at Cambridge infuriated the leaders of the impeachment process in the House of Commons. 'The Parliament was wonderfully exasperated', 'aggravating it as an act of Rebellion.' Whether Parliament should register a formal protest in a letter to the University became in itself an issue at Westminster, with the king insisting that all rights and privileges of the University derived from him.[4] And then the Parliament was dissolved. If only Suffolk could have hung on for another fortnight!

---

[1] BL, MS Harl. 390, fol. 68; printed in Cooper 1845, pp. 187–9, and Heywood and Wright 1854, II, pp. 338–41. The formal communication of the king's 'desire' was contained in a letter from Bishop Neile of Durham to the vice-chancellor of 29 May 1626, CUA, Lett. 12. A1. The Buckingham affair is documented, with voting lists, in Cooper 1845, pp. 185–96 and Heywood and Wright 1854, II, pp. 338–46. There are accounts in Mullinger 1911, pp. 53–64 (somewhat biassed in favour of the Heads, and anxious not to be too much swayed by Mede) and Twigg 1990, pp. 20–4. But the story is told in the greatest detail by Morgan 1983, pp. 15–29.

[2] Morgan 1983, pp. 1–5. On the famous (and apparently quite authentic) 'bookfish', see forthcoming work by Dr Alex Walsham.

[3] Conrad Russell, *Parliaments and English Politics 1621–1629* (Oxford, 1979), pp. 260–322.

[4] Cooper 1845, pp. 190–2.

The crisis was compounded by ideology. In the five months since the York House Conference, it had become clear that Buckingham (and the king) now sided entirely with the so-called Arminian party, and it was the Arminian (or anti-Calvinist) heads of houses, whom Mede called 'the courtiers', Leonard Mawe of Trinity, Matthew Wren of Peterhouse, Thomas Paske of Clare Hall, who became instant electoral agents for the duke. (When the M.P. for Cambridge told the Commons that there were no Arminians in Cambridge, he was told that it was as likely that there were no whores.[5]) Mawe interviewed all sixty of his fellows one by one, some twice, and then marched them in a body towards the Senate House, to an election held only four days after Suffolk's death. Within a month, he had his reward: the bishopric of Exeter. Paske too dragooned his fellows, including one unfortunate individual who had taken a laxative, 'which wrought ere he got home'.[6] But in the event, Buckingham won by a mere six votes (Mede made it only three), which was the worst result possible. His opponent, hastily chosen without his knowledge, was Suffolk's son, Thomas Howard, earl of Berkshire, seen as a kind of hereditary claimant, and 'the duke's profound opposite'. From Emmanuel, there were twelve votes for Berkshire, including that of Anthony Tuckney, only four for the duke.[7] The master, John Preston, abstained. We shall discover in the next section why that was significant. The issue was anything but clear-cut, since Berkshire, too, was seen by some as a 'courtly' candidate. The only person to do well out of this sorry affair was Mr Hobson, the carrier. 'Divers in towne gott hackneyes and fled to avoyd importunitie.'[8]

Buckingham made himself agreeable. On his first, and, as it transpired, only visit to the university, in March 1627, he pronounced two words of Latin, 'placet' and 'admittatur', and promised to provide a magnificent and badly needed new library (Cambridge's envy of the Bodleian knew no bounds), committing £7000 of his own money to the project, which would have involved clearing all the houses between Great St Mary's and Caius. The booksellers and lawyers who faced eviction put their losses at an 'unreasonable' £1695. The University offered compensation totalling £870, but supposed that it would cost at least £1100 to clear the site.[9] But this was fantasy, and reality was what was happening in Caius College itself. Caius had unanimously elected a new master, Thomas Batchcroft, but the Court responded with a royal commission, which asked all kinds

---

[5] Morgan 1983, p. 27.
[6] Ibid., p. 24.
[7] Mullinger 1911, pp. 58–9.
[8] Mede to Stuteville, 3 June 1626, BL, MS Harl. 390, fol. 68v. Writing in 1911, J. B. Mullinger imagined the scholars escaping from Cambridge in cabs. But 'hackneys' were hired horses.
[9] Mede is, again, a chatty informant. See BL, MS Harl. 390, fols. 217, 221, 227v, partly printed in Heywood and Wright 1854, II, pp. 359–61. See also Mullinger 1911, pp. 72–5.

of questions about the conduct of the election and the quality of the man chosen. (Rumour had it that, rich though he was, Batchcroft had failed to grease the chancellor's palm.) Joseph Mede feared 'the utter overthrow of all elections of masters'. 'What a chancellor shall we have! God give them joy that were so eager.' But this reaction was excessive. Charles I, as distinct from 'the system', was less disposed to be free with mandates than his father and Batchcroft was not, after all, opposed. But the university had once again divided, 'courtiers' versus the rest, with as many as 140 signatures procured to a petition or testimonial for Batchcroft, 'very home and downright' in reminding the duke of his solemn promise to defend the privileges of the University.[10] The final irony is that presently Batchcroft received his D.D. – by royal mandate![11]

And then, on 22 August 1628, Buckingham was dead, the victim of an assassin in a Portsmouth inn. He was replaced as chancellor by an Emmanuel man, Henry Rich, earl of Holland and brother of the great puritan patron Robert Rich, earl of Warwick. What lay behind this unopposed election? The by now obsequious University (its heads anyway) had made a pretence of inviting the king himself to assume the office, and Charles, while promising that he would not cease to be chancellor 'in effect', mandated Holland.[12] But it looks very much as if what lay behind these courtesies was a concerted attempt by what we may call (however anachronistically) the religious left to rescue the University from Arminianism and all that Buckingham had stood for. The earl of Warwick's brother was a shrewd choice, for this handsome, courtly, ambivalent man was a great favourite of Charles I's queen, Henrietta Maria. It would hardly be too much to say that here was the Emmanuel connection using its big guns to fight back. Six days after the dreadful deed done in Portsmouth, the earl of Warwick wrote to William Sancroft, master elect of Emmanuel (John Preston having died in July), but still in his Essex parish. 'I have made all the meanes I can to Cambridge to make my Brother Holland Chancellor. I pray you writt to your Colledge about it, and if occation be, that you would goe over, as Dr Sibbes will, to doe your best in it.' Now Richard Sibbes, master of St Catharine's and preacher at Grays Inn, was the prince of godly preachers.[13] It was on the very same day, 28 August, that Charles I 'commended' Holland to 'free

---

[10] Mede to Stuteville, 11 November 1626, BL, MS Harl. 390, fol. 157; CUL, MS Baumgartner (Patrick) 22, fol. 13 (8); Heywood and Wright 1854, II, pp. 349–50; Mullinger 1911, pp. 68–9; Brooke 1985, pp. 121–2; Morgan 1983, p. 34. Mede had found himself pleasantly surprised when a free election occurred at Christ's in May 1622 (Morgan 1983, p. 483), although not, with the passage of time, with the outcome.

[11] CUL, CUA/Lett. 12. C3.

[12] Cooper 1845, pp. 207–8; Heywood and Wright 1854, II, pp. 366–7.

[13] DNB, art. Henry Rich, earl of Holland; earl of Warwick 'to Mr Sandcroft m. of Stanford in Essex', 28 August n.y., BL, MS Harl. 3785, fol. 67, copy, CUL, MS Mm.1.45 (Baker 34), p. 129.

election' by the University, 'whose hearty affection to advance religion and learninge generally in our kingdomes, and especially in the fountaynes, cannot be doubted of'.

What can also be not doubted of, since the smoking gun in the form of incriminating epistolary evidence still exists, is that far from releasing the University and its colleges from the curse of royal mandates, Holland's chancellorship witnessed more intrusive and even corrupt practice than ever before.[14]

Mandates, whether in the case of college elections or for the granting of degrees,[15] were not new in the days of Charles I, nor was sturdy, Medeian, resistance to them. In the later years of Elizabeth I, members of Christ's College had been in trouble with the Vice-Chancellor's Court for words uttered in alleged contempt of such processes: 'the mandatum latelie brought to the said Colledge was a foolish Mandate', 'these foolish letters, meaninge . . . the Queens Mandate': 'whosoever shall but sue for her Majesties letters shall never have my voyce' – evidence that mandates were not a simple matter of political interference, but often procured by interested parties within *academe* itself.[16] By the early seventeenth century, colleges were actually petitioning for the rare privilege of a free election, promising that they would not abuse it. The reign of James I witnessed 'an unprecedented level of intervention', although eventually James seems to have realised that mandates procured by interested and competing parties were not the best way to run a successful university, while Charles, at least initially, was more reserved and punctilious in these matters than his father.[17] Virtually as the condition of his election, Holland naturally made the usual promises to defend statutes and privileges. 'I am tyed by my education to serve you.'[18] Indeed, unlike Buckingham, he was a university man, an alumnus of Emmanuel. His protestations seem to have been sincere, and what he set out to do was as far as possible to route all mandates through himself. But a year after his election, Holland had to admit that so many mandates had lately passed from the Court to the University that his former promises were called to account. If in future mandates came through any other channel than his own office, 'your owne remissnesse in acquainting mee must excuse the neglect of the lybertye you may enioy, by your free Elections'.[19]

[14] The evidence survives in CUL, CUA/Lett.12.B (Letters Concerning Mandates), Lett.12.C (Royal Mandates for Degrees) and Lett.12.D (Letters to Holland, 1629–1635). It is discussed in Morgan 1983, Chapter 7, 'Masters and Elections, Mandates and the Prerogative'.

[15] Technically, peremptory mandates and letters dispensatory (i.e., dispensing from statutes).

[16] CUL, CUA Lett. 10 (Mandates temp. Elizabeth) 9.

[17] Morgan 1983, pp. 468, 483, 484.

[18] Cooper 1845, p. 208.

[19] Holland to the vice-chancellor, heads, regents and non-regents, 29 July 1629, CUL, CUA Lett. 10, D1.

That was all very well. But of course Holland did not attend personally to such matters. They were left to his secretary and man of business, William Sanderson. Holland's policy invested Sanderson with great power, and there is every likelihood that he used that power corruptly. His letters, addressed to the vice-chancellor, Henry Butts of Corpus, suggest a Uriah Heep – like character. Outwardly and ostensibly, Sanderson was all sweetness and light. When, in March 1630, Thomas Ball, John Preston's biographer, resigned his Emmanuel fellowship, the college intended to replace him with Martin Holbech (and did), but were afraid of outside presssure and, according to Sanderson, had misunderstood a letter from the chancellor. Was it likely that Holland would disregard the interests of his own alma mater? 'The care of that Colledge to whose statutes his Lordship once tooke Oath makes him tender what to oppose to others Consciences.'[20] But when approaches were made to Sanderson to place a certain young man in a Trinity scholarship, having first refused, 'because of my promise to take off these trowblesome requests', he was then so far moved by 'the good Mans teares for his sonnes preferment', that he gave in, and on the very same day that he acted in respect of Emmanuel. In a similar case, involving Caius College, 'charyty to the father' persuaded Sanderson to stretch a point. One wonders whether it was only tears which paid for these places and mere charity which responded. Soon Sanderson was complaining that a fellowship election at Christ's had been countermanded by a mandate of which he had known nothing. 'You must receave an expresse letter from my lord heerein, till then bee silent.'[21]

The official Holland line seems to have been that mandates were to be used only to prefer to places or degrees men who were appropriately qualified: in other words, mandates as such were to be allowed, but not letters dispensatory. However, as Sanderson explained to Dr Butts, 'his Majesties especiall Command upon especiall occasion' could 'alter his Lordships resolution'.[22] In view of subsequent events, it is somewhat ironical that Charles I should have dispensed from the Statutes and required the University to confer the degree of B.D. on a young man who was neither a Bachelor nor a Master of Arts. And who was he? Stephen Marshall of Emmanuel, the fiery preacher who in 1642 would proclaim the Civil War before Parliament in his sermon *Meroz Cursed*. But Marshall's patron was Holland's brother, the earl of Warwick.[23]

---

[20] William Sanderson to the vice-chancellor, 12 March 1629(30), ibid., D5.

[21] Sanderson to the vice-chancellor(?), 12 March 1629(30), ibid., D6; Sanderson to the vice-chancellor(?) 26 November 1630, ibid., D11; Sanderson to the vice-chancellor, 11 August 1631, ibid., D17. These cases are discussed in Morgan 1983, pp. 488–90.

[22] Sanderson to the vice-chancellor, ibid., D2.

[23] CUL, CUA/Lett. 12. C7(i). For Marshall, see Webster 1997, passim, and Webster 1994.

Holland's 'resolution' was put to a particular test, and failed it, in March 1632. The occasion was the first, and only, visit of Charles I and Henrietta Maria to Cambridge: a time for feasts, comedies, and special academic acts and congregations, as well as the statutory tour of King's Chapel. The king brought with him a signet letter containing a list of names of no less than sixty individuals who, to mark the occasion, were to receive degrees for which many were statutorily unqualified. There were to be three bachelors of law, five doctors of physic, eight M.A.s, and no less than twenty-three B.D.s.[24] But attention focused on the twenty-one D.D.s, called by Simonds D'Ewes, who was present, 'divers new and unworthy Doctors of Divinity', including, most controversially, Edward Martin, the president of Queens', chaplain to Archbishop Laud and a notorious Arminian.[25] Holland was hardly aware of what was going on, since in the midst of these festivities the poor man fell from his horse, knocked himself out and was 'taken up for dead'; so that the comedies had to be postponed for a fortnight, while the royal party went back to Newmarket. But when he recovered consciousness Holland seems to have made a formal complaint, telling the king that preferment to degrees without the performance of due acts and exercises 'may tend much to the preiudice of young scholars'. Charles passed on his words to the University, giving instructions, as if butter would not melt in his mouth, that henceforth when royal warrants or letters were received, care should be taken to ensure that the persons named were properly qualified.[26]

Did the king know that the whole university had been deeply offended that Dr Butts, the vice-chancellor, had been accused to his face before the whole Regent House of accepting bribes? Did he know that 'all those doctors' had indeed paid large sums of money to William Sanderson for their preferments, so that 'about this time' Holland dismissed him from his service, or so according to D'Ewes?[27] The king was not standing by when Dr Butts left Great St Mary's saying, as others heard: 'I perceive all mine actions are misinterpreted, and therefore I will go home and dye.' But perhaps he was told that on Easter Sunday, which was 1 April, two days after he had written his admonitory letter to the vice-chancellor, Dr Butts, who was due to preach that morning, was found dead in his chamber, hanging by his garters. D'Ewes attributed Butts's suicide to the humiliation which he had suffered in the Regent House, while admitting

---

[24] CUL, CUA/Lett. 12.B1; Mullinger 1911, pp. 115–16.

[25] Halliwell 1845, II, p. 68; Mullinger 1911, p. 115.

[26] Nelson 1989, I, p. 640; Charles I to the vice-chancellor and caput senatus, 30 March 1632, CUL, CUA/Lett. 12.B2.

[27] Halliwell 1845, II, p. 68. As some confirmation of the testimony of D'Ewes as to this point, an anonymous letter written on 4 April 1632 alleged that Butts's willingness to admit to degrees all those named on the king's list was 'by Sanderson's instigation'. (Nelson 1989, I, p. 641.)

that Butts had other reasons for inflicting such a cruel April Fool's joke on himself and the University.[28]

A Note on the Suicide of Dr Butts

The reader may like to know more about the alleged reasons for and the circumstances of Butts's suicide. Butts had just entered on his third consecutive term as vice-chancellor, a fact which caused Professor David Williams (of Emmanuel) to reflect when the same thing happened to him in the early 1990s. It was said that Butts's motive was to enjoy the glory of entertaining the king and queen. But his second term of office had coincided with the worst visitation of the plague in living memory, and he was clearly an exhausted man. The Holland-Sanderson-Butts correspondence makes it clear that he was in poor health and behaving strangely as early as 1630. But some reports suggest that the suicide was precipitated by the poor reception given to one of the two comedies performed before the king and queen. This was *The Rival Friends* by Peter Hausted. It was performed in Trinity Great Hall, like the other, successful play, Thomas Randolph's *The Jealous Lovers*. But the play which failed to amuse, even though it was said to be an anti-puritan piece, was performed by the men of Queens', and either Butts was a principal sponsor of it, or the circumstances were linked with the issue of the hour, the conferment of a D.D. by special mandate on Dr Martin, the Arminian president of Queens'. Either way, Butts was again humiliated, and it was said that 'the killing blow was the dislike of that comedy'. D'Ewes wrote: 'It was certain the King himself, whilst he was at Cambridge, at this time had given him a check or two, which so daunted him, being an ambitious man, and fearing his friends at Court would discountenance him upon it, as it drove him into this extreme desperation.' But the pious and proper D'Ewes thought that the underlying reason for the suicide was that Butts had, lying on his conscience, 'that crying sin of adultery, which he secretly practised; without which, doubtless, the devil could never have brought him to that sudden exigent upon the mere frown of a prince'.[29]

Three Masters: Preston, Sancroft and Holdsworth

In 1622 the fellows of Emmanuel for the first time elected a master, John Preston of Queens'. Whose scheme it was that Laurence Chaderton should step down, after thirty-eight years, allowing this to happen, is not entirely clear. It could have been Chaderton's own idea. But Preston's

[28] Halliwell 1845, II, pp. 68–9.
[29] Ibid.; CUL, CUA/Lett. 12 D4, 11; Nelson 1989, I, pp. 641–2; Cooper 1845, pp. 250–2.

biographer, Thomas Ball, who was Preston's pupil[1] and must have been part of the triumphal progress from Queens' to Emmanuel on that day in October 1622, represents it as a plot by the fellows to take advantage of Preston's powerful Court connections, not least to obtain some favourable relaxation of the uncompromising college Statutes; and that it was necessary to overcome Chaderton's fears about slips betwixt cup and lip, and for his own pension. 'The poor man wist not what to do; to out-live the Mastership he thought was to out-live himself.' A third possibility is that the initiative lay with those Court connections, which is to say, the duke of Buckingham, in which case there was no need to be afraid of an unwelcome intervention by mandate. On 20 September Buckingham had written to Chaderton. 'You shall not need to fear anything.' And so, a statutory seven days after Chaderton's secret resignation,[2] Preston was elected. Joseph Mede wrote: 'Never did I beleeve till now I see it experienced that so many as 12 could keep counsell a week together, and fellows of a Colledge too!'; and, from Suffolk, William Bedell (to Samuel Ward): 'the newes was alltogether unexpected in these parts: whereof I doubt not but that there was some secret motives, and perhaps more conditions than the worlde knowes of'.[3]

John Preston is one of the more enigmatic figures in the history of religion, and of politics, especially if one removes from the competition a number of Jesuits. On the other hand, to comprehend the motivation and strategy of Preston's career will be to have some small understanding of the nature of both religion and politics in seventeenth-century England. Preston was proud to inform King James I that he was a Preston of Preston in Lancashire, but in truth that was four generations back, his great grandfather having fled a blood feud to set up as a modest tenant farmer in Northamptonshire. So, with the help of a wealthy family friend who virtually adopted him, Preston had to make his own way in the world, or rather, in the university, first at King's, where he applied himself to 'the genius of the college', music, as a lutenist finding difficulty

---

[1] *The Life of Doctor Preston* by Thomas Ball, editor, with Thomas Goodwin, of several of Preston's works, was published in successive editions of Samuel Clarke's *General Martyrologie* (from 1651; I use the edition of 1677), and in 1885 was edited and published by E. W. Harcourt from the original MS. Ball went up to Queens' in 1619, was part of the migration to Emmanuel in 1622, and became a fellow in 1625. (Morgan 1957, p. 31.) Ball's chronology is sometimes confused. Ball and Morgan are my sources for Preston, unless otherwise stated. Shuckburgh's account of Preston (Shuckburgh 1902) is useful, and Alexander Gordon's article in the *DNB* excellent.

[2] A letter from Joseph Mede to Sir Martin Stuteville dated 5 October 1622 (BL, MS Harl. 389, fol. 235r) establishes that the election took place on 2 October. This suggests that Chaderton resigned on 25 September. Assuming that he received Buckingham's letter (which is printed in Ball) no later than 21 September, that might mean that it took him four or five days to make up his mind, which may be evidence that the Preston 'plot' was not his idea.

[3] BL, MS Harl. 389, fol. 235r; Shuckburgh 1902, p. 260.

with the fingering. But as a non-Etonian he had no prospects and moved on to Queens' where his formidable intellect and almost self-destructive industry began to be recognised. Aristotle was his 'tutelary saint', and 'what broke others teeth was nuts to him'. He became a fellow at twenty-two. Preston's sights were set on a political or diplomatic career. He thought it beneath him to be a clergyman, 'and the study of Divinity a kind of honest silliness'. He dabbled in medicine and astrology.

In a way, Preston's courtly aspirations would be fulfilled, and his initial worldliness would stay with him. But first he was, as it were, arrested, and converted, by that unexpectedly plain sermon preached in Great St Mary's by John Cotton,[4] which made him a life-long disciple, visiting Cotton at Boston every summer and sending his own choicest pupils to be 'finished' by him. But for a time his conversion to a puritan style of self-consciously regenerate piety (c. 1611) was another well-kept secret. Now Preston turned to divinity, devouring the schoolmen, Scotus, Ockham and Aquinas. Studying the *Summa* while the barber was cutting his hair, he blew away the hairs which fell on the page and carried on reading. Then came Calvin, 'whose very stile and language much affected him'. Out of this formation emerged one of the most learned and sophisticated, as well as moderate, of all the English Calvinist divines, posthumously famous for his sermons.[5] Meanwhile, Preston's worldly prospects looked bright, especially when he played the star role in the famous philosophy act performed before James I on the question, whether dogs can make syllogisms.[6] But the courtiers wondered that this dog didn't bite. 'That a young man should not be ambitious'!

Preston was ambitious. Already suspect as a 'Puritan' (there is no evidence that he was ever a nonconformist),[7] Ball tells us, in a very

---

[4] See pp. 191–2 above.

[5] Nothing was published in Preston's lifetime, but in the decade or so following his death no less than thirty different titles appeared from the press, some running to several editions (*The new covenant, or the saints portion*, nine known editions between 1629 and 1639, *The saints daily exercise*, ten between 1629 and 1635, *Sermons preached before his majestie*, five between 1630 and 1637). In a decade supposedly dominated by Arminianism, this is evidence of the fierceness of the contest for the title of 'orthodox' in Caroline England. With 74 items to his credit in the *Revised Short-Title Catalogue*, Preston evidently rivalled in his popularity with the religious public William Perkins, with 118. The most recent study of Preston's divinity, a piece of revisionism which classifies him as a 'universal redemptionist' (the uninstructed may interpret this as 'low' or 'soft' Calvinist), is the (forthcoming) Cambridge Ph.D. thesis of Jonathan Moore, 'A Softer Calvinism, A Harder Punch? The Theology of John Preston (1587–1628) and the York House Conference, 1626'.

[6] See p. 71 above.

[7] In a letter of 14 April 1623 Joseph Mede shared with his correspondent Sir Martin Stuteville the conceit that there were three sorts of Puritans: (1) 'a Puritan in politicks or the Political Puritan'; (2) an 'Ecclesiastical Puritan'; (3) 'a Puritan in Ethicks or morall Puritan'. (BL, MS Harl. 389, fol. 314.) There was little of no. 2 in Preston, as much of no. 1 as was consistent with his courtly connections, but much of no. 3, although he took tobacco, for medical reasons (Ball 1677).

revealing aside, that he thought 'if he must be a Puritan, and bid farewell to all his Carnal and Court-designes, he would not be of the Lower rank, but would get places if he could'. What did it mean to 'get places'? In the course of his career, Preston would pass up the chance to be Lady Margaret professor, bishop of Gloucester, and even, it appears, Lord Keeper of the Great Seal, Lord Chancellor in all but name. But he competed strenuously for the lectureship at Holy Trinity church (worth no more than £80 a year), conspired to become Master of Emmanuel, and as Master hung on to his influential preachership at Lincoln's Inn. He had made John Davenant (soon to be bishop of Salisbury) President of Queens' (by a clever stratagem executed at Court) and thereafter he always took off his cap to Davenant and secured the best chambers in college for his pupils. And what pupils! Thomas Fuller, who called him a 'perfect politician', also said that he was the 'greatest pupil-monger in England', admitting sixteen fellow commoners in one year, mostly heirs to great estates. According to Ball, 'many had their eyes upon him, for their sons or friends', 'the only tutor'. Apparently Preston was not interested in younger sons.[8] These well-born pupils included the young earl of Lincoln, whose sister we shall bury in Massachusetts in the next chapter,[9] Robert Rich, son of the earl of Warwick, James Fiennes, son and heir of Lord Saye and Sele who would become Preston's closest political ally, and the two sons of Chief Justice Henry Yelverton who declared from the bench on one occasion that 'he had always been accounted for a Puritane, and he thanked God for it'. Among the many who accompanied Preston and the young Fiennes to Emmanuel was Henry Lawrence, later a member of Oliver Cromwell's Council of State. We begin to see what it was to 'get places': something like that enigmatic biblical injunction to make friends of the Mammon of Unrighteousness. But how did all those Cottonians secure 'places' in Emmanuel? Fuller remembered that 'it was much admired where all these should find lodgings in that Colledge, which was so full already'.[10]

The greatest friends that Preston acquired were Prince Charles, heir to the greatest estate of all, and the greatest man of the hour, George Villiers, duke of Buckingham. This came about through an elaborate courtly quadrille. The king, who knew enough about Preston to suspect him of Puritanism, wanted to win him over to conformity and usefulness, and after Preston had given him a singularly tactful sermon, was persuaded that it could be done. The godly party in courtly and political life, whom we may or may not want to call Puritans, those who espoused Calvinist

---

[8] Thomas Fuller, *The History of the Worthies of England* (1662), p. 291.
[9] See below, pp. 228–9.
[10] Morgan 1957, pp. 28–34; Fuller 1662, p. 291.

divinity and were enemies to peace with Spain, and to a Spanish wife for Prince Charles, were responsible for bringing Preston and preachers like him within earshot of the king at his hunting lodges at Royston and Newmarket. Their game plan was something like a mirror image of the king's. So it was that almost behind James's back, and thanks to Buckingham, who was also interested in Preston's usefulness, Preston became Charles's chaplain.

Preston's modern biographer seems to see his preferment as an odd circumstance ('*Prince Charles's Puritan Chaplain*', Morgan 1957) and credits Preston and his friends with the re-invention of Puritanism as a political force, round about 1620. But there was nothing new or unprecedented about these manoeuvres. Fifteen years earlier, skilful lobbying by evangelical Protestants with the right connections had surrounded Charles's elder brother Prince Henry with tutors and chaplains whose lessons and sermons constituted what has been called 'an unambiguous agenda of anti-Catholic militant Protestantism', creating a religious atmosphere at the Court of St James less balanced, more univocal than that of Whitehall. After Henry's death, Charles, whose religious opinions in these early years are virtually an unknown quantity, inherited the religious establishment of St James's, the sermons to which he was exposed echoing those preached at his brother's court. Preston represented continuity, not discontinuity and he was not an anomaly.[11]

The contradictions inherent in the religious politics of St James's and Whitehall came to a head in the early 1620s in the furore over the Spanish match, with its bizarre climax in the romantic journey of Charles and Buckingham to the Spanish court, and the collapse of the match. Opposition to the marriage came from those godly quarters so close to the prince and to Buckingham, and either the prince and the favourite wanted to placate that body of opinion, or they partly and privately were part of it. The preferment of Preston, that consummate politician with so many powerful friends, was part of this politics. But Preston was no inert cipher. He may have written one of the most outspoken attacks on the match, which reads like a godly manifesto, primarily addressed to Buckingham, and a mysterious journey which he undertook to the Netherlands, heavily disguised, may have had as its principal object a meeting with Prince Charles's sister, the dispossessed queen of Bohemia

---

[11] McCullough 1998, pp. 183–209. Contemporaries were as much in the dark about Charles's religion as historians. Mede wrote to Stuteville on 21 June 1623, with the prince and Buckingham still in Spain: 'Mr Wren writes that we have great cause to thank God for the Princes constancie in Religion, whose livelynes and courage therein they his chaplaines do admire . . .' (BL, MS Harl. 389, fol. 342.) But as Dr McCullough points out, Matthew Wren, the future bishop of Ely, was the Arminian cuckoo in this nest, anxiously debriefed by the anti-Calvinist bishops on his return from Spain (pp. 205–6, 208–9).

and Electress of the Palatinate, a piece of anti-match diplomacy.[12] This was the man whom Emmanuel in conditions of great secrecy made its Master in October 1622. Insofar as it was Buckingham who made him, was this his reward for services rendered?

But the days of Preston's political usefulness were already numbered. This was not immediately obvious. His doctorate (1623) was by royal mandate. When the Master of Trinity (John Richardson) died in April 1625, the hot money was on Preston to succeed him, 'a man in speciall favour with the king'.[13] In the same year, Buckingham took Preston sufficiently seriously to dangle before him the great office of Lord Keeper, which Bishop John Williams had occupied after Francis Bacon's impeachment and disgrace. (In the event it went to Thomas Coventry, a good legal friend of Emmanuel.) But Preston no longer believed in Buckingham, who was said by a contemporary to be recovering from his 'godly fit'.[14] When Charles prepared, on the rebound, to marry a French wife, Preston could not approve, and Ball tells us that 'from that time Doctor Preston doubted of the Saint-ship of the Duke of Buckingham'. As for the duke, his affections towards Preston were 'ebbing'. At the feast held at Buckingham's residence of York House to celebrate his election to the chancellorship of the university, Preston caused offence by taking a token sip when it came to drinking the health of the king, apparently a moral rather than a political gesture. In 1625 he had played a strange role in the York House Conference.[15] It was a conference which he feared (rightly) would prove a mistake, and he was a reluctant participant. That the Conference did not end in the conviction of the alleged 'Arminians' whose opinions were on trial was partly due to the moderation of Preston's 'soft' Calvinist position, for which he was blamed and attacked. But the true significance of the Conference was that it signalled a seismic realignment of religious attitudes, with Buckingham and Charles, now on his throne, throwing their weight behind the anti-Calvinists.[16] Preston and Buckingham were now finished with each other. But Preston remained a royal

---

[12] Ball reports that Preston was persuaded to write a paper against the Spanish match which circulated in the House of Lords, of which no copy appears to survive. On the other hand many copies do survive of a paper attributed to the government clerk Thomas Alured, which is the 'manifesto' referred to here, and which Morgan argues, plausibly in my opinion, was in reality the work of Preston, as the spokesman of a party. Morgan is also responsible for the suggestion that Preston's journey to the Netherlands, which Ball implausibly suggests was undertaken to perfect his Latin in order to qualify for the Lady Margaret chair, had an undercover diplomatic motive. (Morgan 1957, pp. 51–62, 83–90.)

[13] Mede to Stuteville, 23 April 1625, BL, MS Harl. 389, fol. 428.

[14] Morgan 1957, p. 60.

[15] For the York House Conference, see p. 203 above.

[16] Preston's role in the Conference, and the theological position from which he argued, have been radically revised by Jonathan Moore, to whom I am grateful for sharing his work with me.

chaplain, and in 1627 preached his last sermons at Court, one of which almost prophetically denounced his former patron's conduct of the disastrous Ile de Rhé expedition.

Preston's mastership saw the fortunes of Emmanuel, in terms of its enrolments, rise to their zenith. But what did he otherwise do for the College? Ball, who wrote 4500 words about Preston at the York House Conference, tells us almost nothing about his government of Emmanuel, except that he doubled the number of academic 'acts' or exercises which students were obliged to undertake, and of this there is no independent, corroborative evidence. Probably he was almost never there. In all his time, Preston signed only four corrective admonitions, three of them on the same day.[17] And the only order he put his name to confirmed the casuistical agreement he had extracted from the fellows before his admission that a clause in the Statutes (cap. 2, *De residentia magistri*), 'nisi violenta detentione impeditus', covered 'service of the King and Prince'.[18] Soon the honeymoon was over, as so often happens in college life. Writing to Preston's successor, Anthony Tuckney, a future master and another of John Cotton's disciples, warned him 'to study the college's peace' and to maintain the lawful privileges of the fellows, especially in small matters. He wrote of 'former broyles and toyles . . . if not in your time, yet I am sure in your Predecessor's, his clashes with the Fellows, especially them who were a means to bring him into his Mastership', something which had proved more damaging to him than to them.[19] Was the statute *De mora sociorum* a small matter? When it was perceived that Buckingham had broken with Preston, the fellows petitioned the Crown directly to have the statute set aside, and it was probably to spite Preston, who, like Chaderton, opposed the change, that Buckingham procured the royal suspension of *De mora sociorum*.[20] But if Preston was distant, in both senses, from his college and its fellows, he remained at the very hub of the godly community and network. Chaderton in his prime had been a pope in Cambridge, but Preston was the puritan pope of all England.[21]

Preston's health had never been good, and there seems to have been a long history of tuberculosis. In July 1628 he died in his native Northamptonshire, aged forty, under the roof of another pope-like figure, John Dod. To the funeral at the puritan shrine of Fawsley, the home of Preston's close political ally, Sir Richard Knightley, came 'a world of

[17] ECA, CHA.1.4A, fol. 8r.
[18] ECA, COL.14.1, p. 27; Shuckburgh 1904, pp. 59–60.
[19] Anthony Tuckney to William Sancroft (the elder), 7 September 1635, BL, MS Harl. 3785, fol. 58, copy in CUL, MS Mm.1.45 (Baker 32), pp. 129–30.
[20] See pp. 27–8 above.
[21] Webster 1997, pp. 9, 13, 38, 67, 76, 77, 81–2.

godly people'. He died a bachelor, but not, in terms of liquidity, a wealthy one, since much of his substance was tied up in the East India Company. A codicil to his will, of which Lord Saye and Sele was an executor, settled a small annuity on the College for the benefit of its scholars. But, as not infrequently happens, nothing came of this for forty years, and fifty years after that the endowment lapsed amidst unsuccessful litigation on the College's part.[22]

For all that 'world' of godly mourners, Preston's funeral happened obscurely, in the country, 'without state', to enable the fellows to hold an election without interference, or so Ball alleges. The all-enveloping sense of political and religious crisis (it was the summer of the Petition of Right) made more acute what in any circumstances would have been a dangerous corner. Before long, William Laud, as bishop of London, would be urging on Charles I the need to provide 'grave and orthodox men', to be governors of Emmanuel and Sidney Sussex, 'which are the Nurseries of Puritanism'.[23] That meant royal mandates, and mandates exercised in the interest of Arminianism. Letters to Emmanuel from the country are evidence of a deep anxiety about the evident threat to religion, nationally, and in the College itself. A Norwich minister wrote about 'fightings without, feares within', John Rogers of Dedham of 'the spirit of Error being much more bold every day to outbrave the blessed Truths that we have been trayned up in'.[24] In the risky July of 1628, the godly, and, it appears, the votes of a majority of the fellows, favoured the candidature of William Sancroft, senior fellow in his time, who had obeyed the founder's statutory wishes by becoming rector of the Essex parish of Stanford-le-Hope. But Sancroft was being 'backward'. His near neighbour, Nathaniel Ward of Stondon Massey (the future and first American satirist,[25]) whose patron was his Emmanuel contemporary, Sir Nathaniel Rich, wrote to communicate the urgent concerns of the godly Essex ministers. It seems that Thomas Hooker had held one of his conferences at Chelmsford, and that if Sancroft had been at home he would have been confronted with their decision face to face. 'My earnest suite to yow is that yow would lay downe all fleshly pleas, all private and personall respects, melancholy and supermodest objections, and make all hast to give way to their motion. The kingdom of Satan finds instruments inough and such as crowd fast inough for advantages against Christ and the truth.' 'Yow have the votes of all that heare of it, and shall have their prayers with strenght. All our feare is that delayes will subvert this good

[22] Shuckburgh 1904, pp. 67–8. See ch. 4, p. 111, above.

[23] Laud's 'considerations' are dated 14 March 1629(30); ECA, COL.9.1A, p. 78.

[24] John Yates to William Sancroft, 30 June 1635, BL, MS Harl. 3783, fol. 45; John Rogers to William Sancroft, 4 September n.y., ibid., fol. 52.

[25] See above, pp. 190–1.

work.'[26] From Emmanuel itself, the Fellows wrote 'charging' Sancroft to accept their call. 'If you fayle us the College sinkes certainly, and way will be made for a mandat[e] to our undooinge.'[27]

The Sancrofts were old, if very minor, gentry, who had lived for ever in and around the small Suffolk village of Fressingfield, a place which William Sancroft's nephew, William Sancroft the younger, Master and Archbishop, would make for ever famous, for that was where his life began and ended. The younger Sancroft had his education at Bury St Edmunds, and it is likely that in the 1590s his uncle had preceded him in a school which was already distinguished, set in a strongly puritan town culturally dominated by a famous preaching exercise every Monday and a precocious parish library.[28] The younger Sancroft (who never seems to have thrown anything away) preserved his uncle's notebooks, which reveal a well-stocked and eclectic mind. Besides commonplaces of a puritan character, including notes on *Piers Plowman* which turn it into a contemporary and godly text ('dumme and idle ministers', 'keeping the word of God from the people'), these include a collection of 348 political 'maxims and sentences', which mingle the conventional wisdom of Polonius with the guile of Machiavelli.[29] Sancroft served an exacting apprenticeship under Ralph Cudworth (the elder) and became in his turn a hard task-master.[30] As Master, Sancroft restored discipline. Whereas only four admonitions had been administered in Preston's six years, Sancroft put his name to twenty-one in his seven, almost all for the usual disorders of drunken and rowdy behaviour.[31] As happens nowadays, many scholars were neglecting formal hall and taking their meals out of college. 'This is to cease.'[32] But Sancroft had his own cross to bear. His nephew composed an elegy 'upon the death of the only sonne of Mr D. Sancroft Master of Emmanuel College in Cambridge'.[33]

The godly honeymoon was again short-lived, and trouble seems to have been stirred up by the conflicting pecuniary interests of Master and

---

[26] Nathaniel Ward to William Sancroft, 'Stondon July' [1627], BL, MS Harl. 3783, fol. 11. Nathaniel Rich wrote to Sancroft from Warwick House, 20 November 1633, referring to 'your selfe amongst many others who syde with God and his truth in theise tymes.' (Ibid., fol. 31.)

[27] Quoted (from Bodl., MS Tanner 155, fol. 21), Twigg 1990, p. 28, Webster 1997, p. 43.

[28] John Craig, 'The "Cambridge Boies": Thomas Rogers and the "Brethren" in Bury St Edmunds', in Wabuda and Litzenberger 1998, pp. 154–76.

[29] Bodl., MSS Sancroft 46 (especially fols. 10–12), Sancroft 55, fols. 38–50v. MS Sancroft 31 contains 64 of the older Sancroft's sermons, in 200 close-written folios.

[30] Evidence in letters from John Stoughton and John Yates to William Sancroft, 13 November 1635, 30 June 1635, BL, MS Harl. 3783, fols. 8–9, 45.

[31] ECA, CHA.1.4A, fols. 8v–10v. These entries are also evidence of Sancroft's fairly constant residence.

[32] ECA, COL.14.1, p. 35.

[33] Bodl., MS Tanner 465, no. 37, fol. 73.

Fellows in a college with a limited endowment. The reasons for Sancroft's 'backwardness' become clear when we find that before his admission, and no doubt as the condition of it, the Fellows agreed to interpret Statute 13 to allow a Master who was beneficed to retain his living 'for a convenient time'.[34] Sancroft's attempt to have the suspension of *De mora* revoked (in about 1630)[35] was already indicative of a divided college, since it was supported by only half the fellowship and made the rather specious claim that if the statute had remained in force it would have prevented 'no small disturbances of the peace of the College which have lately happened' – presumably because some of the other faction would have been obliged to leave.[36] Now it was not only students who were the objects of discipline. In 1632 a fellow, Henry Salmon, was 'peremptorily admonished' for openly resisting the Master, and the censure was only remitted after a visit to the Vice-Chancellor's Court. Two years later, Salmon and the three other senior fellows, including the tutor to the younger Sancroft (who had come up a few months earlier), Ezekiel Wright, were at odds with the Master over the distribution of the proceeds of a lease and of 'sealing money'.[37] By 1635, as Anthony Tuckney's letter (already quoted) makes clear, the College was not a happy place, with the petty row about small revenues not resolved. Even the junior undergraduate William Sancroft had heard that his tutor had 'falne out' with the Master over a lease, and that Ezekiel Wright hoped that his father, the Master's brother, might be prepared to arbitrate. Young Sancroft could only hope that the quarrel would be patched up, 'that at least wee might have no strife in our owne bowells'.[38]

Yet it was a prosperous time for the College. Student numbers were buoyant, and in February 1633 the decision was taken to ease the overcrowding by erecting a new range of buildings, known to more recent generations as Old Court, or the 'Brick Building', the works to be financed in part by increasing room rents. (But it is not at all clear how all this was afforded.) The contracts entered into with the builder, John Westly, and the carpenter, Henry Man, survive, and with the bursarial accounts provide a detailed record of these works, which outran the original estimate of £665, what with the little extra touches which Westley

---

[34] Order dated 5 August 1628, ECA, COL.14.1, p. 29. The 'convenient time' was defined as 'not above that time which the Fellowes are allowed to enioy their places after they have induction into a living.' Sancroft resigned Stanford-le-Hope in 1628–9. (Newcourt 1710, p. 549.)

[35] See above, pp. 27–8.

[36] Shuckburgh 1904, p. 75.

[37] ECA, COL.14.1, p. 41. The original order, assigning three quarters of sealing money to the College, and a quarter to be divided between the Master and Fellows, was made in Chaderton's time, 30 June 1621. (Ibid., p. 24a.)

[38] William Sancroft (the younger) to his father, 17 August 1635, Bodl., MS Tanner 65, fol. 48.

added, and the need to compensate Mr Pit, the nurseryman on whose garden the building impinged.[39] Unfortunately, the result was not a complete architectural success. The acerbic Bishop Bennet reported in 1788 that in spite of all the money spent on it, the Brick Building was by then 'in a tottering state', only kept together by the strength of its chimneys.[40]

In April 1637 Sancroft went home to Suffolk to die,[41] and on April 25th the Fellows elected Richard Holdsworth of St John's, probably the best master that Emmanuel ever had, but who was destined to be violently taken from them. It is understandable that in the divided state of the College an outsider was elected. But how was it managed? Holdsworth was not, on Archbishop Laud's terms, 'orthodox'. Busy as he was, it is inconceivable that the archbishop (and the king) should not have known that there was a vacancy at Emmanuel. In 1633 Holdsworth had been the choice of a majority of the fellows of his own college. But there had been a challenge, the Crown had intervened, and, after eight months of dispute, had mandated the Arminian ceremonialist William Beale.[42] But while Holdsworth was a Calvinist, he was a moderate Calvinist, much like Preston, and distanced himself from more rigid predestinarians.[43] On matters ceremonial too, he trod a discreet line. He could say of Laud: 'His grace delights in gentleness'. As archdeacon of Huntingdon (his compensation prize for missing St John's) he was stricter than his diocesan, John Williams, insisting on the placing of the holy table at the east end and on the receiving of communion at the altar rails. He confessed to 'weakness' when it came to dealing with genuinely tender and scrupulous consciences, but claimed to be 'stout' in his resistance to incorrigible rebels against church discipline. He was pleased to have achieved total altar-drill conformity at St Ives.[44] He refused to read the Book of Sports, so offensive to 'Puritans'.[45] He was chosen to preach one of the fast sermons before the Short Parliament in 1640; and he opposed the controversial continuation of Convocation after the dissolution of that Parliament and was unhappy about the Canons which resulted from it, especially the seventh, which enforced on consciences what he called 'these new taken up ceremonies'. Later, in the early months of 1641, with Charles I attempting to come to some sort of settlement with the increasingly bellicose Long Parliament, Holdsworth was one of the leading proponents, with Archbishop James Ussher and his Cambridge colleague

[39] ECA, COL.14.1, pp. 39–40; *ECM*, 6, 12–16.
[40] ECA, COL.9.1(B), p. 42.
[41] Shuckburgh 1904, p. 79.
[42] *DNB*, art. Holdsworth; Twigg 1990, p. 27.
[43] Milton 1995, p. 423 n.164; Tyacke 1990, p. 54 n.120.
[44] Sharpe 1992, pp. 292, 344; Davies 1992, p. 237.
[45] Ibid., p. 193. This was in his capacity as rector of the London parish of St Peter le Poer.

Ralph Brownrigg, of a scheme of modified or 'reduced' episcopacy which, it was hoped, might stave off the root and branch threat to bishops. He was made a royal chaplain and in October 1641 was one of five anti-Arminian moderates to be offered bishoprics: in his case, Bristol. He was the only one to refuse.[46] We may call Holdsworth a central church-man, an establishment Calvinist, even an extreme moderate. Such men were to suffer most in the upheavals now to come, when Holdsworth, like Bishop Hall, would receive 'hard measure'.

Holdsworth, the son of a vicar of Newcastle, arrived at St John's in 1607 and became a fellow in 1613. Since he wrote very little that was pre-served or published,[47] the main evidence of his prodigious learning is his library, one of the largest of its age. According to a catalogue in the Cambridge University Library, where most of the books still are (and we shall discover later how they came to be there), it contained more than 10,000 volumes.[48] The lawyer and politician Sir Simonds D'Ewes, who became Holdsworth's pupil in 1618, has left a number of snapshots of his 'loving tutor': Holdsworth reading him the standard texts in logic, ethics and moral philosophy, as well as some history, and, at night, Virgil's Eclogues; Holdsworth returning from London late, when D'Ewes (who presumably slept in the same chamber) was already tucked up in bed, friends at once dropping in, so that the seventeen-year-old had to sit up with them half the night; D'Ewes sharing with Holdsworth the sight of Halley's Comet; Holdsworth conducting his pupil home to Suffolk when he went down, and only finding it in him to mention the £13 his father owed him when they were both in the coach, on their way to the Bury lecture.[49]

Holdsworth was a great preacher, although little enough of the evidence for that now exists.[50] D'Ewes remembered that his sermons were 'by

[46] Ibid., pp. 255–9, 261, 262, 277 (following Lambeth Palace Library, MS 943/599); Russell 1991, pp. 109, 110, 240, 246–7, 249–50, 271–2, 412.

[47] Apart from a few posthumously published English sermons, we have only his *Praelectiones Theologicae Habitae in Collegio Greshamensi*, published in 1661.

[48] *DNB*, art. Holdsworth; J. C. T. Oates, *Cambridge University Library, a History* I (Cambridge, 1986), pp. 314–48.

[49] Halliwell 1845, I, pp. 107, 121, 122, 148; Marsden 1851, pp. 3, 37, 54, 64, 117, 121, 124–5.

[50] The only sermon published in Holdsworth's lifetime was *The peoples happinesse; A sermon preached in Maries Cambridge upon Sunday May 27* (Cambridge, 1642), printed at the insistence of the king. A collection of 21 sermons published posthumously in 1651 was very corrupt. (*DNB*, art. Holdsworth.) Bishop Ralph Brownrigg wrote to William Sancroft on 11 June 1651 to inform him that the editor of these sermons, Holdsworth's nephew Richard Pearson, wished to 'peruse' his uncle's papers and copies of sermons left at Cambridge, which Brownrigg hoped he would be enabled to do, 'because their ar many in London whoe have taken his Sermons by their shortwriting, they give out that they will print them as they have allreddy begunn.' (Bodl., MS Tanner 54, fol. 80.) Probably nothing came of this, since the sermons were indeed printed from shorthand notes.

general approbation deemed extraordinary'.[51] From 1624 he was rector of the London parish of St Peter le Poer, and from 1629 Professor of Divinity at Gresham College. Evidently he was one of the most admired London preachers of his day, and by the time he became President of Sion College (a kind of clergy guild) he was their doyen. As Master of Emmanuel, Holdsworth continued to be a high profile public figure, and retained his outside livings and offices. In his case, too, the statute concerning residence was interpreted more liberally than the founder had intended.[52]

Holdsworth was a man who aroused real devotion. When he preached in the young D'Ewes's Suffolk parish, 'so sweetly and profoundly', Simonds 'began to love him even better than ever.'[53] William Sancroft, whose politics were to be so different from those of D'Ewes, told him: 'Your counsell was both card and compasse ... your favor the gale that fill'd my sails.' It was only the hope of living under Holdsworth's 'happy discipline', to receive from him directions 'for study, for life, for all', that had kept him at Emmanuel.[54] In an earlier chapter we encountered those 'Directions' which Holdsworth left behind for posterity.[55] If, wrote this most admirable of college heads, you keep to this plan of study, and 'spend your time according to this Calendar', you will graduate with applause and credit, and will be able to go on to riper studies 'with delight to your self, and advantage over others that have not kept so good a reckoning of their studies.' 'I shall now leave you to your self.'[56]

---

[51] Marsden 1851, p. 34.
[52] ECA, COL.14.1, p. 45.
[53] Marsden 1851, p. 35.
[54] William Sancroft to Richard Holdsworth, 19 August n.y., Bodl. Library, MS Tanner 61, fol. 64v (copy in ECA, COL.9.8); William Sancroft to Bishop Ralph Brownrigg, 14 August 1649, Bodl., MS Tanner 56, fol. 94.
[55] ECM, vols. 1, 4. See above, pp. 74–5.
[56] ECM, 4, 9.

7

Emmanuel, New England and Harvard

The Emmanuel Thirty-Five

One of the most successful, and wealthy, of Elizabethan clergymen was a certain Robert Johnson, like William Cecil, Lord Burghley, a native of Stamford, who put down deep roots in neighbouring Rutland, where he was rector of North Luffenham for fifty years, from 1574 to 1625.[1] The foundations of Johnson's career were laid as chaplain to Sir Walter Mildmay's colleague and Cecil's brother-in-law, Sir Nicholas Bacon, and may have had something to do with those crown livings which were at Bacon's disposal as lord keeper.[2] In addition, Johnson held, from time to time, prebends in no less than four cathedrals, and the arch-deaconry of Leicester to boot. The remainder of his fortune he owed to two advantageous marriages. One might call Johnson worldly, 'cocking abroad with his four several prebends', as Archbishop Parker sourly observed; except that he was a staunch Puritan who used much of his substance to found two still famous schools in his adopted Rutland: Oakham and Uppingham. At the end of his life, this patriarch set up Oakham and Uppingham scholarships in four Cambridge colleges, Emmanuel included.

Johnson and his family became part of the furniture of Emmanuel and part of the early history of America. Robert sent his son Abraham to the college in 1591, the same year that his brother-in-law, the London merchant William Romney, conveyed the advowson of North Luffenham to the college, while selling the remainder of his estate in the parish to

---

[1] Much of this account of the Johnsons is based on 'Isaac Johnson: a memoir' by E. A. I., *ECM*, 17 (1906–7), 59–78. See also Sheils 1979, pp. 3, 38, 46, 62, 134; and Bryan Matthews, *By God's Grace: A History of Uppingham School* (Maidstone, 1984).

[2] Rosemary O'Day, 'The Ecclesiastical Patronage of the Lord Keeper, 1558–1642', *Transactions of the Royal Historical Society*, 5th ser. 23 (1973), 89–109. The livings in question were those valued at less than £20, the great majority of crown livings. Johnson was not formally employed in this department (a certain Bartholomew Kemp was), but I find it hard to believe that he did not profit from his connection with Bacon.

Johnson.[3] Presently Abraham married (as his second wife) Laurence Chaderton's daughter, Elizabeth. He set up as a country gentleman, was sheriff of Rutland, and became a great patron of the preaching ministry in the county.[4] He sent all four of his own sons to Emmanuel. The eldest was Isaac. To cut a long story short, Isaac married, somewhat above his station, Arbella Fiennes, the sister of the earl of Lincoln, who had been a pupil of John Preston's at Queens'. All these young people were in their twenties. The alliance made for some bad blood in the family, and led to Robert disinheriting Abraham in favour of Isaac. Cicely Chaderton, who mostly disapproved, wrote to Isaac in some distress, trying to avert a nasty law suit. She regretted what the old man had done, 'for the blemmish of his reputation, who was soe eminent for wisdome and wealth'.[5] In the late 1620s, Isaac Johnson invested much of his now considerable fortune in a newly founded joint-stock company with interests in Massachusetts Bay and was one of the original 'undertakers' of the Massachusetts Bay Company. In 1630, Isaac and Arbella sailed in what Australians might call the First Fleet, destination Massachusetts, in what since 1616 had been known as New England.[6] It was an event of far greater importance than the more legendary voyage, ten years earlier, to another spot on the North American coastline, of a small company of puritan colonists in a ship called the *Mayflower*.

The first of the eleven ships in the fleet of 1630, named the *Arbella* in Mrs Johnson's honour, carried John Winthrop, the first governor of the infant colony together with its royal charter, in effect the colonial government; as well as Charles Fiennes, Isaac Johnson's brother-in-law and another prominent founder of the Company, Sir Richard Saltonstall, a Yorkshire gentleman, but nephew and heir of a lord mayor of London, whose son had entered Emmanuel in 1627 and who joined him on the voyage. The Saltonstalls would send send nine successive generations in

---

[3] See Sarah Bendall's discussion of these transactions, p. 110 above. When Robert Johnson died, in 1625, the trustees to whom he had enfeoffed his North Luffenham property, assuming that the advowson was included, proceeded to exercise a right of presentation which actually belonged to Emmanuel. But since their candidate was an Emmanuel graduate, Jonathan Tooqué, who had served as Johnson's curate, the College took no legal action.

[4] Sheils 1979, pp. 46, 62, 134.

[5] Cicely Chaderton to Isaac Johnson, 24 August 1625; *Winthrop Papers*, I, pp. 1498–1628 (Boston, Mass., 1929), 323–4. I owe this reference to Arnold Hunt. Joseph Mede reported Archdeacon Johnson's controversial deed of gift on 3 May 1623. He had 'estated' upon his grandson £1000 or £1200 a year. (BL, MS Harl. 389, fol. 322.)

[6] The name was first used by Captain John Smith in *A description of New England* (1616). (Cressy 1987, p. 4.) It was not really, of course, a 'first fleet' at all. Englishmen had been active on the New England coast for more than ten years. John White wrote in *The Planters Plea* (1630) p. 231v: 'It is well knowne before our breach with Spaine, we usually sent over to *New-England* yearly forty or fifty sail of ships of reasonable good burthen for fishing onely.'

the male line to Harvard.[7] Only nine weeks after stepping ashore in America, Lady Arbella died, evidently a victim of scurvy. Isaac followed her to the grave five weeks later, but not before he had named the peninsula of Shawmut, to which the little colony had moved from an earlier settlement at Salem in search of clean water, 'Boston', in honour of John Cotton of Boston, where he had sat under Cotton's preaching. Massachusetts reported to the older, separatist colony at Plymouth Plantation that God's visitation had not spared 'the righteous', who shared with 'the wicked' in these bodily judgments. In December 1630 Joseph Mede, back in Cambridge, reported Mrs Johnson's death. 'Alas, good lady!', adding: 'Divers of the faction, especially women, were dead.'[8]

Why 'the faction'? Why was Mede, a devoutly learned Calvinist, unsympathetic? And what were the motives which had taken that little armada into Massachusetts Bay in the spring of 1630? Because we are dealing with the origins of the United States of America, this question has exercised literally hundreds of its historians. And since America is an idea, and ideal, as much as a place, there has been a heavy emphasis on an ideal, religious motivation behind the great migration, for all that other historians, revisionists, have preferred to stress economic factors.[9] America was a puritan idea, an idea defined by Perry Miller in the most famous of all essays on the subject as the vision of 'a city on a hill', the migration an 'errand into the wilderness' to establish an exemplary christian society, a beacon and model for the degenerate churches of England and Europe.[10] Miller's critics suspect in this thesis the back-projection of American exceptionalism, the 'redeemer nation' with its 'manifest destiny', and they maintain that the motives of the colonists were negative and confused. They took ship hesitantly, and after long debates with the disapproving brethren (such as Mede) whom they left

---

[7] Hardman 1986, pp. 457–60; Morison 1932, p. 32

[8] *Bradford's History of Plimouth Plantation* (Boston, Mass., 1900), pp. 330–2; Joseph Mede to Sir Martin Stuteville, 5 December 1630, BL, MS Harl. 390, fol. 525r. Mede later reported, 20 May 1631, the death of Isaac Johnson. 'And so the lands will come to Mr Samuel Dr Chaddertons grandchild who was once at Dalham [which was Stuteville's parish].' (Ibid., fol. 551r.) But Johnson's two wills, relating to his property in England and New England, which tell a confusing story, show that Mede's assumption was unfounded. (*ECM*, 17, 72–4.) Cf. John Winthrop's obit for Johnson: 'He was a holy man and wise and died in sweet peace, leaving some ['a good' cancelled] part of his substance to the Colonye.' (*Winthrop Papers*, II, 1623–1630 (Boston, Mass., 1931), p. 267.) Johnson's English will of 1627 is printed, ibid., 49–56.

[9] The controversy is reflected in scores of publications. But, for convenience, see Chapter 3, ' "Reasons moving this people to transplant themselves": migrant motives and decisions', Cressy 1987. See also Webster 1997, pp. 270–85.

[10] Perry Miller, *Errand Into the Wilderness* (Cambridge, Mass., 1956, repr. New York, 1964). For a searching critique, see Chapter 3, 'The Errand Into the Wilderness Reconsidered', Theodore Dwight Bozeman, *To Live Ancient Lives: The Primitivist Dimension in Puritanism* (Chapel Hill and London, 1988). See also Michael McGiffert, 'American Puritan Studies in the 1960s', *William and Mary Quarterly*, 3rd ser. 27 (1970), 36–67.

behind, debates and uncertainties which they carried with them and lived with in their new and precarious world. Crossing the Atlantic was not exactly a flight from persecution. But it was a search for spiritual safety in an environment free from bishops and their idolatrous ceremonies and vindictive courts; a calculated and conscientious departure from an England which, for its public sins, seemed as doomed as Sodom and Gomorrah, a move inspired by what has been called exhilarating despair.[11] These puritan migrants sought a place where the 'gospel ordinances', and especially those associated with the Sabbath, could be safely enjoyed. They needed to perpetuate and intensify the shared experience of godliness, the communion of saints. And they needed to resolve conflicts and contradictions which gnawed at the heart of the puritan church within the Church, especially as Laudian policies narrowed their room for manoeuvre. In short, the explanation for New England lay in the immediate English past, not in an American future.[12] And yet, the Autobiography and Journal of the Emmanuel migrant Thomas Shepard suggest that New England made him, quite simply, 'a new man'. The very ocean crossing, a watery Exodus, was for many a powerful metaphor for regeneration.[13]

It will be clear that we are here discussing, primarily, the motives of the migrating ministers, and of godly lay men and women whose religiosity was of an intensity at least equal to that of their preachers and pastors.

As with so many great historical debates, the argument has been bedevilled by badly put 'either or' questions. Human beings are usually motivated by more considerations than one, and the words they choose to explain and interpret their actions (words in this case like 'refuge', 'shelter', 'hiding place', 'wilderness') may not correspond exactly to motive causes. And yet it was those mantra words which would become memory and history, the kind of history written by Cotton Mather.[14] They are a true record to the considerable extent that devout Puritans virtually annexed what might otherwise have taken shape as a more humdrum settlement of fishermen and fur traders, 'ordinary people'.[15] (The Pilgrim Fathers of 1620 had been financed by the fishing and fur

---

[11] Foster 1991, p. 110.

[12] Argued, from varying perspectives, by David Grayson Allen, *In English Ways: The Movement of Societies and the Transferral of English Law and Custom to Massachusetts Bay in the Seventeenth Century* (Chapel Hill, 1981), Bozeman 1988. And note something said by Nathaniel Ward: 'our children for whose sake and safety we came over'. (Morison 1930, p. 224.)

[13] McGiffert 1972, p. 7; Patricia Caldwell, *The Puritan Conversion Narrative: The Beginnings of American Expression* (Cambridge, 1983).

[14] Mather 1852. A reference is implied here to ideas contained in Paul Fussell, *The Great War and Modern Memory* (Oxford, 1977).

[15] Rutman 1965, pp. viii–ix. S. E. Morison wrote: 'Most of the people described in this book would have led obscure lives but for a dynamic force called puritanism.' (Morison, 1930, p. v.)

interest.) At Boston, in 1631, the controversial decision was taken to restrict citizenship ('freedom of the body politic') to members of the newly founded, gathered churches. These were puritan congregations, and they were exclusive rather than inclusive in their membership, which was limited to 'visible saints'. At its most extreme (New England was a laboratory for a variety of ecclesiological experiments) the criterion for membership, based on personal conversion testimony, implied a claim to know the unknowable, about souls and their eternal destiny. Here was the basis, not of democracy, but of a narrow and intolerant theocracy. Soon a disillusioned Sir Richard Saltonstall was complaining of 'your tyranny and persecutions in New England'.[16]

Besides Isaac Johnson and Richard Saltonstall, Winthrop's well-heeled and even aristocratic fleet conveyed three other Emmanuel men to Massachusetts Bay: Simon Bradstreet (resident in the college in 1628–9 but never, strictly speaking, a member), a future governor; Samuel Dudley (Emmanuel 1626), travelling with his father Thomas Dudley, Winthrop's deputy and another future governor; and William Pelham (Emmanuel 1615), one of the Pelhams of Sussex. New England might almost have been called New Emmanuel, or, in Cotton Mather's Bunyan-esque phrase, 'Immanuel's land'.[17] It appears that the first white man to cultivate the land where Boston now stands was an Emmanuel graduate, William Blackstone (or Blaxton), Isaac Johnson's exact contemporary. Blackstone sounds like a loner, a minister turned fur trader. After the arrival of Winthrop's fleet, he found the place too crowded for comfort, sold up and withdrew deeper into the American wilderness, eventually joining himself to the dissident colony established at Providence, Rhode Island, by another stormy petrel of the great migration, Roger Williams, with whom he neither agreed nor was obliged, in the tolerant environment of Providence, to agree.[18]

The king pin behind Massachusetts and all other colonial ventures of the time, including Bermuda, privateering and the slave trade, was Robert Rich, earl of Warwick, who had entered Emmanuel in 1603; and who, as his share of the assets of the New England Council, owned the land taken up by the Massachusetts Bay Company.[19] John Winthrop, the first governor of Massachusetts, had been a student not at Emmanuel but at Trinity, where his father Adam had audited the accounts. But he belonged to the villages and cloth towns of south-west Suffolk,

---

[16] Saltonstall to John Cotton and John Wilson (1652), Robert E. Moody, ed., *The Saltonstall Papers* (Boston, Mass., 1972), I, 148–9.

[17] Mather 1852, pp. 589–90.

[18] Morison 1932, p. 10; *ECM*, 17, 77–8.

[19] A. P. Newton, *The Colonising Activities of the English Puritans: The Last Phase of the Elizabethan Struggle with Spain* (New Haven, 1914); K. O. Kupperman, *Providence Island: The Other Puritan Colony* (Cambridge, 1993); both *passim*.

communities which were so deeply impregnated with Emmanuel-style practical divinity, and he and his father had an insatiable appetite for sermons. To his fellow countryman, Sir William Spring (Emmanuel 1603) he wrote: 'My soule is knitt to you, as the soule of David to Jonathan.'[20] Ezekiel Culverwell, Chaderton's brother-in-law and Cicely's sister, was an important influence in Winthrop's life. 'About 18 yeares of age . . . I married into a family under Mr Culverwell his ministry in Essex; and living there sometimes I first found the ministry of the word come to my heart with power . . . I could no longer dally with Religion.' In his closely monitored, strenuous pilgrimage of a life, Winthrop was the archetypal Puritan.[21] As we know, Puritans were never at peace with themselves. When he boarded the Arbella, Winthrop was a troubled and dis-appointed man, sacked from a minor government post and shaken by bereavement. The Massachusetts plan of action had been hatched at meetings which he attended at the earl of Lincoln's seat of Sempringham and at Cambridge (in Emmanuel?). In the background hovered the earl of Warwick and other puritan grandees, whose eyes were focused on a rocky volcanic island off the coast of what is now Nicaragua, to which yet another puritanical joint-stock company had given the name Providence. It was assumed in these experienced circles that England's transatlantic empire would take shape in the West Indies, not on the barren shores of New England. So it was against Warwick's instincts and advice, but in line with the armchair know-how of the master-mind of the Massachu-setts venture, John White, rector and 'patriarch' of Dorchester,[22] that Winthrop's fleet headed north for Massachusetts Bay. It was third time lucky for White and his associates, for the Massachusetts Bay Company succeeded where the earlier Dorchester Company and New England Company had foundered. Winthrop and company established what is now the most powerful nation on earth, whereas the puritan colony on Providence Island lasted a mere ten years.[23] The Providence Company was an important piece of history, but not of colonial history. As a kind of Cave of Adullam for the opposition to Charles I, it belongs to the pre-history of the Civil War. The secret of Massachusetts's success was

[20] Bremer 1994, p. 6.
[21] Winthrop's life and religious journey is copiously documented (for the most part by himself) in *The Winthrop Papers*, of which six volumes have so far been published (Boston, Mass., 1929–47). See especially, in vol. 1, the Diary of John Winthrop's father, Adam Winthrop and the record of John Winthrop's own 'Experiencia'. Professor Francis Bremer of Millersville University is editing the remaining papers, which include a detailed record of the sermons heard at Boxford and elsewhere in Suffolk by Adam and John Winthrop. Bremer is also preparing a full-scale study of Winthrop.
[22] Frances Rose-Troup, *The Massachusetts Bay Company and its Predecessors* (New York, 1930); Frances Rose-Troup, *John White The Patriarch of Dorchester (Dorset) and the Founder of Massachusetts 1575–1645* (London, 1930); David Underdown, *Fire from Heaven: Life in an English Town in the Seventeenth Century* (London, 1992).
[23] Kupperman 1993. Historians of Virginia might take exception to this.

settlement (rather than tobacco growing and slavery) and self-government. It was a true colony in the ancient Greek sense; and the product of Winthrop's narrow vision, the vision of a small-scale Suffolk squire obsessed with religion.

Samuel Eliot Morison, the historian of Harvard, counted 129 Oxford and Cambridge men who went to New England before 1650. Of these, no less than thirty-five had been at Emmanuel.[24] Between 1611 and 1629 there were only two years when no future colonist entered the college, and between 1620 and 1629 the total was fifteen. An analysis of the Emmanuel 35 might distinguish between the great and good; those who made a conventional career out of New England; a few failures and interesting eccentrics, like Blackstone; while recording eight colonists who made the return migration to old England.[25] The reverse migrants included William Mildmay (Emmanuel 1640), the great-grandson of the founder, who completed his education at Harvard; and such notable ministers as Giles Firmin (Emmanuel 1628) and Nathaniel Ward, who defended the New England Way with witty satire. Ward was the oldest of the Emmanuel New Englanders, born in 1578 and entering the college in 1596. John Philip, brother-in-law of the most learned of all puritan divines, William Ames, was rector of the Suffolk parish of Wrentham. He came to New England in 1638 but after three years, with the political situation in England transformed, returned to Wrentham and presently reorganised that parochial congregation on exclusive New England lines, as a gathered church.

Our category of the great and the good should include Nathaniel Rogers, son of John Rogers of Dedham, whom Cotton Mather called 'one of the greatest men that ever set foot on the American strand';[26] and, among the laity, Daniel Denison (Emmanuel 1626), whose political and military leadership took him to the rank of Major General of all the colonial forces. But the greatest and goodest were John Cotton and Thomas Hooker, who created their own versions of what became known as the New England Way.[27] Cotton, the older man by eighteen months, migrated to Emmanuel from Trinity in 1604, at about the time that Hooker transferred from Queens'. These lifelong friends, Cotton at

---

[24] Morison 1932. No other Cambridge (let alone Oxford) college came anywhere near this number. Trinity sent thirteen men to New England, St John's ten and Magdalene eight. Much of the biographical information in these paragraphs is taken from Morison's monograph, and from the *DNB*.

[25] Hardman 1986, pp. 294–6, 352, 397, 420–5, 438–41, 454–5, 493–7, 497–8.

[26] Mather 1852, p. 419.

[27] For Cotton, see Mather 1852, pp. 252–86, Ziff 1962; for Hooker, *Thomas Hooker: Writings in England and Holland, 1626–1633*, ed. George Williams *et al.*, Harvard Theological Studies 28 (Cambridge, Mass., 1975), Frank Shuffleton, *Thomas Hooker, 1586–1647* (Princeton, 1977), Sargent Bush, Jr., *The Writings of Thomas Hooker: Spiritual Adventure in Two Worlds* (Madison, Wisconsin, 1980).

Boston, Lincolnshire, and Hooker in Essex, were the acknowledged leaders of the godly puritan brotherhood in the 1620s. As Hooker prepared to leave England for ever, his farewell sermon contained the solemn warning that as sure as God was God, God was going from England. 'Well, look to it, for if God is going, and if he do go, there our glory goes also.'[28] It was Cotton who preached the farewell sermon for Winthrop's fleet. When, in 1633, Cotton and Hooker themselves took ship in the *Griffin*, together with Samuel Stone of Towcester (Emmanuel 1620) (Mather called this 'a glorious triumvirate'[29]), many concluded that God indeed was a fellow-passenger. Thomas Shepard wrote: 'I saw the Lord departing from England when Mr Hooker and Mr Cotton were gone, and I saw the hearts of most of the godly set and bent that way, and I did think I should feel many miseries if I stayed behind.'[30] The trickle of immigrants now became a flood, which by 1640 had attracted as many as 21,000 English settlers to New England.[31]

Mather called Cotton 'an extraordinary person', 'the father and glory of Boston'. When Jesus Christ had a more than ordinary thing to be done for his glory in the American wilderness, he sent over 'a more than ordinary man'. Cotton and Hooker were 'the Luther and Melanchthon of New England', 'the oracle of their several colonies'.[32] For in 1636 Hooker and his following had left the vicinity of Cotton's Boston (Newtown, soon to be known as Cambridge), to found a new colony farther south on the Connecticut River, which they called Hartford, after Samuel Stone's birthplace. Hooker and his people sold out to Thomas Shepard and his company, who were now to occupy the new Cambridge, the home of Harvard College, and to enter into 'church fellowship'. Presently Shepard took Hooker's daughter as his second wife.[33] It remains a question too complicated to be entered into here, how much religious differences, especially over church policy and how to deal with dissidence, contributed to this decision to part company. Massachusetts in its early years was rent by bitter religious conflict, involving so-called 'Familists', 'Anabaptists' and the 'Antinomian' followers of one of Cotton's most devoted disciples, Mrs Anne Hutchinson ('disruption personified'), who

---

[28] 'The Danger of Desertion', Hooker 1975, pp. 228–52.
[29] Mather 1852, p. 265.
[30] McGiffert 1972, p. 55.
[31] There are no very reliable statistics for the population of New England in the 1630s. But see Daniel Scott Smith, 'The Demographic History of Colonial New England', *Journal of Economic History*, 32 (1972), 165–83. It has been estimated that upwards of 21,000 men, women and children had arrived by 1640, but that the white population stood at only 13,500. (Cressy 1987, pp. 67–70.) There was, of course, some return migration, and considerable movement between the American colonies. But New England families were fertile and life expectancy higher than in England. In 1700 there was a population of 'more than 90,000'. (Ibid., p. 36.)
[32] Mather 1852, pp. 282, 252, 264, 342.
[33] McGiffert 1972, pp. 64–5, 69.

was placed on trial and forced into exile.[34] Hooker's Connecticut established more liberal criteria for church membership and severed the Massachusetts connection between church membership and citizenship.[35] The formative impact on New England of Cotton and Hooker, as ecclesiastical statesmen, theologians and writers, can hardly be exaggerated. Yet Hooker, who died in 1647 aged sixty-one, spent only fourteen years in America. Five years later, Cotton too was gone, at the age of sixty-eight. By then the great migration was long since over and New England had entered upon the secondary stage of its historical development.

We may notice in conclusion a few more ordinary careers, and one or two misfits.[36] Typical New England ministers out of the Emmanuel stable were Samuel Whiting (Emmanuel 1613), school-friend and chamber fellow of the future master, Anthony Tuckney (according to Mather, 'they continued an intimate friendship . . . when they were a thousand leagues asunder'), who having preached at King's Lynn in Norfolk ministered at Lynn in Massachusetts from 1636 until his death in 1679; John Yonges (Emmanuel 1620), who was pastor at Southold, Long Island, for more than thirty years, Southold having been named for his wife's birthplace, Southwold in Suffolk; Zachariah Symmes (Emmanuel 1617), teacher and pastor at Charlestown for almost forty years; and John Ward (Emmanuel 1622), Nathaniel's son, who was minister at Haverhill, a town named for his Suffolk birthplace, for more than fifty years, preaching his last sermon in 1693, at the age of eighty-eight. Ezekiel Cheever, son of a London spinner and a good classical scholar out of Christ's Hospital, came up to Emmanuel as a sizar in 1633, left for New England in 1637, and served as master of various grammar schools until his death in 1708. 'He held the rod for seventy years', the most famous schoolmaster in New England.

In contrast to these conventionally fruitful careers, Thomas James (Emmanuel 1611), whose prospects must have been good as pastor of the church at Charlestown, was 'a very melancholick man, and full of causeless jealousies'. He fell out with his people, left the church and became a planter and a rolling stone. Edward Browne (Emmanuel 1624) sounds more congenial. He was pastor of Sudbury, but was also a famous fisherman, hunter and Indian fighter, who played the bass viol and left behind many music books. Emmanuel did its fair share of populating the new country. Samuel Dudley (Emmanuel 1626), son of a governor and 'a great power in the community', fathered no less than nineteen children.

But some of the Emmanuel New Englanders were very obscure indeed, and none more obscure than a certain John Harvard, who entered the college in 1627.

---

[34] David Hall, ed., *The Antinomian Controversy* (Middletown, Conn., 1968); Rutman 1965, p. 119.
[35] Foster 1991, p. 156.
[36] Most of this information I derive from Morison 1932.

Harvard[1]

The most surprising thing about the beginnings of Harvard is how little we know, and, it seems, will ever know about the man in whose name the college was established: John Harvard. Not a single letter from or to Harvard has survived, and all that we can say about him is this: his father was a prosperous Southwark butcher and inn-keeper and his mother the thirteenth child of a cattle dealer of Stratford-upon-Avon. (Naturally, the Shakespearean Stratford-Southwark will-o'-the-wisp has lured many sleuths, amateur and otherwise, but they have always drawn a blank.) The great plague of 1625 carried off most of the family, and perhaps made it possible for John, as its residual legatee and worth £300 a year, to enter Emmanuel as a pensioner at the advanced age of twenty, evidently sponsored by the rector of St Saviour's Southwark, Nicholas Morton (Emmanuel 1612), whose son Charles would become vice-president of Harvard. Harvard came to Emmanuel in December 1627, took his B.A. in 1632, and his M.A. in 1635. He left no mark on the college, where his contemporaries included Ralph Cudworth and Benjamin Whichcote. In 1636 he married the sister of another celebrated contemporary, John Sadler, later master of Magdalene, and a year later he took ship for New England. We know a little about what happened to him at Charlestown, where he settled, and occasionally preached, Harvard being described as 'clerk', implying ordination.

In Samuel Eliot Morison's words, Harvard 'did not initiate the foundation that bears his name, or obtain the charter that gave it corporate existence, or provide the funds to set it in motion.'[2] But, like Isaac Johnson, Harvard continued to inherit family property and money, which made him one of the wealthier colonists and the very first of the private benefactors on whom Harvard's greatness has ever depended. On his deathbed in September 1638, the thirty-year-old Harvard left one half of his estate and the whole of his library 'towards the erecting of a Colledge'. That was in money more than £800 (the bulk derived, perhaps, from the sale of the Queen's Head in Southwark), twice the sum which the leading men of the colony had already set aside for a somewhat vaguely defined educational purpose two years earlier. (Whether all these funds were ever received may be another question, and yet another

---

[1] This section has little in the way of annotation. Much of what it contains refers to the writings of the modern historian of Harvard, Samuel Eliot Morison. See Morison 1930, Morison 1932, Morison 1935, Morison 1936. The fullest and best account of early Harvard is in Chapter 6, 'Henry Dunster, President of Harvard', in Morison 1930. And see now Brewer 1997–8.

[2] Morison 1935, p. 210.

what happened to those that were.) Six months after John Harvard's untimely death, the Great and General Court, including some of the Overseers of the college appointed in 1636, ordered 'that the college agreed upon formerly to bee built at Cambridge shalbee called Harvard College.'

At Cambridge! Cambridge, which had first been called Newtown, occupied an excellent site on good land running down to the Charles River, unlike Boston sheltered from storms at sea and invasion. To some it seemed the ideal location for the fortified capital of the little colony, which for four years it was. But when most of the original settlers, Thomas Hooker's company, had driven their cattle away to the richer pastures of Connecticut, and the magistrates had decamped back to Boston, Newtown had to find a new *raison d'être*, and that was as English-speaking America's first campus town, Cambridge.

The annals of Massachusetts suggest that this might never have happened, but for the arrival of Thomas Shepard and his people, for Shepard as the pastor who gathered a model congregation in the little town gained an instant reputation for his orthodox resistance to the religious turmoil tearing Boston apart (in Shepard's words, 'maintained too obscurely by Mr Cotton'[3]), and for his 'soul-ravishing' ministry. The time was right. The religious dissidents of Boston had been defeated and dispersed, and Massachusetts had won its first Indian war.

Harvard College began very badly. Even before John Harvard's bequest, the Board of Overseers had appointed as 'professor' of the embryonic institution Nathaniel Eaton, to whom was entrusted (unwisely as it transpired) the available funds, in order to erect 'such edifices as were meet and necessary for a Colledge', as well as a house for himself. Unfortunately, Eaton and his wife ran the establishment as if it were Dotheboys Hall. Mrs Eaton later admitted that the food was terrible and the beer often non-existent. 'Concerning their beef . . . truly I must confess, to my shame, I cannot remember that ever they had it.' Mackerel were served 'with their guts in them', 'and goats dung in their hasty pudding'. That was what Eaton's pupils got for £15 a year. As for the 'professor', he flogged his charges without mercy, and finally fell foul of the authorities when he beat his usher with a yard-long cudgel. Thomas Shepard, who lived next door and was an overseer, never forgave himself for failing to notice what was going on: 'my ignorance and want of wisdom and watchfulness over him very great, for which I desire to mourn all my life.'[4] Eaton, fined and dismissed, ran away from the colony leaving a trail of bad debts. There followed a series of picaresque scandals, in Virginia, Padua (a source for bogus medical degrees) and England, where the first

[3] McGiffert 1972, p. 65.
[4] Ibid., p. 69.

head of Harvard College died in jail, in 1674. As for the college, it closed its doors.

In 1640 a second and more propitious start was made under Henry Dunster, a newly arrived immigrant and 'a conscionable and industrious man', who stayed the course until an enforced resignation (he had turned Baptist) in 1654. Dunster was the true founder of Harvard. By 1642, there was a proper building, the 'Old College', 'thought by some to bee too gorgeous for a wilderness', accommodating, besides its great hall, what was described as early as 1638 as 'a prity library'. Among the 400 volumes in John Harvard's bequest were the seventeen volumes of Aquinas, published in Venice in 1593, Cardinal Bellarmine and his Protestant opponents, much other Catholic as well as Protestant divinity, and a fair sample of the Classics. One quarter of the books had been printed after 1630. Morison exclaims: 'That such a collection could be brought to a colony only seven years settled . . .'!

It would be convenient to report that 'the lawes liberties and orders of Harvard Colledge' (1642–6) were, like the Statutes of Trinity College Dublin, so many clones of Mildmay's Statutes for Emmanuel. Not so. The circumstances were very different. But, echoing at many points the 1570 Statutes for Cambridge University, they demonstrate the almost seamless web connecting these twin academies, on the banks of the Cam and Charles rivers. The orders required, as a condition of admission, an advanced knowledge of Latin and the rudiments of Greek, acquired at the neighbouring grammar school. 'The students shall never use their mother tongue.' The laws made it clear that an education at Harvard was conducted within a deeply religious alembic. 'Every one shall consider the mayne end of his life and study'; and there was much more that followed from that. And yet no religious test was imposed: a puzzle for Harvard's historians. If it were not for the very recent Hutchinsonian affray in Boston, one might suppose that such tests were unnecessary, in what was, outside the college gates, a tightly regulated bible commonwealth.

Even the charlatan Samuel Eaton was a man of genuine learning, and the academic standards now established at Harvard bear respectable comparison with the Holdsworthian model we have encountered at Emmanuel.[5] We read of lectures and exercises in the hall, and of public declamations in Latin and Greek. Afternoon studies were pleasant: 'History in the Winter, the nature of plants in the Summer'. But in some respects the Harvard curriculum surpassed its English models. Third year students tackled not only Hebrew but 'Chaldee' and Syriac. 'One of the next things we longed for and looked after [after God's worship and 'Civill Government'] was to advance Learning and perpetuate it to

[5] See above, pp. 74–5.

Posterity.'[6] Harvard degrees were from the earliest days recognised in Oxford and Cambridge, and even in other European universities.[7] But other aspects of English college life were not neglected, including the 'salting' of freshmen.[8] In 1650, Harvard received its charter as a corporation consisting of a president, five fellows, and a bursar, the oldest corporation in North America which still exists. There were by now forty undergraduates in residence, and ten graduates studying for the M.A.[9]

So Harvard graduates were as well prepared, mainly for the ministry, as their English counterparts. But a warts and all portrayal of its first alumni would have to record that one of Eaton's pupils, in fact Harvard's second graduate, was, if not another bad egg, something of a curate's egg. In October 1636, John Winthrop received a *cri de coeur* from a brother-in-law in England, asking him to attend to the educational needs of his son, a 'poor boy' and 'reasonable hopefull lad'. This was none other than the future Sir George Downing, Bart., Oliver Cromwell's hatchet man in Scotland, and ambassador in Holland for both the Cromwells and Charles II, a man of many affairs but, according to Pepys, 'a most ungrateful villain'. But at least Harvard had ensured that Downing could sustain a two-hour conversation in Latin with Cardinal Mazarin. It was Downing's grandson, another Sir George and another scoundrel in the family tradition, who founded, or attempted to found, the college which, after thirty years of Chancery litigation, came to bear his name as Downing College. When, in 1807, William Wilkins laid the foundation stone of this, the first new Cambridge college since 1596 and Sidney Sussex, Old England was repaying a remote debt to New England, the Cam to the Charles River.

[6] This description, with the 'Rules and Precepts', is contained in the anonymous pamphlet of 1643, *New Englands First Fruits*, printed as Appendix D in Morison 1935.
[7] Morison 1930, p. 204.
[8] Ibid., pp. 212–13.
[9] Morison 1936, pp. 3–12.

8

The English Revolution and the Strange Death of the Old College

Cambridge, Parliament and the Civil War[1]

The wind having been sown, the whirlwind was duly reaped, and the reapers included many who least deserved their bitter wages. The early 1640s were one of those moments in English history when the centre no longer held, and when moderate men went to the wall: Emmanuel men like Bishop Joseph Hall, who had 'hard measure',[2] and the Master of the College when Parliament went to war against its king, Richard Holdsworth, whose measure was harder still. The man of the hour was an estate manager of very modest means and small reputation, who for reasons hard to fathom was chosen one of the M.P.s for the town of Cambridge in both the parliaments elected in 1640: a certain Oliver Cromwell, who in the election to the Long Parliament was thought to have won by a single vote. It was said that 'by this slender wire was such an Engine moved, that afterwards tore up the Church and State'.[3] Cambridge in the 1640s would be dominated by Cromwell and by his sometime Huntingdon neighbour, later his ideological and political opponent, Edward Montagu, second earl of Manchester. When it came to war between the king and the parliament, what both sides called this 'unnatural war',[4] Cambridge was often in the front line, the key to the wealthy parliamentary heartland of East Anglia. It was from time to time a garrison town for parliamentary soldiery, who misbehaved themselves as soldiers will, a town under martial law and prepared for the worst, with all the stone bridges over the Cam demolished, at one point in the

---

[1]   This chapter is heavily reliant on Twigg 1990.
[2]   See above, p. 89.
[3]   Cooper 1845, p. 297. See John Morrill, 'The Making of Oliver Cromwell', in John Morrill, ed., *Oliver Cromwell and the English Revolution* (London, 1990). Morrill does not claim to have fathomed the mystery of Cromwell's election, but thinks that the explanation may lie in an undocumented connection with the earl of Warwick, brother to the earl of Holland, Cambridge's chancellor.
[4]   Twigg 1990, p. 91.

hostilities a concentration camp for royalist prisoners (in more normal times St John's College). With the town mostly parliamentarian and the university largely royalist, there were sometimes skirmishes and deaths in the streets of Cambridge itself.

Normal academic life was hardly sustainable. For a year or two, the public ceremonies which punctuated the academic year were suspended. Rents were hard to collect and the war years saw a catastrophic fall in college incomes. At Emmanuel, where thirty-three students had matriculated in 1640–1, there was only one matriculant in 1643–4. In the university at large, the equivalent figures were 317 and 45.[5] It was reported from Cambridge in March 1643 that 'the schollers there begin to leave the University'.[6] Here was some anticipation of the Cambridge of 1914–18. A Christ's man, Thomas Smith, later to be university librarian, an enthusiastic student of oriental languages and an admirer of the great Ralph Cudworth, 'the honour of Emanuel College', tells us how England's troubles could become one young man's frustration. He had come to Cambridge from St Paul's School with an exhibition from the Mercers' Company of £10 a year. But 'the wars increasing, charity decreased', and the Mercers told him that since they had to pay so much in war taxation they could no longer support him. For a time Smith was forced to become a schoolmaster, exiled from a Cambridge which was 'my only paradise upon earth'.[7] And yet, somehow or other, learning was sustained, not only the traditional curriculum but the newer studies which were to effect an intellectual revolution, later in the century. By 1648, Smith was back in Cambridge, teaching Greek, Hebrew and Rhetoric, and hoping for a fellowship at Emmanuel, where they were thought to favour 'such as have best skill in the Orientals'. But there was much discouragement. 'A general opinion hath bespread our young scholars (I wish I might not say our Fellowes too) that humane learning is no way profitable, much lesse necessary to Divinity, which they account the only knowledge.'[8] But at Emmanuel, all through these years, payments were made to the lecturers in Greek (William Sancroft) and Hebrew (Ralph Cudworth and Ezekiel Culverwell), while substantial sums were spent on the library.[9]

On the whole, it was probably helpful that Parliament and its committees had no radical plan to 'reform' the university, and little enough time to spend on its affairs. More than half of the M.P.s of 1640 had been

---

[5] Ibid., pp. 83, 291.
[6] Heywood and Wright 1854, II, p. 457.
[7] Thomas Smith to Samuel Hartlib, 18 October 1647, 29 November 1647; Sheffield University Library, Hartlib Papers 15/6, 1B–2A, 5A–6B.
[8] Thomas Smith to Samuel Hartlib, 9 December 1647, 24 April 1648, 11 October n.y., 22 October 1647, ibid., 7B, 17 A–B, 27A–28B, 3A–4B.
[9] ECA, BUR.8.2.

students at Oxford and Cambridge, and they had no desire to reform their *almae matres* out of existence. For the most part a distinction was made between errant individuals and the university and its colleges, and there was no threat to institutions. Most interventions in university and college affairs, which were actually less intrusive than the ceaseless flow of royal mandates under the Stuarts, were motivated by a kind of political necessity: the need to purge societies inclined to royalism of 'malignant' 'delinquents'. There was also a resolve to cleanse the colleges of the 'popish', 'canterburian' abuses of Laudian religion, manifested early in the life of the Long Parliament by a sub-committee of the Grand Committee for Religion, which soon became a full Committee of the House 'to consider of the Abuses in Matters of Religion and Civil Government, either done or suffered by the Universities'; and, in 1643, in William Dowsing's iconoclastic 'visitation'.[10] Dowsing was followed by two more official and momentous visitations, each of which brought about the greatest disruption, both to the colleges of the university and to personal careers, which Cambridge had ever experienced. In January 1644, as part of a general crackdown on dissidence in the eastern counties, the earl of Manchester was empowered to investigate the personnel of the university and other clergy of the region who were scandalous, or 'ill-affected to the parliament, or Fomenters of this unnaturall Warre', who were to be ejected, and their estates and incomes sequestered. Manchester and his committees were also to administer, as a test of loyalty, the Scottish-inspired Solemn League and Covenant, tendering an oath which denounced prelatical episcopacy and endorsed the presbyterian ecclesiastical system. He was assisted in the work by two chaplains, one of them an Emmanuel man, Simeon Ash. There were at least 212 expulsions. (Emmanuel was a rather special case, to which we shall return.) This was called 'new modelling Cambridge'.[11] Five years later, with Charles I defeated and beheaded, and chancellor of the University, the earl of Holland, executed, as it were, in the same breath, the English Republic subjected Cambridge to a new visitation in order to impose the Engagement, a form of words which ran: 'I do declare and promise, that I will be true and faithful to the Commonwealth of England, as the same is now established, without a King or a House of Lords.' This new test resulted in upwards of fifty further expulsions, a rather ineffective purge which has been called 'a sorry showdown'. As we shall see, however ineffective and messy, this exercise was brilliantly successful in driving innumerable small wedges into an academic community which was always competitive and systemically suspicious of motives. Samuel Dillingham wrote to William Sancroft: 'Some have subscribed that were never

---

[10] Twigg 1990, chapter 5; Mullinger 1911, pp. 273–322.
[11] Twigg 1990, pp. 152–3.

dreamed on; others quite contrary: whence I have learned not to think of men by this touchstone.'[12] There was an ironical sting in the tail of these proceedings when Manchester, who had succeeded Holland as chancellor, was in his turn removed, and for refusing the Engagement, to be replaced by Lord Chief Justice Oliver St John.[13]

The impact of these events on Emmanuel can best be traced through the sad but in some ways heroic story of the decline and fall of Richard Holdsworth. We have seen that as the curtain rose on the English Revolution, Holdsworth was something of a trimmer, a friend of the Parliament, but also a royal chaplain who in the crucial summer of 1641 was offered, but refused, a bishopric.[14] It was not long before Holdsworth became an object of suspicion. One way in which some Cambridge colleges and individual members of colleges disclosed their 'delinquency', on the eve of the Civil War, was in responding to the king's request for financial aid, and for the surrender (ostensibly on loan, at interest) of college plate, much of which in the event was prevented from leaving Cambridge, or intercepted, by Cromwell. Three heads of houses, Beale of St John's, Martin of Queens' and Sterne of Jesus, were carried off to the Tower for their part in this affair, and stayed there. Holdsworth was another head who clearly believed that he had no choice but to come to his royal master's assistance, and all of the £100 contributed by Emmanuel appears to have come from his own pockets.[15] But for the moment he retained the confidence of Parliament, enough confidence to be nominated to the Westminster Assembly of Divines, appointed to advise on the post-revolutionary ecclesiastical settlement.

But if the choice had to be made, and it had, Holdsworth was a royalist, and as vice-chancellor he was in an exposed and vulnerable position. In July 1641 his Commencement address was one long lament for what appeared to be the coming eclipse of both University and Church. The speech was heard by members of parliament and was referred to a parliamentary committee.[16] When Charles I returned from Scotland in November, Holdsworth took first place in a volume of congratulatory verses, published by the university printer, Roger Daniel.[17] In March 1642, the king was in Cambridge in person, and Holdsworth chose the anniversary of his accession to preach a robustly royalist sermon in Great St Mary's.[18] As an elegy in doggerel verse later put it: 'The kings day first

---

[12] Ibid., pp. 156–63; Mullinger 1911, pp. 368–92.
[13] See above, pp. 210–13.
[14] See above, pp. 224–5.
[15] Twigg 1990, pp. 70–8.
[16] Mullinger 1911, pp. 215–19.
[17] Cooper 1845, p. 317.
[18] Mullinger 1911, p. 223.

began his night,/And dragd him from his peace to fight.'[19] A year later, Holdsworth was arrested and brought to the bar of the House of Commons for his part in the publication by the university printer, first of an anti-parliamentarian pamphlet denouncing resistance to the crown, and then of a reprint of Charles I's *Declarations*, first published in York on the eve of the Civil War.[20] Holdsworth caused further offence by a sermon preached when held in lax custody in London. In June 1643, a parliamentary committee appointed to consider a petition from Cambridge for 'succour and encouragement', and specifically for relief from taxation, was invited 'to consider the State of Emmanuel College, and . . . of the Carriage and Behaviour of Dr Holdsworth, the Master thereof; by what means he came into that Place, and whether, by his Demeanour since, he hath not forfeited the said Place'.[21] Four months later Samuel Ward of Sidney Sussex died, and the University elected Holdsworth Lady Margaret Professor in his place. There could hardly have been a stronger candidate, but this was the ultimate provocation, and Holdsworth was now imprisoned in the Tower. He was released two years later, but forbidden to travel more than twenty miles from London. In 1647 he managed to kiss hands at Hampton Court and, for what little that was now worth, was made dean of Windsor. In September 1648, he made further unsuccessful efforts to attend the king, now only weeks away from his trial and execution. 'So here is their circle: first we are imprisoned because with the king, and then denied to be with the king because imprisoned.' Holdsworth never saw Cambridge, or his vast library, again, and he died in 1649.[22]

Long before that, Holdsworth had been formally deposed from his mastership in the course of Manchester's visitation. Two fellows of the college, Robert Soresby and Richard Weller, were also ejected, together with three other fellows whose cases were rather different; and we shall return to them.[23] Holdsworth's successor, imposed on the college but an internal candidate (Manchester was civilised in these dealings), was an old-fashioned Calvinist, Anthony Tuckney, a cousin of John Cotton and his successor as vicar of Boston. Morally, Holdsworth remained Master. Sancroft wrote in May 1646: 'We cannot yet with leave enjoy him here, though I dare still hope the time will come when he shall not come to us as a stranger to lodge for a night, but as the soul and life of this body,

---

[19] The late Jeremy Maule, an inexhaustible mine of archival information, discovered these verses in a MS. in the Clark Library in Los Angeles. Unfortunately he failed to provide me with a reference, but it is far more unfortunate that I am now unable to ask him for it.

[20] Twigg 1990, pp. 84–7.

[21] Cooper 1845, pp. 348–9.

[22] Mullinger 1911, pp. 255–7; Holdsworth to Sancroft, 4 September 1648, Cary 1842, II, pp. 11–12; *DNB*, art. Holdsworth.

[23] Mullinger 1911, pp. 312–13. And see p. 252 below.

which hath been in a fainting and swooning condition ever since he was by violent hands snatched from us.'[24] In the best tradition of the college, Holdsworth continued to feed prime gentry pupils to Sancroft. Of one of these he wrote: 'You may please to take notice that he is a baronet'; of another, that he was only a pensioner, 'but a pretty scholar, and a very fine child, and one that I love'. Sancroft duly responded. 'Put him into Sizar Rawlett's study. The income is about fifty shillings.'[25] There were the usual delicate niceties over rooms. Holdsworth wrote about the accommodation of one of his protégés: 'I would be loath to be put to speak to Mr Tuckney; but if there be no remedy, I must.'[26] He urged young Sancroft to make friends with Tuckney, as man to man, if not as Master,[27] and he remained civil to a man who was evidently not only a usurper but an absentee. When, as vice-chancellor, Tuckney began to reside in the college, he visited Holdsworth to ask permission to use his furniture and to penetrate his study: 'which I granted him on this condition, that he would use things well, and carry none with him, not so much as to look in, but only himself, and leave no books abroad'.[28] Holdsworth's divorce from his books must have been the worst of it. He told Sancroft: 'I would fain forget them but I cannot; every book I look on revives the remembrance.'[29]

Outwardly, things could not have been better, or more courteously, managed. Holdsworth wrote: 'The college hath a share of my books which I hope will preserve the whole. The furniture of my lodging it must needs go, it will please me the better if they give it to my successor than to a sequestrator. The college plate for which I stand engaged must be supply'd whatever else miscarry; if other fellows have not restored theirs, it is no example for me nor credit for them. There is as much plate as will satisfy left behind as a pawn. I pray take it into your custody, and now account it not mine but the college's.' The sequestrator got the value of the hay and wood in the outhouses, £2 15s 0d, while Manchester intervened personally to prevent the sequestration of the books.[30] There were 10,000 books, and we have not heard the last of them.[31] Our doggerel elegist has this final comment on Holdsworth: 'Fit for his ruine in this age.'[32]

---

[24] Sancroft to his father, 4 May 1646, Cary 1842, I, pp. 15–19.
[25] Holdsworth to Sancroft, 14 April 1647, 16 April 1647, 30 June 1647, 13 November 1647, 4 September 1648, Sancroft to Thomas Holdsworth, 4 November 1648, ibid., I, pp. 192–4, 273–4, 359–60, II, pp. 11–12, 51–3.
[26] Holdsworth to Sancroft, 16 April 1647, ibid., I, pp. 193–4.
[27] Holdsworth to Sancroft, 18 November 1648, ibid., II, pp. 58–9.
[28] Ibid.
[29] Holdsworth to Sancroft, 14 April 1647, ibid., I, pp. 192–3.
[30] Mullinger 1911, pp. 312–13; ECA, COL.9.1(B) (William Bennet's book), pp. 77–8; Twigg 1990, pp. 117, 152–3.
[31] See pp. 270–1 below.
[32] See n. 19.

Holdsworth's last days coincided with a short-lived, pyrrhic victory for the old college, in many ways its apogee and last stand. Puritan Emmanuel now basked in the sun of the Commonwealth and Protectorate, the old stigma of preciseness turned on its head, as the old guard dictated what was politically, and theologically, correct. But it was a straw's breadth which separated the victims, men such as Holdsworth, from the new victors, a straw's breadth of conscience. In normal times such differences as split them asunder would have been settled over a glass or two of wine, in the parlour. And settled or not, it mattered very little, until the monster of the state, Leviathan, intervened.

One symbol of the new status of Emmanuel was a decision by the parliamentary Committee for the Reformation of the Universities, taken in August 1650, that both Emmanuel and Sidney Sussex should join the rest of the University, for the first time, in enjoying their fair, rotarian, share of the office of proctor, with other minor offices. Strange as it may seem, until this moment, the largest college in the University had been only partly of the University.[33]

William Sancroft, as we shall see,[34] wrote melodramatically of the decapitation of whole colleges. But new heads were stuck on, and most of them were Emmanuel heads. No less than ten heads of houses were imposed on Cambridge by the regime, to replace those ejected in Manchester's purge, with another three elected in 1646 and 1647 to fill places which fell vacant by natural causes. Of these no less than eight were Emmanuel men: in the first tranche, besides Tuckney at Emmanuel itself, Ralph Cudworth at Clare (and from 1654 Master of Christ's), Thomas Hill, who was initially thought of as Holdsworth's replacement at Emmanuel but almost at once was preferred to Trinity, Thomas Horton at Queens', Lazarus Seaman at Peterhouse, William Spurstowe at St Catharine's, and Benjamin Whichcote at King's. Whichcote was uncomfortable about his appointment as Provost of King's. 'Their necessity required me, and I served their necessity.' That statement postdates the Restoration, but, in the eighteenth century, there was said to have survived better evidence for his indecision: 'a short schedule', containing reasons *pro* and *contra*, 'in the course of this deliberation and debate within himself'.[35] When Whichcote's Emmanuel colleague John Worthington displaced Richard Sterne from the Master's Lodge at Jesus, he shared these scruples: 'It was not my seeking.' Whichcote sent him ten reassuring reasons for acceptance, including: 'You had no hand in it', and, 'he

---

[33] Heywood and Wright 1854, II, pp. 528–30.
[34] See pp. 252–3 below.
[35] Twigg 1990, pp. 103–5, 117–18, 178; *Eight Letters of Dr Antony Tuckney and Dr Benjamin Whichcote,* bound with *Moral and Religious Aphorisms . . . of the Reverend and Learned Doctor Whichcote* (1753), p. xviii.

cannot return if you give way.'[36] Whichcote gave half of his annual dividend to his ejected predecessor, Samuel Collins. And, as we have seen, Anthony Tuckney did not presume, at least at first, to move into the Master's Lodge at Emmanuel, or even to return to the college from his London parish.

The strangest of these politically and ideologically inspired acts of intrusion was to make Master of Gonville and Caius another Emmanuel man, William Dell, who came back to Cambridge after an exciting wartime career as an army chaplain and preacher to the New Model Army and confidant of Oliver Cromwell, a man said by Richard Baxter to have neither understood himself nor to have been understood by others, and characterised by Mullinger as 'a divine whose best energies were given to proclaiming his antipathies'. What was particularly odd about Dell's appointment was that he was not sure that Oxbridge should continue to exist in its traditional, pre-revolutionary form. He favoured a radically reformed, modern and practical curriculum, and the creation of universities or colleges in most major towns and cities, including York and Norwich, which would have to wait three hundred years to see his eccentric vision realised. But Caius remembers its Emmanuel cuckoo in the nest with some affection, perhaps because he spent more time in his Bedfordshire parish (where he entertained the tinker preacher John Bunyan) than in Cambridge.[37]

The Emmanuel of William Sancroft the Younger

Colleges, like individual human beings, have their climacterics, times of relatively sudden change, alterations much more than circumstantial, alterations almost of identity. Looking back, observers who believe in progress, or in what is soon to be rather than what has been, will see a hopeful and forward-looking advance. Those who are part of what was, what used to be, will fear the demise of all that they have held dear. Somewhere between the late nineteenth and early twentieth centuries, Corpus Christi, from having been the most evangelical of Cambridge colleges, became in churchmanship avant-garde Anglo-Catholic.[1] So it

---

[36] Crossley 1847, pp. 39–40.
[37] Brooke 1985, pp. 129–31; Mullinger 1911, pp. 364–7.

[1] Brooke 1993, pp. 50–1. The principal source for this section is Sancroft's correspondence in the Tanner MSS., Bodleian Library. There are copies and extensive extracts from the letters in three places: ECA, COL.9.8; George D'Oyly, *The Life of William Sancroft*, 2 vols. (London, 1821); and *Memorials of the Great Civil War in England from 1642 to 1652, Edited from Original Letters in the Bodleian Library*, ed. Henry Cary, 2 vols. (London, 1842). I have sometimes found it convenient to cite these secondary sources.

was, in a more complicated way, with Emmanuel, in the 1640s and 1650s. The old puritan college of Mildmay, Chaderton, Preston and the elder Sancroft strangely died. It was replaced by not one new Emmanuel but two, two colleges which sometimes lived in the mind and spirit of the same individual: the one intellectually expansive and liberal, in touch with strands of thought which are held to constitute the philosophical and scientific revolution of the seventeenth century, a new world of latitude and reason; the other, ardent above all for Church and King, for the sacredness of the Church, a new current of high churchmanship. Both tendencies can be understood as reactions against the single-minded, if not narrow, Calvinism of the old college. The first we shall consider in the next section. But this section belongs to William Sancroft, nephew of the third master and destined to become the sixth, and the seventy-eighth archbishop of Canterbury; and to the beginnings, so far as Emmanuel was concerned, of what we may start to call Anglicanism.

People who never throw anything away are bound to catch the attention of historians. Such a person was Sancroft. The Bodleian Library is bursting at the seams with his correspondence and notebooks, the detritus of a lifetime, to the extent that Sancroft must dominate the history of his college at this critical juncture in its intellectual trajectory.[2] The archive opens in Sancroft's early teens, with schoolboy essays from Bury St Edmunds and early sermon notes, trying out a new pen: 'William Sandcroft is my name and with my pen I writ the same and if my pen it had bin better I would have mended ons my letter.'[3] It closes as the ever active pen of the elderly and deprived archbishop of Canterbury occupied his enforced leisure by filling little notebooks with millions of words of tiny handwriting.[4] Yet this archival accident (for everything *could* have gone up in smoke) is not necessarily distorting. Sancroft was, from the first moment that we observe him, a very considerable figure, in the perception of his elders and mentors, such as Richard Holdsworth, and, it has to be said, of himself.

---

[2] In addition to the Tanner MSS., there are in Bodl. 145 volumes of Sancroft MSS., consisting for the most part of commonplace books and other notebooks, mostly in Sancroft's distinctive hand, but including papers of his uncle, William Sancroft the elder, and several MSS. of Richard Holdsworth. Although many pages are blank, these notebooks must contain some millions of words on subjects which range from the sublime to the ridiculous: sermon notes and divinity commonplaces, but also divinations, dreams and prophecies (MS. Sancroft 51), 105 'Oxford jests', and the 1607 satire known as the 'Great Parliament Fart' (MS. Sancroft 53). There is a stray Sancroft commonplace book in MS. Rawlinson D 816.

[3] School essays, Bodl., MS. Tanner 467, no. 1; Bodl. Libr., flyleaf of MS. Sancroft 62, containing notes of sermons, some of which may have been heard at Bury St Edmunds, as a schoolboy.

[4] The later notebooks suggest that the 'inditing' habits of a lifetime were never abandoned. Sancroft MS. 28 contains notes on the Salem witch trials, dated 1693 (pp. 405 ff.). Sancroft died in November 1693.

The reader will recall that the Sandcrofts (or Sancrofts) were minor Suffolk gentry.[5] Their family home, Ufford Hall in the village of Fressingfield, was an emotional anchor for Sancroft, a lifelong bachelor, and in the days of his greatness it was a kind of Colombey-les-deux-Eglises. As dean of St Paul's, he was there throughout the great plague of 1665, and there again when his cathedral burned down in 1666, only hearing of the event some days later.[6] After being deprived of his archbishopric by the new regime of the Glorious Revolution, he ended his days in Fressingfield exile, at the age of seventy-four building a new house for himself on the old property.[7] Years before, he had written to his brother, longing to hear the latest of 'the story of Fressingfield', 'the marvailes of your dairy, with the wooden looking glass on the shelf'.[8] A friend wrote from London to say that he would leave town tomorrow, 'could I find a Fressingfield among my relations'.[9]

Sancroft's father sent William and his older brother Thomas to Emmanuel in 1633, Thomas, the heir, for 'finishing', William to begin a life dedicated to learning. The father wrote to his brother, the Master: 'William will not hazard the losse of any opportunity that may tend to his furtheraunce.'[10] Returning from the Long Vacation in 1635, William wrote: 'I pray forget not to send our shoes, my brother Thomas his cheese.'[11] Sancroft's progress as a scholar was rapid. He and his chamber fellow and dearest friend, Arthur Bownest, vied with one another in extreme diligence. A set of good resolutions is worth quoting in full:

'August 1. I begin this course of studies, which I purpose to continue all this vacation.

1 I will be at chappell every morning.

2 After chappell, and my private devotions, I will read a chapter in the Greeke Testament and note something in it.

3 The rest of the forenoone, till halfe an houre past 10, I intend for Hebrew.

---

[5] See p. 222 above.

[6] Sancroft's movements at the time of the Great Plague and the Fire of London are documented in his correspondence in BL, MS. Harl. 3785, and in Bodl., MSS. Tanner 45, fols. 17, 28, 53, Tanner 467, fols. 52–4, 56. And see especially MS. Tanner 45, fol. 94, Sancroft to Sir John Breton, 6 September 1666, written from Fressingfield: 'I intend about Michaelmas by God's permission to return to London.' The fire began on 2 September and had engulfed St Paul's two days before this letter, which betrays no knowledge of it, was written. A correspondent wrote to inform him of 'this dismall accident of London' on 11 September. (MS. Tanner 45, fol. 95.)

[7] See p. 278 below.

[8] Sancroft to his brother, Thomas Sancroft, 10 July 1650, Bodl., MS. Tanner 56, fol. 216.

[9] John Gayer to Sancroft, 7 May 1655, BL, MS. Harl. 3783, fol. 128.

[10] Thomas Sancroft the elder to William Sancroft the elder, n.d. (1633), BL, MS. Harl. 3783, fol. 24.

[11] Sancroft to his father, 17 August 1635, Bodl., MS. Tanner 467, fol. 48.

4 From 1 of the clock till 3 I'll read Homer's Odysses.

5 From 3 till 5 Ile studie Ethicks. Arist. Thomas. Pavonius.

6 The rest of my time, and an houre after praiers I reserve for emergent occasions in my study.

7 I will be at praiers in my Tutors chamber constantly.

8 Saterday in the afternoone, and Sunday I'le study Divinitie.

9 Breakefasts are breakestudies. I'll abjure them; all but a draught of College beere and a morsell of bread.' [12]

Sancroft somehow survived the blow of Bownest's death, evidently the greatest emotional crisis of his life,[13] and by 1641 the Master, Holdsworth, regarded him as the strongest candidate for the next vacant fellowship, while encouraging him to take seriously the offer of a chaplaincy in the household of an unnamed earl.[14] He resisted this temptation, a possible path to preferment, became a fellow in 1642, and by 1644 was bursar, reader in both Greek and Hebrew (described in his own bursarial accounts in 1647 as 'head lecturer'), and a tutor whose practice built on Holdsworth's exemplary foundations, and who soon aroused the same devotion in his pupils that Sancroft felt for Holdsworth.[15]

The contents of Sancroft's notebooks, and of his large library, much of which survives in Emmanuel, reveal an extraordinarily wide-ranging and well-stocked mind, full, like his commonplace books, of all kinds of literature (the Greek and Latin classics above all, but also the English poets, Shakespeare, other plays, in Spanish as well as Latin and English), curious scientific observations ('dogs suffer from sea-sickness', 'shells of fishes found 100 200 miles from the sea, on the tops of mountains' 'i granchi (crabbs) never go but side-wise, gambari (lobsters) I have seen go forward and then backe' – these morsels garnered from a book published in Venice in 1646).[16] In his still surviving library, L'Antidemon Historial (Lyon, 1609) sits alongside Segunda Parte del Ingenioso Cavallero Don Quixote Dela Mancha (Brussels, 1616). Until the very year of his (impecunious) death, Sancroft kept up his subscriptions to foreign periodicals, such as Le Journal des Scavans (Amsterdam). Music was a lifelong passion, shared not only within the family circle, which was

---

[12] Bodl., MS. Sancroft 80, p. 3.

[13] See above, p. 62.

[14] D'Oyly 1821, I, pp. 15–18, 23.

[15] DNB, art. Sancroft; ECA, BUR. 8.2; Sancroft to 'Jacobissimo suo' (a pupil), Bodl., MS. Tanner 467, fol. 60r–v; letters from Henry Paman, later a distinguished physician and Fellow of the Royal Society, Sancroft's lifelong friend (Emmanuel, 1643, St John's 1646) to his 'honoured tutor', D'Oyly 1821, I, pp. 50–1, 54–5, 80–4, Cary 1842, II, pp. 249–50, 252–3; and from his brother Clement, 'honoured tutor', Bodl., MS. Tanner 56, fol. 249.

[16] Bodl., MS. Sancroft 28, pp. 190 ff. See above, p. 73, for further discussion of Sancroft's notebooks.

easily converted into a consort of viols, but with his friends the Norths, notable musical practitioners and patrons.[17]

But although Sancroft's piety, and priestly vocation, are not in doubt, he does not seem to have had a profound interest in theology, and the reactionary trajectory which we are about to trace was evidently more political than theological. It used to be thought that Sancroft was responsible for the English translation of a Dutch satire called *Fur Praedestinatus*, and in English *The predestinated thief*, which mounted a tendentious attack on Calvinism as equivalent to the antinomianism which was its perversion. In a manner reminiscent of James Hogg's *The Memoirs and Confessions of a Justified Sinner*, it tells of a criminal condemned to hang who is convinced, in spite of his wicked life, that he is predestined to salvation. But we now know that Sancroft was not the translator.[18] However he was, as we shall see, the author of *Modern Policies, Taken from Machiavel, Borgia and Other Choise Authors* (1652). There is not much, if any, evidence that Sancroft was an anti-Calvinist, but plenty to establish that he was anti-puritan, and indeed anti everything which happened in Church and State from the fateful year of 1640. In the bloody fruition of the regicide, in 1649, he wrote: 'I looke upon the cursed Puritan faction as the ruine of the most glorious Church upon earth (in whose Faith I still live and hope to die).'[19] In 1640 poor Arthur Bownest's mother had written, asking for reliable information about a pond in Cambridge which was blood-red at both ends, but clear in the middle. She thought this a 'prodigious prognostication', and who is to say that she was wrong? Not Sancroft.[20]

The source of what it is only faintly anachronistic to call Sancroft's high churchmanship, more or less contrary to the religion in which he was reared, his uncle's religion, is unknown, but perhaps it was his tutor

---

[17] See Sancroft to his father, 27 November 1648: arriving at Bury 'and going to Mr North with my letter, found there some forty strangers in a room, listening to good voices, well managed, and a lute well strung.' (Cary 1842, II, pp. 63–6.) There is a tradition that Sancroft formed a consort of voices with his Emmanuel colleague John Worthington and Humfrey Babington of Trinity. On leaving Lambeth, the deprived Archbishop Sancroft gave Roger North his bass viol 'which he had at Cambridge and had all his life.' (Crossley 1847, p. 28.)

[18] *Fur Praedestinatus: sive, dialogismus inter quendam Ordinis Praedicantium Calvinistam et Furem* was printed in London in 1651. There is a unique copy of the English edition of 1658, *The predestinated thief*, at Dulwich College. See Thomas Jackson, 'Archbishop Sancroft Not the Author of "The Predestinated Thief"', Dr Williams's Library Pamphlets, G. F. Nuttall, 'Some Bibliographical Notes and Identifications', *Congregational Historical Society Transactions*, 16 (1949–51), 154–5. I owe these references to Dr Nicholas Tyacke.

[19] Sancroft to his brother, 10 July 1650, Bodl., MS. Tanner 56, fol. 216. Sancroft copied out the anti-puritan character satire 'Who is a puritan?' ('Long hath it vext our learned age to scan/Who rightly might be term'd a Puritan . . .') (Bodl., MS. Tanner 465, fol. 82); and composed an 'Epilogue to Tartuffe, spoken by himself', consisting of references to Ben Jonson's *Bartholomew Fair* and *The Alchemist*. (Bodl., MS. Sancroft 53, pp. 5–6.)

[20] Mrs Bownest to Sancroft, 29 July 1640; Bodl., MS. Tanner 467, fol. 71.

Ezekiel Wright, with whom he enjoyed a lasting affinity. In 1663 he wrote: 'Sir, I never pleased myself more [than?] in the relation I once had to you.'[21] Wright was not one of the Emmanuel fellows indicted by a committee of the Long Parliament for Laudian ceremonialism,[22] but along with those who were, Nicholas Hall and the future master, Thomas Holbech, he was soon out of favour with the Parliamentarians. In December 1640 Parliament appointed a committee to review the statutes of Emmanuel.[23] The point at issue, of course, was the ever controversial statute *de mora sociorum*, which Charles I had suspended, with questionable legality, in 1627.[24] It was alleged that a candidate for a fellowship had been illegally elected by the votes of three fellows who, according to *de mora*, were *non socii*: Hall, Holbech and Wright. Although their status remained as uncertain as the validity of *de mora* itself, it is ironical that it was evidently one of these fellowships, perhaps even Wright's, to which Sancroft was presently elected.[25] In 1644 the trio would, it appears, have refused subscription to the Solemn League and Covenant, but rather than suffering deprivation, they were deemed to be no fellows, according to the terms of the disputed statute.[26] It is just possible that the reactivation of the *de mora* issue had to do with the obnoxious churchmanship of our trio, who included Sancroft's tutor.

Sancroft's correspondence leaves us in no doubt about the fierceness of his church-and-king royalism as revolutionary politics led to Civil War. He avoided subscription to the Covenant, which he called 'the thing out of the North':[27] 'to comply would be to throw a foule aspersion upon the whole Church of God in England since the Reformation'.[28] In spite of this, he led a charmed existence as a fellow of Emmanuel for another seven years. But Holdsworth's removal from the mastership drove Sancroft into a kind of hyperbolic despair: 'I had not thought they would have beheaded whole colleges at a blow; nay, whole universities and whole churches too.' 'They' were worse than the Emperor Caligula, who had

---

[21] Sancroft to Ezekiel Wright, 'my ever honoured tutor', from 'your most observant pupil', 17 January 1663, D'Oyly 1821, I, pp. 125–31. There is a copy of Sancroft's letter in ECA COL.9.1A ('William Bennet's Book' vol. 1).

[22] See p. 244 above.

[23] Twigg 1990, pp. 55–6.

[24] See pp. 27–8 above.

[25] Sancroft to his father, 10 September, 12 October 1641, 4 April 1642; D'Oyly 1821, I, pp. 15–18, 23, Bodl., MS. Tanner 467, fol. 50.

[26] Twigg 1990, pp. 55–6, 297. On 17 October 1643, John Almond and John Sadler appealed to Bishop Ralph Brownrigg, deputy vice-chancellor, against the ruling of Robert Soresby, *locum tenens* for the vice-chancellor (Richard Holdsworth) that their fellowships were void according to Statute 26 'for too long absence from the Colledge'. Brownrigg found for the appellants, and declared them 'true and full fellowes'. (ECA, COL. 14.1, pp. 55–7.)

[27] Bodl., MS. Tanner 62, fol. 641.

[28] Sancroft to Richard Weller, 26 May 1645, Bodl., MS. Tanner 60, fol. 161.

lopped off the head of Jupiter in the Capitol, replacing it with his own.[29] 'They' soon became Oliver Cromwell, 'his Mightinesse' for whom Sancroft developed a peculiar hatred.[30] In 1645, he wrote: 'I cannot look upon this bleeding kingdom, this dying church, with the same indifference as I would read the history of Japan or hear the affairs of China related.'[31] Sancroft could not be reconciled to the usurper, Tuckney. Returning to Cambridge from Fressingfield in November 1648, he found 'all well, only that Mr Tuckney was vice-chancellor . . ., my continuing inconvenience'.[32]

In his correspondence with Holdsworth, and other victims of the regime, including his old tutor, Sancroft drew upon primitive sources to extol their triumphant fate as martyrs. Angels would minister to them 'as to the old Egyptian hermits', or to St John on Patmos.[33] When the Covenant threatened, in 1643, he wrote: 'I am going forth, I know not whither: God, I hope, will provide me with a hiding place.'[34] In 1650, with the Engagement hanging over his head, he responded in agitated, theatrical terms to a gentleman who had made a bread-and-butter offer of a domestic chaplaincy. 'Were the Primitive Monkery retrivd', he would become a monk in 'the utmost recesses and solitudes of the desert', 'in the homeliest cell', abandoning a world in which tyrannny and atheism were triumphant.[35] All this was very much in a complex character, for Sancroft would behave in the same way forty years later, when the so-called Glorious Revolution of 1688 pulled the ideological rug from under his church-and-king feet.[36]

But, in the 1640s, Sancroft and the college continued to live, not in the Egyptian desert, but as if things were normal. Sir Thomas Littleton wrote about his son: 'I request . . . that you would provide him of a private lodging, where he may have the commodity of dressing his diet, and a private stable, there or near his lodging, for four or five horses.'[37] The father of another pupil believed that his son was entitled to occupy the

---

[29] Sancroft to Richard Holdsworth, 17 December 1645, Bodl., MS. Tanner 61, fol. 261.
[30] Bodl., MS. Tanner 56, fol. 216.
[31] Sancroft to Richard Weller, 26 May 1645; Bodl., MS. Tanner 60, fol. 161.
[32] Sancroft to his father, 27 November 1648, Cary 1842, II, pp. 63–6. And see Sancroft to Thomas Holdsworth, 21 October 1648: 'But why no news of Mr Tuckney? Did he come? Is he gone?' (Ibid., II, pp. 38–40.)
[33] Sancroft to Ezekiel Wright, n.d., Sancroft to Richard Holdsworth, 1 December 1644; Bodl., MS. Tanner 61, fols. 64, 201. In writing to both correspondents, Sancroft prefaces his reference to ministering angels with: 'Pardon my pious credulity if I think . . .'
[34] Sancroft to 'Mr Need', Bodl., MS. Tanner 62, fol. 641.
[35] Sir Framlingham Gawdy to Sancroft, and Sancroft to Gawdy, Bodl., MS. Tanner 56, fol. 163.
[36] See pp. 277–9 below.
[37] Littleton to Sancroft, 21 May 1646, Cary 1842, I, pp. 54–6.

founder's chambers. 'If you have not already moved it, I pray do it at the next meeting of the fellows.'[38]

1649 must have occasioned more emotional turmoil even than 1641, the year of Bownest's death. In February Sancroft lost his father, 'the sole prop of this now ruined family'.[39] In August, Holdsworth was dead. Sancroft told Holdsworth's closest friend, Bishop Ralph Brownrigg, that he was shedding 'rivers of tears upon his hearse'. It was only his 'high inimitable example' which had reconciled him to his place in Emmanuel.[40] But these sad events were almost eclipsed by the catastrophe of 30 January, the regicide, which, indeed, had served to precipitate the death of Sancroft's father. Sancroft wrote: 'The waters of the ocean we swim in cannot wash out the spots of that blood, than which never any was shed with greater guilt since the Son of God poured out his.' This was 'the martyrdom of the best Protestant in these kingdoms, and incomparably the best king upon earth, Charles, the pious and the glorious . . .'[41]

As the republican Engagement was pressed upon the University, but in a messy and confused way, Sancroft was only one of many who found themselves acting out a novel by Kafka. Everyone acted out of character, and usually out of self-interest. The day of execution for Sancroft was postponed again and again and even he did not know why. He suspected, uncomfortably, that someone was protecting him, and the someone was probably Brownrigg, to whom he wrote in December 1650: 'When the Cedars fall and when Lebanon shudders, who can be sensible that a poor shrub suffers?'[42] On 18 September 1650 he told his brother Thomas that he almost hoped to be dismissed sooner rather than later, for with the return of 'the Man in the North' (Cromwell) things could only be worse. He proposed to hide his head in a hole so obscure that 'our jolly conquerors' would never find him. He had already sent his books to Fressingfield, and now despatched after them his viol, wrapped in towels and napkins.[43] But in the event only a small minority of non-subscribers were ever evicted, and the crude fact was that this often only happened when younger, ambitious men, the latest crop of graduates, took

[38] Francis Gardiner to Sancroft, August 1646, ibid., I, pp. 151–3.
[39] Sancroft to Thomas Holdsworth, 20 February 1649, ibid., II, pp. 121–3.
[40] Sancroft to Bishop Ralph Brownrigg, 14 August 1649, Bodl., MS. Tanner 56, fol. 94.
[41] Sancroft to his father, 10 February 1649, Cary 1842, II, pp. 117–19.
[42] Sancroft to his brother, 13 September, 18 September, 17 November 1650, ibid., II, pp. 232–4, Bodl., MS. Tanner 56 fol. 229 (the letter of 17 November inaccurately in D'Oyly 1821, I, pp. 55–7), Samuel Dillingham to Sancroft, 22 November, 11 December, (?) December, 1650, ibid., fol. 236, Cary 1842, II, pp. 239–49; Sancroft to Brownrigg (draft), December 1650, Bodl., MS. Tanner 56, fol. 238. Brownrigg wrote (over optimistically) on 15 August 1651: ''Tis likely that you shall abide in the College till Michaelmas.' (Bodl., MS. Tanner 54, fol. 183.)
[43] Bodl., MS. Tanner 56, fol. 229.

advantage of the crisis to bid for their fellowships.[44] Those who enquired after Sancroft's fellowship were told (according to a former pupil) 'that they might as well think to remove a mountain as Mr Sancroft'.[45]

But on 10 April 1651, 'upon humble petition of Thomas Brainford', Sancroft was served formal notice (at Fressingfield) that unless he complied with the Engagement forthwith, his place would be deemed vacant.[46] Even this was not final, and it was not until the end of July that Sancroft left Emmanuel, as he must have supposed, for ever.[47] We are fortunate that a German traveller happened to record what he thought was the immediate, provocative cause of Sancroft's expulsion: a sermon in which he let his metaphorical hair down in a savage attack on the republican regime, which he compared with the tyrannies of Diocletian and Caligula, accusing it of an ambition to destroy all Christian learning: 'those bats and night-owls, disgusting birds of bad omen, lovers of the darkness, speaking ill of the sun itself and revolting against the light' (words translated into German and back again).[48] As he went off into Suffolk, Sancroft will have shared the thoughts of his colleague Samuel Dillingham, who wrote that he parted with the university as willingly as he had first embraced it, for it was 'up to the neck in rubbish (and what's Oxford then?)'.[49] No-one seems to have noticed that Sancroft was in serious breach of *de mora*. It was not until 1662 that he would take scarlet, by the royal mandate of Charles II.[50]

The place of Sancroft's rustication was, of course, Fressingfield, where his pupil Thomas Holdsworth addressed him in May 1652: 'Though you be now retired into a Persian-kinglike state, a countrey solitude and privacy, and none fit company for you but le grand Cyrus . . . May it then please your Majesty when it shall descend to converse with mortalls to present my best service.'[51] But this was deceptive. In the same year, Sancroft published his mordant best seller, *Modern Policies*, dedicated to Brownrigg and consisting of such Machiavellian maxims as 'the Politician must have the shadow of Religion, but the substance hurts' – 'there is no superstition in politics more odious then to stand too much upon niceties and scruples' – 'there is no mask that becomes Rebellion and Innovation

---

[44] Sancroft to his brother, 17 November 1650, Cary 1842, II, pp. 234–9; William Sancroft to Bishop Ralph Brownrigg, 24 May 1651, Bodl., MS. Tanner 54, fol. 77.

[45] Henry Paman to Sancroft, 23 March 1651, Cary 1842, II, pp. 252–3.

[46] ECA, COL.9.8; Bodl., MS. Tanner 54, fol. 35v; D'Oyly 1821, I, p. 58.

[47] Sancroft to Thomas Holdsworth, 6 September 1651: 'I have bin turn'd out of my fellowship these 6 weekes.' (Bodl., MS. Tanner 55, fol. 39.)

[48] Christoph Arnold to Georg Richter, 7 August 1651; F. J. M. Blom, *Christoph and Andreas Arnold and England: The Travels and Book-Collections of Two Seventeenth-Century Nurembergers* (Nuremberg, 1982), pp. 63, 81–3. I owe this reference to the kindness of Arnold Hunt.

[49] Samuel Dillingham to Sancroft, 17 July 1651, Cary 1842, II, pp. 282–3.

[50] *DNB*, art. Sancroft.

[51] Thomas Holdsworth to Sancroft, 17 May 1652, BL, MS. Harl. 3783, fol. 89.

so well as Religion'. References to 'necessity' as the 'great patroness of illegal actions' leave us in no doubt that Oliver Cromwell was his target.[52]

In 1658, Sancroft left with his friend Robert Gayer for a continental grand tour: a year in Utrecht, and then Geneva, Padua, Venice and Rome, where, in May 1660, news arrived of the return of the monarchy.[53] Within six months, Sancroft was preaching at Westminster Abbey on the occasion of the consecration of seven bishops. 'Well, blest be the Mercies of God, we are at last restored.'[54]

Emmanuel and the Cambridge Platonists

If Puritanism in its full theological development was a product of Emmanuel, so was the very different, even antipathetic theological and philosophical tendency known as Cambridge Platonism. The literature on the so-called Cambridge Platonists is immense.[1] It is a subject which currently attracts the attention not only of theologians but of philosophers and historians of the seventeenth-century scientific revolution. If, or so it seems, the Cambridge Platonists were actually going nowhere, their intellectual cul-de-sac is nevertheless of some interest, and had abiding influence. Of the most considerable member of this group, it has been said: 'Henry More is that strange and rather sad figure, a major but undisciplined talent in a minor intellectual movement that was destined to be overridden by history . . ., fated to enjoy no moment of triumph.'[2]

But it is the beginning of wisdom to understand that 'the Cambridge Platonists' scarcely existed, except as a collection of Cambridge luminaries living, thinking, teaching and writing from the 1640s to the 1680s, all

---

[52] William Sancroft, *Modern Policies* (1652), Sigs. B3, B4, F3v.

[53] BL, MS. Harl. 3783, fols. 152 ff., *passim*; MS. Harl. 3784, fols. 5, 9; D'Oyly 1821, I, pp. 93–107.

[54] William Sancroft, *A Sermon Preached In St Peter's Westminster* (London, 1660), p. 34.

[1] The foundation of all later studies is John Tulloch, *Rational Theology and Christian Philosophy in England in the Seventeenth Century: II, The Cambridge Platonists* (Edinburgh and London, 1874). Another important classic is Ernst Cassirer, tr. James P. Pettegrove, *The Platonic Renaissance in England* (London, 1953). Sympathetic and somewhat old-fashioned accounts of Cambridge Platonism as religious thought include Frederick J. Powicke, *The Cambridge Platonists: A Study* (London and Toronto, 1926 (Powicke 1926)), W. C. De Pauley, *The Candle of the Lord: Studies in the Cambridge Platonists* (London, 1937), W. K. Jordan, *The Development of Religious Toleration in England*, IV (London, 1940), and G. R. Cragg, *From Puritanism to the Age of Reason* (Cambridge, 1950). For a representative collection of more recent studies, directed towards Cambridge Platonism as philosophy and science, see R. Kroll, R. Ashcraft, P. Zagorin, eds., *Philosophy, Science, and Religion in England 1640–1700* (Cambridge, 1992). There is a selection of Cambridge Platonist writings in Cragg 1968.

[2] Hall 1990, p. 4.

of them associated with Emmanuel, or with its mother house of Christ's, to whom the term has been attributed, posthumously. In their own time, these academics and divines were called (in 1662) 'latitude men', from which we derive the vague, ugly, but useful term, 'latitudinarian', indicative of a liberal rejection of narrowness and sectarian partisanship in religion.[3] But that is not what they called themselves. Indeed, they did not call themselves anything and the existence of 'them' is itself questionable, unless it means no more than kindred spirits, sharing a common intellectual and spiritual climate. We can almost reduce their philosophy, and religion, to an ethic, the belief that it is good to be good (but also natural to be good); and to the urge to know. Henry More's tutor asked him: 'But, young man, what is the Reason . . . that you so earnestly desire to know Things?' More answered: 'I desire, I say, so earnestly to know, that I may know.'[4]

What, the reader may ask, are we to understand, in this context, by Platonism? A bare definition will have to serve. Platonism is an idealist system, a belief in the unity of all things, the unity of an idea not to be apprehended by sense, not material, but amounting to essential reality, and ultimate meaning. It was a kind of wisdom compatible with Christianity but not derivative from or dependent upon Christianity. In the thought of the much later philosophers known as neo-Platonists, idea was equivalent to Soul, a Soul immanent in the Universe. That there were affinities along these philosophical lines linking the 'Platonists' (or, better, Platonisers) or 'latitude men' of Cambridge is not in doubt, but there were also differences amounting almost to contradictions within the minds and personalities of individual Platonists. Henry More of Christ's, the most prolific if not necessarily the most powerful of those minds, was both attracted to and repelled by the exacting rationality of the French philosopher René Descartes. He was, progressively (or regressively?) anti-materialist, anti-mechanistic, his consuming interest Spirit and spirits (not excluding what we should call 'ghosts'); an enemy of enthusiasm in religion who was nevertheless a kind of enthusiast himself, according to his first biographer, 'he, knowing better . . . what was an Enthusiast than they themselves'.[5]

---

[3] The source was a 24-page pamphlet by one S.P. (known to have been Simon Patrick), *A Brief Account of the New Sect of Latitude-Men, Together with Some Reflections upon the New Philosophy* (Cambridge, 1662). That this 'sect' and philosophy was alleged to be 'new' as late as 1662 has had a distorting effect.

[4] Richard Ward, *The Life of Dr Henry More* (London, 1710), p. 9.

[5] Ibid., p. 44; Hall 1990, *passim*; Daniel Fouke, *The Enthusiastic Concerns of Dr Henry More: Religious Meaning and the Psychology of Delusion* (Leiden, 1997). More's spiritual enthusiasms are best explored in *Conway Letters: the Correspondence of Anne, Viscountess Conway, Henry More and their Friends, 1642–1684*, ed. M. H. Nicolson (London, 1930), revised and enlarged edition, ed. Sarah Hutton (Oxford, 1992).

Surprisingly little is known about the sources of the religious and philosophical positions which these men adopted. Plato, and even the less rigorous Plotinus and other neo-Platonists, to whom the Renaissance had given a great run for their money, cannot be shown to have figured prominently on their reading lists.[6] (But More claimed to have been the first person in Cambridge to have secured a copy of Plotinus, 'the first that had either the luck or the courage to buy him'.[7]) Just as significant, evidently, was a fixation, almost, on certain congenial biblical texts and passages: such as the wisdom of Solomon in Proverbs 20.28: 'The spirit of man is the candle of the Lord'; or St Paul in Romans 1.20: 'For the invisible things of him from the creation of the world are clearly seen, being understood by the things that are made'; or the same Apostle, preaching in Athens: 'For in him we live, and move, and have our being' (Acts 17.28).

Rather clearer are the negative impulses and thrusts of Cambridge Platonist ideas, at first a reaction against the reduction of religion to a new and arid scholasticism which undervalued, in its academic formulations, religious experience, especially in the form of Calvinist dogmatics; and against an exclusive revelatory scripturalism. The anti-Calvinism of the tendency is best documented in the case of More, who tells us how as a schoolboy at Eton, and to the consternation of his nearest and dearest, he rejected the doctrine of predestination in its Calvinist form.[8] (One of the ironies of intellectual history is that it took Calvinists to rebel in this way against Calvinism, which is the story of Emmanuel, at this moment in its history. But perhaps More was converted by the Eton luminary John Hales, who was famously said to have 'bid John Calvin good-night' at the Synod of Dort.)

Later, the materialism of Thomas Hobbes, widely equated with atheism, served as a negative point of focus and identification for Cambridge Platonism, 'the means of concentrating its thought and giving dogmatic direction to it'. The fierceness of the Platonists' anti-Hobbism can be illustrated from the writings of Ralph Cudworth: 'He that does not perceive any higher degree of perfection in a man than in an oyster, nay, than in a clod of earth or lump of ice, in a piece of paste or piecrust, hath not the

---

[6] Hall 1990, pp. 8, 59–60. However, there were some relevant resources in the library of Emmanuel. A copy of Plato's *Phaedo* in the Graeco-Latin edition of Marsilio Ficino was among early losses from the collection. The 1637 catalogue includes Plato's *Opera* in both Latin (Basle, 1561?), acquired between 1584 and 1597, and Greek (Basle, 1534), acquired between 1622 and 1626. (Bush and Rasmussen 1986, pp. 21, 133–4, 198.)

[7] *Henry More: The Immortality of the Soul*, ed. A. Jacob (Dordrecht, 1987), p. v.

[8] Ibid., pp. i–ii; Ward 1710, pp. 8–9. On the significance of Eton, see Marjorie Nicolson, 'Christ's College and the Latitude Men', *Modern Philology*, 27 (1929–30), 36. See also Aaron Lichtenstein, *Henry More: The Rational Theology of a Cambridge Platonist* (Cambridge, Mass., 1962), pp. 3–4.

reason or understanding of a man in him.'[9] More was the first English-man to enter into a serious intellectual engagement with Descartes. While still plucking up the courage to writing to 'that gallant Mounsieur', More called him 'the very Miracle of the world'. 'Methinks all that have attempted anything in naturall Philosphy hitherto are mere shrimps and fumblers in comparison of him.' What More particularly admired in Descartes was the mathematical chastity of his mind, his rejection of 'slibber-sauce experiments that are to little purpose'.[10] (So this Cambridge Platonist (and Fellow of the Royal Society) was, on our terms, no scientist.) But later More found that he had misunderstood Descartes, whose mechanistic universe was almost as distasteful as the philosophy of Hobbes.[11] The two points of negative reference were linked, in that the old Calvinism, hermetically sealed within its own dogmatics, was perceived to be incapable of making an adequate response to the challenge of the new philosophy and science, to cope with Francis Bacon as well as with Hobbes and Descartes.

However, it would be wrong to view the new movement simply in terms of negative reaction and generational discontinuity. Paradoxically, 'Platonism', which overflowed with its own piety, was a coming to fruition of the religious hotpot which had been the old Emmanuel.

It is convenient to focus on Benjamin Whichcote, not only because he was an Emmanuel man, but on account of a famous correspondence conducted between Whichcote now, thanks to the interregnal regime, Provost of King's, and his erstwhile tutor, Anthony Tuckney, by the same authority Master of Emmanuel.[12] For this correspondence represents a kind of San Andreas Fault in the intellectual history of the seventeenth century, and not least of Emmanuel College.

But first let us bring Whichcote to that moment in time. Whichcote was the oldest of our group, born in 1609 as the sixth son of a minor Shropshire gentleman and an Emmanuel pensioner in 1629. But that is not the only reason why he is usually given primacy as a father figure in accounts of Cambridge Platonism.[13] If the Platonists of Christ's were compulsive writers, the Emmanuel men, as one might expect, were inveterate preachers. A divine rather than a philosopher, Whichcote became lecturer of Holy Trinity in 1636 and remained in that pulpit for twenty years. Sermons in written form notoriously fail to convey their effect as living

---

[9] Samuel I. Mintz, *The Hunting of Leviathan: Seventeenth-Century Reactions to the Materialism and Moral Philosophy of Thomas Hobbes* (Cambridge, 1962), pp. 80, 97.
[10] Henry More to Samuel Hartlib, 11 December (1648?); Sheffield University Library, Hartlib Papers 18/1/38A–39B.
[11] Hall 1990.
[12] *Eight Letters of Dr Antony Tuckney and Dr Benjamin Whichcote*, Whichcote 1753; extracts from Whichcote's letters in Cragg 1968, pp. 35–49.
[13] *DNB*, art. Whichcote.

utterances, and Whichcote's sermons survive in a very unsatisfactory state.[14] But their impact on his generation was evidently as much personal as intellectual (can we compare him with Simeon, who preached from the same pulpit, or with Newman?). Bishop Burnet testified to the influence of his conviction that Christianity was sent from God 'both to elevate and sweeten human nature; in which he was a great example, as well as a wise and kind instructor'.[15]

Whichcote's Christianity was a reasonable faith, capable of apprehending God rationally. 'If there were no other argument in the world, to prove there is a God, a man is an argument sufficient to himself. For thus a man feels that he is; and he doth prove that by his acting: I act, therefore I am; I do, therefore I have being; and if I am, either I made myself, or was made by another. I did not make myself . . .'[16] God made me. And God did not make 'a sorry worthless piece for no use, when he made man'.[17] He made a reasonable creature, and 'to go against Reason is to go against God'.[18] 'Reason' is a tricky word. Whichcote and his friends were not, on our terms, rationalists. Reason for them was close to what Pascal called the reason of the heart, an inner illumination of the soul.[19] This sort of thing was catching. In 1648, Thomas Smith wrote: 'Most men of parts here have their thoughts so taken up with Platonisme, or other high and aery speculations of Divinity or Philosophy they will scarce vouchsafe to cast a glance on . . . anything which is not in their way or in their aime.' 'Anything' for Smith meant experimental science.[20] It has been said that the religion of Ralph Cudworth, who entered Emmanuel in 1632, and who was to be successively Master of Clare and Christ's, was 'the common faith of all who fell under the influence of Benjamin Whichcote'.[21]

It was 1651, the year of Hobbes's *Leviathan*. Anthony Tuckney, who had been back in Cambridge since 1648, could not have been unaware of what Whichcote had been up to. Whichcote protested that his head had been possessed with these matters 'these manie yeares', and that he had said it all in formal exercises in Emmanuel chapel fourteen years before (1637!). Tuckney retorted: 'You were then but a yonge divine', and recalled that at that time he had found his pupil 'studious and pious and very loving of me', but 'somewhat cloudie and obscure in your expressions'.[22] But it was in 1651 that he was provoked to speak his mind

[14] Cragg 1968, pp. 61–2.
[15] Quoted, De Pauley 1937, p. 2.
[16] Ibid., p. 5.
[17] Quoted, Powicke 1926, p. 61.
[18] Quoted, Cassirer 1953, p. 41.
[19] Ibid., pp. 30–1; Mintz 1962, p. 82.
[20] Charles Webster, *The Great Instauration: Science, Medicine and Reform 1626–1660* (London, 1975), p. 148.
[21] Passmore 1951, p. 1.
[22] *Eight Letters*, Whichcote 1753, pp. 12–13, 28, 36.

by Whichcote's Commencement address as vice-chancellor (it has not survived), which he chose to interpret as a personal attack on his own address of a year before. Hence the Tuckney-Whichcote correspondence, conducted between two men separated by a distance of a quarter of a mile, who could have sorted out their differences face to face but, fortunately for us, evidently found it impossible to do so. The correspondence itself is evidence of the fracture of an old bonding between not only these two but Thomas Hill, now Master of Trinity, who had taken over from Tuckney as Whichcote's tutor, and John Arrowsmith, Master of St John's, three old Calvinist warhorses. As the eighteenth-century editor of the letters suggests, Whichcote's old friends may have come to envy his 'popularity and credit'.[23]

Tuckney and Whichcote each wrote four letters, and here is a bare digest of their exchanges, mapping, as it were, two divergent intellectual and religious worlds. Whichcote had insisted on the sufficiency of scripture (which is to say, without opinionated dogmatic structures erected on Scripture), and that 'good men' can differ in their interpretation of Scripture. Tuckney said that that was to put the orthodox (an unfashionable word, he knew, but he had to use it) 'into a bag' with Papists, Arians, Socinians and the worst of heretics. 'Good men can be wrong.' Whichcote had taught that Christ saves through acting not upon God but upon us, doing for us not without us but within us. 'With God there cannot be reconciliation without our becoming God-like.' Tuckney said that that was a divinity 'which my heart riseth against'. It was a denial of one of the fundamental truths of the Gospel. According to Tuckney, Whichcote was immersed in Philosophy and the Metaphysics to the neglect of Scripture, 'Plato and his schollers above all'. His ministry was in consequence less 'edifying', and he had departed from the 'spirituall, plaine, powerful' tradition for which Cambridge had been famous. Whichcote somethat disingenuously protested that as a tutor at Emmanuel he had been too busy with his pupils to read very much at all, but that Calvin, Beza and Perkins had figured prominently in what he had read. Tuckney accused Whichcote of propagating 'a kind of Moral Divinitie' with only a little tincture of Christ added, 'nay a Platonique faith'. Whichcote suggested that the issue between them concerned the power of reason to judge in matters of faith. 'What does God speak to us but by reason?' 'Sir, I oppose not rational to spiritual; for spiritual is most rational: But I contradistinguish rational to conceited, impotent affected CANTING.' 'Truth is Truth.' Tuckney agreed, but, since truth was truth, he denied an unbridled liberty of prophesying, and denounced 'toleration' (the public issue of the day, in Cromwell's England). Whichcote asked: 'If this libertie may not be allowed to the universities, wherefore

---

[23] Ibid., pp. xxx–xxxiii.

do we study? We have nothing to do but to get good memories and to learn by heart.' And he insisted against what he believed to be a wilful misunderstanding on Tuckney's part on the strength and sovereignty of his own Christian Theism: 'I never leave God oute . . . God is reallie all in all to mee; I hold of Him, derive from Him, live by Him, enjoy my selfe under Him, hope in Him, expect from Him.'[24]

This was the reasonable but passionate message which Whichcote's London auditory at St Lawrence Jewry (but actually gathered at the London Guildhall, during Wren's rebuilding of the church) would hear from him for many years, after his removal from King's, at the Restoration. Whichcote in his London pulpit was a godfather to the Church of Archbishops Tillotson and Tenison. Back in 1651 Whichcote and his old tutor had agreed to differ. Whichcote signing off: 'I think not the worse of You at all, for aught wherein we differ.'[25]

Whichcote's near contemporary at Emmanuel, Ralph Cudworth, and as the son of a former fellow he was an Emmanuel man by inheritance, was more of a philosopher than a divine, in potential if not quite in achievement the greatest philosopher of the school, and certainly its most systematic thinker. From his arrival in 1632 until his death in 1688, he almost never left Cambridge, and he was Master of Christ's for thirty-four years. That is not to say that he, or Henry More, led entirely peaceful lives, for that college had its own politics, in the 1660s as much as in the twentieth century of C. P. Snow. In 1665, the archbishop of Canterbury was informed that Christ's was 'a seminary of heretics'.[26] More, who, although older seems to have been his pupil,[27] called Cudworth 'that silent but rich treasury of all manner of learning and accomplishments',[28] while for a modern author he was an 'inveterate promiser of books he never wrote or could not bring himself to publish, the very type of the perfectionist'.[29] Well, the diffident Cudworth was not quite silent. When over sixty, he published a huge confutation of atheism, part of an intended larger work, called *The True Intellectual System of the Universe* (1678). This has been described as 'monstrously obese' and a 'gigantic fragment',[30] and when we read that the whole enterprise seems now 'a little pointless and its massive scholarship tedious at best and usually

---

[24] Ibid., pp. 1–5, 13, 26, 37–8, 39, 54, 57, 58, 85–6, 108.
[25] *DNB*, art. Whichcote; *Eight Letters*, Whichcote 1753, p. 133.
[26] *Conway Letters* (n. 5), pp. 236–9, 241–3. The best account of these politics, a vendetta mounted primarily by Ralph Widdrington against Cudworth and More, is in Nicolson, 'Christ's College and the Latitude Men'.
[27] Passmore 1951, p. 16.
[28] Henry More to Samuel Hartlib, 11 December (1648?); Sheffield University Library, Hartlib Papers 18/1/38A–39B.
[29] Passmore 1951, p. 17.
[30] John Laird, *Hobbes* (London, 1934), p. 260; Cassirer 1953, p. 42.

wrong',[31] we may be tempted to see in Cudworth the Casaubon of George Eliot's *Middlemarch*. But Cudworth not only drew upon an immense (but increasingly unfashionable) humanistic learning, which embraced a typically Renaissance sense of a perennial and partly cryptic wisdom. He used it to mount the first sustained attack to have been made on Hobbes, while proving himself an acute critic of the sometimes circular arguments of Descartes. Philosophically he was no slouch.[32] In March 1647 Cudworth made one of his rare appearances outside Cambridge, when he preached before Parliament. This was one of the regular series of 'fast sermons', but it was quite unlike most fast sermons. The text was John 2.3–4: 'And hereby we do know that we know him, if we keep his commandments.' Cudworth denounced 'our bookish Christians', 'as if religion were nothing but a little *Book-craft*, a mere *paper-skill*', and ended with a call for Reformation, the conventional theme of such sermons. However, what Cudworth urged was something different from the ordinary, an 'inward Reformation of the heart'.[33] The sermon was so successful that it invited some rather catty comments on how much material good it had done the preacher: to be precise, a pension of £150.[34]

Whichcote and Cudworth were almost contemporaries, no more than six years separating them. The strength of Whichcote's moral and intellectual influence is best demonstrated in his pupils, whom, according to Gilbert Burnet, he 'set ... on reading the ancient philosophers, chiefly Plato, Tully and Plotin'.[35] These were members of the next generation, or cohort, exact contemporaries, as it happens, of William Sancroft, although nothing survives in writing to connect them with Sancroft: evidence, perhaps, that more than one spiritual microclimate could coexist in the same college. Nathaniel Culverwell (yes, one of *those* Culverwells, effectively founder's kin,[36]) came up in 1633, only a year after Cudworth, John Smith in 1636. Not much is known about either. Unlike the long-lived Whichcote and Cudworth (or, for that matter, Sancroft), both died young, Culverwell at thirty-three, Smith at thirty-four. Their writings were published posthumously, Culverwell's by his friend William Dillingham, who was Master of Emmanuel from 1653 to 1662. But in Culverwell and Smith 'the candle of the Lord' burned, and shone, more brilliantly and fiercely than in any other Cambridge Platonist works, for both were brilliant stylists. Both exalted the role, and power, of reason, and both

---

[31] Joseph M. Levine, 'Latitudinarians, Neoplatonists, and the Ancient Wisdom', in Kroll, Ashcroft and Zagorin 1993, pp. 85–108.

[32] Passmore 1951.

[33] Ralph Cudworth, *A sermon preached before ... the House of Commons* (Cambridge, 1647). See Alan Gabbey, 'Cudworth, More and the Mechanical Analogy', in Kroll, Ashcroft and Zagorin 1993, pp. 109–27, at pp. 115–17.

[34] Ibid., p. 125, n. 32.

[35] Quoted, De Pauley 1937, p. 2.

[36] See above, pp. 33–4.

grappled with the problem of reconciling reason with revelation. Culverwell's masterpiece was a work called (in Dillingham's edition) *An Elegant and Learned Discourse of the Light of Nature*. 'To blaspheme reason is to reproach heaven itself and to dishonour the God of Reason, to question the beauty of the image.' This was St John's 'true light, lightening every man coming into the world'. Yet, elsewhere, Culverwell compared this 'lamp of the Lord' unfavourably with revelation, which with the power of the Sun outshone the poor lamp of reason.[37] Smith, as learned a man as Emmanuel produced in these years (he left 600 books to the College), and the most brilliant of the Platonists, exalted rationally based religion as a principle of 'Freedom, Love, Peace, Life and Power', 'the Mother and Nurse of true liberty'.[38] We should add to this roll of honour John Worthington, who entered Emmanuel in 1632, became a fellow in 1642 and Master of Jesus in 1650, and who was editor not only of John Smith but of the works of Joseph Mede of Christ's, an important fellow-traveller of the Platonists.[39] We must, I think, conclude that the Emmanuel of the 1630s received into its bosom and proceeded to form what was intellectually the most fertile of all its many generations.

[37] Powicke 1926, Chapter V; extracts from *An Elegant and Learned Discourse* in Cragg 1968, pp. 53–60.
[38] Cassirer 1953, pp. 162–5; Powicke 1926, Chapter III.
[39] *DNB*, art. Worthington; Crossley 1847.

9

Restoration and Transmogrification

Restoration Emmanuel: A New College

In May 1660 the restoration of the monarchy was celebrated at Cambridge in a manner deemed remarkable 'both for the manner and continuance', the party lasting two whole days. The procession of doctors in scarlet and the proclamations were accompanied by a loud band, with soldiers firing volleys from the roof of King's chapel, 'which, with the ringing of bells and variety of musick, gave a handsome entertainment to the spectators'. There were any number of bonfires, costing Emmanuel £1.10s.4d.[1]

It is said that restored monarchs neither remember nor forget. When Charles II returned from his travels, determined not to repeat them, it was to be business as usual in Cambridge. There was what Mullinger calls 'a shower of mandates', 160 in the first eight months of the reign, and many more to follow, including a D.D. for the well-qualified William Sancroft.[2] In March 1663, Charles's natural son, the duke of Monmouth, later to be the occasion of the last battle fought on English soil but at this time aged fourteen, visited the university, was subjected to the inevitable comedy at Trinity, and received, by royal mandate, the degree of M.A., along with 34 others.[3] In due course, Monmouth became chancellor (replacing the second duke of Buckingham who had succeeded the re-instated earl of Manchester), and the usual more or less empty promises were made about restricting the use of such royal mandates and respecting the liberties of the university.[4]

Had nothing changed? Some things had, and would. William Sancroft was mandated Master of Emmanuel on 31 August 1662, much to his surprise. Nine months later he found himself still a stranger in the college, 'my acquaintance being wholly worne out'. He told his old tutor, Ezekiel Wright: 'I am come into a new college, quite another thing from

---

[1] Cooper 1845, pp. 478–9; Mullinger 1911, pp. 554–5.
[2] Ibid., pp. 557–8; Thomas Buck to Sancroft, 21 March 1661(2), BL, MS. Harl. 3784, fol. 92.
[3] Cooper 1845, p. 509.
[4] Ibid., pp. 559–64.

what I, and much more from what you, left it.'[5] Sancroft was Master for less than three years. Yet no-one did more to create the new college, or at least, the outward face of a new college. He had come hotfoot from Italy and was not so much glad to be back in his old surroundings as appalled to be reminded of Emmanuel's ridiculous apology for a chapel, aligned north to south, and its poky library, defying Vitruvius by lying east to west, which meant that the precious light of early morning was lost. 'I have it in designe to make both a new library and chapel too.' Sancroft was a builder, an architect *manqué*, who in the troubled days of 1650 had sent into Suffolk for his copy of Sir Henry Wootton's *Elements of Architecture*. Wherever he went, he started to build. From Durham, a friend wrote: 'I wish you a large dividend, the better [to] enable you to build.'[6] The new Emmanuel would be symbolised for all time to come by the new chapel with its elegantly flanking cloister and gallery. This creation Sancroft, as dean of St Paul's, did much to fund and, in a sense, to create, not forgetting the part played by Christopher Wren, who would soon be given the rather larger commission of rebuilding Sancroft's cathedral, in a 'Latin' style.

However, the classical sophistication of the new Emmanuel would not hide the fact that its great days were already over. The new regime had confirmed Charles I's suspension of the statute *De mora*, and with that Emmanuel lost its exceptionality, becoming just another college, and potentially a hive for drones.[7] In 1672, the society would number 170, compared with 400 at Trinity, and 372 at St John's. On that crudely statistical scale, Emmanuel still ranked fourth in the university, but it was a trailing fourth, and no longer a finishing school for the sons of the great and good.[8] A French visitor to Cambridge in 1677 wrote that, of the twelve colleges, four were 'worth going to see'. Emmanuel, naturally, was not one of them, even though this was the year in which Wren's new chapel was consecrated.[9]

Back in 1662, when he wrote to his old tutor, Sancroft had a gloomy sense of Ichabod, of glory departed. It was not so much that the old puritan cause, the college's original *raison d'être*, was now marginalised and sent into the wilderness. The Anglican Sancroft was pleased that there was now little left of 'that former singularity, which rendered us heretofore so unhappily remarkable'. 'Blessed is the barren and

5   ECA, COL.9.1A, pp. 222–3; printed in full, D'Oyly 1821, I, pp. 125–31, in part, Shuckburgh 1904, pp. 109–12.
6   Mullinger 1911, pp. 583–4; Sancroft to Thomas Sancroft, 17 November 1650, Bodl., MS. Tanner 56, fol. 229; G(eorge) D(avenport) to Sancroft, n.d. (*c*.1662), BL, MS. Harl. 3784, fol. 64.
7   Mullinger 1911, p. 585.
8   Twigg 1990, p. 289.
9   Cooper 1845, pp. 555–6.

miscarrying womb, rather than she that is always teeming and drawing forth her breasts to the children of disobedience.'[10] (Sancroft's attitude to more novel religious and intellectual tendencies is less clear. But there are hints of it in a letter written to him in January 1664 which assumes that he will know 'how farr Dr More's whimseys have prevailed in the University', and that More's books contain 'strange things'. 'And time it is we sleep not till all is past the remedy.'[11]) More royal mandates and dispensatory letters, some of them doubtless manipulated by Sancroft himself, would now ensure that Emmanuel would become a bastion for church and king, no longer a puritan Cave of Adullam. No less than four royal mandates for fellowships were received at Emmanuel in 1662 and 1663, including a mandate for Edward Maydwell, 'having taken into our Princely consideration his many sufferings', and another for Henry Miles, 'being much impoverished by his sufferings under the late calamityes'.[12] But, as well he might, Sancroft feared that the baby had been thrown out with the bathwater. He told Wright: 'I find not that old genius and spirit of learning generally in the college that made it once so deservedly famous.' In the early months of his mastership, he was involved in the election of seven fellows, but most of them were from other colleges and they were of inferior quality. Sancroft was a practical man, who saw that the problem was at root one of stringent statutes and scarce resources. 'For my part, after many sad thoughts spent in this argument, I am come to a persuasion . . . that 'tis impossible for this college ever to flourish again . . . till the fellowships and scholarships be made competent . . . and . . . till the body of our statutes be changed, which, if it may not be done, I see not but that we are remediless.'[13]

Sancroft inherited a dubious legacy. William Dillingham had become Master of the College in 1653, after Anthony Tuckney's departure for St John's. He was a learned and conservative scholar, who evidently had his doubts about the Whichcote-Cudworth-More tendency, since while he brought to the press Nathaniel Culverwell's *Light of Nature*, he preached a course of sermons which denounced 'natural reason',[14] but as a head of house he was not a success. The college recruited ever fewer, and poorer, students, and the drinking over the road, at the Bird Bolt, was getting out of hand.[15] Ecclesiastically, the College was hopelessly divided. In November 1660, as Sancroft returned from Italy, he was warned that 'half

---

[10] ECA, COL.9.1A, pp. 222–3.
[11] Mark Frank (Master of Pembroke Hall) to Sancroft, 21 January 1663(4?), CUL, MS. Mm.1.45 (Baker 34), p. 119. Frank suspected that these 'strange things' implied Socinianism.
[12] ECA, COL.14.1, pp. 71–4; Shuckburgh 1904, pp. 113–14; Twigg 1990, p. 253.
[13] ECA, COL.9.1A, pp. 222–3.
[14] Twigg 1990, p. 201.
[15] Shuckburgh 1904, pp. 101–3.

the Society are for the Liturgy, and half against it', with the Prayer Book read one week and the puritan Directory the next.[16] In January 1663, one of Sancroft's correspondents sent a donation to an organ fund, remarking that some were inclined to give out of love for the College 'as it is', and others out of spite for the College 'as it was'.[17] Thomas Smith wrote to Sancroft from Christ's, hoping to see him Master of Emmanuel. 'One halfe of the Fellows desire nothing more.'[18]

At the Restoration, ten of the sixteen interregnal Cambridge heads were removed, or resigned, including the Emmanuel worthies Dell of Caius, Sadler of Magdalene, Tuckney of St John's, Whichcote of King's, and Worthington of Jesus; although Cudworth remained undisturbed at Christ's, where he would die in his bed in 1688.[19] Dillingham would certainly have been summarily ejected from Emmanuel in favour of Holdsworth, if Holdsworth had still been alive. As it was, he lasted until St Bartholomew's Day 1662, when, with some two thousand other clergymen of the Church of England, he suffered eviction for rejecting the terms of the Restoration Settlement, in his case refusing to renounce the Solemn League and Covenant. He retired to Oundle, later married a widow with seven children, and eventually conformed, ending his days as a rural incumbent in Bedfordshire. He spent his exile years translating English verse, and especially his beloved George Herbert, into Latin, exchanging his efforts with Joseph Mede's old pupil Sir Justinian Isham, who was similarly engaged. Dillingham's contributions to *Poemata varii argumenti* lurched from the press in 1677. As was becoming almost an Emmanuel tradition, Dillingham had remained on excellent terms with the cuckoo who had thrust him out of the nest, and with whom he had opened a friendly correspondence no later than 1640. Their letters of the 1670s were all about literature. Why should they not have remained friends? They had shared rooms as undergraduates.[20] Four months after his departure from the College, Dillingham wrote a most helpful letter to Sancroft, arranging to clear his rooms, sending his academic robes, 'which you may please freely to make use of', and asking the new Master to look out

---

[16] Thomas Smith to Sancroft, 2 November 1660; CUL, MS. Mm.1.45 (Baker 34), pp. 126–7.

[17] G(eorge) D(avenport) to Sancroft, 15 January 1661(2), BL, MS. Harl. 3784, fol. 96.

[18] Thomas Smith to Sancroft, n.d., CUL, MS. Mm.1.45 (Baker 34), p. 128.

[19] Twigg 1990, pp. 237–43.

[20] A letter to Dillingham of 29 September (1640) strongly suggests that Sancroft, Dillingham and Arthur Bownest roomed together. Sancroft writes (from Fressingfield): 'I know not whether Arthur be in the college or not: if he bee, then I hope that this letter will not be delivered, but that I shall see you both heere at Fressingfield this week.' (Bodl., MS. Tanner 467, no. 2, fol. 19.) See also Shuckburgh 1904, p. 103. The literary correspondence of later years is preserved in BL, MS. Sloane 1710, fols. 204–16v. I have been helped with Dillingham's literary activities (and in much else) by the late and sadly missed Jeremy Maule, who put me on to the Dillingham-Isham correspondence (Northamptonshire Record Office, IC 744), and who is responsible for 'lurched'.

for the material welfare of Emmanuel men recently ejected from their college livings for nonconformity.[21]

Sancroft was not at all sure that he wanted to be Master of Emmanuel. There were protracted negotiations, costing the College more than twenty pounds.[22] In exile he had, so to speak, invested in John Cosin, lending him 119 crowns (where had he found the money?), and now Cosin invited him to preach at his consecration as bishop of Durham, made him his chaplain, tried to marry him off (a vain ambition), gave him a rich Durham prebend and preferred him to Houghton-le-Spring, reputedly the best parochial living in England, its tithes worth more than £400.[23] It is very striking that Cosin, who had been the leading high churchman of Cambridge in the 1630s, should have sought out two Emmanuel men to take to Durham in the early 1660s: for before he preferred Sancroft, John Sudbury had been made dean of Durham (1661/2–1684). The dean was later to endow the Sudbury Prize, which has played a notable role in the history of Emmanuel. Sancroft wrote to his brother, five weeks after the royal die had been cast: 'There are many things that discourage me. I affect not an university life. I never had my health there. The Statutes are very odd and strict in point of residence, and otherwise.'[24]

'Otherwise' meant money. 'The Mastership is not able to maintain itself, and the Statutes permit one not to take any thing else.' And how could one commute between Durham and Cambridge? There was every reason for Sancroft to regard Emmanuel as a story, for him long since concluded. But Bishop Gilbert Sheldon of London (soon to be archbishop), the driving force behind the Restoration Church, whose idea it was that Sancroft should return to his old college and to the centre of affairs, was not to be gainsaid. Sancroft was sternly warned of his duty, just as the godly had once warned his uncle, in the very different circumstances of thirty years earlier. 'I am sorry there are such barrs against your entring into Emmanuel Colledge. We must remove them for you the best way we can'; and, presently: 'This enclosed which the king will send to be there before you will let you into that Colledge without scruple.'

---

[21] Shuckburgh 1904, pp. 104–5.

[22] ECA, BUR.8.2: 'Charges about the Election of a new Master', 29 September 1662–25 March 1663.

[23] Items of the (extensive) Sancroft-Cosin correspondence will be found in BL, MSS. Harl. 3783, fols. 150, 188, 189, 238 (26 June 1659, from Paris, acknowledging receipt of 119 crowns), 241; Harl. 3784, fols. 27, 29, 34; Bodl., MS. Tanner 467, fol. 72; *The Correspondence of John Cosin*, I, Surtees Society, 52 (1868), pp. 286–7, 288–90; II, Surtees Society, 55 (1870), pp. 12–15, 21–3, 25–6, 30–2, 35–7, 142–3. D'Oyly 1821, I, pp. 121–2, prints Cosin's letters to Sancroft of 23 August and 3 September 1661, relating to the 'virtuous person' whom he had lined up for Sancroft to marry. Sancroft to Cosin, 29 August 1662 (MS. Tanner 467, fol. 72) speaks of his 'steddy resolution . . . never to marry.'

For Dean Sudbury and his Prize, see pp. 123, 302; as dean, Hardy 1854, p. 300.

[24] Sancroft to Thomas Sancroft, 4 October 1662; Bodl., MS. Tanner 48, fol. 52. Sancroft signs off with 'my dearest love to all my sisters and brothers and young cousins'.

Sancroft was told that part of his new duties would be to prepare new statutes for cathedral churches and some colleges, Sheldon's 'declining age standing in need of such assistance'. What Sheldon enclosed must have been a draft of the royal letter dated 13 October 1662, which took 'very well' Emmanuel's choice of Sancroft, and which, 'having taken notice of the unusuall severity of your College Statutes' which would 'much discourage' their newly elected Master and render him less useful to the Church, granted a royal dispensation from the Statutes in question.[25] Sancroft's own scruples seem to have been overcome by notes he made of what had been decided in his uncle's time: that the Statutes restrained the Master from accepting any new benefice after his election, but allowed him to hang on to any benefice he already had.[26] So Sancroft retained both his prebend and his parish.[27] Ample funds continued to come south with regularity: on one occasion, Sancroft's share of the latest Durham Chapter dividend, £200, and another £200 from Houghton.[28] This was several years' salary for a Master of Emmanuel. Soon Sancroft was dean of York and within months, dean of St Paul's.[29] A wellwisher wrote: 'The next step will be to a mitre.'[30] The mitre would be St Augustine's, which Sancroft inherited from Sheldon in 1677. This was what it was to be in the fast lane in

'good King Charles's golden days,
When loyalty no harm meant;
A furious High-Churchman I was,
And so I gain'd preferment.'

But for Sancroft, this was the reward of consistency. From youth through to extreme old age, he was no Vicar of Bray.

London as much as Durham kept Sancroft out of Cambridge, but on business which was of the greatest importance for the College: the destination of Dr Holdsworth's famous library, consisting of at least 10,000 books. In a letter to the College of March 1646, Holdsworth had spoken of his 'continued resolution of increasing their Library'. But he had left behind a most unsatisfactory will, in Bishop Bennet's words, 'obscurely

[25] Bishop Gilbert Sheldon to Sancroft, 20 September, 2 October 1662, BL, MS. Harl. 3784, fols. 71, 77; ECA, COL.14.1, p. 70.
[26] ECA, COL.18.24: 'Papers relating to the College Statutes', assigned to the mastership of John Breton, but evidently, from the hand, Sancroft's working notes on the Statutes.
[27] Twigg 1990, p. 252.
[28] R. Wrench to Sancroft, 27 February 1662(3); BL, MS. Harl. 3784, fol. 100.
[29] When Sancroft arrived in York his London appointment was already anticipated. One correspondent 'ernestly' hoped that this would be 'but a step speedily to convey you to an higher Orb[it]', while another thought that even though the dean of St Paul's, John Barwick, had recovered from a dangerous illness, Sancroft would not be at York for long. (Ibid., fols. 112, 115.) Bishop Henchman advised him of his London preferment on the very day that the old dean deceased, 22 October 1664. (Ibid., fol. 190.)
[30] Thomas Page to Sancroft, 27 January 1664; ibid., fol. 123.

expressed and clogged with provisions'. It stipulated that his library should be 'bestowed upon the University of Cambridge', but only if were to please God 'within five years' to make a resettlement of the Church, and if Lambeth Palace Library were to be restored. Otherwise, it was to go to Emmanuel, always provided, and here was the rub, 'that they erect a roome or case fit to retain it'. If none of these conditions was met, its destination was to be Trinity College Dublin.[31] Hence, in part, Sancroft's ambition, disclosed in his letter to Ezekiel Wright, to build both a new library and, while he was about it, 'a Chapel too'. 'I am now in pursuit of Dr Holdsworths numerous Library.'

'Pursuit' was in the Court of Arches, which, after a year of tripartite litigation (Sancroft wrote – 'a whole University, so dreadfull an Adversary'[32]) referred the case to the mutually agreed arbitration of the archbishop of York and the bishops of London and Ely. By now the books were physically in Cambridge, and were sorted out by four representatives from each side.[33] On 19 December 1664, meeting in the dining hall of Doctors' Commons, the bishops came to their decision. All Holdsworth's books, printed and in MS., with the exception of duplicates and triplicates, were assigned to the University, to be 'distinguished from other books there by the name of Dr Holdsworth's Library'. And there, in the 'U.L.', they remain to this day, constituting a substantial portion of the 'Syndicate' class of Rare Books; but, contrary to the terms of the settlement, not preserved as a discrete collection. Emmanuel was compensated with the sum of £220, to be spent on books which, with the duplicates and triplicates, were also to be signalled out as 'Dr Holdsworth's books'. In addition, the College was awarded all costs against the University of Cambridge. Looking into the accounts, Bishop Bennet later concluded that the University had done badly out of this deal, for when legal expenses were taken into account it was nearly £500 out of pocket, which was more than the books were probably worth.[34] That would hardly be our assessment today. It was not until 1671, more than twenty years after Holdsworth's death, that Emmanuel's small share of the books arrived in the College.[35]

---

[31] Holdsworth's will is in PRO, PROB 11/209 (P.C.C. 1649 122 Fairfax), fols. 44v–45r, and the critical codicil headed 'Directions for my Executors ffor my Library' in PRO, PROB 11/312 (P.C.C. 1663 131 Juxon), fol. 202. See also ECA, COL.9.1B (William Bennet's Book no. 2), pp. 77–8. There is a full account of the saga of Holdsworth's library, and of Sancroft's part in it, in Oates 1986, pp. 314–26. Letters from Sancroft of July 1663 and February 1664 indicate how time-consuming the business was: "'Tis our suit with the University about D. Holdsworths Library that hath kept me here so long . . .' (Bodl., MSS. Tanner 155, fol. 200, 47, fol. 62.)

[32] Sancroft to Robert Alfounder, 21 July 1663; Bodl., MS. Tanner 155, fol. 200.

[33] Robert Alfounder to Sancroft, 21 July 1664; BL, MS. Harl. 3784, fol. 186.

[34] ECA, COL.9.1B, p. 107; COL.9.1A, p. 73.

[35] ECA, BUR.8.2: 4 May 1669. 'In Charges for bringing Dr Holdsworths books to Pinder for his paynes 12s.6d'. 8 May 1671: 'To Mr Smith for worke for bringing Dr Holdsworths bookes to Coll. 6d.'

While all this was going on, Sancroft was making expensive improvements to the Deanery in York ('such a dwelling . . . as I am never like to be owner of again'[36]), when, in October 1664, he was suddenly catapulted upstairs to St Paul's. Six months later, he resigned his mastership, and within a week, on 4 May 1665, the Crown intervened with a mandate to elect as his successor John Breton, a staunch high churchman who had missed a fellowship owing to the Interregnum, and who, like Sancroft, was to be relieved of any statutory limitation on his enjoyment of other preferments.[37] The senior fellow, Robert Alefounder, who seems to have been running the College in Sancroft's frequent absences (on 4 April 1665, he had written 'all things in the Colledge are well, and the Society presents you their service'[38]), conveyed his reaction to 'your unexpected and (with your pardon) unwelcome resignation'. He professed himself otherwise pleased with the outcome. 'This I thinke was the onely way to preserve unity among us, and to satisfy owr selves and all other our friends abroad: it is easier to obey then to chuse . . .',[39] a motto nowadays for Trinity College rather than Emmanuel.

But the likelihood is that all this had been stitched up by Sancroft himself. When he had been expected to resign upon his preferment to York, the Master of Pembroke had written: 'Yow will however looke to the maine chance and be able to design a person to succeed you, though not worthy of your self, yet serviceable to your College.'[40] A full year before Sancroft's actual resignation, a correspondent shared with him the sounds coming out of the Cambridge rumour mill concerning the mastership, 'if it must be quitted'. 'I hear Dr Britton [Breton] named, and Dr Holbech I am told desires it, but he never said so much to me.' 'I know not for whom you are.'[41]

John Breton's ten-year mastership could not have begun more inauspiciously. John Sadler was an Emmanuel man and a distinguished and radical lawyer who had been imposed on Magdalene as Master in 1650, and at the Restoration took his leave of Cambridge, retiring to his wife's property in Dorset, 'much disturbed in mind'. There, in 1661, he, and only he, saw a stranger at the end of his bed who had 'great things to tell him', which Sadler, calling for pen and ink, wrote down: 'That there would die in the city of London so many thousands, I have forgot the number and time, tho both were mentioned; that the City would be burnt down, great part of it, and that St Pauls would tumble down, as if beaten down by

---

[36] Bodl., MS. Tanner 47, fol. 377 (D'Oyly 1821, I, pp. 134–5).
[37] ECA, COL.14.1, pp. 76 (Latin text), 77 (English).
[38] Robert Alefounder to Sancroft, 4 April 1665; CUL, MS. Mm.1.45 (Baker 34), p. 132.
[39] Robert Alefounder to Sancroft, 'Trinity even' 1665; BL, MS. Harl. 3784, fol. 276.
[40] Mark Frank to Sancroft, 21 January 1663(4); CUL, MS. Mm.1.45 (Baker 34), p. 119.
[41] G(eorge) D(avenport) to Sancroft, 9 April 1664; Ibid., p. 146.

great guns.'[42] As every schoolboy used to know, in 1665 and 1666 all this would come to pass.

First, 1665, which Daniel Defoe, in the title of a famous book, would call *The Plague Year*. John Tillotson, Sancroft's second-in-command at St Paul's and a future archbishop of Canterbury, described the London scene to his boss, who was away from the city at Tunbridge Wells when disaster struck, and was careful not to return: 'Death stares us continually in the face in every infected person that passeth by us, in every coffin which is dayly and hourely carried along the streets: the Bells never cease to putt us in mind of our mortallity.' The dead lay in heaps and the burying went on day and night. Defoe himself could not have described it better, for Tillotson was the greatest preacher of his age.[43] The plague reached Cambridge from London in early August 1665, and Breton's very first order as Master was to close the College down. This order was renewed on 7 October, and even in January 1666 things were not back to normal. And then, in the summer of 1666, the pestilence returned, and on 17 June all members of the College were again given leave to disperse. 'The greatest danger is near unto us.'[44] The crisis cost money: a total of £61.19s.2d, quaintly distinguished in the bursarial accounts as paid by 'the living College', £36.1s.2d, and by 'the dead College' (presumably endowments, since there were, so far as we know, no plague deaths in Emmanuel) £25.8s.1d.[45] Sancroft, taking what one might call the M25 route around London, dropped in at Emmanuel for a week or so at a time, on his way to or from Fressingfield, which was quite out of communication with the outside world, Bishop Henchman not knowing for some months whether his dean was alive or dead.[46]

The main occasion for these visits would have been early negotiations for the great project of the new chapel, to which Breton was committed no less than his predecessor, although the chapel and its accompanying cloister are fittingly considered to constitute 'Sancroft's memorial'.[47] Sancroft and Wren were already discussing a radical and classical facelift for old St Paul's, updating Inigo Jones whose portico and other improvements had made the old pile somewhat more stately in the 1630s; and

---

[42] 'Mr Sadler's Prophecy', ECA, COL.9.1A, p. 253.

[43] John Tillotson to Sancroft, 14 September 1665; BL, MS. Harl. 3875, fol. 35.

[44] ECA, COL.9.1B, p. 42; ECA, COL.14.1, pp. 97–100.

[45] ECA, BUR.8.2, account of 30 April 1666.

[46] Letters documenting Sancroft's movements in 1665–6: BL, MS. Harl. 3785, fols. 8, 12, 19, 35, 40, 42, 45, 50, 52, 53, 57, 73, 85, 87, 88; Bodl., MS. Tanner 467, fols. 51–4, 56, MS. Tanner 45, fols. 28, 41, 53. He was back in London on 8 April 1666. (MS. Tanner 45, fol. 70.) In Sancroft's prolonged absence from London, initially at Tunbridge Wells, where he went annually to take the cure, increasingly desperate and reproachful letters reached him (or failed to reach him?) from those looking after the shop.

[47] J.B.P. 'Chapters in College History: The Chapel.II' (printing original documents from the College Archives). *ECM*, 8, 95–113.

important decisions about this were taken only days before the Great Fire of 1666 presented Wren (and Sancroft) with the unexpected opportunity of what is nowadays called a brownfield site.[48] Wren had been building a new chapel for Pembroke, the college of his uncle, Bishop Matthew Wren, and his 'blueprint' drawings can still be seen on the plaster wall of the Gray Room of that college, if, in the course of a convivial evening, one pulls back the hinged panelling. Wren's design for Emmanuel, the chapel a centre piece for new cloisters and a gallery above, shows that he at first envisaged a gallery of brick with stone dressings, no doubt intended to harmonise with the older adjacent buildings. But Loggan's print proves that the façade was ashlared and golden from the first. Wren now made and sent down a model in wainscot, which whetted the appetites of Breton and the fellows. But they wondered whether they were in any position to lay a foundation stone. 'The unexpected troubles have raised the price of Lime to be double to what it was a month since.' And would Wren submit to some modification of his design? 'We would wish it could be raised to a greater height, and if it have not an East Window . . . it is thought it will be necessary that the side windows be inlarged.' Sancroft was independently advised of these concerns.[49]

Serious work began early in 1668, when Breton was off to Northamptonshire to bargain for stone. Presently the founder's descendant, the earl of Westmorland, gave forty great oaks for the roof timbers. Meanwhile, Sancroft was busy on the financial front, advising on the mysteries of modern banking, subscribing £600 from his own pocket, and twisting the arms of other benefactors, including 'good Dr Holbech', who would be sure to lay £50 on the foundation stone. The basic structure of the chapel was complete by 1672, the roof leaded, the scroll and festoons on the pediment carved, the ceiling plastered. It was left to Holbech, who succeeded Breton as Master in 1676, to see to the glazing, wainscotting, and paving in the very best black and white marble. Sancroft seems to have paid £300 for the altar furniture and other internal fittings,[50] and, ten years later still, he would provide the altar-piece of carved oak which we still see, replacing an earlier reredos of satin. On 29 September 1677 a ceremony of consecration (what would Chaderton have made of that?) was conducted by Bishop Gunning of Ely. The dinner cost £35.12s, plus £7.19s for wine. The chapel itself had cost the immense sum of £3972, which was more than covered by subscriptions of £4116. But it cost a mere fifteen shillings to remove the corpses of the first and eighth

[48] *The Diary of John Evelyn*, ed. E. S. De Beer (London, 1955), III, pp. 648–9; D'Oyly 1821, I, pp. 139–46.

[49] Breton to Sancroft, 9 February 1667, ECA, COL.9.8, copying Bodl., MS. Tanner 155.105.

[50] Holbech's receipt for £100, 'the last third part' of Sancroft's 'most munificent guift towarde the adorning and furnishing with wainscot of the new erected Chappell', ECA, COL.9.8, copying Bodl., MS. Tanner 155.58.

masters, Chaderton and Breton, out of the old chapel and to inter them in the new, an act of reverence of which the Celtic Church, or the Middle Ages, would have approved. Holbech had written to Sancroft conveying 'the earnest desire of all the Society' to see him at the consecration, and suggesting that he should hitch a lift from London in the coach of his old friend and the College's benefactor, Sir Robert Gayer.[51] But it looks as if Sancroft was unable to make it, since in November Holbech wrote again with a fulsome letter of thanks, reporting on the consecration of 'our (or rather your Chappell)'. Sancroft was now consulted on the conversion of the old chapel into the library, work completed, with minimal structural alteration, in 1679, at a cost of £231.18s.6d.[52]

As we progress towards the so-called Glorious Revolution of 1688, which was to change the constitution of the nation and destroy Sancroft, and ever deeper into the age of the Scientific Revolution, which was to change everything, we find that Emmanuel was still determined to keep one foot, as it were, firmly in the past, its past. One of Holbech's innovations was a course of lectures in Ecclesiastical History, no less than sixty lectures to run over four years, five per term. These were delivered in Latin in the chapel, to last 'not over an hour or under half an hour', with all students under the rank of M.A. obliged to attend. In the first year the course was to reach the Council of Nicaea, in the second the Sixth Ecumenical Council (Constantinople III, 680–1, a curious choice), in the third, the year 1500. The fourth and final year was to be devoted to modern times, the turbulent times of Reformation and Counter-Reformation. The lecturer was to pay particular attention to the ecclesiastical history of the British Isles, and to such matters 'as still remain controversial'. His reward was to be £20 a year, and he was required to place on deposit a transcript of his lectures. With such a subject, one could not be too careful. But if this was still a live subject in 1677, a hundred years later it was dead. By the late eighteenth century it was thought that 'the Ecclesiastical Lecture', being in Latin, had become 'totally disregarded and useless', and the then Master allowed it to be read in English.[53] But was Emmanuel perhaps the very first English place of learning to provide specifically for the teaching of Church History? Was this the root from which in the nineteenth century would grow the Dixie Chair of Ecclesiastical History, still established in Emmanuel, and graced in our own day by one of the authors of this History?

---

[51] Holbech to Sancroft, 7 September 1677, ECA, COL.9.8, copying Bodl., MS. Tanner 155.51.
[52] *ECM*, 8. 95–113; ECA, COL.9.8, copying Bodl., MS. Tanner 155.52; Willis and Clark 1886, II, pp. 702–10.
[53] ECA, COL.9.1A, pp. 164–5. Holbech, who was evidently a man of means, also settled funds on the College to maintain a 'Catechitical' Lecture, a perk worth £20 a year to one of the six senior fellows, to be appointed by the Master. (Ibid., pp. 161–3.)

Revolutionary Politics and Revolutionary Science

The Church of England, and Emmanuel College, now fully and unreservedly part of that Church, had bound itself to the mast of the restored monarchy, ever reminded of the shameful calamity of 1649, prepared to weather any future storms under the ensign of Church and King. No text was more popular with the Anglican preachers of Charles II's golden days than 1 Samuel 15.23: 'For rebellion is as the sin of witchcraft.' But the mast broke, carrying a considerable part of the Church with it, and compromising much of what was left. For Charles II's brother and legitimate successor, James, duke of York, threw the Church over, making no secret of his conversion to Roman Catholicism and prepared, by constitutionally illegal means, at the very least to advance the interests of his coreligionists. The spectre of arbitrary government, indelibly associated in the national, protestant consciousness with 'popery', the provocative cause of the wars of the 1640s, again reared its ugly head, threatening to plunge the nation back into another civil war. This was averted in the so-called Exclusion Crisis of 1679–82, but only because memories of the first civil war were still painfully fresh.[1] But within three years of coming to the throne in 1685, defeating the pretensions of his bastard nephew, the duke of Monmouth, James II had so far alienated his natural supporters, not least in the hierarchy and clergy of the Church of England, that he was driven from his throne and replaced by the joint sovereignty of his daughter Mary, and her Dutch husband, William of Orange: the so-called 'Glorious' or 'Bloodless' Revolution of 1688–9.

Through all these tumultuous and extraordinary events, Emmanuel's most famous son, William Sancroft, rode a kind of ideological roller coaster. As archbishop of Canterbury, he presided in the years following the Exclusion Crisis over a repressively triumphalist Church of England, fiercely intolerant towards the political and religious dissent which had threatened the very foundations of the Restoration regime. The record of his government, copious in the extreme, survives in the Tanner Manuscripts in the Bodleian Library.[2] But when James II issued his Declaration of Indulgence in favour of both protestant and popish dissenters, and required it to be read from all England's pulpits, the worm turned, and Sancroft was one of the Seven Bishops who were committed to the Tower, acquitted, and released amidst widespread national rejoicing. As we

---

[1] Jonathan Scott, *Algernon Sidney and the Restoration Crisis, 1677–1683* (Cambridge, 1991).
[2] Sancroft's archiepiscopal administration, as recorded in the Tanner MSS., is the subject of an Oxford doctoral dissertation by Robert Beddard of Oriel College, which however appears to be currently unavailable for consultation in the Bodleian Library.

know, Sancroft had for many years constructed himself as a kind of reclusive martyr, but to be a popular hero was for him an unfamiliar role. Presently, he had to come to terms with the fact that he was, after all, a Protestant, and he hovered on the edge of a compromising, if not treasonable, correspondence with the princess Mary, in Holland. He wanted to tell Mary that the worst thing to have happened after the murder of Charles I was its sequel: the driving of his sons into foreign exile where they had learned to serve other gods. The heart of the Church of England would break were it not that God had caused 'some Dawn of Light to break forth unto us from the Eastern shore in the Constancy and good Affection of your Roiall Highness and the excellent princ towards us'. 'You have put new life into a dying old man.'[3] An Emmanuel man, Stephen Marshall, had uttered prophetically in a sermon to the Long Parliament in 1643: 'And I suspect, in case the tables were turned and we had a king endeavouring to take down the bishops, . . . the world would hear another Divinity.'[4] In the privacy of his own study, Sancroft thought the unthinkable. The Church might have to go it alone, 'preserving itself independent of the state'.[5]

But Sancroft could not, and did not, accept the revolutionary transfer of sovereignty to William and Mary. There was no difference between William and Cromwell but the name. James Stuart remained 'our Master'. Having with his own hands placed the crown on that head, Sancroft would never be the man to take it off again.[6] He refused the oath of allegiance, becoming the first and foremost of the Anglican sect known as the Non-Jurors, and deprivation by the new rulers rendered his letter of resignation otiose. But even in those challenging circumstances, Sancroft was still the old Sancroft. He was looked to for a lead, addressed as 'the admiration of the present age, . . . Champion of the Church of England doctrine', even one of 'the great Confessors of the Christian Faith'. 'Proceed, pious Prelate, perswade our Clergy, command your sons to stick to the truths of our Church.'[7] Bishop Francis Turner of Ely, an

---

[3] There is a letter from Princess Mary to Sancroft, dated 1 October 1687, in Bodl., MS. Tanner 29, no. 55, fol. 77. The rough draft of Sancroft's reply is in ibid., no. 72, fol. 111. It appears that this reply was never sent. William Stanley, formerly chaplain to the princess, reported in 1715 that he had encouraged his mistress to write to the archbishop 'to encourage her still to give countenance to the church of England', but that 'he was pleased not to write to her'. Stanley alleged that Sancroft later told him he was glad that he had not written because if he had 'they would have said that I had sent to invite them over.' (D'Oyly 1821, I, pp. 372–3.)

[4] Quoted, Collinson 1982, p. 7.

[5] Quoted, Spurr 1991, p. 78.

[6] Robert Beddard, *A Kingdom Without a King: the Journal of the Provisional Government in the Revolution of 1688* (Oxford, 1988), p. 7; Sancroft to Bishop William Lloyd, 2 April 1692, ECA, COL. 9.8, p. 27.

[7] Edmund Elys, rector of East Allington, Devon, to Sancroft, n.d.; Bodl., MS. Tanner 28(2), no. 258, fol. 367. Cf. an anonymous letter to Sancroft of 23 October 1689: 'All the treu

ambitious man who had expected to be Sancroft's successor, wrote: 'I beseech your Grace's Directions.' But in vain. A modern authority writes of this 'strange, obstinate passiveness'.[8] The martyr-hermit fixation now returned with a vengeance. Sancroft waited, uncommunicative and sluggish, occupied with trivial intellectual pursuits, until he was physically thrown out of Lambeth. After a spell in the Temple, where 'company and business' frequently broke in,[9] he retreated to where else?, Fressingfield, where he began to build a new house for himself at the end of his brother's garden. Not that he was wholly inactive, politically. A correspondence survives with a fellow Non-Juror, Bishop William Lloyd of Norwich, in which there are many references to the safe arrival of 'wash balls'. It does not seem very likely that these really were wash balls.[10] And from Fressingfield, Sancroft maintained a very cautious contact with the exiled court at St Germain. When the most distinguished of the Non-Jurors, Jeremy Collier, visited Sancroft on his way to that court (which, however, he never reached), the archbishop 'desired him to let our Master know where I am, and in what condition; a very old infirm man, driven from my own house (and all that belongs to it) into the wilderness . . . confined to the poor house in which I was born'. But he would not risk his life for the cause. For thereby James II would have 'one faithful subject fewer than he had before'.[11] He tried to shake off his two learned chaplains, Henry Wharton and William Needham (an Emmanuel man), who both took the oaths, declaring that 'he must be content to be his own chaplain', but with limited success. Needham hung on the longer, visiting his old master at Fressingfield regularly. There Sancroft led prayers himself, and when he got to the state prayers, prayed 'for the King only, and Royal Family': no prizes for guessing which king. He took two dishes of coffee and a pipe for breakfast, some chicken or mutton at noon, and a cup of wheat beer and a piece of bread, 'if anything', at night.[12] And so Sancroft died, a kind of patriarch of a rump of the old Church of England

members of the Church of England have their eyes now fixt upon you.' (Bodl., MS. Tanner 27, no. 65, fol. 89.)

8   Bishop Francis Turner to Sancroft (from Leamington, Warwickshire), 20 March 1689, Bodl., MS. Tanner 28(2), no. 261, fol. 370; Beddard 1988, pp. 121–2; *The Revolution of 1688*, ed. Robert Beddard (Oxford, 1991), p. 44.

9   'A short account of Arch Bishop Sancroft from Mr Needham', ECA, COL.9.8.

10 ECA COL.9.8 contains transcripts of the Sancroft-Lloyd correspondence, recently acquired by Lambeth Palace Library, made by Barbara Graebe of Fressingfield. There are letters from Lloyd to Sancroft dated 1 April 1687, 5 November 1688, 21 March 1689, 19 October 1689, 5 August 1690, 4 September 1693, 15 September 1693; Bodl., MSS. Tanner 29, no. 3, fol. 5, 28(2), no. 165, fol. 232, no. 266, fol. 377, 27, no. 68, fol. 92, no. 113, fol. 176, 25, no. 60, fol. 90. Am I too suspicious about 'wash balls', for which Sancroft thanks Lloyd in four of his letters. 'I forgot yesterday to pay for my last dozen wash-balls.' How much soap did Sancroft need?

11 Sancroft to Lloyd, 2 April 1692; ECA COL.9.8, p. 28.

12 ECA, COL. 9.8.

in partibus, who failed to do anything much to preserve and perpetuate it, a role which necessarily fell to others, primarily to Bishop Lloyd, to whom he relinquished his archiepiscopal powers and functions (were there any?).[13] This is a remarkable historical example of the sterility of noble principle.

Sancroft did not live long enough to hear of the divine providence visited upon a junior Emmanuel colleague and friend, Richard Kidder, a fellow of the College in the interregnal years. Kidder had the courage to consent to succeeding the saintly and non-juring Bishop Thomas Ken of Bath and Wells, an emblematic, exemplary Anglican figure and one of the Seven Bishops. On the night of 26–27 November 1703, there happened the worst storm in English history, when 10,000 lives are said to have been lost at sea. On land, a great chimney stack fell on Bishop Kidder and his wife in bed in their palace at Wells, crushing them both to death, an awful warning against the virtue of episcopal residence.[14]

This is the story of a college, not of a nation negotiating the most critical corner in its constitutional history, and the reader might justifiably expect these paragraphs to be but the prolegomenon to an account of the impact of James II and of the Revolution which he provoked on Emmanuel. But if the truth be told, there was not much of an impact and nothing to be compared with the *cause célèbre* of James's attempt to convert Magdalen College Oxford into a Catholic seminary.[15] In the University at large, to be sure, there was an impact. Under James, and his extraordinary Commission for Ecclesiastical Causes, royal mandates were more urgently pressed than ever. When the University resisted a mandate to confer an M.A. on a certain Benedictine monk called Alban Francis, the vice-chancellor, John Peachell of Magdalene, a genial drinking companion of Samuel Pepys but hardly the man for this hour, backed by a university delegation which included Isaac Newton, was repeatedly and mercilessly hectored by the notorious Judge Jeffreys (Jeffreys of the 'Bloody Assize') and eventually deprived of his vice-chancellorship and suspended from his mastership. He was replaced as vice-chancellor by John Balderston, who had succeeded Holbech as Master of Emmanuel in 1680. According to Bishop Burnet, Balderston showed great spirit, declaring to the Senate that 'during his magistracy, neither religion, nor the rights of the body, should suffer by his means'.[16] But Balderston was powerless to prevent new statutes being imposed on Sidney Sussex College, excising all unfavourable references to 'popery'. James had used

[13] D'Oyly 1821, II, pp. 30–4. In the formal instrument consigning his powers to Lloyd, dated 9 February 1691(2), Sancroft styles himself 'Ecclesiae Metrop. Cant. humilis minister'.
[14] Rupp 1986, p. 39.
[15] Beddard 1997, pp. 946–7.
[16] Burnet quoted by Cooper 1845, p. 633, who reproduces much of the lively exchanges between Peachell and his colleagues and the Commissioners, pp. 620–32.

his mandatory powers to wish upon Sidney a popish Master in the person of the Caian and recent Catholic convert Joshua Basset, a close associate of Alban Francis and the author of these statutes, dispensing him from taking the customary oaths. Master and Fellows were at once at total loggerheads. In consequence, the Fellows were summoned to face the intimidating wrath of the Ecclesiastical Commission. But Cambridge had responded to James with a defiance which surprised and impressed observers. Isaac Newton, soon to represent Cambridge in Parliament, was distracted from the preparation of the final text of his *Principia Mathematica* to enter the political fray. There were rumours that the Sidney Sussex affair was only the beginning, that all the colleges would be 'dealt with one after another, as the goose . . . was plucked of all her feathers'. But soon everything fell apart for James. Cambridge's stand was seen, with the still larger affair of Magdalen College Oxford, to be part of the turning of the tide. Bishop Turner wrote: 'You have had a most glorious part in this great transaction.'[17]

Amidst the local riots which followed James's precipitate departure from the scene, Joshua Basset too made himself scarce. It would take another 296 years for the next Roman Catholic to become head of a Cambridge house: Sir John Lyons, Master of Trinity Hall in 1984, closely followed in Emmanuel by Lord St John of Fawsley.

Apart from two or three troublesome mandates,[18] Emmanuel seems to have escaped the political hazards of these years more or less scot free. Was this due to the spirit of pugnacious patriotism attributed by Burnet to John Balderston? It is more likely that Sancroft was still able to shield his own college, which in any case no longer mattered as much as it once did. Certainly, if Balderston's mastership opened with something of a bang, it ended with a very long whimper indeed. Elected in 1680 and Master until his death in August 1719, Balderston equalled Laurence Chaderton's record by remaining in office for thirty-nine years. But in no other respect did he resemble Chaderton. It is hard now to say what Balderston's career and life added up to. He published nothing, received no higher preferments, and failed to make it into the *Dictionary of National Biography*. His was one of the most undistinguished masterships, with as few as a dozen undergraduates being admitted in some years. Shuckburgh thought this period 'the least fortunate in the College history'.[19]

In the University, an even longer reign was about to commence. In the midst of the revolutionary events of 1688, Cambridge found itself without a chancellor, and opted for Sancroft, ignoring James's recommendation of

---

[17] Twigg 1990, pp. 276–85; Mark Goldie, 'Joshua Basset, Popery and Revolution', in Beales and Nisbet 1996, pp. 111–30; Cunich, David Hoyle *et al.* 1994, pp. 150–4.
[18] Shuckburgh 1904, pp. 118–19.
[19] Ibid.

Lord Dartmouth. Sancroft insisted upon his total ineligibility, aged and infirm, unable to do the University any service in high places. Nothing deterred, and within six weeks of the landing of Dutch William in Torbay, the Regent House elected the archbishop 'by universal consent'. From Lambeth, silence. In February 1689, the University sought the new chancellor's advice on, of all matters, the reception of the new sovereigns, who were about to visit Cambridge. But Cambridge was not being pig-headed or naive. It was using Sancroft, cynically, as a stopgap to postpone the evil day of having to make a real, and politically divisive, election until it was clear which way the wind was going to blow. Only in March was there recognition that it would be necessary to think of someone else, although 'at present no particular person is named or thought on'. Presently Cambridge thought on a safe, second-rate, candidate, Charles Seymour, 6th duke of Somerset, who would remain chancellor for the next sixty years: one of the more bizarre consequences of the Glorious Revolution.[20]

Dead, Sancroft was of more consequence for Emmanuel than Balderston alive: a replay of the story of Holdsworth's library, but with a happier outcome for the College.[21] But for his deprivation, Sancroft's library, which must originally have rivalled Holdsworth's in size, might have remained at Lambeth, a major accession to the collection originally endowed by Archbishop Bancroft. But now the books which John Evelyn saw being boxed up were intended for Emmanuel. Their first destination seems to have been Fressingfield, where they remained for two years. Not long before Sancroft's death, William Needham was liaising between Fressingfield and the College. Sancroft showed him a roomful of books and asked whether he thought they could be accommodated in the old chapel, now roughly converted for the purposes of a library. Needham thought that they might be shoehorned in, but Sancroft's mind was running, as it had thirty years earlier, on 'a new fabric'; as well it might, since his benefaction was likely to double the size of the existing library, and Needham had more books to fetch from Lambeth. On 16 September 1693, ten weeks before the end, Balderston conveyed his thanks for 'the most valuable treasure of your Grace's books, just now lodged in our Library.'[22] But 'lodged' was the right word. It was not until 1707 that the arrangements proposed by Needham had been made, and a catalogue prepared. The library was uncomfortably full, and in 1712 it was decided

---

[20] Cooper 1845, pp. 642–3; D'Oyly 1821, I, pp. 398–408; letters between the University and Sancroft, November 1688–February 1689, and the formal instrument of Sancroft's election, BL, MS. Harl. 3785, fols. 275–84; Dr John Covel to Sancroft, 1 March 1689, Bodl., MS. Tanner 29, no. 255, fol. 364.

[21] For what follows, see Bennett 1963.

[22] Balderston to Sancroft, 16 September 1693, Bodl., MS. Tanner 25, no. 59, fol. 89.

to sell off such books 'as the Society thinks fit to part with', and to use the proceeds for new acquisitions.

Consequently, we cannot equate the more than five thousand volumes currently in the Emmanuel Library and at last receiving the attention they deserve[23] with Sancroft's library as it may have originally existed. We may note but not make too much of the almost total absence of the great English poets and playwrights who, as we learn from his notebooks, had been Sancroft's lifelong companions. We know from what he said to Needham that it was Sancroft's intention to leave at Fressingfield 'a good Library for a gentleman', 'for the use of the family there', bequeathing to Emmanuel only 'the books of learning'.[24] We know that Sancroft's failure to make a will (not a matter of negligence, but of reluctance to put his affairs into the hands of his usurping successor, Tillotson, and of the Prerogative Court of Canterbury), occasioned some difficulty. This may be the reason why Sancroft's huge archive found its way on to the market, much of it to be snapped up by Bishop Tanner, to the great advantage of the Bodleian Library.[25] (Sancroft had promised his papers to Henry Wharton, who indeed posthumously published, in 1695, his collection of the remains of Archbishop Laud.[26]) But what 'books of learning' Emmanuel received! – books of an eclectic and very European learning, including a heavily annotated Spanish grammar, much literature in that language, and long runs of foreign periodicals. Six months short of his death, the now impecunious Sancroft had written to Sir Henry North: 'I pray, let Mr Berners be paid in the first place for the Journal des Scavans' – to which he had subscribed since 1666.[27]

Nevertheless, one would not necessarily gather from Sancroft's library, nor from anything else preserved in the Emmanuel of this epoch, that a kind of intellectual revolution was in progress in the England of political Restoration and Revolution.[28] The magnitude of that revolution so far as Cambridge was concerned should certainly not be exaggerated. Of 443 Fellows of the Royal Society elected between 1660 and 1686, only 76, or 16%, were Cambridge graduates, and almost half of those were physicians, no longer resident in the University. Isaac Barrow of Trinity, the first Lucasian Professor of Mathematics, resigned his chair within six years in order to devote more time to theology. Soon after publishing *Principia*, his successor, Isaac Newton, left the University for a more

---

[23] A history and catalogue of the library are being prepared for publication. The work was started by Dr Sarah Bendall and is now being continued by Dr Helen Carron.

[24] Needham reports (ECA, COL.9.8) that these were soon sold 'to Bateman the Bookseller'. So much for the cultivation of *belles lettres* at Fressingfield.

[25] Bennett 1962–3, pp. 34–5.

[26] *DNB*, art. Wharton.

[27] *Familiar Letters of Dr William Sancroft Late Lord Archbishop of Canterbury to Mr North Afterwards Sir Henry North of Mildenhall Bart.* (London, 1757), p. 39.

[28] For much of what follows, see Gascoigne 1989.

public life in London. A biographer of Newton has even written of 'the catastrophic decline of the university after the Restoration [which] left it an intellectual wasteland.'[29]

But such judgments usually pay too much attention to the formalities of the syllabus and overlook the more insidious progress of new intellectual tendencies, especially through the relative informalities of the tutorial system. A more recent authority has gone so far as to claim that at the turn of the seventeenth and eighteenth centuries, Cambridge 'almost totally reshaped its curriculum', escaping from the medieval scholastic straitjacket, with Mathematics about to become the new staple of under-graduate education. This was a 'virtual academic revolution', camou-flaged by nominal adherence to the Elizabethan Statutes of the University. But it is the major contention of Dr Gascoigne's history of *Cambridge in the Age of the Enlightenment* that progressive intellectual and pedagogical tendencies were almost confined to certain colleges, notably Trinity, Clare and Corpus Christi, and are to be attributed mainly to the political and religious leanings of those societies. Emmanuel was emphatically not in this vanguard. Consistently Tory in its politics, it was more concerned with the conservation of Anglican orthodoxy than with risky adventures of the mind and spirit. In 1702 Henry Lee, a Fellow of Emmanuel by royal mandate since 1677, and hence a clone of Sancroft, launched an ambitious attack on John Locke's *Essay concerning human understanding* under the title *Antiscepticism*, an attack on 'the inquisitive Genius of this Age'. 'Our Philosophy, our Policy, our religion, must be all new or none at all.' This was ironical and not a plea for novelty. It appears that only medicine, as the least metaphysical of the natural sciences, was congenial to the Church and King tendency: witness the lifelong friendship which existed between Sancroft and his sometime pupil Henry Paman, a friend of the famous physician Sir Thomas Sydenham who made his home at Lambeth while he served as Professor of Physic at Gresham College in the early 1680s, becoming Sancroft's Master of the Faculties.[30]

It is an attractive paradigm favoured by some historians of science that most great new ideas start life as heresies and finish up as new and eventually rather sterile orthodoxies. In the in-between process there may be relatively little intelligent intellectual engagement with the ideas in question. So it was in the nineteenth century with Darwinism, which was at first widely rejected, but later uncritically accepted, with much mis-understanding, leading to the widespread notion that 'Science' had dis-proved 'Religion'. Newton's *Principia*, a comparable case, was at first

---

[29] Quoted ibid, p. 6.
[30] Ibid., p. 61; *DNB*, art. Paman. Paman corresponded with Sancroft, his 'honoured tutor', throughout his life, and in addition to his formal functions, seems to have acted as the archbishop's general man of business (evidence here and there in the Tanner MSS). He left Lambeth with Sancroft and went to live in Covent Garden.

greeted not so much with hostility as with incomprehension. When the Cambridge undergraduates passed Newton in the street, they said: 'There goes the man who has writ a book that neither he nor any one else understands.'[31] Newton was made accessible by popularisers such as the controversial Master of Trinity, Richard Bentley, and William Whiston, and eventually by the codifying efforts of eighteenth-century tutors.[32] This trickle-down treatment had already been meted out to René Descartes. In the 1640s Cartesianism was the most exciting thing since sliced bread, an avant-garde intellectual method promoted in Cambridge by Henry More of Christ's, much as a twentieth-century don might adopt Derrida or Lacan. But by the turn of the century Descartes had become standard tutorial fare, even in darkest Emmanuel. Joshua Barnes, a Fellow from 1678 to 1701, and so presumably another Sancroftian, revised Richard Holdsworth's famous 'Directions' for study, adding to Holdsworth's philosophical set texts for the fourth year the observation that 'because the course of Philosophical Study is now alter'd', students could, if they wished, 'make use of Des Cartes his *Meteorum* or Book of Meteors, also his *De Passionibus* etc., and other *Cartesians*'.[33] But Newtonianism no doubt took a little longer to be digested.

And, in any case, *plus ça change* . . . In 1696, the vice-chancellor circulated a rocket to the colleges, complaining of the 'evill manners' of some of 'the youth'. In the streets, undergraduates, far from doffing their caps to M.A.s and other senior members, pushed them into the gutter and even struck them. They misbehaved in Great St Mary's, in sermon time, 'entertaining them selves with merriment and laughter'. They frequented (and this was hardly news) taverns and alehouses. At Emmanuel, the 'youth' were herded into chapel and subjected to a harangue from the Master (or his deputy?) which must have lasted well over an hour. We have this 'discourse' in full, and for the first time hear the very words in which the student body was addressed on such occasions. 'I hope, or at least could wish, none of our College were guilty of this fault [misbehaviour in church], but I have too much reason to hear it, by observing what I have often seen with grief and shame, and am therefore glad of this opportunity to tell you all of how irreverent many of you have been too often in these Holy places, in this House of God . . . For Gods sake, for our soules sake, gentlemen, if we be *Christians*, if we are Scholars, if we are men, let us speedily mend this fault also, and put on reverent and devout behaviour when we come to Chappell, or to Church, and whatever we do at other times, let us be sober and vigilant

[31] Quoted, Gascoigne 1989, from King's College Cambridge, Keynes MS. 130, p. 142.
[32] 'Newtonian Natural Philosophy Established', chapter 6 of Gascoigne 1989.
[33] ECL, MS. 179.56. See Gascoigne 1989, p. 55.

and devout at that time.'[34] It would be unwise to read this as evidence of a decline in 'manners' as Emmanuel entered an age of reason and some scepticism. But 'whatever we do at other times' may imply a significant concession to changing mores.

William Law and the Serious Call[1]

William Law, like William Sancroft, was born and died (at about the same age as Sancroft) in the same village, in his case King's Cliffe, a little place not far from Stamford, where his life began in 1686 and ended in 1761. Like Sancroft, but without the intervening drama of high office and great affairs, William Law took on a retiring, even monkish, disposition. Although he was a man of the eighteenth century, and placed an indelible mark on its religious sensibility, Law provides a kind of coda to seventeenth-century Emmanuel, a unique consummation equally of the godliness of the old puritan tradition of the College (something he would have been the last to have admitted) and of the Anglican piety of the age of William Sancroft.

There has been a long debate among historians about the calibre of English religious belief and life in the Augustan age, but steadily the weight of informed opinion, thanks to historians as diverse as Norman Sykes and Jonathan Clark, has moved away from the old caricature of a moribund, worldly Church and an almost dechristianised populace, the rich cynically worldly, the poor neglected until Methodism swept in to make all the difference, towards recognition of the persistent and fundamental vitality of its Christianity, and even of the centrality of the Anglican Church in the fabric of what was still, according to Clark, a kind

---

[34] ECL, MS. 179, fols. 8r, 15r. This report, and the recension of Holdsworth's 'Directions', with much other material, appears to have been intended to form a large treatise on pedagogy and discipline, compiled by Joshua Barnes.

[1] William Law's *Works* were privately printed in nine volumes by G. Moreton in 1892 and 1893. A highly disorganised but often richly informative account of Law, and especially of his mystical enthusiasms, is A. C. Walton, *Materials for an Adequate Biography of William Law*, privately printed in 1854. A copy with corrections and additions in Walton's hand is in the Cambridge University Library. A more conventional if now somewhat dated biography is J. H. Overton, *William Law, Nonjuror and Mystic* (London, 1881). Editions of the Serious Call are legion. I have used the edition by Paul G. Stanwood in 'The Classics of Western Spirituality' (London and New York, 1978). *Selected Mystical Writings of William Law* are edited by Stephen Hobhouse (London, 1938). See also *William Law: Selected Writings*, ed. Janet Louth (Manchester, 1990). Reference is made here to Arthur W. Hopkinson, *About William Law* (London, 1948), 'William Law', chapter 15 of Rupp 1986, Henri Talon, *William Law: A Study in Literary Craftsmanship* (London, 1948), and A. Keith Walker, *William Law: His Life and Thought* (London, 1973). The *DNB* article on Law is a useful source.

of confessional state. It is hard to say which side of this argument is strengthened by the obscure life and prominent writings of William Law. Here was a man of the eighteenth century who drank tea and chocolate, enjoyed his evening pipe, and related in his own curious fashion to the new and rising moneyed classes, from which he had come and to which his writings ministered, but who was also some kind of antique saint and an undoubted religious genius. But Law cannot be expected single-handed to redeem the religious reputation of the eighteenth century. He lived a remote life, divorced from the age in which he lived; while the writings for which he is for ever famous, and especially the *Serious Call to a Devout and Holy Life* (1729), in their address to conventional and shallow religion, strengthen and perhaps distort our impression of an age which had forgotten what Christianity was really about, and more profoundly than that, indict a whole nominally Christian civilization which had never chosen to take the Gospels seriously. One of the unforgettable 'characters' who pass before us in the pages of the *Serious Call* is 'Julius', on his own and society's terms an exemplary Christian: 'All the parish supposes Julius to be sick if he is not at church.' 'And yet if Julius was to read all the New Testament from the beginning to the end, he would find his course of life condemned in every page of it.'[2]

Law was the fourth of eight sons (eleven children in all) of a prosperous grocer. That he was sent to Cambridge to become a scholar is indicative of early recognition of remarkable intellectual talents; that he proceeded to Emmanuel College (in 1705) natural for a native of that part of Northamptonshire, Mildmay territory. Not much more is known of his Cambridge career, or, indeed, of an entire life which one authority has declared to be 'not particularly interesting': 'apart from his writings, a dim and unconvincing figure'.[3] He followed a conventional academic career, which in 1711 brought him to ordination and a fellowship. It is not surprising that in late Stuart Emmanuel Law should have acquired the convictions of a high churchman and tory. But unlike most of his contemporaries, he pursued the logic of his principles with single-minded consistency. After the accession of George I and the 1715 Rebellion, the oaths of allegiance and abjuration were again imposed, and Law refused to take them, so becoming a second-generation Non-Juror, the only Fellow to take that course. He had already been degraded by the University for a performance as praevaricator at the Commencement in which he had asked 'whether the sun shines when it is in eclipse?', the sun meaning the Old Pretender. In 1716 he resigned his fellowship and, after two or three years of a shadowy and mostly unrecorded clerical existence, curate here and there, and perhaps some continued residence in Emmanuel, where

---

[2] Law 1978, p. 49.
[3] Hopkinson 1948, p. 25.

there are traces of his presence as late as 1723,[4] was taken on by the Gibbon family of Putney, becoming tutor to Edward Gibbon, the father of the historian. At one point he accompanied his charge back to Emmanuel (where he proved to be a far from satisfactory scholar). William Law is good evidence of the truth of what is sometimes said: that the Non-Jurors in their Never Never Land preserved the lost soul of the old Church of England. But Law cannot be called a leading, or even a typical Non-Juror. He was a spiritual writer who happened to be a Non-Juror, not a Non-Juror who wrote spiritual books.[5]

On the death of his father, Law had inherited an equal share of his estate, a modest but adequate living of £115 a year, and in 1740 he returned to King's Cliffe, where he lived for the remainder of his life, rarely if ever venturing anywhere else. He was joined by two ladies, a widow called Mrs Archibald Hutcheson, who has been described as 'amiable and brainless', and Miss Hester Gibbon, the aunt of the historian, 'infatuated and visionary'.[6] Soon these ladies moved in with Law at Hall Yard House, and made him their chaplain and spiritual director. Together they shared an unvarying daily routine of religious offices and charitable works, with a little daily exercise, Law on his feet, Miss Gibbon on horseback, Mrs Hutcheson in her little carriage, complete with coachman. The ladies were well off and the joint income of this *ménage à trois* was £3000, of which Law had the disposal. But the household reversed the principle of tithing, living on a tenth of this sum and giving nine-tenths away in often promiscuous and undiscriminating charity, which made them far from popular in a village, which, like other parish communities of the age, practised a kind of politics of exclusion, so far as the 'undeserving' poor were concerned.[7] Law went scrupulously to every service in the parish church, where he could exercise no public ministry, but seems to have had little else to do with the rector, a good parish priest called Wilfred Piement, who was incumbent of King's Cliffe for thirty-three years. A major focus of charitable activity was the school for fourteen girls, which Law had set up with £1000 given to him by a well-wisher and admirer, to which Mrs Hutcheson later added a school for boys.

So far we may have given the impression that William Law was a reclusive nonentity, outside his spiritual writings. But long before the return to his native roots, he had become celebrated as a controversialist

---

4 Rupp 1986, p. 218.
5 Hopkinson 1948, p. 11.
6 Ibid., pp. 14–15.
7 Steve Hindle, 'Power, Poor Relief and Social Relations in Holland Fen, c. 1600–1800', *Historical Journal*, 41 (1998), 67–96; Keith Wrightson, 'The Politics of the Parish in Early Modern England', in Paul Griffiths, Adam Fox and Steve Hindle, eds., *The Experience of Authority in Early Modern England* (Basingstoke, 1996), pp. 10–46.

in a great age of religious controversy, one of the most effectively and brilliantly mordant of those who took up their pens in defence of what was orthodox and traditional rather than currently fashionable. His opponents and targets, who included Bishop Benjamin Hoadly and Bernard Mandeville, author of *The Fable of the Bees*, are long-forgotten figures who, it has been said, survive as types,[8] not least in a turn-of-the-millennium Britain dominated by what is politically expedient and controlled by spin doctors. Hoadly was the archetype of what in the next century would be called the Broad Churchman, latitudinarian and un-demanding in his theology, confident about what his contemporary Toland called the reasonableness of Christianity, an apologist for the whig Erastianism which in the age of Robert Walpole stamped on any pretensions the Church of England might have had to a distinct and transcendent existence as a visible spiritual society and a hierarchy. It was as a direct result of what became known as the Bangorian Controversy (Bangor, which in six years Hoadly never visited, being the first of his four episcopal preferments) that Convocation was suppressed, never to meet again until the mid-nineteenth century. Hoadly had published an attack on the non-Jurors which included the dubious casuistry that man's entitlement to God's favour depended, not on principles, but on the sin-cerity of his own conscience. This was followed by his sermon preached before the king on *The Nature of the Kingdom or Church of Christ*, which denied the visibility and the distinct spiritual authority of the Church. When Convocation responded with a censure, the government pro-rogued it *sine die*, a public vindication and implementation of Hoadly's Erastian principles.

Although Hoadly paid him little attention (for who was William Law?) Law's *Three Letters to the Bishop of Bangor* (1717–19) were by far the most telling of the almost two hundred pamphlets generated by the Bangorian Controversy. It was not so much the matter of his polemic, a predictable defence of Church, sacraments, ministry, as its manner and style which raised Law to what his biographer J. H. Overton called 'the very highest rank in controversial divinity'. 'You have at once, my Lord, by these doc-trines condemned the Scriptures, the Apostles, their martyred successors, the Church of England, and your own conduct; and you have thereby given us some reason to suspect, whether you, who allow of no other church but what is founded in sincerity, are yourself really a member of any church.'[9] Law's Remarks on Mandeville's witty fable which argued that private vices were public virtues, for only selfishness made the world go round, was no less sharp-edged in its use of irony. 'If therefore you would prove yourself to be no more than a brute or an animal, how much

---

[8] Hopkinson 1948, p. 31.
[9] Quoted, Talon 1948, p. 15.

of your life you need to alter I cannot tell, but you must at least forbear writing against virtue, for no mere animal ever hated it.'[10] It would be good to read Law against Professor Dawkins's *The Selfish Gene*. Rather more heavy-handed, and hard to stomach, was Law's *The Unlawfulness of Stage Entertainments* (1726), a polemic which went beyond the puritan antitheatricality of William Prynne's *Histriomastix* and was a stern prelude to the unrelenting works of moral persuasion which were to follow. Law condemned the stage, absolutely, not as a mere occasion of sin but, like drunkenness, lewdness, lying and profaneness, grossly sinful in itself. 'It must be as unlawful to go to a Play, as it is unlawful to approve, encourage, assist, and reward a man for *Renouncing* a Christian Life.' 'The Business of Players is the most wicked and detestable Profession in the World.'[11]

If this was a prelude, the overture to Law's *Serious Call* was a little book called *A Practical Treatise on Christian Perfection* (1726). 'Christianity is not a school, for the teaching of moral virtue, the polishing our manners, or forming us to live a life of this world with decency and gentility.' 'It implies an entire change of life, a dedication of ourselves, our souls and bodies unto God, in the strictest and highest sense of the words.' 'Light and darkness are but faint resemblances of that greater contrariety, that is betwixt the Spirit of God, and the spirit of the world.'[12]

In no respect did Law more resemble the Puritans of the Emmanuel past than in his insistence that true religion was something quite different from mere civil politeness. His orchestral masterpiece, the *Serious Call to a Devout and Holy Life*, may have been, as the title-page claimed, *Adapted to the State and Condition of All Orders of Christians*, but it was addressed, not to the great unwashed, not to notorious sinners in the eyes of the respectable world, but to various sections of his own middle class, and to those wallowing in what the Puritans would have called the dangerous delusion of spiritual 'security'. 'To atheists and rakes he has nothing to say.'[13] At the outset Law declares, surprisingly for a high churchman, that prayer, whether public or private, was secondary to being devout. 'It is very observable that there is not one command in all the gospel for public worship; and perhaps it is a duty that is least insisted upon in scripture of any other.' 'Devotion signifies a life given or devoted to God.' 'This and this alone is Christianity.' But of this there was little or nothing to be found 'even amongst the better sort of people'. 'You see them often at church, and pleased with fine preachers; but look into their lives and you see them just the same sort of people as others are that make no pretences

[10] Quoted, ibid., p. 17.
[11] Quoted, Hopkinson 1948, p. 42.
[12] *Selected Writings*, pp. 17, 20.
[13] Talon 1948, p. 35.

289

to devotion.' Law's religion was an austere and demanding Pelagianism, which all too readily lent itself to the pun that Law came before Gospel. 'It seems plain that our salvation depends upon the sincerity and perfection of our endeavours to obtain it.'[14]

The argument is moved forward by the deployment, as in a toy theatre, of a number of brilliantly drawn but somewhat two-dimensional types, or characters. As a literary technique this was an adaptation of the device of the Theophrastan 'character', which we last encountered as deployed by Bishop Joseph Hall.[15] 'Flatus' resembles Toad of Toad Hall (but perhaps was Law's pupil Edward Gibbon), prosperous and healthy but dissatisfied and always pursuing new passions: first, fine clothes, then gaming, next 'the diversions of the town', then hunting, building, learning languages, vegetarianism. At one point, Flatus does what he has never done before: 'He is reasoning and reflecting with himself.' 'Calidus' is a great man in the city. 'Every hour of the day is with him an hour of business; and though he eats and drinks very heartily, yet every meal seems to be in a hurry, and he would say grace if he had time.' He literally has no time for religion, but he is no friend to heretics or infidels, keeps on good terms with the vicar, and gives something to the charity schools. 'Cognatus' is first cousin to Parson Woodforde, 'a sober, regular clergyman of good repute in the world, and well esteemed in his parish. All his parishioners say he is an honest man and very notable at making a bargain . . . and has raised a considerable fortune by good management.' He has done this in order to leave a small fortune to his niece, whom he has educated in expensive finery out of the profits of two livings, whereas his father was 'but an ordinary man'. Had Cognatus ever considered 'how absurd a thing it is to grow rich by the gospel'?[16]

The Theophrastan mode is best suited to the construction of negative, satirical stereotypes, a vehicle for blame rather than praise. The central characters in Law's theatre are two spinster sisters, Flavia and Miranda, who have each been left an income of two hundred pounds a year, which they have enjoyed since they buried their parents twenty years ago. They may or may not be modelled on the Gibbon sisters, Catharine and Hester. Flavia lives a carefully frivolous life, all fashion and gossip. 'I shall not take it upon me to say that it is impossible for Flavia to be saved; but thus much must be said, that she has no grounds from scripture to think she is in the way of salvation.' Miranda, by total contrast, is a real Christian. 'She considers all as due to God, and so does everything in His name and for His sake.' She spends next to nothing on herself. 'To relate her charity would be to relate the history of every day for twenty years; for so long

---

[14] Law 1978, pp. 47, 50–1, 52–3, 66.
[15] See p. 87 above.
[16] Law 1978, pp. 164–6, 80–1, 179–81.

has all her fortune been spent that way.' A rather disturbing part of Miranda's story, for the modern reader, may be that she 'bought' three children from their wicked and warring parents, and brought them up in godly ways. 'When she dies, she must shine amongst apostles and saints and martyrs, she must stand amongst the first servants of God and be glorious amongst those that have fought the good fight and finished their course with joy.'[17] Miranda is scarcely credible. But if she is for real, and to be identified with Miss Hester Gibbon, there are some rather strong indications that that lady, for all her relentless good works, lost sight of charity in the sense of I Corinthians 13, without which, said St Paul, all was but in vain.[18]

For all his claims to be addressing 'all orders and ranks of men and women of all ages', Law cannot escape the charge of having constructed a model of Christian perfection which the Middle Ages had reserved for the religious life, as not attainable in the world. A critic wrote: 'Though you seem to disclaim monastick retirements, yet your principles manifestly serve to promote the same effects.'[19] Arguably, his understanding of Christian vocation, of the value of all legitimate callings, was greatly inferior to that of Martin Luther and the protestant tradition which derives from it, to which George Herbert gave such memorable expression: 'Who sweeps a room as for thy lawes,/Makes that and th'action fine.' The *Serious Call* is about the use of means, and leisure, and has little to offer to the great bulk of the eighteenth-century population who enjoyed neither, infinitely less than John Wesley and the Methodists were about to set out. And it has nothing to say about the skilled craftsmen of Hanoverian England whose work was their prayer.[20] Nevertheless the book proved an inspiration, to the Wesleys amongst others, who walked all the way from Oxford to Putney to consult the oracle.[21] And it left its mark on many who can hardly be said to have made it their rule of life, including Samuel Johnson, who had picked it up as a book to laugh at, but had found that it made him for the first time think in earnest about religion.[22]

Law the Anglican and non-juring controversialist had turned into the moral persuader and advocate of real rather than counterfeit Christianity. He now underwent a further sea-change, turning to the way of the mystics. He had always profited from the great masters of late medieval mysticism, Tauler, à Kempis, and the *Theologia Germanica*, and Malebranche was an early inspiration. But now he fell under the spell of Jacob

---

[17] Ibid., pp. 105–20.
[18] Hopkinson 1948, p. 24. 'Miss Gibbon seems to have been, at times, a particularly bad-tempered woman. See her correspondence with her niece, given by Walton, p. 503.'
[19] Quoted, Talon 1948, p. 48.
[20] Rupp 1986, p. 225.
[21] Walker 1973, pp. 96–7.
[22] Quoted, Rupp 1986, p. 226.

Boehme (or Behmen) (1575–1624), the self-taught German cobbler-seer, eventually developing a one-eyed fixation, as if only Boehme provided access to a true apprehension of God as infinite, all-embracing Love. Only in the twentieth century has Law's infatuation with mysticism (he was not himself a mystical practitioner) been appreciated, by such fellow afficionadi as Dean Inge and Evelyn Underhill, and even by Aldous Huxley, who praised him in *The Perennial Philosophy* as 'one of the great masters of devotion'.[23] But in his own generation the later Law alienated many of his admirers, including John Wesley who had no room for or understanding of mysticism, and who came to blame Law for a rough, morose, sour doctrine which had failed to reveal to Wesley until it was almost, but, thanks to the Moravians, not too late the Gospel of God's free and gracious salvation in Christ. Law had been mistaken if he thought that the young Wesley had saving faith. Perhaps 'you had it not yourself'. Law's response was in character. Speaking of the *Theologia Germanica*, he wrote: 'If that book does not plainly lead you to Jesus Christ, I am content to know as little of Christianity as you are pleased to believe.'[24]

William Law had nobility but he was by no means a flawless or even attractive character. It has been noted that he had little capacity for friendship, preferring a condescending relationship to his social, moral and spiritual inferiors. The household at Hall Place was not so much a mutual admiration society as an environment of uncritical adulation, and it is not clear that this was good for the object of the adulation. The Boswell to his Johnson was 'Christians Awake!' John Byrom: more adulation. After a reputation in his youth of being a ladies' man[25] he appears to have become as asexual as it is possible for a human being to be, which must have cramped his pastoral gifts. He might have been fond of children but were children fond of him? (Rule 16 for his school was that 'every girl . . . must always go to Church at all funerals', while the penalty for lying or cheating was to be chained to a pillar for half a day.) He was in spirit Dominican rather than Franciscan, and comparisons drawn between his exemplary menage and Nicholas Ferrar's Little Gidding are a bit of an insult to Little Gidding. Let us leave him as described by his most eccentrically uncritical biographer, Christopher Walton. Law's days were spent in his study, which was a recess or little cell four foot square, separated from his bed-chamber by a wainscotting, looking out of an old mullion window at the yard and garden which hopeful tramps so often crossed, equipped with almost nothing beyond a chair, a table, the Bible, and the complete works of Jacob Boehme.[26]

---

[23] Ibid., pp. 232–40; George E. Clarkson, *The Mysticism of William Law* (New York, 1992). Huxley is quoted by Walker, p. xii.

[24] Ibid., pp. 134–5; Hopkinson 1948, pp. 99–104.

[25] Rupp 1986, p. 219.

[26] Hopkinson 1948, p. 15.

10

The Society in the Eighteenth Century

The visitor who knew little of the history of Emmanuel might be excused for thinking that its golden age lay between the 1660s and the 1760s. One stands in the entrance, and ahead lies Wren's marvellous chapel and gallery, of the 1660s and 70s. To the right is the Westmorland building, its walls a noble monument of the period 1719–22; on one's left the hall, in outward show of the 1760s. All about one is the fine eighteenth-century façade. The late sixteenth century may still be seen in the Old Library, once the chapel, and the early seventeenth in the splendid, unaltered brick building of the 1630s. But the general effect is similar to that of the Queen's College at Oxford, totally remodelled to be a spectacular stone monument of the late seventeenth and early eighteenth centuries, to give the image of grandeur to what is commonly reckoned the least notable epoch in the history of the university of Oxford. Emmanuel is equally beautiful if not quite so grandiose.[1]

The size of the society
In the early seventeenth century Emmanuel had been one of the largest societies in Cambridge, with over 250 undergraduates. In the eighteenth and for most of the nineteenth it was one of the smallest. By 1719 it was recruiting sometimes as few as 9 a year. In 1743 there were 39 undergraduates in residence, in 1751 less than 30, in 1753, and again in 1763, 34. 'For the twenty-four years from 1743 to 1766 the average number of residents, other than fellows [but including a sprinkling of graduates], was 43', wrote E. S. Shuckburgh.[2] In Richard Farmer's time as tutor and master, from 1767 to 1797, annual admissions of between 14 and 16 were characteristic numbers, though 1778 produced a record crop of 29. In Emmanuel, as in most colleges, there was some revival in the very early nineteenth century.[3] In 1800 the undergraduates numbered 59 in all,

---

[1] See chap. 12. For the Queen's College, see Brooke, Highfield and Swaan 1988, pp. 206–11 and plates 130–3; Colvin 1986, pp. 833–4, 838–9.

[2] Shuckburgh 1904, p. 141; for other details, see ibid. pp. 140–4. The numbers for each year, above and below, are from the 'Register'.

[3] The details which follow are based on *CUC* 1800, pp. 80–1; 1810, pp. 238–9; 1820, pp. 294–7; 1830, pp. 356–60; 1840, pp. 298–301; 1850, p. 402; etc. to 1890, p. 752.

including 16 fellow commoners – the fellow commoners thereafter declined; in 1820 the total had risen to 65, and it fluctuated between about 70 and 80 until the very end of the nineteenth century, falling to 51 in 1840 and rising to 95 in 1850, but then usually in the 80s until about 1890. Between 1880 and 1910, in the age of S. G. Phear and William Chawner, Emmanuel grew fast, nearly trebling in thirty years.[4]

The eighteenth century has traditionally been portrayed as an age of decadence in Cambridge, and this decline in numbers, more marked in Cambridge than in Oxford, has been seen as part of a general torpor.[5] Yet the fall in numbers was most marked when Isaac Newton was in his prime and continued while Richard Bentley dominated the world of classical studies. It is true that when Bentley, as Regius Professor of Divinity, presented 58 candidates for the D.D. to King George II in 1728 – not to increase the divinity faculty but apparently to bolster the number of Whig voters – they hardly reflected theological learning; and George's response was to lend his patronage to the new University of Göttingen in his German territories.[6] Few serious scholars or scientists of the late eighteenth century would have doubted that Thomas Young chose wisely when he studied at Göttingen before his brief residence in Cambridge in the 1790s.[7]

The masters

The central paradox of eighteenth-century Cambridge is that the age of Newton and Bentley carried within it the seeds of a marked decline in numbers, standards and creativity. Yet Bentley had not been long dead when, in 1748, the Mathematical Tripos was planted, the root from which much higher academic attainments in the future were to grow; and there was no generation between 1748 and 1870 in which the supply of men of the highest talent entirely failed.[8] Emmanuel reflected the paradox in miniature: small, conservative and rarely prominent among the wranglers, it witnessed something of a golden age in the history of the college buildings, and two of the eighteenth-century masters of Emmanuel were scholars of real distinction. Little is known of William Savage, master from 1719 to 1736, but William Richardson (1736–75) has left large memorials of his scholarly tastes and his careful administration, and Farmer was a distinguished Shakespearean scholar and one of the

---

[4] From 82 in 1880 (*CUC*, p. 642) to 177 in 1900 (*CUC*, p. 944) to 229 in 1909–10 (*CUC*, p. 1154).

[5] For correctives, see Gascoigne 1989; Searby 1997. For the traditional view in a sophisticated and scholarly form, see Winstanley 1922, 1935.

[6] Monk 1830, pp. 542–3; Brooke, Highfield and Swaan 1988, p. 246.

[7] See below, p. 319.

[8] Gascoigne 1983, 1989 (esp. chap. 9).

notable characters of this *History* – so much so as to demand a separate chapter.[9]

When John Balderston died on 28 August 1719, one of the oldest surviving ex-fellows, George Thorpe, was elected in his place at the respectable age of about 81.[10] He had been a scholar and fellow of Caius in his youth – then a fellow of Emmanuel and a fellow of Caius once more; he had been a chaplain to Archbishop Sancroft, under whose reign he acquired a benefice and a stall in Canterbury cathedral which he kept after his benefactor's 'retirement'. He was himself to be a major benefactor of Emmanuel; nor did he overlook Gonville and Caius. George Thorpe refused the mastership, and died before the year's end; but he was not forgotten. Under his will he was to be commemorated yearly; and on 'Thorpe Day' (in the Michaelmas Term), from the early eighteenth till the late nineteenth century, the society drank from the founder's cup 'in piam memoriam fundatoris nostri et benefactorum nostrorum, praecipue Doctoris Thorpe'.[11]

Next the fellows elected William Savage, a man of about fifty, who had himself been a fellow from 1692 to 1703. He had then held ample preferment in London and Kent and served the Emmanuel lawyer, Sir Nathan Wright, when he was Lord Keeper of the Great Seal in the opening years of the eighteenth century. Next he was chaplain to Francis Atterbury, the leading Tory high churchman of the 1710s and bishop of Rochester, who was imprisoned and exiled for giving some countenance to the Jacobite cause. Thus William Savage was a well attested Tory before his election. In 1720, the year after his election as master, he resigned 'in order to be presented to the living of St Anne's, Blackfriars, thus evading the statute forbidding the master accepting preferment' – and was soon after re-elected master.[12] He largely resided in London at first, and was given express permission to do so, possibly in order to seek funds for the great building operation already under way. Of his rule as master, relatively little is known: he died in 1736, on 1 August, and on the 10th the fellows elected William Richardson.

Richardson's uncle had been a fellow from 1674 to 1685 and a non-juror, who had to resign his living at North Luffenham on that account and devote himself to theological debate.[13] His nephew, born in 1698, was in turn scholar of Emmanuel and a prebendary and precentor of Lincoln. He accepted the Hanoverian regime, yet evidently shared a good many of his uncle's Tory beliefs. Cambridge was already his main place of

---

[9] See chap. 13.
[10] Shuckburgh 1904, pp. 127–8; Venn, *Caius*, I, 387–8.
[11] Shuckburgh 1904, p.127; for his will see ECA SCH.1.17, and below, pp. 341–3.
[12] Shuckburgh 1904, p. 128; on Savage, see ibid. pp. 128–32; *DNB*.
[13] On the Richardsons, see Shuckburgh 1904, pp. 132–8; on their relationship, *DNB*.

residence, it seems, from 1734, when he settled there to use its libraries for his scholarly work, and to enjoy the company of the ageing Thomas Baker – most notable of Cambridge antiquaries of the day and a celebrated non-juror who none the less resided in St John's till his death.[14] Baker and Richardson were both distinguished antiquaries and notable high Tories; and it seems that Richardson's learning and above all his staunch adherence to the Tory cause attracted the notice of the Emmanuel fellowship. It was relatively unusual in Cambridge to elect someone as master who was not (or had not been) a fellow, and the election came (so it seems) as a surprise to Richardson himself. 'He was a most strict and unpleasant Master to his Fellows', wrote William Bennet, 'but had a great regard for the prosperity of the body, with a gentleman-like behaviour, and a liberal mind.' But he fulfilled the duties expected of him, as scholar, Tory and administrator, if not perhaps in a very genial manner, yet with care and conscientious devotion.[15]

There is a remarkable book of room-rents in the College Archives which shows the succession of fellows and students in each of the chambers in the first half of the eighteenth century.[16] Many entries are concluded with a statement in Richardson's writing that the College had taken the rooms in hand. Hitherto the furniture and wainscotting were provided by the inmate and sold to his successor; now – in return for an enhanced rent – the college took seisin of the contents. This is one sign of a tighter financial management in Richardson's time. He was also interested in the details of College history, and his 'Book of admissions' is a record of masters and fellows from the foundation.[17] One has the impression of a precise, businesslike master, whose mind dwelt equally in past and present.

His scholarly achievement chiefly consists in his edition of the *De Praesulibus Angliae commentarius* of Francis Godwin, a work designed to establish the precise episcopal succession of the English bishops – with short biographies of many – and so lay on secure foundations the claims

---

[14] On Baker, see Brooke 1992, pp. 8–9 and refs.

[15] Bennet's Book II (ECA COL. 9.1.B), p. 46, quoted in Willis and Clarke 1886/1988, II, 714–15n.; cf. Shuckburgh 1904, esp. pp. 133–4. He notes that there were several disputes between Richardson and the fellowship. But minor disputes about endowments etc. were the stuff of eighteenth century Cambridge: cf. the much worse disputes in Caius chronicled in Brooke 1985, pp. 168–70. The troubles in Caius were exacerbated by politics: Richardson was at least a staunch Tory. On one issue, the duty of dean, lecturer and steward to treat the fellowship on the day of their election, Richardson quashed a college order, only to substitute another of similar import a fortnight later. It was the procedure, not the wish of the fellows, which he disputed. The issue was characteristically trivial; and I suspect that Shuckburgh (p. 133) had read too much into Richardson's portrait, which suggested to him a man 'neither genial nor conciliatory'.

[16] ECA STE.24.1.

[17] Shuckburgh 1904, p. 133; the 'Book of Admissions' is ECA COL. 9.2.

of the Church of England to the apostolic succession.[18] Godwin had apparently won promotion from the government of Elizabeth I and James I for his scholarly services to the young and struggling Anglican church: he had become bishop successively of Llandaff (1601–17) and Hereford (1617–33). His work was a notable achievement, but its scholarship is deeply flawed. It opens with a long, rambling, credulous study of the episcopacy in the apostolic and sub-apostolic age, and of the early history of Christianity in Britain. Once Bede was there to guide him – still more after the Norman Conquest with the aid of good chronicles and records – he established a tolerably complete succession for most sees. But his work abounds in errors and inaccuracies. To the modern taste Richardson's edition is a curiosity. He left Godwin's introductory chapters untouched: he threw no new light on the early history of Christianity. But he worked minutely over every source Godwin had used and many he had known nothing of; he corrected and clarified and improved the details and especially the dates while rarely altering his characterisation of the bishops; he brought the lists up to date. He was not infallible; but he was far more accurate than Godwin; he had the great advantage of standing on the shoulders of the notable antiquaries of the previous generation, such as Henry Wharton and John Le Neve; and he provided a reasonably correct list of bishops over many centuries until – as a catalogue – it was replaced by William Stubbs' *Registrum Sacrum Anglicanum* in the 1850s. Even Stubbs, great scholar that he was, would have admitted that he took quite a number of details and references over from Richardson. Richardson's Godwin is thus a genuine work of learning, but a perverse one: for his attempt to preserve as much of Godwin's text as he could left a patchwork of scholarship accurate and deplorable. He will leave glaring errors in the text and correct them in discreet notes, with references to authorities to prove his point.[19] The essence of it is that he accepted much higher standards of accuracy, as a scholar of the age of Bentley might; but he hated change for its own sake, just as he hated the whiggery of Bentley.

But what did it mean to be a Whig or a Tory in the eighteenth century? The answer was abundantly clear in the Emmanuel Parlour then and is

---

[18] F. Godwin, *De praesulibus Angliae commentarius*, 2 parts, London, 1616: this was the basis of Richardson's edition. The book had originally been published in English in 1601 (*A Catalogue of the Bishops of England*; 2nd edn, 1615). As a catalogue of bishops it was partially replaced by John Le Neve, *Fasti Ecclesiae Anglicanae* (London, 1716); more effectively by W. Stubbs, *Registrum Sacrum Anglicanum* (Oxford, 1858; 2nd edn, 1897) and by the revised edition of Le Neve's *Fasti* published in many fascicules by the Institute of Historical Research (London, 1962–: in progress). Godwin himself is a shadowy figure: he was made bishop of Llandaff in 1601, the year his book was first published; he certainly lives only in it (*DNB*). But he must have been inspired by devotion to the Anglican tradition established by Matthew Parker and his circle.

[19] Thus Alberic cardinal bishop of Ostia is 'Albertum' in both 1616 (p. 98) and 1743 (p. 69); but Richardson added a footnote variant, 'Albericum', citing the Chronicle of Melrose and Matthew Paris. He could have found better authorities, but at least he cited them.

totally obscure to us now: it has been the theme of one of the most fascinating and inconclusive historical debates of recent generations.[20] In the
late seventeenth century the Tories, or many of them, had been connected
with the Jacobite cause; but after the Hanoverian succession in 1714 and
the failure of the rebellion of 1715 the Stuart pretenders might be toasted
in port, and hankered for by the bolder Tories like Francis Atterbury; but
little by little their support fell away. The Tories remained the party of
'Church and king'. In national politics there were discernible groups who
did not care to deny the label Tory down to about 1750 – though historians differ as to what they stood for or how seriously they cohered. By
1760 everyone was a Whig, in name or fact; and Sir Lewis Namier propounded long ago the doctrine – to which most historians for a while subscribed – that the labels were meaningless at the accession of George III.[21]
In the 1780s and 90s the labels changed, chameleon-like. The young
William Pitt, MP for the University of Cambridge, was in the ascendant,
and he and his followers were in process of becoming Tories. Looking
back from the 1850s, the old Henry Gunning, a disappointed radical in
politics, declared that in the 1790s 'scarcely a Whig was to be found'.[22]
Logically, there seems no close similarity between the Tories of 1700 and
those of 1800; yet political connections are not the fruit of logic but of
prejudice and friendship and aspiration. While the parties changed their
nature in Westminster, they remained more clearly distinct in Cambridge, and especially in Emmanuel; even in 1760 the fellows of
Emmanuel were Tory. It is broadly speaking true that in the 1720s the
Tories ruled Cambridge: their leader among the Heads of House, Thomas
Gooch of Caius, was three times elected Vice-Chancellor to keep the
Whigs at bay.[23] Then he changed sides, became a Whig; Dr Bentley
created Whig voters at random; the clerical dons of Cambridge, seeking
patronage and preferment in Westminster, found that they had to be on
terms with Walpole and Newcastle. By 1748 Newcastle had long been very
powerful in Westminster and strove to be all-powerful in Cambridge: if
ruling England (or the small part of it engaged in government) was his
profession, ruling Cambridge was his hobby.[24] In 1747 the ancient Chancellor of Cambridge, the duke of Somerset, was on his deathbed, and the
duke of Newcastle prepared to succeed him. In this endeavour 'our old
friend' Dr Gooch was prominent:[25] he had already enjoyed promotion to

---

[20] The debate began its modern career with Namier 1929; its most recent phase is represented by the distinguished studies of Linda Colley (Colley 1977, 1982) and Jonathan
Clark (Clark 1978, 1982, 1983, 1985) – I am particularly indebted to the guidance of
Jonathan Clark. For what follows, see Brooke 1985, pp. 162–70.
[21] Namier 1929; for what follows see esp. Clark 1985.
[22] Gunning 1854, I, 189.
[23] Brooke 1985, pp. 163–70; for his conversion to the Whigs, ibid., pp. 167–8.
[24] On Newcastle and Cambridge see Winstanley 1922 – for what follows, esp. pp. 37–54.
[25] Brooke 1985, p. 168.

the sees of Bristol and Norwich, and in 1748 he was translated to Ely. In the same year the Chancellor died and Newcastle was duly elected. There was no opponent, but a number of electors abstained, including, in the words of the waspish Tory William Cole:

> 'all the fellows of pure Emmanuel, the three or four Tories they still have at Peterhouse, all of the same stamp at King's, one or two of Trinity and Pembroke, several of Caius, and Dr Rutherforth and some few of St John's.'[26]

Newcastle was to show in Cambridge the same exquisite arts of corruption which he exercised with passion in Westminster: he was personally incorrupt, but enslaved others to his system of patronage. It may be difficult to discern what a Tory might be in Westminster; but in Cambridge he was a person who resisted the blandishments of the Chancellor; hence Cole's testimonial to 'pure Emmanuel'.

In Caius the survival of the Tory predominance stimulated – or was stimulated by – strife with Sir Thomas Gooch (as he now was), though the Tory leader, James Burrough, was a peaceable man, more noted for his architectural than his political views.[27] In early life he helped James Gibbs design the Senate House; in middle life he presided over the transformation of several colleges. In 1752 he was invited by his fellow-Tory William Richardson to redesign part of the western range of Emmanuel.[28] Perhaps the most important of all Burrough's contributions to Cambridge architecture was his instruction and patronage of James Essex – and it was Essex in the event who transformed the hall and west front of the college in the 1760s and 70s. Meanwhile the duke of Newcastle pulled strings in almost every part of Cambridge, ensuring the appointment of loyal supporters to chairs and headships. But Cambridge was a federation as diverse in its politics as Switzerland; and several colleges rejoiced in their independence of the duke. Of these the most secure was 'pure Emmanuel'.[29] When Newcastle died in November 1768, the duke of Grafton succeeded to some of his influence in the university and a dominant influence in the town – as Fitzroy Street and the Grafton Centre still bear witness;[30] but he never wielded anything like the authority of Newcastle; and by the 1790s the dominant political star was William Pitt.

[26] Winstanley 1922, p. 48; for what follows, see esp. ibid. pp. 35–6 and 35 n.1. In spite of Richardson's opposition to Newcastle, the latter recommended him for a royal chaplaincy (Taylor 1987, p. 93).

[27] On Burrough, see Brooke 1985, pp. 170–4; Colvin 1978, pp. 168–70; Cocke 1984.

[28] For this and what follows, see below pp. 327–31.

[29] See Winstanley 1922, p. 233. Emmanuel and Caius were the two colleges wholly immune from Newcastle's meddling. Gascoigne 1989, pp. 99, 203–4, 206–8, has interesting examples of Emmanuel's consistent Toryism, culminating in Farmer (see below, p. 391).

[30] On the influence of Grafton and his son, Lord Euston, see Brooke, Highfield and Swaan 1988, p. 27 and refs.

The Tories had entered into their inheritance; and in this process – so far as the colleges were concerned – Richard Farmer was to play a leading role.[31]

The tutors

The most powerful figures in a modern college are the bursar and the senior tutor. But in Emmanuel in the eighteenth century – till the death of Richard Farmer – the master was the bursar; and the office of senior tutor only achieved that title in the nineteenth century. In the seventeenth century, under the master, the domestic administration lay in the steward's charge; discipline was the dean's affair; the educational work of the college lay with the tutors. Their office is mentioned in the statutes; but in Emmanuel as in all colleges they were not a formal body of specially appointed college officers. In origin they were the fellows who taught: under the master's direction they recruited and cared for the students, and looked after their affairs. In the vital matter of rooms the steward oversaw an administration which ran itself: rooms passed from one tenant to the next and the new tenant bought the furnishings from his predecessor. This changed for a time under Richardson, who brought more and more of the rooms and their contents into the college's domain, while the steward collected the rents. The tutors meanwhile continued to recruit the students, to draw fees from them, and in general to manage their financial affairs. The college only took cognisance of what the tutors passed on to it. In the early seventeenth century when numbers were booming, most of the fellows were tutors. But as the numbers declined in the late seventeenth and early eighteenth centuries it ceased to be necessary or practical for most of the fellows to be tutors. They took their turns as dean, steward or lecturer; but the teaching work of the college came to be concentrated in fewer and fewer hands. In the end serious teaching came to be the work of private coaches – often themselves fellows of colleges, but employed and paid for by the men not the college.[32] Meanwhile, from the 1720s and 30s it became the norm in the smaller Cambridge colleges for the work to be done by only one or two tutors – so much the norm that it was regarded as part of the institutional framework of Cambridge.[33] But tutors were commonly nominated by the heads of colleges without other formality; and at Emmanuel their appointments are never recorded in the College Order Book until the late nineteenth century.[34] Peter Searby has argued that it was the growing

---

[31] See below, p. 391.
[32] See Brooke, Highfield and Swaan 1988, p. 256, quoting Gunning 1854, I, pp. xix–xx; Searby, 1997.
[33] See the account in Searby, 1997.
[34] See below, Appendix 3. From 1777 we can only reconstruct the list of tutors from the Admissions Register, TUT.23.4, which names them year by year.

necessity for effective instruction in mathematics which explains, in part at least, this concentration of authority into the hands of tiny numbers of tutors. It is interesting to note that the longest serving tutor of all, Henry Hubbard, tutor probably from 1736 to 1767, was algebra lecturer from 1746 to 1768; and Searby's suggestion may well help to explain the appointment of John Oldershaw, tutor from 1783 to 1793, for he had been Emmanuel's sole senior wrangler in 1776.[35] In 1791 Oldershaw was joined in the tutorship by Robert Cory, fifth wrangler in 1780, who was promoted master in 1797, but remained a tutor till 1809.[36] Wrangling apart, they were, like most of their colleagues, men bent on a clerical career; Oldershaw ended archdeacon of Norfolk, Cory master of Emmanuel – and both had livings besides.

Shuckburgh believed that John Wilkinson, fellow from 1728 till his departure to a rectory in 1736, and Henry Hubbard were sole tutors; and the surviving accounts suggest that students' affairs, still in several hands till 1736, were mostly managed by Hubbard from then on.[37] But the studies of Dr Sarah Brewer in the college archives brought forth clear evidence that there were still three tutors in the 1730s, and two from the 1740s on;[38] and two remained the normal number until the late nineteenth century, save in 1813–16 when there was only one.

It is probably significant that Hubbard became tutor in the same year that Richardson became master, for he shared with the master a close interest in university antiquities and meticulous administration. His *Book of Accounts* opens with a list of admissions from 1733 to 1767; from 1736 on he gives a fair amount of information on each. He notes caution money while he was tutor and his receipts in tutorial fees in his early years. He gives precise and fascinating details of his income as a fellow and college officer. As a fellow he received between £28 and £50 a year. This included a basic stipend of £10, to which a variety of sums had come to be added in fellows' dividends over the years. These included dividends from the proceeds of various estates, dividends of entry fines; dividends of the profits of the buttery; and capon dividends – that is, from the money received from tenants in lieu of the capons they were due to provide under long-standing college leases. The entry fines naturally fell very unevenly over the years, and this was the chief reason for the marked fluctuations in fellows' incomes. In addition, Hubbard held college offices from time to time – such as dean and steward, which commonly moved round among the fellowship. In his first golden year,

[35] Shuckburgh 1904, p. 149; 'Register' 1771; Tanner 1917, p. 457. For the list of tutors see n. 34.

[36] 'Register' 1776; Tanner 1917, p. 459.

[37] Shuckburgh 1904, p. 138; on Wilkinson see 'Register' 1722. Hubbard's succession as tutor is revealed by accounts in BUR.8.4; cf. TUT.23.3.

[38] See below, Appendix 3, acknowledging the vital clues provided by Sarah Brewer.

1737–8, he received more than £19 each from the offices of steward, dean and and lecturer; and he was Library Keeper besides at a stipend of £10. The total came to £108.19s.4d.[39] But the most persistent of his college offices was the 'Algebra Lectureship' which he held from 1746 to 1768, earning about £24 a year.[40] In due course he came to play a prominent role in the university: was 'Lady Margaret's preacher for twenty-one years and . . . Registrary for twenty'; and became known as a university character. Late in life 'though in ill-health, he had himself carried into the Senate House in a sedan chair to *non-placet* the M.A. of a man who had publicly cast aspersions on the bishops. Yet the contemporary who commented that Hubbard would die with a *non-placet* on his lips also recorded that he was reckoned a good tempered, cheerful man, and a merry companion.'[41] From his various offices and from any profit he made as tutor he amassed a handsome fortune, from which he intended to provide the college with £1,000 – £400 to enhance the stipend of the senior fellow, £400 to provide an income for the best classic among Dr Thorpe's scholars; and £200 to enlarge the endowment of the Sudbury prize, which became the Sudbury- Hubbard prize and was at that time awarded to the B.A. 'judged to be most worthy of that year for his piety learning and parts'.[42] The rest of his fortune, some £4,000, was destined for his closest friend, Richard Canning, with whom he had been an undergraduate at St Catharine's; but Canning died before him, and it all came to Emmanuel, rendering him a major benefactor.

If the Algebra lectureship indicates Hubbard's dedication to mathematics, his endowment of classics suggests an equal interest in classical learning. The other tutor, apart from Farmer, who has left ample records of his activities, William Bennet, was first and foremost a classic. Frank Stubbings opened his account of Bennet by quoting the words of Roger Ascham which Bennet himself copied on to the endpaper of his manuscript notes on the history of the College. ' "He that is able to maintain his life in learning at Cambridge knoweth not what a felicity he hath". . . . He knew what he was talking about, for he spent twenty-seven years in the College,' from 1763 to 1790.[43] He was a fellow from 1769, a tutor from 1779 or 1780. When Farmer became Master in 1777 he himself continued to act as tutor until 1782 or 1783. His first colleague was Samuel Blackall the elder, tutor 1767–1779 or 1780,[44] when Blackall was succeeded by Bennet, who remained a tutor till 1790. In that year his former pupil, the

---

[39] These details are given in Shuckburgh 1904, pp. 147–8. What never clearly emerges is the value of the tutorship to him.
[40] Shuckburgh 1904, p. 149.
[41] Stubbings 1983b, no.20.
[42] ECA Box 21.B10; cf. Shuckburgh 1904, p. 151. Cf. Stubbings 1983b, no. 20.
[43] Stubbings 1983b, no. 25.
[44] See below, pp. 314–15. For the dates of tutors see n. 34.

Earl of Westmorland, was appointed Lord Lieutenant of Ireland, and took Bennet as his chaplain: he was provided with a Dublin DD and the bishopric of Cork and Ross; the next year, 1791, he married; in 1794 his patron presided over his translation to Cloyne; and bishop of Cloyne he remained till his death in 1820. Among the many promotions of 1790 he had become a Fellow of the Society of Antiquaries of London; and his antiquarian tastes are evident in the copious, beautifully copied extracts from college documents and notes on college history which adorn 'Bennet's Book'.[45] Otherwise his chief interest lay in classical antiquities, and he was deeply interested in the history of Roman roads. He compiled a volume of notes on Roman roads with his friend Thomas Leman, fellow from 1783 to 1796 at latest, with whom he had roamed far and wide in search of them. He also compiled exceedingly thorough lecture notes on classical authors. They are eloquent testimony to the care he took in grounding his pupils in the classics – perhaps the best surviving evidence of what Cambridge classical lectures were in the eighteenth century. They cover in detail Cicero, *De Oratore*, book i; Tacitus, *Germania* and *Agricola*; Sophocles, *Electra*; Longinus, *On the Sublime*, and the Greek *New Testament*.[46]

'I am now beginning to read with you the very best work of the very best author, for though as an orator I esteem him inferior to Demosthenes, in works like the present I believe he has no equal.' Thus Bennet on Cicero, *De Oratore*. 'It appears . . . that [Cicero] esteemed it as his best and most valuable work . . . , nor was his work received with less applause by his contemporaries; Atticus declared it to be the best book his friend ever wrote, and the learned in all ages seem to have agreed in the same opinion . . .'; and he cites the authority of 'the present Lord Mansfield . . . It is particularly in obedience to the decided sentiments of the latter, that I first introduced it into this lecture room, as he recommended it to a young man of fashion at the University, as the first classical book in the world to form both the gentleman and the scholar. I had long before read it with my private pupils, and was happy in having my experience of its use confirmed by his declaration. . . .' He goes on to set the book in the context of

---

[45] COL.9.1A,B.

[46] Bennet's own MSS are Emmanuel College Library MSS 167, Cicero *De Oratore*, bk. i, dated 1786; 163, Sophocles, *Electra*, 1784; 228, on Roman Roads, partly in his hand, partly in Thomas Leman's. The rest are copied, presumably by an amanuensis, MSS 141, Cicero, *De Oratore*, bk. i; 162, Sophocles, *Electra*; 166, Longinus, *On the Sublime*; 168, Tacitus, *Germania* and *Agricola*; 164–5, the New Testament in Greek. The quotation which follows is from MS 167, proem (not paginated), with spelling slightly modernised. The copies have a note that they were 'almost entirely written or compiled' by Bennet; and no. 166 specifies that it was 'given to me upon my coming into the Tutorship' by Bennet, bishop of Cork and Ross (i.e. 1790–4, before his translation to Cloyne). The notes must have been written, it seems, by an amanuensis for Cory, Bennet's successor as tutor, who presumably lectured from them.

Cicero's life and then to gloss the text, chapter by chapter. It is interesting to note the difference between Bennet's private pupils, with whom he read classical texts in tutorials or supervisions, and his college pupils to whom he gave formal lectures.

Of the lectures on Cicero and Tacitus we have Bennet's own copies, brought back to the college on his death in 1820 by Thomas Leman; all the others are in the hand of a copyist, and have a note of Bennet's authorship in another hand – of one who says on the fly-leaf of MS 166 that they were 'given to me upon my coming into the Tutorship' – which seems to mean, were copied by his successor as tutor. When Bennet went to Ireland, he was succeeded as tutor by Robert Cory, the future master, who seems to have paid Bennet the compliment of copying his lecture notes – presumably in order to deliver them himself. Not all tutors were so creative as Bennet or Farmer.

Richard Hurd

Nor were the tutors the only literary figures among the fellows. No fellow of Emmanuel of the eighteenth century before Richard Farmer played so active a role in leading literary circles as Richard Hurd; and of his life and studies we are exceptionally well informed, since many of his letters have survived, and have been admirably edited by Dr Sarah Brewer.[47] He was the son of a yeoman farmer in Staffordshire and an undergraduate at Emmanuel from 1735 to 1741. It is evident that he was well thought of by his teachers, for he was elected fellow in 1742 – and held his fellowship till 1757. Meanwhile he made close friends of two well-to-do families of highly educated men of wealth – the Macros and Sir Edward Littleton, whose personal tutor he became for a while. He also introduced himself to William Warburton, and his friendship with Warburton led him to the centre of the literary circles of London, and eventually into the court itself. In 1742 he was offered a very modest living in Norfolk, which he shared, in effect, with a friend; but for much of the next 15 years he was resident in Emmanuel. Though he never married, he took the Emmanuel living of Thurcaston (Leicestershire) in 1756, resigning his fellowship the next year – but was able to combine residence in the country with frequent appearances in town: first as Whitehall preacher, then as preacher in Lincoln's Inn; above all, he became one of Warburton's chaplains when he was promoted bishop of Gloucester in 1759–60, and archdeacon of Gloucester from 1767. At the turn of 1774 and 1775 Hurd himself became bishop of Lichfield and Coventry, later accepting translation to Worcester; and bishop of Worcester he remained – in spite of the offer of the see

---

[47] Brewer 1995. I am exceedingly grateful to Sarah Brewer for giving me access to her thesis (Brewer 1987) before publication, and allowing me to quote and cite it.

of Canterbury in 1783 – from 1781 to his death in 1808, leaving his mark on the literary world and on his diocese, and on his seat at Hartlebury Castle.

Hurd's letters reveal an extraordinary range of interests, of which the most remarkable and enduring were classical and English poetry, which led him so greatly to admire Warburton's edition of Pope's *Dunciad*, as to imitate his methods in his edition of the *Ars poetica* of Horace – perhaps, after his *Letters on Chivalry and Romance*, his most remarkable achievement.[48] He was also something of a poet himself. One might think of him as a clever dilettante; but there is more to him than that. His classical learning was considerable; his critical acumen not unworthy of a scholar bred in Bentley's Cambridge. His literary taste was discriminating, even if he admired some of his contemporaries' books which seem to us prodigiously dull. His letters about contemporary biblical studies show him no mean student of the Bible. As a young man, furthermore, in the heyday of Cambridge mathematics – shortly before the mathematical tripos was established – he wrote to a friend in 1741.

'The study of logic is almost entirely laid aside in this university, and that of the mathematics taken up in its room. It is looked upon as a maxim here, that a justness and accuracy in thinking and reasoning are better learned by a habit than by rules; and it is an observation founded upon long experience, that no men argue more closely and acutely than they who are well versed in mathematic learning, even though they are ignorant of the rules delivered by the great masters in that other science. Indeed, as our disputations in the schools are always carried on in syllogism, a small part of that study is still requisite; but, as this is very easily learned from any system, we are not very curious in the choice of one . . .'[49]

The centre of his interests in Cambridge lay naturally in Emmanuel. But he was very much alive to what was going forward of a serious educational kind elsewhere in Cambridge, and an early supporter of the reforming tutor, later master, of St John's, William Powell. In 1745 he wrote to his pupil Sir Edward Littleton, after commending him for staying with his regiment engaged in putting down the invasion of the Young Pretender, rather than returning to his studies at Cambridge. 'Mr Powell's lectures, as I told you, began on the 12th [November], and, as I had then expectations of seeing you ev'ry day, your name and mine are amongst the subscribers. Some senior tutors . . . , as you know, were not favorable to Mr Powell's design, and indeed were rather willing, by insinuations and otherwise, to obstruct and discourage it. But I have the pleasure to tell you, that their malice has had but little effect, for instead

---

[48] Brewer 1987, I, pp. xi–xii; Brewer 1995, p. xvi.
[49] Brewer 1995, no. 14 to James Devey, 14 March 1741.

of twenty or thirty which was the largest number Mr Powell durs't flatter himself with the hopes of raising at the first, there are near eighty sub-scribers.'[50] Attempts to improve the standard of university teaching met with much discouragement, but there were plenty of men about like Hurd who would welcome them.

Though earnest in his studies and the teaching of his private pupils, and in the pursuit of his literary interests with his friends and patrons, he was set, like almost all his colleagues, on a clerical career. His first encounters with the duties of a country parson in Norfolk rather alarmed him; and he wrote in haste to his friend John Potter. 'What I am going to ask of you is a very great favor, but I don't on that account despair of obtaining it. To explane myself at once, I am at a terrible loss for sermons: I have hitherto made all I have us'd, but begin now to be tired of it.' And he begged for some good plain sermons. He is nicely poised between feeling that he was a little above spending his days writing country sermons, and the determination to give his flock their due.[51] In later years he was to preach to more educated, or at least to more courtly audiences, and not to be at a loss for words. He was to be remembered as one of the most cultivated of the leading clergy of his age.

William Burdon

The letter book of William Bennet's pupil William Burdon (1764–1818), who was an undergraduate in the 1780s and fellow from 1788 to 1796, opens many windows into the life of the society in the late eighteenth century, and illustrates something of its variety. He never took the mathe-matical tripos and he never took orders. He was a rich coal owner's son from the north-east, who in later life wrote copiously on political and literary themes: though he had enjoyed life to the full in Emmanuel under Farmer, he became a moderate radical in politics and (as we would say) an agnostic. At some date towards the end of his life he made careful copies of a selection of his surviving correspondence – letters by and to him – ranging from schooldays to maturity, from about 1780 to 1800, with an occasional stray from later days.[52]

He was born in 1764, and among the earliest letters is an exchange of 1780 with his aunt Mrs Bower, a lively and devoted friend, who had been alarmed by an early 'propensity to drinking' – a rebuke he received 'with a pleasing pain', acknowledging the concern and affection she showed.[53] Perhaps he learned the lesson: there is no sign of riot in his letters from Cambridge. An undated note from Bennet, his tutor, 'desires his

---

[50] Brewer 1995, no. 67, 24 November 1745.
[51] Brewer 1995, no. 28, to John Potter, 25 August 1742.
[52] Emmanuel College Library ms. 269, acquired in the mid-twentieth century. What seems to be the latest item is of 1813: he died in 1818.
[53] Ms.269, pp. 2–5.

acceptance of Oudendorp's Suetonius, as a testimony from his tutor of his classical merit and very exemplary conduct at lectures.'[54] He soon struck up a friendship with a younger contemporary, Theodore Broadhead (later to be an M.P.), who wrote to him from Surrey as the Michaelmas Term of 1785 approached.

'Hail October with its yellow leaves, now I find the country pleasant and amuse myself with hunting to pass away a few of those hours I am master of. I begin to look forward to a college life, and amuse myself with the thoughts of a quiet game at whist . . . or sitting socially round our fire side in Emmanuel lodgings again with our old friends' – as evidently they did soon after.[55]

They were later to lament together the departure of William Bennet from the College. 'I really don't know a loss the society of Emmanuel College could feel more sensibly', wrote Broadhead, 'than the departure of Mr Bennet. He fill'd his station as Tutor with a dignity that acquired him respect and an affability that endeared him to all who were under his care – he enlivened by his polished vivacity the natural dullness of a college . . .'[56]

On a summer's day in 1788 Burdon was admitted a fellow; and Broadhead wrote to him next morning. 'If your head has got sufficiently free from the fumes of your Fellowship dinner on Wednesday to enable you to decypher a scrawl I hope you will receive with satisfaction the sincere congratulations I now offer you on your coming in with so little trouble. It is rather hard upon a young man that he cannot be made Fellow of a college without submitting to be tortured with a head-ache for the first two or three days.'[57]

A few years later we find Burdon acting private tutor to John and George Beresford, two of the sons of the archbishop of Tuam, young bloods whose debts and mode of life caused him much anxiety. In May 1795 he explained to the father that £300 – a good deal more, no doubt than most of the archbishop's poorer clergy enjoyed – was 'too little for a fellow commoner who lives here a great part of the year.' George 'has lived since he came here in a manner equally moderate and respectable, with a proper attention to his studies and a limited indulgence in pleasure. His acquaintance has been *chiefly* among the young men of his own college, who are by no means expensive, for I gave him every caution against a *large* acquaintance in other colleges . . .' Burdon estimates that college expenses add up to £60 per quarter; and £15 for 'cloathes, linen, wine etc.', that is £75, which leaves 'nothing for any

[54] Ms.269, p. 7.
[55] Ms.269, p. 13.
[56] Ms.269, pp. 164–5.
[57] Ms.269, p. 149.

further expences which with young men are usually called pocket money, such as cards, music, balls, etc. . . .' – and which would add another £15; that is, £90 per quarter, £360 a year.[58] The father was sceptical, but a further letter explaining that George's expenses last quarter were less than his brother's had ever been seems to have worked, for a while later we find Burdon speaking to George of the liberal addition his father had made to his allowance. But the rosy picture painted by the tutor soon faded. Early in 1796 George Beresford was living in London, and the tutor was anxious both about the cost and the manner of his life. In February 1796 he wrote telling him that gaming and Newmarket were his undoing; and a little later, with a sigh of relief, he learned that he had returned to Ireland.[59] Without further effort (so it seems) George took his B.A. in 1796, and added the LL.B. and LL.D. of Trinity College Dublin (where he had also been a fellow commoner) in 1797. By 1798 he was a priest and a prebendary of Tuam, where he went on to be provost from 1816 to his death in 1842. 1796 had not quite seen the end of Burdon's trouble with the Beresfords, however; for about the time of his marriage in 1798 he was still owed £136 by John, and the debts were not finally cleared until 1800.[60]

Meanwhile Burdon was developing dangerously radical opinions. First in university politics: an undated letter to the bishop of Llandaff and regius professor of divinity – Richard Watson, absentee bishop and professor, who had inherited an estate in Westmorland in 1786 which claimed much of his attention – warning him 'that I intend some time during the present term to promote a grace to the university to enable them to inquire whether your Lordship's ill health still prevents you from performing in person the duties of your office as Professor of Divinity . . .' – one of many ineffective attempts to recall Watson to his duty. He remained an absentee professor till his death in 1816.[61]

In the mid 1790s Burdon came seriously to doubt the truth of the Christian faith. In July 1797 he wrote to a Cambridge friend, a printer called Mr Flower, with whom he had had many conversations over the last three years, but not on religion, because in that they differed. Burdon pleads for a liberal view of the place of Christianity among the world's religions. 'I am not the advocate, but I am not the foe of Christianity. I will bear to hear its merits temperately discussed. I once believed it to be true. I now am satisfied to the contrary, and it is not possible to learn it afresh . . .'[62]

Naturally he could not proceed to holy orders, and in due course he resigned his fellowship. But a liberal-minded fellowship – in Farmer's last

---

[58] Ms. 269, pp. 189–93.
[59] Ms.269, pp. 194, 208–10, 215–17, 226–7. For George Beresford's later career, see Venn.
[60] Ms.269, pp. 229–30, 234–8, 243.
[61] Ms.269, pp. 228–9; on Watson and the regius chair, see Winstanley 1935, pp. 106–8; *DNB*.
[62] Ms.269, pp. 230–4.

years and the first of Cory – allowed him still to live in the College. In 1798 new winds blew to carry him back to his northern home. Ten years before he had told his aunt Bower, apropos the forthcoming nuptials of his sister Hannah: 'marriage is at best a lottery, in which there are many blanks to a prize'. In June 1798 he wrote to his father to tell him that he was going to marry Bess Dickson, a lady without fortune – the Burdon fortune sufficed for both – but with many good qualities.[63] So he set up house in Morpeth in Northumberland with his bride; and later that year he wrote to Cory, the Master, thanking him for allowing him to live at Emmanuel 'after I had ceased to be connected with you either by a similarity of right [that is, a fellowship] or by sentiment', and promises a piece of plate. What arrived, so far as we know, was a very modest wine strainer made in 1799; but after the fire of 1811 he was to do better, and to contribute £100 to the restoration of the Westmorland Building.[64]

There was to be an epilogue less flattering to the College. On 19 April 1800 he wrote to the archbishop of Tuam, now seeking advice on the placing of his third son.

John's debts have at last been paid. As for the third son, 'I will tell you plainly that Cambridge is not so bad as Dublin; it is not much better unless he goes there with very strong dispositions to be regular and meets with a tutor who will be a perpetual mentor to him. I am sorry to say that though my partiality for Emmanuel is very great it is not what it has been – nor can I mention any man there among the fellows with whom I should choose to trust a young man either for his private or public tutor; those who are there at present have neither zeal nor knowledge to qualify them for such an employment, and the College is at present nearly empty [in truth there were 49 undergraduates in 1800]. Trinity is in my opinion by much the best college in the University . . . [the fellows] are all elected after a severe examination: at Emmanuel there is no examination'. In view of the generosity of the College in making him a fellow without a distinguished place in tripos, and evidently without examination, this seems ungracious. It is pleasant to record that when the shadows had lengthened he sent his sons George and William Burdon to the College as pensioners in 1815 and 1817; in 1818 he died.[65]

Recruitment

Why then did men come to Emmanuel in the eighteenth and early nineteenth centuries? Some, like Dr Richardson and Thomas Martyn, came because their family had been there before, and it was evidently a

[63] Ms.269, pp. 142, 255–6.
[64] Ms.269, pp. 256–7; Plate Inventory, 7.3; ECA COL.6.1; Venn.
[65] Ms.269, pp. 243–5; Venn. For the numbers in 1800, see CUC 1800, p. 81.

connection which Richardson's uncle and Martyn's father still valued.[66]
Thomas Martyn was the son of John Martyn; and they were successive
professors of botany, spanning between them well over 90 years. In the
manner of eighteenth-century professors, John lectured for two years
only; and his links with Emmanuel were not close. But he remembered
his college in the dedication of one of the plates of his exquisite *Historia
Plantarum Rariorum* – it shows the *Geranium Africanum*;[67] and a sprinkling
of Emmanuel friends contributed to his fine edition of the *Georgics* of
Virgil of 1741, whose preface is dated significantly from Chelsea. Thomas,
his son, spent more of his life in Cambridge: he was a student at
Emmanuel from 1752, a fellow of Sidney from 1758, professor from 1762,
curator of the Botanic Gardens from 1770. He shared his father's antiquarian interests, and wrote both on the plants of Cambridge and the antiquities of Herculaneum. For a time he was an active teacher of botany; but
eventually, in 1798, he retired to his cousin's parsonage at Pertenhall in
Bedfordshire; after a few years he himself became rector and 'ended his
days as a country parson, preaching until his eighty-second year'.[68]

In the next generation all the sons of Cory, the master, were in the
college. We can discern a number of hereditary students; but the evidence
is defective: we cannot tell what proportion of Emmanuel men had had
fathers in the College; unless our material deceives us, it was a small
fraction of the total.

Others came to Emmanuel because they had been pupils of Emmanuel
men. We know that Anthony Askew (1722–1774) was taught by 'that
learned and forceful scholar' and Emmanuel man, Richard Dawes, at
Newcastle Grammar School.[69] From Dawes he may have acquired his
classical tastes, and doubtless heard of Emmanuel. Askew followed in his
father's profession as a physician; and though nominally a student at
Cambridge, his real education was in Leiden, which was a notable centre
for classical studies as well as medical. He early acquired a passion for
collecting books, both in London and Greece; and although his tastes
were wide and deep, they were also directed to a plan for a new edition
of Aeschylus, which never matured. Little of his life was spent in
Emmanuel and very few of his books came to its library. But Richard
Farmer bought his *Liber Amicorum*, a fascinating album of his continental
friends and acquaintances;[70] and Samuel Parr later acquired an eleventh
century manuscript of John Chrysostom, once Askew's; and so both are
now in the College Library.

---

[66] See p. 295.
[67] Martyn 1728, p. 28.
[68] Stubbings 1983b, no. 24.
[69] Stubbings 1977b, p. 306.
[70] See Stubbings 1977b. For what follows, see Stubbings 1983b, no. 22.

Many came to seek a clerical career. This had been a powerful motive from the very foundation of the universities, and remained central to their purposes till the late nineteenth century. It was the heart of the covenant in Emmanuel in its early days, and remained its chief function till the time of William Chawner.[71] This did not prevent budding lawyers and country gentlemen and others from coming too: the numbers of fellow commoners in late eighteenth century Emmanuel – the fruit, evidently, of Richard Farmer's connections and his celebrity for learning, sound Toryism and good fellowship – were considerable. But the lay element, which had been preponderant in Cambridge at large in the late sixteenth and early seventeenth centuries, was in a minority by the early eighteenth. As other professions grew and prospered, very few of them looked to Cambridge as their training ground. The medical profession was an ironical exception. To prosper as a physician and to attract scholarships, a period of residence at Cambridge could be highly desirable. But by the late eighteenth century there was little medical training to be had there in the ordinary sense of the term: that had to be sought elsewhere.[72] It was this curiously paradoxical situation which brought Thomas Young as fellow commoner to Emmanuel in 1797 – intellectually one of the most distinguished of all Emmanuel men.[73] He chose Emmanuel because Farmer had been a friend of his uncle and chief benefactor, Dr Richard Brocklesby, and both had backed his election to the Royal Society in 1794; and also because the one really notable medical scientist in Cambridge at the time, Sir Busick Harwood, was a resident fellow.[74] Harwood had come, not for the science of the College but for its ample rooms and congenial talk – his name may still be read over the original entry to his rooms in front cloister. He and Farmer were among the leading Tories of Cambridge; Harwood fled from the Whiggery of Christ's.

The Emmanuel Parlour lives for us in the flowing conversation of men like Young and Harwood and Samuel Parr, and in the records of wagers in it. A prime source for the manner and substance of conversation in the Parlour should be the Wager Books, which start in 1769. Most of the early bets, alas, are couched in terms so abbreviated as to be unintelligible. But it is clear that many were personal – some remarkably so: in 1774 Alpe bet Blackall the elder that he could arrange the fellowship in order of weight; and the matter was put to the test: his order was Cory [actually 13 stone

---

[71] What follows is based on a scrutiny of the 'Register' for the eighteenth and nineteenth centuries.

[72] Cf. Brooke 1985, pp. 197–9, and Brooke 1993, p. 167n., with reference to the work of Dr J. Kendall.

[73] What follows is chiefly based on Wood and Oldham 1954.

[74] Wood and Oldham 1954, chap. 2, esp. pp. 60ff. On Harwood, see below; *DNB*; Gascoigne 1989, pp. 183n.1, 287–8; Tanner 1917, pp. 87, 95.

10 lb], Askew [13 2½], Farmer [13 3], Alpe [12 9], Blackall [11 11], Drewe [11 2½], Topp [10 9], Cooke [10 6], Bennet [9 9].[75] Others were about how soon fellows would receive wives or benefices. Others celebrated notable events, such as when Cory was elected a member of that venerable dining club (as it now is) the Family, in 1789.[76] A certain number were political, and these tended to increase as the excitement of the French Revolution brought forecasts of Marat's murder and the fall of Robespierre.[77] The tone is set by the rules, which were from to time reviewed and revised. Thus *c.* 1769: 'That no bets be paid in ink where wine may be had . . . That whoever presumes to take salt from any of the saltcellars on the table, at dinner, with anything except the salt spoons, shall be punish'd a shilling for the benefit of the fruit-eaters . . . That any person who leaves his bowls on the Green, and goes out of the Garden shall be punished a shilling . . .' By 1791 the punishments usually took the form of a bottle of wine – three bottles for the major offence of 'destroying or damaging any plant in the garden'. 'That whosoever . . . comes into the hall without shoes [half-boots were added by an amendment of 1795], buckles, shoe-strings, or gown shall be punish'd one bottle . . . That any person being elected into any College or University office, or appointed Lecturer of any church, shall pay one bottle; being made Chaplain to a bishop two bottles, Prebendary of any Church four.' A rule against drinking healths 'unless strangers are present' was 'entirely repeal'd' in 1793.[78]

Harwood was a native of Newmarket who had made a fortune (so it was generally supposed) by performing operations on Indian princes, and he was tempted to spend his life in India. 'He preferred, however, returning to England, and very soon after his arrival, admitted himself a Fellow-Commoner of Christ's College,' wrote Henry Gunning, himself a former undergraduate at Christ's. 'He lived in an expensive style, gave frequent dinners, and also wine parties: to the latter he invited, in their turns, all the undergraduates, and became very popular with men of all ages. He was a person of considerable wit, according to the fashion of those days, but such as would not be tolerated at the present time [1854]: his conversation was profligate and licentious in the extreme, notwithstanding which he was in the habit of living on the most intimate terms with men of the highest station in the University. He took the degree of M.B. in 1785, and in the same year succeeded Dr Collignon as professor of Anatomy. . . . Harwood resided for some years in Christ's College, but afterwards removed to Emmanuel, where he took his doctor's degree in

---

[75] ECA FEL.9.1, p. 80.
[76] ECA FEL.9.2, p. 197.
[77] Quoted Shuckburgh 1904, p. 157.
[78] The rules quoted are in FEL.9.1, p. 3, and FEL.9.3, pp. 3–10.

1790. As he was on the most friendly terms with the master and resident fellows of Christ's College, everyone was astonished at his quitting it; the reason he assigned was, that his accommodations there were insufficient. It is true that he got at Emmanuel, in addition to most excellent rooms, a very extensive garden [Chapman's garden]: this was, without doubt, one of his reasons for removing, but in my opinion not the only one. He had been always considered a very strong Whig, but a late election had proved that Pitt's influence in the University was irresistible, and Whiggism was at a considerable discount; he therefore felt it essential to the promotion of those views (which I believe he at that time began to entertain), to connect himself with another society, where political principles were held diametrically opposite to those in the society he had just quitted. He kept up, however, his connexion with Christ's College, and generally, out of term time, dined there three or four days in the week, and was allowed to pay for this privilege like the other members of the society. His evenings were generally spent in Emmanuel parlour, which, under the presidency of Dr Farmer, was always open to those who loved pipes and tobacco and cheerful conversation. He purchased a house adjoining his garden, in which he placed his man-servant and wife, where his dinners were usually dressed. During term-time covers were daily laid for half-a-dozen, and the professor in the course of his morning walk always contrived to pick up the requisite number of guests. A plain dinner was neatly served up at two o'clock; and as his lectures began at four, there was no great consumption of wine, and the guests, with scarcely an exception, accompanied him to lectures' – a time-honoured method of filling a Cambridge lecture-room. 'He was at that time lecturing on comparative anatomy; and it was no unusual thing to see the turbot on which Mr Orange [his demonstrator] had exercised his skill one day, carved by the professor on the following.' Thus Gunning, who has other improbable tales to tell of Harwood, the most famous his announcement that he was engaged. Gunning encountered Harwood at dinner in Christ's: 'I am going to do a devilish foolish thing ... I am going to be married!' 'As he had always been in the habit of speaking of the marriage state in strong terms of reprobation, we were astonished at this declaration'; and when Harwood attempted to describe her charms, 'his own remarks on the marriage state were too fresh in the memory of all present, and the laugh against him became so hearty and universal, that he left the party unusually early.'[79] In 1800 he was chosen first Downing Professor of Medicine, and held both his chairs till his death in 1814; but it is hard to grudge him this plurality, since he was that rare bird in the eighteenth and very early nineteenth centuries, a professor who lectured –

---

[79] Gunning 1854, I, 53–6; II, 95–8. For correctives, see Williamson 1983; Searby 1997, pp. 198–9.

and rarer still, he advanced the science he professed by conducting some of the early experiments in blood transfusion.

Harwood could enjoy ample rooms because numbers were few; and one reason was that many were excluded. Dissenters and Jews could not in theory come to Cambridge at all. In practice a few came and their faith went unheeded. Thomas Young himself was born a Quaker, and had to practice an occasional conformity to be received. No women came as students to Emmanuel till the 1970s. That is not to say that they played no part in its history. It is said that an unhappy love affair in his early days inspired Richard Farmer to a life of celibacy; and it was celibacy which enabled him to remain fellow and tutor long past the age when most men married. From the foundation till the late nineteenth century the fellows were not permitted to marry. This embargo was universal in Oxford and Cambridge, but – by a curious custom not always justified by college statutes – it was ignored in master's lodges; none the less few masters of Emmanuel of the early generations were married.[80] But the most piquant female influence which we may know or suspect among the fellows of Emmanuel is that of Jane Austen.

Miss Austen herself came from the heart of the Oxford establishment. Her great uncle had been master of Balliol for much of the eighteenth century; her father and eldest brother were fellows of St John's. Two of her five brothers became clergymen; two others admirals.[81] The most deserving of her clergymen, Edmund Bertram of Mansfield Park, went to Oxford, and Fanny Price was able to see the outside of his College as the carriage took her and Edmund from Portsmouth to Northamptonshire: one may suspect that Miss Austen had St John's in her mind. Otherwise, she is very sparing in her information on the forming of her characters. But she specifically tells us that two of her most worthless young men, Mr Wickham in *Pride and Prejudice*, and Mr Crawford in *Mansfield Park*, had been to Cambridge;[82] Fanny Price very wisely preferred the Oxford man. Yet there is some evidence that Jane was not averse to one Cambridge man at least.

Over thirty years ago Frank Stubbings brought to life the Reverend Samuel Blackall in an enchanting article on his relations with Miss Austen.[83] Mr Blackall may serve as a model of the Emmanuel men of his age, for he was a hereditary Emmanuel man who long served the College as fellow and tutor, before receiving his reward in a country living and a wife – even though the wife was not perhaps the lady of his first choice.

Mr Blackall was the son or nephew of another Samuel Blackall, who

[80] See p. 421 n.23.
[81] Chapman 1952, pp. xxxviii (bibliography) and Index 1 (Jane Austen's family).
[82] *Pride and Prejudice*, chap. 35; *Mansfield Park*, chap. 6.
[83] What follows is based on Stubbings 1984b, first published in 1964–5.

had been a fellow from 1772 to 1786 and was Farmer's colleague as tutor in the late 1770s. In 1786 Samuel Blackall senior 'retired to the comfortable College living of Loughborough'.[84] He was one of a multitude of Cambridge men who had the misfortune to be portrayed by the mordant pen of William Cole, the antiquary and vicar of Milton.

'He is a little black man, of no humane aspect, and carries his malignancy in his forehead; he is lame of one leg by some accident, and a great rower on the water; a lively and ingenious man, plays well on the harpsichord, sings well, draws well and etches not amiss.'[85]

We have a very different image of the younger Samuel. He came to Cambridge in 1787 and had a respectable academic career, ending fourteenth wrangler in the Mathematical Tripos in 1791. In 1794 he was ordained and elected a fellow; from 1803 to 1812 he was a tutor.[86] In that year Dr John Askew, former fellow and rector of North Cadbury in Somerset, died, and Blackall was able to take a country living and to marry.

'That Samuel Blackall was' tempted to matrimony 'in 1798', writes Frank Stubbings, 'we happen to know from the letters of Jane Austen. If Blackall was still "gay, gentlemanly, and classical" in 1811, at the age of forty, he can hardly have been less so at the age of twenty-seven; and when, visiting in Hampshire, he met among the unidea'd girls of the country rectories the charm and wit and perspicacity of Jane Austen, his delight in her company naturally led to a little wishful thinking.'[87]

On 17 November 1798 Jane wrote to her sister Cassandra. 'Mrs Lefroy [a neighbouring parson's wife] did come last Wednesday . . . Of her nephew [Tom Lefroy, the best recorded of Jane Austen's admirers] she said nothing at all, and of her friend [Samuel Blackall] very little. She did not once mention the name of the former to *me*, and I was too proud to make any enquiries . . .

'She showed me a letter which she had received from her friend a few weeks ago . . . , towards the end of which was a sentence to this effect: "I am very sorry to hear of Mrs Austen's illness. It would give me particular pleasure to have an opportunity of improving my acquaintance with that family, with a hope of creating to myself a nearer interest. But at present I cannot indulge any expectation of it." This is rational enough; there is less love and more sense in it than sometimes appeared before, and I am very well satisfied. It will all go on exceedingly well, and decline away in a very reasonable manner. There seems no likelihood of his coming into Hampshire this Christmas, and it is therefore most probable that our

---

[84] Stubbings 1984b, p. 78.
[85] Ibid.
[86] Stubbings 1984b, p. 78; ECA TUT.23.2, *sub ann.* 1803–12.
[87] Stubbings 1984b, p. 78; cf. below, p. 404.

indifference will soon be mutual, unless his regard, which appeared to spring from knowing nothing of me at first, is best supported by never seeing me.'

On 3 July 1813 Jane wrote to her brother Frank, one of the future admirals:

> 'I wonder whether you happened to see Mr Blackall's marriage in the papers last January. *We* did. He was married at Clifton to a Miss Lewis, whose father had been late of Antigua. I should very much like to know what sort of a woman she is. He was a piece of Perfection, noisy Perfection himself which I always recollect with regard. – We had noticed a few months before his succeeding to a College living, the very living which we remembered his talking of and wishing for; an exceeding good one, [North] Cadbury in Somersetshire. – I would wish Miss Lewis to be of a silent turn and rather ignorant, but naturally intelligent and wishing to learn; – fond of cold veal pies, green tea in the afternoon, and a green window blind at night.'[88]

In 1798 the tutor's son or nephew, soon to be a tutor himself, was evidently a lively talkative man who took it for granted the girls were less well read than he. But his talk was good and his person memorable, for Miss Austen and her sister were closely interested in his fate fifteen years later. 'By this point in the letter', says Dr Stubbings, 'Jane's feelings, if they were indeed stirred by what might have been, are back in their place and under total control; and she changes the subject to tell her brother that every copy of *Sense and Sensibility* is now sold.' He observes that when they had first met, she was engaged in writing *Northanger Abbey*, and with a delicacy appropriate to such conjectures, hints that Blackall may have helped to inspire the bright young clergyman Henry Tilney and his 'gaily satirical (if sometimes didactic) conversation. . . . However, we need shed no tears on Jane's behalf for what might have been, nor regret that Dr Askew . . . did not vacate North Cadbury sooner. Had he done so, Blackall might have played his hand and won. But then we might not have had the novels.'[89]

In the 1790s a young man called Henry Tilney became a fellow of Caius; he too was later a country parson. He bears an East Anglian name as befitted a Caian – but such are very rare in Miss Austen's novels; and he is the only Henry Tilney in Venn's *Alumni*.[90] It is a striking coincidence

---

[88] Chapman 1952, nos. 11, 81, pp. 27–8, 316–17 (now Le Faye 1995, nos. 11, 86, pp. 19, 216), quoted Stubbings 1984b, pp. 79–80.
[89] Stubbings 1984b, pp. 80–1.
[90] Brooke 1985, p. 185 and n.101.

that he should have been an almost exact contemporary of Miss Austen's only known friend who was a fellow of a Cambridge college. In any case we need not doubt that she would have acknowledged that Cambridge could produce better men than Wickham and Crawford.

The society over which Blackall and his like presided was intimate but not egalitarian. Doubtless in practice there was friendship and fellowship throughout the society. But in Emmanuel in the eighteenth century, and especially in the second half during Farmer's regime as tutor and master, there was a substantial number of fellow commoners, sons of the gentry or men of more mature years come at their own expense. The rest of the undergraduates comprised scholars, pensioners – wholly paid for by their parents – and sizars.[91] In the sixteenth and seventeenth centuries it had been the practice to provide for the servicing of the community by remitting part or whole of the fees of some of the students. They could act as butlers, waiters, valets, chamber servants or the like. Some of them came from modest homes, but there was no necessary social distinction from scholars or pensioners: many went on to become scholars, and masters, like William Savage at Emmanuel. 'Who sweeps a chamber for thy Laws, makes that and th'action fine': thus the aristocratic George Herbert in the 1620s. He corrected 'a chamber' into 'a room as', but we need not doubt he started with a Cambridge sizar in his mind.[92] In the course of the eighteenth century, however, the distinction became more sharply drawn; a social stigma attached to service and to sizarship; they were an inferior breed. In the nineteenth century they disappeared and hired servants replaced them.[93]

At the other end of the spectrum, the fellow commoners were men of substance who paid heavily for their special privileges: they dined with the fellows; they had comfortable quarters; they wore gowns adorned with gold or silver lace and velvet caps. In return they were expected to enhance the college's collection of silver and help it to recruit more of their kind.[94]

The fellow commoners of Trinity and their rivals of Christ Church were sometimes notorious layabouts, who came to university for a spell of hunting, fishing and good fellowship. The eccentric if Reverend John Trusler, who himself entered as a sizar in 1753, gave the whole class a bad name.

'As to the fellow-commoners, they were always at Cambridge called "empty-bottles" from the following circumstance that occurred at Emmanuel. Wine-merchants send their porters occasionally round the

---

[91] On sizars, see Brooke 1985, pp. 117–18, 248.
[92] Charles 1971, fo. 75.
[93] See below, p. 549; but see also above, p. 46.
[94] See below, pp. 402–4.

Colleges to collect the bottles; one of these men, during the hour of lecture, knocked at the lecture-room door by mistake, and called out "empty bottles!" The tutor, then out of humour at being attended by only one fellow-commoner, when there were twenty in college, cried out, "Call again another time; I have now but one." ' But Trusler himself, though a sizar, was no model student. If we may believe his own account he copied a key to one of the college gates and was much sought after by those requiring illicit entry – and this was perhaps in character, since in later life he seems to have been more noted for ingenious inventions than pastoral care. He claims to have been rusticated for failing to translate a great quantity of Caesar in punishment for wearing his cap in a fellow's presence in the court – 'being ... troubled by weak eyes.. when it mizzled'.[95]

I doubt if Mr Trusler is a reliable witness. But there was assuredly much variety; and some fellow commoners were mature men of intellectual distinction. Of the empty bottles George Wright stands as an example, of the more intellectual, Thomas Young. In the Admonition Book under 2 April 1763 it is written that – 'Notwithstanding the many repeated reproofs which have been given to Mr George Wright Fellow Commoner of the College for not attending the service of God in the Chappel, he has yet continued to persevere therein, to the great offence of Almighty God and the scandal of good men, he was this day for such seeming contempt and a total neglect of study and the discipline of the College, admonish'd by the Master before the Society.'[96]

George Wright represents the fellow commoner of legend, the empty bottle. It was certainly not the case, however, that all Emmanuel men of privilege were fellow commoners. William Calvert, elected fellow in 1728, was a pensioner, but a man who moved in the best circles and by 1742 was an M.P., by 1749 Lord Mayor of London, by 1755 M.P. for Old Sarum, most celebrated of pocket boroughs, already deserted before Parliament existed.[97] The Reverend Hugh Wade Gery, rector of Thurning and squire of Bushmead Priory in what once was Huntingdonshire, had started as Hugh Wade, sizar of 1778; elected fellow in 1785, he won the living and married one of the heiresses of Bushmead in 1792; and their marriage was blessed with many children, five of them Emmanuel men.[98] Some of the most distinguished of Emmanuel men came as senior residents: the golden year 1786 brought both Busick Harwood and the distinguished chemist, Smithson Tennant, who was already an FRS on his

---

[95] Trusler's memoirs, quoted by Shuckburgh 1904, pp. 167–8. On Trusler, see 'Register' 1753.
[96] ECA CHA.1.4A, fo. 21v. On Wright, see 'Register' 1761 s.v. Wrighte. Nothing is known of his later career.
[97] 'Register' 1722.
[98] 'Register' 1778.

arrival and resided briefly; much later he was to be professor of chemistry (1813–15).[99]

All these characters are today eclipsed in fame by Thomas Young, a 'man alike eminent in almost every department of human learning', as his epitaph in Westminster Abbey declares.[100] He is best known as a key figure in the history of optics and light: he wrote a paper in 1793 on how the human eye focusses and was elected FRS the next year, aged twenty-one; in his brief stay in Cambridge from 1797 to 1800 he began to develop his theory of light: for years he was to struggle against other scientists to establish the view that light was transmitted by waves, not particles. 'The wave theory of light was probably the greatest achievement of early nineteenth-century theoretical science. It won its way slowly, but after the work of Young and [Augustin] Fresnel its victory was inevitable' – though slow. 'John Herschel was not an easy convert and until 1827 [only two years before Young's death] found it hard to give a complete acceptance.'[101] 'An attractive tradition has it that he first observed the phenomenon of "interference" in the ripples set up by two swans on the Emmanuel pond.'[102] These interests would have filled the time of many lesser men; but he also 'ran the *Nautical Almanack*, and developed a theory of tides; ... advised on the introduction of gas lighting in London; ... was foreign secretary to the Royal Society; ... devised "Young's modulus" to quantify elasticity.' He was also from an early age proficient in languages; and he applied his astonishing linguistic gifts to the famous Rosetta Stone, the main key to the deciphering of Egyptian hieroglyphics – for its inscription is written in Greek as well as in hieroglyphs and demotic script. As with his theory of light, the progress of his work was clouded by controversy; his friend turned rival, Jean François Champollion, refused in the end to acknowledge his debt to Young and the learned world was divided between them. We can now see that the code would not have been broken at that time if both had not contributed their learning and ingenuity to the search.[103]

Young has a large place in the intellectual history of Britain in the first quarter of the nineteenth century; how large a place he has in the history of Emmanuel is a nice question. He resided for three years, but already in 1799 was starting in medical practice in London; his uncle Sir Richard Brocklesby had recently died and left him his fortune. He was a scholar of independent means; and that suited well his independent character. He

---

[99] *DNB*: Tanner 1917, p. 86 and n.5; Gunning 1854, II, 59–62.
[100] Quoted in Stubbings 1983b, no. 33.
[101] Wood and Oldham 1954, p. 204. The Coal Books, ECA STE 12.1, show 'Mr Young' – evidently this Thomas Young – resident for much of the period from mid-1797 to mid-1800, with a brief return in 1802. I am very grateful to Dr John Kendall for this reference.
[102] Stubbings 1983b, no. 33 – also for what follows.
[103] Wood and Oldham 1954, chap. 10.

had come to Cambridge for a degree; he had chosen Emmanuel for its good talk and the fame of Dr Farmer – who sadly died just before Young came into residence. He clearly enjoyed the conversation of the parlour. But it is unlikely that he thought highly of Cambridge or of Emmanuel as places of education. 'Whoever would arrive at excellence', he wrote in a letter to his brother, 'must be self-taught' – and that he was, or believed himself to be.[104]

George Peacock's *Life* of Young, published in 1855, contains a circumstantial account of Young at Emmanuel, claiming to be the work of his tutor. It is curiously unfriendly, even malicious at times, and some of it is hard to reconcile with what we know of Young. An early passage in it reads: 'When the master introduced Young to his tutors he said, "I have brought you a pupil qualified to read lectures to his tutors".'[105] There were but two tutors in 1797, and the master himself, Robert Cory, was one. It would be natural to assume that Cory himself was tutor to so distinguished a fellow commoner; and of the two tutors in 1797, Cory alone survived Young, dying in 1835; the other, Richard Hardy, went to the college living at Loughborough in 1798, and ended his days there in 1827.[106] But Cory had the reputation of being a kindly man, and this sentence suggests a confused memory. It is hard to know how to use it as evidence.

But one of its anecdotes was at least well found: it describes the meeting of Young – the bird of passage – and Samuel Parr, in whose extraordinary character we see, as in a mirror, something of the character of Emmanuel in the age of Farmer and Cory. 'The Whig Dr Johnson' – as Parr came to be remembered – seems an unlikely person to meet in Emmanuel; and it is true that he left the college after only one year's residence as an undergraduate, owing to poverty; and that later on he broke off his visits there in 1784 'in a pet' and transferred to St John's, a society more congenial to a Whig; but the breach was not lasting.

'I remember [Young] meeting Dr Parr in the college Combination Room', wrote his 'tutor', 'and when the Doctor had made, as was not unusual with him, some dogmatical observation on a point of scholarship, Young said firmly: "Bentley, sir, was of a different opinion"; immediately quoting his authority, and showing his intimate knowledge of the subject. Parr said nothing; but when Dr Young retired, asked who he was, and though he did not seem to have heard his name before, he said, "A smart young man, that." '[107]

While Emmanuel in the mid eighteenth century had been remote from

---

[104] Quoted ibid. p. 12.
[105] Quoted ibid. p. 62.
[106] 'Register' 1778; list of tutors, see Appendix 3.
[107] Peacock 1855, p. 116, quoted in Wood and Oldham 1954, pp. 63–4. Cf. Stubbings 1983b, no. 26.

the Whig fountains of patronage, Parr himself at the end of the century was cut off from Tory patrons. He was a not very successful school-master, and a perpetual curate, no more. But he is secure of immortality, like Johnson himself, for his conversation. The Emmanuel Parlour was a Mecca for those who valued talk and tobacco; and he was very much at home there. 'He subscribed £100 after the 1811 fire in the Westmorland Building; he gave the College his portrait by Romney, and two biblio-graphical treasures for the library: an eleventh century MS of St [John] Chrysostom, originally from Mount Athos, which had belonged to Anthony Askew, and an *editio princeps* of Aristophanes ... His great silver-mounted pipe and tobacco-box ... are still in the College's posses-sion.'[108] The pipe and tobacco box are monuments of an age when men could enjoy tobacco without shame. But the Chrysostom and the Aristophanes are reminders of one fundamental reason why Parr was so widely courted and sought after. He was a man of ample, wide and genuine learning.

[108] Stubbings 1983b, no. 26. On Parr see Stubbings 1967–8; Derry 1966.

11

The Buildings – 1719–1871

The Westmorland Building

On 1 March 1718 the Master sent out a letter of appeal.

'This College Sir Walter Mildmay by the encouragement of Q. Eliza-beth founded for the propagating true religion, and for the defence of it against Popery, and all other heresies and errours, and endow'd it according to his abilities, and the account of those times with a tolerable provision for the encouragement of learning. But the materials of his building proving very defective, the ruinous condition to which, notwith-standing the expense and care which have from time to time been bestow'd upon it, a great part of it is at last reduc't, obliges us to look abroad for contributions to enable us to rebuild it in a better manner . . .'[1]

The appeal is both moving and puzzling. Its purpose was to raise funds for replacing the Founder's Building, and the outcome was the stately eighteenth century southern range of the front court now known as the Westmorland Building. Loggan's engraving of *c.* 1690 seems to show the Founder's Building in good shape: there is nothing ruinous about his presentation of it. But the building accounts for the Westmor-land Building survive in profusion and have been studied by Hugh Richmond; and these record the digging and construction of foundations for the new building as well as the shaping of the upper structures.[2] Nevertheless the main form of the Westmorland Building must have been influenced by the layout of the earlier buildings. The east end of the Founder's Building partly survives: behind the war memorial in the cloister there is still a window of the old ground floor room. Presumably the structure was needed to provide support to the cloister and gallery on the one side and the brick building on the other while demolition was in progress. More than this, the book which records the chambers and their occupants and rents in the early and mid-eighteenth century shows that the ground floor chamber between cloister and brick building was con-tinuously occupied while building was in progress; here and at the west

---

[1] ECA BDG.1.Y1; cf. pp. 354–5 below.
[2] The accounts are ECA BDG.1.

end earlier structures evidently survived.[3] The book also shows that the rest of the building was occupied by 1722, although wainscotting and fitting up of chambers continued for some years.[4]

It may be that extensive repairs were needed by 1718: the roof may have been in bad condition, the fine stonework on the front may have weathered. We cannot tell. But we can shrewdly suspect that other motives were at work, helping the governing body to seek a more radical solution than patching and mending.

Wren's gallery and chapel form one of the supreme beauties of Cambridge; and by closing the eastern aspect of the Founder's court it created an enclosed court: its intimacy with the Founder's Range must have driven home the difference in style between the Tudor Gothic of the Founder and Wren's Italian Baroque mode. The ancestry of Wren's work was classical, that of Mildmay's architect, Ralph Symons, gothic. It is a striking fact that down to the 1660s many colleges in Cambridge followed the fashion for red brick building: the last notable example before the late nineteenth century was the rebuilding of St Catharine's in the 1670s and 1680s. When Wren first designed his arcade and gallery they were to have been of red brick, like the brick building of the 1630s, but dressed with stone, like Pembroke chapel; by the time it was built, ashlar prevailed.[5] The taste of the age may well have inspired the fellows of Emmanuel to plan the refacing of the whole court with classical designs and the finest ashlar; and not the taste only. For the fifty years from 1665 to 1715, which had witnessed the first steep decline in the admission of students, had also brought forth building plans of exceptional grandeur in Oxford and Cambridge. In Oxford the period opens with Wren's Sheldonian Theatre and comes to a climax when Dr Radcliffe made his will in 1714, from which were later to emerge a new court in University College and the magnificent Radcliffe Camera. Hawksmoor's new buildings at All Souls were on the drawing board. Meanwhile the Queen's College in Oxford was in the throes of the most complete rebuilding programme of the age, starting with a monumental library in the 1690s, 'worthy of Wren or Hawksmoor'.[6] Nor was Cambridge far behind. Wren had beautified Pembroke and Emmanuel with chapels, and helped to complete Nevile's Court at Trinity with the great classical library which is among the most monumental of all the buildings of Cambridge. In 1712–13 Hawksmoor

---

[3] ECA STE.24.1, p. 35; cf. p. 39 for reoccupation of the first floor chamber by 1721. Ibid. pp. 61, 67, show a similar continuous use of earlier structures at the west end of the range. BDG.1.c.64 contains accounts for wainscotting occupied rooms in the period 1720–2.

[4] STE.24.1, pp. 43, 47, 49, and *passim*; BDG.1.

[5] Willis and Clark 1886/1988, II, 704.

[6] Heyworth 1981, p. 107, quoted in Brooke, Highfield and Swaan 1988, pp. 207–9. The rebuilding of Oxford is illustrated and discussed in ibid. pp. 196–212; and see esp. Colvin 1986. For what follows see *RCHM Cambridge*, I, p. lvi; Willis and Clark 1886/1988, I, 556–9.

was set to work to design a range of buildings to complete the great court of King's. This was part of a grandiose scheme to remodel the whole centre of Cambridge, and nothing came of it. But his idea for a Fellows' Building caught the imagination of the community; and out of it the simpler Gibbs building of the 1720s was to emerge.

Sir Howard Colvin has shown how Oxford – often in spite of inadequate resources – set out on the path of massive and monumental rebuilding in the early eighteenth century. 'The result was to put Oxford, for the first time since the Reformation, in the forefront of English architecture'.[7] A part of the credit for this he assigned to two remarkable devotees of architectural grandeur, Dean Aldrich of Christ Church and George Clarke of All Souls; but 'in an age when a knowledge of architecture was fashionable among the aristocracy and gentry, colleges whose membership was increasingly being drawn from those ranks of society would naturally share the tastes of their class'.[8] Cambridge had made a splendid start in the same direction with Wren's chapels and Trinity Library; and in the 1710s and 20s grandiose plans were afoot. The Senate House is a fragment of a great design completely to remodel the Old Schools: it proceeded slowly through shortage of funds and was stopped in its tracks by the fellows of Caius, who most strenuously objected to losing the open aspect to the south from Caius Court.[9] In the mid-eighteenth century the eastern range of the Old Schools was remodelled by an architect chosen by the duke of Newcastle, Stephen Wright. But the chief influence on Cambridge architecture from the 1720s to the 1760s was James Burrough, tutor and master of Caius and a more modest version of the Oxford paladins, whose work can be seen in Caius, Clare, Peterhouse and Trinity Hall, and who nearly anticipated the work of Essex at Emmanuel. James Essex himself owed much to the patronage, instruction and encouragement of Burrough, and completed what Burrough had begun, working in several colleges – above all in Emmanuel.

The grandeur of Oxford owed much to 'the new element of upper class fellows and undergraduates – above all the gentlemen commoners'.[10] The Garden Quadrangle of New College, begun in the 1680s, completed in the 1700s, was a recognition that gentlemen commoners could not live in medieval chambers. When first planned in 1682–3, it was designed so that each ample chamber allowed for two studies, with two bedrooms attached; but when it was enlarged in 1700–7 individual sets were designed, comprising 'a spacious sitting room with a study and a bedroom to the rear' – and this was to be the model followed (rather

---

[7] Colvin 1986, p. 842.
[8] Colvin 1986, pp. 842–3.
[9] Brooke 1985, p. 171. For what follows, ibid. pp. 171–4; Cocke 1984.
[10] Colvin 1986, p. 843 – and also for what follows.

approximately) in Cambridge, in the Westmorland Building at Emmanuel and the Gibbs building at King's. The new style of accommodation was provided on a scale as grand as in New College, and in the new buildings of Christ Church and Magdalen, Oxford, in the first half of the eighteenth century. It is with these that the Gibbs Building of King's has to be compared, with its large chambers and provision of bedrooms and other quarters besides. But in truth the fall in numbers from the 1660s on had enabled the whole of some college communities to seek more ample quarters. The chambers in Caius Court in Caius had been built for groups of three or four; by the 1690s the better rooms were being wainscotted to provide fine accommodation for fellows; by the early eighteenth century more modest wainscotting was provided for under-graduates as well.[11]

In Caius as in most colleges in which older buildings were preserved, shared rooms were converted into single sets by the simple process of removing partitions from all but one of the studies, leaving a single chamber for an undergraduate with a small bedroom attached. What had been tutor's rooms had cocklofts above which could become tutor's bedrooms; grander fellows, then as now, could add chamber to chamber. The Westmorland Building differed in lay-out from its predecessor in having a new outer wall built eleven feet to the south, so that after the remodelling of the old building each chamber led into two smaller rooms. The accommodation is not so lavish as in the Gibbs Building at King's, but it is ample; and the handsome new Georgian windows made the chambers light and gave the fellows and fellow commoners within delightful views of the court before and the gardens behind – and for the privileged members of the community who enjoyed the founder's rooms at the eastern end, an ample prospect of the pond and the paddock. We need hardly doubt that the provision of more ample accommodation – to do more modestly for Emmanuel what was already afoot in New College and Christ Church and on the drawing board for King's – was the chief motive for the new building. It has been suggested that it was primarily designed for fellow commoners, whom the College could only hope to attract by offering lavish, up-to-date accommodation. This certainly seems to have been the effect. In the five years 1715–19 there was only one fellow commoner in 1715, one in 1718, one in 1719. Any idea of attracting more must have been fairly speculative. But when the Westmorland Building opened, there was a flurry of fellow commoners – five entered in

---

[11] For the fine panelling of some first-floor rooms, see Brooke 1985, p. 156; plain wainscot-ting of various dates in the early-mid eighteenth century survive in many rooms on the ground floor. For all that follows see Willis and Clark 1886/1988, esp. II, 703–17; *RCHM Cambridge*, I, 62–3, 68–9.

1723–4.[12] The chief beneficiaries were the fellows, and it is extremely odd that only one fellow contributed to the appeal to pay for the building – but seventeen ex-fellows subscribed, and at least eight fellow commoners and former fellow commoners.[13] One of these was Colonel John Fane, later Earl of Westmorland, who we know had occupied the founder's chambers in the old Founder's Building between 1704 and 1707, and laid out on it about £30 'in new hanging it, window curtains, glazing, partition etc.'[14] He was later to subscribe £100 to the rebuilding and doubtless discussed with his elder brother, then the earl, the need to provide more amply for their successors.

Its design was dictated by a skilful adaptation marrying the form of the earlier building to a new classical front elevation, with large rectangular windows, ornamental entrance doors and two giant Ionic pilasters. Comparison with Christ Church and King's makes it seem modest and cautious; yet it helps to form one of the loveliest courts in Cambridge; by comparison with most of the collegiate architecture figuring in Loggan's engraving of twenty years before it is monumental, of its age and of its mode; once it was built no fellow – nor, what was perhaps more to the point, no fellow-commoner – could complain that he was inadequately provided. None the less, the fundamental rebuilding helps to establish that complaints of decay and damage in the 1710s told the truth, if – we may reasonably suppose – not the whole truth about the reasons for embarking on the Westmorland Building.

On 10 March 1715 first steps were taken to prepare for a major outlay of funds on the college buildings: a college order asserting that 'the Buildings of the College, in the Walls, Roofs, and Tilings thereof, are at this time much decay'd and out of Repair, in so much that it will require a good sum of Money to repair them as they ought to be'[15] suspended two fellowships then vacant till the work was done. By 1718 something had been saved, and it was time to mount the appeal. They evidently turned first to the Founder's representative, Thomas Fane, twelfth earl of Westmorland – sixth of the new creation of 1624. The earl gave the building £500; he doubtless encouraged others to give; he gave it his name and he gave it his architect.[16] John Lumley came from a family of masons, and worked quite extensively in Bedfordshire, Northamptonshire and Rutland. At the Earl of Westmorland's Northamptonshire seat at Apethorpe, he acted as overseeer, and this may mean that he designed the orangery,

[12] See Register.
[13] ECA COL.6.1 gives details of donors; see pp. 354–5.
[14] ECA STE.24.1, p. 37.
[15] Quoted Willis and Clark 1886/1988, II, 711.
[16] ECA COL.6.1; Colvin 1978, p. 529.

built in 1718, which forms the south side of the second court.[17] It was doubtless on the earl's advice, or instruction, that he designed the Westmorland Building, and adorned its central portal with the Westmorland Coat of Arms and the Fane motto.

James Burrough and James Essex

After the grandiose dreams of Hawksmoor and the splendid mansions of Gibbs, building in Cambridge in the mid and late eighteenth century was dominated by two men of more modest aims and capabilities, but notable skill and taste, James Burrough, tutor and master of Caius, and his protégé, James Essex.[18] Burrough himself as a young fellow had had a hand in designing the Senate House. In 1722 James Gibbs came down from London and 'Mr Burrough's plan of the intended publick buildings' was placed in his hands; and Gibbs was 'retained to supervise and conduct' the operation: we may reasonably ascribe the Senate House to their joint efforts.[19] In course of time Burrough was to play a role in refacing Peterhouse and providing it with a new building by Trumpington Street; in remodelling and refacing the main court of Trinity Hall and Gonville Court in Caius; at the end of his life he made the plan, which Essex was to execute, for Clare Chapel – an imaginatively modified version of Wren's Pembroke Chapel.[20] Burrough found much of Cambridge Gothic and left it classical – in his 'robust, conservative style' which he taught Essex;[21] for his modest, classical ashlar courts were extended by Essex to Christ's and St John's – though he was only allowed to reface one wing of St John's first court. Burrough and Essex were men of very different backgrounds. Burrough was a don – though never in orders – and a tutor, who directed his operations from his chambers in Caius. James Essex the Elder had been a notable craftsman and builder – the woodwork of the Senate House is his principal monument; and he had worked in the Westmorland Building itself; his son grew up to the trade of mason and builder. Burrough and the younger Essex formed a remarkable alliance: Burrough's academic training and architectural knowledge helped to form the mind of Essex, while Essex provided practical knowledge and understanding of materials to the partnership. They shared antiquarian tastes: Burrough wrote a study of the antiquities of Bury St Edmunds, his home town, replete with architectural drawings; Essex in his later years was a Fellow of the Society of Antiquaries. Both could appreciate Gothic buildings, even if their time in Cambridge was

---

[17] Colvin 1978, p. 529.

[18] On Burrough and Essex, see esp. Cocke 1984; Colvin 1978, pp. 168–70, 297–300.

[19] Willis and Clark 1886/1988, III, 44; Brooke 1985, p. 171.

[20] See esp. Cocke 1984, pp. 24–5; Brooke 1985, pp. 171–3; Willis and Clark 1886/1988, I, 35–8, 114–16, 188–9, 227–9.

[21] Cocke 1984, p. 24. For James Essex senior, see ibid. and ECA BDG. 1.E.7–13.

largely spent in indulging the classical tastes of their contemporaries. But Essex came to have much the more varied palette. At Queens' he planned – but only partly executed – a modest version of the Gibbs building at King's in brick, and constructed the celebrated mathematical bridge, designed by W. Etheridge.[22] At St Catharine's he added another wing to match the fine dark-red brick of the late seventeenth-century buildings. In Trinity he restored and remodelled the older part of Nevile's Court with a skill that deceives the eye: he made the court less Jacobean, more classical, more of a piece; he subdued the Jacobean ornament; he showed himself a brilliant adapter as well as a restorer. But perhaps the most notable work of his later years lay in restoring great Gothic monuments, especially the cathedrals of Ely and Lincoln. He restored every part of Lincoln Minster, and showed a deeply sensitive appreciation of Gothic taste far removed from the superficial Gothic fashionable in his day: he was even to add the most genuinely Gothic element to Strawberry Hill.[23] Between the soaring Gothic of Lincoln and the modest classicism of Essex's work at Emmanuel there seems little in common – yet both were characteristic enthusiasms of their age; and the precentor of Lincoln, deeply involved in the patronage of Essex and his work there, was also the Master of Emmanuel. William Richardson, indeed, had been a prebendary of Lincoln since 1724, and in the 1730s commuted between Cambridge and Lincoln; he became precentor in 1760, the year in which Essex began to remodel the hall at Emmanuel, and in 1761 Essex was set to work at Lincoln.[24] Among his interiors, his two most striking monuments are the remodelling of the choir at Lincoln, culminating in his throne for the bishop, and the delicate classical panelling and plasterwork with which he adorned the hall at Emmanuel – the Gothic nave of the church of the Dominican friars recast as Tudor Gothic by Ralph Symons in the 1580s. These two works form a most piquant contrast. Had Richardson not been deeply involved in both – and a celebrated medievalist in his day – we would confidently have asserted that the two idioms reflected the tastes of two different patrons. Something may be attributed to context: Wren and Lumley had brought a classical flavour to Emmanuel; Wren had, indeed, brought it to the library in the cloisters of Lincoln too – but no power on earth could have brought it to the Minster. Something more may be attributed to the wide interests and eclectic tastes of Richardson and Essex.

James Burrough is first recorded to have worked in Emmanuel in 1735, when he was paid seven guineas 'for his assistance in beautifying the

[22] Cocke 1984, pp. 24–5, and p. 47 for Essex's original design for Queens'; Willis and Clark 1886/1988, II, 18.

[23] See esp. Cocke 1984, pp. 26–7, 34, 37–8.

[24] See below, pp. 330–1; Cocke 1984, p. 34. On Richardson and Lincoln, see Thompson 1994, pp. 215, 219.

chappell' – whatever he may have done there.[25] Taste apart, he was a natural friend to the fellows of Emmanuel, for Emmanuel and Caius were the leading Tory colleges of the day. In William Cole's catalogue of the Tories who abstained from voting for the Duke of Newcastle as chancellor in 1748, 'all the fellows of pure Emmanuel' were joined by some at Peterhouse, King's and Caius – and even a few in Trinity and St John's, though John's was one of the duke's principal strongholds.[26] Pembroke was also represented, where toryism was to rise again like the phoenix in the age of the young Mr Pitt of Pembroke. In Caius, Burrough's predecessor as Master, Thomas Gooch, had been a tory, but defected in pursuit of a bishopric in the late 1720s and became a whig; yet Burrough and most of the fellows stayed loyal. Even before Richardson became master, Burrough was evidently an acceptable visitor in the Emmanuel parlour. More was to come. On 22 June 1752 it was noted in the Order Book that 'the Butteries and the contiguous buildings are become very ruinous, and it is hop'd that benefactions may be procur'd to defray the expence of rebuilding the same; agreed that they be pull'd down and rebuilt so soon as money sufficient be rais'd for that purpose; and that the butteries and the end rooms in Bungay court be the first that be gone upon'.[27] That is to say, a plot was afoot to replace the whole western range; but the start should be made at its northern end, in Bungay Court. As in the 1710s, the state of the buildings was the excuse for drastic rebuilding; and doubtless the same mixture of motives prevailed: the need for repairs, changing taste, and the urge for larger and more elegant rooms. The main western range, as shown in Loggan's engraving of c.1690, was evidently a medieval rabbit warren. The Order continues:

'Agreed thereupon that Mr Burrough be desir'd to prepare a plan for the whole of the said intended new Building in conformity to that call'd the Founder's Range' – that is, the Westmorland Building which had replaced the original founder's building – 'and that Mr Devie be join'd to the Master in carrying the said plan into execution, when approv'd by the Society'.[28]

But Richardson had evidently overreached himself. He was a married man, who no doubt found the lodge cabined and confined; so he had hatched the design to incorporate the parlour in the lodge; but on this point the approval of the Society could by no means be achieved. Thus William Bennet:

[25] Willis and Clark 1886/1988, II, 709.
[26] Winstanley 1922, p. 48; see p. 299. On Gooch and Burrough in Caius, see Brooke 1985, pp. 163–71.
[27] Willis and Clark 1886/1988, II, 713 n.6. Here and below 'ruinous' seems to carry a less devastating sense than would be normal today.
[28] Quoted in Willis and Clark 1886/1988, II, 713 n.6.

'The master, according to the plan, was to have had the present Combination Room added to his Lodge, and the passage between them stop'd up. The fellows on the other hand were unwilling to go to the bottom of the hall to a more distant and noisy room. The scheme accordingly went off for some years, and the money, of which a large sum had been subscrib'd (one gentleman alone, Sir Richard Chase of Hartfordshire, having sent five hundred pounds) was return'd to the donors.'[29] We can understand the ambivalence of Bennet's summary of Richardson as master. While observing that his 'economy in college affairs' made possible the large building schemes of his time, and paying tribute to his 'liberal mind' and gentlemanly conduct, he asserts that: 'He was a most strict and unpleasant Master to his Fellows'.[30]

But the urge to modernize the older buildings did not go away; and in 1760 the Society accepted a plan by James Essex for the hall to be 're-paired and fitted up'.[31] 'The hall, which has retained the panelling, plaster ceiling and wrought iron gates designed by Essex', writes Thomas Cocke, 'is his most impressive secular interior to survive'.[32] In Lincoln Cathedral he made the Gothic choir more Gothic still; in the hall at Queens' he boldly set classical panelling in a Gothic setting; in the hall at Emmanuel he set exquisite classical panelling and plaster work in happy companionship with Tudor Gothic windows.

The adaptation of the exterior, and the remodelling of the rooms to the east of the hall – the parlour and what was then the master's lodge – were achieved with all the skill Essex showed in Nevile's Court in Trinity and the front court in Christ's: eighteenth-century ashlar and, where appropriate, eighteenth-century windows, were made to live contentedly with the great Tudor windows of the old hall. All this, completed between 1760 and 1764, made the western range seem more incongruous than ever.

'March 11, 1769. Whereas the building opposite to the chappel is in so ruinous a condition that the Surveyor says that it can stand but very few years, agreed that the butteries and the building running from thence to the street be immediately pulled down, and rebuilt according to the plan drawn by Sir James Burrough some years since.' In the event, Essex was employed to replace the whole western range and provide a new west front and entrance to replace the old college entrance in Emmanuel Street. In this the Ionic motif of the Westmorland Building was repeated, and a

---

[29] Willis and Clark 1886/1988, II, 714, from Bennet's Book II, 45.
[30] See p. 296; Willis and Clark 1886/1988, II, 715n., citing Bennet's Book II, 46.
[31] Willis and Clark 1886/1988, II, 714; RCHM Cambridge, I, 67–8; Cocke 1984, p. 29.
[32] Cocke 1984, p. 29. For what follows, see RCHM Cambridge, I, 67–8; Willis and Clark 1886/1988, II, 714.

fine western range designed with a new north wing to balance the profile of the Westmorland building to the south, and a centre of characteristic dignity and restraint: as at Queens', Essex devised a much quieter version of Gibbs' building at King's – and other similar buildings of the age – and within the court he completed what Wren had begun a hundred years before. The outcome is one of the most dignified and harmonious of college courts – harmonious in spite of the variety of the themes and motifs of three different architects. Clearly the chief credit for this goes to Essex. The College Order was not obeyed, 'the plan of Sir James Burrough being departed from in almost every instance, and in some considerably improved'.[33] Thus William Bennet, and in July 1769 a second order accepted Essex's plan for the western range. Bennet concludes:

> 'When the great repairs of the hall, chapel, and now of the front or cloyster building (in all which £10,000 was expended) are consider'd, it reflects the highest honour on Dr Richardson's Mastership, whose economy in college affairs provided the funds, and whose good sense directed the expenditure' – and he goes on to give Richardson the character quoted above.[34] Be this as it may, the expense of building was beyond the funds raised by subscription – £1796 was spent in the campaign of 1760–4 and £2857 for the rebuilding of the western range in 1769–75. Richardson left the college in debt, and in March 1776 the pattern of earlier generations was repeated: 'we the master and major part of the fellows have determin'd . . . that none of the vacant fellowships can be fill'd up for the present'.[35]

The nineteenth century, to 1871

Before the new west front was finished, the main entrance had been from the north; once this had ceased to be an entry of consequence, future generations could think of enclosing the space between the kitchens and the old library. Bungay Court, at the north-west corner of the precinct, had been partly engulfed by Essex's building; in its place came the New Court further to the east. It was here that the main plans for new building matured in the early nineteenth century. It is striking indeed how much building work took place then, considering how quiescent was the educational and scholarly life of the college.[36] Doubtless an increase in undergraduate numbers, from the low 40s in the mid-eighteenth century to 59 in 1800 and 79 in 1820 – and perhaps the anticipation of more – stimulated the formation of New Court in the 1820s. But before that a stimulus

---

[33] Willis and Clark 1886/1988, II, 714 and n.4.
[34] Willis and Clark 1886/1988, II, 714–15n.; for the order of July 1769, ibid. p. 715.
[35] Willis and Clark 1886/1988, II, 715 and n.
[36] See pp. 401–2; and for what follows, p. 402.

of a different kind had led to a more substantial work. On 15 October 1811 fire broke out in the rooms of George Thomas, a fellow commoner, in the centre of the Westmorland Building, and gutted the building. A major work of restoration and reconstruction was needed, for which £4484 was subscribed – to which Mr Thomas contributed £500; on this occasion even the fellows contributed. 'It was rebuilt in the same style, and with the same internal arrangements, as before the fire' wrote Robert Willis – and indeed the stonework of the original building clearly survived; but burn marks survived here and there and some are still visible.[37]

In the early 1820s there was evidently some difference of opinion where the next new building should be – though agreement that more sets were needed. In 1823 a College Order approved the sealing of a contract with James Webster for the building which now forms the north side of New Court. But then came delay: plans were afoot for a large building adjoining the Brick Building in quite another part of the precinct; Charles Humfrey was employed to make plans. Humfrey was a leading Cambridge architect and developer, responsible for some of the streets to the north east of the college, notably Maids' Causeway and Willow Walk – and later to be Robert Willis's father-in-law; but his plans for Emmanuel came to nothing.[38] Webster's dull design – if he was indeed the architect – was executed; it was characteristic of the 1820s in Cambridge in being a kind of Tudor Gothic finished in stucco – a poor relation of Wilkins' New Court at Trinity, more remotely related to his and other men's work at half a dozen colleges in that age of rapid expansion.[39] Thus was Emmanuel's New Court formed; but not all in one campaign, for at first its new north wing stood unattached, later linked to the kitchens on the one hand and the library on the other. In 1828 arrangements were made for the final destruction of Bungay Court and its replacement by a building running north from the kitchen, thus closing the west side of New Court. This was designed by Arthur Browne, the architect of Magdalene Bridge, though Webster was again the contractor.[40]

Then peace reigned in the buildings of Emmanuel until the advent of Arthur Blomfield in 1871.

---

[37] Willis and Clark 1886/1988, II, 713. *RCHM Cambridge*, I, 68, seems to imply that the staircases survived. For the contribution of the fellows, see ECA COL.6.1.
[38] Willis and Clark 1886/1988, II, 716n. On Humfrey, see Colvin 1978, pp. 438–9.
[39] See e.g. *RCHM Cambridge*, I, p. lxxxiv.
[40] Willis and Clark 1886/1988, II, 716; *RCHM Cambridge*, I, 63, 70–1. On Arthur Browne see Colvin 1978, p. 150.

12

Estates and Finances 1719–1871

When Sir William Blackstone offered his Bursar's prayer at All Souls College, Oxford in 1753, he wished the new incumbent a peaceful year and successful maintenance of the status quo.[1] He could hardly have imagined how the finances and estate management of the Oxbridge colleges were to change over the next century. Changes were already in the air, but they took a while to gather momentum and the pace quickened in the early nineteenth century. Sir William would not, however, have felt totally out of place in 1871: amidst all of the alterations, there were strong threads of continuity.

Sir William wrote at a time when collegiate rental incomes were beginning to increase, when land prices were rising partly as a result of agricultural improvements and inclosure.[2] At St John's in Cambridge, for instance, some of the surplus general funds of the College were invested in property,[3] and at Balliol, Oxford, rental incomes almost tripled between 1726–7 and 1774–5.[4] During the Napoleonic Wars, the uneven rises in rents were transformed into rapid and sustained growth and Fellows' stipends and dividends increased;[5] once hostilities had ceased in 1815, rents slumped as the country entered into a period of agricultural depression. Colleges had to tighten their belts: at Queens', Cambridge, one of the poorest, Fellowships were held vacant, the audit dinners were discontinued in 1821, and economies were made in the number of feasts in 1828.[6] From the 1840s until the end of the period covered by this chapter, agriculture boomed once again and rental incomes increased.[7] Other landowners, too, fared in similar ways.[8]

---

[1] Blackstone 1898, p. 50.
[2] Searby 1997, p. 136.
[3] Howard 1935, p. 73.
[4] Beachcroft 1982, p. 84.
[5] At St Catharine's, Cambridge, the Bursar's stipend increased by £30 in 1810 and the porter's wages were put up in the same year; in the following year, the cook's wages were increased (Rich 1973, p. 200). Howard (1935, p. 137) details how the Fellowship dividend at St John's rose from £40 in 1770 to £160 in 1821.
[6] Twigg 1987, p. 305.
[7] Howard 1935, p. 204.
[8] Beckett 1989, pp. 620–3.

333

Emmanuel's fortunes were not dissimilar from those of some of its sister colleges. As at Jesus and Queens', the balance of income over expenditure hovered around zero (Fig. 7), thus contrasting with Clare and St John's Colleges, where large surpluses were shown for many years in the late eighteenth and early nineteenth centuries.[9] Evidence for periods of financial hardship at Emmanuel can be gleaned from a number of sources. In 1717 George Thorpe, 'sensible of the straitness of the Revenue of the said Emmanuel College', left the manor of Chequer Court near Ash in Kent to his *alma mater* and the property was conveyed to the College two years later.[10] Records were kept of the indebtedness of the College in the 1740s; in 1744 it was decided that, in view of the increasing debt of the garden, the deficit should in future be divided amongst those who used the facility.[11] In 1767 repairs to the Unicorn, the College

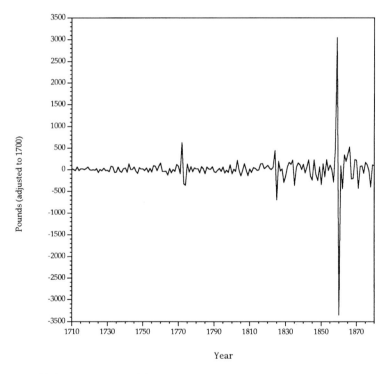

Figure 7 Balance at audit of income over expenditure 1720–1870. *Source*: ECA BUR.0.2, BUR.1.2, BUR.8.4, BUR.8.6–9, BUR.11.2, 6.

[9] Bendall 1992, p. 167. Clare College appears to have been particularly hard-hit by the agricultural depression and was in debt for many years around 1830.
[10] ECA SCH.1.17.
[11] ECA BUR.0.1; ECA COL.14.1 p. 182.

property in Petty Cury, Cambridge, cost £216, and the Society 'made that a pretence for sinking the Branthwaite Scholarships intirely', much to the ire of William Bennet who became a Fellow two years later.[12] From time to time during the eighteenth century, Fellowships were kept vacant and loans were sought to finance both general and particular projects.

Nevertheless, the incomes of Fellows, as distinct from those of the College, increased in the later part of the century. Bennet demonstrated how Fellows benefited from savings in the buttery and from degree money between 1760 and 1779 and added the comment that, 'it is curious enough that a great part of the Society are ignorant from what these Dividends arise, and whether they are imposed upon or no by the Butler in stating them'.[13] Indeed, the resident Fellows profited more than their non-resident colleagues: to receive a buttery dividend, a Fellow had to be resident for the major part of the month from 1734.[14] In 1775 it was decided that capon money should only be divided amongst those who were present at the audit, and a similar decision about sealing money was taken nine years later.[15]

Both the College and the Fellows joined with collegiate and other land-owners in experiencing a rise in real income from their estates in the nineteenth century.[16] Although Emmanuel did not seem to suffer unduly in the immediate aftermath of the French wars, rental income did take a downturn in the later 1820s (see Fig. 8). Payments from the endowment increased, however: in 1807, in view of the 'progressive improvement of the income of the College', it was agreed to pay the Master an additional £160, each Fellow another £40, and the stipends of sizars and scholars were also increased.[17] Similar decisions were taken in 1822, when the cook, the butler and the Master's servant also enjoyed pay rises;[18] in 1837, when a committee was appointed to inquire into the finances and probable expenses of the College and recommended further increases;[19] and in 1856, when there was a 'considerable surplus of income over Expenditure'.[20] It appears that shortly before this last date, Emmanuel's Master was one of the better paid amongst those heads of house who made a return to the Graham Commission in 1852–3 and the Fellows were not badly off (Fig. 9).[21] The trust estates also showed signs of financial well-being: the Johnson exhibitioners enjoyed increased allowances

[12] ECA BUR.8.6; ECA COL.9.1(A) p. 238.
[13] ECA COL.9.1(A) p. 89.
[14] ECA COL.14.1 p. 175.
[15] ECA COL.14.2 ff. 78v, 90v.
[16] Dunbabin 1997, pp. 379–81.
[17] ECA COL.14.2 f. 143r.
[18] ECA COL.14.2 f. 176v.
[19] ECA BUR.11.3; ECA COL.14.2 f. 222r.
[20] ECA COL.14.3 pp. 105–6.
[21] Graham Commission.

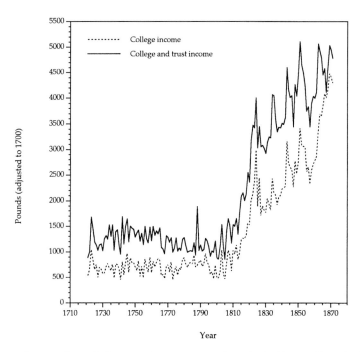

Figure 8   Income from College and trust estates from Lady Day 1720 to Lady Day 1871. *Source*: ECA BUR.1.2, BUR.11.2, 6, FEL.5.7–11, SCH.1.2–18.

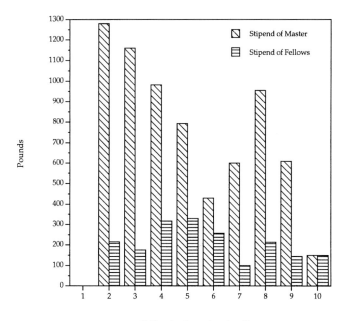

College by decreasing size of income

Figure 9   Stipend of Master and Fellows as reported to Graham Commission 1852 (1. Trinity College (no date); 2. King's College; 3. St John's College; 4. Pembroke College; 5. Christ's College; 6. Peterhouse; 7. Downing College; 8. Emmanuel College; 9. Queens' College; 10. Trinity Hall). *Source*: Graham Commission 1852–3.

in 1802;[22] annual payment to the College from the Thorpe Trust increased from £21 to £24 in 1818 and to £30 in 1845;[23] and the value of the Gillingham Fellowship was increased in 1856.[24]

The relative wealth of Emmanuel compared with other colleges is not easy to determine; it is hard to be sure that comparisons are being made of like with like, and the size of the institution affected the amount of income that was available for disposal. At Lady Day 1770, the income of Emmanuel for the preceding year was £2042,[25] compared with £6449 at St John's (a college with 52 Fellows while Emmanuel had 15)[26] and an average annual income of £1147 for the preceding decade at Queens' (which had 16 Fellows in 1764 and 21 in 1774).[27] Of the ten colleges that made returns to the Graham Commissioners in 1852–3, Emmanuel was eighth, amongst the poorest in terms of gross income (Fig. 10). The

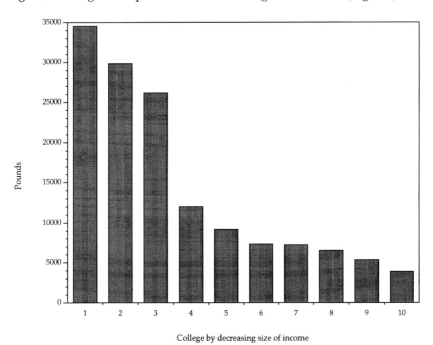

College by decreasing size of income

Figure 10 Gross income of colleges as reported to Graham Commission 1852 (1. Trinity College; 2. King's College; 3. St John's College; 4. Pembroke College; 5. Christ's College; 6. Peterhouse; 7. Downing College; 8. Emmanuel College; 9. Queens' College; 10. Trinity Hall). *Source*: Graham Commission 1852–3.

[22] ECA BUR.11.3.
[23] ECA SCH.1.17; ECA COL.14.3 p. 35.
[24] ECA FEL.5.8.
[25] ECA BUR.0.2.
[26] Howard 1935, p. 101.
[27] Twigg 1987, pp. 185, 458.

College was the fourth largest at the same time, and its per capita income was the lowest (Fig. 11), though it could afford to treat its Master and Fellows relatively well.

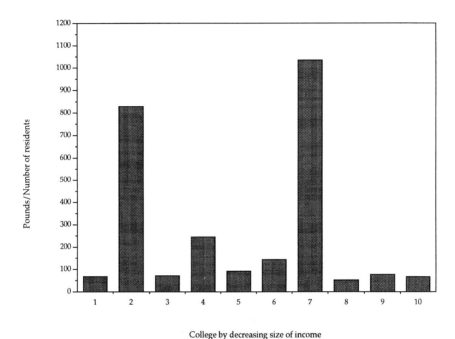

College by decreasing size of income

Figure 11   Per capita income of colleges as reported to Graham Commission 1852 (1. Trinity College; 2. King's College; 3. St John's College; 4. Pembroke College; 5. Christ's College; 6. Peterhouse; 7. Downing College; 8. Emmanuel College; 9. Queens' College; 10. Trinity Hall). *Source*: Graham Commission 1852–3.

To paint the general picture of college finances during the eighteenth and nineteenth centuries, however, it is also necessary to look at the changing distribution of the income. Rental income, though it always made up the bulk of the disposable assets of the College, fluctuated in importance. Before the 1770s it usually formed at least three-quarters of the general endowment; by the 1790s it had dropped to only just over one-half; rents became more important again in the early nineteenth century, though they took a downturn during the agricultural depression (Fig. 12). Transfers from trust estates to the College funds oscillated between 10% and 20% and were especially significant in the later eighteenth century; such transfers all but stopped when the new statutes of 1861 abolished all except the Dixie and Thorpe trusts (Fig. 13). Income from fines fluctuated between about 4% and 14% and, apart from a boom in the later 1820s, generally decreased in the early nineteenth century

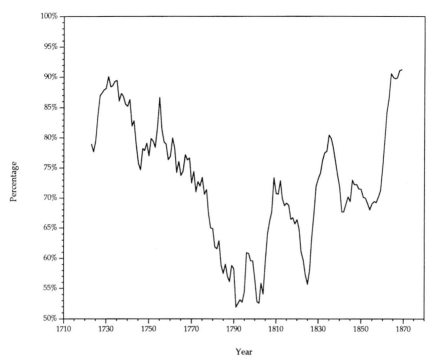

Figure 12   Percentage of College income from rents 1720–1870 (five-year moving averages). *Source*: ECA BUR.1.2, BUR.11.2, 6.

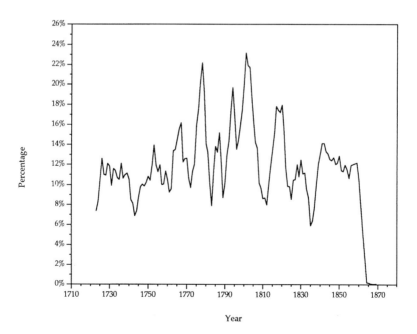

Figure 13   Percentage of College income from trust estates 1720–1870 (five-year moving averages). *Source*: ECA BUR.1.2, BUR.11.2, 6.

(Fig. 14). Investment income, on the other hand, became more important: from barely reaching 4% in the early and mid-eighteenth century, it rose markedly in the 1780s to over 20%, fell to about 12% in the early nineteenth century, and rose in the 1850s before declining once again (Fig. 15). Compared with other colleges, in 1852–3 Emmanuel depended relatively heavily on house property and investment funds for its income, and was less dependent on its farmland and tithes. Indeed, the graph in Fig. 16 shows that it was the college that depended least on farmland and most on house property, although undue importance should not be attributed to these figures as different colleges might have compiled their data in different ways. Emmanuel probably did have a more varied source of income than some of the other colleges.

New Acquisitions 1719–1871

In contrast to the early years of the College, relatively few new benefactions arrived during the eighteenth and nineteenth centuries. Emmanuel had been established and was running satisfactorily; further donations were not essential to its existence. As with other colleges, Emmanuel was given property, or funds to buy land, from time to time, and three major

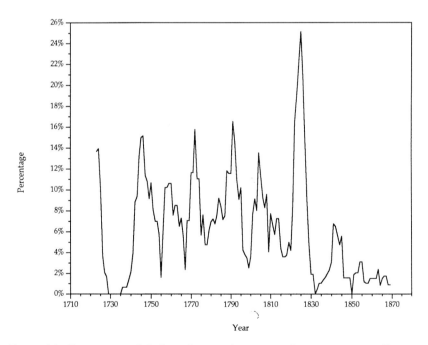

Figure 14 Percentage of College income from entry fines 1720–1870 (five-year moving averages). *Source*: ECA BUR.1.2, BUR.11.2, 6.

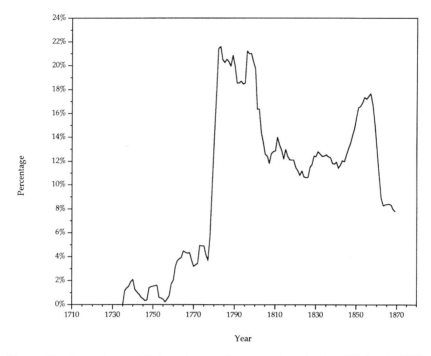

Figure 15   Percentage of College income from investments in public funds 1720–1870 (five-year moving averages). *Source*: ECA BUR.1.2, BUR.11.2, 6.

new estates were acquired between 1719 and 1738 through bequests from two former Fellows and from a member of the College. For nearly a century thereafter, however, no new estates were given or bequeathed – the licence of mortmain to hold land to the annual value of £500 which had been purchased in 1729 was noted as not being full in 1787[28] – and it was not until 1832 that the next major accession to the College's property portfolio was made. Experiences of other colleges varied: although St John's, likewise, did not acquire any new properties between 1729 and 1817, Gonville and Caius continued to add to its estates throughout the period.[29] The story of Emmanuel does not end here: monetary gifts, some of them substantial, were also received. Some were solicited for specific purposes, others were unprompted.

George Thorpe made a handsome bequest. He was one of the Fellows who was elected under William Sancroft the younger's Mastership in a move to alter the character of Restoration Emmanuel. The newly elected Fellow came from Caius in 1663 and returned there in 1667; indeed,

[28] ECA Charter Cabinet Drawer 4; ECA COL.9.1(A) p. 83. See p. 98.
[29] Howard 1935, pp. 286–93; Gross 1912.

341

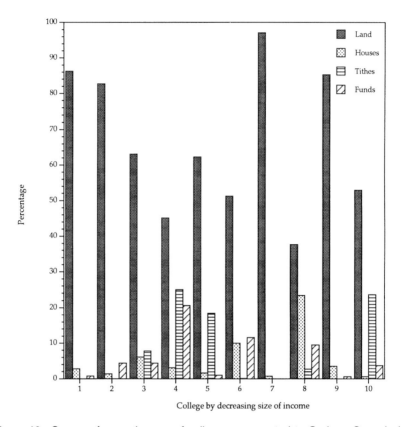

Figure 16   Source of gross income of colleges as reported to Graham Commission 1852 (1. Trinity College; 2. King's College; 3. St John's College; 4. Pembroke College; 5. Christ's College; 6. Peterhouse; 7. Downing College; 8. Emmanuel College; 9. Queens' College; 10. Trinity Hall). *Source*: Graham Commission 1852–3.

Emmanuel was lucky to be the College which largely benefited under his will – Caius might have expected to have been the main beneficiary. Instead, Thorpe just left some books for the Caius Library.[30] A Prebendary of Canterbury from 1680–1719, Thorpe made his will in March 1717 and left the manor and farm of Chequer Court at Ash-next-Sandwich in Kent to Emmanuel to endow five divinity scholarships, to make a contribution towards the general purposes of the College, and to pay for a commemoration service and dinner either on 24 November (the anniversary of Sancroft's death)[31] or on the day of his own death (in fact, only three

---

[30] Venn, *Caius*, I, pp. 387–8.

[31] The significance of this date had been forgotten by the 1780s: William Bennet, in his descriptions of the College estates, said that 24 November was 'probably his [Thorpe's] birth day' (ECA COL.9.1(A) p. 122).

days earlier). Thorpe also decreed that his estate should be well administered, with properly kept and audited accounts, regular holding of the
manorial court, and accumulation of a reserve fund from surplus
income.[32] Two years after he made his will, on 28 August 1719, the
Fellows elected Thorpe, who was in his 80s, Master of Emmanuel. He
declined, and died nearly three months later.[33]

Richard Gillingham was admitted a sizar at Emmanuel in 1687 and
then went into the church. Though he had been a poor student, by the
time he died in 1721 he was in a position to leave £1600 to his college to
endow a Fellowship. A Chancery decree was sought to settle the gift;[34]
the money was used to buy an estate at St Cross in Suffolk on 29 January
1723[35] and the remainder was invested in funds. Thus, by 1733 the Trust
was able to receive an annual income of £55 from rents and £14 from
investment in the South Sea Annuities.[36] Gillingham's bequest was,
however, divisive. His Fellowship, which received the total income from
the estate and investments (less expenses), was more valuable than those
of the foundation Fellows (who received £10 a year).[37] Consequently, in
1732 an order was passed that, 'it will much conduce to the peace, and
tranquility of the College' if the Fellowship were offered to each of the
existing Fellows in turn, in order of seniority.[38] By 1751, second thoughts
had occurred and the Master and Fellows decided 'unanimously' that to
dispose of the Fellowship in such a way was inconsistent with the intention of Gillingham's will and the consequent decree in Chancery. In the
future, new Fellows were to be elected to fill vacancies; John Brigham,
whose turn it had been to succeed into the Fellowship, did not sign the
order.[39] The decision in itself led to further problems and to disputes over
the privileges to which the Gillingham Fellow was entitled. Eventually,
the Masters of Christ's and Corpus were called upon to adjudicate and
they determined in 1756 that the Gillingham Fellow was to have a status
equal to those on the foundation.[40] Murmurs of discontent still rumbled
on: thus in 1772, it was decided that the Gillingham Fellow was only
entitled to a share of sealing money when there were insufficient foundation Fellows to make a majority without him;[41] he was allowed a share of
the profits of coals 16 years later.[42]

[32] ECA SCH.1.17.
[33] Shuckburgh 1904, p. 127; Venn; see also p. 295.
[34] ECA COL.14.1 p. 139.
[35] ECA COL.9.1(B) pp. 61–2.
[36] ECA FEL.5.7.
[37] ECA BUR.8.4.
[38] ECA COL.14.1 pp. 171, 173.
[39] ECA COL.14.1 p. 174.
[40] ECA COL.14.2 ff. 43v–45v.
[41] ECA COL.14.2 f. 71v.
[42] ECA COL.14.2 f. 98r.

The four middle Fellows profited from the benefaction of John Brown. An undergraduate at Pembroke College, he moved to Emmanuel to a Fellowship in 1687 and continued a Fellow until 1715; the previous year, he had been presented to the College living of Wallington in Hertfordshire and he remained there until his death in 1736.[43] Under his will, £1000 in Old South Sea Annuities was left to Emmanuel to augment the Mastership, £500 in South Sea trading stock to augment the stipends of the four middle Fellows (the four seniors already benefited from the Pinchbeck tithes), £500 in the same stock to endow two Greek scholarships, £50 to the College library and first choice of his books. Pembroke College was not entirely forgotten: it was to have second choice of the books and the profits of the sale of the remainder were to be divided between the two Colleges.[44] In addition, an estate in Canterbury was left to the Dean of the Cathedral there to send a scholar from the King's School to either of Brown's colleges; under the constraints of the Mortmain Act, this part of the bequest could not take place.[45] Two years later, in 1738, Emmanuel bought a messuage, lands and the impropriation of Rushall, Langmere and Dickleburgh in Norfolk (and near St Cross) for £1780,[46] leaving £276 in stock.[47] The purchase included the advowson of Rushall, which the College could not hold under the 1735 Mortmain Act and so asked that it be settled on the Vicar of Fressingfield.[48]

No further estates were acquired until 1832, although there had been a possibility that the College might receive land in Lincolnshire and Suffolk to endow two Fellowships and four scholarships under the will of Thomas Fynn, a Fellow from 1710 to 1715, which was proved in 1741.[49] Emmanuel was lucky to receive lands in Hornchurch, Navestock, Stapleford Abbots and Stratford in Essex as a bequest from Henry Lusby. Although he had not been educated at Cambridge University, Lusby wanted to leave property to one of the colleges there. His will was drawn up by John Roberts who, as a friend of Richard Foley (Fellow 1825–42), advised that Emmanuel be the lucky recipient. The estates were left to Mrs Elisabeth Gray for her lifetime; she died in 1832 and the College received lands to the annual value of £330 (net of land tax).[50]

Other gifts and bequests were made which were not invested in property. Nicholas Aspinall died in 1727 and left £100 for an exhibition;[51] Dr Michael Smith left £700 in 1773 to buy lands to endow a scholarship, to

[43] Venn.
[44] ECA Box 9.Oa21.
[45] ECA SCH.1.4; ECA COL.9.1(A) p. 233.
[46] ECA Box 20.K1–3.
[47] ECA SCH.1.4.
[48] ECA Box 20.K1.
[49] ECA Box 9.Oa22.
[50] ECA Box 16.A2; ECA Es.1.1; ECA FEL.5.11.
[51] ECA Box 9.Oa20.

help to repair the chapel and to augment the Fellows' commons on Commencement Sunday and the money was invested in securities.[52] Five years later, a much more significant bequest was made. Henry Hubbard, who came to a Fellowship at Emmanuel from St Catharine's in 1732 and was Tutor for many years, intended to leave £1000 in stocks to his second college.[53] Various members of the College received small bequests besides: all of the Fellows were left books and Richard Farmer and John Askew were left other items too, and Hubbard's bedmaker and servant in the College kitchens were also beneficiaries.[54] In fact, Hubbard's residuary legatee predeceased his potential benefactor and the College received £5800.[55] The bequest made a significant impact: the stipend of the Master (£60) was increased by £40, the four senior Fellows each enjoyed a doubling of their stipends with an additional £10, and a Fellowship that had been left vacant to help to pay for the costs of the new entrance range to the College was filled again.[56] In the early nineteenth century, Bishop Hurd, a former Fellow, left £2000 in 4% consols in 1808,[57] another former Fellow, William Hardyman, left £1000 in 1829 which endowed a prize to the best commencing classic each year[58] and smaller gifts were made by David Pyke Watts in 1806[59] and the Reverend Octavius Glover in 1865.[60] From time to time the College received gifts and bequests from others, too: appeals were made to fund specific projects such as the Essex building; money, books, plate and other items were also donated.

The financial resources of the College therefore increased partly as a result of gifts and bequests which were made to it during the eighteenth and nineteenth centuries. Many of these donations were, however, appropriated for specific purposes: the Master and Fellows enjoyed increased stipends, more scholarships became available and building projects were supported. Benefactions contributed far less to the sums that were available to support the general running of the College – the only major bequest which did so was that of Henry Lusby – and the growth in real income demonstrated in Fig. 8, therefore, reflects other forces at work.

---

[52] ECA COL.9.1(A) p. 239; ECA BUR.11.3; ECA COL.14.2 f. 76v.
[53] To Hubbard's bequest of £200 to enlarge Dean Sudbury's endowment of an annual award of £6 for a piece of plate, John Cooke subsequently left £200 to augment further the plate money; he died shortly before February 1850 (ECA Box 9.Oa27).
[54] ECA Box 9.Oa24.
[55] ECA BUR.11.3; ECA COL.9.1(A) p. 90; see also p. 302.
[56] ECA COL.14.2 ff. 79r, 81v.
[57] ECA COL.14.2 f. 146v.
[58] The bequest was subject to a life interest and so did not arrive at Emmanuel until 1837 (ECA Box 9.Oa27; ECA COL.14.2 ff. 198r, 222v).
[59] An exhibition worth £10 a year (ECA COL.14.2 f. 142r).
[60] £100 to promote the study of Hebrew (ECA COL.14.3 p. 171).

College Finances and Their Administration

The Bursars and their accounts

The practice that had become established in the mid-seventeenth century, of the Master taking on the Bursarship, continued until the final years of the eighteenth century; regular payment of a stipend for performance of bursarial duties, however, only started in mid-century. Only on Farmer's death, in 1797, did the Master exercise his right to delegate the office to a Fellow. The rate of turnover of Bursars varied from college to college: at Gonville and Caius, Bursars rarely held office for longer than three or four years;[61] at St John's, the Senior Bursars tended to hold office for a little longer, though none surpassed the 30-year tenure of Charles Blick from 1816 to 1846.[62] William Holme, Robert Birkett and William Castlehow each ran the finances of Emmanuel for periods exceeding ten years (see Appendix 2). From 1756, the Master was paid £20 a year out of the study rents for his duties as Bursar;[63] the stipend continued at this level when the office was delegated to Tyson in 1797, was doubled in 1804[64] and again in 1818,[65] was increased to £100 in 1835[66] and to £130 in 1856.[67] Payment of the Senior Bursar at St John's similarly started in the 1750s (though he and his predecessors had previously invested cash balances in public funds for their own emolument):[68] in 1757, he was allowed £30 annually in addition to existing perquisites; over time, he was paid sums in lieu of these allowances and his stipend eventually stabilised at £160.[69] St John's was a larger and richer college so it is hardly surprising that its Bursar was better paid than his counterpart at Emmanuel.

The bursarial Masters – William Savage, William Richardson and Richard Farmer – all appear to have taken seriously their duties as the College's financial officer. They kept the accounts in their own hands (there was no Bursar's clerk), summarised the terms of the endowments of the various trust estates at the front of the account book of each one, and generally kept a close eye on what went on. The accounts of receipts and divisions of fines for the renewal of leases, for example, contain many notes by William Savage commenting on and explaining the levels at

[61] Hall 1990a, pp. 123–4.
[62] Howard 1935, p. 284. Blick's long tenure was not in the College's best interest; he mismanaged the finances and was not re-elected in 1846 (Howard 1935, pp. 159–62, 171–2).
[63] ECA COL.14.2 f. 46r.
[64] ECA COL.14.2 f. 136v.
[65] ECA COL.14.2 f. 166v.
[66] ECA COL.14.2 f. 212r.
[67] ECA COL.14.3 p. 106.
[68] Miller 1961, p. 50.
[69] Howard 1935, pp. 134–5.

which they were set.[70] William Richardson made similar notes and he seems to have examined drafts of leases carefully. In the register of leases, he wrote 'I do not understand this' and 'what?' by a lease to Charles Clarke of land in Godmanchester in 1744,[71] and he commented on a lease of land at Mitcham and Clapham in Surrey, dated 26 January 1736,[72] that a clause against alienation should be included: this was done when the lease was renewed in 1742.[73] Richardson also compiled an historical register which gave details, amongst others, about the College's estates[74] and, when he started a new rental in 1736, he changed the layout so that the rents due, the number of quarters owed and the sums received could be entered separately.[75] Less laudably, many accounts for trust estates were not balanced annually: while Savage had provided yearly summaries for the Gillingham Fellowship accounts, Richardson only did so when the page was full.[76] Similarly, the Dixie accounts were only settled in 1741 and 1775.[77]

Farmer has been accused of having been 'a poor man of business',[78] but there is much evidence that he, too, paid close attention to his bursarial duties. Like Richardson, Farmer also made additions in the register of leases: for example, he filled in gaps that had been left by the scribe in a lease of land at Gransden in 1784,[79] and he habitually wrote 'examined' at the end of each entry. He restored the practice of balancing the accounts of trust estates annually and he numbered carefully the vouchers for expenditure; these were examined at each audit and compared with entries in the Bursar's long book. Indeed, these vouchers demonstrate the detailed involvement of Farmer in his College's finances. He seems to have paid tradesmen himself on many occasions and wrote out the receipts to be signed. He also amplified the detail on some vouchers to state more precisely what specific items of expenditure were for: when a plumber worked in the lodge in 1786–7, for instance, Farmer inserted that the bill was for 'Lead-Pipes, &c'.[80] He chased up outstanding bills, if necessary: in 1778, he asked for a bill for wax candles and ordered some more:

> I do not see by our Agent's Account which I have
> just now received that you \are/ paid for the last

[70] ECA BUR.3.2.
[71] ECA BUR.6.4 pp. 45–7.
[72] ECA BUR.6.3 pp. 697–9.
[73] ECA Box 28.A18.
[74] ECA COL.9.2.
[75] ECA BUR.11.3.
[76] ECA FEL.5.7.
[77] ECA SCH.1.15.
[78] Shuckburgh 1904, p. 134.
[79] ECA BUR.6.4 pp. 405–8.
[80] ECA BUR.0.3(c).

> Parcel of Wax-Candles. please to call on Mr
> Nicholls, N.88 Queen-street, Cheapside, & \He will/
> pay you & likewise for the usual Quantity, which I
> wish for as soon as possible. We must have 2 Pair
> of large Tapers. Pray, send 2 or 3 Pounds of the
> smallest sort immediately.[81]

Criticism of Farmer's business methods is not, however, totally un-founded. There are gaps in the accounts of some of the trust estates during his Mastership and an explanatory note in the Dixie accounts that, 'The Fellows, being generally non-resident, & paid by Drafts, &c: & the Scholars, as Pupils, having their stipends deducted in the Quarterly Bills, I continued the Account in my private Books'.[82] For other trust estates, such as for Shernborne and Rushall, the accounts were kept in very summary form.[83] This was not the way to conduct College affairs and it is indisputable that when he died the accounts were in a muddle. Six hundred and eighty-two pounds were received by the College from the estate,[84] the Sudbury plate was not awarded in 1797 as it was 'Included in the late Master's Accounts towards making up the deficiencies of the pre-ceding years',[85] and Mr Tyson was asked to accept a piece of plate to the value of 20 guineas in 1799, partly 'in consideration of the extraordinary trouble which . . . [he had] experienced in settling the Accounts of the College with the Administrator of the late Master'.[86]

Never again was the Master to be Bursar: henceforward the office was delegated and, simultaneously, account keeping became more rigorous. The numbers of vouchers that were presented at each audit immediately grew, to perhaps half as many again as during Farmer's Mastership.[87] From 1799, those accounts that were not audited in public were to be examined on the day preceding the Easter Audit by the two senior resident Fellows and signed on behalf of the College.[88] London bankers, Messrs Hoare and Co., were appointed in 1834;[89] and a structured break-down of receipts was introduced into the new rental which was started in 1844 when the previous volume became full.[90] The new statutes of 1861 resulted in the passing of College orders that the financial year was to start at the Easter Audit, that the two auditors should be paid £5 each and

---

81 ECA BUR.0.3(a).
82 ECA SCH.1.15.
83 ECA SCH.1.3–4.
84 ECA BUR.11.3.
85 ECA SCH.1.12.
86 ECA COL.14.2 f. 121r.
87 ECA BUR.0.3(d).
88 ECA COL.14.2 f. 120r.
89 ECA COL.14.2 f. 211r.
90 ECA BUR.11.4: the headings in the rental were arrears, rents, when payment was due, reductions allowed, sums received, and monies now due.

that a scholarship fund should be created.[91] The format of the rental changed slightly as income was included from all of the trust estates except the Dixie and Thorpe trusts; the rental was first signed by the auditors in 1867, and in 1869 the balances of separate accounts were also given.[92] Records of expenditure, too, became more refined with the new statutes. For the first time, a breakdown was given by subject – insurances, leases, materials and repairs, tradesmens' bills – and, again from 1867, the accounts were signed by the auditors.[93] The build-up of College reserves commenced in 1867 with the decision to allocate £850 annually to a repair fund from which to pay insurance premiums and landlord's repairs;[94] before then, only minor accumulations had occurred as with the Gillingham Fellowship in 1732[95] and the Johnson exhibition in 1802.[96]

The Bursars took their duties as seriously as had their magisterial predecessors. William Holme, Bursar from 1809 to 1826, clearly had a grip on the College's finances. He demonstrated his tight control from the start: after less than a year in office, he was writing sternly to the tenant of Rushall in Norfolk about his 'pretended' estimate for repairs to the house, brew-house, dairy and granary. Holme presumed that Thomas Smith 'did not mean to mock' the College, but how else could it agree on such 'vague unmeaning statements?' So long as there was a 'particle of common sense' amongst the Fellowship, the Society could never allow College property to be 'squandered away';[97] and three years later in 1813, Holme queried a small bill for repairs and deducted 19s 11½d from the tenant's claim.[98] He continued as he had started: he demanded precise information from tenants (such as the types of pollards to be felled for repairs at Stondon in 1817),[99] he paid close attention to leases and their covenants (in 1825, he specified how covenants should be altered in a lease of Lydden and Ewell in Kent),[100] he ensured that he understood how rents and fines were calculated (as at Holborn in 1823),[101] and he took care that the College's rights were vigorously defended by the tenants (especially at Hyde Farm between 1822 and 1825 and at Lydden and Ewell in 1824).[102] William Castlehow similarly stands out in the estate correspondence as a Bursar who was particularly concerned with the

[91] ECA COL.14.3 pp. 144–5, 147–8.
[92] ECA BUR.11.4.
[93] ECA BUR.8.9.
[94] ECA COL.14.3 p. 184.
[95] ECA COL.14.1 pp. 171, 173.
[96] ECA BUR.11.3.
[97] ECA Nf.5.8.
[98] ECA Nf.5.13.
[99] ECA Es.4.4k.
[100] ECA Ke.6.487.
[101] ECA Lo.11.135.
[102] ECA Sr.17.41–64 *passim*; ECA Ke.6.475–81.

management of the College's property. (It was during his period of office that the bath house was repaired and the 'Pond in the Fellows' Garden' – the swimming pool – was cleaned out and bricked, and so Castlehow's name and the date, June 1855, are recorded in the pool today.)[103] Nor were the other Bursars negligent. They tried to become familiar with the College's estates: Holland visited the London estates in September 1829 (though he had already been in office for two-and-a-half years by this time);[104] when George John Archdall took over in 1832, he was soon invited to the next rent day at Sutton Coldfield so that he could meet the tenants;[105] and Thomas Hewitt inspected the Old Bailey property in 1865 shortly after he had taken up his post.[106]

Not surprisingly, hiccups occurred from time to time. Bursars asked their predecessors for advice: William Holme requested help from both Tyson and Smythies over the College's ownership of land in Gransden in 1826.[107] Thus, doubts and uncertainties could easily arise over the exact extent of holdings; additionally, the College could lose track of its dues. In 1823, the Haberdashers' Company rediscovered the two exhibitions due to Emmanuel that had been endowed by Lady Romney in 1643, and they were re-established soon afterwards.[108] Henry Holland's bursarship, too, was not without its failings: in 1831 and 1832, he received £25 from the Old Bailey estate which he did not pass on to the College.[109]

Private landowners, like colleges, used unsophisticated methods of accountancy in the early to mid-eighteenth century based on the 'charge' and 'discharge' method. Under this system, all receipts ('charges') appeared on one side, all payments ('discharges') on the other and incomes and expenditures were not normally grouped together; hence, it was not possible to see the profitability of particular enterprises or estates.[110] During the eighteenth century, estate accounts came to be presented more systematically under various heads of income and expenditure;[111] Guy's Hospital broke down its accounts in this way from 1760[112] and St John's College, Cambridge, did so from 1770.[113] It was another 70 years before Emmanuel followed suit and Queens' College did not start to reform its accounts until 1851.[114]

[103] ECA COL.14.3 p. 101.
[104] ECA BUR.0.4(d); ECA COL.14.2 f. 191r.
[105] ECA Wa.1.88, 90.
[106] ECA Lo.11.129a.
[107] ECA Box 14.C8, C11.
[108] ECA BUR.0.4(c).
[109] ECA BUR.11.3.
[110] Martin 1979, p. 26; Pollard 1965, pp. 210–1.
[111] Mingay 1963, pp. 174–5.
[112] Trueman 1980, p. 35.
[113] Howard 1935, pp. 90–106.
[114] Twigg 1987, p. 307.

The use of firms of bankers to provide financial facilities hitherto available from goldsmiths, private individuals and, informally, from merchants, developed from the late seventeenth century in the metropolis and from the mid-eighteenth century in the provinces. Colleges took advantage of these new opportunities at varying times: in Oxford, two colleges opened accounts with bankers during the 1720s,[115] Christ Church commenced its bank book in 1764[116] and by the third quarter of the eighteenth century a number of colleges in Oxford had opened bank accounts in London.[117] At Cambridge, St John's used a firm of London bankers from 1765 but St Catharine's did not open an account until 1845, 11 years after Emmanuel.[118]

Fellowship dividends remained sacrosanct: until the mid-nineteenth century, surpluses were divided and reserves were only built up in a half-hearted way, if at all. Thus, although St Catharine's built up an improvement fund from 1853, the annual rate of transfer had been much reduced by 1867: the Fellows had been overwhelmed by a desire to increase their dividends.[119] Pembroke College established a repair fund in 1844, and a reserve fund was created at Caius in 1860.[120] Emmanuel took part in the trend and followed a few years later; it was not usual for private landlords to have repair and improvement accounts before the 1870s.[121]

The Bursar's power was limited: many decisions, some of them quite trivial, were taken by the Master and Fellows at College meetings. The Society authorised repairs and improvements. Sometimes these were major, such as building a farmhouse at Cuckoo Farm, Pinchbeck in 1846 at a cost to the College of over £400;[122] on other occasions they were minor, for instance allowance of £14 8s 3d for drainage tiles and £7 15s for a new pump there in 1850.[123] Approval also had to be given for ploughing up pasture: Robert Everitt was allowed to break up nine acres at Pinchbeck in 1844 and the tenant at Rushall was given permission to plough up about half of this amount two years later.[124] Not only were all new leases and renewals sealed in the presence of the Master and Fellows, but permission also had to be given for the Bursar to enter into negotiations beforehand.[125] Auditing occupied a significant amount of time: at Christ

[115] Martin and Highfield 1997, p. 276.
[116] Bill 1956, p. 9.
[117] Dunbabin 1986, p. 285.
[118] Howard 1935, p. 80; Jones 1936, p. 262.
[119] Rich 1973, p. 208.
[120] Attwater 1936, p. 113; Brooke 1985, p. 251.
[121] Holderness 1972, p. 435.
[122] ECA COL.14.3 p. 44; ECA BUR.8.9.
[123] ECA COL.14.3 p. 66.
[124] ECA COL.14.3 pp. 34, 41.
[125] For example, the Master was to treat about the renewal of The Ball in Gracechurch Street in 1786 (ECA COL.14.2 f. 94r).

Church, Oxford, the annual audit took six men eight hours spread over two days in 1801; similar details are not available for Emmanuel, a smaller landlord, but the Master and all of the Fellows were involved to some extent and the two auditors must have spent more time than their colleagues in examining the accounts. Some colleges only sealed leases at regular times of the year such as at audits; at Emmanuel, however, sealing was executed whenever necessary.[126]

While, therefore, Emmanuel was not at the forefront of changes in accounting procedures and financial management, nor was it particularly laggardly in following current trends. It was fortunate in having a sequence of responsible and adequately assiduous Masters and Bursars; Farmer, perhaps, did not follow proper practices but there is no evidence that he actually did the College serious harm. His death, at a time of wartime uncertainties and inflation, saw the start of many alterations but at the same time a strong element of continuity remained.

Financing extraordinary expenditures

It might be assumed that a consequence of the failure among colleges to build up their reserves would be the impossibility of financing any non-routine activities, such as the construction of new buildings; however, this was not so. Loans and grants were sought from a variety of sources; Fellows might be expected, either during their time in the College or after they had left, to contribute personally to generate necessary funds as a trade-off for the preservation of dividends; and by holding Fellowships vacant, the endowment could also make its contribution.

Throughout the eighteenth century, Fellowships were held vacant from time to time: savings were therefore made on stipends, and allowances were diverted to the use of the College. In January 1726, it was decided to elect no more Fellows for the time being as the College was in debt from building the Westmorland Building;[127] continuing indebtedness, need for repairs and legal expenses led to a decision to reduce the number of Fellows to seven in 1737;[128] three Fellowships were to remain vacant in 1739;[129] one outstanding vacancy and a new one were to be filled in 1742;[130] and by 1745 the College was out of debt and the remaining two vacancies were filled.[131] All remained quiet until construction of the Essex front led to a need to hold Fellowships vacant again in

---

[126] Dunbabin 1986, pp. 272, 283–4.
[127] ECA COL.14.1 p. 161.
[128] ECA COL.14.1 p. 177.
[129] ECA COL.14.1 p. 179.
[130] ECA COL.14.2 f. 14v.
[131] ECA COL.14.2 f. 20r.

1776;[132] Hubbard's bequest two years later enabled the Fellowship to be restored to its full strength.[133] Two legal suits occasioned the holding of a Fellowship and the Gillingham Fellowship vacant in 1798;[134] a Gillingham Fellow was elected in 1801,[135] and the vacant foundation Fellowship was filled in the following year.[136] Extraordinary expenditures on trust estates were on occasion financed by vacancies which might or might not have been caused deliberately: in 1736, vacancies of the Ash exhibitions were used to pay for legal expenses at Shernborne to defend rights to a sheep walk and to cultivate 12 acres.[137] Use of vacancies in these ways, largely in the eighteenth and early nineteenth centuries and mostly in connection with buildings and repairs, occurred in other colleges, too. Sidney Sussex, for example, used the practice: by 1756, there were only four Fellows left, six vacancies were filled in 1758 but Fellowships were suspended again from 1774 to 1781.[138] Later, Sidney partly financed Wyatville's rebuilding work in the 1820s and 1830s by holding Fellowships vacant once more.[139]

Colleges also financed extraordinary activities through loans, from members of the College, from friends to it, from public funds and by internal transfers. In 1726, the wish to save interest payments on a loan from a former Fellow led to the early acceptance of a fine for the renewal of 11–12 St Andrew's Street before the new lease could be sealed.[140] The inclosure of Shernborne in the 1770s led to a need for borrowing: Richardson, the Master, lent £400 in 1771, a further £300 in the following year and made the loan up to £1100 in 1775, all at 4% interest.[141] He then died, and to pay off the debt to the late Master, further sums had to be borrowed, at 4% and 5%.[142] In 1824, an Act of Parliament was passed to enable colleges to borrow money from the Public Works Commissioners for the erection of new buildings for the accommodation of students, and to mortgage rents for the same purpose.[143] Emmanuel sold stocks to enable the building of New Court in the following year.[144] St Catharine's borrowed from its Fellows in similar ways;[145] Queens' borrowed considerable sums in the

---

[132] ECA COL.14.2 f. 79r.
[133] ECA COL.14.2 f. 81v.
[134] ECA COL.14.2 f. 117r.
[135] ECA COL.14.2 f. 129r.
[136] ECA COL.14.2 f. 131v.
[137] ECA SCH.1.2; ECA Box 22.A14.
[138] Scott-Giles 1975, pp. 75, 84.
[139] Salt 1992, p. 150.
[140] ECA BUR.3.2 ff. 23v, 28v.
[141] ECA COL.14.2 ff. 70v, 72v, 78r.
[142] ECA COL.14.2 ff. 81r, 82v; ECA SCH.1.3. The loans were finally paid off in 1819 (SCH.1.3).
[143] 5 George IV, Cap.36.
[144] ECA COL.14.2 f. 186v.
[145] Rich 1973, p. 197.

early nineteenth century.[146] Loans were also made from one fund to another. The building of the Founder's Range was helped with loans of £250 from the Library and £300 from the Dixie estate, at interest, from 1722; these sums were finally paid off to the Dixie estate in 1743 and to the Library two years later.[147] The College lent sums to the trust estates on occasion: from 1797 to 1800, it helped the Whichcote and Sudbury estate;[148] in 1802, it contributed towards repairs at the Gillingham estate.[149]

At Emmanuel, as elsewhere, appeals were made for specific purposes, especially for building. Around the time when Savage became Master, money was needed for rebuilding the Founder's Range. On St David's Day 1718, a letter was written and impressed with the Master's personal seal:

> To all whose generosity, or regard for a learned education, especially to those, whose gratefull sense of having had the advantage of it in Emmanuel College will admit of an address of this nature, The Mr and Fellows of the said College find themselves under a necessity of applying for assistance towards the repairing thereof . . .

The materials of the Range had proved 'very defective' and, despite the College's best endeavours, the building had fallen into a 'ruinous condition'. The Master continued to explain that the Society was obliged to appeal for contributions to enable rebuilding 'in a better manner',

> the smallness of our revenue not allowing us to lay up any Fund that can be answerable to such a charge.
>
> And we are in hopes that the present concern for religion is not sunk so far below the piety of former times, as to render this application fruitless, that is made in behalf of a Seminary founded for such excellent purposes; which has producet [sic] many signal instances of piety and learning, and may furnish posterity with many more for the defence of the reformed religion, if supported by the timely and generous assistance of the well wishers to the Church of England.[150]

Similar appeals were made to finance the Essex Building in the 1770s and in the aftermath of the 1811 fire in the Westmorland Building.

Substantial sums were raised in these ways from members of the College and well-wishers to it. £2386 7s was donated for the Westmorland Building in 1719 from 68 persons; only one current Fellow contributed (William Draper, Dixie Fellow, gave £16) but he was joined by 17

[146] Twigg 1987, pp. 304–5.
[147] ECA BUR.8.4; ECA SCH.1.15.
[148] ECA SCH.1.12.
[149] ECA BUR.8.7.
[150] ECA BDG.1.Y1. See p. 322.

who had resigned their Fellowships. Of these, only three gave sums equal to or less than those of Draper; the rest contributed more and four donated £50 each, including John Alleyn, Rector of the valuable College living of Loughborough.[151] The Master and two Fellows gave towards the Essex Building (Richardson, Master, gave £200, Henry Hubbard donated £150 and Richard Farmer £25), with ten former Fellows (of whom five gave £100 apiece) and 26 others. The appeal after the 1811 fire attracted 52 donations: two-thirds of the current Society contributed (three gave £50 each, the rest £21), with a further 12 gifts from former Fellows (two gave £100, two £50 including the Rector of Loughborough and many others £21).[152] There was, however, an embarrassment in the 1750s when building plans were postponed and donations had to be returned.[153]

Fellows thus played a small part and in general gave – and in many cases could probably only afford – low sums. At the same time, however, they ensured that their dividends were protected and, indeed, every effort was made to guarantee them. Even when, for various reasons, fines were not received when they might have been expected, dividends were advanced by the College. At Sutton Coldfield in 1721, for example, no fine was taken as the rent was raised, but a dividend was allowed out of the estate;[154] exactly one hundred years later, the affairs of the tenant of the Horseshoe in Godmanchester were in Chancery and so the College advanced the dividend once again.[155] The most usual causes of the College lending Fellows their dividends were delays in fixing the fine or refusal of terms for renewal. Thus, when the tenant of the Four Swans in Bishopsgate Street refused the terms for renewal in 1808 and again in 1817, the dividend was advanced on both occasions.[156] The College was cautious and adopted the custom of advancing only the sum offered by the tenant rather than that demanded by the landlord.[157] In addition, the College's London agents recommended in 1807 that a percentage should be deducted from the value of the estate as the land should not be taken as security for its full value: 10% was suggested.[158] The Fellows also made sure that they enjoyed any increased benefits that accrued from particular estates and when rents were raised, as of the Four Swans in 1722, one-third of the fine was divided instead of one-quarter.[159] By the second decade of the nineteenth century, the proportion of fines to be divided had slightly increased: fines below £20 were divided in their entirety

[151] Which was worth 800 guineas a year in 1773 (ECA COL.9.1(A) p. 68).
[152] ECA COL.6.1.
[153] ECA BUR.11.3; BUR.8.6. See pp. 329–30.
[154] ECA BUR.3.2 f. 13.
[155] ECA BUR.3.3.
[156] ECA BUR.3.3.
[157] ECA Sr.1.8.
[158] ECA Sr.1.6.
[159] ECA BUR.3.2 f. 11v.

(compared with £10 in the seventeenth century), £20 was divided of fines between £20 and £80, and one-quarter was divided of fines above £80.[160] At some colleges, however, the Fellows did allow their incomes to be reduced from time to time. At Sidney, payments into the Treasury in 1814 and 1820 were linked to the nominal rent roll rather than to actual receipts, and so the spending power of the College, rather than of the Fellows, was protected.[161] When St John's suffered from mounting arrears of rent in the 1830s, it preferred to reduce dividends rather than to redirect income from building;[162] many similar reductions were made as a result of the agricultural depression in the closing decades of the century.

Investments in public funds
Although the bulk of collegiate incomes in the eighteenth and nineteenth centuries continued to come from rents, investments in public funds made increasingly significant contributions from the late eighteenth century. Private landowners led the trend;[163] colleges followed behind. Throughout the period, freehold land remained the proper form of investment of the basic endowment; funds such as South Sea stock and, later, turnpike and canal bonds and consols were essentially the destination of surplus balances.[164] Most such investments were seen as purely temporary and stocks were sold to finance inclosure and to redeem the land tax.[165]

At Emmanuel, investment in funds started with that of the remainder of Richard Gillingham's bequest in South Sea annuities, from which income was first received in 1732.[166] John Brown's gift of stock followed four years later and interest was received from 1737 (though in 1738 the bulk of the bequest was invested in land).[167] Meanwhile, the College had also taken out its first investment in funds in 1737[168] and letters of attorney were first issued to agents to receive dividends on the College's behalf in 1739.[169] Emmanuel invested in funds earlier than some other colleges: at Queens', for instance, a donation of stock in the early eighteenth century was reinvested in land and there was little interest in

[160] ECA BUR.3.3.
[161] Salt 1992, p. 149.
[162] Howard 1935, p. 168.
[163] Beckett 1986, p. 69.
[164] Dunbabin 1986, pp. 273–4.
[165] Howard 1935, p. 123. See pp. 377, 382.
[166] ECA FEL.5.7.
[167] ECA SCH.1.4.
[168] ECA BUR.11.3.
[169] ECA COL.14.2 p. 1.

securities before the late eighteenth century;[170] St John's first invested in funds in 1749;[171] Caius bought its first stocks in 1766.[172] Investments in funds at Emmanuel increased in the nineteenth century but they were still treated gingerly: Holme was reassured in 1824 that it was not improper or regarded as gambling to sell and reinvest at a more favourable price; a transaction eventually took place in 1828.[173] Some of the income so deployed came from the sale of small pieces of land to the railways, as at Mitcham in 1806 and Sutton Coldfield in 1861,[174] and from the sale of the lease of the Sempire Lands in 1823.[175] Other sums came from the investment of surplus balances, notably from the Dixie estate; the investments in this trust were still temporary as they were then used to buy advowsons.[176]

Estate management

Despite, therefore, changes in the makeup of the external revenue of the College, the bulk still came from landed property, which had to be managed. There are elements both of continuity and of change in practices of estate management during the eighteenth and nineteenth centuries. A hint of developments to come can be seen from a College order which was passed in the early years of Savage's Mastership, in 1721, that,

> for the future all matters agreed and resolved upon by the Society concerning the management, or disposal of the estate or revenue, or in any wise relating to the interest of the College, so that they may be of consequence to it, shall be entered in this book of orders by the Senior Fellow present, & subscribed by all the members of the Society that are concerned in making such agreements & resolucions.[177]

Much stemmed from such sentiments; and books to help in estate management, renewing leases and calculating fines were bought within the next decade.[178] As can be seen in Fig. 17, expenditure on management of the College's resources tended to increase during the period and was especially high in the years after Farmer's death at the outset of the Napoleonic Wars. Although these figures partly reflect increased expenditure on the Bursar's stipend, they also demonstrate that more was being spent on

---

[170] Twigg 1987, p. 301.
[171] Howard 1935, p. 80.
[172] Gross 1912, p. viii.
[173] ECA Lo.2.7; ECA COL.14.2 f. 196r.
[174] ECA BUR.11.3; ECA SCH.1.15.
[175] ECA BUR.11.3.
[176] ECA SCH.1.15. See p. 407.
[177] ECA COL.14.1 p. 135.
[178] In 1725 and 1731 (ECA BUR.8.4). The 1731 purchase was Edward Laurence's *A Dissertation on Estates upon Lives and Years, Whether in Lay or Church-Hands* (see Bendall 1992, p. 164).

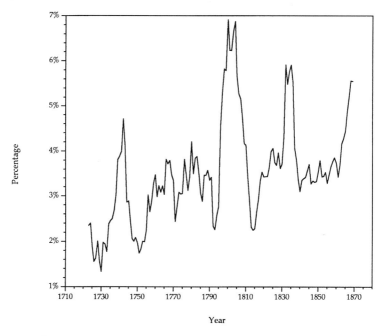

Figure 17 Percentage of College and trust income spent on agency and management 1720–1870 (five-year moving averages). *Source*: ECA BUR.1.2, BUR.8.4, 6–9, BUR.11.2, 6, FEL.5.7–11, SCH.1.2–18.

the use of agents and on management of estates, both directly by the College itself and also by agents on its behalf.

Agents, surveyors and rent collectors

As in earlier years, colleges used agents to receive their rents for them and to manage their estates. In the eighteenth and nineteenth centuries there was increasing reliance on professional agents, who also came to collect investment income on behalf of their clients. Expenditure on agents accordingly increased: the annual salary of Emmanuel's Receiver of Rents rose from £6 to £10 in 1779,[179] and doubled to £20 in 1849.[180] Payment for collecting rents from the Thorpe estate doubled to £4 per annum in 1819 and further increased to £6 in 1845;[181] at Rushall, too, the rent collector enjoyed salary increases[182] and the Dixie estate first bore the costs of an agent and rent collector from 1827.[183]

[179] ECA BUR.8.6.
[180] ECA BUR.8.9.
[181] ECA SCH.1.17.
[182] ECA SCH.1.4–5.
[183] ECA SCH.1.15.

In increasing their dependence on agents, colleges were participating in a current trend: from the mid-eighteenth century, the number of competent estate stewards increased in response to, and resulted in, growing demand for their services by both private and institutional landlords. Lawyers came to be replaced by men who were trained in land agency and who managed and administered estates rather than supervised their legal and financial aspects. These land agents were increasingly business-like and worked for a number of employers, and the relationship between landlords, agents and tenants was critical.[184] For example, the Corporation of the Sons of the Clergy began to keep a closer watch over its tenants and leases in the 1730s and appointed a more efficient bailiff to supervise the running of its Stowe estate in 1735.[185] Secretaries who managed episcopal estates became increasingly efficient and served for longer periods, and problems of corruption decreased.[186] From the 1780s, Thomas William Coke depended less on his steward at Holkham in Norfolk to let farms on the estate and employed outside valuers and agents instead; when Francis Blaikie became agent in 1816, methods of estate management were revised and letter books were introduced in which copies of all in- and out-going correspondence were kept.[187] By this time, many professional stewards ran estates, took initiatives, made all of the day-to-day decisions and framed long-term policies,[188] with the chief concern still being to find able tenants.[189]

Much of Emmanuel's business was conducted by firms of London agents. There is little evidence that the early employees were much more than rent collectors. George Lightfoot of Blackfriars, for instance, was a grocer but he also collected rents for the College from 1730 and administered the bequest of John Brown.[190] A succession of firms followed:

1746   Richard Grainger (gentleman) – Bankrupt 1749,[191]
1749   John Shepherd of Smithfield[192] – Dismissed,
1762   Charles Bathurst of London,[193]
1763   William Currie (factor) of Thames St[194] – Died
and replaced by brother Luke (died 1773).[195]

---

[184] Beckett 1989, pp. 590–6.
[185] Cox 1978, p. 60.
[186] Virgin 1989, p. 60.
[187] Parker 1975, pp. 101, 136.
[188] Hainsworth 1987, p. 162.
[189] Spring 1963, p. 178.
[190] ECA BUR.0.9; BUR.8.4; BUR.6.3 ff. 701v–2v, 704v–5r.
[191] ECA COL.14.2 f. 23v.
[192] ECA COL.14.2 f. 27v.
[193] ECA COL.14.2 ff. 54v, 55r.
[194] ECA COL.14.2 f. 57v.
[195] ECA COL.14.2 f. 65v.

Letters of attorney were sealed to Nathaniel Nicholls of London, gentleman and attorney, in 1773 when Currie died, and Nicholls and his successors managed the College's property and finances until the middle of the nineteenth century. The partners became increasingly business-like and in 1807 announced that they would keep a register of reports that they had made to the College and a portfolio of plans.[196] They practised under various names:

by 1795   Nicholls and Nettleshipp,[197]
1806   Thomas Nettleshipp and his brother William,[198]
1822   William retired, Henry Bicknell a partner,[199]
1834   Henry Bicknell alone,[200] retired 1858.[201]

Mark Anthony Reyroux took over in 1858,[202] and Messrs Smith, Payne and Smith (London agents of the Cambridge bankers Mortlock and Co.) were appointed to receive dividends.[203] Reyroux soon made his mark and improved the College's control over the collection of quit rents: those of Letchworth and Leesthorpe, which it had been customary to collect once every four years were, he recommended, to be called in yearly in the future.[204]

   Although the College's London agents managed many of its estates in Essex and Surrey as well as in London, they did not have a monopoly over estate business for Emmanuel, even in the capital. Other properties were looked after by different firms and, as in previous years, Fellows and other non-professional agents also acted as rent collectors from time to time. In London and Surrey, George Gwilt (an architect who achieved sufficient distinction to be buried in St Saviour's Southwark in 1856 and was a son of the county surveyor for Surrey)[205] surveyed and valued for the Nettleshipps from 1799. He then came to manage some of the properties of Emmanuel: he was appointed rent collector for the land in Threadneedle Street in 1831,[206] and granted power of attorney for the care of certain London estates in 1835.[207] George offered his resignation in 1850; his son, Alfred, replaced him, first temporarily and then in 1854 on a permanent basis.[208] When Henry Bicknell retired in 1858, Alfred hoped,

[196] ECA Lo.2.1a.
[197] ECA BUR.0.9.
[198] ECA COL.14.2 f. 141v.
[199] ECA Es.2.1h.
[200] ECA COL.14.2 f. 210r.
[201] ECA Lo.1.69.
[202] ECA COL.14.3 p. 121.
[203] ECA COL.14.3 p. 123.
[204] ECA BUR.0.5(b).
[205] Bendall 1997, G347, G347.1; *DNB*.
[206] ECA COL.14.2 f. 203v.
[207] ECA COL.14.2 f. 213v.
[208] ECA Lo.1.1–2; ECA COL.14.3 pp. 68, 95.

in vain, to take over management of the rest of the London property.[209] By this time the situation had become very complicated and even responsibility for a particular estate had become divided: in the previous year, Gwilt had taken over the management of part of the College's property in St Dunstan's Alley whilst the remainder was left in Bicknell's care.[210]

Elsewhere, the Lusby estate was managed by John Roberts until 1850 and then by Edward Phillips;[211] and the Sutton Coldfield estate was looked after by W. S. Perkins from 1828 to 1864 and then by his son, Edward.[212] Rents were also collected by tenants, Fellows and others: after commutation, the tenants of Little Melton and Rushall collected the tithes there for the College in 1844,[213] and in 1797 Henry Yeats Smythies, shortly to become Bursar, collected the quit rents at Lavenham (they were only collected once every seven years as they were 'so trifling').[214] Another type of non-professional agent, a housekeeper, was employed from 1824 to look after the minutiae of the Threadneedle Street property on a daily basis.[215]

Lack of proper agents gave rise to problems from time to time. Collection of the Fleet rents caused many difficulties over the years: in 1802, arrears of nearly 60 years were recovered after distraining on the lessee[216] and the Nettleshipps complained about the difficulty of collecting the College's dues in 1813 and 1816; indeed, they wished that the rents could be sold.[217] Two years later, the collector had further problems, as happened again in 1825 when it was difficult to discover which lands were liable to the rent charge.[218] If only there had been a vigilant local agent, the problems could have been avoided. Similarly, the collector of the quit rents at Lavenham had problems in 1864 as some of the land had changed hands without the purchasers having been informed of their liabilities. Closer observation of land transactions in the area would clearly have been an advantage.[219] Lack of an agent led to disagreements elsewhere, too. In 1824, for instance, it proved very difficult to persuade the College that it was liable for a chief rent at Sutton Coldfield.[220]

This description of who managed the College's estates shows that on the whole the agents performed satisfactorily: many dynasties were

[209] ECA Lo.8.80a–b, 81b.
[210] ECA Lo.11.130, 132.
[211] ECA COL.14.2 f. 208r; COL.14.3 p. 65.
[212] ECA SCH.1.15–16; ECA COL.14.3 p. 166.
[213] ECA COL.14.3 p. 30.
[214] ECA Sf.1.11; ECA COL.14.2 f. 113v.
[215] ECA Lo.8.33.
[216] ECA BUR.11.3; ECA COL.14.2 f. 131v.
[217] ECA Sr.17.17a, 19.
[218] ECA Li.10.288B–D, 290.
[219] ECA Sf.1.13.
[220] ECA Wa.1.31–2, 37.

employed and there are few tales of malpractice despite some problems in the mid-eighteenth century. Guy's Hospital had a similar experience: it drew up rules for agents to follow in the daily administration of its estates after problems of demotion, bankruptcy and dismissal in the early eighteenth century. Again, there was a dynastic pattern to those who were engaged.[221] At Emmanuel, sometimes particular individuals were singled out for praise: Nathaniel Nicholls, for instance, received a 'present' of ten guineas in 1784 for extra business at the Catherine Wheel,[222] and George Quested of Canterbury, agent for the College at Chequer Court and Lydden and Ewell in Kent, was in 1858 given a piece of plate worth £15 for his 'gratuitous services'.[223] Quested had previously been the College's tenant at Chequer Court, from 1821 to 1847 (Plate 24 shows the map that he drew of the estate in 1824);[224] after his death, his daughter was helped with a gratuity of £20 in 1875.[225]

On occasion, however, agents did not behave satisfactorily and some had to be dismissed. In 1721, discretion was given to a Fellow, William Whitehead, either to continue or remove the letters of attorney to John Austen (tenant of The Ball, Gracechurch Street) to manage the Hyde Farm estate.[226] The porter at South Sea Chambers gave trouble in 1851: many complaints were received that he was inattentive and did not keep the premises clean.[227] A few years later, it was evident that something had gone wrong in supervision of the College's property at the Old Bailey when part of the premises were condemned as uninhabitable by the Commissioners of the Police in 1860 and rebuilding was necessary.[228]

The favour of the Gwilt family waxed and waned. George Gwilt fell out of favour in his management of affairs at the Four Swans, Bishopsgate in 1832: his advice of an appropriate level of fine was not accepted, much to his chagrin for, Gwilt claimed, if he had been given the opportunity to discuss the matter for half an hour with the Master, the College would have been £100 a year better off. Gwilt reminded the College of the proverb 'it is naught, it is nought [*sic*] said the buyer, but when he goeth away, he boasteth',[229] but in vain: management of the property passed to Philip Hardwick, whose lower valuation had been accepted.[230] After Gwilt resigned in 1850, it proved very difficult to settle the final account between him and the College and in 1853 he was threatened with legal

221 Trueman 1980, p. 37.
222 ECA BUR.8.6.
223 ECA COL.14.3 p. 121.
224 ECA BUR.6.5 pp. 450–2; ECA COL.14.3 p. 50.
225 ECA COL.14.3 p. 268.
226 ECA BUR.0.9.
227 ECA Sr.17.73.
228 ECA Lo.8.91.
229 ECA Lo.5.16, quoting *Proverbs* 20:14.
230 ECA COL.14.2 f. 207r; ECA Lo.5.15.

proceedings.[231] Gwilt's son, Alfred, also had a contretemps with the College, over the letting of the Old Bailey property on a building lease in 1865. Alfred, similarly, lost the management of the estate, this time to Messrs Reyroux and Bromehead.[232] Gwilt was also reprimanded for not sending in bills as expenses occurred.[233] In other ways, however, the Gwilts' relationship with the College was harmonious. In 1829, for instance, George responded to a request from the Master's wife, Mrs Cory, as to whether there was anything new in the 'musical line'. Gwilt offered a 'little piece' which his daughter had brought home a few days before as 'it is going here . . . "from morn to noon from noon to dewy eve" ', and so it might be equally acceptable to the young ladies at Emmanuel.[234] Then, in 1848, he bought land in front of the College's land at Mitcham in Surrey: Emmanuel had sold the land to the Surrey Iron Railway Company in 1804,[235] but had declined to repurchase the property when the company was dissolved 42 years later. Gwilt stepped in; after his death in 1856, his son Alfred repeatedly advised successive Bursars that it would be a good idea for the College to repossess the land.[236] Eventually, £550 was paid to do so in 1867.[237] Here, then, is evidence that, despite recent problems over the Old Bailey property, Alfred Gwilt could still have a beneficial effect on his employer's property.

Agents and Bursars liaised closely: whilst the former offered detailed advice, final decisions remained with the latter. There are numerous instances of agents suggesting covenants for leases, levels of rents and fines, repairs and improvements to property and the suitability of prospective tenants. In 1806, for instance, Thomas Nettleshipp reminded Smythies that he had always strongly urged that attention be paid to repairs on the various estates.[238] George Gwilt recommended in 1818 that the value of the College's properties would be much enhanced if they were let in smaller portions; he singled out Threadneedle Street.[239] Similarly, in 1852 Alfred Gwilt informed the landlord that up to £100 would have to be spent in repairs and decorations there in order to be competitive with new and more commodious office accommodation nearby.[240] In 1741, James Hanson recommended appropriate covenants for a lease of Chequer Court.[241] Estate correspondence also deals with management of

---

[231] ECA BUR.0.5(a).
[232] ECA COL.14.3 p. 172; ECA Lo.11.129a.
[233] ECA Lo.11.131.
[234] ECA Lo.11.122c.
[235] ECA COL.14.2 f. 137r.
[236] ECA Lo.11.132; ECA Sr.17.78.
[237] ECA COL.14.3 p. 186.
[238] ECA Lo.8.3.
[239] ECA Lo.8.9.
[240] ECA Lo.8.54a.
[241] ECA Box 17.C9.

woodland, breaking-up of pasture, necessity for fencing and appropriate materials for the same, frequency of survey, and so the list continues.

Agents rarely acted without reference to the College: in 1823, for instance, Nettleshipp and Bicknell asked whether plans were wanted in a lease of the Gracechurch Street property; the agents thought that they might not be needed.[242] Similarly, the Bursar was asked to contradict, if necessary, tentative suggestions that had been made to tenants: in 1809, Thomas and William Nettleshipp were inclined to agree to a tenant's request to have an additional year for repairs and had altered the lease accordingly, but Smythies was asked to reverse this action if he objected.[243] Likewise, when a lease at Lydden and Ewell in Kent was about to be renewed in 1824, the Bursar was asked to tell the agent if he had been wrong to suggest to the tenant that he might have first refusal.[244] The negotiations over this transaction provide further evidence of bursarial control. Holme wrote to the agent, Thomas Knocker, in 1825 to ask how the lease should describe a stable or cowshed with a yard for foddering stock in severe weather, and to say that the new lease must be more specific than the old one: underwood as well as timber must be reserved to the College and there was no need to allow timber for repairs as they should be done at once and not form part of the lease.[245] In 1848 the next tenant fell into arrears and George Quested wrote to ask for authority to claim the rent and for advice on how he should act in the future.[246] If agents did not keep the Bursar fully informed, they could come unstuck. Alfred Gwilt lost the management of the Old Bailey property in 1865 for precisely this reason.

Normally, the agents seem to have had their employer's interests very much in mind. Thus in 1824, Nettleshipp and Bicknell were worried that South Sea Chambers were partly built on land owned by Christ's Hospital. They tried to get as long a lease as possible from the Hospital but feared that they would be lucky to obtain 60 years and might even have to take 21; in the event, 40 years were settled upon.[247] At Sutton Coldfield, W. S. Perkins negotiated on the College's behalf in the sale of land to the turnpike road commissioners in 1828: they offered £150 per acre but Perkins said that the College would not accept less than £200 per acre.[248] Occasionally, agents had to go to considerable expense when acting for the College: in 1866, Alfred Gwilt had to defend an action that

[242] ECA Lo.11.7.
[243] ECA Sr.1.10.
[244] ECA Ke.6.477.
[245] ECA Ke.6.487.
[246] ECA Ke.6.493–4.
[247] ECA Lo.8.13; Lo.2.7; ECA COL.14.2 f. 192r.
[248] ECA Wa.1.72. The College eventually received £189 12s in 1834 for sale of the land and a blacksmith's shop (ECA SCH.1.15).

had been brought against him by the tenant of South Sea Chambers, who claimed that he had been put to unnecessary expense in rebuilding. Gwilt won but was ordered to pay £300 costs; there is no evidence that he was ever reimbursed for this sum.[249]

Agents were responsible for ensuring that tenants fulfilled their obligations to defend the landlord's property against encroachment. If tenants informed the College of infringement of its rights, then agents investigated, as happened at Godmanchester in 1857.[250] A similar request for help came from the tenants at Lydden and Ewell, who did not have a cordial relationship with their vicar in the early nineteenth century. The incumbent claimed land in 1805 and 1806,[251] and the problem arose again in 1823–4 when there was a new 'eccentric' vicar and William Holme was Bursar. He did not agree to a 'hasty decision' by the agent, Thomas Knocker, who recommended that the land be given up.[252] George Quested was called in and eventually the College agreed to a boundary for the sake of peace; the matter was only finally settled, however, by the death of the occupier.[253]

Surveys

Together with the increased dependence of landlords on agents and estate managers during the eighteenth and nineteenth centuries, was a growth in the numbers of surveyors who were employed. Many landowners started to have their estates surveyed on a regular basis: the Haberdashers from 1753;[254] the Corporation of the Sons of the Clergy from 1760;[255] St John's College, Cambridge from the 1770s;[256] the Duchy of Cornwall from 1771 (which employed its first full-time surveyor in 1844);[257] the Drapers' Company from 1817;[258] to name a few. Valuations and maps were produced, in increasing numbers.[259]

Emmanuel participated in this trend and was one of the earlier Cambridge colleges to have its estates mapped, starting in 1720 with Heber Lands' map of Hyde Farm.[260] A number of men were employed from the 1770s: the Cambridge surveyors Joseph Freeman (1773 to 1797), Alexander Watford (1798 to 1801) and William Custance (1802 to 1820)

[249] ECA Lo.11.132.
[250] ECA BUR.0.5(a).
[251] ECA Ke.6.460–1.
[252] ECA Ke.6.478.
[253] ECA Ke.6.479–81; ECA Box 17.A21.
[254] Archer 1991, p. 111.
[255] Cox 1978, p. 74.
[256] Howard 1935, p. 150.
[257] Haslam 1991, pp. 63, 69.
[258] Curl 1979, p. 25.
[259] Bendall 1992, Chapter 7.
[260] ECA SUR.43.

travelled all over the College's property.[261] Men local to particular estates were employed, too. George Gwilt, for instance, was employed by the Nettleshipps to survey in London and they also used William Forster, Francis Whishaw and William Neale.[262] Likewise, the Worcestershire surveyor Henry Jacob surveyed at Sutton Coldfield in 1812 and 1813.[263] Emmanuel never, however, commissioned a systematic series of surveys or maps of its estates, unlike some of its neighbours. Nor did the College officers go on regular or annual progresses of the estates, as did those of St John's in the early nineteenth century.[264] The failure of Emmanuel and its agents to carry out annual inspections was commented on by Francis Whishaw in his survey of Stondon in 1814: he feared that farming covenants had not been observed but in the absence of yearly visits could not substantiate this supposition.[265]

Visits and surveys were made when the need arose. Chequer Court in Kent was the only estate to be visited regularly: under the terms of George Thorpe's will, a court had to be held there at least once every seven years.[266] Usually the Master went, accompanied by two Fellows. Elsewhere, journeys and inspections were occasional. The Rushall estate in Norfolk, for example, was visited by two Fellows Christopher Hand and Gervase Holmes before it was bought in 1738.[267] Repair and building work led to many visits by agents, surveyors and College officers. The tenant of St Cross in Suffolk asked for the Bursar to visit in 1817 as the buildings had to be repaired that summer, and a similar request was made in 1848.[268] Improvements were also inspected once they had been completed: Birkett was invited to visit Sutton Coldfield partly for this purpose in 1847.[269]

Surveys were frequently carried out before estates were let. Gonville and Caius College decided in 1776 that estates should be mapped and valued before fines were set; at Queens' College, two-thirds of the maps that were drawn before 1836 were associated with the renewal of leases.[270] Maps were drawn for Emmanuel, too. In 1818, for instance, a plan was needed before a lease of land in Threadneedle Street was made as the description of the estate had hitherto been copied from lease to lease and had now reached the most 'profound obscurity' and George

[261] Bendall 1992, p. 186.
[262] ECA Sr.1.1–2, 20.
[263] ECA Wa.1.4–7.
[264] Howard 1935, pp. 156–8.
[265] ECA Es.4.3.
[266] ECA SCH.1.17.
[267] ECA SCH.1.4.
[268] ECA Nf.5.20, 58.
[269] ECA Wa.1.132.
[270] Bendall 1992, p. 173.

Gwilt could 'make nothing of it'.[271] In many other cases, however, the land was surveyed and valued but not mapped. Normally, the College paid for the costs of the survey if the tenant accepted the terms for a new lease; if he declined, he paid.[272] In 1833, failure to put this understanding into writing led to a dispute between the College and its prospective tenant at Bishopsgate Street, who refused to pay all of the surveyor's charges.[273]

Surveys that were carried out before leases were granted sometimes revealed areas where tenants should assert their landlord's rights as, for example, to a vault under Leadenhall Market in 1830.[274] Similarly, at Mitcham and Clapham in 1801 the tenant, William Cole, had failed to defend the College's title to five small pieces of land.[275] Thomas Nettleshipp changed his mind over whether or not attempts should be made to recover the fields. In 1802, he advised that it would not be worth-while; by 1812, however, he felt that perhaps the plots should be mentioned as his firm 'must not always Act for Corporate Bodies who have the Interest of Posterity in their hands as we would for those who are in themselves absolute Lords of the soil'.[276] In 1817, the Nettleshipps suggested that the College might be able to get rid of the dispute by selling the land to redeem land tax.[277] The affair continued, however, with complaints of trespass in 1819 (to which Emmanuel responded that it could not interfere),[278] and in 1823 Nettleshipp and Bicknell changed their tune again and advised the College to forget about the disputed lands.[279] Not until 1825 was the business finally settled, by a new tenant who went to law to establish the College's right of way.[280] This protracted affair, which involved visits by the Bursar in 1812 and 1818 and three journeys to the area in 1822,[281] demonstrates the consequences of a lack of close supervision by agents, and also that they did not always defend the College's property interests with the vigour that one might expect.

Rents and fines
The growing numbers of surveys and valuations that were carried out before leases were renewed took place against a background of both continuity and change. The College's estate income barely increased in real

[271] ECA Lo.8.9.
[272] ECA Lo.2.15.
[273] ECA Lo.5.21.
[274] ECA Lo.11.11.
[275] ECA Sr.1.1.
[276] ECA Sr.17.13.
[277] ECA Sr.17.20a.
[278] ECA Sr.17.28.
[279] ECA Sr.17.40, 52.
[280] ECA Sr.17.64.
[281] ECA BUR.0.4.(b–c); ECA Sr.17.45, 48.

terms in the eighteenth century; in the nineteenth, there was marked growth and the balance between rental and income from fines changed after 1830 (Figs 8, 12 and 14). For much of the period, therefore, the practice of letting estates at low reserved rents and charging fines on each renewal remained unaltered. Much of the estate correspondence and survey and valuation work was thus carried out within this basic framework. The breakdown of the system and replacement of it with rack rents was a major change.

Agents and surveyors for much of the period, therefore, were concerned to establish the full rental value of an estate so that appropriate levels of fines and rents could be set. The College became less and less prepared merely to base its demands on those that had been made in the past. It was not always easy, however, to discover the full rental value and it was clearly in the tenant's best interest to try to conceal it from his landlord. For example, in 1745 the College discovered that the Harrow in Gracechurch Street was sub-let for £58 (and the passage into Leadenhall Market for an additional £10) rather than £45 as had previously been advised. The true value of the premises was found out too late as the fine had already been fixed.[282] At Threadneedle Street, on the other hand, the misrepresentation of the true value of the property in 1731 was realised in time to set a fine higher than that which accorded to the tenant's calculations (though lower than the sub-letting suggested).[283] When the property in question was an inn, the tenant was a little more vulnerable. In 1729, William Savage stayed at the Four Swans Inn in Bishopsgate. Mr Hill, the landlord, was 'very communicative the first night, after coming home from the Tavern', and so Savage discovered the terms on which the sub-tenant held the estate, estimated the value of it and discovered the income of the innkeeper from the premises.[284] By such enquiries, surveys and knowledge of rental values of nearby properties, appropriate levels of fines could be determined. The College could be surprised at the value of its property: in 1807, Smythies expressed alarm at the level of the proposed fine of £1435 for the Four Swans (renewed at a fine of £100 in 1792).[285] George Gwilt explained his reasoning in some detail: the first step had been to fix a rental for the business of a grocer, or a similar trade, on an extensive scale. Gwilt had carried this out through knowledge of the costs of a building of more or less the same dimensions that he had recently completed for a grocer. The annual rental depended on the state of repair of the premises: Gwilt had then deducted the reserved rent and made an allowance for repairs. The number of years for which

---

[282] ECA BUR.3.2 f. 49v.
[283] ECA BUR.3.2 f. 45v.
[284] ECA BUR.3.2 ff. 37v–38r.
[285] ECA COL.14.2 f. 105r.

the lease was to be renewed also affected the fine. In the event, the terms were declined by the tenant.[286] The system was so deeply rooted that in at least one instance a fine was taken by mistake: when the Holborn estate was to be re-let in 1795, the lessee paid a fine of £190 10s to renew. The error was soon detected – the estate had always been let at a rack rent, as was more appropriate to trust estates whose incomes were not intended to swell the Fellowship dividend – and the property was not re-let until 1800.[287]

Changes were on the way, however, and the days of the beneficial lease were numbered. Indeed, the system had quietly been altering for some time as all of the new acquisitions of the eighteenth or early nineteenth centuries had been let on rack rents *ab initio*. In the 1750s, Balliol College, Oxford, was one of the first colleges to decide to let beneficial leases run out;[288] St John's and St Catharine's, Cambridge, did so in the 1770s;[289] Gonville and Caius acted similarly in 1816 and Trinity Hall in 1840;[290] and at Christ's, the changeover was managed by James Cartmell during his Mastership of 1849 to 1881 and the revenue of the college materially increased for a time.[291] By the time when colleges were reporting to the Graham Commissioners in 1852–3, all of those who made returns, except for Magdalene and Downing, said that they were either in the process of or had completed converting from beneficial leases to letting property at rack rents. The two exceptions had never used the system of beneficial leases in any case. While some colleges such as Peterhouse and King's said that they had no particular system in hand for making the change, many others had.[292]

Emmanuel decided to substitute rack rents for reserved rents in 1837.[293] Changes had already taken place in a few instances: 38 acres at Gransden had been let at rack rent from some time during Richardson's Mastership;[294] Little Melton had been let at rack rent in 1821, after inclosure;[295] and, most recently, George Gwilt had advised in 1831 that the value of the Bishopsgate Street estate would be better realised by letting it at rack rent. His advice was taken.[296] After 1837, change was not automatic and some beneficial leases were still renewed. Fifteen years later, however, the only remaining beneficial leases were for

[286] ECA Lo.2.1–2; ECA BUR.3.3.
[287] ECA Lo.11.139; ECA BUR.6.6 pp. 88–94.
[288] Dunbabin 1986, p. 281.
[289] Howard 1935, p. 115; Jones 1936, p. 230.
[290] Gross 1912, pp. ix–x; Crawley 1977, p. 257.
[291] Peile 1910–13, II, pp. 436–7.
[292] Graham Commission, pp. 197–9.
[293] ECA COL.14.2 f. 222v.
[294] ECA BUR.3.2 f. 19r.
[295] ECA Box 20.D17; ECA COL.14.2 f. 173v.
[296] ECA Lo.2.14; ECA Box 26.G9.

houses,[297] and when such leases were renewed the College considered the advantage of changing to rack rents.[298]

The mechanisms of change were not straightforward as both college and Fellows lost their incomes from fines and thus had to endure reduced revenues for a considerable period. The new system was expected to be more advantageous: when, in the past, estates had been let at rack rents, they had been much improved and become more productive and so were better able to respond sensitively to changing economic conditions. The benefits were set out for the Fellows of Queens' College in 1818 or thereabouts:[299] it had been difficult to levy fines that reflected the true value of the estates and sometimes to find tenants to buy a new lease (this problem had been exacerbated by the inflation of the Napoleonic Wars). Examples of this problem can be seen at Emmanuel: we have already seen that the tenant refused to pay a fine of £1435 to renew his lease of Bishopsgate Street in 1807 and renewal, this time for £3668, was refused again in 1817.[300] Consequently, money had to be borrowed to pay fellowship dividends.

Some colleges made a habit of compensating Fellows for their loss of dividends when fines ceased to be collected: at Pembroke, for instance, a loan was made from the Building Fund at 4% interest to pay Fellows sums in lieu of some of the fines; Queens' acted similarly. Of the colleges that made returns to the Graham Commissioners, however, most – including Emmanuel – said that no compensation had been paid.[301] Nevertheless, after the conversion to rack rents at Gransden a sum in lieu of a fine was advanced in 1798,[302] and at Little Melton in 1820 a dividend was paid.[303] A different way of smoothing over the change was made in 1845 at Sutton Coldfield, where rents were calculated so that the increase over 21 years would make up for a decrease in fines at 4% interest.[304] The 1858 and 1860 Universities and College Estates Acts saw the final death blow to beneficial leases: they could no longer be granted or revived, and colleges were empowered to borrow on mortgage sufficient sums to indemnify Fellows for their loss of fines.[305]

The changeover from beneficial leases to rack rents accounts for part of the increase in rental income in real terms in the early nineteenth century. However, the rise in receipts started before many of the changes took

---

[297] Graham Commission, p. 198.
[298] For example, in the renewal of 10–12 St Andrew's Street in 1859 and of Petty Cury in 1860 (ECA BUR.0.5(c)).
[299] Queens' College Archives, Account Book 'Coll. No. 2' pp. 2–7.
[300] ECA BUR.3.3.
[301] Graham Commission, pp. 197–9.
[302] ECA Box 14.C17(2).
[303] ECA BUR.3.3.
[304] ECA Wa.1.121a, 125.
[305] Shadwell 1898, pp. 23–5; Dunbabin 1997, p. 386.

place; it also occurred in trust estates, most of which had never been let under beneficial leases (Fig. 8). Development of the estates themselves also had a part to play.

Repairs and improvements

A contrast can be drawn between the eighteenth and nineteenth centuries in terms of expenditure on maintenance and improvement of the College's estates: another indication of the ways in which attitudes to estates changed. Figure 18 shows the situation clearly: of estate income, an increasing proportion was spent on repairs and improvements from the 1790s. In this respect, Emmanuel was not particularly out of line with other landowners, though it was a relatively low spender. In the late seventeenth and early eighteenth centuries, landlords rarely spent as little as 4%–5% of their gross income on repairs;[306] Emmanuel only spent in the region of 2%. Levels of landowner investment increased thereafter.[307] Guy's Hospital which, like Emmanuel, was a maintaining rather than an improving landlord, spent on average 9.5% of its gross income on improvements and repairs between 1762 and 1815; the Duke of Kingston, however, spent between 1% and 5%.[308] Emmanuel spent 2.5% on average, though this figure is probably artificially low as a result of negligible expenditure (or, alternatively, a lack of data) during the years of Farmer's Mastership. Records of expenditure resume immediately after Farmer's death in 1797, and between then and 1815 levels rose to an average of 5.5% per annum. This was the period of the French Wars, when agricultural conditions were favourable and so some private landlords tended to leave investment to their tenants;[309] nevertheless, expenditure by Emmanuel increased, perhaps in an attempt to catch up on repairs and improvements that had been neglected in previous years. At Holkham in Norfolk, Thomas Coke similarly invested during this period,[310] and Sarah Wilmot has shown how interest in agricultural improvements dwindled during the depression of the 1820s.[311] Thus, while some private landowners spent more on their estates during periods of agricultural depression in an attempt to attract and maintain tenants, others – and Emmanuel – behaved differently.[312]

Whence came the initiative for repairs and improvements? If Emmanuel was an unadventurous landlord and a relatively low spender on repairs and improvements, one might expect it to have been reactive, not

---

[306] Clay 1985, p. 247.
[307] Beckett 1989, p. 601.
[308] Trueman 1980, p. 41.
[309] Beckett 1986, p. 179.
[310] Wade Martins 1980, p. 97.
[311] Wilmot 1990, p. 24.
[312] Beckett 1986, p. 179.

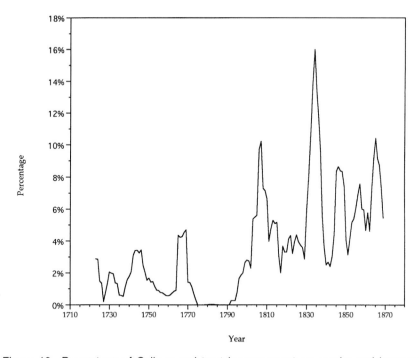

Figure 18 Percentage of College and trust income spent on repairs and improvements 1720–1870 (five-year moving averages). *Source*: ECA BUR.1.2, BUR.8.4, 6–9, BUR.11.2, 6, FEL.5.7–11, SCH.1.2–18.

proactive. This, indeed, seems to have been the case. Agents identified the need for repairs and improvements on many occasions, often in their surveys prior to the renewal of leases. Thus when Francis Whishaw surveyed Whipples Farm at Stondon in 1811, he recommended that a plot of meadow that had been broken up should be laid down to pasture again and pointed out considerable repairs that were needed to the farm buildings.[313] Thomas Nettleshipp reported the results of the survey to Holme and advised that the tenant be made to carry out repairs, and that a coppice should be grubbed up and converted to tillage.[314] Failure to inspect in-between lease renewals occasionally led to problems: at Hyde Farm in 1845, for instance, Samuel Martin claimed that he had not realised that he was responsible for repairs to the estate as no-one had come to inspect them for nearly 30 years.[315]

Tenants, too, provided a stimulus to repair and improvement work.

[313] ECA Es.4.3.
[314] ECA Es.4.4a, 4c; ECA Sr.17.8.
[315] ECA Sr.1.57.

They asked for meetings to see and authorise necessary repairs: at St Cross, the tenants asked the Bursar to visit them in 1817 and 1848 for this purpose.[316] Heavy expenditure on the farm buildings at Shernborne between 1832 and 1834 (£2300) arose after repeated requests from the tenant for inspections and help, and complaints that the barns did not protect the corn from winter storms.[317] Tenants could ask for improvements to buildings: at Lydden and Ewell in 1825, the lessee asked for a lodge to be built so that he could keep stock in it over the winter and manure the land more effectively,[318] and a similar request was made by the tenant at Rushall in 1850.[319] More radical changes were also suggested from time to time. In 1825, Frederick Silver, tenant of Hyde Farm, suggested that the farm be developed on a building lease as there was at that time a favourable opportunity to arrange access to such a development. The College could not agree to the proposal as the tenant was not prepared to invest sufficiently in the project.[320] Circumstances changed, so that by 1869, when it was itself considering a similar development, one of the drawbacks was the quantity of building land already on the market.[321] At Sutton Coldfield four years earlier, the letting of building leases was likewise proposed but again there was already much land on offer on such leases in the parish.[322] Thus in the 1860s, Emmanuel was suffering from following, rather than setting, the trend.[323]

Repairs and improvements also occurred as a result of developments in the areas surrounding the estates or as part of national trends. Poor drainage in Pinchbeck was blamed for causing, in part, the insolvency of Cawood Robinson, tenant of Cuckoo Farm in 1818;[324] two years later, neighbouring owners met to decide whether to introduce steam drainage in the South Fen. Nothing material had happened by 1822, when there were bad floods in January; plans were finally approved and, after delays and unexpected expenses, drainage was eventually completed in 1826.[325] Inclosure was an improvement that had to be decided upon by all of the proprietors who would be affected. Emmanuel was involved in many inclosures, but there is no evidence that it actually initiated any of them; at Queens', the impetus often came from the tenants.[326] Emmanuel did, however, expect to participate fully in the process once it was under way,

---

[316] ECA Nf.5.20, 58.
[317] ECA Nf.6.89, 92; ECA SCH.1.3.
[318] ECA Ke.6.482.
[319] ECA Nf.5.61a.
[320] ECA Sr.1.38–47.
[321] ECA Sr.1.66–9, especially Sr.1.67.
[322] ECA Wa.1.163.
[323] See p. 378.
[324] ECA Li.2.28.
[325] ECA Li.9.23–5, 27; Li.2.1, 28–9, 34, 36–7, 41–3, 45, 47, 49.
[326] Twigg 1987, p. 302.

and William Holme was clearly displeased when his College did not appear among the list of proprietors in the proposed inclosure of Sutton Coldfield in 1824.[327] Emmanuel also took part in national fashions in improvements. Draining of farm land by pipes became widespread in England from the 1840s and Emmanuel participated at Godmanchester from 1858 and at Molland Farm in Kent in 1859.[328] Despite the slower adoption of underdraining in East Anglia compared with elsewhere in England, the improvement was carried out on Emmanuel's land at Shernborne and St Cross in the 1850s.[329]

Wherever the initiative for repairs and improvements came from, the College kept close control over them once they had been approved. Every item – plans, estimates, materials – had to be authorised by the landlord. In 1846, for example, the Society saw and approved plans for a new farm-house and premises at Cuckoo Farm, Pinchbeck.[330] The College was concerned with quality. There is much evidence amongst estate corre-spondence of insistence that new buildings should be erected properly and the work supervised and approved. In 1855, William Castlehow enjoined Alfred Gwilt to make sure that good and substantial cottages were built at Mitcham and Clapham in Surrey.[331] The cost of materials had to be balanced against the durability of the result: for example, the College agents advised that the sea wall at Ripple should be repaired in stone rather than in planks in 1833, and that the slope of the river front should be faced in stone in 1861.[332] At Sutton Coldfield in 1843, a pump needed mending. The tenant could patch it up at his own expense; alter-natively, the College could make a contribution for an effective repair. The latter option was chosen.[333] At Mitcham and Clapham in 1851 the tenant was made to put in cast-iron rather than wooden posts for a fence so that it would last 50–60 years,[334] and in 1866, a similar decision was taken to use more expensive but durable materials in repairs to a well on the estate.[335] When at Shernborne in 1824 the field barn needed repair, the agent advised that to spend too little would be 'picking the pockets of the College';[336] the following year the tenant recommended that repairs be carried out in brick nogging rather than in more expensive and less durable boards. The College, however, preferred the latter.[337] For repairs

[327] ECA Wa.1.35, 38a.
[328] ECA BUR.8.9; ECA Box 13.C18.
[329] ECA BUR.6.6 pp. 304–8, 344; BUR.6.7 pp. 175–80; Phillips 1989, pp. 242–3.
[330] ECA COL.14.3 p. 44.
[331] ECA Sr.17.77.
[332] ECA Es.2.3B; ECA Lo.11.125.
[333] ECA Wa.1.112; ECA COL.14.3 p. 42.
[334] ECA Sr.17.72.
[335] ECA Lo.11.132.
[336] ECA BUR.0.10.
[337] ECA Nf.6.71–2.

to Stratford wharf in 1854, the cheaper, timber, option was chosen rather than more expensive brick.[338]

Finance of repairs and improvements was an important consideration. For all landowners, the landlord usually provided the fixed capital and the tenant the working capital: thus, Emmanuel paid for sheds, tenants for cows.[339] Tenants were responsible for routine repairs, though landlords were often obliged to carry out work on run-down premises before they were re-let. For more substantial improvements, investment by the landlord could be high. Often, landowners paid for materials, tenants contributed the labour.[340] This happened, for instance, in the financing of a new bullock shed at Emmanuel's estate at Great Melton in 1858.[341]

Emmanuel frequently made allowances to tenants for repairs. Fines might not be levied as, for example, at Eltisley in 1746, when no fine was collected because the tenant was bound by new covenants in his lease about management of timber, sowing grass, spreading muck and rebuilding or repairing the barn.[342] Similarly, at Godmanchester in 1809 the tenant was leased the estate at no fine so long as he paid for the costs of inclosing and fencing the College's allotment there.[343] On other occasions the fine was reduced: the tenants of 11–12 St Andrew's Street hoped, in vain, that their fine would be lowered from £240 to £180 as they had spent over £600 on renovations.[344] Alternatively, allowances were made from rent: at Stondon in 1847, up to £9 was to be deducted to pay for a new barn floor in oak.[345] On occasions, a lease was extended so that the tenant could get a return on improvements: Thomas Smith was allowed a lease of Rushall for nine rather than the usual seven years in 1810, so that he could enjoy the benefits of draining and claying the land, demolishing the old backhouse and dairy and tiling the farmhouse.[346] He was, in addition, allowed £150 spread over three years for rebuilding and reroofing work.[347] The tenant of the King's Head, Threadneedle Street, asked for a similar extension in 1823, for 61 years, so that he could rebuild the premises.[348] His wish was not granted, however; 40 years was the maximum length of lease that the College could grant legally. At other times, the beneficiaries of rents were granted extensions of their awards so that improvements could be paid for. When, for instance, drainage was

---

[338] ECA BUR.0.5(b).
[339] Beckett 1989, p. 597.
[340] Howell 1986, pp. 61–2.
[341] ECA COL.14.3 p. 120.
[342] ECA Box 12.C11.
[343] ECA BUR.6.5 pp. 223–30.
[344] ECA Ca.1.9–10.
[345] ECA Es.4.9b.
[346] ECA Nf.5.2.
[347] ECA SCH.1.5.
[348] ECA Lo.8.11.

carried out at Witham in Lincolnshire in 1798, one year's rent was lost in paying for the work. As the income was used to pay exhibitioners, those affected were allowed to hold their awards for an additional year in compensation.[349]

Landlords often provided the capital for repairs and improvements and tenants then paid interest on the loans. The lessee at Bishopsgate Street preferred this method of finance in 1831;[350] and it was used elsewhere. When construction of a new warehouse at 21 St Andrew's Street was agreed in 1845, for instance, the tenant was to pay 5% interest;[351] and in 1855, the tenant at Cuckoo Farm in Pinchbeck was charged 4% interest for alterations to the house.[352] The College tried to spread the capital costs, but not always successfully. At Sutton Coldfield in 1833, for instance, land had to be drained. Hopes to let it at a low rent and for the tenant to carry out the work were dashed as times were hard and it proved impossible to let the estate under such terms. In the end, the land was let at a higher rent and the College paid for drainage.[353]

The College did not always agree to pay, or only did so very reluctantly. It was not, for example, inclined to support financially such improvements as insertion of a sewer in Gracechurch Street in 1834,[354] or a proposed building lease for Bishopsgate Street in London, which fell through in 1865 when the builder could not find sufficient funds.[355] At Cowbit Farm in Pinchbeck, on the other hand, Emmanuel did eventually contribute £300 at 7% interest towards the cost of the farmhouse.[356] The contribution was made grudgingly as the tenant had previously offered to erect the house at his own expense and only asked for financial help when the building was almost complete. The College questioned whether the farmhouse did in fact add to the value of the estate as was claimed; the tenant was reminded of the original agreement but got away with his action in the end, though he had to pay a higher interest rate rather than the 5% that he had asked for.[357]

Many improvements were thus partly paid for by the College; when the landlord bore the entire cost, loans sometimes had to be sought, from special funds and from elsewhere. Thus, in 1863 £300 was borrowed by the College from the scholarship fund to pay towards the cost of new farm buildings at South College Farm, Pinchbeck. An identical sum was lent by the College at 4% interest, and the tenant was to pay

[349] ECA SCH.1.7.
[350] ECA Lo.5.7.
[351] ECA COL.14.3 p. 37.
[352] ECA COL.14.3 p. 96.
[353] ECA Wa.1.90.
[354] ECA Lo.11.13–14.
[355] ECA Box 26.G20; Peace 1908, p. 20.
[356] ECA Li.2.12.
[357] ECA Li.2.3, 5, 7–11.

£59.[358] Others, too, including the Master and Fellows, lent the College money from time to time.[359]

Financing patterns were therefore complex; the ways in which inclosures were paid for demonstrate this. The College paid at Shernborne; it also did so at Sutton Coldfield in 1824, when money from the sale of land to the turnpike road commissioners was used to pay the expenses.[360] We have already seen how elsewhere the tenants paid, as at Godmanchester. At Gransden, too, in 1843 the tenant had to pay the costs.[361] At Pinchbeck, however, the College contributed towards the costs of hedging.[362] When farmhouses were built in the decades following inclosure, the College normally helped its tenants either by a loan or by buying the buildings at the end of the lease.[363]

The major improvements on Emmanuel's property – inclosure, new farm buildings, drainage and introduction of building leases – were all adopted by other landlords. Inclosure could be very expensive: though Emmanuel had problems financing the process at Shernborne, it was worth the cost as the rent rose from £140 in 1749 to £320 in 1770.[364] Queens' was concerned about the high costs in 1818 and was reluctant in the following year to embark on inclosing Oakington, which eventually took place in 1834, at vast expense.[365] Similarly, St Catharine's had difficulty in 1828 in paying for rebuilding the Bull Inn as the College was spending so much on inclosures.[366] St John's was involved in inclosures in 21 parishes between 1798 and 1813 and had to sell stock to pay for them, and in inclosure of a further eight parishes between 1839 and 1845. Between 1770 and 1813, that College spent over £8000 on inclosure and fencing,[367] costs that Emmanuel sometimes passed on to its tenants, especially in the early nineteenth century. St John's spent substantial sums on new farm buildings after inclosure;[368] Emmanuel did likewise as, for example, at Pinchbeck and Great Melton, but on a lesser scale than its neighbour. Nor was Emmanuel alone in investing in drainage of its land: St John's did so too, especially in the late 1840s and 1850s.[369]

As at most other colleges, the development of land on building leases by Emmanuel did not take place on any large scale until the 1860s, when

---

[358] ECA COL.14.3 p. 158; ECA Li.5.10a.
[359] See also p. 353.
[360] ECA Wa.1.73.
[361] ECA Box 14.F1.
[362] ECA Box 18.E2.
[363] As, for example, at South College Farm, Pinchbeck, in 1848 (ECA COL.14.3 p. 52).
[364] ECA BUR.6.4 pp. 72–5, 261–71; see p. 353.
[365] Twigg 1987, p. 303.
[366] Rich 1973, p. 200.
[367] Howard 1935, pp. 154–6, 163.
[368] Howard 1935, p. 155.
[369] Howard 1935, pp. 181–2.

projects at the Old Bailey, Hyde Farm and Sutton Coldfield were discussed. Earlier proposals had been made in the 1820s of developments at Hyde Farm and Threadneedle Street but these had come to nought, and in 1831 a beachman at Pakefield in Suffolk had asked to have a building lease of part of the land so that he could construct a warehouse there.[370] Caius College had let its first building lease in 1799 and developed its Barnwell Estate in Cambridge from 1827, though the major construction work took place in the 1880s.[371] St John's College, Oxford, similarly made out its first building leases in the 1820s.[372] At this time, however, colleges could not easily follow private landowners in such developments as leases could not be made out for longer than 40 years, too short a time for tenants to realise an adequate profit on their investments. In Oxford, Magdalen College got around the problem in 1776–7 by securing a private Act of Parliament to issue 99-year building leases for its land at Southwark. Between 1846 and 1855, five colleges in Oxford followed this example, including St John's who took out legislation in 1855 to build on its land in North Oxford, and an Act of 1853 enabled Sidney Sussex, Cambridge to develop its estate at Cleethorpes, Lincolnshire.[373] Three years later, however, the 1858 Universities and Colleges Estates Act enabled colleges to grant building leases for up to 99 years.[374] Developments were thus facilitated: St John's, Cambridge, took action immediately; Emmanuel followed suit slightly later, though most activity took place after the period covered by this chapter.[375]

The use of covenants to enforce repairs and improvements of estates altered during the eighteenth and nineteenth centuries, but most especially amongst private landowners. Farming covenants were going out of fashion amongst these landlords in the nineteenth century,[376] though Thomas Coke extended and tightened such clauses at Holkham at the turn of the two centuries.[377] Guy's Hospital, too, used increasingly detailed covenants at the end of the eighteenth century.[378] Emmanuel continued to use covenants to regulate major repairs and improvements, though repetition of clauses from one lease to the next suggests that the requirements were not always enforced. At Sutton Coldfield, for example, a covenant in a lease of 1764 that the Bull's Head Inn should be demolished within two years and a new dwelling house built at a cost of

[370] ECA Sf.1.57a.
[371] Gross 1912, pp. 18–19, 27.
[372] Hinchcliffe 1992, p. 13.
[373] Dunbabin 1997, p. 428; Hinchcliffe 1992, p. 36; Ambler and Dowling 1996, pp. 183–4.
[374] Shadwell 1898, p. 24.
[375] Howard 1935, p. 191. See pp. 491–5.
[376] Beckett 1989, p. 614.
[377] Wade Martins 1980, pp. 74–5.
[378] Trueman 1980, pp. 38–9.

at least £150, was repeated in 1785.[379] Tenants increasingly had to pay to insure their premises. Covenants to do so became common in the nineteenth century: they were introduced into leases of Emmanuel Street in 1826, when the fine for numbers one and nine was reduced as the tenant had to start paying for insurance, and similarly in 1828 for numbers two to eight.[380] In 1830, the tenant at South College Farm, Pinchbeck, recommended that the College's barns there should be insured; a fire had occurred nearby in the previous week.[381] Agents, too, recommended insurance, as at Rushall in 1865.[382] The College was also increasingly being recommended to specify the insurance office rather than to leave it to the discretion of the tenant: George Gwilt advised in this way in 1823 for the Holborn estate.[383]

Rents: increases, arrears and abatements

Increased active management of Emmanuel's estates by visits and surveys, and repairs and improvements to the properties, all played their part in contributing to the increased rental income of the College. Many landlords experienced a doubling of rental income from estates after they were inclosed: Christ Church, Oxford, found that their receipts doubled or trebled and Sidney Sussex College similarly enjoyed an increase.[384] Inclosure brought benefits to Emmanuel, too: at Pinchbeck, for example. The tithes there had been let for £90 in 1784;[385] in 1811 – after inclosure – a great increase in income from the estate took place as the College had been allotted, in lieu of tithes, three farms with a combined rental income of £1219. Elsewhere increases were substantial, though less dramatic: we have seen how the rent at Shernborne rose nearly threefold between 1749 and 1770, and at West Street, Godmanchester, the rent of £26 13s 4d in 1800 was increased to £40 12s 4d in 1805.[386] Lucky landowners also experienced growth in rents from the development of mineral resources on their estates. St John's, for instance, let its first mineral lease in 1816; three years later, it received £97 but by 1826 its income had risen to £718.[387] Corpus Christi received £8900 between 1858 and 1871 from coprolites.[388] Perhaps the most spectacular example amongst the Cambridge colleges, however, is that of Sidney Sussex, where the discovery of minerals on its estates at Dudley in the second decade of the nineteenth

---

[379] ECA Box 29.B20; ECA BUR.6.5 pp. 3–9.
[380] ECA BUR.3.3; ECA Box 4.E2.
[381] ECA Li.5.2.
[382] ECA Box 20.K11.
[383] ECA Lo.11.153.
[384] Bill 1956, p. 7; Salt 1992, p. 149.
[385] ECA Box 18.A9, C1, D1, E1.
[386] ECA Box 13.C1; ECA BUR.6.5 pp. 223–30.
[387] Howard 1935, p. 122.
[388] Bury 1952, p. 63.

century encouraged the College to think of its future. The increased income that was enjoyed went a long way towards payment for Wyatville's remodelling and refurbishment of the College in the following two decades.[389] Emmanuel optimistically introduced covenants about mineral rights into its leases from 1856, but nothing came of them. Nor did Emmanuel benefit from developing its timber resources in the way that St John's did.[390]

From time to time, Emmanuel received complaints about the rents that it charged: sometimes, personal circumstances of the tenants made them unable to pay; on other occasions, claims were made that the College was out of line with others in the area. Some tenants lived beyond their means. In 1805, the Horseshoe Inn, Godmanchester, was re-let after the former lessee had become bankrupt.[391] At Sutton Coldfield, the tenant of the College's new allotment ruined himself by building too expensive a house on land adjoining that which he rented from Emmanuel; he, too, was declared bankrupt and fled to America in 1833.[392] Many complaints were made that the College charged higher rents than surrounding landlords. In 1827, for instance, the tenant of Shernborne successfully asked for an abatement in rent: he had taken the farm from Michaelmas 1824 so as to be close to his son-in-law who farmed nearby, despite the advice from every farmer in the neighbourhood that the rent was too high.[393] When the tenant at Stratford Wharf asked for an extension to his lease in 1858, he claimed that competition from the railways decreased the value of the premises. A surveyor was sent, who recommended that the lease be renewed as he thought that it would be difficult to find an enterprising man with sufficient capital to take on the premises should they became vacant.[394] By 1866, however, the College's agent was reporting that the wharf was considerably under-let, so clearly the tenant was doing well out of his property.[395] The wishes of tenants were not always met. In 1848, the lessee of the Four Swans in Bishopsgate Street asked for a reduction of rent and extension of the lease. George Gwilt surveyed the premises and advised the Bursar that no reduction was 'needful, necessary or reasonable': it was well-known that the original lease had been disposed of twice or thrice by the tenant for nearly treble the rent due to the College, and there was every appearance that the inn was thriving as Birkett had tried to stay there on more than one occasion and there had been no

---

[389] Salt 1992, pp. 119–24.
[390] Howard 1935, p. 121.
[391] ECA Box 13.C2.
[392] ECA Wa.1.90.
[393] ECA BUR.6.6 pp. 110–16; ECA Nf.6.82.
[394] ECA Es.5.1, 3.
[395] ECA Es.1.39b.

accommodation available.[396] Rises of taxation also led to difficulties in payment of rent as, for example, on the Lusby estate in 1855.[397]

Problems were both short- and long-term. In 1823 at Gransden, for instance, the tenant apologised for not sending his entire rent, but his shepherd had lost 11 sheep going to St Ives fair as it was very wet and dark, and he had not found them until it was too late to complete the journey.[398] Other difficulties in payment of rent were more long-standing. Sea erosion at Pakefield in Suffolk caused continuing problems in the 1820s:[399] in 1823, the tenant said that not more than four acres were left, the sea was carrying away hundreds of loads of beach material in each high tide, and there was just room for a carriage to pass from one field into the other.[400] By the following year, a fence had to be thrown down to enable passage between the two fields;[401] and two years later the tenant claimed that there were little more than three acres left and that he had to throw down many yards of the bank so as to make a road on his neighbour's land. He had also suffered a personal misfortune and had lost a leg.[402]

The most sustained period of difficulty was during the agricultural depression that followed the Napoleonic Wars. Other landowners suffered in similar ways: the Corporation of the Sons of the Clergy, for instance, reduced its rents by one-third during this period.[403] Almost every year from 1816 to 1836 allowances were made by Emmanuel to its East Anglian tenants at Shernborne, St Cross and Rushall, and abatements were made to the rent due from Lydden and Ewell in Kent in the mid-1820s.[404] Tenants at Pinchbeck, Lincolnshire, also had problems at this time and the combination of low corn prices and poor drainage led to the bankruptcy of Cawood Robinson, tenant of Cuckoo Farm, in 1818.[405] The depression also affected the tenants at Sutton Coldfield in 1822.[406] Nor was London immune from difficulties: in 1816 houses were hard to let,[407] and a factor in settling the rent of the Four Swans, Bishopsgate in 1832 was the depreciation in property values in general and of taverns in particular.[408] No general policy was adopted for granting abatements during these hard times: the rent was often reduced by 10% and

[396] ECA Lo.1.85.
[397] ECA BUR.0.5(b).
[398] ECA Hu.2.2.
[399] ECA SCH.1.14a.
[400] ECA Sf.1.53.
[401] ECA Sf.1.54.
[402] ECA Sf.1.56.
[403] Cox 1978, p. 101.
[404] ECA SCH.1.3; SCH.1.5; SCH.1.10; ECA FEL.5.7.
[405] ECA Li.2.1, 3, 8, 10, 18–19, 31, 36–7, 40.
[406] ECA Wa.1.45.
[407] ECA Lo.11.4.
[408] ECA Lo.5.12.

occasionally by 15%. In 1822, the owner of lands at Little Welnetham in Suffolk, which were liable to a rent charge to the College, asked for an allowance if Emmanuel maintained a general policy; he had to grant 25% to his tenants.[409] For East Anglian estates, attention was paid to the abatements current in the area. Thus, in 1830 Henry Holland was advised, in response to his enquiry, that reductions in the 'Windham' (Wymondham) area were between 5% and 10%;[410] when an abatement of 10% each on the land and tithes was granted at Melton in 1834, George Archdall had likewise asked what were the general levels of allowances in the area.[411]

Sales and purchases of land

For most of the eighteenth and nineteenth centuries, colleges had difficulty in rationalising their land holdings or selling unproductive properties; changes did, however, gradually start to occur. Acts of Parliament were the only means of alienating property until the end of the eighteenth century when a redefinition of the land tax in 1798 offered a small opportunity for change. The Universities and Colleges Estates Act of 1858 broadened the scope for colleges.

In 1798, new ways to raise finance were being sought by the government – there was the threat of a French invasion – income tax was introduced and redemption of land tax was offered.[412] The Act of that year encouraged redemption of land tax, and under the Consolidation Act of 1802 colleges were enabled to sell any part of their landed estate to redeem tax on other portions.[413] Many colleges took advantage of this legislation: at Cambridge, St John's did so,[414] Pembroke sold land at Sawston in 1799,[415] and St Catharine's sold land in 1801 and 1805.[416] Emmanuel did not take the opportunity to sell land to raise the necessary income, but agreed to sell its fee-farm rent in 1799,[417] and sold consols to redeem the land tax at Stondon in 1799;[418] that of The Chalice (St Andrew's Street) was redeemed in 1839.[419] In 1810, in connection with the renewal of the lease of the Catherine Wheel in Smithfield, William Holme agreed with the Nettleshipps that the College should not dispose of land to redeem the land tax; to sell old houses, he felt, would be less objectionable.[420]

---

[409] ECA BUR.0.4(a).
[410] ECA BUR.0.4(d).
[411] ECA Nf.1.18.
[412] Turner 1986, pp. 1–2.
[413] Shadwell 1898, pp. 7–8.
[414] Howard 1935, p. 126.
[415] Attwater 1936, p. 105.
[416] Jones 1936, p. 272.
[417] ECA COL.14.2 ff. 118r–v.
[418] ECA COL.14.2 f. 123r.
[419] ECA Box 2.B4.
[420] ECA BUR.0.10.

During the nineteenth century, under individual Acts of Parliament, small pieces of land were sold to turnpike road commissioners or to railway developments; these sales were forced upon the College. Thus, in 1802 and 1834 land was sold at Sutton Coldfield for road improvement (the College was advised to use income from the later sale to pay costs of inclosure),[421] and land at Lydden and Ewell was purchased by the commissioners of the turnpike from Dover to Barham Downs in 1808.[422] Property was also sold to railway companies, as at Hornchurch in 1847 and Sutton Coldfield in 1861.[423] Estates did not necessarily benefit from such disposals: in 1864, uncertainty over the threat of compulsory purchase caused problems in the development of land at the Old Bailey where the tenements were in a bad state of repair. The next year, the decision was taken to rebuild as the College would probably receive more compensation than if it did not do so.[424] Railway schemes were opposed on the College's behalf, as at Stratford in 1843 and Hyde Farm (Surrey) in 1866, for instance.[425]

Redemption of various charges was also possible during the late eighteenth and early nineteenth centuries. In 1788, the annual payment of 3s 4d for the site of the College was compounded for £5;[426] most redemptions, however, took place in the following century. Tithes payable by Emmanuel were commuted between 1839 and 1848, at annual costs of over £40 in 1843 and over £20 in 1839, 1840 and 1844.[427] Copyholds were enfranchised at Great Gransden in 1851–2 and on the Lusby estate in 1863–4.[428] Inclosure at Sutton Coldfield provided the opportunity to redeem the rent charge there in 1830,[429] and the College sold its lease of the Sempire Lands in Cambridge in 1820 and 1823 and invested the proceeds in stocks.[430]

Such sales, of small pieces of land or of minor dues for trifling sums, were insignificant; not until the 1858 Universities and Colleges Estates Act did much change. The Act enabled colleges to sell, enfranchise and exchange all or any part of their landed property, subject to consent from the Copyhold Commissioners. Monies realised from such sales were to be paid to the Commissioners (and then their successors, the Board of Agriculture) to invest on behalf of the college until they were laid out in the purchase of other land.[431] Attitudes of colleges did not change overnight,

[421] ECA SCH.1.15; ECA Wa.1.73.
[422] ECA SCH.1.10.
[423] ECA Es.2.174; ECA COL.14.3 pp. 149–50, 154.
[424] ECA Lo.11.130.
[425] ECA COL.14.3 p. 26; ECA Lo.11.132.
[426] ECA BUR.0.3(c).
[427] ECA BUR.8.9; ECA FEL.5.7; FEL.5.11; ECA SCH.1.3; SCH.1.5; SCH.1.17.
[428] ECA BUR.8.9.
[429] ECA Wa.1.78.
[430] ECA COL.14.2 ff. 174r, 178r.
[431] Shadwell 1898, p. 22.

but during the next decade Emmanuel took the opportunity to sell its rent charges at Little Welnetham in Suffolk in 1860 and at Babraham in 1866, and to sell its estate at Pakefield in 1869 before it was entirely eroded away by the sea.[432]

Purchase of land remained subject to the law of mortmain, which was not repealed until the 1960 Charities Act, but certain exceptions were introduced. In 1856, land could be bought for college buildings, and under the 1858 Act no licence was necessary to reinvest monies derived from the sale of other college estates.[433] Emmanuel started to purchase estates in the nineteenth century, though initially on a tiny scale. In 1826, an opportunity to buy the vicarial tithes and glebe at Rushall was not taken advantage of;[434] in the next few years, however, some small purchases were made. These were all of land adjoining existing College property: one-ninth of Stratford Wharf was bought in 1834, next to land that had been bequeathed to the College two years earlier;[435] wasteland next to the College garden was bought from the Cambridge Corporation in 1838;[436] and as a result of inclosure land was bought at Sutton Coldfield in 1844.[437]

From the late 1850s, more substantial estates were bought. The first hint of such purchases occurs in 1857, when the Society approved the acquisition of Hall Farm, Little Plumstead near Norwich.[438] Nothing came of this, but two years later Molland Farm, adjacent to existing College property at Ash in Kent, was bought for £13,700.[439] More purchases were made during the 1860s: land at Mitcham in Surrey in 1867 (the vendor was Alfred Gwilt, the College's agent)[440] and in 1870;[441] Hook End Farm, Stondon in 1867;[442] and in the previous year houses in St Andrew's Street, Cambridge, using income from the sales of the Babraham rent charge and of land to the Kettering and Thrapston Railway.[443]

Emmanuel as a Landlord

Good tenants were an essential part of successful estate management; it was, therefore, important to choose them with care and to maintain good

---

[432] ECA BUR.11.4; ECA COL.14.3 pp. 180, 203.
[433] Shadwell 1898, pp. 19–22.
[434] ECA Nf.5.44.
[435] ECA Box 16.D43.
[436] ECA Box 1.F15.
[437] ECA Box 29.Aa29.
[438] ECA COL.14.3 p. 114.
[439] ECA BUR.8.9.
[440] ECA COL.14.3 p. 186; see p. 363.
[441] ECA Sr.17.80; ECA BUR.8.9.
[442] ECA BUR.8.9.
[443] ECA COL.14.3 p. 180; ECA Box 2.F6; ECA BUR.8.9.

relations with them thereafter. As amongst private owners, colleges rarely dismissed tenants and leases were frequently renewed or made out again to existing holders or their descendants.[444] Opportunities did arise, however, to let properties afresh and inevitably some tenants were unsatisfactory.

When a new tenant had to be found, the vacancy was often advertised. In 1821, for instance, the estate at Ripple in Essex was repossessed and Thomas Nettleshipp advised that the vacancy be announced in the Chelmsford papers.[445] This method was not always successful: in August 1830, only one response was made to an advertisement of a tenancy at Threadneedle Street and that applicant did not call again so George Gwilt offered to try once more.[446] On other occasions, College tenants offered to take land nearby: John Robinson, tenant of South College Farm in Pinchbeck, asked to become the lessee of the adjoining Cowbit Farm in 1815 when the existing tenant fell into financial difficulties.[447] He was unsuccessful, but did eventually become tenant of Cuckoo Farm in the parish in 1834.[448] Tenants also recommended their successors in some instances: at Lydden and Ewell, for example, the lessee wanted to leave in 1825 as his son had obtained a larger farm some distance away. The wish that the property would be let to William Darling Davis of Lydden, a carpenter, who agreed to a plan to build a lodge for livestock, was accepted by the Society.[449]

Announcement of a forthcoming vacancy had to be made with caution, especially if the existing tenant was not aware that he was about to be dispossessed. In 1842, for example, the College's agent at Sutton Coldfield advised that consideration of renewal of leases should be left until three to four months before the existing leases expired. Otherwise, those tenants who thought that the rent was too high and decided not to offer to renew would be given an opportunity to get as much out of the land as possible before the lease ended.[450] Similar considerations were made in other cases, too, sometimes for complex reasons. When the tenant at Holborn died in 1812, for instance, the College was advised that the estate should be let separately so as to avoid loss of money to a middleman.[451] In fact, though, Emmanuel itself was tempted to buy the lease. As the tenements were in need of repair, the Nettleshipps suggested that notice be given to do so but that an offer for the property should not be made in

---

[444] Beckett 1989, p. 616.
[445] ECA Sr.17.37.
[446] ECA Lo.8.30a.
[447] ECA Li.10.101.
[448] ECA BUR.0.4(e).
[449] ECA Ke.6.485; ECA Box 17.A20.
[450] ECA Wa.1.113.
[451] ECA Lo.11.141–2.

the College's name as it would appear as if the landlord was trying to depreciate the value of the land.[452] In the event, the lease was sold at a price beyond the College's limit.[453]

Prospective tenants often had letters of recommendation to support their applications. In 1816, for instance, the lessee at Stondon fell into difficulties and the lease was assigned to John Playle. The Nettleshipps advised Holme to write to the rector of the parish in which Playle lived, as the College might receive a more candid reference than its agents. Holme did so and received a reassuring reply.[454] On other occasions agents passed on comments and advice about possible new tenants. At Lydden and Ewell in 1842, for example, the landlord of the local pub wanted to take the farm. Quested, the College's agent, did not know the man but thought that he might be acceptable as he had access to plentiful supplies of manure as coaches changed horses at his pub.[455] A land surveyor was employed to let the land at Ripple in 1825 and he recommended that jobbers who did not graze their own cattle should be avoided as tenants since if they were to fall into arrears there might not be sufficient stock on the land upon which to distrain.[456] The assignee of Hyde Farm in 1809 was a man of credit and fortune and so a suitable tenant, despite his being an attorney;[457] and when the Four Swans Inn at Bishopsgate was passed to Henry Pearce, the College was assured that he had managed the inn for 20 years, was a careful man and was supposed to have saved money.[458] Security was also sought for rent as, for instance, at Cuckoo Farm in Pinchbeck in 1818.[459]

Despite these safeguards, not all tenants were entirely satisfactory. They could fail to pay their rents: in 1826, Cawood Robinson had to pay 5% interest on arrears of his rents at Pinchbeck.[460] The editor of the *Morning Chronicle*, James Perry, was tenant at Mitcham and he had to be reminded to pay his rent. The agents supposed that he generally thought more of politics: he eventually remembered his dues on one of his walks into the City to pick up news.[461] The tenant at Shernborne was given permission to resign his lease in 1818 on condition that he paid all of his arrears within ten days and sent a substantial advance on what was due for the current year.[462] He did not do this; the following year, he offered

[452] ECA Lo.11.146a.
[453] ECA Lo.11.147.
[454] ECA Es.4.4j; ECA BUR.0.10.
[455] ECA Box 17.A21.
[456] ECA Box 15.A32; ECA Es.4.6b.
[457] ECA Sr.1.9.
[458] ECA Lo.2.12.
[459] ECA Hu.3.3; ECA BUR.0.4(c); ECA Li.2.34.
[460] ECA Li.2.52.
[461] ECA Es.4.4h.
[462] ECA Nf.6.24.

to pay a reduced rent and to leave at Michaelmas but failed to agree on terms for a reduction.[463] In the end, he became insolvent and went to gaol and the College lost one quarter's income from the property.[464] Tenants could neglect their estates and fail to keep covenants. At Eltisley in 1810, for example, the College paid £106 in a successful suit for breach of covenants;[465] in 1801, a survey revealed that the tenant of the Old Bailey property had not kept the premises in good repair;[466] and in 1757 the felling, without permission, of at least £100 worth of timber by the tenant at Hyde Farm was noted. As he had died since then and as his executor was a bankrupt, there was no probability of redress.[467]

Not all tenants were pleasant characters. Lessees could be indolent (Benjamin Rouse of Chequer Court in 1815, for instance);[468] they could be 'of the radical genus and moreover very troublesome' (such as two of those who leased parts of South Sea Chambers, Threadneedle Street, in 1835);[469] they could be overactive and erect buildings without permission, as at St Andrew's Street in 1824;[470] or they could be obstreperous. George Boggas, tenant of Shernborne, was one such person and did his best to impede the progress of inclosure there and in 1768 he ploughed and sowed crops despite the fact that the allotments had already been staked out. Thus he created confusion and delayed execution of the award.[471] Such tenants harmed the estates. In 1831, for example, the lessee of the Four Swans asked for favourable terms because trade had declined. The fall in business could partly be attributed to the depression, partly to better transport and partly to increased availability of alternative accommodation which decreased the attractiveness of inns and stabling. In addition, however, the discourtesy of the innkeeper's predecessors had driven customers away.[472]

If tenants lived far distant from the properties that they leased, problems could arise. In 1817, for instance, Thomas Nettleshipp did not know how the tenant of Threadneedle Street could be asked to lay down the cost of a survey before mentioning the fine that would be expected, as he lived so far away.[473] Similarly, when the tenant of Lydden and Ewell wanted to assign his lease in 1819, he hoped that a licence would be granted without visiting the estate as he lived too far off to attend and

[463] ECA Nf.6.26–7.
[464] ECA SCH.1.3.
[465] ECA BUR.0.4(a).
[466] ECA Sr.1.1.
[467] ECA BUR.3.2 f. 68v.
[468] ECA Ke.5.1a.
[469] ECA Lo.8.35.
[470] ECA Ca.1.8.
[471] ECA Box 22.A13.
[472] ECA Lo.5.7.
[473] ECA Sr.17.21.

was planning to move even further away at Michaelmas.[474] One of the problems of the poorly farmed land at Hyde Farm in 1801 was that the tenants had not lived on the estate for the past 60 years.[475]

The College tried to keep its tenants at arm's length; like other landlords such as Guy's Hospital, much correspondence was carried out through agents.[476] Direct contact was not usually recommended. In 1811, for instance, the College was advised not to communicate with the tenant at Stondon; he was being made to carry out repairs and kept in ignorance of a decision not to renew his lease.[477] Tenants occasionally did write to the College directly. Sometimes this was to avoid the agents, especially if the tenant knew that he was not regarded with favour by them; this was so in the case of William Cole, who caused much damage to the Hyde Farm estate in the late eighteenth century.[478] Tenants also wrote from time to time to try to negotiate more favourable terms for their leases: such a communication might have been the cause of a reduction in the proposed rent at Holborn from £210 to £205 a year in 1825, but requests like this were rarely very successful.[479] At other times tenants were advised by agents to write to the Bursar: Henry Bicknell recommended the lessee of the Old Bailey to explain directly to the College why he could not pay his rent in 1856 and 1857.[480] On some estates, direct correspondence was much more usual as, for example, at Pinchbeck, where a tenant advised his landlord on a mode of management of South College Farm in 1825 and recommended five years later that insurance be taken out.[481]

College tenants must have found their landlord exasperating from time to time. Rent could be expected at a different time from that customary for the area: at Lydden and Ewell in 1805, the tenant wrote to explain that it was not usual to pay Michaelmas rent before Christmas, and in Essex, similarly, rent was not normally paid as soon as the College required it.[482] The main problems, however, were caused by slowness in decision-making. Between June and October, very little could be authorised as few Fellows were in Cambridge. Delays could be highly inconvenient: in 1804, a quick decision on renewal of the Catherine Wheel in London was asked for as the lease to the under-tenant was expiring and James Williams, the tenant, needed to know the fine that he would be charged

[474] ECA Ke.6.467–8.
[475] ECA Sr.1.1.
[476] Trueman 1980, p. 38.
[477] ECA Es.4.4a.
[478] ECA Sr.17.13.
[479] ECA Lo.11.155–6.
[480] ECA Lo.11.123a; Lo.1.68.
[481] ECA Li.5.1b, 2.
[482] ECA Ke.6.460; ECA Es.1.21.

before he could renew his sub-letting.[483] The need to sow turnips at Shernborne necessitated an instant decision on who would be the new tenant there in 1824;[484] and when a barn floor at Melton had to be repaired in July 1862, a quick reply was imperative as otherwise the work could not be carried out before the harvest.[485] Sometimes, tenants had to take risks as a result of such delays. In December 1837, for instance, a tenant at Sutton Coldfield wanted to make a fold yard and to build a brick shed on his allotment so that he could make manure and shelter his team and servants during storms. He asked for an allowance of £20 and a reply within ten days. The Bursar answered that the Fellows had gone down, but that he would recommend the request, which could hardly fail, to the Society in January; he suggested that the tenant might like to chance it.[486] Whether he did or not, the expenditure was approved on 30 January, he received his £20 and a good shed was built.[487]

Despite these frustrations, the College did its best for its tenants. Some were entertained to dinners, though not on a grand scale. In 1797, for instance, tenants were fed beef, pickles and apple pie on one occasion, lamb at Midsummer and mutton chops and pickles in October. The following year, ham, beef and pickles were provided in April, veal cutlets, bacon, shoulder of lamb and salad in May, lamb and salad in June and duck, mutton and potatoes in September – the total expenditure for these two years, though, was only £1 1s 10d.[488] The tenant at Rushall invited the tithe payers there to a substantial tea in 1855, with which they 'seemed much pleased', and thenceforward the College spent £3 annually on similar refreshments.[489] Individual tenants asked for the College's patronage from time to time: the tenant at Shernborne asked for advice on how to vote in a forthcoming by-election in 1817. Holme replied that the College was decidedly for the government.[490] At Pinchbeck, where the College generally managed its property without an intermediary, relationships were closer. Cawood Robinson asked for the College to use its influence to reappoint him a drainage commissioner there in 1819;[491] Clement Laxton requested aid in sending his nephew to Christ's Hospital in 1856;[492] and at Christmas 1844 and 1845 John Robinson sent a haunch of mutton to his landlord.[493]

[483] ECA Lo.11.133a.
[484] ECA Nf.6.66–7.
[485] ECA BUR.0.5(c).
[486] ECA Wa.1.102.
[487] ECA COL.14.2 f. 225r; ECA SCH.1.15; ECA Wa.1.104.
[488] ECA BUR.0.3(d).
[489] ECA BUR.0.5(b); ECA SCH.1.5.
[490] ECA Nf.6.19.
[491] ECA Li.2.35.
[492] ECA BUR.0.5(b).
[493] ECA Li.5.3b, 4.

The College also helped the local communities, especially their schools and churches. For instance, it gave two guineas for schoolbooks at Rushall in 1847, £25 for a new school there in 1855 and £2 annually to the national school from 1861.[494] Small pieces of land were given for schools: at Chequer Court in 1858, and at Melton in 1861, for example.[495] Churches in parishes where the College owned land were also supported: £10 was given towards reseating Godmanchester church in 1852; a new harmonium at Ewell received a donation of £2 in 1860; and £100 was promised towards building a church at Cowbit once the whole sum had been raised and proper contracts drawn up.[496] Local charities, too, were supported, such as the Harleston rifle corps in 1859 and Great Melton clothing club in 1868.[497] Other colleges, such as St John's, played similar roles in local affairs.[498]

Masters, Bursars, Fellows, rent collectors, agents and tenants in 1871 were all very different people from their predecessors in the early eighteenth century. Much had changed: letting arrangements, communications, finances, agricultural techniques and methods of administration had all altered. Long-established practices died hard, however, and much remained the same. The College still relied on land and property for its income, few estates were bought or sold, decision-making was very similar to that of earlier centuries and the College was still seen as a patron of local affairs. Whispers of changes to come, however, were in the air in 1871.

---

[494] ECA COL.14.3 pp. 50, 100, 142.
[495] ECA Ke.5.35; ECA Nf.3.33.
[496] ECA COL.14.3 pp. 81, 140; ECA Li.10.125–6.
[497] ECA SCH.1.5; ECA COL.14.3 p. 190.
[498] Howard 1935, pp. 143–5.

13

Richard Farmer

'I have not time to teach with precision: be contented therefore with a few cursory observations, as they may happen to arise from the Chaos of Papers, you have so often laughed at . . .'

Thus Richard Farmer in his open letter to his friend Joseph Cradock, *An Essay on the Learning of Shakespeare*.[1] It was the only book he published, and it is no more than a large pamphlet: brilliant, witty, deeply learned, perhaps a little perverse. Such was Richard Farmer, the central character in the history of Emmanuel in the late eighteenth century – a man too deeply occupied in the affairs of the college and of his pupils to have limitless time for study; a man too given to reading to have much time for writing.[2] In his day the College Parlour was the heart of Cambridge society; and his cheerful, friendly, ceaseless conversation won golden opinions from men of very different stamps. Farmer was a Tory, on very friendly terms with William Pitt, prime minister and MP for the University, in whose company most of 'the rulers of the University could not forget they were in the presence of a man who had the power of dispensing Bishoprics and Deaneries'; but not Farmer, who was said to have refused two bishoprics, though he certainly accepted a canonry at St Paul's, with the prebend of Consumpta-per-Mare, from the all-powerful minister and MP; and 'was always particularly affable' when Pitt 'came to visit his constituents'.[3] Yet Farmer the Tory was congenial both to Samuel Parr, 'the Whig Dr Johnson', and to Henry Gunning, the waspish radical who as Esquire Bedell personified the traditions and ceremonies of the University, and who in his *Reminiscences* damaged the reputation of many of the leading characters of the Cambridge he had known, and destroyed the fame of the University he loved and served (in other respects) so faithfully. The age of Farmer was to Gunning 'the very worst part of our history' –[4] all the more credit to Farmer that he is so amiably portrayed. The Master, indeed, regularly invited Gunning to college

---

[1] Farmer 1767, p. 3.
[2] Shuckburgh 1884, p. 36, cited Thackeray for this dilemma. On Farmer, see Sherbo 1992; McKitterick 1986, chap. 8; Shuckburgh 1884; Roberts 1961.
[3] Gunning 1854, I, 181–2, cf. p. 184.
[4] Gunning 1854, I, pp. xix–xx.

feasts, and enjoyed pulling his leg: when he found his pipe failed to balance on his finger, he would say: '"This is a Whig pipe, Master Gunning; it has got a twist the wrong way".'[5]

Yet the portrait we have of this remarkable man is very incomplete. We know him as a Shakespearean scholar, bibliomaniac, senior librarian or Protobibliothecarius of the University Library; we know him as a very active member of a distinguished literary circle. But he was first and foremost a family man and a college man; and we rarely encounter him with his family or his pupils. His father was a woolman and maltster in Leicestershire, and he retained so great an affection for his homeland that he embarked on an ambitious scheme for a *History of the Town of Leicester*.[6] At the end of his book on Shakespeare he threatens Cradock with more on the theme 'when I am fairly rid of the Dust of Antiquity, which is at present very thick about me, and indeed more in quantity, than I expected'.[7] Thus Farmer in 1767; in the mid 1770s the scheme was abandoned and his materials handed over to John Nichols, whose massive *History and Antiquities of the County of Leicester* is a masterpiece among the great county histories of the age; how much of it we owe to Farmer cannot be known.[8] He was always close to his family, and his mother outlived him; his own substantial fortune went to them;[9] his immense collection of books – which could have adorned either the College or the University Library and added greatly to their riches – was sold for the family's benefit.[10]

He was born in 1735 and came to Emmanuel in 1753. He was evidently a natural scholar, but no mathematician: in the Mathematical Tripos in 1757 he scraped a second, as we should say – he was not among the Wranglers, that is, but low among the Senior Optimes.[11] Yet by 1759 he was a fellow; by 1761 a tutor of the College. The affairs of many of the undergraduates and the organisation of their teaching (in so far as the College arranged it) were in his hands. In 1775 he became master, but remained tutor till 1782 or 1783. 'He lectured in Euclid, and the Greek Testament, besides Aristophanes, Cicero *De Officiis*, Plautus *Amphitryon*, Horace, and Grotius.'[12] As tutor, he handled the accounts of his students.

---

[5] Gunning 1854, I, 178.
[6] Shuckburgh 1884, p. 47. For his father's occupations, see Hubbard's *Book of Accounts*, quoted in Shuckburgh 1884, p. 140.
[7] Farmer 1767, p. 50.
[8] Nichols 1795–1815, esp. (for Farmer) I, p. v and n.8; cf. Sherbo 1992, chap. 4.
[9] Shuckburgh 1884, pp. 38, 49; Sherbo 1992, p. 17.
[10] On his library, see Lloyd 1977; McKitterick 1986, esp. pp. 296–7; Shuckburgh 1884, p. 54.
[11] Tanner 1917, p. 448. For his early career, see Sherbo 1992, chap. 1; Shuckburgh 1884, pp. 46–9, corrected by Shuckburgh 1904, p. 139.
[12] Shuckburgh 1884, pp. 46–7; cf. Sherbo 1992, p. 22 for sources; for what follows, see pp. 347–8. On Farmer as tutor, see Sherbo 1992, p. 22; on the tutors, see above, pp. 300–4, and Appendix 3.

In money matters, he was strangely inconsistent: in some respects careful in keeping accounts, concerned to ensure some regularity in his own and the College's affairs – and yet often careless of the difference between his own and the College's, and the University's, finances – and leaving a legacy of prosperous chaos at his death. His genial spirit seems to have made him a popular tutor, though Emmanuel remained small, with an intake of only about ten a year, as in his predecessor's time, throughout his tutorship. As Master, it is evident that his genial, easy-going ways combined with personal ascendancy and friendliness left little scope for the disputes with the Fellows which had punctuated Richardson's regime. He was the last Master to manage the financial affairs of the College: he was himself the Bursar. When he died, the accounts were in such confusion – and the difficulty of sorting them out with Farmer's heirs so great – that Tyson the Bursar was given a handsome piece of plate worth 20 guineas two years after Farmer's death – when he retired to a country living – particularly on account of the pains he had been at to settle the affairs of the College with the late Master's administrator.[13]

If we know little of Farmer the tutor, we fare better with Farmer the Anglican clergyman. He was a conventional figure of the Anglican establishment of his day. 'He had a deep-rooted dislike of Dissenters,' wrote Henry Gunning, 'whom he was most anxious to exclude from office, because he *conscientiously* believed them to be disaffected to the existing government'. As a fellow he was ordained, and like many Cambridge dons he served for many years a local curacy; Farmer's was at Swavesey, 'about nine miles' from Cambridge. 'He made a point of attending in all weathers. He began the service punctually at the appointed time, and gave a plain practical sermon, strongly enforcing some moral duty. After service he chatted most affably with his congregation, and never failed to send some small present to such of his poor parishioners as had been kept from church through illness. After morning-service he repaired to the public house, where a mutton-chop and potatoes were soon set before him: these were quickly despatched, and immediately after the removal of the cloth, Mr Dobson (his Churchwarden) and one or two of the principal farmers, made their appearance, to whom he invariably said, "I am going to read prayers, but shall be back by the time you have made the punch". Occasionally another farmer accompanied him from church, when pipe and tobacco were in requisition until six o'clock.' He then rode back to Cambridge, and slept in his chair from 7.30 to 9.00, 'when resuming his wig he started for the Parlour, where the fellows were in the

---

[13] Shuckburgh 1904, p. 134.

habit of assembling on a Sunday evening.'[14] In 1780 he was appointed chancellor of Lichfield, and in 1782 he succeeded to the 9th Prebend at Canterbury, which he held from 1782 to 1788, when Pitt arranged his translation to a resident canonry at St Paul's.[15] That was the extent of his ambition. He was ready to fulfil the duties of curate at Swavesey, and eager to be a canon of Canterbury and St Paul's – which involved a part of each year in residence – but he reckoned himself unfitted for the spiritual authority, or the courtly life, of a bishop. Thus Gunning: 'he would have made, I have heard him remark, "a very indifferent Bishop." He felt he could not discharge the duties of the Episcopacy with that dignity and decorum which the office demanded', but he was happy to be a canon of St Paul's, 'an appointment he considered far more suitable, and in which situation he was very popular. Consistently with his love of good fellowship, he gave excellent dinners to the Minor Canons on a Sunday, at one o'clock', and at nine he had a supper reminiscent of the cheer of the Emmanuel parlour. 'Farmer's mornings were usually spent in examining the old bookstalls in the neighbourhood of St Paul's. . . . His residence in town rarely prevented his being present on Feast-days at his own College. I well remember his exclaiming, on entering the vestry at [Great] St. Mary's on Ascension-Day, – "I have had hard work to be with you in time, Mr Vice-Chancellor, for at three o'clock this morning I was blowing my pipe with the worshipful Company of Pewterers!" '[16]

Residence at St Paul's was the culmination of many visits to London, to which he was drawn by two of his closest interests. He was an avid collector of historical portraits – 'iconomania' as contemporaries called it –[17] which led him to seek the acquaintance of London painters, engravers and dealers: 'Farmer had his foragers, his jackalls and his avant-couriers' at work on his behalf, in the characteristic phrase of his friend William Cole, the Cambridge antiquary, who refers elsewhere to this hobby as 'the rage for head-hunting'.[18] Thus he helped to found the systematic study of historical portraiture, and has a role in the prehistory of the National Portrait Gallery. In London he sat for Romney.[19] He gave work to London engravers, and to local craftsmen too: Joseph Freeman surveyed the college estates, repaired and improved old portraits in the

[14] Gunning 1854, I, 178–9. For the conflicting accounts of Farmer's preaching, see Sherbo 1992, pp. 57–8. He served Swavesey for many years and seems to have regarded clerical work as a normal and necessary part of a conscientious clergyman-fellow's duty in life. Gunning's view was that 'few parishes [in the Cambridge region] were so well satisfied with their pastor as Swavesey' (Gunning 1854, I, 180).

[15] Horn 1974, p.33; Horn 1969, p. 31; Shuckburgh 1884, p. 48; Hardy 1854, I, 586; Sherbo 1992, pp. 24–5.

[16] Gunning 1854, I, 184–5.

[17] See Owst 1949, esp. p. 85.

[18] Owst 1949, pp. 76, 83.

[19] Owst 1949, p. 89.

1 Miniature of Queen Elizabeth on her Letters Patent of 11 January 1584, granting licence to Sir Walter Mildmay for the foundation of the College. Most probably by Nicholas Hilliard.

2 The Westmorland Building – a reconstruction of the 'Founder's Range' begun in 1719. Over the door, the arms of Thomas Fane, 6th Earl of Westmorland (direct descendant of the Founder), the chief contributor to the cost.

3 The west front of the College; architect James Essex, completed 1775. Coloured aquatint from Ackermann's *Cambridge*, 1815.

4 The Chapel and Gallery from the south-west; architect Sir Christopher Wren, completed *c.* 1677.

5 The Great Pond, formerly the Dominicans' fishpond, with Emmanuel House (1894) and part of the Hostel (1886–94).

6c Screens in the Old Library,
originally the Chapel.
All of the late sixteenth century.

6b The original Hall screens,
masked by the eighteenth-
century panelling.

6a The Hall roof-trusses.

7 The Hall, interior.

8a The chapel, interior, after the refurbishment by A. W. Blomfield in 1884.

8b The Master's Lodge of 1874, by A. W. Blomfield.

9a The Chapel ceiling, designed by James Grove.

9b Detail of the communion rail in the Chapel.

10b The gable end of the Brick Building of the 1630s, commonly called Old Court.

10a The Elizabethan pulpit from the original Chapel (now the Old Library), now in Trumpington Church.

11a Lime-wood carving over the Gallery entrance-door, showing the arms of John Breton (Master 1665–75), William Sancroft (Master 1662–5) and Thomas Holbech (Master 1675–80).

11b Silver caudle-cup and cover, 1677, given by Sir William Temple.

12. North Court. One of several alternative designs by Leonard Stokes, c. 1910. As built, the gate-tower was omitted, and the left-hand range reduced to one storey.

13 The Founder's Tomb in St Bartholomew the Great, Smithfield, City of
London. Drawing by John Carter, 1784.

14a The Founder, from the full-length portrait painted for the College in 1588, now in the Old Library.

14b Binding, by Jean de Planche, of Theodore Beza, *Tractationes Theologicae*, vol. II (Geneva, 1573). The book, dedicated to Mildmay, is shown in the Founder's portrait.

14c Inscription in the Founder's hand on the title page of the French Bible (Geneva, 1588), presented to him by the ministers of the church at Geneva.

15a Ralph Symons, architect of the original buildings of the College.

15b Joseph Hall, Bishop of Exeter (1627–41) and Norwich (1641–56). Engraving by John Payne, 1628. Reproduced from vol. II of Hall's collected *Works*, 1647.

15c William Sancroft, by Bernard Lens the elder, painted in 1650.

15d William Bennet, Bishop of Cork (1790–4), and Cloyne (1794–1820), probably by G. C. Stuart.

16a Silhouette of Robert Towerson Cory, Master, 1797–1835. By Auguste Édouart, 1829.

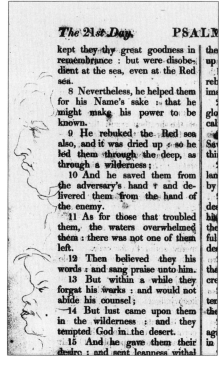

16b Caricatures in the margin of Psalm 106 in a Prayer Book of 1829 from the College Chapel, now owned by Mr John Harding.

16c Sketch of George Archdall-Gratwicke, Master, 1835–71, made in 1859 by Frank Besant, then an undergraduate at Emmanuel.

16d James Bennet Peace as rowing coach; from Herbert G. Jones, *Friends in Pencil*, Cambridge, 1893.

17a Edward Welbourne, Master 1951–64.

17b Richard Farmer, Master 1775–97. Drawing by John Downman, 1778, in the Fitzwilliam Museum.

17c Leonard Hugh Graham Greenwood, Fellow 1909–65. Chalk drawing by Luis Vargas, 1959.

17d Sir Frederick Gowland Hopkins (1861–1947). Charcoal drawing by Edmond Kapp, 1943, in the Fitzwilliam Museum.

18a The Founder's Cup:
silver-gilt tazza, made at
Antwerp, 1541. The finial is
enamelled with the Founder's
arms on one side and his
monogram on the òther.

18b The Founder's Cup: repoussé
decoration inside the bowl,
showing the poet Arion being
rescued by a dolphin, surrounded
by a frieze of fantastic
sea-creatures.

19 The Chapel Plate of 1637: all except the first were purchased from the legacy of the elder William Sancroft (Master 1628–37).
a One of a pair of double-gilt chalices, with paten covers; and one of three 'livery-stoops' (i.e. serving-flagons).

19b One of two parcel-gilt alms-dishes; and one of two silver-gilt patens.

20 Silver tea service, made by Paul Storr, 1817 (see p. 402): the tea-pot was given by George Porcher, the sugar-basin and cream-jug by George Collins Poore.

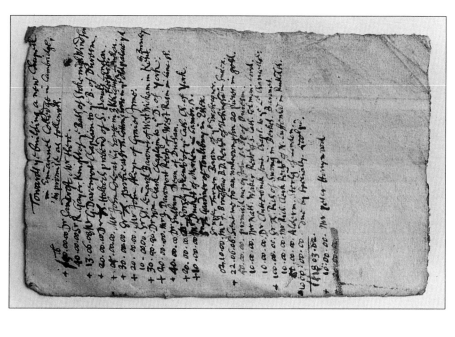

21c A first list, in William Sancroft's hand, of subscriptions towards the building of the Wren Chapel.

21a College Orders of 10 December 1588, signed by Laurence Chaderton, first Master, and the first twelve Fellows of the College.

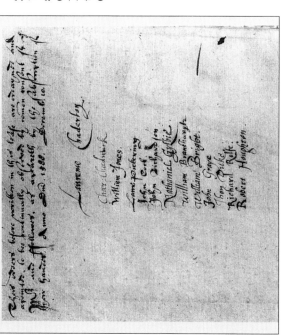

21b Entries in the College Admissions Register. The second line reads 'John Harvard Midlsex: Decemb: 19 [fee paid] £0 - 10s - 0d.'

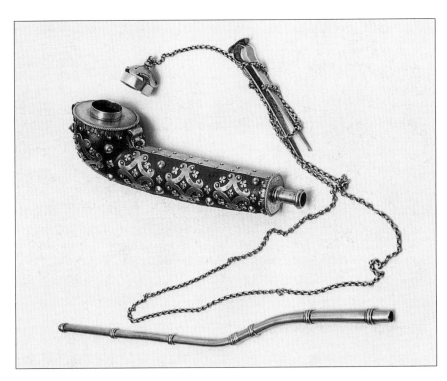

22a Samuel Parr's German silver tobacco pipe, *c.* 1790.

22b Samuel Blackall's woods (perhaps *c.* 1795), still used for playing bowls in the Fellows' Garden.

23 The Four Swans Inn, Bishopsgate, London, given to the College by the Founder in 1585. From a drawing of *c.* 1850.

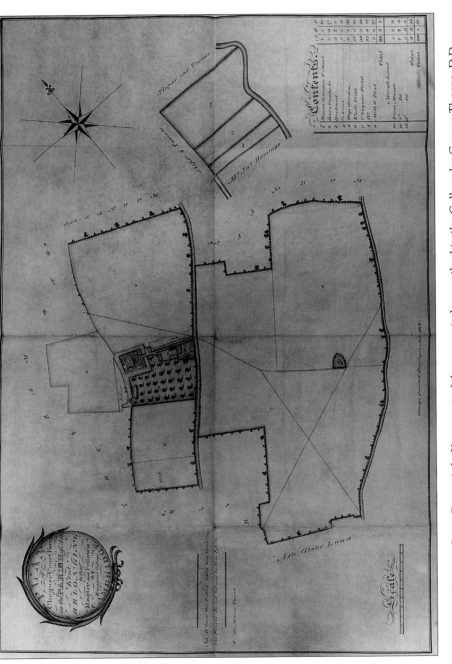

24 Map of Chequer Court Farm, Ash, Kent, part of the property bequeathed to the College by George Thorpe, D.D. (1638–1719). Drawn in 1824 by George Quested, surveyor, tenant of the farm.

Gallery, and provided numerous copies for Farmer's chambers and the Parlour.[20]

His love of books and his study of Shakespeare brought contact with literary circles in London, and especially with the editors of Shakespeare – brief contact with Samuel Johnson himself, acquaintance with Edmund Malone, close friendship with George Steevens and Isaac Reed.[21] Reed's diary is a prime source for Farmer's visits to London, his delight in the London theatre and similar indulgence nearer home at Stourbridge Fair, and for Farmer's favourite relaxation – pottering in his library with Reed and Steevens, visiting the other libraries of Cambridge and exploring the City; and the conversation of the Parlour.

Brief as it is, Farmer's *Essay on the Learning of Shakespeare* is sufficient alone to establish his fame as a scholar. Other students of Shakespeare, taking note of the immense depth of reading presupposed in his plays, had reckoned him a learned man, and cited sources in Latin, Italian and French he must have used. From an early age Farmer had collected voraciously English literature, middle and early modern; and this gave him a unique insight into the materials in the vernacular accessible to the poet. He was able to show that all the sources hitherto identified were available in English. He can dismantle the absurd conjectures of the learned by a hearty gust of common sense. For *unyoke* in Hamlet 'Homer and his Scholiast' had been quoted; but 'if it be not sufficient to assert it, with Dr Warburton, a phrase taken from Husbandry . . . we may produce it from a Dittie of the workmen of Dover, preserved in the additions to Hollinshed, "My bow is broke, I would *unyoke* . . ." '.[22]

Sometimes it is by subtle and penetrating textual and source criticism that he shows that Shakespeare used the English version. 'I myself will engage to give you quotations from the elder English writers (for to own the truth, I was once idle enough to collect such)' – thus the ageing young man of 32, the veteran tutor who had spent seven years at his last – 'Mr Theobald informs us that the very names of the gates of Troy, have been barbarously demolished by the Editors [of Shakespeare]: and a deal of learned dust he makes in setting them right again . . . But had he looked into the *Troy boke* of Lydgate, instead of puzzling himself with Dares Phrygius, he would have found this horrid demolition to have been neither the work of Shakespeare nor his Editors.'[23] Richard Bentley had made Cambridge illustrious as a centre of classical studies; and though Bentley had died when Farmer was a boy, and the age of silver had followed the age of gold, he shows himself a worthy successor of Bentley

[20] Owst 1949, pp. 80–1; Bendall 1992, pp. 118–19.
[21] Sherbo 1992, pp. 40–2, and *passim*; Reed 1946, *passim*.
[22] Farmer 1767, pp. 12–13.
[23] Farmer 1767, pp. 8, 22.

in the brilliance and originality of his scholarship and the polemical vigour and precision of his arguments. Farmer had been trained as a classic, and added to his knowledge of ancient literature a passionate interest in English, and in collecting books. When he defended a reading in *Much Ado* out of the *Arcadia* of Sir Philip Sidney, he characteristically added:

> 'I know it may be objected . . . that the *Arcadia* was not published before 1613, and consequently too late for this imitation: but I have a copy in my own possession, printed for W. Ponsonbie, 1590, 4to. though it hath escaped the notice of the industrious Ames, and the rest of our typographical Antiquaries.'[24]

By learning Farmer meant classical learning, and by the end of his book he had saved Shakespeare from almost all of it – even of the 'little Latin and less Greek' attributed to him by Ben Jonson.

'I hope, my good friend, you have by this time acquitted our great Poet of all piratical depredations on the Ancients: he remembered perhaps enough of his schoolboy learning to put the *Hig, hag, hog*, into the mouth of Sir Hugh Evans [in *The Merry Wives of Windsor*]; and might pick up in the course of his conversation a familiar word or two of French or Italian; but his Studies were most demonstratively confined to Nature and his own Language . . . Those who apply solely to the ancients for this purpose, may with equal wisdom study the *Talmud* for an exposition of *Tristram Shandy*.'[25] Perhaps; but like almost all polemic, his arguments carry him some distance beyond his goal.

'The late Dr Johnson . . .,' wrote William Bennet in a gloss on Cicero's *De Oratore* for use in his Emmanuel lectures, 'congratulated our Master Dr Farmer on the victory his pamphlet . . . had gain'd over all his adversaries, and Dr F. observ'd that some opponents . . . remain'd yet cavilling and refusing to be silenc'd. "Sir", replied Johnson, in the metaphorical style and strength of his Rambler, "the muscles will quiver when the life has departed." '[26] The muscles have quivered to some purpose, so that Samuel Schoenbaum can assert that in the twentieth century 'Farmer's ninety[27] small pages would be answered by T. W. Baldwin's fifteen hundred large ones'.[28] A variety of sources in French and Italian have since been found for which no English version can have been available to Shakespeare. He used anything that was grist to his mill; he had an extraordinary range of knowledge, including some languages at least

---

[24] Farmer 1767, pp. 22–3.

[25] Farmer 1767, p. 49.

[26] Quoted in Stubbings 1965–6, p. 71, from Emmanuel College MS 167.

[27] He is citing the enlarged third edition of 1789: there were five editions in all, two in 1767, 1789, 1800, 1821.

[28] Schoenbaum 1991, p. 104, citing Baldwin 1944. See also Sherbo, chap. 5.

other than English. If a busy working actor-playwright made most use of the material in English that he could lay hands on, that is no surprise; it is not the same as asserting that he had only Nature and English to guide him.

Farmer's virtuosity as a bibliophile was brought to trial when he first met Johnson, who visited Cambridge – chiefly perhaps in order to meet Farmer – in 1765. Fifty-three or so years later Baptist Noel Turner of Emmanuel, who was present, recalled the scene.

'In the height of our convivial hilarity our great man exclaimed: "Come now, I'll give you a test; now I'll try who is a true antiquary amongst you. Has anyone . . . ever met with the History of Glorianus and Gloriana?" Farmer, drawing the pipe out of his mouth, followed by a cloud of smoke, instantly said, "I've got the book". "Gi'e me your hand, gi' me your hand," said Johnson, "you are the man after my own heart.". . .' The story has an epilogue; for no one, not even Farmer, had truly seen a book of that name; but Dr Frank Stubbings detected in the sale catalogue of his books an edition of 1642 of Friedrich Dedekind's *Grobianus* (1549), a satirical guide to bad manners, to which the author subsequently added *Grobiana*, 'setting forth the rules and sleights of misdeportment for young women.'[29]

Farmer had all the learning and devotion to books which might have qualified him as a great librarian. He had two weaknesses: a lack of system and too great a devotion to reading. He presided over three libraries: his own, his College's and the University Library. They were all one to him, save that it seems never to have occurred to him to make any provision for the survival of his own, which went under the auctioneer's hammer when he was dead. It contained a unique collection of English literature, including twelve Caxtons, a First Folio of Shakespeare, a first edition of Paradise Lost, and an infinite number of less eminent rarities. Yet the University Library 'bought not a single fifteenth- , sixteenth- or early seventeenth-century English book during his librarianship'.[30] He was liable to keep among his own books some he had bought for the Library – while claiming reimbursement, sometimes more than once: not through dishonesty, but by carelessness. Under his instructions, others bound and re-ordered the University Library; and he himself added greatly to its holdings in some regions; but he made no attempt at all to duplicate the special rarities of his own collection for the sake of posterity. In 1784 a German scholar called Wendeborn came to Cambridge with an introduction to Farmer.

---

[29] Stubbings 1977a; cf. Stubbings 1965–6, pp. 69–70. Another version of the story is quoted in Schoenbaum 1991, p. 103, from James Northcote's *Life of Sir Joshua Reynolds* (2nd edn, London, 1818, I, 152).

[30] McKitterick 1986, p. 297. For Farmer's own library see above, n.10.

'He at first received me somewhat coldly, as a stranger; but when we had spoken together for some ten minutes, he took me by the arm, went with me into the College garden, showed me his own library as well as that of the College, and when he found that I desired to see the University Library at once went with me to it through several streets [to the Old Schools, where the Library then was], in his slippers, gave me a general view of it, and instructed the superintendent to have books and manuscripts which I wished to see sent to the hotel where I had put up. In the afternoon I had to eat with him and the Fellows of the College in their "Hall" or great dining room, and afterwards spent several evenings with him in the Combination-room . . . They were merry evenings, and Dr Farmer, a learned and good-humoured man, made them very pleasant by his conversation, his wit, and his joviality. . . .'[31]

In the same Hall on 29 September 1784, to celebrate the bi-centenary of the College, there gathered 'three turtles from the western Indies', a choir from the Chapel Royal directed by the Professor of Music, and 138 Fellows and guests, notable among them the young Mr Pitt, graduate of Pembroke, aged 25, recently elected MP for the University, Prime Minister and Chancellor of the Exchequer. Farmer presided: it was the crowning moment of his mastership.[32] But he is not to be judged by feasts and junketing alone. Careless in dress and manners he may have been; fond of his pipe and the parlour he undoubtedly was; but he was not the coarse-grained, indolent eighteenth-century mandarin he has sometimes been portrayed. He had a sensibility, a sensitivity even, which called out an answering chord in so unlikely a friend as Thomas Gray the poet, of Peterhouse and Pembroke; in Gray's later years a close friendship formed between 'a cheerful, companionable, hearty, open, downright man, of no great regard to dress or common forms of behaviour; the other of a most fastidious and recluse distance of carriage, rather averse to all sociability, but of the graver turn: nice and elegant in his person, dress and behaviour, even to a degree of finicalness and effeminacy'.[33]

In spite of his dedication to St Paul's and its bookstalls, Farmer is seen at his most characteristic in his own Library and among his own pupils and Fellows in Emmanuel; and we have a few – tantalisingly few – glimpses of both these interests in his fascinating correspondence with Thomas Percy (1729–1811). They were alike in their devotion to early

---

[31] Stubbings 1977–8.

[32] See *Cambridge Chronicle* 1784; Gunning 1854, I, 186–7. A satirical account of the festivity was printed under the pretence of being *An Account off the Festivation and Jubilee, holden at Emanuel Colledge, ynne Cambridge, September 29, 1684*, of which a copy is preserved in the Emmanuel College Library, bound up with a list of those actually present on 29 Sept. 1784 (amounting to 138). This mentions the three turtles ('several' in Gunning).

[33] William Cole, quoted in Shuckburgh 1884, p. 50, and Sherbo 1992, p. 37 (see ibid., p. 203, chap. 2, n.1).

English literature; utterly unlike in their capacity to publish, for Percy was a prolific author: the *Reliques of Ancient English Poetry* was only one – though the most remarkable – of many books. Percy had the singular merit of not living in Cambridge and rarely visiting it, so that they had to correspond, and some of their correspondence survives. 'I haunt you upon Paper like your Evil Genius'; wrote Percy on 28 February 1764; 'and break in upon your Philosophical and Tutorial persuits with my old ballads; as Punch interrupts the most solemn scenes of the puppet-show with his impertinent ribaldry.'[34] Two letters from Farmer to Percy illustrate his pursuits to perfection.

On 25 February 1765 Farmer wrote to Percy to tell him of Dr Johnson's visit and answer an enquiry about one Dr Wingfield whom he supposed dean of Worcester and his ancestor. Percy subsequently discovered he had misnamed the dean, but not before Farmer had searched Le Neve's *Fasti*, Thomas's *Survey of the Cathedral-Church of Worcester*, Godwin, Dugdale, Wharton, Inett etc. in vain. He was a true antiquary, not easily diverted from the chase. But the opening and the heart of the letter relate to Johnson.[35]

'Since I last heard from you, I have had the unexpected pleasure of Mr Johnson's Company at Cambridge – a Character the most extraordinary, that it has ever been my fortune to meet with. – I admire him, and I pity him: You will not ask me a reason for the former – his Compass of knowledge, and his manner of expressing that knowledge are really admirable, but he has pitiable infirmities both in body and mind. I can excuse his Dogmatism and Prejudices; but he throws about rather too much of what some Frenchman calls the Essence of But: in plain English, he seems to have something to except in every man's Character. Hurd for instance comes off badly, and Shenstone still worse.[36] . . . He was in good spirits, and seem'd pleased with us: the latter he confirm'd, by promising another visit towards summer. I wish, you may contrive to meet him; but it must be in No term, for his hours are not very Academic and I have been obliged to work double tides ever since . . .'

Farmer's Academic hours remind us of his tutorial duties, which we encounter in another letter to Percy, in which he thanks him for recommending Mr Nott to the College: his father has entered him as Fellow-Commoner – and Farmer was doubtless the more pleased, since these well-to-do students brought patronage and plate to the College.[37] It is followed by a dazzling display of bibliographical virtuosity, starting with: 'I have luckily found for you Wyatt's Psalms' which he had found

---

[34] *Percy Letters*, p. 66.
[35] *Percy Letters*, pp. 84–6, no. 24 (the orthography slightly adapted).
[36] For Hurd see above, p. 304. William Shenstone (1714–63), a versifier and friend of Percy, had been a contemporary of Johnson at Pembroke College, Oxford.
[37] *Percy Letters*, pp. 166–72, no. 54.

by persistent search in the University Library though the book was not catalogued, for he had followed a clue which hinted to him it should be there. This very rare collection of metrical psalms of 1549 by Thomas Wyatt was lent to Percy and returned; and it is still in the University Library. The letter concludes with comments on a liturgical pamphlet. Here are gathered a sheaf of his interests, as tutor, divine and bibliophile. Farmer was exceptionally gifted, in the variety of his interests a character-istic example of an eighteenth century savant – a brilliant scholar whose learning bore little relation to the studies of Cambridge undergraduates, and whose books were not the kind he sought for the University Library. But in the literary circles of men like Johnson and Percy, and in the Society of Antiquaries, he helped to preserve the good name of Cam-bridge and Emmanuel for learning in an epoch when relatively few sought their education there. Farmer died in 1797, and the new century brought a marked increase in the flow of students, though none for a while, perhaps, with his flair.

14

1797–1871

The masterships of Robert Towerson Cory (15 September 1797–April 1835) and George Archdall, later Archdall-Gratwicke (30 April 1835– 16 September 1871) between them spanned 74 years, which saw some activity in College building and estate management, but in learning were the most silent in the history of the College. 'The mastership of . . . Cory was not a period of much movement . . .; the mastership of Dr Archdall-Gratwicke was not an eventful one', wrote Shuckburgh.[1] Cory had been a tutor under Farmer, and was a well-established college man; but he lacked Farmer's panache or fame. Archdall was also an established college figure – he had come to the college in 1811 aged 24, after some years of internment in France: in later years he delighted to tell stories about Napoleon gathered during his French adventure. He had been a fellow since 1817, and bursar; he was a Bachelor of Divinity from 1825, and (as was the custom with clerical heads of house) took the D.D. on his election as master; from 1842 he was a canon of Norwich Cathedral. The most remarkable events of his long reign were two changes of statutes. The first, of 1844, was conservative. 'The number of the statutes is reduced from the original forty-four to thirty-four, chiefly by the omission of certain detailed provisions on discipline, and on stipends and allowances, which by lapse of time were socially or economically outmoded. The new book rationalised *de facto* changes, but it was concerned to preserve the *status quo ante*, not to look forward. Archdall' – from 1863, by royal licence, Archdall-Gratwicke – 'was already a man of seventy-four or so when the 1861 Commissioners brought change from outside'. As in all colleges, the new statutes deriving from the First Royal Commission cleared away much ancient lumber: the provision that only one scholar and one fellow might come from each county disappeared, and the scholarships and exhibitions were simplified. It became possible for a layman to hold a fellowship for ten years, or longer if assistant tutor, tutor or bursar; and fifteen years' service in a college office entitled a man to a fellowship for life – so long as not more than two such fellowships

---

[1] Shuckburgh 1904, pp. 169, 176. For Cory and Archdall see ibid. chap. 9, esp. pp. 169, 177, and pp. 163, 175, 179 for these dates – and for what follows.

were held at one time. A breath of the new more secular world is felt, but a gentle breath. It was still assumed that most fellows will be clerics, and that they will marry and go out to serve livings; the lifelong professional academic still lay unperceived in the future, if not very far in the future. In Caius the statutes of 1860 allowed any fellow to marry. Emmanuel eschewed this revolutionary step; but they tested the water. A new statute allowed the election of men of literary distinction who were married, so long as their number never exceeded one sixth of the whole body – nor had they any claim to college livings. 'One is not surprised to find', writes Frank Stubbings, that this new freedom 'had no practical result until after [Archdall-Gratwicke's] death'. He was remembered as 'a man of singular good sense, with the charm of an old time courtesy'.[2] He was remembered for little else.

Distinguished recruits were rare, and 'the numbers continued small: the entrances from 1801 to 1810 averaged 14.7; from 1811 to 1820' – when the University was growing fast – '21; from 1821 to 1830, 21.8; from 1831 to 1840, 17.1'.[3] 'On a hunting morning same dozen horses, it is said, would be in waiting at the college gates';[4] but it was rare for an Emmanuel man to enter for the mathematical tripos – or for the classical tripos, after it opened in 1824. It was not a college of hard reading men. Yet the tutors were not the nonentities William Burdon had described in 1800. They included Jane Austen's lively friend Samuel Blackall, and, briefly, James Slade, a notable minor theologian, who settled in Lancashire and won some celebrity for teaching the poor of Bolton, and writing on church reform.[5]

For a while after 1797 the community contained a fair sprinkling of fellow commoners, as in Farmer's day. They can still be traced by their plate – by knives and forks and coffee pots and every kind of plate, above all, by their tea-pots. The eighteenth-century rule that fellow-commoners justified their places at high table by presenting plate was still honoured; and in 1816 Mr Tighe presented two teapots; soon after, four identical teapots from the workshop of Paul Storr are the memorial to three fellow commoners and one mature pensioner.[6] By 1820 the Emmanuel Parlour must have been awash with tea. Tea-drinking was so prevalent at this period in Evangelical Magdalene that its students are supposed to have 'absolutely rendered unnavigable with tea-leaves' the river below the

---

[2] The quotations are from Stubbings 1983b, no. 35. For the statutes see *Statutes* 1861, p. 21; Shuckburgh 1904, pp. 177–8.
[3] Shuckburgh 1904, p. 170.
[4] Ibid.
[5] See above, pp. 314–17; *DNB*; Venn.
[6] These items are 17.9–18 in Joan Stubbings' catalogue of the College plate, ECA FUR.8.12 (1) and (2). For tea drinking at Magdalene, see E. Duffy in Cunich *et al.* 1994, p. 190.

College, and in 1828 the first Magdalene Boat Club was called 'The Tea Kettle'.

The fellow-commoners went into a variety of professions; some were country gentlemen, some men of affairs, some – like the rank and file of pensioners and scholars – became clergymen; one, George Tufnell, was briefly a soldier, and then took orders.[7] The most interesting of the donors was Frederick Thackeray, who followed his father to become a leading surgeon at Addenbrookes.[8] But his early career was checked by an astonishing professional confrontation. In 1803–4 the vice-chancellor was the master of Caius, Dr Davy, M.D., a practising physician; and he and the regius professor of physic of the day, Sir Isaac Pennington, joined forces to reinterpret an ancient statute to the effect that a candidate who had practised 'any trade or profession whatsoever' might not proceed to a medical degree. By this means they prevented anyone who had practised as a surgeon from proceeding M.D., while welcoming practising physicians. It was a strange manoeuvre in the long campaign between physicians and surgeons. Frederick Thackeray's father, in Henry Gunning's words, 'had sent him and his two brothers to Edinburgh, as well as to Paris, for the express purpose of improving themselves, and of acquiring that professional knowledge for which our University was confessedly an indifferent school' – and so remained till the late nineteenth century.[9] But when Thackeray came to Emmanuel in 1800 as fellow commoner, he presently found his way ahead barred, because he had not only studied, he had (in a modest way) practised the art, or trade, of surgery. But by 1815 new winds were blowing even in the ancient medical faculty, and he was able to resume his studies; in 1819 he presented his teapot; and in 1820 he proceeded M.D.

An exceptionally vivid source for the varieties of student aspiration in the Emmanuel of the 1810s survives in the diaries of the fellow-commoner John Barber Scott of Bungay, and in the revision of them made by the author himself to form a kind of autobiography. From this 'autobiography' Frank Stubbings has abstracted all that relates to Emmanuel, and we are able to discern the portrait of a young man in whom the temptations which beset a well-to-do fellow-commoner fought for mastery with academic ambition.[10] In 1809 his name 'was put upon the boards of Emmanuel as a pensioner', and he embarked on a course of moderate

---

[7] Joan Stubbings' catalogue, no. 18.

[8] Frederick Thackeray's teapot is 17.15, given in 1819.

[9] Gunning 1854, II, 193, quoted Brooke 1985, pp. 198–9, where the incident is discussed; cf. Winstanley, 1940, pp. 161–3. For the revival of the medical school, see Brooke 1993, pp. 166–73.

[10] The following extracts are all from Frank Stubbings's notes. Some of them have been printed in Ethel Mann's volume of extracts, Mann 1930; and further volumes of extracts are in prospect. Although Scott incorporated much material from the original diary, these extracts also contain much later reflection on the errors of his youth.

study punctuated with 'gaieties and flirtations', but also with bouts of ill-health which led him reluctantly to accept translation into the more luxurious life of a fellow commoner – though 'I felt less confident of being able to read for honours.' When he returned for a new session in October 1810, 'the aspect of my College pleased me. The tone of Emmanuel society at that time was gay, gentlemanly and classical. The senior Tutor, Samuel Blackall, was eminently so. The kindness, mildness and quiet piety of the other Tutor, James Slade, won my affection and respect . . . The Master, Dr Cory, was timid, unused to the world, troublesomely doubtfully conscientious, but very kindly disposed.' Scott found himself popular with dons and undergraduates alike, and gathered a large acquaintance from many colleges. 'Sir Busick Harwood, professor of Anatomy, invited me to a supper party of 20.' Blackall examined him and 'pronounced me first in mathematics' of his own and the previous year; Slade 'also reported favourably on my classical acquirements'. In 1811, in spite of the support of his tutors and good advice from his father, 'I was constantly suspended as it were between virtue and industry, and idleness and dissipation . . . I was not undistinguished – ingloriously alas! – for street and college rows. Meanwhile my turn came to write a Latin Declamation' – and but for the intrusion of a friend from Suffolk when he was learning it, so that he could not recite it all from memory in College chapel, he might have won the prize. We hear much of balls – after a Huntingdon ball he and a friend 'astonished the Natives by levelling their iron palisades and wrenching their knockers – all out of pure exuberance of health strength and spirits'. At about the same time 'I attended Harwood's lectures on anatomy and Blackall's on optics. Rode to races on the hills' – and galloped to Newmarket. 'At the request of my tutors I did compose a Greek Sapphic ode of 30 stanzas' for a university prize; and the classical tutor told him that if he had brought it to him in time for correction, he might have won the prize. In June 1811 the duke of Gloucester was installed as chancellor, and Scott describes the ceremonies and celebrations – 'concerts, orations, balls, dinners, suppers and public breakfasts' with lively enthusiasm. In the long vacation Blackall invited him on a tour 'to the seat of war in Portugal'; but he chose instead two months of quiet study – 'read some of Newtons Principia but having no help could not make it out . . . – went over to Conic Sections – read much of Herodotus attentively with maps and Beloes translation, and notes – began Italian grammar and read Roscoe's Life of Lorenzo de Medici – and in miscellaneous reading Tom Jones – Pope's Letters – Delolmes Constitution of England (in part) and Burrows' History of the Stuarts.'[11]

---

[11] This is from fo. 87 of the 'diary'; the passages quoted below are between fos. 87 and 113. 'Delolme' was Jean Louis de Lolme; his book, *Constitution de l'Angleterre* (1771) was translated into English as *The Constitution of England* (1775).

On 16 October 1811 a friend came 'to tell me that the Westmoreland Buildings of Emmanuel, in which my rooms were situated, were wholly burnt out . . . The fire which had arisen in G. Thomas's rooms, probably in consequence of his dropping a spark from his candle into his portmanteau which stood near the curtains, had entirely destroyed the fine range of buildings except the outer walls . . . I dug among the ruins in the forlorn hope of finding some relics of my property' – but all his books and furniture were destroyed – and he had to be content that winter with cold rooms in the Brick Building. In retrospect he speaks with gloom of how the misfortune encouraged them to idleness and dissipation; but in a letter to his father of 6 December 1811 he speaks with enthusiasm of dinners he had attended and given. 'I flatter myself my dinner on Tuesday was very handsome. The first course consisted of fish and soups only; the second of turkey, roast beef, haricoes, curry etc. etc.; the third of game and sweets' – twelve sat down to it, including Blackall, and the port and claret provided by his father were much enjoyed. 'Your enclosing a £50 note in your next letter will oblige.'

But in 1813 he was hard at work on mathematics in particular, only occasionally visiting Newmarket or travelling elsewhere. In January 1814, 'in the second week of this year, I was a prey to headaches and languor and all the complaints incidental to a hard reading man'. He went through the snow to the Senate House examination, and secured a good II.1 – 6th Senior Optime, to his own satisfaction, though to his father's disappointment. 'And considering in what idle and dissipated society I was thrown . . . by being sent up as a Fellow Commoner of Emmanuel with almost unlimited command of money, and how idle I consequently was for two years', and interrupted by illness even in the eighteen months' hard reading, 'I felt and still feel I had good cause to be satisfied'. The College allowed him to stay in his old rooms for two more terms of study free 'from mathematical drudgery'. 'I turned to subjects I best liked. Among these were Sir Joshua Reynolds' Lectures on Painting. I also read Mme de Staël's "L'Allemagne" with great interest.' In the summer he travelled – and visited Napoleon on Elba – and in November finally gave up his rooms; but not his studies, for he planned to take orders, and 'attended divinity lectures by Fawcett with that view', finally leaving Cambridge in June 1815. In 1815–16 he spent some months in Edinburgh studying philosophy and natural sciences, and from 1816 to 1818 travelled on the continent. There followed three years' careful study of scripture – he learned Hebrew and read deeply in the Old and New Testaments. His final decision was against taking orders.[12]

Scott's account of himself is a remarkable commentary on Cambridge in this era: on the temptations that surrounded a young man of means –

---

[12] Cited from Frank Stubbings's transcripts.

and the opportunities for serious study of a wide range of subjects, including both mathematics and divinity. It is in marked contrast to the brief account of Emmanuel by a man who came up in 1859, and later recalled only his sporting life – loading the tutor's gun when he went shooting, supplying the pond with fish from the fens, hunting 'once a week with the Suffolk', and 'boating and cricket', for the era of more organised sports had arrived – the boat clubs in the 1820s, cricket by the middle of the century.[13]

The relative paucity of men who secured high honours made for some difficulty, it seems, in the recruitment of fellows; in 1813 they even took the step of electing a Caian, E. V. Blomfield, brother of the celebrated bishop of London. But Blomfield died in 1816, and the experiment was not repeated till many years later. In 1827 a college order attempted to list the essential qualifications for a fellow: he must be a wrangler (a first in the maths tripos) or a senior optime (a second), or a first or second in the classical tripos, or have won some other University honour open to competition. There had been some successes – Foley in 1823 was 6th wrangler; and some scrapes – Fearon in 1824 was a low second in maths and a third in classics.[14] In after life the roles were reversed: Foley was a rector all his days, succeeding Samuel Blackall in North Cadbury; Fearon rose to be archdeacon of Leicester. The new fellows of the late 1820s and early 1830s included some wranglers, and some seconds.[15] In the mid 1820s and again in the mid 1830s for some years there were no Emmanuel wranglers. Meanwhile another college order had attempted to provide another hurdle in the fellowship stakes: all candidates, after being placed in their tripos order, were sat down to a general knowledge examination, in which they had to show 'a competent proficiency in every one of the subjects: viz., Mathematics and Natural Philosophy; Hebrew, Greek, Latin; Elements of Theology, especially the Greek Testament'.[16] This may partly reflect the weakness of the candidates; but it also represents the clear notion that the triposes did not contain all that was necessary for salvation, nor even all one learned at Cambridge; that a reading man should be proficient in a wide range of disciplines. The same order concluded that if no local candidate could be found, recourse be had to

[13] ECA TUT. 18.6, anonymous reminiscences.
[14] Shuckburgh 1904, pp. 171–3; Tanner 1917, pp. 482–3, 602. For Blomfield, see Venn, *Caius*, II, 148 and ECA COL.14.2 fo.156b; Shuckburgh 1904, p. 172, alleges that the new rule was broken in 1829 by the election of Colbeck and Bunch, and in 1831 of Dickson – but all three were senior optimes. Emmanuel had no wranglers between 1824 (Warden, who somehow was not made a fellow) and 1828 (Tuck, who *was* elected a fellow: Tanner 1917, pp. 483–7). For the degrees of Emmanuel fellows between 1750 and 1870 see Appendix, p. 732, in Searby 1997. Five had only ordinary degrees in the period 1781–1810. There is a marked improvement in the mid and late nineteenth century.
[15] Tanner 1917, pp. 487–92.
[16] Quoted Shuckburgh 1904, p. 172.

another college 'as directed by the statutes'. But this was not a popular option before the 1870s: only W. P. Anderson and J. B. Pearson came under this rubric, both from St John's in the 1850s.[17] After 1870 Fenton Hort and many others ushered in a new age, in which teaching fellows especially were frequently recruited from elsewhere.

However chosen, the fellows of the early nineteenth century were – with hardly an exception – all potential clergymen. They served their turn as fellows of Emmanuel and filled a variety of offices; a few of them became tutors and so seriously involved in college teaching and the welfare of the undergraduates; and then they took a college living and were free to marry. Thus to the fellowship the college livings seemed a most valuable part – perhaps the most valuable of all – of the college properties; and they took great pains, still in the nineteenth century, to enhance them, especially by use of the Dixie Fund, in agreement with the current representative of the family who had to be involved in presentations to such livings. The advowson of Boddington in Northamptonshire was purchased in 1823 and Brantham in Suffolk in 1836: they were valued in 1841 at £757 and £1,117 per annum, which put them well above the middle range of incomes, between Loughborough at £1,848 and Thurning at £181 and Little Melton at £110.[18] The purchases went on: East Bergholt (Suffolk) in 1836; Little Bentley and North Benfleet in Essex in 1839 and 1841; Lechlade in Gloucestershire in 1852; Winteringham in Lincolnshire in 1854; Whitestone in Devon in 1870; Bletchingley in Surrey in 1876.[19] By then the test acts had been abolished; fellows no longer had to take orders; there was already a significant lay element in the fellowship, and secularisation was on the way. As the college livings reached their peak, their crucial importance to the fellowship began to wane.

Of their importance in the first half of the century there is no question. Of the eleven fellows who are listed in the *Cambridge University Calendar* for 1806, all pursued clerical careers.[20] William Pemberton alone remained a fellow till his death, at a comparatively early age, in 1816. He had been elected in 1796, and in later years, from 1808, combined his college duties with the curacy of St Andrew the Great, a hundred yards from the college. He was University Registrary from 1809 till his death, and a tutor from 1812. John Gilbert was to be presented in 1809 by the college as master of Bungay School and vicar of the small parish annexed to the

---

[17] Shuckburgh 1904, p. 173. For the syllabus, see Searby, 1997; Wordsworth 1877.

[18] ECA Box 6.C.20; 6.D.5 (Boddington and Brantham). For the valuation of 1773 see Bennet's Book (ECA, COL 9.1 (A)), pp. 68–71; for 1841, *CUC*, p. 302 (this was the first year in which values were recorded in *CUC*). The Dixie Fund had been aimed to advance the study of divinity (see pp. 109, 169, 425n.).

[19] ECA Box 6.D.5; 7.F.11; 8.B.59; 7.E.11; 11.C.29; 11.B.9; 6.B.26.

[20] *CUC* 1806, p. 243. Details of the fellows' careers are from Venn; for Pemberton, see also tutors' list (p. 582) and Tanner 1917, p. 51.

mastership. In 1812 he married and received a Norfolk living from another patron; and in due course he became a country squire and died in ripe old age at the Manor House at Chedgrove in 1862. Robert Watkinson already had a lien with Charterhouse when elected fellow in 1800; he was a master there on and off until 1826; then he married and settled to an Essex living, not one of Emmanuel's, remaining there till his death in 1869. Perhaps the most remarkable character in the fellowship was John Griffith, who came as a sizar from Carmarthenshire in 1791, was elected fellow in 1797, and married in 1809 before he was entitled to a college living. He held various curacies in and about Ely and ended vicar of Fulbourn; he was 'a remarkable personality and an esteemed preacher; long remembered for his rich store of anecdotes'. He never lost contact with Ely, where he had been prison chaplain, and had received the ropes of hanged felons as perquisites of his office: he left his housekeeper his collection of them, and she in turn sold them as a cure for sore throats. He was the moving spirit in the founding of the first National School at Ely; and at St Mary's Ely he is buried.[21]

The six senior fellows of 1806 all took college livings in their turn. The turn was not a simple matter of rote, for some livings were much more valuable than others, and some fellows had their own choice of the county in which they preferred to live. Hardyman, the senior, already non-resident, took North Luffenham in the same year 1806 (£624 in the list of 1841). In 1809 Henry Smythies, second senior in 1806, took Stan-ground, which was a plum (£1,300), while Fressingfield cum Withersdale in Suffolk, worth only £597 in the list of 1841, went to Thomas Allsopp, fifth on the list of 1806. Curiously the third, another absentee, James Dunn, who had been for some while a curate in Kent, had to be content with the yet poorer living of Preston in Suffolk in 1810 (£402) – which he was, however, able to combine with a Norfolk living to make a competent livelihood. Samuel Blackall had told Jane Austen in 1798 that he had a fancy to North Cadbury;[22] and in 1812 he at last had his reward: it was not a rich living (£700), and we may presume that he had other reasons for preferring Somerset to the East Anglian villages he might have aspired to. Long after all these events, William Holme, who had served the college as bursar, was rewarded with the richest of all, the rectory of Loughborough (£1,848) in 1827. And finally, in 1832, Henry Holland, junior fellow in 1806, after serving curacies here and there, was presented to the moderate living of Thurcaston (£676). These long delays help to

---

[21] Venn. The residents and non-residents have been distinguished below by signatures to college orders: the distinction cannot be precisely drawn – attendance at meetings shows curious fluctuations.

[22] See above, p. 316.

explain the eagerness of the nineteenth century fellows to add to the stock of livings.

The year 1835 saw the death of R. T. Cory and the election of G. Archdall to succeed him as master – and Archdall's marriage to a parson's daughter from Sussex.[23] Of the thirteen fellows listed in that year all but four achieved college livings. Of the four, Ralph Clutton rose to be vicar of Saffron Walden in 1844; Robert Andrews went to live at Middleton with his brother-in-law, and died in his rectory in 1888, aged 89, having resigned his fellowship in the early 1870s – we do not know why. Thomas Dickson had already moved to Lancashire where he was perpetual curate of Whittle-le-Woods and held other preferment; Robert Birkett went further north and settled in his father's vicarage in Westmorland. The nine who received college livings were given them approximately in chronological order from 1837, when John Weller, senior fellow, went to Luffenham, to 1849 when Roger Buston, junior fellow in 1835, went to Twyford. William Colbeck indeed a little anticipated his natural turn when he took Fressingfield cum Withersdale in 1846; for Henry Fearon, his senior, was waiting for the supreme reward of Loughborough. This he achieved in 1848; but an arrangement had been made ten years earlier whereby a part of this large parish was separated to form Emmanuel Church in Loughborough – which also became a college living, and Robert Bunch one its first incumbents.[24]

The problems and possibilities in the choosing of fellows are particularly well illustrated in the case of Harold Browne, the one really distinguished, and well documented, fellow of the 1830s.[25] Browne was born of well-to-do parents living in Aylesbury, and spent four years at Eton and nearly a year with a private tutor at Postford House near Albury on the Surrey Downs, who prepared him after a fashion for Cambridge while the village parson drove home the evangelical teaching of his early life.[26] In 1827 he was entered a pensioner at Emmanuel – the reason for the choice is not known; nor did it at first stimulate the young man's academic interests.

'Emmanuel, like Eton,' he himself wrote later in life, 'was then a very idle though a very gentlemanlike college. I am ashamed to say that, notwithstanding all the good impressions of Postford and Albury, the idle habits of Eton came back upon me at Cambridge. Notwithstanding my idleness, I had always been very fond of literature and of literary society,

---

[23] Venn.

[24] Bunch is wrongly called rector of Loughborough in Venn. The parish of Loughborough was divided in 1838 by the creation of Emmanuel Church – both old and new were in the patronage of the College. ECA Box B. A.95.

[25] For what follows see Kitchin 1895, esp. pp. 22–40.

[26] Kitchin 1895, pp. 8–22. Kitchin (p. 21) gives him 'about a year' at Postford, but he was still at Eton early in 1827 and at Emmanuel by late November (Kitchin 1895, pp. 8, 22).

and felt great interest in mathematics. My tutor assured me I could be Senior Wrangler if I would read, but I could not bring myself to read steadily, and cared more to pull stroke of our College boat, and to have her successful in the boat-races, than to take a distinguished degree. My classical studies I utterly neglected all through my undergraduateship. When it was too late I bitterly regretted the time I had lost. I felt that I might have done more if I had worked . . . and I determined to be a harder working man for the future, and by God's help I became so.'[27]

Meanwhile he earned a reputation as a friendly and peaceable man – a peacemaker indeed – among his fellows, which he kept all his days; but life and popularity came easily to him, more easily than mathematics, and he had to be content with being 24th wrangler in 1832. Ill-advisedly he went on to the Classical Tripos, in which he secured a third.[28] 'Happily for himself and the English Church' wrote Dean Kitchin, his biographer, 'Harold Browne was not hampered by lack of means; for his parents . . . were only too glad to give him another chance of winning University distinctions'; and he set to work to study theology. Cambridge made no provision in its triposes until the 1870s for theology; and even the Theological Examination in which one might attain honours only dated from 1856. But it had considerable provision for the small number who wished to study theology seriously on their own. In 1833 Browne was one of the first Crosse Scholars; in 1834 he won a Tyrwhitt Hebrew Scholarship; in 1835 the Norrisian Prize, receiving personal compliments from the master of Trinity. And so he read and studied, and taught a little; and in the Long Vacations he went on reading parties with friends and pupils to Wales, to Scotland, to Devon, and to Germany and Switzerland.[29] In these years he laid the foundation of the deep, if fairly conventional, learning in biblical and patristic studies which was to qualify him for the Hulsean Professorship twenty years later. He was also undergoing a kind of conversion. He had been brought up an evangelical, and confirmed in his Calvinism by the parson of Albury; in the early 1830s he was deep in the fathers, feeling the urge, becoming common in his day, for a genuine return to the early church, 'to primitive practice . . . Then . . . came the "Tracts for the Times", which he . . . gladly accepted, because they too, in the main, advocated a return to primitive Christianity.' Thus far, Dean Kitchin; Browne himself declared that 'Something of the kind was in the air before Newman arose, a great genius, to put it into form and shape . . . Then came out the "Tracts for the Times" . . . no wonder that many of us were very much struck and carried away by the zeal of the Tract-writers, because they so turned our attention, especially to the primitive

---

[27] Kitchin 1895, pp. 22–3.
[28] Kitchin 1895, p. 28; Tanner 1917, pp. 491, 606.
[29] Kitchin 1895, pp. 28–30.

antiquity.'[30] From this time on, Browne was a high churchman, a tractarian – though never a ritualist, and always taking an independent view, from distant Cambridge, of the Oxford movement, especially when some of its leaders approached, then joined, the Church of Rome. He retained, furthermore, some sympathy for the evangelical associates of his early life, and always strove to avoid being a party man; only for liberals had he little sympathy, even though a scholar himself. When *Essays and Reviews* appeared in 1860, the manifesto of a mild liberalism as it seems to us, the mark of the beast as it seemed to many traditionalists at the time, Professor Browne (as he then was) preached a course of sermons in Great St Mary's arguing for traditional interpretations of the messianic prophecies in the Old Testament.[31] Yet he strongly deprecated the exaggerated language of many of the critics of *Essays and Reviews*.

Harold Browne is our one clear guide to the churchmanship of Emmanuel in the 1830s, and a confusing one. He had come to the college an Evangelical, and it was presumably not uncongenial to men of evangelical temper – though it had housed no Simeon as King's had, nor had the reputation of being a leading evangelical college, as had Queens' and Magdalene, or as Caius was to have soon after.[32] Doubtless the religious practice of the chapel conformed to the Book of Common Prayer, and celebration of the eucharist was from the north side of the altar; the chapel had no pictures or ornaments or stained glass; and when Hort set to work in the 1870s and 80s to devise glass and wall-painting, he encountered a natural prejudice against any change in the old arrangements in even so liberal-minded a clergyman as S. G. Phear.[33] It was in the sermons and the general conversation of the College that differences in churchmanship would have appeared; and we have no sermons from Emmanuel of this date to contradict the natural assumption that the college remained conservative, prayer book, middle of the road; just as it remained (on the whole) faithful to the Tory politics of Dr Farmer. In 1828 the College subscribed £100 towards the newly founded King's College London, the Church's answer to godless University College. A petition against Catholic emancipation was prepared in 1829, but not in the event sealed.[34] It is in any case striking that Browne's conversion from low to high made no difference to his standing in the College. In 1834 he became an Assistant Tutor, presumably engaged in teaching. The progress of his theological studies had evidently been studied and admired by Dr Archdall who encouraged him to extend his teaching in the college in

---

[30] Kitchin 1895, p. 50.
[31] Kitchin 1895, p. 208.
[32] Brooke, Highfield and Swaan 1988, p. 257, citing Twigg 1987, pp. 170–8, and Gunning 1854, I, 262–3; Brooke 1985, pp. 218–19.
[33] See below, p. 511.
[34] Shuckburgh 1904, p. 174.

1836, albeit Algebra and Euclid were mingled with the Greek New Testament.[35]

Meanwhile his progress in Emmanuel was hindered by the county rule: he could not be elected fellow while another Buckinghamshire man held office. He consulted Samuel Lee, regius professor of Hebrew at Cambridge, as to whether to put in for an Oxford fellowship, and received a hesitant encouragement. 'At Oxford your Hebrew will tell much better than at Cambridge, as will also your theology. It is a great pity that Colleges generally do not break down that foolish consideration of county preference.'[36] In 1836 Browne became a tutor at Downing, which he combined with teaching in Emmanuel – 'He was probably glad to retain some hold on his own College when he adventured himself so far out of the University world as to the precincts of Downing.'[37] After some previous rebuffs, the bishop of Ely agreed to ordain him deacon in November 1836, and he became chaplain as well as tutor in Downing – and curate in Fen Ditton.[38]

In 1837 John Weller, senior fellow and the fellow from Buckinghamshire, took the rectory of Luffenham, and the way was open for Browne's return to Emmanuel: by the end of the year he was elected fellow, and in 1838, still a junior fellow, he was made Senior Tutor, a striking indication of the master's trust in him.[39] But influences from another direction were already threatening to abbreviate his tenure of his fellowship. In the same year 1838 'he went down into Cornwall' to visit his Emmanuel friend Philip Carlyon in Truro, and met his sister Elizabeth; and 'when the summer vacation of 1839 came round, he found it necessary (at least so he professed) to make a second visit to Cornwall, that he might see something more of that picturesque county'; and in June 1840 Browne and Miss Carlyon were married.[40] Marriage terminated his fellowship, and his career in Emmanuel; he and his wife settled down to pastoral work in Stroud and Exeter; and he had a spell as Vice-Principal – in effect head – of St David's Lampeter, a theological college on the way to becoming a liberal arts college, established in enchanting collegiate buildings of the 1820s. In 1849 he became vicar of Kenwyn and Kea in Cornwall, and lived in the ample vicarage which later became for a while the palace of the bishops of Truro, set on a hill above the little city. Through all these rapid changes his mind was never far from Cambridge, and in 1853 he applied for and won the Norrisian Chair of Divinity. This

---

[35] Kitchin 1895, pp. 37, 43.
[36] Kitchin 1895, pp. 34–5.
[37] Kitchin 1895, p. 37.
[38] Kitchin 1895, pp. 46, 59–60.
[39] Kitchin 1895, p. 60. This is the earliest reference to the phrase 'Senior Tutor' in Emmanuel which I have encountered: in general it found fortune in the late nineteenth century.
[40] Kitchin 1895, pp. 61–6. For what follows, see Kitchin 1895, pp. 67–161.

was before the days of professorial fellowships; and although he resumed his links with Emmanuel and was an influential figure there all his days, he was never again a fellow. As a theologian he combined much of the old world with a little of the new: he was a reasonable interpreter of the thirty-nine articles, a man deeply read in the fathers and in the biblical learning of his day. He was able to combine his Cambridge chair with his Cornish living – later with a canonry at Exeter and a Devon living – until 1864. The combination seems to us bizarre, and caused comment at the time, for it is evident that Browne could not combine the offices so easily as – for instance – J. B. Lightfoot combined a chair at Cambridge with a canonry in St Paul's. But it is clear that the bishop of Exeter, Henry Phillpotts, though an Oxford man, felt strongly the value of having a Cambridge professor among his clergy, and one like himself who was a high churchman not enamoured of everything in the 'Tracts for the Times', even if Browne could only visit his living for any length of time in the long vacations.[41]

The Norrisian chair, though recently augmented by a legacy from Benedict Chapman, the old-world clerical master of Caius, had a very modest stipend. In 1855 Browne was a candidate in a celebrated election to the Lady Margaret Professorship, described in the eighteenth century as 'a valuable sinecure', and in the 1850s, if no sinecure, still very valuable, worth at least £1,500 a year.[42] The election was a *cause célèbre*; the electors were numerous and the vice-chancellor, the new master of Caius, Dr Guest, proceeded according to a time-consuming form; Professor Whewell, the master of Trinity, grew impatient of the tedious delays, and took a walk – only to find on his return that a speedier formula had been found, that Harold Browne and William Selwyn had tied for first place, and that Guest had given his casting vote to Selwyn. If Whewell had been there it would have gone the other way – and the Selwyn Divinity School might not have been built. For William Selwyn, who was as generous as he was undistinguished, gave nearly half his salary to Browne till he became a bishop – and then put it into a fund from which was paid most of the cost of building the Divinity School in the 1870s.[43] So Browne remained Norrisian professor till the day when he became bishop of Ely in 1864; and in Ely till he was translated to Winchester in 1873. He died in 1891 leaving the memory of a firm high churchman who none the less sought reconciliation between all parties within the Church. He had softened the polemics which accompanied the publication of *Essays and Reviews*; and he had played a pacific role in the adventures of

---

[41] Kitchin 1895, pp. 179–97. On Phillpotts, see *DNB*: he is chiefly remembered as the bishop who precipitated the Gorham case.

[42] For what follows, see Kitchin 1895, pp. 169–75. For the Lady Margaret Chair, Winstanley 1935, p. 359 n.10.

[43] Rupp 1981; Brooke 1993, pp. 141–2.

Bishop Colenso of Natal – persecuted for holding liberal views on the Pentateuch, which Browne disapproved, but he equally deprecated the virulence of the attacks made upon him. He was a peacemaker all his days; he even joined in the consecration of Bishop Temple, who had contributed, modestly, to *Essays and Reviews*.[44] With Browne's brief tenure of a fellowship at Emmanuel, the curtain lifts for a moment, then quickly falls again.

If we look forward to the fellowship in 1859, which argued and passed – in collaboration with the Statutory Commissioners – the new statutes of 1861, we still find the whole fellowship clerical; still containing a majority, now only a small one, who came to enjoy college livings.[45] Even Octavius Glover, who sailed the high seas as chaplain of H.M.S. *Clio* and held office in the Collegiate School on Vancouver Island, British Columbia in the early 1860s (while still a fellow of Emmanuel), returned to be rector of Emmanuel church, Loughborough in 1870, for 35 years or so. William Castlehow went to North Cadbury in 1861; Philip Dennis to North Luffenham in 1862; John Fuller to Thurcaston in 1864, all in proper order; and so the story goes on. Fuller had matriculated in Trinity, but rapidly moved to Emmanuel, where he was a fellow from 1848, tutor from 1850; and in the 1860s he married Emmeline, daughter of Richard Okes, provost of King's, who bore him numerous offspring to fill empty rooms in Emmanuel in due time. A striking difference from twenty years earlier is the number of wranglers in the list. These included Samuel Phear, fourth wrangler in 1852, and Robert Braithwaite Batty, second wrangler in 1853.[46]

Phear was to be the central figure in the creation of a new Emmanuel in the 1870s and 80s; meanwhile he was the type of which Cambridge revolutionaries were made: that is to say, he came from the heart of the establishment.[47] He was a fellow in 1853, then Senior Tutor and Bursar. He had some theological interests, for Harold Browne made him his examining chaplain at Winchester in 1873. He also had scientific interests, natural for a wrangler – but in an exceptional degree; he was to help, perhaps substantially, in developing scientific education in Cambridge. In the late 1850s there was a sprinkle of Emmanuel men among those taking firsts in Natural Sciences, and in 1864 Phear himself examined for it. More than that one cannot say, for Emmanuel did not reappear among the Firsts until 1876, in the person of William Napier Shaw.[48] But Phear was one of those who came to believe fervently that the college should be a centre of

---

[44] Kitchin 1895, pp. 200–23, 290–336.
[45] What follows is based on *CUC* 1859, p. 375, and Venn.
[46] Tanner 1917, pp. 511–12.
[47] Cf. Brooke 1993, pp. 34–5 on Augustus Austen-Leigh of King's.
[48] See below, pp. 522–3. Tanner 1917, pp. 738–9, 741, 746.

teaching in a variety of subjects: in 1859 the professional don is already a gleam in the eye.

If we look on again to 1871, to the fellowship which elected Phear master, we find quite a radical change in the making.[49] Of the eleven fellows five were survivors from 1859; the next three were clergymen; the final three were laymen, the first of a great multitude which has taken over the home of the godly preachers. Of the clergy, Arthur Chapman was a fellow from 1862–1913, one of the first of many of this age and later to be a fellow for life – hitherto his kind, though not unknown, were rare. He is remembered by his garden, then a private enclosure outside his rooms. But he was also a notable scholar – eleventh wrangler and Tyrwhitt Hebrew Scholar, college lecturer in Hebrew and Mathematics – a combination peculiar to Cambridge in the nineteenth century. Though uncreative as a scholar he was noted for learning, and for helping Phear, and more particularly Hort, to bring in the new world. Alfred Rose, after a brief curacy at Ramsgate, was likewise a fellow for life, dying in college in 1919 aged 79. Thomas Pitts represented tradition: after a spell of teaching at Haileybury, he went to two college livings, first to Thurning, then to Loughborough; a son and a grandson came to the College. Two of the laymen became equity draftsmen: they remind us that law was reviving as a subject of study. The senior of the three laymen had an interesting history: he was Evelyn Shuckburgh, the college historian. He was a fellow from 1866 – when he had achieved a first in classics, in the eleventh place – to his marriage in 1874, when he went to teach at Eton. In 1884 he returned to Emmanuel as librarian, and although he was not reelected to a fellowship he remained a member of the community till his death in 1906, dedicating his history in 1904 to the master, William Chawner, 'from a friend of many years'. Shuckburgh was a very assiduous student of the college records, and acknowledged particular help from J. B. Peace, fellow and bursar, and author of numerous historical articles in the college *Magazine*. In the History and his other writings Shuckburgh's learning is deployed in a manner at once admirable and frustrating – for he almost never gives a reference to the source of any of the innumerable facts he notes, and checking them can often be exceedingly difficult. He also shared the current prejudice against the eighteenth century, which led him to underestimate Farmer; and the assumption that no one was interested in his own day – that it was not history – which has done so much to obscure the late nineteenth century in Cambridge. None the less it is a remarkable achievement. Shuckburgh was a classic all his days, author of numerous translations from the classics and of textbooks on

---

[49] What follows is mainly based on *CUC* 1871, p. 466, and Venn. On Chapman see Stubbings 1984–5; Tanner 1917, pp. 268, 521.

ancient history; he knew better how to handle the history of remoter ages than his own.[50]

We have entered the world of lay fellows, of fellows dedicated to the college for life; we are about to elect Dr Phear as master. We are at the end of a chapter.

---

[50] On Shuckburgh see esp. P. Giles in *DNB*, 2nd Supplement III (1912), 311–13.

15

1871–1914

S. G. Phear

In 1871 Dr Archdall-Gratwicke died, and the Reverend Samuel George Phear, BD, was elected master in his place.[1] At first sight Phear might seem to belong to an old and dying world: he was a clerical fellow and a bachelor; he sprang from a family of Cambridge tutors. His father had been fellow and tutor of Pembroke and lived out his days in the college living of Earl Stonham in Suffolk. His brothers were lawyers, the eldest a judge in India and Ceylon after a brief spell as fellow and tutor of Clare; the second was a fellow of Caius and a barrister. Phear was fourth wrangler, a good cricketer, a good college man, fellow and senior tutor of Emmanuel. In his early years college and university alike had an eminent past and a modest present fame. Emmanuel was still a small college – one of the smallest in undergraduate numbers – when he was elected master in 1871.[2] He lived to see both the college expand nearly threefold in numbers and the university enter the modern world; and he played a leading part in both adventures. He was the stuff of which the academic revolutionaries of late nineteenth century Cambridge were made: like Augustus Austen-Leigh of King's and Ernest Stewart Roberts of Caius he was so obviously and so deeply a dedicated college man that he was able to shift (not without grumbles) the more conservative fellows to accept a brave new world. 'Many members of the College were not much enamoured of Dr Phear's innovations, and it was not without considerable perseverance that he was able to initiate successfully the policy which developed the college to a size never reached' since the seventeenth century. Thus Peter Giles, in his sympathetic memoir – almost the only account of Phear of any substance which survives.[3]

Phear's celibacy was, indeed, not wholly voluntary: in 1870 he was engaged to be married, and had been presented to the college living of

---

[1] On Phear, see Giles 1919, on which much of what follows is based; see also Shuckburgh 1904, pp. 179–84. For his family, see Venn; Venn, *Caius*, II, 272, 426. The marble Buddha which currently sits outside the Welbourne Room was a gift from his brother (a judge in India) to Phear on his election – and from Phear to the College on his retirement.

[2] See p. 402.

[3] Giles 1919, p. 211.

Emmanuel church, Loughborough; but the sudden death of his fiancée sent him back to Cambridge for life, alternately pursuing with fervour his visionary schemes, and sinking into sorrow and depression in recalling the wife he had lost.[4]

Nor was he solely a product of the vicarage. Fourth wrangler in 1852, he was soon a fellow and a college officer: 'and in those days when it was the fashion of the University to find a man and train him to hold some office in the future, he was early marked out as one who might do good work in the Natural Sciences'.[5] So Phear went to Germany to pursue his studies: in 1859 he was 'at Heidelberg and Berlin with Liebig and other famous professors'.[6] From 1864, when Phear became senior tutor, he was entangled in college administration and never pursued scientific research any further; but he retained a lively interest in developing the teaching and study of science in Cambridge; he was a member of the Syndicate which set up the Cavendish Laboratory in 1870; in later years 'he was very proud of the fact that Emmanuel was the first college to possess electric light, and nothing was more likely to provoke spirited remonstrance than a report that electric light had been installed at a still earlier period elsewhere'. In the twentieth century national and university politics have often been entirely separate in the minds of dons. But, just as Farmer had been a Tory in politics and conservative in university affairs, so Phear was a radical in both. With characteristic selflessness he presided over the scheme to amalgamate Emmanuel and Christ's in 1878, which would have made the master of Christ's head of both colleges. Most characteristic of all was his selection of teaching fellows in divinity, mathematics, science and classics. He took the initiative in proposing Fenton Hort in 1872 to revive theology in Emmanuel – and in Cambridge at large – and to be Emmanuel's first married fellow. His second protégé was the distinguished mathematician from St John's, G. A. Greenhill. His own interest in the Cavendish bore fruit in 1876–7, when William Napier Shaw secured a first in physics and a fellowship, and set to work in the Cavendish lab under Clerk Maxwell, Lord Rayleigh and J. J. Thomson, eventually rising to be assistant director.[7] Nor were the classics neglected: here Phear's choices suggest that he had been talking to E. S. Roberts, the tutor, later master, of Caius whom he so much resembles. At least it was from Caius that Emmanuel recruited two new classics: James Adam in 1884, and Peter Giles, by now fellow of Caius, in 1890. They brought the languages of ancient Greece and modern Aberdeenshire – in which Giles

---

[4] Ibid. For the date, see e.g. *CUC* 1880, p. 558.
[5] Giles 1919, p. 211, from which the quotations which follow also come.
[6] Justus von Liebig was professor at Munich from 1852, so it seems likely that Phear went also to Munich – unless Liebig was giving a course at Berlin.
[7] On Shaw see below, pp. 522–3; Tanner 1917, p. 746. For Phear and the Cavendish, see Brooke 1993, p. 173.

was especially adept – into Emmanuel. Adam was a notable exponent of Plato, an apostle of the doctrine that Plato was a Christian before Christ; Giles was one of the most distinguished pupils of the pioneer Cambridge philologists Edward Cowell and John Peile – and like Peile both were stalwart supporters of the entry of women to Cambridge. Adam died in 1907 comparatively young; Giles lived on to be master of Emmanuel and vice-chancellor in the crucial years after the Great War.[8]

Meanwhile, in 1875, the Lecture Fund was set up, 'out of which the Lecturers or Assistant Tutors . . . are to be paid . . .'. In 1885, 'a slight increase was made in the tuition fee, in order that the Lecturers might do for their men what had formerly been done at much greater cost by private Tutors': in this deadpan fashion Shuckburgh noted the most remarkable change in college teaching in late nineteenth-century Cambridge.[9] In a classic – if perhaps excessively critical – account of college teaching in Caius in the 1850s, John Venn likened it to the education of Sam Weller in *Pickwick Papers*, whose father 'let him run about the streets and pick up information for himself': tutors lectured, perfunctorily; serious study depended on coaches whom the students chose, and paid for, themselves.[10] The movement for reviving college teaching started in Trinity – where tutorial teaching had survived to a greater extent than elsewhere – and its central figure was Henry Jackson.[11] But it was rapidly taken up by a group of energetic tutors in other colleges; Roberts of Caius and Phear and Chawner of Emmanuel were outstanding examples.[12]

To William Chawner we shall return. Phear meanwhile fell ill in 1895, and sickness and depression made him decide 'that the important decisions which must be taken should be taken by a younger man'; and so he resigned the mastership, living quietly in St Peter's Terrace till his death in 1918, just after the armistice.[13] The story is told that Perowne, the master of Corpus, described Phear's resignation as 'a most immoral proceeding'. Perowne was the most conservative of masters, whose aim was to preserve Corpus as an evangelical seminary. On his death in 1906 it ceased to be either a seminary or evangelical: Perowne doubtless had the strongest motives to follow the Cambridge tradition that masters did not retire, but died in harness.[14] However that may be, Phear had done his

---

[8] On Adam, see *DNB*; Venn; Venn, *Caius*, II, 443, etc.; Dawkins 1935, pp. 415–16 (stressing Phear's initiative in the appointment of both Adam and Giles). Adam is recorded in a fine monument in the College Library Reading Room. On Giles, see below, pp. 440–3.

[9] College Orders, 11 October 1875; 20 June 1885 (£6 to £7); Shuckburgh 1904, p. 183.

[10] Venn 1913, p. 262; Brooke 1985, p. 218. But in some colleges efforts were made to help students to find private tutors: see Searby 1997, pp. 120–33.

[11] Brooke 1993, pp. 70–3.

[12] Brooke 1985, chap. 12, esp. pp. 234–6.

[13] Giles 1919, p. 211.

[14] Nor could they look forward to pensions before the 1920s. The story is in Venn.

work: he could contemplate in his later years a college which reflected his purposes and his dreams.

Phear was in the saddle as senior tutor and master from 1864 to 1895, over a generation which saw perhaps the most dramatic transformation in college and university since the seventeenth century; and the story we have outlined illustrates many elements in the transformation. In 1884 the College looked back over three hundred years of achievement; and it characteristically celebrated the event by installing electric light in the Chapel, the hall and elsewhere – a remarkable symbol of the coming of a new world.[15] Yet we must not exaggerate the transformation, as a comparison with Pembroke underlines. The buildings of Pembroke are now predominantly nineteenth century, and the fellows only just stopped Waterhouse from building an apse and a campanile on to Wren's exquisite chapel.[16] In Emmanuel much new building was needed in the wake of the changes of this age; but its outer face and front court are still essentially eighteenth century in character, little altered since the death of Richard Farmer save by such repair and restoration as was needed after the fire of 1811. The buildings, as always, are a parable, not always easy to interpret; but they remind us that much of the old Emmanuel was preserved.

The abolition of celibacy

One of the most powerful assumptions in Cambridge before the 1860s was that the fellows of colleges were celibate while the masters could marry; hence, in part, the ample lodges provided for them. In 1561 Queen Elizabeth I, who was a convinced Protestant, yet with some old fashioned views of her own, issued a decree that there should be no married clergy in cathedral closes or Oxbridge colleges. The effects of the decree were whittled away, until in 1570 one part only survived: in that year the new statutes of the university of Cambridge – mainly the work of one or two heads of house[17] – decreed that *fellows* might not marry; and such was the universal law in Cambridge – and also, in effect, in Oxford – till 1860. Some college statutes, meanwhile, decreed that the whole community should be celibate; but these statutes were somehow overlooked. The statutes of the founder of Emmanuel were quite explicit that no member of the community should be married – and that the head was one of the members.[18] But when Mildmay chose Chaderton as master, he chose a

---

[15] J. B. Peace in *ECM* 16 (1905–6), 63–79, esp. pp. 64–6.

[16] Brooke 1993, pp. 65–6. See pp. 510–11 and 510 n.2.

[17] P. Collinson in McKitterick 1991, p. 11. On the decree of 1561, see Brooke 1985, p. 68.

[18] Stubbings, 1983a, pp. 89, 147–8 (chap. 42): 'There are many and grave causes why we should suffer noone . . . among the members of our College to be married'. Cf. pp. 30, 115, chap. 2, which talks of the head being 'united with the other members' ('*caeteris* uniatur membris'), which is scarcely ambiguous. Dr Caius spelt out the same point more

married man; and according to a letter written by Ralph Brownrigg in 1659 (when the matter was under discussion), Chaderton himself had in his presence asserted 'with some warmth that "he had never received any dispensation from the founder in that matter; nor had it ever occurred to the founder to forbid matrimony to the masters of that college" '.[19] One is reminded of the words Mildmay is said to have addressed to Chaderton before the foundation: 'If you will be no master, I will be no founder'[20] – and possibly of those of St Francis on his deathbed, when his anxious companions announced the arrival of the lady Jacoba of Settesoli whom he had invited to call on him, contrary to his own regulation that no women were allowed in the house where he lay – 'The regulation is not to be observed with *this* lady'.[21] Perhaps a little nearer home is the paradox of St John Fisher's statute for St John's in which he prescribes residence for the master; yet he appointed as master his own archdeacon of Rochester, who was by definition only a very occasional visitor.[22] By Chaderton's time the custom that heads of house might marry was well established; the paradox that some elements in college statutes were obeyed to the letter and others ignored was not an eighteenth-century abuse, but had been hallowed by the most devout of the founding fathers of the sixteenth century.[23]

The first Royal Commission and Statutory Commission on the Universities sat in the 1850s and early 1860s and abolished many outdated rules and hallowed traditions. The Statutory commissioners seem to have expected to see a sharp decline at least in the rules enjoining celibacy. In many colleges the relaxation was modest until the Second Commission of the 1870s; after the new statutes which followed, they were largely swept away. In Caius the celibacy laws departed entirely in 1860.[24] In Emmanuel in 1861 a concession was made that one sixth of the fellows,

specifically still: 'We ordain that all members of your College, master, fellows, scholars and pensioners, be celibate' (quoted Brooke 1985, p. 68). The first married master of Caius was the Emmanuel puritan William Dell (ibid. p. 131), who may well have known how things stood at his old college. In any case the distinction was customary in the Cambridge colleges.

[19] Dillingham 1700, p. 21; translated in Shuckburgh 1884, pp. 8–9 (here slightly adapted).

[20] See above, p. 42; Shuckburgh 1884, p. 7.

[21] Brooke, R. B., 1970/1990, pp. 266–7 (slightly adapted).

[22] M. Underwood in Bradshaw and Duffy 1989, p. 36; Mayor 1859, p. 352 – the statute is verbally very similar to those of Christ's and Emmanuel.

[23] A complete list of married masters cannot be compiled with certainty. The following are known to have been married, though it is not in all cases clear that they were married while master: Chaderton, Tuckney and Dillingham in the seventeenth century; Richardson in the eighteenth; Cory and Archdall-Gratwicke in the nineteenth; and all the masters since 1911, save Lord St John.

[24] Brooke 1985, p. 224 and n.4. For a full statement of intended statutes on this issue see Parliamentary Papers 1861, H.C.XX [2852], *Report of the Cambridge University Commissioners*, pp. 17–24 (a reference I owe to the kindness of Dr Peter Searby). The exact outcome needs further research.

that is, two at most, might be married; and the very limited nature of the concession – and the ten-year gap before it was implemented – have suggested to some that the old master, Archdall-Gratwicke, personally resisted the innovation.[25] It was first invoked in the election of Fenton Hort to the fellowship in 1872; and in the statutes of 1882 all barriers were removed. 1861 saw two other radical changes: the bizarre prescription that prevented more than one fellow coming from any single county was abolished, and a lay element was admitted to the fellowship.[26] The first fellow elected under this rubric was William Chawner in 1871, by a symbolic coincidence the year that saw Parliament abolish religious tests for admission to college and university offices in Oxford and Cambridge.[27]

The abolition of celibacy reflected a changing view of the fellow's role. In the days of Hubbard and Farmer a small number of fellows had been lifelong bachelors and stayed the course in the college. This tradition was still strongly represented in Phear himself and A. T. Chapman, a bachelor fellow from 1862 till 1913 – and interestingly, like Phear, a strong supporter of reforming causes. Yet he is also and chiefly remembered for the garden outside his rooms, still 'Chapman's garden'.[28] Most of the fellows came and went early in life, passing on to a college living – or the mastership – which enabled them to marry. A few went on to quite other careers; but for most the fellowship was a kind of apprenticeship for a country living, and indeed sometimes combined with pastoral care in a local church.[29] A small number of fellows of the old school actively taught; a rather larger number dedicated some of their energies to learning. But neither was strictly necessary, and some fellows were altogether non-resident. The new conception of the age of Phear was to revive the fellows' original function of teaching; it was envisaged that the fellowship would still contain bright young men serving their apprenticeship who might go on to other careers. It would also contain more or less permanent college officers – tutors, bursars and deans, guardians of education, finance, and discipline, which meant first and foremost regular attendance at chapel.[30] One of the most powerful social movements of the nineteenth century was the growth of the professions, which became more numerous, more organised, and a great deal more professional.[31] Not the least of these was the profession of university teacher. In the wake of the second Royal Commission of the 1870s, the Oxford and

---

[25] Cf. Stubbings 1983b, no. 35. For the statute, see *Statutes* 1861, p. 21.
[26] *Statutes* 1861, esp. p. 16, c. 14.
[27] See Brooke 1993, pp. 99–106; and on Chawner, see below, pp. 429–36.
[28] Stubbings 1984–5; Brooke 1993, p. 58.
[29] See p. 393.
[30] Brooke 1993, chap. 2 and pp. 111–19; and see below, pp. 433–5.
[31] Perkin 1989.

Cambridge Act of 1877 set up the statutory commissions which established the new statutes of the years which followed; and in the Act the function of the colleges and so by implication of the dons was defined as 'education, religion, learning and research'.[32] As the university and colleges became increasingly secularised, religion came to be a more precarious or controversial element in the list; for a century research held a very ambivalent place in it: some rejoiced that the college was a home of research, others viewed this incursion of novel approaches to learning with reserve, and probably still do. But education and learning became the keynotes of what was rapidly becoming – not the apprenticeship of young clergymen – but a profession for life.[33] The careers of Hort, Chawner and Shaw[34] illustrate admirably the inwardness of this remarkable transition.

F. J. A. Hort

When Fenton Hort came to Emmanuel as fellow and lecturer in divinity in 1872 at the age of 43, he brought with him an exceptionally wide and vivid experience of the intellectual and religious movements of the mid and late nineteenth century, and a mind of extraordinary acuteness and dedication to the service of the College.[35] He was a college lecturer from 1872 to 1878, then Hulsean professor of Divinity and from 1887 Lady Margaret's professor of Divinity;[36] yet he remained a fellow till his death in 1892, leaving an indelible mark on the college.[37]

As a boy he had sat at Dr Arnold's feet at Rugby; as an undergraduate he had been an Apostle[38] and a close friend and disciple of F. D. Maurice; as student and fellow of Trinity he formed the fundamental alliance with J. B. Lightfoot and B. F. Westcott which was to make Cambridge a theological centre of international repute. Hort's mind was a palimpsest, reflecting the deep convictions and vivid impressions of a multitude of influences, including those of his many friends. An evangelical from his mother's knee, he early acquired the liberal outlook of Maurice, and later the love of the beauty of holiness, which we normally associate with high church circles, and still glows from the windows of Emmanuel college chapel.

After the mathematical tripos (in which illness prevented him from being a wrangler) he took in quick succession the classical tripos and that

---

[32] Brooke 1993, pp. 103–4.
[33] Engel 1983; Rothblatt 1981; Brooke 1993, pp. 7–19.
[34] On Shaw see below, pp. 522–3.
[35] Hort 1896, II, chap. 8, esp. p. 172.
[36] Tanner 1917, p. 74.
[37] For what follows, see esp. Hort 1896; Rupp 1977, chap. 10; and cf. Brooke 1993, pp. 9–13.
[38] For the literature on the celebrated, 'secret' discussion society of the Apostles, see Brooke 1993, p. 127 n.70. See now Lubenow 1998.

in natural sciences, at the moment of its birth in 1851.[39] In later life, when driven by illness from Cambridge and the Greek New Testament, he studied alpine flowers with a like scientific intensity. Gordon Rupp, Dixie Professor and fellow of Emmanuel in the 1960s and 70s, in an inspired lecture on Hort, observed how he 'brought to single words the loving attention which he gave to his Alpine flowers . . . As a daisy by the river's brim held mysteries for him beyond the wisdom of Solomon to conceive, so for him a Biblical word was something [from] which you might extract layer under layer of meaning.'[40] He greeted Darwin's *Origin of Species* with enthusiasm – 'it is a treat to read such a book'; he rebuked his friends for harbouring doubts that scholarship and biblical inspiration were allies. 'I am not able to go as far as you in asserting the absolute infallibility of a canonical writing', he wrote to Westcott, and to Lightfoot in almost identical words.[41] He did less than justice to Lightfoot at least in uttering these words, but they reveal his own attitude none the less surely.

Yet he held together in early years much of the old world with the new. In 1857, the year of his marriage, he published a pamphlet which was a lively and vigorous defence of the traditional Cambridge *cursus honorum*: that fellows should be celibate clergy – as a newly married man he admitted marriage to be the 'greatest of human blessings', but for a don one which should follow a celibate apprenticeship – and trained in the traditional Cambridge mode, with a broad arts base and the maths tripos. He expresses fervent opposition to the specialised study of theology.[42] By 1872 his mind had passed on: he agreed to be Emmanuel's first married fellow and to become one of the founders of the Theological Tripos, first sat in 1874; Hort was first an examiner in 1878.[43]

He was a fellow of Trinity from 1852 to 1857; then married and settled in the Trinity living of St Ippolyts near Hitchin, returning to Cambridge on his election to Emmanuel early in 1872. He was thus at hand when Emily Davies founded what was to be Girton College in Hitchin in the late 1860s; and he was one of her first lecturers – though only briefly, for his lectures were evidently too specialised for the students.[44] Even in Emmanuel he had few students for the tripos in early days; and as professor his lectures never (it seems) commanded large audiences. He was too deep a scholar: he is said to have lectured for a whole term on ten verses of an Epistle.[45]

---

[39] Hort 1896, I, 92–3; Tanner 1917, p. 737.
[40] Rupp 1977, p. 158.
[41] Hort 1896, I, 414, 422; cf. Brooke 1993, pp. 10, 137.
[42] Hort 1896, I, 362–8.
[43] Tanner 1917, pp. 812–14.
[44] Brooke 1993, p. 309 and refs. in n.26.
[45] Neill and Wright 1988, p. 98.

Yet his interests were anything but narrow. His immortal fame as a scholar rests on his textual introduction to Westcott and Hort's *Greek New Testament*, which came out in 1881 on the eve of the Revised Version of the Bible, in which Hort was deeply involved; and the introduction is a model of acuteness and clarity.[46] But in his heart he yearned – it seems – to be a church historian and systematic theologian.[47] Of original theology the only substantial remnants are his Hulsean lectures, *The Way, the Truth and the Life*, which Rupp called 'a not so minor spiritual classic',[48] and has seemed to many a pioneer study in the theology of the Holy Spirit. His scheme for a history of the church issued in many articles, and inspired the windows which still adorn Emmanuel college chapel. Above all, it issued in the Dixie Professorship.

In 1867 the tiny provision for the study of history in the moral sciences tripos in Cambridge was stifled on the initiative of F. D. Maurice; and when J. R. Seeley returned to Cambridge as Regius Professor of Modern History in 1869 he had urgently to seek to revive it. In 1870 the Law and History Tripos was founded, in 1875 the History Tripos sole, at first a very modest star in the constellation of triposes.[49] If its early prestige owed much to the Regius Professors, Seeley and Acton, its academic content and formation were equally indebted to the first two Dixie Professors, Mandell Creighton from Merton, Oxford, and H. M. Gwatkin from St John's, Cambridge. In 1870 Hort's friend J. B. Lightfoot gave a generous fillip to the study of history by founding the Lightfoot Scholarships, to encourage the study of history – and especially ecclesiastical history, 'the most important and instructive part of history' in his eyes.[50] In the 1870s the Second Royal Commission sought ways to encourage or compel the colleges to come to the assistance of the University and help equip it for the modern world. To some this meant the formation of labs or the support of scientific education. In Emmanuel in the late 1870s Hort was the architect of a scheme for a chair in medieval history. When this was turned down by the Governing Body in favour of a chair in ecclesiastical history, Hort, echoing Lightfoot, proposed a chair in 'the History of the Christian Church in connexion with General History' – but 'Ecclesiastical History' prevailed.[51]

The Dixie Professorship was woven into the new statutes of 1882, and in 1884 Mandell Creighton, former tutor of Merton and rector of the

---

[46] Westcott and Hort 1881; Neill and Wright 1988, pp. 74–81.
[47] For his scheme for a great church history, see his letter of 1852 (aet. 24) in Hort 1896, I, 233–5.
[48] Rupp 1977, p. 153.
[49] Brooke 1993, p. 228.
[50] Clark 1904, pp. 329–30.
[51] ECA COL.19.26, discussion of Statute's Clauses IV.1, 2. Chairs of Comparative Philology and Mental Philosophy and Logic were also considered. It was reckoned that ecclesiastical history accorded best with the terms of the Dixie Trust.

ample Merton living of Embleton in Northumberland, was elected to the chair.[52] The original stipend of the professor of £500 per annum, which accompanied a fellowship at Emmanuel, with its dividends and allowances; the £500 was paid out of the Dixie fund, and hence the name of Sir Wolstan Dixie, Mildmay's friend, master of the Skinners' Company and Lord Mayor in the 1580s, was given to the chair.

Creighton's major historical work, *A History of the Papacy from the Great Schism to the Sack of Rome*, was written partly at Embleton, partly in Cambridge, and was an achievement on the grand scale, for Creighton did nothing by halves. He was profoundly interested in education in a very wide sense, a man of liberal outlook who sought good relations between folk of different views and persuasions, and intellectual partnership in marriage. He combined deep academic interests with a strong pastoral sense – he was reluctantly, but surely, drawn into leadership in the church and became an outstanding bishop. Lord Acton, the Catholic historian, later Regius Professor of Modern History, reckoned Creighton, the Anglican divine, too gentle with the popes of the Renaissance.[53] But fairmindedness was Creighton's leading quality; and he showed it alike in his handling of extreme ritualists and anti-ritualists as bishop and as editor of the *English Historical Review*. He and Acton indeed had much in common, especially in their faith in the value of historical scholarship; and first Creighton, then Acton, worked to create a history tripos which reflected it. Its progress in Emmanuel, in spite of the dreams of Hort and the example of Creighton, was slow. In the 1890s George Green, a schoolmaster who also looked after the historians in Caius for a while, was given the task of directing historical studies in Emmanuel. It was not until 1900 that Emmanuel produced its own historian in F. W. Head.[54] Meanwhile, Emmanuel rarely figures in the Tripos lists for History or Theology in the 1870s or 80s – a first and a third in theology in 1875 are the only Emmanuel entries in Hort's years as college lecturer, though the numbers were to increase a little in the late 1880s. But in truth one finds only a selection of the Emmanuel men of this era in tripos lists: down to the early 1880s the majority were still poll men, taking a general degree; then the number of honours students gradually

---

[52] On Creighton see Creighton 1904; Chadwick 1959. On the origin of the Dixie Chair, see ECA COL.19.26 (as above); on Hort's involvement, Whitney 1919, p. 7: 'Emmanuel College, under the wise leadership of Dr Phear, first brought Dr Hort back to Cambridge, and then, upon lines laid down by that greatest scholar of a famous trio, devoted a large part of the Dixie trust to the needs of Ecclesiastical History in the University'.

[53] Creighton 1882–94, originally *A History of the Papacy during the period of the Reformation*, renamed in the reprint of 1897; cf. Chadwick 1959, esp. p. 16. For Creighton on marriage, see Brooke 1993, p. 257.

[54] See below, pp. 436–7. On the early history of the Tripos see esp. Slee 1986; on G. E. Green, Brooke 1993, pp. 230–1; *CUC* 1892–3, p. 755 and 1893–4, p. 774; ECA TUT.4.1, minute of Education Board of 21 June 1893.

increased.[55] If Emmanuel produced few theologians, it produced many clergymen.[56] But its academic progress is more clearly visible in the list of fellows than among the undergraduates: the leaders of Emmanuel had a vision of a new Cambridge and a new Emmanuel; as one contemplates the fellows and encounters the names of Hort and Creighton, of Creighton's successor as Dixie, H. M. Gwatkin, of Adam and Giles, the classical lecturers, of Sir Napier Shaw and Sir Gowland Hopkins among the scientists, one can see that by 1900 the College could hold its own among the academic societies of Cambridge. Emmanuel produced its own modest share of first rate scholars; but of the names just listed only Shaw had been an undergraduate in the college. They reflect the enlightened recruitment of the age of Phear and Chawner.

Hort's colleagues remembered him in the Jerusalem Chamber in Westminster Abbey, where he was said to have spoken 'for three years out of the ten' in which the Revised Version of the Bible was in the making; they remembered him 'as he rounded at full pace some buttress of books in the University Library'; they remembered him in his room in the Divinity School, as 'book after book came down from the shelves . . . fact after fact was verified'; they remembered him in the Alps, a tireless walker while his health lasted, and a dedicated botanist to the end.[57] He was a cosmopolitan scholar; his work spread far outside the college. He knew all too little how to say no, and his energies were widely diffused. But he was a loyal and devoted fellow of Emmanuel; he rarely missed a college meeting; he threw himself heart and soul into the revision of the statutes and into such schemes as the foundation of the Dixie chair; and he left his mark indelibly in the chapel.[58]

The Dixie livings

In the late 1870s, in the wake of the Second Royal Commission, new statutes were discussed, including a new disposal of the Dixie Fund and the Dixie livings. What was finally agreed was that the Dixie fellows, as a separate group, should cease to be; that once the current incumbents had departed, the rights of the Dixie heir – that is, the current representative of Sir Wolstan Dixie, donor of the Fund – with a significant exception, would cease. Without any such pause new Dixie exhibitions would replace the old scholarships and exhibitions; and the newly created Dixie Professor of Ecclesiastical History would receive a professorial fellowship

[55] Tanner 1917, p. 812 – and *passim*, checked by Register. Cf. Chawner 1909, p. 8: 'poll men . . . supply a large proportion of candidates for holy orders'.
[56] See below, pp. 436–8.
[57] See e.g. Hort 1896, II, 236–7 (Dean Burgon on the RV); Rupp 1977, pp. 154, 157; Brooke 1993, pp. 10–12.
[58] See below, pp. 510–12.

and a stipend of £500 a year from the College.[59] The Dixie heir retained the right of nomination to the rectories of Boddington, Brantham and North Benfleet – and to this right is attached a curious tale. It was the heir's duty to find a graduate of Emmanuel who was either kin to Sir Wolstan Dixie, or had been at the school founded by Sir Wolstan at Market Bosworth for at least a year. The fortunes of two of these livings, Boddington and Brantham, well illustrate the outcome of this clause; and they also illustrate the changing circumstances of college livings in and after the 1880s – after the abolition of celibacy and the growing lay element in the fellowship had ended the close links between fellows and livings which had been an essential part of the character of the College from the foundation. For from the 1880s the fellows needed no livings to enable them to marry – and an increasing proportion were no longer Anglican clergymen. To Brantham in 1887 Sir Beaumont Dixie had successfully nominated John Plummer Boyer, an Emmanuel man and a kinsman, and the College had duly presented him. But in 1890 J. P. Boyer died, aged only 33, and Sir Beaumont nominated Charles Edward Pochin Boyer – apparently J.P.'s brother, also an Emmanuel man – in his place.[60] The College presented the new Boyer to the bishop, who refused to institute him, on the grounds that Sir Beaumont was a Roman Catholic – as the College evidently did not know. In the wake of the Gunpowder Plot of 1605 acts had been passed – subsequently confirmed by further acts in Queen Anne's reign – that if the right of presentation lay with a Roman Catholic, it should pass to the universities of Oxford and Cambridge – Cambridge taking the north and east, Oxford the south and west. C. E. P. Boyer fought the issue in the courts: the Dixie heir, he claimed, had only the right of nomination; presentation lay with the College, and so was valid. But it was decided in the Court of Arches, and confirmed by the Judicial Committee of the Privy Council – still at that time the final court of appeal in ecclesiastical suits – that the disabling acts referred to nomination as well as presentation; and since the current Dixie was (in learned counsel's words) a 'Popish recusant convict', his nomination was invalid. Meanwhile the three months within which Sir Beaumont had to nominate and the six months in which the College had to present had passed; and the bishop of Norwich triumphantly installed his candidate, H. R. Cole of St John's. Cole had been curate at Lowestoft, and was installed as curate of Brantham in 1891–2 while the dispute was being settled – and promoted rector in 1892 at its close. He held the living till his death in

---

[59] *Statutes* 1882, Appendix A, B, pp. 47–51 – also for what follows.

[60] For the two Boyers, see Venn. For the nominations and the drama of 1890–1, ECA Box 6 B26, D19. Ibid. C23 and COL.17.2 give Council's opinions (1890–4). The series of acts disabling Catholics from presenting to livings began with 3 James I, c.5; and the involvement of the universities was abolished in the 1980s.

1924; but meanwhile a lesser drama had been enacted at Boddington.[61] In 1894 the College took Counsel's opinion on how it should proceed in future. This was to the effect that while the Dixie heir was a Roman Catholic, his rights went to the universities – but only the right to nominate; the College could still present if it did so within the period prescribed; advice which left the College with little but perplexity. At Boddington (in Northamptonshire), the sitting rector, R. H. Woodcock, was already in 1894 asking for an exchange: agriculture was depressed (and with it tithes, the main source of his income), the living insufficient to make ends meet. His efforts continued from time to time, and in 1913 an arrangement was made, involving the rector, the University of Oxford and the College. But it fell through and the vacancy only came in 1917. In September of that year, to the College's surprise, Sir Beaumont indignantly declared that he had ceased to be a Roman Catholic; and he nominated the Reverend Wolstan Dixie Churchill – whose name seemed destined to prepare him for the living; but in the event he decided not to come. The College failed to find a substitute and the bishop presented Mr W. T. Gibbings. Light is thrown on Mr Churchill's reluctance by a letter from Mr Gibbings of 1929: he sought the College's approval in his efforts to sell the rectory, which was very large, and provided with '*no* modern conveniences, *no* water laid on – *no* bath room – no lighting etc.'. Doubtless in earlier times, when College livings had been commonly occupied by ex-fellows, such difficulties had involved the direct aid of the College. In this and other cases, the College archives reveal a sympathetic attitude on the part of the College authorities; but the rectory outlasted Mr Gibbings. In 1951 neither the College nor the bishop of Peterborough could fill the living, which lapsed to the archbishop – as we know from a letter from Bishop Spenser Leeson sent in January 1952. At last a rector has been found; the old rectory is to be sold, and arrangements are in hand to combine it with Aston-le-Walls. In 1979 the new scheme was finally confirmed, with Emmanuel as sole patrons. By such revised schemes the Dixie heir has finally lost his right to nominate.

William Chawner

One of the many schemes of the 1870s which Hort supported was the plan to amalgamate Emmanuel with Christ's. The act of 1877 had specifically foreseen the possibility that colleges might be merged, and gave the statutory commissioners leave to accept such plans. In the event abortive schemes to yoke St Catharine's to King's and Christ's with Emmanuel were seriously canvassed.[62] These plans reveal how radical were the ideas of reform which were in the air in the 1870s. They also reflect the

---

[61] On Cole, see Venn. On Boddington, below, see ECA Box C24.
[62] On these schemes and their context, see Brooke 1993, pp. 44–5, 86–7.

desperate search for money to support an impoverished university full of academic ambition. It was widely believed that university provision for teaching and research, and especially scientific laboratories, could only be financed if the colleges pooled their resources; and that the smaller colleges could only become efficient teaching institutions once again if they merged. For new triposes were springing up, bringing new demands for college lecturers; and it seemed evident to the more radical fellows of Emmanuel and Christ's that a merger would equip both colleges more effectively to face the challenges of the day.

The fellow who proposed that the governing body formally discuss the idea of a merger was William Chawner.[63] Chawner was one of the first lay fellows of the college; but the research of his early years lay in fact in early church history, issuing in a book on *The Influence of Christianity upon the Legislation of Constantine the Great*. After serving the college in a variety of offices, especially as Assistant Tutor, he spent a year as a master at Winchester, then returned to Emmanuel in 1875, on Phear's invitation, to be senior tutor.[64] He and Phear worked closely together to revive college teaching; and under his tutorship the great expansion really got under way. He and Phear seem to have wished to revive the office of tutor in its original sense, and to make the tutors the nucleus of the teaching staff. When Chawner was master (from 1895) and Napier Shaw senior tutor, the tutors became in effect directors of studies in the leading disciplines studied in the college. But the tide in Cambridge was flowing in a different direction, and the Cambridge tutor was becoming divorced from teaching, in marked contrast to his counterparts in Oxford. In Emmanuel the formal link between tutors and disciplines has survived from the 1890s; but the number of tutors has remained – as in all colleges – relatively few while the disciplines have proliferated. So directors of studies and tutors now hold entirely separate offices, and the Emmanuel tutor is not substantially different in function from his colleagues in other colleges.[65]

Charles Raven described Chawner as master as 'a great administrator, officially something of a martinet, privately a charming host and delightful companion, obviously the strongest member of the governing body'.[66] Chawner and Phear were the central figures in the revival of Emmanuel: neither was a scholar of note, but both were determined to make the college a centre of education, learning and perhaps research. Religion is another matter; for Chawner is remembered above all for the powerful

---

[63] ECA COL.18.15c (Alfred Rose's notes of meetings on the revision of statutes), p. 30.

[64] Material on Chawner – save for the 'affair' of 1909–11 – is scarce: see esp. Peace 1911.

[65] See e.g. *CUC* 1900, p. 899, where the disciplines of the four tutors are noted. Gold 1945, p. 205, ascribes the extension of the number of tutors to four to Shaw, but gives Chawner the credit for initiating the system.

[66] Raven 1928, p. 133.

attack he mounted in his last years against the traditional religious beliefs and practices of Emmanuel.

All that lay well in the future when Chawner opened the discussion on a merger with another college on 16 February 1878.[67] On 23 February the proposal 'that it is desirable to take steps towards effecting a complete union of our own College with some other College or Colleges . . .' was carried by 7 votes to 3, with four fellows absent – one known to be favourable, one unfavourable. The known opponents were clerical fellows, some elderly; the supporters included a majority of the clergy, including Phear, Chapman and Hort, as well as the laymen, such as Chawner and Shaw. The scheme was swiftly submitted to Christ's – we may be fairly sure that there had been informal talks already; a joint committee was set up, and a 'draft scheme of union' printed for private circulation.[68] This envisaged security of tenure for existing fellows and tutors, but a radical longer term future in which there would be a 'single hall and chapel . . . either by new buildings or by enlargement of the existing building'. On 13 June the master and nine fellows gathered to discuss and vote on the draft scheme, though it is evident from the voting that three had departed before the final votes were taken. The meeting expressed general support for most of the paper: the final votes were, for the substantive scheme, 6 in favour, none against, with one abstaining; for the temporary arrangements to cover the process of integration, 5 for, none against, and 2 abstaining. The most contentious matter was the name of the united college. In the end, by 6 votes to 3, with one fellow abstaining, 'The New College of Christ's and Emmanuel' found favour over 'St Andrew's College' – there was little support for 'Christ-Emmanuel College'.[69] The scheme envisaged that James Cartmell, master of Christ's, would be first master, with Phear as vice-master, and that Phear would succeed.

The rest is silence. All that we know is that the scheme foundered, and that the master of Christ's – in spite of the efforts to conciliate him – led the opposition. Cartmell 'successfully opposed a proposal for the entire amalgamation of Christ's with Emmanuel – a proposal which found warm support in both Colleges', wrote John Peile, Cartmell's successor.[70] Cartmell died in 1881, and after an interval the scheme was revived; all that we have is an appreciative letter of 1893 from Peile to Chawner on the readiness of the fellows of Emmanuel to make him master of the joint college; but it also makes clear that the scheme had once more failed.[71] In

[67] ECA COL.18.15C, p. 30; the original of the resolution of 23 Feb. is in Christ's College Library, MSS, Box 89; a copy is ECA COL.19.10a; cf. COL.18.15c, p. 35.
[68] ECA COL.19.10b–c, esp. 10c, clauses 9–10; cf. COL.19.10d (on the chapel); COL.18.15c, pp. 70, 72, 80–6.
[69] ECA COL.19.10e (copy of original in Christ's College Library, MSS, Box 89).
[70] Peile 1910–13, II, 436–7.
[71] ECA COL.19.10f; for what follows see Brooke 1993, chap. 18.

the late nineteenth century the urgent need to provide effective college teaching, and the insistent demands of the university, seemed to make such mergers desirable, though their supporters had a great weight of sentiment and tradition against them. In the 1950s and 60s the immense expansion of the post war years in university staff and postgraduate students, and the wish to provide more amply for women in Cambridge, led to the rapid growth of the old and the foundation of many new colleges; and there arose a generation which could reasonably be grateful to James Cartmell for his foresight, if such it was.

The scheme to merge Christ's and Emmanuel is (or was until recently) an almost forgotten incident; not so the adventure of Chawner's later years as master, 'the Chawner affair'. In 1909 he printed and circulated (in his own words) 'to all Undergraduates and to nearly all the Fellows of the College and to about 100 friends and acquaintances . . . in and out of Cambridge' a pamphlet called *Prove all Things* in which he firmly rejected traditional Christianity and prophesied its downfall.[72] He speaks with warm approval of 'the growing conviction . . . that the canons of criticism require us to abandon as un-historical the miraculous events in the life of Jesus – the Virgin Birth, the Resurrection and the Ascension'; and there is some circumstantial evidence in the accompanying pamphlets that he had come more or less to a Unitarian position.[73] It is hard to tell how recent was his conversion; harder still to believe that its author had been a close colleague of Fenton Hort. He had resigned as tutor in 1890 and spent a year in Germany studying principally philosophy. He returned, intending to spend his time in 'study and research'.[74] But he was soon accepting college offices again, and from 1895 he was master, deeply involved in college and university administration. *Prove all Things* is extraordinarily one-sided as an attack on orthodoxy. He points to numerous signs of decline in religious belief and observance in England, France and Germany; he quotes with approval the view that in France 'it is a bar to promotion' in army or civil service 'to be known to attend regularly at mass'.[75] To a later generation the notorious anti-clericalism of that era in France seems redolent of religious persecution, whatever our beliefs or lack of them; to Chawner it was simply a sign of the times; and of the times he approved. He was getting on in years and far from well, and some have attributed his desire to let everyone know his opinions to

---

[72] Chawner 1909, reprinted with significant omissions in 1911; supplemented meanwhile by Chawner 1909a and Chawner 1911. On 'the Chawner affair' see Cupitt 1970–1; *ECM* 54 (1972), 17–30; Dillistone 1975, pp. 69–76; ECA COL.19.7–9; Brooke 1993, pp. 123–6.

[73] Chawner 1909, esp. p. 14. In Chawner 1909a, pp. 23–4, he concluded a selection of the letters he had received with one especially supportive which seems clearly to come from a Unitarian; and the climax of Chawner 1911 (pp. 22–3) likewise speaks with approval of the Unitarians. So also Cupitt 1970–1, p. 7.

[74] Peace 1911, p. 368.

[75] Chawner 1909, p. 6.

sickness; to C. E. Raven, who was appointed dean at the age of 24 and came into the crisis which the pamphlet created like a lamb to the slaughter, it seemed that he 'had caught late in life the scepticism that affects most of us at eighteen; and like measles at his age it was a bad attack.'[76] But as a defence by a senior academic of intellectual honesty as a central virtue of college and university it must win our sympathy. If we look beyond the motives, now irrecoverable, to the historical setting, the affair is extraordinarily piquant and revealing. There is a sense in which Chawner, a layman in a fellowship (in his early years) still predominantly clerical – and the first lay master of what had been a thoroughly clerical college – blurted out in later life the instinctive anti-clericalism of the devout layman. There is a sense too in which we can see him as a central figure in the Cambridge establishment proclaiming that the University has become secular. To the word he might have objected, for he believed himself an exponent of *true* religion. Hitherto, he observed – until the abolition of religious tests in 1871 and the freeing of headships and fellowships from religious ties completed (more or less) in the wake of the Oxford and Cambridge Act of 1877[77] – nearly all heads and a number of fellows had to be in Holy Orders. 'This last bulwark of clericalism has now for about thirty years been almost completely swept away. Since the Statutes of 1882 our College has wholly ceased to be a sectarian institution. Any member of the Governing Body, either Master or Fellow, any Scholar on the Foundation may profess what creed he will or may abjure all creeds. They may be all Roman Catholics or all atheists. The College is in no sense attached to the Church of England'. Yet Anglicans still have some privileges, the service of the Church of England is read twice daily in chapel, 'and the Governing Body may compel those [members of the college] who are *in statu pupillari* to attend, and instruction is ordered to be given them in the tenets of their faith'. 'The Universities Act of 1877 defines a College as "a place of education, religion, learning and research" ' – but he denies with fervour that 'religion' means the traditional modes of the Church of England.[78]

In *Prove all Things* as originally delivered and published he had denounced compulsory chapel. But it was the business of the dean, supported by the tutors and other college officers, to enforce the current regulations which made some attendance at College chapel compulsory. It is hard for us to enter a world of ideas in which even men of such liberal outlook as the young clerical fellows of Emmanuel could regard enforced attendance at chapel as an essential part of the life of the college; and its demise was not far off – it barely survived the First World War in most

[76] Raven 1928, p. 133; Dillistone 1975, pp. 70–1; cf. Cupitt 1970–1, p. 5.
[77] I am summarising Chawner 1911, p. 20.
[78] Chawner 1911, pp. 20–1.

colleges. Meanwhile it remained a problem in all the older colleges of Oxford and Cambridge and some of the younger. They were religious foundations and the common life of chapel and hall was fundamental to them. The act of 1871 had abolished religious tests, but the act of 1877 had reiterated the colleges' religious purpose. Nor was religion the whole of it, for early rising to attend chapel was thought by many to be an essential element in student discipline; and King's for a time substituted signing a book at an early hour for chapel going to those who had or claimed conscientious scruples.[79] In 1908 F. M. Cornford, in his *Microcosmographia Academica*, had cynically observed that –

> 'The most valuable rules are those which ordain attendance at lectures and at religious worship. If these were not enforced, young men would begin too early to take learning and religion seriously; and that is well known to be bad form.'[80]

But to Christians of good will striving to preserve the element of religion in the college's purpose – and regarding it as peculiarly fundamental to the traditions and nature of Emmanuel – compulsory chapel seemed an inescapable prop, even if an embarrassing one. Furthermore, it was part of the rules of the College, and dean and tutors were enjoined to its enforcement. This created a position of extreme embarrassment for the young dean, Charles Raven.

On 18 May 1910 'the master circulated among resident Undergraduates' an address by the former President of Harvard commending the Unitarian position, and this seems to have been the spark which set the straw alight.[81] On 31 May seven of the fifteen or so members of the Governing Body[82] signed a letter representing 'their conviction that his recent practice of issuing to the undergraduates pamphlets and circulars dealing with questions of religious controversy is detrimental to the general interests of the College and specifically and gravely embarrassing to other officers of the College in the discharge of their statutory duties'. The protest was followed by letters from two other fellows, the senior fellow, A. T. Chapman, and L. H. G. Greenwood. The master was evidently shaken, but not diverted from his courses. He asked the senior

---

[79] For all this, see Brooke 1993, pp. 111–19.

[80] Cornford 1908, pp. 18–19 (edn. of 1987, p. 10).

[81] Chawner, quoted in Cupitt 1970–1, p. 7.

[82] Cupitt 1970–1, pp. 7–8, seems to make the Governing Body 13 strong (i.e. 14, including the Master). *CUC* 1909–10, pp. 1104–5, gives 16 fellows, but these included West Watson, bishop of Barrow, presumably too far away to vote, and Phear who, as ex-Master, may have stood aloof; it also includes Gowland Hopkins, who resigned in 1910 (see p. 524), but not Raven, who was elected early in 1910. My count (excluding Hopkins) would be 15 (i.e. 16 with the Master). The signatories thus did not form a majority, though we must not assume, as Cupitt points out, 'that the other . . . members of the Governing Body endorsed the Master's action' (loc. cit.).

tutor, the Reverend F. W. Head, which college officers were embarrassed and why, and Head made particular mention of the dean, who had to maintain college services and discipline, and himself as tutor, whose duty it was to support the dean. Chawner next sought Counsel's opinion, which was delivered on 22 July: he had committed no breach of the statutes, he was told, but his public statements condemning the current rules for chapel attendance were 'a breach of his duty as master'.[83] In the light of this the master made a formal reply to the seven fellows, conceding that he had been wrong to speak publicly on chapel attendance, but conceding no more. Early in the following year he reissued *Prove all Things* for public sale, carefully removing the offending sentences on chapel attendance, together with another pamphlet, *Truthfulness in Religion*, in which he restated his position and specifically defended his efforts to advance the cause of true religion – that is, as he makes clear at the end, of Unitarianism.[84] These demarches had a curious sub-plot and a dramatic conclusion.

Just over a week before the protest was sent, on 23 May 1910, the Governing Body elected L. H. G. Greenwood (already a fellow), to the Tutorship in Classics: he was to prove a steady, reliable, effective college teacher, if not deeply inspired or productive as a scholar. His rival had been the brilliant young King's classic, J. T. Sheppard. In later years Sheppard was to claim that he was refused election because he was thought 'a militant atheist'; but Sheppard, who was certainly anti-clerical in youth and probably in some sense agnostic, warmly denied the charge of atheism.[85] We may reckon it most improbable that at this juncture, with Chawner in the chair, there was any discussion of religious issues, though they may well have been in the minds of some of the Governing Body; and Greenwood, I am told, was also an agnostic. In the event Sheppard was to have his reward in his own college, King's, where he was soon a teaching fellow and later provost.

Early in 1911, after issuing his pamphlets, the master set off on holiday, and on 29 March, at Vence in the Alpes Maritimes, he suddenly died.[86] In his place the fellows elected Peter Giles, a respected peace-maker, not one of the signatories of the letters, but a master calculated to quieten the storms of the previous months.

Later in the year there appeared in the *Cornhill Magazine* a whimsical skit on the Chawner affair, 'The conversion of the master', by William Dampier Whetham of Trinity and his wife Catherine – Kitty Holt, of Liverpool and Newnham, niece of Beatrice Webb. The master of St

[83] Cupitt 1970–1, p. 8.
[84] Chawner 1911, pp. 22–3.
[85] Brooke 1993, p. 125; ECA COL.11.3, pp. 53, 119; TUT.4.2, pp. 295–7, 317–19.
[86] Peace 1911, p. 368.

Cuthbert's, Oxbridge, ceases to believe in the supernatural, and propagates his views to the embarrassment of dean and tutor. But on a holiday in Ireland he is bequeathed a curse, with which he finds to his alarm he can cause the death of cats; and his alarm is turned to horror when the curse is still with him on his return to his master's lodge – and he mistakenly fears he has harmed the tutor's baby. He hastens back to Ireland to a Catholic priest expert in exorcism. On his return to Oxbridge, even the cats survive his curse, to his intense relief; and he is last heard of reading a paper to the 'Freshmen's Christian Union' on 'The necessity of the supernatural element in religion'; the matriculations in the college take a turn for the better.[87] While the fellows of Emmanuel wept, their colleagues elsewhere in the city were considerably entertained.

The clergy of Emmanuel 1900–1914

Four of the signatories to the protest to Chawner had been Anglican clergymen; but none of them was a reactionary 'clerical', and Head and Raven were among the youngest of the fellows. In 1896 Head had been the first Emmanuel man to be given a first class in the History Tripos; he went on to research and to win the Prince Consort Prize and Seeley Medal for a study of 'The Fallen Stuarts' in 1900; in the same year he was elected fellow of Emmanuel, and although G. E. Green was nominally college lecturer in History still, Head was Emmanuel's first professional historian. But he had already embarked on another career, as a pastor: in 1902–3 he was ordained and became dean and tutor; in 1907 senior tutor. He was away in the YMCA and the army during the Great War, then returned to be Senior Tutor through the post-war generation. In 1922 he became vicar of Christ Church Greenwich; and after a spell when he and Raven were both canons of Liverpool, he went to Australia in 1929 as archbishop of Melbourne. 'The call of daily duty had made him deaf, if with regret, to the call for scholarship.' Thus Edward Welbourne, his former pupil, in his all-too-brief memoir.[88] Welbourne dwells on his modesty and simplicity. 'He had perhaps become a don too soon in life. He was perhaps not well informed about many of the worlds from which the undergraduates were beginning to come. He held to a view that every freshman was a possible ordinand, that Emmanuel remained what it perhaps still remains, a seminary of evangelicals, that its purpose was to send ordinary men into the world to do its necessary work. At a time when it was fast turning into a college of scientists, men who aspired to careers in research, this seemed a little, and obstinately, blind.' This

---

[87] Whetham 1911. On Mrs Whetham, Catherine Holt, see Brooke 1993, pp. 313–14.

[88] *ECM* 33 (1950–1), 74–5, on p. 75, from which the following quotations are also taken. For the details of his career, see the brief and moving memoir by his wife, Head 1943, esp. pp. [i], 2–7; Tanner 1917, p. 911.

perhaps tells us as much about Welbourne as about Head, for the exaggeration, the love of paradox, are characteristic – as also the warmth and affection with which he extols 'his example of punctuality and regularity, and the putting of duty before self'.

If Head was an evangelical with some knowledge of scholarly standards, the ageing Dixie Professor, H. M. Gwatkin (1844–1916), was a scholar to the fingertips, and a liberal, a modernist, of stoutly Protestant views. He was a man of exceptional gifts: it was said of him that he had taken three triposes in one year and lost a sense with each: it was certainly the case that he took Maths and Classics and Moral Sciences in 1867, and the Theological Examination (with prizes in Hebrew and Biblical Greek) the next year;[89] and that in later life his sight and his hearing were impaired and even his speech was eccentric. Yet he overcame these defects to be a distinguished scholar and much-valued teacher. He had been an undergraduate and fellow of St John's, and had hopes of election to the Dixie chair in 1884; though disappointed, he made friends with Creighton, and by 1891 was his obvious successor as Dixie professor and professorial fellow; thus he came to Emmanuel in his late 40s. In politics and religion he was a staunch liberal, but his liberality did not extend to Roman Catholics or Anglo-Catholics; the evangelical tone of Emmanuel in this era was to his taste.[90] His most lasting book was his early *Studies of Arianism* (1882); but his *Early Church History* (1909) was well known in its day; and he was a theologian as well as a historian and published Gifford Lectures on *The Knowledge of God* (1906). In a Cambridge in which professional historians were still scarce, he was widely respected, and helped to form the new professional historians and teachers of the next generation, including the medievalist Zachary Brooke of St John's and Caius, and Edward Welbourne of Emmanuel.

One of the most remarkable of his disciples was Charles Raven. Raven had been an undergraduate in Caius, where he was converted from classics to theology by the ferocious classical teaching of W. T. Lendrum and the first stirrings of religious vocation.[91] In his theological studies he encountered Gwatkin, and was deeply influenced by him. Thus Raven's inveterate prejudice against the middle ages owed something to Gwatkin's early inspiration; and, more creatively, Gwatkin taught him that a scholar may be a theologian, a historian and a natural scientist. Gwatkin was deeply interested in entomology and zoology all his life, and his vast collection of the *radulae* of snails went to join the treasures of the South Kensington Natural History Museum.[92] It may well have been Gwatkin

---

[89] Stubbings 1983b, no. 38; Tanner 1917, pp. 526, 628, 707, 809.
[90] Stubbings 1983b, no. 38. On Gwatkin there is an unpublished life by H. D. Hazeltine, together with an archive of letters, papers etc., in ECA.
[91] Dillistone 1975, pp. 40–9; for Lendrum cf. Brooke 1985, p. 237.
[92] Dillistone 1975, pp. 52–3; Stubbings 1983b, no. 38.

who first proposed Raven's name to the Emmanuel Governing Body.

Charles Raven was an inspired preacher, a scholar and a prophet; a man of the deepest integrity and independence of mind – yet mercurial, warm hearted, dependent on others to an exceptional degree. His early experience of Emmanuel was traumatic: he was immediately involved in the Chawner affair and lived through 1910 and the early months of 1911 in constant expectation of having to depart. Although his life was less fraught after Chawner's death the early impression seems never to have left him: after war service he returned to the College in 1919 for the briefest of spells: in 1920 he took the College living of Bletchingley, soon to be followed by a canonry in Liverpool; and when he returned to Cambridge as professor in 1932, he became a fellow not of Emmanuel but of Christ's.[93] None the less, Emmanuel had given him his first taste of high table life in Cambridge, and the opportunity to spread his wings as scholar and lecturer. Of his scholarship the first fruits comprised the book *Apollinarianism*, not published until 1923, but in the making long before under the inspiration of Gwatkin and his close colleague Professor Bethune-Baker. Meanwhile, like Gwatkin, he developed a passionate interest in natural history; and in the long run his most enduring book was probably his study of the great seventeenth century naturalist *John Ray* (1942), a masterpiece in the history of scientific and religious thought and the middle ground that linked them. In the 1920s Raven sought a new reformation – a revival of the Church in a strongly ecumenical sense, though with a liberal protestant inspiration behind it; and he wrote a prophetic book in support of the ordination of women. But he was at his most profound in seeking a union of religion and science; both the influence of Gwatkin and the traumatic experience of the Chawner affair taught him to seek above all a genuine meeting place for modern thought and Christian faith.[94] In his interest in science and religion, and the dedicated pacifism of his later years, he had a close ally in another of the signatories of 1910, Alex Wood.

Alex Wood

Wood was a presbyterian layman; yet he offers a fitting coda to this brief encounter with the devout among the fellows of Emmanuel in 1910. For in him one meets the new world created by the ending of religious tests in 1871 in a much more constructive form than in the pamphlets of Chawner, and in harness with the growing interest in science. No doubt there were many agnostics among the young scientists of Emmanuel in the early twentieth century; but doubtless too there were some who

---

[93] The inner story of this choice – by Raven and Christ's – seems not to be known.
[94] Dillistone 1975 *passim*; cf. Brooke 1993, pp. 147–50; on the ordination of women see Raven 1928a.

followed Raven and Wood in seeing science as a stimulus to faith, not its enemy. He was a native of Partick, and had studied in Glasgow at the feet of Lord Kelvin, whose characteristics deeply influenced him: 'the prayer with which Kelvin opened his lectures; the sense of high vocation which he impressed upon his classes; the combination in him of profound theoretical knowledge with a shrewd insight into the practical applications of his researches', as Raven said in his memoir of Wood.[95] Alex Wood was a devout member of the Church of Scotland; he was an elder of St Columba's, the presbyterian church in Downing Street, close to Emmanuel; he was bursar of the presbyterian theological College, Westminster, and took a deep interest in its affairs. He was an ardent pacifist, and a leading figure – with Raven – of the Peace Pledge Union; he and his wife played an active role in the boys' clubs of Cambridge; he became a local Councillor in the 1920s and a leader among the Labour councillors. With all this he miraculously succeeded in being an effective member of the Cavendish lab and a dedicated college man. Other Emmanuel scientists had more eclat in the scientific community: from the creative biochemistry of Gowland Hopkins to the explosive physical chemistry of Norrish. But Wood was a respected physicist, who did valuable work on acoustics and sound; and a central figure in college teaching, and a tutor for thirty years.

---

[95] Raven 1954, p. ix. On Alex Wood see Brooke 1993, p. 393 and refs. in n. 18, esp. Raven 1954; on the Peace Pledge Union see esp. Dillistone 1975, pp. 234–5. A road and a hall were named after him to commemorate his services to the city.

16

The Masters, 1911–1964

Peter Giles

Three masters spanned the half century of this chapter, Peter Giles, T. S. Hele, and Edward Welbourne. Giles was a considerable scholar and a Fellow of the British Academy; he was also an outsider, a migrant from Aberdeen and Caius. But by 1911 when he was elected master he had been twenty years a fellow of Emmanuel and was well known as a devoted college man and college teacher. Hele and Welbourne were in the nineteenth century tradition of masters: dedicated college men, little known in the scholarly world outside Cambridge. Hele was for many years a leading figure in university affairs. That can hardly be said of Welbourne, who was never vice-chancellor, nor craved for influence in the university. He was well known in Cambridge as a remarkable charac-ter; he had a small number of devotees who thought his lectures among the most interesting (as they were certainly among the most extraordi-nary) in the history faculty – but no man since Laurence Chaderton has been more widely known among the whole community of Emmanuel men, or, perhaps, more widely loved.

Let us start with Welbourne on Giles. 'He was the genuine poor Scot who had gone to the university [of Aberdeen] with his bag of oatmeal, but he had been taught his philology by a Yorkshire woolcomber who, illiterate until his twenties, became an Oxford professor. Except for the fact that most people found his Aberdeen accent difficult, which troubled me not at all, and that he aged rather fast and was handicapped by the general belief in Cambridge that all Scots were good men of business (which was not true of him), he was an excellent master, though apt in his old age not to open his post and unwilling to let anyone else open it.'[1]

Giles was born in Aberdeenshire of poor parents, and had the good fortune to be taught in a good school and to study and work among those who encouraged and helped poor boys of promise. With the aid of a bursary he went to Aberdeen University, and eked out his narrow means by teaching in his vacations. A strenuous course was rewarded with

[1] *ECM* 46 (1963–4), 9.

prizes and scholarships, and in the autumn of 1882 he followed James Adam to Cambridge and Caius.[2]

In Caius Giles was a pupil of the genial tutor, later master, E. S. Roberts, the very type of the college tutor in the heyday of the revival of college teaching – himself a notable classic, author of work on Greek epigraphy.[3] In the 1880s E. B. Cowell, professor of Sanskrit in Cambridge, was at the height of his influence in comparative philology; and he had an able younger colleague in classical philology in John Peile, later master of Christ's. In 1886 Giles had a break in his studies, and was encouraged by Roberts to visit Freiburg and sit at the feet of Karl Brugmann; he visited Brugmann again in Leipzig the next year. In 1887 Giles was elected fellow of Caius, in 1890 of Emmanuel. There he stayed for the rest of his life, fellow till 1911, master from 1911 till his death in 1935. He was a philologist with a real interest in literature, much less in Greek philosophy, which was Adam's bent. I myself possess detailed notes of his undergraduate lectures on Greek syntax taken by my father in 1904, which are of an extremely formal nature – with some references to advanced literature but no hint of a lighter touch. Already in 1891, supported by references from Scotland and Germany as well as from Cambridge, he was appointed University Reader in Comparative Philology. From the late 1880s to 1895 he was deeply involved, with much encouragement from Peile, in writing his *Manual of Comparative Philology for the Use of Classical Students*. This showed above all the value of his German visits: under the influence of Brugmann he made English scholars fully acquainted with the doctrines of the Neo-Grammatiker, and especially with novel ideas about the nature of phonetic law. Soon after he was at work on Theocritus; and in the next decade Giles laid the foundations of an edition of his works which he was never able to complete. His involvement in teaching, and in college and university administration, gradually absorbed more and more of his time; and the volume of his later original published work was never large – though its range is wide, taking in early Scottish literature and Walter Scott. But he was a widely known and respected philologist, and a Fellow of the British Academy from 1927.[4]

'With his election as master in 1911', wrote L. H. G. Greenwood, 'began a long reign of beneficent activity in the college and in the university. The master's lodge, a somewhat severe establishment in the reign of his bachelor predecessor, became the scene of regular and generous hospitality: there was always a welcome there from himself and Mrs Giles, for young and old members of the college alike, and for many others as well. His conduct of college meetings was marked by a kindly consideration

[2] Dawkins 1935, pp. 406–8.
[3] Brooke 1985, chap. 12, esp. pp. 234–6. For what follows, cf. Brooke 1993, pp. 427–31.
[4] For all this see Dawkins 1935, esp. pp. 416–22, 430.

that was not unwelcome after the sometimes ruthless efficiency of William Chawner, whose great services to the college Giles was, in spite of his very different temperament and outlook, one of the first to recognise. It was his way to accept without demur what he perceived to be the wishes of his colleagues, though he had a curious reluctance to be content with any decision, on a grave matter, that was not unanimous or nearly so. His two years as Vice-Chancellor, the two that followed the end of the [Great] War, were years of great strain; but his discharge of his duties added much to his reputation in university circles and outside them.'[5]

While he was Vice-Chancellor, the university was reviving after the war, coping with enormously increased numbers, and adjusting to a new world. This involved preparing evidence for the Royal Commission – after which Giles was to be himself a Statutory Commissioner, one of those responsible for vetting the new university and college statutes. He presided over the Syndicate which paved the way for the arrival in Cambridge of the Ph.D. in 1920, a crucial step in preserving the international standing of Cambridge as a centre of research – however little some of Giles's colleagues, including Edward Welbourne, approved of it.[6] In his work for the Royal and Statutory Commissions he was a close ally of the master of Caius, Sir Hugh Anderson, the central figure in the Cambridge committee of the Royal and the Statutory Commissions.[7] One of the most crucial tasks in which Giles and Anderson worked together was in guiding opinion in Cambridge on the future of the University Library, still cabined, cribbed, and confined in the Old Schools. Giles presided over the Sub-Syndicate which in November 1918 recommended 'a whole series of daring measures – underground stores, a new bookstore on the west court, a reading room in the east court, and so forth'.[8] Before the Great War the Bodleian had faced similar problems and burrowed deep under Oxford. Similar measures were suggested in Cambridge. But in 1919–21 new winds were to blow; and Giles and Anderson were among those who were gradually converted to the idea that a new site must be found for the Library. No one then knew how it was to be financed; and in the discussions and intrigues which led to the appointment of Sir Giles Scott as architect and the successful appeal to the Rockefeller Foundation for funds, Anderson filled the central role. But Giles had played a crucial part in the years immediately following the War.[9]

Within the walls of Emmanuel, he presided over the growth of the college and the many changes of the 1920s; and his era is particularly

---

[5] ECM 29, *Supplement* (1935) [henceforth *Suppl.* – memoirs of Giles], p. 170.
[6] Margaret Wallace in *Suppl.*, pp. 165–8.
[7] *Suppl.*, p. 165; Brooke 1993, chap. 11; for what follows, ibid., chap. 12.
[8] Brooke 1993, p. 373.
[9] Ibid., pp. 370–7.

associated with great building projects, with the north court and the new library, which belong to another page.[10]

Characteristically, throughout his time as Vice-Chancellor, he 'attended College Chapel at 7.45 in the morning and lectured in college every day at 9.00' – that is, gave his university lectures. In the chapel his ashes were laid on 20 October 1935 – the 75th anniversary of his birth.[11]

T. S. Hele

Hele was a north countryman from Carlisle, educated at Carlisle Grammar school and Sedbergh – 'the school of his loyalties, where a clumsy unathletic boy learned by feats of endurance to laugh at pain and exhaustion, and where an eager, intellectually curious, ambitious boy learned also, in the fashion of the times, to belittle his ability, to conceal a massive and midnight industry behind a pose of improvisation, but where he also was prepared to make his way into class I in both parts of the Natural Sciences Tripos, and a little to bewilder himself, who meant to become a doctor, by becoming a scientist.'[12] In fact he qualified as a doctor at St Bartholomew's and spent some years in medical work and research in London and Bristol; but in 1911 he was summoned back to a fellowship in Emmanuel and a college lectureship in natural sciences. This he combined till the First World War with research under the guidance of Gowland Hopkins. The war took him abroad in the RAMC; and when he returned to Cambridge he was quickly caught up in college teaching and administration and much else.

'An exigent college, which heaped its duties on the willing horse, the administrative care of the new biochemistry laboratory, and service on numerous boards, completed the damage the war had begun, and he said himself – so often that many people believed too well what he said – that a failure as research worker had become a failure as a university teacher.'[13] This was the characteristic utterance of a modest man who used to attribute his OBE – awarded, probably, for his work for the RAMC in Salonika – to a 'recognition of his performance as Malvolio in an army production of *Twelfth Night* behind the lines'. Before the cult of research tightened its grip on the universities in the mid and late twentieth century it was possible to recruit teachers without a creative gift in research; and there were and are many who started on the path of research as well as teaching whose energies became wholly absorbed in teaching or administering college and university. The truth is that in all

---

[10] See pp. 513–17.

[11] Dawkins 1935, p. 432.

[12] *ECM* 35 (1952–3), 1–2 (by E. Welbourne – ex inf. Frank Stubbings). For what follows, see Venn, *ECM*, 35, 1–4.

[13] Ibid., p. 2. I owe the story of Malvolio, below, to his daughter Mrs Carroll Holland; and much help besides to Carroll and her elder sister, Dr Priscilla Hele.

recent generations a university teacher has been confronted by three tasks, any one of which can monopolise his time and his interest if he so wills it. Hele became a quintessential college man. 'He soon moved into Emmanuel House, which overlooks the pond, and there, and later in the Master's Lodge, he shared a happy family life with his pupils, breaking down their shyness by hilarious parlour games, and maybe by unexpected encounters with natural history, for his children were given an interest in biology which both their parents shared.'[14] His daughter Mrs Carroll Holland writes: 'Lab animals from the Biochemistry department were brought home as temporary pets and we children benefited from meeting all sorts of creatures – at that time many of them virtually unknown – such as hamsters, marmosets, axolotls, salamanders and south American bull-frogs as well as the run-of-the-mill experimental rats. Also, damaged or orphaned birds and animals were brought to Emmanuel House where they were nursed back to health again. I don't think it's just my imagination, but the unsuspecting visitor could well find a large bull-frog established in an armchair, a bedraggled white hen, which had fallen into the pond, drying out in front of the gas fire or a young barn owl perched on the curtain rail. In retrospect we must have been quite an eccentric household.' And Carroll's elder sister Dr Priscilla Hele recalls 'the toy train parties. Every Sunday afternoon, autumn and winter during term, undergraduates would start showing up at about 2 pm to set up the track on the drawing room floor. It was an elaborate track, with a lot of points to switch. About half a dozen wind-up trains were run very competitively over this track, with mad switching at the points. After tea and after dark the lights were turned out, and the trains ran with lighted sparklers in their funnels. Joy and mayhem. I don't know why Emmanuel House didn't get burnt down.'

Hele lived in Emmanuel House as senior tutor, and his concern for undergraduates was wide and deep. 'He deplored the ragging (debagging and tossing in the Pond) of the scholarship students who lived together in the cheaper accommodation of the Hostel. A few years later he told me that this ragging was due to resentment and prejudice at the working-class origins of the scholarship students.' His fervour in condemning prejudice and unfairness extended outside the college to the treatment of academic women in the university in his day.[15] Hele 'was a magnificent medical educator' and ever more deeply absorbed in running the College, until 1935 when his experience and service were recognised in his election as master.

In Cambridge colleges in the present century, three kinds of men have

---

[14] *ECM* 35, pp. 1–2; Mrs Carroll Holland, personal communication; the quotation in the next sentence is from *ECM* 35, 1–2.

[15] Dr Priscilla Hele, personal communication. The following phrase is from *ECM* 35, 1–2.

been elected masters: devoted college tutors or bursars, little known in the outside world; eminent scholars and scientists; and notable public figures with a special interest in Cambridge. Hele and Welbourne belong to the first group; Sir Gordon Sutherland, who came from outside Emmanuel and Cambridge to be master in 1964, to the second; Derek Brewer to the second – though he was also a dedicated servant of the college; Peter Wroth to the second; Lord St John of Fawsley to the third – he is very evidently a public figure, but a man of such wide interests as to overflow the bounds of any category.

Hele had not been long elected when the Second World War broke out, and much of his time as master, and all his time as vice-chancellor, was occupied with the special problems of war-time Cambridge. 'The necessary and at times drastic reforms which this most conservative of men had in his mind, and which would have made of his mastership a magnificent period in the history of Emmanuel, were put aside by the onset of the war.'[16] Perhaps it would be truer to say of him, with his daughter Priscilla, that 'he described himself as "a Victorian Liberal". He was outspoken in his dislike of prejudice, unfairness and favouritism'. During the war his first wife died, bringing domestic sorrow, restored by a happy second marriage; but after the war Hele fought bravely against declining health and advancing age, and only survived his retirement in 1951 by just over a year. 'He became, with age, at times scandalously outspoken, as experience confirmed the prejudices of his youth and he saw society losing its battle with a plague of paper administration which he looked on as a biological degeneracy of society. . . . Those who say that modern Cambridge has lacked its characters, cannot have met this large untidy laughing man, his unpunctuality growing as he grew older and less able to estimate the time it would take him to hobble from place to place . . . a country G.P. out of place, maybe, but a country G.P. of the days when a doctor was an educated man, and a friend of all the world.'[17]

Edward Welbourne

If Hele was a personality, his successor was one of the notable eccentrics of Cambridge history. On 27 November 1951 at 4.00 p.m. 25 out of the 28 members of the Governing Body gathered to discuss the election of a master to succeed T. S. Hele. By 5.15 Edward Welbourne had been elected – it was one of the shortest college elections recorded.[18] It was about the first election in Cambridge after the publication of C. P. Snow's *The Masters*, and I was told at the time that some fellows of Emmanuel were determined to avoid any suspicion of the intrigues which fill that

[16] *ECM* 35, 2–4.
[17] *ECM* 35, 2–4.
[18] ECA COL.17.4.

celebrated mirror of Cambridge life by an ex-fellow of neighbouring Christ's. In any case, Welbourne was greatly loved, and immensely popular with the undergraduate community. He had long been director of studies in history and a tutor, and since 1935 Senior Tutor.

'The portrait of Welbourne painted for the College', writes Ronald Gray, 'gives little idea, with its mild eyes and rosy cheeks, of the cheerful, prejudiced, limited but uncommonly generous and illuminating old devil Welbourne was. His head was extraordinarily large, and so was his chin ... He wore roughish clothes, rather hairy tweeds, usually with a cardigan. . . . In later years he walked with a slight stoop but never complained of the piece of shrapnel that circulated in him from a war wound. He never mentioned ... how he came by his Military Cross'.[19] He will be remembered above all for his ceaseless flow of talk – whether in the court, where he spent long hours catching acquaintances old and new; or in supervisions. He avoided outside commitments; he did little formal entertaining – 'he gave no private parties or dinners'[20] – and so had ample time for the innumerable chance encounters which made him the central figure of the college, and for endless supervisions.

'I heard tales', writes Gray, '. . . of how a supervision might go on for several hours, in the course of which he might be brandishing a poker drawn from the fire to illustrate some point, while dealing with interruptions from the Head Porter, his secretary, the telephone, and perhaps leaving his pupil for half an hour at a time while dealing with some emergency. Supervisions seldom ended at any definite moment . . .; the final words might be shouted from the platform of a bus he had just boarded.'[21]

Gray, a modern linguist, could feel the influence of Welbourne's acuteness and scepticism – not in religious matters, but in accepted and traditional views, whether of economic history or of Goethe – and the latter in spite of Welbourne's very slight interest in literature. David Newsome, one of the most distinguished of his pupils, described the supervisions from within.

'I normally went to him at 4.00 p.m. on Fridays, when he offered me tea, and the supervision lasted until hall at 7.30. He never set an essay title. "Bring me another", he would say at the close of each supervision. "Read away!" would be the first words one heard on entering his room, the following week. In fact I succeeded in reading an essay to him only

---

[19] From a paper by Ronald Gray, 'A Past Master, 1894–1966', pp. 55–6, generously put at our disposal by the author and subsequently published in *ECM* 78 (1995–6), 50–9. I have made copious use of this paper, of Frank Stubbings' memoir in *ECM* 48 (1965–6), 6–12, and of Newsome 1984. There is a lively and appreciative account in Parkinson 1966, unreliable in detail.

[20] Ronald Gray (n.19), p. 50.

[21] Ibid., p. 56.

once, and on this occasion he fell asleep. It was normally sufficient to read just the first sentence to let loose the stream of paradox which flowed on undisturbed, except when he paused to munch moodily at a Marie biscuit. "Ah, well," he would say, before flinging himself into some bewildering non-sequitur, which somehow, through devious routes, brought him back to the main track. It was always brilliant, but frequently baffling . . . Looking at some notes which I attempted to take after one supervision (ostensibly on the Counter-Reformation), I find that we covered *inter alia* the childhood of Ribbentrop, the *real* story behind the building of the American railways, why London footmen were usually Irish, the origin of the Lyons Corner Houses, Luther's consumption of liver sausage and the religious significance of porridge. Somehow it all got back to the Council of Trent.'[22] He was a man of extraordinarily ingenious mind, acute, iconoclastic, much too diffuse to be creative; but his ideas were shot through with brilliant insights based on wide reading and down-to-earth study of practical things. 'He once passed me a *History of the Sulphuric Acid Industry in Cheshire* with the words "If you want to get a First in Tripos, you'd better read this. It's all in here" '.[23]

'The decline of religion in the nineteenth century was due – he would not stoop to saying partly due – to the invention of the water closet . . .' So Gray reports. Better sanitation meant less disease – and 'with the invention of the W.C. interest in the after-life declined, along with interest in religion'.[24]

'He could be mischievous – he could be perverse; he was certainly wonderfully stimulating . . .' writes David Newsome. 'He reached his position of authority through voracious reading. His method, as one would expect, was unusual. I have heard it said that he read a book a day and two on Sundays. He skipped and "gutted" as his fancy moved him. His discerning eye picked out the relevant fact, the injudicious slip which provided the clue to all – a clue which would have eluded ninety-nine out of a hundred readers. And the information would be docketed away in his mind. He ranged far and wide in his reading. One week he would collect a "bag of books" (a favourite phrase) on the lesser councils of the Church, the next he would be studying the processes of glass-blowing; he would then turn to some dozen different volumes of reminiscences of the Peninsular War. It seemed to be without order or logic, the connecting links as tenuous and obscure as the sequence of his conversation. But he had read most of the books which the specialist had read, and sometimes a few which they had not, and he could take on all comers.'[25]

---

[22] Newsome 1984, p. 106.
[23] Ibid., p. 107.
[24] Gray, p. 54.
[25] Newsome 1984, pp. 107–8.

The range of his reading and the cast of his mind prevented him from any large-scale writing, after his early Prince Consort essay, *The Miners' Unions of Northumberland and Durham*, which set him on the academic path. This added an edge to his jibes at research and specialism and Ph.Ds.; though it must be said that they were only part of the larger world of prejudice in which he revelled.

'While never disguising his prejudices, he gave vent to them with such vehemence in his emphasis on the conspiratorial element in history, that left his pupils, as often as not, with the impression that he who would slake his thirst at the fountain of history must imbibe a witches' brew, compounded of the venom of sinister papists, court toadies, pretentious *arrivistes*, hot-headed Welshmen and power-hungry Jews. There is more to history than this, and Welbourne well knew it – but he did not always choose to say so.'[26] I was myself introduced to Welbourne by an old friend who was both a scholar and a Welshman, James Conway Davies; and it was characteristic of him not to let his prejudices affect his friendships or his courtesy to guests in hall and parlour. Yet Ronald Gray reminds us that 'the prejudices were not harmless'; a widely respected tutor and head of house could not but help to confirm other men's views – and 'what he said about Jews was too much like the unthinking view of many ordinary students'.[27]

He controlled many or most of the admissions to Emmanuel over a long period, and deliberately avoided elitism of background or academic quality. He relied on intuition and experience – as some would say, on strange quirks of experience. He was always for the underdog and the good grammar school boy – he had himself been at De Aston's School, Market Rasen, in Lincolnshire; he was no respecter of persons. 'He had little regard for brilliance in examinations,' writes Ronald Gray, 'though he himself had won an open scholarship and a First in both parts of the History Tripos. I demonstrated in 1962 that most holders of scholarships and other awards based on examinations in my own subject over the previous ten years had gained Firsts or Two-Ones. The rest, men admitted by him on his own judgement or his own principles, just under half the total, had never gained either Firsts or Two-Ones. Nearly half of them had gained Thirds, and over a third had been "allowed a special examination" [an ordinary degree] . . . When this was reported to the Governing Body, he merely observed, "Gray has proved that by statistics". His genial contempt was not meant to question my argument; it was meant to sweep it away, and it did so . . .'[28]

---

[26] Newsome 1984, p. 107. On his prejudices see esp. Gray, pp. 51 (an almost definitive list), 52–3.

[27] Gray, p. 52.

[28] Gray, p. 54.

Frank Stubbings, in his perceptive memoir, quoted Welbourne's own summary of his philosophy of a college education:

> We are content to see men turn into themselves and admit to themselves their abilities and their limitations. We hope they leave us with some understanding of the nature of knowledge and of the difference between knowledge and memorised verbal formulae, with some experience of the nature of understanding and its difference from acceptance of authority and, still more, from rejection of authority through even greater, if similar, credulity, with some ability to reach agreement, at first with their friends, and as time passes with others, and to understand that argument and explanation is not for victory but to reach agreement. We hope that they will be able to resist the stream of propaganda of a world deluged with propaganda, even though the channels of that propaganda seem always to narrow. We hope, therefore, that they will have been encouraged in honesty and stoutness of heart, and that some will have come to see how far they need to believe, and that some will have acquired a better command both of the spoken and of the written word than is common.[29]

'At Governing Body meetings', writes Gray, 'he was at his least effective ... Often several motions would be in progress at once, some seconded, some not, and if anyone asked for a clear ruling he would answer (with a smile) "I was waiting for somebody to say that" '[30] – though he had his own methods for getting his way when he wanted to. In looking after the college buildings – though no handy man himself – he showed a very practical interest, in which sewers and sanitation figured prominently. 'This was the countryman in him', comments Ronald Gray; but it invaded his academic work too.[31] Newsome remembers 'him talking over coffee for quite an hour on the history of hat-making, following an idle enquiry about the headgear of the Mongols. This was real knowledge, and to find out the truth you might have to talk with a master-craftsman himself, which to Welbourne was sheer delight.' And his handling of the college buildings won great respect from the foreman of Rattee and Kett.[32]

Like Hele, Welbourne carried the Senior Tutorship into the Master's office – though not into the Lodge, where he never lived; his family stayed in Great Shelford, but he himself spent the day, and often the night too, in college, talking and reading; in an eccentric and exaggerated and

[29] *ECM* 48 (1965–6), 11–12.
[30] Gray, p. 58.
[31] Gray, p. 57; what follows is from Newsome 1984, p. 111.
[32] Gray, pp. 57–8.

highly individual way he illustrated the qualities of the leading tutors of Cambridge of the period 1870–1950, who believed in education and learning and sometimes in religion, but had perhaps more in common with exceptionally clever schoolmasters than with the professional academics of the late twentieth century. It was fitting that a school-master-don, David Newsome – but one who has had in abundance the creative gift Edward Welbourne lacked – should have described in vivid and affectionate detail the bewildering experience of being taught by him.[33]

'The essential Welbourne' wrote Frank Stubbings 'was especially apparent to those who had the good fortune to hear him talk to the William Law Society, about a year before his death, taking as his subject "Sectarianism". He did not willingly give talks or papers to societies, and it was therefore an unusual occasion. One who was present writes:

> Most people there realised it was going to be Welbourne's last big intellectual ramble and wanted to go on it with him. He got through what he had prepared and then talked at random about anything which came to mind. 'Sectarianism' was a wonderful subject for him ... he was able to make it include everything he wanted to talk about and most of the things those who knew him best wanted him to talk about. He aired most of his sympathies and antipathies, and on that occasion the former were more than the latter. He talked for two and a half hours and then I had to stop him for the sake of some who, in my overcrowded room, were acutely uncomfortable. He revealed more strikingly than I ever heard him before his apprecia-tion of the many-sidedness of human life and his wonderful under-standing of and compassion for all kinds of human beings.'[34]

---

[33] Newsome 1984.
[34] *ECM* 48 (1965–6), 6–7. The 'one who was present' was the Chaplain, the Reverend J. H. Lang (ex inf. Frank Stubbings).

17

Estate Management and Finance in the Modern World

Whispers of changes in the ways in which collegiate finances and estates were managed and organised, in the air in 1871, were soon to become clearly audible. During the past 100 years or so the nature of Emmanuel's investments, the attitude towards changes to this portfolio, the rules governing its use and the management of it have all altered. No longer is Emmanuel's income largely derived from agricultural rents, nor are sales and purchases few, nor is the College's estate management tightly constrained by legislation specifically aimed at colleges and universities. The College now holds a wide range of investments: in real estate, such as farm land, shops and industrial premises; and in the stock market. These assets are now regarded as being tradeable and, since 1964, colleges have had a much freer hand in choosing and managing their capital assets. The path of change has not always been smooth, and Emmanuel has been subjected to both external pressures and internal demands.

The overall parameters and underlying precepts have, however, remained constant. Emmanuel's investments are held in trust for future generations. The College is obliged by laws of trusteeship both to preserve its capital for future generations and also to spend an appropriate proportion of its income for the present members in residence. The long term view, therefore, still prevails and the College's assets are actively and professionally managed.

The Bursars and their Advisers

Attitudes to estate management have changed during the past century. In 1874, the Royal Commissioners praised the care and vigilance of college bursars in their estate management: many, though not Emmanuel's, collected rents themselves and only employed solicitors and land agents as the need arose.[1] By the early twentieth century, however, the current

---

[1] Royal Commission 1874, p. 36.

practices were being questioned,[2] and in 1922 the Commissioners found only a few instances of efficient estate management, though no radical changes were recommended. Few colleges – Trinity Hall was an exception[3] – had bursars who had any professional expertise in estate management, and Emmanuel was one of the many colleges that relied on an untrained bursar and professional advisers.[4] There was much to be said for the system, for a bursar's and agents' areas of expertise could be complementary, and a bursar was responsible for the overall financial administration in his college, rather than just for estate business.[5] The bursar should, the Commissioners recommended, be assisted by an Estates Committee; Emmanuel already conformed to this practice.[6] Since the 1920s, as affairs have become more complex, colleges have increasingly turned to the employment of full-time bursars with professional qualifications: Emmanuel did so for a five-year period from 1992 to 1997.

Since the 1870s, Emmanuel has inevitably seen Bursars come and go, though the turnover has been less frequent than in the earlier decades of the nineteenth century. The Reverend Alfred Rose, Bursar from 1872 to 1893,[7] was the last clergyman (so far) to hold the office.[8] His successor, James Bennett Peace, combined his College duties with a University Demonstratorship and then Lectureship in mechanical engineering and latterly with being University Printer.[9] It was during his bursarship that evidence first comes readily to light of much more active estate management, both of agricultural and of urban properties, and of the conversion of the Hyde Farm estate from the former to the latter category. Peace clearly had a good working relationship with the College's tenants: in 1916, the lessee of South College Farm in Pinchbeck, Lincolnshire, hoped that Peace would continue as Bursar as he was such a good and fair person with whom to deal;[10] when there was a hint of his resignation in 1919, he received letters from tenants that expressed, in strong terms, the hope that he might continue;[11] he finally gave up the office in the following year and a tribute to him was paid by the tenant of the farm at Great Melton in Norfolk.[12]

During his last year as Bursar, Peace was assisted by Robert Gardner;[13]

[2] Tillyard 1913, pp. 309–15.
[3] Crawley 1977, p. 191.
[4] Royal Commission 1922, pp. 222–3.
[5] Royal Commission 1922, p. 222; Howard 1935, p. 266.
[6] Royal Commission 1922, pp. 223–4; see p. 455.
[7] ECA COL.14.3 pp. 230–1; COL.14.4 p. 84.
[8] The Reverend J. S. Boys Smith was Senior Bursar of St John's College from 1944 to 1959 (CUC).
[9] Venn.
[10] ECA Li.6.435.
[11] ECA Li.9.71–2.
[12] ECA Nf.1.126; ECA COL.14.5 p. 306.
[13] ECA COL.14.5 p. 280.

in 1920, Gardner succeeded to the position and so began an epic reign in the Bursary of 40 years. He witnessed many changes – the Royal Commission and new statutes of 1926, the depression of the 1930s, the Second World War – and oversaw the investment in a wider range of stocks and shares in the 1950s, and many changes to individual properties. 'Modest, punctual, thorough, fore-thoughtful, unsparing of himself, tough physically and mentally, clear in mind, brought up in a world which accepted as man's lot duty, retaining . . . kindness and gentleness . . .' – thus his obituary in *The Times*[14] – these qualities appear time and again throughout the estate papers and correspondence. Before meetings, Gardner would prepare detailed notes that summarised succinctly the issues to be discussed and the background to them. He kept a close eye on the activities on the College's estates by tenants and agents. In 1925, for instance, he wrote to Mathews and Sons at Sutton Coldfield about alterations to 10 Mill Street that,

> If I remember rightly, this shed was separate from the shop and living quarters and was passed as one went through to the lane behind. Its structure did not seem to be very substantial. I should have thought that it would have been advisable to include it in any scheme of rebuilding.[15]

A few years later, when the development of land nearby at Maney on building leases was being considered, Gardner typically asked to see plans of the different types of houses proposed and the general layout of the estate as 'I am interested in house building.'[16] Gardner was a sympathetic person with whom to deal and, like Peace, had a good relationship with the College's agents and tenants; in 1956, when the College decided to sell its farm at Great Melton in Norfolk, he consoled the widow of the late tenant that 'in my own family affairs in recent years similar difficulties have arisen, and that contrary to our expectations "manna" has always "dropped from the sky"';[17] and he hoped to be able to visit her when he was next in the area.[18]

From 1948, Gardner had an Assistant Bursar, A. J. Ward,[19] and it was he who was to take over the Bursarship on Gardner's retirement in 1960. For 14 years, Ward masterminded the College's finances, and the times were not quiet ones. The amendment in 1964 of the 1925 Universities and College Estates Act, the sale of some of Emmanuel's properties in Cambridge and London, and the Leasehold Reform Act were just some of the

[14] *ECM* 54, 1971–2, pp. 9–11.
[15] ECA Wa.6.292.
[16] ECA Wa.10.164.
[17] ECA Nf.2.465.
[18] ECA Nf.2.512.
[19] ECA COL.11a.4.

major developments with which he had to cope. 'None failed to respect his preparedness and clarity of mind', wrote F. H. Stubbings on Ward's death in 1984,

> More than one City lawyer or investments adviser has been astonished to find this seemingly umbratile don, patently tailored far from Savile Row, display a knowledge and acumen to match the best in Lombard Street. His Bursarship (though he would have been first to disclaim the credit) saw some major financial transactions and some unprecedented growth; it also saw major building developments; and throughout he kept a firm hand on the present and a sharp eye to the future . . .
>
> Gus Ward was in many ways unworldly, simple in his pleasures, a lifelong teetotaller – though it is not true that it was he who invested the Parlour wine-account capital in the Metropolitan Water Board. Though shy of formal sociabilities he enjoyed family life, living in the country at Fen Drayton and sailing on the Great Ouse. He was the protagonist of lunch-time bowls in the Fellows' Garden – whatever the weather – and proved this as much a mathematician's game as chess (another pastime of his). He had joined in youth the Salvation Army, playing a horn in the band, and maintained an active loyalty to that body, bringing to bear valuable skills of mind and experience.[20]

The bursarship of John Reddaway (1974–83) saw a new hard-headed approach to the College's financial affairs. Shortly after his successful negotiations for the purchase of Park Terrace, thus bringing to reality a Bursarial dream of very many years,[21] he was appointed Secretary to the University of Cambridge Local Examinations Syndicate. David Livesey took over as Bursar and carried on from where Reddaway had left off. Bursarial business, and the Bursary, expanded, the first College Accountant was appointed and computer systems were introduced. In 1992, Livesey followed Reddaway's example and resigned the Bursarship on his appointment to high University office, as Secretary-General of the Faculties. Tony Cramp generously ran the Bursary until the appointment, later in the year, of the College's first full-time professionally qualified Bursar: an Emmanuel graduate, Stephen Brooker, who held the reins until 1997. In that year, the Assistant Bursar and Director of Studies in Economics, Michael Gross, took over.

When the Bursar was absent on leave or, as in 1925, through ill health, deputies had to be appointed. They did not always find their new duties

---

[20] ECA COL.9.3.

[21] Others, too, participated in the wish to buy the property: see p. 571 for the contribution that Derek Brewer, Master at the time, played in the negotiations.

straightforward, and P. W. Wood wrote in 1926, after he had received an alarming report about conditions at one of the College's farms in Pinchbeck, that the report was not flattering to the College as landlord, that it was to be expected that other farm properties had been equally neglected, and that he would be happier when the bursarial work was in 'more competent hands' than his.[22]

The Bursars were never entirely left on their own: advice was always to hand and, as business became more complicated, so more support was available. Assistance came from within the College, from Fellows and staff, from within the University, and from the College's own professional agents.

From 1907 onwards, the Bursar was advised by, and was responsible to, an Estates Committee of the Governing Body. The Committee's remit was to advise on management of the estates and to oversee repairs and improvements to them, and consisted of the Master, the Bursar and one other Fellow (initially, P. W. Wood).[23] Under the reforms of 1926, duties of the Bursar and Steward were divided along the lines laid down by the Royal Commission: the Bursar was responsible for the external revenue accounts, the Steward for those of internal revenue.[24] The Estates Committee now consisted of four Fellows besides the Master and Bursar; it was to manage all affairs regarding the College's properties and estates except for purchases, sales and extraordinary alterations to the College's fabric and grounds.[25] In 1963, the Committee was given authority to order the College seal to be used, without reference to the Governing Body, for certain routine transactions.[26]

Particular members of the Estates Committee brought to it specific expertise. James Line, Steward from 1924 to 1952, was also a University Lecturer in the Faculty of Agriculture and Forestry. He reported on conditions on many of the College's estates, especially the Sutton Coldfield estate near his home town of Birmingham.[27] He did not, however, confine his advice to Warwickshire: when modernisation of Great Melton Farm in Norfolk was being considered in 1949 and 1950, he asked the advice of the Executive Officer of the local Agricultural Executive Committee, whom he knew well.[28] On other occasions, he obtained unofficial soil analyses for tenants and investigated why their crops had failed.[29] Line was not soft: he could be very critical of farmers,[30] suspicious of agents

---

[22] ECA Li.2.310.
[23] ECA COL.14.4 p. 401.
[24] ECA COL.11.5 p. 196.
[25] ECA COL.11.5 p. 220.
[26] ECA COL.11.13 (26 July 1963).
[27] ECA Wa.2.137.
[28] ECA Nf.2.142.
[29] ECA Ru.1.202, 215.
[30] ECA Ke.1.410.

and advised against some requests for rent reductions during the depression of the inter-war years.[31] Line collaborated with Wilfred Mansfield, who was equally tough. From 1929, Mansfield was a University Lecturer in the same Faculty as Line; three years later, Mansfield became Director of the University Farm. He advised the College on estate business from 1930, and in 1936 he was elected a Fellow and appointed Adviser in Agriculture,[32] an office which he held until 1950. Thereafter he continued to help, but in an honorary capacity.[33] His advice remained valuable, and in 1959 a decision about improvements to one of the Pinchbeck farms was delayed until he returned to Cambridge.[34]

Help and advice came from others within the College, too. The Master was naturally expected to take an interest in estate business: in 1905, while he was in Egypt, Chawner had to be consulted about developments on the Hyde Farm estate. Peace must have enjoyed the reply, as in addition to advice, he received a colourful description of an excursion on the Nile.[35] Fellows could have particular expertise to offer: Frederick Tom Brooks, Reader and later Professor of Botany, advised in 1935 about the planting of cherry orchards at Ash in Kent, for example.[36] From 1937,[37] Gardner and then Ward received the invaluable help of Ronald Fuerni, Bursar's Clerk. He retired in 1974 but continued to come into College to help to catalogue the College Archives until his death in 1982. Fuerni's 'impeccable calligraphy' appears throughout bursarial documents; he sorted, filed, catalogued and indexed meticulously; he had a thorough knowledge of the College's affairs and an outstanding memory; and was also a skilled photographer. He clearly greatly eased the Bursar's burden.[38]

Bursars at Emmanuel shared their expertise with their colleagues within the University and at Oxford, through both informal and formal networks. From time to time, informal advice was received and passed on. The request from farmers for permission to form limited liability companies gave colleges particular problems: in 1944, Gardner asked his counterpart at Gonville and Caius College[39] why he thought that such arrangements would be undesirable. Then, some years later, the Bursar of St John's benefited from Gardner's explanation of why Emmanuel did

[31] ECA Ke.1.180; ECA Wa.11.397, 409.
[32] ECA COL.14.7 p. 22.
[33] ECA COL.11a.5.
[34] ECA Li.7.426.
[35] ECA Sr.3.253, 255.
[36] ECA Ke.5.309.
[37] ECA STE.25.2.
[38] Obituary in *ECM* 65, 1982–3, pp. 24–6, which reprints an appreciation by A. J. Ward, first published in *ECM* 57, 1974–5, pp. 17–18.
[39] E. P. Weller, a professional estate manager and the college's first professional bursar: Brooke 1985, pp. 266, 272.

not allow its tenants to sub-let their farms to their own farming companies.[40] Bursars also shared their experiences more formally, through meetings of the inter-collegiate Bursars' Committee. The Committee discussed issues of common concern such as town planning proposals within Cambridge; legislation and its effect upon colleges, and especially the working and revision of the 1925 Universities and College Estates Act; tithes; the procedures for claiming compensation for damage by enemy action during the Second World War; farming methods and improvements; investment policy; and much more. The minutes are full of advice by Maynard Keynes on many matters: the relative value of real estate and gilt-edged securities, the merits of investing in long- or short-dated securities, and the worth of particular Government stocks.[41] The Oxford and Cambridge Joint Standing Committee gave an opportunity for Bursars of Cambridge colleges to exchange their concerns with their colleagues at Oxford. Common problems were compared and contrasted: the Bursars at Oxford, for example, were in 1954 far more wary of the proposed repeal of the 1925 Universities and College Estates Act than were those at Cambridge, and prolonged discussions ensued.[42]

The Bursar sought advice from firms of agents and solicitors. Figure 19 shows that Emmanuel, one of the colleges of medium wealth in terms of external revenue received, spent relatively high sums on agency and management around 1905. Expenditure had risen markedly during the previous decade partly as a result of the development of the Hyde Farm estate. In 1902, a small economy was made when it was decided that the College should collect the rents from Chequer Court in Ash (Kent) itself, as many small matters were constantly arising and the adjoining farm of Molland had always been managed directly by the Bursar. After some discussion, it was agreed that the Kentish agents should continue to collect the rents at Lydden so as to maintain the connection with the College; the decision proved to be wise as within three years the agents were asked to manage all of the Kent farms on the College's behalf.[43] Expenditure on agency and management then fell and was abnormally low until the mid-1920s. The illness of Gardner in 1925 led to the decision to hand the management of the Pinchbeck farms over to agents.[44] In 1937, however, shortly after the appointment of Mansfield as Adviser in Agriculture, the College office was reorganised. Management of the estates at Pinchbeck, Melton, Godmanchester and Gransden was taken over by the College, partly in order to establish closer connections with its tenants.[45]

[40] ECA Li.3.268–9; Li.7.404, 408–9.
[41] Cambridge University Archives Min.VII.73.
[42] Cambridge University Archives EXR.57; especially EXR.57.44.
[43] ECA Ke.1.10–12, 28.
[44] ECA Li.2.306.
[45] ECA COL.14.7 p. 80; ECA Li.1.150.

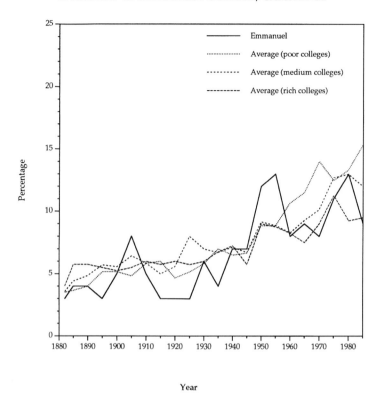

Figure 19 Average percentage of external revenue spent on agency and management 1882–1985 (see pp. 463–4 for a definition of 'poor', 'medium' and 'rich' colleges). *Source: Reporter.*

Despite this move, expenditure on agency and management rose during the War years and continued to do so thereafter.

By 1950, there was concern over the high levels of expenditure on agency and management, considerably greater than those of other colleges – at St John's the Bursar himself collected rents over large parts of the estate and inspected principal areas annually[46] – and the Estates Committee was asked to consider whether costs might be reduced.[47] Expenditure continued to rise for a few years, and in 1953 a decision was made to ask for five-yearly inspections of the Pinchbeck estate.[48] Costs fell during Ward's bursarship, perhaps too low in some instances as when an estate was bought without an independent valuation and subsequently proved

[46] Boys Smith 1983, pp. 122–5.
[47] ECA COL.11a.5.
[48] ECA Li.1.239.

to be a poor investment.[49] Thereafter, as in other colleges, increasing proportions of income were spent on managing the endowment revenue,
though efforts were made to keep levels of expenditure down and management of suitable estates was taken over by the College as the opportunity arose.[50]

A close relationship was maintained with the agents. Presents of
apples and cherries were received from the College's agents in Kent over
two decades from 1945, for example.[51] Gardner developed and maintained a particularly close personal relationship with Lewis O. Mathews,
who managed the Dixie estate at Sutton Coldfield. When Mathews died,
a warm letter was sent to his son and successor, Roger, expressing the
College's:

> profound sympathy on the death of your father . . . We wish to place
> on record with you our appreciation of the invaluable services
> rendered by your father to the College over so long a period . . . To
> two Bursars, the late Mr Peace and myself, your father was literally
> a guide, philosopher and friend in all matters connected with that
> estate. The College placed implicit trust in the soundness of your
> father's judgment, and invariably paid him the compliment of fol-
> lowing his advice.
>
> Personally I owe much to your father. He did all in his power to
> make the visit of my colleagues and myself to Sutton Coldfield
> pleasant and profitable. His death leaves the College with a real
> sense of loss, and of appreciation of his unfailing help in the man-
> agement of an important estate where difficult problems constantly
> arose.[52]

Gardner's words were genuine, for advice from agents was not invariably taken, second opinions could be sought, and occasionally complaints
were made that firms had acted without proper authority from the
College.[53]

As a last resort, help could be sought from the Ministry of Agriculture.
When a housing subsidy for a new foreman's cottage at Pinchbeck was
reduced, for instance, the Ministry was asked to assist in 1935, though
little comfort could be offered.[54] A few years earlier, in 1929, difficulties
were encountered in the degree of rounding of corners on a housing
estate at Wylde Green, Sutton Coldfield, and the Ministry of Agriculture
sought informal advice from the Ministry of Health on the College's

---

[49] ECA Yk.3.2.
[50] ECA He.1.132.
[51] ECA Ke.1.393, 518, 570, 579.
[52] ECA Wa.2.247.
[53] ECA Ke.4.125; Ke.1.375–6; ECA Wa.2.261.
[54] ECA Li.3.63.

behalf.[55] Aid to colleges was not, however, the main role of the Ministry of Agriculture, and Bursars frequently found a need to be advised about, rather than from, it.

The Ministry of Agriculture and its Influence

Ever since the 1858 Universities and Colleges Estates Act, colleges were subject to control by the Copyhold Commissioners and their successors, the Ministry of Agriculture, over transactions in land.[56] Little changed until 1964. The 1898 Universities and Colleges Estates Act[57] extended the powers of colleges in the light of the 1882–90 Settled Land Acts, in requirements for a surveyor's report and in borrowing of funds, but the Board of Agriculture controlled the College's capital investments.

The Universities and Colleges Estates Acts, 1858 to 1898, were consolidated and amended in 1925.[58] This Act stipulated that land could only be sold or exchanged with the consent of the Minister of Agriculture (after examination of a detailed report by a surveyor) and payment of receipts to him. Sales and rents had to be for the best reasonable sums, though, with the consent of the Minister, from one to five acres could be granted at lower prices for public or charitable purposes. Leases could not be granted for longer than 99 years for building leases, 60 years for mining leases and 21 years for all others, though the Minister could authorise variations. Capital money could be invested in securities as authorised by laws of trusteeship, with the consent of the Minister. Colleges were given wider powers than ordinary Trustees and were empowered to use capital money to repay loans or to pay for certain improvements, but it had to be replaced, often via sinking funds, within specified times so as to maintain a fair division between income and capital. Sinking funds also had to be set up if freehold land subject to a lease was sold, so that the same benefit might be received as would have been expected from the reversion of the lease. These funds were seen as being necessary to preserve the monetary value of property since if old-fashioned buildings were sold in the 1920s, under the low interest rates and inflation then prevailing, the money in the sinking fund might well be needed to add to the proceeds of the sale to get back the original capital. A further consequence of low interest rates was that no requirement was made that large increases of capital value should be achieved.[59]

Continual correspondence therefore passed between the College and the Ministry. Approval from the Ministry could never be taken for

---

[55] ECA Wa.7.456, 458.
[56] See p. 383.
[57] 61 and 62 Vict. Cap.55.
[58] 15 Geo.V Cap.24.
[59] ECA BUR.19.4.4.

granted: in 1909, the proposed purchase of a farm in Essex was deemed to be of 'doubtful expediency' and so was not proceeded with.[60] If practices in a particular area were different from the norm, Ministry officials usually picked up variations and queried them, as in the redemption of quit rents at Ash in Kent in 1913, for instance.[61] The Ministry maintained vigilance in ensuring that land was sold at the best possible price: an explanation had to be given of why the farm at Rushall in Norfolk was sold in 1918 at a much lower rate than that of an earlier sale of part of the estate in 1915.[62] Purchase prices, too, were examined carefully, and the acquisition of land at public auction was not regarded favourably.[63] An Emmanuel man at the Ministry, A. T. A. Dobson, gave a personal touch to the successful request for permission to purchase 58 St Andrew's Street in 1926 at rather a high price, which was justified by the importance of the site to the College.[64]

The system did not always run smoothly. The Ministry had dual responsibilities, both to the College and to the wider farming community. These interests were sometimes in conflict, as when one of the most valuable and productive fields of one of the Kentish farms was the subject of a compulsory purchase order in 1947 so as to enable expansion and development of the local market-gardening industry. The Ministry decided against the College in this instance.[65] Nor did the Ministry's vigilance always save the College from making mistakes. In 1954, for example, the Ministry gave special permission for some of the College's property to be let on an abnormally long building lease, 150 years, with no provision for rent review.[66] The need to seek permission from the Ministry could cause vexatious delays: when a College tenant generously gave his landlord property in Pinchbeck, it took over two years for approval to be received from the Ministry and caused some embarrassment to those concerned in Cambridge with the negotiations.[67] The cumbersome procedures could be more than a mere irritation, and in 1898 the sale of land at Grove Park, Bromley, fell through because in the meantime the prospective purchaser had bought land elsewhere.[68]

Ministry requirements for the establishment of sinking funds, and changes of policy about this and other matters, caused severe problems, especially in the 1950s. Rules concerning sinking funds prevented many sales that, in retrospect, could have been to the College's advantage.

[60] ECA Es.6.391a.
[61] ECA Ke.1.87, 89–90.
[62] ECA Nf.5.382–3.
[63] ECA Li.1.144b.
[64] ECA Ca.6.269–70.
[65] ECA Ke.5.422.
[66] ECA Ca.9.13b, 26.
[67] ECA Li.4.19, 22, 75.
[68] ECA Ke.7.205.

Concern about the high proportion of the College's investments in land let on building lease led to investigations in 1953 of whether any of the Hyde Farm estate should be sold.[69] The requirement to take out a sinking fund to produce the difference between the sale price at that time and the likely price at the end of the leases in 1995 made any disposals uneconomic.[70] In 1959, the sale of two flats at 50 years' purchase was finally approved by the Ministry (slightly to the surprise of the College's solicitors), but in the following year the official in charge decided that a higher premium should be transferred to a sinking fund when proceeds from any sales were reinvested, sale prices became prohibitively high and it proved impossible to dispose of the estate.[71] Changes of policy by the Minister caused problems on other occasions, too, as at Sutton Coldfield when abnormally long extensions of leases were approved in 1953 and 1958 but were then not allowed for the intermediate property in 1962. Thus, it was not possible to ensure that leases of adjacent premises all fell in at the same time so as to allow redevelopment in the future.[72]

It is, therefore, hardly surprising that from 1953 efforts were made, especially by the bursars of Cambridge colleges, to have the system changed. Prolonged negotiations took place and, after some disappointments, matters looked promising in the autumn of 1963, when the Minister told the Vice-Chancellor that a Private Member's Bill was to be introduced in the next session of Parliament.[73] By December, Ward was able to write that 'we have grounds for hope that this whole system may soon be modified or even done away with'.[74] The 1925 Universities and College Estates Act was finally amended with effect from 16 August 1964: many of the provisions about the general management of collegiate finances remained unaltered, but the main result was to curtail severely the involvement of the Minister in transactions. Colleges were thus enabled to act much more freely on ordinary matters and capital monies held on their behalf by the Ministry of Agriculture were handed over to the institutions concerned. The *Universities and College Estates Acts, 1925 and 1964*, referred to in Emmanuel as 'The Bursar's Bible', remain the Statutes under which colleges operate to this day.[75] Emmanuel acted cautiously under its hard-won freedom. The College continued to require reports on possible purchases to be drawn up in the same form as they would have been for the Ministry, giving the surveyor's general opinion of properties as investments, the chances of their appreciation in value in

[69] ECA Sr.5.652.
[70] ECA Sr.5.653, 661f.
[71] ECA Sr.6.377, 380, 526b.
[72] ECA Wa.10.467, 579, 593, 596–7.
[73] ECA Lo.10.353b.
[74] ECA Sr.7.134.
[75] ECA BUR.19.4.4.

the foreseeable future, assesment of prices and so on.[76] For major property decisions, independent advice from two firms was sought if thought desirable.[77] The College was basically, however, on its own.

Accounts and Finances

In 1852–3, Emmanuel was among the poorest of the colleges; by 1871, it was still well down in the list ranked by size of income (Fig. 20); in 1920, however, it was fifth (Fig. 21). Thereafter, whether in terms of external revenue or of University tax (a measure of wealth which is an indication of bursarial acumen as much as of a college's riches), Emmanuel's place has been, together with Christ's, Clare, Corpus, Jesus, Peterhouse and Sidney Sussex, amongst those colleges of medium wealth and has usually

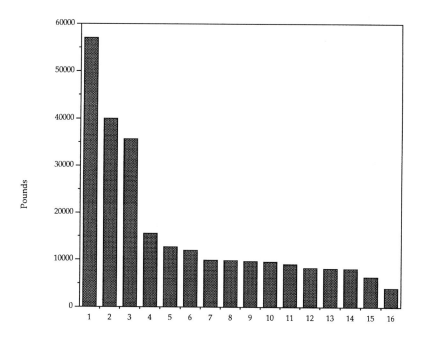

College by decreasing size of income

Figure 20   Collegiate incomes 1871 (1. Trinity College; 2. St John's College; 3. King's College; 4. Gonville and Caius College; 5. Pembroke College; 6. Clare College; 7. Christ's College; 8. Jesus College; 9. Emmanuel College; 10. St Catharine's College; 11. Downing College; 12. Peterhouse; 13. Queens'; 14. Corpus Christi; 15. Trinity Hall; 16. Magdalene). *Source*: Royal Commission 1873–4.

[76] ECA Mi.1.6b.
[77] ECA Lo.2.188.

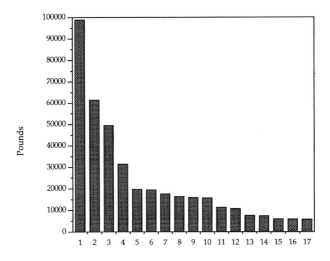

College by decreasing size of income

Figure 21   Collegiate incomes 1920 (1. Trinity College; 2. St John's College; 3. King's College; 4. Gonville and Caius College; 5. Emmanuel College; 6. Sidney Sussex College; 7. Jesus College; 8. Clare College; 9. Corpus Christi College; 10. Christ's College; 11. Pembroke College; 12. Peterhouse; 13. Downing College; 14. Queens' College; 15. Trinity Hall; 16. Magdalene College; 17. St Catharine's College).
Source: Royal Commission 1922.

been towards the top of its group (Table 1). Competition has rarely been possible with any of the richest colleges – Trinity, St John's, King's and Gonville and Caius – and Emmanuel has always been comfortably ahead of its poorest colleagues – Downing, Magdalene, Pembroke, Queens', St Catharine's and (until recently) Trinity Hall.

Emmanuel has rarely, however, felt that it has been in a financially secure position and the accounts have been kept under close scrutiny: in 1932, the Governing Body asked the Bursar and the Treasurer to report to it on the general financial position and liabilities of the College.[78] From the mid-1960s, serious attempts have been made to reduce expenditure: in his audit speech in 1966, the Bursar stated that 'the years of considerable surplus and of ability cheerfully to face large expenditures for special repairs or improvements are at an end, and will not return for some time', and a Finance Committee was established to examine the principles governing the use of the endowment and to report on the audit and estimates.[79] In the following year, the Master reported that a comparison of Emmanuel's accounts with those of another college suggested that his

[78] ECA COL.14.6 p. 292.
[79] ECA COL.11.13 (28 November 1966).

Table 1   Colleges listed by Increasing Amount of External Revenue 1925–85
(*Source: Reporter*)

1925	1930	1935	1940	1945
Magdalene	St Catharine's	St Catharine's	St Catharine's	St Catharine's
St Catharine's	Magdalene	Magdalene	Magdalene	Magdalene
Trinity Hall	Trinity Hall	Trinity Hall	Trinity Hall	Trinity Hall
Queens'	Downing	Downing	Downing	Downing
Downing	Queens'	Queens'	Pembroke	Pembroke
Peterhouse	Pembroke	Pembroke	Queens'	Queens'
Jesus	Peterhouse	Peterhouse	Peterhouse	Peterhouse
Pembroke	Corpus Christi	Christ's	Christ's	Christ's
Corpus Christi	Sidney Sussex	Corpus Christi	Corpus Christi	**Emmanuel**
Christ's	Christ's	Clare	**Emmanuel**	Clare
Sidney Sussex	Clare	Sidney Sussex	Clare	Corpus Christi
Clare	Jesus	**Emmanuel**	Sidney Sussex	Sidney Sussex
Emmanuel	**Emmanuel**	Jesus	Jesus	Jesus
Caius	Caius	Caius	Caius	Caius
King's	St John's	St John's	St John's	St John's
St John's	King's	King's	King's	King's
Trinity	Trinity	Trinity	Trinity	Trinity

1950	1955	1960	1965	1970
Magdalene	Magdalene	Queens'	Clare	Queens'
St Catharine's	Trinity Hall	Magdalene	Queens'	Magdalene
Trinity Hall	Queens'	Pembroke	Downing	Downing
Downing	Downing	Downing	Magdalene	Pembroke
Pembroke	St Catharine's	Trinity Hall	Pembroke	Trinity Hall
Queens'	Pembroke	St Catharine's	Trinity Hall	St Catharine's
Peterhouse	Peterhouse	Sidney Sussex	St Catharine's	Sidney Sussex
Emmanuel	Christ's	Corpus Christi	Sidney Sussex	Corpus Christi
Christ's	Sidney Sussex	Christ's	Corpus Christi	Christ's
Sidney Sussex	Corpus Christi	Clare	Christ's	Peterhouse
Corpus Christi	**Emmanuel**	Peterhouse	Peterhouse	Jesus
Clare	Clare	**Emmanuel**	**Emmanuel**	Clare
Caius	Jesus	Jesus	Jesus	**Emmanuel**
Jesus	Caius	Caius	Caius	Caius
St John's	St John's	King's	King's	King's
King's	King's	St John's	St John's	St John's
Trinity	Trinity	Trinity	Trinity	Trinity

1975	1980	1985
Queen's	Queens'	Queens'
Downing	Magdalene	St Catharine's
Pembroke	Pembroke	Pembroke
Magdalene	St Catharine's	Magdalene
Trinity Hall	Downing	Downing
Clare	Clare	Trinity Hall
St Catharine's	Trinity Hall	Clare
King's	Corpus Christi	Sidney Sussex
Christ's	Sidney Sussex	Corpus Christi
Corpus Christi	Christ's	**Emmanuel**
Sidney Sussex	**Emmanuel**	Peterhouse
Jesus	Jesus	Christ's
Peterhouse	Peterhouse	Jesus
Emmanuel	King's	King's
Caius	Caius	Caius
St John's	St John's	St John's
Trinity	Trinity	Trinity

College's finances were not being run as efficiently as they might be.[80] In 1971, income for the next five years was not expected to keep pace with inflation, and therefore there was little room to finance capital or increased expenditures;[81] and in 1980 the Governing Body was asked to suggest ways of reducing expenditure from the Endowment.[82] Threats to income continued thereafter: the failure of the College fee (the sum that is charged to each Junior Member – and is usually paid by the state – to pay for running a college as a teaching institution) to maintain its real value has put great pressure on both the fee-financed and endowment accounts, and now, in the 1990s, there is considerable concern over the changes that are being introduced and will affect the entire system of financing education at Oxford and Cambridge.

Collegiate accounts became increasingly uniform and comparisons between colleges might, therefore, be expected to become more straightforward. At the time of the 1873 Royal Commission, there was no uniformity in account keeping and no colleges employed professional auditors.[83] During the following two decades, more or less uniform accounts were published, largely to enable the University to start taxing incomes and so to obtain financial help for faculties and chairs.[84] As a result of the 1922 Royal Commission, a model form of accounts was prescribed.[85] From 1926, therefore, under its new statutes, Emmanuel adopted a new accounting system. It was not, however, devised to show profit or loss and balance sheets, but to ensure that income was spent on proper purposes.[86] Monies are transferred from one account to another, and the overall picture is still obscure and not easy to assess. The Governing Body of Emmanuel has considered simplifying its accounts on average about once every decade, but to no avail.[87] In 1922, Emmanuel was one of 13 colleges that employed non-professional auditors; thereafter, all were to use professional firms.[88]

Two major changes have taken place between the 1920s and 1990s. First, since the audit meeting of the Governing Body in 1962, a regular budget has been introduced and thus income and expenditure can be matched more closely.[89] Second, these years have seen the final death of

---

[80] ECA COL.11.14 (4 December 1967).
[81] ECA COL.11.14 (22 June 1971).
[82] ECA COL.11.16 (25 February 1980).
[83] Royal Commission 1873–4, pp. 34–5.
[84] Dunbabin 1975, p. 632; Brooke 1993, pp. 78–9.
[85] Royal Commission 1922, pp. 210–1.
[86] Brooke 1993, pp. 359–61.
[87] ECA COL.14.8 (2 December 1940); COL.11.12 (29 November 1954); COL.11.13 (28 November 1966).
[88] Royal Commission 1922, p. 158.
[89] ECA COL.11.13 (3 December 1962).

the fellowship dividend. The 1882 statutes, in common with those of other colleges,[90] limited the maximum dividend payable to Senior and Junior Fellows to £250: the precise sum to be paid was ⁵⁄₆₀ of the income remaining after various allocations had been made. The value of the dividend declined in real terms (Fig. 22), and the 1926 statutes increased the proportion of the sum divided to ⁷⁄₇₉ for Official Fellows and ⁶⁄₇₉ for Research Fellows and set limits of £350 and £300 respectively. Decline continued and, through changes in stipends paid by the University, Fellows with dividends were only £50 better off than University Teaching Officers who had no such entitlement. With the introduction of full-time

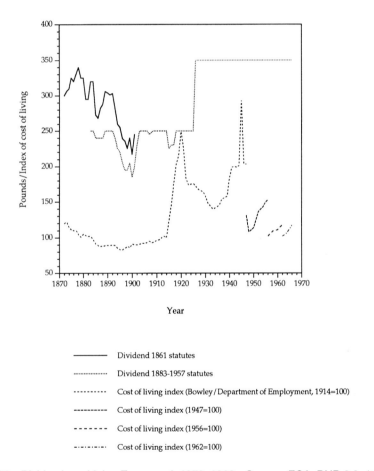

Figure 22   Dividends paid by Emmanuel 1872–1966. *Source*: ECA BUR.8.9–11, COL.11.13.

[90] Bury 1952, p. 89; Howard 1935, p. 219.

University stipends in 1947 and increased financial assistance to it from the government (through the University Grants Committee), colleges were reimbursed for all except for the £50 difference. After the University had introduced payment of full stipends to all, irrespective of enjoyment of a Fellowship with dividend, had discontinued the refund, and had thus transferred to itself responsibility for adequate remuneration of most Fellows of colleges, in 1966 the Governing Body agreed (not unanimously) to give up its statutory right.[91]

The framework can be thus described, under the headings of finances looked after by a bursar helped by advisers, control by the Ministry of Agriculture, and the emergence of Emmanuel as one of the moderately wealthy colleges. A more detailed picture of the College's fortunes will emerge as its sources of income are examined in closer detail: its investments, and its agricultural and urban properties.

Investment in the Stock Market

Over the past century, there have been two major changes in practices of investment by colleges in legal tender. The overall composition of collegiate portfolios has changed and the balance between real estate and stocks and shares has swung to and fro. The nature of holdings in the money markets has also altered over the years: most colleges only invested in trustee securities – gilt-edged, local authority and colonial stocks – until the 1950s and indeed a few (though not Emmanuel) had to change their statutes before they were able to place money in equities and industrial shares.

Changes took place gradually and the timing varied from college to college.[92] In 1871 Emmanuel, one of the colleges of average wealth, was also one with an average percentage of income from legal tender of just under 10% (Fig. 23). By 1920, though the College itself had risen in the list of colleges ranked by affluence, it had a relatively low proportion of its assets invested in the money markets (Fig. 24). The decline of Emmanuel's position as an investor in stocks and shares during these years can be seen in Fig. 25. While some colleges, such as Trinity Hall, were selling land and reinvesting in trustee securities from the second decade of the twentieth century[93] others, including Emmanuel, waited until the end of the First World War. Indeed, in 1911 the College was reluctant to sell a piece of land at Sutton Coldfield because only a relatively low return would be received if the income from the sale were invested in trustee

[91] Boys Smith 1983, pp. 266–7; ECA COL.11.13 (24 October 1966).
[92] For the chronology in Oxford, see Dunbabin 1994, pp. 668–71.
[93] Crawley 1977, p. 187.

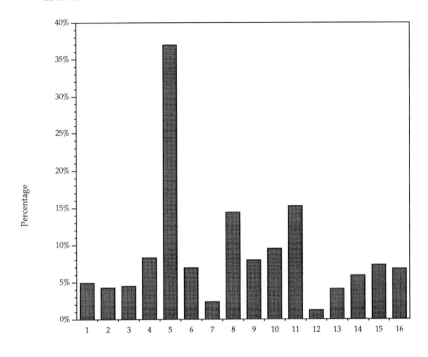

College by decreasing size of income

Figure 23 Percentage of collegiate incomes from stocks and securities 1871 (1. Trinity College; 2. St John's College; 3. King's College; 4. Gonville and Caius College; 5. Pembroke College; 6. Clare College; 7. Christ's College; 8. Jesus College; 9. Emmanuel College; 10. St Catharine's College; 11. Downing College. 12. Peterhouse; 13. Queens'; 14. Corpus Christi; 15. Trinity Hall; 16. Magdalene).
Source: Royal Commission 1873–4.

securities. Reinvestment in a ground rent was also unattractive: income, although higher, would still have been low.[94]

After the War, the balance of rates of return changed. In the immediate post-war years, a combination of exceptionally high prices for agricultural land and unusual facilities for investment of money in sound and long-dated securities at remunerative rates of interest gave an opportunity for colleges to profit and some did so (Fig. 26).[95] St Catharine's doubled its income by selling over half of its real estate in 1919 and 1920. Sentiment was not forgotten, however, and the Bursar expressed the hope in 1922 'that, when concrete estate becomes prosaic stocks and shares, the names and intentions of the donors will not be forgotten'.[96] Maynard

[94] ECA Wa.9.18.
[95] Royal Commission 1922, p. 219.
[96] Jones 1936, pp. 401–4.

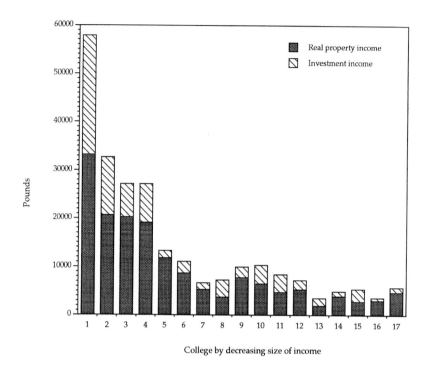

Figure 24   Income from real property and investments 1920 (1. Trinity College; 2. St John's College; 3. King's College; 4. Gonville and Caius College; 5. Emmanuel College; 6. Sidney Sussex College; 7. Jesus College; 8. Clare College; 9. Corpus Christi College; 10. Christ's College; 11. Pembroke College; 12. Peterhouse; 13. Downing College; 14. Queens' College; 15. Trinity Hall; 16. Magdalene College; 17. St Catharine's College). *Source*: Royal Commission 1922.

Keynes counselled caution: he felt in 1924 that the recent tendency among colleges to sell land and invest in gilt-edged securities was getting some into a dangerous position for, on past experience, the value of legal tender always declined in the long term.[97]

Other colleges moved into the stock market on a lesser scale. St John's did so in the 1920s,[98] as did King's. At the latter college, the influence of Keynes was great. A member of the college's Estates Committee in 1911, Second Bursar from 1919 and First Bursar from 1924 until his death in 1946, he first acted in a significant way in 1920 when he invested £30,000 of the college's money in foreign government and other government non-trustee securities. He was very active on the college's behalf: almost 30% of the shares that comprised the college Chest were held for three

---

[97] Keynes 1981, pp. 320–1.
[98] Miller 1961, p. 122.

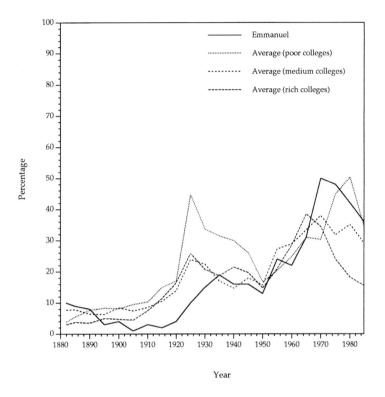

Figure 25 Average percentage of income from stocks and shares 1882–1985.
Source: *Reporter*.

months or fewer. He also speculated (it is safer, he claimed, to be a specu-
lator who runs risks of which he is aware than to be an investor, who is
unaware of the hazards) in currency and commodities, and by 1945 had
easily out-performed the London Industrial Shares Index. Keynes was
sure that his good results were achieved because a large proportion of the
assets of King's was held in fewer than 50 securities, for 'to carry one's
eggs in a great number of baskets, without having time or opportunity to
discover how many have holes in the bottom, is the surest way of increasing risk and loss'.[99]

Emmanuel was recommended by its agents to take advantage of the
changes in relative rates of return from securities and land after the First
World War. Thus, in 1920 the College's property at Lydden and Ewell in
Kent was sold and the proceeds were partly invested in stock.[100] Figure 26

[99] Keynes 1983, pp. 88–91, 99, 113.
[100] ECA Ke.6.527.

471

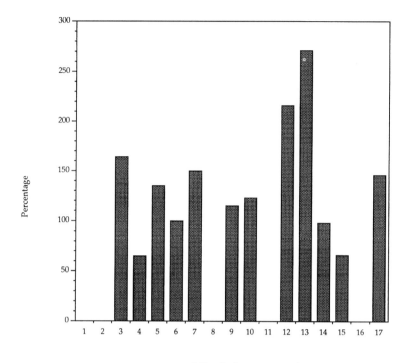

College by decreasing size of income

Figure 26   Percentage increase to net rental income by sale of real estate 1918–20 and reinvestment in money markets (1. Trinity College; 2. St John's College; 3. King's College; 4. Gonville and Caius College; 5. Emmanuel College; 6. Sidney Sussex College; 7. Jesus College; 8. Clare College; 9. Corpus Christi College; 10. Christ's College; 11. Pembroke College; 12. Peterhouse; 13. Downing College; 14. Queens' College; 15. Trinity Hall; 16. Magdalene College; 17. St Catharine's College). For 1, 2, 8, 11, 16 no data is available. *Source*: Royal Commission 1922.

shows how Emmanuel acted compared with the other colleges. Although the percentage of income from stocks and shares did rise from the 1920s, levels rose more slowly than at other colleges (Fig. 25). Suggestions by agents were not always acted upon: in 1919, the College was recommended to sell its farms at Stondon in Essex. They had large outgoings and were unlikely to have a development value, and a higher and steadier income could have been obtained from securities.[101] Emmanuel did not act on this advice; neither did it accept an offer for part of its farm at Upminster;[102] nor a couple of years later did it agree to the suggestion that it should sell its land at Pinchbeck and invest the proceeds in

[101] ECA Es.4.71.
[102] ECA Es.7.23–4.

securities which would, it was thought, probably increase the return three-fold.[103]

Formal advice on investments could be obtained from a number of sources. Firms of stockbrokers advised colleges on their investment portfolios: Emmanuel sought professional opinion about its holdings in 1925 and at intervals thereafter.[104] Within the College, the Estates Committee oversaw the investment policy until the 1950s.[105] The election of Charles Frederick Carter, University Lecturer in Statistics, to a Fellowship in 1947 brought to the College a Fellow with financial expertise and a permanent investment sub-committee of the Estates Committee was established in 1950.[106] When he left in 1951 to take up the chair of Applied Economics at Queen's University, Belfast, the Governing Body decided that the sub-committee should become a committee in its own right and Carter was invited to visit the College and to advise from time to time.[107] Elected to an Honorary Fellowship of Emmanuel in 1965, a couple of years after his appointment as Vice-Chancellor of the University of Lancaster, Carter has had a distinguished career: he was knighted in 1978 and became President of the Policy Studies Institute in 1989.[108]

The years following the Second World War were ones of significant changes. In 1946, after the Estates Committee had taken advice on whether the College, as a trustee, might invest in equities and had considered the practices at King's and Trinity colleges, the Governing Body agreed that money in Emmanuel's free control might be so invested.[109] Not until 1950, however, did the College finally decide to purchase industrial shares and to reduce the proportion of gilt-edged and similar stocks to about one-half of the total holdings in the money markets. Investments were consolidated in a general investment fund at about the same time.[110] The increasing importance of investment in the money markets during the 1950s can also be seen by the formulation of a new statute 'Of the Investment and Application of Capital Moneys', approved by the Privy Council on 22 December 1955. This addition clarified rather than changed Emmanuel's powers of investment: whilst other colleges added similar statutes in the 1950s,[111] for a few – Gonville and Caius, Jesus and Trinity Hall, for example – such additions were permissive as under their 1926 statutes these colleges had been prohibited from investing in equities and industrial shares. Emmanuel broadened its investments relatively early,

[103] ECA Li.1.22b.
[104] ECA BUR.1.1.
[105] ECA BUR.14.1.2–3.
[106] ECA BUR.14.1.3.
[107] ECA COL.11a.5 (3 December 1951).
[108] *Who's Who* (1990).
[109] ECA BUR.14.1.3; ECA COL.10.10 (13 May 1946).
[110] ECA COL.11a.5 (9 October 1950, 20 November 1950).
[111] Brooke 1993, p. 74.

and a good start was made by purchase of shares in International Business Machines in 1951. The investment proved very advantageous to the College: the holding increased and when it was sold in 1959, the value had risen nearly seven-fold.[112] Figure 25 shows how the College was thus enabled to catch up with others in the percentage of its income which was received from legal tender. Thereafter, percentages varied according to the contemporary perception of how the College's investment portfolio should best be balanced.

Investment in Real Estate

The management of investments in the stock exchange was castigated by Maynard Keynes to his Estates Committee in 1938 as being a 'low pursuit', having very little of social value and at its best being a game of skill. Real estate, though less profitable and more troublesome than investments in ordinary shares, provided an opportunity of becoming involved in a constructive and socially beneficial enterprise, where a college had the chance of exercising a genuine entrepreneurial function and in which members of the college could reasonably be usefully interested.[113] Real estate, for Emmanuel as for King's, remained an integral part of the investment portfolio, in which business concerns and sentiment had to be nicely balanced. Although in 1872 Emmanuel was one of the colleges with the lowest acreages of land (Fig. 27), it was heavily dependent upon real estate and was indeed the college that received the highest percentage of income from landed property in 1920 (Fig. 28). These bald figures, however, conceal distinctions that should be made between the College's agricultural and urban properties and movement between them.

Agricultural properties
In 1871, nearly all colleges received over half of their rental incomes from agricultural land (Fig. 29). Emmanuel did so, too, though it was one of those that did not rely particularly heavily on income from its agricultural estates compared with other sources of revenue. Thereafter, along with other colleges, farm land provided decreasing proportions of external revenue; Emmanuel consistently received less than the average of other colleges (Fig. 30).

Sales
Decreasing returns from agricultural properties were partly a reflection of two factors: sales of land and, from time to time, decreasing income

---

[112] ECA BUR.19.1.1; BUR.12.8.
[113] Keynes 1983, p. 109.

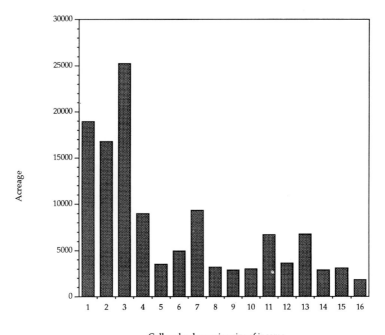

College by decreasing size of income

Figure 27   Size of collegiate estates 1872 (1. Trinity College; 2. St John's College; 3. King's College; 4. Gonville and Caius College; 5. Pembroke College; 6. Clare College; 7. Christ's College; 8. Jesus College; 9. Emmanuel College; 10. St Catharine's College; 11. Downing College. 12. Peterhouse; 13. Queens'; 14. Corpus Christi; 15. Trinity Hall; 16. Magdalene). *Source*: Royal Commission 1873–4.

from the farms that remained. The farm at St Cross in Suffolk was sold in 1874,[114] and the Governing Body approved the sale of Papley Grove Farm, Eltisley, in 1899,[115] but substantial sales of agricultural land were few before the 1920s. The preceding decade had, however, seen renewed, but vain, attempts to sell the marshland at Ripple, Essex;[116] and successful sales of Shernborne, Norfolk, to the Crown in 1912,[117] and the purchase by the Admiralty of land at Rushall in Norfolk in 1915 and of the remainder in 1918.[118] The years also saw the loss of the rent charges from Fleet, Lincolnshire: an attempt had been made to receive them in 1895 and 1906, but by 1920 they were deemed to be irrecoverable.[119] During the 1920s, in

[114] ECA BUR.6.7 pp. 237–9.
[115] ECA COL.14.4 p. 204.
[116] ECA Es.1.117; in 1905, the hope had been expressed that it might be possible to sell the land (Es.2.106).
[117] ECA Box 22.A15.
[118] ECA Nf.5.276, 369.
[119] ECA Li.10.298, 318, 335.

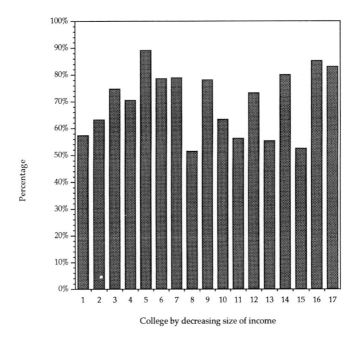

Figure 28   Percentage of net external income from property 1920 (1. Trinity College; 2. St John's College; 3. King's College; 4. Gonville and Caius College; 5. Emmanuel College; 6. Sidney Sussex College; 7. Jesus College; 8. Clare College; 9. Corpus Christi College; 10. Christ's College; 11. Pembroke College; 12. Peterhouse; 13. Downing College; 14. Queens' College; 15. Trinity Hall; 16. Magdalene College; 17. St Catharine's College). *Source*: Royal Commission 1922.

common with another 11 colleges in Cambridge and seven in Oxford,[120] more sales were achieved: the estate at Lydden and Ewell in Kent was sold in 1920;[121] the farm at Braintree in Essex (of which Emmanuel was owner with three other colleges) in 1921;[122] Lees Farm, Navestock, Essex in 1923[123] and the Ripple marshland finally in the same year.[124] Heavy bills for repairs led to the sale of the Horseshoe, Godmanchester, in 1925 (the property had been vacant for many years);[125] Whipples farm, Stondon in 1927, despite the poor state of the land market;[126] and Mitchell's farm, Stapleford Abbots, in 1930.[127] The development of land for building

---

120 Dunbabin 1994, p. 658.
121 ECA Ke.6.527.
122 ECA Es.2.168.
123 ECA Es.3.71.
124 ECA Es.2.156; the small marsh had been sold in 1920 (Es.2.106, 123).
125 ECA Hu.3.313, 403, 406.
126 ECA Es.4.86b, 91c.
127 ECA Es.3.158, 164, 168.

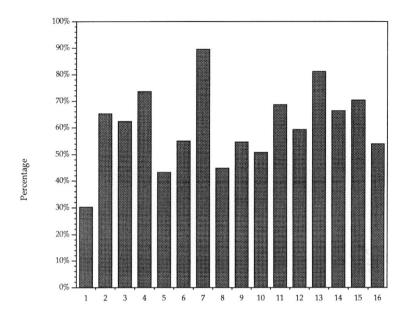

College by decreasing size of income

Figure 29   Percentage of rental income derived from land 1871 (1. Trinity College; 2. St John's College; 3. King's College; 4. Gonville and Caius College; 5. Pembroke College; 6. Clare College; 7. Christ's College; 8. Jesus College; 9. Emmanuel College; 10. St Catharine's College; 11. Downing College; 12. Peterhouse; 13. Queens'; 14. Corpus Christi; 15. Trinity Hall; 16. Magdalene). *Source*: Royal Commission 1873–4.

purposes led to further sales at about this time: at Chequer Court in Kent in 1927,[128] and at Bromley and Hornchurch in 1930.[129]

Little agricultural land was then sold until after the Second World War (apart from some of the Lands in Ming at Pinchbeck to prevent further loss of any of the rents).[130] The cottages and fields at Gransden were finally sold in 1945.[131] In the following year, a decision to sell some of the less remunerative agricultural properties led to the disposal of the farm at Godmanchester: there was no farmhouse, the fields were scattered and a new implement shed was needed.[132] The 1947 Town and Country Planning Act[133] led to the sale of Page's and Tye's Farms, Upminster, two

[128] ECA Ke.5.226X-Y.
[129] ECA Ke.7.474; ECA Es.2.328, 341, 380.
[130] ECA Li.8.486.
[131] ECA Hu.2.358, 437.
[132] ECA Hu.4.366, 371, 384.
[133] 10 and 11 Geo.VI Cap.51.

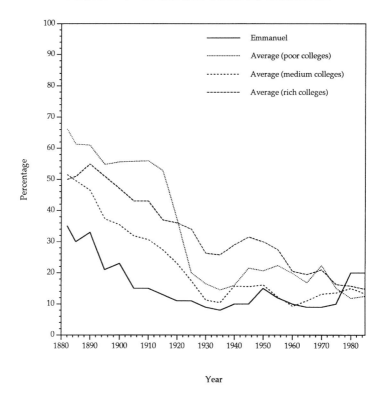

Figure 30 Average percentage of income from lands let at rack rent 1882–1985.
Source: *Reporter.*

years later: the Act had put paid to any hopes for future development of the area as a building estate.[134] Further sales of some of the College's historic estates took place in the 1950s: of Great Melton in 1952 and 1956,[135] and of the wood at Gransden in 1957 (after having decided to get rid of it 'by hook or by crook':[136] attempts had been made since 1925 to sell it or even, in 1926, to give it away as the costs of upkeep were so high).[137] Since the sale of the farmhouse, marshland and some cottages at Chequer Court in 1965,[138] disposal of the ancient estates has continued so that by the 1990s, historic farm land forms a very small part of the College's investment portfolio.

Not all sales were of entire estates. Sometimes, parts were sold, usually for public purposes and often under compulsory purchase orders. When

[134] ECA Es.7.507, 518, 525.
[135] ECA Nf.2.295, 354, 465, 491, 494, 512.
[136] ECA Hu.1.864, 911.
[137] ECA Hu.1.303, 306, 311.
[138] ECA Box 17.J4–5; ECA Ke.6.320, 336.

possible, the Bursar was careful to discover the views of the tenant who would lose part of his farm land. Thus, requests to purchase the College's land at Upminster in 1921 and at Chequer Court in 1933 were refused as in both cases the tenant was not keen for the sale to go ahead.[139]

The College had (and still has) a duty to ensure that the best possible prices for its sales is realised, and the Ministry of Agriculture assiduously checked that this was done. On occasion, pleasant surprises occurred, as when land at Bromley was sold in 1930. After the College had been advised to accept offers as low as £1700 because the land was difficult to drain and would therefore be unsuitable for building, £4050 was finally received. This dramatic rise in price took place as the purchaser had ascertained that drainage would be possible and he was anxious to acquire the land and so prevent its sale for a greyhound racing track.[140] On the other hand, the College must have wondered whether Chequer Court farmhouse was sold as advantageously as possible in 1965, as in 1970 it was resold for well over three times as much.[141]

The agricultural depression

Although sales can, therefore, help to explain the decreased proportion of rental income from farm land in the 1920s and 1950s, they do not account for the very marked decrease in the 1880s and 1890s. These were the years of the agricultural depression, the impact of which varied considerably from college to college and was less severe at Emmanuel than at some of the others. Much depended on the reliance of a college on agriculture: those that owned potential building land fared better. At Oxford, Merton, Magdalen, Brasenose and St John's colleges all had considerable amounts of non-agricultural property and enjoyed rises in income; Worcester, Wadham, University and Lincoln colleges, however, all suffered badly, and many colleges reduced expenditure on their fabric, postponed or cancelled building projects, and either had to sell stock to pay stipends or had to reduce dividends.[142]

Emmanuel did have its fair share of problems, however. Arrears mounted (Fig. 31) and abatements increased (Fig. 32). As in earlier times of hardship, the College was anxious not to act in a way dissimilar from other landowners in a particular area:[143] in 1904, for instance, Peace asked the agents in Essex how others were reacting to the previous year's wet season, and whether applications for abatements should be expected.[144] Fellowship dividends fell (Fig. 22), as they did at St John's, Downing and

[139] ECA Es.7.30; ECA Ke.5.289–91.
[140] ECA Ke.7.422, 454, 474, 506.
[141] ECA Ke.6.456.
[142] Engel 1978, pp. 442–3; Dunbabin 1997, pp. 403–6.
[143] See p. 382.
[144] ECA Es.1.74–5.

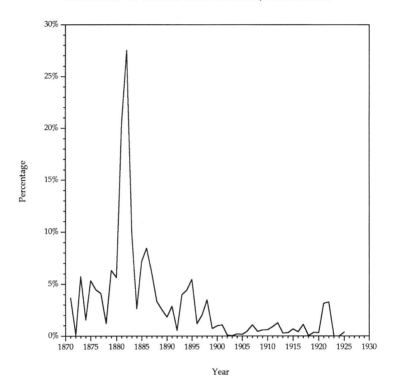

Figure 31   Indebtedness to the College 1871–1925 (as a percentage of total of income and sums in arrear). *Source*: ECA BUR.0.1, BUR.1.2–3.

Magdalene. Indeed, at this last college, one of the poorest in Cambridge, income was so low that for many years all repairs were in effect paid for out of the fines levied upon undergraduates who missed compulsory chapel.[145] At Emmanuel, development of the Hyde Farm estate and rising values of City property helped to cushion the effects of the depression from the mid-1890s and in 1902 the College felt sufficiently wealthy to ask – and receive – permission from the Vice-Chancellor, as Visitor, to increase the size of the fellowship by two, to transfer annually larger sums to the Scholarship, Reserve and Education funds, and to make transfers to the Studentship fund.[146]

Depression occurred again in the early 1930s, especially from 1929 to 1933.[147] Tenants on many of the College's estates experienced problems: rents were abated at Godmanchester, Ash (Kent), Pinchbeck and

[145] Dunbabin 1975, p. 641; Hyam 1992, p. 4.
[146] ECA COL.14.4 pp. 266–8.
[147] Whetham 1978, pp. 229–32.

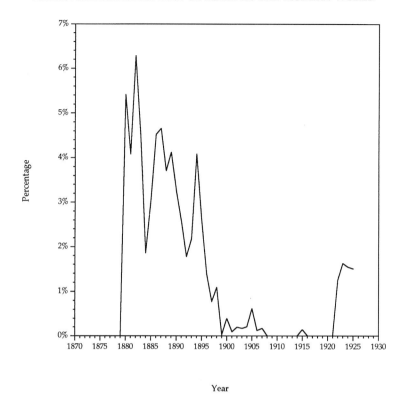

Figure 32 Percentage of income lost through rent abatements 1871–1925.
Source: BUR.1.2–3.

Roughley (Sutton Coldfield).[148] Tithes were abated at Little Melton and
Rushall; as in the earlier depression, the College kept a check on the
action of other landowners and when the managers of Queen Anne's
Bounty refused to grant an abatement at Rushall in 1935, Emmanuel
followed suit.[149] The depression created difficulties in the letting of farms:
at Gransden, a suggestion was even made that the farm should be re-let at
no rent in 1928 as it would be hard to find a new tenant; the farm was
eventually leased out at a reduced rent in 1929.[150] At Pinchbeck, the
tenant of Laurel House Farm was allowed to continue as a yearly tenant
in 1933 on account of the hard times.[151] The depression led, less directly,

[148] ECA Hu.4.180a, 203; ECA Ke.1.165–6, 178–81, 183, 186; Ke.4.155; ECA Li.8.86, 92; ECA
Wa.11.383–4, 393, 412.
[149] ECA Nf.3.400, 421, 459, 481, 591, 601, 646; Nf.4.380, 403, 421, 439, 455.
[150] ECA Hu.2.71b, 98, 185.
[151] ECA Li.7.39b.

to a need for other help to College tenants: assistance was given towards the costs of labour for repairs at Melton in 1931 and 1932, for example.[152] In the latter year, the College received a request for assistance in repairs to Dunsby Fen School at Pinchbeck. In easier times, it would have been in the best interest of local farmers to have kept the school viable as labourers would have refused work unless their children could have been educated in the district; the depression, however, had caused so much unemployment that labourers could not afford to be choosy and so farmers had little incentive to support local education.[153]

The wars

The two World Wars affected Emmanuel's agricultural estates. Labour problems were particularly acute in the 1914–18 war: in 1916, for instance, the tenant at Great Melton complained that he now had only one man working for him and he had to be his own yardman and milkman. 'I wish this dreadful war was over', he lamented.[154] Similar problems were experienced at Pinchbeck, where the tenant of South College Farm feared that his foreman – who was also acting as horseman – would be called up and force the abandonment of the farm.[155] In 1915, the tenant had bought a self-binder as he could not find sufficient labour to help with the harvest, though he feared that recent thunder storms would render his new machine useless and put him at the mercy of a few men who would charge exorbitant prices.[156] The following year, he had a poor harvest as he could not grow labour-intensive crops.[157] The aftermath of the Second World War also created labour problems and made it difficult to take up market-gardening on the College's Kentish estates.[158] Local War Agricultural Executive Committees were established: in Kent, the local Committee took possession of some of the Ash Levels in 1943 so as to make them more productive,[159] and in the following year it requested repairs to farm buildings at Molland.[160] Bomb damage on the College's agricultural estates was limited – cottages at Upminster were destroyed in 1944 and finally rebuilt in 1949[161] – though Emmanuel took care of heraldic stained glass from the farm at Molland on the tenant's behalf.[162]

[152] ECA Nf.1.280–1, 313.
[153] ECA Li.10.197.
[154] ECA Nf.1.121.
[155] ECA Li.6.439.
[156] ECA Li.6.415.
[157] ECA Li.6.441.
[158] ECA Ke.1.404; though arable farming was becoming much less labour-intensive at this time.
[159] ECA Ke.1.366.
[160] ECA Ke.1.383.
[161] ECA Es.7.470, 494, 502, 507.
[162] ECA Ke.4.362; *ECM* 32, 1950–1, pp. 14–17.

After both wars, the opportunity was taken to increase rents: substantial increases were recommended at Pinchbeck in 1921, from £687 12s 6d to £1410;[163] by 1925, however, when authorisation was given to re-let the estates, the rental value had decreased to £1200.[164] After the Second World War, the College had its properties surveyed but the disastrous harvest of 1946 led to a delay in rental increases for one year.[165]

Repairs and improvements

Other developments on the College's agricultural estates led to periodic reductions in income from them. The need for expenditure of more than one year's rent on repairs at Whipples and Hook End farms, Stondon, in 1902, was understandably not greeted with enthusiasm by the Bursar.[166] The World Wars led to accumulations of repair and improvement work: in 1923, the College agreed to spend more than its usual share on repair work to a barn at Cowbit, Pinchbeck, which had first been discussed in 1912 and had been delayed by the First World War.[167] There was little large-scale expenditure on estate improvements in the later inter-war years, apart from the improvement of milking accommodation at Ash in 1934 and the planting of cherry orchards there.[168] The Second World War prevented expenditure on improvements:[169] in 1939, suspension of grants under the Housing (Rural Workers) Act meant that a scheme to recondition cottages at Laurel House Farm, Pinchbeck, had to be curtailed.[170] In the immediate post-war years attempts were made to catch up. Thus at Emmanuel, as at other colleges, expenditure rose markedly (Fig. 33). A newly acquired farm in Rutland proved to be very expensive: £3758 8s 10d was spent between 1947 and 1949[171] but the tenant proved to be 'insatiable' and, despite efforts to hold him back, nearly £9000 was invested in the farm by the College.[172] Funds were thus absorbed which could have been spent on other properties: the farm buildings, cow-house and dairy at Great Melton were modernised, however, at a cost of about £1700 in 1952.[173]

Housing shortages in rural areas led to a demand for cottages for farm workers. Emmanuel was not alone in finding cottage provision a burden, for there were constant demands for building, repairing and improving

[163] ECA Li.1.22b.
[164] ECA Li.1.25, 26a.
[165] ECA Ke.1.397, 418; ECA Li.1.214, 217.
[166] ECA Es.1.60.
[167] ECA Li.2.292, 296.
[168] ECA Ke.1.216–18, 222, 253, 255a, 259.
[169] ECA Li.1.217.
[170] ECA Li.7.165.
[171] ECA Ru.1.186.
[172] ECA Ru.1.311, 387.
[173] ECA Nf.2.273.

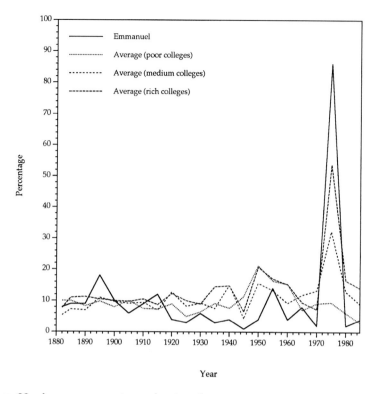

Figure 33 Average percentage of external revenue spent on estate repairs and improvements 1882–1985. *Source*: *Reporter*.

such accommodation.[174] In 1899, James Robinson, tenant of South College Farm in Pinchbeck, was impatient to hear whether the College would build a pair of cottages for him as he had severe problems in finding labour;[175] the buildings were approved at a cost not exceeding £300 so long as the rent of the farm were increased by £10 yearly.[176] Cottages were built on other estates, too, in the years which followed: at Shernborne, Norfolk, in 1904 and 1910, for example.[177] The decision to replace some run-down cottages at Upminster, Essex, in 1913 committed the College to more than it had bargained for. A local architect felt strongly that the old cottages should have been repaired and a lengthy correspondence ensued in *Country Life*, in which Emmanuel was condemned for having made a 'ghastly confession of incompetence'. 'In the

[174] Whetham 1978, pp. 47–8.
[175] ECA Li.6.20.
[176] ECA COL.14.4 p. 187.
[177] ECA Nf.6.120, 200.

middle of a landscape which Constable would have loved to paint', wrote the architect, 'now gleams this vulgar excrescence of Collegiate vacuity'.[178] Two weeks later, an artist indicated the effect imagined by a correspondent of building similar cottages in Front Court.[179] The Bursar even received an abusive postcard.[180] The *Essex Times*, on the other hand, praised Emmanuel for having erected commodious, substantial and modern cottages. The writer explained that the main entrances were at the sides as neither the Crown nor colleges favoured front doors as these made it easy for neighbours to gossip, pass the time of day and 'discuss the affairs of all and sundry'.[181] After the destruction of the cottages by a flying bomb in 1944 it was, however, acknowledged that they had been very ugly.[182]

In 1922, the Royal Commission pressed for provision of better cottages by colleges: many estates had high percentages of small cottages, though Emmanuel was by no means the worst landlord in this respect (Fig. 34). The 1926 Housing (Rural Workers) Act[183] made available grants for improvements and subsidies could be obtained for building new accommodation. A new foreman's cottage at Pinchbeck, built in 1929, subsequently caused problems as the annual subsidy of £11 and to be paid for 40 years, was reduced in 1934, to the College's dismay.[184] Caution had to be exercised in the late 1940s, when an application to build a pair of cottages at Cuckoo Farm, Pinchbeck, was refused as it would have been impossible to have prevented their being requisitioned, irrespective of the labour needs of the farm.[185] In the 1950s and early 1960s, many farmhouses and cottages were modernised, and electricity and bathrooms installed, especially when grants were available.[186] From time to time, grants were problematic: councils sometimes insisted on prohibitively high standards of repair,[187] and improvements to cottages at Pinchbeck in 1957 were held up when the local Council changed its policy and refused to offer help.[188]

Tenants and local communities

Emmanuel invested more than money in its agricultural estates: it also tried to help tenants and the local community through other methods. A particularly close relationship was maintained with the lessees at

[178] *Country Life* 4 October 1913, p. 470.
[179] ECA Es.6.518, 540b.
[180] ECA Es.6.548.
[181] ECA Es.6.543c.
[182] ECA Es.7.470, 473.
[183] 16 and 17 Geo.V Cap.56.
[184] ECA Li.3.53, 63.
[185] ECA Li.3.334.
[186] ECA Ke.4.417; ECA Li.1.235b.
[187] ECA Ru.1.327.
[188] ECA Li.7.386.

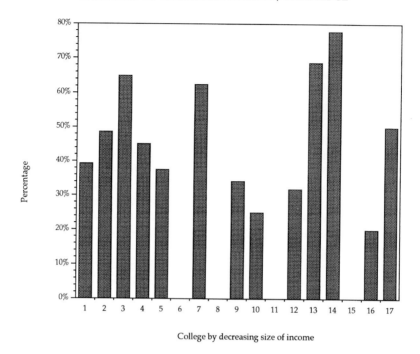

College by decreasing size of income

Figure 34   Percentage of cottages on estates with not more than two bedrooms, 1920 (1. Trinity College; 2. St John's College; 3. King's College; 4. Gonville and Caius College; 5. Emmanuel College; 6. Sidney Sussex College; 7. Jesus College; 8. Clare College; 9. Corpus Christi College; 10. Christ's College; 11. Pembroke College; 12. Peterhouse; 13. Downing College; 14. Queens' College; 15. Trinity Hall; 16. Magdalene College; 17. St Catharine's College). For 6, 8, 11, 15 no data is available. *Source*: Royal Commission 1922.

Pinchbeck. The pair there from the 1930s to 1950s were, indeed, Emmanuel's 'star' tenants. They had excellent relations with the College, had progressive ideas, invested in their farms themselves – indeed, one gave his landlord some of his own land – and every effort was made to treat them similarly.[189] One was the nephew of an Emmanuel man and subsequently sent his son to the College.[190] Glimpses of close relations with other tenants can be seen from time to time, such as the gift of produce: a hare, apples, plums and potatoes.[191] One of the more unusual pieces of estate correspondence was the request in 1907 by one of the Pinchbeck tenants for the Bursar to ascertain whether Pharaoh really did drown with all his host in the Red Sea, as opinions are 'so conflicting' (we have, alas, no record of the reply).[192] From time to time, of course, some tenants

[189] ECA Li.1.230; Li.2.436a; Li.4.8b, 75; Li.7.96a, 262.
[190] *ECM* 24, 1923–4, pp. 3–4.
[191] ECA Li.2.260; Li.5.137; Li.6.512.
[192] ECA Li.6.173.

were troublesome: the decision not to renew the tenancy of Cuckoo Farm at Pinchbeck in 1892 led to many requests, in vain, from members of the Robinson family for the Bursar to reconsider;[193] and Peace must have become very tired of reading the tirades of the two Robinson brothers against each other at the turn of the century.[194]

The College also felt a responsibility towards local communities in general. Thus, coronation festivities were supported in 1902 and 1911 at Stondon, Melton and Rushall.[195] The First World War led to a request for help towards war memorials.[196] Education was a local cause that the College supported by giving sites for schools, as at Shernborne in 1875[197] and Pinchbeck in 1891. In the latter case, Emmanuel insisted that parents be represented on the management committee.[198] Despite the decision in 1904 to stop general subscriptions to schools,[199] assistance continued to be forthcoming when particular needs were identified. Parish activities were supported, too: in 1901, the College offered a substantial subscription towards the cost of a parish room at Godmanchester (because of the requirements of the Board of Agriculture, land could not have been sold for this purpose at a greatly reduced price).[200] Individuals from Emmanuel made their own contribution to the local community, as in 1919 when the Bursar became, for a while, the Chairman of the Star Lode Drainage Board in Pinchbeck.[201] Distance made such an appointment impractical, however, and in 1934 a tenant was appointed to represent the College on the Deeping Fen Drainage Board.[202]

Purchases

Despite the overall trend of decreasing proportions of rental income coming from agricultural estates, some farm land was bought from time to time. The prospect of future development for building led to the purchase of Page's Farm, Upminster, in 1898, when the College considered investing in land.[203] Opportunities to extend and consolidate existing holdings were often taken: at Upminster, Tye's Farm was bought in 1902 and a road frontage in 1913;[204] and the Pinchbeck estate was added to by the purchase of a farm there in 1903.[205]

[193] ECA Li.2.63–7, 69.
[194] ECA Li.6.18, 20, 31.
[195] ECA Es.4.34; ECA Nf.3.35; Nf.5.191.
[196] ECA Hu.1.178.
[197] ECA Nf.6.250.
[198] ECA Li.10.141, 145–7.
[199] ECA Nf.6.122.
[200] ECA Hu.3.21–2.
[201] ECA Li.9.73.
[202] ECA Li.9.124a.
[203] ECA Es.6.194, 198.
[204] ECA Es.6.281, 438, 467a.
[205] ECA Li.6.130, 132.

The period of the inter-war agricultural depression was an attractive one, in terms of capital rather than income, for investing in farm land as prices were low. Corpus Christi College in Cambridge transferred capital from gilt-edged securities to land at this time, especially in eastern England, and continued to do so during the Second World War;[206] King's did so, too;[207] whilst St John's started in 1919 a policy of concentrating its land holdings in high quality land that could be managed conveniently and made extensive purchases between 1932 and 1939.[208]

Emmanuel took little advantage of the favourable conditions for investment until the very end of the Second World War. In 1929, the tenants at Pinchbeck were asked to look out for land that they would like to farm,[209] and purchase of farm land was actively considered. In the following year, however, the Governing Body decided, by 12 votes to three, not to buy agricultural land unless it had the prospect of value as building land and was adjacent to College property.[210] By 1940, policy had changed and the Governing Body hoped that some stocks could be reinvested in agricultural land.[211] Nothing happened, and one year later the Bursar wrote to the College's agents in Essex that it was not considering the purchase of agricultural land at that time.[212] One wartime purchase was made, of a farm in Leicestershire in 1944 (a special allowance of petrol was needed so that the Estates Committee could inspect the property before buying it).[213] In 1946, proceeds from the sale of the historic agricultural land at Eltisley and Gransden, together with the greater part of a bequest from Miss E. B. Allix, were invested in a farm in Rutland.[214] After a small farm was bought in Lincolnshire in 1953,[215] further substantial agricultural purchases were not made until the 1970s. Emmanuel did not have the same emotional attachment to these twentieth-century purchases as to its historic estates, and the new acquisitions were seen as tradeable commodities. Few of them are still owned in the 1990s; capital from the sales has been reinvested in land, buildings, or stocks and shares, according to the market at the time.

Tithes

Besides the decline in the proportions of income from rental of farm land during much of the past 100 years, other income from agricultural estates

[206] Bury 1952, pp. 164–5, 171–2.
[207] Keynes 1983, p. 90.
[208] Miller 1961, p. 122; Boys Smith 1983, p. 108.
[209] ECA Li.1.61.
[210] ECA COL.14.6 p. 160.
[211] ECA COL.14.8 (6 May 1940).
[212] ECA Es.1.228.
[213] ECA Box 19.B11; ECA Le.1.28.
[214] ECA Ru.1.4ii.
[215] ECA Box 18.H44.

has also decreased. Rent charges, quit rents and copyholds have been redeemed or enfranchised; the tithe question has been particularly troublesome.

Unlike some other colleges, Emmanuel never received a large income from tithes,[216] and it must have been glad that this was so in the early decades of the twentieth century. Tithe payments were often very unpopular and proposals were made by the government in 1925 to compel owners to accept in lieu a fixed money annuity. Many Oxbridge colleges were seriously affected, as Maynard Keynes wrote in a letter to *The Times* on 21 November of that year.[217] Emmanuel experienced the unpopularity of tithe payments at first hand in 1932, when it became necessary to distrain against one of the payers at Little Melton in Norfolk, who was Secretary of the East Anglian Tithe Payers' Association. Much ill-feeling was caused, and the removal of corn, appropriately described as the 'Tithe War', had to be effected with considerable assistance from the police.[218] Threatening letters were received by the Bursar:

> The Tithe owners will be shown up in Public, and so will their
> Collectors it may not be safe for you to go out, as your life will be in
> Danger from now on. So Beware Mr Gardner.
> You Collect money which is not yours unjustly, Dishonestly.[219]

Collection remained difficult: in 1934, Emmanuel was due to receive tithes from three parishes to the value of £334 6s 0d and £138 8s 1d was in arrears. Generous allowances and abatements had to be made, but smaller tithe payers used the agricultural depression as an excuse for evading their legal liabilities.[220] The 1936 Tithe Act[221] finally ordered the redemption of all tithes (though not of all of the obligations attached and Emmanuel is still responsible for the upkeep of some chancels).[222] Peace ensued.

Houses and Urban Property

The decline in relative importance of agricultural land as a source of external revenue implies that the balance of collegiate investment portfolios changed and that there was a movement away from farm land to other forms of real estate. In 1871, Emmanuel stood out among the

---

[216] See p. 342.
[217] Keynes 1981, pp. 451–3; Dunbabin 1994, p. 663.
[218] ECA Nf.3.333–4.
[219] ECA T.R.1.1a.
[220] ECA T.R.1.6.
[221] 26 Geo.V and 1 Edw.VIII Cap.43.
[222] Kain and Prince 1985, p. 68.

Cambridge colleges in receiving a high proportion of its external income from urban property (Fig. 35). During the following decades, the College's fortunes were to be affected by increasing its holdings of house property, both by the conversion of agricultural land into building estates and by purchases of urban land. Developments on the estates themselves and external circumstances both influenced receipts from urban property, sometimes in dramatic ways. The College was an urban landlord, and had to meet new challenges.

Building leases
By 1871, some colleges had taken steps to develop suitable land on building leases. The 1858 Universities and Colleges Estates Act had made the granting of 99-year leases a possibility, and colleges came to take

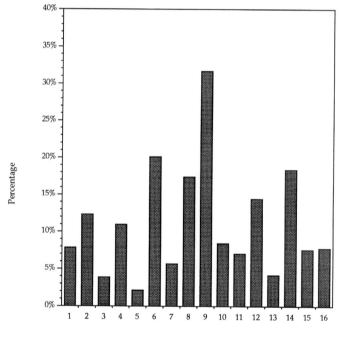

College by decreasing size of income

Figure 35 Percentage of rental income derived from houses 1871 (1. Trinity College; 2. St John's College; 3. King's College; 4. Gonville and Caius College; 5. Pembroke College; 6. Clare College; 7. Christ's College; 8. Jesus College; 9. Emmanuel College; 10. St Catharine's College; 11. Downing College; 12. Peterhouse; 13. Queens' College; 14. Corpus Christi College; 15. Trinity Hall; 16. Magdalene College). *Source*: Royal Commission 1873–4.

advantage of the opportunity.[223] Emmanuel had made some moves by 1871, though some other colleges had much higher percentages of their urban property let on long leases at this time (Fig. 36). The times were ripe for house-building:[224] St John's developed its land at Sunningdale, Kentish Town and part of its Cambridge estate in the 1880s and 1890s;[225] and Sidney Sussex, faced with falling income from its agricultural property in 1890, developed its Cleethorpes estate for building purposes.[226] These developments were time-consuming and were not entered into lightly.

Emmanuel let part of its land at Bishopsgate, London, on an 80-year building lease in 1873,[227] but it was the developments of the 1890s that

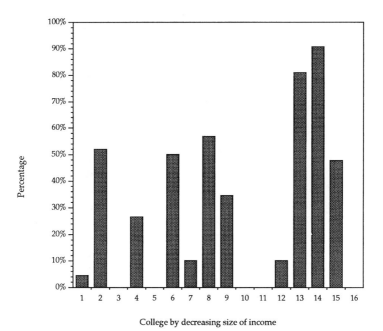

College by decreasing size of income

Figure 36   Percentage of house income derived from letting beneficial and long leases 1871 (1. Trinity College; 2. St John's College; 3. King's College; 4. Gonville and Caius College; 5. Pembroke College; 6. Clare College; 7. Christ's College; 8. Jesus College; 9. Emmanuel College; 10. St Catharine's College; 11. Downing College; 12. Peterhouse; 13. Queens' College; 14. Corpus Christi College; 15. Trinity Hall; 16. Magdalene College). For 3, 5, 10, 11, 16 no data is available. *Source*: Royal Commission 1873–4.

[223] See p. 378.
[224] Rodger 1982, pp. 60–6.
[225] Howard 1935, pp. 234–5.
[226] Scott-Giles 1975, p. 107; Ambler and Dowling 1996, pp. 187–8.
[227] ECA Box 26.K2.

491

were to make the College join Sidney Sussex in being the two colleges most heavily dependent on ground rents for their incomes, far more so than average, and especially in the first decade of the twentieth century (Fig. 37). A small-scale development took place at Maryland Park, Stratford, in 1895, when 18 houses and three shops were built,[228] but development of the Hyde Farm estate at Balham had the most significant impact on Emmanuel's finances.

The possibility of developing the land at Hyde Farm for building purposes had been considered from 1869, but a quarter of a century was to pass before the opportunity could be realised.[229] In 1878, the future looked promising,[230] and the land was let for seven years from 1880, on the proviso that it might be taken in hand by the College at any time if required for building.[231] Temporary sub-lettings of the land proved to be unsatisfactory and troublesome, and the College received many complaints about such activities as declamations by atheist lecturers who used blasphemous and indecent language, carpet-beating and pigeon-shooting.[232] The use of part of the land as a pig farm gave rise to many complaints, and 33 of those who were affected signed a letter in 1884 about the nuisance that was caused.[233] The creation of a fair ground three years later provided further aggravation: 'We might as well live in the East End', wrote one neighbour to the College's solicitors in 1887.[234] The estate was not ripening as expected, and in 1891 it was being developed as a sports ground.[235] Meanwhile, efforts were being made to improve the poor access to the land and properties were bought and exchanged to improve the situation.[236]

In 1895 conditions became more favourable and steps were taken to develop this, the last major housing undertaking in Balham.[237] A committee of the Governing Body (the Master, the Bursar, Rose the former Bursar and Napier Shaw the Senior Tutor) was set up to oversee the developments. They recommended that 1100 houses should be built, supervised by a firm of agents, Wilkinson and Son.[238] One-fifth of the estate was let first, to Arthur William Webb in 1896;[239] an agreement to develop the remainder was finally made with Ernest Hayes Dashwood in 1898. The

228 ECA Es.6A.2.
229 ECA Sr.1.66–9.
230 ECA Sr.1.118.
231 ECA Sr.1.125b.
232 ECA Sr.1.130, 138.
233 ECA Sr.1.163.
234 ECA Sr.1.170b.
235 ECA Sr.1.185, 194.
236 ECA Sr.1.124; ECA Box 28.Aa20, Aa26; Box 28.K6, K8.
237 Gower 1990, p. 25.
238 ECA Sr.2.58–9.
239 ECA Box 28.Ab; ECA Sr.2.62.

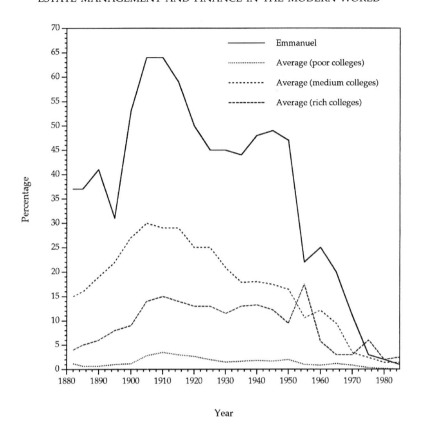

Figure 37   Average percentage of income from houses let on long leases 1882–1985.
Source: Reporter.

estate was to be developed in four parts, with each house let individually by the College until the ground rent had been secured; the rest of the houses were let *en bloc* to Dashwood at a nominal rent.[240] Although the daily details of development were administered by the Wilkinsons, the Bursar, too, was involved in much work. He saw plans for the buildings – and criticised them when necessary[241] – was concerned with building lines and, above all, had to deal with the signing of the leases. This process taxed the College's administration to the full and many complaints were made by the developers about delays in sealing that held up letting the properties and paying the builders.[242] By January 1903, the agents were able to report that all of the rents had been secured: 449

[240] ECA Sr.2.237a, 246, 252.
[241] ECA Sr.3.84.
[242] ECA Sr.2.337, 339, 346b, 347.

493

houses were let directly by the College, and four leases covered all of the rest.[243] A Development Account was set up by the College in 1899 to which expenses were charged, and 10% of the gross rents were paid into this fund;[244] the deficit in the account peaked at £2931 in 1914 and decreased to £900 in 1926.[245]

Building leases on other estates followed, but none were on quite the same scale. At Sutton Coldfield, 20 acres at Wylde Green were advertised for development in 1899 but negotiations fell through and the land was finally let in 1907;[246] six-and-a-half acres at Maney were let in 1901.[247] The inter-war years saw further developments: for example in Cambridge in 1931 and 1937,[248] and at Sutton Coldfield. Road-making was expensive, so development there of the interior of the Wylde Green estate was not finally put in train until 1929.[249] Although these developments were more piecemeal, the College remained as interested in them as it was in Hyde Farm. Concern was expressed in 1922 over the quality of the houses being erected at Wylde Green, for instance, and James Line's father sent a report on them;[250] ten years later, Gardner was asking to see plans for further houses to be built there as the College was keenly interested in the development.[251]

Other attempts proved abortive or were long delayed. A plan to build shops and lodging houses in Emmanuel Street in Cambridge in 1897 was finally abandoned in 1902, at a considerable cost to the College.[252] The possibility of selling land at Ash in Kent for development was considered in 1901, but the agents did not recommend doing so as much building land was already on the market.[253] By 1906, the College's agents had been thinking about developing the land at Mitcham in Surrey 'for some time', a scheme for development was drawn up in 1909 but nothing happened until the estate was finally sold for building purposes in 1927, after the adjoining tube station had been opened.[254] An offer in 1924 for land at Little Sutton, Sutton Coldfield, first advertised in 1910, was withdrawn and the estate was sold with outline planning permission in 1954–5;[255] while the First World War affected a

[243] ECA Sr.3.80.
[244] ECA Sr.2.270.
[245] ECA Sr.4.268.
[246] ECA Wa.7.124–5, 200, 206–7, 218; ECA Box 29.F12–13.
[247] ECA Box 29.F11, F19.
[248] ECA Box 2.H8, H11; Box 5.F47.
[249] ECA Wa.7.410c, 430, 458.
[250] ECA Wa.7.132.
[251] ECA Wa.7.558.
[252] ECA Ca.11.6–10, 21, 23–4, 26–7.
[253] ECA Ke.1.9.
[254] ECA Sr.17.84, 230b, 253–4; Sr.19.2–3, 136.
[255] ECA Wa.2.137; Wa.11.87, 103a, 104, 109, 123, 131a, 145.

possible development at Bishopsgate and negotiations were not reopened in the 1920s.[256] The Second World War delayed until 1954 the development of a site in Cambridge, which had first been seriously discussed in 1936.[257] This was the last major building lease to be made out and, as Fig. 37 shows, houses on long leases provided much reduced percentages of revenue thereafter.

Purchases of urban land

Whilst income from ground rents fell markedly after the Second World War, that from other urban properties rose (Fig. 38). Although Emmanuel was not out of line in receiving relatively low sums from houses at rack rent until the 1930s, the College then lagged behind many other colleges

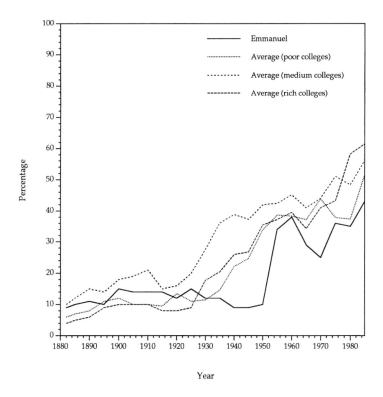

Figure 38   Average percentage of income from houses let at rack rent 1882–1985.
Source: Reporter.

[256] ECA Lo.2.95, 105.
[257] ECA Ca.8.7; Ca.9.78b.

until the 1950s, in increasing its revenue from such premises. By this time many colleges were seeking to diversify their investment portfolios: the two St John's Colleges in both Cambridge and Oxford, and Queens' College, Cambridge, are some examples.[258]

Major changes to Emmanuel's holdings of urban property did not take place until after the Second World War. Houses had been acquired by Emmanuel in the first half of the twentieth century, mainly in Cambridge to consolidate the College's holdings, though Chawner's villa in Hampshire was also bought, in 1937, from the Chawner Trust.[259] The agreement by the Governing Body in 1947 to consider the purchase of first-class shop property marks a change in emphasis.[260] Possibilities were discussed from 1950, including those of acting in conjunction with another college;[261] but Emmanuel eventually acted on its own in 1953 with the purchase of three shops in Chertsey, Surrey.[262] Investment in industrial and commercial premises was attractive in the mid-1960s and, to obtain a better balance in its portfolio,[263] the College bought shops in Barnet and Harrow in 1965.[264] The proceeds from the sale of a farm in 1967 were reinvested in commercial property and equities,[265] and shops were bought near Sheffield in 1967,[266] a warehouse in Camberwell in 1968,[267] and shops in London and Ealing in 1969.[268] In 1970, a factory and office block was purchased in Sheffield,[269] and a warehouse in Kent.[270] Further purchases took place of houses in Cambridge itself, especially for housing junior members and for letting to a few of the College staff. The only addition to the College's property portfolio through a bequest was that of some rent charges in 1964, the Forder Bequest.[271]

College finances and urban estates

The financial health of Emmanuel inevitably both reflected and influenced developments on the College estates. Rent reviews, repairs and improvements all had their effects.

Adjustments to rent levels ideally took place in accordance with rates of inflation. In the first decade of the twentieth century, when the cost of

[258] Miller 1961, p. 122; Boys Smith 1983, p. 110; Hinchcliffe 1992, p. 196; Twigg 1987, p. 367.
[259] ECA Box 17.J37, J40.
[260] ECA COL.14.9 (21 April 1947).
[261] ECA BUR.14.1.3–4.
[262] ECA Box 19.C18; ECA Sr.20.6.
[263] ECA Mi.1.3.
[264] ECA Box 16B.A37; Box 19.L37.
[265] ECA Ru.1.598.
[266] ECA Yk.3.1a, 2, 9.
[267] ECA Box 19.F10–11.
[268] ECA Box 25.K24; ECA Lo.13.3.
[269] ECA Yk.4.193, 196.
[270] ECA Ke.9.7.
[271] ECA Box 16A.A10.

living was rising very slowly (Fig. 22), there was evidence that rents were too high. The lessee of Stratford Wharf had to give up his tenancy in 1904 as his income from it was less than expenditure on rents, rates and repairs. The premises proved very difficult to let as business was bad and there were many vacant properties in the London area: a considerable amount had to be spent on repairs before a new lease was settled in 1908.[272] On the Hyde Farm estate, the developer E. H. Dashwood told the College's solicitors in 1910 that half of numbers 35 to 43 Emmanuel Road, which had been built a few years later than the rest of the estate and were let to him at a higher ground rent than the rest, had never been sub-let and that he had decided to lower the rent to that of adjoining properties. 'For some time past', he complained, 'people have remarked the fact that new houses should stand empty for years and this is not a nice joke about the estate.'[273]

After the Second World War, rent levels on the College's urban estates, as on its agricultural properties, were reviewed. Increases of 30% to 40%, and in one case of 70%, were recommended for the premises in Cambridge in 1946.[274] The post-war years were inflationary and upward rent reviews took place, though the College endeavoured to keep its demands moderate. 'Whatever rents were finally agreed', wrote the Bursar to the College's London solicitors in 1955 when redevelopment of its property in Threadneedle Street was being considered, 'the College would not in any way press for the highest figure obtainable . . . to "seem grasping" is the last thing we would wish to appear.'[275] Nevertheless, rents were increased and work in the College kitchens in the early 1950s was partly financed by such means.[276] St John's College in Cambridge similarly introduced rent increases gradually: they started in 1948 and by about 1955, rental income began to reflect the real value of the land.[277]

Rents could only be revised, however, within certain constraints. The College imposed its own boundary conditions when leases were drawn up. In times of low inflation, the question of incorporating rent reviews into building leases was, it seems, rarely considered. When redevelopment at Bishopsgate was being discussed in 1914, which involved buying adjoining property for £19,200 and granting a building lease at a ground rent of £3200 for 99 years, P. W. Wood wrote to the Bursar that 'I hope the Governing Body of 2014 will be properly grateful' and an immediate

[272] ECA Es.5.25, 83, 194.
[273] ECA Sr.4.19b.
[274] ECA Ca.1.113–19.
[275] ECA Lo.10.37.
[276] *ECM* 38, 1955–6, p. 3.
[277] Boys Smith 1983, pp. 119–21.

increase of income was of secondary importance.[278] Even if the development had taken place, no opportunity to express gratitude remains as the property has since been sold. This type of long-term view would have had its problems, as no provision for rent review would have been built into the lease and in the second half of the century the income from the property would have declined markedly in real terms. At the time, however, inflation was not a factor to be considered and it had not been necessary to think about it for very many years; other colleges similarly did not think at that time about the likelihood of very great rises in the cost of living.[279] The letting by Emmanuel of a building lease in the 1950s, again without provision for rent review, is, however, rather more surprising. External constraints were also imposed upon the College by legislation. The Rent Restrictions Acts[280] affected the College on a number of occasions: in 1930, for instance, the Acts made it impossible to obtain vacant possession of Severn House, near the Hyde Farm estate, and so to sell it or to develop the site on a building lease.[281]

Improvements and repairs affected rent levels. It has already been shown how the letting of the Hyde Farm estate on building leases, together with developments in the City, enabled the fellowship to be enlarged and other expenditures to be increased in 1902. Sidney Sussex College was similarly encouraged and a building programme was embarked upon in the light of the prospect of increased income from development of its Cleethorpes estate.[282] Repairs and improvements at Emmanuel were paid for from the Repair Fund, and since 1926, statutory transfers of sums not exceeding 25% of gross receipts from lands and houses at rack rent have been so transferred.[283] Modernisation and general repairs have thus preserved and enhanced the College's capital and have enabled rents to be maintained at their existing levels or increased. Opportunities were taken to carry out improvements when leases expired or when property was purchased. Thus when the 80-year building lease of 69 Bishopsgate and 7 Union Court in London expired in 1953, it was decided to install central heating, provide additional lavatory accommodation and redecorate so as to extend the life of the building. The College was very pleased with the letting that was subsequently made, though the repairs proceeded slowly and the full rental was not received until 1956.[284] The purchase of property could also result in substantial improvements being carried out. After

[278] ECA Lo.2.57, 95.
[279] Scott-Giles 1975, p. 119.
[280] Such as 5 and 6 Geo.V Cap.97; 10 and 11 Geo.V Cap.17; 13 and 14 Geo.V Cap.32; 23 and 24 Geo.V Cap.32; 2 and 3 Geo.VI Cap.71.
[281] ECA Sr.10.243, 293.
[282] Scott-Giles 1975, p. 107; Ambler and Dowling 1996, p. 191.
[283] ECA COL.14.5 pp. 441–2.
[284] ECA Lo.7.128, 383, 507.

number 3 Petty Cury, Cambridge, was bought in 1927, for instance, the property was redeveloped as a bookshop for Heffers and alterations were carried out to number 4 next door, including addition of a lift at Heffers' expense. The work was completed in 1930, at a cost of about £7800 (about £1800 over contract), and an additional rent of £110 was paid by the tenants.[285]

Routine repairs also had to be carried out from time to time, and the Hyde Farm estate provides a good example of how policies were formulated and adapted to changing circumstances. A visit by the Bursar and the College agents to the estate in 1907 showed that several houses were falling out of repair. The agents were therefore asked to carry out a survey and they reported that several of the flats were empty though the single houses were let well. The houses built and owned by E. H. Dashwood were in general of a better quality and, as he had a builder's yard on the estate, were more adequately maintained than the other properties. In those parts of the estate that were not well looked after, the class of tenant was deteriorating. A scheme of regular periodical inspection, street by street, was introduced. In the first year the agents were instructed to be quite strict in ensuring that repairs were properly carried out, so as to set a good example for the future.[286] It may be no coincidence that later in the same year the College Estates Committee was established, with particular responsibility to oversee repairs and improvements on all of the College's property.[287] By 1915, the agents were able to report that the Hyde Farm estate had a much better appearance and that it was now well tenanted;[288] in 1919, despite difficulties in obtaining labour for repairs during the war years, the estate was in even better shape, there was not an empty house on it and the incoming tenants were of 'a superior standard'.[289] By 1937, however, the houses were beginning to show their ages and the Bursar asked the agents whether the estate should be sold, as the property did not comply with modern standards: of 977 houses, 413 were without bathrooms. Although there was a market for ground rents at the time, it would have been difficult for the College to have reinvested at a profit and so the advice not to sell was heeded.[290] The Second World War created further problems with carrying out repairs, but every effort was made to ensure that the property did not deteriorate more than the wartime circumstances compelled;[291] and in

[285] ECA Ca.14.238, 265, 332, 421, 436b, 451.
[286] ECA Sr.3.357a, 358, 361, 363.
[287] ECA COL.14.4 p. 401.
[288] ECA Sr.4.107.
[289] ECA Sr.4.142.
[290] ECA Sr.5.77, 81, 83.
[291] ECA Sr.5.161.

1956 the Bursar asked the agents whether they should resume the pre-War periodical inspections of the estate.[292]

Developments on estates thus affected the College's income; projects and developments in the College itself similarly affected those on its properties. Thus in 1910, expenditure on the new lecture rooms at Emmanuel depleted the bank balances. As stipends and other dues had to be paid, the Bursar inquired at Midsummer of the rent collectors for the Hyde Farm estate whether they could advance payments on account, so as to prevent the need to sell stock or to incur an overdraft.[293] Building in College – North Court – made the Bursar cautious about buying land and redeveloping its property at Bishopsgate in 1913.[294] Growth of the College in the years after the First World War, increased demands for University education, the need to endow fellowships and encourage research, as well as the increased cost of repair and maintenance of buildings, compelled the Bursar in 1920 to ask the Ministry of Agriculture to waive its requirements for a sinking fund to be set up on the sale of the Gracechurch Street estate. The Ministry refused, but in the following year announced that it would consider revising the terms of any sinking funds that had been arranged during the past 12 months, and a new rate of transfer was agreed.[295] Repairs and building plans in College in the mid-1950s led to a similar disinclination to invest in the urban estates. The College was very concerned about the wisdom of its ownership of Hyde Farm, a large leasehold estate of small houses, and about the uncertainty of the legal, economic and physical conditions when the leases fell in, and was actively considering its future. Even so, the Estates Committee in 1957 did not feel that the College was in a position to try to purchase the interests of head lessees.[296] The increased rent from letting an estate in Cambridge on a building lease a few years previously had provided welcome income to help to pay for costly repairs within the College.[297]

External influences on urban estates

The economic and legal context within which the College operated inevitably imposed conditions upon it and affected its estates in a variety of ways. Town planning, the two World Wars and legislation all created their own problems and opportunities. Estates were also affected by others changes, such as car ownership and design: by 1934 few undergraduates were permitted to own cars and the garages owned by the

[292] ECA Sr.6.148.
[293] ECA Sr.4.15.
[294] ECA Lo.2.42.
[295] ECA Lo.11.106, 116, 119.
[296] ECA Sr.6.205, 229a.
[297] ECM 38, 1955–6, p. 1.

College were not deep enough to take full-sized vehicles, so the premises were difficult to let. Indeed, one potential tenant took over an hour to get out again because of the limited turning space.[298]

Planners caused the Bursar and his advisers considerable headaches over the years. In Sutton Coldfield, problems were encountered over renewal of the licence for the College Arms in 1907 and 1908 because the magistrates wished to reduce the number of public houses in the area.[299] Plans for a new road in 1938 that would divide one of the College's fields at Walmley nearby, prevent development of the land to its fullest capacity, and impose the construction costs on Emmanuel, led to investigations of the possible sale of three fields. The discussions were unsuccessful, but the planning proposal had involved considerable expenditure of time and money on behalf of the College.[300] These frustrations were, however, insignificant compared with some of the protracted negotiations and sales under the threat, or as a result, of compulsory purchase orders. From 1953 to the mid-1960s, discussions about the Lion Yard development in Cambridge threatened much of the College's property and led to the sale of its land in Petty Cury in 1962.[301] In London, the land at Bishopsgate was included in the Comprehensive Development Area in 1963 and the College's appeal against this decision was unsuccessful. Discussions about redevelopment were hindered by the 1965 Control of Office and Industrial Development Act.[302] The College did not want to sell its property, but after Office Development Permits had been granted to the developers in 1967 there was a real threat of compulsory purchase and, with regret, the estate was sold in 1968. The sale of one of the Founder's benefactions was agonising, the more so since two days later it became apparent that, as a result of a misunderstanding, a higher counter offer was now being made, but the College stood by its decision.[303] Emmanuel was not alone in selling its City property: Gonville and Caius College was compelled to do so in 1956.[304]

The sorry tale of the College's land at the corner of High Street and Mill Street, Sutton Coldfield, shows how severe the effect of town planning could be. In 1939, the leases of this site, a commanding corner position close to the town centre with excellent possibilities for development as a shopping centre, had fallen in. It was, therefore, decided to redevelop: detailed negotiations were entered into with a developer and plans were

---

[298] ECA Ca.12.16, 55b.
[299] ECA Wa.6.15b, 44.
[300] ECA Wa.8.512a, 515a.
[301] ECA COL.11.13 (7 May 1962).
[302] 13 and 14 Eliz.II Cap.33.
[303] ECA Lo.2.155, 157a, 213–14, 218a, 224, 260–1, 263, 266.
[304] Brooke 1985, p. 252.

approved.[305] The Second World War, however, intervened and plans were shelved;[306] afterwards, planners cast their blight. Uncertainty over their intentions prevented the College from reacting in 1960 to proposals to sell or develop the site in any positive way;[307] considerable alarm was felt in 1962 when the draft town plan re-zoned the property as flats, which would have resulted in a substantial decline in the capital value of the land.[308] The threat was not realised,[309] and in 1964 the College agreed to sell part of the land, the unremunerative section, to a property company, but to remain in possession of the main rents and so be able to redevelop separately from the company.[310] In 1967, the company was refused planning permission and the area was re-zoned for public buildings, an unsatisfactory position for the College as it was at that time unlikely that Sutton Coldfield Council would soon be given money for civic buildings. Emmanuel was, therefore, left with land with an uncertain future and under threat of compulsory purchase.[311] Hopes were raised in 1972, when the reorganisation of local government meant that Sutton Coldfield would be absorbed into the City of Birmingham and so the site would not be needed for local authority purposes.[312] Efforts were made to obtain planning permission for redevelopment before Birmingham Council took control in April 1974; this council was controlled by Socialists, and would, it was feared, be unlikely to grant consent.[313] Approval was obtained with just days to spare on 22 March 1974,[314] but changes in plans for a relief road to the town centre caused the development to be put in abeyance in 1975.[315] Redevelopment was considered once again in the 1980s; the site was finally sold in 1987, with the possibility that it would be used for sheltered housing.[316] A war and constant changes in planning prospects thus converted this prime shopping site into a white elephant.

Both the World Wars caused redevelopment plans to be postponed and had other effects on the College's urban properties. The 1914–18 war affected proposed developments in Bishopsgate, which were eventually abandoned,[317] and also led to the delay in the purchase of 58 St Andrew's

[305] ECA Wa.3.32, 34, 63, 76.
[306] ECA Wa.3.82.
[307] ECA Wa.3.93e.
[308] ECA Wa.3.94.
[309] ECA Wa.3.122.
[310] ECA Wa.3.129a, 130.
[311] ECA Wa.3.137, 142a.
[312] ECA Wa.3.157.
[313] ECA Wa.3.184a.
[314] ECA Wa.3.214.
[315] ECA Wa.3.263–4.
[316] ECA Wa.3.322a; ECA BUR.14.1.8.
[317] ECA Lo.2.95.

Street, Cambridge, until 1926.[318] The 1939–45 war also affected developments in Cambridge, as well as in Sutton Coldfield. Damage by enemy action in the First World War was limited to that caused by an unexploded shell at Stratford Wharf in 1917 and to three panes of broken glass from an air raid at Gracechurch Street.[319] The Second World War, however, was much more destructive. In 1942, houses at Maryland Park, Stratford, were destroyed;[320] in 1944 came the destruction of one-eighth of 7 Union Court, Bishopsgate, and a further three-eighths were rendered unsafe.[321] The greatest devastation occurred at Hyde Farm: 50 properties were totally destroyed[322] and others were damaged. The Universities and Colleges (Emergency Provisions) Act, 1939,[323] enabled the use of capital to make good deficits in revenues caused by the war and extended periods of loans; the cost of repairing war damage was met by the Landlord and Tenant (War Damage) Acts.[324] The College and its agents became involved in lengthy correspondence with one of the head lessees, who could not be persuaded to follow the correct procedures for declaring and claiming compensation for war damage.[325] Colourful and idiosyncratic letters were sent by the lessee which, if their abusive language could be ignored, provided 'comic relief' in difficult times.[326] Apart from this lessee, who regularly asked for relief with his rents,[327] few problems were encountered over collecting the College's dues, either at Hyde Farm or in Sutton Coldfield.[328]

The aftermath of the Second World War brought its own problems. Compensation from the War Damage Commission was slow to arrive: a final settlement for the Bishopsgate property was not achieved until 1958.[329] Bomb sites at Hyde Farm were requisitioned by the local council for temporary housing and were subject to threats of compulsory purchase, both at the end of the war and when the pre-fabricated housing came to an end of its useful life ten years later. These enforced sales were avoided,[330] and the 35 remaining bomb sites were sold to a private developer in 1955.[331] Other premises were requisitioned too: Severn House

[318] ECA Ca.6.266, 284.
[319] ECA Es.5.348b; ECA Lo.11.73.
[320] ECA Es.6A.581.
[321] ECA Lo.6.624a, 628. There was also minor damage to 42 Threadneedle Street (Lo.9.402, 404).
[322] ECA Sr.5.587a.
[323] 2 and 3 Geo.VI Cap.106.
[324] 2 and 3 Geo.VI Cap.72; 4 and 5 Geo.VI Cap.41.
[325] ECA Sr.5.380.
[326] ECA Sr.5.302.
[327] ECA Sr.5.350a.
[328] ECA Wa.2.274, 319.
[329] ECA Lo.7.655.
[330] ECA Sr.5.434a; Sr.6.106.
[331] ECA Sr.6.128–9.

nearby was let to the army in 1942; after the war, the property was requisitioned by Wandsworth Borough Council and was sold to London County Council for redevelopment in 1955.[332] Building restrictions delayed repairs to damage after the war: to the 12 rooms in Bishopsgate that remained unfit for letting as offices in 1946, for instance;[333] and a licence for repairs to the club house at Hyde Farm was only obtained in 1951 after some difficulty.[334]

The impact of legislation on the capital value of the College's estates and their management can thus be seen from wartime Acts and the Town and Country Planning Acts. Other Acts that governed the relationship between landlords and their tenants were also influential. Ever since the First World War, Rent Acts limited raising of rents of some properties to changes of tenancy,[335] and the 1927 Landlord and Tenant Act[336] stipulated that all covenants against under-letting or assigning should only be effective in the last seven years of a lease. Until the end of a lease drew near, a landlord therefore had very limited control over who occupied the property or held the tenancy. In many ways, however, the Act that had the greatest effect upon the College's urban property was the 1967 Leasehold Reform Act.[337] The legislation had been on the horizon for some time. After the Second World War, the Government considered the position of freehold and leasehold property, and negotiations for a building lease from Emmanuel in 1948 were held up while the Government's plans remained unclear.[338] Warnings of legislation with far-reaching consequences, giving almost unbelievable privileges to lease-holders, were given by the College's agents in Sutton Coldfield in 1951.[339] An emergency meeting of the College Estates Committee discussed the Government's white paper on leasehold reform in 1953,[340] and grave doubts over what the value of the Hyde Farm estate would be in 1995 when the leases fell in led the Committee to consider the sale of the property.[341] By 1957, the chances were remote of the College being free to deal with the estate as it wished at the end of the lease.[342] Considerable efforts were made to decrease the College's holdings of ground rents, but requirements by the Ministry of Agriculture for sinking funds to be set up made sales uneconomic. 'For my own sake and that of my successors I

[332] ECA Sr.10.637, 651, 670.
[333] ECA Lo.6.649a.
[334] ECA Sr.16.415.
[335] Hinchcliffe 1992, p. 199.
[336] 17 and 18 Geo.V Cap.36.
[337] 15 and 16 Eliz.II Cap.88.
[338] ECA Ca.8.214.
[339] ECA Wa.10.515.
[340] ECA Lo.7.101.
[341] ECA Sr.5.661h.
[342] ECA Sr.6.223.

could wish . . . that we had not been saddled with it [the Hyde Farm estate]',[343] lamented the Bursar in 1963. The 1964 Universities and College Estates Act and its removal of Ministry requirements for sinking funds offered hope but this was dashed as, just as steps were being taken towards selling the estate, further legislation affecting leasehold property was announced.[344]

The Leasehold Reform Act was finally passed in 1967 and the 'near deluge' of applications from tenants at Hyde Farm to purchase their properties under the Act started.[345] In the first 18 months, so many requests were received that only those who were qualified to buy – tenants who had been the occupying lessee for five years – were dealt with;[346] 'sometimes I feel inclined to wish that we had never had it [the property]', confessed the Bursar again.[347] By October 1969, the situation had eased and sales were also made to lessees who would in the future become entitled to purchase under the Act.[348] The estate was thus gradually sold off, at prices much lower than would have been realised under free negotiations, but always maintaining the policy that sales should be to occupiers rather than to head lessees (who then could sell to those in residence at a profit),[349] and to treat all applicants equally and fairly.[350] By 1978, only just over 10% of the houses remained.[351]

So vanished, on the Hyde Farm estate as at Sutton Coldfield and Stratford, part of the College's endowment, which had been carefully managed and developed over the years. Even the threat of compulsory purchase at Sutton Coldfield in 1970 could hardly have been worse than the Leasehold Reform Act, felt the Bursar,[352] and the Act certainly eroded confidence in the security of long-term rent charges.[353] St John's College, Cambridge, had been more fortunate with its Kentish Town Estate. As many of the leases were due to fall in during the 1960s, sinking fund requirements by the Ministry in the 1950s were not prohibitive. The college was, therefore, able to sell when it saw the wisdom of so doing and a majority of houses was sold by 1965, safely before the Leasehold Reform Act. Erosion of that college's endowment by an estimated £3.5 million was thus prevented.[354]

[343] ECA Sr.7.101a.
[344] ECA Sr.7.216.
[345] ECA Sr.7.443.
[346] ECA Sr.7.488.
[347] ECA Sr.7.470.
[348] ECA Sr.8.39.
[349] ECA Sr.6.534.
[350] ECA Sr.8.65.
[351] ECA Sr.8.270.
[352] ECA Wa.9.368.
[353] ECA Ha.3.259.
[354] Boys Smith 1983, pp. 170–7.

Sales

The last 100 years have thus been a period of many sales of urban property. Changing economic circumstances, compulsory purchase orders and the Leasehold Reform Act have all taken their toll. As with the College's agricultural estates, few of the historic properties now remain and new acquisitions have been seen as commodities that can be bought and sold as market conditions dictate.

Before the Second World War, the College sold its property in the City at Holborn in 1909 (after an offer had been received that was too good to refuse)[355] and at Gracechurch Street in 1920.[356] The wharf at Stratford was sold in 1928 to the tenant, to avoid high expenditure on repairs.[357] After the Second World War, the influence of external circumstances can been seen most clearly. Vacant bomb sites were sold, as at Maryland Park in 1959.[358] After the sale of Bishopsgate in 1968, the last remaining ancient City estate, Threadneedle Street, was sold in 1970 as part of comprehensive redevelopment of the area.[359] The Sutton Coldfield estate was steadily sold off, partly through the Leasehold Reform Act, partly through changing circumstances. In 1944 the Smithy, Maney, was sold after the tenant had died. Representations by locals that a proposed development on a building lease was inappropriate as the building was the oldest house in the Borough led to the sale of the property to the local Council on favourable terms, on condition that the house and site were maintained in their present state.[360] Many of the mid- and late-twentieth-century purchases were only owned by Emmanuel for relatively short periods. Chawner's villa in Hampshire was sold in 1949, 12 years after its purchase, as poor and unsightly development in the vicinity had marred its attractions.[361] Shops in Barnet, Chertsey, Harrow and Sheffield, warehouses in Kent and Camberwell, and industrial premises in Sheffield have all been sold again after periods of ownership ranging from under ten to about 30 years. The proceeds from recent sales have been reinvested as thought appropriate at the time: income from the Bishopsgate sale was partly put back into real estate and was partly used to finance capital projects within the College, including the extension to the Library.[362]

---

[355] ECA Lo.11.297.
[356] ECA Lo.11.112.
[357] ECA Es.5.498, 505.
[358] ECA Es.6A.665.
[359] ECA Lo.10.454a.
[360] ECA Wa.9.135, 140, 169.
[361] ECA Ha.2.43, 541.
[362] ECA COL.11.14 (14 April 1969).

Emmanuel as landlord of its urban estates

As with its agricultural estates, the College took seriously its duties as landlord of its urban property. The interests of the tenants were respected and every effort was made to keep a good relationship with them. In redevelopment plans at Cambridge, London and Sutton Coldfield, long-established tenants were disturbed with reluctance.[363] Land or subscriptions were given for churches in Sutton Coldfield;[364] and donations were given to war and other memorials.[365]

The development of land on building leases gave the College the greatest opportunities for social enterprises on its estates. Some were positive, others negative. Two sites were reserved for public purposes when the Hyde Farm estate was laid out: one for a church and the other for an institute. In the event, it was felt that it would be better to enlarge St Thomas' Church nearby, and so £1500 was given to the church's building fund and the southern site was developed.[366] The nature of the development, however, caused problems. Lengthy negotiations were entered into over the building of a public house, but terms acceptable to both parties could not be agreed upon as the College insisted on the right to take over direct control of the premises in the case of unsatisfactory or disorderly management.[367] The lessee did not agree, nor did he accept the suggestion that the public house be managed by a trust such as that organised by Earl Grey and suggested by the College, and so houses were built on the site instead in 1905.[368] In the following year, approval for an off-licence was given, with wide powers for the College to withdraw its consent if the shop proved detrimental to the estate,[369] but the promise of temperance legislation in 1908 led the developers to refrain from applying for a licence.[370] The same policy of wishing for direct control over licensed premises was shown at Sutton Coldfield in the same decade.[371]

The northern reserved site on the Hyde Farm estate provided a chance for close involvement by members of the College in social work. Other colleges, such as St John's and Corpus Christi, had missions and Emmanuel was to follow suit.[372] An old member of the College, H. C. Turner, took the initiative, a meeting was held in the College Hall in 1909 and a sports and recreational club was founded.[373] Accommodation soon

---

[363] ECA Ca.8.406; ECA Lo.10.12; ECA Wa.3.40, 50, 59.
[364] ECA Wa.7.9; Wa.9.3b, 9.
[365] ECA Sr.13.160; ECA Wa.3.89.
[366] ECA Sr.13.68.
[367] ECA Sr.3.244.
[368] ECA Sr.3.260.
[369] ECA Sr.3.344.
[370] ECA Sr.3.386b.
[371] ECA Wa.9.211; Wa.11.179, 187.
[372] ECA Sr.14.4–5.
[373] ECA Sr.3.401; Sr.14.6, 19.

became a problem, and in 1911 a decision was taken to build a club house on the remaining reserved site.[374] The architect was Leonard Stokes, who lived nearby[375] and was already employed by Emmanuel on the new lecture rooms at Cambridge.[376] College involvement was great at this time. The Master was President of the Hyde Farm Association, which was formed to bring into closer relationship members of the College and residents on the estate;[377] the Bursar took great interest in the building plans, down to details such as the colour of the paint and the position of light switches; the Hyde Farm Committee suggested rules for the club; and the premises included a sitting room and three bedrooms for members of the College to share in the life of the estate and work of the club and church.[378] Books and games (draughts, for instance) were donated and the club grew rapidly.[379] Although the College Association became defunct in 1914 and attempts to revive it in 1920 proved unsuccessful,[380] College control continued: repeated applications to be allowed to play tennis on Sundays were turned down in the late 1920s.[381] Permission was finally granted in 1935 for tennis to be played on Sunday afternoons: the College was especially anxious that Bible classes should not be disturbed.[382] The club was closed in 1940 for the duration of the War and in 1947 the need for such a social organisation no longer existed.[383] The premises were let to the school next door and were finally sold to London County Council in 1964.[384]

The last century has, therefore, been a time of considerable change, not only of properties but also of attitudes. Periods of depression and inflation have come and gone, the bulk of the College's historic land (apart from its site) has been sold, and the portfolio of investments has broadened from farm land and land let on building leases to include shops, industrial premises and shares. While legislation has been enacted that has made the College able to carry out its daily estate business without reference to higher authority, the general environment of the post-war decades has produced its own checks and controls. The underlying ethos has, however, remained constant: the College's investments exist to be

---

[374] ECA Sr.14.163.
[375] Gower 1990, p. 30.
[376] See pp. 514–16.
[377] ECA Sr.14.29.
[378] ECA Sr.14.56.
[379] ECA Sr.14.297, 356b.
[380] ECA Sr.15.84.
[381] ECA Sr.15.119.
[382] ECA Sr.15.285.
[383] ECA Sr.16.33, 227.
[384] ECA Sr.16.373, 557.

managed, sensitively and properly, to maintain Emmanuel as a place of education, religion, learning and research.

It was in this spirit that the 400th anniversary of the College's foundation was marked. Ever since the Second World War, Emmanuel had its eye on the property adjoining the College in Park Terrace.[385] Three-and-a-half decades later, negotiations looked promising and the Governing Body took the hard decision, after much debate, to commit itself to a major capital investment in the property.[386] Following in the footsteps of Sir Walter Mildmay, the College appealed for financial help over the purchase. As did its Founder, so too was Emmanuel 400 years later to receive support from those 'far-sighted and generous private benefactors who until the early years of this century were entirely responsible for the creation or maintenance of Cambridge colleges'.[387] The appeal was well supported by Old Members and some foundations, the houses were purchased and gradually the College was able to take more and more over for its own use during the following decade. In the long-term, all of the properties and the land behind them will be occupied by the College and there will be exciting possibilities for use of the area. For its Quatercentenary, Emmanuel was thus enabled significantly to extend its site from that which Sir Walter had given 400 years earlier and so to expand its facilities for enjoyment by future generations.

[385] ECA COL.14.9 (17 March 1947).
[386] ECA COL.11.16 (17 December 1981).
[387] Derek Brewer in ECM 64, 1981–2, p. 3.

18

The Buildings, 1871–1996

The Chapel

The 1870s and the early 1880s marked the era of Arthur Blomfield in Emmanuel. He was the son of Bishop Blomfield of London, the celebrated leader of episcopal reform; and he was by the late 1860s a possible rival to Alfred Waterhouse as the leading architect for Cambridge building. From 1869 to 1876 he was engaged in refurnishing and redecorating Trinity Chapel and adorning it with new glass – and in much other, lesser work in Trinity; in 1870 he gave Corpus chapel a new east end in the Early English taste; in the 1870s he was active in Emmanuel; in the 1880s he was the architect of Selwyn.[1] His major work in Trinity comprised wall-paintings and windows based on a scheme devised by the great theologians Westcott and Lightfoot. In 1872 the third of the theological triumvirs, F. J. A. Hort, former fellow of Trinity, became a fellow of Emmanuel; and it was no doubt owing to his influence that, after flirting with Waterhouse for advice on hall and library and Master's Lodge, and a survey of the college buildings, the College turned to Blomfield to assist in the Master's Lodge, the library and above all in refurbishing the chapel. Wren's masterpiece – the most celebrated of the college buildings – had a narrow escape indeed.[2] Blomfield admitted at an early stage that his plans for the chapel would be expensive – 'it would be a serious question whether it would not be better to undertake the small additional outlay which would be required to build an entirely new one'. 'One hopes', comments Frank Stubbings with charity, 'that this last comment was designed to check, and not to encourage, any notion of scrapping the existing chapel', and Blomfield admitted that 'there are many reasons for preserving the present building, if some of its more glaring defects can be remedied'.[3] Among these he reckoned the plasterwork and ornaments of the ceiling, 'not even good in their kind', the lack of decoration and

---

[1] Pevsner 1970, pp. 64, 197–8, and see below. For his work in Trinity chapel, see esp. Willis and Clark 1886/1988, II, 587–95.

[2] For all this, see esp. Stubbings 1977c, pp. 16–23. For Waterhouse's survey – an event which may give us a *frisson* in view of what he was doing in Pembroke at the time – see Cunningham and Waterhouse 1992, p. 240 no. 345.

[3] Stubbings 1977c, p. 18.

embellishment – bare walls, plain glass in the windows – the east end, which he wished to replace with three windows and an inlaid wood or marble reredos; and the ante-chapel, which he reckoned too dark. His radical suggestions, after initial acceptance, evidently divided the governing body, and after long discussion, nothing was done until 1883–4. Then, at long last, he was allowed to execute a part of his plans, much modified, by a series of compromises between those who lived in the world of Wren and those who lived in the world of Blomfield. The chapel was spared, the ante-chapel lit with two oval windows, the east end slightly modified, the windows filled with stained glass and the walls with historical inscriptions. The east end illustrates the nature of the compromise. Wren's scheme, and the picture, were preserved; and so was much of the exquisite altar rails – only the centre was removed elsewhere. But the altar and baldachino were raised a few inches so that certain features of the new ecclesiological tastes, doubtless shared by Blomfield and Hort – and some others among the fellowship – could be incorporated. Hitherto, two steps had supported the altar table; now a third was added – 'that being the "correct" number';[4] and a new altar table was devised which looked as if it were attached to the wall – in the new taste – but was not actually fixed and could be moved; and thus it conformed to the existing law and the traditions of Emmanuel, and, as we know from Hort's explanation to Westcott, to the personal anxieties of the master.[5]

Hort set to work, in close consultation with Westcott, to devise a scheme for the windows and walls illustrating the history of the Church and the College. Though the idea was inspired by Trinity, and the windows made by the same firm, Heaton, Butler and Bayne, the effect is very different. The walls had large, simple inscriptions listing major historical figures; and these disappeared in 1927. The windows of Emmanuel chapel are much more to our taste than the inscriptions – or the windows of Trinity. In each two elegant figures have a more ample space than in the Gothic lights of Trinity; and they stand at leisure portrayed in a manner peculiarly fitting to their seventeenth-century setting – though the figures themselves range from the third to the eighteenth century, from Origen and Augustine to William Law; and 'their background detail', as Dr Stubbings observes, 'is early Jacobean rather than late seventeenth century in inspiration'.[6] Hort's notebooks and some of his correspondence with Westcott survive to show how carefully he worked out the scheme and sought for suitable models for the designer. It was a remarkably ecumenical selection, in which Augustine and Eriugena and Anselm mingle with creative figures of varied persuasion

---

4 Stubbings 1977c, p. 22.
5 ECA, CHA.2.4.
6 Stubbings 1977c, p. 22.

from the sixteenth century: Colet and Tyndale, Fisher and Cranmer; and these are followed by the divines of Emmanuel, by implication, colleagues to them all: Chaderton, Bedell, Harvard, Whichcote, John Smith, Sterry, and William Law. This notable group from the College itself seem to follow quite naturally from their predecessors, 'men, it is lightly said, who might have belonged to Emmanuel had it existed'.[7]

1871–1914

Blomfield was also employed to provide the new master, Samuel Phear, with a more commodious and convenient Lodge – a building stigmatised by Pevsner in 1954, rather unkindly, as 'an uncommonly ugly brick villa of 1873–4'[8] – and then removed in the 1960s to make way for the present Master's Lodge.

The period between the 1880s and the Great War saw major building enterprises planned and executed, especially under the energetic and able direction of J. B. Peace as bursar – powerfully supported by William Chawner as master. Between 1880 and 1910 the number of undergraduates rose from 82 to 229; the number of married fellows began – slowly at first, but surely, to multiply; the college began once more to take on a teaching function; and Cambridge became a great centre of sport.[9] Of these major events in the history of Cambridge and Emmanuel the new buildings of the age are striking witnesses. Student numbers inspired the building of the hostel in 1888 and its extension in 1894, and, even more dramatically, North Court in 1910–14; from 1890 the Senior Tutor was no longer a bachelor, and in 1894 he was provided with an official residence in Emmanuel House; in 1895 came the Boathouse; in 1910 the pavilion and groundsman's cottage by the Driftway, now (since the early 1930s) Wilberforce Road.[10]

The first step to meet growing numbers came in 1886–8, when the central building of the hostel was provided by one of the least inspired of Cambridge architects, W. M. Fawcett – author of the old Cavendish laboratory of the 1870s and much other mediocre work besides. One of the principal preoccupations of late nineteenth century Oxbridge was the provision of college lodgings for the less well off: Selwyn College had been founded for them, and so too had the short-lived colleges called Cavendish and Ayerst.[11] Meanwhile the traditional colleges sought to provide cheaper living, and the hostel had its own spartan breakfast room from the start. In 1894 it was greatly extended by J. L. Pearson, now

---

[7] Stubbings 1986, p. 1; cf. Stubbings 1977c, pp. 21–2. Hort's notebook and correspondence are in ECA, CHA.2.4.

[8] Pevsner 1954, p. 58; Shuckburgh 1904, p. 15.

[9] See pp. 538–41.

[10] *ECM* 6 (1894–5), p. 113, and facing; ECA Em.23.

[11] Brooke 1993, pp. 91–5, 594; Searby 1984; see also Welbourne, quoted below, pp. 535–6.

towards the end of a notable career which had produced Truro Cathedral and much else besides, including elegant country houses. The extensions of the hostel on either side show him a master of the Queen Anne or Dutch red-brick style: they are worthy successors to Basil Champneys' early villas at Newnham.[12] The 1890s also witnessed the first married Senior Tutor, the notable scientist William Napier Shaw. As married fellows multiplied it was felt particularly essential that the tutors – or at least the senior tutor – should retain a living presence in the college. In the ample precincts of Jesus a tutor's house was built; and in Caius a house was formed for the senior tutor when he married in 1886 in the very heart of the college.[13] When Napier Shaw became the first married senior tutor in 1890 he lived in the old house beside the hostel. But this was not thought sufficient; and in 1894 Pearson provided Emmanuel House for him and his successors on the same site, a more handsome and attractive rival to Blomfield's Master's Lodge. It remained the senior tutor's home till T. S. Hele moved into the Lodge and Edward Welbourne succeeded him as senior tutor in 1935. In 1936–7 Emmanuel House was converted into sets of rooms.[14] After it was built in 1894, the next step was to provide the college boathouse by the river: this followed in 1895.[15] This accomplished, the college could turn to more academic provisions.

As the nineteenth century drew to a close the horse-drawn trams spread over Cambridge; and in 1899 a scheme was afoot to extend the tramway from St Andrew's Street through to Drummer Street. Since Emmanuel Street was not wide enough, we find Chawner in 1899 expressing support for the idea of a new road further north – roughly where Bradwell's Court now is – and firm opposition to any suggestion of widening Emmanuel Street by eroding the college precincts. In 1902 the Borough Corporation made an agreement with the college to close Emmanuel Street; but this was never acted on. For when the time came to implement it, the corporation held an acrimonious debate, on 22 February 1906, in which it was suggested that the closing only served the college's interest, not the town's. The closure was proposed and an amendment moved to refer the proposal back to the committee whence it came: by 22 votes to 21 (with two abstentions) the amendment was carried, and an embarrassed letter went from the Town Clerk to the College explaining what had occurred. After being told how much useless expense the college had been to in preparations for the closure, the Corporation was soon in a mood to offer compensation, and the Bursar, J. B. Peace,

---

[12] On Pearson, see Quiney 1979; Girouard 1979, pp. 164–70, 440; on Newnham, Brooke 1993, pp. 314–15 and refs.

[13] Brooke 1985, p. 249.

[14] *ECM* 30, 2 (1936–7), 85–6. For Shaw's residence in the old Emmanuel House see College Order of 4 March 1885 (ECA COL.14.3).

[15] *ECM* 6 (1894–5), 113 and facing.

characteristically snatched victory from the jaws of defeat by suggesting the town approve – and provide – a subway under Emmanuel Street. Schemes for building where the street lay had to be abandoned; but the subway opened a path to what was to become North Court.[16]

This was one step in more extensive plans. In October 1906 the college's Building Committee suggested that the key needs were lecture rooms – they already had in mind to place these in the south-west of the paddock – and thirty sets of rooms on the site by Emmanuel Street. In the months which followed the architect J. W. Simpson provided a report – what would today be called a feasibility study – offering three alternative schemes, built into a report of the Building Committee in June 1907. The most modest scheme provided the lecture rooms, and sets for thirty on the west side of Chapman's Garden. The more ambitious introduced the idea of a new Library in this region, with up to 90 sets, 30 on Chapman's Garden, 60 on the paddock – or alternatively, 60 or even the whole 90 on Emmanuel Street.[17] The vastly expanded college was not merely a hostel or group of hostels: it was an active centre of teaching. Space for lectures in most colleges was cramped and inadequate; college libraries were only slowly coming to provide space and books for undergraduates to study the rapidly expanding disciplines.[18] In Emmanuel the Old Library provided virtually no space at all for undergraduate books, and this urgent need was met for the time being by the provision of a Junior Students' Library at the foot of F staircase in Old Court, facing the paddock.[19] So it was decided to concentrate on the lecture rooms first – but without losing sight of the possibility of a new library and the necessity of more students' sets.

The crucial report was dated 6 June 1907, and later that month letters were sent to a variety of architects, mostly suggested by the President of the RIBA.[20] These included J. W. Simpson, but among the first to be approached was also Leonard Stokes. When the Michaelmas Term opened Stokes was evidently already the favoured candidate – though it was to be many months before the Governing Body ceased considering others. The surviving correspondence suggests that Peace had been impressed by what he learned of Stokes – and reasssured by what the Town Clerk of Chelsea and the authorities of a school in Lincoln told him in October about whether Stokes was good to work with: above all, a

---

[16] All these events are laid out in letters, reports and press cuttings in ECA Ca.10, esp. nos. 1, 37.i, ii, 42.1, 47 (5a–d, 7c, 12c show possible plans for the new road). On 17 May 1906 the corporation decided to construct the subway at a cost not exceeding £250.

[17] ECA Em.12.41.i–xvii. The report of 6 June 1907 was signed by Chawner (master), Rose (divine), Adam (classical don), Peace (bursar), Seward and Head (see pp. 436–7, 524–5).

[18] See Brooke 1993, chaps. 5–7, 15.

[19] Stubbings 1981, p. 6.

[20] Em.12, esp. 42–3; 78 shows that Stokes's name was suggested by 'the President', i.e. of the RIBA.

good listener.[21] Leonard Stokes (1858–1925) had indeed much experience of schools and churches;[22] and in Emmanuel he was to have to listen to a ceaseless discussion over several years. Rarely have college buildings been so closely debated through so many changes of plan and design as Leonard Stokes' Lecture Rooms – now the nucleus of the Library – and North Court. It is clear that many fellows expressed their views, and there was real debate, all of it carefully monitored and controlled by J. B. Peace. At the end of October 1907 Stokes was invited to build a block comprising three lecture rooms and two class rooms. But he had got wind meanwhile of the larger schemes and on 18 November produced a grandiose sketch – another feasibility study – for a semi-circle of buildings starting with a library in Chapman's garden and stretching right out into the paddock and round into the fellows' garden. On 23 November Peace wrote to Stokes tactfully but firmly concentrating his mind on the lecture rooms. The committee 'think you may take it as an instruction that no large plan of building on the Paddock or Fellows' Garden will be entertained by the Governing Body of the present generation. If there were no other reason the funds for such an enterprise are wholly wanting.'[23] The financial disclaimer may seem disingenuous in the light of the adventures in North Court which were so soon to follow; but it was doubtless wise not to let an architect see a crock of gold prematurely; and several of Peace's letters on the lecture room building were designed to dampen Stokes' enthusiasm for exuberant adornment. Stokes proved extremely adaptable. By 26 May 1908 he had three schemes, two classical and one 'gothic' – though it had been emphasised from the outset that in a college founded in 1584 medieval gothic would be out of place.[24] The early discussions were somewhat confused by the notion that there should be some link between the brick building and the new block – a building at an angle with the end of the brick building to link the two and provide some of the needed sets; and the prospects for a new library became more than a gleam in the eye when an ex-fellow, Thomas Hewitt, gave £1,000 towards a library building fund.[25] Through many months requests went to Stokes to produce new alternative plans and modify the old, and it is clear that he was indeed a good listener, very sensitive to the conflicting claims that the fellows of Emmanuel laid before him.[26] In the final outcome the ornament is restrained, and the eclectic style shows a

---

[21] Em.12.72; cf.74.
[22] On him see Gray 1985, pp. 337–42.
[23] Em.12.75–6, 82.ii; the sketch is in Map Drawer, BNB 94.
[24] In the report of 6 June 1907: Em.12.41; for Stoke's schemes see Em.12.124, etc., and his plans Lib.1,4,6,8–9.
[25] Stubbings 1981, p. 6; for the other building, see e.g. Em.12.104.i, 145, 181.
[26] See esp. Em.12.124–45. The plans (see n.24) all show an eclectic element; and all presuppose a building of red brick with stone facings.

classical symmetry, and stonework reminiscent of the eighteenth century buildings not far away; with windows distantly echoing the tudor gothic of the hall, and red brick to match the brick building. The upper lecture room, with its woodwork, is remarkably good.

Meanwhile the corporation had in 1906–7 agreed to provide a subway, but plans were slow to mature for the building to lie beyond it. In 1909 a series of schemes for the North Court were presented. The first included a tower beside Emmanuel Street and a court similar to the lecture rooms of red brick and stone. In the end the present North Court emerged, after much debate, and was being finished as the war clouds gathered. As late as 1913 Peace was still urging Stokes to subdue the ornaments on his chimney pieces and elsewhere.[27] This illustrates the care that the architect and his patrons took both in the main design and in detail; the woodwork is of exceptional quality for a college building of the nineteenth or twentieth century. Though all of stone the exterior is remarkably similar to that of the lecture room block, showing 'the same happy mixing of . . . motifs [such as hooded doorways in shallow bays with concave sides] with others of remote Tudor Gothic or Georgian derivation', in Pevsner's words.[28] The court is connected to the main college buildings by means of the subway. There are ambiguities of scale between the western cloister which has a modest second storey for utilities, a massive four-storey northern wing and a three-storey east wing which has a symmetrical elevation to Drummer Streeet. But the court remains one of the best college buildings of its age, a notable monument both to Leonard Stokes and to J. B. Peace.

The Library

The years between the wars saw modest extension of the buildings in the precinct such as the squash courts (1933) – and above all the conversion of the lecture rooms into the Library. Stokes himself had died in 1925, but his practice continued in the able hands of his partner George Drysdale; and to Drysdale was given the brief to create a library out of Stokes's lecture rooms; the transformation was largely financed from a legacy promised by three Emmanuel brothers, A. E., C. H. and W. B. Allcock.[29] The new university statutes of 1926 envisaged faculty teaching, and more and more university lectures took place outside colleges – though most college lecture rooms only became finally redundant in the 1960s. While Emmanuel was contemplating its need for a library, the university was laying plans for the Mill Lane Lecture Rooms (1931–3), which transformed

---

[27] Ca.10.1,5a–d,7c,12c etc.; Box 15.379.
[28] Pevsner 1954, p. 62; 1970, p. 74.
[29] Stubbings 1981, p. 8. The legacy was finally received in 1947, and partly used 'to replace funds that had been drawn upon' in 1930 (ibid.).

the prospects for arts faculties. The conversion of Stokes's building was accomplished with extraordinary fidelity and skill: the symmetry was maintained, and the changed function closely studied; in the provision of space for a large reading room and stacks and special collections. But the college library of 1930 could not be adapted to the needs of the much larger and more diverse college of the 1960s and 70s; and once again an extension was needed, which Cruickshank and Seward provided in 1974 with like ingenuity, though in harmony with, yet also in contrast to, the work of Stokes and Drysdale – and also very much in keeping with its new neighbour, South Court.

Since the bequest of Archbishop Sancroft in 1693, Emmanuel has enjoyed one of the most distinguished collections of books in the old colleges – not so grandly housed as those in the old Library of St John's or the Wren Library of Trinity – or the Cockerell Building now the Library of Caius – but a very fine collection of early printed books lovingly cared for (since the 1870s) by a succession of librarians who were also bibliophiles. Until 1930 the undergraduates were less well provided. 'In 1874 it had been agreed that Scholars of the college be allowed to take out books in their own names, a privilege they had lost for two centuries or more. This was something, but one reason why the needs of junior students were still inadequately met was that there was no room in the [Old Library, which remained until 1930 the] library building, to do much about it, apart from the erection of an iron gallery around the room to give access to additional shelves against the upper parts of the walls. Hence the creation of a separate "Junior Students' Library" on the ground floor of F staircase in Old Court, facing the Paddock. By 1904 this contained about 2,000 volumes (as against over 23,000 in the Old Library).'[30] But this was no more than a book stack – there was no undergraduate reading room; and in spite of much talk of a new library building, no answer to this fundamental need was found until 1930. The new Library of that era transformed the provision both for the older books and for the younger readers: since 1930 Emmanuel has had one of the best stocked, best housed and best managed of college libraries. The grand lecture room, much enlarged, makes a stately reading room; the extension of 1972–4 gives ample space to house the rapidly expanding stock of books to be expected in an active college library of the late twentieth century. But the quality of the Library in recent decades is also a monument to its librarians. H. S. Bennett and Frank Stubbings (1933–59, 1959–80) have both been distinguished bibliographers with a strong interest in the older books under their care; they have been scholars, Bennett a noted medievalist, heir of G. G. Coulton in expounding medieval social history to the English Faculty; Stubbings a classic, especially expert in the archaeology

---

[30] Stubbings 1981, pp. 5–6.

of ancient Greece, and a much respected public orator. They have also been teachers and devoted college men who cared for the needs of the whole community. Under their care the library became a haven for generations of Emmanuel students; and their zeal and scholarship helped to inspire a notable succession of benefactions, carefully described in Frank Stubbings' *Brief History of Emmanuel College Library* (1981).

The greatest of these is the Graham Watson Collection, a monument to a very generous and devoted Emmanuel man, happily still living, still augmenting his collection. It was very much to the College's credit, and to the Librarian's, that Mr Watson found a college library a fitting home for a collection which would much have graced a national library. The college (inspired by Dr Stubbings) had the foresight to provide a room when the alterations completed in 1974 were under way. 'Thus was received . . .' (in Frank Stubbings' own words) 'the greatest gift ever made to the library since the arrival of Sancroft's books, and surely one of the most princely ever made to any Cambridge library. The unifying theme of the approximately 1,700 volumes is that the great majority are illustrated with hand-coloured engravings, mostly produced in that golden age of book-illustration between about 1770 and 1840. The subject-matter is widely varied; and the artistic quality is of the highest. The books give a vividly full picture of the world of the romantic movement, of Wordsworth and the pursuit of the picturesque; of Jane Austen and the quiet cultivated life of the small country estate; of ambitious improvement, in architecture and landscape gardening, on the large ones; of the Regency and Brighton Pavilion; of the grand tour, now taking in Greece and the Levant; of a growing consciousness of antiquity, and of fresh exploration and discovery in the plant and animal kingdoms; of the Napoleonic wars, which despite their menace of doom still gave scope for the glamour of heroic action and military splendours. The books are in splendid condition, sumptuously bound; and they are housed in mahogany glazed bookcases of the finest period of English cabinet-making. They are treasures of art as well as a rich mine of social history.'[31] They will remind future generations of a golden age in the Emmanuel Library.

1959–1996

The last four decades – as in many colleges – have seen almost constant activity in refurbishing the old and providing new buildings. In the 1950s and early 60s much repair work was needed, and the Westmorland Building was re-roofed and extensively refaced. The first major change was the new kitchen, with a secondary dining hall and the Robert Gardner room above by Robert Hurd, an Edinburgh architect and former student at the College. This work replaced an ancient structure, much

---

[31] Stubbings 1981, pp. 15–16; see now Stubbings 1993.

modified, set between an inner wall of the 1580s and an outer wall of the 1820s. 'We are grateful to our architects for preserving the [inner] kitchen wall . . .', wrote Edward Welbourne in 1958, as the building went up. 'From the street . . . there will be visible our new kitchen with its upstairs hall. We wait for the sharp criticism, which will no doubt come' – as it assuredly did when the building was complete in 1959, for a well-known, if not very distinguished, piece of Regency Cambridge had disappeared – 'but already some murmurs of approval are to be heard, and already, even with the workmen still at work, it becomes plain that we shall have increased the efficiency of our domestic life.'[32]

In 1964, as Welbourne was retiring, a new Master's Lodge was built. Of it Lord St John has written: 'The Master's Lodge, wisely central, externally simple and austere, completed by [Tom] Hancock in 1964, has hitherto not been universally admired, but I cannot regret its harsh crimson elephant of a predecessor designed by the Victorian architect, Sir Arthur Blomfield, with its draughty state apartments and fleet of chilly servantless bedrooms. Any architect commissioned to create a contemporary Master's lodge faces one supreme dilemma: an official residence has somehow to be combined with a private home. Hancock resolved it brilliantly, . . . by providing an upper public floor which is linked by a broad staircase with the private areas on the lower level and, on the top storey, with five bedrooms and bathrooms.'[33] To this shell each Master adds his own possessions; the study has 'one wall, virtually of glass, providing an excellent panorama of the college's greatest treasure: the Wren chapel.'[34]

The main purpose of recent building, however, has been to provide more living space for students, both undergraduate and postgraduate. In Welbourne's reviews of the year in the College Magazine, a recurrent theme was the need for the college to replace the old lodgings: their landladies were retiring and not being replaced; the young married women of the next generation found other employment more profitable, students less congenial than their predecessors.[35] Thus Welbourne in the mid and late 1950s; the emancipated students of the late 1960s and later found the old rules irksome, and the discipline of the lodging house keepers unacceptable. So more and more of the colleges created their own hostels or built afresh. Already in 1953 Emmanuel had leased a former nurses' hostel in the Newmarket Road, and subsequently bought and extended it. The new building was designed by T. A. Bird and R. M. T. Tyler in 1960 with a three storey L shaped block, forming a small court at the rear of the

---

[32] *ECM* 40 (1957–8), 6; cf. Taylor and Booth 1970, p. 20.
[33] See Lord St John in *House and Garden* 1993, pp. 130–3. Cf. Taylor and Booth 1970, p. 20.
[34] See Lord St John, loc. cit., pp. 131–2.
[35] *ECM* 38 (1955–6), 4; 40 (1957–8), 1–2, 4.

old hostel. In 1962 the Senior Tutor, Peter Hunter Blair, wrote in the College Magazine: 'Barnwell Hostel has now been inhabited for a full academical year by 37 undergraduates, 8 in the old building and 29 in the new.'[36]

But he also gave the more dramatic news that the New Theatre, whose 'towering blank wall' had hitherto dominated the south-western corner of the college precinct itself, had been demolished;[37] and on this site Tom Hancock, architect of the new Master's Lodge, was commissioned to build South Court, opened in 1966. 'The new building . . .', wrote Frank Stubbings in 1964, 'will be externally of brick with stone facings' – like the Library, but much lighter in colour and of the 1960s, though unpretentious and modest in style for its period. It 'will consist of two ranges running roughly southwards from the further side of Chapman's Garden across the theatre site. . . . The two will be joined at the garden end by an assembly room.' The main blocks are of three, sometimes four storeys, the assembly room of one only, with 'glass walls on three sides, which helps to prevent the mass of the new building forming a "wall" on the south side of Chapman's Garden'.[38]

South Court thus converts a bleak presence of the outer world into a new court within the precinct. Less dramatically, but with a similar intent, the charming early nineteenth-century artisan dwellings at the opposite corner of the precinct were translated into East Court by the careful and modest adaptation designed by Nicholas Hare in 1981, with an extension in 1986.

In the 1990s a new building by Michael Hopkins rose in the forecourt of the Master's Lodge, which provides a whole range of public rooms – an auditorium, common rooms, practice rooms and so forth – and a new profile on Emmanuel Street. It was opened by the Queen on 19 April 1995. 'The new Queen's Building of Emmanuel College . . .', wrote the architectural critic Clare Melhuish, 'is Michael Hopkins and Partners' first collegiate building and fourth in a sequence of buildings exploring the use of load-bearing masonry. It is a compact golden-coloured structure with rounded ends and a detached circular glass-block stair-tower, which stands adjacent to the 1960s designed Master's Lodge . . . As always with Hopkins, it presents a well-mannered, context-sensitive, modern identity realised in high quality materials . . . All the internal spaces above ground level are extremely light, enjoying wonderful views through large, regularly spaced windows into the leafy Fellows' Garden on the far side, and across College buildings, including the Wren Chapel, on the near side. The sense of light and space is enhanced by the light, reflective colours in

---

[36] *ECM* 44 (1961–2), 3–4; cf. Taylor and Booth 1970, p. 90.
[37] Ibid., p. 3.
[38] *ECM* 46 (1963–4), 60; cf. Taylor and Booth 1970, pp. 21–2.

the materials used – the pale gold Ketton limestone, shiny stainless steel roof trusses, American white oak timberwork, and opalescent glass block for the stair-tower ... In contrast to the lightness of the interior, the exterior has an appearance of anchored solidity ... The proximity of the site to the street and its passing traffic made it particularly important to maximise the density of the structure. It was this which promoted the decision to build in stone as much as' the context – and the neighbour-hood of the Chapel.[39] Its completion in 1995 was a fitting climax to the mastership of Lord St John, who had devoted much care to the choice of the architect and the search for funds – with a coda in the opening of the Douglas Finlay Museum of College Life by the Prince of Wales at the very end of Lord St John's tenure in September 1996.

Meanwhile, of all the schemes to extend and enlarge the college the most dramatic has been the acquisition of Park Terrace, achieved in the master-ship of Derek Brewer. The precinct has been dedicated to education, learning and religion for well over 750 years, and its medieval wall has only occasionally been breached for minor extensions. The southern wall will survive almost intact; but it is no longer the boundary of the college, whose southern face looks over Parker's Piece, comprising one of the finest rows of domestic dwellings of the early nineteenth century in Cambridge. The acquisition was made in 1983, and formed a fitting memorial to the College's quatercentenary in 1984, a splendid enhancement in the late twentieth of the noble precinct which unknown benefactors provided for the Order of Preachers in the thirteenth century.

[39] Quoted from *Building Design*, 26 May 1995, in *ECM* 77 (1995), 30–2.

19

The Scientists of Emmanuel

Considering the number and distinction of Emmanuel's scientists, it is hard to realise that experimental science in Cambridge only dates from the foundation of the Cavendish Laboratory in the early 1870s, and experimental science only impinged on Emmanuel with the election as fellow of one of the first stars of the Cavendish, William Napier Shaw, in 1877. We have encountered Thomas Martyn and his fine botanical studies in the eighteenth century; we have listened to the broad talk of Busick Harwood in the Parlour; we have admired Thomas Young. But these were harbingers only. In the 1860s and 1870s S. G. Phear was taking a close interest in the revival of scientific teaching in Cambridge, and he was one of the syndicate which sat in 1868–9 to consider what could be done in Cambridge for experimental science – and to answer the challenge of Oxford's Clarendon Lab, already building. The Syndicate included a small group of scientists led by Sir George Stokes, Lucasian Professor of Applied Mathematics, and an even smaller group of college tutors including Phear of Emmanuel and Campion of Queens'.[1] They defined the need but could not compass the means, until in October 1870 the chancellor of the university, William Cavendish, seventh Duke of Devonshire, aristocrat, wrangler and industrialist, offered the money to build the first Cavendish Laboratory. The Cavendish was small at first, its students relatively few in number; but it was already in the 1870s a portent of great changes and remarkable growth to come. Shaw was one of the first beneficiaries – and then one of the architects of its growing stature.

Shaw was born in Birmingham of prosperous nonconformist parents, who doubted the value and feared the temptations of university life.[2] But his teachers at King Edward's Birmingham were convinced of his talent and fostered his interest in chemistry and physics; and by their persuasions he was allowed to take a mathematical scholarship at Emmanuel – one would like to know why Emmanuel was chosen – with a view to reading for the Indian Civil Service. But with Phear's encouragement he

---

[1] For all this, see Brooke 1993, pp. 173–4.
[2] For this and what follows see Gold 1945–8; Stubbings 1983b, no. 39.

aimed for the mathematics tripos, instructed by E. J. Routh, the celebrated mathematical coach, under whose guidance he became 16th wrangler in 1876. Then he returned to chemistry and physics, and by the end of the year had a first in the Natural Sciences Tripos and a distinction in physics. This led, first to his fellowship in 1877, then to two crucial visits to Germany. In 1878 he was at Freiburg sitting at the feet of Professor Warburg, from whom Clerk Maxwell, the Cavendish Professor, hoped he might obtain 'a specimen of psilomelane for it is disobedient to Ohm's law'; then in 1879, he studied in Berlin under von Helmholtz.[3] Later the same year came an epoch in Emmanuel and Cambridge science: Napier Shaw was one of the first to be appointed to a college lectureship in Natural Sciences, and under his direction the number of students taking that tripos slowly but steadily grew. In the same year, 1879, he was appointed by the new Cavendish Professor, Lord Rayleigh, demonstrator in the Cavendish Laboratory, and rose steadily under Rayleigh's successor J. J. Thomson – who was several years Shaw's junior in age: university lecturer in 1887, Assistant Director in 1898. Down to 1898 his closest colleague was R. T. Glazebrook, later Sir Richard; and together they produced a *Manual of Physics* which remained standard in university departments for many years. Shaw was much engaged in research on terrestrial magnetism and hygrometry, especially on the theory of ventilation, and increasingly involved in the Meteorological Council. The winter of 1898–9 was exceptional and stimulated him to a variety of original observations; and these in their turn stimulated the Council to offer him the post of Secretary. At the turn of 1899 and 1900 he left Cambridge, and worked as Secretary and Director of the Meteorological Council and Office till his retirement in 1920, after inspiring a remarkable range of studies and greatly expanding the activities of his Office.[4] In his retirement he completed a vast *Manual of Meteorology* (1926–31) and a shorter and livelier *Drama of Weather* (1933).[5]

Thus Shaw played a leading role in two very different worlds: as a creative figure in college and lab in Cambridge, and in the ethereal world of weather. In Emmanuel he rowed in the college eight, and served his turn as Praelector, Steward, Senior Tutor and treasurer of the amalgamated clubs. He succeeded Chawner as Senior Tutor in 1890 and developed that close link between the tutorial system and the revival of college teaching which was a special mark of Emmanuel in the 1890s.[6] His lasting monument is the boathouse, in whose planning he played a leading role.

His creative work in science teaching in Emmanuel was followed by

---

[3] Gold 1945–8, p. 204.
[4] Gold 1945–8, pp. 207–21.
[5] Gold 1945–8, pp. 227–30. There is a Napier Shaw Library in the Cavendish.
[6] See p. 430. On Shaw at Emmanuel, see Stubbings 1983b, no. 39; Gold 1945–8, p. 205.

that of two of the most eminent scientists who have taught in Emmanuel, Frederick Gowland Hopkins the biochemist and Albert Charles Seward the palaeobotanist, both of whom were appointed to teach there as Shaw was preparing to depart. Hopkins taught for Emmanuel from 1898 till 1910, and latterly was a tutor as well; in these years he created medical and biochemical teaching in the College. He was one of the notable characters of early twentieth century Cambridge, an extraordinary mixture of inconsistent qualities: 'timid, insecure, sensitive, kindly, homely', yet also a brilliant scientist who came in due course to be 'conscious of his own powers, and exerted a natural leadership among his colleagues all the more effective because they knew his warmth and simplicity and kindliness'.[7] He had begun as a humble hospital chemist in Guy's, slowly acquiring academic degrees. Then, in his late thirties, he caught the attention of Sir Michael Foster, professor of physiology. Foster himself was not a creative scientist; but he had brought to Cambridge in the 1870s the tradition of T. H. Huxley, and a powerful determination to bring Cambridge physiology to the forefront of international departments; and he had a genius for discovering talent. Hopkins was perhaps the most remarkable case of all, for superficially he lacked Foster's own most vital qualities, his vigour and confidence and drive. Soon after he arrived in Cambridge he met the neurophysiologist Hugh Anderson, later to be master of Caius and the mandarin of the university of the 1920s; and throughout their lifelong friendship Anderson preserved the impression of Hopkins as ' "the worm" who must be fortified by the best claret and the most ribald insults before an important meeting "to put some spunk in him" '.[8]

Hopkins was a great creative scientist, not a teacher of undergraduates. Emmanuel gave him a living wage, but loaded him with pupils; meanwhile he was struggling to develop his research, which was entering a crucial phase. The result was a breakdown; and his career was rescued by Walter Morley Fletcher (later to be founder of the Medical Research Council) who induced Trinity to give Hopkins a praelectorship in biochemistry which involved no teaching at all.[9] This was in 1910; by 1914 he was professor of biochemistry, free to develop his brilliant investigations, including the discovery of vitamins. Emmanuel had played a crucial part in establishing him in Cambridge, and he had set on foot teaching in medical sciences and chemistry; but it was doubtless for the benefit of both that he went to Trinity, for Emmanuel was able to recruit scientists better adapted to teaching undergraduates.

The other most notable figure of this period was A. C. Seward, who

[7] Brooke 1993, pp. 195–8. On Hopkins see esp. Needham and Baldwin 1949.
[8] Maisie Anderson, quoted Brooke 1993, p. 196. On Foster see esp. Geison 1978.
[9] Brooke 1993, p. 196.

moved from St John's to Emmanuel, already an established University Lecturer in Botany, soon after the arrival of Hopkins. He taught for only a few years before becoming professor of Botany in 1906 and master of Downing in 1915. But he remains a symbol of the quality Emmanuel sought in its scientists. He was a celebrated lecturer – Sir Harry Godwin has described how he prepared himself for his first lectures by studying Seward's technique from the room beneath; and he was a man of pastoral gifts, who was to know all the undergraduates of Downing individually, as well as a creative palaeobotanist, and a great master of fossils.[10]

The pattern of scientifc advance in Emmanuel is interesting: first the new physics, attracting the involvement of Phear and the educational reformers; then botany, one of the sciences longest established in Cambridge in the chair and the Garden, one of the first of the major biological sciences to grow to maturity; and medical sciences and chemistry, close allies, for it was the rapid advance of the medical school in the late nineteenth century which first created the major need for teaching in chemistry.[11] From the early 1900s on the pattern grows more complex: the natural sciences tripos had become a giant and a steady flow of teachers in it a natural element in the teaching resources of a college like Emmanuel which had long taken the natural sciences seriously. Soon the mantle of physics teaching – and the sciences tutorship – fell on the young Alex Wood, a central figure in Emmanuel and in many other regions of Cambridge for many years to come. We have met him as Raven's friend and ally in the Chawner affair, at the opening of his career; in later years he and Raven were to share a passionate dedication to pacifism; we have met him too as an elder in the Presbyterian St Columba's, the nearest major city church to the college, and bursar of Westminster College; and as leader of the Labour councillors in the city in the 1920s. Meanwhile he made a name for himself by quiet, unspectacular but useful work in acoustics in the Cavendish; and was the leading teacher of natural sciences in Emmanuel for a generation.[12]

Some of those recruited to teach the sciences had little pretension to be research scientists. One such was James Line, who was recruited to teach botany in the College shortly after the First World War. He gradually established himself as fellow and college lecturer – and was for a number of years a very active Steward. Meanwhile his interests had shifted to agriculture; and his teaching continued, only interrupted by agricultural war work in the Second World War, until his retirement. He never attempted extensive research, but his cheerful, energetic, efficient

---

[10] Brooke 1993, p. 162; on Seward, see Godwin 1985, pp. 40–1; Thomas and Bower 1939–41; Stubbings 1983b, no. 41.
[11] Brooke 1993, pp. 156–7, 160–2, 164–9.
[12] See p. 438–9.

presentation of his subject made him a valued teacher. He was a strange combination – like Hopkins – of inconsistent parts. In a moving memoir, his son Timothy recalled him as 'the agriculturist, with hundreds of Cambridge undergraduates passing through his lectures; the outdoors person, with his love of sailing, [and] striding over the Welsh mountains; or the rigid religious zealot, following exactly the teachings of the Exclusive Plymouth Brethren'. He had been brought up a Brother, but learned in Cambridge and the First War a wider view of life, and married a devout Anglican; Dorothy Line's heroic loyalty to her husband and her Church preserved an essentially happy family life through the early storms which blew when the Brethren reclaimed him. But in his last years the horizons narrowed: the Exclusive Brethren (in marked contrast to the Open Plymouth Brothers) attempted to shut out their members from every body save the Body of Christ, and membership of university and college became impossible to him. He was even made to live as if apart from his wife, though under the same roof. After Dorothy's death there was a happier epilogue: he remarried, and his second wife, Mary Bolt – who had been catering manager when Line was Steward – was herself one of the sect, so they could enjoy each other's company in extreme old age without any trouble to his conscience. To be subjected to the rigid, fundamentalist views of the Brethren was an astonishing end for a professional scientist; yet such it was, and he had to sever his ties with the college he had loved and served.[13]

Very different from Line in their approach to science – and very different from each other in character and appearance – were the three notable scientists who became professorial fellows between the two world wars, Sir Bennett Melvill Jones, C. E. Tilley and R. G. W. Norrish.

Bennett Melvill Jones had been an undergraduate in Emmanuel from 1906 to 1909, reading Engineering; in the years that followed he became a pioneer aeronautical engineer, testing current theories of flight on his own account, and designing airships for Armstrong Whitworth. During the First World War he designed air instruments and guns, and himself became a skilled pilot and gunner. In 1918–19 he was translated from Lieutenant-Colonel in the Royal Flying Corps to lecturer in Cambridge and fellow of Emmanuel; and almost at once was chosen first holder of the Francis Mond Chair of Aeronautical Engineering. His meteoric rise followed the pattern of his profession; but aeroplanes, though widely seen as the carriages of the future in war and peace, remained in the 1920s and 30s wayward, perilous machines. He was a man of singular courage,

---

[13] This is partly based on an unprinted memoir by Timothy Line kindly given me by his sister Jaqueline Line, with much other information, and on her own study, Line 1993; partly on personal knowledge: Dorothy Line was a close friend of my mother. See also the account by Ronald Gray in *ECM* 73 (1990–1), 133–4.

who enjoyed flying with a small number of chosen colleagues; he found the answer to numerous problems of aerodynamics by exploring dangerous paths with his friends.[14] Very characteristic of him was his manner of combating the stall, leading to the downward spin which was the cause of most disasters in the air in that epoch. He flew with J. A. G. Haslam at the controls, while Jones observed the effect of deliberately courting a stall: 'free flying experiment' he wrote in 1930, 'provides the essential cutting edge of aeronautical research'.[15] And so we no longer fear a stall when we set off into the air. His other most celebrated contribution lay in streamlining aircraft to avoid the effects of drag. But some of his most important work lay in helping and encouraging other engineers. In 1920 he was inclined to deny the possibility of a jet engine as a practical method of propelling aircraft. But in the 1930s he was quick to see the value of Frank Whittle's projects. In 1935, Whittle tells us, Jones said to him 'I think you are on the right track, young man, but don't expect the sky to be black with jet aircraft for at least ten years'.[16] In fact it took much longer, and would probably have been still further delayed, but for the firm and prophetic support Melvill Jones gave to the development of jet engines, not only for military but for civil flight.

Tilley was an Australian who had studied at Adelaide and Sydney before he came to Cambridge in 1920 'bearing with him an extensive collection of metamorphic rocks' from South Australia. He rose from research student to demonstrator in 1923, and by 1928 was Lecturer in Petrology in the Sedgwick Museum. In these years plans were afoot for reorganising the various strata in geology, and in 1931 a separate department combining mineralogy and petrology was established with Tilley as its first professor; in the same year Emmanuel made him a professorial fellow. In lab and college he had curiously different reputations. Among his neighbours on the Downing Site he was regarded by some as an arrogant scientist who reckoned geology an old-fashioned descriptive science; petrology was the way of analysis and advance. In 1961 he retired, and in 1980 geology and petrology and other neighbours were to be gathered into one Department of Earth Sciences.[17] Meanwhile, Tilley had transformed mineralogy and petrology 'from the old world of minerals and crystals to the new modes of crystallographic and paragenetic research into rocks and minerals', with characteristic vigour.[18] 'A new building, largely to his design, was ready for occupation in 1933 and Tilley moved in. His aim from the first was to produce a laboratory of the

---

[14] On all this, see Hall and Morgan 1977, especially, on the 'stall', pp. 269–70; on streamlining, pp. 262–5; on Whittle and the jet engine, pp. 270–2.
[15] Hall and Morgan 1977, p. 259.
[16] Hall and Morgan 1977, p. 271.
[17] Deer and Nockolds 1974, esp. p. 382; Brooke 1993, pp. 157–60.
[18] Brooke 1993, p. 159.

top rank both in teaching and research and in this he succeeded, with absolute dedication and not a little ruthlessness. He made it quite clear that the facilities of the department were there to be used and that time was not to be wasted – "The hours of this Department are from 9 to 7" one research student was told on returning from a mid-week excursion to London.'[19] Through his own hard work and strong determination, especially to apply the techniques of physical chemistry to the study of rocks, many of the problems then confronting students of metamorphic and igneous rocks melted away; though he was keenly aware at the end of his life that basalt and many another had still many secrets to yield. In the lab he was an imperious, successful, head of department, yet admired: 'the methods he used in his research – the extensive collection in the field, the accurate petrographic investigation accompanied by chemical analysis of suitable specimens and the more important minerals, the search for relevant literature – and the love of rocks both as subjects for research and as objects of beauty when seen in thin section under the microscope, these he has passed on to numerous students, now scattered over the globe, who remember him with gratitude.'[20] In the College he was more relaxed, and was remembered as 'a very kindly man with a somewhat roguish sense of humour'; his popularity, and the admiration in which he was held, were reflected in his election as vice-master, an office he held from 1952–8[21] – or perhaps the fellowship sought in the vice-master as marked a contrast to Edward Welbourne, elected master in 1951, as could be found.

R. G. W. Norrish had a much longer association with Emmanuel and with Cambridge. He was born in Panton Street, close to the new Chemistry Laboratories of the 1950s; he was a pupil at the Perse School; as a schoolboy he already had his private lab – and his apparatus is preserved in the Science Museum in South Kensington.[22] He was nearly 63 years a member of Emmanuel, from 1915 when he entered as scholar, to 1978 when he died, senior fellow. He was a man of the lab, a Nobel Prize-winner, a man of the world; but a devout college man too; characteristically, he and his wife found a house as close to the college as could be: from the 1930s they lived in Park Terrace. He had an international reputation as a physical chemist and a bon viveur – for his 'generous and occasionally overwhelming hospitality'. His many international tours were marked by parties in his honour and suited to his tastes. 'Back in England he derived much pleasure as a host in College and at home, and the visits of distinguished foreign scientists, not all of them chemists, usually led to

[19] Deer and Nockolds 1974, esp. p. 382.
[20] Deer and Nockolds 1974, p. 396.
[21] *ECM* 55 (1972–3), 5–6.
[22] Dainton and Thrush 1981, pp. 380, 383.

a party at which few could match the Professor in stamina.'[23] In College above all, but also in London, at Royal Society soirées and meetings of the Savage Club, he showed his enjoyment of human society and good liquor.

His early work revealed Norrish 'as an unusually gifted and energetic experimentalist, capable of making significant advances in photochemistry and kinetics.' This led to a research fellowship in Emmanuel in 1924 and to his first post in Physical Chemistry in 1926, and, as his research and fame advanced, he was elected to the chair in 1937.[24] After his early work with E. K. Rideal he and his many collaborators investigated the photochemistry of numerous compounds. His studies carried him on to many areas of physical chemistry, including polymerisation studies – 'stimulated by his industrial connections, particularly with the Distillers' Company', a natural ally; and sensitised explosions. 'Norrish had a sense of the dramatic' which issued in enjoyment of the company of actors at the Savage Club, and in chemical explosions.[25] But in the late 1930s 'his touch and inspiration seemed to wane' and he became preoccupied with minor elements in his research; and so the Second World War formed a kind of caesura in his work. In the late 1940s he set vigorously to work to help physical chemists from all over the country to recover their enthusiasm for the subject through summer schools, and in the process he began to revive his own research. In the years which followed he scored his greatest successes and paved the way for his and George Porter's Nobel Prizes. George Porter was his pupil and brought to their joint study of flash photolysis and kinetic spectroscopy expertise in electronics learned in the navy during the war. Norrish and Porter, with other younger chemists, who included Brian Thrush of Emmanuel, worked together to develop this very fruitful field. 'Norrish saw flash photolysis as a means of identifying the intermediates in photochemical processes and in chain reactions which he had postulated from his earlier work with conventional techniques.' He and Porter developed these techniques to study a variety of chemical reactions, including such difficult customers as 'vibrationally excited molecules' and 'electronically excited atoms'.[26]

His chief hero was Rutherford, and he 'never tired of playing his gramophone records of Rutherford lecturing at Göttingen, as much for his own as his guests' pleasure'. The symbol of the crocodile, which Kapitza applied to Rutherford, represented in Russian folklore the father of the family, rigid, unbending, ever marching forward with gaping jaws;[27] it would apply well to Norrish too. He had extraordinary knowledge and insight, surpassing experimental gifts, but no subtlety. He loved

---

[23] Dainton and Thrush 1981, pp. 383, 412.
[24] Dainton and Thrush 1981, p. 383.
[25] Dainton and Thrush 1981, pp. 391–2, 395–6.
[26] Dainton and Thrush 1981, pp. 400, 404–5, 411.
[27] Dainton and Thrush 1981, p. 407; Brooke 1993, pp. 191–2.

to welcome and entertain scientists from all over the world; yet a part of him was afraid that *his* discoveries, *his* scientific secrets, would be stolen.[28] Nor was his conversation at high table and in the parlour that of a great scientist expounding the subtleties of his mind, or eliciting the skills of his younger colleagues – as was the conversation of Sir Ronald Fisher and Joseph Needham in Caius in the 1940s and 50s. He was a personality, a lively, convivial talker, with many interests; a man of power, but not a great intellectual force. All the originality of his mind was poured into work in the laboratory, which was immensely successful, whether one views his own researches, or the daily rounds of the research students, with whom he kept up a constant dialectic which compelled them to keep on their toes, or in his undergraduate lectures – not universally popular, but deeply influencing those who had talents akin to his.[29]

It is thus more than chance that two of Emmanuel's most eminent scientists of recent times, Lord Porter and Professor Brian Thrush, have been pupils of Norrish. George Porter was briefly a fellow of Emmanuel, before setting forth to a chair in Sheffield, and then to be director of the Royal Institution. He has won fame both for the fundamental scientific research which won him the Nobel Prize, jointly with Norrish and M. Eigen, in 1967, and for his exceptional gifts in explaining modern science to a wider audience from his chair in the Royal Institution. Brian Thrush has worked mainly in Cambridge – though he has travelled far, lecturing in the 1990s, for example, in Poona and South Africa and examining in Singapore – and has been Head of the Department of Chemistry, and in Emmanuel, where he has been vice-master. Among his marks of recognition has been the Rank Prize for Opto-Electronics, 'for discovering the fundamental process which made possible efficient lasers in the far ultraviolet'.[30]

Since the turn of the century the Natural Sciences Tripos has been a giant, gathering innumerable students; and more recently Engineering has grown enormously too, claiming one tenth of the University's students, staff and resources. Engineering has spilt over into the social sciences, giving birth – in its Cambridge context – to management sciences, under the leadership of Stephen Watson, formerly professorial fellow of Emmanuel and Director of the Judge Institute of Management Sciences.[31] Not long ago, a gigantic crane stood aloft over the old Addenbrookes, symbol or symptom of a new world of management sciences come to replace what was the heart of the old hospital.

[28] Dainton and Thrush 1981, pp. 407–9.
[29] Dainton and Thrush 1981, p. 410, citing Professor Peter Gray.
[30] *ECM* 74 (1991–2), 80.
[31] Called after its principal benefactor, Mr Paul Judge.

Naturally there has been a notable growth in the number of scientists in the fellowship – and also in scientists who have gone out from the College to ply their crafts elsewhere. Emmanuel has not attempted the scientific bias of some college high tables; but it has played its role. The alumni have included distinguished physicists such as E. C. Stoner, who died Cavendish Professor of Physics in Leeds in 1968; biochemists such as Robin Hill, later honorary fellow, and Malcolm Dixon, later a fellow of King's; biologists such as G. E. Hutchinson and physiologists such as Peter Baker – to name a few. Baker was a precocious scientist who studied earwigs as a schoolboy and the Loch Ness monster as an undergraduate; then, as a research student, he was one of those who 'struck gold' in the nerve fibres of the giant squid, and went on to advance knowledge of a variety of regions of physiological research; a man of immense energy, much of it spent in Emmanuel, where he was a fellow from 1962 to 1974, teaching medical students and – for a time – filling the role of Domestic Bursar, where his pace was too fast for some of his colleagues. In 1974 he moved to a chair in King's College, London, in time to prepare the King's Medical School for defence against the processes of 'rationalisation' which have mesmerised the University of London in recent years. The combination of research and teaching and university politics sadly proved too much for his strength, and he died young in 1987, the day before his 48th birthday.[32]

Robin Hill was a man of research, and never a teacher: he and Malcolm Dixon both started their careers in biochemistry under the baton of Gowland Hopkins; Hill 'was an immensely shy man who found lecturing excruciatingly painful'. He was one of those who revolutionised 'knowledge of how photosynthesis works', for which he was rewarded by long support from the Agricultural Research Council, which enabled him to continue working in Cambridge – and ultimately with the Copley Medal of the Royal Society and the honorary fellowship of Emmanuel.[33]

G. E. Hutchinson was one of the founders of the modern science of ecology. He was a native of Cambridge who had discovered his environment among the butterflies and other insects of Wicken Fen; he enjoyed a distinguished undergraduate career at Emmanuel, but his later life and achievements all belonged elsewhere. By 1928 he was established at Yale, where he was to be for many years Sterling Professor of Zoology. 'Hutchinson was admired as limnologist, biochemist, ecologist, evolutionist, art historian and ranks among our zoological giants'.[34] He became in due course an honorary fellow of Emmanuel, and the last rites were performed for him in the College Chapel.

[32] Knight and Hodgkin 1990, esp. pp. 2, 20–4.
[33] Derek Bendall, quoted in ECM 73 (1990–1), 123–5; D. Bendall 1994.
[34] Quoted from The Times obituary (4 June 1991) in ECM 73 (1990–1), 128.

It is fitting that we should close this survey of Emmanuel scientists with an eminent engineer, Professor John Eirwyn (Shôn) Ffowcs Williams, the present Master. He has played a leading role in a branch of acoustics peculiarly vital to modern life, the diminution of noise – a branch of learning, one might think, especially appropriate to the head of a Cambridge college. He is the son of a Welsh-speaking Methodist minister, who learned English at the Quaker School at Great Ayton in Yorkshire, and then became an engineering apprentice; taking A levels and the London external Degree in his spare time, and eventually winning a scholarship to Southampton University. His early research on the noise created by jets and rockets brought contact with Sir Gordon Sutherland and a place in the National Physical Laboratory – briefly, for he was soon in a leading acoustics consultancy in Cambridge, Massachusetts. There followed a return to England – a Readership and Professorship at Imperial College, and the formation of a research team closely linked to industry and aimed in particular to bring peace to Concorde. Since 1972, Ffowcs Williams and his team have been in Cambridge, UK, he as Rank Professor of Engineering; and a period of notable stability has followed the migrations of his earlier life. He came – as so many professorial fellows have come to their Cambridge colleges – knowing nothing of Emmanuel and little of Cambridge. He has explored many regions of the university and played a leading role in its affairs. Yet he has also been a very active college man, with a deep insight into the way a college works and how its noise levels may be modified. He is a striking example of the union of brilliant scientific and subtle human gifts – in notable contrast to some other notable scientists who have been heads of colleges, including Sir Gordon Sutherland, the eminent scientist who helped to bring him to Emmanuel.[35]

[35] Based on the Master's own account in *ECM* 78 (1995–6), 1–5. For Sir Gordon Sutherland, see below, pp. 555–8.

20

Undergraduates and Dons, 1910–1960[1]

Before 1914

For the years immediately before the Great War we have an incomparable source in the reminiscences of Edward Welbourne, later Senior Tutor and Master.[2] It is impossible to quote Welbourne without rambling; yet however strange the path he takes, his perambulations are always shot through with shrewd observation and vivid memory.

'Whenever I give myself time to remember, I see clearly that it was a miracle that I went to Cambridge' – he came from a relatively humble background and all his life tried to make Emmanuel a home for the unprivileged. 'My college has at all times . . . stood somewhat on the flank of the university. In the days when people reached Cambridge by train, it was the first college which was encountered, for the modest gate of Downing is generally passed unobserved. There was then a horse tram, which stopped at Christ's . . . The town was smaller, quieter, visited by few tourists. Undergraduates commonly walked on the road, leaving the pavements to the shopping women' – and he goes on to inveigh against the commercial development of central Cambridge after 1919 which crowded the narrow streets with shops and shoppers. 'What did I, or maybe two out of three of the undergraduates know of that mysterious university written about by novelists and journalists, where rich young men idled gorgeously? . . . Noone has ever been poorer than the son of a country parson, or the son of a widow who hoped to see her son turn into a parson, scratching his way through the three years of Cambridge as best he could, with a scholarship which perhaps half paid his way and here and there an odd grant from some semi-charitable source . . . And for one young man who spent his three years in the Pitt Club there were five or six who lived as I came to live, counting every penny.' Welbourne himself was a police officer's son from a modest Lincolnshire grammar school. 'If Emmanuel was dominated by this penniless class' – including many who

---

[1] This chapter is an attempt to evoke the nature of life in Emmanuel by a series of vignettes based on reminiscences, some contemporary, most written many years later with some benefit of hindsight. I am especially indebted to Mr Graham Watson and Mr Harry Whitcut for their generous help.

[2] ECA COL.9.29, slightly edited.

'used the university to which their careers as parsons and schoolmasters compelled them to come' – 'every other college into which I penetrated had its share of them . . . Already the social need to play games was a burden, for games demanded an apparatus of proper clothes . . .' which inhibited expense even on books. 'But it was not the narrow poverty of the working class. It was that of a definitely middle class group . . . living a negative life because it could do no other. Yet it gained hugely by its three years, and understandably came to remember them as its once enjoyed paradise . . . For it escaped from the isolations of an isolated home' in a country village; 'it escaped from the isolation of being a parson's son, a doctor's son, a schoolmaster's son in a late Victorian industrial town. . . . Cambridge for them was a kindly jail. Noone imposed himself on their solitude – noone had a right to do so. There at every man's door was his outer door, his oak, which he could if he wished "sport", and then he was alone in his own world, inviolate. The old discipline of chapel attendance was fast going into decline'[3] – though 'Emmanuel had a large number of members of the CICCU, the almost fundamentalist evangelical group which spent much of its time in prayer meetings . . . Noone need know when they went to bed, when they rose, whether they ate breakfast, or lunch . . . The five obligatory dinners could be eaten in silence in a full hall. Lectures existed', intercollegiate lectures planned to enable the 'smaller colleges to provide adequate teaching'; but they were not compulsory, 'though a tutor could make [them] so if he was that kind of tutor. Most college teaching was given individually, and in some subjects this was its strength' since the undergraduate 'was witheld by no shame from exhibiting his ignorance in front of a group'. But the life was not necessarily solitary. 'In all colleges there were small groups, sometimes of school friends, sometimes of men whom some chance encounter had made friends, sometimes of men devoted to some common cause, who lived in close intimacies . . . There was a slight tendency stronger in some colleges than in others . . . derived from the lesser public schools, for a kind of snobbery based on athletic eminence, but it was in no way dominant.

'I sent my tin trunk in advance, and with a Gladstone bag in my hand . . . I found my way to my rooms – ground floor rooms in the middle stair, O, of New Court, then a little enclosed court pervaded by kitchen smells. . . . I was reading history. There were several . . . men . . . reading history as a necessity because they were no good at classics, and as a method of evading theology because they were going into the church and were evangelicals, who knew that theology was forbidden by God' – thus Welbourne characteristically sets the traditionalist evangelicals of his early days apart from the liberal evangelicals who flourished in the

---

[3] See pp. 433–4.

Divinity School. 'I found friends mostly among the men from overseas: a silent Scot, still speaking some form of Scots, from South Africa ... destined to be a Presbyterian minister, ordered by his mother to join the movement for the emancipation of women. We rowed in a boat together. A loquacious New Zealander, who after a short time found that his Scottish belief – for he too was a Scot – that everyone like himself was reading medicine was wrong, and that we were not idle Englishmen absenting ourselves ... from the lab ...

'We all lunched on the remnants of our commons, that daily loaf, pint of milk and pat of butter, which was just going out of fashion as the economical demanded half commons and [so saved] a penny or so ... But my ignorance of petty economies commended me to my bedmaker, a little woman in a black bonnet called Mrs Humphreys, served by a similar but oppressed woman, her sister-in-law, who did the dirty work and was hardly allowed to make contact with the gentlemen. The bulk of the college behaved well towards the servants, though here and there a man incited to suspicion by his upbringing made futile efforts to prevent his bedmaker making anything out of him.' The rest accepted that the women supplemented their wages by acting as agents of local tradesmen. 'I was aware how much work these women did, for each two looked after eight men, and could in no way control the work which resulted from entertainment. It was pure fortune whether every man on the stair had a breakfast party on the same day, or left the crockery of the whole court on the floor after being the host of a late coffee drinking. There was a formal round of breakfast parties', the food being supplied from the kitchen, 'very rarely lunch parties, almost never dinner parties. In the main we lunched on bread, butter, jam and cheese, and as time went on I bought more and more fruit ... and in the summer cream cheeses. We were saved from malnutrition by an admirable institution, college hall, where for half a crown we could eat as many helpings as we liked of the meat course.

'Half my friends were in the hostel: they had gone to Emmanuel because it [the Hostel] existed. The caution money, payment in advance, the furniture at no certain price, the complete lack of certainty what a term's bill would be: all abolished by this Victorian experiment.[4] They were in the main from the careful middle class, parsons' sons, widows' sons, public school men, many of them ordinands, others potential schoolmasters' – two professions now, where they had often been one in the nineteenth century.[5] 'To a certain extent they were a race apart, losing something by their compelled communal life, cut off from the easy life of

[4] For the hostel, see pp. 512–13.
[5] See Brooke 1993, pp. 246–7. On the numerous clergy's sons in public schools – clearly the folk Welbourne has particularly in mind here – see Brooke 1993, ibid.

the university. But to a good many other men in the college they were fortunate, for they lived better and cheaper than did anyone else.' It also
broke down the rigid division operating elsewhere between different
years.

'The years were kept apart by a kind of pretence that seniority would
bring privilege. I imagine there was some conscious imitation from the
public schools . . . The years not only dined apart in hall' because several
sittings were required, 'but sat separately in chapel. The first war made
an end of the rigidity of the system. Set against it was the remaining tradition of the college when it had been smaller, and more civilised. The
senior men all ceremonially called on every freshman, or tried to do so,
and to some extent entertained them, and we in turn, with much leaving
of cards which in fact none of us understood, returned calls and entertained in our turn. No doubt when the college had consisted of some
fifteen men a year it had been an extremely friendly college, but in my
year we were over seventy and the system was already in decay.'

Thus far Edward Welbourne. Two notable omissions we must immediately fill: music and sport.

Music and Edward Naylor

Music in Cambridge has a long and distinguished history; but within
many colleges the musical tradition – even of chapel music – is surprisingly recent. Thus the flourishing music of Caius of recent generations
began when Charles Wood became 'organist scholar' in 1889, and from
then till his death as professor of music in 1926 was a central creative
figure in the college.[6] Edward Naylor came to Emmanuel as undergraduate organist in 1884; and after a spell in the Royal College of Music and as
an organist in London, he returned to Emmanuel in 1898 as chapel
organist, and remained there till his death in 1934. By then many pupils
and colleagues had joined him in appreciating and performing music; but
he was throughout the creative inspiration. From 1901 he was college
lecturer, and it is strange that he was never a fellow – Wood was a fellow
of Caius from 1894; and it may reflect a dying notion among the Governing Body that music was not a fully academic subject. If so, they
repented with style, for in 1920 he was made an honorary fellow.

Raymond Hockley has summarised his life thus.[7]

'From his birth in 1867 Edward Naylor was surrounded by musicians. His grandfather sang bass, an uncle sang tenor, another uncle

---

[6] Brooke 1985, pp. 242–4.
[7] What follows is from Hockley 1974–5: we look forward to Canon Hockley's full biography, which is nearing completion; he has most generously shown me draft chapters
from it. Meanwhile Hockley 1974–5 gives a fine summary, and a full appreciation (on
pp. 11–14) of Naylor's opera, the *Angelus*.

and a cousin were cathedral organists, his father was organist of York Minster and composer of considerable ability, and his younger brother was also a professional organist and composer. The young Edward had little formal education but his father's careful teaching enabled him to enter Emmanuel, when he was only just seventeen, to read for an ordinary degree. His subjects were classics and theology, and it was not until his extra fourth year that he read music. On leaving Cambridge he went to the Royal College of Music where he studied composition, the organ and the viola. He returned briefly to Cambridge in 1891 to take the Mus.B. and again in 1898 to take the Mus.D. While in London Naylor began to reveal the many sides of his musical talent. He wrote a large number of compositions, many of which were performed; he published the first fruit of his research in his book *Shakespeare and Music*; he performed on the organ regularly; and he gained a considerable reputation as a lecturer on music at Toynbee Hall. In 1898 he was appointed organist at Emmanuel and soon afterwards was invited to give a series of lectures on music. It says much for the perception and educational benevolence of the Governing Body that he was the first, and for many years the only, College lecturer in music at Cambridge. The remainder of Naylor's life was devoted to teaching, lecturing, performing, composing and musical research. The *Angelus* [an opera – his most ambitious composition] was performed at Covent Garden in 1909 and revived by the Carl Rosa Company in 1921. His setting of the Requiem Mass, *Pax Dei*, was first performed at Cambridge in 1913. His *Tokugawa Overture*, composed for the opening concert of the Nanki Auditorium, the Marquis Tokugawa's Concert Room in Tokyo, was first performed there in 1920. He published a critical account of the famous manuscript in the Fitzwilliam Museum, *An Elizabethan Virginal Book*, in 1905, and his second Shakespearean book, *Shakespeare Music*, in 1913. In addition the Chapel organ was rebuilt to his design and the standard of the Chapel music vastly improved; and he continued to pour out a steady stream of Church music.'

And here is his quality as appreciated by one of his contemporaries, the mathematician G. T. Bennett.

'One noticed first the rich and sensitive equipment he possessed for the art he practised: a musician from his soul to his finger-tips. His fine ear was not merely an instant detector of all musical nuances of pitch and quality of tone, but possessed a most remarkable power of harmonic analysis. It was quite easy for him to identify the pitches of an incredible number of partials in a complex tone, and he would amuse himself on occasion by making out a complete list, whether for a glass lampshade or a bath exhaust-pipe. What he did in a few moments a physical laboratory might have accomplished expensively in a week or so. His hands rivalled his ears, and his pianoforte touch was a joy to hear. Beyond all sophistications of phrasing and accent and balance of tone there was the elastic playing of the individual note. The magic went beyond that: for, when making his pianoforte do duty for an orchestra, he seemed able at will to make clear in some mysterious way that it was, say, the horns that were speaking. And his accompaniments were ideal. Where lesser men were 'at the piano' his playing gave the composer's balanced contribution to the undivided whole: he played, it seemed, not as a pianist but as a composer. His organ-playing had the same qualities; and he somehow made a present to the instrument of the power of accentuation that it does not rightly possess. In the chapel services he perhaps encouraged rather force-fully the laggard voices of the pious; but his occasional recitals were little feasts of taste and beauty. His excursions to King's, when Dr Mann came down from his organ-loft to conduct his Festival Choir, were not only opportunities for the collaboration of fast and firm friends but musical occasions notable for fine performances of great works.'[8]

In the 1920s recognition came from the university as well as the college: as the faculty of Music was formed in the process of University reorganisation in the mid 1920s, he became a university lecturer in 1925 and a member of the Faculty Board in 1926. Sadly, his eyesight was deteriorating, and he withdrew from the public view in his later years; but he could still play piano and organ in the college, from a remarkable musical memory, till retirement in 1932 – he died in 1934. By then music had come to hold an indelible grip on the college; his memory and the tradition he formed live on.

Sport and the college staff
Rowing is easily the most venerable of the organised sports of Cambridge; and the Emmanuel Boat Club, like so many – including the Cambridge University Boat Club itself – was founded in the 1820s, apparently in 1827.[9] Through the nineteenth century the boats, the bumps and the boathouses gradually evolved. 'Emmanuel is not one of the great names in the rowing world' – thus Geoffrey Wynne Thomas, the club's historian – 'but the Boat Club has a not undistinguished record.' Writing in 1978, he could boast of 20 Blues, 12 Goldie Caps and 67 Trial Caps: this

---

[8] *ECM* 29 (1933–4), 2–7, at pp. 3–4. For a later, much less professional but very vital element in college music, provided by L. H. G. Greenwood, see pp. 546, 554.
[9] All that follows is based on Wynne Thomas 1978. On its author, see below, pp. 542–4.

may seem 'a small contribution to university rowing' in 150 years, but it places Emmanuel in the middle rank – well below the leaders, Trinity, Jesus, Trinity Hall and the Lady Margaret Boat Club of St John's, well above the tail.[10] The 1890s witnessed its climacteric. In 1890 'the May Boat was said to be the fastest on the river over a full course, especially the last part, with staying power, steady swing and leg-drive. They made two bumps, and were the first Emmanuel Boat to go to Henley.' In 1891–2 the Amalgamated Clubs were set up in Emmanuel, as in many colleges about this time, to provide funds for the Boat Club, and also football, cricket, athletics, tennis, music – and the Reading Room. In 1892 James Adam, the classical fellow, composed the Latin words of the Boat Club Song, 'Fit via vi', and an undergraduate called Arnold Culley set them to music in 1893. Hitherto boats and changing rooms had been hired from one of the boat-builders on the Cam. In 1893 the site of the boathouse was acquired, and in the summer of 1895 the College Magazine carried a drawing of the building about to rise, with a call for subscriptions; it was opened in 1897. Already Billy Taylor had been appointed first College Boatman in 1896, and he held sway there till his retirement in 1935, when he was succeeded by George Hones, long his assistant, later a keen coach as well as boatman, who held office till his death in 1962. Meanwhile, between 1896 and 1899, the First Lent Boat entered the First Division, rising 13 places in four years.[11]

The Boat Club, as in all colleges, has had its ups and downs. In abeyance during the First World War, it took some reviving in 1919 and 1920. In 1919, 'Owing to the devotion which the college now displays to reading, work, laboratories, and lectures, it was found difficult to per-suade the proper proportion of men to row . . .'[12] – the eternal sports-man's lament; and still it is heard, for even in the 1990s, when every student enters hoping for a reasonable class in tripos, the pass man is extinct and the third an endangered species, very high standards are sought and found in the Emmanuel Boat Club.

Continuity owed much to Taylor and Hones and their successors; also to the steady support of the Treasurers of the Amalgamated Clubs on the river and the Sports Ground; also to the lasting enthusiasm of old members, first among them Geoffrey Wynne Thomas, captain in 1926–7, coach, on and off, for over fifty years thereafter. The long service of the boatmen can be matched elsewhere in the college staff. In 1887 Allison E. Shaw became a porter, in 1893 head porter. When he retired in 1930 Sidney Freestone had already been on the staff since 1911, a porter (war service apart) since 1914. He succeeded Shaw as head porter in 1930,

[10] Wynne Thomas 1978, p. 5.
[11] Wynne Thomas 1978, pp. 6–9, 12, 14; *ECM* 6 (1895), frontispiece and p. 9.
[12] Wynne Thomas 1978, p. 6.

retiring in 1958.[13] But all these records are beaten by the Mannings, father and son, who lived in the groundsman's cottage on Wilberforce Road from 1910, when it was first built, until Mr John Manning's retirement in 1980.[14]

The years before the First World War witnessed the opening of the playing fields and the building of the pavilion and groundsman's cottage. Early in this century the Amalgamated Clubs expanded their activities, and the ground by the Driftway, now Wilberforce Road, was opened in 1908; over it presided the elder Mr Manning till his retirement in 1947. From 1910 he lived in the cottage, and he and his wife – and in more recent times the younger Mr and Mrs Manning – looked after the sportsmen of the college, the groundsman providing admirable conditions for football, cricket, hockey, tennis and athletics – and his wife tea and refreshments for the teams. In early days the lawns were kept in trim by horse-drawn mowers – and the elder Mr Manning appropriately passed the First World War as a saddler in the Royal Artillery Depot at Woolwich. In 1926 came the revolution: one of the first Ransome motor mowers and rollers entered the ground, and soon after the horses departed. The groundsman's cottage and pavilion form a social centre crucial to college life far from the old Dominican precinct; and the Mannings, husbands and wives, entered whole-heartedly into it. By chance I myself was brought up in a house nearly opposite the cottage and well remember the elder Manning – 'the salt of the earth' as my father regarded him; and I have no doubt that later generations have regarded Mr and Mrs John Manning, happily still alive, as we regarded his parents. The groundsman is an occasional visitor to the college itself. Mr John Manning has also been on numerous tours with the cricket club as umpire – with their first base in Eastbourne College where the master in charge of Cricket was an old member of the college and Seaford College which had an Emmanuel headmaster – spreading their bats through Kent and Sussex and Hampshire, engaging in convivial as much as sporting events. But during term John Manning was available six days a week and 24 hours a day in Wilberforce Road. He has also refereed soccer and hockey matches past counting, and helped the sporting teams in innumerable ways – and so become well-acquainted with generations of notable sportsmen. These have included undergraduates like Peter Wroth, a keen sportsman of the early 1950s, whose advent as master (though sadly brief) came as a particular thrill to Mr Manning; and the county cricketers brought into the college by David Newsome.[15] He also

---

[13] *ECM* 40 (1957–8), frontispiece and pp. 4, 35–6. Among the Treasurers of the Amalgamated Clubs Mr Robert – Bobbie – Gardner is especially remembered (see pp. 452–3).

[14] What follows is largely based on personal knowledge, and the kind help of Mr and Mrs John Manning. See also ECM 61 (1977–8) 52; 62 (1978–9), 54.

[15] See p. 560.

witnessed the arrival of the first women hockey players – but had retired before they spread their wings to all other parts of the ground.

In such a book as this the college staff, on whom so much of its life depends, get far less than their share of space: the boatmen, the head porters and the groundsmen must represent for us the numerous members of staff who provided much that is essential to the idea of a college as it has been known to its members: all the other members of the staff, caterers and tutorial administrators and secretaries, assistant librarians and archive assistants, and all those who help in kitchen and hall and master's lodge – an army more numerous than the fellows. Without the fellows Emmanuel would hardly be an academic institution; without the staff it could not be a college.

The Great War, 1914–1918

In August 1914 the war began, and in a wave of enthusiasm in many and deep anxiety in not a few, many hundreds – eventually nearly 15,000 – of the young men of Cambridge joined the forces. By the Easter Term of 1916 the number of male undergraduates had fallen from nearly 4,000 (3,699 in 1909–10) to 575 – the number of women stayed at about 400.[16] Nearly 1,000 Emmanuel men joined the British forces.[17] Empty rooms and a flock of sheep on the paddock were reminders that the young men were elsewhere. The newly completed North Court was requisitioned by the Army; and of the military presence a Silver fusilier, a present from the invaders, remains as a reminder.

'What a rotten place Cambridge must be', wrote a young magistrate from India called Geoffrey Stevens early in 1916, 'with only sixty weeds up' – doubtless a very unfair summary of the unfit and the medical and other students who kept the College alive in these years. But he also justly observed that if life in Emmanuel was lonely, so was his, '25 miles from anywhere'.[18]

Stevens was writing to P. W. Wood, mathematical lecturer and tutor, who remained throughout the war a central pillar in Emmanuel, and for long afterwards the mathematical Wood and the classical Greenwood were the fellows best known to the undergraduates. The dossier of letters to Wood during the war is striking testimony to the affection in which his pupils held him – and reflects the range of sentiment of Emmanuel men under pressure of war. We encounter Rollo Atkinson, in November 1915, talking in a friendly, affectionate, slightly cynical way about his general – followed by a very moving letter to Atkinson's father from the general

---

[16] Brooke 1993, p. 331 and references; *CUC* 1919–20, p. 427.
[17] *CUC* 1919–20, p. 427, gives 936.
[18] ECA COL.24 contains a dossier of letters written to P. W. Wood, or collected by him, during the war.

reporting his death in February 1916. We encounter the ordinand whose course was interrupted by the call to do military service; the soldier suffering from shell-shock whose mother sent frequent bulletins to Wood of her son's deteriorating condition. T. Davenport wrote in November 1915: 'It is a relief to me in these days to find someone who is not "flag-wagging" and dressed in red, white and blue. It is tiring to hear what a noble thing it is to die for one's country when this is precisely the very thing we are all trying to avoid . . .' But Davenport soon went to France where he was wounded. In September 1916 a vicar wrote to say that his son had been killed leading his company, 'a sad knock' for his mother already suffering nervous prostration: in a second letter, 'I think he had the best courage, of daring to do to the utmost what he naturally feared.'

Yet the pathetic hope that the war would soon be over lived on. In yet another letter of November 1915, Second Lieutenant W. D. Womersley wrote that he was 'looking forward to returning to Cambridge for next summer term – maybe I am thinking a year too soon' – more truly three years too soon – 'But a year more or less doesn't seem to matter much in the army.' Thus a window is opened into the sufferings of the soldiers and their sympathetic audience in Cambridge.[19]

The 1920s

For the space between the two World Wars I have used the evidence of two witnesses, both of whom remained very loyal to Emmanuel in after years, both of whom looked back from a distance in time with affection to their undergraduate days: Dr Geoffrey Wynne Thomas, a medical student and captain of the Emmanuel Boat Club in his prime, and a Rowing Blue, who continued to coach Emmanuel boats to a ripe old age – and wrote about 1980 – and Graham Watson, a very notable benefactor to the College library who wrote in the 1990s.[20]

Wynne Thomas observed some of the changes of the intervening years with distaste. 'The basic collegiate system remains, but the colleges are now co-ed . . . A sort of hybrid oak seems to have grown from Sir Walter's acorn . . . [In the 1920s] women were seldom seen in the courts of the colleges, apart from mothers or sisters, except during May Week, whereas now they swarm . . . Occasionally during the Long Vac a mixed double might be played on the Paddock tennis courts. . . . But generally, apart from lectures, the sexes seldom mixed . . .

'The modern undergraduate is just as stupid (or clever) as the old ones of my day. [I doubt if Geoffrey Wynne Thomas would have been impressed at being told that if the tripos results may be trusted the

---

[19] ECA COL.24.
[20] For Geoffrey Wynne Thomas, ECA TUT.18.14; and from Graham Watson, personal communications generously provided for my use.

academic prowess of Emmanuel at least has risen considerably.] Basically, under the long hair, dirty jeans and sandals they are much the same, but the lunatic fringe is larger and more obtrusive . . .' He notes occasional eccentricites of dress in the 1920s: 'trousers in lavender, fawn and other pastel shades . . . Hair was worn "short back and sides" and a few people sported small side-burns . . . College life differed from the present in that the College was smaller and there were fewer dons.[21] The first year was spent in digs, and sometimes the second year also, but the third year was always spent in college . . . Hall in the evenings was the only meal taken there, breakfast and lunch being eaten in one's rooms. Breakfast would be carried by a gyp or kitchen servant on a tray, on his head, covered with a green baize. Lunch, usually bread and cheese, would come out of the gyp room, but lunch (and dinner) could be ordered from the kitchen . . . Hall was presided over by a tall, frock-coated man with a small spade beard, known as Pharaoh, from his striking resemblance to the ancient Egyptian monarchs. His real name was Townsend. He noted down the names of all in hall, for there was no voucher system . . . Pharaoh asked you your name when you first arrived as a fresher and only once was ever known to ask a second time.

'The bedders were usually older than at present' – or seemed so – 'and invariably wore a hat . . . One particularly stately one was Mrs Cornwall, the Duchess, who worked on D staircase. I was looked after by her during one Long Vac term, and very good she was. Shoes were cleaned for you . . . and coal was carried for you, all rooms having open grates. Water was drawn from the gyp room by the bedder for use in the jug and basin in the bedroom . . .'

Wynne Thomas was a highly successful medical student, but pre-eminently a rowing man, and 'bump suppers were noisy affairs, but lasted a much shorter time than nowadays. Speeches were few and short, after which the crews took to the streets and other colleges, frequently noisy but rarely belligerent . . .

'Discipline outside the college was maintained by the proctors aided by their bulldogs [bullers]. Cap and gown had to be worn after dark, and many were the chases of fleet-footed undergraduates by the panting bullers. Speed was of the essence. . . .' The penalty for lesser crimes was a fine of 6s.8d. 'Being sent down was a penalty only for the most heinous of crimes, and rarely exercised. Failure in exams didn't really matter, provided that your parents could pay the fees . . . The tolerance and humour of the progs [proctors], bullers and police on such occasions as Guy Fawkes night were proverbial, and reflected the respect of the

---

[21] The master and 16 fellows and 286 undergraduates in June 1919: *CUC* 1919–20, pp. 881–3, 937.

seniors for the juniors, and vice versa' – a sentiment which can be echoed in Cambridge reminiscences back to the sixteenth century.[22]

Like many students, Wynne Thomas joined in the efforts to break the General Strike of 1926: he describes it as a 'chance to show' they were 'not all "idle, upper class" ' – though to the eyes of the students of the 1960s or later they were showing themselves solidly middle class in supporting the government against working folk. 'On the first day, the queue of volunteers for stokers, engine-drivers, bus-drivers or any other job was at least a quarter of a mile long.' He got a job as a lorry-driver's mate at the station, delivering bacon and groceries, and the women folk 'of Mill Road and that area' hurled abuse at him. Later on he met a train at Stowmarket which was driven by D. R. Goodfellow, captain of the college boat club – who succeeded in getting the train to Norwich. 'It was a great adventure and very instructive'. Through all this he somehow did his academic work, helped on one occasion by H. E. Tunnicliffe of Caius, who hypno-tised him 'to do six hours good work a day. It certainly produced the right result, as even Anatomy lost most of its terrors and became a pleasure.'

'University rags were not uncommon, were usually funny, and rarely ... caused damage ... One of the best ... was conducted in the tunnel [to North Court]. On going to my bath in North Court from New Court one morning in 1926, I found the walls decorated with railway posters: "St Pancras for Scotland", "Go by LMS" etc.; and the underground sign of a circle crossed by the name "Emmalebone". It had all been done with great care and attention to alignment and proportion and symmetry' – but in paint, 'which was only removed with some difficulty ...' Those were 'care-free, happy days, when the horror of the 1914–18 war had faded and the world was bright for the young, and the dark clouds of the 1939–45 war had not yet gathered.'

The dons of the 1920s

Both Geoffrey Wynne Thomas and Graham Watson have much to say of the dons. Thus Wynne Thomas: 'In the May term the dons would fre-quently take coffee in the fellows' garden, and ... the butler, Page, carrying the silver coffee pots at shoulder height, and advancing with stately tread, was a sight to be remembered. Page was the perfect Jeeves in looks, manners, skill and urbanity ... The dons lived a more leisurely and civilised life then. There was not the exam rat-race, and there was time for quiet conversation and reflection. ... As a result, their relation-ship with the undergraduates was one of mutual respect, though perhaps less close than today. The master rarely had much contact with us,

[22] Cf. Venn 1912, p. 17.

although on one occasion I dined at the Lodge and went to the Festival Theatre' with the master and his wife.

Wynne Thomas made many contacts among the fellows. He speaks of Hugh Burnaby, dean from 1921 to 1956,[23] 'a shy, very hard-working man ... I think everyone liked him, but we wished he had been a little more forceful in his methods'. None the less, outside the chapel, where he was much respected, he entered whole-heartedly into a wide range of other activities: as coach of the second boat; as manager of theatricals; as a star of Greenwood's musical evenings, when he 'frequently sang negro spirituals in his beautiful light tenor' voice. Wynne Thomas speaks of J. P. Whitney, Gwatkin's successor as Dixie professor, as 'an elderly man [he was born in 1857], white-haired and of great charm' – he invited Wynne Thomas to lunch, which he reckoned a notable privilege. 'Jock Wallace, an engineer, was always ready to talk, owned a Lagonda car, and was a very friendly extrovert character'. Of G. T. Bennett, a distinguished mathematician elected as long ago as 1893, whom he found an entertaining neighbour at a graduation lunch, he tells the story that Bennett, a notable cyclist and of ingenious mind, 'placed a mirror below his saddle so that by putting his head right down he could see where was going and thus reduce head-resistance'.[24] He none the less lived to a great age. But both Wynne Thomas and Watson speak most of P. W. Wood, the mathematician, and L. H. G. Greenwood, the classic.

'The senior tutor was P. W. Wood,' wrote Wynne Thomas, 'a man with a dry sense of humour and considerable understanding of the undergraduates'; and he goes on to describe Wood dressing him down – as captain of the boat club – after a bump supper night in which a fellow student had been thrown into the pond. 'After about five minutes of stern reprimand I was told I could go. As I left the room he said quietly "I'd have done the same thing myself" '. Watson recalls that Wood 'had both cultivated and grown into the widely held image of what a learned university don must look like. Though a fit man he had a slight stoop, thinning grey hair, very sharp features with a prominent nose' and a pronounced sniff. 'As I was his worst pupil [a doubtful claim, we may think] it has seemed to me strange that we should have developed a relationship in which he was constantly kind and supportive. His wife was a lively American, the antidote to his rather gloomy attitude; and both as an undergraduate and later I often visited them in St Paul's Road ...'

Watson owed his introduction to Greenwood to W. W. Grave, the first professional modern linguist in the fellowship, whose own expertise lay

---

[23] See *ECM* 38 (1955–6), 15–19.
[24] He also has brief mentions of T. S. Hele, Alex Wood, Robert Gardner, Ronald Norrish, Melvill Jones, W. W. Grave (see pp. 438–9, 443–5, 452–3, 526–30, 545–6), and a research fellow called Lavington.

in Spanish and Italian – who later, after a period as vice-chancellor of the University of the West Indies, became University Registrary, and Censor and Master of Fitzwilliam, which he converted into a college – and was to be, in his 90s, the doyen of both societies. Grave 'often came to my room in the evening for I was keen on languages, and on some occasion he must have brought an invitation from Leo [Leonard Greenwood] to join others on a Sunday evening after hall for music and talk in his room' – Greenwood's Sunday evenings were major events in the social life of the college. He goes on to describe Greenwood's small house at Crantock in Cornwall – 'a village where for some years he had been taking parties for walking holidays. So in about 1928 he invited me to join him there in June. . . . It was a wonderful unspoilt place [and] he was a generous host, subject to certain disciplines. To avoid embarrassment over names, regular visitors had' the names of beasts: 'so he was Lion (he was Leo anyway), I was Whale (I never knew why), Grave was Seal . . . There was always grace to be sung before all meals (composed by himself) . . . You were awoken with a whistle and "Dominus vobiscum" and what would have happened had anyone shirked bathing before breakfast I never had cause to know.' A species of golf of his own devising, coast walks and cream teas – and presumably some reading – provided the rest of the menu for these holidays 'as near perfection as one could wish for'.

The Second World War
Thus was Emmanuel in the 1920s, and thus it remained in all essentials until 1939. The outbreak of the war did not lead to the immediate exodus of 1914–15: though many volunteered, conscription came in at once, recruitment was more orderly, much more attention was paid to the likely talents of academic recruits, and in a more technological age scientists of many different kinds were reserved for the exercise of their skills.

Harry Whitcut read engineering from 1941 to 1943, and was then a research scientist for a number of years, later a business man in great chemical firms; finally he and his wife, also a Cambridge graduate, have retired to the Cumbrian fells where he does much service for the local community. Looking back to the 1940s, he writes thus:

'Undergraduates were of four types: scientists, who were allowed two years and then had to go where they were sent (I was sent to Farnborough, the air force research station); arts men, who were only allowed one year; foreigners who, we thought rather unfairly, could stay as long as they wished; and six-month short course armed forces officers, whom the rest of us thought the most unfortunate, being effectively under the control of' some military unit. 'Everyone, unless physically fourth-rate, had to do some war work. I joined the air squadron; and, as I rowed, fire watched one night a week at the boathouse. I also worked in an armaments factory during the long vacation, but this probably had more to do with reading engineering ... At one point undergraduates were asked to go to the Pye factory to work a full shift on Sundays. Many, certainly in the hundreds, volunteered, including me, and we were all given mass production tasks for which little training was necessary. At the end of the first Sunday we were told that the undergraduate shift had produced three times the amount of a normal shift. After three weeks, however, the idea was abandoned as the undergraduates could not stand the boring repetitive work' and stayed away.

'Our instructors in the air squadron were mainly pilots who were given the job for a few months as a reward. One day we were told of a marvellous device, actually a simple slide rule which was strapped to a pilot's knee, and "could work out one's speed, for example if I fly 60 miles in 20 minutes then [twiddling a dial] my speed is 179 miles per hour." All the students burst out laughing as they had done the sum mentally more quickly, but our instructor became furious as "this instrument is never wrong". We never could convince him that *he* was wrong.'

Whitcut's director of studies was Jock Wallace, the engineering fellow, actually in his fifties but seeming older to his pupils. According to his own account, he 'answered engineering tripos questions on the paper itself, writing very small in the margins'. 'We used to see him going across to the cake shop opposite to buy one bun for his tea, and said to ourselves, "poor old man earning a little to eke out his pension".' In this and other ways they underestimated a remarkable character and a very experienced teacher; and 'later we discovered that he was very rich' having lucrative industrial connections.

'At the beginning of my stay we had to wear squares and gowns [in the streets] after dinner, but owing to the presence of many Americans who collected squares, these became unobtainable and were no longer required.' On one occasion 'a group of American airmen, seeing a group of undergraduates one evening all wearing squares, fell on them, but, to the university's delight, had unfortunately picked the entire university boxing team returning from a meeting.

'Emmanuel had handed over two sets of buildings, the north court to the air force [though G. T. Bennett stayed on in their midst] and Emmanuel House and the Hostel to a hospital. Taken together with the removal of some railings for conversion into armaments this meant that climbing into college after midnight was much simplified.

'There were of course very few cars. Then, as now, everyone used a bicycle, but travel was generally difficult. For example we had to do our surveying course in flat Cambridge rather than travel to a more hilly area; the mountaineering club could not go abroad, and neither could anyone else, so I had my first introduction to the Lake District and North Wales. The only train journeys one made, which took a very long time in awful overcrowding, were home for vacations or to such events as climbing. Even so, going to North Wales or other mountains involved long walks or, very occasionally, a hitch.

'I spent the first year in digs but the second in college. Our chief bedder, a formidable lady, obviously thought that the standard of under-graduates had fallen and frequently told us "how her young gentlemen in the past always dressed for dinner and gave banquets in their rooms".

'Food rationing was a constant preoccupation. I think that the college did very well, but effectively all meals had to be in hall, even if one lived in digs, as I did for my first year. So every morning one saw a procession of people carrying their jars of milk, butter and jam to hall. There was a riot, however, when Cottage Cream Pie was served once again. This seemed to consist of potatoes and was served with more potatoes. I well remember the envy we felt when reading the mountaineering club diary of past meets when they had *sent jam back* to the grocers. Clothes were also rationed, so that gowns were bought second hand as indeed were bicycles. So was fuel: if one was fortunate enough to have a window backing onto the college coal dump, then a quick excursion through the window was made for a few extra lumps. Similarly the baths in the bath house had holes bored in their overflows, brass tubes, so that one could only have a very shallow bath. A generous tip to the attendant, however, produced a tube without a hole.'

The 1950s

The war ended in 1945, rationing in the early 1950s; national service lingered until the early 60s. The end of national service brought two generations at once to the gates – and the pressures of the sixties meant that the urge to increase was no temporary affair. Looking forward to this world from the late 1950s, the master, Edward Welbourne, in one of his rambling yet incisive 'Reviews', spelt out what the pressure to increase involved, in buildings and in teaching resources. With Welbourne we began this survey, and he shall conclude it.[25]

'Gone are the days when the middle class, pushing into a university which was almost entirely a seminary for the established Church, a place where country parsons' sons spent three years before they returned to the country to be country parsons themselves, was prepared to pay lodging rents which encouraged jerry builders to run up lodging houses, and respectable women to buy second hand furniture, retire into the

---

[25] *ECM* 40 (1957–8), 1–9: the quotations are from pp. 1–4, 6–8.

basement, and, with the help, maybe, of a husband in a steady job, earn a living without making the social sacrifice of going out to work. Modern health regulations forbid the use of the basements, social change provides good part-time work, more highly esteemed than letting lodgings, and better paid, and young women work out the sum and see that lodging rents barely meet the hire purchase payments for the furniture and that in the middle of the town there are other uses for old houses; and on its out-skirts, houses which can let one bed-sitting-room collect in the fifty-two weeks of the year more from a young girl [who works in an office] than in half a year from an undergraduate.

'. . . Suddenly those who have built the laboratories saw that to fill them they must build bedrooms, and that colleges are not, as reformers thought, a relic of hated feudalism, where the harsh discipline necessary for young priests killed freedom of mind, in whose defence revolutionary youth would man the barricades and make the fortunes of cafe pro-prietors – they were the expedient of a medieval society in which no one expected a scholar to be rich enough to pay his way and where his very poverty drove him into a squalor which was no help to learning. The garrets of romance, into which urban life drove students, can only be the top floor of some other building. We had our garrets too, even in college, let cheaply to the sizars, youths who worked their way through college, until Victorian egalitarianism abolished this. But the finance of the college always depended on new benefaction for extension and for major repair . . .

'It is plain to any visiting old member that we have been spending. On what? On putting our buildings into an order which will make them of use for a good many more years. Have we still a need? Yes, to put right some of our old roofs, to replace most of the electric wiring. Have we any other need? Yes, of an addition, whether in college or out, of new rooms so that we can maintain our admissions. Have we any other need? Yes, the old one, of fellowships, to launch some of our better men into life, to help the provision of that college teaching which most old members know was what was most valuable in their university life. The state grant to the university . . . has greatly strengthened the university teaching staff, but in many subjects it cannot provide the college teaching still necessary, and the rapid growth of the university staff has been more to make Cambridge University a place of research, than to make it a teaching university.[26] It becomes plainer every year that unless we add to our college rooms, and add to our fellowships, we must reduce our admissions.'

He then turned aside to talk of current events, both among senior and

[26] This was a half-truth: and see below, pp. 562–3.

junior members, and of the building of South Court.[27] Next – 'Our athletic achievements have been repeated. We may begin to be thought too much given to athletic feats. . . . Also, we had the best string quartet we have ever had. The additional hall [in South Court] will make college concerts, college plays and some other necessary college activities less troublesome to arrange. But, and for a second year, we had a poor tripos year, especially when measured by the standards of a few years ago. There is no one explanation. A strengthened college teaching staff is needed' – more rooms for fellows were needed, and more for undergraduates in the centre, better work places than distant lodgings. 'Maybe even we have become too games conscious, and perhaps schoolmasters and parents and applicants have thought so and gone elsewhere . . . By what seems to be the cycle of university life, we have moved to a success on the river we have perhaps never had before. However, the freshman's year had its due quota of men in the first class and it seems probable that a year hence, or maybe a year later, we shall recover our academic strength. This is no complaint against the undergraduates who are leaving us. There is no exact correspondence between academic success and success in life . . . What to a large extent seems to have happened is that other colleges have become the social mixture Emmanuel has long been. . . .' And he returned to the theme of increased competition for entry – and the sad effect this had had that some old members found their sons turned away.

'How, but for the increase of our annual admission from about 110 to about 150, we should have fared, we cannot even guess . . . It is not often remembered that the upper forms of all types of school are fuller than they have ever been, and every type of school and indeed every type of applicant, is apt to feel that his kind is not having its fair share. It is still a cause of regret that the old ordinary degree has gone. Now the stout third class man goes too. But often the efficiency of the schools and the pace of work brings here, for a probable second class, men who once would have contented themselves with an ordinary degree. It is not the college which conducts the examinations, nor the college which sets the pace of public teaching, though it is on the shoulders of the college that responsibility lies when a man is admitted who finds himself unable to achieve today's pace. It is only proper to make plain to old members that if we have raised our admission demand, it is in the interest of the candidates themselves. The tripos system makes a simple standard of competitive admission impossible and the search for soft options, so that a place can be found, is rarely wise and seldom successful. There is a new phenomenon. We begin to see boys who have done science creditably at school and who wish to give it up. There is another, the continuing notion that the vacations are holidays, or opportunities for earnings.

[27] See p. 520.

They can be so used to men's loss. There is another, the decline in reading. Perhaps the greater efficiency, or at least the more elaborate provision, of university teaching removes the sense of need to read. Our library provision, indeed the general library provision of the university, is immensely better than it was even in very recent years. No library provision can be a sufficient substitute for what to many seems an extravagance in book buying. Perhaps the scholar's garret has some greater value than better common rooms. We have lost by the loss of the privacy of life.'

In this bewildering kaleidoscope, one may catch fleeting glimpses and penetrating insights into the changing pattern of life in Emmanuel over the previous fifty years, and especially into the predicaments of the mid-twentieth century, as the college prepared to face the new world of the 1960s.

21

From the 1960s to the 1990s[1]

The old world

We are now too near the present to see events clearly in perspective, and the college historian who is an outsider must tread as delicately as Agag. Yet the period from the mid-sixties to the nineties is a fascinating epoch in the history of Cambridge and Emmanuel – it has seen the student revolution, the admission of women, the rapid expansion of the fellowship, a new look in admissions, adaptation to the later twentieth century, the conquest of Park Terrace: a challenging agenda.

Peter Bayley, now Drapers Professor of French, fellow of Caius and ex-fellow of Emmanuel, was an undergraduate from 1963 to 1966, and recalls a traditional Emmanuel, little changed from earlier decades. Translation from home and grammar school in Cornwall to Cambridge 'represented an almost unimaginable freedom and space in which to grow both intellectually and personally', yet 'in cold fact the Emma of my undergraduate years was very distinctly pre-student revolt. . . . I suspect that college life was indistinguishable (apart from the effects of the abolition of National Service)[2] from what it had been at least since rationing ended. It was sober, orderly, well-behaved; it had a very strong sense of its own historical identity (almost any convention could be defended by a mention of "our Puritan tradition" and the Harvard Scholar was a revered figure) and thought of itself as somewhat shut off from the rest of the university. The Jacobean ditty about "the pure house of Emmanuel" still struck a chord. Partly this was the effect of geography: before South Court was built and the Bus Station extended and developed, the college seemed to exist in a green oasis of quiet. As a freshman I lived alone in vile digs in Pretoria Road (Welbourne had a ludicrous theory that

---

[1] In this chapter I have been especially indebted to Peter Bayley, David Newsome, Gerard Evans, Ronald Gray, Derek Brewer, and Lord St John of Fawsley.

[2] After the end of the war, National Service survived for fluctuating periods of approximately 18 months to 2 years until the early 1960s. From 1945 there was an element of undergraduates straight from school, and a majority of veterans. Since the 1960s the practice of intercalating a year off between school and university has meant that while some have come at 18 or so, many freshers are a year older. 'War-time' rationing survived well into the 1950s.

landladies provided a comforting bridge between life at home and living in college) and had to cycle every morning for breakfast come rain, shine or snow. One passed through Midsummer Common and Christ's Pieces as through continuous countryside. On the other side lay Parker's Piece. [Those who have lived beyond Parker's Piece may not share this pastoral recollection. C.B.] Inside the college, life revolved around the Paddock (for access to the Library and the Junior Reading Room at the end of Old Court) – another vast green space. It was a distinctly un-urban idyll.

'But undoubtedly the major factor in giving us this sense of an identity apart was Edward Welbourne's admissions policy. We had all been admitted by him, most (though not me) after a memorable interview: there was much swapping of anecdotes about these encounters among my contemporaries, and his letters announcing the result were treasured. He favoured the sons of Emmanuel men (all but a few of my closest friends were such), and was suspicious of the products of the grander public schools.' [The class of 1963 were recruited in fact from Public Boarding Schools and Grammar Schools in about equal numbers, with a smaller number from Public day schools][3] 'and their fathers were schoolmasters, clergymen, doctors, solicitors, civil servants. There was an almost universal notion that we were in some way being trained for public service (presumably in these very same professions); and Welbourne openly regretted the disappearance of the Indian Civil Service as a career. . . .

'Undergraduate social life mirrored these rather earnest policies . . . There was nothing like the current JCR (though . . . one could use the pretty inaccessible attic of the Old Library then called the JCR). Hall was obligatory (noone ever cooked in a gyp room) but perfunctory: my chief memory is of watery soups and endless braised celery; the servants were either townie youths or immensely aged retainers (one of these, much loved, was Sidney; he was nearly blind and discovered whether a water glass was empty by enquiring "avez-voo?" and sticking his fingers into it when clearing away – which he did during rather than after meals). After hall, people took turns in inviting their friends to coffee. Strong drink featured hardly at all. The centre of life was the Reading Room, handsomely furnished as a miniature Union chamber; and the elected officers of the debating society had something of the status of today's union officers. These elections were hotly contested, and the debates – largely on themes of public policy, but with occasional light relief – massively attended. Some of our stars rose to prominence in the Union . . .

---

[3] For these categories, see below, Appendix 4; the figures (very approximately) were 40 from Public Boarding Schools, 14 from Public Day, 37 from Grammar Schools: i.e. 91 from British schools out of total admissions of 116, which included at least 13 postgraduates from other universities.

'But the purpose of leisure activities was very definitely not to produce stars but to enable everyone to join in. I know virtually nothing about organised sport; but in the Easter Term the Paddock was laid out for lawn tennis and anyone could play, and there was croquet outside the Library. This sense of communal activity was most apparent in music, rather to the horror of the professional musicians in my year ... The termly concerts were attended by everyone, but the standard was appalling. The presiding genius was Leo Greenwood, despite his great age.[4] Amateur music-making took place over markedly astringent claret in his rooms in Emmanuel House, and he was the organiser of the annual Messiah in which everyone was encouraged to sing.

'Greenwood was one of very few dons whom most undergraduates knew: his funeral, in the snow, was a memorable event ... One of the forums for meeting the dons was the William Law Society, traditionally run by the dean (Howard Root, whose role as an observer at Vatican II made him a glamorous figure)[5] and regularly attended by Greenwood and the vice-master, Edward Wilson. Links with tutors were formal, if frequent (there were still absits as well as exeats);[6] I do not recall any contemporary seeking "counselling" from a tutor, though many did so from their friends. Some of the younger dons, such as Robert Coleman – who organised the public-spirited team which Emma annually turned out to run the Societies' Fair – were notably friendly, and the master [Edward Welbourne to 1964] was famous for random conversations in the courts; but there was a definite divide. Christian names were never used.'

Peter Hunter Blair was the senior tutor, a man deeply loved by the small circle who came to know him well, and a greatly respected historian of Anglo-Saxon England: in his last years he was to enjoy an Indian summer – lifted from the sadness of his first wife's illness and death by a new marriage, and enjoying at last the recognition his careful scholarship deserved: he was not elected FBA until 1980.[7] In the 1960s he seemed to the young Bayley an austere, even frightening figure; and his man-to-man talk to the freshmen on 'what was expected of us, and the limits of toleration' made a great impression. 'The porters would call us "sir", but we would obey them; ... gate-hours were firmly enforced, but there was nothing to stop us from climbing in if we could escape detection. We

---

[4] See above, p. 546.
[5] Root went to be professor of theology in Southampton University at the turn of 1965–6, to be succeeded by Don Cupitt, one of the most widely known and admired of Emmanuel's deans.

    Among the many college societies of that era, the best recorded is the Mildmay Essay Club, founded in 1883, and still flourishing (see Shallcross 1983).
[6] 'Absit' meant permission for a brief absence during term; 'exeat' means permission to leave college for the vacation.
[7] Hunter Blair 1983–4; Clemoes 1984. His first wife's death in 1963 was followed by his second's soon after; his fortunes were happily revived by his marriage to Pauline in 1969.

could run away from the proctor's bulldogs, and they had no jurisdiction in college. But we were gentlemen' – if we were caught, we must tell the truth.

From 1966 to 1969 Peter Bayley was a research student and 'virtually lost contact with the college. . .'. Accommodation for Emmanuel graduates was only provided in the Barnwell Hostel at a later date[8] – 'and so I moved into "the town" and eventually migrated to the Jesus graduate hostel at Little Trinity. I also spent over half of my three years in Paris, and my supervisor was an Oxford don. So my contact with Emma was limited to a few obligatory dinners and to formal lunches with the graduate tutor . . . All this remoteness meant that I had a sharp sense, when I returned as a fellow, of the changes that had taken place. My absence coincided, of course, with the general "student revolution" . . . : it was an almost unimaginably different world that I found in 1969 – and I think the change was largely wrought by David Newsome.'

Sir Gordon Sutherland

For many years the masters of Emmanuel had been former senior tutors or at least pillars of the fellowship. In Cambridge at large it was canvassed already in the 1920s, and widely canvassed in the twenty years after the second World War by many, especially the younger dons, that academic eminence must be sought in a head before all else; or, following the example of Peterhouse in the 1920s and early 30s which elected first a notable public figure then a field-marshal, that one should seek a head whose name carried weight in the world as well as in the parlour. Such a division of opinion, when it is first carried into action, naturally leads to anxieties and regrets; for it goes to the heart of a community and its values and personal relations. In the 1980s and 90s all communities contemplate a wide range of choice; but in 1964 the election of Sir Gordon Sutherland – an eminent scientist and public figure who had no previous links with Emmanuel – represented a new departure.

Sutherland was a scientist and a scientific administrator of great distinction, and a conscientious leader in many fields of enterprise, including (as a young man) rock-climbing in the Cairngorms and roof-climbing in Cambridge.[9] Born in Caithness, he received at St Andrews a thorough grounding in a range of sciences with their centre in theoretical physics, before moving to Cambridge and Trinity for graduate work and research. 'By the end of my first year in Cambridge', he said himself, 'it was clear to me that I did not have the mathematical ability to be a first rate theoretical

[8] See pp. 519–20.
[9] Sheppard 1982, p. 596. What follows is based on the Royal Society memoir, Sheppard 1982, and the sympathetic notices by Sir David Williams and Professor Brian Thrush in *ECM* 62 (1979–80), 12–19.

physicist and I decided to switch (at least, partly) to experimental work'.[10] He was soon immersed in infrared spectrosocpy, which was to be the central interest of his life as a research scientist. First in Cambridge, then in Ann Arbor, Michigan (1931–3), then in Cambridge once more, he pursued the ramifications of his field widely and deeply; and from 1935 he was a fellow of Pembroke and began to gather a circle of colleagues and pupils to extend the range of his work. The war of 1939–45 was both a stimulus and a check: it provided remarkable opportunities for him to use his skills in Cambridge and elsewhere; but it hindered the development of more advanced techniques. In the late 1940s he was one of a number of physicists and chemists who worked out new methods of research, new technology for speeding it, and the almost infinite variety of uses to which infrared spectroscopy could be harnessed. From 1949 to 1956 he was in Ann Arbor once more, as professor. One of his research group of that era has written of him:

'It was always Gordon's hallmark to encourage a deep understanding of phenomena and also to listen carefully to ideas presented by his colleagues. He certainly was generous in encouraging' younger scientists '. . . His was, in fact, a deeper generosity – that of the spirit – and as a result the research group was a harmoniously functioning one'.[11] He and his colleagues spread their interests from many aspects of physics through physical chemistry to biophysics and biochemistry – a characteristic example of the defiance of boundaries which has marked so many leading scientists.

In 1956 he returned to England to be Director of the National Physical Laboratory in Teddington, to which he brought a number of distinguished colleagues who helped him to build up its reputation as a centre for basic as well as applied research – on the pattern of similar institutes in America.[12] He had remarkable gifts as a planner and scientific policymaker. But in the age of rapid university expansion in the early 1960s, public policy tended to see the universities as the home of basic research and to concentrate applied research in government labs. The future became less serene in Teddington, and 'there is no doubt that Sutherland was very pleased to return to Cambridge in 1964 . . . He was delighted to be invited to be the master of Emmanuel', an offer the more flattering in that he had no previous connection with the college.[13] He entered whole-heartedly into his new tasks; and his talented Swedish wife greatly

---

[10] Sheppard 1982, p. 592.
[11] Quoted Sheppard 1982, p. 609.
[12] Brian Thrush cites the United States National Bureau of Standards, N. Sheppard the National Research Council of Canada at Ottawa (*ECM* 62 (1979–80), 18; Sheppard 1982, p. 610).
[13] Sheppard 1982, p. 613.

helped him in entertaining students. Brian Thrush says of him: 'Gordon Sutherland was a modest and rather shy man; those who penetrated his natural reserve found a generous spirited friend whose wide range of interests and achievements provided the basis for many fascinating conversations.'[14] But his shyness inhibited such close relations with others of the rapidly growing fellowship; and the transition from the NPL 'to Emmanuel was not easy', wrote Sir David Williams, for he 'had to come to terms with the vagaries of government by Governing Body'.[15] The difficulty of passing from the more or less autocratic direction of a large laboratory to the game of manipulating and being manipulated which tends to be the role of a head of house in twentieth century Oxbridge has baffled others of like eminence.[16] But Sutherland brought very positive gifts too: Williams notes 'a blend of caution and optimism' in his attitude to many aspects of college affairs, from finance to the admission of women – his slow conversion to firm support for admission helped those colleagues who had to tread a similar path.[17] He took a particular interest in the college's relations with Harvard, and played a leading role in the moves which led, by Dr Herchel Smith's generosity, to the foundation of the Herchel Smith Scholarship to Harvard. He entered university affairs with vigour, helping the foundation of Wolfson College, and sitting on a number of committees, syndicates and boards. Most characteristic was his concern for the Fitzwilliam Museum, for he shared with his wife, the daughter of a Swedish artist, an enthusiastic and instructed interest in many varieties of artistic creation: he himself collected Chinese porcelain, and was also a trustee of the National Gallery.[18] He retired in 1977 to enjoy a sadly brief spell as life fellow, dying in 1980.

However difficult the opening of Sutherland's reign, the college to which Peter Bayley returned in 1969 was in many respects more notably a community than hitherto.[19] Partly this was the new tutorial style of Newsome and his colleagues. 'The younger generation of fellows, typified by David Williams [later Vice-Chancellor] was now much closer to the undergraduates. South Court, too, had made an immense difference, not least because of its bar – widely patronised by the younger fellows as well as by the junior members, and very much the social centre of the college. There was now a graduate hostel,[20] and the BAs were much more prominent in college life. The new chaplain, Raymond Hockley,[21] and

---

[14] *ECM* 62 (1979–80), 19.
[15] *ECM* 62 (1979–80), 13. Cf. Sheppard 1982, p. 614.
[16] Sir Neville Mott describes a similar experience on becoming master of Caius in 1959 in Mott 1986, esp. pp. 128–9; cf. Brooke 1993, p. 266.
[17] *ECM* 62 (1979–80), 14.
[18] *ECM* 62 (1979–80), 19.
[19] In his personal communication: see p. 552.
[20] For the South Court and the Barnwell Hostel, see pp. 519–20.
[21] Later precentor of York Minster (and see p. 536).

first full-time domestic bursar, Ned Foxton, kept virtual open house. New fellows were encouraged to join in and do things . . . The governing body and its disputes loomed importantly in people's lives' – effective chairmanship was not one of Sutherland's strongest points. 'How sad it was that so few had the chance to get to know the charming and talented Lady Sutherland. The generational conflict was beginning to be focussed on the question of admitting women. But corporate togetherness was much sustained by the daily post-lunch bowls in the fellows' garden – apparently the only indulgence of the spartan bursar, Gus Ward. Though no longer vice-master, Edward Wilson was the centre of parlour conversation – often prolonging it over generously poured single malts in his own rooms overlooking the Paddock – and maintained an amusing duet with the star entertainer among the younger conversationalists, Gerard Evans. Life, perhaps especially for a resident fellow, was extremely comfortable materially: the delicious breakfasts served in the elegantly redecorated fellows' breakfast room, the hours in the swimming pool jealously preserved for fellows' use alone on summer afternoons, the circle around the generously stoked Parlour fire on winter evenings, are some of the memories I retain of what was virtually life in a first-class country hotel. But it was also extraordinarily stimulating intellectually; and my brief time there was mightily and memorably enjoyable.'

David Newsome
David Newsome, the distinguished historian of the Victorian Church, was senior tutor from 1965 to 1970 and headmaster of Christ's Hospital and Wellington College over the next twenty years; while senior tutor he was able to publish the masterpiece of historical biography, *The Parting of Friends* – on the Wilberforces and the Mannings (1966) – which established his fame as a historian. Let us return to the 1960s, and listen to the witness of the senior tutor himself, which David Newsome has generously provided.

'I became senior tutor at a pretty dramatic time in the history of Cambridge. I was very young to carry such a senior appointment (at 36), and actually found myself running the tutorial show after only one year as an assistant tutor in charge of admissions. I had very little idea of what I was letting myself in for. Only six years before (when I returned as an official fellow), I was struck by the apathy within the undergraduate body. In 1965, a new world seemed to have come into existence. My first inkling of the new problems that I would have to tackle came a few weeks before the start of the new academic year. One of our major scholars, due to come into residence that September, was charged in London with a heroin offence, and I had to make a snap decision whether to allow him to take up his place. One lives and learns, and I had a lot to learn about drugs, which – up till then – were a problem unknown, I suspect, to any senior tutor. I let the lad come into residence, after seeing him with his father and laying down certain stringent conditions. He broke them within a few weeks, by which time I had three serious drug offenders on my hands. All three were eventually sent down; and I realised then that the mass of the undergraduates were a hundred per cent behind me in taking tough action.

'I can honestly say that the five years of my senior tutorship coincided with the stormiest period of Cambridge history before or since. It was the time of student unrest, "sit-ins", demonstrations orchestrated by semi-professional *enragés*.[22] . . . One of the disturbing aspects of this movement was that one could never count on the trouble-makers actually going down after they had taken their degrees. They stayed on unofficially, many of them lodging in basements in the Warkworth Street area, so that they could influence the next batch of freshmen to carry on the fight. One was sometimes faced with very difficult decisions over admissions. What should one do with a candidate who had all the hallmarks of a trouble-maker, and yet possessed the credentials for acceptance?

'In twenty years as headmaster of very large boarding-schools, I never met with anything approaching the range of crises and problems that I had to deal with as senior tutor – some tragic (two suicides, and two attempted suicides), some rather exciting and comic: a threatened march on the college by disaffected occupants of the Senate House in order to tear down our gates – I was of the conservative school that refused to countenance the abolition of gate-hours – which was thwarted by fear of confronting the posse of muscular young men whom I enrolled to protect our property.

'I would not wish to give the impression that Emma had more of its fair share of trouble-makers than other colleges. The vast majority of the junior members were sane, stable, and supportive to tradition and the old ways. We were thought by the student politicians to be very much "anti-progressive", which was probably true. Certainly there was a marked divide among those who attended Tutorial Reps.[23] Those who fought to preserve the status quo (on the grounds that traditions abandoned through the pressure of a transitory generation, and a minority at that, could never be recovered) were a group consisting of Gus [Augustus] Caesar of St Catharine's, Babbage of Magdalene, Richard Bainbridge of Corpus and myself . . .' – though these alignments did not reflect unanimous opinion among the dons of any college.

'Times were changing in other respects. Although my disposition was to stand by the ancient ways, I actually was responsible for a number of

---

[22] For recent literature on this, see Brooke 1993, pp. 521–6, 555–9 and references.
[23] The inter-collegiate committee of senior tutors or their representatives.

innovations, especially related to admissions, with a view to broadening our entry.

'1 I introduced the policy of making conditional offers' – to be carried much further when David Williams and Alan Baker were senior tutors in the 70s.[24]

'2 I also introduced the policy of inviting a group of about twenty headmasters (ten from schools who regularly sent us boys, and ten from schools who never sent us candidates) to spend a relaxed weekend at Emmanuel, avoiding the conference atmosphere, and laying stress on informal chats over dinner and the like and with individual directors of studies. This was a great success.

'3 I made a point of marketing the college outside – by visiting schools to give prizes away, or to talk to common rooms about admissions procedure . . .

'4 More questionable – though I still think that it was a rewarding policy – I insisted that the senior tutor should always have within his gift at least three admissions each year, which he would resolve himself without necessarily gaining the acquiescence of the directors of studies . . . I brought in some outstanding talent on this ticket – usually musicians or sportsmen, I must admit – but they all brought distinction to the college and none ever let me down. [Newsome's sportsmen were long remembered by Mr and Mrs Manning at the sports ground in Wilberforce Road.]

'5 Since I found myself running a practically new and raw team of tutors, I introduced the practice of a weekly tutorial lunch – that is, the tutors would lunch together alone in the Gardner Room to discuss individual problems and college policy . . .

'The concept of the tutorial function was changing, marked by a reluctance to take on disciplinary responsibilities and embarrassment over the pastoral or paternalistic role'. To this Newsome himself gave a new orientation by encouraging closer relationships – what has been called the avuncular style – between dons, especially the younger dons, and students. The reluctance Newsome describes 'was not unrelated to the issue of student politics of the time. I suspect I was about the last senior tutor to impose the punishment of gating' – confining to the college for a day or a week. 'My gating of six undergraduates caught climbing over the wall in the small hours led to a cartoon in *Varsity*' of the senior tutor of Emmanuel hiding in a dustbin to ambush offenders. 'All the young men concerned became firm friends . . .' Newsome retains his sense that much was lost in the changes of the sixties and seventies, and reckons a later generation 'yearned for the sort of Cambridge that you and I remembered as undergraduates [I of the 1940s, he of the early 50s] but in

[24] See below, pp. 564–5.

many respects it proved impossible to put the clock back – over [the wearing of] gowns, gate-hours etc.'

His is not the style of the senior tutors of the 1990s – but one might search in vain for a tutor who could boast with him of knowing every junior member 'at least by sight. After matriculation one year, when the 120 freshmen signed the college book in the Gallery and also had their photographs taken, to be lodged in their files, the photographer got in a terrible muddle so that the photos were unidentified and were passed to the head porter without any crib' – and he came in alarm to the senior tutor, who arranged them all in order though they had only been in residence three weeks.

The enlarging of the fellowship

In 1919 the fellowship had numbered sixteen; in 1939 twenty-two. After the war there was a slow but steady advance in numbers, which became a canter in the 1970s and 80s. There were 37 in 1960, 62 in 1990. Almost every college has shown a similar growth. Thus Caius had 28 fellows in 1919, 31 in 1939, 51 in 1960 – and passed the 100 mark in the early 1990s. Even Peterhouse, with 8 fellows in 1919 and 9 in 1939, has grown to 18 in 1960, and 31 in 1990.[25] There have been many pressures to produce this effect. The college has deliberately increased the number of research fellows, thus contributing generously, as do all Cambridge colleges according to their means, to the opportunities for young scholars to develop their skills and compass a substantial piece of research at the outset of their careers. At the other end professorial fellows have increased; and the early retirements of the 1980s brought more retired fellows. The growth of academic bureaucracy has bred professional administrators – in Emmanuel, a small number only so far. The whole nature of the college staff has indeed altered: bedmakers and gyps have declined in numbers in a world unaccustomed to servants; economy drives have reduced the number of porters; secretaries have appeared to service tutors and bursars – and been converted into computer experts of varying skills and grades. This process has modified the fellowship only modestly so far.[26]

Far and away the largest increase has been in teaching fellows, from 10 or 11 when Welbourne was first senior tutor in the late 1930s, to 45 under the senior tutorship of Gerard Evans in the early 1990s – a figure he persuaded the Governing Body officially to adopt. Teaching has become more professional; disciplines have multiplied; students look to be effectively directed within their colleges; the vast increase in university teachers has created a much larger pool of talent than existed fifty years ago.

[25] These figures are computed from *CUC*.
[26] See e.g. p. 454.

There have been some casualties in the process. The old private coach, who lived or partly lived by piece-work teaching, has disappeared. There is much freelance teaching by scholars who have no posts and by research students: but it is usually a great deal more specialised, and more related to special needs, than the teaching of the erstwhile coaches who often taught over a wide area, and were rarely creative scholars.[27]

Bertram Goulding Brown (1881–1964) 'represented the unprivileged Cambridge teacher: he was one of the survivors of the ancient order of coaches; he had no fellowship; he had no scholarly reputation outside his immediate circle. He had settled in Cambridge after unsuccessfully competing for a Trinity fellowship in 1906; he lectured for the English tripos during the Great War on Donne; he became librarian of the Seeley' – the History Faculty library; he directed studies for Downing and Emmanuel. 'His professional income was sparse; his home and family were supported by private means. He was not wholly without privileges: he enjoyed dining rights in Emmanuel, and a room, in which he taught for forty years. "To enter Goulding Brown's room as a freshman . . . was to imbibe at once the ethos of *semper eadem*" ' – David Newsome writes as one who entered it in the early 1950s.[28]

' "Neither furniture nor furnishings had changed since he first took root there during the 1914 war. Perhaps the vast library had increased . . . There were cabinets of various sizes, containing faded letters and spidery notes; old pipes reposing in sombre ashtrays; a mantlepiece cluttered with Christmas cards from ten years back; by the fire, two chairs – one high-backed and ample, from which the frail Edwardian figure, with long thin legs crossed above the knee and at the ankles, surveyed you solemnly as you fumbled for your essay; the other – reserved for pupils – a huge wicker monstrosity, its seat only inches from the floor, so that the act of sitting seemed like dropping into a void."

' "The Middle Ages were studied according to an established pattern, based on the classics of his own youth; most moderns were dismissed, Gaillard Lapsley as 'ingenious'. Yet the fare was never stale and the lesson was worth learning: the books he admired were of lasting worth." '

Goulding Brown was a college lecturer, but never a fellow: normally now the two offices go together, and the basic college teaching in almost all disciplines can be provided from within the fellowship – even if specialised college teaching is compassed by an ever more complicated series of exchanges. A student may be supervised in several different colleges, but at least he will probably have a director of studies who is a fellow of

---

[27] For a notable exception, the medievalist G. G. Coulton, see Brooke 1993, pp. 276–7 and refs. (where he is wrongly stated to have studied at St John's: he was an undergraduate at St Catharine's, and in later life a fellow of St John's).

[28] This and the next two paragraphs are from Brooke 1993, p. 279, quoting Newsome 1984, pp. 104–6.

his own. This is in a sense the logical outcome of the policies of Phear and Chawner, to produce effective teaching within the college staff. But the numbers involved are much larger than they dreamed of, partly owing to the great proliferation of triposes and subjects – and the poll man and his general degree have disappeared. Partly it reflects growing specialisation in teaching. Down to the 1950s history dons, such as Welbourne and Goulding Brown, taught history: the weakness of the method was that supervisors could be alarmingly ignorant of some of the fields they taught; its strength, that they often understood the student's problems more clearly, and could make their pupils really explain what they were trying to say. This was especially true of special subjects, the most specialised of all – in which in those days some supervisors in a sense learned with their pupils and lifted them to new heights of historical understanding. Since the 1950s supervision has become a specialism – and college teaching of special subjects wholly forbidden, on the specious ground that it may be unfair if some colleges can command expertise in the subject. History has become in a sense more professional – in another sense less so, since the good students are more spoonfed than before. Similar changes have taken place in almost all disciplines; and to provide even a nucleus of profes-sional teaching in a college demands a larger teaching staff.

At the same time, in the 1950s – and even more in the 60s and 70s – the university staff expanded very rapidly, and whole new disciplines appeared. The college fellowship had always been a mark of distinction separating the elite (or the fortunate) from the rank and file of coaches and private tutors; but in the 1920s a new distinction arose, between those who were university teachers and fellows – and those who had university posts, but none in a college. The Cambridge Committee of the Asquith Commission on Oxbridge of the early 1920s – which issued in the new university and college statutes of 1926 – had deliberately separated the university and the college sector as much as possible, in the hope of attracting as much government money to the impoverished university sector as could be. They never intended that the staff should become two separate bodies, but that was the effect. In 1928–9 there were already 29% of university teaching officers without fellowships; in the post-war years the figure rose steeply, to 46% in 1961–2. The heroic measures of the 1960s brought the figure down to 16% by 1989 – but nowhere near the Oxford percentage, which has been reduced more or less to zero.[29] These measures were the subject of earnest discussion by the Bridges Commit-tee, and after its report in 1962, by the whole university and all the colleges. Bridges urged the colleges to open their gates to many new fellows; some of the committee also strongly urged the founding of new colleges – also much needed to provide a collegiate home for the rapidly

[29] Brooke 1993, pp. 574–5.

increasing number of postgraduate students and visiting scholars. The most dramatic outcome was the foundation of a posse of new colleges in the 1960s and 70s.[30] One of these, Wolfson College, had a specific provision at the outset that half its fellowships should go to UTOs (university teaching officers) elected by seniority – and though this was soon modified, the principle remained intact. Most of the older colleges protested that their character would be altered, their buildings would overflow – yet something they would do to help.

They did far more than might have been expected, especially where they saw a teaching need. For if the need is urgent a college may have to provide the whole salary of a college lecturer; if there is an eligible university lecturer free to take a fellowship and college lectureship, he or she can be hired much more economically, for the university pays most of the salary. Thus conscientious adherence to Bridges could often go hand in hand with enlightened self-interest. However motivated, the increase in teaching fellows has been the main cause of the growth in the fellowship – and so of one of the most striking changes in the history of the college. But we observed at the outset that growth was not confined to the teaching fellows. The inner core of tutors and teaching fellows has always tended to regard professorial fellows – or fellows of academic distinction in fields in which the college has few candidates or none – as drones. In the last twenty years there has been a vast increase in the number of university professors, by the founding of new chairs and the conferment of strangely called *ad hominem* professorships on many men, and a few women too. Professorial fellows, retired fellows, research fellows: all these have contributed to the growth. In many colleges there has been earnest debate as to the best size for the fellowship. Some think that the colleges have a duty to provide for the UTOs; some think any substantial increase means reducing standards of entry to the fellowship; some think it means raising them – welcoming in scholars of real distinction even if they have few college pupils; some worry greatly about the effect on the community of a large increase; some take thought for the size of the combination rooms or the parlours; some attempt to compute the relative claims of fellows and students for rooms in college. There have been no simple answers, no clear-cut victories in these arguments: they will go on so long as the colleges survive. Meanwhile the historian notes that fellowships have grown.

Admissions

Emmanuel has been the pioneer among the Cambridge colleges in abandoning an admission system based on the Colleges' Entrance Examination, for which all entrants competed – most of them after spending a

---

[30] Brooke 1993, chap. 18.

third year in their sixth forms preparing for it. The new path to admission is based on conditional offers made after interview to sixth-formers who have not yet taken their A-levels: they are conditional on specified A-level results. The tradition of Welbourne's day had been to admit a high proportion of grammar school boys: the transition in most regions from grammar to comprehensive schools might have tended to reduce the proportion of entrants from the public sector. 'The college recognised', writes Gerard Evans, senior tutor from 1986 to 1994, 'that far fewer candidates (especially in state schools) were in a position to take the third year in the sixth form, which was normally needed to prepare for the Cambridge Colleges' Entrance Examination.' Already 'in the late 1960s some offers were made to pre-A-level candidates, and thereafter an increasing proportion came in by that method: in 1970 10% of the applicants were pre-A-level; by 1983 65% of applicants were, securing 50% of places.' In 1984 came an announcement by Alan Baker, then senior tutor, that the college was withdrawing altogether from the Entrance Exam. 'It will be the first Cambridge – indeed, Oxbridge – college to do so.' 'Applicants for admission to Emmanuel will be assessed on their headteachers' reports and on interviews by the college's tutors and directors of studies': thus the press release of 7 February 1984. Since 1984 all Cambridge colleges have adopted the conditional offer as the normal mode of entry.

Summing up the achievement of the 25 years to 1994, and looking forward, and commenting on the more structured links with the student body, some wrought by tutorial contact with the students, some by representation of the Emmanuel College Students' Union and the Middle Common Room on the Governing Body, Gerard Evans wrote thus:

'Partly as a result of the student protest movement, the college has developed a system whereby students, through representation and consultation, play a greater role in the college's decision-making process. Throughout the period, tutorial concerns have been to secure a wider social and geographical spread from which our students are drawn, to maintain and increase the effective teaching fellowship, to maintain and improve care for student welfare, both individual and collective, and to extend and modernise the facilities available for student use. Important objectives of the current [1994] Development Fund therefore include:

'(1) to maintain and increase the teaching fellowship;
'(2) to establish more research studentships, and to make available more generous funds for the relief of hardship;
'(3) to provide improved physical facilities: the new building[31] will include a theatre, a new MCR and quiet reading room for

---

[31] See pp. 520–1.

students, and music practice rooms, but additional provision of
public rooms and teaching rooms must also be met.'

And beside all these he has stressed, among the achievements of the
1970s and 80s, 'the admission and integration of women into the college.'

The admission of women

Most people of good will agreed, as the second World War drew to a
close, that there must be more space for women in Oxford and Cambridge than heretofore. The only problem was how to provide it. The one
solution which was almost unthinkable was that women should enter the
colleges of men – almost, but not quite. On 6 December 1947, Peter
Hunter Blair recorded in his diary that his 'Placet' as proctor to the Grace
proposing the admission of women to the University 'was literally the
last word in an argument that has been going on for half a century and
more . . . Shall we be arguing about co-educational Colleges after another
half century?'.[32] When Churchill College was on the drawing board in the
late 1950s an enterprising woman suggested to Winston that it ought to
take women, and Lady Churchill and he (it is said) were quite taken with
the idea. But the great man was very quickly put in his place by his
advisers: the funds had been raised for a *male* college: some donors would
not countenance a mixed community. The first fruit of endeavours to
improve the lot of women in Cambridge and to increase their numbers
was the foundation of New Hall in 1954. In the 1960s came new graduate
colleges which were mixed, and Lucy Cavendish, which provided fellowships for underprivileged women scholars and student places for mature
women who had missed their chance earlier in life.[33] In 1966 the Franks
Report drew attention to the proportion of women students in Oxford,
still only 18% – while in Cambridge in the early 1960s Newnham, Girton
and New Hall accounted for less than 10% of all students entering the
University.[34] The demand for equal opportunities was in the wind, and
much discussed. There was at this time intense debate within many
colleges already as to their role and destiny – and the meaning of the new
relationships of the sexes, the new-found adulthood of the students, for
the future. Then in the late 1960s came widespread student demand for
the admission of women to male colleges. It is true that the evidence
is confused and incomplete as to the extent of student demand for
'co-residence'; but there is no doubt of the contrast between the situation
in the 1960s and 70s and in 1897 and 1921 when the votes of the Senate
against admitting women to the university had been anticipated by far

---

[32] Clemoes 1984, p. 455. For what follows, see Brooke 1993, p. 569 and n.6.
[33] Brooke 1993, pp. 527–8, 569–73.
[34] Franks 1966, I, 51 (no. 101), II, 81 (no. 142); *CUC* 1967–8, p. 481.

larger majorities among the students in the university to the same end.[35] The historian is bound to observe that a very major change in the ethos and institutions of Oxford and Cambridge took place with extraordinary rapidity: the first woman fellow of King's was elected in 1970, and by 1979 most Cambridge colleges were mixed; by 1987 this included all the men's colleges – only Newnham, New Hall and Lucy Cavendish remained for women alone.[36]

The extent of the novelty in Emmanuel is well illustrated by the Founder's Statute which declared: 'None shall hold secret converse with a woman anywhere, especially in any of the rooms of the said college, which we desire no woman ever to enter, if she be alone, nor to remain in the same, except in time of sickness, in a manner known and approved of by the master or his deputy.'[37] Apart from masters' wives[38] and bed-makers, and tutors' wives in Emmanuel House, it was a male society. 'One or two married fellows lived in college', writes Ronald Gray, 'after 1945, at a time of housing shortage, until the late 1950s. But the atmosphere of the fellows' parlour was then rather that of a London Club in the old days'.[39] As in most of the male colleges, fellows' wives dined only on special occasions – dinner in the master's lodge or (from the 1960s) the annual ladies' night in hall and gallery. Gradually it came to be accepted that women might dine at high table – and so eventually fellows' wives found their way there: the story was repeated, with many variations, in all the older men's colleges: the women's colleges entertained men with a readier grace. But in the late 60s and early 70s a much more radical change was in the wind; and for its progress in Emmanuel we have the guidance of Ronald Gray.

Whatever the situation elsewhere in Cambridge, 'there was no strong pressure from students at Emmanuel. A referendum held in 1973 was answered by only 35% of the undergraduates and 20% of the graduates, although a large majority favoured the introduction of co-residence even if it meant a reduction in the number of men'. Meanwhile, 'in 1969 seven fellows [had] raised the question of co-education, and two of them were asked to write a report, which was discussed the next year and met a divided reception, almost entirely according to age. All but one fellow of those over 50 were opposed, all but one of those under 50 more or less in favour of admitting women somehow, somewhen' – in contrast to Caius where there were some strong supporters among the older fellows, some leading opponents among the younger. Like many colleges, Emmanuel

---

[35] Cf. Brooke 1993, pp. 528–30 with ibid. pp. 325–6.
[36] Brooke 1993, pp. 529n., 531n. New Hall now admits men to their fellowship.
[37] Stubbings 1993a, p. 62 (no. 22), quoted by Ronald Gray in 'The admission of women, 1969–97', a paper generously offered for my use, since published in *ECM* 1996, pp. 67–75.
[38] See p. 421 n.23.
[39] See n.37.

had specifically forbidden the admission of women in a statute passed in 1926 and confirmed in 1952[40] – in the wake of the admission of women to the university in 1948. 'To change the statute required a vote of not less than two-thirds of the' whole fellowship and this took time to achieve.[41] A new statute was agreed in 1974 – and approved by university and Privy Council; but this did not in itself decree that women be admitted; rather it laid down that they be not admitted unless a vote of two thirds of the governing body as normally defined, excluding the older life fellows and the fellows most recently elected, decree that they should. And such a vote was passed on 5 May 1975.[42]

Meanwhile, as in all the male colleges, the debate had wavered this way and that. The two sides produced arguments which now seem of very various weight; and it is extremely difficult, nearly twenty years after the change took place, to rehearse the arguments without caricaturing them. It was one of the most fundamental debates in the history of the college, though conducted without forming any deep fissures. Here are a few elements in the discussion. The founder had intended it to be for men – and this had the support of 390 years' of tradition. To admit women would alter the character of the society unpredictably yet irrevocably. The sporting prowess of the college would be threatened (a prediction hardly fulfilled, since women in Cambridge are now adept at most sports formerly supposed to be manly). Women ' "had different ways of doing things" . . . "Perhaps I should add", wrote one very senior fellow, "that celibacy is not always a road to the madhouse. Many of the greatest men in the arts led largely celibate lives . . ." – But celibacy was not the question being discussed'. On the other side it was canvassed that women should have more opportunities in Cambridge, should be treated equally, that the ethos of the age was for the more informal mingling of the sexes in every branch of education. Gerard Evans describes the case thus: 'some felt that co-residence would create a more natural environment, or make the college a less "hearty" and more civilised place'. Ronald Gray reckons the decisive factor in Cambridge at large was government pressure: this was the time when the Equal Opportunities Act was being framed, and institutions favouring a particular sex were under

---

[40] The Royal Commission, keen to encourage the admission of women to the *University*, had suggested their formal exclusion from male colleges to allay the fears of the opponents of their policies (Brooke 1993, pp. 326–7). The statute exluding women was c.2 of the 1926 *Statutes*, confirmed in 1952 (see *Statutes* 1957, pp. (i), 1).

[41] Since 1926, with the passing of statutes in conformity to the Oxford and Cambridge Act of 1923, in all colleges the 'governing body' invited to change a statute had to comprise all the fellows of whatever grade or status.

[42] Governing body minute 127 of 5 May 1975. For the issue at large I am much indebted to Ronald Gray's paper; for these final details, to the help of Frank Stubbings. Inverted commas below signify quotations from Gray – representing the arguments, not necessarily his own opinions.

scrutiny. It could well have been supposed so; but in the event the Act itself made specific provision for institutions such as Oxbridge colleges whose statutes confined them to one sex. Meanwhile, it was perhaps the fundamental attitudes which gave birth to the acts – the assumptions of the 1960s and 70s – which seem to have weighed most with many proponents of co-residence. But it is impossible to enter the human mind, or to tell how much was due to conviction, how much to expediency, how much to fashion. The argument I myself heard most often canvassed elsewhere was that once colleges began to go mixed they became immediately more attractive to good candidates – or a high minded variant of this argument which observed that this was particularly true of candidates from comprehensive schools entirely unused to single-sex institutions; and that therefore the old way was socially divisive. One can only canvas the arguments. The result is beyond doubt: with remarkable speed the colleges changed their statutes.

'More serious arguments insisted', writes Ronald Gray, 'that the college should try to move together, without rancour, which it did', in spite of the very deep feelings and convictions affected. 'Despite the uncommonly large number of votes needed, Emmanuel too swung into line' – not among the first, but not far behind them – 'strongly influenced by a new attitude on the part of some of the most senior members. On 11 March 1974 the statutory majority was achieved' creating the new statute; 'and on 5 May 1975 a motion definitely admitting women was passed, about three quarters of the ordinary governing body being in favour'. The first woman graduate came in 1975, the first women research fellow in 1976;[43] the first women undergraduates were admitted in 1979.

'Since 1979 about a third of the undergraduates admitted have been women, and about a third of the research fellows also, though there is no declared policy in either case' – nor can there be for fellows; for the law forbids discrimination in appointments in favour of either sex. There has been much discussion as to why it is that while the number of women undergraduates in Cambridge has increased very substantially since the changes of the 1970s, the number of women fellows has grown much more slowly. Some purely speculative explanations have been given. What is not in doubt is that for teaching fellowships all colleges seek to appoint those who have university posts – the whole structure of the university is built on the assumption that they will, and the colleges have to pay far less to a fellow who already has a university stipend. And it is notorious that there are far fewer women than men who are university

---

[43] Two women graduate students were admitted in 1976. The proportion of women undergraduates 'has reached 35–40%, and might have been higher if women candidates had been more numerous in science subjects, especially engineering' (ex inf. Gerard Evans in 1994). In 1998 the proportion is 44%. For women in Cambridge generally, see Mason 1993.

teaching officers. But it seems likely that the historian of the future will discern another, even more fundamental, reason. Undergraduates stay only three years, or four at most; a new generation, with a new balance between the sexes, comes quickly. Fellows stay in their posts much longer; the opportunities for enlarging the new element in the fellowship are less – and every time an appointment is made by an advertisement drawn up according to the law of the land, men have as much chance as women to win the prize: this inhibits any deliberate attempt to redress the balance. However this may be, there are now about 15% of the fellows of Cambridge colleges who are women: in Emmanuel there are 11 out of a fellowship of 81, and they include a fellow Women's Adviser. 'So', writes Ronald Gray, 'although women undergraduates [present and past] filled the hall at a dinner to celebrate the tenth anniversary of women being admitted, women fellows had nothing much to celebrate on what was their own thirteenth anniversary.'

Professor Derek Brewer

In 1977 the fellows chose a new master who was at once one of their number and an eminent scholar. Like Welbourne, Derek Brewer had been fellow and tutor; but he was unlike him in many other ways, for his influence – and the presence of the college – was deeply felt in the university during his reign; and he knew the world as well as Cambridge, since he has travelled the globe, lecturing especially in the United States and Japan.

Brewer was educated at The Crypt Grammar School, Gloucester and Magdalen College, Oxford and had had three years war service in the infantry; and he was a senior lecturer in English at Birmingham University – as well as a professor in Japan for two years – before coming to Emmanuel as fellow and tutor in 1965; he subsequently became Reader in the university, and an *ad hominem* Professor in 1984. In the university he has been a member of many committees and chairman of not a few – most notably of the Library Syndicate, over which he presided for 13 years. He was twice Chairman of the English Faculty Board. He was also a key member of the Council of the Senate, the summit of the university's central committees. He has continued to lecture in Japan and the U.S.A., not to mention Taiwan and many parts of Europe: he has renewed the personal links of Emmanuel and Harvard. He is a leading expert on Middle English literature, a world authority on Chaucer; yet this is only a part of his wide interests, recognised by his Presidency of the English Association, and seven honorary degrees in Britain, the United States, France, Belgium and Japan. He has nine times been awarded the Seatonian Prize for a poem on a sacred subject. He revived and edited the *Cambridge Review* from 1981–6. He founded, and has – with his wife Elisabeth – helped to sustain, the academic publishing house of Boydell and Brewer.

He has found time and energy to trek with Elisabeth in the Himalayas.

In spite of all this Brewer was from 1977 to 1990 an extremely active Master, presiding over a period of marked development in the college's history: the first generation of women students, a rapidly expanding fellowship, the celebrations of the quatercentenary, including a visit by the Queen. The Master founded the Emmanuel Society in 1989, which has 'brought wider horizons and greater interest in the college'.[44] Above all, 'it was clear that college accommodation needed improvement and extension', and Derek Brewer 'led the attempt to do this by acquisition of the handsome row of early nineteenth century buildings overlooking Parker's Piece called Park Terrace – a kind of extended row of "stair-cases" offering in total some 140 rooms for junior and senior members'; and he 'managed a Quatercentenary Appeal to which old members generously contributed' to finance the acquisition of Park Terrace and other good causes besides: visiting fellowships, research funds and scholarships.

In his own words, 'this has been a period in which Cambridge and Emmanuel have turned their faces much more to the outside world, and the outside world has correspondingly taken more interest in Cambridge. As far as old members, and the worlds of business, industry and the professions are concerned, this has been wholly beneficial. Continual government interference has not been always helpful, though some innovations introduced by government have been valuable. Government, or rather tax-payers', funds have been much reduced, and we can now see the end of the whole post-war era of generous government funding both for research and for students. This is too complex and vexed a field to be more than noted – and to remark that the whole ethos of university education, teaching and research is being changed, not always for the better, if not quite always for the worse.

'Throughout this period the college, like other colleges, has made great efforts, with some success, to broaden the field of undergraduate entry. The admission of women has been unequivocally a good thing. Socially the college has never been elitist. Intellectually, we are bound to be, and we require high intellectual achievements for admission . . . Choice and discrimination are essential. But this again is a complicated question that continually engages our minds.

'In the end we try to combine what is valuable in tradition with what is valuable and necessary in innovation. It is regrettable that we have almost entirely lost any sense of religious vocation, privilege and gratitude' – and Derek Brewer enters a pessimistic judgement on the degree of involvement or sense of obligation felt by some recent undergraduates

---

[44] The words in inverted commas, here and hereafter, are from a memorandum generously provided by Derek Brewer himself.

571

and younger fellows. 'We live in a time when institutions as such are distrusted and little cherished, despite the fact that for most of us they are the frail vessels that sustain us in the rough seas of life . . . Nevertheless there is always the saving remnant, the salt that gives savour. Colleges and universities will always attract those whose dominant passion, so little understood by many others, is the intellectual life. Of them we still have many, and many who will see the survival of the institution as of high value both for individuals and society.'

Peter Wroth

Derek Brewer, the English scholar, was succeeded by Peter Wroth, a distinguished engineer, a man who seemed a young 61 – who had indeed been a very active sportsman. After the sorrowful illness and death of his first wife he had recently remarried, and seemed set for a new life in the Emmanuel Lodge. Very sadly, it lasted only four months: he was admitted Master in October 1990 and died of cancer in February 1991.

Peter Wroth had been undergraduate and postgraduate at Emmanuel, then for many years in the 1960s and 70s fellow of Churchill College, and tutor for advanced students at a time when Churchill was a pioneer among colleges in providing for rapidly growing numbers of postgraduates.[45] From 1979 to 1990 he was professor of Engineering Science in Oxford and fellow of Brasenose, returning to Emmanuel as Master in 1990. He was one of those who helped to make soil mechanics a fundamental branch of civil engineering. In his own words, his early research was in the period when soil mechanics 'was progressing from being a black art towards becoming an inexact science.'[46] Of his work for Emmanuel, Alan Baker, vice-master, spoke thus:

> 'Peter taught us to take ourselves seriously – for example he committed to memory the Latin sentence which he was required by College statute to use for the admission of new fellows. But he also taught us not to take ourselves *too* seriously – he persuaded the fellows after our Christmas dinner to engage in a light-hearted competition writing limericks based upon somewhat *risqué* black-and-white photographs. Peter's calm, confident leadership was founded not only upon his own ideas and initiatives but also upon his willingness to listen to the opinion of others, and to learn about their aspirations for themselves and for the college. . . .'[47]

---

[45] This, and what follows, are based on his own account, *ECM* 72 (1989–90), 5–9; and the addresses from the Memorial Service in *ECM* 73 (1990–1), 9–20. He was a pupil of the notable Emmanuel engineer K. H. Roscoe.
[46] *ECM* 72 (1989–90), 6.
[47] *ECM* 73 (1990–1), 12–13: words spoken at the Memorial Service.

Lord St John of Fawsley

Cambridge has been surprisingly shy of statesmen as heads of house. But the new master elected in 1991 was as much a man of arts and libraries as of the Palace of Westminster, and one of his most characteristic achievements as a cabinet minister was the creation of the Office of Arts and Libraries. His own library is legendary, and he remained (among many other duties) Chairman of the Royal Fine Art Commission. His own mark was very clear on the decor of the master's lodge and the new building which has risen in its forecourt.[48]

'My roots are in Cambridge and now I return home', he wrote on entering office. 'Cambridge was my first choice of university and I became an undergraduate at Fitzwilliam shortly after the war. One of the most delightful things that has happened to me since becoming master of Emmanuel is that my old college has elected me to an honorary fellowship. While in Cambridge I became interested in politics, haunting the Union, of which I became president, and for which I have always felt a strong affection. After I graduated in law I migrated to Christ Church at Oxford where I passed a happy two years . . ., and was tempted by the walled garden of academic life. Yet in the end the bright lights and the grand surface shine of London won and I passed to Westminster by means of the New World (Yale) and *The Economist* of which I became political editor and started work on my edition of Walter Bagehot. And so through governments and cabinets and royal commissions, home to Cambridge. I can truthfully say with Mary Queen of Scots that in my end is my beginning. My road back has been an ecumenical one' – for a leading Catholic layman – 'since my contemporary links with Emmanuel were re-established in 1989 when I accepted an invitation of the far-sighted Derek Brewer to become a member of the committee of honour sponsoring the Cranmer Quincentenary Exhibition at the British Library'.

In his introduction to the *Emmanuel College Magazine* for 1992–3, the Master spoke in glowing terms of the Development Plan and the new building which forms its centre; and he went on to survey the precinct which the college has inherited from the Dominican friars and Sir Walter Mildmay and four centuries of masters, fellows and benefactors:

'One of the great delights of life at Emmanuel is the enjoyment of the beauty of its buildings and gardens. The perception of beauty is as much part of education as are less aesthetic forms of learning and this is well understood by our junior members. Undergraduates, also, have eyes. Appreciation of the visual environment needs only

[48] See pp. 520–1.

three things, all free, namely to look, to see what one is looking at, and then to judge its merits. Until this becomes a part of education in all our institutions of learning, we shall never achieve a worthy contemporary built environment.'[49]

In 1996 Lord St John retired. We have already met his successor among the scientists of Emmanuel;[50] and for the present and future, he shall speak for himself.

[49] *ECM* 75 (1992–3), 7–8.
[50] See p. 532.

Epilogue

by

The Master, J. E. Ffowcs Williams

To be Master of Emmanuel as it enters the new millennium is both a privilege and a challenge. I doubt if the buildings and gardens of the College can ever have looked more beautiful than they do now. Undergraduate applications run at an all time high in both quality and numbers and the achievement of Junior Members across the broad scope of university life is a source of immense satisfaction to all. The fact that the College contributes so well to a university whose work and achievement is absolutely outstanding is what makes the post a privilege. The challenge comes from managing a change that is driven by the different expectations of modern society and by the Government's desire to see student numbers grow without a corresponding increase in public funding. Cost effectiveness, accountability and demonstrations of value, measured through assessment exercises that are applied uniformly across the broad spectrum of higher education, are very much the order of the day.

It is not a time when it is easy to be different – but it is in being different that our strength lies. It is not an accident that Cambridge University graduates people largely destined for abnormal success in life, nor is that bias at all undesirable in a healthy society. By and large, our members must have an exceptional ability, because acceptance into any group selected on demonstrated merit makes an intellectual bias inevitable. Emmanuel is today amongst the most effective centres of higher education because its intake is so strong and because its students are supported by a diverse group of gifted teachers that were similarly selected on grounds of merit.

I believe that society benefits disproportionately from the investment made in the education of exceptionally good students and that it is correct for the College to protect its ability to stand out in providing for its members the very best support – even though to be distinct is far more difficult to justify now that issues of transparency and accountability are becoming common to those in receipt of public funds.

The tendency to specialise and the desire to provide cover for all subjects from within the Fellowship has driven a huge increase in the size of the Fellowship even over the period that I have been a member. Given the emphasis we now place on maintaining the size of the College at a comfortable human scale it is hard to see that the pressures for growth can be so dominant in future – but there will always be a need for new and different facilities. Future improvements will, I hope, encroach no further on the open spaces and gardens of Emmanuel which are generally admired and which provide much needed tranquillity in the heat and rush of examination time.

Ever since I've known the College it has impressed me as a very friendly place. Whether the warmth of the society is a result or a cause of success is hard to say. Similarly, one can speculate on the degree to which the effectiveness of college staff causes or results from the good atmosphere in College, but there can be no mistaking the advantages brought to Emmanuel by its wonderful staff.

The modern tendency to judge University teachers by the success of their research and by the value of the sponsorship they attract for that research puts strains on the collegiate university. Time spent in college does not score on that basis so that the enormous benefit of being taught by Fellows active in research and at the cutting edge of the subject is more difficult to provide. College Fellowship is also much more difficult to sustain for those reluctant to teach because of research demands. As a professor I had twenty-five years in College with negligible teaching duties and know how different the College appears from that position. The sparkle of undergraduate life, which is the dominant aspect from the viewpoint of Tutorial Fellows, was hardly visible. College life revolved around the Governing Body and its committees, which, for me, was about as demanding as the social side of the Fellowship was wonderful. One saw how easy it is for the College to get things wrong, to make a mistake over matters of policy or resources, but also realised that the processes of College governance are so inherently conservative that mistakes hardly matter. The friendship of Sir Gordon Sutherland was what first brought me to Emmanuel and the marvellous wit and sparkle of Gerard Evans is what made the most impact on me once I got here. Friendships made in College are very strong. My view of undergraduate life was mainly provided by sharing a set of rooms with David Williams, then Senior Tutor, and I am left with the clearest impression from that period of his amazing memory for names, the respect he held for each undergraduate and the friendly formality of his interaction with them. Those qualities were still there when David became the University's first permanent Vice-Chancellor and brought a wonderful human touch into the new administration.

The Mastership of course provides a completely different perspective of the College. The social side of the Fellowship features more because the

Master sees so much of the Fellows through their committee work, contact which leads inevitably to a sharing of hopes and objectives. Parlour life provides a rich variety of informal conversations with Fellows and their guests, conversations which can be incredibly bright and stimulating, though obviously that is not always the case.

The best aspects of junior member activities, ones giving rise to celebration, are the ones the Master sees most. Difficult areas requiring a degree of moderation are scarcely visible to the Master, being handled by the Senior Tutor and his team, the Master becoming aware of them at meetings of the Master and Tutors' Committee. Apart from appreciating the strength and cultural diversity of the college this view allows him to see the care and detailed attention given by senior members to their students. Despite the much increased workload caused by the research emphasis for University teachers there is still clear evidence that teachers at Emmanuel know their students in very great depth and find enjoyment in their teaching duties. I cannot believe that there was ever more individual attention provided for undergraduates than there is today nor that more was known of them by our tutorial predecessors.

To keep the College working so well in the different conditions that lie ahead is today's main aim. A strong Bursarial team is vital to ensuring that our resources are properly applied and a commitment to develop resources to provide for future needs is equally important. The College is very well positioned at the beginning of the new millennium in both its Bursarial and Development sides and as Master I am much more aware of the privilege of my post than I am apprehensive of its challenges. I am greatly enjoying the privilege of writing the last word in this History of our wonderful College.

Appendix 1

The Masters

1584 LAURENCE CHADERTON
1622 JOHN PRESTON
1628 WILLIAM SANCROFT (the elder)
1637 RICHARD HOLDSWORTH
1644 ANTHONY TUCKNEY
1653 WILLIAM DILLINGHAM
1662 WILLIAM SANCROFT (the younger)
1665 JOHN BRETON
1675 THOMAS HOLBECH
1680 JOHN BALDERSTON
1719 WILLIAM SAVAGE
1736 WILLIAM RICHARDSON
1775 RICHARD FARMER
1797 ROBERT TOWERSON CORY
1835 GEORGE ARCHDALL-GRATWICKE
1871 SAMUEL GEORGE PHEAR
1895 WILLIAM CHAWNER
1911 PETER GILES
1935 THOMAS SHIRLEY HELE
1951 EDWARD WELBOURNE
1964 SIR GORDON BRIMS BLACK McIVOR SUTHERLAND
1977 DEREK STANLEY BREWER
1990 CHARLES PETER WROTH
1991 LORD ST JOHN OF FAWSLEY
1996 JOHN EIRWYN FFOWCS WILLIAMS

Appendix 2

The Bursars

† The Bursar was also Master

1601	WILLIAM BEDELL[1]
1610–22	† LAURENCE CHADERTON[2]
1622 (Mich. audit)–1628 (Easter audit)	† JOHN PRESTON
1628 (Mich.)–1637 (Easter)	† WILLIAM SANCROFT (the elder)
1637 (Mich.)–1641 (Mich.)	RICHARD CLERK
1642 (Easter)	THOMAS HOLBECH
1642 (Mich.)–1643 (Easter)	JOHN ALMOND
1643 (Mich.)–1644 (Easter)	RICHARD WELLER
1644 (Mich.)–1645 (Easter)	WILLIAM SANCROFT (the elder) (There seems to have been an overlap between Sancroft and Dillingham, as both were paid a stipend of £4 in 1645.)[3]
1645 (Easter)–1650 (Easter)	WILLIAM DILLINGHAM
1650 (Mich.)–1653 (Easter)	† ANTHONY TUCKNEY
1650 (Mich.)–1653 (Mich.)	WILLIAM DILLINGHAM was paid for helping with the accounts.[4]
1654 (Easter)–1662 (Easter)	†WILLIAM DILLINGHAM
1662 (Mich.)–1668 (Mich.)	ROBERT ALEFOUNDER (William Sancroft (the younger), Master, signed the indenture of the Easter audit 1663.)
1669	JOHN KENT
1670 (Easter)–1673 (Mich.)	MICHAEL STUKELEY
1674 (Easter)–1675 (Mich.)	† JOHN BRETON

[1] ECA COL.9.19A.
[2] ECA BUR.0.2 gives Bursars from Chaderton to Farmer.
[3] ECA BUR.8.2.
[4] ECA BUR.8.2.

1676 (Easter)–1677 (Mich.)	† THOMAS HOLBECH
1678 (Easter)–1680	JOHN BALDERSTON[5]
1680–1719	† JOHN BALDERSTON
1719–36 (Easter)	† WILLIAM SAVAGE
1736 (Mich.)–1774 (Mich.)	† WILLIAM RICHARDSON
1775 (Easter)–1797	† RICHARD FARMER
1797–9	WILLIAM RICHARDSON TYSON[6]
1799–1809	HENRY YATES SMYTHIES
1809–26	WILLIAM HOLME
1827–32	HENRY EVELEIGH HOLLAND
1832–5	GEORGE JOHN ARCHDALL
1835–50	ROBERT BIRKETT
1850–61	WILLIAM CASTLEHOW
1861–3	PHILIP GRETTON DENNIS
1863–4	JOHN FULLER
1864–70	THOMAS HEWITT
1870–2	SAMUEL GEORGE PHEAR
1872–93	ALFRED ROSE
1893–1920	JAMES BENNET PEACE
1920–60	ROBERT GARDNER
1960–74	AUGUSTUS JOHN WARD
1974–83	JOHN REDDAWAY
1983–91	DAVID ANTHONY LIVESEY
1992	ALFRED BERNARD CRAMP
1992–7	STEPHEN MICHAEL BROOKER
1997–	MICHAEL JOHN GROSS

[5] ECA BUR.8.2.
[6] Hereafter, Bursars are listed in the College Order Books and Governing Body minutes, ECA COL.11 and COL.14.

Appendix 3

The Tutors of Emmanuel, 1731–1777

It is surprisingly difficult to compile an accurate list of tutors for the mid-eighteenth century. Tutors were not formally appointed by the governing body, so there are no college orders for their appointment till the late nineteenth century; and the word itself was ambiguous, since private tutors, who were hired by the students or their parents, flourished beside the official college tutors – and they cannot always be readily distinguished. Furthermore, E. S. Shuckburgh, in his history of the College, attempted to reconstruct the dates of tutorships from some surviving accounts, coming to the misleading conclusion that Henry Hubbard, the dominant figure of the mid-century, was for many years sole tutor (Shuckburgh 1904, p. 138). Mercifully, for the period from 1777 on, the College matriculation book (TUT.23.4) gives the names of the tutors each year, and there were always two – save in 1813–16, when there was only one – until the late nineteenth century. Dr Sarah Brewer, who worked extensively in the archives for her study of Richard Hurd, pointed out that the Commons Accounts Books from the 1730s to the 1760s (STE.15.8–9) regularly record the matriculation of individual students in the college hall, commonly naming the tutors who were present. From these details it is clear that in the 1730s, and down to 1740 or a little later, there were three tutors; thereafter, it seems that there were normally two, and they commonly hunt in pairs in the notes on the account. There are some sports. On 13 June 1732 Mr CHRISTOPHER HAND appears as tutor to one student; on 27 May 1745 Mr JOHN TOOKE acts surety for a matriculand, but is not called tutor – and the same with Mr JAMES BICKHAM on 28 June 1745. Finally, on 14 October 1756, Mr ROBERT RICHARDSON, the junior fellow and the master's son, acts tutor to Mr Potter (Brewer 1987, no. 127 has another reference to Richardson as tutor, possibly as private tutor, in 1752). Hand and Richardson appear to be official tutors from the context, but evidently acting more in the capacity of private tutors to individuals. These apart, the list is as follows (the biographical details are from Venn, *Alumni*, unless otherwise stated).

ARNALD, RICHARD, occ[urs] 15 March 1731 – 15 May 1733
[Rector of Thurcaston, 1733–56, when he died.]

WHITEHEAD, WILLIAM, occ. 23 March – 1 November 1731
[Vicar of Stanground, 1731–54, when he died.]

WILKINSON, JOHN, occ. 25 June 1731 – 10 July 1736
[Rector of Wallington, 1736–59, when he died.]

SMALLEY, NATHANIEL, occ. 26 April 1732 – 2 March 1740
[Vicar (or rector?) of Preston, Suffolk, 1742–76, when he died.]

HUBBARD, HENRY, occ. 2 June 1737 – 2 February 1767
[Hubbard evidently succeeded Wilkinson, who departed for a rectory in 1736. The evidence of the accounts studied in Shuckburgh 1904, p. 138, strongly suggests that Hubbard was acting as tutor before the end of 1736. Hubbard and Lyne occ. frequently together – then Hubbard and Bickham, Hubbard and Farmer. Hubbard was evidently succeeded by Blackall.]

LYNE, MATTHEW, occ. 17 January 1739 – 26 October 1745
[Lyne died on 2 November 1745 (STE.15.9; cf. Brewer 1995, No. 67 and nn.]

BICKHAM, JAMES, occ. 26 December 1745 – 11 July 1761
[Bickham evidently succeeded Lyne, and was succeeded in his turn by Farmer. He was rector of Loughborough, 1762–85, when he died.]

FARMER, RICHARD, occ. 9 October 1761 – 1782 or 1783 [TUT.23.4. Farmer was Master from 1775.]

BLACKALL, SAMUEL [the elder], 21 November 1767 – 1779 or 1780 [TUT.23.4.]

Appendix 4

Notes on the Changing Patterns of Schools and Fathers' Professions in the late 19th and 20th Centuries

In Brooke 1985, pp. 307–15 an attempt was made to plot the background from which Caians sprang, and their own careers, in a series of tables arranged in the customary groups of five years. What follows provides such comparisons as are possible for the students of Emmanuel over the same period. For those who matriculated down to 1900 the source is Venn; from 1901 on I have had the benefit of the admirable register begun by Frances Willmoth and completed by Janet Morris.

The limitations of current knowledge need to be emphasised. For the years 1886–90 the records of origin are very incomplete: where a parent was a doctor or a clergyman, this showed in his style, so that we have fairly complete figures for these two categories, but only haphazard knowledge of others. For the schools, the information in Emmanuel records was also very fragmentary; but the editors of Venn were able to fill many gaps from school registers and the like. This has given a marked bias to all figures based on Venn in favour of Public Schools, which may for Emmanuel be wholly misleading. It is quite likely that most of those whose schools are not known came from grammar or secondary schools. This bias in the data provided by Venn, and some comparable figures, are noted in Brooke 1993, pp. 247–9, 599–600.

On the other hand, it is possible to give a table of the destiny of Emmanuel students of 1886–90, such as is not possible in the present state of knowledge for the twentieth century.

TABLE 2
Schools from which Emmanuel men have come

The analysis is almost exactly as in Brooke 1985, pp. 308–9, q.v. for some details – save that postgraduates arriving from outside Cambridge and Emmanuel are included. 'The pattern of English secondary schools has

584

changed dramatically over the last hundred years; yet if the tables are to reveal anything there must be some measure of comparison. I have therefore chosen three categories, with shifting frontiers and meaning indeed, but with less shift than others one can choose – the Public Schools in the sense of boarding schools . . .; what used to be called Public day schools, most of which were Direct Grant schools between the 1940s and the 1970s, though many were already Independent; and the Grammar Schools and other Secondary Schools which do not readily fall under the second category, the majority of which (though with many exceptions) are now Comprehensive.' Thus Brooke 1985 (p. 308): needless to say the changes of the last ten years have made such comparisons increasingly hazardous. It cannot be too strongly emphasised that the categories have shifted too much for the figures to be precise, and that I shall have made errors in analysis and in computation. In the Caius tables I gave percentages, but in this case they seem to me so misleading as best avoided: percentages can only be useful if based on precise information. For the period 1886–90 the information is heavily biassed – not by anyone's intention, but by the nature of the evidence – as has been explained above. In the Caius tables I included overseas postgraduates both under 'overseas' and under 'from another university': in these tables they only appear under the second heading. All institutions of higher education have been included under 'universities'. In the early years those from other universities sometimes came to take another first degree; later on the vast majority are postgraduate students.

With all qualifications made, the tables show a less pronounced preponderance of category 1 than in Caius in 1907–11, but a very similar swing towards category 3 in 1967–71.

All figures are annual averages.

Annual Average of	Average total per year	1 Public Boarding	2 Public Day	3 Grammar & Secondary	4 Educated Overseas	Educated in another university	Educated privately	Not Known
1886–90	47	18.2	5.0	4.4	0.2	1.0	0.2	18
1907–11	73.6	31	8.8	18	5.2	5.4	5.2	0.2
1932–6	109.2	41.8	11.6	36.2	10.2	5.0	4.4	0
1951–5	148.2	48.2	15.4	50.4	6.8	25.6	0.2	1.6
1967–71	147.6	28.8	27.0	67.2	1.6	22.0	0	1.0

TABLE 3

Fathers' Professions

As for Caians, the tables have to be compiled from sources which give too little evidence of mothers' occupations to be tabulated, and use categories which are not as precise as to satisfy a social scientist: it is impossible to categorise students' parents by income group or class (whatever that now means). The business entries are doubtless particularly misleading, owing to the shifting use of words and the ambiguity of 'director', 'manager' etc. The entries for 1886–90 are haphazard, save for physicians and clergy (see above). Those for later years are much more complete, save that in the 1950s and 60s it was common not to record the origin of students who came to Emmanuel as postgraduates; this lacuna puts a bias in the table, since they may well have come from more varied backgrounds.

The proportion of fathers who were clergy in the period down to 1911 is strikingly high – much higher than among the Caians; and so is the proportion of clergy among the professions of Emmanuel men of 1886–90. These were even higher than appears, since in these tables we have put clergy known to have been professional schoolmasters under schoolteachers. One of the most marked signs of the secularisation of British society in the late nineteenth and early twentieth centuries was the separation of the clerical and teaching professions, which were often indistinguishable in the nineteenth century. As with the Caians, the range of social origin evidently became much wider in the second half of the twentieth century: this is clearly illustrated by this table, however imprecise its details.

| | Annual averages of – | | | | |
	1886–90	1907–11	1932–6	1951–5	1967–71
Unknown	26.8	9.4	11.2	10.6	53.2
Accountants	0	1.0	3.0	3.2	2.6
Architects (including naval architects)	0	0.2	0.6	1.0	0
Armed forces	1.4	1.4	4.0	5.0	1.8
Artists, designers	0	0.2	0.8	0.4	0.6
Bankers, Bank managers	0	1.2	2.0	3.8	2.8
Builders	0	0.6	2.0	1.2	0.2
Business: manufacturers	0.8	3.4	4.6	1.2	1.4
merchants, shipowners	0	4.6	5.4	4.6	1.4
directors, managers	0	3.2	7.8	18.6	25.0
Civil servants, including diplomats	0	1.2	6.0	12.8	10.8

Indian Civil Service	0.4	2.0	2.4	0.8	0.2
Clergy (of all denominations, lay missionaries)	11.4	9.2	10.6	5.2	1.6
Clerks	0	1.0	1.8	3.6	2.4
Craftsmen	0	2.6	2.4	3.4	1.6
Engineers	0.2	3.2	7.4	12.2	10.2
Factory workers	0.2	0.8	1.0	3.2	2.0
Farmers	0	1.8	4.2	5.6	2.2
Foremen	0	0.4	0	0.4	0.8
Insurance	0	0.6	1.2	1.4	2.0
Journalists	0	0	0	0.2	0.6
Land, estate agents, surveyors	0	1.0	1.4	2.6	2.6
Landowners, 'gentlemen'	0.6	3.2	0.8	0.8	0.2
Lawyers: barristers	0.6	1.0	1.2	1.0	0.2
solicitors	1.0	3.8	3.2	2.6	2.0
Merchant navy	0	0.2	0.2	1.0	0
Musicians	0.4	0.4	0.2	0.4	0.2
Physicians, surgeons, dentists	1.6	6.4	7.4	9.6	7.0
Police	0	0.2	0.4	0.8	0.2
Sales managers, supervisors	0	0	0.4	0	0.4
Schoolteachers	0.4	3.4	5.4	11.2	11.0
Scientists in business etc.	0	1.4	2.2	3.4	4.4
Shopkeepers	0.2	1.0	5.4	6.0	3.4
Stockbrokers	0.2	0.4	0.6	0.6	0
Tailors	0	0.2	0.2	0	0
University teachers, and higher education	0.4	0.6	1.4	3.0	5.8
Other	0	2.0	2.2	7.0	5.0

TABLE 4

The destiny of Emmanuel students, 1886–90

	Annual averages
Unknown	8
Architects	0.2
Armed forces	1.0
Business: merchants	0.2
directors, managers	0.2
Civil servants, diplomats	0.8
Indian Civil Service	3.8
Clergy (of any denomination)	14.6
Engineers	1.0
Farmers	0.2
Insurance	0.2

TABLE 4 (*continued*)

	Annual averages
Landowners, 'gentlemen'	0.2
Lawyers: barristers	1.4
solicitors	1.6
Musicians	0.2
Physicians, surgeons, dentists	6.2
Schoolteachers	6.0
Stockbrokers	0.2
Tea planters	0.4
University teachers and higher education	0.6

Appendix 5

Outline History of the College Estates to 1871[1]

The following list does not give each tenant; it mentions, however, most of those about whom something is known. The dates are those from which leases ran, not those of sealing. All manuscript sources are in Emmanuel College Archives, unless otherwise indicated.

† Lord of the Manor   § Lay Rector

Crown

1585   Queen Elizabeth granted annuity of £16 13s 4d to maintain 5 scholars. (Charter Cabinet drawer 9)

1653   Allowed £17 9s 4d from fee-farm rents. (BUR.11.2)

1661   Payment from the Exchequer resumed. (BUR.11.2)

Sancroft Educational Foundation – Harleston School

1688   William Sancroft (the younger) granted annuity of £54 to pay for a schoolmaster and chaplain at Harleston (Norfolk). He had received sum in settlement of debt from Robert Welsted, a London goldsmith. Half the arrears already due to Sancroft to be paid to the Library and half to be divided among Master and Fellows. (Box 9.Mc5; BUR.6.3 p. 203)

1718   First chaplain appointed (had been difficulties in collection of annuity). (BUR.0.8; Candler 1896, p. 167)

1719   Exchequer paid £900 to discharge all liability. Sum administered by schoolmaster, William Smith, rather than invested in land. (Candler 1896, p. 167)

1764   Money invested by College in Government securities, to produce an annual income of £10. (Candler 1896, p. 167)

---

[1] Since 1871, many of the estates listed here have been sold, others bought, and land-holdings reorganised. Land has come to be seen as a tradeable asset and has formed a smaller percentage of the College's endowment. The recent history of particular plots of land has become too complex to be listed clearly in the format of this Appendix and much of the information is confidential. For these reasons, this Appendix covers the period discussed in the first three chapters about the College's estates.

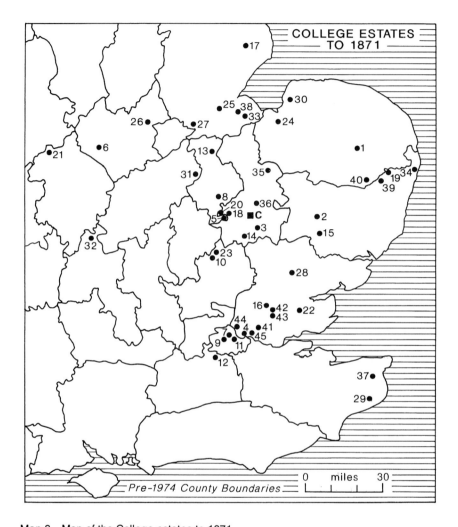

Map 3   Map of the College estates to 1871.

1. Little Melton (Norfolk) land and tithes (1584–)
2. Little Welnetham (Suffolk) rent charge (1585–1859)
3. Babraham (Cambs) rent charge (1585–1862)
4. Ripple (Essex) (1585–)
5. Gransden (Hunts) rent charge (1585–99), manor and land (1599–)
6. Market Bosworth and Brascote (Leics) rent charge (1585–1617)
7. London Bishopsgate Street Four Swans and tenements to North and West (1585–), Gracechurch Street The Ball and The Harrow (1585–), Thames Street rent charge (1594–), Threadneedle Street (1588–)
8. Godmanchester (Hunts) Horseshoe Inn and meadow (1585–), West Street (1585–)
9. London Holborn (1670–), Old Bailey St Dunstan's Alley (1586–) and house (1670–)
10. Letchworth (Herts) (1586–)

590

11. London West Smithfield (1587–)
12. Mitcham (Surrey) Hyde Field Farm (1587–), Mitcham and Clapham Farm (1587–)
13. Stanground (Hunts) rent charge (1588–)
14. Fowlmere (Cambs) rent charge (1588–)
15. Lavenham (Suffolk) rent charge (1588–)
16. Stondon (Essex) Whipples Farm (1588–), Hook End Farm (1867–)
17. Skendleby (Lincs) rent charge (1589–1613)
18. Caxton (Cambs) tithes (1590–1605)
19. Bungay (Suffolk) rent charge (1592–)
20. Eltisley (Cambs) (1593–)
21. Sutton Coldfield (Warwicks) (1594–)
22. Woodham Ferrers (Essex) rent charge (1594–1613)
23. Radwell (Herts) rent charge (1606–13)
24. King's Lynn (Norfolk) (1607–)
25. Pinchbeck (Lincs) tithes (Cowbit, Cuckoo and South College and Laurel House Farms from 1811) (1617–)
26. Leesthorpe (Leics) rent charge (1618–)
27. Witham on the Hill (Lincs) rent charge (1625–1709)
28. Braintree (Essex) (1632–)
29. Lydden and Ewell (Kent) (1639–)
30. Shernborne (Norfolk) manor and land (1654–)
31. Thurning (Nhants) (1664–)
32. Drayton (Oxon) rent charge (1668–)
33. Fleet (Lincs) (1674–)
34. Pakefield (Suffolk) (1674–1869)
35. Littleport (Cambs) rent charge (1681–)
36. Waterbeach (Cambs) rent charge (1681–)
37. Ash (Kent) manor and Chequer Court (1719–), Molland Farm (1859–)
38. Whaplode and Holbeach (Lincs) (1709–)
39. St Cross (Suffolk) (1723–)
40. Rushall (Norfolk) land and tithes (1738–)
41. Hornchurch (Essex) (1832–)
42. Navestock (Essex) Lees Farm and meadow (1832–)
43. Stapleford Abbots (Essex) Mitchell's Farm (1832–)
44. Stratford (Essex) Maryland Point and Wharf (1832–)
45. Dagenham (Essex) (1865–)
C. Cambridge Emmanuel Street Pensionary (1587–), Emmanuel Street East End (1612–), Petty Cury The Unicorn (1621–), St Andrew's Street nos 11–12 Wolfe's House (1607–), no. 10 (1867–), no. 21 The Chalice (1585–), nos 63–4 St Nicholas Hostel (1585–), Sempire Lands (1668–1823)

Cambridge – College

Brew-house

1628   Let at £13 6s 8d rent. (BUR.11.0.C f. 2v)

1647   New house built next to brew-house. (BUR.8.2)

1651   Rent increased to £24 6s 8d. (COL.9.1(A) p. 149; BUR.11.0.C f. 2v)

1676   Rent increased to £28 rent + 2 fat capons or 5s for each. (BUR.6.3 pp. 2–7)

1710   Lease to Mary Terry not sealed as Terry did not agree to clause to ensure better drink. (BUR.6.3 pp. 422–7)

1713 Let to Mary Terry and John Brooke (brewer). (BUR.6.3 pp. 457–62)

1714 Tenants became bankrupt; College had to pay £37 arrears of duty in 1715. (COL.9.10.31; COL.14.1 pp. 121–2)

1720 Let to Richard Thurlbourne, bookseller. (Box 1.F5)

1727 Let in 2 parts: 1st to William Thurlbourne (son of Richard) at fine of only £9 as tenant spent much on repairs, rent £4. 2nd part let to Ann Robson for £3, fine £8 as tenant spent much on repairs, allowed to use path through Master's garden. (BUR.3.2 ff. 25v, 26v; Box 1.F6–7)

1728 1st part let to Charles Chambers of Grevile St., London. (Box 1.F8; BUR.3.2 f. 32v)

1729 2nd part let to Ann Robson, allowed to enclose small part of stable yard. (Box 1.F9)

1738 1st part let to Mr Sindrey; note by transcript of lease hoping that would never renew without deleting clause giving access through College as it gives scholars entrance at all hours without having to pass through the gates and so irregularities pass unknown. (BUR.3.2 f. 32v)

1795 Let to Henry Mason, innholder, for 40 years, tenant to build stable and coachhouse within 3 months, ground rent 1s/year for 14 years, then fine set by College. (Box 1.F12)

1837 Wasteland bought from Corporation for £50. (BUR.8.9)

Emmanuel House

1779 Let to Robert Masters, rector of Landbeach, rent £16. (Box 1.F10)

1793–1859 Let to Rev. James Goodwin, executors and descendants. (Box 5.H2–3; Box 1.F14; COL.14.3 pp. 42, 130)

1832 Licence to sub-let a tenement to Weston Hatfield, printer. (BUR.6.6 pp. 163–4)

1838 Licence to sub-let to John Challice, drawing-master. (BUR.6.6 pp. 201–2)

1859 Claim for £76 for breach of covenants. College agreed to connect 2 houses to mains sewers. (COL.14.3 p. 130)

1860 College agreed to repairs of roofs and exteriors. (COL.14.3 p. 136)

Cambridge – Emmanuel Street

East end, including The White Horse, bounded by Emmanuel Street to South, St Nicholas Hostel to North, Barnwell Fields (Drummer Street) to East. C and D on Map 4.

1612 College purchased 9 messuages, gardens and 2 barns from John Atkinson for £400 (C on Map 4). (Box 4.A14)

1615 First of 11 tenements let separately; tenement 6 let to John

Brasbone for 40 years for Laurence Chaderton's use. (BUR.11.0.C ff. 2r–v)

1650   Repairs carried out. (BUR.8.2)

1660   Tenements 6–11 let to Daniel Johnson for 40 years, £10 16s 8d rent. (BUR.11.0.C f. 2v)

1668   Repairs carried out. (BUR.8.2)

1673   Waste ground (D on Map 4) leased from Cambridge Corporation. A 'summerhouse', or stable or outhouse stood on the ground. (Box 4.C1)

1677   The White Horse on corner of Emmanuel Street and Drummer Street, 'now new builded', with malthouse, offices, stables and orchard let to James Everard, £12 rent. (Box 4.C2; BUR.8.2)

1687   About £12 spent by College on repairs to White Horse. (BUR.8.2)

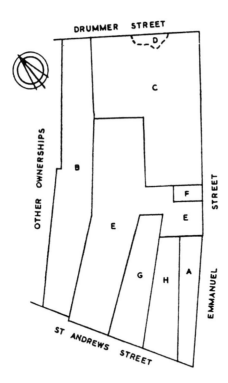

Map 4   The Emmanuel Street/St Andrew's Street site (A. The Pensionary; B. St Nicholas Hostel; C. Purchased from John Atkinson 1612; D. Waste ground; E. Purchased from Henry Rance 1890; F. Purchased from Cambridge Corporation 1898; G. Purchased from Executors of Mrs Sarah Francis 1901; H. Purchased from St John's College 1926). *Source*: *ECM*, 37 (1954–5), p. 22.

1690   Repairs carried out. (BUR.8.2)

1724   Nos 11–12 let to Nicholas Sanderson, Professor of Mathematics; College already spent £80 on premises, Sanderson to pay £4 interest. (BUR.6.3 pp. 536–8)

1729   Summerhouse let to Richard Cooper, bricklayer. (Box 4.C4)

1732   White Horse and summerhouse let to Thomas Whitstone, tenant to demolish outbuildings and allowed to demolish cottage, rent £17. (Box 4.C5(1); BUR.6.3 pp. 661–4)

1739   White Horse and summerhouse let to Robert Simpson, Esquire Bedell, with no fine as tenant had spent large sums on house. (Box 4.C5)

1741–57   Nos 11–12 let to John Wright, cook. (BUR.6.4 pp. 6–8, 82–3)

1766–80   White Horse let to Martha Swann and her devisees, rent £17. (Box 4.C6–7)

1771   Nos 11–12 let to John Beverley, College to repair. (BUR.6.4 pp. 248–51)

1773   John Beverley also leased no. 13. (Box 4.B3)

1779–1840   Nos 11–16 let to Charles Day, joiner and cabinet-maker, then to his executor Peete Musgrave, woollen draper and then to Rev. Thomas Musgrave, Lord Almoner and Professor of Arabic, rent £21. (Box 4.B4–10)

1790–1835   White Horse alienated to Rev. George Borlase and then let to him and widow Anne, rent £17. (BUR.6.5 pp. 22–3; BUR.6.6 pp. 180–1; Box 4.C8–12)

1792   Wasteland leased from Corporation for 999 years. (Box 8.H11)

1808   Nos 11–16 valued by William Custance who advised College to rebuild as 3–4 houses as would be expensive to repair. (Ca.11.2)

1809   White Horse valued by William Custance, in pretty good repair. (Ca.11.3)

1822   White Horse valued by F. W. Smith. (Ca.11.5a–b)

1823   Nos 11–16 valued by F. W. Smith, in need of repair. (Ca.1.7)

1835–42   White Horse let to William Searle of Chesterton, to his widow and then to Elliot Macro Smith of Cambridge, auctioneer. (Box 4.C13–15; BUR.6.6 pp. 209–11)

1840–63   Nos 11–16 alienated and then let to John Gillam Bell of Cambridge, seedsman. (BUR.6.6 pp. 207–9; Box 4.B11)

1842   White Horse alienated to Francis John Gunning. (BUR.6.6 pp. 211–14)

1847–1914   White Horse alienated and then let to Clement Francis and his widow. (BUR.6.6 pp. 247–9; Box 4.C16–18)

1849   White Horse valued by Elliot Smith. (BUR.8.9)

1863   White Horse let with brewery (East part of St Nicholas Hostel), rent increased to £27, used as attorney's and solicitor's office. (Box 4.C18)

West end, Pensionary and Roxton Hall, bounded by St Andrew's Street to West, Emmanuel Street to South. A on Map 4.

1587   Given by Edward Leeds (Box 4.D7); had been let to architect of Emmanuel, Ralph Symons, for 60 years from 1586 and Symons had and was to build upon it. Part of property sub-let to Andrew Symonds and Robert Serle. (Box 4.D4–6)

1588   Sir Walter Mildmay bought remainder of lease from Symons and granted it to College (Box 4.D9–10). Let as 6 tenements for £12. House at corner of St Andrew's Street and Emmanuel Street known as Roxton Hall. (BUR.11.0.B f. 4v)

1594   Under-lease of 2 rooms to Andrew Symonds assigned to College. Sub-tenant was Richard Brigg, under-cook at College. (Box 4.D11)

1616   Tenement 4 let with covenant to accommodate 6 scholars or more in 2 chambers and others above. (BUR.11.0.C f. 1v)

1616   Tenement 5 let with covenant to accommodate 1 or 2 scholars. (BUR.11.0.C f. 2r)

1640   Repairs carried out. (BUR.8.2)

1669   Roxton Hall, 'lately builded', let to Ralph Flyer, Doctor of Physic of King's College. (Box 4.E1)

1772   Nos 1–8 let to Charles Humfrey, carpenter; no. 9 let to Thomas Thackeray. (Box 4.E7–9)

1784–1849   Nos 2–8 let to Charles Humfrey, then to executor, then to Humfrey's widow and then to descendant. (BUR.6.4 pp. 420–2; Box 4.E2, E14, E17–20)

1797–1855   Nos 1 and 9 let to Thomas Thackeray and descendants. (Box 4.E10–13, E21)

1797   One of Thackeray's houses newly built. (BUR.0.3(d))

1798   Nos 2–8 valued by Alexander Watford. (Ca.11.1)

1812   All valued by William Custance; nos 2–8 in very bad repair. (Ca.1.4; Ca.11.4)

1826   Nos 1 and 9 valued by F. Smith. (Ca.1.12)

1849   Nos 2–8 passed to Charles Cave of Threadneedle St, banker. (BUR.6.6 pp. 266–6 [*sic*])

1852   Nos 2–8 passed to William Waters of Brunswick Place, Cambridge. (BUR.6.6 pp. 284–6)

1855   Nos 1 and 9 passed to Samuel Peed, solicitor. (BUR.6.6 pp. 308–10)

1866–8   Dilapidations surveyed and College spent £900; total annual rental £164. (BUR.0.5(d–e); BUR.8.9; REF.2.1)

Cambridge – Petty Cury (The Unicorn)

1621   Purchased by College from Nathaniel Harrison for £480 (£200 bequeathed by William Branthwaite to endow 2 scholarships, £20 given by Mr Herne, schoolmaster of Merchant Taylor's School, and rest by College to restore the fellowship endowed by Sir Francis Hastings' rent charge). Annual quit rent of 6s 8d payable to St John's College. Let as 7 tenements for £39 7s. (Box 3.A16, A18)

1628–37 Goods of tenants distrained and problems with arrears and debts. (Box 3.A20; BUR.0.9; BUR.8.2; BUR.11.1; COL.9.10.103)

1639 Repairs and building carried out. (BUR.0.9; BUR.8.2)

1644 All let to Thomas Glover for £15; he spent £300 on rebuilding. (BUR.11.0.C f. 1r; COL.9.1(A) p. 147)

1676 Let to Thomas Morin of St Giles, Cripplegate, brewer; same rent but 2 capons or 5s for each at audit added. (Box 3.A21)

1681 Let to Benjamin Spence, chandler. (Box 3.A22)

1763 Distrained for rent. (BUR.6.4 p. 181)

1767 College spent £216 on estate so wanted to stop paying 2 scholarships. (BUR.8.6; COL.9.1(A) p. 238)

1769–79 Let to Uriah Matthews of Grantchester, miller and then to grandson. (Box 3.B3–5)

1781 Let separately as inn and 4 messuages, total rental £15. Inn let to Richard Wheeler, basket maker. (Box 3.B6–9; BUR.6.4 pp. 377–81)

1781–1810 1 messuage fronting street let to John Blackman, saddler, then to widow and descendants. (Box 3.B7–8, B19–20; BUR.6.5 pp. 111–14)

1790–1804 Inn assigned and then let to John Forlow, brewer. (COL.14.2 f. 101v; BUR.6.5 pp. 68–71)

–1791 Messuage fronting street let to Francis Herring, breeches maker. (BUR.6.5 p. 25)

1794–1846 Yard, formerly coal warehouse, now workshop, let to Richard Wheeler and executors. (Box 3.B10, B15–16, B23; COL.14.2 ff. 215r, 227, 228r)

1804–37 Inn alienated and let to William and Ambrose Harbord Steward, brewers, and then also to Benjamin Cotton, rent £3. (BUR.6.5 pp. 192–4; Box 3.B13–14, B24)

1806 2 messuages valued by William Custance. (Ca.14.1)

1807 Inn and warehouse valued by William Custance; £200 spent by tenant on rebuilding warehouse. (Ca.14.2)

1809 Messuages fronting street valued by William Custance, part a shop, houses in indifferent repair. (Ca.14.3)

1810–24 1 messuage fronting street alienated and then let to George Chapman, publican. (BUR.6.5 pp. 266–7; Box 3.B25–6)

1820 2 messuages valued by William Custance. (Ca.14.4)

1822 Premises valued by Elliot Smith: inn and shop out of repair. (Ca.14.5, 6, 8a; BUR.0.4(c))

1823–68 Other messuage fronting street let to William Mitchell, innholder and executors. (Box 3.B27–8, B32–3, C4–5, C8–9)

1824–45 1 messuage fronting street alienated and then let to Edward and Sarah Felton, plumber and glazier. (BUR.6.5 pp. 531–4; Box 3.B29)

1834–68+ 2 messuages alienated to Thomas John Ficklin, surgeon. Then inn let to him 1837, 1 messuage fronting street alienated to him 1845, yard alienated to him 1846, 2nd messuage fronting street alienated to him 1868. (BUR.6.6 pp. 177–8, 194–6, 240–1, 351–4; Box 3.C6–7, C10; COL.14.3 pp. 42, 181)

1846 Premises surveyed by Elliot Smith and mapped by John Smith. (BUR.8.9)

1853 Messuage fronting street valued by E. and J. Smith. (BUR.0.5(a))

1860–1 Valued, surveyed and mapped by Richard Harwood. Alternative valuation for converting fine into ground rent not taken up. (BUR.0.5(c))

Cambridge – St Andrew's Street

Nos 11–12 (Wolfe's House)

1607 College bought from Michael Wolfe for £130. Let for £8 10s. (Box 2.D5, D9)

1630 Let to Edward Gibson; £100 to be spent by tenant on building within 3 years. (BUR.11.0.C f. 1v)

1686 Let to Edmund Greene, brewer, as 3 messuages 'new builded'. (BUR.6.3 pp. 121–4)

1726 Let to Catherine Edwards, widow. (Box 2.D12)

1758 Let to Rev. Dr John Newcome, Master of St John's. (Box 2.D13)

1769–92 Let to Jonathan Munns, tin plate worker. (Box 2.D14; BUR.6.5 pp. 15–18, 33–4)

1801 Valued by Alexander Watford. (Ca.1.1)

1810 Let to Richard Foster, merchant and brewer. (Box 2.E2–3)

1812–56 Let to Samuel Chase, Dissenting Minister, then to sisters Harriet and Elizabeth Ann Fysh, then to Rev. Frederick Fysh. (Box 2.E4–13)

1824 Valued by F. W. Smith, 1 building in bad repair and some buildings illegally erected on garden wall. Tenants had spent upwards of £600 on repairs but College refused to allow reduced fine. (Ca.1.8–10)

1850 1 house sub-let to Charles Pashler, hosier. (Box 2.E14)

1851 1 house sub-let to James Miller, plumber and glazier. (Box 2.E15)

1856–9 2 houses assigned to James Miller and then mortgaged to John Gillam Bell, solicitor. 1 tenement assigned to Joshua Harper, staymaker, mortgaged to Clement Francis and then let to Harper. (Box 2.E16–17, E19–22, E25–8)

1856   3 tenements in rear assigned to Robert Sayle, draper. (Box 2.E23–4)

1859   2 tenements assigned and then let to Robert Sayle, draper. Surveyed by Richard Harwood who supervised building of draper's shop and gave alternative valuation of converting fine into ground rent. (Box 2.E30–1; BUR.0.5(c))

Nos 10–12

1867   No. 10 and 2 tenements in Blue Lion Yard conveyed to College by Elizabeth Jane King for £860. Paid for from sale of Babraham rent charge and land to Kettering and Thrapston Railway. Let to Robert Sayle, draper. (Box 2.F6, G1; COL.14.3 p. 180)

No. 21 (The Chalice)

1585   Bequeathed by Henry Harvey, Master of Trinity Hall. Let for £6. (Box 2.A5–6)

1636   Let to Thomas Bendish of Helions Bumpstead. Sub-let to James Hawkes, chandler. (Box 2.A9)

1641   Let to William Winch of St Faith's Parish London, silkman. Sub-let to James Hawkes. (Box 2.A10)

1658–1700   Let to Ann Hawkes, widow of James (who bought lease). (BUR.11.0.C f. 1v)

1700   Let to James Fletcher, grocer. (Box 2.A12)

1708   Let to Elizabeth Chess, widow of Peter, haberdasher of hats. (BUR.6.3 pp. 379–82)

1723–1837   Let to Michael Headley, tallow chandler, then to Peter Headley, tallow chandler, then to widow Frances, then to Miss Sarah Headley and husband Rev. James Speare. (Box 2.A13–21, B1–3; BUR.3.3; BUR.6.4 pp. 193–6, 355–8; BUR.6.5 pp. 154–6)

1801   Rent increased from £6 to £9 10s. (BUR.6.5 pp. 154–6)

1802   Valued by William Custance: old buildings. (Ca.1.3)

1823   Valued by Elliot Smith: chandling office in yard, £200–£250 needed to put into repair. (Ca.1.6)

1839   Land tax redeemed for £58 3s 1d. House and brewery. (BUR.8.9; Box 2.B4)

1842–67   Let to Edward Jay, grocer. (Box 2.B5–7)

1845   New warehouse cost College £200, Jay paid 5% interest. (BUR.8.9; COL.14.3 p. 37)

1848   Agreed to rebuild garden wall for £16. (COL.14.3 p. 56)

1862   Surveyed by Richard Harwood. (BUR.0.5(d))

1866–7   Jay in arrears with rent. (BUR.0.5(d))

1867   Let to James Baker, grocer, allowed to let warehouses at rear quarterly. (Box 2.B8)

Nos 63–4 (St Nicholas Hostel). B on Map 4.

1585 Bought by College from Symon Watson for £150 (using £140 given by Sir Henry Killigrew). Let for £7. (Box 4.H9)

1585 Let to Laurence Chaderton, who spent 100 marks on repairs and so rent for half year reduced to 6s 8d. (BUR.11.1 p. 9)

1594 Sold to John Norket, alderman and John Brasbone, scrivener, for £200 and made over to Chaderton, who lived there. In this way, College received loan of £200. (Box 4.H12, H15)

1603 Given by Chaderton to College; he remained tenant. (Box 4.H16)

1613 Rent raised from 10s to £7 as John Spenluffe's rent charge was sold. (BUR.11.1)

–1677 Let to Laurence Chaderton and then to daughter Elizabeth (first Johnson and then Salmon). (BUR.11.0.C f. 1v; COL.9.1(A) p. 111)

1679 Let to Sir Thomas Slater (for no fine) as soon as he had spent £30 on building barn and stable. Slater and previous tenant, the late William Lendall, spent £206 0s 10d between them on repairs. (Box 4.K1; COL.14.1 preliminary pp. 15–16)

1782–92 Alienated and then let to Thomas Johnson, brewer and widow. (BUR.6.4 pp. 370–1; Box 4.K4)

1792–1824 Alienated to Edward Ind, brewer and trustees. (BUR.6.5 pp. 49–50)

1801 Valued by Alexander Watford. (Ca.1.2)

1812 Valued by William Custance. No great business as a brewery; could convert into building land at good price. (Ca.1.5)

1824 Let to Peter Grain and to Elliot Smith, auctioneer. Rent increased to £30, fine reduced to £1100 if tenant build within one year. Valued by Elliot Smith. (BUR.3.3; BUR.6.5 pp. 523–6; Ca.1.11)

1827–52 2 newly erected tenements and brewhouse let separately to Peter Grain and Elliot Smith. (Box 4.K5–10)

1852 Surveyed and valued by Elliot and John Smith. No. 63 let to Henry Rance, solicitor. (Box 4.K15–16; BUR.0.5(a))

1852–65 No. 64 let to Thomas and George Bradwell, builders. (Box 4.K12–13)

1852–+ Brew-house assigned and let to Clement Francis; tenant to spend at least £800 on buildings. Let with White Horse from 1865. (BUR.6.6 pp. 280–1; COL.14.3 pp. 84–5; Box 4.K18–19)

1865 No. 64 assigned to Henry Rance. (Box 4.K20)

1866 Nos 63–4 let to Henry Rance, solicitor. Valued by Mr Wentworth. (Box 4.K21; COL.14.3 p. 181)

Cambridge – Sempire Lands

1668 Lease of 21 acres South of Cambridge and partly in Coe Fen Leys given by Thomas Holbech; landlord was Peterhouse and

Emmanuel paid 19s 6d and 6 bushels of wheat, 1 quarter of malt and 1 quarter of oats in rent. Income (£10 10s) to go towards new Chapel. (BUR.8.2; Box 2.J2(1); BUR.6.3 pp. 190–2)

1671 Rent first received by College. (BUR.36.2 f. 2)

1798 Surveyed and mapped by Alexander Watford. (BUR.0.10; BUR.8.7)

1801 Agreed to extinguish common rights. (COL.14.2 f. 128r)

1809 Valued by William Custance. (BUR.8.7; BUR.0.4(a))

1810–15 Inclosed. (BUR.0.4(a–b); BUR.8.8)

1819 Sub-let to Richard Hopkins, brewer. (BUR.6.5 pp. 426–30)

1820 Part of lease surrendered to Hopkins for £205 and invested in 3% consols. (Box 2.J13; COL.14.2 f. 174r)

1823 Sold rest of lease for £500; invested in stock. (BUR.11.3; COL.14.2 f. 178r)

Cambridgeshire – Babraham (3 on Map 3)

1585 Robert Taylor gave rent charge of £20 arising from manor. (BUR.11.0.A f. 1v; BUR.2.6 f. 257r)

1631 Sub-poena served to recover rents. (BUR.8.2)

1862 Sold rent charge for £596 13s 4d. Used money to purchase premises at 10 St Andrew's Street and Blue Lion Yard. (BUR.6.6 pp. 412–16; COL.14.3 p. 180)

Cambridgeshire – Caxton (18 on Map 3)

1590 John Sleigh bequeathed lease of impropriated revenues of rectory and £50 for renewal (though only £40 10s was received). Of annual income, £15 due to Dean and Canons of Windsor, £14 13s 4d for incumbent's stipend, 3s 10d to Archdeacon of Ely and 20d to Dean and Chapter of Ely. Remainder divided among Master and Fellows, until at least 1598. (BUR.0.9; BUR.8.1; BUR.11.1; Ibish 1985, pp. 104–6)

1605 Lease not renewed.

Cambridgeshire – Eltisley (20 on Map 3)

1593 About 200 acres of arable land let by William Marshall to Gawan Pelset on 20 September; rent of £30 to be paid to College. (Box 12.B17). College bought estate for £900 on 29 September. (Box 12). Tenant carried out extensive repairs. (Box 12.B17). Woods let separately for £4 for 51 years, then for £2 for 10 years. (Box 12.B19)

1623 Problems over collection of rent of 6 acres. (Box 12.C3)

1649 Wood and arable let for £34 for 7 years, then for £32, and 2 fat capons or 6s for each at audit added. (Box 12.C4)

1677 Allowed tenant costs of law suit and arbitration. (BUR.8.2)

1686 Letters of attorney issued to recover arrears. (BUR.6.3 p. 129; BUR.8.2)

1694 Let for very low fine of £5 because tenant had paid taxes for 7 years though there had been no express covenant in lease. Rent still £32. (Box 12.C7; BUR.3.1)

1741 Arrears so crops seized. (COL.14.2 p. 10)

1746 Let with no fine as new covenants to improve land, tenant allowed £6 towards removing, repairing or rebuilding barn. (Box 12.C11)

1749–78 Let to Samuel and then to Evan Mortimer. Allowed 2 years' rent towards cost of rebuilding house, barns and stables in more convenient place. Valued n.d. (Box 12.C10, C13–14)

1770 Threatened to seize crops. (COL.14.2 f. 68v; BUR.6.4 p. 235)

1777 Surveyed by Joseph Freeman. (BUR.8.6)

1778–96 Let to Arthur George Karr of Birchin Lane, London, wine merchant. (Box 12.C15; COL.14.2 ff. 92v, 105r)

1800 Surveyed and mapped by Alexander Watford. (BUR.0.10)

1801 Surveyed by William Custance; in need of repairs. (Box 12.C17)

1802–10 Sued Sir Richard Hetley for breach of covenants. Defendant to pay 12d damages, 40s costs and to repair for £800; cost College £106. (COL.14.2 f. 130v; BUR.0.4(a); Cb.2.1)

1815 Allotted 7a.2r.3p. on inclosure of Papworth. Surveyed by William Custance and vacancy advertised. Let at rack rent for £100. (Box 12.C17)

1822 Distrained upon tenant. (BUR.0.4(d); Cb.2.2)

1827 Prospective tenant withdrew as open field land and titheable, so hard to improve. (Cb.2.6–7)

1828 Let for £75. Expenditure by College on repairs. (Box 12.C18; BUR.8.8)

1833 Expenditure by College on repairs. (BUR.8.8)

1836 College agreed to build or repair barns. (COL.14.2 f. 215r)

1837–82 Let to Mr Sadler. First land, then 3 cottages and 47a. from 1855. (COL.14.2 f. 218v; COL.14.3 p. 96; BUR.6.7 pp. 50–5)

1837–55 3 cottages and 47a. let to Mr Warwick. (COL.14.2 f. 218v; BUR.0.5(a))

1838 Expenditure by College on repairs. (BUR.8.9)

1843 Tithes commuted. (BUR.8.9)

1854 Valued by Robert Emson. Warwick's property in dilapidated state and served notice to quit. (Box 12; BUR.0.5(a))

1864 College agreed to inclosure. Had owned 157a.2r.6p. in open fields, 45a. old inclosures, 10a. wood and spinney. (Box 12)

1865 College spent £425 on new farmhouse; £109 on drainage tiles. (BUR.8.9; Box 12)

1866   College spent £562 on farm buildings, £230 on draining. Surveyed by R. Harwood. (BUR.8.9)

Cambridgeshire – Fowlmere (14 on Map 3)

1588   Thomas Skinner gave rent charge of £8 arising from manors of Fowlmere and Lavenham (Suffolk). (Box 1.A6)
1620   Distrained for arrears. (BUR.8.1)
1627   Charterhouse became responsible for this half of rent charge. (BUR.11.1)
1648   Rent in arrears. (BUR.8.2)

Cambridgeshire – Littleport (35 on Map 3)

1681   Thomas Holbech gave rent charge of £41 13s 5d, together with £9 from lands at Waterbeach. Of the income, £20 to be paid yearly to Catechist and Ecclesiastical Lecturer, half of remainder was for the Master and rest for repairs of the College. (Box 1.C7)

Cambridgeshire – Waterbeach (36 on Map 3)

1681   Thomas Holbech gave rent charge of £9 arising from lands called Highelman and Lowelman, part of manors of Waterbeach and Denny, together with £41 13s 5d from Littleport. See under Littleport for how money was to be divided. (Box 1.C6)
1808   Owner of estate wanted College to redeem rent charge by purchase of land tax or to move charge to another freehold estate in parish. (BUR.0.10)
1847   Distrained for 9 years' arrears. (BUR.0.4(f))

Essex – Braintree (Hobbes) (28 on Map 3)

1632   Thomas Hobbes bequeathed remainder of rents to maintain 2 or 3 scholars at St Catharine's College or Emmanuel, with preference to sons of 'godly poor ministers'. Two scholarships allotted to each college. Land originally let for £35 but then for £30; of this sum, £6 paid to Vicar of Braintree, £5 to Catechist at St Catharine's College and £3 to an Exhibitioner at Pembroke College. (SCH.1.1; Jones 1936, p. 238)
c. 1770   Rental income only £4/year for 2 exhibitioners. (COL.9.1(A) p. 224)
1778–96   Gap in accounts.

Essex – Dagenham (45 on Map 3)

1865 1a.2r.12p. acquired under award of common rights of manor of Stapleford Abbots. (Es.2.169a)

1866 Let to Philip Taylor of Black Bush Farm, Stapleford Abbots. (BUR.6.7 pp. 41–4)

Essex – Hornchurch (Lusby) (41 on Map 3)

1832 5 cottages and meadow conveyed to College by will of Henry Lusby. Annual income £71 10s. (Box 16.A2; Es.1.1; FEL.5.11)

1832–60+ 2 meadows let to Charles Cove, builder. Already been tenant for 20 years in 1833 and father had been tenant for about 20 years beforehand. (Es.2.172; COL.14.3 pp. 67, 145)

1835–6 College spent £1537 on buildings; Charles Cove had offered to estimate for work but had not been employed. (BUR.8.8; Es.2.172; FEL.5.11)

1847 Distrained for arrears without success. Sold 2a.1r. to Thames Haven and Dock Railway for £550. (Es.1.7; Es.2.174)

1850 Distrained for arrears. (Es.1.16b)

1858 Property alleged to be let at highest rents of area. (BUR.0.5(b))

1860 Surveyed by Mr Carter. (FEL.5.11)

1866 Surveyed. (Es.1.39b)

Essex – Lusby Estate

1830 Henry Lusby died, left property to Mrs Elisabeth Gray for her life and after her death to College. She died in 1832. (FEL.5.11)

1832 Conveyed to College by will of Henry Lusby. Total value £332 12s 0d less £2 12s land tax. (Box 16.A2; proved 28 Oct. 1830; Es.1.1)

1834–50 Managed by John Roberts of Middle Temple. (BUR.6.6 pp. 171–3)

1850– Managed by Edward Phillips of 3 Harcourt Buildings, Temple. (COL.14.3 p. 64)

Essex – Navestock (Lusby) (42 on Map 3)

1832 Conveyed to College by will of Henry Lusby. (Box 16.A2; Es.1.1)

1840 Tithes commuted. (FEL.5.11)

Lees Farm (Homestead and c.26a.)

1832 Let for £30. (FEL.5.11)

1833 Valued. (FEL.5.11)

1846 Tithes apportioned. (Es.2.91a)

Meadow (2 cottages and c.10a., West Hatch Farm)

1832   Let for £23. (FEL.5.11)

1850   Valued by Thomas Champness; arable in need of manuring and underdraining. (Es.2.92)

1863–4   Copyholds at Navestock and Stapleford Abbots enfranchised for £442 15s 2d. (BUR.8.9)

1866   Surveyed. (Es.1.39b)

Essex – Ripple (4 on Map 3)

1585   Sir Walter Mildmay bought 23 acres of marsh at Ripple from John Digge and gave to College. Let for £20. Soon afterwards, College discovered that 6 of these acres were owned by the Crown. (Box 15.A3–4, A8)

1585–1627+   Let to Valentine Dale, then to daughter Dorothy, Lady North, and then to her son (and member of Emmanuel), Sir John. (Box 15.A5, A6(1), A10; BUR.0.9)

1602   Six leasehold acres let for 4 years for £6, rest let for 21 years for £14. (Box 15.A6(1))

1604   Lease of 6 acres (from Queen Elizabeth to Thomas Warren for 21 years from 1592) assigned to College by Edmund Pye. (Box 15.A9)

1620   College leased 6 acres from Prince of Wales for 12s. (Box 15.A13)

1654   Rent raised to £25. (BUR.11.2)

1660   Bequest of Henry Gale, minister of Hemmington (Northamptonshire), of £54 15s used to pay part of fine to renew lease of 6 acres from Sir Thomas Fanshaw, to endow an exhibition for a scholar from Oundle school. (Box 15.A17; COL.9.10.13 and 22)

1661   Rent raised to £28 (£20 for 17 acres, £8 for 6 acres). (BUR.11.2)

1666   College failed to pay Lady Day rent for 6 acres and Sir Thomas Fanshaw reentered; College agreed to pay arrears, divide and ditch land, and make a gate. College's tenant was to carry out the work, in consideration for which he would be allowed £3 from next half year's rent. (Box 15.A19)

1681   Let to John Booth of London, innholder. Two fat capons or 5s for each at audit added to rent. (Box 15.A22)

1682   College leased 6 acres from Sir Thomas Fanshaw, with covenant to divide and ditch this land from College ground within one year. Half year's rent remitted to tenant. Spent £27 16s on repairs. (Box 15.A16, A20–1; BUR.8.2; SCH.1.1)

1713   Let to Joseph Marlow of London, goldsmith. Whole fine divided as only received once every 21 years. (Box 15.A23; BUR.3.1)

1733   Mapped. (BUR.8.4; ESS.22)

1735–57   Let to Joshua Smart of Romford, grazier. (Box 15.A26)

1758   Distrained on Smart. (BUR.8.6)

1786   Surveyed by Joseph Freeman. (BUR.0.9; BUR.8.6)

1806   Asked for allowance towards new flood gates. (Lo.8.3)

1811   Surveyed by Francis Whishaw; suspected exchange had occurred. (BUR.0.4(a); BUR.8.8; Es.4.3; Es.2.1d)

1812–21   Tenant in arrears, safe man but negligent; tried to distrain but found no cattle. (Es.2.1e–f; Es.4.g–i; Lo.2.6; Sr.17.11, 15, 25a; COL.14.2 f. 173v)

1825   John Wiggins, land surveyor, employed to let estate. (Es.4.6b; BUR.0.4(c); Box 15.A32)

1833   Ordered to rebuild sea wall; advised to use stone rather than planks. (Es.2.3b)

1848   Tithes at Barking commuted. (BUR.8.9)

1861–6   Needed to rebuild sea wall; resistance from adjoining landowner. (Lo.11.125, 132)

Essex – Stapleford Abbots, Mitchell's Farm (Lusby) (43 on Map 3)

1832   Homestead and about 40a. conveyed to College by will of Henry Lusby. Rent £60. (Box 16.A2; Es.1.1; FEL.5.11)

1843   College spent £326 8s 4d on rebuilding after fire. (BUR.8.9; Es.1.2)

1850   Surveyed by Thomas Champness. (FEL.5.11)

1851   Ejected tenant for bad management. Farmhouse barely habitable. College took action in Queen's Bench and not stopped until 3 days before trial when all legal expenses had been incurred. (Es.1.18a; FEL.5.11; BUR.0.5(a))

1853   Expenditure on repairs. (FEL.5.11; BUR.0.5(a))

1857   Repairs needed to barn floor. (Es.2.93a)

1863–4   Copyholds at Navestock and Stapleford Abbots enfranchised for £442 15s 2d. (BUR.8.9)

1864   Tenant allowed to plough up pasture so long as reinstated before end of lease. (Box 16.F18)

Essex – Stondon (16 on Map 3)

1588   Sir Walter Mildmay bought Whipples Farm for £260 and gave to College. Already let for 21 years from 1572; Mildmay granted lease in reversion to Edmund Downing and John Sale for 21 years (not taken up). Rent was £10. (Box 15.D2, D5; BUR.11.0.B f. 4v)

1639–1717+   Let to Richard Harrington of Finchingfield; Mr Sandars paid fine and family were tenants thenceforward. (Box 15.D10–13; BUR.6.3 ff. 496–7; BUR.11.1)

1652   Two fat capons at audit added to rent. (Box 15.D11)

1729 Covenant that tenant to sow grass seed, College to put buildings into repair. (Box 15.D14)

1770 Surveyed by John Smith. 45a.0r.27p. Needed repairs. (Box 15.D16; BUR.8.6)

1771–1811 Let to Rev. Rice Evans of Fox Hatch near Ongar, then to Thomas, then to William, son of Rice. Sub-let. (Box 15.D17–19; COL.14.2 f. 93r; Sr.17.6)

1778 Valued by Joseph Freeman. 48a.0r.4p. (Box 15.D18)

1789 Valued by Joseph Freeman. Much out of repair but well managed. (Box 13.B35)

1799 Land tax redeemed for £80 13s 4d; invested in 3% consols. (Es.4.4e; COL.14.2 f. 123r)

1800 Surveyed and mapped by Alexander Watford. (BUR.0.10; Es.4.2)

1801 College advised to fell timber soon as it was being injured by the poor. (Sr.1.1)

1810 Timber surveyed by Francis Whishaw. (BUR.8.8; BUR.0.4(a))

1811 Surveyed by Francis Whishaw: 48a.1r.15p. In need of repairs, proper management, drainage. Let at rack rent £73. (Es.4.3, 4c; Sr.17.8; BUR.0.4(a); Box 15.D20)

1816 Distrained on tenant. (Es.4.4i)

1817 College agreed to allow timber for repairs. (Es.4.4k)

1820–4 Requests from tenant for rent reduction and repairs. (Es.2.1h; Es.4.4l–m; Lo.11.5, 135–6; Sr.17.40)

1825 Surveyed by William Cantis. 47a.3r. Repairs needed, lay 3 pieces to permanent pasture. Let for £50. (Box 15.D21; Es.4.4b–c, 5; BUR.8.8)

1827 Proposed allowance to tenant for repairs. (Es.4.8b)

1830–90 Assigned and let to James Webb. (COL.14.2 f. 202v; Box 15.D22–3)

1833 Expenditure by College on repairs. (BUR.0.4(e))

1839 Allowed tenant £25 for repairs. (Box 15.D22)

1847 Allowed tenant new oak barn floor. (Es.4.9b)

1850 Tithes commuted. (BUR.0.5(a))

1853 Allowed tenant £50 for repairs. (Box 15.D23)

1858–9 College paid part of costs of fire, £386 on new farm buildings and £49 17s 3d on repairs. (BUR.0.5(c); BUR.8.9; COL.14.3 p. 127; Es.4.9c)

1867 College agreed to spend £420 on new farmhouse, tenant to pay additional £20 a year. (COL.14.3 p. 182)

Hook End Farm

1867 Bought for £2535, costs of £41 13s 6d, new house for £50. (BUR.8.9)

1871 Surveyed by Mr Sworder. (BUR.8.9)

Essex – Stratford (Lusby) (44 on Map 3)

1832   Conveyed to College by will of Henry Lusby. (Box 16.A2; proved 28 Oct. 1830; Es.1.1)
1836   Small piece of land conveyed to Stratford Road Commissioners; sum received spent on replacing buildings destroyed in altering bridge. (COL.14.2 f. 216v)
1843   College gave £5 5s towards plate to John Tucker for defeating proposed railway. (COL.14.3 p. 26)

2 Forest Lane, Maryland Point

1832   Let to Mrs French for £60. (FEL.5.11)
1843   Surveyed by Ford and Gayen. (Es.1.2)
1844   College spent £160 on repairs. (BUR.8.9)
1850   Rent reduced to £50. (Box 16.B18)
1856   Surveyed by Thomas Champness. (Es.6.1)
1866   Used as a school. (Es.1.39b)
1867   Let to Rev. James McQuoin of Stratford, rent £62. (BUR.6.7 pp. 100–5)
1871   Advertised vacancy and let. (BUR.0.5(f); Box 16.B20)

Wharf

1832   Conveyed to College ⅝ coal wharf and 3 cottages adjoining by will of Henry Lusby, rent £90. (Es.1.1; FEL.5.11)
1834   Bought ⅑ of wharf for £346 18s 9d. (BUR.8.8; Box 16.D43)
1835   Mapped by J. Blore. (FEL.5.11)
1836   Bought ⅜ of wharf. College spent £90 on buildings. (Box 16.D48; FEL.5.11)
1837   College agreed to spend £400 on buildings on wharf, tenant to spend like sum and pay £90/year instead of £70. (COL.14.2 f. 218r)
1838–(?91)   Let to C. W. Tanner; rent £90. (Box 16.D49–51; COL.14.3 p. 17)
1848   Rent increased by £30/year as 5% interest on £600 spent on new warehouse. (BUR.8.9; COL.14.3 p. 52)
1854   College spent £196 16s on new timber wharfing (£250 authorized); had considered brick but too expensive. Surveyor was C. Dyson. (BUR.8.9; BUR.0.5(a–b); COL.14.3 p. 89)
1858   Let to C. W. Tanner; rent £130; 14 years; tenant to insure for £2000. (Box 16.D50–1)
   Surveyed by Thomas Champness: more repairs to wharfing soon be needed, should be paid for by tenant; value of wharfs reduced by railways though this one well situated; would be difficult to find man with large enough capital to undertake

business if vacant. Tanner built 3 new coalsheds for £200. (BUR.0.5(b); Es.5.1–6)

Tanner proposed (to Phillips) College spend £200 on new coal sheds and tenant pay 6% outlay; or Tanner spend £200 and allow for improvements at end of term; Champness thought 6% good rate and buildings great acquisition; maybe Tanner could pay 8%; Castlehow replied College not likely to agree: Champness' report did not encourage outlay; wait until Oct. (Es.5.4)

1859   Tanner paid for survey. (FEL.5.11; Es.5.9)

1865   College advised to buy houses adjoining wharf; no reply and sold for more than expected. (BUR.0.5(d))

1866   College agreed to allow Mr Tanner to enlarge water accommodation; wharf considerably under-let. (COL.14.3 p. 178; Es.1.39b)

Essex – Woodham Ferrers (22 on Map 3)

1594   College bought rent charge of £13 6s 8d from William Fludd of Upton (Norfolk), using £200 obtained from sale of St Nicholas Hostel. (Box 4.H12; BUR.11.1)

1613   Payments by William Fludd ceased: he paid rent charge until 1608, and then repaid a bond of £35 in instalments. (BUR.11.1)

Hertfordshire – Letchworth (10 on Map 3)

1586   Robert Snagge gave rent charge of £6 13s 4d. (Box 1.A4)

1858   Rent charge to be collected annually instead of once every 4 years. (BUR.0.5(b))

Hertfordshire – Radwell (23 on Map 3)

1606   John Parker bequeathed annuity of £20: £10 for one Fellow, £5 each to 2 scholars. (Box 9.Oa.6)

1613   Rent charge commuted for 200 marks. (Box 1.A9(1))

Huntingdonshire – Godmanchester (8 on Map 3)

Horseshoe Inn, 20 acres of meadow and 2 closes of pasture

1585   Sir Walter Mildmay bought estate and conveyed to College. Let for £22, of which £20 to be paid to schoolmaster of Godmanchester grammar school. (Box 13.A13, A22)

1629–91+   Let to Conny family (Robert, haberdasher to 1650; John from 1661, of Rochester 1670, of Canterbury 1691, latterly Doctor of Physick). (BUR.11.0.C f. 3v; Box 13.B2, B7–10; BUR.11.2)

1649–51   Repairs carried out. (BUR.8.2)

1670   Two fat capons or 5s for each at audit to be added to rent after 6 years. (Box 13.B7)

1698–1719   Let to Katharine Pell, widow and innholder, and then to James Pell, grocer. (BUR.6.3 pp. 245–9, 348–52; Box 13.B13)

1749–90   Let to Original Jackson and then to son John. (COL.14.2 f. 27v; Box 13.B18, B21)

1763   Tenant allowed to demolish barn and to pay College value of materials. (COL.14.2 f. 56v)

1774   Letters of attorney to receive arrears from John Jackson. (BUR.6.4 pp. 322–3)

1778   Valued by Joseph Freeman. (Box 13.B23)

1789   Surveyed by Joseph Freeman. (BUR.8.6)

1790   Inn and meadows let separately to William Fisher of Cambridge, banker, at least £300 to be spent by tenant on premises. (Box 13.B29–32)

1801   Meadows assigned to Henry Sweeting. (BUR.6.5 pp. 142–3)

1804   College gave £30 towards repairs to school. (BUR.8.7)

1805   Fisher became bankrupt. Valued by William Custance. Too many outbuildings, let oxyard at rack rent to tenant. Inn let to John Stephen Dind, dancing master; rent increased to £13. Meadows let with West Street. (Box 13.C2–5, C20)

1808   College gave £15 towards repairs at school. (BUR.8.7)

1812–58   Assigned and let to Robert Matson, farmer. (Box 13.C8, C11–12)

1819   Surveyed by William Custance. (BUR.8.8; Box 13.C20)

1821   Tenant's affairs in Chancery. College had no intention of extending lease. (BUR.3.3; Hu.3.316)

1859   Let to Richard Farey of Warboys, farmer, rent increased to £20. (Box 13.C17; BUR.6.6 pp. 359–61)

1860   Mortgaged to Martha Brown of Brampton (Huntingdonshire), widow. (BUR.6.6 pp. 391–2)

1871   Assigned from executors to Mrs Martha Brown to William Fowler of Huntingdon, solicitor. (BUR.6.7 pp. 180–1)

West Street, messuage and land

1585   Sir Walter Mildmay bought estate and conveyed to College. Let for £26 13s 4d. (Box 13.A13, A22)

1612–92+   Let to John Shepherd and then to brother Thomas (of Hilton, Huntingdonshire 1656, of Doctors Commons, London 1677, of Northampton 1692). (Box 13.B11, D2; BUR.6.3 pp. 27–30; BUR.11.1)

1656   £100 spent by College in rebuilding. (BUR.11.2)

1677   Two fat capons or 5s for each at audit added to rent. (BUR.6.3 pp. 27–30)

1716   Tenant allowed one year off fine because of loss of sheep. (BUR.3.1)

1723–93+ Let to Alured Clarke and descendants. (BUR.6.3 pp. 527–30, 650–3; BUR.6.4 pp. 196–8; Box 13.B15–16, B19–20, B22, B25–6, B33; COL.14.2 f. 96v)

1730 Buildings now or about to be erected to be kept in repair, tenant asked for lower fine. (BUR.6.3 pp. 650–3; BUR.3.2 f. 43v)

1780 Tenant asked, successfully, for fine to be lowered as had been increased when rents being reduced. (Box 23.B24)

1786 Surveyed by Joseph Freeman. (BUR.8.6)

1800–46+ Let to George Maule and Henry Sweeting of Huntingdon, then to Sweeting alone. (Box 13.C1, C4–7, C9–10; BUR.6.5 pp. 212–13, 223–30; COL.14.3 p. 44)

1801 Valued by Alexander Watford. (Box 13.C20)

1805 Valued by William Custance: 77a.0r.5p. plus 18a.2r.13p. meadows added. Inclosure cost £497 18s 8d and College paid £270. (Box 13.C4–5, C20; BUR.8.7)

1809 81a.3r.26p. allotted on inclosure + 11a.0r.34p. let in 1 lease; no fine so long as costs of inclosure and fencing paid by Sweeting; rent £40 12s 4d. (BUR.6.5 pp. 223–30; COL.14.2 f. 147r)

1812 Rent reduced to £39 8s 4d. (Box 13.C6–7)

1819 Valued by William Custance. Land valuable as near town. (Hu.4.3; Box 13.C20)

1826 Valued by William Cantis. 95a.0r.28p. Tenant asked for reduced fine, in vain. (Hu.4.3–4, 6; Box 13.C20)

1846 Let at rack rent £200. (COL.14.3 p. 44)

1846 Valued by Emson. (BUR.8.9)

1847 Sold 3a.2r.33p. to Great Northern Railway Co. for £760. (COL.14.3 p. 47)

1851–91 Let to Henry Markham and then to William Markham of Godmanchester, farmers. (Box 13.C14–16, C18)

1851 Rent reduced to £170. (Box 13.C14–15)

1857 Valued by James Witt. Investigation by Clement Francis about encroachment by owners of estate about to be sold by trustees of late Mr Sweeting. (BUR.0.5(a–6))

1858 Rent £210, covenant introduced about mineral rights. (Box 13.C16)

1858–62 College provided draining tiles for 21a. (BUR.8.9; Box 13.C18)

1860 College spent £20 4s 11d on materials for new hovel. (BUR.8.9)

1861 Claim for reimbursement for land tax. (Hu.3.14–16)

1864 Conveyed 1a.1r.7p. to Kettering and Thrapston railway. (COL.14.3 p. 166)

† Huntingdonshire – Gransden (5 on Map 3)

1585 Edward Leeds gave rent charge of £16 arising from estate. (Box 1.A3)

1599   Rent charge extinguished on purchase of manor. (BUR.11.0.B f. 1v; BUR.11.1)

Copyholds

1599   College bought manor and land from Edward Leeds; entire purchase cost £340. Let for £5 17s. (Box 14.A11; BUR.11.0.C f. 3r.)

Messuage, 18 acres of arable, ½ acre of meadow

1599   College bought from Edward Leeds (see under Copyholds). Let for £5, with covenants for tenant to keep court and provide refreshment. (Box 14.A11)

1629–1790   Let to James Kettle, yeoman to 1689, then to Timothy Kettle, grocer, then to Charles Kettle, gent. (Box 14.D4, D7, D10–11, D16–17, D20–1, E1, E4, E7–8, E10, E12, E14, E16, E18, E20–1; BUR.11.1)

1770   Surveyed by Smith. (BUR.8.6)

1778   Surveyed by Joseph Freeman. (BUR.8.6)

1790–1826   Let to Charles Kettle's executors John Spring of Gransden, carpenter and Samuel Flinders of Waresley, farmer, and then to Spring alone. (Box 14.E24, E27–8, E30)

1791   Surveyed by Joseph Freeman. (BUR.8.6)

1796   Surveyed by Joseph Freeman. (BUR.8.7)

1797   Let with Berry Closes. (Box 14.E27–8)

1798   Valued by Alexander Watford: 34a.1r.0p. (Box 14.C)

1799   Visited by Alexander Watford in connection with land tax. (BUR.0.10)

1812   Surveyed by William Custance: 72a.1r.0p. Manor house let as double cottage, barn roof needed repair. (Box 14.C; BUR.8.8)

1815   Wood surveyed by William Custance. (BUR.8.8; BUR.0.4(b))

1823   James Spring apologised for not sending more rent: shepherd lost 11 sheep going to St Ives fair as very wet and dark and did not find them until too late. (Hu.2.2)

1823–6   Dispute over ownership of lands of Horseshoe public house. Lands mapped by Alexander Watford (the younger). Advice from lawyer that would be hazardous and expensive to recover possession, if had been lost. (Box 14.C; BUR.0.4(c))

1825   Surveyed by William Cantis: 73a.1r.0p. Notice to John Spring to repair manor house and then to him and James Spring to quit. (Box 14.C; BUR.8.8; Hu.2.4–5)

1827   Additions made to farm buildings. (BUR.0.4(d))

1833   Rent reduced to £30. (COL.14.2 f. 211r)

1836   College agreed to build or repair barns. (COL.14.2 f. 215r)

1843   Sealed inclosure bill. Farmhouse and 77a.1r.31p. including new inclosures (68a.3r.31p.) let to William Webb, Master of Clare Hall, rent £40, tenant allowed to convert farmhouse into 2 cottages, tenant to pay costs of inclosure. (Box 14.F1; COL.14.3 p. 23)

1851–69 Copyholds enfranchised. (COL.14.3 pp. 63, 151, 167, 206; BUR.8.9)

1862 Copyholds enfranchised. (COL.14.3 p. 151)

1863 Valued by Witt. (BUR.8.9)

1864 Let to Theodore Vincent Webb of Great Gransden, rent £60, introduced covenant about mineral rights. (Box 14.F2)

38 acres arable and pasture

1599 College bought from Edward Leeds (see under Copyholds). Let for £4 1s. (Box 14.A11)

1651 Rent reduced to £4. (BUR.11.0.C f. 3r)

After 1725 Let at rack rent. (BUR.3.2 f. 19)

1797 Let to John Spring (tenant of 18a), rent £14. (Box 14.E29)

1798 Valued by Alexander Watford. (Box 14.C)

Berry Closes (7 acres) and Meadow (7 acres, 1 rood)

1599 College bought from Edward Leeds (see under Copyholds). Let for £8. (Box 14.A11)

1619 Let with covenant to plant 252 willow trees. (BUR.11.0.C f. 3r)

1634 and 1644 Let with covenant to plant 240 willows 7 feet high. (Box 14.D6, D8–9)

1634–98+ Let to Timothy Griffin until 1684, then to Charles Griffin of London, grocer. (Box 14.D6, D8–9, D12–13, D15, D18–19, E2)

1695 Fine set in Master's absence, too low as misinformation from tenant. (BUR.3.1)

1709– Let to tenants of messuage and 18a. (Box 14.E2, E5–6, E9, E11, E13, E15, E17, E19, E22–3, E25–6)

Huntingdonshire – Stanground (13 on Map 3)

1588 Sir Walter Mildmay gave rent charge of £8 arising from rectory land. (Box 1.A5)

Kent – Ash (37 on Map 3)

† *Chequer Court (Thorpe) (See Plate 24)*

1719 Conveyed to College by will of George Thorpe of 7 March 1717. (Box 17.C7)

1721–1816 College paid £2/year for collecting rents. (SCH.1.17)

1721 College paid for frame to map of estate. (BUR.8.4)

1722 Richard May in debt for £114 for timber and £50 for ½ year's rent. Spent £37 on repairs. (BUR.0.8; SCH.1.17)

1741   Seized effects of Richard May for 3½ years rent; lost £200 13s 10d by him. (SCH.1.17; Box 17.C10)

1741–62+   Let to William Sayer of Ash, yeoman, rent £100, tenant to rebuild barn and repair buildings, allowed £100 from 1st 2 years' rent and £20 from 3rd year's rent towards costs. (SCH.1.17; Box 17.C9–12)

1742   College paid arrears of quit rent 1733–41. (Box 17.C10)

1744   College spent £173 16s on repairs (new barn). (SCH.1.17)

1778   Letters of attorney issued to seize on Benjamin Rouse. (BUR.0.3(b))

1780   Letters of attorney issued to recover arrears from Benjamin Rouse. (COL.14.2 f. 85v; BUR.6.4 pp. 366–7)

1788–1820   Let to Benjamin Rouse, brothers Francis and Richard joined in security 1788 (similar lease of 1783 not executed). (Box 17.C13, D1–2)

1794   College spent £24 on repairs. (SCH.1.17)

1797   Site of mill let to Benjamin Rouse senior and junior. (Box 17.C14)

1809   Rent £180. (Box 17.D1–2)

1815   Benjamin Rouse not best of farmers, probably indolent, threatened with distraint. (Ke.5.1a–b)

1817–44   College paid £4/year for collecting rents. (SCH.1.17)

1818   Payment to College increased from £21 to £24. (SCH.1.17)

1819   Very unproductive crop of corn, Rouse said had lost £200–£300 that year. (Ke.5.11)

1820   Benjamin Rouse died indebted for £275; widow Susannah wanted to continue to occupy to Bursar's surprise as Rouse had been tardy in paying rent so better to dispose of lease to respectable person. (Ke.5.2, 11)

1821–47   Assigned and then let to George Quested of Littlebourne, nephew and godson of Susannah Rouse. (BUR.6.5 pp. 450–2; Box 17.D3, D4)

1821   Quested had won silver medal from Board of Agriculture and Silver Cup from Kent Association. Tenant agreed to pay Rouse's debts and so left Rouse's sister's quarter share in mill in Chequer field. Tenant had to repair barn floors and build new lodge for stock. (Ke.5.9, 14, 16)

1822   Quested pulled down and rebuilt old oast and 2 good lodges, hoped for ½ expenses. Given £50. (Ke.5.19; SCH.1.17)

1823   Rent £200, covenants to repair barn floors and roofs, and build brick wall round farmyard, beer cellar under farmhouse and lean-to. (Box 17.D3)

1824   Tenant allowed £32 towards improvements and repairs. Problems from flooding. Asked to sub-let 10a. marsh to brother Thomas as had to give up as was Commissioner for Sewer of East Kent and so must be disinterested. (SCH.1.17; Box 17.A21; Ke.5.23b)

1825   Sale of agricultural produce almost at standstill in December as millers waited for introduction of larger imperial bushel on 1 Jan. (Ke.5.26)

1826   Built new lead pump. (Ke.5.27b)

1829   Very wet harvest and could not sell hops and corn, so rent late. (Ke.5.29, 31)

1832   College spent £224 on repairs. (SCH.1.17)

1836   Surveyed by Mr Murton. (SCH.1.17)

1837   Rent £220. (Box 17.D4)

1840   College gave £30 towards a chapel at Ash. (SCH.1.17)

1841   College gave 4a.5r.38p. for infant school. (BUR.6.6 pp. 358–9)

1844   Tithes commuted. (SCH.1.17)

1845–   College paid £6/year for collecting rents. (SCH.1.17)

1845   Payments to College and scholars increased from £24 to £30. (SCH.1.17; COL.14.3 p. 35)

1847   Licence to Mr Quested to assign to Isaac Rowe. (COL.14.3 p. 50)

1849   Rent £220. (Box 17.D5)

1850   College spent £92 on repairs. (SCH.1.17)

1851   College spent £89 on repairs to barn floor and kitchen. (SCH.1.17; BUR.0.5(b))

1852–4   Allowed tenant abatement of 10% on 90a. arable (£16). (SCH.1.17)

1853   College spent £31 on repairs. (SCH.1.17)

1856   College spent £26 on repairs (mostly to carpenter). (SCH.1.17; BUR.0.5(b))

1858   College gave piece of plate worth £15 to Mr Quested of Canterbury for gratuitous services. Conveyed land for infant school. (COL.14.3 p. 121; SCH.1.17; Ke.5.35)

1860   Gave £2/year from Thorpe Fund and £3 from College to Ash charities. (SCH.1.17; COL.14.3 p. 135)

1861   College spent £23 on new millstones. (SCH.1.17)

1862   Exchanged land to straighten boundary. (COL.14.3 p. 151)

1863   Tenant to pay interest of 5%/year on sums spent by College on new stables and to live in farmhouse. (Box 17.D6–7)

1864–5   College spent £288 on repairs. (SCH.1.17)

1870   Gave £25 towards school (½ from Thorpe, ½ from College). (COL.14.3 p. 216)

§ *Molland Farm*

1859   Bought for £13,700 + costs. College spent £21 9s 8d on draining tiles. (BUR.8.9; Box 17.H6)

1861   Surveyed by George Quested. (BUR.8.9)

1863   Let yearly. College spent £32 16s 5d on repairs. (Box 17.H8; COL.14.3 p. 160; BUR.8.9)

1864 College spent £81 on repairs. (BUR.8.9)

1868 Allowed tenant £50 for new wall, tenant paying £5/year interest for £100 spent on new buildings. (COL.14.3 pp. 195, 197)

1869 New lodge estimated at £107 4s 10d. (BUR.0.5(e))

1871 College spent up to £300 on oast, tenant paying not less than 5% interest. (COL.14.3 p. 218)

Kent – Lydden and Ewell (Richards) (29 on Map 3)

1639 Walter Richards bequeathed messuage, stable, malthouse and about 37 acres to maintain 2 scholars paying them yearly £6 each, plus £4 towards charges of B.A. degree and £3 for books in following year if they promised to remain in College, plus £6 towards charges of M.A. degree and £4 for books in following year if they promised to remain for 5 years. During these 5 years, they were to receive £8. (Box 17.A12, A14; SCH.1.23F)

1649 Let by Sible Richards, widow, for £17 rent. (Box 17.A13)

1650 Mrs Richards died and rents came to College. (Box 17.A14)

1651 Rent increased to £18. (COL.9.1(A) p. 115)

1672 Tenant allowed £4 9s because of poverty. (SCH.1.1)

1673 Rent reduced to £10, let to Samuel Lucas of Dover, baker. Allowed to demolish messuage. (Box 17.A15)

1674 Law suit with previous tenant. (SCH.1.1)

1676 Decided to divide reduced rents equally between the 2 exhibitioners, except if one were M.A. and the other B.A., former was to receive 4/7 and latter 3/7. (SCH.1.1)

1694 Let to Thomas Reeve of Dover, mariner. Power of attorney granted to recover arrears. (BUR.6.3 pp. 204–8; SCH.1.1)

1696–7 One year's rent spent by College on repairs. (SCH.1.1)

1697 Rent reduced to £8. (BUR.6.3 pp. 243–5)

1737–75 College paid rent collector 6s 8d/year. (SCH.1.10)

1741–180(?4) Let to John Belsey of Coldred (Kent), yeoman and then to Henry Belsey. (Box 17.A17–19; COL.14.2 f. 91r)

1776–96 Gap in accounts. (SCH.1.10)

1784 Valued by Robert Petman: 33a.3r. As fields all distant from each other, difficult to get manure for improvements. (Ke.6.457)

1804 Valued by William Custance: 36a. Let for £40. Most of land in village so could be let in parcels. (BUR.6.5 pp. 194–7; Ke.6.458; SCH.1.10)

1805–6 Land claimed by Vicar of Lydden. (Ke.6.460–1)

1808 College compensated for land taken by turnpike Dover–Barham Downs £22 17s 6d + £5 14s 6d interest. (SCH.1.10)

1816 Valued by William Custance. (BUR.0.4(b))

1817 Tenant accused of malpractice. (Ke.6.466)

1819 Permission granted to tenant to assign lease after he had paid for fencing. (Ke.6.467–8; BUR.6.5 pp. 387–90)

1821 Tenant allowed abatement. (Ke.6.472–3)

1822–3 Tenant allowed 20% abatement. (SCH.1.10)

1823–4 New incumbent at Lydden and dispute reopened over piece of land. George Quested surveyed. Settled by death of sub-tenant. (Ke.6.475–81; Box 17.A21)

1824 Tenant allowed abatement of 10%. (SCH.1.10)

1825 Rent reduced to £35. Tenant to build lodge for sheep at cost of £30. (Ke.6.482–5, 487–8a; Box 17.A20)

1826 Allowed £4. (SCH.1.10)

1827–8 Tenant asked for permission to plough up 10a. meadow; surveyor advised to break up in 2 stages and re-sow about 5a. broken up by mistake. (Ke.6.489; Box 17.A21)

1842 Tithes commuted at Lydden. (SCH.1.10)

1843 Tithes commuted at Ewell. (SCH.1.10)

1848 Distrained on tenant, College lost £27 3s 5d. (SCH.1.10; Ke.6.495a, 496)

1850 New letting agreement by George Quested: rent payable half-yearly. (SCH.1.10)

1856 Specification for new barn: £133 10s – £148 13s. (Ke.6.501a)

1861–2 Tenant allowed to fell sufficient trees to build lodge as no place to store corn after threshed. Forgiven for selling oaks and buying more suitable timber. (BUR.0.5(c–d))

Leicestershire – Leesthorpe (26 on Map 3)

1618 Lady Grace Mildmay bequeathed rent charge of £8 to maintain 4 scholars. (Box 9.Oa10)

1778–95 Gap in accounts.

1858 Rent charge to be collected yearly rather than once every 4 years. (BUR.0.5(b))

Leicestershire – Market Bosworth and Brascote (6 on Map 3)

1585 Sir Francis Hastings gave rent charge of £8. (Box 1.A10; BUR.11.0.A f. 2r)

1617 Rent charge sold for £100 to buy lands worth £8/year. (Box 1.A10)

Lincolnshire – Fleet (33 on Map 3)

1609 Moses Wilton bequeathed 20 acres to maintain 2 scholars from Moulton school. No evidence that bequest ever came to College. (Maddison 1891, pp. 31–4)

1674 William Sancroft (the younger) conveyed rents to value of £20 17s 9½d, to be received after his death, to be used for Chapel and Library. (Box 1.B7–8; BUR.36.2)

1736 Problems of keeping track of change of tenants, College might have had to go to Court of Equity to recover arrears. (BUR.0.9)

1740 Letters of attorney to John Richards of Spalding to receive arrears. (BUR.6.3 f. 711r–v)

1774 Letters of attorney to John Atkinson of Spalding to receive rents. (BUR.6.4 p. 315)

1775 Thomas Lombe took advice about quit rents. (BUR.0.3(a))

1802 College received arrears of nearly 60 years – £358; paid Nettleshipp and Bicknell £64 5s 6½d for recovery (BUR.0.9; BUR.8.7; BUR.11.3; COL.14.2 f. 131v)

1805 College received arrears of £7. (BUR.11.3)

1813 Rents troublesome to collect, Thomas Nettleshipp wished they could be sold. (Sr.17.17a)

1816 Rents still troublesome. (Es.4.4h; Sr.17.19)

1818–25 College received arrears of £38 12s. Wanted to distrain for remainder. (Li.10.288b–e, 290)

§ **Lincolnshire – Pinchbeck** (25 on Map 3)

1602 Edmund English bequeathed £1000 to found 2 fellowships of £10/year each and 6 scholarships of £5/year. (Box 18.B20)

1617 College bought tithes of wool and lamb for £555 from Anthony Oldfield and tithe of corn for £600 from Matthew Robinson. Court of Chancery decreed that terms of will be altered to provide for 9 scholarships worth £5 6s 8d each. A tenth of £5 12s was due to the Crown. (Box 18.B4, B8; BUR.11.0.C f. 4r; BUR.8.1)

1618 Richard Dawson bequeathed remainder of lease of impropriation to College on condition that it pay his widow £61 10s outstanding and purchase the advowson. No evidence that College obeyed these conditions. (Box 9.Oa.8)

1622 Let for £80. (Box 18.A1)

1625 Chaderton asked Dymoke Walpole to pay arrears; he asked for time, and reminded College that he had settled advowson upon it. (Box 18.B11, B12)

1632 William Howard of Cambridge, goldsmith, granted power of attorney to sue for arrears from Thomas Ogle. (Box 18.B13)

1636 Sub-poena served to recover arrears. (BUR.8.2)

1638 College resumed Chancery proceedings to recover arrears. (Box 18.B14)

1652 Rent reduced to £60 and 2 fat capons at audit. (Box 18.A2)

1670–1724 Let to John Wimberley of Pinchbeck, then to son Bevil of

Long Sutton, then to Bevil's son Bevil of Weston 1714.
(Box 18.A3–6)

1677 Rent in arrears. (BUR.8.2)

1678 Rent reduced to £50 and 2 fat capons or 5s for each at audit. Power
of attorney granted to recover arrears. College spent £33 on
chancel repairs. (Box 18.A4; BUR.6.3 pp. 35–6; BUR.8.2)

1681 Rent in arrears. (BUR.8.2)

1693 Rent in arrears. (BUR.8.2)

1695 College received arrears of £121, including cost of repairs to
chancel. (BUR.8.2; BUR.11.2)

1697 College sued for arrears. (BUR.0.9)

1714 Repairs carried out. (BUR.8.2)

1735–1806 Let to John Healey of Pinchbeck, yeoman, then to widow
Ann and to son John, tenant to maintain chancel (put into repair
by College). (Box 18.A7; BUR.6.4 pp. 142–4)

1735 Rent £60. (Box 18.A7)

1756 Rent £80. (BUR.6.4 pp. 142–4)

1778 Surveyed by Joseph Freeman. Meeting about inclosure. (BUR.8.6;
BUR.0.3(a))

1779 Dividend increased to £68/year as great improvements (£20 to
Master, £12 to 4 senior fellows). (COL.14.2 f. 84v)

1784 Rent £90. (Box 18.A9)

1795–8 College subject of suit in Exchequer; judgement awarded
against College but without costs. (BUR.0.3(d))

1800 Meeting about inclosure and drainage attended by Bursar.
Alexander Watford, surveyor, spent 4 days at Spalding.
(Box 18.G1; BUR.0.10)

1801 Sealed bill for draining, inclosing etc. lands and commons.
(COL.14.2 f. 128v)

1805–9 Negotiations about inclosure. Advice by Christopher Pemberton
and William Custance. Custance made out allotments, let farms,
collected arrears of tithes. (BUR.0.4(a); Box 18.G3; BUR.8.7)

1810–11 Visited by William Custance to settle rents and covenants, and
to execute leases. (BUR.0.4(a))

1815 Tithes collected by John Robinson. Land still had to be
ring-fenced. (Li.10.100–4)

1819 Appointed Charles Green of Spalding as inclosure agent. (Li.1.1)

1820 Inclosure award settled; advice taken over payment for fencing
allotments. (Box 18.G4)

1820–2 Advice taken over fencing allotments. (BUR.0.4(c); Li.1.4)

1829 College gave £20 to poor of Pinchbeck. (BUR.8.8)

Cowbit Farm (in North Fen, 'West Pinchbeck')

1811–35 142a.0r.27p. let to Eusebius Dandy of Spalding, innkeeper, and then to son Henry Bennett Dandy, farmer, rent £274. (Box 18.D1, D2)

1811   Tenant to divide into 4 with hedges within 4 years. Had intended to let from 1808. Allowed half of costs of bridge (£21 13s). (Box 18.D1; COL.14.2 f. 151r; BUR.0.4(a))

1815   Dandy bankrupt, John Robinson asked to become tenant. (Li.10.101)

1821   Tenant asked for 3 months to pay rent as corn market very depressed and did not want to sell at low prices. (Li.2.1)

1822   Tenant to build farmhouse within 1 year, liable for ⅕ repairs of chancel. (Box 18.D2)

1823–5   Negotiations over allowance for house despite tenant's offer and agreement to build it at own expense. Had built barn and shepherd's house, planted fences and hedgerows, exceptionally well managed, considerable expenditure on improvements for which not allowed. Given £300 by College at 7% interest. (Li.2.3, 5, 7–12; BUR.8.8)

1833   College called on sureties to pay rent. (Li.2.18)

1836   Rent £270. College paid £135 for farm buildings. (Box 18.D3; COL.14.2 ff. 215r, 216v)

1844   Allowed tenant to break up 9a. grass. (COL.14.3 p. 34)

1846   College to pay not more than 2s 6d/acre towards opposing Black Sluice Drainage Act (with South College Farm). Gave £66 5s. (COL.14.3 p. 44; BUR.8.9)

1847   Valued by Mr Nockolds (paid in 1849). (COL.14.3 p. 50; BUR.8.9)

1848   Allowed tenant £135 in repairing and extending farm buildings. College paid excess of 1s 6d/acre to Black Sluice Drainage Commissioners. (COL.14.3 p. 52; Box 18.D4)

1852–6   New buildings and repairs. Specification for building brewhouse, dairy, cellar and rainwater tank: £152 15s. College agreed to spend £85 on back kitchen, dairy and cellar, tenant to pay £4 additional rent. College spent £145 13s. (Li.2.21; COL.14.3 p. 89; BUR.8.9; BUR.0.5(b))

1856–8   College spent about £86 on drainage tiles. (BUR.8.9)

1856   Tenant died leaving widow and 5 children, brother asked for help to send one boy to Christ's Hospital. (BUR.0.5(b))

1858   Valued by James Witt, 142a.0r.27p. Rent £270 for 1st 1½ years, then £290, College to have mineral rights. College spent £43 8s 4d on repairs. (Box 18.D5; COL.14.3 p. 125; BUR.8.9)

1859   Tenant asked College to consider building 2 small cottages for about £140. (BUR.0.3(c))

1861   College agreed to give £100 to Cowbit church when all money raised and proper contracts drawn up, College 2nd largest landed proprietor. (Li.10.125–6)

1865   Distrained for arrears. (COL.14.3 p. 169)

Cuckoo Farm (in South Fen)

1811–31+ 169a.0r.16p. let to Cawood Robinson of Gosberton and Peregrine Emmitt of Spalding, farmers, then to Robinson alone, rent £245. (Box 18.C1–3; Li.2.26)

1811 Tenants to subdivide into 7 within 4 years. Had intended to let from 1808. (Box 18.C1–2; COL.14.2 f. 151r)

1816 Permission given to tenant to reserve 14a. coleworts for seed notwithstanding covenants to contrary in lease. (Nf.6.15)

1818 Cawood Robinson bankrupt. (Li.2.28, 31, 33; Hu.3.3; BUR.0.4(c))

1819 Cawood Robinson asked College to use its influence to have him reappointed as Drainage Commissioner. (Li.2.35)

1820–6 Deeping Fen drained. College owned 169a.16p. so paid £126 16s 6d drainage tax. Sealed drainage bill 1823. (Li.2.1; Li.9.23–5, 27–9, 33–4, 37–9, 41–3, 45, 47–9, 51–2; Box 18.G5; COL.14.2 f. 179v; BUR.8.8; BUR.0.4(c))

1822–3 Tenant had problems in paying rent, very wet and low prices, asked permission to postpone laying down 2 pieces of land. College agreed to abate £45 if rent paid in good time. (Li.2.36–40)

1825–6 Problems in paying rent. Added 5% interest 1826. (Li.2.47–8, 51–3)

1829–33 Problems in paying rent, College distrained 1831. (Li.2.54–5; BUR.0.4(e))

1831 Rent £255. (Box 18.C4)

1833 Tenant asked for allowance in drainage tax 1826–32, other proprietors allowed half. (Li.2.56b)

1834–92 Let to John Robinson and then to William Robinson. (COL.14.2 f. 209v; COL.14.3 pp. 43–4; BUR.0.4(e); Box 18.C5, C7)

1835–8 New farm buildings. College agreed to spend £500, tenant to pay 6% interest. College spent £162 18s 3d. (COL.14.2 ff. 212r, 213r, 226r; Li.2.57; BUR.8.9)

1846–7 Rent £260. College agreed to build farmhouse and premises, tenant to pay 5%. College spent £405 3s 2d on house and £51 10s 4d on fold yard wall and gates. Allowed tenant £50 towards pulling down old cottage and replacing with stable with granary over. (COL.14.3 pp. 44, 49; Li.5.6; BUR.8.9)

1847–58 Repairs cost College £817 17s 2d. Drainage tiles. College paid for painting of outside of house. New cart shed, pig sty and gig house 1854. (Li.2.60; BUR.8.9; COL.14.3 p. 71)

1848 Rent £280, College paid excess over 2s/acre to Deeping Fen General Annual Drainage Rate. (Box 18.C5)

1852–4 Drainage Commissioners decided needed new sluice, opposed Vernatt's sluice bill. (BUR.8.9; BUR.0.5(b); Li.9.42b)

1858 Valued by James Witt, 169a.0r.16p. Rent £280 for 3½ years, then £322, College to have rights to minerals and coprolites. Repairs and additions to cost £220, tenant to pay interest on all but £135 included in rent. (Li.2.60; Box 18.C6; COL.14.3 p. 125)

1858–63 College spent £307 on new barns, stable, chaff house, granary, dairy, including £5 for blue slating instead of grey. (BUR.8.9; BUR.0.5(c))

1866 College spent £300 on new farmhouse. (BUR.8.9)

1868 Sold 3a.1r.28p. to Spalding and Bourn Railway for £650. (COL.14.3 p. 193; Li.2.61)

1870 Rent £326, allowed tenant tiles for underdraining. (Box 18.C7)

South College and Laurel House Farms (in North Fen, 'West Pinchbeck')

1808 John Robinson asked for bridge. (Box 18.G3)

1811–1906 388a.3r.17p. let to John Robinson of Pinchbeck, farmer, then to nephew John 1848, then in 1870 to John Robinson junior and James Robinson. (Box 18.C4A, E1–6)

1811 Rent £700, tenant to subdivide within 4 years, had intended to let from 1808. (COL.14.2 f. 151r; Box 18.E1)

1822 Rent £740, tenant to fence 2 fields within 1 year, tenant to pay ⅗ costs of repairing chancel, College pay £20 towards hedging. (Box 18.E2)

1825 Discussion about fencing allotments. (Li.5.1b)

1830 Tenant asked for contribution to poor relief. Recommended College to insure 3 barns. (Li.5.2)

1844–5 John Robinson sent haunch of mutton after Christmas. (Li.5.3b–4)

1846 College opposed Black Sluice Drainage (with Cowbit Farm). Started to excavate for Black Sluice. (Li.5.6; COL.14.3 p. 44; BUR.8.9)

1847 Valued by Mr Nockolds (paid in 1849). (COL.14.3 p. 50; BUR.8.9)

1848–57 College spent £546 7s 9d on repairs, new cart shed, rebuilding calf house, drainage tiles, painting outside, bridge, new stable and chaff house. 423a. (Li.5.9; BUR.8.9; COL.14.3 pp. 80, 109)

1848 Rent £780, 3 farm homesteads, College paid excess of 1s 6d to Black Sluice Drainage Commissioners. College spent £314 on purchasing buildings and £50 on repairs. (Box 18.E4; BUR.8.9; COL.14.3 p. 52)

1858 Valued by James Witt: 423a.3r.17p. Rent £780 for 1½ years, then £854, College rights to minerals and coprolites, College provided tiles for underdraining, new buildings. (COL.14.3 p. 125; BUR.0.5(c); Box 18.E5; Li.5.9; BUR.8.9)

1859–63 College spent £120 on drainage tiles. (BUR.8.9)

1863 College spent £300 on new farm buildings at no interest, £300 at 4% (borrowed from Scholarship Fund), tenant paid £59. (COL.14.3 p. 158; BUR.0.5(d); Li.5.10a)

1866 College spent £753 on new farmhouse. (BUR.8.9; COL.14.3 p. 177)

1870   Rent £901, tenant liable for repair to gears of pump and underdrains, allowed tiles. (Box 18.E6)

Lincolnshire – Skendleby (17 on Map 3)

1589   John Spenluffe bequeathed rent charge of £4. (BUR.11.0.B f. 5r.; BUR.0.9; Ibish 1985, p. 145)
1601   Sued for arrears. (BUR.11.1)
1612   Distrained for arrears. (BUR.8.1)
1613   Rent charge sold and rent of St Nicholas Hostel raised from 10s to £7 a year in compensation. (BUR.11.1)

Lincolnshire – Whaplode and Holbeach (38 on Map 3)

1709   234a.1r. purchased for £1940 using money from commutation of Robert Johnson's rent charge issuing from land at Witham on the Hill. Purchase price had been reduced from £2000 as estate was mortgaged. (SCH.1.24)
1778–96   Gap in accounts. (SCH.1.7)
1798   £1/acre levied for drainage so lost 1 year's rent, allowed exhibitioners to hold exhibitions for 5 years. (SCH.1.7)
1802   Rents improved so allowance to exhibitioners increased to £11 and rest kept in reserve. (BUR.11.3)
1819   College paid ¼ expences of inclosure (£60/4). (SCH.1.7)

Lincolnshire – Witham on the Hill (Johnson) (27 on Map 3)

1625   Archdeacon Robert Johnson bequeathed £25/year each to Emmanuel, Clare, St John's and Sidney Sussex colleges to maintain 4 scholars in each college, with preference to those educated at Oakham or Uppingham schools. (Box 9.Ma2)
1676   Master and Fellows ordered that if any exhibitioner should leave College for more than 6 months within one year of election, he would forfeit exhibition. (SCH.1.1)
1694   Proceedings taken out in Court of Chancery to recover arrears. (SCH.1.24)
1703   Sued for arrears. (SCH.1.1)
1709   Rent charge commuted for £2100 and used to purchase estate at Whaplode and Holbeach. (BUR.6.3 pp. 412–18; SCH.1.24)

London – Bishopsgate Street (7 on Map 3)

Four Swans (No. 82, later no. 67)

1585   Sir Walter Mildmay bought property and tenement to North from

John Morley and Roger Rant for £200 and conveyed them to College. Let for £14. (Box 26.E7–8)

1662 Let with tenement to North to John Brunning, merchant. (Box 26.F7–8)

1669 Repairs carried out. (BUR.8.2)

1675–1705 Let to Elizabeth Brand (widow of Low Leyton, Essex 1693), then to Benjamin Brand of London in 1701 and to Isaac Brand, draper in 1704. (BUR.6.3 pp. 302–6; BUR.11.2; Box 26.F9–10)

1693 Two fat capons or 5s for each at audit added to rent. (Box 26.F9)

1703 Rent of 2 properties raised to £30. (Box 26.F9–10)

1704 Sub-let for £200 per annum. (BUR.6.3 pp. 302–6)

1722 Rent raised to £30 so ⅓ fine divided, sub-let for £200. (BUR.6.3 ff. 509v–11r; BUR.3.2)

1729 Terms of sub-tenant discovered after Master stayed in inn. (Box 26.F13; BUR.3.2 ff. 37v–38r)

1743 Corner house to be rebuilt by tenant within 1st 5 years of lease for £400. (Box 26.F15)

1765–1826 Alienated to Richard Wright of Bishopsgate, innholder, then let to relatives and descendants. (BUR.6.4 pp. 192–3; Box 26.F18–21; COL.14.2 f. 92v)

1807–8 Surveyed and valued by George Gwilt: stabling and two substantial houses. Fine surprisingly high, terms for renewal declined by tenant. (Lo.2.1a–b, 2; Sr.1.6; BUR.3.3)

1817–18 Surveyed and valued by George Gwilt; terms for renewal declined by tenant. (Box 26.G1; BUR.3.3; Lo.2.3–4; Lo.5.1, 3; BUR.8.8)

1820 Surveyed by George Gwilt, petition from tenant as neighbour blocked light. (Lo.2.6; Lo.5.2; BUR.0.4(c))

1826 Assigned to Thomas Parsons of Bishopsgate St, victualler. (Box 26.G5; Lo.2.8)

1828 Parsons became bankrupt. Assigned to Henry Pearce, innkeeper for 20 years. Gwilt considered possibility of granting separate lease of corner house. (Box 26.G7; Lo.2.11a–b, 12)

1831–3 Negotiated over new lease. Surveyed and valued by George Gwilt, recommended tenant to spend £1000 on repairs, but tenant in debt. Surveyed by Philip Hardwick at lower value, appointed receiver of rents. Gwilt upset that advice not taken. Rent £420. (Lo.2.14–15; Lo.5.5–6, 7, 8b, 9–16, 20–1; COL.14.2 f. 207r; BUR.8.8; Box 26.G9)

1848 Tenant asked in vain for reduction in rent. But original lease disposed of 2–3 times for £1000 or £1200, and Bursar applied for accommodation on more than one occasion and could not stay as all beds (c. 40) full. (Lo.1.85)

1852 New scullery to be built by tenant for not more than £30. (Box 26.G19; Lo.1.52)

1853 Allowed tenant £200 for repairs over 4 years (COL.14.3 p. 91; Lo.1.58; BUR.8.9)

1865 Building lease to Major John Frederic Wieland of 37 Marlborough Road, St John's Wood and Harefield not executed as builder could not find financial support. (Box 26.G20; *ECM* 19 1908, p. 20)

1867 Distrained for arrears. (COL.14.3 p. 183)

Tenement to North of Four Swans

1585 Sir Walter Mildmay bought property with the Four Swans from John Morley and Roger Rant for £200 and conveyed them to College. Let for £4. Under lease from 1581 with covenants to build one storey 8 feet high on front of tenement within 10 years, and to glaze windows looking into Four Swans. (Box 26.D2, E7–8)

1628–38+ Let to Benjamin Brand (of Edwardston, Suffolk 1628), and also to wife Frances in 1638, when Brand was a woollendraper? (Box 26.F3, F5)

1662 Let with the Four Swans. (See above)

Tenement to West of Four Swans (Coach and Horses)

1585 John Morley gave to College. Let for £8. (Box 26.E9)

1608 Let to Thomas Hardwen, cook, with covenant to spend £140 on rebuilding tenement within first 3 years. (Box 26.F1)

1662 Two fat capons or 5s for each at audit added to rent. (Box 26.F6)

1698 Let to William Crouch, upholder. Called the Coach and Horses. (BUR.6.3 pp. 241–3)

1725–97 Let to Michael Lovell of London and then to William Lovell of St James, Clerkenwell, both upholders. (Box 26.F11, F14, F16; BUR.3.2 f. 19v)

1778–1832 Let to tenants of Four Swans. (COL.14.2 f. 83r; Box 26.F22–4, G2–3, G6, G8)

1778 Surveyed by William Jupp. (BUR.0.3(b))

1817 Surveyed by George Gwilt. Substantially built, brick, recently erected, very advantageously situated in most preferable part of street. (Lo.2.5)

1832 Let with Four Swans. (See above)

London – Gracechurch Street (7 on Map 3)

1834 Inhabitants asked for contribution towards sewer. College not favourable. (Lo.11.13–14)

The Ball (on the South) (No. 74)

1585 Given by Thomas Smith. Let for £4. (Box 25.A6)

1629 Margaret Perkins, widow, asked successfully to have lease renewed. (BUR.0.9; BUR.11.0.C f. 5r; BUR.11.1)

1656   Let to James Pye, merchant. Two fat capons or 5s for each at audit added to rent. (Box 25.B2)

1666   Burned down in Fire of London. 1668 court ordered tenant, John Wing, scrivener, to rebuild and that lease should be extended by 40 years. (Box 25.B3)

1708   Let with covenant that tenant should rebuild property if there were a fire. (Box 25.B6; BUR.6.3 pp. 400–6)

1714   Let to John Austen for 5 years at a peppercorn rent, on condition that he repair premises, and pay all arrears of former tenant, the late John Wing and costs of recovery. College would pay to rebuild premises if they were burned down. (BUR.6.3 p. 477)

1741   Distrained for arrears. (COL.14.2 p. 9)

1748   Let to Abraham North of London, turner, rent £4, tenant to spend £50 on repairs in 1st 7 years and another £50 before end of lease. (Box 25.B7)

1786   Surveyed by William Jupp. (COL.14.2 f. 94r; BUR.8.6; BUR.0.3(c))

1788–90   Problems about dilapidations. (BUR.0.3(d))

1822–3   Bursar asked for survey and report, lease not renewed since 1790. Surveyed by George Gwilt. (Lo.11.5, 7; BUR.8.8; Box 25.B10–11)

The Harrow (on the North) (No. 75, Red Lion)

1585   Given by Thomas Smith. Let for £4. (Box 25.A6)

1629–63+   Let to Laurence Chaderton and then to daughter Elizabeth Salmon. (Box 25.C2–3)

1663   Two fat capons or 5s for each at audit added to rent. (Box 25.C3)

1666   Burned down in Fire of London. Rebuilt, called the Blue Lion, let to Thomas Salter, girdler, and lease made up to 60 years. (Box 25.C4)

1708–28   Called the Red Lion. Let to Captain Robert Sandes of Rotherhithe and then to widow. (BUR.6.3 pp. 372–8; Box 25.C5; BUR.3.2)

1745   Discovered terms of sub-letting but after fine had been fixed. (BUR.3.2 f. 49v; Box 25.C11)

1759–1834+   Let to Samuel Bosanquet of St Bartholomew behind the Exchange, then to son Samuel of Forest House near Leyton, then to his son Samuel. (Box 25.C12–20; COL.14.2 f. 98v; BUR.6.5 pp. 354–60)

1802   Surveyed by George Gwilt, included small shop in passage to Leadenhall Market. (Lo.11.1–2b)

1816   Accepted tenant's offer of fine as house ageing, repairs increasing and hard to let house property in London. (Lo.11.4)

1830–4   Surveyed by George Gwilt, terms for renewal declined, tenant should assert College's claim to vault under Leadenhall Market. (Lo.8.30d; Lo.11.11–12; Lo.1.16)

1845–57 Gwilt negotiated over sale of 1 Ship Tavern Passage to City of London Commissioners of Sewers. Invested proceeds in consols. (Lo.1.85; Lo.11.15a, 18, 20; COL.14.3 pp. 72, 114)

1856 Let at rack rent £180 for 21 years. (Box 25.C21)

1862 Evicted tenant and relet for £190. (Box 25.D3–4; Lo.11.125)

London – Holborn (Whichcote and Sudbury) (9 on Map 3)

1670 College bought tenements for £1350, using part of William Larkin's bequest of £1006 13s 4d and John Sudbury's gift of £503 6s 8d. Rest of money used to buy tenements in Old Bailey. Two-thirds to be regarded as benefaction of Benjamin Whichcote (executor to Larkin's will) and divided between Master and Fellows, College, and 4 scholars. Of the remainder, half was to support a Greek lecturer, and rest to be divided between Master, College, and provision of piece of plate to most worthy of commencing B.A.s. Entire property let for £80. (Box 21.B10; BUR.2.6 ff. 209–11; SCH.1.11)

1705 £232 17s 2d spent by College on repairs. (Box 21.B11)

1711 £40 spent by College on repairs and insurance. (SCH.1.1)

1721–71+ Let to John Walker of St Giles in the Fields, ironmonger, and then to William Walker of Holborn, ironmonger. (BUR.6.3 ff. 513r–517v; BUR.6.4 pp. 106–10)

1721 £115 rent but £30 in 1st ½ year as 1 house needed more spending on repairs than trust estate could advance, other 5 houses also much out of repair, tenant to repair roof within 20 years, College insure for £1200 for 7 years, then tenant. (BUR.6.3 ff. 513r–517v)

1751 Surveyed. Rent £90, peppercorn 1st ½ year as houses empty for a time, tenant to spend £600 on repairs to ground floors, party walls, chimneys, wainscotting, staircases, window frames, plastering, painting, drains. (BUR.8.6; BUR.6.4 pp. 106–10)

1778 Valued by Joseph Freeman. (Box 15.D18)

1781 Let without fine and reserved rent not increased because considerable expenditure by tenant on repairs. (Lo.11.139; COL.14.2 f. 87r)

1795 Fine charged by mistake. (Lo.11.139)

1797 Estate owed College £160, advanced rent to scholars 1785–96, no cup awarded. (SCH.1.12)

1799 Surveyed by Nicholls and Nettleshipp and George Gwilt. 6 tenements, no. 246 in occupation of Cannon Hooper, hosier, no. 247 in tenure of Hughes, brazier, no. 248 Boak and White, hosiers, no. 249 Hooper, glass shop, 250 Knowsley milliner, 251 Eaton [tenant?], chemist. (Lo.11.139–40, 142)

1800 Rent £100/year, estate to clear itself of debt. (SCH.1.12; BUR.6.6 pp. 88–94; Lo.11.141)

1812   Tenant died, College advised to let separately. Surveyed by George Gwilt, in deplorable state of repair. College wanted to buy lease but sold beyond limit. (Lo.11.141–3, 145b, 146a, 147; BUR.0.4(b); BUR.8.8)

1819   Alienated to William Hughes of High Holborn, press maker. Executors considered selling leases separately. (COL.14.2 f. 170r; Lo.11.149–51)

1820   Distrained for rent. (Lo.2.6)

1823–5   Valued by George Gwilt, College should name insurance company. Negotiated over rent, let for £205. (Lo.11.153–6; BUR.0.4(c); BUR.6.6 pp. 88–94; BUR.8.8)

1833   Tenant asked for rent reduction as depression. (Lo.11.158)

1864–5   Let separately, 4 for £80, 1 for £120. College spent £46 10s 1d on repairs. (COL.14.3 pp. 165, 168; BUR.8.9)

1866   Conveyed freehold hereditaments (no. 246) to Pneumatic Despatch Company for £450. (COL.14.3 p. 179)

1870   College agreed to spend not more than £150 on new drains. (COL.14.3 p. 211)

London – Old Bailey (9 on Map 3)

1670   College bought house for £160 using part of benefactions of William Larkin and John Sudbury. See under Holborn for use of rest of money. (BUR.2.6 f. 207r.)

St Dunstan's Alley – 10, then 6, tenements, no. 19 Old Bailey and 1–5 St Dunstan's Court

1586   John Howson gave 10 tenements. Let for £7. (COL.8.1; BUR.11.0.A f. 5r)

1653   Let to William Evans, draper. (Box 25.E2)

1666   Burned down in Fire of London. Rebuilt by Robert Reynolds as 6 tenements and court ordered 1668 that lease be extended to 60 years. (Box 25.E4)

1708–45+   Let to Charles Kipling, gunmaker. In several occupations. Rent £7. (BUR.6.3 pp. 396–400, 520–3)

1763–6   Let to Thomas Moore of St Sepulchre, London, gingerbread baker. (BUR.6.4 pp. 189–91)

1766   Alienated to Thomas King of St Dunstan's Court, tailor. (BUR.6.4 p. 204)

1795–6   Recovered possession and relet. (BUR.0.9)

1801   Surveyed by George Gwilt, not kept in proper repair. Advised that lessee should give £40–£50 to exonerate from repairs and should engage to spend £400 on repairs in 1st 2 years. (Sr.1.1)

1825   Reserved rent £105. (Lo.11.122c)

1828 Distrained for rent. (Es.4.8d; BUR.0.4(d))

1829 Exterior surveyed by George Gwilt. (Lo.11.122c)

1843 College lost £25 from H. E. Holland, former Bursar, and unlikely to recover rent owed. Rent of no. 19 £65. (BUR.11.3; COL.14.3 pp. 20, 26, 124)

1848 Surveyed by George Gwilt as tenant of no. 19 had requested reduction in rent (not granted). (Lo.1.85)

1850 Tenant of no. 19 allowed expenditure under City Sewers Act. (Lo.1.52; BUR.0.5(a))

1857/8 Alfred Gwilt proposed to sub-tenant that premises should be rebuilt, but could not afford it. (Lo.8.91)

1860 Part of premises condemned by Commissioners of Police and rebuilt. (Lo.8.91, 95)

1864–5 Threat of compulsory purchase by Midland Railway so let for one year. Alfred Gwilt negotiated to let on building lease. College refused to ratify agreement as said that terms unacceptable and Gwilt had acted without authority. Management placed in hands of Messrs Reyroux and Bromehead. Let to Alfred Tylor and William Henry, braziers and brass founders of Warwick Lane, London for 80 years, tenants to spend £2000 on new building, rent £300. (Lo.11.126–7, 129a–b, 130, 132; COL.14.3 pp. 171–2; BUR.6.7 pp. 27–33; BUR.0.5(d–e))

St Dunstan's Alley – White Lion (no. 20 Old Bailey and 3 tenements behind)

1727 Surveyed and in good repair. (BUR.0.9; BUR.8.4)

1729–45+ Let to John Walter of St Sepulchre, merchant taylor and then to widow, rent £8. (BUR.6.3 pp. 621–4; BUR.6.4 pp. 51–3)

1798 Recovered possession. (SCH.1.12)

1808 Same tenant as remaining houses. (COL.14.2 f. 147r)

1825 Rent £52. (BUR.6.6 pp. 87–8)

1825–61 Sub-let to Thomas Nutman, corn dealer and then to Benjamin Nuttman. (BUR.6.6 pp. 87–8; COL.14.2 f. 185v; COL.14.3 p. 24; Lo.11.122b)

1843 Rent £90. (COL.14.3 p. 24)

1848 Allowed tenant £30 towards new sewer. (COL.14.3 p. 56)

1856–7 Problems in paying rent. (Lo.1.68; Lo.11.123a)

1857 Management taken over by Alfred Gwilt. (Lo.11.132)

1861 Tenant evicted, let for £80, Elliotts Court kept in hand. (Lo.11.125, 131)

London – West Smithfield (Half of the Catherine Wheel and 2 tenements) (11 on Map 3)

1587 Nicholas Fuller gave property. Let for £8. (BUR.11.0.A f. 4v)

1652 Owner of other half of the Catherine Wheel and tenant of College's half claimed ownership of whole; College sued for rent. (Box 25 Letter from William Dillingham to Robert Alefounder 1664)

1695 Two tenements now divided into 4. (Box 25.F2(1))

1707 Rent increased to £12. (Box 25.F21)

1727 Repairs inspected. (BUR.8.4)

1735 Let to Matthew Shelswell, salter, rent £20. (BUR.6.3 pp. 688–91)

1740–67 Let to John Shepherd, upholder. (BUR.6.4 pp. 1–3)

1775–7 Surveyed by William Jupp. (BUR.0.3(b))

1779 Resurveyed by Jupp. (BUR.0.3(b))

1804 Surveyed by George Gwilt, need to rebuilt fronts of 4 houses, renewal urgent as lease to undertenant about to expire. (BUR.8.7; Lo.11.133a)

1804–63 Let to James Williams (then Sir James), stationer. (COL.14.2 f. 138r; BUR.6.6 pp. 10–15; BUR.3.3)

1822 Surveyed by George Gwilt: 4 houses, paper manufactory, warehouse, stabling, coach houses. Piece let to Vicar and Churchwardens of St Sepulchre's church for warehouse. (BUR.6.6 pp. 15–16; Lo.11.143; BUR.0.4(c))

1823–3 Problems about an encroachment. (Sr.17.49; Lo.11.135)

1842 Surveyed by George Gwilt. (Lo.8.42)

1864 Compensated for land taken by Corporation of London for half of West Smithfield under Metropolis Dead Meat and Poultry Act. (Lo.11.138; BUR.0.5(e))

London – Thames Street (Drapers' Key) (7 on Map 3)

1594 Lady Agnes Dixie gave rent charge of £8/year to endow lectureships in Greek and Hebrew. (Box 1.A7)

London – Threadneedle Street, nos 41–2 (7 on Map 3)

No. 41 (rear tenements)

1588 John Barnes bequeathed 7 tenements to one of colleges in Oxford or Cambridge; Emmanuel chosen by Walter Dunch. 5 rear tenements let for £16 13s 4d. (Box 27.A24, A26)

1599 One tenement let to John Ampleforde, draper, and occupied by Robert Lerry, glazier. (Box 27.B3)

1605–76 Increasing parts of rear tenements let to George (leatherseller), then to Margery (widow) and then to William Ivatt. From 1663, Ivatt only responsible for paying rent in 1669 and 1672–6. (Box 27.B7–8, B10; BUR.11.0.C f. 5r; BUR.11.2)

1617 One tenement let to Henry Bishop, waxchandler. (Box 27.B4)

1622 Two tenements let to Robert Washbourne, mercer. (Box 27.B6)

1637 Renewal of William Ivatt's lease of large rear tenement delayed because of arguments among Fellows about division of entry fine. Ivatt had repaired property. (Box 27.B15)

1662 Two tenements let to John Tomlins, grocer. Two fat capons or 5s for each at audit added to rent. (Box 27.B13)

1666 Four of 5 rear tenements burned down in Fire of London. Court decreed in 1668 that William Ivatt's son William should rebuild, pay all arrears without abatement, and lease to be made up to 50 years. After 40 years, 2 capons or 5s for each at audit to be added to rent. Part of one tenement built on land not owned by College. In 1672, Court solved differences between Ivatt and neighbours over tenancy and rent of new building. (Box 27.B15, C1–2)

1677–1722 All tenements let to Ralph Lee, then to widow Ann, and then to her children Ann and Mary. Rent unchanged, 4 fat capons or 5s for each at audit to be paid, and four times sealing fees. Covenant to protect house against claimants to ground not owned by College. (Box 27.C1–3; BUR.11.2)

1702 Sub-let: new large house for £80, other new house for £30, smith's shop for £16. All surveyed and mapped for new lease. (Box 27.B15)

1731–96 Let to John Martin of Overbury (Worcestershire), then to Joseph Martin of London, banker. (Box 27.C4–9; BUR.3.2 f. 45v; COL.14.2 ff. 23r, 99v)

1796 Alienated to William Curtis, Lord Mayor of London. (COL.14.2 f. 110v)

1806–9 Surveyed by George Gwilt: 3 houses, considerable repairs needed. Negotiated over terms for lease. Converted into counting house and chambers. (Lo.8.2–5)

1818 Surveyed by George Gwilt, would increase value if let in 3 leases, plan needed as description just copied from lease to lease. (Lo.8.9)

1824 Lease by College from Christ's Hospital of ground and buildings on which South Sea Chambers partly built. (COL.14.2 f. 192r; Lo.2.7; Lo.8.13)

1825 Surveyed by George Gwilt. Needed repairs to value of £500. Offers to renew from occupier of no. 39 (cook's shop), a doctor and others. (Lo.8.15, 17, 18b, 19a, 19c)

1829–31 George Gwilt surveyed and determined rental from resident housekeeper. Negotiated over leases. In 1831 some still empty, though let. George Gwilt appointed rent collector. (Lo.8.22–4, 26–9, 30a, 30d, 31; Lo.11.122c; Box 27.C10; BUR.8.8; COL.14.2 f. 203v)

1832 Housekeeper paid £54 12s/year. (Lo.8.32b)

1834 Housekeeper P. Elliott dismissed after 10 years in service as paid too much. New housekeeper paid £20. (Lo.8.33–4)

1835 Problems with tenants. (Box 27.C11; Lo.8.35)

1841 Porter's salary increased to £25/year. (COL.14.3 p. 12)

1851–4 Gwilt made alterations to increase rental, College spent £166 on repairs and plumbing, porter not kept premises clean. (Lo.8.52, 54a, 55b–c, 59b–c, 63; Sr.17.73, 75)

1855 South Sea Chambers let to Oriental Bank Corporation, rent £5. (Box 27.D1)

1855–61 Davis and Son demolished old houses 39–40, negotiated over rebuilding and compensation from Commissioners of Sewers. Rent £420, tenant to spend £5000 within 1 year. 1858 received £2835 as compensation of which £1800 to College. Building finished after delays. (Lo.8.81c; Lo.8.65b, 80b, 81a, 82, 91, 95; Lo.11.125; BUR.0.5(b–c); BUR.11.4; BUR.8.9; COL.14.3 p. 118; Box 27.D5)

1859 Exchanged piece of ground with Christ's Hospital. Paid 2 years' arrears, £240, tenant offered to pay old rent until new building roofed and then new rent £420. (Box 27.D3–4; BUR.8.9; Lo.8.94a)

1866 Exchanged land South Sea Chambers with Oriental Bank. Action against Alfred Gwilt by Mr Davis who thought had been put to unnecessary expense: verdict in Gwilt's favour but cost him £300. (Box 27.D6–7; Lo.11.132)

No. 42 (front tenements)

1588 John Barnes bequeathed 7 tenements to one of colleges in Oxford or Cambridge (see under no. 41). Two front tenements let for £4 and £3. (Box 27.A24, A26)

1655 Repairs to one of tenements. (BUR.8.2)

1666 Two tenements burned down in Fire of London. Rebuilt as one brick messuage by Thomas Williamson, weaver. Court decreed in 1668 he should pay arrears of rent and that 40 years be added to first lease and 32 years to second. Double sealing fees would be charged on renewal. (BUR.6.3 pp. 336–44)

1695 Lease assigned to Thomas Mann, draper. (BUR.6.3 p. 217)

1719–1843 Occupied by and then let to Joseph Marston, apothecary, then to Gervas Marston of Cheshunt (Hertfordshire), then to his executor Richard Gervas Ker and then to Ker's devises Phoebe, Martha and Ann Porter of Borlingham (Worcestershire). (BUR.6.3 ff. 504r–6r; Box 27.E2–7; COL.14.2 ff. 83v, 134r; Sr.17.16)

1799 Surveyed by George Gwilt, £100 needed to be spent on repairs. (Lo.8.1)

1817–18 Valued by George Gwilt, needed repairs, terms for renewal not accepted by tenant. (BUR.3.3; Lo.2.3; Lo.8.6–8; Sr.17.21)

1823   Tenant of King's Head wanted to rebuild and asked for lease of 61 years. (Lo.8.11)
1843   King's Head Inn rent £90. (Box 27.E8–9)
1866   Tenant asked for power to turn into offices or commercial use other than inn if he wished. (Lo.11.132)

Norfolk – King's Lynn (24 on Map 3)

1607   John and Elizabeth Titley left money to King's Lynn corporation to endow 2 scholarships of £4/year each for students from King's Lynn grammar school, and annuities of £2 to be divided among Master and Fellows, and £1 to College. (BUR.2.6 pp. 133–4; COL.9.2 p. 56; Ibish 1985, pp. 128–32)

§ Norfolk – Little Melton (1 on Map 3)

1584   Francis Chamberlain conveyed impropriated rectory and advowson of Little Melton, and 3 tenements, and 83a.2r. (including 22a.1r.20p. of glebe) in Great and Little Melton and Hethersett. Let for £8 plus 12 quarters of wheat and one of malt, or best market price for them on Saturday before rents due. (Box 20.C1; COL.8.1 ff. 6v–7r)
1601   Income from estate first arrived at College. (BUR.11.1)
1613   Let, with covenants that tenant had to pay legal costs of maintaining tithe, any charges for repairing chancel of Little Melton and, after 9 years, to augment vicar's stipend to £20. (Box 20.D1)
1631   Sub-poena served to recover rents. (BUR.8.2)
1641   Dispute between College and parishioners over vicarial tithes. (Box 20.B15; Box 25.E4, G1)
1649–1751   Let to members of Benton family: John Benton of Great Dunham, clerk to 1678, then to widow Susan (of Norwich) and Richard Stibbart (carpenter of 'Dersingham'), then in 1695 to Susan's son-in-law John Back (woolcomber of Fulmodeston), then to John Back (butcher of Great Melton) in 1719 and to Matthew Back in 1748. (BUR.11.1–2; BUR.6.3 pp. 39–43; Box 20.D2–8; COL.9.1(A) p. 101; BUR.3.2 f. 65v)
1656   Sued for arrears. (BUR.8.2)
1662   College denied legal obligation to contribute towards vicar's stipend, but agreed to give £8/year as gift. (Box 20.B11–13)
1677   Rent increased to £12, corn rents increased to 16 quarters of wheat and one of malt (or their monetary equivalents), and 2 fat capons or 5s for each at audit. (BUR.6.3 pp. 39–43)
1686   Fine for renewal of lease set low because Susan Benton was a minister's widow and in poor circumstances. (BUR.3.1)

1741   40a. Gt Melton, 42 pieces in Hethersett and Little Melton.
        (Box 20.D7; BUR.3.2 f. 65v)

1749   108a.3r.: 59a. inclosed in Gt Melton and 20a. in open fields, 21a.2r.
        glebe in Little Melton in 35 pieces, 8a.1r. in Hethersett in 8 pieces.
        (BUR.3.2 f. 80v)

1754   Terrier. (Box 20.C3)

1776   Surveyed by John Hinde. (BUR.8.6)

1798   Tithes valued by Alexander Watford, farm and glebe surveyed by
        Thomas Smith: 49a.0r.10p., 17a.3r.0p. rectory land in Little Melton,
        rectory lands in Hethersett and Great Melton likely to be
        exchanged under Hethersett inclosure. (Box 20.C4–5; BUR.0.3(d))

1799   Rent £22. (Box 20.C12, D16)

1800   Inclosure of Hethersett. (Box 20.C12)

1806   Valued by William Custance. (BUR.8.7)

1814–17 Inclosed Little Melton, paid for fencing. College awarded
        17a.3r.29p. + 1a.0r.16p. (BUR.8.8; Nf.3.1–2; Box 20.C9, C11)

1817   Could not let farm because so run down. Advertised oak trees.
        (Nf.1.1c; BUR.0.4(b))

1818   Surveyed by William Custance. (BUR.8.8)

1818–26 Inclosed Great Melton; exchanged land. Paid for fencing and
        gates. Cost of inclosure to College £108 19s 8d. (Box 20.C12, C14;
        COL.14.2 ff. 167r, 169r; BUR.8.8)

1819   Mapped by Robert Corby. (BUR.8.8; Box 20.C12)

1819–20 Negotiated over lease and terms for building farmhouse (cost
        College £552 including superintendence). (Box 20.C12; Nf.1.2, 4b,
        7–8, 14a; Nf.3.7; BUR.8.8)

1820   Tithes let at rack rent £155, land let at rack rent of £140.
        (Box 20.D17; Box 20.E1; BUR.3.3)

1821   Tenant asked for £5 abatement for tithes. (Nf.3.8)

1822   Allowed tenant 10% abatement for tithes. (Nf.3.9)

1823   College paid for new granary and coal shed. Tenant asked for
        abatement for tithes. (BUR.8.8; Nf.3.11a)

1823–32 Repeated offers to lease tithes from College. (Nf.3.13, 15, 19,
        20–1)

1825–6 Problems in making tenant repair roof of chancel. (Nf.2.526–8)

1826   College spent £27 16s 7½d on estate. (BUR.8.8)

1830   Great Melton mapped by Robert Corby. (BUR.8.8; BUR.0.4(d))

1832   Rent of land £150. (Box 20.E2)

1834   Allowed tenant 10% abatement on farm and 10% on tithes, others
        in area made 10%–15% deductions. (Nf.1.18)

1840   Commuted tithes Great Melton. (BUR.8.9)

1841   College spent £29 1s 6d on wall and shed. Agreed to join with
        landowners of Little Melton to ask for compulsory settlement of
        tithes. (BUR.8.9; COL.14.3 pp. 10, 12)

1848   Commuted tithes Hethersett. (BUR.8.9)

1854   Tenant asked for repairs to window sills and painting. College ascertained that land tax had not been redeemed. (BUR.0.5(a); Nf.1.21)

1857–8   Spent £14 12s on horse shed and £19 17s 11d on new bullock lodge. College paid for materials, tenant for labour. (BUR.8.9; COL.14.3 p. 120)

1861   Allowed 30p. for village school, rent to be paid to College tenant. (COL.14.3 p. 144; Nf.3.33)

1862   College spent £21 0s 5d on barn floor. (BUR.8.9)

1866   Bursar allowed to spend up to £60 on repairs. (COL.14.3 p. 179)

1868   Report by James and James Beadon Witt. Rent £160. (BUR.0.5(e); Box 20.E5–6)

§ Norfolk – Rushall (Brown) (40 on Map 3)

1736   John Brown, Rector of Wallington (Hertfordshire) left £1000 Old South Sea Annuities for augmentation of Mastership, £500 in South Sea trading stock for 4 middle fellows, £500 in same stock for 2 Greek scholarships, estate in Canterbury to send scholar to Emmanuel or Pembroke but Dean of Cathedral could not accept trust as subject to restraint of mortmain, £50 to College Library and books, sold remainder not taken by Pembroke and divided profit between 2 Colleges: £6 6s 3d each. (SCH.1.4; Box 9.Oa21)

1738   Bought messuage, lands, impropriation in Rushall, Langmere and Dickleburgh for £1780 plus costs, £275 14s 3d left in stock. As could not hold any more advowsons, asked that gift of Rushall be settled on vicar of Fressingfield. College paid for repairs, usually under £10/year. Rent £85 10s. (Box 20.K1–3; SCH.1.4; BUR.6.4 pp. 20–3)

1740–1   College spent £72 on repairs. (SCH.1.4)

1742   Recommended rent. (Box 20)

1744–70   College paid £2 12s 6d for collection of rents. (SCH.1.4)

1747   Altered farming covenants. (BUR.6.4 pp. 77–80)

1748   College spent £25 on repairs, including £5 allowed to tenant towards loss by cattle. (SCH.1.4)

1764   Letters of attorney to recover arrears. (BUR.6.4 p. 188)

1770   College spent £27 on repairs. (SCH.1.4)

1771   Paid collector £3 for receiving rents. Rent £105. College spent £27 on repairs. (SCH.1.4; BUR.6.4 pp. 255–60)

1772   Paid collector £4 for receiving rents. College spent £26 on repairs. (SCH.1.4)

1773   Mapped by Isaac Lenny: 98a.2r.33p. (Box 20)

1778–96   No accounts of receipts. (SCH.1.4)

1779 Surveyed by Joseph Freeman. (BUR.0.3(a))

1797 1st payment to Master. (SCH.1.4)

1798–188(?2) Land let to Thomas Smith of Rushall, farmer, then to nephew John Stanton. Tithes let to Smith from 1801. (Box 20.K6, K8–10; Nf.4.32, 33; COL.14.3 pp. 24, 41, 76)

1798 Valued by Alexander Watford. College spent £29 on repairs. (SCH.1.4; BUR.0.3(d))

1801 College spent £31 on repairs. Rent of tithes £140. (SCH.1.4)

1802 Surveyed by William Custance. (SCH.1.4)

1805 Surveyed by William Custance. (SCH.1.5)

1806–7 College spent £133 on repairs. (SCH.1.5)

1809 Surveyed by William Custance: 98a.1r.32p., tenant to take down and rebuild in better situation brewhouse, dairy, granary, allowed £150 for expence. (SCH.1.5; BUR.8.7)

1810 Rent £270 (farm £130, tithes £140). Let for 9 years not 7 as tenant had to underdrain and demolish old backhouse and dairy and tile house. Tenant submitted estimates. (Box 20.K8; Nf.5.2, 8)

1811–13 Allowed tenant £150 over 3 years for rebuilding brewhouse, dairy, granary and reroofing house. (SCH.1.5)

1812 Tenant asked permission to lay down 6a. next to yard for pasture and break up 6a. elsewhere as now had good backhouse and dairy and intended to keep more cows. (Nf.5.11)

1816 Tenant asked for repairs to barn doors and floor and cowhouse floor. (Nf.5.19)

1818 College supported request to make inclosed water pond in front of house a public pond. (Nf.5.22–3)

1819 Let for 12 years as new backhouse and tiling expensive. (Box 20.K9; Nf.5.23, 25)

1820–4 Problems in paying rent as poor harvest and low prices. Tenant asked for reduction 1821. Hard to collect tithe. Allowed tenant 10% abatement 1822, 15% 1823, 5% 1824. (Nf.5.27a, 28, 29a, 30–1, 33–6, 38, 40–1; SCH.1.5)

1825 College's support asked for in appeal against county rate. (Nf.1.16)

1826 Vicarial tithes and glebe offered to College. (Nf.5.44)

1830–1 Problems in paying rent, allowed tenant 10% abatement on land 1830, on tithes 1831. (SCH.1.5; Nf.5.51a)

1832 College spent £6 on repairs to stables. (SCH.1.5; Nf.5.52)

1835–6 Allowed tenant 10% abatement. (SCH.1.5)

1837 College spent £20 on repairs. (SCH.1.5)

1839 Surveyed by Mr Colchester. Great tithes let for £300/year. (BUR.8.9; COL.14.3 p. 5)

1840–1 Trust spent £38 17s 10½d on repairs and charged College £10/year until debt liquidated. (SCH.1.5)

1843   Rent £220. Tithes commuted. (COL.14.3 p. 24; SCH.1.5)

1844–63   College paid collector £12/year for receiving tithes. (SCH.1.5)

1844   Commuted tithes at Dickleburgh. Tithes collected by tenants. College agreed to spend £28 8s 6d on repairs. (SCH.1.5; COL.14.3 pp. 30, 32)

1846   Allowed tenant to break up 4a.–5a. in Langmere. (COL.14.3 p. 41)

1847 and 1850   Problems in collecting rent charge because of agricultural depression. (Nf.4.37; Nf.5.61a)

1848 and 1850   Repairs needed to house and barn. (Nf.5.56, 61a)

1853   Exchanged land with vicar so tithe apportionment altered. (SCH.1.5; COL.14.3 pp. 36, 89)

1854–5   House repaired and built new horse shed, chaff bin, harness house and cow shed, with College contribution. (SCH.1.5; BUR.0.5(b))

1854   Dickleburgh inclosed. (Nf.5.64)

1855–   College spent £3/year on refreshments to tithe payers. (SCH.1.5; BUR.0.5(b))

1859   College gave £25 towards new schools at Rushall and £5 to Harleston rifle corps. (SCH.1.5)

1865–8   Surveyed by James Witt and James Beadon Witt: 69a.0r.12p. Rushall, 29a.1r.10p. Dickleburgh and Langmere, more drainage needed, farm buildings repaired as a result of report. (Box 20.K11; BUR.8.9; BUR.0.5(e))

† Norfolk – Shernborne (30 on Map 3)

1654   Francis Ash conveyed manor and 678a.2r., manor house and outbuildings, 2 tenements and foldcourse for 800 sheep to College, valued at £225 6s 10d. Of this, £6 to be paid to the Master, £24 to the Fellows, £10 to Library, £100 to 10 Exhibitioners, £20 to a lecturer at Ashby-de-la-Zouch, £10 to a lecturer at Aldermanbury, £13 6s 8d to schoolmaster at Derby, £6 13s 4d to usher at Derby school, £4 to be divided between manciple, cooks and porter, and remainder to College. (Box 9.Ma3; Box 22.A4)

1660   £48 17s 6d spent by College in managing farm. (BUR.0.2)

1661   Annual income only £185, and decided to abate rent proportionally. Tenant allowed £92 17s 5d for repairs. (Box 22.A5; BUR.6.3 f. 242r)

1672   Farm taken in hand. Yielded £120 a year. (SCH.1.1)

1673   Let for £150. (SCH.1.1)

1679   Rent reduced to £145. (BUR.6.3 pp. 51–8)

1685–6   One year's rent spent on manor house. (SCH.1.1)

1689   Farm taken in hand. Made a profit of £17 11s 4d. (SCH.1.1)

1690   Power of attorney granted to recover arrears. (BUR.6.3 p. 174)

1691   Let for £120 to Thomas Houghton of Burnham Overy. (BUR.6.3 pp. 193–202)

1698   Rent increased to £130. (BUR.6.3 pp. 258–65)

1700   College spent £75 18s 3d on repairs to dairy and manor house and taxes. (SCH.1.1)

1713   College spent £101 16s 2d on repairs and up to £37 16s 9½d on building a new dovehouse; tenant paid remainder. (Box 22.A11; BUR.6.3 pp. 443–51)

1715   College spent £40 on repairs. (Box 22.A11)

1728   Rent £140. (BUR.6.3 pp. 631–6)

1735–45   Law suit about 12a. claimed by parson and rights to sheep walk. College owed £129 19s, charges of law suit paid for by vacancies and contributions from Fellows and exhibitions. Repairs needed. (Box 22.A14; SCH.1.2; COL.14.2 p. 1; BUR.6.4 pp. 72–5)

1743   Surveyed: 1353a.3r.24p. by measure, 1603a.2r.20p. by estimation. Allowed £8 for chimney, £5 for granary. (SCH.1.2; Box 22.A9; COL.14.2 f. 16v)

1749   Tenant allowed to demolish gelding stable and given allowance towards cleaning moat, altered farming covenants to include turnips and clover. (BUR.6.4 pp. 72–5; COL.14.2 f. 25v)

1766–70   Inclosed. Paid for by sale of stock and loans from Master and then others. Paid off in 1819. Allotted 507a.0r.26p. Tenant obstructed execution of award. Cost College £928 10s 4d. Exchanged lands. (SCH.1.2; COL.14.2 ff. 63r, 65r, 66v, 67v, 68, 70v, 76v, 78r, 81r, 82v; Box 22.A13; Box 9.Ma5; BUR.6.4 p. 229; SCH.1.2–3)

1769–70   Negotiated over lease. Rent £320, allowed tenant £105 off 1st year's rent to leave with clover and/or rye and turnips, College to inclose. (Box 22.A13; COL.14.2 f. 66r; BUR.6.4 pp. 261–71)

1771–2   Repaired: tenant paid £389 5s ½d, College spent £261 4s 8d. Had to enforce repairs from tenant. (Box 22.A11; COL.14.2 f. 72r)

1782–96   Disbursements not all recorded. (SCH.1.2)

1782   Complaint about rent. (Box 22.A12)

1791   Rent £285. (BUR.6.5 pp. 75–9)

1793–4   Accounts audited and settled by Joseph Freeman. (Box 22.A12)

1797–9   College spent £79 on repairs. (SCH.1.2)

1803   College spent £114 on repairs. William Custance surveyed, sold timber and viewed repairs. (SCH.1.3)

1804   Surveyed by William Custance. (SCH.1.3)

1805   College spent £22 on repairs. (SCH.1.3)

1807   College spent £23 on repairs. (SCH.1.3)

1811   Surveyed and valued by William Custance. (BUR.0.4(a))

1812   Lecturer at Ashby-de-la-Zouch asked to benefit from increased rents as stipends reduced on inclosure. Told not possible. (Box 9.Ma.5)

1813–31 College spent average of £76 10s/year on repairs. (SCH.1.3)

1813 Rent £735. Mapped. (SCH.1.3; BUR.6.5 pp. 340–7)

1813–15 College spent £793 on repairs and improvements. (SCH.1.3; Nf.6.4, 7–9)

1814–21 Problems in paying rent. Allowed tenant reductions of £100 1814 and to alter cropping sequence, £200 1815, £120 1816, £220 1818 and 1819. Allowed £100 from 1819. Tenant asked to quit. Insolvent 1821, owed £809 12s. (Nf.6.12, 14, 18, 21–2, 24–32, 35, 37–8, 41; SCH.1.3; COL.14.2 f. 168r; BUR.0.4(c))

1817 Tenant asked for advice on how to vote and told to vote for the government. (Nf.6.19)

1818 Tenant informed College that its trees had been felled by adjoining owner. (Nf.6.23)

1819 Surveyed by William Custance. (BUR.0.4(b))

1821 Relet, rent £630. In poor repair. (Nf.6.33, 39–41; BUR.6.5 pp. 452–60)

1822 Allowed tenant £300 off rent. Problems in paying rent. (SCH.1.3; Nf.6.44–6, 48–9)

1823 Barns needed repair; spent £39. (SCH.1.3; Nf.6.54–5)

1824 Problems in paying rent. Relet, rent £525. College spent £44 on repairs. Surveyed by Charles Burcham. (Nf.6.4, 60–1, 63–4, 66–7, 75–8; BUR.6.6 pp. 110–16; SCH.1.3; COL.14.2 f. 189r)

1825 Barn repaired, College spent £107. (Nf.6.71–2; SCH.1.3)

1826–33 Abated £25/year (as wheat under 8s/bushel). (SCH.1.3; Nf.6.89–92)

1827–8 Problems in paying rent. (Nf.6.82, 84–7)

1830 Allowed tenant 10% because of depression. (SCH.1.3)

1832 Rent £450. College spent £743 on repairs. (BUR.6.6 pp. 166–71)

1832–5 College spent £2300 on repairs (£450 on rebuilding farmhouse). (SCH.1.3; BUR.0.4(e))

1834 College owed £659. (SCH.1.3)

1835 College owed £404. (SCH.1.3)

1836 College owed £152. (SCH.1.3)

1840 Commuted tithes at Ingoldisthorpe and Dersingham. (SCH.1.3)

1845–8 College spent £141 on repairs. (SCH.1.3)

1845 College paid for draining tiles. (SCH.1.3)

1850–2 College spent £72 on repairs. (SCH.1.3)

1856 Valued by James Witt: 587a.3r.6p. Let to John Marsters of King's Lynn, miller and merchant. Rent £545. College had mineral rights. Agreed to buy 2r.33p. in Ingoldisthorpe occupied by former tenant. (BUR.8.9; BUR.0.5(b); BUR.6.6 pp. 339–44; COL.14.3 pp. 110–1)

1857 Tenant had to drain 2 lands within 2 years, College provided tiles. College spent £284 on repairs. (BUR.6.6 p. 344; SCH.1.3)

1858 College spent £23 on repairs. (SCH.1.3)
1863 Valued by Messrs Witt. (BUR.8.9; BUR.0.5(d))
1864 Rent £600. College spent £50 on repairs. (BUR.8.9)
1865 College spent £28 8s 3d on repairs. (BUR.8.9)
1869 College agreed to spend £182 16s on repairs to farmhouse, tenant pay £5/year additional rent. (COL.14.3 p. 199)

Northamptonshire – Thurning (31 on Map 3)

1664 John Wells left 30 acres to rector to pay £5 annually to an exhibitioner. (COL.9.10.18; COL.9.1(A) p. 237)
1834 College bought 1a.2r.22p. of land adjoining rectory for £140, let for £6/year to incumbent. (BUR.8.8; BUR.0.4(e); COL.14.2 f. 209v)
1868 Commuted annual payment by rector to 1s/year during his lifetime. (COL.14.3 p. 196)

Oxfordshire – Drayton (32 on Map 3)

1668 Lord Saye and Sele gave rent charge of £12/year arising from about 20 acres of meadowland to support 2 poor scholars. Gift arose from John Preston's bequest of £200 to buy lands for this purpose. (SCH.1.1; Box 1.B2; BUR.6.3 pp. 371–2; SCH.1.23D2–3)
1708 Richard Dodwell of Oxford granted power of attorney to recover arrears of £138. (BUR.6.3 pp. 371–2)

Suffolk – Bungay (19 on Map 3)

1592 Thomas Popeson gave rent charge of £6 and the Town of Bungay gave an equal sum from Cappilles Close, Hempishall, to maintain 10 poor scholars and pay them 4d/week. A Fellow was to choose 7 scholars from Bungay school and receive £1 6s 3d in costs; College to nominate schoolmaster. Scholars to enjoy free tuition and rooms, and left-overs from the Fellows' table. (Box 19.A2; BUR.11.0.C f. 5v)
1694 Rent for 5 years abated by £24 because of a fire. (BUR.11.2)
1721 Thomas Fynn, graduate of College and rector of Henstead appointed receiver of rents. (COL.14.1 p. 137)

Suffolk – Lavenham (15 on Map 3)

1588 Thomas Skinner gave rent charge of £8 arising from manors of Lavenham and Fowlmere (Cambridgeshire). (Box 1.A6)
1605 Sued for arrears. (BUR.8.1)
1612 Distrained for arrears. (BUR.8.1)

1617–19   At least £12 spent by College in distraining for non-payment of rent. (Box 22.C9; BUR.8.1; BUR.11.1)

1657   In arrears. (BUR.8.2)

1685   Distrained for arrears. (BUR.8.2)

1699   Letters of attorney issued to recover arrears. (BUR.6.3 p. 270)

1705   College spent £49 18s 6d in Chancery proceedings to recover arrears. (Box 22.C23, C26; BUR.8.2)

1753   Letters of attorney to collect rents and arrears. (BUR.6.4 p. 125)

1797   Henry Yeats Smythies, Fellow, appointed receiver of quit rents. Only collected once every 7 years as so trifling. (COL.14.2 f. 113v; Sf.1.11)

1822–3   Threatened to distrain for arrears. (BUR.0.4(c))

1829   George William Andrews of Sudbury, solicitor, appointed receiver of quit rents. (COL.14.2 f. 199v)

1864   Difficult to collect rents from those who had bought lands subject to charge without having had notice of it. (Sf.1.13)

Suffolk – Little Welnetham (2 on Map 3)

1585   Sir Robert Jermyn gave rent charge of £8 arising from land called Chocke Smythes. (Box 1.A1)

1822   Asked College for abatement as agricultural depression. (BUR.0.4(a))

1859   Sold rent charge for £200. (BUR.1.2; BUR.6.6 pp. 385–6)

Suffolk – Pakefield (Collins) (34 on Map 3)

1674   Anne Hunt bequeathed 2 acres to maintain 2 poor scholars, with preference to those born in hundreds of Mutford and Lothingland in Suffolk, or to kin of John Collins (her late son). Let for £10. Quit rent of 3s 3d/year to manor of Mutford. (Box 9.Oa17; SCH.1.1, 14a)

1700   Let to Richard Bell of Ludham, Norfolk. (BUR.6.3 pp. 278–80)

1702   Rent abated by £3 because of expenditure by tenant on repairs and of erosion of estate by the sea. (SCH.1.1)

1721   Rent £9. (BUR.6.3 ff. 518r–19r)

1732   Letters of attorney to receive arrears and find new tenant. (BUR.6.3 p. 671)

1749   Rent £7. (BUR.6.4 pp. 94–5)

1778–96   Gap in accounts.

1795   Let to John Mortlock of Cambridge. (BUR.6.5 pp. 98–100; COL.14.2 f. 110v)

1816–24+   Let to Jabez Aldred of Lowestoft, fisherman, rent £10. (Box 22; BUR.6.5 pp. 362–5)

1821–3　Abated £3/year because of land swept away and badness of times. (SCH.1.14a)

1823　Rent reduced to £7 as land eroded by the sea. (Sf.1.53)

1824　Asked for reduction of rent as land eroded by the sea. (Sf.1.54)

1825–6　Abated £2 for sea erosion for 2 years. (Sf.1.55–6; SCH.1.14a)

1827–9　Abated £2/year for sea erosion. (SCH.1.14a)

1829　Rent £6 6s. (SCH.1.14a)

1831　Beachman asked to have building lease of part of land for warehouse. Mapped by Richard Barnes. (Sf.1.57a; SCH.1.14a)

1832　Exhibitioners' payments reduced to 1s 6d/week. (SCH.1.14a)

1835　Rent collected by Reeve and Norton, Lowestoft. (SCH.1.14a)

1854　Rent collected by Edmund Norton. (SCH.1.14a)

1864　Paid R. H. Reeve £1 1s commission for collecting rent. (SCH.1.14a)

1869　Sold for £375 to Mr George Buller with costs of £65. (BUR.8.9; COL.14.3 p. 203)

Suffolk – St Cross (Gillingham) (39 on Map 3)

1723　Purchased from £1600 left by Mr Gillingham to buy lands with income of £60/year. Quit rent of £1 1s 4d. (COL.9.1(B) pp. 61–2; FEL.5.7)

1729–34　£83 spent on repairs. (FEL.5.7)

1732　Three years' arrears due, used for College when estate repaired. Decided to offer fellowship to Fellows in order of seniority as more valuable than foundation fellowships. (COL.14.1 pp. 171, 173)

1737　Decided that Gillingham Fellow had no right to Brown's benefaction. (COL.9.1(B) p. 65)

1739　Arrears from accidental losses so reduced payment to Gillingham Fellow. (COL.14.2 p. 5)

1740–2　Complaints about rent. Recommended reduction to £50 in 1742. (Box 20)

1746　Recommended demolition of buildings. (Box 20)

1750　Fellowship kept vacant half a year because of expenditure on repairs. (COL.14.2 f. 31r)

1751　Ordered that elect new Fellow when vacancies, not signed by John Brigham whose turn it was to succeed. (COL.14.1 p. 174)

1752　Rent £63. (Box 20)

1756　After disputes over privileges of Gillingham Fellow, decided that of status equal to other Fellows. (COL.14.2 ff. 43v–45v)

1764　Letters of attorney to recover arrears. (BUR.6.4 p. 188)

1772　Decided that Gillingham Fellow only had right to sealing money when insufficient foundation Fellows to make majority without him. (COL.9.1(B) p. 66) *c.* 1773   Mapped by Isaac Lenny. (Box 20)

1778–96   Gap in accounts. (FEL.5.7)

1779   Surveyed by Joseph Freeman. (BUR.0.3(a))

1788   Gillingham Fellow allowed share in profits of coals. (COL.9.1(B) p. 66)

1798   Valued by Alexander Watford. Rent £80. (BUR.6.5 pp. 121–4; FEL.5.7; BUR.0.3(d))

1802   Surveyed by William Custance. College spent £34 and £21 16s 4d on repairs. Fellowship had been sequestered for nearly 4 years. (FEL.5.7; BUR.8.7; COL.14.2 f. 133r)

1806   College spent £26 on repairs. Surveyed by William Custance. (FEL.5.7)

1809   Surveyed by William Custance: farmhouse and 74a. (BUR.8.7; FEL.5.7)

1810   Rent £100. (BUR.6.5 pp. 306–15)

1817   College spent £45 on repairs. (FEL.5.7; Nf.5.20)

1822–3   Allowed tenant £10/year for bad harvest. (FEL.5.7)

1824   Allowed tenant £5 for bad harvest. (FEL.5.7)

1830   Allowed tenant 10% abatement (£10). (FEL.5.7)

1832   College spent £109 on repairs. (FEL.5.7)

1835–6   Allowed tenant 10% abatement (£10). (FEL.5.7)

1840   Tithes commuted. (FEL.5.7)

1843   Rent £220. (COL.14.3 p. 24)

1844   Tithes commuted. (FEL.5.7)

1847   College spent £23 on repairs. (FEL.5.8)

1848   South side of house very dilapidated. (Nf.5.58)

1850   College spent £42 on repairs. (FEL.5.8)

1855   College spent £92 on repairs. (FEL.5.8)

1857–8   College spent £54 on repairs. (FEL.5.8)

1860–1   Tenant had problems paying rent. Then declared bankrupt. (BUR.0.5(c); Sf.1.73–4)

1863–4   College spent £210 on new farm buildings. (BUR.8.9; COL.14.3 p. 159)

1869   Rent £110. (BUR.6.7 pp. 175–80)

1870   College agreed to spend £49 5s on farm buildings. (COL.14.3 p. 210)

Surrey – Mitcham (Hyde Farm Estate) (12 on Map 3)

Hyde Field Farm (61a.2r.6p.)

1587   Entire estate bought for £500 10s, using £440 from legacy of Joyce Frankland, £60 given by Sir Walter Mildmay and 10s from College. Let for £20; 11s 2d due to the Crown. (Box 28.A7)

1589   John King, butcher and tenant, entered into covenants with sub-tenants about coppice and they were to hedge and inclose it. (Box 28.Aa21)

1629   Let to George Smith of Broughton (Oxfordshire). (Box.28.A21)

1630   Smith allowed £5. (BUR.8.2)

1631   Smith wrote, apologising for arrears of rent. (BUR.0.9)

1635   College sued for £40 arrears of rent; received £22. (BUR.0.9; BUR.8.2; BUR.11.1)

1650–74+   Let to William Whitaker (B.A. Emmanuel) of Hornchurch (Essex) and then of Bermondsey and his wife (and then widow), Elizabeth. (BUR.11.1; Box 28.A12, Aa5, Aa8)

1658   Two fat capons or 5s for each at audit added to rent. Tenant spent over £200 on building house, barn, stables and outbuildings, so fine lowered in compensation. (Box 28.Aa5)

1681–1721+   Let to Robert Ford, embroiderer of London. (Box 28.Aa9, Aa11, Aa13; BUR.6.3 pp. 345–8)

1685   Quit rent of £1 3s 10d claimed from College by mistake. (Box 28.A21; BUR.0.9; BUR.8.2)

1721   Mapped by Heber Lands, 61a.2r.6p., altered covenants, barren estate. (BUR.0.9; Box 28.Aa21; BUR.8.4)

1728–63+   Let to William Westbrook of London, goldsmith and executors. (Box 28.A15, Aa14; BUR.3.2 f. 31v; BUR.6.4 pp. 12–15)

1757   Surveyed. Tenant had illegally felled £100 worth of timber, Master not optimistic about success of recovery. (BUR.3.2 f. 68v; BUR.8.6)

1762   Surveyed. (BUR.8.6)

1763–1806   Let to William Cole of Clapham. (Box 28.A21, A22, Aa15; COL.14.2 ff. 82r, 91v, 104r; COL.9.1(A) p. 97; BUR.0.9)

1778   Not kept in repair; roads very bad. (BUR.0.9)

1780   Valued by Joseph Freeman. (COL.14.2 f. 83r)

1798   Valued by Alexander Watford. (BUR.0.9; BUR.8.7)

1799   Rent £30. (Box 28.Aa15)

1801   Surveyed by William Forster: tolerably well managed, needed drainage, tenant not resident, farmhouse out of repair. (Sr.1.1)

1806   Repairs needed. (Lo.8.3; Sr.1.2)

1807   Valued by Francis Whishaw. Negotiated over renewal of lease. (Lo.2.1a; Sr.1.3–8)

1809–(?45)   Alienated and then let to Frederick Silver, attorney. (Sr.1.9–11; Box 28.Aa17, Aa22, Aa23)

1812   Tenant asked for lease for lives instead of years. (Sr.1.13)

1814   Surveyed and mapped by Edward Neale: 63a.2r.13p. (Sr.1.19–21, 23a–b, 24–5; BUR.0.4(b))

1823–4   Negotiated for renewal. (Sr.1.29–32, 35)

1825   Tenant wanted to lease for lives and develop as building estate. Refused. (Lo.8.19c; Sr.1.38–40, 42–7)

1826 Problems in receiving rent. Fire. (Sr.1.48–9, 57)

1831 Tenant happy to receive proposals to renew lease and improve estate. (Sr.1.53)

1844 Surveyed by George Gwilt. Plan of farm buildings. (Sr.1.60a)

1845–6 Claimed against Silver for dilapidations. (Sr.1.56, 60a)

1845 Rent £120. (COL.14.3 p. 34)

1848–51 Repairs surveyed by George Gwilt. (Sr.1.57, 60a)

1849 Problems in recovering insurance. (BUR.0.4(f))

1850 George Gwilt negotiated lease of meadow at Balham and boundary. (Sr.1.59b)

1851 Plan: 62a.1r.17p. (Sr.1.60a)

1856 3a. meadow at Balham let for £18. Tenant to underdrain. (COL.14.3 p. 114; BUR.3.3; Sr.17.78)

1866 College advised to oppose proposed railway. (Lo.11.132)

1868 College agreed to apply for exchange under inclosure. (COL.14.3 p. 193)

1869 Surveyed by Reyroux and Phillips, Edward Ryde and William Longmire for possible development on building lease. (COL.14.3 p. 204; Sr.1.66–9)

1870 Small plots let. (Box 28.Aa25, Aa30–3)

Mitcham and Clapham Farm

1587 Part of estate bought for £500 10s (see above, Hyde Field Farm). (Box 28.A7)

1614 Let to Jacob Proctor, merchant tailor of London. Contained 10 acres of meadow, 32 acres of pasture, 2 acres in Balham meadow. (Box 28.Aa3)

1687 Let to Nathaniel Wright, brewer of Southwark. Described as about 24 acres of meadow, 15 acres of arable and another 5 acres. (Box 28.Aa10)

1702 John Cole, yeoman of Mitcham, mortgaged estate to John Hall. (BUR.6.3 pp. 451–7)

1712 Let to John Hall, draper of London. Mapped and contained 38a.2r.9p. Occupied by Jacob Collins and under-tenants. (BUR.6.3 pp. 451–7)

1720 College paid for frame to map of estate. (BUR.8.2)

1721–31 Let to John Gopsill of Southwark, linen draper. (COL.9.1(A) p. 95; BUR.6.3 pp. 608–11)

1735 38 ¼a. (BUR.3.2 f. 57r)

1773–1802 Let to William Cole. (COL.14.2 ff. 75v, 87r, 98r, 107v; COL.9.1(A) p. 95)

1780 Valued by Joseph Freeman. (COL.14.2 f. 87r)

1798 Valued by Alexander Watford. (BUR.0.9; BUR.8.7)

1801　Valued by William Forster. 39a.1r.38p. Landmarks had to be replaced, under-let without permission. (Sr.1.1; Sr.17.3a)

1802–25　Let to James Perry, Editor of *Morning Chronicle* and executors. (Box 28.Bb3–4; COL.14.2 f. 154r; Sr.17.48–9)

1802　Tenant spent over £2000 on estate. (Sr.17.10)

1803　Small pices of land not included in lease as thought could not recover. (Sr.17.13)

1804　Sold land to Surrey Iron Railway Company for £110 18s 1½d; to James Perry for £98; and invested £285 6s 9d in 3% consols. (BUR.11.3; COL.14.2 f. 137r; Sr.17.2)

1806　Plan omitted small piece of land Balham hill, fit spot for cockney's country house. (Sr.1.2)

1810–11　Surveyed by Francis Whishaw. Tenant claimed not derived any benefit from £2000 spent on estate. (Es.2.1d; Sr.17.6–8, 10; BUR.8.8; BUR.0.4(a))

1811–25　Dispute over encroachment, finally reinstated for College by new tenant. (Es.2.1d; Sr.17.7, 9, 11, 14, 19–22, 24, 25a, 26–9, 40–1, 43, 45–6, 50, 52–4; BUR.0.4(b))

1816　Delays in paying rent. (Es.4.4h)

1818　Valued by William Neale: 33a.1r.24p., house needed repair and painting, 2 cottages in good repair. (Sr.17.23a; BUR.0.4(c); BUR.8.8)

1820　Lease not renewed. (BUR.3.3; Sr.17.30–1)

1820–2　Dispute over felling of trees. Surveyed by William Cantis. (Sr.17.32–5, 37, 42–6; BUR.0.4(c); BUR.8.8)

1822　Considered letting in 3 pieces. (Sr.17.42)

1825–41+　Assigned and then let to Henry Flood of Upper Tooting, merchant. (Box 28.Bb5; BUR.6.5 pp. 534–5; Sr.17.57–8, 64; COL.14.3 p. 12)

1825　Surveyed and valued by George Gwilt. Allowed tenant £36 for repairs. (BUR.0.4(c); Sr.17.65–6; BUR.8.8)

1839　Commuted tithes at Clapham. (BUR.8.9)

1847　Tenant paid for dilapidations. George Gwilt investigated encroachment. (Sr.17.69–70)

1848　Bygrove Cottage let separately, rent £70. Commuted tithes at Mitcham. (BUR.8.9; COL.14.3 p. 52)

1848–67　George Gwilt bought land from Surrey Iron Railway (dissolved 1846) refused by College. Leased by Alfred Gwilt to College, then sold to College for £569 1s 3d. (Lo.11.132; BUR.0.4(f); Sr.17.78; COL.14.3 p. 186; BUR.8.9)

1849–51　Negotiated over boundary. (BUR.0.4(f); Lo.1.85; Sr.17.70, 72)

1850　Tenant of Bygrove Cottage bankrupt and relet. (BUR.0.5(a); Lo.1.1, 85)

1851　Rent £10. (Sr.17.73)

1854 Ejected tenant. (Sr.17.75)

1855–8 Cambridge Cottages built. (Sr.17.77; Box 28.Bb8–9; Lo.8.65b; COL.14.3 p. 120)

1857 Sold 25p. Mitcham to London and Crystal Palace Railway for £111 4s 4d. (BUR.11.4; COL.14.3 p. 117)

1866 Spent £20 on well at Bygrove. (BUR.8.9; Lo.11.132)

1868 Quit rents Mitcham conveyed for £27 1s. (BUR.8.9; Box 28.Aa39)

1870 Bought land Merton for £1800. (BUR.8.9; Sr.17.80)

Warwickshire – Sutton Coldfield (Dixie) (21 on Map 3)

1594 143a.3r.16p. purchased by College for £500, out of £600 bequeathed by Sir Wolstan Dixie to buy lands worth £30 a year to found 2 Fellowships and 2 scholarships. Let for £33; chief rent payable of 19s 4d. (Box 29.B1; Box 29.B13; COL.9.10.102)

1598 First income received from estate, after legal proceedings had been taken out against tenants. (Box 29.B22, B24; BUR.11.1)

1601 First lease sealed, after prolonged negotiations with tenants. (Box 29.B22, B24, B25/6)

1602 Sir Anthony Mildmay adjudicated between College and tenants. (Box 29.B22(lxxxix–lxxx))

1604 College re-entered on property for non-payment of rent. (Box 29.B7)

1607 Agreement with Sir Wolstan Dixie about management of estate and its profits. (Box 29.B11, B26)

1614 College claimed arrears of £23 10s. (Box 29.B22(lxxxvi))

1621 College re-entered on property for non-payment of rent. (Box 29.B8)

1623 Maney House let to Edward Willoughby for £29. (BUR.11.0.C f. 6r)

1629–31 Tenant apologised for arrears of rent. (Box 29.B22(viiic–viic))

1640 Wolstan Dixie wrote asking that College should improve land and tenements. (Box 29.B11)

1648 Maney House let to Rowland Thornton of Coleshill, with covenant for tenant to spent £25 on repairs to house and buildings. (Box 29.B25/7)

1653 College sued for arrears. (Box 29.B22(iiic))

1678 Dixie took out Chancery proceedings against College, claiming that income from estate had not been properly applied. (Box 29.B14)

1696 Chancery proceedings resumed. (Box 29.B26)

1701 Lord Keeper Wright's decree about proper running of estate. (Box 29.B21)

1710 Maney House let to John Davis of Market Bosworth, with covenant to put premises into repair within 12 months. Rent one peppercorn in 1st year, £10 in 2nd year, then £40. (Box 29.B25/12)

1722   Estate borrowed £300 from College, paid £12/year interest. (Box 29.B21)

1734   Paid £80 for building. (Box 29.B21)

1742   Surveyed by William Tranter: 143a.3r.16p. (Box 29.B19)

1774–88   Surveyed. (SCH.1.15)

1778–97   Summary acounts kept. (SCH.1.15)

1802   Surveyed by William Custance: 142a.0r.29p. In bad condition, repairs needed. Sold ground for road improvement for £3 3s. Dilapidations valued by Mr Wyatt. (SCH.1.15; Wa.1.1b)

1803   Visited by Bursar and William Custance in order to let. Let to 10 tenants, rent £309 4s, fines £534 17s. (Wa.1.2; SCH.1.15)

1805   Spent £20 on repairs. (SCH.1.15)

1807   Spent £60 on repairs. (SCH.1.15)

1810   25 square yards taken for turnpike. (Wa.1.3)

1811–12   Mapped by Henry S. O. Jacob: 148a.1r.21p. (BUR.0.4(a); Wa.1.5)

1812–15   Dispute over piece of land. Surveyed by William Custance. (BUR.0.4(b); SCH.1.15)

1813   Surveyed and viewed by Richard Court and Jacob. (Wa.1.6, 8)

1818   Tenant died in debt, advised over letting. (Wa.1.16–17)

1819–24   Arrears of payment of chief rent; 11 years paid 1821. Settled 1824. (Wa.1.19, 24–5, 28, 31, 32, 37, 38a, 42–3, 45; BUR.0.4(c))

1819–20   Sketch map. Tenant breached covenants. (BUR.0.4(b–c); Wa.1.43–4, 48–9)

1821   Distrained for rent. (Wa.1.21)

1822   Tenants asked for abatement. Requested permission to straighten watercourse. (Wa.1.45, 55)

1823   Surveyed by William Cantis. (SCH.1.15)

1823–33   Inclosed. Cost £450. (Wa.1.29b, 35, 38a, 52, 62–3, 72–3, 75–82, 86, 89, 93, 99; COL.14.2 ff. 182v, 196v; Box 29.K9; SCH.1.15)

1824   Surveyed by Solomon Smith. Let to 14 tenants, rent £334 6s, fines £505 4s. (Wa.1.2, 12–13, 28, 30, 56–7, 60, 65; SCH.1.15)

1825   Timber sold for £420. (Wa.1.66i, 67)

1826–7   College paid Solomon Smith £5/year to receive rents. College spent £166 on repairs. (SCH.1.15)

1828–64   College paid W. S. Perkins £10/year for receiving rents. (SCH.1.15–16)

1828–34   Sold blacksmith's shop and land to Sutton and Birmingham turnpike road commissioners for £189 12s. (Wa.1.72, 75, 81; SCH.1.15)

1830   Sold chief rents for 25 years' purchase in land. (Wa.1.78)

1833   Tenant bankrupt. (Wa.1.90)

1834   Tenant drowned himself. (Wa.1.96)

1835   Several tenants applied for new gates. (Wa.1.98)

1837–8   Tenant allowed £20 for shed. (Wa.1.102, 104; SCH.1.14; COL.14.2 f. 225r)

1842–5   College advised over reletting: to leave renewal until 3–4 months before expire, otherwise opportunity to exhaust land. Rents increased and fines reduced. (Wa.1.113, 117, 119, 121a, 125)

1843   Allowed new pump. (Wa.1.112)

1844   Bought 45a.2r.14p. Nicklins Field under inclosure act £109. (SCH.1.15; Box 29.Aa29)

1846   Sold 350 yards for lane widening. (SCH.1.15; Wa.1.124a)

1846–7   College spent £654 on repairs. (SCH.1.15; COL.14.3 p. 42; Wa.1.132)

1848   More repairs and improvements. (Wa.1.133–5)

1849   College spent £84 on repairs. (SCH.1.15)

1852   College allowed 10% off some rents. College spent £21 on repairs. Sealed inclosure award. (COL.14.3 pp. 77, 81; SCH.1.15)

1854   Mapped by John Holbeche. (SCH.1.15)

1857   Made allowances to tenants for repairs. (COL.14.3 pp. 116–17)

1860–1   Sold 3a.0r.14p. to North Western Railway Company for £1080 12s 6d, invested in 3% consols. (SCH.1.15; COL.14.3 pp. 149–50, 154; Wa.1.156–7)

1864–8   Edward Perkins collected rents. (SCH.1.15; COL.14.3 p. 166)

1865   Surveyed for development on building lease. (SCH.1.15; Wa.1.163)

1866   Exchanged 4a.0r.12p. Little Sutton with Charles Loveridge; he paid College £200 to invest. (Box 29.Bb8; COL.14.3 p. 176)

1868   Exchanged Blakes Pieces (College lost 11a.2r.30p, gained 10a.3r.5p. in 2 closes) with John de H. Chadwick for £415 11s. College spent £127 on repairs. Surveyed. (Box 29.Dd8, Dd11; COL.14.3 p. 191; SCH.1.16)

1869–71   College spent £16/year on receiving rents. (SCH.1.16)

1869   College spent £90 on repairs. Surveyed by Mr Cooper. (SCH.1.16)

1870   Bought The Plough and Harrow Inn and 5a.2r.7p., Muffins Den and 2a.3r.36p. Nicklins Field (adjoining property bought 1838) from Charles Webb (Box 29.Aa27): 9 messuages, 10a £1650. (Wa.1.164)

White Hart

1623   Built in stone after burned down. Let to Edward Willoughby, part sub-let to William Spooner, blacksmith, and John Underhill. £11 rent. (Box 29.B25/1)

1641–70   Let to William Pargiter despite request from Edward Willoughby that his lease be renewed. Then let to Robert Pargiter of Greteworth, Northamptonshire and to widow Phillis. (Box 29.B22, B25/2–3; BUR.11.1)

1659   Two fat capons or 5s for each at audit added to rent. (Box 29.B25/2)

1680   Rent increased to £14. (Box 29.B25/4–5)

1696   Letters of attorney issued to recover arrears. (BUR.6.3 pp. 233–4)

1699   Rent increased to £26. Let to Charles Chadwick (member of Emmanuel). (Box 29.B17, B17(a))

1721   Rent increased to £30. (BUR.3.2 f. 13)

1743   Rent £70, College paid £135 and premises put into repair. (Box 29.B18; COL.14.2 f. 13v)

1764   To be put into repair. (Box 29.B20). Letters of attorney to terminate lease or pay double rent, leave in good repair apart from barn to be pulled down under 1743 lease. (BUR.6.4 p. 179)

1785   Tenant to spend £70 on repairs. (BUR.6.5 pp. 3–9; COL.14.2 f. 87r)

Bibliography and List of Abbreviations

Books and documents from the College Archives (ECA), a few short papers in the *Emmanuel College Magazine* (*ECM*), and items cited in full in only one footnote are not necessarily listed here.

Ambler and Dowling 1996
    R. W. Ambler and A. Dowling, 'The growth of Cleethorpes and the prosperity of Sidney, 1616–1968', in Beales and Nisbet 1996, pp. 177–93

Anderson 1969 B. L. Anderson, 'Provincial aspects of the financial revolution of the eighteenth century', *Business History*, 11 (1969), 11–22

Archer 1991 I. W. Archer, *The History of the Haberdashers' Company*, Chichester, 1991

Aston and Faith 1984
    T. H. Aston and R. Faith, 'The endowments of the University and colleges to circa 1348', in *The History of the University of Oxford*, I, *The Early Oxford Schools*, ed. J. I. Catto, Oxford, 1984, pp. 265–309

Atherton 1996 I. Atherton and B. A. Holderness, 'The Dean and Chapter estates since the Reformation', in *Norwich Cathedral: Church, City and Diocese 1096–1996*, eds. I. Atherton *et al.*, London, 1996, pp. 665–87

Attwater 1936 A. Attwater, *Pembroke College Cambridge: a Short History*, Cambridge, 1936

Atwell 1658 G. Atwell, *The Faithfull Surveyour: Discovering Divers Errours in Land-measuring . . .* [Cambridge], 1658

Aylmer 1986 G. E. Aylmer, 'The economics and finances of the colleges and University *c.*1530–1640', in McConica 1986, pp. 521–58

Baker 1971 J. N. L. Baker, *Jesus College, Oxford 1571–1971*, Oxford, 1971

Baldwin 1944 T. W. Baldwin, *William Shakespere's Small Latine and Lesse Greeke*, Urbana, Ill., 1944

Ball 1677 T. Ball, *The Life of Doctor Preston*, in Clarke 1677, pp. 75–114

Barker 1913   E. Barker, *The Dominican Order and Convocation*,
        Oxford, 1913

Barrington 1983 *Barrington Family Letters*, ed. A. Searle, Camden 4th
        ser. 28 (1983)

Beachcroft 1982 G. Beachcroft, 'Balliol College accounts in the
        eighteenth century', in *Balliol Studies*, ed. J. Prest,
        London, 1982, pp. 77–87

Beales and Nisbet 1996
        D. E. D. Beales and H. B. Nisbet, eds., *Sidney Sussex
        College Cambridge: Historical Essays in Commemoration
        of the Quatercentenary*, Woodbridge, 1996

Beckett 1986   J. V. Beckett, *The Aristocracy in England 1660–1914*,
        Oxford, 1986

Beckett 1989   J. V. Beckett, 'Landownership and estate
        management', in *The Agrarian History of England and
        Wales*, VI, *1750–1850*, ed. G. E. Mingay, Cambridge,
        1989, pp. 545–640

Beckett 1990   J. V. Beckett, 'Estate management in
        eighteenth-century England: the Lowther-Spedding
        relationship in Cumberland', in Chartres and Hey
        1990, pp. 55–72

Beddard 1988   R. Beddard, *A Kingdom without a King: the Journal of
        the Provisional Government in the Revolution of 1688*,
        Oxford, 1988

Beddard 1997   R. Beddard, 'James II and the Catholic challenge', in
        Tyacke 1997, pp. 907–54

Bendall 1992   (A.) S. Bendall, *Maps, Land and Society: a History, with
        a Carto-bibliography of Cambridgeshire Estate Maps,
        c. 1600–1836*, Cambridge, 1992

Bendall 1994   D. S. Bendall, 'Robert Hill', *BMFRS*, 40 (1994), 141–70

Bendall 1997   (A.) S. Bendall, ed., *Dictionary of Land Surveyors and
        Local Map-Makers of Great Britain and Ireland
        1530–1850*, 2nd edn, London, 1997

Bendall (forthcoming)
        (A.) S. Bendall, 'Estate management and map-making
        in Oxford and Cambridge 1580–1640', *History of
        Universities*, 15 (1999)

Bendall and Stubbings 1989–90
        (A.) S. Bendall and F. H. Stubbings, 'The College
        charter,' *ECM*, 72 (1989–90), 26–32

Bennett 1962–3 H. S. Bennett, 'Archbishop Sancroft's library', *ECM*,
        45 (1962–3), 32–6

Bernard 1990   G. Bernard, 'The Church of England, *c.* 1529–*c.* 1642',
        History, 75 (1990), 183–206

Berthier 1889   J. S. Berthier, ed., *B. Humberti de Romanis Opera, de Vita Regulari*, 2 vols., Rome, 1889

Bill 1956   E. G. W. Bill, 'Some notes on methods of accounting at Christ Church', paper presented to a summer school of the Institute of Chartered Accountants, Christ Church, Oxford, 7 September 1956

BL   British Library

Blackstone 1898   W. Blackstone, *Dissertation on the Accounts of All Souls College Oxford*, London, 1898

BMFRS   *Biographical Memoirs of Fellows of the Royal Society*

Bodl.   Bodleian Library, Oxford

Bowden 1967   P. Bowden, 'Agricultural prices, farm profits and rents', in *The Agrarian History of England and Wales*, IV, *1500–1640*, ed. J. Thirsk, Cambridge, 1967, pp. 593–695

Boys Smith 1983   J. S. Boys Smith, *Memories of St John's College Cambridge 1919–1969*, Cambridge, 1983

Bozeman 1988   T. D. Bozeman, *To Live Ancient Lives: the Primitivist Dimension in Puritanism*, Chapel Hill and London, 1988

Bradshaw and Duffy 1989

    B. Bradshaw and E. Duffy, eds., *Humanism, Reform and the Reformation: the Career of Bishop John Fisher*, Cambridge, 1989

Bremer 1993   F. J. Bremer, ed., *Puritanism: Transatlantic Perspectives on a Seventeenth-Century Anglo-American faith*, Boston, 1993

Bremer 1994   F. J. Bremer, *Congregational Communion: Clerical Friendship and the Anglo-American Community, 1610–1692*, Boston, 1994

Brewer 1987   S. Brewer, 'The Early Letters of Richard Hurd from 1739 to 1762', Birmingham University Ph.D. thesis, 1987

Brewer 1995   S. Brewer, ed., *The Early Letters of Bishop Richard Hurd, 1739–1762* (Church of England Record Society, 3), Woodbridge, 1995

Brewer 1997–8   D. Brewer, 'Emmanuel and Harvard', *ECM*, 80 (1997–8), 54–69

Brodrick 1885   G. C. Brodrick, *Memorials of Merton College with Biographical Notices of the Wardens and Fellows*, Oxford, 1885

Brooke 1971   C. N. L. Brooke, *Medieval Church and Society*, London, 1971

Brooke 1985   C. N. L. Brooke, *A History of Gonville and Caius College*, Woodbridge, 1985

Brooke 1985a	C. N. L. Brooke, 'The churches of medieval Cambridge', in *History, Society and the Churches: Essays in Honour of Owen Chadwick*, eds. D. Beales and G. Best, Cambridge, 1985, pp. 49–76
Brooke 1987	C. N. L. Brooke, 'Reflections on the monastic cloister', in *Romanesque and Gothic: Essays for George Zarnecki*, Woodbridge, 1987, I, 19–25
Brooke 1989	C. N. L. Brooke, 'Oxford and Cambridge: the medieval universities', *Cambridge Review*, 110 (1989), 162–5
Brooke 1992	C. N. L. Brooke, 'Cambridge and the Antiquaries, 1500–1840', *Proceedings of the Cambridge Antiquarian Society*, 79 (1992 for 1990), 1–14
Brooke 1993	C. N. L. Brooke, *A History of the University of Cambridge*, IV, *1870–1990*, Cambridge, 1993
Brooke and Keir 1975	
	C. N. L. Brooke and G. Keir, *London 800–1216: the Shaping of a City*, London, 1975
Brooke, Highfield and Swaan 1988	
	C. N. L. Brooke, J. R. L. Highfield, and W. Swaan, *Oxford and Cambridge*, Cambridge, 1988
Brooke, R. B. 1959	R. B. Brooke, *Early Franciscan Government: Elias to Bonaventure*, Cambridge, 1959
Brooke, R. B. 1970/1990	
	R. B. Brooke, ed., *Scripta Leonis, Rufini et Angeli Sociorum S. Francisci*, Oxford Medieval Texts, Oxford, 1970, corr. repr., 1990
Brooke, R. B. 1975	R. B. Brooke, *The Coming of the Friars*, London, 1975
Brooks 1986	C. W. Brooks, *Pettyfoggers and Vipers of the Commonwealth: the 'Lower Branch' of the Legal Profession in Early Modern England*, Cambridge, 1986
Bury 1952	P. Bury, *The College of Corpus Christi and of the Blessed Virgin Mary: a History from 1822 to 1952*, Cambridge, 1952
Bush 1980	S. Bush Jr., *The Writings of Thomas Hooker: Spiritual Adventure in Two Worlds*, Madison, 1980
Bush and Rasmussen 1986	
	S. Bush Jr. and C. J. Rasmussen, eds., *The Library of Emmanuel College Cambridge 1584–1637*, Cambridge, 1986
Bushell 1938	W. D. Bushell, *Hobson's Conduit: the New River at Cambridge Commonly Called Hobson's River*, Cambridge, 1938
Cambridge Chronicle 1784	
	Extract from Saturday 2 October 1784, repr. under

title 'The Bicentenary Celebrations' in *ECM Quatercentenary Issue* (1984), p. 74

Candler 1896   C. Candler, *Notes on the Parish of Redenhall with Harleston in the County of Norfolk*, London, 1896

Cardwell 1849   E. Cardwell, *History of Conferences . . . Connected with the Revision of the Book of Common Prayer*, Oxford, 1849

Cary 1842   H. Cary, ed., *Memorials of the Great Civil War in England from 1642 to 1652, Edited from Original Letters in the Bodleian Library*, 2 vols., London, 1842

Cassirer 1953   E. Cassirer, *The Platonic Renaissance in England*, tr. J. P. Pettegrove, London, 1953

Chadwick 1959   (W.) O. Chadwick, *Creighton on Luther*, Inaugural Lecture, Cambridge, 1959

Chapman 1952   R. W. Chapman, ed., *Jane Austen's Letters to her Sister Cassandra and Others*, 2nd edn, London, 1952

Charles 1971   A. M. Charles, ed., *The Williams Manuscript of George Herbert's Poems: a Facsimile Reproduction*, Durham, N.C., 1971

Charlton 1965   K. Charlton, *Education in Renaissance England*, London, 1965

Chartres and Hey 1990

   J. Chartres and D. Hey, eds., *English Rural Society 1500–1800: Essays in Honour of Joan Thirsk*, Cambridge, 1990

Chawner 1909   W. Chawner, *Prove all Things*, Cambridge, 1909

Chawner 1909a   W. Chawner, *A Supplement to a Paper entitled Prove all Things*, Cambridge, 1909

Chawner 1911   W. Chawner, *Truthfulness in Religion*, Cambridge, 1911

Clark 1904   J. W. Clark, *Endowments of the University of Cambridge*, Cambridge, 1904

Clark 1906   J. W. Clark, *The Riot at the Great Gate of Trinity College February 1610–11*, Cambridge 1906

Clark 1978   J. C. D. Clark, 'The decline of party, 1740–1760', *English Historical Review*, 93 (1978), 499–527

Clark 1982   J. C. D. Clark, *The Dynamics of Change: the Crisis of the 1750s and English Party Systems*, Cambridge, 1982

Clark 1983   J. C. D. Clark, 'The politics of the excluded: Tories, Jacobites and Whig patriots, 1715–1760', *Parliamentary History*, 2 (1983), 209–22

Clark 1985   J. C. D. Clark, *English Society 1688–1832: Ideology, Social Structure and Political Practice during the Ancien Regime*, Cambridge, 1985

Clarke 1677	S. Clarke, *A General Martyrologie* . . . [Part II], *The Lives of 32 English Divines*, 3rd edn, London, 1677
Clay 1985	C. Clay, 'Landlords and estate management in England', in *The Agrarian History of England and Wales*, V ii, *1640–1750: Agrarian Change*, ed. J. Thirsk, Cambridge, 1985, pp. 119–251
Clemoes 1984	P. Clemoes, 'Peter Hunter Blair 1912–1982', *Proceedings of the British Academy*, 70 (1984), 451–61
Cliffe 1984	J. T. Cliffe, *The Puritan Gentry: the Great Puritan Families of Early Stuart England*, London, 1984
Cobban 1969	A. B. Cobban, *The King's Hall within the University of Cambridge in the Later Middle Ages*, Cambridge, 1969
Cocke 1984	T. Cocke, *The Ingenious Mr Essex, Architect, 1722–1784* (Catalogue of an Exhibition at the Fitzwilliam Museum), Cambridge, 1984
Colley 1977	L. Colley, 'The Loyal Brotherhood and the Cocoa Tree: the London Organisation of the Tory Party, 1727–60', *Historical Journal*, 20 (1977), 77–95
Colley 1982	L. Colley, *In Defiance of Oligarchy: the Tory Party 1714–60*, Cambridge, 1982
Collinson 1957	P. Collinson, 'The Puritan Classical Movement in the Reign of Elizabeth I', University of London Ph.D. thesis, 1957
Collinson 1967	P. Collinson, *The Elizabethan Puritan Movement*, London and Berkeley, 1967, repr. Oxford, 1990, 1991
Collinson 1979	P. Collinson, *Archbishop Grindal 1519–1583: The Struggle for a Reformed Church*, London and Berkeley, 1979
Collinson 1982	P. Collinson, *The Religion of Protestants: the Church in English Society 1559–1625*, Oxford, 1982
Collinson 1983	P. Collinson, *Godly People: Essays on English Protestantism and Puritanism*, London, 1983
Collinson 1983a	P. Collinson, 'The Jacobean religious settlement: the Hampton Court conference', in *Before the English Civil War*, ed. H. Tomlinson, Basingstoke, 1983, pp. 27–51
Collinson 1991	P. Collinson, 'Andrew Perne and his times,' in McKitterick 1991, pp. 1–34
Collinson 1994	P. Collinson, *Elizabethan Essays*, London and Rio Grande, Ohio, 1994
Collinson 1994a	P. Collinson, 'The Elizabethan exclusion crisis and the Elizabethan polity', *Proceedings of the British Academy*, 84, *1993 Lectures and Memoirs* (1994), 51–92
Collinson 1995	P. Collinson, *Archbishop Laud*, St John's College, Oxford, 1995

Collinson 1997
P. Collinson, 'Hooker and the Elizabethan establishment', in *Richard Hooker and the Construction of Christian Community*, ed. A. S. McGrade, Tempe, Arizona, 1997, pp. 149–87

Colvin 1978
H. M. Colvin, *A Biographical Dictionary of British Architects, 1600–1840*, London, 1978

Colvin 1986
H. M. Colvin, 'Architecture', in Sutherland and Mitchell 1986, pp. 831–56

Complete Peerage
G. E. C[ockayne], *The Complete Peerage of England Scotland Ireland Great Britain and the United Kingdom Extant Extinct or Dormant*, ed. V. Gibbs . . . [*et al.*], 12 vols., London, 1910–59

Connor 1987
R. D. Connor, *The Weights and Measures of England*, London, 1987

Conway Letters
Conway Letters: the Correspondence of Anne, Viscountess Conway, Henry More and their Friends, 1642–1684, ed. M. H. Nicolson, London, 1930, rev. and enlarged edn, ed. S. Hutton, Oxford, 1992

Cooke 1962
C. A. Cooke, 'The management of College estates', *Journal of the Chartered Land Agents' Society*, 61 (1962), 513–20

Coolidge 1970
J. S. Coolidge, *The Pauline Renaissance in England: Puritanism and the Bible*, Oxford, 1970

Cooper 1845
C. H. Cooper, ed., *Annals of Cambridge*, III, Cambridge, 1845

Cormack 1997
L. B. Cormack, *Charting an Empire: Geography at the English Universities 1580–1620*, Chicago, 1997

Cornford 1908
F. M. Cornford, *Microcosmographia Academica*, Cambridge, 1908 (also cited from edn of 1987)

Costello 1958
W. J. Costello, S.J., *The Scholastic Curriculum at Early Seventeenth-Century Cambridge*, Cambridge, Mass., 1958

Country Life

Cox 1978
N. Cox, *Bridging the Gap: a History of the Corporation of the Sons of the Clergy over 300 Years 1655–1978*, Oxford, 1978

Cragg 1968
G. R. Cragg, *The Cambridge Platonists*, New York, 1968

Crawley 1977
C. Crawley, *Trinity Hall: the History of a Cambridge College 1350–1975*, Cambridge, 1977

Creighton 1882–94
M. Creighton, *A History of the Papacy during the Period of the Reformation*, 5 vols., London, 1882–94; 2nd edn, renamed *A History of the Papacy from the Great Schism to the Sack of Rome*, 6 vols., London, 1897

Creighton 1904   L. Creighton, *Life and Letters of Mandell Creighton*, 2 vols., London, 1904

Cressy 1987   D. Cressy, *Coming Over: Migration and Communication between England and New England in the Seventeenth Century*, Cambridge, 1987

Crossley 1847   J. Crossley, ed., *Diary and Correspondence of John Worthington*, I, (Chetham Society Pubns, 13), Manchester, 1847

CUC   *Cambridge University Calendar* (cited by year)

CUL   Cambridge University Library

Cunich *et al.* 1994   P. Cunich, D. Hoyle, E. Duffy and R. Hyam, *A History of Magdalene College, 1428–1988*, Cambridge, 1994

Cunningham and Waterhouse 1992
        C. Cunningham and P. Waterhouse, *Alfred Waterhouse, 1830–1905*, Oxford, 1992

Cupitt 1970–1   D. Cupitt, 'The Chawner affair', *ECM*, 53 (1970–1), 5–11

Curl 1979   J. S. Curl, *Moneymore and Draperstown: the Architecture and Planning of the Estates of the Drapers' Company in Ulster*, Belfast, 1979

Curtis 1959   M. H. Curtis, *Oxford and Cambridge in Transition 1558–1642: an Essay on Changing Relations between the English Universities and English Society*, Oxford, 1959

Cust and Hughes 1989
        R. Cust and A. Hughes, eds., *Conflict in Early Stuart England: Studies in Religion and Politics 1603–1642*, London, 1989

Dainton and Thrush 1981
        F. Dainton and B. A. Thrush, 'Ronald George Reyford Norrish', *BMFRS*, 27 (1981), 379–424

Davies 1992   J. Davies, *The Caroline Captivity of the Church: Charles I and the Remoulding of Anglicanism 1625–1641*, Oxford, 1992

Dawkins 1935   R. M. Dawkins, 'Peter Giles', *Proceedings of the British Academy*, 21 (1935), 406–32

Deer and Nockolds 1974
        W. A. Deer and S. R. Nockolds, 'Cecil Edgar Tilley', *BMFRS*, 20 (1974), 381–400

De Pauley 1937   W. C. De Pauley, *The Candle of the Lord: Studies in the Cambridge Platonists*, London, 1937

Derry 1966   W. Derry, *Dr Parr: a Portrait of the Whig Dr Johnson*, Oxford, 1966

Dillingham 1700   W. Dillingham, *Vita Laurentii Chadertoni . . .*, Cambridge, 1700

Dillistone 1975   F. W. Dillistone, *Charles Raven*, London, 1975

DNB   *Dictionary of National Biography* (reference by name)

DNB, Missing Persons
     Dictionary of National Biography: Missing Persons, ed. C. S. Nicholls, Oxford, 1993

Doolittle 1986   I. G. Doolittle, 'College administration', in Sutherland and Mitchell 1986, pp. 227–68

D'Oyly 1821   G. D'Oyly, *The Life of William Sancroft, Archbishop of Canterbury*, 2 vols., London, 1821

Duffy 1992   E. Duffy, *The Stripping of the Altars*, New Haven, 1992

Dunbabin 1975   J. P. D. Dunbabin, 'Oxford and Cambridge college finances 1871–1913', *Economic History Review*, 28 (1975), 631–47

Dunbabin 1986   J. P. D. Dunbabin, 'College estates and wealth 1660–1815', in Sutherland and Mitchell 1986, pp. 269–307

Dunbabin 1994   J. P. D. Dunbabin, 'Finance since 1914', in *The History of the University of Oxford*, VIII, *The Twentieth Century*, ed. B. Harrison, Oxford, 1994, pp. 639–82

Dunbabin 1997   J. P. D. Dunbabin, 'Finance and property', in *The History of the University of Oxford*, VI, *Nineteenth-Century Oxford*. Part 1, eds. M. G. Brock and M. C. Curthoys, Oxford, 1997, pp. 375–437

Duncan 1986   G. D. Duncan, 'An introduction to the accounts of Corpus Christi College', in McConica 1986, pp. 574–96

Duncan 1986a   G. D. Duncan, 'The property of Balliol College *c*. 1500–*c*. 1640', in McConica 1986, pp. 559–73

ECA   Emmanuel College Archives

ECL   Emmanuel College Library

ECM   *Emmanuel College Magazine*

Eden 1983   P. Eden, 'Three Elizabethan estate surveyors: Peter Kempe, Thomas Clerke and Thomas Langdon', in *English Map-Making 1500–1650: Historical Essays*, ed. S. Tyacke, London, 1983, pp. 68–84

Eland 1935   'The annual progress of New College by Michael Woodward, Warden 1659–1675', ed. G. Eland, *Records of Buckinghamshire*, 13 (1935), 77–137

Emden 1963   A. B. Emden, *A Biographical Register of the University of Cambridge to 1500*, Cambridge, 1963

Engel 1978   A. Engel, 'Oxford college finances 1871–1913: a comment', *Economic History Review*, 31 (1978), 437–45

Engel 1983   A. Engel, *From Clergyman to Don: the Rise of the*

Academic Profession in Nineteenth-Century Oxford,
Oxford, 1983

Farmer 1767   R. Farmer, *An Essay on the Learning of Shakespeare:*
addressed to Joseph Cradock Esq., 1st edn, Cambridge,
1767 (cited from this edn; there was a 2nd edn of
1767, a 3rd of 1789, and posthumous edns of 1800 and
1821)

Feingold 1984   M. Feingold, *The Mathematicians' Apprenticeship:*
Science, Universities and Society in England, 1560–1640,
Cambridge, 1984

Fincham 1990   K. Fincham, *Prelate as Pastor: the Episcopate of James I,*
Oxford, 1990

Fincham 1993   K. Fincham, ed., *The Early Stuart Church, 1603–1642,*
Basingstoke, 1993

Fincham and Lake 1985
K. C. Fincham and P. Lake, 'The ecclesiastical policy
of King James I', *Journal of British Studies*, 24 (1985),
169–207

Fincham and Lake 1993
K. C. Fincham and P. Lake, 'The ecclesiastical policies
of James I and Charles I', in Fincham 1993,
pp. 23–49

Fincham and Lake 1996
K. C. Fincham and P. Lake, 'Popularity, prelacy and
puritanism in the 1630s: Joseph Hall explains
himself', *English Historical Review*, 111 (1996), 856–81

Firmin 1670   G. Firmin, *The Real Christian, Or, A Treatise of Effectual*
Calling, London, 1670

Forbes 1928   M. D. Forbes, ed., *Clare College 1326–1926: University*
Hall 1326–1346 Clare Hall 1346–1856, I, Cambridge,
1928

Foster 1991   S. Foster, *The Long Argument: English Puritanism and*
the Shaping of New England Culture, 1570–1700, Chapel
Hill and London, 1991

Franks 1966   *University of Oxford, Report of Commission of Enquiry*
[Franks Report], 2 vols., Oxford, 1966

Fuller 1655, 1840 T. Fuller, *The History of the University of Cambridge,*
Since the Conquest, [London], 1655 and 1840 edns both
cited

Fuller 1662   T. Fuller, *The History of the Worthies of England,*
London, 1662

Galbraith 1925   G. R. Galbraith, *The Constitution of the Dominican*
Order, 1216 to 1360, Manchester, 1925

Gascoigne 1983   J. Gascoigne, 'Mathematics and meritocracy: the

emergence of the Cambridge mathematical tripos',
Social Studies of Science, 14 (1983), 547–84

Gascoigne 1989   J. Gascoigne, *Cambridge in the Age of the Enlightenment: Science, Religion and Politics from the Restoration to the French Revolution*, Cambridge, 1989

Geison 1978   M. F. Geison, *Michael Foster and the Cambridge School of Physiology*, Princeton, 1978

Giles 1919   P. Giles, 'Samuel George Phear', *Cambridge Review*, 14 February 1919, 211–12

Girouard 1979   M. Girouard, *The Victorian Country House*, 2nd edn, New Haven, 1979

Godwin 1601   F. Godwin, *A Catalogue of the Bishops of England*, London, 1601 (2nd edn, 1615)

Godwin 1616, 1743   F. Godwin, *De Praesulibus Angliae commentarius*, 2 parts, London, 1616; ed. W. Richardson, London, 1743

Godwin 1985   H. Godwin, *Cambridge and Clare*, Cambridge, 1985

Gold 1945–8,   E. Gold, 'William Napier Shaw', *Obituary Notices of Fellows of the Royal Society*, 5 (1945–8), 203–30

Gower 1990   G. Gower, *Balham: a Brief History*, Wandsworth, [1990]

Graham Commission

   Report of Her Majesty's Commissioners Appointed to Inquire into the State, Discipline, Studies, and Revenues of the University and Colleges of Cambridge, London, 1852

Gray 1985   A. S. Gray, *Edwardian Architecture*, London, 1985

Gray 1992   M. Gray, 'Exchequer officials and the market in Crown property, 1558–1640', in *The Estates of the English Crown, 1558–1640*, ed. R. W. Hoyle, Cambridge, 1992, pp. 112–62

Gray and Brittain 1960

   A. Gray and F. Brittain, *A History of Jesus College Cambridge*, London, 1960

Gross 1912   E. J. Gross, 'Chronicle of the College estates', in Venn, *Caius*, IV ii, 1912

Gunning 1854   H. Gunning, *Reminiscences of the University, Town, and County of Cambridge from the year 1780*, 2 vols., London, 1854

Habakkuk 1940   H. J. Habakkuk, 'English landownership 1680–1740', *Economic History Review*, 10 (1940), 2–17

Habakkuk 1952–3   H. J. Habakkuk, 'The long-term rate of interest and the price of land in the seventeenth century', *Economic History Review*, 5 (1952–3), 26–45

Hainsworth 1987   D. R. Hainsworth, 'The estate steward', in *The*

Professions in Early Modern England, ed. W. Prest,
London, 1987, pp. 154–80

Hainsworth and Walker 1990

*The Correspondence of Lord Fitzwilliam of Milton and
Francis Guybon his Steward 1697–1709*, eds. D. R.
Hainsworth and C. Walker, Northampton, 1990

Hall 1863   J. Hall, *Works*, ed. P. Wynter, 10 vols., Oxford 1863

Hall 1990   A. R. Hall, *Henry More: Magic, Religion and
Experiment*, Oxford, 1990

Hall 1990a   C. Hall, 'College officers: the bursars, stewards and
registraries of Gonville and Caius College,' *The Caian*
(1990), 114–26

Hall and Morgan 1977

A. Hall and M. Morgan, 'Bennett Melvill Jones',
BMFRS, 23 (1977), 253–82

Halliwell 1845   J. O. Halliwell, ed., *The Autobiography and
Correspondence of Sir Simonds D'Ewes Bart. During the
Reigns of James I and Charles I*, 2 vols., London, 1845

Hardman 1986   S. Hardman, 'Return Migration from New England to
England, 1640–1660', University of Kent at
Canterbury Ph.D. thesis, 1986.

Hardy 1854   T. D. Hardy, ed., J. Le Neve, *Fasti Ecclesiae Anglicanae*,
3 vols., London, 1854

Harrison 1930   G. B. Harrison, ed., *Advice to his Son by Henry Percy
Ninth Earl of Northumberland (1609)*, London, 1930

Harrison 1958   W. J. Harrison, *Life in Clare Hall Cambridge 1658–1713*,
Cambridge, 1958

Haslam 1991   G. Haslam, 'Patronising the plotters: the advent of
systematic estate mapping', in *Maps and History in
South-West England*, eds. K. Barker and R. J. P. Kain,
Exeter, 1991, pp. 55–71

Hasler 1981   P. W. Hasler, *The House of Commons 1558–1603*, (The
History of Parliament), London, 1981

Head 1943   E. M. Head, *F. W. Head, Archbishop of Melbourne*,
London, 1943

Heal and Holmes 1994

F. Heal and C. Holmes, *The Gentry in England and
Wales 1500–1700*, Basingstoke, 1994

Heywood and Wright 1854

J. Heywood and T. Wright, eds., *Cambridge University
Transactions During the Puritan Controversies of the 16th
and 17th Centuries*, 2 vols., London, 1854

Heyworth 1981   P. Heyworth, *The Oxford Guide to Oxford*, Oxford,
1981

Hill 1956   C. Hill, *Economic Problems of the Church from Archbishop Whitgift to the Long Parliament*, Oxford, 1956

Hinchcliffe 1992   T. Hinchcliffe, *North Oxford*, New Haven, 1992

Hinnebusch 1951   W. A. Hinnebusch, *The Early English Friars Preachers*, Rome, 1951

Hockley 1974–5   R. Hockley, 'Edward Woodall Naylor', *ECM*, 57 (1974–5), 8–16

Holderness 1972   B. A. Holderness, 'Landlords' capital formation in East Anglia 1750–1870', *Economic History Review*, 25 (1972), 434–47

Hooker 1975   *Thomas Hooker: Writings in England and Holland, 1626–1633*, ed. G. Williams *et al.*, Cambridge, Mass., 1975

Hopkinson 1948   A. W. Hopkinson, *About William Law*, London, 1948

Horn 1969, 1974   J. Le Neve, *Fasti Ecclesiae Anglicanae, 1541–1857*, I, III (by J. M. Horn), London, 1969, 1974

Hort 1896   A. F. Hort, *Life and Letters of Fenton John Anthony Hort*, 2 vols., London, 1896

Howard 1935   H. F. Howard, *An Account of the Finances of the College of St John the Evangelist in the University of Cambridge 1511–1926*, Cambridge, 1935

Howell 1986   D. W. Howell, *Patriarchs and Parasites: the Gentry of South-West Wales in the Eighteenth Century*, Cardiff, 1986

Hoyle 1990   R. Hoyle, ' "Vain projects": the Crown and its copyholders in the reign of James I', in Chartres and Hey 1990, pp. 73–104

Hoyle 1991   D. M. Hoyle, ' "Near Popery yet no Popery": theological debate in Cambridge 1590–1644', University of Cambridge Ph.D. thesis, 1991

Hughey 1941   R. Hughey, ed., *The Correspondence of Lady Katharine Paston 1603–1627*, (Norfolk Record Society, XIV), Norwich, 1941

Hull 1987   F. Hull, 'Aspects of local cartography in Kent and Essex, 1585–1700', in Neale 1987, pp. 241–52

Hunt 1983   W. Hunt, *The Puritan Moment: the Coming of Revolution in an English County*, Cambridge, Mass., 1983

Hunter Blair 1983–4   Pauline Hunter Blair, 'Days in the life of an idle don: extracts from the diary kept by Peter Hunter Blair from 1947–1960', *ECM*, 66 (1983–4), 16–22

Hyam 1992   R. Hyam, *Godliness, Hunting and Quite Good Learning: the History of Magdalene College, 1792–1992*, Cambridge, 1992

Ibish 1985	J. S. Ibish, 'Emmanuel College: the founding generation, with a biographical register of members of the College 1584–1604,' Harvard University Ph.D. thesis, 1985
Jones 1936	W. H. S. Jones, *A History of St Catharine's College Once Catharine Hall Cambridge*, Cambridge, 1936
Jordan 1959	W. K. Jordan, *Philanthropy in England 1480–1660: a Study of the Changing Pattern of English Social Aspirations*, London, 1959
Jordan 1960	W. K. Jordan, *The Charities of London 1480–1660: the Aspirations and the Achievements of the Urban Society*, London, 1960
Jordan 1961	W. K. Jordan, *Social Institutions of Kent 1480–1660*, *Archaeologia Cantiana*, 75 (1961)
Kain and Prince 1985	R. J. P. Kain and H. C. Prince, *The Tithe Surveys of England and Wales*, Cambridge, 1985
Kendall 1979	R. T. Kendall, *Calvin and English Calvinism to 1649*, Oxford, 1979, also cited from edn. of 1981
Keynes 1981	*The Collected Writings of John Maynard Keynes*, XIX, *Activities 1922–1929. The Return to Gold and Industrial Policy*, ed. D. Moggridge, London, 1981
Keynes 1983	*The Collected Writings of John Maynard Keynes*, VII, *Economic Articles and Correspondence. Investment and Editorial*, ed. D. Moggridge, London, 1983
Kitchin 1895	G. W. Kitchin, *Edward Harold Browne, D.D.*, London, 1895
Knappen 1933	M. M. Knappen, *Two Elizabethan Puritan Diaries*, Chicago, 1933
Knappen 1939	M. M. Knappen, *Tudor Puritanism: a Chapter in the History of Idealism*, Chicago, 1939
Knowles 1948–59	(M.) D. Knowles, *The Religious Orders in England*, 3 vols., Cambridge, 1948–59
Knowles and Hadcock 1971	(M.) D. Knowles and R. N. Hadcock, *Medieval Religious Houses, England and Wales*, 2nd edn, London, 1971
Kroll, Ashcraft and Zagorin 1992	R. Kroll, R. Ashcraft and P. Zagorin, eds., *Philosophy, Science and Religion in England 1640–1700*, Cambridge, 1992
Kupperman 1993	K. O. Kupperman, *Providence Island: the other Puritan Colony*, Cambridge, 1993
Lake 1982	P. Lake, *Moderate Puritans and the Elizabethan Church*, Cambridge, 1982

Lake 1988   P. Lake, *Anglicans and Puritans? Presbyterianism and English Conformist Thought from Whitgift to Hooker*, London, 1988

Lake 1995   P. Lake, 'Predestinarian propositions', *Journal of Ecclesiastical History*, 46 (1995), 110–23

Law 1978   W. Law, *A Serious Call to a Devout and Holy Life*, ed. P. G. Stanwood, London and New York, 1978

Law 1990   *William Law: Selected Writings*, ed. J. Louth, Manchester 1990

Lawrence 1985   H. Lawrence, 'John Norden and his colleagues: surveyors of Crown lands', *Cartographic Journal*, 22 (1985), 54–6

Leader 1988   D. R. Leader, *A History of the University of Cambridge*, I, *The University to 1546*, Cambridge, 1988

Leedham-Green 1986
                   E. S. Leedham-Green, *Books in Cambridge Inventories*, 2 vols., Cambridge, 1986

Le Faye 1995   D. Le Faye, ed., *Jane Austen's Letters*, Oxford, 1995

Lehmberg 1964   S. E. Lehmberg, *Sir Walter Mildmay and Tudor Government*, Austin, Texas, 1964

Line 1993   J. Line, *James and Dorothy: the Story of a Mixed Marriage, 1917–1981*, Bath, 1993

Little 1943   A. G. Little, 'The friars and the foundation of the Faculty of Theology in the University of Cambridge', in Little, *Franciscan Papers, Lists, and Documents*, Manchester, 1943, pp. 122–43

Lloyd 1977   L. J. Lloyd, 'Dr Richard Farmer, 1735–97', *The Book Collector*, 26 (1977), 524–36

Longden 1940   H. I. Longden, *Northamptonshire and Rutland Clergy from 1500*, Northampton, 1940

Lubenow 1998   W. Lubenow, *The Cambridge Apostles, 1820–1914*, Cambridge, 1998

Mabbut 1700   G. Mabbut, *Tables for Renewing and Purchasing of the Leases of Cathedral-Churches and Colleges, According to Several Rates of Interest . . .*, 2nd edn, Cambridge, 1700 [Sometimes misattributed to Isaac Newton]

McCabe 1982   R. A. McCabe, *Joseph Hall: a Study in Satire and Meditation*, Oxford, 1982

McConica 1986   J. McConica, ed., *The History of the University of Oxford*, III, *The Collegiate University*, Oxford, 1986

McCullough 1998   P. McCullough, *Sermons at Court: Politics and Religion in Elizabethan and Jacobean Preaching*, Cambridge, 1998

McGiffert 1972   M. McGiffert, *God's Plot: the Paradoxes of Puritan Piety,*

Being the Autobiography and Journal of Thomas Shepard, Amherst, 1972

McIntosh 1987   M. McIntosh, 'New College, Oxford and its Hornchurch estate, 1391–1675', in Neale 1987, pp. 171–83

McKeon 1829   H. McKeon, *An Inquiry into the Rights of the Poor in the Parish of Lavenham in Suffolk*, London, 1829

McKitterick 1986   D. McKitterick, *Cambridge University Library: A History. The Eighteenth and Nineteenth Centuries*, Cambridge, 1986

McKitterick 1991   D. McKitterick, ed., *Andrew Perne: Quatercentenary Studies*, Cambridge, 1991

Maddison 1891   A. R. Maddison, ed., *Lincolnshire Wills. Second Series A.D. 1600–1617*, London, 1891

Mann 1930   E. Mann, ed., *J. B. Scott, An Englishman at Home and Abroad, 1792–1828*, London, 1930

Manningham 1722   T. Manningham, *The Value of Church and College Leases Consider'd: and the Advantages of the Lessees Made Very Apparent*, 2nd edn, London, 1722 [Sometimes misattributed to Isaac Newton]

Marsden 1851   J. H. Marsden, *College Life in the Time of James the First As Illustrated by An Unpublished Diary of Sir Symonds D'Ewes*, London, 1851

Martin 1979   J. Martin, 'Estate stewards and their work in Glamorgan, 1660–1760: a regional study of estate management', *Morgannwg*, 23 (1979), 9–28

Martin and Highfield 1997

   G. H. Martin and J. R. L. Highfield, *A History of Merton College, Oxford*, Oxford, 1997

Martyn 1728   J. Martyn, *Historia Plantarum Rariorum*, London, 1728

Mason 1993   J. Mason, 'Women in Cambridge: some quandaries', *Cambridge Review*, 114 (1993), 67–74

Mather 1852   C. Mather, *Magnalia Christi Americana; Or, the Ecclesiastical History of New England*, Hartford, 1852 (1853), repr. 1979, I

Mayor 1859   J. E. B. Mayor, ed., *Early Statutes of the College of St John the Evangelist in the University of Cambridge*, Cambridge, 1859

Mayr-Harting 1988

   H. Mayr-Harting, 'The foundation of Peterhouse, Cambridge (1284), and the Rule of St Benedict', *English Historical Review*, 103 (1988), 318–38

Meersseman 1946   G. Meersseman, 'L'architecture dominicaine au xiiie siècle, législation et pratique', *Archivum Fratrum Praedicatorum*, 16 (1946), 136–90

Miller 1961   E. Miller, *Portrait of a College: a History of the College of Saint John the Evangelist Cambridge*, Cambridge, 1961

Miller and Johnson 1938

P. Miller and T. H. Johnson, *The Puritans*, New York, 1938

Mills and Oliver 1967

P. Mills and J. Oliver, *The Survey of Building Sites in the City of London after the Great Fire of 1666*, introduction by P. E. Jones and T. F. Reddaway, London, 1967

Milton 1995   A. Milton, *Catholic and Reformed: the Roman and Protestant Churches in English Protestant Thought 1600–1640*, Cambridge, 1995

Mingay 1963   G. E. Mingay, *English Landed Society in the Eighteenth Century*, London, 1963

Mintz 1962   S. I. Mintz, *The Hunting of Leviathan: Seventeenth-Century Reactions to the Materialism and Moral Philosophy of Thomas Hobbes*, Cambridge, 1962

Monk 1830   J. H. Monk, *The Life of Richard Bentley, D.D.*, London and Cambridge, 1830 (cited from one-vol. edn)

Morgan 1957   I. Morgan, *Prince Charles's Puritan Chaplain*, London, 1957

Morgan 1974   V. Morgan, 'Cambridge University and "The Country" 1560–1640', in Stone 1974, I, pp. 183–245

Morgan 1983   V. Morgan, 'Country, court and Cambridge University, 1558–1640: a study in the evolution of a political culture', University of East Anglia Ph.D. thesis, 1983

Morgan 1986   J. Morgan, *Godly Learning: Puritan Attitudes Towards Reason, Learning and Education, 1560–1640*, Cambridge, 1986

Morison 1930   S. E. Morison, *Builders of the Bay Colony*, London, 1930

Morison 1932   S. E. Morison, *English University Men who Emigrated to New England before 1646*, Cambridge, Mass., 1932

Morison 1935   S. E. Morison, *The Founding of Harvard College*, Cambridge, Mass., 1935

Morison 1936   S. E. Morison, *Harvard College in the Seventeenth Century*, Cambridge, Mass., 1936

Mott 1986   N. Mott, *A Life in Science*, London, 1986

Mullinger 1911   J. B. Mullinger, *The University of Cambridge*, III, *From the Election of Buckingham to the Chancellorship in 1626 to the Decline of the Platonist Movement*, Cambridge, 1911

Munby 1989   L. Munby, *How Much is That Worth?* Chichester, 1989

Myers 1975   A. R. Myers, *Parliaments and Estates in Europe to 1789*, London, 1975

Namier 1929   L. B. Namier, *The Structure of Politics at the Accession of George III*, 2 vols., London, 1929

Neale 1957   J. E. Neale, *Elizabeth I and her Parliaments, 1584–1601*, London, 1957

Neale 1987   K. Neale, ed., *An Essex Tribute: Essays Presented to Frederick G. Emmison as a Tribute to his Life and Work for Essex History and Archives*, London, 1987

Needham and Baldwin 1949
          J. Needham and E. Baldwin, eds., *Hopkins and Biochemistry 1865–1947*, Cambridge, 1949

Neill and Wright 1988
          S. C. Neill and T. Wright, *The Interpretation of the New Testament, 1861–1986*, 2nd edn, London 1988

Nelson 1989   A. H. Nelson, ed., *Records of Early English Drama: Cambridge*, Toronto, 1989

Nelson 1994   A. H. Nelson, *Early Cambridge Theatres: College, University, and Town Stages, 1464–1720*, Cambridge, 1994

Newcourt 1708–10 R. Newcourt, *Repertorium Ecclesiasticum Parochiale Londinense*, 2 vols., London, 1708–10

Newsome 1984   D. H. Newsome, 'Two Emmanuel Historians', *ECM*, 48 (1965–6), 21–34, cited from repr. in *ECM Quatercentenary Issue* (1984), 104–14

Nichols 1795–1815 J. Nichols, *The History and Antiquities of the County of Leicester*, 4 vols. in 8, London, 1795–1815

Norden 1607   J. Norden, *The Surveyors Dialogue*, London, 1607

Northcote 1818   J. Northcote, *The Life of Sir Joshua Reynolds*, 2nd edn, 2 vols., London, 1818

Norton, Park and Binski 1987
          C. Norton, D. Park, and P. Binski, *Dominican Painting in East Anglia: the Thornham Parva Retable and the Musée de Cluny Frontal*, Woodbridge, 1987

Oates 1986   J. C. T. Oates, *Cambridge University Library: a History. From the Beginnings to the Copyright Act of Queen Anne*, Cambridge, 1986

OED   *Oxford English Dictionary*, 2nd edn prepared by J. A. Simpson and E. S. C. Weiner, Oxford, 1989

Oschinsky 1971   D. Oschinsky, *Walter of Henley and Other Treatises on Estate Management and Accounting*, Oxford, 1971

Owst 1949   G. R. Owst, 'Iconomania in eighteenth-century

	Cambridge', *Proceedings of the Cambridge Antiquarian Society*, 42 (1949), 67–91
Parker 1975	R. A. C. Parker, *Coke of Norfolk: a Financial and Agricultural Study 1707–1842*, Oxford, 1975
Parkinson 1966	C. N. Parkinson, *A Law unto Themselves: Twelve Portraits*, London, 1966
Passmore 1951	J. A. Passmore, *Ralph Cudworth: an Interpretation*, Cambridge, 1951, repr. Bristol, 1990
Patterson 1997	W. B. Patterson, *King James VI and I and the Reunion of Christendom*, Cambridge, 1997
PCC	Prerogative Court of Canterbury (Wills in the PRO)
Peace 1908	J. B. P[eace], 'The history of a City freehold', *ECM*, 19 (1908), 1–20
Peace 1911	J. B. Peace, 1911, 'The Master of Emmanuel', *Cambridge Review*, 27 April 1911, 368–9
Peel 1915	A. Peel, ed., *The Seconde Parte of a Register*, 2 vols., Cambridge, 1915
Peile 1910–13	J. Peile, *Biographical Register of Christ's College, 1505–1905*, 2 vols., Cambridge, 1910–13
Percy Letters	*The Correspondence of Thomas Percy and Richard Farmer*, ed. C. Brooks, Louisiana, 1946
Perkin 1989	H. Perkin, *The Rise of Professional Society: England since 1880*, London, 1989
Pevsner 1954, 1970	N. Pevsner, *The Buildings of England: Cambridgeshire*, 1st edn, Harmondsworth, 1954, 2nd edn, 1970
Phillips 1989	A. D. M. Phillips, *The Underdraining of Farmland in England during the Nineteenth Century*, Cambridge, 1989
Pollard 1965	S. Pollard, *The Genesis of Modern Management: a Study of the Industrial Revolution in Great Britain*, London, 1965
Pollock 1993	L. A. Pollock, *With Faith and Physic: the Life of a Tudor Gentlewoman, Lady Grace Mildmay, 1552–1620*, London, 1993
Porter 1958	H. C. Porter, *Reformation and Reaction in Tudor Cambridge*, Cambridge, 1958, corr. repr. 1972
Postgate 1964	M. R. Postgate, 'The open fields of Cambridgeshire', University of Cambridge Ph.D. thesis, 1964
Powicke 1926	F. J. Powicke, *The Cambridge Platonists: a Study*, London and Toronto, 1926
PRO	London, Public Record Office
Quiney 1979	A. Quiney, *John Loughborough Pearson*, New Haven, 1979
Raban 1982	S. Raban, *Mortmain Legislation and the English Church 1279–1500*, Cambridge, 1982

Rackham 1927   H. Rackham, ed., *Early Statutes of Christ's College,
                  Cambridge with the Statutes of the Prior Foundation of
                  God's House*, Cambridge, 1927
Raven 1928   C. E. Raven, *A Wanderer's Way*, London, 1928
Raven 1928a   C. E. Raven, *Women and Holy Orders*, Cambridge, 1928
Raven 1954   C. E. Raven, 'Alex Wood – a memoir', in Wood and
                  Oldham 1954, pp. ix–xvi
RCHM Cambridge   *Royal Commission on Historical Monuments for England,
                  City of Cambridge*, 2 parts, London, 1959
Read 1946   *Isaac Read Diaries, 1762–1804*, ed. C. E. Jones,
                  Berkeley, 1946
Reeve 1890   E. H. L. Reeve, *Stondon Massey, Essex*, Colchester,
                  1890
'Register'   The relevant entries in Venn rearranged under years
                  to make a working Register of Emmanuel alumni
                  down to 1900 [see p. xvi]
Reporter   *Cambridge University Reporter*
Rich 1973   E. E. Rich, 'The nineteenth century', in *St Catharine's
                  College Cambridge 1473–1973: a Volume of Essays to
                  Commemorate the Quincentenary of the Foundation of the
                  College*, ed. Rich, [Cambridge, 1973], pp. 164–247
Roberts 1961   S. C. Roberts, *Richard Farmer (1735–1797)* (Arundell
                  Esdaile Memorial Lecture, 1960), London, 1961
Rodger 1982   R. Rodger, 'Rents and ground rents: housing and the
                  land market in nineteenth-century Britain', in *The
                  Structure of Nineteenth Century Cities*, eds. J. H.
                  Johnson and C. G. Pooley, London, 1982, pp. 39–74
Rolph 1979   R. S. Rolph, 'Emmanuel College, Cambridge, and the
                  Puritan Movements of old and new England,'
                  University of Southern California Ph.D. thesis, 1979
Rothblatt 1981   S. Rothblatt, *The Revolution of the Dons: Cambridge and
                  Society in Victorian England*, 2nd edn, Cambridge, 1981
Royal Commission 1874
                  *Report of the Commissioners Appointed to Inquire into the
                  Property and Income of the Universities of Oxford and
                  Cambridge, and of the Colleges and Halls therein; together
                  with Returns and Appendix*, London, 1874
Royal Commission 1922
                  *Royal Commission on Oxford and Cambridge
                  Universities. Report*, London, 1922
Rupp 1972   E. G. Rupp, *William Bedell 1571–1642*, lecture given in
                  Emmanuel College, 1 December 1971, Cambridge,
                  1972
Rupp 1977   E. G. Rupp, *Just Men: Historical Pieces*, London, 1977

Rupp 1981   E. G. Rupp, 'A Cambridge centenary: the Selwyn
                   Divinity School, 1879–1979', *Historical Journal*, 24, 2
                   (1981), 417–28
Rupp 1986   E. G. Rupp, *Religion in England 1688–1791*, Oxford,
                   1986
Russell 1991   C. Russell, *The Fall of the British Monarchies,
                   1637–1642*, Oxford, 1991
Rutman 1965   D. B. Rutman, *Winthrop's Boston: Portrait of a Puritan
                   Town 1630–1649*, Chapel Hill, 1965
Salt 1992   P. Salt, 'Wyatville's remodelling and refurbishment
                   of Sidney Sussex College, 1820–1837', *Proceedings of
                   the Cambridge Antiquarian Society*, 81 (1992), 115–55
Scarisbrick 1984   J. J. Scarisbrick, *The Reformation and the English People*,
                   Oxford, 1984
Scheeben *et al.* 1935
                   H. C. Scheeben *et al.*, eds., *Monumenta Historica s.
                   patris nostri Dominici*, II (Monumenta Ordinis
                   Praedicatorum Historica, 16), Rome, 1935
Schoenbaum 1991   S. Schoenbaum, *Shakespeare's Lives*, 2nd edn, Oxford,
                   1991
Schofield 1987   J. Schofield, *The London Surveys of Ralph Treswell*,
                   London, 1987
Scott-Giles 1975   C. W. Scott-Giles, *Sidney Sussex College: a Short
                   History*, Cambridge, 1975
Scott Pearson 1925 A. F. Scott Pearson, *Thomas Cartwright and Elizabethan
                   Puritanism,1535–1603*, Cambridge, 1925
Searby 1984   P. Searby, 'A failure at Cambridge: Cavendish
                   College, 1877–1892', *Proceedings of the Cambridge
                   Antiquarian Society*, 72 (1984 for 1982–3), 106–20
Searby 1997   P. Searby, *A History of the University of Cambridge*, III,
                   1750–1870, Cambridge, 1997
[Seward 1799   W. Seward], *Biographiana*, 2 vols., London, 1799
Shadwell 1898   C. L. Shadwell, *The Universities and College Estates Acts,
                   1858 to 1880: their History and Results*, Oxford, 1898
Shallcross 1983   J. R. Shallcross, *Ancient and Honourable: the Mildmay
                   Essay Club 1883–1983*, Cambridge 1983
Sharpe 1992   K. Sharpe, *The Personal Rule of Charles I*, New Haven,
                   1992
Sheils 1979   W. J. Sheils, *The Puritans in the Diocese of Peterborough
                   1558–1610*, Northampton, 1979
Sheppard 1982   N. Sheppard, 'Gordon Brims Black McIvor
                   Sutherland', *BMFRS*, 28 (1982), 589–626
Sherbo 1992   A. Sherbo, *Richard Farmer, Master of Emmanuel College,
                   Cambridge: a forgotten Shakespearean*, Newark, 1992

Shuckburgh 1884   E. S. Shuckburgh, *Laurence Chaderton, D.D. . . . Richard Farmer, D.D. . . .: an Essay*, Cambridge, 1884

Shuckburgh 1902   E. S. Shuckburgh, ed., *Two Biographies of William Bedell, Bishop of Kilmore*, Cambridge, 1902

Shuckburgh 1904   E. S. Shuckburgh, *Emmanuel College*, London, 1904

Skinner 1996   Q. Skinner, *Reason and Rhetoric in the Philosophy of Hobbes*, Cambridge, 1996

Slee 1986   P. R. H. Slee, *Learning and a Liberal Education: the Study of Modern History in the Universities of Oxford, Cambridge and Manchester, 1800–1914*, Manchester, 1986

Smalley 1960   B. Smalley, *English Friars and Antiquity in the early Fourteenth Century*, Oxford, 1960

Southern 1986   R. W. Southern, *Robert Grosseteste*, Oxford, 1986

Spring 1963   D. Spring, *The English Landed Estate in the Nineteenth Century: its Administration*, Baltimore, 1963

Spurr 1991   J. Spurr, *The Restoration Church of England, 1646–1689*, New Haven, 1991

Statutes   *Statutes of Emmanuel College*. For the Founder's Statutes, *see* Stubbings 1983a; the *Statutes* of 1861, 1882, 1926 and 1957 are also cited.

Stone 1974   L. Stone, ed., *The University in Society*, 2 vols., Princeton, 1974

Storey 1979   R. L. Storey, 'The foundation and the medieval college 1379–1530', in *New College Oxford 1379–1979*, eds. J. Buxton and P. Williams, Oxford, 1979, pp. 3–43

Stubbings 1965–6   F. H. Stubbings, 'Dr Johnson in Cambridge', *ECM*, 48 (1965–6), 64–71

Stubbings 1967–8   F. H. Stubbings, 'Samuel Parr recalled', *ECM*, 50 (1967–8), 5–14

Stubbings 1971   F. H. Stubbings, 'A Cambridge pocket-diary, 1587–1592', *Transactions of the Cambridge Bibliographical Society*, 5 (1969–71), 191–202

Stubbings 1977a   F. H. Stubbings, 'Glorianus and Gloriana', *Transactions of the Cambridge Bibliographical Society*, 6 (1977 for 1972–6), 129–30

Stubbings 1977b   F. H. Stubbings, 'Anthony Askew's Liber Amicorum', *Transactions of the Cambridge Bibliographical Society*, 6 (1977 for 1972–6), 306–21

Stubbings 1977c   F. H. Stubbings, *Emmanuel College Chapel, 1677–1977*, Cambridge, 1977

Stubbings 1977–8   F. H. Stubbings, 'Visiting scholar, 1784', *ECM*, 60 (1977–8), 20–1

Stubbings 1981   F. H. Stubbings, *A Brief History of Emmanuel College Library*, Cambridge, 1981

Stubbings 1983a   F. H. Stubbings, ed., *The Statutes of Sir Walter Mildmay Kt . . . authorised by him for the Government of Emmanuel College founded by him*, Cambridge, 1983

Stubbings 1983b   F. H. Stubbings, *Forty-Nine Lives: an Anthology of Portraits of Emmanuel Men*, Cambridge, 1983

Stubbings 1984a   F. H. Stubbings, 'The Black Friars' church and the college hall', *ECM Quatercentenary Issue* (1984), 14–23

Stubbings 1984b   F. H. Stubbings, 'Samuel Blackall and Jane Austen', *ECM*, 47 (1964–5), 40–5, repr. *ECM Quatercentenary Issue* (1984), 77–81

Stubbings 1984–5   F. H. Stubbings, 'Who was Chapman?', *ECM*, 67 (1984–5), 17–21

Stubbings 1987–8   F. H. Stubbings, 'Sempire land and college organists', *ECM*, 70 (1987–8), 12–15

Stubbings 1993   F. H. Stubbings, *The Graham Watson Collection of Colour-Plate Books at Emmanuel College Cambridge*, Cambridge, 1993

Sutherland and Mitchell 1986
   L. S. Sutherland and L. G. Mitchell, eds., *The History of the University of Oxford*, V, *The Eighteenth Century*, Oxford, 1986

Talon 1948   H. Talon, *William Law: a Study in Literary Craftsmanship*, London, 1948

Tanner 1917   J. R. Tanner, ed., *The Historical Register of the University of Cambridge*, Cambridge, 1917

Taylor 1987   S. J. C. Taylor, 'Church and State in England in the mid-eighteenth century: the Newcastle years 1742–1762', University of Cambridge Ph.D. thesis, 1987

Taylor and Booth 1970
   N. Taylor and P. Booth, *New Cambridge Architecture*, 3rd edn, London, 1970

Thomas and Bower 1939–41
   H. H. Thomas and F. O. Bower, 'Albert Charles Seward', *Obituary Notices of Fellows of the Royal Society*, 3 (1939–41), 867–80

Thompson 1994   D. M. Thompson, 'Historical survey, 1750–1949', in *A History of Lincoln Minster*, ed. D. Owen (Cambridge, 1994), 210–318

Thompson 1976   E. P. Thompson, 'The grid of inheritance: a comment,' in *Family and Inheritance: Rural Society in Western Europe, 1200–1800*, eds. J. Goody, J. Thirsk and E. P. Thompson, Cambridge, 1976, pp. 328–60

Thomson 1940   G. S. Thomson, *The Russells in Bloomsbury 1669–1771*, London, 1940

Tillyard 1913   A. I. Tillyard, *A History of University Reform from 1800 AD to the Present Time, with Suggestions Towards a Complete Scheme for the University of Cambridge*, Cambridge, 1913

Trueman 1980   B. E. S. Trueman, 'Corporate estate management: Guy's Hospital agricultural estates, 1726–1815', *Agricultural History Review*, 28 (1980), 31–44

Turner 1986   M. Turner, 'The land tax, land and property: old debates and new horizons', in *Land and Property: the English Land Tax 1692–1832*, eds. M. Turner and D. Mills, Gloucester, 1986, pp. 1–35

Twigg 1987   J. Twigg, *A History of Queens' College, Cambridge, 1448–1986*, Woodbridge, 1987

Twigg 1990   J. Twigg, *The University of Cambridge and the English Revolution, 1625–1688*, Cambridge, 1990

Twigg 1997   J. Twigg, 'College finances, 1640–1660', in Tyacke 1997, pp. 773–802

Tyacke 1973   N. Tyacke, 'Puritanism, Arminianism and Counter-Revolution', in *The Origins of the English Civil War*, ed. C. Russell, Basingstoke, 1973, pp. 119–43

Tyacke 1990   N. Tyacke, *Anti-Calvinists: the Rise of English Arminianism c. 1590–1640*, rev. edn, Oxford, 1990

Tyacke 1993   N. Tyacke, 'Archbishop Laud', in Fincham 1993, pp. 51–70

Tyacke 1997   N. Tyacke, ed., *The History of the University of Oxford*, IV, *Seventeenth-Century Oxford*, Oxford, 1997

Tyacke 1997a   N. Tyacke, 'Religious controversy', in Tyacke 1997, pp. 569–619

Tyler 1975   R. Tyler, ' "The children of disobedience": the social composition of Emmanuel College, Cambridge, 1596–1645', University of California Ph.D. thesis, 1975

Usher 1905   R. G. Usher, ed., *The Presbyterian Movement in the Reign of Queen Elizabeth as Illustrated by the Minute Book of the Dedham Classis, 1582–1589*, Camden 3rd ser. VIII (1905)

Usher 1910   R. G. Usher, *The Reconstruction of the English Church*, 2 vols., London and New York, 1910

Usher 1992   B. Usher, 'The silent community: early puritans and the patronage of the arts', in *The Church and the Arts: Studies in Church History*, 28, ed. D. Wood, Oxford, 1992, pp. 287–302

VCH Cambs   *Victoria History of the Counties of England. Cambridgeshire*, III, ed. J. P. C. Roach, Oxford, 1959

VCH Rutland   *Victoria History of the Counties of England. Rutland*, II,
                   ed. W. Page, London, 1935
Venn   J. and J. A. Venn, eds., *Alumni Cantabrigienses*, 2 parts
                   (to 1751, 1752–1900), 4 and 6 vols., Cambridge,
                   1922–54 (reference by name)
Venn 1912   J. Venn, 'John Caius', repr. with corrections from
                   Venn, *Caius*, III, in J. Caius, *Works*, ed. E. S. Roberts,
                   Cambridge, 1912, pp. 1–78
Venn 1913   J. Venn, *Early Collegiate Life*, Cambridge, 1913
Venn, *Caius*   J. Venn et al., *Biographical History of Gonville and Caius
                   College*, 8 vols., Cambridge, 1897–1998
Vicaire 1964   M.-H. Vicaire, O.P., *Histoire de S. Dominique* (2 vols.,
                   Paris, 1957), here cited from Eng. trans. by K. Pond,
                   London, 1964
Virgin 1989   P. Virgin, *The Church in an Age of Negligence:
                   Ecclesiastical Structure and Problems of Church Reform
                   1700–1840*, Cambridge, 1989
Wabuda and Litzenberger 1998
                   S. Wabuda and C. Litzenberger, eds., *Belief and
                   Practice in Reformation England: a Tribute to Patrick
                   Collinson from his Students*, Aldershot, 1998
Wade Martins 1980
                   S. Wade Martins, *A Great Estate at Work: the Holkham
                   Estate and its Inhabitants in the Nineteenth Century*,
                   Cambridge, 1980
Walker 1973   A. K. Walker, *William Law: his Life and Thought*,
                   London, 1973
Walton 1854   A. C. Walton, *Materials for an Adequate Biography of
                   William Law*, privately printed, 1854
Walton's Lives   ed. S. B. Carter, London, 1951
Walz 1951   A. Walz, ed., *Beati Iordani de Saxonia Epistulae*
                   (Monumenta Ordinis Praedicatorum Historica, 23),
                   Rome, 1951
Ward 1710   R. Ward, *The Life of Dr Henry More*, London, 1710
Webster 1993   T. Webster, 'The godly of Goshen scattered: an Essex
                   clerical conference in the 1620s and its diaspora',
                   University of Cambridge Ph.D. thesis, 1993
Webster 1994   T. Webster, *Stephen Marshall and Finchingfield*,
                   Chelmsford, 1994
Webster 1997   T. Webster, *Godly Clergy in Early Stuart England: the
                   Caroline Puritan Movement, c. 1620–1643*, Cambridge,
                   1997
Welbourne 1963–4   E. Welbourne, 'Reminiscence', *ECM*, 46 (1963–4),
                   1–13

Westcott and Hort 1881

    B. F. Westcott and J. F. A. Hort, eds., *The New Testament in Greek*, 2 vols., Cambridge, 1881

Whetham 1911   W. C. D. Whetham and C. D. Whetham, 'The conversion of the Master', *Cornhill Magazine*, New Series, 31 (1911), 651–64

Whetham 1978   E. H. Whetham, ed., *The Agrarian History of England and Wales*, VIII, *1914–39*, Cambridge, 1978

Whichcote 1753   *Moral and Religious Aphorisms Collected from the Manuscript Papers of the Reverend and Learned Doctor Whichcote* (ed. Samuel Salter) . . . *To which are Added Eight Letters which Passed between Dr Whichcote, Provost of King's College, and Dr Tuckney, Master of Emmanuel College in Cambridge*, London, 1753

White 1992   P. White, *Predestination, Policy and Polemic: Conflict and Consensus in the English Church from the Reformation to the Civil War*, Cambridge, 1992

Whitney 1919   J. P. Whitney, *The Study of Ecclesiastical History Today: an Inaugural Address*, Cambridge, 1919

Who's Who

Williamson 1983   R. Williamson, 'Sir Busick Harwood: a re-appraisal', *Medical History*, 27 (1983), 423–33

Willis and Clark 1886/1988

    R. Willis and J. W. Clark, *The Architectural History of the University of Cambridge and of the Colleges of Cambridge and Eton*, Cambridge, 1886, repr. with introduction by D. Watkin, 1988

Wilmot 1990   S. Wilmot, *'The Business of Improvement': Agriculture and Scientific Culture in Britain, c. 1770–c. 1870* [London], 1990

Winstanley 1922   D. A. Winstanley, *The University of Cambridge in the Eighteenth Century*, Cambridge, 1922

Winstanley 1935   D. A. Winstanley, *Unreformed Cambridge*, Cambridge, 1935

Winstanley 1940   D. A. Winstanley, *Early Victorian Cambridge*, Cambridge, 1940

Winstanley 1947   D. A. Winstanley, *Later Victorian Cambridge*, Cambridge, 1947

Winthrop Papers   *The Winthrop Papers*, ed. G. W. Robinson *et al.*, 6 vols., Boston, Mass., 1929–47

Wood and Oldham 1954

    A. Wood and F. Oldham, *Thomas Young, Natural Philosopher, 1773–1829*, Cambridge, 1954

Wordsworth 1877   C. Wordsworth, *Scholae Academicae*, Cambridge, 1877

Wright 1898–1905　J. Wright, *The English Dialect Dictionary*, London,
6 vols., 1898–1905

Wyatt 1996　　　T. S. Wyatt, 'The building and endowment of the
college', in Beales and Nisbet 1996, pp. 43–53

Wynne Thomas 1978
G. Wynne Thomas, *'Fit Via Vi!' The Story of the E.B.C.,
1827–1977*, Cambridge, 1978

Ziff 1962　　　　L. Ziff, *The Career of John Cotton: Puritanism and the
American Experience*, Princeton, 1962

Zutshi and Ombres 1990
P. Zutshi and R. Ombres, 'The Dominicans in
Cambridge 1238–1538', *Archivum Fratrum
Praedicatorum*, 60 (1990), 313–73

Index

Footnotes have only been indexed separately, and indicated by 'n', if the term does not occur elsewhere on the page. County names have been given for small towns and villages; the pre-1974 counties have been used. London is defined as the area covered by the 1855 Metropolis Management Act. Colleges are in Cambridge unless otherwise indicated, as are university posts.

The following abbreviations are used:

b	bursar
f	fellow
hon. f	honorary fellow
m	master
t	tutor

Abbot, George, archbishop of
  Canterbury, 185
Aberdeen University, 440
Aberdeenshire, 418–19, 440
absentee landowners, leases,
  covenants, 134; *see also*
  landowners
accountancy, treatises about, 128–9
accounting practices, 95–6, 350
Ackermann, *Cambridge, Plate 3*
Acton, Lord (Sir John Emerich Edward
  Dalberg), regius professor of
  modern history, 425, 426
Acts of Parliament: and building
  leases, 378; and college estates,
  382, 383, 504; and land tax, 382;
  individual Acts: 13 Elizabeth
  Cap.10, 100, 130; 14 Elizabeth
  Cap.11, 130; 18 Elizabeth Cap.11,
  130; 19 Charles II Cap.3, *see*
  Rebuilding A.; 5 George IV
  Cap.36, 353; *see also* Charities A.;
  City of London Sewers A.; Control
  of Office and Industrial
  Development A.; Corn Rent A.;
  Equal Opportunities A.; Housing
  (Rural Workers) A.; Landlord and
  Tenant A.; Landlord and Tenant
  (War Damage) A.; Leasehold

Reform A.; Metropolis Dead Meat
  and Poultry A.; Oxford and
  Cambridge A.; religious tests,
  abolition of; Rent A.; Rent
  Restrictions A.; Settled Land A.;
  Tithe A.; Town and Country
  Planning A.; Universities and
  Colleges (Emergency Provisions)
  A.; Universities and Colleges
  Estates A.
Adam, James (f), 418–19, 427, 441,
  514n, 539
Adelaide University, 527
Admiral of the Fleet, *see* Austen, Sir
  Francis
Admiralty, purchase of land from
  Emmanuel College, 475
Aeschylus, 310
agents, 359, 452; *see also* Emmanuel
  College, agents; estate stewards;
  landowners; valuers; *and see also*
  under particular landowners and
  estates
agricultural depression, 134–5, 371,
  508; in late seventeenth century,
  144, 153; in early nineteenth
  century, 333, 334n, 356, 381–2; in
  late nineteenth century, 429,
  479–80; in twentieth century,

War II; brewery on, 594, 596, 597, 599, 600; building developments on, 454, 476–7, 478, 480, 487, 488, 490–5, 498, 499, 501–2, 507, 643, *see also* leases (building leases); charges due, 95, 124, 142, 143, 361, 383, 461, 589–649 *passim*; churches on, 390, 614, 619; college as tenant, 364, 593, 594, 599–600, 604; sub-let, 120, 155; *see also* Cambridge, Sempire Lands, Caxton, Ripple; copyholds, 489, 604, 605, 612; coronation festivities on, 487; customs on, 139, 146, 388, 479, 481, 589–649 *passim*; decisions at college meetings about, 351, 374, 388–9, *see also* governing body; direct farming by college, 163–4, 636; drainage on, 351, 373, 374, 375–6, 601, 610, 614, 618, 619, 620, 621, 622, 635, 638, 644; encroachments to, 365, 367; farm cottages on, 374, 459, 482, 483–6; fire of London and, 149–50, 625, 627, 630, 631; garages, 500–1; gifts of, 100–13, 340–1, 344, 461, 486; inclosure of, 353, 369, 373–4, 375, 377, 383, 384, 387, 592, 600, 601, 610, 611–12, 618, 622, 633, 636, 637, 644, 647, 648; industrial premises on, 451; inns on, 592–4, 596, 608–9, 611, 622–4, 632, 648; inspection of, 132, 142, 366, 372, 458, 488, 499, 500; insurance of, 349, 379, 607, 621, 626, 627, 644; law suits concerning, 131–2, 137–8, 162–3, 353, 589–649 *passim*; leasehold reform and, 504–5; letting of, 363, 366–7, 481, 589–649 *passim*, *see also* leases; licensed premises on, 507; local charities and communities on, 390, 487, 507–8, 614, 618, 621, 635, *see also* churches, schools; lord of the manor, college as, *see* Ash-next-Sandwich (Chequer Court farm), Great Gransden, Shernborne; management of 126–56, 333–90, 451–509; costs of, 357–8, 457–9; manorial courts, *see* lord of the manor, visits, leases (covenants); maps showing location of, 590–1, 593; maps of, 132–3, 155, 360, 365–7, 597, 601,

604, 606, 607, 611, 612, 630, 633, 634, 638, 641, 642, 643, 644, 645, 647, 648; purchases of, 105, 107, 109, 110, 113–17, 120, 167, 340–1, 343, 344, 356, 363, 366, 384, 451, 455, 458–9, 461, 483, 487–90, 506, 589–649 *passim*; of commercial and industrial premises, 496, 629; of Park Terrace, *see* Park Terrace; of shops, 496, 499; of urban land, 111, 113, 123, 167, 384, 451, 454, 490, 496, 497, 500, 502–3, 509, 521; records, 96–7, 347, 357, 360; repairs and improvements, 137, 349, 351, 363, 364, 366, 371–9, 455, 456, 476, 482, 483–5, 498–9, 500, 506, *see also* 589–649 *passim*, drainage, farm cottages, inclosure, war damage, leases (building leases, covenants); sales of, 100, 111, 357, 382–4, 451, 453, 455, 461, 462, 468, 474–9, 487, 494, 498, 499, 501, 506, 508, 627; after World War I, 471–3, 476–7, 506; after World War II, 477–8, 488, 496, 500, 503, 506; and sinking funds, 461–2, 500, 504–5; to railways, 357, 363, 383, 610, 621, 645, 646, 648; to redeem land tax, 367, 382; to turnpike roads commissioners, 364, 377, 383, 615, 647; under compulsory purchase orders, 461, 478–9, 501, 502, 503, 505, 506, 628, 629; under leasehold reform, 504–5, 506; schools and, 390, 482, 487, 607, 614, 634, 635; sea erosion of, 163, 605, 640–1; shops on, 451, 589–649 *passim*; surveys of, 132, 138, 365–7, 372, 380, 387, 394, 462; taxation of, 95, 124, 142–3, 381; land tax, 382, 598, 602, 606, 610, 611; timber resources and sales, 137, 147, 380, 387; town planning and, 501–2; trust estates, 158, 336, 338–9, 347–8, 349, 353, 354, 369, 371, *see also* Ash-next-Sandwich, Braintree, Chawner trust, Dagenham, Dixie trust, Holbeach, Hornchurch, London (Holborn), Lusby estate, Lydden and Ewell, Navestock, Pakefield, Rushall, St Cross, Shernborne, Stapleford Abbots, Stratford, Sutton Coldfield,

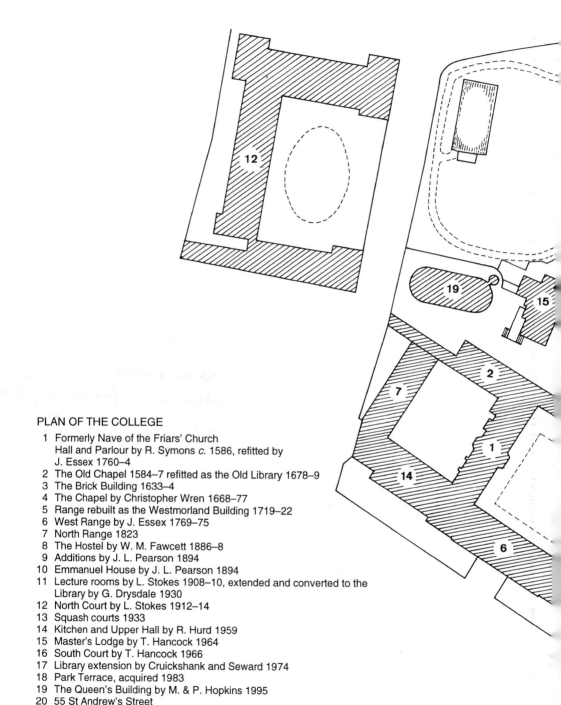

PLAN OF THE COLLEGE

1 Formerly Nave of the Friars' Church
   Hall and Parlour by R. Symons *c.* 1586, refitted by
   J. Essex 1760–4
2 The Old Chapel 1584–7 refitted as the Old Library 1678–9
3 The Brick Building 1633–4
4 The Chapel by Christopher Wren 1668–77
5 Range rebuilt as the Westmorland Building 1719–22
6 West Range by J. Essex 1769–75
7 North Range 1823
8 The Hostel by W. M. Fawcett 1886–8
9 Additions by J. L. Pearson 1894
10 Emmanuel House by J. L. Pearson 1894
11 Lecture rooms by L. Stokes 1908–10, extended and converted to the
   Library by G. Drysdale 1930
12 North Court by L. Stokes 1912–14
13 Squash courts 1933
14 Kitchen and Upper Hall by R. Hurd 1959
15 Master's Lodge by T. Hancock 1964
16 South Court by T. Hancock 1966
17 Library extension by Cruickshank and Seward 1974
18 Park Terrace, acquired 1983
19 The Queen's Building by M. & P. Hopkins 1995
20 55 St Andrew's Street
21 East Court

EMMANUEL COLLEGE